AF678927

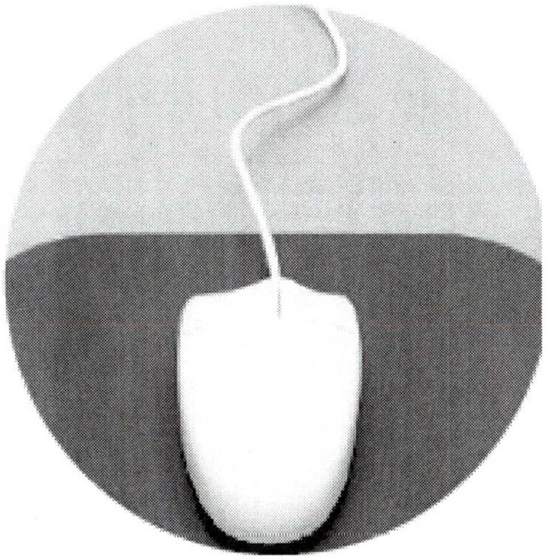

Customer Support Information

Plunkett's Companion to the Almanac of American Employers 2012

Please register your book immediately...

if you did not purchase it directly from Plunkett Research, Ltd. This will enable us to fulfill your requests for assistance. Also, it will enable us to notify you of future editions.

Your purchase includes access to Book Data and Exports online

As a book purchaser, you can register for free, 1-year, 1-seat online access to the latest data for your book's industry trends, statistics and company profiles. This includes tools to export company data. Simply send us this registration form, and we will send you a user name and password. In this manner, you will have access to our continual updates during the year. Certain restrictions apply.

____ YES, please register me as a purchaser of the book.
I did not buy it directly from Plunkett Research, Ltd.

____ YES, please register me for free online access. I am the actual, original purchaser. (Proof of purchase may be required.)

Customer Name ____________________

Title ____________________

Organization ____________________

Address ____________________

City ____________________ State ________ Zip ____________

Country (if other than USA) ____________________

Phone ____________________ Fax ____________________

E-mail ____________________

Return to: Plunkett Research®, Ltd.

Attn: Registration
P.O. Drawer 541737, Houston, TX 77254-1737 USA
713.932.0000 · Fax 713.932.7080 · www.plunkettresearch.com
customersupport@plunkettresearch.com

* Purchasers of used books are not eligible to register. Use of online access is subject to the terms of the end user license agreement.

PLUNKETT'S COMPANION TO THE ALMANAC OF AMERICAN EMPLOYERS: Mid-Size Firms 2012

The only guide to America's hottest, fastest-growing mid-sized companies

Jack W. Plunkett

Published by:
Plunkett Research®, Ltd., Houston, Texas
www.plunkettresearch.com

PLUNKETT'S COMPANION TO THE ALMANAC OF AMERICAN EMPLOYERS: Mid-Size Firms 2012

Editor and Publisher:
Jack W. Plunkett

Executive Editor and Database Manager:
Martha Burgher Plunkett

Senior Editor and Researcher:
Jeremy Faulk
Jill Steinberg

Editors, Researchers and Assistants:
Keith Beeman, III
Kalonji Bobb
Elizabeth Braddock
Raul R.C. Chavez
Xiaowen Chen
Jamey Crane
Jillian Claire Lim
Larissa Matin
Isaac Snider
Suzanne Zarosky

Enterprise Accounts Managers:
Emily Hurley
Kelly Burke

Information Technology Interns:
Danil K. Safin
Yuxin Zhai

Video & Graphics Manager:
Geoffrey Trudeau

Special Thanks to:
National Association for Convenience and Petroleum Retailing
National Restaurant Association
U.S. Bureau of Labor Statistics
U.S. Census Bureau
U.S. Department of Agriculture, Economic Research Service (ERS)
U.S. Department of Commerce
U.S. National Science Foundation
Willard Bishop, Inc.

Plunkett Research®, Ltd.
P. O. Drawer 541737, Houston, Texas 77254 USA
Phone: 713.932.0000 Fax: 713.932.7080
www.plunkettresearch.com

Published by:
Plunkett Research®, Ltd.
P. O. Drawer 541737
Houston, Texas 77254-1737

Phone: 713.932.0000
Fax: 713.932.7080
Internet: www.plunkettresearch.com

ISBN13 # 978-1-60879-664-9
(eBook Edition # 978-1-60879-926-8)

LIMITED WARRANTY; DISCLAIMER OF LIABILITY:

While Plunkett Research, Ltd. ("PRL") has made an effort to obtain the information presented in this book (the "Data") from sources deemed reliable, PRL makes no warranties, expressed or implied, regarding the Data contained herein. The Data is provided to the End-User "AS IS" without warranty of any kind. No oral or written information or advice given by PRL, its employees, distributors or representatives will create a warranty or in any way increase the scope of this Limited Warranty, and the Customer or End-User may not rely on any such information or advice.

Customer Remedies: PRL's entire liability and your exclusive remedy shall be, at PRL's sole discretion, either (a) return of the price paid, if any, or (b) repair or replacement of the product that does not meet PRL's Limited Warranty and that is returned to PRL with sufficient evidence of or receipt for your original purchase.

NO OTHER WARRANTIES: TO THE MAXIMUM EXTENT PERMITTED BY APPLICABLE LAW, PRL AND ITS DISTRIBUTORS DISCLAIM ALL OTHER WARRANTIES AND CONDITIONS, EITHER EXPRESSED OR IMPLIED, INCLUDING, BUT NOT LIMITED TO, IMPLIED WARRANTIES OR CONDITIONS OF MERCHANTABILITY, FITNESS FOR A PARTICULAR PURPOSE, TITLE AND NON-INFRINGEMENT WITH REGARD TO THE PRODUCT, AND THE PROVISION OF OR FAILURE TO PROVIDE SUPPORT SERVICES.

LIMITATION OF LIABILITY: TO THE MAXIMUM EXTENT PERMITTED BY APPLICABLE LAW, IN NO EVENT SHALL PRL BE LIABLE FOR ANY SPECIAL, INCIDENTAL OR CONSEQUENTIAL DAMAGES WHATSOEVER (INCLUDING, WITHOUT LIMITATION, DAMAGES FOR LOSS OF BUSINESS PROFITS, BUSINESS INTERRUPTION, ABILITY TO OBTAIN OR RETAIN EMPLOYMENT OR REMUNERATION, ABILITY TO PROFITABLY MAKE AN INVESTMENT, OR ANY OTHER PECUNIARY LOSS) ARISING OUT OF THE USE OF, OR RELIANCE UPON, THE DATA, OR THE INABILITY TO USE THIS DATA OR THE FAILURE OF PRL TO PROVIDE SUPPORT SERVICES, EVEN IF PRL HAS BEEN ADVISED OF THE POSSIBILITY OF SUCH DAMAGES. IN ANY CASE, PRL'S ENTIRE LIABILITY UNDER ANY PROVISION OF THIS END-USER LICENSE AGREEMENT SHALL BE LIMITED TO THE AMOUNT ACTUALLY PAID BY YOU FOR THE PRODUCT.

PLUNKETT'S COMPANION TO THE ALMANAC OF AMERICAN EMPLOYERS
Mid-Size Firms 2012

CONTENTS

Continued on next page

Continued from previous page

INTRODUCTION

As the name implies, this volume is designed to be used in conjunction with THE ALMANAC OF AMERICAN EMPLOYERS. The main volume of THE ALMANAC covers highly successful firms of 2,500 or more employees. This "companion" volume focuses on mid-size firms, from 100 to 2,500 employees.

PLUNKETT'S COMPANION TO THE ALMANAC OF AMERICAN EMPLOYERS is an easy-to-use solution to what would otherwise be a complicated problem: How can you tell, among all of America's mid-size companies, which firms are most likely to be hiring? Among those hot firms, which are the best to work for? No other source provides this book's easy-to-understand comparisons of growth, treatment of employees, salaries, benefits, pension plans, profit sharing and many other items of great importance to job seekers.

Especially helpful is the way in which PLUNKETT'S COMPANION TO THE ALMANAC OF AMERICAN EMPLOYERS enables readers with no business background to readily compare the growth potential and benefit plans of mid-size employers. You'll see the mid-term financial record of each firm, along with the impact of earnings, sales and growth plans on each company's potential to provide employment or advancement opportunities.

Information is presented in a way that addresses the differing interests of individual employees. You'll find dozens of categories of data that you may want to consider. While the book is aimed primarily at job seekers, it will also be of tremendous value to researchers, marketing executives and personnel professionals. PLUNKETT'S COMPANION TO THE ALMANAC OF AMERICAN EMPLOYERS is the premier guide to the most successful mid-size employers in the nation, their policies and their performance.

PLUNKETT'S COMPANION TO THE ALMANAC OF AMERICAN EMPLOYERS is your opportunity to gain valuable knowledge in a matter of minutes. Five hundred of the most successful mid-size corporate employers in America are analyzed in this book. Tens of thousands of pieces of information, gathered from a wide variety of sources, have been researched for these corporations and are presented here in a form that can be easily understood by job seekers of all types.

Thanks to PLUNKETT'S COMPANION TO THE ALMANAC OF AMERICAN EMPLOYERS' exclusive data system, potentially confusing considerations have been reduced to simple groups of focused data. By scanning the data groups and the long list of unique indexes, you can find the best employer to fit your personal needs.

The MID-SIZE EMPLOYERS 500 are among the best companies to work for in America. Which companies offer the best benefits, are the biggest employers or earn the most profits? Where are these companies operating? What firms have the highest potential salaries? All of these things and more are made easy for the reader to determine.

Thousands of observations are made that will be of great interest to prospective employees. For many of the firms, you'll find comments about such items as plans for growth, increases or decreases in the number of employees and charitable programs. You'll also find notes about special programs for the convenience of employees, such as health and recreation facilities, job training or career paths. Finally, you'll find basic information on each company, including the home office address and telephone number; regional, national and international locations; a description of the business; and a list of selected subsidiaries and trade names. In addition, you'll find fax numbers, Internet addresses and toll-free phone numbers for most of the firms.

Whether you are currently employed by one of these corporate giants or are considering applying for a job with one, you'll be able to see how each company compares with the others, even if you don't have the slightest understanding of accounting, finance or employee benefits.

Whatever your purpose for researching corporate employers, you'll find this book to be an indispensable guide. Nonetheless, as is true with all resources, this volume has limitations that the reader should be aware of:

- Financial data and other corporate information can change quickly. A book of this type can be no more current than the data that was available as of the time of editing. Consequently, the financial picture, management and ownership of the firm(s) you are studying may have changed since the publishing date of this book. For example, this almanac includes the most up-to-date sales figures and profits available to the editors as of early 2012. That means that we have typically used corporate financial data as of mid-2011.

- Corporate mergers, changes in corporate financial ratings or stability, acquisitions and downsizing are occurring at a very rapid rate. Such events may have created significant change, subsequent to the publishing of this book, within a company you are studying.

- Some of the companies in THE MID-SIZE EMPLOYERS 500 are so large in scope and in variety of business endeavors conducted within a parent organization that we have been unable to completely list all subsidiaries, affiliations, divisions and activities within a firm's corporate structure.

- This volume is intended to be a general guide to major employers in numerous industries. That means that researchers should look to this book for an overview and, when conducting in-depth research, should contact the specific corporations and related industry associations in question for the very latest changes and data. Where possible, we have listed contact names, toll-free telephone numbers and Internet site addresses for the companies, government agencies and industry associations involved so that the reader may get further details without unnecessary delay.

- We have used exhaustive efforts to locate and fairly present accurate and complete data. However, when using this book or any other source for business and industry information, the reader should use caution and due diligence by conducting further research where it seems appropriate. We wish you success in your endeavors, and we trust that your experience with this book will be both satisfactory and productive.

- To obtain the best results and to best understand the fields in the company profiles, you should first read the chapter titled "How to Use This Book."

Good luck in your job search. Be patient, do your research and use this book as an important start in the right direction.

Jack W. Plunkett
Houston, Texas
March 2012

HOW TO USE THIS BOOK

Dozens of excellent books already exist to help you choose a career, write a resume, apply for a job, dress for the office and so on. This is not the purpose of PLUNKETT'S COMPANION TO THE ALMANAC OF AMERICAN EMPLOYERS. Instead, this book's job is to help you sort through America's mid-size corporate employers to determine which may be the best for you, or to see how your current employer compares to others. Whether you are entering the job market and looking for your first position, or you are thinking about switching companies in mid-career to find more promising vistas, this book will be a valuable guide.

The two primary sections of the book are devoted first to general information for job seekers (trends analysis and advice on conducting employer research, along with resources and contacts) and then to the "Individual Data Listings" for THE MID-SIZE EMPLOYERS 500. If time permits, you should begin your research in the front chapters of this book. Also, you will find lengthy indexes in Chapter 5 and in the back of the book.

GENERAL INFORMATION FOR JOB SEEKERS

Chapter 1: Major Trends Affecting Job Seekers. This chapter presents an encapsulated view of the major trends in business and the economy that are creating rapid changes in the employment picture at mid-size corporations.

Chapter 2: Statistics. This chapter presents in-depth statistics on employment by education level, sex, race, unemployment rates, fastest-growing industries and more.

Chapter 3: Research–7 Keys for Job Seekers. This chapter provides a definitive list of items that job seekers should look for when conducting research into mid-size corporate employers.

Chapter 4: Important Contacts for Job Seekers. This chapter covers contacts for important government agencies, organizations, job banks, reference sources and more. Included are Internet sites and contact addresses for a wide variety of uses.

THE MID-SIZE EMPLOYERS 500

Chapter 5: THE MID-SIZE EMPLOYERS 500: Who They Are and How They Were Chosen.

The companies compared in this book were chosen from all industries, on a nationwide basis. They were individually chosen from the most successful U.S. employers, from approximately 100 to 2,500 employees in size, based on selected types of business and industry sectors. For a complete description, see Chapter 5.

Individual Data Listings:

Look at one of the companies in THE MID-SIZE EMPLOYERS 500's Individual Data Listings. You'll find the following information fields:

Company Name:

The company profiles are in alphabetical order by company name. If you don't find the company you are seeking, it may be a subsidiary or division of one of the firms covered in this book. Try looking it up in the Index by Subsidiaries, Brand Names and Selected Affiliations in the back of the book.

Industry Code:

Industry Group Code: An NAIC code used to group companies within like segments. (See Chapter 5 for a list of codes.)

Suggested Career Paths:

A grid arranged into six major career categories and several sub-categories. A "Y" indicates that the firm is suggested for certain types of employees, by job discipline.

Types of Business:

A listing of the primary types of business specialties conducted by the firm.

Brands/Divisions/Affiliations:

Major brand names, operating divisions or subsidiaries of the firm, as well as major corporate affiliations—such as another firm that owns a significant portion of the company's stock. A complete Index by Subsidiaries, Brand Names and Selected Affiliations is in the back of the book.

Contacts:

The names and titles up to 27 top officers of the company are listed, including human resources contacts.

Address:

The firm's full headquarters address, the headquarters telephone, plus toll-free and fax numbers where available. Also provided is the World Wide Web site address.

Financials:

Annual Sales (2011 or the latest fiscal year available to the editors, plus up to four previous years): These are stated in thousands of dollars (add three zeros if you want the full number). This figure represents consolidated worldwide sales from all operations. These numbers may be estimates.

Annual Profits (2011 or the latest fiscal year available to the editors, plus up to four previous years): These are stated in thousands of dollars (add three zeros if you want the full number). This figure represents consolidated, after-tax net profit from all operations. These numbers may be estimates.

Stock Ticker, International Exchange, Parent Company: When available, the unique stock market symbol used to identify this firm's common stock for trading and tracking purposes is indicated. Where appropriate, this field may contain "private" or "subsidiary" rather than a ticker symbol. If the firm is a subsidiary, its parent company is listed.

Total Number of Employees: The approximate total number of employees, worldwide, as of the end of 2011 (or the latest data available to the editors).

Apparent Salaries/Benefits:

(The following descriptions generally apply to U.S. employers only.)

A "Y" in appropriate fields indicates "Yes."

Due to wide variations in the manner in which corporations report benefits to the U.S. Government's regulatory bodies, not all plans will have been uncovered or correctly evaluated during our effort to research this data. Also, the availability to employees of such plans will vary according to the qualifications that employees must meet to become eligible. For example, some benefit plans may be available only to salaried workers—others only to employees who work more than 1,000 hours yearly. Benefits that are available to employees of the main or parent company may not be available to employees of the subsidiaries. In addition, employers frequently alter the nature and terms of plans offered.

NOTE: Generally, employees covered by wealth-building benefit plans do not *fully* own ("vest in") funds contributed on their behalf by the employer until as many as five years of service with that employer have passed. All pension plans are voluntary—that is, employers are not obligated to offer pensions.

Pension Plan: The firm offers a pension plan to qualified employees. In this case, in order for a "Y" to appear, the editors believe that the employer offers a defined benefit or cash balance pension plan (see discussions below). The type and generosity of these plans vary widely from firm to firm. Caution: Some employers refer to plans as "pension" or "retirement" plans when they are actually 401(k) savings plans that require a contribution by the employee.

- Defined Benefit Pension Plans: Pension plans that do not require a contribution from the employee are infrequently offered. However, a few companies, particularly larger employers in high-profit-margin industries, offer defined benefit pension plans where the employee is guaranteed to receive a set pension benefit upon retirement. The amount of the benefit is determined by the years of service with the company and the employee's salary during the later years of employment. The longer a person works for the employer, the higher the retirement benefit. These defined benefit plans are funded entirely by the employer. The benefits, up to a reasonable limit, are guaranteed by the Federal Government's Pension Benefit Guaranty Corporation. These plans are not portable—if you leave the company, you cannot transfer your benefits into a different plan. Instead, upon retirement you will receive the benefits that vested during your service with the company. If your employer offers a pension plan, it must give you a summary plan description within 90 days of the date you join the plan. You can also request a summary annual report of the plan, and once every 12 months you may request an individual benefit statement accounting of your interest in the plan.

- Defined Contribution Plans: These are quite different. They do not guarantee a certain amount of pension benefit. Instead, they set out circumstances under which the employer will make a contribution to a plan on your behalf. The most common example is the 401(k) savings plan. Pension benefits are not guaranteed under these plans.
- Cash Balance Pension Plans: These plans were recently invented. These are hybrid plans—part defined benefit and part defined contribution. Many employers have converted their older defined benefit plans into cash balance plans. The employer makes deposits (or credits a given amount of money) on the employee's behalf, usually based on a percentage of pay. Employee accounts grow based on a predetermined interest benchmark, such as the interest rate on Treasury Bonds. There are some advantages to these plans, particularly for younger workers: a) The benefits, up to a reasonable limit, are guaranteed by the Pension Benefit Guaranty Corporation. b) Benefits are portable—they can be moved to another plan when the employee changes companies. c) Younger workers and those who spend a shorter number of years with an employer may receive higher benefits than they would under a traditional defined benefit plan.

ESOP Stock Plan (Employees' Stock Ownership Plan): This type of plan is in wide use. Typically, the plan borrows money from a bank and uses those funds to purchase a large block of the corporation's stock. The corporation makes contributions to the plan over a period of time, and the stock purchase loan is eventually paid off. The value of the plan grows significantly as long as the market price of the stock holds up. Qualified employees are allocated a share of the plan based on their length of service and their level of salary. Under federal regulations, participants in ESOPs are allowed to diversify their account holdings in set percentages that rise as the employee ages and gains years of service with the company. In this manner, not all of the employee's assets are tied up in the employer's stock.

Savings Plan, 401(k): Under this type of plan, employees make a tax-deferred deposit into an account. In the best plans, the company makes annual matching donations to the employees' accounts, typically in some proportion to deposits made by the employees themselves. A good plan will match one-half of employee deposits of up to 6% of wages. For example, an employee earning $30,000 yearly might deposit $1,800 (6%) into the plan. The company will match one-half of the employee's deposit, or $900. The plan grows on a tax-deferred basis, similar to an IRA. A very generous plan will match 100% of employee deposits. However, some plans do not call for the employer to make a matching deposit at all. Other plans call for a matching contribution to be made at the discretion of the firm's board of directors. Actual terms of these plans vary widely from firm to firm. Generally, these savings plans allow employees to deposit as much as 15% of salary into the plan on a tax-deferred basis. However, the portion that the company uses to calculate its matching deposit is generally limited to a maximum of 6%. Employees should take care to diversify the holdings in their 401(k) accounts, and most people should seek professional guidance or investment management for their accounts.

Stock Purchase Plan: Qualified employees may purchase the company's common stock at a price below its market value under a specific plan. Typically, the employee is limited to investing a small percentage of wages in this plan. The discount may range from 5 to 15%. Some of these plans allow for deposits to be made through regular monthly payroll deductions. However, new accounting rules for corporations, along with other factors, are leading many companies to curtail these plans—dropping the discount allowed, cutting the maximum yearly stock purchase or otherwise making the plans less generous or appealing.

Profit Sharing: Qualified employees are awarded an annual amount equal to some portion of a company's profits. In a very generous plan, the pool of money awarded to employees would be 15% of profits. Typically, this money is deposited into a long-term retirement account. Caution: Some employers refer to plans as "profit sharing" when they are actually 401(k) savings plans. True profit sharing plans are rarely offered.

Highest Executive Salary: The highest executive salary paid, typically a 2011 amount (or the latest year available to the editors) and typically paid to the Chief Executive Officer.

Highest Executive Bonus: The apparent bonus, if any, paid to the above person.

Second Highest Executive Salary: The next-highest executive salary paid, typically a 2011 amount (or the latest year available to the editors) and typically paid to the President or Chief Operating Officer.

Second Highest Executive Bonus: The apparent bonus, if any, paid to the above person.

Other Thoughts:

Apparent Women Officers or Directors: It is difficult to obtain this information on an exact basis, and employers generally do not disclose the data in a public way. However, we have indicated what our best efforts reveal to be the apparent number of women who either are in the posts of corporate officers or sit on the board of directors. There is a wide variance from company to company.

Hot Spot for Advancement for Women/Minorities: A "Y" in appropriate fields indicates "Yes." These are firms that appear either to have posted a substantial number of women and/or minorities to high posts or that appear to have a good record of going out of their way to recruit, train, promote and retain women or minorities. (See the Index of Hot Spots For Women and Minorities in the back of the book.) This information may change frequently and can be difficult to obtain and verify. Consequently, the reader should use caution and conduct further investigation where appropriate.

Growth Plans/ Special Features:

Listed here are observations regarding the firm's strategy, hiring plans, plans for growth and product development, along with general information regarding a company's business and prospects.

Locations:

A "Y" in the appropriate field indicates "Yes." Primary locations outside of the headquarters, categorized by regions of the United States and by international locations. A complete index by locations is also in the front of this chapter.

Chapter 1

MAJOR TRENDS AFFECTING JOB SEEKERS

Major trends sweeping through business and the economy that affect job seekers of all types:

1) U.S. Job Market Overview
2) Cost Control is a Major Concern at Employers/ Downsizing and Consolidation Through Mergers Continue
3) Unemployment Will Remain High, But Opportunities are Available to Diligent Job Seekers
4) Consumers Spend Less, Save More, Affecting a Wide Variety of Companies
5) Technology Continues to Create Sweeping Changes in the Workplace
6) Continued Growth in Outsourcing, Including Supply Chain and Logistics Services
7) Millions Working as Temps
8) Offshoring and the Globalization of Business
9) Older Americans Will Delay Retirement and Work Longer/Many Employers Find Older Employees Desirable
10) Employment Sectors that Will Offer an Above-Average Number of Job Opportunities in 2012:

- Biotechnology
- Consulting
- Consumer Products
- Cosmetics
- Cruise Lines
- Data Processing Services
- Elder Care, Home Health Care, Nursing Homes and Assisted Living Communities
- Electronic Games, Games for Cell Phones
- Energy Conservation Products and Services
- Food Processing
- Health Care Services
- Health Care Products
- Health Care Technology, Including Computerized Patient Records
- Health Foods, Organic Foods, Enhanced Foods
- Hotels
- Insurance
- Internet Services, Server Hosting, Cloud Computing
- Nanotechnology and MEMS Technologies
- Oil & Gas Exploration and Production
- Oil & Gas Field Services and Technologies
- Online Search Services with Advertising Revenues
- Online-based Business and Consumer Services including Social Media and Software-as-a-Service
- Outsourcing, Including Outsourced Business and Computer Services
- Pharmaceuticals—Generics
- Radio Frequency ID Tags (RFID)
- Restaurants
- Retailing—Basic, Including Drugstores and Supermarkets
- Retailing—Discount and Warehouse Clubs
- Software—Corporate
- Software—Predictive Analytics
- Supply Chain Services That Create Cost-Savings
- Water Filtration and Conservation Equipment
- Wireless and Cellular Communications
- Wireless—Remote Wireless Sensors and Networks

1) U.S. Job Market Overview

Job seekers in 2012 will continue to face a difficult job market, although a higher level of hiring may begin if the economy is stable. Many types of employers restructured and downsized thanks to the deep financial crisis of 2007-09. By 2011, most employers had pushed productivity about as far as they can, and future growth in business will require more employees. That brings up a big question: when, how and where will businesses begin to grow again? Meanwhile, job seekers who want good positions will be forced to be better prepared and to do better research than in the boom years that ended in 2007. They will also have to work harder to find good jobs. The fact remains that there are millions of Americans either out of work or underemployed. Competition for job openings will remain fierce. For example, Southwest Airlines reported that it received 143,143 resumes during 2010 while hiring only 2,188 new employees.

Job seekers in 2012 should be prepared for the fact that nearly all industry sectors suffered ill effects from economic and financial market problems that originated when the housing bubble finally popped in mid-2007 and the financial meltdown accelerated in 2008 and early 2009. America's unemployment level will remain disturbingly high for some time to come.

The good news is that a select set of employers and growth companies will offer good job opportunities. In this period of challenges, a few companies will enjoy booming business. Sectors such as cloud computing and health care will continue to grow and hire. A few companies with exciting new technologies or cost-saving services will see terrific growth. Salesforce.com, a highly innovative provider of online business services, is a good example.

Solid companies that do a terrific job of providing the day-to-day needs of consumers and business will continue to hire—Costco, Amazon.com and Southwest Airlines are good examples. Other industry sectors that fall into this category include insurance firms such as USAA and GEICO along with electric and gas utilities.

Oil and gas exploration and production will continue to be a bright spot for hiring, even if oil prices decline somewhat. Oil field services firm Halliburton recently announced plans to hire 11,000 people, largely to work in America's rapidly expanding shale oil and gas fields. The development of vast new shale oil and shale gas areas in dozens of states is opening up excellent job opportunities, fueling growth at providers of related services and supplies, and encouraging business investment of many kinds. At the same time, this new supply of oil and gas is holding down market prices, providing relief to consumers' budgets.

Other firms will hire only limited numbers of employees, while some will downsize. Many companies that specialize in the manufacture or sale of luxury items have learned to adapt to two big changes. First, many companies have changed their strategies in order to offer a range of products with luxury features that include items with lower price points. Next, companies like Tiffany and Coach have successfully increased their sales of luxury items in emerging markets such as China.

Growing numbers of consumers will prefer to buy from firms that sell goods and services online, offering savings of time, money and car travel. This boosts companies like Amazon.com that offer low prices combined with deep selections and great customer service. Virtually all major retailers, including giants like Wal-Mart and Home Depot, are working hard to provide better online services and choices to their customers.

The travel industry has stabilized to a large degree. Airlines are in better financial shape than they were two and three years ago. Hotels are enjoying higher occupancy rates. Travel firms that do best will be those that have everyday low prices, like JetBlue, along with those that offer all-inclusive prices that seem like bargains, such as popular cruise lines such as Carnival. In fact, the cruise industry did quite well through the recession, and it is likely to create many jobs over the near future as a large number of new ships continue to enter the fleet. Meanwhile, travel has become the single most successful sector at selling products and services via the Internet.

The automobile sector has stabilized, but it now operates at much lower volume than it enjoyed during the boom. New cars have been selling relatively well in recent months, and hiring may be strong at car dealers and car manufacturers alike.

Residential real estate remains very depressed. Homeowners may make repairs or do light remodeling rather than move up to larger homes. The massive number of unsold homes on the market will continue to put a serious damper on the real estate and construction sectors in 2012.

Banking companies will continue to be challenged, and some, like Bank of America, will have lay offs.

Americans who find themselves in the market for a job will need to understand the changes surging through the economy in order to determine which companies to pursue and which to avoid. The U.S. employment market has evolved dramatically, and job seekers must be both knowledgeable and nimble in order to position themselves to find promising careers.

In order to create a robust job market, corporate investment, profits, productivity and revenues must align themselves correctly. These economic indicators were positive during the 2003 to mid-2007 period, and millions of new American jobs were created. As 2007 was winding down, the residential real estate crash, high levels of consumer debt and difficult credit markets were combining to restrain the economy. Millions of workers were laid off, and hiring slowed to a trickle. Unfortunately, 2008-2009 saw these problems spread throughout most U.S. business sectors. The banking, investment, retailing and automobile sectors were under extreme stress, and many major bankruptcies ensued.

One of the results of this tough recession was a new emphasis on increased productivity and cost-effectiveness at employers of most types. Direct results included reduced spending, investment and hiring, and in many cases layoffs.

In 2012, executives will be under the usual pressure to maintain profitability. If the economy begins to improve, they may also start to see some signs of potential growth in selected business sectors, which would encourage hiring. However, better economic conditions may not appear any time soon. Meanwhile, many major corporations are sitting on huge piles of cash. When CEOs become more confident about the future, that cash could fuel job-creating investments. The bottom line: new grads will find it difficult to land their dream jobs, and job seekers of many types will continue to be challenged to find appropriate positions. Nonetheless, there will still be job opportunities for those who are diligent in seeking good employers in stronger business sectors.

Economic Factors Affecting the Job Market

Business Productivity: Productivity has been rising in recent years. That is, business can be produced—whether it is goods or services—by utilizing fewer workers than before. This will be extremely beneficial to the U.S. economy in the long run, but it can hurt the job market over the short term. Productivity is boosted by new technologies, improved management methods and other factors, sometimes as simple as reorganizing the staff and redesigning the workflow to increase output. It can also receive a quick boost from restrained corporate hiring. If rising productivity occurs along with rapidly rising sales and profits, then the job market will improve.

Corporate Sales: A trend of rising sales encourages hiring. The rapid drop in sales at businesses of nearly all types in 2008-2009 caused employers to slash head count. During 2010-2011, the trend was toward somewhat higher sales in most sectors. Reasonable sales growth in 2012 could lead to slightly increased hiring. It remains to be seen whether this will occur.

Corporate Profits: When profits increase sharply, companies are inclined to increase both business investment and hiring. Profitability took a deep downturn in 2008. Many employers were able to post reasonable profits during 2009, but this was generally the result of deep cuts in spending and hiring. The job market suffered as a result. Growth in profits was exceptionally high during 2010 and much of 2011. However, this profitability was often the result of improved business overseas, restrained spending, or both. Hiring will rebound when corporate sales, and accompanying profits, show significant growth, encouraging executives to forecast an extended period of increased demand for their products and services.

In order to compete effectively in today's job market, one of the most important things you can do is arm yourself with knowledge. It is vital for the job seeker to use the best reference tools possible in order to seek out employers that offer a reasonable balance of financial stability, opportunities for advancement and good pay. Excellent job opportunities always exist if you know where to look. Many of America's most successful firms currently need large numbers of new employees.

Thousands of companies, in technical and non-technical sectors, will need large numbers of new hires. In particular, companies that offer products or services that save time and/or money will prosper—for example, many types of companies that offer services that help businesses operate more efficiently, will be hiring. Meanwhile, large companies that are not increasing their overall numbers of employees will be hiring on a regular basis due to normal attrition—that is, the loss of employees due to retirement, relocation or other personal circumstances. For example, massive companies like Walgreen's or Kroger typically need to hire tens of thousands of workers yearly due to normal attrition.

2) Cost Control is a Major Concern at Employers/Downsizing and Consolidation Through Mergers Continue

For most firms during the current, difficult economic environment, executives have been focusing on cost control as a means to maintain profits and financial stability. Throughout the world of business and industry, expenses of virtually all types have been the focus of cuts or better management, from travel budgets to advertising to investments in equipment. Employee costs have been targeted as well. This means that hiring has been restrained at best, since the economic crisis began in late 2007, while many companies have announced big layoffs. Others have cut work hours or even cut pay rates.

Often, companies have merged with others in order to seek operating efficiencies or gain access to needed capital. By 2010, financing was once again available for large corporate mergers and acquisitions, and the number of mergers announced during 2011 was high. This may continue into 2012. A consolidation of companies via a merger may enable the firms to combine customer bases, administrative staff, sales offices and production facilities, while cutting employees who hold duplicated jobs, in hopes of thereby creating more efficient, more profitable firms. These employee reductions often number in the thousands. Mergers may be spurred by economic difficulties and falling profits, or they may involve large firms seeking to acquire companies that have the potential to boost growth and accelerate profits. For example, extreme duress in the home construction market in 2007-2009 instigated the merger of two massive construction firms, Centex and Pulte. On the other hand, prosperous software giant Oracle has been on a buying spree, acquiring companies that it feels will boost Oracle's own growth.

Because they face tough, global competition, manufacturing firms are frequently involved in such mergers. Good jobs in the U.S. manufacturing sector can still be found, despite intense competition from manufacturers in China and other offshore markets. Factories are running with fewer people thanks to immense investments in technology. Output per employee is up spectacularly over the past few decades—to the extent that millions of manufacturing jobs were lost due to a in productivity. In addition, fewer employees are needed to manage non-production functions, such as logistics, administration and marketing. Of course, some American manufacturing industries have been in deep, long term decline, particularly the automobile and textile industries.

Meanwhile, some of the loss in manufacturing employment has been exaggerated by the fact that firms now outsource a good deal of their non-manufacturing operations to services companies. For example, many computer departments, company cafeterias, distribution centers and engineering needs are now outsourced to outside companies that specialize in such work, thus dramatically reducing the number of in-house jobs at manufacturing firms. This is the long term trend of outsourcing in action.

Another extremely important factor in the loss of U.S. manufacturing jobs is the movement of production to foreign nations where costs are often much lower.

Also, companies in both manufacturing and service sectors have caught on to management by teams, vastly enhanced supply chain technology (such as the use of the Internet for ordering and tracking components), along with networked management, distribution and manufacturing systems, which all add up to the fact that fewer mid-management, white-collar types are needed to communicate with the people doing the day-to-day work. Production workers have been encouraged to communicate among themselves. In many cases, workers are taking on unprecedented responsibilities, setting their own goals and schedules, tracking costs and output, thereby boosting profits. Historically, these were the tasks of middle managers. Today, vast numbers of those management jobs have been eliminated.

Businesses without factories are also undergoing re-engineering and leaps in productivity. For example, by upgrading software and linking desktop computers to central databases, a major U.S. insurance firm was able to go from 3,000 employees issuing new policies to only 700. At the same time, it was able to reduce the time necessary to write a new policy from 15 days to only five. Customers applying for insurance policies today are likely to do so online, thus automating the process and reducing the need for employees. Today's corporations are searching hard for innovative ways to get more work done with fewer people. Using online methods is a foundation of this trend.

3) Unemployment Will Remain High, But Opportunities Are Available to Diligent Job Seekers

If you are looking for a job, you might as well face the fact that 2012's employment market will be challenging. Employers will be cautious about hiring new people or investing in new facilities until a reasonable level of confidence in the future emerges.

The U.S. unemployment rate in August 2007 was down to 4.6%. By August 2008, the unemployment rate shot up to 6.1%, and it reached 7.6% in early 2009. By the end of 2009, unemployment had soared to 10%, and 8 million jobs were eliminated during the Great Recession. The job market will take years to recover fully. Nonetheless, many job seekers will be able to find satisfying jobs if they apply themselves to the job hunt, make sure their resumes and self-marketing skills are in superb shape, network effectively and do thorough research. The number of people applying for each job opening is very high. Consequently, it is vital for a job seeker to understand how to best apply for a job online, how to conduct research that will help him or her to shine during an interview and how to create an effective list of prospective employers.

It is also important for job seekers to face the fact that locale has a lot to do with the unemployment rate. Today's dim real estate market exaggerates that factor. That is, one of the reasons that unemployment is so high is that the currently dismal market for homes makes it much more difficult for a job seeker to sell a house in one city in order to relocate to another city for a new job. Meanwhile, there is wide variance in the unemployment rate from state to state and city to city. For example, in August 2011, America's national average unemployment rate was 9.1%. However, it was dramatically higher in many states, including two that were among the hardest hit by the real estate collapse: Florida at 10.7% unemployment and California at 12.1%. Meanwhile, some states have vastly lower unemployment rates, including Nebraska at 4.2%, South Dakota at 4.7% and Louisiana at 7.2%. Job seekers living in states with the lowest unemployment rates are going to face much less competition when applying for job openings.

Internet Research Tip:
The latest rankings of states by unemployment rate can be found at the Bureau of Labor Statistics, www.bls.gov.

4) Consumers Spend Less, Save More, Affecting a Wide Variety of Companies

After piling on debt, running up their credit cards, signing mountains of mortgages and buying new cars at a soaring rate from 2002 through 2007, consumers have completely reversed course. Personal savings rates are much higher. Consumer debt has declined. House sales are dismal, and millions of people continue to face foreclosure on home mortgages. Saving money is in; spending money is out. Welcome to a new era of reduced personal circumstances, increased frugality and worried consumers. Even people with high, steady incomes are spending less. The financial crisis, high levels of consumer debt, high unemployment rates and uncertainty have put the brakes on conspicuous consumption.

While increased personal savings and lower debt levels will be very good for America over the long run, it is a difficult adjustment for the nation to make, and, for the near term at least, it puts a damper on the job market.

These changes have been tough on manufacturers, distributors, personal services providers, transportation companies and retailers alike. In sum, this means that many employers have not only been unable to hire new people, they have cut both work hours and total staff counts.

Smart job seekers will be aware that today's frugal consumer is not a short-term change. It is going to take years for consumers to pay down debts and rebuild personal savings. Hopefully, the housing market will be stabilizing during this period. The end result should be a new era of economic growth, but it will be a lengthy recovery in the meantime. The most successful employers will be those that provide lasting value, low prices, good service, cost-saving strategies and innovative technologies. Excellent examples are Wal-Mart (low prices), Costco (good service and low prices), Amazon (innovative use of technology to provide convenience and cost-savings), travel firms like JetBlue and Carnival Cruise Lines (good service, low prices, high value) and car makers like Honda, Kia and Hundai (lasting value, low prices).

5) Technology Continues to Create Sweeping Changes in the Workplace

Technology has introduced vast changes throughout industries of all types, greatly boosting productivity and reallocating (or eliminating) workers. A major cause of change for employees, and therefore job seekers, is the tidal wave of new technologies that continues to revolutionize the workplace at all levels. Prospering companies are using new technologies to communicate with customers, automate back-office tasks and industrial operations, and push ahead with research and development. There is a never-ending stream of technological innovation. For example, employers have already harnessed the power of networked desktop computers. Today, they are rapidly adopting the use of mobile computing devices such as tablets, Internet-based telephone systems (VOIP and unified communication systems), cloud computing and video conferencing technologies.

The trend of using new practices and technologies while cutting layers of management is largely about communication. This is true whether it is communication between the top offices and the factory floor, communication with customers, communication between the computers in one corporate office with those in another, or communication from desk-to-desk and office-to-office in massive service businesses.

These new technologies mean continuous retraining for much of the workforce. Job seekers who want the best posts must have the training and skills that will let them utilize new technologies effectively. Even in today's era of high unemployment, hundreds of thousands of jobs are remaining unfilled at many companies because of a shortage of technically qualified people. Workforce development is a critical need nationwide.

Jobs in America are shifting to new categories of work based on technologies that didn't exist 20 and 30 years ago. For example, the job title "webmaster" was coined in the 1990s to describe the employee in charge of a firm's Internet sites and intranet operations. Services firms, as well as manufacturers, are placing more and more employees in recently created technical and service positions, while many of the tasks once performed in-house are now provided by outsourced services providers. In the telecommunications industry, digital technology has completely changed the list of job titles while enabling phone service providers to reduce the ratio of employees to customers. In the meantime, hundreds of thousands of jobs have been created at cellular telephone companies. Now, Internet-based telephony, competition from cable providers, fiber to the premises and wireless networks such as Wi-Fi and LTE continue to force telecommunications firms to evolve.

Another excellent example: Retailing, shipping and warehousing are about to see a technology revolution due to the introduction of Radio Frequency Identification Tags (RFID). This breakthrough in inventory management is based on the placement of microchips in product packaging, combined with the use of special sensors in stores and warehouses that alert a central inventory management system of product purchases and the need to restock inventory. From loading docks to shelves to cash registers to parking lots, radio frequency readers will eventually track the movement of each pallet or individual item. Many bar codes will eventually be replaced by RFIDs, with electronic product codes stored on these microchips. The chips can even eliminate the need to scan each item at checkout. Checkout stations will be equipped with readers that automatically calculate purchases. Benefits can include less shoplifting and few inventory errors. Another benefit is that firms will be able to reduce overall inventory thanks to better tracking.

As online ordering, tracking and inventory management continue to become more sophisticated and cost-effective, purchasing executives at firms of all types and sizes will accelerate the use of Internet-based systems for management of their supply chains. There are significant opportunities here for e-commerce services and software companies. Likewise, there is great promise for third-party logistics (3PL) companies that combine the power of Internet-based information with strategically located warehouses to fulfill the inventory needs of manufacturers.

6) Continued Growth in Outsourcing, Including Supply Chain and Logistics Services

Part of the re-engineering process at employers has been a boom in "outsourcing," or the use of outside specialty firms to do chores that firms formerly performed through in-house departments. For example, Pitney Bowes takes over the mailrooms, desktop printers and copiers at major corporations. As part of this turnkey service, Pitney

Bowes supplies its own copiers and desktop printers, and then buys toner and paper by the truckload at the best possible price. It trains its employees to keep track of every single copy so its clients can control costs. Copy department employees are transferred from the client firm to Pitney Bowes, the outsourcing firm. There, these employees learn that the head of a Pitney Bowes' copy department can rise to be a regional manager, a vice president or an even higher position within the company. The client firm's costs are lowered and its profits increase. The outsourcing provider makes a tidy profit through its focused expertise. Xerox offers similar services, to the extent that providing services, instead of selling copiers, is now the major part of this firm's business.

One of the largest fields of outsourcing growth has long been in computer departments. IBM, Accenture and Hewlett-Packard (HP) are among the global leaders in this area. However, many other business functions are commonly outsourced. ServiceMaster takes over janitorial tasks, building management and maintenance functions for giant corporate office campuses and industrial facilities. Another company outsources all of the food warehousing and distribution for nationwide restaurant chains. Why? Because it can run trucks and warehouses more efficiently while its clients concentrate on running restaurants.

While the 1960s, '70s and '80s saw many firms frantically trying to do all tasks in-house, recent trends are quite different. As a period noted for rising productivity and efficiency, the 1990s and 2000s combined were an era of specialization and focus. Companies may do a better job by focusing on their core tasks, while allowing outside firms to provide support and maintenance needs. That trend will continue to be powerful over the long term. Outsourcing, which rapidly gained popularity, will persist in leading the way to higher efficiency and profits. Many outsourced services companies continue to grow, and they will create (and displace) large numbers of jobs.

Some companies combine outsourcing services with temporary workers. Spherion, a major temporary help firm and one of America's largest employers, is also a leading outsourcing company. Spherion's outsourcing division takes over all human resources administration functions for large clients. This means that Spherion's employees do all of the recruiting, employee records management, benefits management and so on for its client companies. This is a logical extension of Spherion's human resources expertise and good cross-marketing to its roster of corporate clients.

One of the fastest-growing fields in outsourcing has been supply chain and logistics management. Companies offering services in this field include giant transportation companies like UPS. "Supply chain" refers to the entire set of providers of supplies and services that are involved in creating and delivering a component or end product. For example, for an automobile manufacturer like Ford, the supply chain includes companies that make tires, batteries, interior components and engine parts, as well as the trucks and trains that ship these parts and the warehouses that hold them. This supply chain supports Ford's own manufacturing and assembly plants. At the end of Ford's business chain lie the automobile dealers that receive completed cars and deliver them to the end customers. Another example: For a clothing store chain like The Gap, the supply chain includes clothing designers, clothing manufacturers and the warehouses and transportation systems that deliver completed clothes to the stores. The Gap's supply chain is located across dozens of nations.

Logistics is the art of moving goods through the supply chain. Supply chains are so complex and so critical to a company's operations that there are countless ways to automate, improve efficiencies and cut costs. Many manufacturers and retailers are outsourcing all or part of their logistics needs to firms that specialize in creating efficiencies and saving costs. Logistics and supply chain companies have been growing rapidly over the past several years, and creating large numbers of jobs. A concept you should be familiar with is Third Party Logistics ("3PL"), a system whereby a specialist firm in logistics provides a variety of transportation, warehousing and logistics-related services to its clients. These tasks were previously performed in-house by the client. When 3PL services are provided within the client's own facilities, it can also be referred to as "Insourcing." In other words, you might find yourself working for UPS at a site within a distribution company that has no other ties to UPS.

7) Millions Working as Temps

More and more, major firms are using temporary workers to fill short-term needs, thereby cutting overall employment costs, since temps usually do not receive extensive benefits, bonuses or training. In addition to employees who are placed in temporary jobs by agencies, there are millions of people employed as "independent contractors" and "contract workers." Temporary staffing companies operate offices throughout the U.S., in cities small and large. To a growing extent, they hire and place workers via their sophisticated Internet sites.

The largest temporary help agencies tend to have vast global operations. Adecco is a Swiss staffing firm with extensive operations in the U.S., Europe and elsewhere, employing hundreds of thousands of people. Manpower, based in the U.S., does a major part of its business in dozens of nations worldwide.

Demand for temporary workers slows dramatically during economic downturns. The use of temps enables employers to increase the workforce quickly when orders from customers increase, and reduce the workforce rapidly when sales decrease. Temporary workers are also an extremely efficient way to meet needs for one-time projects, fill the slots of permanent employees who are on leave and screen potential candidates for full-time positions by first hiring them on a temporary basis.

In addition, some Americans prefer to work as temporary employees, feeling that this gives them more flexibility in their working lives. Unfortunately, many other people who end up working in temporary positions would greatly prefer to be employed full-time. Many of these workers have significant experience as well as college degrees. A large percentage of temps work in professional specialties, such as law, finance, engineering or accounting. Also, the number of information technology temps has increased dramatically in the past several years.

> ***Internet Research Tip:***
> For data on the temporary staffing industry and the temporary workforce in the U.S., see the American Staffing Association (www.americanstaffing.net).

8) Offshoring and the Globalization of Business

Competition from workers in such nations as Mexico, Indonesia, Thailand, and, in particular, China, means that fewer pure manufacturing jobs will be available in the U.S., where pay is high and employee benefit costs are immense compared to those of competing nations. In fact, the costs of Social Security taxes, Medicare taxes, employer-sponsored health care, vacations, holidays, retirement plans and other benefits have risen so high (an amount typically equal to 38% to 45% of wages) that they provide considerable incentive for firms to hold down the number of employees working in U.S. locations. Instead, companies are utilizing workers in other nations. Depending on their experience and job title, a typical factory worker in China may earn only $300 monthly for long hours of hard work. These employees often receive dormitory-style housing and cafeteria meals as well. Otherwise, employee benefit costs are nominal.

While lower employee pay is a factor in some offshoring, proximity to growing foreign markets is another. Giant multinational companies ranging from IBM to Kraft to General Motors find that a vast portion of their business now lies overseas, often in the rapidly-growing, emerging nations that offer lower operating costs. Many of the world's largest companies find that they need to have local operations throughout much of the world.

"Offshoring" is the word used to describe the movement of jobs of all types away from industrialized nations, like America, to less developed countries, like India, the Philippines, Indonesia and China. For example, U.S. financial services companies are sending hundreds of thousands of jobs overseas to India and the Philippines, in such areas as call centers and financial analysis. Moving jobs to other nations poses serious job displacement problems in the U.S. (At the same time, there is a positive factor to the growth of these emerging economies: Increased exports of U.S. goods and services of all types are creating jobs and profits in America.)

Globalization has a profound effect on Americans—consumer prices become lower, while the U.S. job market changes considerably. Consumer goods are quite inexpensive due to the vast variety of items the U.S. imports from other nations, and prices for many categories of these goods have declined dramatically. Americans can purchase consumer electronics like DVD players and color televisions at extremely low prices, and the price of many types of apparel is much lower thanks to globalization. For example, over 90% of the shoes sold in America are manufactured in low cost nations, especially China.

More than ever before, the world is one vast marketplace. Globalization of business supply chains is a strong trend today and will grow even stronger in the future. Consider the rapid globalization of the automobile industry. The entire global automobile sector is dominated by only a handful of companies, including Toyota, GM, Ford, Daimler, Honda, Volkswagen and Nissan, as well as the increasingly successful Korean automakers Kia and Hyundai. Car manufacturers in China are growing more dominant as well. Car manufacturers commonly have engineering teams collaborating from offices in multiple nations, while parts and components may be imported from a wide variety of suppliers in various countries to undergo final assembly at home.

American companies in many industry sectors have been merging and consolidating on a global basis at a rapid clip. That consolidation will continue. One benefit is that U.S. firms can enter into foreign markets through international acquisitions.

Trade is not necessarily always stable. While global economies are undeniably linked, they do not march hand-in-hand. The nose-dive taken by many Asian economies in the late 1990s occurred during one of the biggest economic booms in U.S. history. The strength of America as a consumer market was a platform that helped to stabilize and regenerate Asian businesses that were having difficulties. Likewise, China's economic stimulus during the economic crisis of 2007-2009 helped to boost business in many nations that were undergoing difficult national recessions.

U.S. firms hold leadership positions in several key product and service sectors vital to the rest of the world, including health technology, computers, e-commerce, software and entertainment of all types. The message is clear: global trade and export markets are extremely vital to the health of American business and industry. A study of 2006 results showed that U.S. corporations listed in the Standard & Poor's 500 created, on average, 49% of their revenues from foreign nations, up from 30% in 2001.

A growing middle class in India, China and other emerging nations has been creating demand for goods exported from the U.S., including consumer products bearing desirable brands, as well as luxury automobiles. Also, U.S.-based firms have been enjoying great success in franchising and licensing their methods to startup businesses in China, India and elsewhere, in everything from hotels to fast food to services. American brands such as Nike and Buick are big sellers in China.

Meanwhile, the U.S. is also exporting its newfound expertise in the booming superstore and discount retailing sectors. For instance, hundreds of Wal-Mart's stores are in foreign locations such as Argentina, Brazil, Canada, China,

Korea, Mexico, and the U.K., and Wal-Mart is entering India in a big way through a joint venture. Eventually, Wal-Mart may bring its brand of retailing to virtually all of the world's major markets.

9) Older Americans Will Delay Retirement and Work Longer/Many Employers Find Older Employees Desirable

Certain large employers, particularly national retail chains, have discovered that older workers provide a terrific pool of potential employees. This may be positive for older workers, but to younger job seekers it means more competition for work.

While 2006 marked the year that the first Baby Boomers turned 60, many members of this immense generation are not planning to retire any time soon. The job market has been made more difficult by the fact that many of America's workers who want to retire will be reluctant (or unable) to do so, because the value of their investments in real estate, stocks, bonds or pension plans is down considerably from the levels they saw during the last boom, and these older workers lost confidence in financial markets at the same time that they lost retirement dollars. Some would-be retirees will be working much later in life than they had planned. This trend is also accelerated by the fact that today's senior citizens will enjoy much longer life spans than earlier generations. Many will continue to work simply because they want to remain active, contributing members of society.

The phrase "Baby Boomer" generally refers to the 78 million Americans born from 1946 to 1964. The term evolved to describe the children of soldiers and war industry workers who were involved in World War II. When those veterans and workers returned to civilian life, they started or added to families in large numbers. As a result, this generation is one of the largest demographic segments in the U.S. Baby Boomers make up about 24% of the U.S. population.

Most recently, 2011 marked the year when millions began turning traditional retirement age (65). As Baby Boomers continue to age, America will be experiencing extremely rapid growth in the senior portion of the population. Many Baby Boomers will leave their traditional, long-term jobs and turn to part-time work. Others will continue in their full-time jobs as long as possible.

A survey released in June 2009 by the AARP (a non profit group that represents Americans who are 50 and older) found that 20% of the group's members said they were likely to work until they were in their 70s. 40% of couples surveyed said that one or both spouses will work part-time in retirement. In the first part of 2008, a Bureau of Labor Statistics survey found that 30% of people between the ages of 65 and 69 were either employed or seeking work. This trend is powerful enough that AARP publishes an annual list of "Best Employers for Workers over 50." The 2011 list included several health care firms, including Scripps Health, Kaiser Permanente and West Virginia University Hospitals.

By the early 2000s, many employers were already developing human resources strategies aimed at hiring or retaining older workers. On the lower end of the pay scale, retailers like Home Depot, a firm that has been known to need tens of thousands of new hires in one year, have found older people to be ideal employees. They have knowledge that is extremely useful for providing advice and service to shoppers. They are experienced workers who understand the need to show up on time. Wal-Mart has hundreds of thousands of employees age 55 or older.

On the higher end of the employment scale, older workers with long-term experience in scientific and engineering tasks will be vital in keeping the gears of business and industry turning. During the 2000s boom, when the airline industry saw good growth, rules were altered in the U.S. to enable commercial airline pilots to keep flying until age 65, instead of facing forced retirement at age 60 as they had in the past. A serious shortage of experienced pilots was averted. (Granted, airlines soon went into a tailspin during the Great Recession, along with the rest of the travel industry, and they mothballed a lot of airplanes while cutting the number of routes and flights. Nonetheless, older, experienced pilots will eventually be in high demand.) Heavy industry is an even better example. The National Science Foundation estimated that 38% of America's scientists and engineers were 50+ years old as of 2006. These older workers may not be good at creating the latest electronic games, but they are undeniably the people who have the experience and the knowledge necessary to successfully operate the laboratories, factories, refineries and legacy systems that keep industry humming. They are going to be extremely difficult to replace in America, because younger generations have been shunning degrees in science and engineering for softer disciplines. Energy industry firms like ExxonMobil, Halliburton and Schlumberger, and chemicals firms like global giant BASF, are dealing with this challenge along two lines: First, how to document and pass along the immense treasure of work-related knowledge that these employees have, and second, how to keep these employees interested in working later into their lives. BASF, a firm with about $90 billion in annual revenues and an employee base of 90,000 scattered around the world, estimates that by 2020, 50% or more of its employees will be 50 to 65 years old. It has implemented measures ranging from making the workplace more comfortable and safe for older workers, to an intense knowledge transfer program where older workers mentor younger staff members.

10) Employment Sectors that Will Offer an Above-Average Number of Job Opportunities in 2012

Job seekers should remain aware of the fact that certain industries will have above-average likelihood to offer job openings. This is due to a number of circumstances, including shifts in consumer tastes and requirements, normal employee turnover and attrition, structural changes within industries, global economic conditions and national policies and priorities.

Below is a list of industries particularly recommended to job seekers.

Employment Sectors that Will Offer an Above-Average Number of Job Opportunities in 2012:

- Biotechnology
- Consulting
- Consumer Products
- Cosmetics
- Data Processing Services
- Elder Care, Home Health Care, Nursing Homes and Assisted Living Communities
- Electronic Games, Games for Cell Phones
- Energy Conservation Products and Services
- Food Processing
- Health Care Services
- Health Care Products
- Health Care Technology, Including Computerized Patient Records
- Health Foods, Organic Foods, Enhanced Foods
- Hotels
- Insurance
- Internet Services, Server Hosting, Cloud Computing
- Nanotechnology and MEMS Technologies
- Oil & Gas Exploration and Production
- Oil & Gas Field Services and Technologies
- Online Search Services with Advertising Revenues
- Online-based Business and Consumer Services including Social Media and Software-as-a-Service
- Outsourcing, Including Outsourced Business and Computer Services
- Pharmaceuticals—Generics
- Radio Frequency ID Tags (RFID)
- Restaurants
- Retailing—Basic, Including Drugstores and Supermarkets
- Retailing—Discount and Warehouse Clubs
- Software—Corporate
- Software—Predictive Analytics
- Supply Chain Services That Create Cost-Savings
- Water Filtration and Conservation Equipment
- Wireless and Cellular Communications
- Wireless—Remote Wireless Sensors and Networks

Chapter 2

STATISTICS

Contents:

U.S. Employment Overview: 2011-2012

(Labor Counts In Thousands; Seasonally Adjusted)

	Jan-11	Nov-11	Jan-12
Civilian Labor Force, Total	153,250	153,937	154,395
Employed	139,330	140,614	141,637
Unemployed	13,919	13,323	12,758
Persons 16 Years of Age and Over, Not in Labor Force	85,454	86,503	87,874
Unemployment Rate, All Workers	9.1%	8.7%	8.3%
Adult Men (20 years and over)	8.9%	8.3%	7.7%
Adult Women (20 years and over)	7.9%	7.8%	7.7%
Teenagers (16 to 19 years)	25.4%	23.7%	23.2%
White	8.1%	7.6%	7.4%
Black or African American	15.7%	15.5%	13.6%
Asian (not seasonally adjusted)	6.9%	6.5%	6.7%
Hispanic or Latino	12.0%	11.4%	10.5%
Average Hourly Earnings, Private Industry[P]	$22.86	$23.23	$23.29
Weekly Earnings, Private Industry[P]	$784.10	$799.11	$803.51
Average Work Week, Private Industry (Hours)[P]	34.3	34.4	34.5
Nonfarm Employment[P]	130,456	131,963	132,409
Goods-Producing	17,821	18,114	18,266
Construction	5,456	5,520	5,572
Manufacturing	11,627	11,780	11,862
Private Service-Providing	90,386	91,845	92,170
Retail Trade	14,550	14,725	14,741
Professional & Business Services	17,055	17,521	17,654
Education & Health Services	19,696	20,046	20,110
Leisure & Hospitality	13,138	13,436	13,499
Government	22,249	22,004	21,973

P = Preliminary figures (for January 2012).

Source: U.S. Bureau of Labor Statistics
Plunkett Research, Ltd.
www.plunkettresearch.com

U.S. Civilian Labor Force: 1997-January 2012

(Persons 16 & Older; In Thousands)

Year	Civilian Workforce Level
1997	136,297
1998	137,673
1999	139,368
2000	142,583
2001	143,734
2002	144,863
2003	146,510
2004	147,401
2005	149,320
2006	151,428
2007	153,124
2008	154,287
2009	154,142
2010	153,889
2011	153,617
2012*	153,485

* As of January; not seasonally adjusted.

Source: U.S. Bureau of Labor Statistics
Plunkett Research, Ltd.
www.plunkettresearch.com

Number of People Employed and Unemployed, U.S.: January 2011 vs. January 2012

(Persons 16 & Older; In Thousands; Not Seasonally Adjusted)

Occupation	Employed		Unemployed		Unemp. Rates	
	Jan-11	Jan-12	Jan-11	Jan-12	Jan-11	Jan-12
Total*	**137,599**	**139,944**	**14,937**	**13,541**	**9.8**	**8.8**
Management, professional and related	51,866	53,152	2,557	2,410	4.7	4.3
Management, business and financial	21,139	22,255	1,177	1,044	5.3	4.5
Professional and related	30,727	30,897	1,380	1,366	4.3	4.2
Service	23,819	24,334	2,773	2,876	10.4	10.6
Sales and office	33,497	33,305	3,364	2,972	9.1	8.2
Sales and related	15,268	15,585	1,574	1,398	9.3	8.2
Office and administrative support	18,229	17,721	1,790	1,574	8.9	8.2
Natural resources, construction and maintenance	12,205	12,561	2,623	2,152	17.7	14.6
Farming, fishing and forestry	893	845	233	243	20.7	22.3
Construction and extraction	6,587	6,887	1,960	1,557	22.9	18.4
Installation, maintenance and repair	4,725	4,828	430	353	8.3	6.8
Production, transportation and material moving	16,211	16,592	2,411	2,016	12.9	10.8
Production	8,032	8,274	1,122	959	12.3	10.4
Transportation and material moving	8,180	8,318	1289	1,057	13.6	11.3

* Persons with no previous work experience and persons whose last job was in the Armed Forces are included in the unemployed total. Updated population controls are introduced annually with the release of January data.

Note: The labor force includes all persons classified as employed or unemployed. Employed persons include persons 16 years and older in the civilian noninstitutional population who, during a reference week, (a) did any work at all (at least 1 hour) as paid employees, worked in their own business, profession, or on their own farm, or worked 15 hours or more as unpaid workers in an enterprise operated by a member of the family, and (b) all those who were not working but who had jobs or businesses from which they were temporarily absent because of vacation, illness, bad weather, childcare problems, maternity or paternity leave, labor-management dispute, job training, or other family or personal reasons, whether or not they were paid for the time off or were seeking other jobs. Each employed person is counted only once, even if he or she holds more than one job. Excluded are persons whose only activity consisted of work around their own house (painting, repairing, or own home housework) or volunteer work for religious, charitable, and other organizations.

Unemployed persons include persons 16 years and older who had no employment during the reference week, were available for work, except for temporary illness, and had made specific efforts to find employment sometime during the 4-week period ending with the reference week. Persons who were waiting to be recalled to a job from which they had been laid off need not have been looking for work to be classified as unemployed.

Source: U.S. Bureau of Labor Statistics

Plunkett Research, Ltd.

www.plunkettresearch.com

Unemployed Jobseekers by Sex, Reason for Unemployment & Active Job Search Methods Used: 2010 Average

Sex and reason	*(Thousands of persons)*		Methods used as a percent of total jobseekers							Average number of methods used
	Total unem-ployed	Total job-seekers	Emp-loyer directly	Sent out resumes or filled out app-lications	Placed or ans-wered ads	Friends or relatives	Public employ-ment agency	Private employ-ment agency	Other	
Total, 16 years and over	**14,825**	**13,394**	**53.6**	**55.2**	**18.4**	**28.8**	**22.2**	**8.9**	**15.4**	**2.03**
Job losers and persons who completed temporary jobs*	9,250	7,819	55.6	54.1	20.5	32.5	26.3	10.7	16.4	2.17
Job leavers	889	889	53.1	58.0	18.6	25.1	20.7	8.3	14.9	2.00
Reentrants	3,466	3,466	50.0	55.9	15.6	23.5	17.0	6.4	14.9	1.84
New entrants	1,220	1,220	51.5	58.4	12.9	22.9	12.3	5.1	11.3	1.75
Men, 16 years and over	**8,626**	**7,638**	**54.9**	**52.7**	**18.1**	**30.4**	**23.0**	**9.0**	**15.7**	**2.04**
Job losers and persons who completed temporary jobs*	5,919	4,932	56.4	51.8	19.7	33.2	26.5	10.5	16.6	2.15
Job leavers	457	457	54.2	56.0	17.9	27.9	19.5	7.9	14.3	1.98
Reentrants	1,608	1,608	51.1	52.6	15.2	25.0	17.2	6.6	15.1	1.84
New entrants	641	641	52.7	57.9	13.4	23.9	12.3	4.7	11.0	1.76
Women, 16 years and over	**6,199**	**5,756**	**52.0**	**58.5**	**18.8**	**26.7**	**21.2**	**8.8**	**15.1**	**2.02**
Job losers and persons who completed temporary jobs*	3,331	2,888	54.3	57.9	21.9	31.2	25.8	11.0	16.1	2.19
Job leavers	432	432	52.0	60.2	19.3	22.2	21.9	8.7	15.7	2.01
Reentrants	1,858	1,858	49.1	58.7	15.8	22.1	16.8	6.2	14.6	1.84
New entrants	579	579	50.1	58.9	12.3	21.7	12.3	5.6	11.5	1.73

Note: Figures are 2010 annual averages, calculated using month-by-month survey data from January through December. The jobseekers total is less than the total unemployed because it does not include persons on temporary layoff. The percent using each met

* Data on the number of jobseekers and the jobsearch methods used exclude persons on temporary layoff.

Source: U.S. Bureau of Labor Statistics
Plunkett Research, Ltd.
www.plunkettresearch.com

U.S. Labor Force Ages 16 to 24 Years Old by School Enrollment, Educational Attainment, Sex, Race & Ethnicity: October 2010

(Numbers in Thousands, Latest Year Available)	Civilian non-institutional population	Total in Labor Force	Percent of Populace	Employed		Unemployed		Not in Labor Force
				Total	Percent of Populace	Number	Rate (%)	
Total, 16 to 24 years	37,616	20,764	55.2	16,945	45.0	3,820	18.4	16,851
Educational Attainment								
Enrolled in school	21,854	8,411	38.5	7,098	32.5	1,314	15.6	13,443
Enrolled in high school[1]	9,612	2,125	22.1	1,576	16.4	548	25.8	7,488
Men	4,965	1,055	21.3	760	15.3	295	28.0	3,910
Women	4,647	1,069	23.0	817	17.6	253	23.6	3,578
White	7,225	1,757	24.3	1,359	18.8	398	22.6	5,468
Black or African American	1,608	266	16.5	141	8.8	125	46.9	1,342
Asian	335	30	8.9	21	6.3	9	(2)	305
Hispanic or Latino ethnicity	1,805	314	17.4	187	10.4	127	40.4	1,491
Enrolled in college	12,242	6,287	51.4	5,521	45.1	766	12.2	5,955
Enrolled in 2-year college	3,512	2,129	60.6	1,772	50.4	358	16.8	1,383
Enrolled in 4-year college	8,729	4,158	47.6	3,750	43.0	408	9.8	4,571
Full-time students	10,680	4,967	46.5	4,331	40.6	635	12.8	5,713
Part-time students	1,562	1,320	84.5	1,190	76.2	130	9.9	242
Men	5,710	2,707	47.4	2,286	40.0	421	15.5	3,003
Women	6,531	3,579	54.8	3,235	49.5	345	9.6	2,952
White	9,461	5,145	54.4	4,569	48.3	576	11.2	4,316
Black or African American	1,630	680	41.7	562	34.5	119	17.4	949
Asian	777	254	32.8	229	29.5	25	9.9	522
Hispanic or Latino ethnicity	1,501	792	52.8	690	46.0	102	12.9	709
Not enrolled in school	15,762	12,353	78.4	9,847	62.5	2,506	20.3	3,409
16 to 19 years	3,134	2,067	65.9	1,357	43.3	710	34.4	1,068
20 to 24 years	12,627	10,286	81.5	8,491	67.2	1,796	17.5	2,341
Sex								
Men	8,274	6,937	83.8	5,341	64.6	1,596	23.0	1,337
Less than a high school diploma	1,731	1,267	73.2	864	49.9	403	31.8	464
High school graduates, no college[3]	3,870	3,193	82.5	2,400	62.0	793	24.8	677
Some college or associate degree	1,784	1,610	90.3	1,328	74.5	282	17.5	174
Bachelor's degree and higher[4]	890	867	97.4	749	84.1	118	13.6	23
Women	7,488	5,416	72.3	4,506	60.2	910	16.8	2,072
Less than a high school diploma	1,299	644	49.6	444	34.2	200	31.0	655
High school graduates, no college[3]	3,125	2,147	68.7	1,671	53.5	476	22.2	978
Some college or associate degree	1,894	1,539	81.2	1,374	72.6	164	10.7	356
Bachelor's degree and higher[4]	1,170	1,087	92.9	1,017	86.9	70	6.5	83
Race								
White	12,330	9,913	80.4	8,140	66.0	1,773	17.9	2,417
Black or African American	2,438	1,679	68.9	1,126	46.2	553	33.0	759
Asian	348	280	80.5	224	64.4	56	20.0	68
Hispanic or Latino ethnicity	3,503	2,631	75.1	2,023	57.7	608	23.1	872

Note: Detail for the above race groups do not sum to totals because data are not presented for all races. Persons whose ethnicity is identified as Hispanic or Latino may be of any race. Because of rounding, sums of individual items may not equal totals.

[1] Includes a small number of persons who are in grades below high school. [2] Data not shown where base is less than 75,000. [3] Includes persons with a high school diploma or equivalent. [4] Includes persons with bachelor's, master's, professional, and doctoral degrees.

Source: U.S. Bureau of Labor Statistics

Plunkett Research, Ltd.

www.plunkettresearch.com

Mean Hourly Earnings & Weekly Hours, Private Industry & State & Local Government: 2010

(By Worker & Establishment Characteristics, Latest Year Available)	Civilian		Private Industry		State & Local Gov't	
	Hourly Earnings[1]	Weekly Hours[2]	Hourly Earnings[1]	Weekly Hours[2]	Hourly Earnings[1]	Weekly Hours[2]
Total	**$21.29**	**35.1**	**$20.47**	**34.9**	**$26.08**	**36.2**
Worker Characteristics[3,4]						
Management, professional & related	34.49	36.7	34.99	37.0	33.02	35.9
Management, business & financial	38.81	39.3	39.42	39.7	35.32	37.4
Professional & related	32.55	35.6	32.57	35.7	32.50	35.6
Service	12.14	30.7	10.62	29.7	19.32	36.4
Sales & office	16.44	34.7	16.35	34.5	17.39	36.4
Sales & related	17.11	32.3	17.11	32.3	16.65	33.9
Office & administrative support	16.09	36.1	15.90	36.0	17.42	36.5
Natural resources, construction & maintenance	21.21	39.0	21.24	39.0	20.97	38.8
Construction & extraction	21.18	39.0	21.31	39.0	20.13	38.7
Installation, maintenance & repair	21.40	39.2	21.34	39.2	21.98	39.2
Production, transportation & material moving	16.00	37.1	15.88	37.2	19.52	34.4
Production	16.26	38.9	16.18	38.8	21.69	39.5
Transportation & material moving	15.73	35.4	15.55	35.6	18.86	33.1
Full time	22.77	39.5	22.01	39.6	26.75	38.9
Part time	12.10	20.7	11.78	21.0	16.39	18.3
Union	26.04	36.6	23.13	36.3	29.72	37.0
Nonunion	20.46	34.8	20.19	34.8	23.12	35.6
Time	21.06	34.9	20.16	34.7	26.07	36.2
Incentive	26.04	38.4	26.03	38.4	--	--
Establishment Characteristics						
Goods producing	--	(6)	22.04	39.4	--	(6)
Service Producing	--	(6)	20.09	34.0	--	(6)
1 to 49 workers	17.86	33.5	17.80	33.6	19.61	33.0
50 to 99 workers	19.24	34.3	19.10	34.2	21.40	35.8
100 to 499 workers	20.88	35.9	20.42	35.8	24.31	36.0
500 workers or more	27.02	36.9	26.65	37.0	27.68	36.7

Note: The survey covers all 50 states and the District of Columbia. Data were collected between December 2009 and January 2011. The average month of reference was July 2010. Dashes indicate that data did not meet publication criteria.

[1] Earnings are the straight-time hourly wages or salaries paid to employees. They include incentive pay, cost-of-living adjustments and hazard pay. Excluded are premium pay for overtime, vacations, holidays, nonproduction bonuses and tips. The mean is computed by totaling the pay of all workers and dividing by the number of workers, weighted by hours.

[2] Mean weekly hours are the hours an employee is scheduled to work in a week, exclusive of overtime.

[3] Employees are classified as working either a full-time or a part-time schedule based on the definition used by each establishment. Union workers are those whose wages are determined through collective bargaining. Wages of time workers are based solely on hourly rate or salary; incentive workers are those whose wages are at least partially based on productivity payments such as piece rates, commissions, and production bonuses.

[4] A classification system including about 800 individual occupations is used to cover all workers in the civilian economy.

[5] Estimates for goods-producing and service-providing industries are published for private industry only. Industries are determined by the 2007 North American Industry Classification System (NAICS).

[6] Estimates for goods-producing and service-providing industries are published for private industry only. The NCS uses the 2007 North American Industry Classification System (NAICS) to determine the industry of each sampled establishment.

Source: U.S. Bureau of Labor Statistics

Plunkett Research, Ltd. www.plunkettresearch.com

Medical Care Benefits in the U.S.: Access, Participation and Take-Up Rates, March 2011

(All workers = 100 percent)

Characteristics	Private Industry			State/Local Government		
	Access	Particip-ation	Take-up Rate[1]	Access	Particip-ation	Take-up Rate[1]
All workers	72%	54%	75%	87%	72%	83%
Worker Characteristics						
Management, professional and related	88%	68%	78%	89%	73%	82%
Service	48%	33%	70%	81%	68%	84%
Sales and office	72%	50%	70%	88%	75%	84%
Natural resources, construction and maintenance	77%	57%	80%	95%	82%	86%
Production, transportation and material moving	76%	59%	78%	82%	69%	84%
Full time	88%	67%	77%	99%	82%	83%
Part time	24%	14%	58%	26%	18%	69%
Union	93%	77%	82%	95%	78%	82%
Nonunion	69%	50%	73%	81%	67%	83%
Wage percentiles[2]						
Lowest 10 percent	22%	12%	56%	54%	43%	81%
Lowest 25 percent	39%	24%	62%	69%	57%	82%
Second 25 percent	77%	56%	73%	91%	77%	84%
Third 25 percent	87%	69%	79%	94%	79%	84%
Highest 25 percent	93%	74%	80%	97%	79%	81%
Highest 10 percent	94%	75%	79%	97%	79%	82%
Establishment Characteristics						
1 to 99 workers	57%	42%	73%	74%	63%	85%
1 to 49 workers	53%	38%	72%	67%	57%	85%
50 to 99 workers	69%	51%	74%	84%	72%	86%
100 workers or more	86%	66%	77%	89%	74%	82%
100 to 499 workers	82%	60%	74%	85%	71%	84%
500 workers or more	90%	71%	79%	91%	74%	82%

Note: For this table, a worker with access to medical care benefits is defined as having an employer-provided medical plan available for use, regardless of the worker's decision to enroll or participate in the plan. Farm and private household workers, the self-employed and Federal government workers are excluded from the survey.

[1] The take-up rate is a rounded estimate of the percentage of workers with access to a plan who participate in the plan.

[2] The percentile groupings are based on the average wage for each occupation surveyed, which may include workers both above and below the threshold. The percentile values are based on the estimates published in the "National Compensation Survey: Occupational Earnings in the United States, 2010."

Source: U.S. Bureau of Labor Statistics
Plunkett Research, Ltd.
www.plunkettresearch.com

Retirement Benefits in the U.S.: Access, Participation and Take-Up Rates, March 2011

(All workers = 100 percent)

Characteristics	Private Industry			State/Local Government		
	Access	Particip-ation	Take-up Rate[1]	Access	Particip-ation	Take-up Rate[1]
All workers	64	49	76	90	85	95
Worker Characteristics						
Management, professional and related	80	68	85	92	87	95
Service	40	22	56	84	79	95
Sales and office	69	52	76	90	86	95
Natural resources, construction and maintenance	62	49	79	94	90	96
Production, transportation and material moving	66	51	77	87	84	96
Full time	73	59	80	99	94	95
Part time	37	20	54	41	37	91
Union	90	83	93	97	92	95
Nonunion	61	45	74	84	79	95
Wage percentiles[2]						
Lowest 10 percent	28	10	35	60	56	94
Lowest 25 percent	39	19	50	74	70	94
Second 25 percent	66	48	73	94	89	95
Third 25 percent	74	61	83	95	91	96
Highest 25 percent	84	75	89	98	93	95
Highest 10 percent	87	79	90	97	92	94
Establishment Characteristics						
1 to 99 workers	49	34	69	78	75	96
1 to 49 workers	45	32	70	73	70	95
50 to 99 workers	62	41	66	87	84	97
100 workers or more	81	66	82	91	87	95
100 to 499 workers	77	59	76	87	84	96
500 workers or more	86	76	88	93	88	95

Note: Benefits may include defined benefit pension plans as well as defined contribution retirement plans. Workers are considered as having access or as participating if they have access to or participate in at least one of these plan types. Farm and private household workers, the self-employed and Federal government workers are excluded from the survey.

[1] The take-up rate is a rounded estimate of the percentage of workers with access to a plan who participate in the plan.

[2] The percentile groupings are based on the average wage for each occupation surveyed, which may include workers both above and below the threshold. The percentile values are based on the estimates published in the "National Compensation Survey: Occupational Earnings in the United States, 2010."

Source: U.S. Bureau of Labor Statistics

Plunkett Research, Ltd.

www.plunkettresearch.com

Top 30 U.S. Occupations by Numerical Change in Job Growth: 2010-2020

(By Thousands of Employees)

Occupation	Employment		Change		Training*
	2010	2020	Number	Percent	
Registered nurses	2,737	3,449	**712**	26.0	Associates's degee
Retail salespersons	4,262	4,968	**707**	16.6	Short-term on-the-job training
Home health aides	1,018	1,724	**706**	69.4	Short-term on-the-job training
Personal care aides	861	1,468	**607**	70.5	Short-term on-the-job training
Office clerks, general	2,951	3,440	**490**	16.6	Short-term on-the-job training
Combined food preparation and serving workers, including fast food	2,682	3,080	**398**	14.8	Short-term on-the-job training
Customer service representatives	2,187	2,526	**338**	15.5	Short-term on-the-job training
Heavy and tractor-trailer truck drivers	1,605	1,935	**330**	20.6	Short-term on-the-job training
Laborers and freight, stock, and material movers, hand	2,068	2,387	**319**	15.4	Short-term on-the-job training
Postsecondary teachers	1,756	2,062	**306**	17.4	Doctoral or professional degree
Nursing aides, orderlies, and attendants	1,505	1,807	**302**	20.1	Postsecondary non-degree award
Childcare workers	1,282	1,544	**262**	20.4	Short-term on-the-job training
Bookkeeping, accounting, and auditing clerks	1,898	2,157	**259**	13.6	Moderate-term on-the-job training
Cashiers	3,363	3,613	**250**	7.4	Short-term on-the-job training
Elementary school teachers, except special education	1,477	1,725	**249**	16.8	Bachelor's degree
Receptionists and information clerks	1,049	1,297	**249**	23.7	Short-term on-the-job training
Janitors and cleaners, except maids and housekeeping cleaners	2,310	2,557	**246**	10.7	Short-term on-the-job training
Landscaping and groundskeeping workers	1,152	1,392	**241**	20.9	Short-term on-the-job training
Sales representatives, wholesale and manufacturing, except technical and scientific products	1,430	1,653	**223**	15.6	Moderate-term on-the-job training
Construction laborers	999	1,211	**212**	21.3	Short-term on-the-job training
Medical secretaries	509	719	**210**	41.3	Moderate-term on-the-job training
First-line supervisors of office and administrative support workers	1,424	1,628	**203**	14.3	None
Carpenters	1,002	1,198	**196**	19.6	Apprenticeship
Waiters and waitresses	2,260	2,456	**196**	8.7	Short-term on-the-job training
Security guards	1,036	1,231	**195**	18.8	Short-term on-the-job training
Teacher assistants	1,288	1,479	**191**	14.8	Short-term on-the-job training
Accountants and auditors	1,217	1,408	**191**	15.7	Bachelor's degree
Licensed practical and licensed vocational nurses	752	921	**169**	22.4	Postsecondary non-degree award
Physicians and surgeons	691	859	**168**	24.4	Doctoral or professional degree
Medical assistants	528	690	**163**	30.9	Moderate-term on-the-job training

* An occupation is placed into 1 of 11 categories that best describes the postsecondary education or training needed by most workers to become fully qualified in that occupation. For more information about the categories, see Measures of Education and Training, on the Internet at www.bls.gov/emp/ep_projections_methods.htm.

Source: U.S. Bureau of Labor Statistics
Plunkett Research, Ltd.
www.plunkettresearch.com

Top 30 U.S. Occupations by Percent Change in Job Growth: 2010-2020

(Employment in Thousands)

Occupation	Employment		Change		Training*
	2010	2020	Number	Percent	
Personal care aides	861	1,468	607	**70.5**	Short-term on-the-job training
Home health aides	1,018	1,724	706	**69.4**	Short-term on-the-job training
Biomedical engineers	16	25	10	**61.7**	Bachelor's degree
Helpers--brickmasons, blockmasons, stonemasons, and tile and marble setters	29	47	18	**60.1**	Short-term on-the-job training
Helpers--carpenters	47	72	26	**55.7**	Short-term on-the-job training
Veterinary technologists and technicians	80	122	42	**52.0**	Associate degree
Reinforcing iron and rebar workers	19	28	9	**48.6**	Apprenticeship
Physical therapist assistants	67	98	31	**45.7**	Associate degree
Helpers--pipelayers, plumbers, pipefitters, and steamfitters	58	84	26	**45.4**	Short-term on-the-job training
Meeting, convention, and event planners	72	103	31	**43.7**	Bachelor's degree
Diagnostic medical sonographers	54	77	23	**43.5**	Associate degree
Occupational therapy assistants	29	41	12	**43.3**	Associate degree
Physical therapist aides	47	67	20	**43.1**	Moderate-term on-the-job training
Glaziers	42	60	18	**42.4**	Apprenticeship
Interpreters and translators	58	83	25	**42.2**	Bachelor's degree
Medical secretaries	509	719	210	**41.3**	Moderate-term on-the-job training
Market research analysts and marketing specialists	283	399	117	**41.2**	Bachelor's degree
Marriage and family therapists	36	51	15	**41.2**	Master's degree
Brickmasons and blockmasons	89	125	36	**40.5**	Apprenticeship
Physical therapists	199	276	77	**39.0**	Doctoral or professional degree
Dental hygienists	182	250	69	**37.7**	Associate degree
Bicycle repairers	10	14	4	**37.6**	Moderate-term on-the-job training
Audiologists	13	18	5	**36.8**	Doctoral or professional degree
Health educators	63	87	23	**36.5**	Bachelor's degree
Stonemasons	16	21	6	**36.5**	Apprenticeship
Cost estimators	185	253	68	**36.4**	Bachelor's degree
Medical scientists, except epidemiologists	100	137	36	**36.4**	Doctoral or professional degree
Mental health counselors	120	164	44	**36.3**	Master's degree
Pile-driver operators	4	6	2	**36.0**	Moderate-term on-the-job training
Veterinarians	61	83	22	**35.9**	Doctoral or professional degree

* An occupation is placed into 1 of 11 categories that best describes the postsecondary education or training needed by most workers to become fully qualified in that occupation. For more information, see Measures of Education and Training, on the Internet at www.bls.gov/emp/ep_projections_methods.htm.

Source: U.S. Bureau of Labor Statistics
Plunkett Research, Ltd.
www.plunkettresearch.com

Occupations with the Largest Expected Employment Increases, U.S.: 2008-2018

(By Increase in Number Employed, in Thousands)

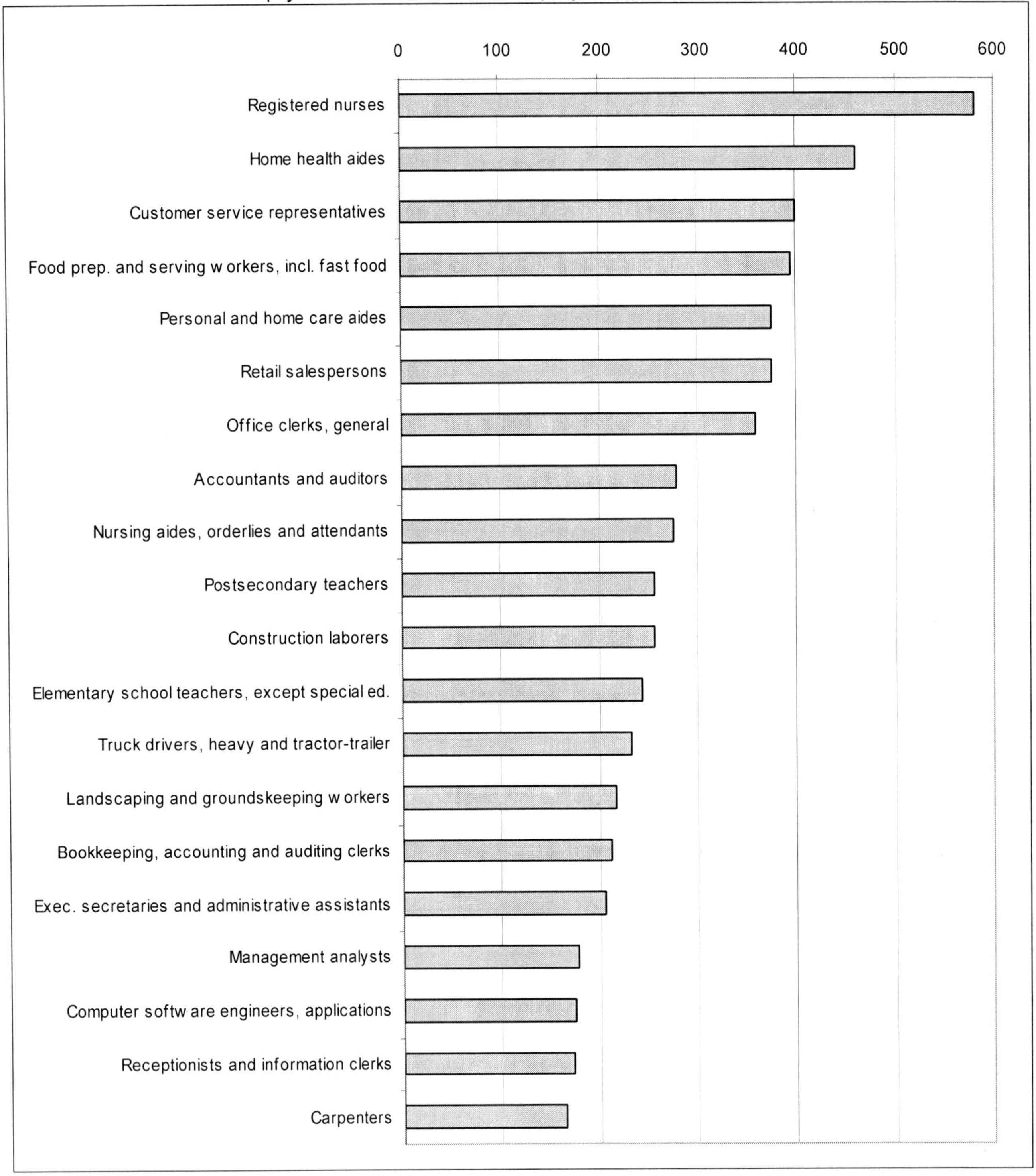

Source: U.S. Bureau of Labor Statistics
Plunkett Research, Ltd.
www.plunkettresearch.com

Occupations with the Fastest Expected Decline, U.S.: 2008-2018

(By Percent Change and Number of Jobs Lost, in Thousands)

Occupation	Change		Wages (May 2008 Median)	Training*
	Percent	Number		
Textile bleaching and dyeing machine operators and tenders	-45%	-7.2	$23,680	Moderate-term on-the-job training
Textile winding, twisting, and drawing out machine setters, operators, and tenders	-41%	-14.2	$23,970	Moderate-term on-the-job training
Textile knitting and weaving machine setters, operators, and tenders	-39%	-11.5	$25,400	Long-term on-the-job training
Shoe machine operators and tenders	-35%	-1.7	$25,090	Moderate-term on-the-job training
Extruding and forming machine setters, operators, and tenders, synthetic and glass fibers	-34%	-4.8	$31,160	Moderate-term on-the-job training
Sewing machine operators	-34%	-4.8	$19,870	Moderate-term on-the-job training
Semiconductor processors	-32%	-10.0	$32,230	Postsecondary vocational award
Textile cutting machine setters, operators, and tenders	-31%	-6.0	$22,620	Moderate-term on-the-job training
Postal Service mail sorters, processors, and processing machine operators	-30%	-54.5	$50,020	Short-term on-the-job training
Fabric menders, except garment	-30%	-0.3	$28,470	Moderate-term on-the-job training
Wellhead pumpers	-28%	-5.3	$37,860	Moderate-term on-the-job training
Fabric and apparel patternmakers	-27%	-2.2	$37,760	Long-term on-the-job training
Drilling & boring machine tool setters, operators, & tenders, metal & plastic	-27%	-8.9	$30,850	Moderate-term on-the-job training
Lathe & turning machine tool setters, operators, & tenders, metal & plastic	-27%	-14.9	$32,940	Moderate-term on-the-job training
Order clerks	-26%	-64.2	$27,990	Short-term on-the-job training
Coil winders, tapers, and finishers	-25%	-5.6	$27,730	Short-term on-the-job training
Photographic processing machine operators	-24%	-12.5	$20,360	Short-term on-the-job training
File clerks	-23%	-49.6	$23,800	Short-term on-the-job training
Derrick operators, oil and gas	-23%	-5.8	$41,920	Moderate-term on-the-job training
Desktop publishers	-23%	-5.9	$36,600	Postsecondary vocational award

* An occupation is placed into 1 of 11 categories that best describes the postsecondary education or training needed by most workers to become fully qualified in that occupation. For more information about the categories, see Measures of Education and Training, on the Internet at www.bls.gov/emp/ep_projections_methods.htm.

Source: U.S. Bureau of Labor Statistics

Plunkett Research, Ltd.

www.plunkettresearch.com

Chapter 3

RESEARCH: 7 KEYS FOR JOB SEEKERS

How to use your library, college placement office, the Internet and other resources to become well-informed about a company and its industry before you ask for an interview

Research is the key to finding appropriate job openings, targeting the best possible employers and performing well when you go to job interviews. Learn what's unique about a company compared to other firms in its industry. Learn why it's prospering–or why it isn't. Where is this company going? Is it favored by stock investors? Is it privately-owned by a family, or has it been acquired by private equity investors who plan to resell it over the mid-term? What are its hottest-selling products and services? Is it investing in research and new facilities so that it may prosper in the future? Also, as many people who have been laid off from failing startup firms have learned the hard way, determining a company's level of financial stability can be one of the most important factors in making a career decision.

The more you're willing to dig deep at the library or your college's career planning office, and the more adept you are at using the Internet for research, the better your chances of success in a job search. If you are willing to ask questions of businesspeople and of employees who currently work for your target employers, you will enhance your job search even further. The two secrets to successful job research are tenacity and focus. Know what to look for and where to find it.

Once you've landed an interview, you should research both the prospective employer and its industry even further. In this manner, you'll know what questions to ask before you agree to take the job, and you'll present yourself as a knowledgeable potential hire who is truly interested in the company and its business.

Here are the seven keys for research that can lead you to a great employer:

1) Financial Stability

Check bond ratings, credit ratings, debt level, growth in sales and growth in profits, along with the views of stock analysts and business journalists.

2) Growth Plans

Look for new plants, stores or offices to be opened; new technologies, products or divisions to be launched; or plans for strategic acquisitions. (See 3, 4 and 5 below.) Is the employer's growth strategy focused primarily on offshoring work to overseas locations or outsourcing work to outside services providers? Or, does it have a balanced growth strategy that will create good opportunities in its American operations?

3) Research and Development Programs

How much does the firm invest in R&D? Is this research and development budget growing? For many types of companies, research is a vital investment in the future.

4) Product Launch and Production

Does the company have the ability to successfully launch new products and services (see 5 below) or to invest in and utilize cutting-edge technologies needed to maintain a competitive edge?

5) Marketing and Distribution Methods

Does the firm utilize an in-house sales force? Does it work through outside dealers and distribution partners? What are its advertising methods? Is it increasing its market share, or are competitors taking customers away? Is the company growing its international sales? Is it adept at using the Internet as a powerful sales tool? Is it successful at selling into growing international markets, such as Brazil, China and India?

6) Employee Benefits

Are wealth-building benefit plans offered? Will the company match all or part of your deposits to a 401(k) savings plan? Check for tuition reimbursement, pension plans, profit sharing, ESOP stock ownership plans, discount stock purchase plans, stock options or performance-based bonuses.

7) Quality-of-Work Factors

Does the company offer continual training, wellness programs, child care, elder care support, promote-from-within policies, flexible work schedules, performance reviews, product discounts or on-site health clubs? Is it a corporate culture that fits your lifestyle?

As a serious job seeker, you should conduct in-depth research and make detailed notes about these key factors for each firm you are considering. Then compare each company's finances, plans and programs to others in the same industry. You'll begin to see what makes some firms outstanding and why those outstanding companies are the best places to make a career investment. For example, if you compare two discount store giants, Wal-Mart and Costco, you will find that Wal-Mart is by far the larger firm, but Costco has an outstanding record of providing superior employee pay and benefits.

Your research goal should be twofold: First, determine whether this is a firm you want to work for. Are the salaries and benefits appealing? Are layoffs likely? Is it planning to expand its workforce in lower-cost nations like India and then lay off U.S. employees? A growing company will offer opportunities for you to advance when it launches new locations, services, technologies or product lines. Second, develop a personal understanding of the company and its industry so you can better sell yourself as a potential employee.

Other Considerations:

Women and Minorities:

Certain industries have a greater tendency to offer advancement opportunities for women or minorities. Historically, the banking and insurance segments have tended to promote both women and minorities, as have retailing, electric utilities, apparel, consumer goods, packaged food and beverages, education, publishing and telephone companies.

Major employers in many other industries are making serious efforts to hire, develop and promote women and minorities for top officers' positions. A study published in September 2011 by Catalyst, a New York-based research group that focuses on women's issues in the workplace, found that 2.8% (14 companies) of the *Fortune 500* firms had female CEOs, up from about 1% in 2001. Some technology companies have been terrific places for women who want to advance, and many tech companies, such as Hewlett-Packard, Xerox and eBay, have been known to post women to CEO spots.

Catalyst reported in another study published in 2011 that 15.7% of members of boards of directors in the Fortune *500* firms were women, up from 9.6% in 1995. (You can access the results of Catalyst studies at www.catalyst.org.) Obviously, women are making slow progress in gaining representation in the highest ranks of corporate America, and they fall far short of parity with men in that regard.

Black Enterprise magazine publishes an annual list of the "Most Powerful African Americans in Corporate America," (see www.blackenterprise.com). Meanwhile, the Executive Leadership Council, www.elcinfo.com, a Washington, D.C.-based nonprofit group that conducts programs aimed at filling more executive posts with African Americans, has a unique statistic to report. Its membership is composed of senior-level black executives who have jobs that are no more than three levels below the CEO spot at Fortune 500 companies. When the group was founded in 1986, it had only a handful of members. Today, its membership is about 380 people employed in high-level executive jobs at major corporations.

The Hispanic Association on Corporate Responsibility (www.hacr.org) promotes Hispanic advancement in the areas of employment, procurement, philanthropy and governance. Another nonprofit agency, National Hispanic Corporate Achievers (hispanicachievers.org), provides an educational forum for Hispanics working for *Fortune 1000* companies.

Tips on Using Business Magazines, Newspapers and Trade Journals to Find Job Leads and Do Employer Research

Many job seekers overlook the tremendous advantages offered by industry magazines (called "trade journals") and other publications when conducting research.

Industry-specific trade journals frequently have classified ads in the back that list job openings. An example of a great magazine to study is *American Banker,* which can be found at major libraries. Additional information is available at www.americanbanker.com.

Journalists at trade journals and business newspapers continuously interview industry-leading executives regarding their companies' growth plans. New projects and company expansion plans described in these articles provide terrific job leads.

You can also get great contact information from these publications. Read the latest business stories about companies and industries that interest you and you will learn vital information. Best of all, you can glean from stories and interviews the names and titles of executives who lead projects, divisions and subsidiaries.

There are literally hundreds of these trade journals—at least one for each industry sector and sometimes dozens covering the largest industries.

Other great resources include business newspapers such as the *Dallas/Ft. Worth Business Journal*, *The Wall Street Journal*, the business pages of major newspapers like *The New York Times* and publications written for major investors like *Investor's Business Daily*. At www.bizjournals.com, you can gain access to news stories from business journals from all over the U.S.

Quality-of-Life Benefits:

Many companies offer benefits that help employees balance their personal and professional lives. The concept is that employees who are healthy and comfortable with their personal and family lives make better, more productive employees. To that end, many companies include fitness programs and family services such as extended maternity leaves and child care or elder care, whether on-site or off-site in the form of referral services. Other popular family-friendly benefits include flextime, flexible benefits spending accounts, adoption assistance and telecommuting. In many cases, benefits are listed on employers' web sites.

Work-Life has become a popular phrase for family-friendly benefits and programs among major employers such as Intel, Abbott Laboratories, Baxter International and Aramark. For additional information, you can study such organizations at the Alliance for Work-Life Progress site at www.awlp.org.

Growth Potential and Job Stability:

A firm's growth potential should be among your top priorities. Companies are always trying to maintain or increase productivity, or the ratio of revenues per employee. If a company's sales are sliding, or if it is running out of cash, the job picture starts to collapse. A little extra research into a company's finances and true potential for growth might save you from a future layoff.

Of course, employers sometimes have to resort to layoffs due to conditions outside of their control. For example, travel industry companies worldwide cut hundreds of thousands of jobs in the revenue slump following the September 11, 2001 attacks on New York City and Washington, D.C.

As a job seeker, you're forced to look out for your own best interests while you sort through thousands of potential employers in dozens of industries. This means that good research is vital. For example, if you put salary at the top of your list, you may have the wrong priorities. From time to time, some of the highest-paying firms have been among those cutting the largest numbers of employees. If you are looking for job stability, your biggest challenge is to pick companies that are more likely to hire now and less likely to have layoffs in the future. That's why a firm's growth outlook should be one of your guiding lights.

However, the goal is *internal* growth caused by expanding sales. Generally less appealing are firms that post a quick spike in growth through big mergers. (In many cases, merged companies lay off people who suddenly find themselves filling jobs duplicated in newly consolidated offices. Also, companies that grow excessively through acquisitions may be taking on loads of debt that can become hard to handle later. However, there are occasional exceptions to this rule, where firms are enjoying soaring demand for products or services and find it difficult to hire quickly enough to keep up.) Companies that are growing rapidly through internal expansion include those opening new stores, distribution centers or offices, developing exciting new products, moving into new markets (including international markets) and creating hot new technologies, retail formats or services. Those types of expansion frequently mean great career opportunities, including the chance for rapid job promotion.

Where can you look for growth companies? If you're tenacious, you can find opportunities where others will find only rejection. Identifying real prospects for growth takes more than a quick glance.

Here's an extremely important point for you to remember: You should look for opportunities in growing divisions that serve special niches, even when the company as a whole is cutting jobs. For example, a firm's online division may be growing, even while its traditional units are shrinking.

Additional key factors for strong corporate growth, and thereby the best job prospects, include:

1) Companies or divisions with a growing share of a promising market.

Management's ability to anticipate or create change in the marketplace makes for a growing company with great prospects. For example, Sam Walton revolutionized the department store business by realizing that consumers want everyday low prices on name-brand merchandise. He created Wal-Mart, while competitor Sears suffered by maintaining an old-fashioned policy of special sales events on private-label goods. Wal-Mart rapidly became one of the largest creators of new jobs in the private sector. Sears was forced to slash its ranks.

Microsoft made its way to the top with unique products serving a soaring market when it developed highly functional software for personal computers. The software giant created thousands of millionaire employees through the immense increase in the value of its stock plans. HEB, an innovative grocer in Texas, has evolved continually over the decades, constantly introducing improvements to store layouts, and even creating an exciting new HEB Marketplace concept that is a retail industry leader. HEB has large numbers of job openings of many types on a continuous basis.

The point to these stories is that you shouldn't invest your career in a company with mediocre prospects. With perseverance, you can target your own list of employers that are posting growth due to competitive advantages or growing market demand. Your best bets are companies taking reasonable risks in order to move ahead. Those risks may include investments in advertising, research and development, new technology, improved techniques on the manufacturing floor, testing of new products and the opening of new retail store formats. For example, Chico's FAS stores scored a hit by filling a niche in the women's apparel market, and Genentech became a leader in the biotechnology field by risking vast amounts on research. Also, don't overlook the potential of the export market—many American firms find much of their growth by creating products and services that enjoy demand overseas as well as in the U.S.

2) Sales and profits: past and present.

The companies most likely to move along at a good clip are those with an exciting mid-term history. Firms with an average annual growth in sales of 10% to 15% or more over the past several years are generally very promising. Companies that managed to get through the recent recession with only minor drops in revenues may be remarkably stable. Many small and mid-size firms grow at much faster rates and find themselves hiring continuously.

3) Beware of fads.

Unfortunately, a few companies post meteoric growth in businesses that turn out to be mere fads. The restaurant industry suffers from this problem on a regular basis. In recent years, companies selling bagels, frozen yogurt, rotisserie chicken and the like enjoyed impressive, nationwide growth only to collapse like a house of cards a couple of years later.

How to Find and Use Expert Opinions:

Superior sources used by sophisticated job researchers include reports written by: 1) stock analysts; 2) professional market research firms; and 3) journalists at business magazines and industry "trade magazines." Many major libraries have large collections of industry-specific trade magazines that can give you clues that competing job seekers will overlook. For example, *Retail Traffic Magazine*, www.retailtrafficmag.com, publishes lists of the fastest-growing retail chains. Virtually every other industry is covered by one or two trade magazines that will give you leads to growing companies. Many articles in these magazines contain the names of executives you may want to contact. Also, most industry trade magazines publish help-wanted ads in the back. The *Gale Directory of Publications and Broadcast Media* is a good index to magazines, organized by industry. You can find this directory in major libraries. Also, it's easy to do an online search for trade magazines, and most of them have terrific web sites that are filled with extremely useful information. For example, a recent search on Google for "pet industry trade magazine" quickly turned up leads to the top magazines for that sector.

Next, move on to reports from experts. Marketing and investment professionals are looking for some of the same clues you should use as a job seeker, and reports written by full-time analysts who cover specific companies or industries can help you find firms that are growing and hiring. You can purchase reports for publicly-traded firms at Yahoo! Finance, http://finance.yahoo.com. First, look up a company by name or ticker symbol. Once you are on the page for that company, look down the left hand column for the link to "Research Reports."

Professionally written market research can be found at Marketresearch.com, www.marketresearch.com. This market research broker charges varying fees for access to the reports. However, many of the reports are reasonably priced, and the insight you gain into industries, markets and leading companies can be extremely helpful. Web sites such as this offer the ability to search for reports by a wide variety of criteria, including company name and industry.

Internet Research Tip:

Be sure to create Google "Alerts" to follow your targeted employers and profession. Google will email results to you daily.

By going to the "more" link at the top of the Google home page, and then selecting "even more" from the drop down list, you can access Google's "Alerts" tool. Here you can arrange to receive email updates on topics of your choice. For example, you can set a general alert about an industry or locale: sales jobs in California, for example. Or something like: opportunities in the American wireless industry. Or even: sales jobs at automobile dealers.

You can use alerts to track specific jobs or employers. For example: openings at Intel. Or: regional sales manager opening Los Angeles. Finally, don't forget that you may want to put a search phrase within quotes to get an exact match to part of your phrase. For example: "loan officer" wanted.

Other Basic Resources:

Annual Reports/10-Ks/S-1s: Companies that sell their stocks to the public, including most of the firms covered in this book, publish annual reports that contain a wealth of information. Annual reports and 10-Ks cover yearly results, financial statements, management practices and other vital information for publicly held firms. S-1s provide the same type of information on companies that are selling stock to the public for the first time. You can find copies of these reports at large libraries. Online, the best place to acquire this information is at the site of the U.S. Securities and Exchange Commission. They have a user-friendly service that enables you to search for companies and access their financial reports at www.sec.gov. (Look for the "Filings & Forms" section, and then see "Search for Company Filings.") Look especially at the five-year "summary financial statement" in the back of these reports. Also, look for growth in sales and earnings. If these are falling, dig deeper to find out why. Faltering sales or profits can lead to layoffs or to a merger with another firm (which could result in deep job cuts).

Also, you can find a wealth of financial information on publicly-traded firms at Yahoo! Finance, http://finance.yahoo.com.

See Chapter 4, "Important Contacts for Job Seekers," for additional places to get basic corporate data.

Tips on Utilizing Financial Documents Filed by Publicly Held Firms

(Access these documents at the Securities Exchange Commission, www.sec.gov.)

10-K (also called Annual Report on Form 10-K): This is an annual filing required by federal law. It follows a standard format. Information includes a complete description of the business, risk factors, historical financial data and much more. It is vital reading for job seekers. You will find that these documents are written in dry, legal language, but they contain a wealth of information.

DEF 14A Proxy Statement: This is an annual document that gives shareholders certain options to consider at their annual meeting. It names the firm's board of directors and top management. It also gives the dollar value and description of salaries, bonuses, pension plans, stock options and other benefits enjoyed by the company's five highest-paid officers. Job seekers can learn a great deal about a firm's management, pay and benefits from this document. Included is a list of the people or organizations that own more than 5% of the company's stock.

S-1: This is a new registration document for companies that are going public for the first time. In other words, they are creating an IPO (initial public offering). The information includes all of the data found in the 10-K and proxy statement filed annually by companies that have been public for more than one year.

10-Q: This is a quarterly report detailing a company's latest sales, profits and balance sheet.

More Ways to Research an Employer's Financial Stability and Growth Plans:

1) Check out its bond rating.

There's no sense in trying to become a financial analyst on your own. Instead, go to your library and turn to the *Bond Guide* published by Standard & Poor's (New York, NY). This monthly booklet rates thousands of corporate bonds, based on a company's ability to pay principal and interest when due. If you're considering a major corporation with a bond rating of less than BB (an indicator that a company's debt is riskier than "investment grade"), you should do a lot more investigating before you continue chasing a job at that company.

2) Talk to vendors and current employees.

Talk to employees who work for the employer, or talk to people who do business with it. No one knows what's really going on better than people who are on the scene. If there are problems that are not yet known by the media, or if there are exciting new developments that have not yet been announced, you may find out a lot just by asking around. While you're at it, ask about corporate culture—how well are employees treated?

Popular Job-Search Internet Sites

CareerBuilder	www.careerbuilder.com
Monster	www.monster.com

Tips on Finding Information on Privately Held Employers

Our subscription service, Plunkett Research Online, and our printed Plunkett's industry almanacs, are among the world's most highly regarded sources of profiles of privately-held companies. Check with your library to see if you have access to these tools.

Study back-issue indexes and archives to major newspapers to see what journalists are reporting about a prospective private employer. Many libraries have recent issues of *The Wall Street Journal, The New York Times* and other important business newspapers. At major public and university libraries, you may be able to access online databases like ProQuest. These databases have excellent search engines that lead you into online archives of the best publications, including *The Wall Street Journal*, as well as many trade magazines and local business journals.

For smaller firms, go online and try American Journalism Review at www.newslink.org, where you'll be able to search news sites including hometown newspapers across the nation. Likewise, search local business newspapers at www.bizjournals.com, where you'll find links to dozens of major business weeklies like the *Houston Business Journal.*

Finally, invest in a credit report. If you really want reassurance, go to Experian SmartBusinessReports, www.smartbusinessreports.com. You can use its links to order a credit report on the employer. These reports are reasonably priced from about $20 to $45, and they can help you determine whether the company is paying its bills on time or has other problems. This could be vital in helping you determine whether to accept a job at a privately-held firm.

3) Use Internet search engines.

Look up your firm and industry in an Internet search engine such as Google. There, you may find unusual articles that were recently written about a company's product breakthroughs, treatment of women or minorities, human interest stories, training programs or stories written from other unique slants.

4) Study other business books and guides.

Search at a library or at an online bookseller like Amazon.com for recent books regarding major companies. For example, if you want to apply to biotech leader Genentech for a job, don't fail to read *The Billion Dollar Molecule: One Company's Quest for the Perfect Drug.* With a little research, you can turn up many other excellent books about specific companies, from banks like Bank of America to publishers like Gannett.

Great Places for Industry Research

Plunkett Research, www.plunkettresearch.com. Go to the specific industry of your choice to see an overview of trends and statistics. At our subscription service, www.plunkettresearchonline.com, subscribers have access to thousands of pages of industry analysis, statistics, contacts and company profiles, along with multiple search and export tools.

Quintessentialcareers.com, www.quintessentialcareers.com. Offers a "Career Resources Toolkit."

Wetfeet.com, www.wetfeet.com. Publishes snapshots of hundreds of employers.

Vault.com, www.vault.com. This site publishes insights about careers with hundreds of leading firms.

5) Explore industry-specific web sites.

See Chapter 4 in this book, "Important Contacts for Job Seekers," for hundreds of sites from dozens of different industry sectors. In particular, study the industry associations for the sector you want to work in.

6) Research benefits and pension plans.

For additional information about corporate pension plans, start with the government agency charged with protecting and regulating pensions: the Pension Benefit Guaranty Corporation, 1200 K St. NW, Washington, D.C. 20005-4026, 202-326-4000, www.pbgc.gov. They can answer certain questions over the telephone.

The U.S. Department of Labor publishes a useful book titled "Protect your Pension." They can be contacted at: U.S. Department of Labor, Employee Benefits Security Administration, 200 Constitution Ave. NW, Room N5635, Washington, D.C. 20210, 866-444-3272 or 202-219-8776, www.dol.gov/ebsa/publications/main.html.

The Social Security Administration, 800-772-1213, www.ssa.gov, can provide you with information regarding your potential Social Security benefits.

NOTE: Generally, employees covered by wealth-building benefit plans do not fully own ("vest in") funds contributed on their behalf by the employer until as many as five years of service with that employer have passed. All pension plans are voluntary—that is, employers are not obligated to offer pensions.

Pension Plans: The type and generosity of these plans vary widely from firm to firm. Caution: Some employers refer to plans as "pension" or "retirement" plans when they are actually 401(k) savings plans that require a contribution by the employee.

Defined Benefit Pension Plans: Pension plans that do not require a contribution from the employee are infrequently offered. However, a few companies, particularly larger employers in high-profit-margin industries, offer defined benefit pension plans where the employee is guaranteed to receive a set pension benefit upon retirement. The amount of the benefit is determined by the years of service with the company and the employee's salary during the later years of employment. The longer a person works for the employer, the higher the retirement benefit. These defined benefit plans are funded entirely by the employer. The benefits, up to a reasonable limit, are guaranteed by the Federal Government's Pension Benefit Guaranty Corporation. These plans are not portable—if you leave the company, you cannot transfer your benefits into a different plan. Instead, upon retirement you will receive the benefits that vested during your service with the company. If your employer offers a pension plan, it must give you a "summary plan description" within 90 days of the date you join the plan. You can also request a "summary annual report" of the plan, and once every 12 months you may request an "individual benefit statement" accounting of your interest in the plan.

Defined Contribution Plans: These are quite different. They do not guarantee a certain amount of pension benefit. Instead, they set out circumstances under which the employer will make a contribution to a plan on your behalf. The most common example is the 401(k) savings plan. Pension benefits are not guaranteed under these plans.

Cash Balance Pension Plans: These plans were recently invented. They are hybrid plans—part defined benefit and part defined contribution. Many employers have converted their older defined benefit plans into cash balance plans. The employer makes deposits (or credits a given amount of money) on the employee's behalf, usually based on a percentage of pay. Employee accounts grow based on a predetermined interest benchmark, such as the interest rate on Treasury Bonds. There are some advantages to these plans, particularly for younger workers: a) The benefits, up to a reasonable limit, are guaranteed by the Pension Benefit Guaranty Corporation. b) Benefits are portable—they can be moved to another plan when the employee changes companies. c) Younger workers and those who spend a shorter number of years with an employer may receive higher benefits than they would under a traditional defined benefit plan.

ESOP Stock Plan (Employees' Stock Ownership Plan): This type of plan is in wide use. Typically, the plan borrows money from a bank and uses those funds to purchase a large block of the corporation's stock. The corporation makes contributions to the plan over a period of time, and the stock purchase loan is eventually paid off. The value of the plan grows significantly as long as the market price of the stock holds up. Qualified employees are allocated a share of the plan based on their length of service and their level of salary. Under federal regulations, participants in ESOPs are allowed to diversify their account holdings in set percentages that rise as the employee ages and gains years of service with the company. In this manner, not all of the employee's assets are tied up in the employer's stock.

Savings Plan, 401(k): Under this type of plan, employees make a tax-deferred deposit into an account. In the best plans, the company makes annual matching donations to the employees' accounts, typically in some proportion to deposits made by the employees themselves. A good plan will match one-half of employee deposits of up to 6% of wages. For example, an employee earning $30,000 yearly might deposit $1,800 (6%) into the plan. The company will match one-half of the employee's deposit, or $900. The plan grows on a tax-deferred basis, similar to an IRA. A very generous plan will match 100% of employee deposits. However, some plans do not call for the employer to make a matching deposit at all. Other plans call for a matching contribution to be made at the discretion of the firm's board of directors. Actual terms of these plans vary widely from firm to firm. Generally, these savings plans allow employees to deposit as much as 15% of salary into the plan on a tax-deferred basis. However, the portion that the company uses to calculate its matching deposit is generally limited to a maximum of 6%. Employees should take care to diversify the holdings in their 401(k) accounts, and most people should seek professional guidance or investment management for their accounts. (Note: when profits are down, many employers exercise their right to suspend their contributions to 401(k)s. Employees may continue to make contributions, but they will not be matched by the employer in these cases.)

Stock Purchase Plan: Qualified employees may purchase the company's common stock at a price below its market value under a specific plan. Typically, the employee is limited to investing a small percentage of wages in this plan. The discount may range from 5% to 15%. Some of these plans allow for deposits to be made through regular monthly payroll deductions. However, new accounting rules for corporations, along with other factors, are leading many companies to curtail these plans—dropping the discount allowed, cutting the maximum yearly stock purchase or otherwise making the plans less generous or appealing.

Profit Sharing: Qualified employees are awarded an annual amount equal to some portion of a company's profits. In a very generous plan, the pool of money awarded to employees would be 15% of profits. Typically, this money is deposited into a long-term retirement account. Caution: Some employers refer to plans as "profit sharing" when they are actually 401(k) savings plans. True profit sharing plans are rarely offered.

Plunkett Research Online and Plunkett's Industry Reference Books:

1) Internet-Based Services: Plunkett Research Online is a reference service that is subscribed to by the nation's leading university placement offices, libraries and information offices. You can use it to filter prospective employers by location, industry, size and more. You can then export contact information for those companies into spreadsheets or text files. In addition, you can use the site to research the latest editions of our industry analysis. Many additional tools for job seekers are included. For an extensive online tour, see www.plunkettresearch.com.

2) Printed Almanacs: Plunkett Research also publishes industry-specific almanacs for the most important industries. These are top-notch resources for job seekers.

Industry-Specific Books from Plunkett Research:

- Plunkett's Advertising & Branding Industry Almanac
- Plunkett's Airline, Hotel & Travel Industry Almanac
- Plunkett's Almanac of Middle Market Companies
- Plunkett's Apparel & Textiles Industry Almanac
- Plunkett's Automobile Industry Almanac
- Plunkett's Banking, Mortgages & Credit Industry Almanac
- Plunkett's Biotech & Genetics Industry Almanac
- Plunkett's Chemicals, Coatings & Plastics Industry Almanac
- Plunkett's Consulting Industry Almanac
- Plunkett's E-Commerce & Internet Business Almanac
- Plunkett's Energy Industry Almanac

- Plunkett's Engineering & Research Industry Almanac
- Plunkett's Entertainment & Media Industry Almanac
- Plunkett's Food Industry Almanac
- Plunkett's Games, Apps & Social Media Industry Almanac
- Plunkett's Green Technology Industry Almanac
- Plunkett's Health Care Industry Almanac
- Plunkett's Insurance Industry Almanac
- Plunkett's InfoTech Industry Almanac
- Plunkett's Investment & Securities Industry Almanac
- Plunkett's Nanotechnology & MEMS Industry Almanac
- Plunkett's Outsourcing & Offshoring Industry Almanac
- Plunkett's Real Estate & Construction Industry Almanac
- Plunkett's Renewable, Alternative & Hydrogen Energy Industry Almanac
- Plunkett's Retail Industry Almanac
- Plunkett's Sports Industry Almanac
- Plunkett's Telecommunications Industry Almanac
- Plunkett's Transportation, Supply Chain & Logistics Industry Almanac
- Plunkett's Wireless & Cellular Telephone Industry Almanac

Publications from Plunkett Research Written Especially for Job Seekers:

- The Almanac of American Employers
- Plunkett's Companion to the Almanac of American Employers

Our books will give you in-depth coverage of specific industries and the leading firms in those industries, along with trends and developments in technology and services. You will find these books in public and academic libraries, college placement offices, human resources offices, corporate libraries and government agency libraries. For sample chapters and additional details, you can preview as well as purchase these books at www.plunkettresearch.com.

The Almanac of American Employers provides profiles and detailed listings of 500 hand-picked, U.S. employers of 2,500 employees or more in size

Plunkett's Companion to The Almanac of American Employers is our book that provides profiles on 500 additional, rapidly growing corporate employers. This companion book covers smaller firms than those in the main volume of *The Almanac of American Employers.*

Chapter 4

IMPORTANT CONTACTS FOR JOB SEEKERS

Contents:

I. Accountants & CPA Associations

American Institute of CPAs (AICPA)
1211 Ave. of the Americas
New York, NY 10036-8775 US
Phone: 212-596-6200
Fax: 1-800-362-5066
Toll Free: 888-777-7077
E-mail Address: *service@aicpa.org*
Web Address: www.aicpa.org
American Institute of CPAs (AICPA) provides information and news for CPAs, news from the organization and a search for accounting firms on its web site.

Council of Petroleum Accountants Societies, Inc. (COPAS)
3900 E. Mexico Ave., Ste. 602
Denver, CO 80210 US
Phone: 303-300-1131
Fax: 303-300-3733
Toll Free: 877-992-6727
E-mail Address: *Execdir@copas.org*
Web Address: www.copas.org
The Council of Petroleum Accountants Societies, Inc. (COPAS) provides a forum for discussing and solving the variety of problems related to accounting for oil and gas. COPAS also provides valuable educational materials related to oil and gas accounting.

International Accounting Standards Board (IASB)
30 Cannon St.
London, EC4M 6XH UK
Phone: 44-20-7246-6410
Fax: 44-20-7246-6411
E-mail Address: *iasb@iasb.org.uk*
Web Address: www.iasb.org
The International Accounting Standards Board (IASB) website hosts an electronic subscription service to the International Financial Reporting (IFRS) Standards as well access to IFRS summaries.

II. Advertising/Marketing Associations

4A's (American Association of Advertising Agencies)
405 Lexington Ave., Fl. 18
New York, NY 10174-1801 US
Phone: 212-682-2500
E-mail Address: *nhill@aaaa.org*
Web Address: www.aaaa.org
The 4A's is the national trade association representing the advertising agency industry in the U.S.

Advertising Women of New York (AWNY)
25 W. 45th St., Ste. 403
New York, NY 10036 US
Phone: 212-221-7969
Fax: 212-221-8296
E-mail Address: *awny@awny.org*
Web Address: www.awny.org
Advertising Women of New York (AWNY) provides a forum for personal and professional growth, serves as a catalyst for the advancement of women in the communications field and promotes and supports philanthropic endeavors through the AWNY Foundation. The web site also provides content from Women Executives in Public Relations (WERP), such as its a dynamic job board.

American Institute of Graphic Arts (AIGA)
164 5th Ave.
New York, NY 10010 US
Phone: 212-807-1990
Fax: 212-807-1799
E-mail Address:
steve_rogenstein@aiga.org

Web Address: www.aiga.org
The American Institute of Graphic Arts (AIGA) strives to further excellence in communication design, both as a strategic tool for business and as a cultural force.

American Marketing Association (AMA)
311 S. Wacker Dr., Ste. 5800
Chicago, IL 60606 US
Phone: 312-542-9000
Fax: 312-542-9001
Toll Free: 800-262-1150
E-mail Address: *info@ama.org*
Web Address: www.marketingpower.com
The American Marketing Association (AMA) serves marketing professionals in both business and education and serves all levels of marketing practitioners, educators and students.

Cable & Telecommunications Association for Marketing (CTAM)
201 N. Union St., Ste. 440
Alexandria, VA 22314 US
Phone: 703-549-4200
E-mail Address: *info@ctam.com*
Web Address: www.ctam.com
The Cable & Telecommunications Association for Marketing (CTAM) is dedicated to the discipline and development of consumer marketing excellence in cable television, new media and telecommunications services.

Direct Marketing Association (DMA)
1120 Ave. of the Americas
New York, NY 10036-6700 US
Phone: 212-768-7277
Fax: 212-302-6714
E-mail Address: *customerservice@the-dma.org*
Web Address: www.the-dma.org
The Direct Marketing Association (DMA) is the oldest and largest trade association for users and suppliers in the direct, database and interactive marketing fields.

III. Aerospace & Defense Industry Associations

American Institute of Aeronautics and Astronautics (AIAA)
1801 Alexander Bell Dr., Ste. 500
Reston, VA 20191-4344 US
Phone: 703-264-7500
Fax: 703-264-7551
Toll Free: 800-639-2422
E-mail Address: *chrish@aiaa.org*
Web Address: www.aiaa.org
The American Institute of Aeronautics and Astronautics (AIAA) is a nonprofit society aimed at advancing the arts, sciences and technology of aeronautics and astronautics. The institute represents the U.S. in the International Astronautical Federation and the International Council on the Aeronautical Sciences.

IV. Airline & Air Cargo Industry Associations

International Air Transport Association (IATA)
800 Place Victoria
P.O. Box 113
Montreal, QC H4Z 1M1 Canada
Phone: 514-874-0202
Fax: 514-874-9632
E-mail Address: *corpcomms@iata.org*
Web Address: www.iata.org
The International Air Transport Association (IATA) represents about 230 airlines in order to offer the highest standards of passenger and cargo service.

V. Alternative Energy-Ethanol

Renewable Fuels Association (RFA)
425 3rd St. SW, Ste. 1150
Washington, DC 20024 US
Phone: 202-289-3835
Fax: 202-289-7519
Web Address: www.ethanolrfa.org
The Renewable Fuels Association (RFA) is a trade organization representing the ethanol industry. It publishes a wealth of useful information, including a listing of biorefineries and monthly U.S. fuel ethanol production and demand.

VI. Alternative Energy-Solar

Solar Energy Industries Association (SEIA)
575 7th St. NW, Ste. 400
Washington, DC 20004 US
Phone: 202-682-0556
Fax: 202-682-7779
E-mail Address: *info@seia.org*
Web Address: www.seia.org
Established in 1974, the Solar Energy Industries Association is the American trade association of the solar energy industry. Among its operations is a web site that provides news for the solar energy industry, links to related products and companies and solar energy statistics.

VII. Alternative Energy-Wind

American Wind Energy Association (AWEA)
1501 M St. NW, Ste. 1000
Washington, DC 20005 US
Phone: 202-383-2500
Fax: 202-383-2505
E-mail Address: *windmail@awea.org*
Web Address: www.awea.org
The American Wind Energy Association (AWEA) promotes wind energy as a clean source of electricity worldwide. Its website provides excellent resources for research, including an online library, discussions of legislation, and descriptions of wind technologies.

VIII. Banking Industry Associations

American Bankers Association (ABA)
1120 Connecticut Ave. NW
Washington, DC 20036 US
Fax: 202-663-7578
Toll Free: 800-226-5377
E-mail Address: *smarshall@aba.com*
Web Address: www.aba.com
The American Bankers Association (ABA) represents banks of all sizes on issues of national importance for financial institutions and their customers. The site offers financial information and solutions, financial news and member access to further advice and content.

IX. Biotechnology & Biological Industry Associations

Biotechnology Industry Organization (BIO)
1201 Maryland Ave. SW, Ste. 900
Washington, DC 20024 US
Phone: 202-962-9200
Fax: 202-488-6301
E-mail Address: *info@bio.org*
Web Address: www.bio.org
The Biotechnology Industry Organization (BIO) represents members involved in the research and development of health care, agricultural, industrial and environmental biotechnology products. BIO has both small and large member organizations.

X. Booksellers Associations

American Booksellers Association, Inc.
200 White Plains Rd., Ste. 600
Tarrytown, NY 10591 US
Fax: 914-591-2720
Toll Free: 800-637-0037

E-mail Address: *info@bookweb.org*
Web Address: www.bookweb.org
The American Booksellers Association is a nonprofit association representing independent bookstores in the United States.

XI. Broadcasting, Cable, Radio & TV Associations

Academy of Television Arts and Sciences
5220 Lankershim Blvd.
North Hollywood, CA 91601-3109 US
Phone: 818-754-2800
Fax: 818-761-2827
E-mail Address: *support@emmys.org*
Web Address: www.emmys.tv
The Academy of Television Arts and Sciences is a nonprofit corporation devoted to the advancement of telecommunications arts and sciences and to fostering creative leadership in the telecommunications industry. It is one of three organizations that administer the Emmy Awards. It is responsible for prime time Emmys.

American Federation of Television and Radio Artists (AFTRA)
260 Madison Ave., Fl. 7
New York, NY 10016-2401 US
Phone: 212-532-0800
Fax: 212-532-2242
E-mail Address: *info@aftra.org*
Web Address: www.aftra.org
The American Federation of Television and Radio Artists (AFTRA) represents actors and other professional performers and broadcasters in television, radio, sound recordings, non-broadcast/industrial programming and new technologies such as interactive programming and CD-ROMs.

American Women in Radio and Television, Inc. (AWRT)
1760 Old Meadow Rd., Ste. 500
McLean, VA 22102 US
Phone: 703-506-3290
Fax: 703-506-3266
E-mail Address: *info@awrt.org*
Web Address: www.awrt.org
American Women in Radio and Television (AWRT), founded in 1951, is a national nonprofit organization dedicated to advancing the role of women in electronic media and related fields.

Association of America's Public Television Stations (APTS)
2100 Crystal Dr., Ste. 700
Arlington, VA 22202 US
Phone: 202-654-4200
Fax: 202-654-4236
E-mail Address: *jeffrey@apts.org*
Web Address: www.apts.org
The Association of America's Public Television Stations (APTS) is a nonprofit membership organization formed to support the continued growth and development of strong and financially sound noncommercial television service for the American public.

Broadcast Education Association (BEA)
1771 N St. NW
Washington, DC 20036-2891 US
Phone: 202-429-3935
E-mail Address: *tbailey@nab.org*
Web Address: www.beaweb.org
The Broadcast Education Association (BEA) is the professional association for professors, industry professionals and graduate students interested in teaching and research related to electronic media and multimedia enterprises.

National Academy of Television Arts and Sciences
111 W. 57th St., Ste. 600
New York, NY 10019 US
Phone: 212-586-8424
Fax: 212-246-8129
E-mail Address: *info@emmyonline.tv*
Web Address: www.emmyonline.org
The National Academy of Television Arts and Sciences is dedicated to the advancement of the arts and sciences of television and the promotion of creative leadership for artistic, educational and technical achievements within the television industry. It is responsible for awarding the Emmy Awards.

National Association of Broadcasters (NAB)
1771 N St. NW
Washington, DC 20036 US
Phone: 202-429-5300
Fax: 202-429-4199
E-mail Address: *nab@nab.org*
Web Address: www.nab.org
The National Association of Broadcasters (NAB) represents broadcasters for radio and television. The organization also provides benefits to employees of member companies and to individuals and companies that provide products and services to the electronic media industries.

National Association of Television Program Executives (NATPE)
5757 Wilshire Blvd., Penthouse 10
Los Angeles, CA 90036-3681 US
Phone: 310-453-4440
Fax: 310-453-5258
E-mail Address: *info@natpe.org*
Web Address: www.natpe.org
The National Association of Television Program Executives (NATPE) is the leading association for content professionals in the global television industry.

National Cable and Telecommunications Association (NCTA)
25 Massachusetts Ave. NW, Ste. 100
Washington, DC 20001-1413 US
Phone: 202-222-2300
E-mail Address: *rstoddard@ncta.com*
Web Address: www.ncta.com
The National Cable and Telecommunications Association (NCTA) is the principal trade association of the cable television industry in the United States.

Radio Television News Directors Association (RTNDA)
1025 F St. NW, Fl. 7
Washington, DC 20004 US
Phone: 202-659-6510
Fax: 202-223-4007
Toll Free: 800-807-8632
E-mail Address: *stefanib@rtnda.org*
Web Address: www.rtnda.org
The Radio Television News Directors Association (RTNDA) is the world's largest professional organization exclusively committed to professionals in electronic journalism.

Syndication Network Television Association (SNTA)
1 Penn Plz., Ste. 5310
New York, NY 10119 US
Phone: 212-259-3740
Fax: 212-259-3770
E-mail Address: *mburg@snta.com*
Web Address: www.snta.com
The Syndication Network Television Association (SNTA) is an organization of national and independent television stations that syndicate television shows.

Women in Cable & Telecommunications (WICT)
14555 Avion Pkwy., Ste. 250
Chantilly, VA 20151 US
Phone: 703-234-9810
Fax: 703-817-1595
E-mail Address: *lvega@wict.org*
Web Address: www.wict.org
Women in Cable & Telecommunications (WICT) exists to advance the position and influence of women in media through leadership programs and services at both the national and local level.

XII. Careers-Airlines/Flying

Aviation/Aerospace Jobs Page
601 SW 9th St., Stes. J & K
c/o NationJob, Inc.
Des Moines, IA 50309 US
Fax: 515-283-1223
Toll Free: 888-526-5967
E-mail Address: *customerservice@nationjob.com*
Web Address: www.nationjob.com/aviation
The Aviation/Aerospace Jobs Page, a division of NationJob, Inc., features detailed aviation and aerospace job listings and company profiles.

AviationJobSearch.com
London Rd. Sayers Common
West Sussex, BN6 9HS UK
Phone: 01273-837538
Web Address: www.aviationjobsearch.com
AviationJobSearch.com lists jobs related to the airline industry.

Avjobs, Inc.
P.O. Box 630830
Littleton, CO 80163 US
Phone: 303-683-2322
Fax: 888-624-8691
E-mail Address: *info@avjobs.com*
Web Address: www.avjobs.com
Avjobs, Inc. is a group of employers dedicated to helping individuals obtain aviation, airline, aerospace and airport careers.

Flightdeck Recruitment Ltd.
82c E. Hill
Colchester, Essex CO1 2QW UK
Phone: 44-1206-383730
Web Address: www.flightdeckrecruitment.com
Flightdeck Recruitment Ltd. provides a link between aviation recruiters who are looking for flight deck crew and pilots or flight engineers who are seeking employment.

XIII. Careers-Apparel

24 Seven Fashion Recruitment
120 Wooster St., Fl. 4
New York, NY 10012 US
Phone: 212-966-4426
Fax: 212-966-2313
Web Address: www.24seveninc.com
24 Seven Fashion Recruitment is an employment agency serving the fashion, beauty, entertainment, advertising, marketing and retail industries.

Fashion Career Center
E-mail Address: *fashioncc@fashioncareercenter.com*
Web Address: www.fashioncareercenter.com
The Fashion Career Center site provides employees and employers with a place to meet and access information about employment in the fashion industry. The FashionCareerCenter.com web site offers links to fashion jobs and fashion schools, as well as offering fashion career advice.

XIV. Careers-Banking

National Banking & Financial Service Network (NBFSN)
3075 Brickhouse Ct.
Virginia Beach, VA 23452-6860 US
Phone: 757-463-5766
Fax: 757-340-0826
E-mail Address: *susan@nbn-jobs.com*
Web Address: www.banking-financejobs.com
The National Banking & Financial Service Network (NBFSN) is made up of recruiting firms in the banking and financial services marketplace. The web site provides job listings.

XV. Careers-Biotech

BiotechEmployment.com
Phone: 561-630-5201
E-mail Address: *jobs@Biotechemployment.com*
Web Address: www.biotechemployment.com
BiotechEmployment.com is an online resource for job seekers in biotechnology. The site's features includes resume posting, job search agents and employer profiles. It is part of the eJobstores.com, Inc., which includes the Health Care Job Store sites.

Chase Group (The)
Phone: 913-663-3100
Fax: 913-663-3131
E-mail Address: *chase@chasegroup.com*
Web Address: www.chasegroup.com
The Chase Group is an executive search firm specializing in biomedical and pharmaceutical placement.

XVI. Careers-Coatings

CoatingsJobs.com
Web Address: www.coatingsjobs.com
CoatingsJobs.com connects coatings industry job seekers and employers. The web site offers job postings, resume postings, information for job seekers and an employment newsletter.

XVII. Careers-Computers/Technology

ComputerJobs.com, Inc.
1995 N. Park Pl., Ste. 425
Atlanta, GA 30339 US
Toll Free: 800-850-0045
Web Address: www.computerjobs.com
ComputerJobs.com is an employment web site that offers users a links to computer-related job opportunities organized by skill and market.

Dice
4101 NW Urbandale Dr.
Urbandale, IA 50322 US
Phone: 515-280-1144
Fax: 515-280-1452
Toll Free: 877-386-3323
E-mail Address: *dicemedia@dice.com*
Web Address: www.dice.com
Dice.com provides free employment services for IT jobs. The site includes advanced job searches by geographic location and category, availability announcements and resume postings, as well as employer profiles, a recruiter's page and career links. It is maintained by Dice Holdings, Inc., a publicly traded company.

Institute for Electrical and Electronics Engineers (IEEE) Job Site
445 Hoes Ln.
Piscataway, NJ 08855-1331 US
Phone: 732-981-0060
Toll Free: 800-678-4333
E-mail Address: *candidatejobsite@ieee.org*
Web Address: careers.ieee.org
The Institute for Electrical and Electronics Engineers (IEEE) Job Site provides a host of employment services for technical professionals, employers and recruiters. The site offers job listings by geographic area, a resume bank and links to employment services.

Pencom Systems, Inc.
152 Remsen St.
Brooklyn, NY 11201 US
Phone: 718-923-1111
Fax: 718-923-6066
Toll Free: 800-736-2664
E-mail Address: *tom@pencom.com*
Web Address: www.pencom.com
Pencom Systems, Inc., an open systems recruiting company, hosts a career web site geared toward high-technology and scientific professionals, featuring an interactive salary survey, career advisor,

job listings and technology resources. Its focus is the financial services industry within the New York City area.

XVIII. Careers-Contract and Freelance

Guru.com
5001 Baum Blvd., Ste. 760
Pittsburgh, PA 15213 US
Phone: 412-687-2228
Fax: 412-687-4466
Toll Free: 888-678-0136
E-mail Address: *pr@guru.com*
Web Address: www.guru.com
Guru.com provides contract job access for freelancers and contract workers, in fields ranging from interior design to architecture, marketing and web design, among others. Employers can post projects, and freelancers can offers bids on prospective jobs. Many tools are provided to enable freelancers to be completely informed about the scope of the work needed.

XIX. Careers-First Time Jobs/New Grads

Alumni-Network Recruitment Corporation
Phone: 905-465-2547
E-mail Address: *karen@alumni-network.com*
Web Address: www.alumni-network.com
Alumni-Network Recruitment Corporation is a professional search and recruiting firm, specializing in ERP, E-Commerce and Engineering.

Black Collegian Online (The)
140 Carondelet St.
New Orleans, LA 70130 US
Phone: 504-523-0154
Web Address: www.blackcollegian.com
The Black Collegian Online features listings for job and internship opportunities, as well as other tools for students of color; it is the web site of The Black Collegian Magazine, published by IMDiversity, Inc. The site includes a list of the top 100 minority corporate employers and an assessment of job opportunities.

CollegeGrad.com, Inc.
234 E. College Ave., Ste. 200
State College, PA 16801 US
Phone: 262-375-6700
Toll Free: 1-800-991-4642
Web Address: www.collegegrad.com
CollegeGrad.com, Inc. offers in-depth resources for college students and recent grads seeking entry-level jobs.

Job Web
62 Highland Ave.
Bethlehem, PA 18017-9085 US
Phone: 610-868-1421
Fax: 610-868-0208
Toll Free: 800-544-5272
E-mail Address: *callen@naceweb.org*
Web Address: www.jobweb.com
Job Web, owned and sponsored by National Association of Colleges and Employers (NACE), displays job openings and employer descriptions for college students and recent graduates. The site also offers a database of career fairs, searchable by state or keyword; sample resumes; and other career related information.

MBAjobs.net
Web Address: www.mbajobs.net
MBAjobs.net is an international service for MBA students and graduates, employers, recruiters and business schools. It aims to match MBA graduates with employers and provides links to online MBA programs.

MonsterCollege
799 Market St., Ste. 500
San Francisco, CA 94103 US
Toll Free: 800-999-8725
E-mail Address: *info@college.monster.com*
Web Address: www.college.monster.com
MonsterCollege provides information about internships and entry-level jobs, as well as career advice and resume tips, to recent college graduates.

National Association of Colleges and Employers (NACE)
62 Highland Ave.
Bethlehem, PA 18017-9085 US
Phone: 610-868-1421
Fax: 610-868-0208
Toll Free: 800-544-5272
E-mail Address: *mcollins@naceweb.org*
Web Address: www.naceweb.org
The National Association of Colleges and Employers (NACE) is a premier U.S. organization representing college placement offices and corporate recruiters who focus on hiring new grads.

XX. Careers-General Job Listings

6FigureJobs
25 3rd St., Ste. 230
Stamford, CT 06905 US
Toll Free: 800-605-5154
Web Address: www.6figurejobs.com
6FigureJobs offers executives a database of high-level positions. Membership is free for qualified individuals.

Career Exposure, Inc.
3934 SW Corbett Ave.
Portland, OR 97239 US
Phone: 503-221-7779
Fax: 503-221-7780
E-mail Address: *pr@careerexposure.com*
Web Address: www.careerexposure.com
Career Exposure, Inc. is an online career center and job placement service, with resources for employers, recruiters and job seekers.

CareerBuilder, Inc.
200 N. LaSalle St., Ste. 1100
Chicago, IL 60601 US
Phone: 773-527-3600
Toll Free: 800-638-4212
Web Address: www.careerbuilder.com
CareerBuilder, Inc. focuses on the needs of companies and also provides a database of job openings. The site has over 1 million jobs posted by 300,000 employers, and receives an average 23 million unique visitors monthly. The company also operates online career centers for 140 newspapers and 9,000 online partners. Resumes are sent directly to the company, and applicants can set up a special e-mail account for job-seeking purposes. CareerBuilder is primarily a joint venture between three newspaper giants: The McClatchy Company, Gannett Co., Inc. and Tribune Company.

CareerOneStop
Toll Free: 877-348-0502
E-mail Address: *info@careeronestop.org*
Web Address: www.careeronestop.org
CareerOneStop is operated by the employment commissions of various state agencies. It contains job listings in both the private and government sectors, as well as a wide variety of useful career resources and workforce information. CareerOneStop is sponsored by the U.S. Department of Labor.

Careers Organization (The)
155 108th Ave. NE, Ste. 810
Bellevue, WA 98004 US
Phone: 510-663-7000
Fax: 510-663-7001
E-mail Address: *support@careers.org*
Web Address: www.careers.org
The Career Organization is an online career resource center with links to jobs and other career-related web sites, as well as information regarding colleges and online degree programs.

CollegeRecruiter.com
3109 W. 50 St., Ste. 121
Minneapolis, MN 55410-2102 US
Phone: 952-848-2211
Fax: 702-537-2227
E-mail Address:
Steven@CollegeRecruiter.com
Web Address: www.collegerecruiter.com
CollegeRecruiter.com provides college students with internship, part-time and summer job listings. Recent graduates can search for career opportunities by category and location.

ContractJobHunter
C. E. Publications, Inc.
P.O. Box 3006
Bothell, WA 98041-3006 US
Phone: 425-806-5200
Fax: 425-806-5585
E-mail Address: *staff@cjhunter.com*
Web Address: www.ceweekly.wa.com
ContractJobHunter is a web-based version of the magazine Contract Employment Weekly Online. It posts job listings and links to contract firms in the engineering, IT and technical fields. Libraries for reference materials and resume writing guidelines are also offered. The site is a service of C. E. Publications, Inc.

EmploymentGuide
150 Granby St.
Norfolk, VA 23510 US
Toll Free: 877-876-4039
Web Address:
www.employmentguide.com
EmploymentGuide offers general career resources along with lists of position openings, company profiles and a resume database. It also circulates a free print publication.

EscapeArtist.com Inc.
832-1245 World Trade Ctr.
Panama, WTC-0832 Republic of Panama
Phone: 507-317-6937
Fax: 507-317-6938
Web Address: www.escapeartist.com
EscapeArtist.com provides job searches for overseas positions, as well as international working condition resources and immigration information.

ExecuNet, Inc.
295 Westport Ave.
Norwalk, CT 06851 US
Toll Free: 800-637-3126
E-mail Address:
member.services@execunet.com
Web Address: www.execunet.com
ExecuNet, Inc. is an executive career management information and contact service.

HigherEdJobs.com
328 Innovation Blvd., Ste. 300
State College, PA 16803 US
Phone: 814-861-3080
Fax: 814-861-3082
E-mail Address:
sales@HigherEdJobs.com
Web Address: www.higheredjobs.com
HigherEdJobs.com lists job vacancies in colleges and universities.

IMDiversity, Inc.
140 Carondelet St.
New Orleans, LA 70130 US
Phone: 504-598-3357
Fax: 504-523-0271
E-mail Address:
support@imdiversity.com
Web Address: www.imdiversity.com
IMDiversity, Inc. provides job listings and career development information for minorities in the U.S., with a particular focus on African Americans, Asian Americans and Pacific Islanders, Latino/Hispanic Americans, Native Americans and women.

Indeed.com
177 Broad St., Fl. 6
Stamford, CT 06901 US
Web Address: www.indeed.com
Indeed.com provides extensive lists of jobs of all types, with links directly to the employers. It covers over 50 countries, including the U.S., Canada, India, Mexico.

Job Search USA
E-mail Address:
contactjsu@jobsearchusa.org
Web Address: www.jobsearchusa.org
Job Search USA is a major job posting site that contains job opportunities classified by a variety of keywords.

JobCentral
9002 N. Purdue Rd., Ste. 100
Indianapolis, IN 46268 US
Phone: 317-874-9000
Fax: 317-874-9100
Toll Free: 866-268-6206
Web Address: www.jobcentral.com
JobCentral, operated by the nonprofit DirectEmployers Association, Inc., links users directly to job opportunities posted on the sites of participating employers, thus bypassing the usual job search sites. This saves employers money and allows job seekers to access many more job opportunities.

Jobs in Logistics
Toll Free: 877-562-7678
Web Address: www.jobsinlogistics.com
Jobs in Logistics provides contacts for job seekers in the transportation and logistics fields.

JobsInTheMoney.com
1040 Avenue of the Americas, Ste. 16B
New York, NY 10018 US
Phone: 212-448-8287
Fax: 212-725-9127
Toll Free: 800-380-9040
E-mail Address: *help-usa@efinancialcareers.com*
Web Address:
www.efinancialcareers.com
efinancialcareers.com provides employment listings in the finance industry, as well as job tools such as salary surveys, resume writing assistance and industry news. It is owned by Dice, a part of Dice Holdings, Inc.

LaborMarketInfo (LMI)
P.O. Box 826880, MIC 57
c/o Employment Dev. Dept., Labor Market Info. Div.
Sacramento, CA 94280-0001 US
Phone: 916-262-2162
Fax: 916-262-2352
Toll Free: 800-480-3287
Web Address:
www.labormarketinfo.edd.ca.gov
LaborMarketInfo (LMI) provides job seekers and employers a wide range of resources, namely the ability to find, access and use labor market information and services. It provides statistics for employment demographics on both a local and regional level, as well as career searching tools for California residents. The web site is sponsored by California's Employment Development Office.

MediaBistro.com
475 Park Ave. S., Fl. 4
New York, NY 10016 US
Phone: 212-389-2000
Fax: 866-880-1429
E-mail Address:
laurelT@mediabistro.com
Web Address: www.mediabistro.com
MediaBistro.com provides news and information on current events relating to the media industry. It also offers an array of employment resources, including job listings within the industry.

Monster Worldwide, Inc.
622 Third Ave., Fl. 39
New York, NY 10017 US
Phone: 212-351-7000
Fax: 646-658-0540
E-mail Address:
matthew.henson@monster.com
Web Address: www.monster.com

Monster Worldwide, Inc., parent company of Monster.com, provides online career and personnel services. The firm operates in 50 countries.

MyResumeAgent.com
1 Phoenix Mill Ln., Fl. 3
Kennedy Information, Inc.
Peterborough, NH 03458 US
Phone: 603-924-0900
Toll Free: 800-531-0007
E-mail Address:
feedback@myresumeagent.com
Web Address: www.myresumeagent.com
MyResumeAgent.com allows senior-level professionals to have their resumes sent to executive placement firms for a fee. The site is owned by Kennedy Information, Inc.

NationJob, Inc.
920 Morgan St., Ste. T
Des Moines, IA 50309 US
Fax: 515-243-5384
Toll Free: 888-292-7731
E-mail Address:
customerservice@nationjob.com
Web Address: www.nationjob.com
NationJob.com is an online job search portal. The web site allows users to search through listings or develop a profile of the ideal job based on the criterion of location, industry, salary; and, if they provide an e-mail address, wait for appropriate listings to be sent to them through the firm's PJScout feature.

NETSHARE, Inc.
83 Hamilton Dr., Ste. 202
Novato, CA 94949 US
Toll Free: 800-241-5642
E-mail Address: *netshare@netshare.com*
Web Address: www.netshare.com
Netshare provides access to exclusive listings of executive jobs that pay $100,000 and up.

Net-Temps, Inc.
55 Middlesex St., Ste. 220
North Chelmsford, MA 01863 US
Fax: 978-251-7250
Toll Free: 800-307-0062
E-mail Address: *service@net-temps.com*
Web Address: www.net-temps.com
Net-Temps, Inc. offers a web site, operated by professional career consultants, that features job listings and job seeking tips.

Recruiters Online Network
3599 E. Normandy Park Dr.
Medina, OH 44256 US
E-mail Address:
recruitersonline@earthlink.net
Web Address: www.recruitersonline.com
The Recruiters Online Network provides job postings from thousands of recruiters, Careers Online Magazine, a resume database, as well as other career resources.

True Careers, Inc.
Web Address: www.truecareers.com
True Careers, Inc. offers job listings and provides an array of career resources. It is partnered with CareerBuilder.com, which powers its career information and resume posting functions.

USAJOBS
1900 E St. NW
Washington, DC 20415 US
Phone: 202-606-1800
Web Address: usajobs.opm.gov
USAJOBS, a program of the U.S. Office of Personnel Management, is the official job site for the U.S. Federal Government. It provides a comprehensive list of U.S. government jobs, allowing users to search for employment by location; agency; type of work; or by senior executive positions. It also has special employment sections for individuals with disabilities, veterans and recent college graduates; an information center, offering resume and interview tips and other information; and allows users to create a profile and post a resume.

XXI. Careers-Health Care

Health Care Source
400 TradeCenter, Ste. 3900
Woburn, MA 01801 US
Phone: 781-368-1033
Fax: 800-829-6600
Toll Free: 800-869-5200
E-mail Address:
info@healthcaresource.com
Web Address: www.healthcaresource.com
Health Care Source is a leading provider of talent management, recruitment and employment services for healthcare providers.

MedicalWorkers.com
191 University Blvd., Ste. 252
Denver, CO 80206 US
Phone: 720-227-9364
E-mail Address: *cs@medicalworkers.com*
Web Address: www.medicalworkers.com
MedicalWorkers.com is an employment site for medical and health care professionals.

MedJump.com
7119 E. Shea Blvd., Stes. 109-535
Scottsdale, AZ 85254 US
E-mail Address: *info@medjump.net*
Web Address: www.medjump.com
MedJump.com is dedicated to empowering health care and medical-related professionals with the necessary tools to market their abilities and skills.

Medzilla, Inc.
P.O. Box 1710
Marysville, WA 98270 US
Phone: 360-657-5681
Fax: 775-514-9440
E-mail Address: *info@medzilla.com*
Web Address: www.medzilla.com
Medzilla, Inc.'s web site offers job searches, salary surveys, a search agent and information on employment in the biotech, pharmaceuticals, healthcare and science sectors.

Monster Career Advice-Healthcare
622 3rd Ave., Fl. 39
New York, NY 10017 US
Phone: 212-351-7000
Fax: 646-658-0540
Toll Free: 800-666-7837
Web Address: career-advice.monster.com/Healthcare/job-category-3975.aspx
Monster Career Advice-Healthcare, a service of Monster Worldwide, Inc., provides industry-related articles, job listings, job searches and search agents for the medical field.

NationJob Network-Medical and Health Care Jobs Page
601 SW 9th St., Stes. H&J
Des Moines, IA 50309 US
Fax: 515-243-5384
Toll Free: 800-292-7731
E-mail Address:
customerservice@nationjob.com
Web Address:
www.nationjob.com/medical
The NationJob Network-Medical and Health Care Jobs Page offers information and listings for health care employment.

Nurse-Recruiter.com
36 Washington St., Ste. 170
Wellesley, MA 02481 US
Toll Free: 877-562-7966
E-mail Address:
support@nurserecruiter.com
Web Address: www.nurse-recruiter.com
Nurse-Recruiter.com is a nurse-owned, web-centric company devoted to bringing health care employers and the nursing community together.

PracticeLink
Fax: 877-847-0120
Toll Free: 800-776-8383
E-mail Address:
physicianhelpdesk@practicelink.com

Web Address: www.practicelink.com
PracticeLink, one of the largest physician employment web sites, is a free service used by more than 18,000 practice-seeking physicians annually to quickly search and locate potential career opportunities. PracticeLink is financially supported by more than 700 hospitals, medical groups, private practices and health care systems that advertise more than 5,000 opportunities.

RPh on the Go USA, Inc.
5510 Howard St.
Skokie, IL 60077-2620 US
Phone: 847-588-7170
Fax: 847-588-7060
Toll Free: 800-553-7359
E-mail Address:
lbalaguer@rphonthego.com
Web Address: www.rphonthego.com
RPh on the Go USA, Inc. places temporary and permanent qualified professionals in the pharmacy community.

XXII. Careers-Interview Tips for Consulting Jobs

McKinsey & Company Interviewing Tips
55 E. 52nd St
New York, NY 10022 US
Phone: 212-446-7000
Fax: 212-446-8575
Web Address:
www.mckinsey.com/careers/how_do_i_apply/how_to_do_well_in_the_interview.aspx
The McKinsey & Company Interviewing Tips site is an excellent resource for preparing for a consulting interview.

XXIII. Careers-Job Listings for Seniors

Dinosaur Exchange
Dino-X Ltd., P.O. Box 100
Sydney Vane House Admiral Park
St. Peter Port, Guernsey GY1 3EL
Channel Islands
E-mail Address:
CustomerSupport@dinosaur-exchange.com
Web Address: www.dinosaur-exchange.com
Dinosaur Exchange, opened in 2003, is a job forum for the elderly, which allows seniors to post resumes and be contacted by employers. Dino-X Ltd. owns and operates the web site.

Employment Network for Retired Government Experts (ENRGE)
Zavala, Inc.
P.O. Box 1532
N. Falmouth, MA 02556 US
Phone: 508-564-4140
Web Address: www.enrge.us
The Employment Network for Retired Government Experts (ENRGE) helps government employees to remain active in their professions after retirement. ENERGE is the business name of Zavala, Inc.

Senior Job Bank
NHC Group, Inc.
P.O. Box 508
Marlborough, MA 01752 US
Toll Free: 888-501-0804
Web Address: www.seniorjobbank.org
The Senior Job Bank web site offers an easy, effective and free method for senior citizens to find occasional, part-time, flexible, temporary or full-time jobs. The site is owned and managed by NHC Group, Inc.

Seniors4Hire.org
7071 Warner Ave. F466
Huntington Beach, CA 92647 US
Phone: 714-848-0996
Fax: 714-848-5445
E-mail Address: *info@seniors4hire.org*
Web Address: www.seniors4hire.org
Seniors4Hire.org is an online career center with job postings, employment resources and information on community service employment programs for older workers, retirees and senior citizens. The site is owned and operated by The Forward Group.

YourEncore
20 N. Meridian St., Ste. 800
Indianapolis, IN 46204 US
Phone: 317-226-9301
Fax: 317-226-9312
E-mail Address:
General.Information@yourencore.com
Web Address: www.yourencore.com
YourEncore is a program that seeks to employ retirees by matching them with member companies. The web site utilizes retirees mainly in the areas of engineering, science and product development.

XXIV. Careers-Job Reference Tools

CareerXroads (CXR)
Mark Mehler
P.O. Box 253
Kendall Park, NJ 08824 US
Phone: 732-821-6652
E-mail Address: *mmc@careerxroads.com*
Web Address: www.careerxroads.com
CareerXroads (CXR) publishes an annual guide on job and resume web sites. It was cofounded by Gerry Crispin and Mark Mehler.

Job-Hunt.org
186 Main St.
NETability, Inc.
Marlborough, MA 01752 US
Phone: 508-624-6261
E-mail Address: *info@job-hunt.org*
Web Address: www.job-hunt.org
Job-Hunt.org, rather than collecting resumes or posting job vacancies, offers a vast list of job listing web sites and links to helpful job search tools. It is owned by NETability, Inc.

JobStar
E-mail Address:
electrajobstar@earthlink.net
Web Address: jobstar.org
JobStar has a salary info link to over 300 different salary information and salary survey sites. It also contains job listings focused on the California market.

MBA Career Services Council (CSC)
E-mail Address:
kip.harrell@thunderbird.edu.
Web Address: www.mbacsc.org
The MBA Career Services Council (CSC) is a global professional association for individuals in the field of MBA career services and those that recruit directly from graduate management programs.

NewsVoyager
Web Address: www.newsvoyager.com
NewsVoyager, a service of the Newspaper Association of America (NAA), links individuals to local, national and international newspapers, allowing job seekers to search through thousands of classified sections.

Quintessential Careers (QC)
EmpoweringSites.com
DeLand, Fl 32720 US
Phone: 386-740-8872
Fax: 386-740-9764
E-mail Address:
randall@quintcareers.com
Web Address: www.quintcareers.com
Quintessential Careers (QC) provides a large collection of data and links for job seekers, including advice, tools and job postings; it also offers a guide to researching companies. QC is a subsidiary of EmpoweringSites.com.

Vault.com, Inc.
75 Varick St., Fl. 8
New York, NY 10013 US
Phone: 212-366-4212
Fax: 212-366-6117
Web Address: www.vault.com
Vault.com, Inc. is a comprehensive career web site for employers and employees, with job postings and valuable information on a wide variety of industries. Its features and content are largely geared toward MBA degree holders.

WetFeet.com
Web Address: www.wetfeet.com
WetFeet.com provides an excellent combination of links and resources for job seekers. The site is owned by Universum.

What Color is Your Parachute?
E-mail Address:
rnbolles@jobhuntersbible.com
Web Address: www.jobhuntersbible.com
The What Color is Your Parachute? official web site, JobHuntersBible.com, is based on the "Job-Hunting on the Internet" chapter of Richard (Dick) Bolle's best-selling book. Designed to aid job hunters and career changers who want to use the Internet as part of their job search, the site provides links to job listing, resume, career counseling, contacts and research sites.

XXV. Careers-Restaurants

FoodService.com
Phone: 678-256-8014
Toll Free: 800-896-4442
E-mail Address:
customercare@Foodservice.com
Web Address: www.foodservice.com
FoodService.com, managed and run by Food Service Interactive, LLC, offers web site design and job search services for the food service industry.

Resources in Food, Inc. (RIF)
1007 N. Main St.
Columbia, IL 62236 US
Phone: 618-281-3100
Fax: 866-281-7374
Toll Free: 877-743-1100
E-mail Address: *rifchicago@rifood.com*
Web Address: www.rifood.com
Resources in Food (RIF) provides professional management placement for the hospitality industry.

XXVI. Careers-Science

Chem Jobs
730 E. Cypress Ave.
Monrovia, CA 91016 US
Phone: 626-930-0808
Fax: 626-930-0102
E-mail Address: *info@chemindustry.com*
Web Address: www.chemjobs.net
Chem Jobs is a leading Internet site for job seekers in chemistry and related fields, with a particular focus on chemists, biochemists, pharmaceutical scientists and chemical engineers. The web site is powered by Chemindustry.com.

New Scientist Jobs
Quadrant House
84 Theobald's Rd.
Sutton, SM2 5AS UK
E-mail Address: *nssales@elsevier.com.*
Web Address: www.newscientistjobs.com
New Scientist Jobs is a web site produced by the publishers of New Scientist Magazine that connects jobseekers and employers in the bioscience fields. The site includes a job search engine and a free-of-charge e-mail job alert service.

Science Jobs
E-mail Address: *webmaster@science-jobs.org*
Web Address: www.science-jobs.org
Science Jobs is a web site that contains many useful categories of links, including employment newsgroups, scientific journals and placement agencies. It also links to sites containing information regarding internship and fellowship opportunities for high school students and undergrads.

XXVII. Careers-Sports

Jobs in Sports
2506 N. Clark St., Ste. 225
Chicago, IL 60614 US
E-mail Address:
comments@jobsinsports.com
Web Address: www.jobsinsports.com
Jobs in Sports is an employment web site that provides job listings in areas including sports marketing, sports media, sales, health and fitness, computers and administration, as well as other job resources.

Sports Careers
7010 E. Chauncey Ln., Ste. 115
Phoenix, AZ 85054 US
E-mail Address:
support@sportscareers.com
Web Address: www.sportscareers.com
Sports Careers offers a range of services to help individuals and employers in the sports industry, including job listings, a resume bank, industry contacts and salary information.

Sports Job Board
Web Address: www.sportsjobboard.com
The Sports Job Board is an employment web site for the sports industry.

WomenSportsJobs.com
Women's Sport Services, LLC
P.O. Box 11
Huntington Beach, CA 92648 US
Phone: 714-848-1201
Fax: 714-848-5111
E-mail Address:
Feedback@WSServices.com
Web Address:
www.womensportsjobs.com
WomenSportsJobs.com is an employment web site specializing in jobs for women in the sports industry. The site is managed by Women's Sport Services, LLC.

Work in Sports LLC
7335 E. Chauncey Ln., Ste. 115
Phoenix, AZ 85054 US
Phone: 480-905-7221
Fax: 480-905-7231
Web Address: www.workinsports.com
Work in Sports LLC is an online employment resource for the sports industry that posts hundreds of jobs on its web site.

XXVIII. Careers-Telecommunications

Call Center Careers
6525 Gunpark Dr.
Ste. 570, PMB 127
Boulder, CO 80301 US
Phone: 303-527-1440
Fax: 303-530-0154
Toll Free: 877-562-8588
E-mail Address:
sales@callcentercareers.com
Web Address: www.callcentercareers.com
Call Center Careers provides recruiting and staffing services to the call center industry.

XXIX. Careers-Video Games Industry

GameJobs
Web Address: www.gamejobs.com
GameJobs.com is independently owned and operated by the Crest Group, LLC., the managers of the Interactive Entertainment Merchants Association (IEMA), a non-profit retail trade association

Video Game Jobs-About.com Career Planning
Web Address:
http://careerplanning.about.com/od/occupations/a/videogamecareer.htm
A useful page on About.com that contains advice and links for people interested in working in the video games industry.

XXX. Chemicals Industry Associations

American Chemical Society (ACS)
1155 16th St. NW
Washington, DC 20036 US
Phone: 202-872-4600
Toll Free: 800-227-5558
E-mail Address:
executivedirector@acs.org
Web Address: www.acs.org
The American Chemical Society (ACS) is a nonprofit organization aimed at promoting the understanding of chemistry and chemical sciences. It represents a wide range of disciplines including chemistry, chemical engineering and other technical fields.

XXXI. Communications Professional Associations

Association for Women In Communications (AWC)
3337 Duke St.
Alexandria, VA 22314 US
Phone: 703-370-7436
Fax: 703-370-7437
E-mail Address: *info@womcom.org*
Web Address: www.womcom.org
The Association for Women In Communications (AWC) is a professional organization that works for the advancement of women across all communications disciplines by recognizing excellence, promoting leadership and positioning its members at the forefront of the communications industry.

Health and Science Communications Association (HeSCA)
39 Wedgewood Dr., Ste. A
Jewett City, CT 06351 US
Phone: 860-376-5915
Fax: 860-376-6621
E-mail Address: *hesca@hesca.org*
Web Address: www.hesca.org
The Health and Science Communications Association (HeSCA) is an organization of communications professionals committed to sharing knowledge and resources in the health sciences arena.

Health Industry Business Communications Council (HIBCC)
2525 E. Arizona Biltmore Cir., Ste. 127
Phoenix, AZ 85016 US
Phone: 602-381-1091
Fax: 602-381-1093
E-mail Address: *info@hibcc.org*
Web Address: www.hibcc.org
The Health Industry Business Communications Council (HIBCC) seeks to facilitate electronic communications by developing appropriate standards for information exchange among all health care trading partners.

International Association of Business Communicators (IABC)
1 Hallidie Plz., Ste. 600
San Francisco, CA 94102 US
Phone: 415-544-4700
Fax: 415-544-4747
Toll Free: 800-776-4222
E-mail Address: *jugalde@iabc.com*
Web Address: www.iabc.com
The International Association of Business Communicators (IABC) is the leading resource for effective business communication practices.

XXXII. Computer & Electronics Industry Associations

Electronics Technicians Association (ETA)
5 Depot St.
Greencastle, IN 46135 US
Phone: 765-653-8262
Fax: 765-653-4287
Toll Free: 800-288-3824
E-mail Address: *eta@eta-i.org*
Web Address: www.eta-i.org
The Electronics Technicians Association (ETA) is a nonprofit professional association for electronics technicians worldwide. The organization provides recognized professional credentials for electronics technicians.

Semiconductor Industry Association (SIA)
1101 K St. NW, Ste. 450
Washington, DC 20005 US
Phone: 202-446-1700
Fax: 202-216-9745
Toll Free: 866-756-0715
E-mail Address: *mailbox@sia-online.org*
Web Address: www.sia-online.org
The Semiconductor Industry Association (SIA) is a trade association representing the semiconductor industry in the U.S. Through its coalition of more than 60 companies, SIA members represent roughly 80% of semiconductor production in the U.S. The coalition aims to advance the competitiveness of the chip industry and shape public policy on issues particular to the industry.

TechAmerica
601 Pennsylvania Ave. NW
North Bldg., Ste. 600
Washington, DC 20004 US
Phone: 202-682-9110
Fax: 202-682-9111
E-mail Address: *csc@techamerica.org*
Web Address: www.techamerica.org
TechAmerica was formed from the combination of former technology and electronics industry associations AeA and Information Technology Association of America (ITAA). The combined organization represents nearly 1,200 member companies of all sizes from the public and commercial sectors of the industry.

XXXIII. Consulting Industry Associations

American Association of Healthcare Consultants (AAHC)
5938 N. Drake Ave.
Chicago, IL 60659 US
Fax: 773-463-3552
Toll Free: 888-350-2242
E-mail Address: *info@aahcmail.org*
Web Address: www.aahc.net
The American Association of Healthcare Consultants (AAHC) is a professional society for credentialed consultants practicing in health care organization and delivery.

Association of Internal Management Consultants (AIMC)
824 Caribbean Ct.
Marco Island, FL 34145 US
Phone: 239-642-0580
Fax: 239-642-1119
E-mail Address: *info@aimc.org*
Web Address: www.aimc.org
The Association of Internal Management Consultants (AIMC) is a professional association representing in-house management consultants. Members work in for-profit corporations, government agencies, educational institutions and nonprofit organizations.

Institute of Management Consultants USA (IMC)
2025 M St. NW, Ste. 800
Washington, DC 20036-3309 US
Phone: 202-367-1134
Fax: 202-367-2134
E-mail Address: *gail@imcusa.org*
Web Address: www.imcusa.org

The Institute of Management Consultants USA (IMC) certifies management consultants in accordance with the strict international standards of the International Council of Management Consulting Institutes.

Investment Management Consultant Association (IMCA)
5619 DTC Pkwy., Ste. 500
Greenwood Village, CO 80111 US
Phone: 303-770-3377
Fax: 303-770-1812
E-mail Address: *imca@imca.org*
Web Address: www.imca.org
The Investment Management Consultant Association (IMCA) provides information and communication for investment management consultants.

XXXIV. Consulting Industry Resources

Consulting Magazine
1 Washington Park, Ste. 1300
100 Enterprise Dr., Ste. 600
Newark, NJ 07102 US
Phone: 212-563-6054
Fax: 212-564-0465
E-mail Address:
consultingmag@kennedyinfo.com
Web Address: www.consultingmag.com
Consulting Magazine is a leading publication for the consulting industry, and features information on consulting careers, thought leadership and corporate strategies. The magazine is published by Kennedy Information, Inc., a BNA Company.

XXXV. Corporate Information Resources

bizjournals.com
120 W. Morehead St., Ste. 400
Charlotte, NC 28202 US
Web Address: www.bizjournals.com
Bizjournals.com is the online media division of American City Business Journals, the publisher of dozens of leading city business journals nationwide. It provides access to research into the latest news regarding companies both small and large. The organization maintains 42 websites and 64 print publications and sponsors over 700 annual industry events.

Business Wire
44 Montgomery St., Fl. 39
San Francisco, CA 94104 US
Phone: 415-986-4422
Fax: 415-788-5335
Toll Free: 800-227-0845
Web Address: www.businesswire.com
Business Wire offers news releases, industry- and company-specific news, top headlines, conference calls, IPOs on the Internet, media services and access to tradeshownews.com and BW Connect On-line through its informative and continuously updated web site.

Edgar Online, Inc.
11200 Rockville Pike, Ste. 310
Rockville, MD 20852 US
Phone: 301-287-0300
Fax: 301-287-0390
Toll Free: 888-870-2316
Web Address: www.edgar-online.com
Edgar Online, Inc. is a gateway and search tool for viewing corporate documents, such as annual reports on Form 10-K, filed with the U.S. Securities and Exchange Commission.

PR Newswire Association LLC
350 Hudson St., Ste. 300
New York, NY 10014 US
Fax: 800-793-9313
Toll Free: 800-776-8090
E-mail Address:
information@prnewswire.com
Web Address: www.prnewswire.com
PR Newswire Association LLC provides comprehensive communications services for public relations and investor relations professionals, ranging from information distribution and market intelligence to the creation of online multimedia content and investor relations web sites. Users can also view recent corporate press releases from companies across the globe. The Association is owned by United Business Media plc.

Silicon Investor
100 W. Main
P.O. Box 29
Freeman, MO 64746 US
E-mail Address: *bobz@talkzilla.com*
Web Address: siliconinvestor.advfn.com
Silicon Investor is focused on providing information about technology companies. Its web site serves as a financial discussion forum and offers quotes, profiles and charts.

XXXVI. Disabling Conditions

Job Accommodation Network (JAN)
P.O. Box 6080
Morgantown, WV 26506-6080 US
Phone: 304-293-7186
Fax: 304-293-5407
Toll Free: 800-526-7234
E-mail Address: *jan@jan.wvu.edu*
Web Address: janweb.icdi.wvu.edu
The Job Accommodation Network (JAN) is a free consulting service that provides information about job accommodations, the Americans with Disabilities Act and the employability of people with disabilities.

XXXVII. Electronic Health Records/Continuity of Care Records

American Health Information Management Association (AHIMA)
233 N. Michigan Ave., Fl. 21
Chicago, IL 60601-5800 US
Phone: 312-233-1100
Fax: 312-233-1090
E-mail Address:
alan.dowling@ahima.org
Web Address: www.ahima.org
The American Health Information Management Association (AHIMA) is a professional association that consists health information management professionals who work throughout the health care industry.

American Medical Informatics Association (AMIA)
4915 St. Elmo Ave., Ste. 401
Bethesda, MD 20814 US
Phone: 301-657-1291
Fax: 301-657-1296
E-mail Address: *mail@amia.org*
Web Address: www.amia.org
The American Medical Informatics Association (AMIA) is a membership organization of individuals, institutions and corporations dedicated to developing and using information technologies to improve health care.

College of Healthcare Information Management Executives (CHIME)
3300 Washtenaw Ave., Ste. 225
Ann Arbor, MI 48104 US
Phone: 734-665-0000
Fax: 734-665-4922
E-mail Address: *staff@cio-chime.org*
Web Address: www.cio-chime.org
College of Healthcare Information Management Executives (CHIME) was formed with the dual objective of serving the professional development needs of health care CIOs and advocating the more effective use of information management within health care.

Healthcare Information and Management Systems Society (HIMSS)
230 E. Ohio St., Ste. 500
Chicago, IL 60611-3270 US

Phone: 312-664-4467
Fax: 312-664-6143
E-mail Address: *himss@himss.org*
Web Address: www.himss.org
The Healthcare Information and Management Systems Society (HIMSS) provides leadership in the optimal use of technology, information and management systems for the betterment of health care.

XXXVIII. Energy Associations-Electric Power

American Public Power Association (APPA)
1875 Connecticut Ave. NW, Ste. 1200
Washington, DC 20009-5715 US
Phone: 202-467-2900
Fax: 202-467-2910
E-mail Address: *mrufe@appanet.org*
Web Address: www.appanet.org
The American Public Power Association (APPA) is a nonprofit service organization for the country's community-owned electric utilities, dedicated to advancing the public policy interests of its members and their consumers.

Edison Electric Institute (EEI)
701 Pennsylvania Ave. NW
Washington, DC 20004-2696 US
Phone: 202-508-5000
E-mail Address: *feedback@eei.org*
Web Address: www.eei.org
The Edison Electric Institute (EEI) is an association of U.S. shareholder-owned electric companies as well as worldwide affiliates and industry associates. Its web site provides energy news and a link to Electric Perspectives magazine.

Women's International Network of Utility Professionals (WINUP)
P.O. Box 817
Fergus Falls, MN 56538-0817 US
Phone: 218-731-1659
E-mail Address: *tdrexler@otpco.com*
Web Address: www.winup.org
The Women's International Network of Utility Professionals (WINUP) provides networking and support for women in the utility industry.

XXXIX. Energy Associations-Natural Gas

American Gas Association (AGA)
400 N. Capitol St. NW, Ste. 450
Washington, DC 20001 US
Phone: 202-824-7000
E-mail Address: *rshelby@aga.org*
Web Address: www.aga.org
The American Gas Association (AGA) represents a large number of natural gas providers, advocating for these companies and providing a broad range of programs and services for members.

XL. Energy Associations-Other

American Association of Blacks in Energy
1625 K St. NW, Ste. 450
Washington, DC 20006 US
Phone: 202-371-9530
Fax: 202-371-9218
E-mail Address: *info@aabe.org*
Web Address: www.aabe.org
The American Association of Blacks in Energy is dedicated to ensuring the input of African Americans and other minorities in discussions and developments of energy policies, regulations, research and development technologies and environmental issues.

XLI. Energy Associations-Petroleum, Exploration, Production, etc.

American Association of Professional Landmen (AAPL)
4100 Fossil Creek Blvd.
Fort Worth, TX 76137 US
Phone: 817-847-7700
Fax: 817-847-7704
E-mail Address: *aapl@landman.org*
Web Address: www.landman.org
The American Association of Professional Landmen (AAPL) promotes the highest standards of performance for all land professionals and seeks to advance their stature and to encourage sound stewardship of energy and mineral resources.

American Petroleum Institute (API)
1220 L St. NW
Washington, DC 20005-4070 US
Phone: 202-682-8000
Web Address: www.api.org
American Petroleum Institute (API) represents U.S. oil and gas industries and its web site includes in-depth sections for energy consumers and energy professionals.

Independent Petroleum Association of America (IPAA)
1201 15th St. NW, Ste. 300
Washington, DC 20005 US
Phone: 202-857-4722
Fax: 202-857-4799
E-mail Address: *rcarter@ipaa.org*
Web Address: www.ipaa.org
The Independent Petroleum Association of America (IPAA) provides a forum for the exploration and production segment of the independent oil and natural gas business. It also provides information on the domestic exploration and production industry.

International Association of Drilling Contractors (IADC)
10370 Richmond Ave., Ste. 760
Houston, TX 77042 US
Phone: 713-292-1945
Fax: 713-292-1946
E-mail Address: *info@iadc.org*
Web Address: www.iadc.org
The International Association of Drilling Contractors (IADC) represents the worldwide oil and gas drilling industry and promotes commitment to safety, preservation of the environment and advances in drilling technology.

XLII. Engineering, Research & Scientific Associations

American Association of Petroleum Geologists (AAPG)
1444 S. Boulder Ave.
Tulsa, OK 74119 US
Phone: 918-584-2555
Fax: 918-560-2665
Toll Free: 800-364-2274
E-mail Address: *lnation@aapg.org*
Web Address: www.aapg.org
The American Association of Petroleum Geologists (AAPG) is an international geological organization that supports educational and scientific programs and projects related to geosciences.

American Institute of Chemical Engineers (AIChE)
3 Park Ave.
New York, NY 10016-5991 US
Phone: 203-702-7660
Fax: 203-775-5177
Toll Free: 800-242-4363
E-mail Address: *steps@aiche.org*
Web Address: www.aiche.org
The American Institute of Chemical Engineers (AIChE) provides leadership in advancing the chemical engineering profession. The organization, which is comprised of more than 40,000 members from over 90 countries, provides informational resources to chemical engineers.

American Society for Healthcare Engineering (ASHE)
155 N. Wacker Dr., Ste. 400
Chicago, IL 60606 US
Phone: 312-422-3800
Fax: 312-422-4571
E-mail Address: *ashe@aha.org*
Web Address: www.ashe.org
The American Society for Healthcare Engineering (ASHE) is the advocate and resource for continuous improvement in the health care engineering and facilities management professions.

American Society of Agricultural and Biological Engineers (ASABE)
2950 Niles Rd.
St. Joseph, MI 49085 US
Phone: 269-429-0300
Fax: 269-429-3852
E-mail Address: *hq@asabe.org*
Web Address: www.asabe.org
The American Society of Agricultural and Biological Engineers (ASABE) is a nonprofit professional and technical organization interested in engineering knowledge and technology for food and agriculture and associated industries.

American Society of Civil Engineers (ASCE)
1801 Alexander Bell Dr.
Reston, VA 20191-4400 US
Phone: 703-295-6300
Fax: 703-295-6222
Toll Free: 800-548-2723
E-mail Address: *member@asce.org*
Web Address: www.asce.org
The American Society of Civil Engineers (ASCE) is a leading professional organization serving civil engineers. It ensures safer buildings, water systems and other civil engineering works by developing technical codes and standards.

American Society of Safety Engineers (ASSE)
1800 E. Oakton St.
Des Plaines, IL 60018 US
Phone: 847-699-2929
Fax: 847-768-3434
E-mail Address:
customerservice@asse.org
Web Address: www.asse.org
The American Society of Safety Engineers (ASSE) is the world's oldest and largest professional safety organization. It manages, supervises and consults on safety, health and environmental issues in industry, insurance, government and education.

Association of Federal Communications Consulting Engineers (AFCCE)
P.O. Box 19333
Washington, DC 20036 US
E-mail Address: *secretary@afcce.org*
Web Address: www.afcce.org
The Association of Federal Communications Consulting Engineers (AFCCE) is a professional organization of individuals who regularly assist clients on technical issues before the Federal Communications Commission (FCC).

Institute of Industrial Engineers (IIE)
3577 Parkway Ln., Ste. 200
Norcross, GA 30092 US
Phone: 770-449-0460
Fax: 770-441-3295
Toll Free: 800-494-0460
E-mail Address:
executiveoffices@iienet.org
Web Address: www.iienet2.org
The Institute of Industrial Engineers (IIE) is dedicated to the professional needs of industrial engineers.

National Society of Professional Engineers (NSPE)
1420 King St.
Alexandria, VA 22314-2794 US
Phone: 703-684-2800
Fax: 703-836-4875
Toll Free: 888-285-6773
E-mail Address: *memserv@nspe.org*
Web Address: www.nspe.org
The National Society of Professional Engineers (NSPE) represents individual engineering professionals and licensed engineers across all disciplines. NSPE serves approximately 45,000 members and has more than 500 chapters.

Society of Automotive Engineers (SAE)
755 W. Big Beaver, Ste. 1600
Troy, MA 48084 US
Phone: 248-273-2455
Fax: 248-273-2494
Toll Free: 877-606-7323
E-mail Address: *automotive_hq@sae.org*
Web Address: www.sae.org
The Society of Automotive Engineers (SAE) is a resource for technical information and expertise used in designing, building, maintaining and operating self-propelled vehicles for use on land, sea, air or space.

Society of Broadcast Engineers, Inc. (SBE)
9102 N. Meridian St., Ste. 150
Indianapolis, IN 46260 US
Phone: 317-846-9000
Fax: 317-846-9120
E-mail Address: *mclappe@sbe.org*
Web Address: www.sbe.org
The Society of Broadcast Engineers (SBE) exists to increase knowledge of broadcast engineering and promote its interests, as well as to continue the education of professionals in the industry.

Society of Cable Telecommunications Engineers (SCTE)
140 Philips Rd.
Exton, PA 19341-1318 US
Phone: 610-363-6888
Fax: 610-363-5898
Toll Free: 800-542-5040
E-mail Address: *scte@scte.org*
Web Address: www.scte.org
The Society of Cable Telecommunications Engineers (SCTE) is a nonprofit professional association dedicated to advancing the careers and serving the industry of telecommunications professionals by providing technical training, certification and standards.

Society of Hispanic Professional Engineers (SHPE)
5400 E. Olympic Blvd., Ste. 210
Los Angeles, CA 90022 US
Phone: 323-725-3970
Fax: 323-725-0316
E-mail Address: *shpenational@shpe.org*
Web Address: oneshpe.shpe.org
The Society of Hispanic Professional Engineers (SHPE) is a national nonprofit organization that promotes Hispanics in science, engineering and math.

Society of Manufacturing Engineers (SME)
1 SME Dr.
Dearborn, MI 48121 US
Phone: 313-425-3000
Fax: 313-425-3400
Toll Free: 800-733-4763
E-mail Address:
communications@sme.org
Web Address: www.sme.org
The Society of Manufacturing Engineers (SME) is a leading professional organization serving engineers in the manufacturing industries.

Society of Motion Picture and Television Engineers (SMPTE)
3 Barker Ave., Fl. 5
White Plains, NY 10601 US
Phone: 914-761-1100
Fax: 914-761-3115
Web Address: www.smpte.org
The Society of Motion Picture and Television Engineers (SMPTE) is the leading technical society for the motion imaging industry. The firm publishes recommended practice and engineering guidelines, as well the SMPTE Journal.

Society of Women Engineers (SWE)
230 E. Ohio St., Ste. 400

Chicago, IL 60611 US
Phone: 312-596-5223
Toll Free: 877-793-4636
E-mail Address: *hq@swe.org*
Web Address:
societyofwomenengineers.swe.org
The Society of Women Engineers (SWE) is a nonprofit educational and service organization of female engineers.

SPIE
1000 20th St.
Bellingham, WA 98225-6705 US
Phone: 360-676-3290
Fax: 360-647-1445
Toll Free: 888-504-8171
E-mail Address:
CustomerService@spie.org
Web Address: www.spie.org
SPIE is a nonprofit technical society aimed at the advancement and dissemination of knowledge in optics, photonics and imaging.

XLIII. Entertainment & Amusement Associations-General

International Association of Amusement Parks and Attractions (IAAPA)
1448 Duke St.
Alexandria, VA 22314 US
Phone: 703-836-4800
Fax: 703-836-6742
E-mail Address: *dmandt@iaapa.org*
Web Address: www.iaapa.org
The International Association of Amusement Parks and Attractions (IAAPA) is dedicated to the preservation and prosperity of the amusement industry.

International Special Events Society (ISES)
401 N. Michigan Ave.
Chicago, IL 60611-4267 US
Phone: 312-321-6853
Fax: 312-673-6953
Toll Free: 800-688-4737
E-mail Address: *info@ises.com*
Web Address: www.ises.com
The International Special Events Society (ISES) is comprised of over 7,200 professionals in over 38 countries representing special event planners and producers (from festivals to trade shows), caterers, decorators, florists, destination management companies, rental companies, special effects experts, tent suppliers, audio-visual technicians, event and convention coordinators, balloon artists, educators, journalists, hotel sales managers, specialty entertainers, convention center managers, and many more professional disciplines.

XLIV. Film & Theater Associations

Academy of Motion Picture Arts and Sciences (AMPAS)
8949 Wilshire Blvd.
Beverly Hills, CA 90211-1972 US
Phone: 310-247-3000
Fax: 310-859-9619
Web Address: www.oscars.org
The Academy of Motion Picture Arts and Sciences (AMPAS) is a professional honorary organization, founded to advance the arts and sciences of motion pictures. Besides hosting the Academy Awards and selecting the winners of the Oscars, AMPAS organizes smaller events highlighting the art of filmmaking, including lectures and seminars, and is currently building the Academy Museum of Motion Pictures.

Alliance of Motion Picture and Television Producers (AMPTP)
15301 Ventura Blvd.
Encino, CA 91403 US
Toll Free: 818-995-3600
Web Address: www.amptp.org
The Alliance of Motion Picture and Television Producers (AMPTP) is the primary trade association with respect to labor issues in the motion picture and television industry.

American Cinema Editors, Inc. (ACE)
100 Universal City Plz.
Verna Fields Bldg. 2282, Rm. 190
Universal City, CA 91608 US
Phone: 818-777-2900
Fax: 818-733-5023
E-mail Address:
amercinema@earthlink.net
Web Address: www.ace-filmeditors.org
American Cinema Editors (ACE) is an honorary society of motion picture editors that seeks to advance the art and science of the editing profession.

American Society of Cinematographers (ASC)
1782 N. Orange Dr.
Hollywood, CA 90028 US
Phone: 323-969-4333
Fax: 323-882-6391
Toll Free: 800-448-0145
E-mail Address: *office@theasc.com*
Web Address: www.theasc.com
The American Society of Cinematographers (ASC) is a trade association for cinematographers in the motion picture industry.

Art Directors Guild (ADG)
11969 Ventura Blvd., Fl. 2
Studio City, CA 91604 US
Phone: 818-762-9995
Fax: 818-762-9997
E-mail Address: *nick@artdirectors.org*
Web Address: www.artdirectors.org
The Art Directors Guild (ADG) represents the creative talents that conceive and manage the background and settings for most films and television projects.

Association of Cinema and Video Laboratories (ACVL)
630 9th Ave.
Chip Wilkinson, Pres., ACVL
New York, NY 10036 US
Phone: 212-586-4822
Fax: 212-582-3744
E-mail Address: *cfw2447@rcn.com*
Web Address: www.acvl.org
The Association of Cinema and Video Laboratories (ACVL) is an international organization whose members are pledged to the highest possible standards of service to the film and video industries.

Independent Film & Television Alliance (IFTA)
10850 Wilshire Blvd., Fl. 9
Los Angeles, CA 90024-4321 US
Phone: 310-446-1000
Fax: 310-446-1600
E-mail Address: *info@ifta-online.org*
Web Address: www.ifta-online.org
The Independent Film & Television Alliance (IFTA), formerly the American Film Marketing Association (AFMA), is a trade association whose mission is to provide the independent film and television industry with high-quality, market-oriented services and worldwide representation.

International Alliance of Theatrical Stage Employees (IATSE)
1430 Broadway, Fl. 20
New York, NY 10018 US
Phone: 212-730-1770
Fax: 212-921-7699
E-mail Address: *webmaster@iatse-intl.org*
Web Address: www.iatse-intl.org
The International Alliance of Theatrical Stage Employees (IATSE) is the labor union representing technicians, artisans and crafts workers in the entertainment industry, including live theater, film and television production and trade shows.

International Animated Film Society (ASIFA-Hollywood)
2114 W. Burbank Blvd.
Burbank, CA 91506 US
Phone: 818-842-4691

E-mail Address: *info@asifa-hollywood.org*
Web Address: www.asifa-hollywood.org
International Animated Film Society (ASIFA-Hollywood) is a nonprofit organization dedicated to the advancement of the art of animation.

International Documentary Association (IDA)
1201 W. 5th St., Ste. M270
Los Angeles, CA 90017 US
Phone: 213-534-3600
Fax: 213-534-3610
E-mail Address: *amina@documentary.org*
Web Address: www.documentary.org
The International Documentary Association (IDA) is a nonprofit member service organization, providing publications, benefits and a public forum to its members for issues regarding nonfiction film, video and multimedia.

Motion Picture Association of America (MPAA)
15301 Ventura Blvd., Bldg. E
Sherman Oaks, CA 91403 US
Phone: 818-995-6600
Fax: 818-285-4403
Web Address: www.mpaa.org
The Motion Picture Association of America (MPAA) serves as the voice and advocate of the U.S. motion picture, home video and television industries.

Motion Picture Editors Guild (MPEG)
7715 Sunset Blvd., Ste. 200
Hollywood, CA 90046 US
Phone: 323-876-4770
Fax: 323-876-0861
Toll Free: 800-705-8700
E-mail Address: *mail@editorsguild.com*
Web Address: www.editorsguild.com
The Motion Picture Editors Guild's (MPEG) web site provides an online directory of editors, a discussion forum and links to related magazines and other organizations that serve the motion picture industry.

Producers Guild of America, Inc. (PGA)
8530 Wilshire Blvd., Ste. 450
Beverly Hills, CA 90211 US
Phone: 310-358-9020
Fax: 310-358-9520
E-mail Address: *info@producersguild.org*
Web Address: www.producersguild.org
The Producers Guild of America, Inc. (PGA) is a nonprofit organization for career professionals who initiate, create, coordinate, supervise and control all aspects of the motion picture and television production processes.

Screen Actors Guild (SAG)
5757 Wilshire Blvd., Fl. 7
Los Angeles, CA 90036-3600 US
Phone: 323-954-1600
Fax: 323-549-6603
Toll Free: 800-724-0767
E-mail Address: *saginfo@sag.org*
Web Address: www.sag.org
The Screen Actors Guild (SAG) represents its members through negotiation and enforcement of collective bargaining agreements that establish equitable levels of compensation, benefits and working conditions for performers. Established in 1933, the guild has 23 branches that represent 120,000 actors worldwide.

Women In Film (WIF)
8857 W. Olympic Blvd.
Ste. 201
Beverly Hills, CA 90211-3605 US
Phone: 310-657-5144
Fax: 310-657-5154
E-mail Address: *info@wif.org*
Web Address: www.wif.org
Women In Film (WIF) strives to empower, promote and mentor women in the entertainment, communication and media industries through a network of contacts, educational programs and events.

XLV. Fitness Industry Associations

American Fitness Professionals and Associates (AFPA)
1601 Long Beach Blvd.
P.O. Box 214
Ship Bottom, NJ 08008 US
Phone: 609-978-7583
Fax: 609-978-7582
Toll Free: 800-494-7782
E-mail Address: *afpa@afpafitness.com*
Web Address: www.afpafitness.com
American Fitness Professionals and Associates (AFPA) offers health and fitness professionals certification programs, continuing education courses, home correspondence courses and regional conventions.

XLVI. Food Industry Associations, General

Institute of Food Technologies (IFT)
525 W. Van Buren, Ste. 1000
Chicago, IL 60607 US
Phone: 312-782-8424
Fax: 312-782-8348
Toll Free: 800-438-3663
E-mail Address: *info@ift.org*
Web Address: www.ift.org
The Institute of Food Technologies (IFT) is devoted to the advancement of the science and technology of food through the exchange of knowledge. The site also provides information and resources for job seekers in the food industry. Members work in food science, food technology and related professions in industry, academia and government.

XLVII. Food Industry Resources, General

Food Manufacturing
1 University, Ste. B6000
Advantage Business Media
Rockaway, NJ 07886-0912 US
Phone: 973-920-7000
Fax: 973-920-7531
E-mail Address: *mbotta@reedbusiness.com*
Web Address: www.foodmanufacturing.com
Food Manufacturing is a trade magazine for companies and employees in the food manufacturing industry. It is published by Advantage Business Media.

XLVIII. Food Processor Industry Associations

Grocery Manufacturers Association (GMA)
1350 I St. NW, Ste. 300
Washington, DC 20005 US
Phone: 202-639-5900
Fax: 202-639-5932
E-mail Address: *info@gmaonline.org*
Web Address: www.gmaonline.org
The Grocery Manufacturers Association (GMA), formerly the National Food Products Association (NFPA), is the voice of the food, beverage and consumer products industry on scientific and public policy issues involving food safety, food security, nutrition, technical and regulatory matters and consumer affairs.

National Frozen and Refrigerated Foods Association (NFRA)
4755 Linglestown Rd., Ste. 300
Harrisburg, PA 17112 US
Phone: 717-657-8601
Fax: 717-657-9862
E-mail Address: *info@nfraweb.org*
Web Address: www.nfraweb.org
The National Frozen and Refrigerated Foods Association (NFRA) promotes the sales and consumption of refrigerated and frozen foods through education, research, training, sales planning and menu

development, providing a forum for industry dialogue.

XLIX. Food Service Industry Associations

International Flight Services Association (IFSA)
1100 Johnson Ferry Rd., Ste. 300
Atlanta, GA 30342 US
Phone: 404-252-3663
Fax: 404-252-0774
E-mail Address: *ifsa@kellencompany.com*
Web Address: www.ifsanet.com
The International Flight Services Association (IFSA), formerly the International Inflight Food Service Association, informs the public with respect to educational and career opportunities within the multi-billion-dollar inflight and railway food service industry.

L. Games Industry Associations

Entertainment Software Association (ESA)
575 7th St. NW, Ste. 300
Washington, DC 20004 US
Phone: 202-223-2400
E-mail Address: *esa@theesa.com*
Web Address: www.theesa.com
The Entertainment Software Association (ESA) is a U.S. trade association for companies that publish video and computer games for consoles, personal computers and the Internet. The ESA owns the E3 Media & Business Summit, a major invitation-only annual trade show for the video game industry.

Fantasy Sports Trade Association (FSTA)
Phone: 312-771-7019
E-mail Address: *megan@fsta.org*
Web Address: www.fsta.org
The Fantasy Sports Trade Association (FSTA) was founded in 1997 to provide a forum for interaction between companies in a unique and growing fantasy sports industry. FSTA represents more than 100 member companies.

Game Manufacturers Association (GAMA)
280 N. High St.
Columbus, OH 43215 US
Phone: 614-255-4500
Fax: 614-255-4499
E-mail Address: *ed@gama.org*
Web Address: www.gama.org
The Game Manufacturers Association (GAMA) is an international nonprofit trade association serving the hobby games industry. It hosts two annual events, the GAMA Trade Show and Origins Game Fair, and publishes a quarterly information newsletter, GAMATimes.

International Game Developers Association (IGDA)
19 Mantua Rd.
Mt. Royal, NJ 08061 US
Phone: 856-423-2990
Fax: 856-423-3420
E-mail Address: *Gordon@igda.org*
Web Address: www.igda.org
The International Game Developers Association (IGDA) represents members involved in the video game production industry. The firm aims to promote professional development within the gaming industry and advocates for issues that affect the game developer community, including anti-censorship issues.

LI. Grocery Industry Associations

Food Marketing Institute (FMI)
2345 Crystal Dr., Ste. 800
Arlington, VA 22202 US
Phone: 202-452-8444
Fax: 202-429-4519
E-mail Address: *fmi@fmi.org*
Web Address: www.fmi.org
The Food Marketing Institute (FMI) is a nonprofit association conducting programs in research, education, industry relations and public affairs on behalf of its 1,500 members.

LII. Health & Nutrition Associations

American Dietetic Association (ADA)
120 S. Riverside Plz., Ste. 2000
Chicago, IL 60606-6995 US
Fax: 312-899-4899
Toll Free: 800-877-1600
E-mail Address: *foundation@eatright.org*
Web Address: www.eatright.org
The American Dietetic Association (ADA) is the world's largest organization of food and nutrition professionals, with nearly 65,000 members. In addition to services for its professional members, this organization's web site offers consumers a respected source for food and nutrition information.

LIII. Health Care Business & Professional Associations

Advanced Medical Technology Association (AdvaMed)
701 Pennsylvania Ave. NW, Ste. 800
Washington, DC 20004-2654 US
Phone: 202-783-8700
Fax: 202-783-8750
E-mail Address: *info@advamed.org*
Web Address: www.advamed.org
The Advanced Medical Technology Association (AdvaMed) strives to be the advocate for a legal, regulatory and economic climate that advances global health care by assuring worldwide access to the benefits of medical technology.

American Academy of Medical Administrators (AAMA)
701 Lee St., Ste. 600
Des Plaines, IL 60016-4516 US
Phone: 847-759-8601
Fax: 847-759-8602
E-mail Address: *info@aameda.org*
Web Address: www.aameda.org
The American Academy of Medical Administrators (AAMA) is an association for health care leaders to enhance their profession and community health.

American Academy of Nursing (AAN)
888 17th St. NW, Ste. 800
Washington, DC 20006 US
Phone: 202-777-1170
Fax: 202-777-0107
E-mail Address: *info@aannet.org*
Web Address: www.aannet.org
The American Academy of Nursing (AAN) works to help nursing leaders transform the health care system in order to optimize public well-being.

American Association of Medical Assistants (AAMA)
20 N. Wacker Dr., Ste. 1575
Chicago, IL 60606 US
Phone: 312-899-1500
Fax: 312-899-1259
Web Address: www.aama-ntl.org
The American Association of Medical Assistants (AAMA) seeks to promote the professional identity and stature of its members and the medical assisting profession through education and credentialing.

American College of Health Care Administrators (ACHCA)
1321 Duke St., Ste. 400
Alexandria, VA 22314 US
Phone: 202-536-5120
Fax: 866-874-1585

E-mail Address: *elollis@achca.org*
Web Address: www.achca.org
The American College of Health Care Administrators (ACHCA) offers educational programming and career development for health care administrators.

American College of Healthcare Executives (ACHE)
1 N. Franklin, Ste. 1700
Chicago, IL 60606-3529 US
Phone: 312-424-2800
Fax: 312-424-0023
E-mail Address: *ache@ache.org*
Web Address: www.ache.org
The American College of Healthcare Executives (ACHE) is an international professional society of health care executives that offers certification and educational programs.

American Dental Association (ADA)
211 E. Chicago Ave.
Chicago, IL 60611-2678 US
Phone: 312-440-2500
E-mail Address: *online@ada.org*
Web Address: www.ada.org
The American Dental Association (ADA) is a professional association of dentists committed to the public's oral health, ethics, science and professional advancement.

American Medical Technologists (AMT)
10700 W. Higgins Rd., Ste. 150
Rosemont, IL 60018 US
Phone: 847-823-5169
Fax: 847-823-0458
Toll Free: 800-275-1268
E-mail Address: *membership@amt1.com*
Web Address: www.amt1.com
American Medical Technologists (AMT) is a nonprofit certification agency and professional membership association representing individuals in health care.

American Medical Women's Association (AMWA)
100 N. 200th St., Fl. 4
Philadelphia, PA 19103 US
Phone: 215-320-3716
Fax: 215-564-2175
Toll Free: 866-564-2483
E-mail Address: *info@amwa-doc.org*
Web Address: www.amwa-doc.org
The American Medical Women's Association (AMWA) is an organization of women physicians and medical students dedicated to serving as the unique voice for women's health and the advancement of women in medicine.

American Occupational Therapy Association, Inc. (AOTA)
4720 Montgomery Ln.
P.O. Box 31220
Bethesda, MD 20824-1220 US
Phone: 301-652-2682
Fax: 301-652-7711
Web Address: www.aota.org
The American Occupational Therapy Association, Inc. (AOTA) advances the quality, availability, use and support of occupational therapy through standard-setting, advocacy, education and research on behalf of its members and the public.

American Organization of Nurse Executives (AONE)
325 7th St. NW
Liberty Pl.
Washington, DC 20004 US
Phone: 202-626-2240
Fax: 202-638-5499
E-mail Address: *aone@aha.org*
Web Address: www.aone.org
The American Organization of Nurse Executives (AONE) is a national organization of nurses who design, facilitate and manage health care.

American Public Health Association (APHA)
800 I St. NW
Washington, DC 20001-3710 US
Phone: 202-777-2742
Fax: 202-777-2534
E-mail Address: *comments@apha.org*
Web Address: www.apha.org
The American Public Health Association (APHA) is an association of individuals and organizations working to improve the public's health and to achieve equity in health status for all.

American School Health Association (ASHA)
7263 State Rte. 43
P.O. Box 708
Kent, OH 44240 US
Phone: 330-678-1601
Fax: 330-678-4526
E-mail Address: *asha@ashaweb.org*
Web Address: www.ashaweb.org
The American School Health Association (ASHA) advocates high-quality school health instruction, health services and a healthy school environment.

Dental Trade Alliance (DTA)
2300 Clarendon Blvd., Ste. 1003
Arlington, VA 22201 US
Phone: 703-379-7755
Fax: 703-931-9429
E-mail Address: *info@dentaltradealliance.org*
Web Address: www.dentaltradealliance.org
The Dental Trade Alliance (DTA) represents dental manufacturers, dental dealers and dental laboratories.

Health Industry Distributors Association (HIDA)
310 Montgomery St.
Alexandria, VA 22314-1516 US
Phone: 703-549-4432
Fax: 703-549-6495
E-mail Address: *rowan@hida.org*
Web Address: www.hida.org
The Health Industry Distributors Association (HIDA) is the international trade association representing medical products distributors.

Healthcare Financial Management Association (HFMA)
2 Westbrook Corporate Ctr., Ste. 700
Westchester, IL 60154 US
Phone: 708-531-9600
Fax: 708-531-0032
Toll Free: 800-252-4362
Web Address: www.hfma.org
The Healthcare Financial Management Association (HFMA) is one of the nation's leading personal membership organizations for health care financial management executives and leaders.

Medical Device Manufacturers Association (MDMA)
1350 I St. NW, Ste. 540
Washington, DC 20005 US
Phone: 202-354-7171
Web Address: www.medicaldevices.org
The Medical Device Manufacturers Association (MDMA) is a national trade association that represents independent manufacturers of medical devices, diagnostic products and health care information systems.

Medical Group Management Association (MGMA)
104 Inverness Ter. E.
Englewood, CO 80112-5306 US
Phone: 303-799-1111
Fax: 303-643-4439
Toll Free: 877-275-6462
E-mail Address: *service@mgma.com*
Web Address: www.mgma.com
Medical Group Management Association (MGMA) is one of the nation's principal voices for medical group practice.

National Association of Health Services Executives (NAHSE)
1140 Connecticut Ave. NW, Ste. 505
Washington, DC 20036 US
Phone: 202-429-6060
Fax: 301-429-6767

E-mail Address: *nahsehq@nahse.org*
Web Address:
www.netforumondemand.com
The National Association of Health Services Executives (NAHSE) is a nonprofit association of black health care executives who promote the advancement and development of black health care leaders and elevate the quality of health care services rendered to minority and underserved communities.

Regulatory Affairs Professionals Society (RAPS)
5635 Fishers Ln., Ste. 550
Rockville, MD 20852 US
Phone: 301-770-2920
Fax: 301-770-2924
E-mail Address: *raps@raps.org*
Web Address: www.raps.org
The Regulatory Affairs Professionals Society (RAPS) is an international professional society representing the health care regulatory affairs profession and individual professionals worldwide.

LIV. Health Insurance Industry Associations

America's Health Insurance Plans (AHIP)
601 Pennsylvania Ave. NW, Ste. 500
Washington, DC 20004 US
Phone: 202-778-3200
Fax: 202-331-7487
E-mail Address: *ahip@ahip.org*
Web Address: www.ahip.org
America's Health Insurance Plans (AHIP) is a prominent trade association representing the private health care insurance system.

LV. Hearing & Speech

Hearing Industries Association (HIA)
1444 I St. NW, Ste. 700
Washington, DC 20005 US
Phone: 202-449-1090
Fax: 202-216-9646
E-mail Address:
mspangler@bostrom.com
Web Address: www.hearing.org
The Hearing Industries Association (HIA) represents and unifies the many aspects of the hearing industry.

LVI. Hotel/Lodging Associations

American Hotel and Lodging Association
1201 New York Ave. NW, Ste. 600
Washington, DC 20005-3931 US
Phone: 202-289-3100
Fax: 202-289-3199
E-mail Address:
informationcenter@ahla.com
Web Address: www.ahla.com
The American Hotel and Lodging Association is a federation of state lodging associations throughout the U.S.

LVII. Human Resources Industry Associations

Society for Human Resource Management (SHRM)
1800 Duke St.
Alexandria, VA 22314 US
Phone: 703-548-3440
Fax: 703-535-6490
Toll Free: 800-283-7476
E-mail Address: *shrm@shrm.org*
Web Address: www.shrm.org
The Society for Human Resource Management (SHRM) addresses the interests and needs of HR professionals through advocacy, publications, research and other resource materials.

LVIII. Industry Research/Market Research

Forrester Research
400 Technology Sq.
Cambridge, MA 02139 US
Phone: 617-497-7090
Toll Free: 866-367-7378
Web Address: www.forrester.com
Forrester Research is a publicly traded company that identifies and analyzes emerging trends in technology and their impact on business. Among the firm's specialties are the financial services, retail, health care, entertainment, automotive and information technology industries.

MarketResearch.com
11200 Rockville Pike, Ste. 504
Rockville, MD 20852 US
Phone: 240-747-3000
Fax: 240-747-3004
Toll Free: 800-298-5699
E-mail Address:
customerservice@marketresearch.com
Web Address: www.marketresearch.com
MarketResearch.com is a leading broker for professional market research and industry analysis. Users are able to search the company's database of research publications including data on global industries, companies, products and trends.

Plunkett Research, Ltd.
P.O. Drawer 541737
Houston, TX 77254-1737 US
Phone: 713-932-0000
Fax: 713-932-7080
E-mail Address:
customersupport@plunkettresearch.com
Web Address: www.plunkettresearch.com
Plunkett Research, Ltd. is a leading provider of market research, industry trends analysis and business statistics. Since 1985, it has served clients worldwide, including corporations, universities, libraries, consultants and government agencies. At the firm's web site, visitors can view product information and pricing and access a large amount of basic market information on industries such as financial services, infotech, e-commerce, health care and biotech.

LIX. Insurance Industry Associations

American Insurance Association (AIA)
1130 Connecticut Ave. NW
Ste. 1000
Washington, DC 20036 US
Phone: 202-828-7100
Fax: 202-293-1219
E-mail Address: *info@aiadc.org*
Web Address: www.aiadc.org
The American Insurance Association (AIA) is a leading property and casualty insurance trade organization, representing companies that offer all types of property and casualty insurance.

LX. Insurance Industry Associations-Agents & Brokers

Council of Insurance Agents & Brokers (CIAB)
701 Pennsylvania Ave. NW, Ste. 750
Washington, DC 20004 US
Phone: 202-783-4400
Fax: 202-783-4410
E-mail Address: *ciab@ciab.com*
Web Address: www.ciab.com
The Council of Insurance Agents & Brokers (CIAB) is an association for commercial insurance and employee benefits intermediaries in the U.S. and abroad.

Independent Insurance Agents & Brokers of America, Inc. (IIABA)
127 S. Peyton St.
Alexandria, VA 22314 US
Fax: 703-683-7556
Toll Free: 800-221-7917
E-mail Address: *info@iiaba.org*

Web Address: www.independentagent.com
Independent Insurance Agents & Brokers of America (IIABA) represents its over 300,000 members who are independent insurance agents and brokers.

Professional Insurance Agents (PIA)
25 Chamberlain St.
P.O. Box 997
Glenmont, NY 12077-0997 US
Fax: 888-225-6935
Toll Free: 800-424-4244
E-mail Address: *pia@pia.org*
Web Address: www.piaonline.org
Professional Insurance Agents (PIA) is a group of voluntary, membership-based trade associations representing professional, independent property and casualty insurance agents.

LXI. Magazines, Business & Financial

Blooomberg Businessweek Online
P.O. Box 8418
Red Oak, IA 51591-1418 US
Fax: 712-623-5229
Toll Free: 800-635-1200
E-mail Address: *bwzcustserv@cdsfulfillment.com*
Web Address: www.businessweek.com
Business Week Online offers an investor service, global business advice, technology news, small business guides, career information, business school advice, daily news briefs and more.

Forbes Online
90 5th Ave.
New York, NY 10011 US
Phone: 212-366-8900
E-mail Address: *dweathers@forbes.net*
Web Address: www.forbes.com
Forbes Online offers varied stock information, news and commentary on business, technology and personal finance, as well as financial calculators and advice.

Fortune
Time & Life Bldg.
Rockefeller Ctr.
New York, NY 10020-1393 US
Phone: 212-522-6724
Fax: 212-522-6412
Toll Free: 800-777-1444
E-mail Address: *Katy_Reitz@timeinc.com*
Web Address: money.cnn.com/magazines/fortune
Fortune, one of the world's premiere business magazines, contains news, business profiles and information on investing, careers, small business, technology and other details of U.S. and international business. Fortune is a publication of Cable News Network (CNN), a Time Warner company.

Investor's Business Daily (IBD)
12655 Beatrice St.
Los Angeles, CA 90066 US
Phone: 310-448-6600
Toll Free: 800-831-2525
E-mail Address: *ibdnews@investors.com*
Web Address: www.investors.com
Investor's Business Daily (IBD) offers subscribers information and articles on the stock market, educational resources, advice from analyst William O'Neil, personal portfolios and updates on events and workshops.

Wall Street Journal Online (The)
200 Liberty St.
New York, NY 10281 US
Phone: 212-416-2000
Toll Free: 800-568-7625
E-mail Address: *onlinejournal@wsj.com*
Web Address: www.wsj.com
The outstanding resources of The Wall Street Journal are available online for a nominal fee.

LXII. MBA Resources

MBA Depot
Web Address: www.mbadepot.com
MBA Depot is an online community and information portal for MBAs, potential MBA program applicants and business professionals.

LXIII. Online Recruiting & Employment ASPs & Solutions

Insala
1331 Airport Fwy., Ste. 313
Euless, TX 76040 US
Phone: 817-355-0939
Fax: 817-355-0746
E-mail Address: *info@insala.com*
Web Address: www.insala.com
Insala provides job search software solutions for the outplacement industry.

Kenexa
650 E. Swedesford Rd., Fl. 2
Wayne, PA 19087 US
Phone: 877-971-9171
Fax: 610-971-9181
Toll Free: 800-391-9557
E-mail Address: *contactus@kenexa.com*
Web Address: www.kenexa.com
Kenexa is a back-end recruiting and job-posting service that is used by many companies in building a workforce. Products and services include recruitment software solutions, talent consulting and recruitment process management.

Workstream, Inc.
2600 Lake Lucien Dr., Ste. 410
Maitland, FL 32751 US
Phone: 407-475-5500
Fax: 407-475-5502
Toll Free: 866-953-8800
E-mail Address: *info@workstreaminc.com*
Web Address: www.workstreaminc.com
Workstream, Inc. creates workforce management solutions through a combination of technology and services designed to integrate an organization.

LXIV. Outsourcing Industry Associations

International Association of Outsourcing Professionals (IAOP)
2600 South Rd., Ste. 44-240
Poughkeepsie, NY 12601 US
Phone: 845-452-0600
Fax: 845-452-6988
E-mail Address: *kim.maneeley@iaop.org*
Web Address: www.outsourcingprofessional.org
The International Association of Outsourcing Professionals (IAOP) represents outsourcing leaders and experts from companies of all sizes and industries around the world.

LXV. Pensions, Benefits & 401(k)s Associations

Profit Sharing/401(k) Council of America (PSCA)
20 N. Wacker Dr., Ste. 3700
Chicago, IL 60606 US
Phone: 312-419-1863
Fax: 312-419-1864
E-mail Address: *psca@psca.org*
Web Address: www.psca.org
The Profit Sharing/401(k) Council of America (PSCA) is a national nonprofit association of 1,200 companies and their 6 million employees. The group expresses its members' interests to federal policymakers and offers practical, cost-effective assistance with profit sharing and 401(k) plan design, administration, investment, compliance and communication. Its web site offers a thorough glossary, statistics and educational material.

LXVI. Pensions, Benefits & 401(k)s Resources

Employee Benefits Security Administration (EBSA)
200 Constitution Ave. NW
Washington, DC 20210 US
Phone: 202-693-8700
Fax: 202-693-8736
Toll Free: 866-444-3272
Web Address: www.dol.gov/ebsa
The Employee Benefits Security Administration (EBSA) is a division of the U.S. Department of Labor, whose web site features a wealth of benefits information for both employers and employees. Included are the answers to such questions as to how a company's bankruptcy will affect its employees and what one should know about pension rights.

Pension Benefit Guarantee Corporation (PBGC)
1200 K St. NW
Washington, DC 20005-4026 US
Phone: 202-326-4000
Fax: 202-326-4344
Toll Free: 800-400-7242
E-mail Address: *participant.pro@pbgc.gov*
Web Address: www.pbgc.gov
The Pension Benefit Guarantee Corporation (PBGC) is a U.S. Government agency that guarantees a portion of the retirement incomes of about 44 million American workers in about 30,000 private defined benefit pension plans. Its web site contains information regarding this guarantee, along with information on retirement planning and links to several related organizations.

LXVII. Pharmaceutical Industry Associations (Drug Industry)

American Pharmaceutical Association (APhA)
2215 Constitution Ave. NW
Washington, DC 20037 US
Phone: 202-628-4410
Fax: 202-783-2351
Toll Free: 800-237-2742
E-mail Address: *infocenter@aphanet.org*
Web Address: www.pharmacist.com
American Pharmaceutical Association (APhA) is a national professional society that provides news and information to pharmacists.

Pharmaceutical Research and Manufacturers of America (PhRMA)
950 F St. NW, Ste. 300
Washington, DC 20004 US
Phone: 202-835-3400
Fax: 202-835-3414
Web Address: www.phrma.org
Pharmaceutical Research and Manufacturers of America (PhRMA) represents the nation's leading research-based pharmaceutical and biotechnology companies.

LXVIII. Pilots Associations

Airline Pilots Association (ALPA)
1625 Massachusetts Ave NW
Washington, DC 20036 US
Phone: 703-689-2270
Web Address: www.alpa.org
ALPA is an association for professional airline pilots in the United States, in Canada and internationally.

LXIX. Printers & Publishers Associations

International Publishing Management Association (IPMA)
710 Regency Dr., Ste. 6
Kearney, MO 64060 US
Phone: 816-902-4762
Fax: 816-902-4766
E-mail Address: *ipmainfo@ipma.org*
Web Address: www.ipma.org
The International Publishing Management Association (IPMA) is an exclusive not-for-profit organization dedicated to assisting in-house corporate publishing and distribution professionals.

MPA-The Association of Magazine Media
810 7th Ave., Fl. 24
New York, NY 10019 US
Phone: 212-872-3700
E-mail Address: *mpa@magazine.org*
Web Address: www.magazine.org
MPA-The Association of Magazine Media (formerly the Magazine Publishers of America, Inc.) is the industry association for consumer magazines in all formats, including printed, mobile and online.

National Association of Printers & Lithographers (NAPL)
75 W. Century Rd., Ste. 100
Paramus, NJ 07652 US
Phone: 201-634-9600
Fax: 201-634-0234
Toll Free: 800-642-6275
E-mail Address: *dlospaluto@napl.org*
Web Address: www.napl.org
The National Association of Printers & Lithographers (NAPL) focuses on helping graphic arts professionals increase their expertise.

Newspaper Association of America (NAA)
4401 Wilson Blvd., Ste. 900
Arlington, VA 22203-1867 US
Phone: 571-366-1000
Fax: 571-366-1195
E-mail Address: *Jeff.Sigmund@naa.org*
Web Address: www.naa.org
The Newspaper Association of America (NAA) is a nonprofit organization representing the newspaper industry.

LXX. Real Estate Industry Associations

Institute of Real Estate Management (IREM)
430 N. Michigan Ave.
Chicago, IL 60611 US
Fax: 800-338-4736
Toll Free: 800-837-0706
E-mail Address: *custserv@irem.org*
Web Address: www.irem.org
The Institute of Real Estate Management (IREM) seeks to educate real estate managers, certify their competence and professionalism, serve as an advocate on issues affecting the real estate management industry and enhance its members' professional competence so they can better identify and meet the needs of those who use their services.

National Association of Real Estate Brokers (NAREB)
9831 Greenbelt Rd., Ste. 309
Lanham, MD 20706 US
Phone: 301-552-9340
Fax: 301-552-9216
E-mail Address: *NAREB3@comcast.net*
Web Address: www.nareb.com
The National Association of Real Estate Brokers (NAREB) is a national trade organization dedicated to bringing together the nation's minority professionals in the real estate industry.

National Association of Real Estate Companies (NAREC)
216 W. Jackson Blvd., Ste. 625
Chicago, IL 60606 US
Phone: 312-263-1755
Fax: 312-750-1203
E-mail Address: *info@narec.org*
Web Address: www.narec.org
The National Association of Real Estate Companies (NAREC) is composed of representatives of publicly and privately owned real estate companies, significant

subsidiaries of publicly owned companies and public accounting firms.

National Association of Realtors (NAR)
430 N. Michigan Ave.
Chicago, IL 60611-4087 US
Phone: 202-383-1176
Toll Free: 800-874-6500
E-mail Address: *lsalvant@realtors.org*
Web Address: www.realtor.org
The National Association of Realtors (NAR) is composed of realtors involved in residential and commercial real estate as brokers, salespeople, property managers, appraisers and counselors and in other areas of the industry. NAR also sponsors Realtor.com, operated by Move, Inc.

Women's Council of Realtors (WCR)
430 N. Michigan Ave.
Chicago, IL 60611 US
Toll Free: 800-245-8512
E-mail Address: *wcr@wcr.org*
Web Address: www.wcr.org
The Women's Council of Realtors (WCR) is a community of female real estate professionals.

LXXI. Recording & Music Associations

American Federation of Musicians (AFM)
1501 Broadway, Ste. 600
New York, NY 10036 US
Phone: 212-869-1330
Fax: 212-764-6134
E-mail Address: *presoffice@afm.org*
Web Address: www.afm.org
The American Federation of Musicians (AFM) is the largest union in the world for music professionals, serving musicians throughout the U.S. and Canada.

American Society of Composers, Authors & Publishers (ASCAP)
1 Lincoln Plz.
New York, NY 10023 US
Phone: 212-621-6000
Fax: 212-621-8453
Web Address: www.ascap.com
American Society of Composers, Authors & Publishers (ASCAP) is a membership association of U.S. composers, songwriters and publishers of every kind of music, with hundreds of thousands of members worldwide.

Content Delivery & Storage Association (CDSA)
39 N. Bayles Ave.
Port Washington, NY 11050 US
Phone: 516-767-6720
Fax: 516-883-5793
E-mail Address:
mporter@CDSAonline.org
Web Address: www.cdsaonline.org
The Content Delivery & Storage Association (CDSA), formerly the International Recording Media Association, is a worldwide trade association encompassing organizations involved in every facet of recording media, including entertainment, information and software content storage. CDSA is under the management of the Media & Entertainment Services Alliance (MESA).

International Association of Audio Information Services (IAAIS)
3920 Willshire Dr.
Lawrence, KS 66049 US
Toll Free: 800-280-5325
E-mail Address:
Stuart.Holland@state.mn.us
Web Address: www.iaais.org
International Association of Audio Information Services (IAAIS) is an organization that provides audio access to information for people who are print-disabled.

Music Publisher's Association of the United States (MPA)
243 5th Ave., Ste. 236
New York, NY 10016 US
Phone: 212-327-4044
E-mail Address: *admin@mpa.org*
Web Address: mpa.org
The Music Publisher's Association of the United States (MPA) serves as a forum for publishers to deal with the music industry's vital issues and is actively involved in supporting and advancing compliance with copyright law, combating copyright infringement and exploring the need for further reform.

Recording Industry Association of America (RIAA)
1025 F St. NW, Fl. 10
Washington, DC 20004 US
Phone: 202-775-0101
Web Address: www.riaa.com
The Recording Industry Association of America (RIAA) is the trade group that represents the U.S. recording industry.

Society of Professional Audio Recording Services (SPARS)
9 Music Sq. S., Ste. 222
Nashville, TN 37203 US
Fax: 214-722-1442
Toll Free: 800-771-7727
E-mail Address: *info@spars.com*
Web Address: www.spars.com
The Society of Professional Audio Recording Services (SPARS) is an organization for members of the recording industry to share practical business information about audio and multimedia facility ownership, management and operations.

Songwriters Guild of America
5120 Virginia Way, Ste. C22
Brentwood, TN 37027 US
Phone: 615-742-9945
Fax: 615-630-7501
Toll Free: 800-524-6742
E-mail Address:
corporate@songwritersguild.com
Web Address: www.songwritersguild.com
The Songwriters Guild of America is the nation's largest and oldest songwriters' organization, providing its members with information and programs to further their careers and understanding of the music industry.

LXXII. Satellite-Related Professional Organizations

Satellite Broadcasting & Communications Association (SBCA)
1100 17th St. NW, Ste. 1150
Washington, DC 20036 US
Phone: 202-349-3620
Fax: 202-349-3621
Toll Free: 800-541-5981
E-mail Address: *info@sbca.org*
Web Address: www.sbca.com
The Satellite Broadcasting & Communications Association (SBCA) is the national trade organization representing all segments of the satellite consumer services industry in America.

Society of Satellite Professionals International (SSPI)
55 Broad St., 14th Fl.
The New York Information Technology Ctr.
New York, NY 10004 US
Phone: 212-809-5199
Fax: 212-825-0075
E-mail Address: *rbell@sspi.org*
Web Address: www.sspi.org
The Society of Satellite Professionals International (SSPI) is a nonprofit member-benefit society that serves satellite professionals worldwide.

LXXIII. Securities Industry Associations

North American Securities Administrators Association, Inc. (NASAA)
750 1st St. NE, Ste. 1140
Washington, DC 20002 US
Phone: 202-737-0900
Fax: 202-783-3571
E-mail Address: *bw@nasaa.org*
Web Address: www.nasaa.org
The North American Securities Administrators Association (NASAA) is the oldest international organization committed to investor protection. Its web site provides information on franchising and raising capital, as well as state blue sky securities laws and resources for small investment advisors.

Securities Industry and Financial Markets Association (SIFMA)
120 Broadway, Fl. 35
New York, NY 10271-0080 US
Phone: 212-313-1200
Fax: 212-313-1301
E-mail Address: *inquiry@sifma.org*
Web Address: www.sifma.org
The Securities Industry and Financial Markets Association (SIFMA), formed by the merger of the Securities Industry Association (SIA) and the Bond Market Association, brings together the shared interests of more than 650 securities and bond industry firms to accomplish common goals.

LXXIV. Software Industry Associations

Software & Information Industry Association (SIIA)
1090 Vermont Ave. NW, Fl. 6
Washington, DC 20005-4095 US
Phone: 202-289-7442
Fax: 202-289-7097
E-mail Address: *lgreenback@siia.net*
Web Address: www.siia.net
The Software & Information Industry Association (SIIA) is a principal trade association for the software and digital content industry.

LXXV. Stocks & Financial Markets Data

Reuters.com
3 Times Sq.
New York, NY 10036 US
Phone: 646-223-4000
E-mail Address:
general.info@thomsonreuters.com
Web Address: www.reuters.com
Reuters.com, a service of Thomson Reuters, offers information on business and world markets, political and international news and company-specific stock information.

Yahoo! Finance
701 1st Ave.
Yahoo! Inc.
Sunnyvale, CA 94089 US
Phone: 408-349-5080
Web Address: finance.yahoo.com
Yahoo! Finance provides a wealth of links and a supreme search guide. Users can find just about any financial information concerning both U.S. and world markets. Tax, insurance information, financial news and community research can be conducted through this site, as can searches for other aspects of the financial world.

LXXVI. Telecommunications Industry Associations

CompTel
900 17th St. NW, Ste. 400
Washington, DC 20006 US
Phone: 202-296-6650
Fax: 202-296-7585
E-mail Address: *gnorris@comptel.org*
Web Address: www.comptel.org
CompTel is a trade organization representing voice, data and video communications service providers and their supplier partners. Members are supported through education, networking, policy advocacy and trade shows.

National Association of Telecommunications Officers and Advisors (NATOA)
2121 Eisenhower Ave., Ste. 401
Alexandria, VA 22314 US
Phone: 703-519-8035
Fax: 703-997-7080
E-mail Address: *jharman@natoa.org*
Web Address: www.natoa.org
The National Association of Telecommunications Officers and Advisors (NATOA) works to support and serve the telecommunications industry's interests and the needs of local governments.

Telecommunications Industry Association (TIA)
2500 Wilson Blvd., Ste. 300
Arlington, VA 22201 US
Phone: 703-907-7700
Fax: 703-907-7727
E-mail Address: *gseiffert@tiaonline.org*
Web Address: www.tiaonline.org
The Telecommunications Industry Association (TIA) is a leading trade association in the information, communications and entertainment technology industry. TIA focuses on market development, trade promotion, trade shows, domestic and international advocacy, standards development and enabling e-business.

United States Telecom Association (USTelecom)
607 14th St. NW, Ste. 400
Washington, DC 20005 US
Phone: 202-326-7300
Fax: 202-315-3603
E-mail Address: *osc@ustelecom.org*
Web Address: www.ustelecom.org
The United States Telecom Association (USTelecom) is a trade association representing service providers and suppliers for the telecom industry.

LXXVII. Temporary Staffing Firms

Adecco
Saegereistrasse 10
Glattbrugg, CH-8152 Switzerland
Phone: 41-44-878-88-88
Fax: 41-44-829-89-24
E-mail Address:
investor.relations@adecco.com
Web Address: www.adecco.com
Adecco maintains human resources and staffing services offices in 70 countries. It provides temporary and permanent personnel.

Advantage Resourcing, Inc.
6-10-1 Roppongi, Minato-ku
Roppongi Hills Mori Twr. 35F
Tokyo, 106-6135 Japan
Phone: 81-03-3405-9229
E-mail Address:
info@advantageresourcing.com
Web Address: www.hirethinking.com
Advantage Resourcing, Inc., formerly Radia Holdings, Inc., provides integrated human resources services throughout Asia, North America, Europe and Australia. It is one of the largest staffing providers in Japan, with over 80 branches and satellite offices. In the U.S., the firm maintains over 230 locations in 34 states.

Allegis Group
7301 Parkway Dr.
Hanover, MD 21076 US
Phone: 410-579-4800
Fax: 410-540-7556
Toll Free: 877-388-3823
Web Address: www.allegisgroup.com

The Allegis Group provides technical, professional and industrial recruiting and staffing services. Allegis specializes in information technology staffing services. The firm operates in the United Kingdom, Germany and The Netherlands as Aerotek and TEKsystems, and in India as Allegis Group India. Aerotek provides staffing solutions for aviation, engineering, automotive and scientific personnel markets.

CDI Corporation
1717 Arch St., Fl. 35
Philadelphia, PA 19103-2768 US
Phone: 215-282-8050
Toll Free: 800-996-7566
E-mail Address:
Vince.Webb@cdicorp.com
Web Address: www.cdicorp.com
CDI Corporation specializes in engineering and information technology staffing services. Company segments include CDI IT Solutions, specializing in information technology; CDI Engineering Solutions, specializing in engineering outsourcing services; AndersElite Limited, operating in the United Kingdom and Australia; and MRINetwork, specializing in executive recruitment.

Express Employment Professionals
8516 NW Expressway
Oklahoma, OK 73162 US
Phone: 405-840-5000
Toll Free: 800-222-4057
E-mail Address:
jennifer.anderson@expresspros.com
Web Address: www.expresspros.com
Express Employment Professionals operates through a network of over 550 locations in the United States, Canada, South Africa and Australia. Services include temporary and flexible staffing, evaluation and direct hire, professional and contract staffing, human resource services and online payroll processing (U.S. only).

Glotel Inc.
8700 W. Bryn Mawr Ave., Ste. 400N
Chicago, IL 60631 US
Phone: 312-612-7480
Fax: 312-715-0756
E-mail Address: *info@glotelinc.com*
Web Address: www.glotel.com
Glotel is a global technology staffing and managed projects solutions company specializing in the placement of contract and permanent personnel within all areas of technology. Glotel has a network of offices throughout Europe, the U.S. and Asia-Pacific.

Harvey Nash
1680 Rte. 23 N, Ste. 300
Wayne, NJ 07470 US
Phone: 973-646-2100
Fax: 973-696-3985
E-mail Address: *info@harveynash.com*
Web Address: www.harveynash.com
Harvey Nash provides professional recruitment, interim executive leadership services and outsourcing services. The firm specializes in information technology staffing on a permanent and contract basis in US, UK and Europe. It also offers outsourcing services including offshore software development services, information technology systems management, workforce risk management and managed services for network administration.

Hays plc
250 Euston Rd.
London, NW1 2AF UK
Phone: 44-20-7383-2266
Fax: 44-20-7388-4367
E-mail Address: *feedback@hays.com*
Web Address: www.hays.com
Hays plc is a global leader in specialist recruitment. It places professional candidates in permanent, temporary and interim positions across numerous fields, including accountancy and finance; education; health care; IT and telecom; manufacturing and engineering; pharmaceuticals; professional services; retail, sales and marketing; and support services.

Hudson Highland Group, Inc.
560 Lexington Ave., Floors 4 & 5
New York, NY 10022 US
Phone: 212-351-7400
Fax: 917-256-8592
E-mail Address:
media.relations@hudson.com
Web Address: www.hudson.com
Hudson Highland Group, Inc. provides permanent recruitment, contract and human resources consulting and inclusion solutions. Services range from single placements to total outsourced solutions. The company employs more than 2,000 professionals serving clients and candidates in 20 countries.

Kelly Services, Inc.
999 W. Big Beaver Rd.
Troy, MI 48084-4782 US
Phone: 248-362-4444
E-mail Address: *kfirst@kellyservices.com*
Web Address: www.kellyservices.com
Kelly Services is a staffing solutions company providing approximately 530,000 employees to client companies in more than 25 countries worldwide.

Kforce, Inc.
1001 E. Palm Ave.
Tampa, FL 33605 US
Phone: 813-552-5000
Toll Free: 877-453-6723
Web Address: www.kforce.com
Kforce, Inc. is one of America's largest temporary placement firms, with more than 70 offices in 44 cities across the U.S. It specializes in employees for the following types of jobs: finance and accounting, scientific, technology, health care, clinical research, mortgages, title insurance and real estate.

Labor Ready, Inc.
P.O. Box 2910
Tacoma, WA 98401-2910 US
Phone: 253-383-9101
Fax: 877-733-0399
Toll Free: 877-733-0430
Web Address: www.laborready.com
Labor Ready, Inc. specializes in temporary staffing in construction, manufacturing, hospitality services, transportation, landscaping, warehousing, retail and more with almost 700 branches throughout the U.S., Canada and Puerto Rico.

Manpower, Inc.
100 Manpower Pl.
Milwaukee, WI 53212 US
Phone: 414-961-1000
Web Address: www.manpower.com
One of the largest temporary staffing providers in the world, Manpower places approximately 2 million workers annually in a variety of positions around the world.

Michael Page International plc
Page House, 1 Dashwood Lang Rd.
Addlestone, Weybridge
Surrey, KT15 2QW UK
Phone: 44-1932-264-144
Fax: 44-1932-264-297
E-mail Address: *ukpr@michaelpage.co.uk*
Web Address: www.michaelpage.co.uk
Michael Page International is one of the world's leading professional recruitment consultancies specializing in the placement of candidates in permanent, contract, temporary and interim positions. The Group has operations in the US, UK, Continental Europe, Asia-Pacific and a regional presence in France and Australia. In the US, the firm's focus is on the areas of financial services, supply chain, executive searches, marketing, legal and administrative support.

MPS Group, Inc.
1 Independent Dr.
Jacksonville, FL 32202 US
Phone: 904-360-2000

Fax: 904-360-2972
Web Address: www.mpsgroup.com
MPS Group is a leading provider of staffing, consulting, and human resource solutions with offices throughout the United States, Canada, the United Kingdom and continental Europe. Primary brands include Accounting Principals, Badenoch, Entegee Engineering Technical Group, Soliant Health and Modis International IT solutions.

Pasona Group Inc. (Japan)
Otemachi 2-6-4 Chiyoda-ku
Tokyo, 100-8228 Japan
Web Address: www.pasonagroup.co.jp
Pasona, Inc. provides personnel services, ranging from temporary staffing/contracting, placement/recruiting and outplacement to outsourcing and training.

Randstad USA
2015 S. Park Pl. SE
Atlanta, GA 30339 US
Phone: 770-937-7000
Fax: 770-937-7001
Toll Free: 877-922-2468
Web Address: www.us.randstad.com
Randstad provides staffing services in the office, industrial, technical, creative and professional markets. It specializes in temporary and permanent staffing; recruitment and consultant services; and human resource services. It operates in 83 countries, primarily in Europe, Asia and the U.S. Brands include Capac, Yacht, and Tempo-Team.

Robert Half International Inc. (RHI)
2884 Sand Hill Rd.
Menlo Park, CA 94025 US
Phone: 650-234-6000
E-mail Address: *webmaster@rhi.com*
Web Address: www.rhi.com
Robert Half International Inc. (RHI) specializes in accounting and finance positions. It also places workers in administrative, information technology, legal, advertising and marketing positions on temporary or permanent bases.

Robert Walters plc
55 Strand
London, WC2N 5WR UK
Phone: 44-20-7379-3333
Fax: 44-20-7509-8714
E-mail Address:
contact@robertwalters.com
Web Address: www.robertwalters.com
Robert Walters PLC is a professional recruitment specialist, outsourcing and human resource consultant. The firm provides services for the temporary, contract and permanent placement of individuals in the sectors of finance, operations, legal, information technology, marketing and administration support. It has 43 offices in 20 countries including the US.

Spherion Corporation
2050 Spectrum Blvd.
Fort Lauderdale, FL 33309 US
Phone: 954-308-7600
Toll Free: 800-774-3746
E-mail Address: *help@spherion.com*
Web Address: www.spherion.com
Spherion Corp., a subsidiary of SFN Group, provides temporary staffing, recruitment and employee consulting.

Synergie SA (France)
112 Rue de Chemin Vert
Paris, 75011 France
Phone: 33-1-43-57-22-97
Fax: 33-1-40-21-35-75
Web Address: www.synergie.fr
Synergie provides human resource management services that include temporary placement, consulting and training. The firm is most active in France, but also operates through a network of 550 agencies in throughout Europe and Canada.

Tempstaff Co., Ltd. (Japan)
Shinjuku Maynds Twr. 2-1-1
Yoyogi, Shibuya-ku
Tokyo, 151-0053 Japan
Phone: 81-3-5350-1212
Web Address: www.tempstaff.co.jp
Tempstaff Co., Ltd. provides temporary and permanent placement and recruiting and outsourcing services. It has 263 offices in Japan and 12 overseas offices located in Los Angeles, Seattle, Shanghai, Suzhou, Guangzhou, Hong Kong, Taiwan, Korea, Singapore and Indonesia.

Volt Information Sciences, Inc.
1065 Ave. of the Americas, Fl. 20
New York, NY 10018 US
Phone: 212-704-2400
Fax: 212-704-2413
E-mail Address:
mediarelations@volt.com
Web Address: www.volt.com
Volt Information Sciences, Inc. provides temporary staffing services, professional search, managed services programs, vendor management systems and recruitment process outsourcing, as well as a wealth of additional support services, in North and South America, Europe and Asia through approximately 400 locations.

LXXVIII. Testing Resources

CPP, Inc.
1055 Joaquin Rd., Fl. 2
Mountain View, CA 94043 US
Phone: 650-969-8901
Fax: 650-969-8608
Toll Free: 800-624-1765
E-mail Address: *custserv@cpp.com*
Web Address: www.cpp.com
CPP, Inc. (formerly known as Consulting Psychologists Press) publishes the Meyers-Briggs Type Indicator, Strong Inventory Test and other psychological assessment-related products. CPP also provides information about the tests and, through division Davies-Black Publishing, offers business-related books and services, including those covering career management and leadership development.

LXXIX. Textile & Fabric Associations

International Textile and Apparel Association (ITAA)
6060 Sunrise Vista Dr., Ste. 1300
Citrus Heights, CA 95610 US
Phone: 916-723-1628
Fax: 719-722-8149
E-mail Address: *info@itaaonline.org*
Web Address: www.itaaonline.org
The International Textile and Apparel Association (ITAA) is a nonprofit educational and scientific corporation dedicated to providing opportunities to scholars in the retail, textile and apparel industries.

LXXX. Travel Business & Professional Associations

American Society of Travel Agents (ASTA)
1101 King St., Ste. 200
Alexandria, VA 22314 US
Fax: 703-739-3268
Toll Free: 800-275-2782
E-mail Address: *askasta@astahq.com*
Web Address: www.asta.org
The American Society of Travel Agents (ASTA) is one of the world's largest associations of travel professionals.

Association of Corporate Travel Executives (ACTE)
515 King St., Ste. 440
Alexandria, VA 22314 US
Phone: 703-683-5322
Fax: 703-683-2720
E-mail Address: *info@acte.org*
Web Address: www.acte.org

The Association of Corporate Travel Executives (ACTE) serves the specialized travel interests of corporate purchasers and travel service suppliers from nearly 50 countries.

Association of Retail Travel Agents (ARTA)
4320 North Miller Rd.
c/o Travel Destinations, Inc.
Scottsdale, AZ 85251 US
Fax: 615-985-0600
Toll Free: 800-969-6069
E-mail Address: *info@artaonline.com*
Web Address: www.artaonline.com
The Association of Retail Travel Agents (ARTA) is one of the largest nonprofit associations in North America to exclusively represent travel agents.

Association of Travel Marketing Executives (ATME)
P.O. Box 3176
West Tisbury, MA 02575 US
Phone: 508-693-0550
Fax: 508-693-0115
E-mail Address: *admin@atme.org*
Web Address: www.atme.org
The Association of Travel Marketing Executives (ATME) is a global professional association of senior-level travel marketing executives dedicated to providing cutting-edge information, education and opportunities for meaningful networking with peers.

National Society of Minorities in Hospitality
107 S. West St.
PMB 119
Alexandria, VA 22314 US
Phone: 703-549-9899
Fax: 703-997-7795
E-mail Address: *hq@nsmh.org*
Web Address: www.nsmh.org
The National Society of Minorities in Hospitality strives to establish a working relationship between the hospitality industry and minority students.

Network of Executive Women in Hospitality, Inc. (NEWH)
P.O. Box 322
Shawano, WI 54166 US
Fax: 800-693-6394
Toll Free: 800-593-6394
Web Address: www.newh.org
The Network of Executive Women in Hospitality, Inc. (NEWH) brings together professionals from all facets of the hospitality industry by providing opportunities for education, professional development and networking. Although primarily a U.S.-based organization, NEWH does have international chapters in Toronto and London.

Society of Incentive and Travel Executives
401 N. Michigan Ave.
Chicago, IL 60611 US
Phone: 312-321-5148
Fax: 312-527-6783
E-mail Address: *Marcie_Valerio@site-intl.org*
Web Address: www.site-intl.org
The Society of Incentive and Travel Executives is a worldwide organization of business professionals dedicated to the recognition and development of motivational and performance improvement strategies in the travel industry.

LXXXI. Travel Industry Associations

Destination Marketing Association International
2025 M St. NW, Ste. 500
Washington, DC 20036 US
Phone: 202-296-7888
Fax: 202-296-7889
Toll Free: 888-275-3140
E-mail Address: *info@destinationmarketing.org*
Web Address: www.destinationmarketing.org
The Destination Marketing Association International, formerly the International Association of Convention & Visitor Bureaus, strives to enhance the professionalism, effectiveness and image of destination management organizations worldwide.

International Association of Conference Centers (IACC)
243 N. Lindbergh Blvd.
St. Louis, MO 63141 US
Phone: 314-993-8575
Fax: 314-993-8919
E-mail Address: *info@iacconline.org*
Web Address: www.iacconline.com
The International Association of Conference Centers (IACC) is a nonprofit, facilities-based organization founded to promote a greater awareness and understanding of the unique features of conference centers around the world.

National Tour Association (NTA)
546 E. Main St.
Lexington, KY 40508 US
Phone: 859-226-4444
Fax: 859-226-4414
Toll Free: 800-682-8886
E-mail Address: *questions@ntastaff.com*
Web Address: www.ntaonline.com
The National Tour Association (NTA) is an association for travel professionals who have an interest in the packaged travel sector of the industry.

U.S. Travel Association
1100 New York Ave. NW, Ste. 450
Washington, DC 20005-3934 US
Phone: 202-408-8422
Fax: 202-408-1255
E-mail Address: *feedback@tia.org*
Web Address: www.tia.org
The U.S. Travel Association is the result of a merger between the Travel Industry Association (TIA) and the Travel Business Roundtable. It is a nonprofit association that represents and speaks for the common interests and concerns of all components of the U.S. travel industry.

LXXXII. U.S. Government Agencies

Bureau of Economic Analysis (BEA)
1441 L St. NW
Washington, DC 20230 US
Phone: 202-606-9900
E-mail Address: *customerservice@bea.gov*
Web Address: www.bea.gov
The Bureau of Economic Analysis (BEA), an agency of the U.S. Department of Commerce, is the nation's economic accountant, preparing estimates that illuminate key national, international and regional aspects of the U.S. economy.

Bureau of Labor Statistics (BLS)
2 Massachusetts Ave. NE
Washington, DC 20212-0001 US
Phone: 202-691-5200
Toll Free: 800-877-8339
Web Address: stats.bls.gov
The Bureau of Labor Statistics (BLS) is the principal fact-finding agency for the Federal Government in the field of labor economics and statistics. It is an independent national statistical agency that collects, processes, analyzes and disseminates statistical data to the American public, U.S. Congress, other federal agencies, state and local governments, business and labor. The BLS also serves as a statistical resource to the Department of Labor.

Equal Employment Opportunity Commission (EEOC)
1801 L St. NW
Washington, DC 20507 US
Phone: 202-663-4900
Toll Free: 800-669-4000
E-mail Address: *info@eeoc.gov*

Web Address: www.eeoc.gov
The Equal Employment Opportunity Commission (EEOC) is a Federal Government agency focused on practices and programs that foster equal opportunity at work and elsewhere. Its web site features details about various protective laws regarding employment. It also provides information on how to file a discrimination claim.

FedStats
Web Address: www.fedstats.gov
FedStats compiles information for statistics from over 100 U.S. federal agencies. Visitors can sort the information by agency, geography and topic, as well as perform searches.

National Labor Relations Board (NLRB)
1099 14th St. NW
Washington, DC 20570-0001 US
Phone: 202-208-3000
Fax: 202-208-3013
Toll Free: 866-667-6572
Web Address: www.nlrb.gov
The National Labor Relations Board (NLRB) provides case reports on labor disputes, searchable by company or union.

U.S. Census Bureau
4600 Silver Hill Rd.
Washington, DC 20233-8800 US
Phone: 301-763-4636
Toll Free: 800-923-8282
E-mail Address: *pio@census.gov*
Web Address: www.census.gov
The U.S. Census Bureau is the official collector of data about the people and economy of the U.S. Founded in 1790, it provides official social, demographic and economic information. In addition to the Population & Housing Census, which it conducts every 10 years, the U.S. Census Bureau numerous other surveys annually.

U.S. Department of Commerce (DOC)
1401 Constitution Ave. NW
Washington, DC 20230 US
Phone: 202-482-2000
Fax: 202-482-5168
E-mail Address: *kgriffis@doc.gov*
Web Address: www.commerce.gov
The U.S. Department of Commerce (DOC) regulates trade and provides valuable economic analysis of the economy.

U.S. Department of Labor (DOL)
200 Constitution Ave. NW
Frances Perkins Bldg.
Washington, DC 20210 US
Phone: 202-693-4676
Toll Free: 866-487-2365
Web Address: www.dol.gov
The U.S. Department of Labor (DOL) is the government agency responsible for labor regulations.

U.S. Securities and Exchange Commission (SEC)
100 F St. NE
Washington, DC 20549 US
Phone: 202-942-8088
Toll Free: 888-732-6585
E-mail Address: *publicinfo@sec.gov*
Web Address: www.sec.gov
The U.S. Securities and Exchange Commission (SEC) is a nonpartisan, quasi-judicial regulatory agency responsible for administering federal securities laws. These laws are designed to protect investors in securities markets and ensure that they have access to disclosure of all material information concerning publicly traded securities. Visitors to the web site can access the EDGAR database of corporate financial and business information.

LXXXIII. Waste Industry Associations

Air & Waste Management Association
420 Fort Duquesne Blvd.
1 Gateway Ctr., 3rd Fl.
Pittsburgh, PA 15222-1435 US
Phone: 412-232-3444
Fax: 412-232-3450
Toll Free: 800-270-3444
E-mail Address: *info@awma.org*
Web Address: www.awma.org
The Air & Waste Management Association provides training, information and networking opportunities to environmental professionals worldwide.

LXXXIV. Water Resources Associations

American Water Resources Association (AWRA)
P.O. Box 1626
Middleburg, VA 20118 US
Phone: 540-687-8390
Fax: 540-687-8395
E-mail Address: *info@awra.org*
Web Address: www.awra.org
The American Water Resources Association (AWRA) represents the interests of professionals involved in water resources.

LXXXV. Wireless & Cellular Industry Associations

Cellular Telecommunications & Internet Association (CTIA)
1400 16th St. NW, Ste. 600
Washington, DC 20036 US
Phone: 202-736-3200
Fax: 202-785-0721
E-mail Address: *PChandler@ctia.org*
Web Address: www.ctia.org
The Cellular Telecommunications & Internet Association (CTIA) is an international nonprofit membership organization that represents a variety of wireless communications sectors including cellular service providers, manufacturers, wireless data and Internet companies. CTIA's industry committees study spectrum allocation, homeland security, taxation, safety and emerging technology.

Wireless Communications Association International (WCAI)
1333 H St. NW, Ste. 700 W
Washington, DC 20005-4754 US
Phone: 202-452-7823
E-mail Address: *susan@wcai.com*
Web Address: www.wcai.com
The Wireless Communications Association International (WCAI) is the principal nonprofit trade association representing the wireless broadband industry.

LXXXVI. Writers, Photographers & Editors Associations

American Society of Journalists and Authors, Inc. (ASJA)
1501 Broadway, Ste. 302
New York, NY 10036 US
Phone: 212-997-0947
Fax: 212-937-2315
E-mail Address: *director@asja.org*
Web Address: www.asja.org
The American Society of Journalists and Authors (ASJA) is of the nation's leading organizations of independent nonfiction writers.

American Society of Magazine Editors (ASME)
810 7th Ave., 24th Fl.
c/o Magazine Publishers of America (MPA)
New York, NY 10019 US
Phone: 212-872-3736
E-mail Address: *asme@magazine.org*

Web Address: www.magazine.org/asme
The American Society of Magazine Editors (ASME) is a professional organization for editors of print and online magazines. ASME is part of the Magazine Publishers of America (MPA).

American Society of Newspaper Editors (ASNE)
11690B Sunrise Valley Dr.
Reston, VA 20191-1409 US
Phone: 703-453-1122
Fax: 703-453-1133
E-mail Address: *asne@asne.org*
Web Address: www.asne.org
The American Society of Newspaper Editors (ASNE) is an association that brings together editors of daily newspapers and people directly involved with developing content for daily newspapers.

International Women's Writing Guild (IWWG)
P.O. Box 810
Gracie Sta.
New York, NY 10028-0082 US
Phone: 212-737-7536
Fax: 212-737-9469
E-mail Address: *dirhahn@iwwg.org*
Web Address: www.iwwg.com
The International Women's Writing Guild (IWWG) is a network for the personal and professional empowerment of women through writing.

Media Communications Association International (MCAI)
2810 Crossroads Dr., Ste. 3800
Madison, WI 53718 US
Phone: 608-443-2464
Fax: 608-443-2474
E-mail Address: *execdirect@mca-i.org*
Web Address: www.mca-i.org
The Media Communications Association International (MCAI) is the leading global community for media communications professionals seeking to drive the convergence of communications and technology for the growth of the profession.

National Association of Hispanic Journalists (NAHJ)
529 14th St. NW
1000 National Press Bldg.
Washington, DC 20045-2001 US
Phone: 202-662-7145
Fax: 202-662-7144
Toll Free: 888-346-6245
E-mail Address: *nahj@nahj.org*
Web Address: www.nahj.org
The National Association of Hispanic Journalists (NAHJ) is dedicated to the recognition and professional advancement of Hispanics in the news industry.

National Association of Science Writers, Inc. (NASW)
P.O. Box 890
Hedgesville, WV 25427 US
Phone: 304-754-5077
Fax: 304-754-5076
E-mail Address: *director@nasw.org*
Web Address: www.nasw.org
The National Association of Science Writers (NASW) exists to foster the dissemination of accurate information regarding science through all media devoted to informing the public.

National Conference of Editorial Writers (NCEW)
3899 N. Front St.
Harrisburg, PA 17110 US
Phone: 717-703-3015
Fax: 717-703-3014
E-mail Address: *ncew@pa-news.org*
Web Address: www.ncew.org
The National Conference of Editorial Writers (NCEW) strives to stimulate the conscience and quality of editorial writing.

National Federation of Press Women (NFPW)
P.O. Box 5556
Arlington, VA 22205 US
Fax: 703-812-4555
Toll Free: 800-780-2715
E-mail Address: *presswomen@aol.com*
Web Address: www.nfpw.org
The National Federation of Press Women (NFPW) is an organization of professional journalists and communicators.

National Writers Union (NWU)
113 University Pl., Fl. 6
New York, NY 10003 US
Phone: 212-254-0279
Fax: 212-254-0673
E-mail Address: *nwu@nwu.org*
Web Address: www.nwu.org
The National Writers Union (NWU) is a labor union that represents freelance writers in all genres, formats and media. It is committed to improving the economic and working conditions of freelance writers.

Society of Children's Book Writers and Illustrators (SCBWI)
8271 Beverly Blvd.
Los Angeles, CA 90048 US
Phone: 323-782-1010
Fax: 323-782-1892
E-mail Address: *scbwi@scbwi.org*
Web Address: www.scbwi.org
The Society of Children's Book Writers and Illustrators (SCBWI) serves people who write, illustrate or share a vital interest in children's literature, including publishers, librarians, booksellers and agents.

Chapter 5

THE MID-SIZE EMPLOYERS 500: WHO THEY ARE AND HOW THEY WERE CHOSEN

Note: financial data given for each of the MID-SIZE EMPLOYERS 500 firms is for the year ended December 31, 2011, a fiscal year ended in 2011 or the latest figures available to the editors. Telephone numbers, addresses, contact names, Internet addresses and other vital facts were collected in late 2011.

The companies chosen to be listed in PLUNKETT'S COMPANION TO THE ALMANAC OF AMERICAN EMPLOYERS are not the same as the "Fortune 500" or any other list of corporations. The MID-SIZE EMPLOYERS 500 were chosen specifically for their likelihood to provide new job openings to the greatest number of employees. Complete information about each firm can be found in the "Individual Data Listings," beginning about the middle of this book. They are in alphabetical order.

THE MID-SIZE EMPLOYERS 500 includes companies from all parts of the United States and from a broad range of selected industry segments: banks, retailers, service companies, wholesalers and distributors, insurance companies and others, as well as industrial companies, technology firms and manufacturers.

Simply stated, the list contains 517 of the most successful, mid-size employers in the United States today. In particular, the list contains companies that we have selected to have qualities that we feel will be of greatest interest to job seekers of today who are looking for opportunities to obtain employment with mid-size corporations.

In order to make this reference guide as useful as possible, we have altered the company selection criteria that were used in early editions. Rather than focusing largely on mid-term growth histories, we are instead focusing more on type of business and industry sector served. This is because some sectors may not be hiring in large numbers today. Consequently, we have deleted some truly outstanding companies due to the state of their particular markets. However, job seekers should bear in mind the fact that firms of many types will continue to restrain hiring. In addition, frequent layoffs have become standard in corporate America. (See Chapter 1 "Trends" for further thoughts about layoffs and other trends.)

To be included in our list, the firms generally were selected on the following criteria:

1) U.S.-based companies. (However, a small number of companies may be subsidiaries of foreign-based firms.)

2) Between approximately 100 and 2,500 employees. A small number of firms may have slightly lower or higher counts.

3) Selected Type of Business and/or Industry Sector: Companies were chosen based on our analysis of the business potential of their products, services and industrial sectors in light of today's economy.

The companies were chosen in this manner for the following reasons:

500 COMPANIES (the actual count is 517 companies) so there is a broad base among which to make comparisons and from which you can study potential employers.

MID-SIZE EMPLOYERS (between 100 and 2,500 employees) so the information can supplement the main volume of The Almanac of American Employers which focuses on employers with more than 2,500 employees.

COMPANIES THAT OPERATE IN PROMISING BUSINESS SECTORS because:

1) Companies that are stable or enjoying growing business are much more likely to have job openings. (See Chapter 1, "Trends.")

2) These companies may be much more likely to offer advancement opportunities. Current employees may benefit from promote-from-within policies when new plants, new stores, new product lines or new offices are opened.

A low score in any part of this book should not be taken as a slur against the company so ranked; it should be taken as evidence of the obvious: some companies are better to work for than others, depending, of course, on what you value. It is not easy to get into the MID-SIZE EMPLOYERS 500, and the mere presence of a company on the list can be taken as evidence that it has excelled in many ways. To start with, it has to have generated enough business to employ large numbers of people–never a simple task. Nonetheless, job seekers should use caution. Situations can change quickly at corporate employers, and job seekers should make certain they are armed with the latest information prior to making a final decision.

INDUSTRY LIST, WITH CODES

This book refers to the following list of unique industry codes, based on the 2007 NAIC code system (NAIC is used by many analysts as a replacement for older SIC codes because NAIC is more specific to today's industry sectors, see www.census.gov/NAICS). Companies profiled in this book are given a primary NAIC code, reflecting the main line of business of each firm.

Agriculture

Agriculture

11511 Agricultural Crop Production Support, Seeds, Fertilizers

Farming

1113 Fruit & Tree Nut Farming
112310 Egg Production
311612 Meat Production
311615 Poultry Production

Apparel

Apparel & Shoe Manufacturing

315 Apparel Manufacturing-General
315211 Apparel Manufacturing-Athletic
31522 Apparel Manufacturing-Men's & Boy's Clothing
315299 Apparel Manufacturing-Uniforms
3162 Shoe Manufacturing-General
316219 Shoe Manufacturing-Athletic Shoes & Misc. Shoes, Incl. Children's

Automotive

Automotive Manufacturing

33611 Automobiles, Manufacturing
336211 Motor Vehicle Body Manufacturing
3363 Automobile Parts Manufacturing

Toys, Sporting Goods & Miscellaneous Manufacturing

336991 Motorcycle, Bicycle, & Parts Manufacturing

Automotive Distribution

423120 Automobile Parts, Wholesale Distribution

Automotive Services

8111 Automotive Repair & Maintenance
811191 Automotive Oil Change & Lubrication Shops

Energy

Fuel Mining & Extraction

211111 Oil & Natural Gas Exploration & Production
213111 Drilling Services--Oil & Gas Wells
213112 Oil Field Services

Utilities

221 Utilities-Electric & Gas
2211 Utilities-Electric
221113 Utilities-Nuclear Generation
221119 Utilities-Alternative Energy Generation
221210 Utilities-Gas

Petroleum-Refining & Manufacturing

324110 Petroleum Refineries

Manufacturing

332410 Nuclear Reactor Manufacturing

Manufacturing, Electrical

33591 Battery Manufacturing

Entertainment

Publishing

511130 Books, Publishing

Film, Video & Music Recording

512110 TV/Video/Theatrical, Production
532230 Video Rental

Broadcasting

515111 Radio Broadcasting

Gambling & Recreation

329999 Gambling Equipment
713210 Casinos/Horse Racing, Gambling

Hotels & Accommodations

721211 RV Parks & Campgrounds

Financial Services

Banking, Credit & Finance

522110 Commercial Banking
522291 Finance--Consumer
522320 Payment & Transaction Processing Services
522320A Payment & Transaction Processing--Benefits Management

Stocks & Investments

523110 Investment Banking
523120 Stock Brokerage
523210 Stocks, Bonds & Commodities Exchanges
523910 Venture Capital/Private Equity Investments/Hedge Funds

Code	Industry
523920	Investment Management/Mutual Funds/Pension Funds
	Insurance
524113	Insurance-Life
524114	Insurance-Health, HMO's & PPO's
524126	Insurance--Property & Casualty, Specialty, Surety
524130	Insurance-Reinsurance
524210A	Insurance Intermediary-Online

Food & Restaurants

Code	Industry
	Food Service
722110	Restaurants

Health Care

Code	Industry
	Health Products, Manufacturing
325411	Medicinals & Botanicals, Manufacturing
325412	Drugs (Pharmaceuticals), Discovery & Manufacturing
325412A	Drug Delivery Systems
325412B	Veterinary Products Manufacturing
325413	Diagnostic Substances Manufacturing
325414	Biological Products, Manufacturing
334510	Diagnostic and Other Electromedical Equpment Manufacturing
33911	Medical/Dental/Surgical Equipment & Supplies, Manufacturing
423450	Medical/Dental/Surgical Equipment & Supplies, Distribution
541711	Biotechnology Research
	Equipment Rental
5324	Equipment Rental
	Health Care-Clinics, Labs and Organizations
6211	Physician Practice Management
6214	Clinics--Outpatient Clinics & Surgery
621410	Fertility Clinics
6215	Diagnostic Devices, Manufacturing
621511	Laboratories & Diagnostic Services--Medical

InfoTech

Code	Industry
	Computers & Electronics Manufacturing
33411	Computer Networking & Related Equipment, Manufacturing
334111	Computer Hardware, Manufacturing
334112	Computer Storage Equipment & Misc Parts, Manufacturing
334119	Computer Accessories, Monitors, Printers Manufacturing
334310	Audio & Video Equipment, Consumer Electronics
33441	Semiconductors (Microchips)/Integrated Circuits/Components, Manufacturing
334419	Contract Electronics Manufacturing
3345	Instrument Manufacturing, including Measurement, Control, Test & Navigational
	Computers & Electronics, Distribution
423430	Computer & Telecommunications Equipment Distribution
	Software
511201	Computer Software, Accounting, Banking & Financial
511210	Computer Software, Publisher
511210A	Computer Software, Supply Chain & Logistics
511210B	Computer Software, Network Management, System Testing, & Storage
511210C	Computer Software, Telecom, Communications & VOIP
511210D	Computer Software, Healthcare & Biotechnology
511210E	Computer Software, Security & Anti-Virus
511210F	Computer Software, Multimedia, Graphics & Publishing
511210G	Computer Software, Games & Entertainment
511210H	Computer Software, Business Management & ERP
511210I	Computer Software, Operating Systems, Languages & Development Tools
511210J	Computer Software, Data Base & File Management
511210K	Computer Software, Sales & Customer Relationship Management
511210L	Computer Software, Content & Document Management
511210P	Computer Software, Educational & Training
	Information & Data Processing Services
518210	Data Processing Services
	Information Services-Professional
541512	Consulting--Computer, Telecommunications & Internet
541513	Computer Programming & Software Design

Internet

Code	Industry
519130	Internet Publishing & Web Search Portals
541511	Computer Program or Software Development, Custom

Manufacturing

Code	Industry
	Food Products Manufacturing
311	Food Products, Manufacturing
3112	Grain Distribution, Milling & Oilseed Processing
311230	Breakfast Cereal Manufacturing
311320	Chocolate & Confectionery Manufacturing
31141	Frozen Food Manufacturing
3115	Dairy Products, Manufacturing
31191	Snack Products, Manufacturing
31194	Seasonings, Flavorings & Dressings Manufacturing
	Beverage & Tobacco Manufacturing
3121	Beverages--Soft Drinks & Juices Manufacturing
312120	Beverages--Breweries
312130	Beverages--Wineries
	Textiles Manufacturing
313	Textiles, Fabrics, Sheets/Towels, Manufacturing
	Chemicals
325	Chemicals, Manufacturing
	Plastics & Rubber
3261	Plastic Products, Manufacturing
	Construction
326199	Building Products & Construction Materials in Plastic, Manufacturing
	Nonmetallic Minerals/Rock/Aggregate
327	Nonmetallic Mineral, Rock & Aggregate Manufacturing
335991	Carbon Products, Manufacturing

Fabricated Metals

332	Steel & Metals--Fabricated Metals Components, Manufacturing

Machinery & Manufacturing Equipment

33313	Machinery-Mining & Oil & Gas Field, Manufacturing
333295	Semiconductor Manufacturing Equipment
334413	Solar Cells, LEDs & Other Semiconductor Products

Electrical Equipment, Appliances, Tools

335	Electrical Equipment, Manufacturing

Real Estate

Real Estate

531110	Real Estate Investment Trusts - Residential
531120	Real Estate Investment Trusts - Nonresidential

Retailing

Automobiles & Parts Stores

441110	Auto Dealers, Retail

Food & Beverage Stores

445110	Grocery Stores/Supermarkets
445110E	Grocery Stores/Supermarkets-Online

Drug Stores, Beauty Supply & Health Items Stores

446110E	Drug Stores-Online
446191	Health Supplement Stores

Apparel & Accessories Stores

448	Apparel Stores, General
448310E	Jewelry Stores-Online

Sporting Goods, Hobbies, Books & Music Stores

451110	Sporting Goods Stores
451110E	Sporting Goods Stores-Online
451220E	Music Stores-Online

Miscellaneous Retailers

453910	Pets/Pet Supplies Stores
45399	Other Retailers, Misc. Retailers
453998	Auctions

Nonstore Retailers

454113	Mail Order and Non-Store Selling, Incl. TV Shopping
454319	Other Fuel Dealers, Retail

Services

Construction

237	Construction, Heavy & Civil Engineering
237130	Construction, Power & Communication Lines and Structures
2389	Construction--Other Special Trade Contractors

Real Estate

5311	Real Estate Operations & Development--General

Consulting & Professional Services

541330	Engineering Services
541360	Surveying & Mapping--Geophysical
54161	Consulting--Management & Business
541612	Consulting-Human Resources
541613	Consulting--Marketing
541614	Logistics Outsourcing
541690	Consulting--Scientific & Technical
541712	Research & Development-Physical, Engineering & Life Sciences
541810E	Advertising/Marketing--Online
541870	Advertising Material Distribution Services
541910	Market Research

Personnel, Administrative & Support Services

561	Staffing or Outsourcing
561210	Facilities Support Services

Travel Agencies

5615E	Travel Services-Online

Educational

611410	Business Training, Distance Learning

Telecommunications

Telecommunications Equipment

3342	Communications Equipment, Manufacturing
334210	Telecommunications Equipment Manufacturing
334220	Radio & Wireless Communication, Manufacturing
334290	Security, Detection & Intercom System Manufacturing

Telecommunications

517110	Telecommunications Service Wired, Satellite or Cable
5172	Telecommunications Service Cellular, U.S. & Non-U.S.
561499	Teleconferencing

Transportation

Aerospace

33641	Aerospace & Aircraft Related Manufacturing

Air

481111	Air Transportation

Ships

483111	Shipping-Deep Sea
48321	Shipping-Inland

Truck

484	Truck Transportation
4842	Truck Transportation-Specialized
4885	Freight Forwarding & Support Services

Wholesale Distribution-Other

Distribution-Durable Goods

4233	Lumber & Construction Materials, Wholesale Distribution
4236	Electronic Parts & Equipment, Distribution

Distribution-Nondurable Goods

4244	Food Distribution
424710	Petroleum Bulk Stations & Terminals Distribution
4248	Wines & Spirits, Distribution
486	Petroleum Products (except Bulk Stations/Terminals) Distribution & Pipelines

INDEX OF COMPANIES WITHIN INDUSTRY GROUPS

Company	Industry Code	2010 Sales (U.S. $ thousands)	2010 Profits (U.S. $ thousands)
Advertising Material Distribution Services			
DIGITAL GENERATION INC	541870	247,528	41,569
Advertising/Marketing--Online			
24/7 REAL MEDIA INC	541810E		
ACXIOM DIGITAL INC	541810E		
AKQA INC	541810E		
CHOICESTREAM INC	541810E		
CONSTANT CONTACT INC	541810E	174,231	2,914
COUPONS INC	541810E		
ONSTREAM MEDIA CORPORATION	541810E	16,694	-9,281
VIBRANT MEDIA INC	541810E		
Aerospace & Aircraft Related Manufacturing			
AVIALL INC	33641		
Agricultural Crop Production Support, Seeds, Fertilizers			
AMERICAN VANGUARD CORP	11511	229,620	10,984
CF INDUSTRIES HOLDINGS INC	11511	3,965,000	440,700
SCOULAR COMPANY (THE)	11511	4,000,000	
Air Transportation			
ALLEGIANT TRAVEL COMPANY	481111	663,600	65,700
Apparel Manufacturing-Athletic			
PATAGONIA INC	315211	330,000	
Apparel Manufacturing-General			
G-III APPAREL GROUP	315	800,864	31,718
JOE'S JEANS INC	315	98,176	2,601
VOLCOM INC	315	323,181	22,290
Apparel Manufacturing-Men's & Boy's Clothing			
PERRY ELLIS INTERNATIONAL INC	31522	729,217	13,167
Apparel Manufacturing-Uniforms			
SUPERIOR UNIFORM GROUP INC	315299	105,878	3,807
Apparel Stores, General			
TRUE RELIGION APPAREL INC	448	363,714	43,496
Auctions			
SOTHEBYS	453998	774,309	160,950
Audio & Video Equipment, Consumer Electronics			
DOLBY LABORATORIES INC	334310	922,713	283,447
SRS LABS INC	334310	31,220	3,006
VOX INTERNATIONAL CORPORATION	334310	550,695	22,483
Auto Dealers, Retail			
AMERICA'S CAR-MART INC	441110	338,930	26,799
Automobile Parts Manufacturing			
DORMAN PRODUCTS INC	3363	455,716	46,138
FUEL SYSTEMS SOLUTIONS INC	3363	430,632	40,284
MOTORCAR PARTS OF AMERICA INC	3363	142,250	9,646
SPARTAN MOTORS INC	3363	480,736	4,141
STRATTEC SECURITY CORP	3363	207,964	3,941

Company	Industry Code	2010 Sales (U.S. $ thousands)	2010 Profits (U.S. $ thousands)
Automobile Parts, Wholesale Distribution			
AMERICAN TIRE DISTRIBUTORS	423120		
HAHN AUTOMOTIVE WAREHOUSE INC	423120		
Automobiles, Manufacturing			
WABASH NATIONAL CORP	33611	640,372	-167,214
Automotive Oil Change & Lubrication Shops			
LUCOR INC	811191	2,027,000	
Automotive Repair & Maintenance			
AAMCO TRANSMISSIONS INC	8111		
CALIBER HOLDINGS CORP	8111		
MIDAS INC	8111	192,400	-13,400
STERLING AUTOBODY CENTERS	8111		
ZIEBART INTERNATIONAL CORP	8111		
Battery Manufacturing			
ULTRALIFE CORPORATION	33591	178,577	-6,179
Beverages--Breweries			
BOSTON BEER COMPANY INC (THE)	312120	505,870	50,142
Beverages--Soft Drinks & Juices Manufacturing			
MONSTER BEVERAGE CORP	3121	1,303,942	212,029
NATIONAL BEVERAGE CORP	3121	592,465	32,853
Beverages--Wineries			
KENDALL-JACKSON WINE ESTATES LTD	312130		
Biological Products, Manufacturing			
ANIKA THERAPEUTICS INC	325414	55,557	4,316
GENENCOR INTERNATIONAL INC	325414		
GTC BIOTHERAPEUTICS INC	325414	7,226	-31,053
LIFECELL CORPORATION	325414		
LIFECORE BIOMEDICAL INC	325414		
SERACARE LIFE SCIENCES INC	325414	50,380	6,705
Biotechnology Research			
AMAG PHARMACEUTICALS INC	541711	66,245	-81,153
Books, Publishing			
EDUCATIONAL DEVELOPMENT CORP	511130	28,671	1,914
MARVEL ENTERTAINMENT LLC	511130		
Breakfast Cereal Manufacturing			
MALT-O-MEAL COMPANY	311230		
Building Products & Construction Materials in Plastic, Manufacturing			
TREX COMPANY INC	326199	317,690	-10,066
Business Training, Distance Learning			
BLACKBOARD INC	611410	447,318	16,644
ECOLLEGE.COM	611410		
HEALTHSTREAM INC	611410	65,754	4,154
Carbon Products, Manufacturing			
CALGON CARBON CORPORATION	335991	482,341	34,850
Casinos/Horse Racing, Gambling			
MTR GAMING GROUP INC	713210	434,697	-5,116

Company	Industry Code	2010 Sales (U.S. $ thousands)	2010 Profits (U.S. $ thousands)
Chemicals, Manufacturing			
ARIZONA CHEMICAL COMPANY	325		
INNOPHOS HOLDINGS INC	325	714,231	45,155
INNOSPEC INC	325	683,200	73,700
KRONOS WORLDWIDE INC	325	1,499,700	130,600
QUAKER CHEMICAL CORP	325	544,063	31,807
STEPAN COMPANY	325	1,431,122	65,427
ZEP INC	325	568,512	13,504
Chocolate & Confectionery Manufacturing			
TOOTSIE ROLL INDUSTRIES INC	311320	521,448	53,714
TOPPS COMPANY INC (THE)	311320		
Clinics--Outpatient Clinics & Surgery			
CRITICAL CARE SYSTEMS	6214		
HEALTHTRONICS INC	6214	197,005	55,008
HEARUSA INC	6214	83,502	-7,737
NOVAMED INC	6214	92,640	
US PHYSICAL THERAPY INC	6214	211,233	15,645
Commercial Banking			
CAPITOL FEDERAL FINANCIAL INC	522110	408,462	67,840
FIRST FINANCIAL BANCORP (OH)	522110	490,333	57,386
FNB CORP	522110	489,693	74,652
HANCOCK HOLDING COMPANY	522110	489,507	52,206
HUDSON CITY BANCORP INC	522110	2,947,490	537,206
SVB FINANCIAL GROUP	522110	709,261	94,951
Communications Equipment, Manufacturing			
ARRIS GROUP INC	3342	1,087,506	64,128
COMTECH TELECOMMUNICATIONS CORP	3342	778,205	60,630
EMS TECHNOLOGIES INC	3342	355,225	14,065
PHAZAR CORP	3342	7,639	-938
Computer & Telecommunications Equipment Distribution			
PC CONNECTION INC	423430	1,974,198	22,961
SCANSOURCE INC	423430	2,114,979	48,812
TESSCO TECHNOLOGIES INC	423430	522,032	9,139
Computer Accessories, Monitors, Printers Manufacturing			
INTERMEC INC	334119	679,111	-5,325
SYNAPTICS INC	334119	514,890	52,965
Computer Hardware, Manufacturing			
ADEPT TECHNOLOGY INC	334111	51,627	-1,428
CRAY INC	334111	319,388	15,062
SMART MODULAR TECHNOLOGIES INC	334111	703,090	52,571
SUPER MICRO COMPUTER INC	334111	721,438	26,915
Computer Networking & Related Equipment, Manufacturing			
COMVERGE INC	33411	119,389	-31,351
EMULEX CORP	33411	399,150	23,620
FORTINET INC	33411	324,696	41,245
INTERACTIVE INTELLIGENCE GROUP INC	33411	166,315	14,901
NETGEAR INC	33411	902,052	50,909
RIVERBED TECHNOLOGY INC	33411	551,889	34,158

Company	Industry Code	2010 Sales (U.S. $ thousands)	2010 Profits (U.S. $ thousands)
Computer Program or Software Development, Custom			
EPAM SYSTEMS	541511		
Computer Programming & Software Design			
ARGON ST INC	541513		
Computer Software, Accounting, Banking & Financial			
ACI WORLDWIDE INC	511201	418,424	27,195
EBIX INC	511201	132,188	59,019
S1 CORPORATION	511201	209,086	-6,283
Computer Software, Business Management & ERP			
NETSUITE INC	511210H	193,149	-27,480
PEGASYSTEMS INC	511210H	336,599	-5,891
ULTIMATE SOFTWARE GROUP INC	511210H	227,811	2,157
Computer Software, Content & Document Management			
ROVI CORPORATION	511210L	541,490	212,884
Computer Software, Data Base & File Management			
EMBARCADERO TECHNOLOGIES INC	511210J		
Computer Software, Educational & Training			
PLATO LEARNING INC	511210P		
ROSETTA STONE INC	511210P	258,686	13,284
Computer Software, Games & Entertainment			
GLU MOBILE INC	511210G	64,345	-13,423
TAKE-TWO INTERACTIVE SOFTWARE INC	511210G	862,200	-28,802
ZYNGA INC	511210G	597,000	91,000
Computer Software, Healthcare & Biotechnology			
ALLSCRIPTS HEALTHCARE SOLUTIONS INC	511210D	704,502	62,870
ERESEARCH TECHNOLOGY INC	511210D	140,992	9,871
QUALITY SYSTEMS INC	511210D	291,811	48,379
TRIZETTO GROUP INC (THE)	511210D		
Computer Software, Multimedia, Graphics & Publishing			
REALNETWORKS INC	511210F	401,733	5,038
Computer Software, Network Management, System Testing, & Storage			
F5 NETWORKS INC	511210B	881,972	151,153
NETSCOUT SYSTEMS INC	511210B	260,342	27,917
NETWORK ENGINES INC	511210B	221,620	1,529
Computer Software, Operating Systems, Languages & Development Tools			
WIND RIVER SYSTEMS INC	511210I		
Computer Software, Publisher			
BOTTOMLINE TECHNOLOGIES INC	511210	157,990	3,954
CONCUR TECHNOLOGIES INC	511210	292,936	20,581
CYBERSOURCE CORP	511210		
ONLINE RESOURCES CORP	511210	149,513	5,376
SS&C TECHNOLOGIES HOLDINGS INC	511210	328,905	32,413
Computer Software, Sales & Customer Relationship Management			
LIVEPERSON INC	511210K	109,862	9,259
RIGHTNOW TECHNOLOGIES INC	511210K	185,522	28,390
SELECTICA INC	511210K	15,159	-4,644

Company	Industry Code	2010 Sales (U.S. $ thousands)	2010 Profits (U.S. $ thousands)
Computer Software, Security & Anti-Virus			
ARCSIGHT INC	511210E	181,384	28,387
BLUE COAT SYSTEMS INC	511210E	496,137	42,879
RSA SECURITY INC	511210E	729,400	
VASCO DATA SECURITY INTERNATIONAL INC	511210E	107,963	12,390
WEBSENSE INC	511210E	332,762	18,652
Computer Software, Supply Chain & Logistics			
ARIBA INC	511210A	361,146	16,386
MANHATTAN ASSOCIATES INC	511210A	297,117	28,061
Computer Software, Telecom, Communications & VOIP			
ARUBA NETWORKS INC	511210C	266,534	-33,998
INTEGRAL SYSTEMS INC	511210C	177,895	-2,396
NOTIFY TECHNOLOGY CORP	511210C	7,246	616
OPENTV CORP	511210C		
SEACHANGE INTERNATIONAL INC	511210C	201,665	1,323
Computer Storage Equipment & Misc Parts, Manufacturing			
ISILON SYSTEMS INC	334112		
QUANTUM CORP	334112	681,427	16,634
Construction, Heavy & Civil Engineering			
STERLING CONSTRUCTION COMPANY	237	459,893	26,224
Construction, Power & Communication Lines and Structures			
AMERICAN TOWER CORP	237130	1,985,335	373,606
CROWN CASTLE INTERNATIONAL CORP	237130	1,878,658	-311,259
SBA COMMUNICATIONS CORP	237130	626,619	-194,674
SOLARRESERVE	237130		
Construction--Other Special Trade Contractors			
ORION MARINE GROUP INC	2389	353,135	21,882
Consulting--Computer, Telecommunications & Internet			
DIAMOND ADVISORY SERVICES	541512	209,944	12,373
KEYNOTE SYSTEMS INC	541512	79,851	1,686
LCC INTERNATIONAL INC	541512		
PERFICIENT INC	541512	214,950	6,480
Consulting-Human Resources			
KORN/FERRY INTERNATIONAL	541612	599,649	5,298
Consulting--Management & Business			
ADVISORY BOARD COMPANY (THE)	54161	239,323	11,433
CORPORATE EXECUTIVE BOARD COMPANY (THE)	54161	438,907	40,363
CRA INTERNATIONAL INC (CHARLES RIVER)	54161	287,424	1,960
MANAGEMENT NETWORK GROUP INC (THE)	54161	67,243	-2,903
Consulting--Marketing			
GALLUP ORGANIZATION (THE)	541613		
Consulting--Scientific & Technical			
AMERESCO INC	541690	618,226	28,726
ENERNOC INC	541690	280,157	9,577
RECYCLED ENERGY DEVELOPMENT LLC	541690		
Contract Electronics Manufacturing			
KEY TRONIC CORP	334419	199,620	8,690

Company	Industry Code	2010 Sales (U.S. $ thousands)	2010 Profits (U.S. $ thousands)
Dairy Products, Manufacturing			
DANNON COMPANY INC (THE)	3115		
GREAT LAKES CHEESE COMPANY INC	3115		
WHITEWAVE FOODS COMPANY	3115		
Data Processing Services			
AKAMAI TECHNOLOGIES INC	518210	1,023,586	171,220
EQUINIX INC	518210	1,220,334	36,881
INVESTMENT TECHNOLOGY GROUP INC (ITG)	518210	570,754	23,980
J2 GLOBAL COMMUNICATIONS INC	518210	255,394	83,047
NEUSTAR INC	518210	488,845	106,209
NIC INC	518210	161,534	18,363
PREMIERE GLOBAL SERVICES INC	518210	441,753	4,831
TRANSCEND SERVICES INC	518210	94,307	8,520
Diagnostic and Other Electromedical Equipment Manufacturing			
BIOSITE INC	334510		
CALIPER LIFE SCIENCES INC	334510	123,696	4,276
CEPHEID	334510	212,468	-5,917
GEN-PROBE INC	334510	543,327	106,937
LUMINEX CORPORATION	334510	141,557	5,231
Diagnostic Devices, Manufacturing			
MEDTOX SCIENTIFIC INC	6215	97,101	3,017
Diagnostic Substances Manufacturing			
CHOLESTECH CORP	325413		
IMMUCOR INC	325413	329,073	82,583
MERIDIAN BIOSCIENCE INC	325413	143,000	26,647
NEOGEN CORPORATION	325413	140,509	17,521
QUIDEL CORP	325413	113,339	-11,271
TECHNE CORP	325413	269,047	109,776
Drilling Services--Oil & Gas Wells			
UNIT CORP	213111	881,845	146,484
Drug Delivery Systems			
IMPAX LABORATORIES INC	325412A	879,509	250,418
NEKTAR THERAPEUTICS	325412A	159,039	-37,938
NOVEN PHARMACEUTICALS INC	325412A		
Drug Stores-Online			
DRUGSTORE.COM INC	446110E	456,507	-3,550
Drugs (Pharmaceuticals), Discovery & Manufacturing			
AKORN INC	325412	86,409	21,824
ALEXION PHARMACEUTICALS INC	325412	540,957	97,030
APP PHARMACEUTICALS INC	325412		
ASTEX PHARMACEUTICALS INC	325412	52,972	16,273
BIOMARIN PHARMACEUTICAL INC	325412	376,267	205,819
CAMBREX CORP	325412	226,236	9,647
CARACO PHARMACEUTICAL LABORATORIES LTD	325412	233,674	-8,660
CELLDEX THERAPEUTICS INC	325412	46,793	-2,533
CERUS CORPORATION	325412	23,109	-16,911
CUBIST PHARMACEUTICALS INC	325412	636,458	94,325

Company	Industry Code	2010 Sales (U.S. $ thousands)	2010 Profits (U.S. $ thousands)
HI-TECH PHARMACAL CO INC	325412	163,691	31,121
JAZZ PHARMACEUTICALS INC	325412	173,781	32,778
MEDICINES CO (THE)	325412	437,645	104,635
MEDICIS PHARMACEUTICAL CORP	325412	699,968	123,335
MILLENNIUM PHARMACEUTICALS INC	325412		
MYRIAD GENETICS INC	325412	362,648	152,303
PAR PHARMACEUTICAL COMPANIES INC	325412	1,008,874	92,731
QUESTCOR PHARMACEUTICALS INC	325412	115,131	35,071
REGENERON PHARMACEUTICALS INC	325412	459,074	-104,468
SALIX PHARMACEUTICALS	325412	336,973	-27,061
SCICLONE PHARMACEUTICALS INC	325412	85,112	21,081
SCIOS INC	325412		
SEATTLE GENETICS	325412	107,470	-66,265
SPECTRUM PHARMACEUTICALS INC	325412	74,113	-48,844
STIEFEL LABORATORIES INC	325412		
UNITED THERAPEUTICS CORP	325412	603,831	105,916
VIROPHARMA INC	325412	439,012	125,608
XOMA LTD	325412	33,641	-68,756
Egg Production			
CAL-MAINE FOODS INC	112310	910,143	67,823
Electrical Equipment, Manufacturing			
IROBOT CORP	335	400,952	25,514
POWERSECURE INTERNATIONAL INC	335	97,514	3,462
TII NETWORK TECHNOLOGIES INC	335	54,498	2,230
UQM TECHNOLOGIES INC	335	8,692	-4,141
Electronic Parts & Equipment, Distribution			
BRIGHTSTAR CORPORATION	4236		
Engineering Services			
KIMLEY-HORN AND ASSOCIATES INC	541330		
Equipment Rental			
UNIVERSAL HOSPITAL SERVICES INC	5324	317,400	-29,100
Facilities Support Services			
SHARED TECHNOLOGIES	561210		
Fertility Clinics			
INTEGRAMED AMERICA INC	621410	243,169	4,725
Finance--Consumer			
ENCORE CAPITAL GROUP INC	522291	381,308	49,052
Food Distribution			
AMCON DISTRIBUTING CO	4244	1,010,538	8,966
Food Products, Manufacturing			
B&G FOODS INC	311	513,337	32,379
HANOVER FOODS CORPORATION	311		
Freight Forwarding & Support Services			
FEDEX SUPPLY CHAIN SERVICES INC	4885		
HUB GROUP INC	4885	1,833,737	43,458
Frozen Food Manufacturing			
MICHELINAS INC	31141		

Company	Industry Code	2010 Sales (U.S. $ thousands)	2010 Profits (U.S. $ thousands)
Fruit & Tree Nut Farming			
CALAVO GROWERS INC	1113	398,351	17,764
DIAMOND FOODS INC	1113	680,162	26,211
Gambling Equipment			
WMS INDUSTRIES INC	329999	765,100	112,900
Grain Distribution, Milling & Oilseed Processing			
RICELAND FOODS INC	3112		
Grocery Stores/Supermarkets			
ARDEN GROUP INC	445110	417,065	18,085
NUGGET MARKET	445110		
SPROUTS FARMERS MARKET LLC	445110	575,000	
Grocery Stores/Supermarkets-Online			
FRESHDIRECT LLC	445110E	300,000	
PEAPOD LLC	445110E		
Health Supplement Stores			
MEDIFAST INC	446191	257,552	19,611
Instrument Manufacturing, including Measurement, Control, Test & Navigational			
AMERICAN SCIENCE & ENGINEERING INC	3345	242,093	36,176
ILLUMINA INC	3345	902,741	124,891
NANOMETRICS INC	3345	188,065	55,948
Insurance Intermediary-Online			
EHEALTH INC	524210A	160,404	17,482
Insurance-Health, HMO's & PPO's			
DELPHI FINANCIAL GROUP INC	524114	1,737,248	173,147
HEALTH INSURANCE PLAN OF GREATER NEW YORK	524114		
METROPOLITAN HEALTH NETWORKS INC	524114	368,186	25,700
Insurance-Life			
AMERICAN FIDELITY ASSURANCE COMPANY	524113	846,000	
GREAT AMERICAN FINANCIAL RESOURCES INC	524113		
INDEPENDENCE HOLDING CO	524113	435,368	23,413
PHOENIX COMPANIES INC (THE)	524113	2,084,900	-12,600
PROTECTIVE LIFE CORP	524113	3,097,755	260,241
Insurance--Property & Casualty, Specialty, Surety			
AMTRUST FINANCIAL SERVICES INC	524126	1,002,457	146,340
CRUM & FORSTER HOLDINGS INC	524126		
HCC INSURANCE HOLDINGS INC	524126	2,303,254	345,096
HORACE MANN EDUCATORS CORPORATION	524126	974,800	80,900
MAPFRE USA CORP	524126		
PHILADELPHIA CONSOLIDATED HOLDING CORP	524126	2,108,038	265,585
PMA COMPANIES INC	524126		
PROASSURANCE CORP	524126	692,065	231,598
STATE AUTO FINANCIAL CORP	524126	1,355,110	24,500
Insurance-Reinsurance			
EVEREST RE GROUP LTD	524130	4,705,807	610,754
ODYSSEY RE HOLDINGS CORP	524130	2,383,938	333,275
REINSURANCE GROUP OF AMERICA INC	524130	8,261,730	574,402
TRANSATLANTIC HOLDINGS INC	524130	4,362,153	402,201

Company	Industry Code	2010 Sales (U.S. $ thousands)	2010 Profits (U.S. $ thousands)
Internet Publishing & Web Search Portals			
BANKRATE INC	519130	220,300	-38,900
COSTAR GROUP INC	519130	226,260	13,289
EDGAR ONLINE INC	519130	19,468	-8,649
HEALTH GRADES INC	519130		
INFOSPACE INC	519130	246,835	13,703
INTERACTIVE DATA CORPORATION	519130	796,645	-71,789
IVILLAGE INC	519130		
SHUTTERFLY INC	519130	307,707	17,127
WEBMD HEALTH CORP	519130	534,519	54,072
WEBMEDIA BRANDS INC	519130	8,987	-3,020
WIKIMEDIA FOUNDATION	519130	16,578	
XO GROUP INC	519130	112,881	3,654
Investment Banking			
CANTOR FITZGERALD LP	523110		
EDELMAN FINANCIAL GROUP (THE)	523110	168,843	9,696
EVERCORE PARTNERS INC	523110	378,897	8,954
GLEACHER & COMPANY INC	523110	282,227	-20,621
HOULIHAN LOKEY HOWARD & ZUKIN INC	523110		
KBW INC	523110	425,857	26,628
MESIROW FINANCIAL HOLDINGS INC	523110	526,403	
MOELIS & COMPANY	523110		
PIPER JAFFRAY COMPANIES	523110	530,074	18,929
ROBERT W BAIRD & CO INC	523110		
Investment Management/Mutual Funds/Pension Funds			
AFFILIATED MANAGERS GROUP	523920	1,358,242	287,328
EATON VANCE CORP	523920	1,121,661	174,298
WADDELL & REED FINANCIAL INC	523920	1,032,162	156,959
Jewelry Stores-Online			
BLUE NILE INC	448310E	332,889	14,142
Laboratories & Diagnostic Services--Medical			
BIO REFERENCE LABORATORIES INC	621511	458,024	26,381
CELSIS INTERNATIONAL PLC	621511		
CRYOLIFE INC	621511	116,645	3,744
GENOMIC HEALTH INC	621511	178,101	4,288
Logistics Outsourcing			
LOGISTICARE INC	541614		
Lumber & Construction Materials, Wholesale Distribution			
LB FOSTER COMPANY	4233	475,050	20,492
Machinery-Mining & Oil & Gas Field, Manufacturing			
TESCO CORPORATION	33313	378,665	7,045
Mail Order and Non-Store Selling, Incl. TV Shopping			
SPORT SUPPLY GROUP INC	454113		
Market Research			
FORRESTER RESEARCH INC	541910	250,726	20,507
HARRIS INTERACTIVE INC	541910	138,415	-2,166
Meat Production			
CACTUS FEEDERS INC	311612	750,000	

Company	Industry Code	2010 Sales (U.S. $ thousands)	2010 Profits (U.S. $ thousands)
Medical/Dental/Surgical Equipment & Supplies, Distribution			
CHINDEX INTERNATIONAL INC	423450	171,191	8,204
Medical/Dental/Surgical Equipment & Supplies, Manufacturing			
ABAXIS INC	33911	124,557	13,023
ALIGN TECHNOLOGY INC	33911	387,126	74,253
AMERICAN MEDICAL SYSTEMS HOLDINGS INC	33911	542,316	87,010
ANALOGIC CORP	33911	423,597	15,555
ARTHROCARE CORP	33911	355,379	37,084
ATRION CORPORATION	33911	108,569	20,952
CANTEL MEDICAL CORP	33911	273,952	19,941
CARDIONET INC	33911	119,924	-19,860
COHERENT INC	33911	605,067	36,916
CYBERONICS INC	33911	167,776	78,449
DJO GLOBAL INC	33911	965,973	-50,750
ENVIRONMENTAL TECTONICS CORP	33911	42,271	6,453
EXACTECH INC	33911	190,483	10,465
HAEMONETICS CORPORATION	33911	645,430	58,370
ICU MEDICAL INC	33911	284,582	30,929
I-FLOW CORPORATION	33911		
INTUITIVE SURGICAL INC	33911	1,413,000	381,800
IRIDEX CORP	33911	43,694	3,046
IRIS INTERNATIONAL INC	33911	107,672	3,042
LAKELAND INDUSTRIES INC	33911	94,141	1,030
MAKO SURGICAL CORP	33911	44,296	-38,687
MENTOR CORP	33911		
MERIT MEDICAL SYSTEMS INC	33911	296,755	12,460
MICROTEK MEDICAL HOLDINGS INC	33911		
NATIONAL DENTEX CORP	33911		
NATUS MEDICAL INC	33911	218,655	11,919
NUVASIVE INC	33911	478,237	78,285
SCHICK TECHNOLOGIES INC	33911		
SPECTRANETICS CORP	33911	117,917	-13,063
STAAR SURGICAL CO	33911	54,958	53
SYNOVIS LIFE TECHNOLOGIES INC	33911	68,565	4,876
THERAGENICS CORP	33911	82,184	2,070
THORATEC CORPORATION	33911	382,973	53,166
UTAH MEDICAL PRODUCTS INC	33911	25,121	6,014
VENTANA MEDICAL SYSTEMS INC	33911		
WRIGHT MEDICAL GROUP INC	33911	518,973	17,841
ZOLL MEDICAL CORP	33911	443,989	18,919
Medicinals & Botanicals, Manufacturing			
CHATTEM INC	325411		
MARTEK BIOSCIENCES CORP	325411	434,752	27,900
SCHIFF NUTRITION INTERNATIONAL INC	325411	204,887	18,446
USANA HEALTH SCIENCES INC	325411	517,644	45,651
Motor Vehicle Body Manufacturing			
SUPREME INDUSTRIES INC	336211	220,889	-11,529

Company	Industry Code	2010 Sales (U.S. $ thousands)	2010 Profits (U.S. $ thousands)
Motorcycle, Bicycle, & Parts Manufacturing			
ZAP JONWAY	336991	3,816	-19,018
Music Stores-Online			
AUDIBLE INC	451220E		
Nonmetallic Mineral, Rock & Aggregate Manufacturing			
AMCOL INTERNATIONAL CORP	327	852,538	29,924
Nuclear Reactor Manufacturing			
GENERAL ATOMICS	332410		
Oil & Natural Gas Exploration & Production			
BERRY PETROLEUM CO	211111	669,955	82,524
CABOT OIL & GAS CORP	211111	884,035	103,386
CARRIZO OIL & GAS INC	211111	139,462	9,950
CLAYTON WILLIAMS ENERGY INC	211111	331,631	36,938
CONTINENTAL RESOURCES INC	211111	839,065	168,255
DENBURY RESOURCES INC	211111	1,921,791	285,527
EOG RESOURCES INC	211111	6,099,896	160,654
PETROLEUM DEVELOPMENT CORPORATION	211111	347,647	6,214
PIONEER NATURAL RESOURCES COMPANY	211111	2,471,590	605,208
PLAINS EXPLORATION AND PRODUCTION COMPANY	211111	1,544,595	103,265
PRIMEENERGY CORPORATION	211111	118,169	2,753
QUICKSILVER RESOURCES INC	211111	928,331	435,069
SANDRIDGE ENERGY INC	211111	903,400	190,600
SOUTHWESTERN ENERGY CO	211111	2,610,663	604,118
SWIFT ENERGY CO	211111	438,429	46,294
TARGA RESOURCES PARTNERS LP	211111	5,460,200	134,000
XTO ENERGY INC	211111		
Oil Field Services			
CARBO CERAMICS INC	213112	473,082	78,716
HELIX ENERGY SOLUTIONS GROUP INC	213112	1,199,838	-126,988
RPC INC	213112	1,096,384	146,742
Other Fuel Dealers, Retail			
CLEAN ENERGY FUELS CORP	454319	211,834	-44,568
Other Retailers, Misc. Retailers			
GAIAM INC	45399	274,268	4,275
LESLIE'S POOLMART INC	45399		
Payment & Transaction Processing Services			
ATHENAHEALTH INC	522320	245,538	12,704
CARDTRONICS INC	522320	532,078	41,133
COMDATA CORP	522320		
Payment & Transaction Processing--Benefits Management			
BIOSCRIP INC	522320A	1,638,623	-69,142
CATALYST HEALTH SOLUTIONS INC	522320A	3,764,092	80,957
Petroleum Bulk Stations & Terminals Distribution			
GLOBAL PARTNERS LP	424710	7,801,559	27,038
NUSTAR ENERGY LP	424710	4,403,061	238,970
Petroleum Products (except Bulk Stations/Terminals) Distribution & Pipelines			
ENERGY TRANSFER PARTNERS LP	486	5,884,827	617,222

Company	Industry Code	2010 Sales (U.S. $ thousands)	2010 Profits (U.S. $ thousands)
GENESIS ENERGY LP	486	2,101,324	-48,459
MAGELLAN MIDSTREAM PARTNERS LP	486	1,557,447	311,580
TRANSAMMONIA INC	486	8,500,000	
Petroleum Refineries			
HOLLYFRONTIER CORPORATION	324110	8,322,929	133,051
Pets/Pet Supplies Stores			
PETMED EXPRESS INC	453910	238,266	26,002
Physician Practice Management			
CONTINUCARE CORP	6211	310,791	22,176
Plastic Products, Manufacturing			
POLYPORE INTERNATIONAL INC	3261	616,600	63,600
ROGERS CORPORATION	3261	379,188	34,571
Poultry Production			
CAGLE'S INC	311615	307,091	2,537
Radio & Wireless Communication, Manufacturing			
ALIEN TECHNOLOGY CORPORATION	334220		
CLEARONE COMMUNICATIONS INC	334220	41,284	2,374
GLOBECOMM SYSTEMS INC	334220	227,817	7,902
VIASAT INC	334220	688,080	30,839
Radio Broadcasting			
CUMULUS MEDIA INC	515111	263,333	29,402
Real Estate Investment Trusts - Nonresidential			
HOSPITALITY PROPERTIES TRUST	531120	1,085,488	21,351
SENIOR HOUSING PROPERTIES	531120	339,009	116,485
SL GREEN REALTY CORP	531120	1,101,246	270,826
SOVRAN SELF STORAGE INC	531120	192,072	40,642
SUN COMMUNITIES INC	531120	263,140	-2,883
SUPERTEL HOSPITALITY INC	531120	84,114	-10,585
Real Estate Investment Trusts - Residential			
AVALONBAY COMMUNITIES INC	531110	895,266	175,331
ESSEX PROPERTY TRUST INC	531110	415,732	50,782
INVESTORS REAL ESTATE TRUST	531110	242,775	4,585
MID-AMERICA APARTMENT COMMUNITIES INC	531110	401,549	29,761
UDR INC	531110	632,249	-112,362
Real Estate Operations & Development--General			
AMERICAN CAMPUS COMMUNITIES INC	5311	344,991	16,210
Research & Development-Physical, Engineering & Life Sciences			
ALBANY MOLECULAR RESEARCH INC	541712	198,066	-62,871
ARRAY BIOPHARMA INC	541712	53,880	-77,631
FUEL TECH INC	541712	81,795	1,735
PACIFIC BIOMARKERS INC	541712	9,665	-1,383
VERENIUM CORPORATION	541712	52,073	19,933
Restaurants			
INTERNATIONAL DAIRY QUEEN INC	722110		
RV Parks & Campgrounds			
KAMPGROUNDS OF AMERICA INC	721211		

Company	Industry Code	2010 Sales (U.S. $ thousands)	2010 Profits (U.S. $ thousands)
Seasonings, Flavorings & Dressings Manufacturing			
NUTRASWEET COMPANY (THE)	31194		
Security, Detection & Intercom System Manufacturing			
DEI HOLDINGS INC	334290		
LOJACK CORPORTATION	334290	146,600	-18,600
Semiconductor Manufacturing Equipment			
AMTECH SYSTEMS INC	333295	120,019	9,563
Semiconductors (Microchips)/Integrated Circuits/Components, Manufacturing			
CIRRUS LOGIC INC	33441	220,989	38,398
EMCORE CORP	33441	191,278	-23,694
MINDSPEED TECHNOLOGIES INC	33441	178,179	21,070
QUALCOMM ATHEROS INC	33441	926,832	54,373
SIGMA DESIGNS INC	33441	206,083	2,455
SILICON LABORATORIES INC	33441	493,341	73,242
SPIRE CORPORATION	33441	79,842	-408
VARIAN SEMICONDUCTOR EQUIPMENT ASSOCIATES INC	33441	831,780	159,584
Shipping-Deep Sea			
ALEXANDER & BALDWIN INC	483111	1,646,200	92,100
GENCO SHIPPING & TRADING LIMITED	483111	448,687	147,409
GULFMARK OFFSHORE INC	483111	359,766	-34,745
Shipping-Inland			
KIRBY CORP	48321	1,109,557	116,249
Shoe Manufacturing-Athletic Shoes & Misc. Shoes, Incl. Children's			
ROCKY BRANDS INC	316219	252,792	7,684
Shoe Manufacturing-General			
ICONIX BRAND GROUP INC	3162	332,559	110,480
KENNETH COLE PRODUCTIONS INC	3162	411,652	2,084
STEVEN MADDEN LTD	3162	635,418	75,725
Snack Products, Manufacturing			
GOLDEN ENTERPRISES INC	31191	128,441	4,209
JOHN B SANFILIPPO & SON INC	31191	561,633	14,425
Solar Cells, LEDs & Other Semiconductor Products			
HELIOVOLT CORP	334413		
SOLFOCUS INC	334413		
Sporting Goods Stores			
SPORTSMAN'S GUIDE INC (THE)	451110		
Sporting Goods Stores-Online			
GOLFSMITH INTERNATIONAL HOLDINGS INC	451110E	351,851	-5,493
Staffing or Outsourcing			
ALLIED HEALTHCARE INTERNATIONAL INC	561	271,079	10,056
Steel & Metals--Fabricated Metals Components, Manufacturing			
AROTECH CORPORATION	332	73,741	-917
Stock Brokerage			
GFI GROUP INC	523120	862,113	25,615
KNIGHT CAPITAL GROUP INC	523120	1,149,056	91,638
RV Parks & Campgrounds			
KAMPGROUNDS OF AMERICA INC	721211		

Company	Industry Code	2010 Sales (U.S. $ thousands)	2010 Profits (U.S. $ thousands)
NEW YORK MERCANTILE EXCHANGE INC	523210		
Surveying & Mapping--Geophysical			
DAWSON GEOPHYSICAL COMPANY	541360	205,272	-9,352
Telecommunications Equipment Manufacturing			
ADTRAN INC	334210	605,674	113,989
ANAREN INC	334210	168,789	13,712
CHANNELL COMMERCIAL CORP	334210		
RAYTHEON APPLIED SIGNAL TECHNOLOGY INC	334210	225,229	13,223
TEKELEC	334210	423,963	15,009
XETA TECHNOLOGIES INC	334210	85,678	1,373
Telecommunications Service Cellular, U.S. & Non-U.S.			
PURPLE COMMUNICATIONS INC	5172		
Telecommunications Service Wired, Satellite or Cable			
ATLANTIC TELE-NETWORK INC	517110	619,145	38,454
COGENT COMMUNICATIONS	517110	263,416	669
ECHOSTAR CORP	517110	2,350,369	204,358
GENERAL COMMUNICATION INC (GCI)	517110	651,250	8,955
HICKORY TECH CORPORATION	517110	162,247	12,094
IBASIS INC	517110		
INTERNAP NETWORK SERVICES CORP	517110	244,164	-3,622
KNOLOGY INC	517110	459,546	-281
NTELOS HOLDING CORP	517110	545,684	46,345
SHENANDOAH TELECOMMUNICATIONS CO	517110	194,889	18,075
SYNIVERSE TECHNOLOGIES	517110		
TERREMARK WORLDWIDE INC	517110	292,347	-31,673
UNITED ONLINE INC	517110	920,553	50,454
Teleconferencing			
ACME PACKET INC	561499	231,232	43,037
TELIRIS	561499		
WEBEX COMMUNICATIONS INC	561499		
Textiles, Fabrics, Sheets/Towels, Manufacturing			
CULP INC	313	206,416	13,188
OMNOVA SOLUTIONS INC	313	846,200	107,900
Travel Services-Online			
TRAVELZOO INC	5615E	112,784	13,157
Truck Transportation			
ECHO GLOBAL LOGISTICS INC	484	426,400	8,400
Truck Transportation-Specialized			
FROZEN FOOD EXPRESS INDUSTRIES INC	4842	368,822	-11,930
TV/Video/Theatrical, Production			
DREAMWORKS ANIMATION SKG INC	512110	784,791	170,639
LUCASFILM LTD	512110		
RENTRAK CORP	512110	91,076	576
Utilities-Alternative Energy Generation			
SACRAMENTO MUNICIPAL UTILITY DISTRICT	221119		
RV Parks & Campgrounds			
KAMPGROUNDS OF AMERICA INC	721211		

Company	Industry Code	2010 Sales (U.S. $ thousands)	2010 Profits (U.S. $ thousands)
CENTRAL VERMONT PUBLIC SERVICE CORP	2211	341,925	20,954
DPL INC	2211	1,883,100	290,300
IDACORP INC	2211	1,036,029	142,798
TAMPA ELECTRIC COMPANY	2211		
UIL HOLDINGS CORPORATION	2211	997,666	54,854
WESTAR ENERGY	2211	2,056,171	202,926
Utilities-Electric & Gas			
ATLANTIC CITY ELECTRIC COMPANY	221		
AVISTA CORPORATION	221	1,558,740	92,425
NORTHWESTERN CORPORATION	221	1,110,720	77,376
UNISOURCE ENERGY CORPORATION	221	1,453,677	111,477
WGL HOLDINGS INC	221	2,708,876	111,205
Utilities-Gas			
EQT CORPORATION	221210	1,322,708	227,700
LACLEDE GROUP INC (THE)	221210	1,735,029	54,040
NEW JERSEY RESOURCES CORPORATION	221210	2,639,304	117,457
PIEDMONT NATURAL GAS COMPANY INC	221210	1,552,295	141,954
SOUTHERN UNION COMPANY	221210	2,489,913	216,213
SOUTHWEST GAS CORP	221210	1,830,371	103,877
Utilities-Nuclear Generation			
GREEN MOUNTAIN POWER CORPORATION	221113		
Venture Capital/Private Equity Investments/Hedge Funds			
COMPASS DIVERSIFIED HOLDINGS	523910	1,657,609	-44,770
KKR & CO LP (KOHLBERG KRAVIS ROBERTS & CO)	523910	382,287	333,178
Veterinary Products Manufacturing			
HESKA CORP	325412B	55,655	18
Video Rental			
NETFLIX INC	532230	2,162,625	160,853
REDBOX AUTOMATED RETAIL LLC	532230	1,160,110	
Wines & Spirits, Distribution			
NATIONAL WINE & SPIRITS INC	4248		
YOUNG'S MARKET COMPANY LLC	4248	2,300,000	

ALPHABETICAL INDEX

FRESHDIRECT LLC
FROZEN FOOD EXPRESS INDUSTRIES INC
FUEL SYSTEMS SOLUTIONS INC
FUEL TECH INC
GAIAM INC
GALLUP ORGANIZATION (THE)
GENCO SHIPPING & TRADING LIMITED
GENENCOR INTERNATIONAL INC
GENERAL ATOMICS
GENERAL COMMUNICATION INC (GCI)
GENESIS ENERGY LP
GENOMIC HEALTH INC
GEN-PROBE INC
GFI GROUP INC
G-III APPAREL GROUP
GLEACHER & COMPANY INC
GLOBAL PARTNERS LP
GLOBECOMM SYSTEMS INC
GLU MOBILE INC
GOLDEN ENTERPRISES INC
GOLFSMITH INTERNATIONAL HOLDINGS INC
GREAT AMERICAN FINANCIAL RESOURCES INC
GREAT LAKES CHEESE COMPANY INC
GREEN MOUNTAIN POWER CORPORATION
GTC BIOTHERAPEUTICS INC
GULFMARK OFFSHORE INC
HAEMONETICS CORPORATION
HAHN AUTOMOTIVE WAREHOUSE INC
HANCOCK HOLDING COMPANY
HANOVER FOODS CORPORATION
HARRIS INTERACTIVE INC
HCC INSURANCE HOLDINGS INC
HEALTH GRADES INC
HEALTH INSURANCE PLAN OF GREATER NEW YORK
HEALTHSTREAM INC
HEALTHTRONICS INC
HEARUSA INC
HELIOVOLT CORP
HELIX ENERGY SOLUTIONS GROUP INC
HESKA CORP
HICKORY TECH CORPORATION
HI-TECH PHARMACAL CO INC
HOLLYFRONTIER CORPORATION
HORACE MANN EDUCATORS CORPORATION
HOSPITALITY PROPERTIES TRUST
HOULIHAN LOKEY HOWARD & ZUKIN INC
HUB GROUP INC
HUDSON CITY BANCORP INC
IBASIS INC
ICONIX BRAND GROUP INC
ICU MEDICAL INC
IDACORP INC
I-FLOW CORPORATION
ILLUMINA INC
IMG WORLDWIDE INC
IMMUCOR INC
IMPAX LABORATORIES INC
INDEPENDENCE HOLDING CO
INFOSPACE INC
INNOPHOS HOLDINGS INC
INNOSPEC INC
INTEGRAL SYSTEMS INC
INTEGRAMED AMERICA INC
INTERACTIVE DATA CORPORATION
INTERACTIVE INTELLIGENCE GROUP INC
INTERCONTINENTALEXCHANGE INC (ICE)
INTERMEC INC
INTERNAP NETWORK SERVICES CORP
INTERNATIONAL CREATIVE MANAGEMENT INC (ICM)
INTERNATIONAL DAIRY QUEEN INC
INTUITIVE SURGICAL INC
INVESTMENT TECHNOLOGY GROUP INC (ITG)
INVESTORS REAL ESTATE TRUST
IRIDEX CORP
IRIS INTERNATIONAL INC
IROBOT CORP
ISILON SYSTEMS INC
IVILLAGE INC
J2 GLOBAL COMMUNICATIONS INC
JAZZ PHARMACEUTICALS INC
JOE'S JEANS INC
JOHN B SANFILIPPO & SON INC
KAMPGROUNDS OF AMERICA INC
KBW INC
KENDALL-JACKSON WINE ESTATES LTD
KENNETH COLE PRODUCTIONS INC
KEY TRONIC CORP
KEYNOTE SYSTEMS INC
KIMLEY-HORN AND ASSOCIATES INC
KIRBY CORP
KKR & CO LP (KOHLBERG KRAVIS ROBERTS & CO)
KNIGHT CAPITAL GROUP INC
KNOLOGY INC
KORN/FERRY INTERNATIONAL
KRONOS WORLDWIDE INC
LACLEDE GROUP INC (THE)
LAKELAND INDUSTRIES INC
LB FOSTER COMPANY
LCC INTERNATIONAL INC
LESLIE'S POOLMART INC
LIFECELL CORPORATION
LIFECORE BIOMEDICAL INC
LIVEPERSON INC
LOGISTICARE INC
LOJACK CORPORTATION
LUCASFILM LTD
LUCOR INC
LUMINEX CORPORATION
MAGELLAN MIDSTREAM PARTNERS LP
MAKO SURGICAL CORP
MALT-O-MEAL COMPANY
MANAGEMENT NETWORK GROUP INC (THE)
MANHATTAN ASSOCIATES INC
MAPFRE USA CORP
MARTEK BIOSCIENCES CORP
MARVEL ENTERTAINMENT LLC
MEDICINES CO (THE)
MEDICIS PHARMACEUTICAL CORP
MEDIFAST INC
MEDTOX SCIENTIFIC INC
MENTOR CORP
MERIDIAN BIOSCIENCE INC
MERIT MEDICAL SYSTEMS INC
MESIROW FINANCIAL HOLDINGS INC
METROPOLITAN HEALTH NETWORKS INC
MICHELINAS INC
MICROTEK MEDICAL HOLDINGS INC
MID-AMERICA APARTMENT COMMUNITIES INC
MIDAS INC
MILLENNIUM PHARMACEUTICALS INC
MINDSPEED TECHNOLOGIES INC
MOELIS & COMPANY
MONSTER BEVERAGE CORP
MOTORCAR PARTS OF AMERICA INC
MTR GAMING GROUP INC
MYRIAD GENETICS INC
NANOMETRICS INC
NATIONAL BEVERAGE CORP
NATIONAL DENTEX CORP
NATIONAL WINE & SPIRITS INC
NATUS MEDICAL INC
NEKTAR THERAPEUTICS
NEOGEN CORPORATION
NETFLIX INC
NETGEAR INC
NETSCOUT SYSTEMS INC
NETSUITE INC
NETWORK ENGINES INC
NEUSTAR INC
NEW JERSEY RESOURCES CORPORATION
NEW YORK MERCANTILE EXCHANGE INC
NIC INC
NORTHWESTERN CORPORATION
NOTIFY TECHNOLOGY CORP
NOVAMED INC
NOVEN PHARMACEUTICALS INC
NTELOS HOLDING CORP
NUGGET MARKET
NUSTAR ENERGY LP
NUTRASWEET COMPANY (THE)
NUVASIVE INC
ODYSSEY RE HOLDINGS CORP
OMNOVA SOLUTIONS INC
ONLINE RESOURCES CORP
ONSTREAM MEDIA CORPORATION
OPENTV CORP
ORION MARINE GROUP INC

PACIFIC BIOMARKERS INC
PAR PHARMACEUTICAL COMPANIES INC
PATAGONIA INC
PC CONNECTION INC
PEAPOD LLC
PEGASYSTEMS INC
PERFICIENT INC
PERRY ELLIS INTERNATIONAL INC
PETMED EXPRESS INC
PETROLEUM DEVELOPMENT CORPORATION
PHAZAR CORP
PHILADELPHIA CONSOLIDATED HOLDING CORP
PHOENIX COMPANIES INC (THE)
PIEDMONT NATURAL GAS COMPANY INC
PIONEER NATURAL RESOURCES COMPANY
PIPER JAFFRAY COMPANIES
PLAINS EXPLORATION AND PRODUCTION COMPANY
PLATO LEARNING INC
PMA COMPANIES INC
POLYPORE INTERNATIONAL INC
POWERSECURE INTERNATIONAL INC
PREMIERE GLOBAL SERVICES INC
PRIMEENERGY CORPORATION
PROASSURANCE CORP
PROTECTIVE LIFE CORP
PURPLE COMMUNICATIONS INC
QUAKER CHEMICAL CORP
QUALCOMM ATHEROS INC
QUALITY SYSTEMS INC
QUANTUM CORP
QUESTCOR PHARMACEUTICALS INC
QUICKSILVER RESOURCES INC
QUIDEL CORP
RAYTHEON APPLIED SIGNAL TECHNOLOGY INC
REALNETWORKS INC
RECYCLED ENERGY DEVELOPMENT
REDBOX AUTOMATED RETAIL LLC
REGENERON PHARMACEUTICALS INC
REINSURANCE GROUP OF AMERICA INC
RENTRAK CORP
RICELAND FOODS INC
RIGHTNOW TECHNOLOGIES INC
RIVERBED TECHNOLOGY INC
ROBERT W BAIRD & CO INC
ROCKY BRANDS INC
ROGERS CORPORATION
ROSETTA STONE INC
ROVI CORPORATION
RPC INC
RSA SECURITY INC
S1 CORPORATION
SACRAMENTO MUNICIPAL UTILITY DISTRICT
SALIX PHARMACEUTICALS
SANDRIDGE ENERGY INC
SBA COMMUNICATIONS CORP
SCANSOURCE INC
SCHICK TECHNOLOGIES INC
SCHIFF NUTRITION INTERNATIONAL INC
SCICLONE PHARMACEUTICALS INC
SCIOS INC
SCOULAR COMPANY (THE)
SEACHANGE INTERNATIONAL INC
SEATTLE GENETICS
SELECTICA INC
SENIOR HOUSING PROPERTIES
SERACARE LIFE SCIENCES INC
SHARED TECHNOLOGIES
SHENANDOAH TELECOMMUNICATIONS CO
SHUTTERFLY INC
SIGMA DESIGNS INC
SILICON LABORATORIES INC
SL GREEN REALTY CORP
SMART MODULAR TECHNOLOGIES INC
SOLARRESERVE
SOLFOCUS INC
SOTHEBYS
SOUTHERN UNION COMPANY
SOUTHWEST GAS CORP
SOUTHWESTERN ENERGY CO
SOVRAN SELF STORAGE INC
SPARTAN MOTORS INC
SPECTRANETICS CORP
SPECTRUM PHARMACEUTICALS INC
SPIRE CORPORATION
SPORT SUPPLY GROUP INC
SPORTSMAN'S GUIDE INC (THE)
SPROUTS FARMERS MARKET LLC
SRS LABS INC
SS&C TECHNOLOGIES HOLDINGS INC
STAAR SURGICAL CO
STATE AUTO FINANCIAL CORP
STEPAN COMPANY
STERLING AUTOBODY CENTERS
STERLING CONSTRUCTION COMPANY
STEVEN MADDEN LTD
STIEFEL LABORATORIES INC
SUN COMMUNITIES INC
SUNOCO LOGISTICS PARTNERS LP
SUPER MICRO COMPUTER INC
SUPERIOR UNIFORM GROUP INC
SUPERTEL HOSPITALITY INC
SUPREME INDUSTRIES INC
SVB FINANCIAL GROUP
SWIFT ENERGY CO
SYNAPTICS INC
SYNIVERSE TECHNOLOGIES
SYNOVIS LIFE TECHNOLOGIES INC
TAKE-TWO INTERACTIVE SOFTWARE INC
TAMPA ELECTRIC COMPANY
TARGA RESOURCES PARTNERS LP
TECHNE CORP
TEKELEC
TELIRIS
TERREMARK WORLDWIDE INC
TESCO CORPORATION
TESSCO TECHNOLOGIES INC
THERAGENICS CORP
THORATEC CORPORATION
TII NETWORK TECHNOLOGIES INC
TOOTSIE ROLL INDUSTRIES INC
TOPPS COMPANY INC (THE)
TRANSAMMONIA INC
TRANSATLANTIC HOLDINGS INC
TRANSCEND SERVICES INC
TRAVELZOO INC
TREX COMPANY INC
TRIZETTO GROUP INC (THE)
TRUE RELIGION APPAREL INC
UDR INC
UIL HOLDINGS CORPORATION
ULTIMATE SOFTWARE GROUP INC
ULTRALIFE CORPORATION
UNISOURCE ENERGY CORPORATION
UNIT CORP
UNITED ONLINE INC
UNITED THERAPEUTICS CORP
UNIVERSAL HOSPITAL SERVICES INC
UQM TECHNOLOGIES INC
US PHYSICAL THERAPY INC
USANA HEALTH SCIENCES INC
UTAH MEDICAL PRODUCTS INC
VARIAN SEMICONDUCTOR EQUIPMENT ASSOCIATES INC
VASCO DATA SECURITY INTERNATIONAL INC
VENTANA MEDICAL SYSTEMS INC
VERENIUM CORPORATION
VIASAT INC
VIBRANT MEDIA INC
VIROPHARMA INC
VOLCOM INC
VOX INTERNATIONAL CORPORATION
WABASH NATIONAL CORP
WADDELL & REED FINANCIAL INC
WEBEX COMMUNICATIONS INC
WEBMD HEALTH CORP
WEBMEDIA BRANDS INC
WEBSENSE INC
WESTAR ENERGY
WGL HOLDINGS INC
WHITEWAVE FOODS COMPANY
WIKIMEDIA FOUNDATION
WIND RIVER SYSTEMS INC
WMS INDUSTRIES INC
WRIGHT MEDICAL GROUP INC
XETA TECHNOLOGIES INC
XO GROUP INC
XOMA LTD
XTO ENERGY INC
YOUNG'S MARKET COMPANY LLC
ZAP JONWAY
ZEP INC
ZIEBART INTERNATIONAL CORP
ZOLL MEDICAL CORP
ZYNGA INC

INDEX OF U.S. HEADQUARTERS LOCATION BY STATE

To help you locate members of THE MID-SIZE EMPLOYERS 500 geographically, the city and state of the headquarters of each company are in the following index.

PETROLEUM DEVELOPMENT CORPORATION; Denver
SPECTRANETICS CORP; Colorado Springs
TRIZETTO GROUP INC (THE); Denver
UDR INC; Highlands Ranch
UQM TECHNOLOGIES INC; Longmont
WHITEWAVE FOODS COMPANY; Broomfield

CONNECTICUT
ALEXION PHARMACEUTICALS INC; Cheshire
COMPASS DIVERSIFIED HOLDINGS; Westport
INDEPENDENCE HOLDING CO; Stamford
ODYSSEY RE HOLDINGS CORP; Stamford
PHOENIX COMPANIES INC (THE); Hartford
PRIMEENERGY CORPORATION; Stamford
ROGERS CORPORATION; Rogers
SS&C TECHNOLOGIES HOLDINGS INC; Windsor
UIL HOLDINGS CORPORATION; New Haven

DELAWARE
DELPHI FINANCIAL GROUP INC; Wilmington

DISTRICT OF COLUMBIA
ADVISORY BOARD COMPANY (THE); Washington
BLACKBOARD INC; Washington
COGENT COMMUNICATIONS; Washington
COSTAR GROUP INC; Washington
GALLUP ORGANIZATION (THE); Washington
WGL HOLDINGS INC; Washington

FLORIDA
ARIZONA CHEMICAL COMPANY; Jacksonville
BANKRATE INC; North Palm Beach
BRIGHTSTAR CORPORATION; Miami
CONTINUCARE CORP; Miami
EXACTECH INC; Gainesville
HEARUSA INC; West Palm Beach
MAKO SURGICAL CORP; Ft. Lauderdale
METROPOLITAN HEALTH NETWORKS INC; Boca Raton
NATIONAL BEVERAGE CORP; Ft. Lauderdale
NOVEN PHARMACEUTICALS INC; Miami
ONSTREAM MEDIA CORPORATION; Pompano Beach
PERRY ELLIS INTERNATIONAL INC; Miami
PETMED EXPRESS INC; Pompano Beach
SBA COMMUNICATIONS CORP; Boca Raton
SUPERIOR UNIFORM GROUP INC; Seminole
SYNIVERSE TECHNOLOGIES; Tampa
TAMPA ELECTRIC COMPANY; Tampa
TERREMARK WORLDWIDE INC; Miami
ULTIMATE SOFTWARE GROUP INC; Weston

GEORGIA
ARRIS GROUP INC; Suwanee
CAGLE'S INC; Atlanta
COMVERGE INC; Norcross
CRYOLIFE INC; Kennesaw
CUMULUS MEDIA INC; Atlanta
EBIX INC; Atlanta
EMS TECHNOLOGIES INC; Norcross
IMMUCOR INC; Norcross
INTERCONTINENTALEXCHANGE INC (ICE); Atlanta
INTERNAP NETWORK SERVICES CORP; Atlanta
KNOLOGY INC; West Point
LOGISTICARE INC; Atlanta
MANHATTAN ASSOCIATES INC; Atlanta
PREMIERE GLOBAL SERVICES INC; Atlanta
RPC INC; Atlanta
S1 CORPORATION; Norcross
THERAGENICS CORP; Buford
TRANSCEND SERVICES INC; Atlanta
ZEP INC; Atlanta

HAWAII
ALEXANDER & BALDWIN INC; Honolulu

IDAHO
IDACORP INC; Boise

ILLINOIS
AKORN INC; Lake Forest
ALLSCRIPTS HEALTHCARE SOLUTIONS INC; Chicago
AMCOL INTERNATIONAL CORP; Hoffman Estates
APP PHARMACEUTICALS INC; Schaumburg
CELSIS INTERNATIONAL PLC; Chicago
CF INDUSTRIES HOLDINGS INC; Deerfield
DIAMOND ADVISORY SERVICES; Chicago
ECHO GLOBAL LOGISTICS INC; Chicago
FUEL TECH INC; Warrenville
HORACE MANN EDUCATORS CORPORATION; Springfield
HUB GROUP INC; Downers Grove
JOHN B SANFILIPPO & SON INC; Elgin
MESIROW FINANCIAL HOLDINGS INC; Chicago
MIDAS INC; Itasca
NOVAMED INC; Chicago
NUTRASWEET COMPANY (THE); Chicago
PEAPOD LLC; Skokie
RECYCLED ENERGY DEVELOPMENT LLC; Westmont
REDBOX AUTOMATED RETAIL LLC; Oak Brook Terrace
STEPAN COMPANY; Northfield
TOOTSIE ROLL INDUSTRIES INC; Chicago
VASCO DATA SECURITY INTERNATIONAL INC; Oakbrook Terrace
WMS INDUSTRIES INC; Waukegan

INDIANA
INTERACTIVE INTELLIGENCE GROUP INC; Indianapolis
NATIONAL WINE & SPIRITS INC; Indianapolis
SUPREME INDUSTRIES INC; Goshen
WABASH NATIONAL CORP; Lafayette

KANSAS
CAPITOL FEDERAL FINANCIAL INC; Topeka
MANAGEMENT NETWORK GROUP INC (THE); Overland Park
NIC INC; Olathe
WADDELL & REED FINANCIAL INC; Overland Park
WESTAR ENERGY; Topeka

MARYLAND
CATALYST HEALTH SOLUTIONS INC; Rockville
CHINDEX INTERNATIONAL INC; Bethesda
EDGAR ONLINE INC; Rockville
INTEGRAL SYSTEMS INC; Columbia
MARTEK BIOSCIENCES CORP; Columbia
MEDIFAST INC; Owings Mills
TESSCO TECHNOLOGIES INC; Hunt Valley
UNITED THERAPEUTICS CORP; Silver Spring

MASSACHUSETTS
ACME PACKET INC; Bedford
AFFILIATED MANAGERS GROUP; Prides Crossing
AKAMAI TECHNOLOGIES INC; Cambridge
AMAG PHARMACEUTICALS INC; Cambridge
AMERESCO INC; Framingham
AMERICAN SCIENCE & ENGINEERING INC; Billerica
AMERICAN TOWER CORP; Boston

ANALOGIC CORP; Peabody
ANIKA THERAPEUTICS INC; Bedford
ATHENAHEALTH INC; Watertown
ATLANTIC TELE-NETWORK INC; Beverly
BOSTON BEER COMPANY INC (THE); Boston
CALIPER LIFE SCIENCES INC; Hopkinton
CELLDEX THERAPEUTICS INC; Needham
CHOICESTREAM INC; Cambridge
CONSTANT CONTACT INC; Waltham
CRA INTERNATIONAL INC (CHARLES RIVER); Boston
CUBIST PHARMACEUTICALS INC; Lexington
EATON VANCE CORP; Boston
ENERNOC INC; Boston
FORRESTER RESEARCH INC; Cambridge
GLOBAL PARTNERS LP; Waltham
GTC BIOTHERAPEUTICS INC; Framingham
HAEMONETICS CORPORATION; Braintree
HOSPITALITY PROPERTIES TRUST; Newton
IBASIS INC; Burlington
INTERACTIVE DATA CORPORATION; Bedford
IROBOT CORP; Bedford
LOJACK CORPORTATION; Westwood
MAPFRE USA CORP; Webster
MILLENNIUM PHARMACEUTICALS INC; Cambridge
NATIONAL DENTEX CORP; Natick
NETSCOUT SYSTEMS INC; Westford
NETWORK ENGINES INC; Canton
PEGASYSTEMS INC; Cambridge
RSA SECURITY INC; Bedford
SEACHANGE INTERNATIONAL INC; Acton
SENIOR HOUSING PROPERTIES; Newton
SERACARE LIFE SCIENCES INC; Milford
SPIRE CORPORATION; Bedford
STERLING AUTOBODY CENTERS; Natick
VARIAN SEMICONDUCTOR EQUIPMENT ASSOCIATES INC; Gloucester
ZOLL MEDICAL CORP; Chelmsford

MICHIGAN
AROTECH CORPORATION; Ann Arbor
CARACO PHARMACEUTICAL LABORATORIES LTD; Detroit
NEOGEN CORPORATION; Lansing
SPARTAN MOTORS INC; Charlotte
SUN COMMUNITIES INC; Southfield
ZIEBART INTERNATIONAL CORP; Troy

MINNESOTA
AMERICAN MEDICAL SYSTEMS HOLDINGS INC; Minnetonka
FAIR ISAAC CORPORATION; Minneapolis
HICKORY TECH CORPORATION; Mankato
INTERNATIONAL DAIRY QUEEN INC; Minneapolis
LIFECORE BIOMEDICAL INC; Chaska
MALT-O-MEAL COMPANY; Minneapolis
MEDTOX SCIENTIFIC INC; St. Paul
MICHELINAS INC; Duluth
PIPER JAFFRAY COMPANIES; Minneapolis
PLATO LEARNING INC; Bloomington
SPORTSMAN'S GUIDE INC (THE); St. Paul
SYNOVIS LIFE TECHNOLOGIES INC; St. Paul
TECHNE CORP; Minneapolis
UNIVERSAL HOSPITAL SERVICES INC; Edina

MISSISSIPPI
CAL-MAINE FOODS INC; Jackson
HANCOCK HOLDING COMPANY; Gulfport
MICROTEK MEDICAL HOLDINGS INC; Columbus

MISSOURI
LACLEDE GROUP INC (THE); St. Louis
PERFICIENT INC; St. Louis
REINSURANCE GROUP OF AMERICA INC; Chesterfield

MONTANA
KAMPGROUNDS OF AMERICA INC; Billings
RIGHTNOW TECHNOLOGIES INC; Bozeman

NEBRASKA
AMCON DISTRIBUTING CO; Omaha
SCOULAR COMPANY (THE); Omaha
SUPERTEL HOSPITALITY INC; Norfolk

NEVADA
ALLEGIANT TRAVEL COMPANY; Las Vegas
SOUTHWEST GAS CORP; Las Vegas
SPECTRUM PHARMACEUTICALS INC; Henderson

NEW HAMPSHIRE
BOTTOMLINE TECHNOLOGIES INC; Portsmouth
CRITICAL CARE SYSTEMS; Nashua
PC CONNECTION INC; Merrimack

NEW JERSEY
ATLANTIC CITY ELECTRIC COMPANY; Mays Landing
AUDIBLE INC; Newark
B&G FOODS INC; Parsippany
BIO REFERENCE LABORATORIES INC; Elmwood Park
CAMBREX CORP; East Rutherford
CANTEL MEDICAL CORP; Little Falls
CRUM & FORSTER HOLDINGS INC; Morristown
EVEREST RE GROUP LTD; Liberty Corner
HUDSON CITY BANCORP INC; Paramus
INNOPHOS HOLDINGS INC; Cranbury
KNIGHT CAPITAL GROUP INC; Jersey City
LIFECELL CORPORATION; Branchburg
MEDICINES CO (THE); Parsippany
NEW JERSEY RESOURCES CORPORATION; Wall
PAR PHARMACEUTICAL COMPANIES INC; Woodcliff Lake
SCIOS INC; New Brunswick

NEW MEXICO
EMCORE CORP; Albuquerque

NEW YORK
24/7 REAL MEDIA INC; New York
ACI WORLDWIDE INC; New York
ALBANY MOLECULAR RESEARCH INC; Albany
ALLIED HEALTHCARE INTERNATIONAL INC; New York
AMTRUST FINANCIAL SERVICES INC; New York
ANAREN INC; E. Syracuse
BIOSCRIP INC; Elmsford
CANTOR FITZGERALD LP; New York
CKX INC; New York
COMTECH TELECOMMUNICATIONS CORP; Melville
DANNON COMPANY INC (THE); White Plains
EVERCORE PARTNERS INC; New York
FRESHDIRECT LLC; Long Island
FUEL SYSTEMS SOLUTIONS INC; New York
GENCO SHIPPING & TRADING LIMITED; New York
GFI GROUP INC; New York
G-III APPAREL GROUP; New York
GLEACHER & COMPANY INC; New York
GLOBECOMM SYSTEMS INC; Hauppauge
HAHN AUTOMOTIVE WAREHOUSE INC; Rochester
HARRIS INTERACTIVE INC; New York
HEALTH INSURANCE PLAN OF GREATER NEW YORK; New York
HI-TECH PHARMACAL CO INC; Amityville

ICONIX BRAND GROUP INC; New York
IMG WORLDWIDE INC; New York
INTEGRAMED AMERICA INC; Purchase
INVESTMENT TECHNOLOGY GROUP INC (ITG); New York
IVILLAGE INC; New York
KBW INC; New York
KENNETH COLE PRODUCTIONS INC; New York
KKR & CO LP (KOHLBERG KRAVIS ROBERTS & CO); New York
LAKELAND INDUSTRIES INC; Ronkonkoma
LIVEPERSON INC; New York
MARVEL ENTERTAINMENT LLC; New York
MOELIS & COMPANY; New York
NEW YORK MERCANTILE EXCHANGE INC; New York
REGENERON PHARMACEUTICALS INC; Tarrytown
SCHICK TECHNOLOGIES INC; Long Island City
SL GREEN REALTY CORP; New York
SOTHEBYS; New York
SOVRAN SELF STORAGE INC; Williamsville
STEVEN MADDEN LTD; Long Island City
TAKE-TWO INTERACTIVE SOFTWARE INC; New York
TELIRIS; New York
TII NETWORK TECHNOLOGIES INC; Edgewood
TOPPS COMPANY INC (THE); New York
TRANSAMMONIA INC; New York
TRANSATLANTIC HOLDINGS INC; New York
TRAVELZOO INC; New York
ULTRALIFE CORPORATION; Newark
VIBRANT MEDIA INC; New York
VOX INTERNATIONAL CORPORATION; Hauppauge
WEBMD HEALTH CORP; New York
WEBMEDIA BRANDS INC; New York
XO GROUP INC; New York

NORTH CAROLINA

AMERICAN TIRE DISTRIBUTORS; Huntersville
CULP INC; High Point
KIMLEY-HORN AND ASSOCIATES INC; Cary
LUCOR INC; Raleigh
PIEDMONT NATURAL GAS COMPANY INC; Charlotte
POLYPORE INTERNATIONAL INC; Charlotte
POWERSECURE INTERNATIONAL INC; Wake Forest
SALIX PHARMACEUTICALS; Morrisville
STIEFEL LABORATORIES INC; Research Triangle Park
TEKELEC; Morrisville

NORTH DAKOTA

INVESTORS REAL ESTATE TRUST; Minot

OHIO

DPL INC; Dayton
FEDEX SUPPLY CHAIN SERVICES INC; Hudson
FIRST FINANCIAL BANCORP (OH); Cincinnati
GREAT AMERICAN FINANCIAL RESOURCES INC; Cincinnati
GREAT LAKES CHEESE COMPANY INC; Hiram
MERIDIAN BIOSCIENCE INC; Cincinnati
OMNOVA SOLUTIONS INC; Fairlawn
ROCKY BRANDS INC; Nelsonville
STATE AUTO FINANCIAL CORP; Columbus

OKLAHOMA

AMERICAN FIDELITY ASSURANCE COMPANY; Oklahoma City
CONTINENTAL RESOURCES INC; Enid
EDUCATIONAL DEVELOPMENT CORP; Tulsa
MAGELLAN MIDSTREAM PARTNERS LP; Tulsa
SANDRIDGE ENERGY INC; Oklahoma City
UNIT CORP; Tulsa
XETA TECHNOLOGIES INC; Broken Arrow

OREGON

RENTRAK CORP; Portland

PENNSYLVANIA

AAMCO TRANSMISSIONS INC; Horsham
CALGON CARBON CORPORATION; Pittsburgh
CARDIONET INC; Conshohocken
DORMAN PRODUCTS INC; Colmar
ENVIRONMENTAL TECTONICS CORP; Southampton
EPAM SYSTEMS; Newtown
EQT CORPORATION; Pittsburgh
ERESEARCH TECHNOLOGY INC; Philadelphia
FNB CORP; Hermitage
HANOVER FOODS CORPORATION; Hanover
LB FOSTER COMPANY; Pittsburgh
PHILADELPHIA CONSOLIDATED HOLDING CORP; Bala Cynwyd
PMA COMPANIES INC; Blue Bell
QUAKER CHEMICAL CORP; Conshohocken
SUNOCO LOGISTICS PARTNERS LP; Philadelphia
VIROPHARMA INC; Exton

SOUTH CAROLINA

SCANSOURCE INC; Greenville

SOUTH DAKOTA

BLACK HILLS CORP; Rapid City
NORTHWESTERN CORPORATION; Sioux Falls

TENNESSEE

CHATTEM INC; Chattanooga
COMDATA CORP; Brentwood
HEALTHSTREAM INC; Nashville
MID-AMERICA APARTMENT COMMUNITIES INC; Memphis
WRIGHT MEDICAL GROUP INC; Arlington

TEXAS

AMERICAN CAMPUS COMMUNITIES INC; Austin
ARTHROCARE CORP; Austin
ATRION CORPORATION; Allen
AVIALL INC; Dallas Fort Worth Airport
CABOT OIL & GAS CORP; Houston
CACTUS FEEDERS INC; Amarillo
CARBO CERAMICS INC; Houston
CARDTRONICS INC; Houston
CARRIZO OIL & GAS INC; Houston
CIRRUS LOGIC INC; Austin
CLAYTON WILLIAMS ENERGY INC; Midland
CROWN CASTLE INTERNATIONAL CORP; Houston
CYBERONICS INC; Houston
DAWSON GEOPHYSICAL COMPANY; Midland
DENBURY RESOURCES INC; Plano
DIGITAL GENERATION INC; Irving
EDELMAN FINANCIAL GROUP (THE); Houston
ENERGY TRANSFER PARTNERS LP; Dallas
EOG RESOURCES INC; Houston
FROZEN FOOD EXPRESS INDUSTRIES INC; Dallas
GENESIS ENERGY LP; Houston
GOLFSMITH INTERNATIONAL HOLDINGS INC; Austin
GULFMARK OFFSHORE INC; Houston
HCC INSURANCE HOLDINGS INC; Houston
HEALTHTRONICS INC; Austin
HELIOVOLT CORP; Austin
HELIX ENERGY SOLUTIONS GROUP INC; Houston
HOLLYFRONTIER CORPORATION; Dallas
KIRBY CORP; Houston
KRONOS WORLDWIDE INC; Dallas
LUMINEX CORPORATION; Austin
NUSTAR ENERGY LP; San Antonio
ORION MARINE GROUP INC; Houston

UTAH

VIRGINIA

VERMONT

WASHINGTON

WISCONSIN

WEST VIRGINIA

INDEX BY REGIONS OF THE U.S. WHERE THE FIRMS HAVE LOCATIONS

WEST

CARBO CERAMICS INC
CARDIONET INC
CATALYST HEALTH SOLUTIONS INC
CEPHEID
CERUS CORPORATION
CF INDUSTRIES HOLDINGS INC
CHANNELL COMMERCIAL CORP
CHOICESTREAM INC
CHOLESTECH CORP
CIRRUS LOGIC INC
CLAYTON WILLIAMS ENERGY INC
CLEAN ENERGY FUELS CORP
CLEARONE COMMUNICATIONS INC
COHERENT INC
COMDATA CORP
COMTECH TELECOMMUNICATIONS CORP
COMVERGE INC
CONCUR TECHNOLOGIES INC
CONSTANT CONTACT INC
CORPORATE EXECUTIVE BOARD COMPANY (THE)
COSTAR GROUP INC
COUPONS INC
CRA INTERNATIONAL INC (CHARLES RIVER)
CRAY INC
CRITICAL CARE SYSTEMS
CROWN CASTLE INTERNATIONAL CORP
CRUM & FORSTER HOLDINGS INC
CUBIST PHARMACEUTICALS INC
CUMULUS MEDIA INC
CYBERONICS INC
CYBERSOURCE CORP
DANNON COMPANY INC (THE)
DAWSON GEOPHYSICAL COMPANY
DEI HOLDINGS INC
DELPHI FINANCIAL GROUP INC
DENBURY RESOURCES INC
DIAMOND FOODS INC
DIGITAL GENERATION INC
DJO GLOBAL INC
DOLBY LABORATORIES INC
DREAMWORKS ANIMATION SKG INC
DRUGSTORE.COM INC
EATON VANCE CORP
EBIX INC
ECHOSTAR CORP
ECOLLEGE.COM
EDELMAN FINANCIAL GROUP (THE)
EDGAR ONLINE INC
EDUCATIONAL DEVELOPMENT CORP
EHEALTH INC
EMBARCADERO TECHNOLOGIES INC
EMCORE CORP
EMULEX CORP
ENCORE CAPITAL GROUP INC
ENERGY TRANSFER PARTNERS LP
ENERNOC INC
EOG RESOURCES INC
EQUINIX INC
ESSEX PROPERTY TRUST INC
EVERCORE PARTNERS INC
EVEREST RE GROUP LTD
F5 NETWORKS INC
FAIR ISAAC CORPORATION
FEDEX SUPPLY CHAIN SERVICES INC
FORRESTER RESEARCH INC
FORTINET INC
FROZEN FOOD EXPRESS INDUSTRIES INC
FUEL SYSTEMS SOLUTIONS INC
GAIAM INC
GALLUP ORGANIZATION (THE)
GENENCOR INTERNATIONAL INC
GENERAL ATOMICS
GENERAL COMMUNICATION INC (GCI)
GENESIS ENERGY LP
GENOMIC HEALTH INC
GEN-PROBE INC
G-III APPAREL GROUP
GLEACHER & COMPANY INC
GLU MOBILE INC
GOLFSMITH INTERNATIONAL HOLDINGS INC
GREAT LAKES CHEESE COMPANY INC
HAEMONETICS CORPORATION
HANOVER FOODS CORPORATION
HARRIS INTERACTIVE INC
HCC INSURANCE HOLDINGS INC
HEALTH GRADES INC
HEARUSA INC
HESKA CORP
HOLLYFRONTIER CORPORATION
HORACE MANN EDUCATORS CORPORATION
HOSPITALITY PROPERTIES TRUST
HOULIHAN LOKEY HOWARD & ZUKIN INC
HUB GROUP INC
IBASIS INC
ICU MEDICAL INC
IDACORP INC
I-FLOW CORPORATION
ILLUMINA INC
IMG WORLDWIDE INC
IMPAX LABORATORIES INC
INDEPENDENCE HOLDING CO
INFOSPACE INC
INNOSPEC INC
INTEGRAL SYSTEMS INC
INTEGRAMED AMERICA INC
INTERACTIVE DATA CORPORATION
INTERACTIVE INTELLIGENCE GROUP INC
INTERMEC INC
INTERNAP NETWORK SERVICES CORP
INTERNATIONAL CREATIVE MANAGEMENT INC (ICM)
INTERNATIONAL DAIRY QUEEN INC
INTUITIVE SURGICAL INC
INVESTMENT TECHNOLOGY GROUP INC (ITG)
INVESTORS REAL ESTATE TRUST
IRIDEX CORP
IRIS INTERNATIONAL INC
IROBOT CORP
ISILON SYSTEMS INC
J2 GLOBAL COMMUNICATIONS INC
JAZZ PHARMACEUTICALS INC
JOE'S JEANS INC
JOHN B SANFILIPPO & SON INC
KAMPGROUNDS OF AMERICA INC
KBW INC
KENDALL-JACKSON WINE ESTATES LTD
KENNETH COLE PRODUCTIONS INC
KEY TRONIC CORP
KEYNOTE SYSTEMS INC
KIMLEY-HORN AND ASSOCIATES INC
KKR & CO LP (KOHLBERG KRAVIS ROBERTS & CO)
KNIGHT CAPITAL GROUP INC
KORN/FERRY INTERNATIONAL
KRONOS WORLDWIDE INC
LB FOSTER COMPANY
LCC INTERNATIONAL INC
LESLIE'S POOLMART INC
LIVEPERSON INC
LOGISTICARE INC
LOJACK CORPORTATION
LUCASFILM LTD
MAGELLAN MIDSTREAM PARTNERS LP
MALT-O-MEAL COMPANY
MAPFRE USA CORP
MARTEK BIOSCIENCES CORP
MARVEL ENTERTAINMENT LLC
MEDICIS PHARMACEUTICAL CORP
MEDIFAST INC
MENTOR CORP
MERIT MEDICAL SYSTEMS INC
MESIROW FINANCIAL HOLDINGS INC
MIDAS INC
MINDSPEED TECHNOLOGIES INC
MOELIS & COMPANY
MONSTER BEVERAGE CORP
MOTORCAR PARTS OF AMERICA INC
MYRIAD GENETICS INC
NANOMETRICS INC
NATIONAL BEVERAGE CORP
NATUS MEDICAL INC
NEKTAR THERAPEUTICS
NETFLIX INC
NETGEAR INC
NETSCOUT SYSTEMS INC
NETSUITE INC
NEUSTAR INC
NIC INC
NORTHWESTERN CORPORATION
NOTIFY TECHNOLOGY CORP
NOVAMED INC
NUGGET MARKET
NUSTAR ENERGY LP
NUVASIVE INC
ODYSSEY RE HOLDINGS CORP
ONLINE RESOURCES CORP
ONSTREAM MEDIA CORPORATION

OPENTV CORP
PACIFIC BIOMARKERS INC
PATAGONIA INC
PEGASYSTEMS INC
PERFICIENT INC
PERRY ELLIS INTERNATIONAL INC
PETROLEUM DEVELOPMENT CORPORATION
PHILADELPHIA CONSOLIDATED HOLDING CORP
PIONEER NATURAL RESOURCES COMPANY
PIPER JAFFRAY COMPANIES
PLAINS EXPLORATION AND PRODUCTION COMPANY
PREMIERE GLOBAL SERVICES INC
PRIMEENERGY CORPORATION
PROTECTIVE LIFE CORP
QUAKER CHEMICAL CORP
QUALCOMM ATHEROS INC
QUALITY SYSTEMS INC
QUANTUM CORP
QUESTCOR PHARMACEUTICALS INC
QUICKSILVER RESOURCES INC
QUIDEL CORP
RAYTHEON APPLIED SIGNAL TECHNOLOGY INC
REALNETWORKS INC
REDBOX AUTOMATED RETAIL LLC
RENTRAK CORP
RIGHTNOW TECHNOLOGIES INC
RIVERBED TECHNOLOGY INC
ROBERT W BAIRD & CO INC
ROSETTA STONE INC
ROVI CORPORATION
RPC INC
RSA SECURITY INC
S1 CORPORATION
SACRAMENTO MUNICIPAL UTILITY DISTRICT
SBA COMMUNICATIONS CORP
SCHIFF NUTRITION INTERNATIONAL INC
SCICLONE PHARMACEUTICALS INC
SCOULAR COMPANY (THE)
SEACHANGE INTERNATIONAL INC
SEATTLE GENETICS
SELECTICA INC
SENIOR HOUSING PROPERTIES
SHARED TECHNOLOGIES
SHUTTERFLY INC
SIGMA DESIGNS INC
SILICON LABORATORIES INC
SMART MODULAR TECHNOLOGIES INC
SOLARRESERVE
SOLFOCUS INC
SOUTHERN UNION COMPANY
SOUTHWEST GAS CORP
SPECTRANETICS CORP
SPECTRUM PHARMACEUTICALS INC
SPROUTS FARMERS MARKET LLC
SRS LABS INC
SS&C TECHNOLOGIES HOLDINGS INC
STAAR SURGICAL CO
STATE AUTO FINANCIAL CORP
STEPAN COMPANY
STERLING AUTOBODY CENTERS
STERLING CONSTRUCTION COMPANY
STEVEN MADDEN LTD
STIEFEL LABORATORIES INC
SUN COMMUNITIES INC
SUPER MICRO COMPUTER INC
SUPERIOR UNIFORM GROUP INC
SUPERTEL HOSPITALITY INC
SUPREME INDUSTRIES INC
SVB FINANCIAL GROUP
SYNAPTICS INC
SYNOVIS LIFE TECHNOLOGIES INC
TARGA RESOURCES PARTNERS LP
TECHNE CORP
TERREMARK WORLDWIDE INC
TESSCO TECHNOLOGIES INC
THERAGENICS CORP
THORATEC CORPORATION
TOPPS COMPANY INC (THE)
TRANSATLANTIC HOLDINGS INC
TRANSCEND SERVICES INC
TRAVELZOO INC
TREX COMPANY INC
TRIZETTO GROUP INC (THE)
TRUE RELIGION APPAREL INC
UDR INC
ULTRALIFE CORPORATION
UNIT CORP
UNITED ONLINE INC
UNIVERSAL HOSPITAL SERVICES INC
UQM TECHNOLOGIES INC
US PHYSICAL THERAPY INC
USANA HEALTH SCIENCES INC
UTAH MEDICAL PRODUCTS INC
VARIAN SEMICONDUCTOR EQUIPMENT ASSOCIATES INC
VERENIUM CORPORATION
VIASAT INC
VIBRANT MEDIA INC
VOLCOM INC
VOX INTERNATIONAL CORPORATION
WABASH NATIONAL CORP
WADDELL & REED FINANCIAL INC
WEBEX COMMUNICATIONS INC
WEBMD HEALTH CORP
WEBSENSE INC
WHITEWAVE FOODS COMPANY
WIKIMEDIA FOUNDATION
WIND RIVER SYSTEMS INC
XETA TECHNOLOGIES INC
XO GROUP INC
XOMA LTD
XTO ENERGY INC
YOUNG'S MARKET COMPANY LLC
ZIEBART INTERNATIONAL CORP
ZOLL MEDICAL CORP
ZYNGA INC

SOUTHWEST

AAMCO TRANSMISSIONS INC
ACI WORLDWIDE INC
ADTRAN INC
ADVISORY BOARD COMPANY (THE)
AKAMAI TECHNOLOGIES INC
ALEXANDER & BALDWIN INC
ALLEGIANT TRAVEL COMPANY
ALLSCRIPTS HEALTHCARE SOLUTIONS INC
AMCOL INTERNATIONAL CORP
AMCON DISTRIBUTING CO
AMERESCO INC
AMERICAN CAMPUS COMMUNITIES INC
AMERICAN FIDELITY ASSURANCE COMPANY
AMERICAN MEDICAL SYSTEMS HOLDINGS INC
AMERICAN TIRE DISTRIBUTORS
AMERICAN TOWER CORP
AMERICA'S CAR-MART INC
AMTECH SYSTEMS INC
AMTRUST FINANCIAL SERVICES INC
ARCSIGHT INC
ARGON ST INC
ARIBA INC
ARTHROCARE CORP
ATRION CORPORATION
AVIALL INC
B&G FOODS INC
BANKRATE INC
BERRY PETROLEUM CO
BIOSCRIP INC
BLACK HILLS CORP
BLACKBOARD INC
BLUE COAT SYSTEMS INC
CABOT OIL & GAS CORP
CACTUS FEEDERS INC
CALAVO GROWERS INC
CALGON CARBON CORPORATION
CALIBER HOLDINGS CORP
CAL-MAINE FOODS INC
CANTOR FITZGERALD LP
CARBO CERAMICS INC
CARDTRONICS INC
CARRIZO OIL & GAS INC
CATALYST HEALTH SOLUTIONS INC
CF INDUSTRIES HOLDINGS INC
CIRRUS LOGIC INC
CLAYTON WILLIAMS ENERGY INC
CLEAN ENERGY FUELS CORP
CLEARONE COMMUNICATIONS INC
COHERENT INC
COMDATA CORP
COMTECH TELECOMMUNICATIONS CORP
CONCUR TECHNOLOGIES INC
CONTINENTAL RESOURCES INC
CORPORATE EXECUTIVE BOARD COMPANY (THE)
COSTAR GROUP INC
CRA INTERNATIONAL INC (CHARLES RIVER)
CRITICAL CARE SYSTEMS

CROWN CASTLE INTERNATIONAL CORP
CRUM & FORSTER HOLDINGS INC
CUMULUS MEDIA INC
CYBERONICS INC
DANNON COMPANY INC (THE)
DAWSON GEOPHYSICAL COMPANY
DELPHI FINANCIAL GROUP INC
DENBURY RESOURCES INC
DIGITAL GENERATION INC
EBIX INC
ECHOSTAR CORP
EDELMAN FINANCIAL GROUP (THE)
EDUCATIONAL DEVELOPMENT CORP
EMCORE CORP
EMULEX CORP
ENCORE CAPITAL GROUP INC
ENERGY TRANSFER PARTNERS LP
EOG RESOURCES INC
EVERCORE PARTNERS INC
F5 NETWORKS INC
FAIR ISAAC CORPORATION
FEDEX SUPPLY CHAIN SERVICES INC
FORRESTER RESEARCH INC
FORTINET INC
FROZEN FOOD EXPRESS INDUSTRIES INC
GALLUP ORGANIZATION (THE)
GENERAL ATOMICS
GENESIS ENERGY LP
G-III APPAREL GROUP
GOLFSMITH INTERNATIONAL HOLDINGS INC
GREAT AMERICAN FINANCIAL RESOURCES INC
GULFMARK OFFSHORE INC
HCC INSURANCE HOLDINGS INC
HEALTHTRONICS INC
HELIOVOLT CORP
HELIX ENERGY SOLUTIONS GROUP INC
HOLLYFRONTIER CORPORATION
HORACE MANN EDUCATORS CORPORATION
HOSPITALITY PROPERTIES TRUST
HOULIHAN LOKEY HOWARD & ZUKIN INC
HUB GROUP INC
IDACORP INC
I-FLOW CORPORATION
IMG WORLDWIDE INC
INDEPENDENCE HOLDING CO
INTEGRAMED AMERICA INC
INTERCONTINENTALEXCHANGE INC (ICE)
INTERMEC INC
INTERNAP NETWORK SERVICES CORP
INTERNATIONAL DAIRY QUEEN INC
IRIDEX CORP
JOE'S JEANS INC
JOHN B SANFILIPPO & SON INC
KAMPGROUNDS OF AMERICA INC
KBW INC
KENNETH COLE PRODUCTIONS INC
KEY TRONIC CORP
KEYNOTE SYSTEMS INC
KIMLEY-HORN AND ASSOCIATES INC
KKR & CO LP (KOHLBERG KRAVIS ROBERTS & CO)
KNIGHT CAPITAL GROUP INC
KORN/FERRY INTERNATIONAL
KRONOS WORLDWIDE INC
LACLEDE GROUP INC (THE)
LB FOSTER COMPANY
LCC INTERNATIONAL INC
LESLIE'S POOLMART INC
LOGISTICARE INC
LOJACK CORPORTATION
LUMINEX CORPORATION
MAGELLAN MIDSTREAM PARTNERS LP
MEDICIS PHARMACEUTICAL CORP
MEDIFAST INC
MENTOR CORP
MERIT MEDICAL SYSTEMS INC
MESIROW FINANCIAL HOLDINGS INC
MICROTEK MEDICAL HOLDINGS INC
MID-AMERICA APARTMENT COMMUNITIES INC
MIDAS INC
NATIONAL BEVERAGE CORP
NATIONAL DENTEX CORP
NETFLIX INC
NETSCOUT SYSTEMS INC
NETSUITE INC
NEW JERSEY RESOURCES CORPORATION
NIC INC
NOVAMED INC
NUSTAR ENERGY LP
ORION MARINE GROUP INC
PATAGONIA INC
PC CONNECTION INC
PEGASYSTEMS INC
PERFICIENT INC
PERRY ELLIS INTERNATIONAL INC
PHAZAR CORP
PHILADELPHIA CONSOLIDATED HOLDING CORP
PIONEER NATURAL RESOURCES COMPANY
PIPER JAFFRAY COMPANIES
PLAINS EXPLORATION AND PRODUCTION COMPANY
POWERSECURE INTERNATIONAL INC
PRIMEENERGY CORPORATION
PROTECTIVE LIFE CORP
QUAKER CHEMICAL CORP
QUALITY SYSTEMS INC
QUANTUM CORP
QUICKSILVER RESOURCES INC
RAYTHEON APPLIED SIGNAL TECHNOLOGY INC
REDBOX AUTOMATED RETAIL LLC
RICELAND FOODS INC
RIGHTNOW TECHNOLOGIES INC
RIVERBED TECHNOLOGY INC
ROBERT W BAIRD & CO INC
ROGERS CORPORATION
ROSETTA STONE INC
ROVI CORPORATION
RPC INC
S1 CORPORATION
SANDRIDGE ENERGY INC
SCANSOURCE INC
SCOULAR COMPANY (THE)
SENIOR HOUSING PROPERTIES
SHARED TECHNOLOGIES
SHUTTERFLY INC
SILICON LABORATORIES INC
SMART MODULAR TECHNOLOGIES INC
SOUTHERN UNION COMPANY
SOUTHWEST GAS CORP
SOUTHWESTERN ENERGY CO
SOVRAN SELF STORAGE INC
SPARTAN MOTORS INC
SPORT SUPPLY GROUP INC
SPROUTS FARMERS MARKET LLC
STATE AUTO FINANCIAL CORP
STERLING AUTOBODY CENTERS
STERLING CONSTRUCTION COMPANY
STEVEN MADDEN LTD
SUN COMMUNITIES INC
SUNOCO LOGISTICS PARTNERS LP
SUPREME INDUSTRIES INC
SVB FINANCIAL GROUP
SWIFT ENERGY CO
SYNAPTICS INC
TARGA RESOURCES PARTNERS LP
TEKELEC
TERREMARK WORLDWIDE INC
TESCO CORPORATION
THERAGENICS CORP
TOPPS COMPANY INC (THE)
TRANSAMMONIA INC
TRIZETTO GROUP INC (THE)
TRUE RELIGION APPAREL INC
UDR INC
ULTRALIFE CORPORATION
UNISOURCE ENERGY CORPORATION
UNIT CORP
UNIVERSAL HOSPITAL SERVICES INC
US PHYSICAL THERAPY INC
VARIAN SEMICONDUCTOR EQUIPMENT ASSOCIATES INC
VENTANA MEDICAL SYSTEMS INC
WABASH NATIONAL CORP
WADDELL & REED FINANCIAL INC
WESTAR ENERGY
WHITEWAVE FOODS COMPANY
WIND RIVER SYSTEMS INC
XETA TECHNOLOGIES INC
XO GROUP INC
XTO ENERGY INC
YOUNG'S MARKET COMPANY LLC
ZIEBART INTERNATIONAL CORP
ZYNGA INC

MIDWEST

24/7 REAL MEDIA INC
AAMCO TRANSMISSIONS INC
ACI WORLDWIDE INC
ADTRAN INC
ADVISORY BOARD COMPANY (THE)
AKAMAI TECHNOLOGIES INC
AKORN INC
ALEXANDER & BALDWIN INC
ALIEN TECHNOLOGY CORPORATION
ALLEGIANT TRAVEL COMPANY
ALLSCRIPTS HEALTHCARE SOLUTIONS INC
AMCOL INTERNATIONAL CORP
AMCON DISTRIBUTING CO
AMERESCO INC
AMERICAN CAMPUS COMMUNITIES INC
AMERICAN FIDELITY ASSURANCE COMPANY
AMERICAN MEDICAL SYSTEMS HOLDINGS INC
AMERICAN TIRE DISTRIBUTORS
AMERICAN TOWER CORP
AMERICAN VANGUARD CORP
AMERICA'S CAR-MART INC
AMTRUST FINANCIAL SERVICES INC
APP PHARMACEUTICALS INC
ARIBA INC
ARIZONA CHEMICAL COMPANY
AROTECH CORPORATION
ARRIS GROUP INC
AVALONBAY COMMUNITIES INC
AVIALL INC
B&G FOODS INC
BIOSCRIP INC
BLACK HILLS CORP
BLACKBOARD INC
BOSTON BEER COMPANY INC (THE)
BRIGHTSTAR CORPORATION
CABOT OIL & GAS CORP
CACTUS FEEDERS INC
CALAVO GROWERS INC
CALGON CARBON CORPORATION
CAL-MAINE FOODS INC
CAMBREX CORP
CANTEL MEDICAL CORP
CANTOR FITZGERALD LP
CAPITOL FEDERAL FINANCIAL INC
CARACO PHARMACEUTICAL LABORATORIES LTD
CATALYST HEALTH SOLUTIONS INC
CELSIS INTERNATIONAL PLC
CEPHEID
CF INDUSTRIES HOLDINGS INC
CLEAN ENERGY FUELS CORP
COHERENT INC
COMDATA CORP
CONCUR TECHNOLOGIES INC
CONTINENTAL RESOURCES INC
CORPORATE EXECUTIVE BOARD COMPANY (THE)
COSTAR GROUP INC
CRA INTERNATIONAL INC (CHARLES RIVER)
CRAY INC
CRITICAL CARE SYSTEMS
CROWN CASTLE INTERNATIONAL CORP
CRUM & FORSTER HOLDINGS INC
CUBIST PHARMACEUTICALS INC
CUMULUS MEDIA INC
CYBERONICS INC
DANNON COMPANY INC (THE)
DAWSON GEOPHYSICAL COMPANY
DELPHI FINANCIAL GROUP INC
DIAMOND ADVISORY SERVICES
DIAMOND FOODS INC
DIGITAL GENERATION INC
DORMAN PRODUCTS INC
DPL INC
EBIX INC
ECHO GLOBAL LOGISTICS INC
ECHOSTAR CORP
EDELMAN FINANCIAL GROUP (THE)
ENCORE CAPITAL GROUP INC
ENERGY TRANSFER PARTNERS LP
EOG RESOURCES INC
EQT CORPORATION
EQUINIX INC
EVERCORE PARTNERS INC
EVEREST RE GROUP LTD
EXACTECH INC
F5 NETWORKS INC
FAIR ISAAC CORPORATION
FEDEX SUPPLY CHAIN SERVICES INC
FIRST FINANCIAL BANCORP (OH)
FNB CORP
FORTINET INC
FROZEN FOOD EXPRESS INDUSTRIES INC
FUEL SYSTEMS SOLUTIONS INC
FUEL TECH INC
GAIAM INC
GALLUP ORGANIZATION (THE)
GENENCOR INTERNATIONAL INC
GENERAL ATOMICS
G-III APPAREL GROUP
GLEACHER & COMPANY INC
GOLDEN ENTERPRISES INC
GOLFSMITH INTERNATIONAL HOLDINGS INC
GREAT AMERICAN FINANCIAL RESOURCES INC
GREAT LAKES CHEESE COMPANY INC
HAEMONETICS CORPORATION
HAHN AUTOMOTIVE WAREHOUSE INC
HARRIS INTERACTIVE INC
HCC INSURANCE HOLDINGS INC
HEARUSA INC
HESKA CORP
HICKORY TECH CORPORATION
HOLLYFRONTIER CORPORATION
HORACE MANN EDUCATORS CORPORATION
HOSPITALITY PROPERTIES TRUST
HOULIHAN LOKEY HOWARD & ZUKIN INC
HUB GROUP INC
IDACORP INC
IMG WORLDWIDE INC
INDEPENDENCE HOLDING CO
INNOPHOS HOLDINGS INC
INTEGRAMED AMERICA INC
INTERACTIVE DATA CORPORATION
INTERACTIVE INTELLIGENCE GROUP INC
INTERCONTINENTALEXCHANGE INC (ICE)
INTERMEC INC
INTERNAP NETWORK SERVICES CORP
INTERNATIONAL DAIRY QUEEN INC
INVESTMENT TECHNOLOGY GROUP INC (ITG)
INVESTORS REAL ESTATE TRUST
IRIDEX CORP
JOE'S JEANS INC
JOHN B SANFILIPPO & SON INC
KAMPGROUNDS OF AMERICA INC
KBW INC
KENNETH COLE PRODUCTIONS INC
KEYNOTE SYSTEMS INC
KIMLEY-HORN AND ASSOCIATES INC
KIRBY CORP
KNIGHT CAPITAL GROUP INC
KNOLOGY INC
KORN/FERRY INTERNATIONAL
KRONOS WORLDWIDE INC
LACLEDE GROUP INC (THE)
LAKELAND INDUSTRIES INC
LB FOSTER COMPANY
LCC INTERNATIONAL INC
LESLIE'S POOLMART INC
LIFECORE BIOMEDICAL INC
LOGISTICARE INC
LOJACK CORPORTATION
MAGELLAN MIDSTREAM PARTNERS LP
MALT-O-MEAL COMPANY
MANAGEMENT NETWORK GROUP INC (THE)
MANHATTAN ASSOCIATES INC
MAPFRE USA CORP
MARTEK BIOSCIENCES CORP
MEDICIS PHARMACEUTICAL CORP
MEDIFAST INC
MEDTOX SCIENTIFIC INC
MENTOR CORP
MERIDIAN BIOSCIENCE INC
MESIROW FINANCIAL HOLDINGS INC
MICHELINAS INC
MID-AMERICA APARTMENT COMMUNITIES INC
MIDAS INC
MOELIS & COMPANY
MTR GAMING GROUP INC
NATIONAL BEVERAGE CORP
NATIONAL DENTEX CORP
NATIONAL WINE & SPIRITS INC
NATUS MEDICAL INC

NEOGEN CORPORATION
NETFLIX INC
NIC INC
NORTHWESTERN CORPORATION
NOTIFY TECHNOLOGY CORP
NOVAMED INC
NUSTAR ENERGY LP
NUTRASWEET COMPANY (THE)
ODYSSEY RE HOLDINGS CORP
OMNOVA SOLUTIONS INC
ONLINE RESOURCES CORP
PATAGONIA INC
PC CONNECTION INC
PEAPOD LLC
PEGASYSTEMS INC
PERFICIENT INC
PERRY ELLIS INTERNATIONAL INC
PHILADELPHIA CONSOLIDATED HOLDING CORP
PIONEER NATURAL RESOURCES COMPANY
PIPER JAFFRAY COMPANIES
PLATO LEARNING INC
PMA COMPANIES INC
PREMIERE GLOBAL SERVICES INC
PRIMEENERGY CORPORATION
PROASSURANCE CORP
PROTECTIVE LIFE CORP
QUAKER CHEMICAL CORP
QUALITY SYSTEMS INC
QUANTUM CORP
QUIDEL CORP
RECYCLED ENERGY DEVELOPMENT LLC
REDBOX AUTOMATED RETAIL LLC
REINSURANCE GROUP OF AMERICA INC
RICELAND FOODS INC
RIGHTNOW TECHNOLOGIES INC
RIVERBED TECHNOLOGY INC
ROBERT W BAIRD & CO INC
ROCKY BRANDS INC
ROGERS CORPORATION
ROSETTA STONE INC
ROVI CORPORATION
SCANSOURCE INC
SCOULAR COMPANY (THE)
SENIOR HOUSING PROPERTIES
SHARED TECHNOLOGIES
SOUTHERN UNION COMPANY
SOVRAN SELF STORAGE INC
SPARTAN MOTORS INC
SPORT SUPPLY GROUP INC
SPORTSMAN'S GUIDE INC (THE)
SS&C TECHNOLOGIES HOLDINGS INC
STATE AUTO FINANCIAL CORP
STEPAN COMPANY
STERLING AUTOBODY CENTERS
STEVEN MADDEN LTD
SUN COMMUNITIES INC
SUNOCO LOGISTICS PARTNERS LP
SUPERTEL HOSPITALITY INC
SUPREME INDUSTRIES INC
SVB FINANCIAL GROUP
SYNOVIS LIFE TECHNOLOGIES INC
TARGA RESOURCES PARTNERS LP
TECHNE CORP
TEKELEC
THORATEC CORPORATION
TOOTSIE ROLL INDUSTRIES INC
TOPPS COMPANY INC (THE)
TRANSAMMONIA INC
TRANSATLANTIC HOLDINGS INC
TRAVELZOO INC
TRIZETTO GROUP INC (THE)
TRUE RELIGION APPAREL INC
ULTIMATE SOFTWARE GROUP INC
UNITED ONLINE INC
UNIVERSAL HOSPITAL SERVICES INC
US PHYSICAL THERAPY INC
VASCO DATA SECURITY INTERNATIONAL INC
VOX INTERNATIONAL CORPORATION
WABASH NATIONAL CORP
WADDELL & REED FINANCIAL INC
WEBMD HEALTH CORP
WESTAR ENERGY
WIND RIVER SYSTEMS INC
WMS INDUSTRIES INC
XETA TECHNOLOGIES INC
XO GROUP INC
XTO ENERGY INC
ZIEBART INTERNATIONAL CORP

SOUTHEAST

AAMCO TRANSMISSIONS INC
ACI WORLDWIDE INC
ACXIOM DIGITAL INC
ADTRAN INC
ADVISORY BOARD COMPANY (THE)
AKAMAI TECHNOLOGIES INC
ALEXANDER & BALDWIN INC
ALLEGIANT TRAVEL COMPANY
ALLSCRIPTS HEALTHCARE SOLUTIONS INC
AMCOL INTERNATIONAL CORP
AMCON DISTRIBUTING CO
AMERESCO INC
AMERICAN CAMPUS COMMUNITIES INC
AMERICAN FIDELITY ASSURANCE COMPANY
AMERICAN TIRE DISTRIBUTORS
AMERICAN TOWER CORP
AMERICAN VANGUARD CORP
AMERICA'S CAR-MART INC
AMTRUST FINANCIAL SERVICES INC
ARCSIGHT INC
ARGON ST INC
ARIBA INC
ARIZONA CHEMICAL COMPANY
AROTECH CORPORATION
ARRIS GROUP INC
ARUBA NETWORKS INC
ATHENAHEALTH INC
ATRION CORPORATION
AVIALL INC
B&G FOODS INC
BANKRATE INC
BIOSCRIP INC
BLACK HILLS CORP
BOTTOMLINE TECHNOLOGIES INC
BRIGHTSTAR CORPORATION
CABOT OIL & GAS CORP
CAGLE'S INC
CALAVO GROWERS INC
CALGON CARBON CORPORATION
CAL-MAINE FOODS INC
CANTEL MEDICAL CORP
CANTOR FITZGERALD LP
CARBO CERAMICS INC
CARDIONET INC
CARRIZO OIL & GAS INC
CATALYST HEALTH SOLUTIONS INC
CF INDUSTRIES HOLDINGS INC
CHATTEM INC
CLAYTON WILLIAMS ENERGY INC
CLEAN ENERGY FUELS CORP
COHERENT INC
COMDATA CORP
COMTECH TELECOMMUNICATIONS CORP
COMVERGE INC
CONCUR TECHNOLOGIES INC
CONSTANT CONTACT INC
CONTINENTAL RESOURCES INC
CONTINUCARE CORP
COSTAR GROUP INC
CRA INTERNATIONAL INC (CHARLES RIVER)
CRITICAL CARE SYSTEMS
CROWN CASTLE INTERNATIONAL CORP
CRUM & FORSTER HOLDINGS INC
CRYOLIFE INC
CUBIST PHARMACEUTICALS INC
CUMULUS MEDIA INC
CYBERONICS INC
DELPHI FINANCIAL GROUP INC
DENBURY RESOURCES INC
DIAMOND FOODS INC
DIGITAL GENERATION INC
DORMAN PRODUCTS INC
EATON VANCE CORP
EBIX INC
ECHOSTAR CORP
EDELMAN FINANCIAL GROUP (THE)
EMS TECHNOLOGIES INC
ENVIRONMENTAL TECTONICS CORP
EOG RESOURCES INC
EQT CORPORATION
EVEREST RE GROUP LTD
EXACTECH INC
FAIR ISAAC CORPORATION
FEDEX SUPPLY CHAIN SERVICES INC
FNB CORP
FORTINET INC
FROZEN FOOD EXPRESS INDUSTRIES INC
GALLUP ORGANIZATION (THE)
GENERAL ATOMICS

GENESIS ENERGY LP
G-III APPAREL GROUP
GLEACHER & COMPANY INC
GOLDEN ENTERPRISES INC
GOLFSMITH INTERNATIONAL HOLDINGS INC
GREAT AMERICAN FINANCIAL RESOURCES INC
GULFMARK OFFSHORE INC
HANCOCK HOLDING COMPANY
HCC INSURANCE HOLDINGS INC
HEALTHSTREAM INC
HEALTHTRONICS INC
HEARUSA INC
HELIX ENERGY SOLUTIONS GROUP INC
HORACE MANN EDUCATORS CORPORATION
HOSPITALITY PROPERTIES TRUST
HOULIHAN LOKEY HOWARD & ZUKIN INC
HUB GROUP INC
IBASIS INC
IDACORP INC
IMG WORLDWIDE INC
IMMUCOR INC
INDEPENDENCE HOLDING CO
INNOPHOS HOLDINGS INC
INTEGRAMED AMERICA INC
INTERACTIVE INTELLIGENCE GROUP INC
INTERCONTINENTALEXCHANGE INC (ICE)
INTERMEC INC
INTERNAP NETWORK SERVICES CORP
INTERNATIONAL DAIRY QUEEN INC
IRIDEX CORP
JOE'S JEANS INC
JOHN B SANFILIPPO & SON INC
KAMPGROUNDS OF AMERICA INC
KBW INC
KENNETH COLE PRODUCTIONS INC
KEYNOTE SYSTEMS INC
KIMLEY-HORN AND ASSOCIATES INC
KIRBY CORP
KNIGHT CAPITAL GROUP INC
KNOLOGY INC
KORN/FERRY INTERNATIONAL
KRONOS WORLDWIDE INC
LAKELAND INDUSTRIES INC
LB FOSTER COMPANY
LCC INTERNATIONAL INC
LESLIE'S POOLMART INC
LIVEPERSON INC
LOGISTICARE INC
LOJACK CORPORTATION
MAGELLAN MIDSTREAM PARTNERS LP
MAKO SURGICAL CORP
MANHATTAN ASSOCIATES INC
MARVEL ENTERTAINMENT LLC
MEDICIS PHARMACEUTICAL CORP
MEDIFAST INC
MERIDIAN BIOSCIENCE INC
MESIROW FINANCIAL HOLDINGS INC
METROPOLITAN HEALTH NETWORKS INC
MICROTEK MEDICAL HOLDINGS INC
MID-AMERICA APARTMENT COMMUNITIES INC
MIDAS INC
NATIONAL BEVERAGE CORP
NATIONAL DENTEX CORP
NEKTAR THERAPEUTICS
NETFLIX INC
NIC INC
NOVAMED INC
NOVEN PHARMACEUTICALS INC
NUSTAR ENERGY LP
NUTRASWEET COMPANY (THE)
NUVASIVE INC
ODYSSEY RE HOLDINGS CORP
OMNOVA SOLUTIONS INC
ONSTREAM MEDIA CORPORATION
ORION MARINE GROUP INC
PATAGONIA INC
PC CONNECTION INC
PEGASYSTEMS INC
PERFICIENT INC
PERRY ELLIS INTERNATIONAL INC
PETMED EXPRESS INC
PHILADELPHIA CONSOLIDATED HOLDING CORP
PIEDMONT NATURAL GAS COMPANY INC
PLAINS EXPLORATION AND PRODUCTION COMPANY
PMA COMPANIES INC
POWERSECURE INTERNATIONAL INC
PREMIERE GLOBAL SERVICES INC
PRIMEENERGY CORPORATION
PROASSURANCE CORP
PROTECTIVE LIFE CORP
QUALITY SYSTEMS INC
QUANTUM CORP
REDBOX AUTOMATED RETAIL LLC
RENTRAK CORP
RICELAND FOODS INC
ROBERT W BAIRD & CO INC
ROSETTA STONE INC
RPC INC
SBA COMMUNICATIONS CORP
SCANSOURCE INC
SCOULAR COMPANY (THE)
SENIOR HOUSING PROPERTIES
SHARED TECHNOLOGIES
SOUTHERN UNION COMPANY
SOUTHWESTERN ENERGY CO
SOVRAN SELF STORAGE INC
SPORT SUPPLY GROUP INC
STATE AUTO FINANCIAL CORP
STEPAN COMPANY
STERLING AUTOBODY CENTERS
STEVEN MADDEN LTD
STIEFEL LABORATORIES INC
SUN COMMUNITIES INC
SUPERIOR UNIFORM GROUP INC
SUPERTEL HOSPITALITY INC
SUPREME INDUSTRIES INC
SVB FINANCIAL GROUP
SWIFT ENERGY CO
SYNIVERSE TECHNOLOGIES
SYNOVIS LIFE TECHNOLOGIES INC
TAMPA ELECTRIC COMPANY
TARGA RESOURCES PARTNERS LP
TERREMARK WORLDWIDE INC
THERAGENICS CORP
TOOTSIE ROLL INDUSTRIES INC
TOPPS COMPANY INC (THE)
TRANSAMMONIA INC
TRANSATLANTIC HOLDINGS INC
TRANSCEND SERVICES INC
TRAVELZOO INC
TRUE RELIGION APPAREL INC
UDR INC
ULTIMATE SOFTWARE GROUP INC
ULTRALIFE CORPORATION
UNIT CORP
UNITED ONLINE INC
UNITED THERAPEUTICS CORP
UNIVERSAL HOSPITAL SERVICES INC
US PHYSICAL THERAPY INC
VERENIUM CORPORATION
VOX INTERNATIONAL CORPORATION
WABASH NATIONAL CORP
WADDELL & REED FINANCIAL INC
WEBMD HEALTH CORP
WHITEWAVE FOODS COMPANY
WIND RIVER SYSTEMS INC
WRIGHT MEDICAL GROUP INC
XTO ENERGY INC
ZEP INC
ZIEBART INTERNATIONAL CORP

NORTHEAST

24/7 REAL MEDIA INC
AAMCO TRANSMISSIONS INC
ACI WORLDWIDE INC
ACME PACKET INC
ACXIOM DIGITAL INC
ADEPT TECHNOLOGY INC
ADVISORY BOARD COMPANY (THE)
AFFILIATED MANAGERS GROUP
AKAMAI TECHNOLOGIES INC
AKORN INC
AKQA INC
ALBANY MOLECULAR RESEARCH INC
ALEXANDER & BALDWIN INC
ALEXION PHARMACEUTICALS INC
ALLIED HEALTHCARE INTERNATIONAL INC
ALLSCRIPTS HEALTHCARE SOLUTIONS INC
AMAG PHARMACEUTICALS INC
AMCOL INTERNATIONAL CORP
AMERESCO INC

AMERICAN CAMPUS COMMUNITIES INC
AMERICAN FIDELITY ASSURANCE COMPANY
AMERICAN SCIENCE & ENGINEERING INC
AMERICAN TIRE DISTRIBUTORS
AMERICAN TOWER CORP
AMERICAN VANGUARD CORP
AMTECH SYSTEMS INC
AMTRUST FINANCIAL SERVICES INC
ANALOGIC CORP
ANAREN INC
ANIKA THERAPEUTICS INC
APP PHARMACEUTICALS INC
ARCSIGHT INC
ARGON ST INC
ARIBA INC
AROTECH CORPORATION
ARRAY BIOPHARMA INC
ARRIS GROUP INC
ARUBA NETWORKS INC
ATHENAHEALTH INC
ATLANTIC CITY ELECTRIC COMPANY
ATLANTIC TELE-NETWORK INC
AUDIBLE INC
AVALONBAY COMMUNITIES INC
AVIALL INC
B&G FOODS INC
BIO REFERENCE LABORATORIES INC
BIOSCRIP INC
BLACKBOARD INC
BLUE COAT SYSTEMS INC
BOSTON BEER COMPANY INC (THE)
BOTTOMLINE TECHNOLOGIES INC
CABOT OIL & GAS CORP
CAGLE'S INC
CALAVO GROWERS INC
CALGON CARBON CORPORATION
CALIPER LIFE SCIENCES INC
CAL-MAINE FOODS INC
CAMBREX CORP
CANTEL MEDICAL CORP
CANTOR FITZGERALD LP
CARDIONET INC
CARDTRONICS INC
CARRIZO OIL & GAS INC
CATALYST HEALTH SOLUTIONS INC
CELLDEX THERAPEUTICS INC
CELSIS INTERNATIONAL PLC
CENTRAL VERMONT PUBLIC SERVICE CORP
CEPHEID
CF INDUSTRIES HOLDINGS INC
CHINDEX INTERNATIONAL INC
CHOICESTREAM INC
CKX INC
CLEAN ENERGY FUELS CORP
COGENT COMMUNICATIONS
COHERENT INC
COMDATA CORP
COMPASS DIVERSIFIED HOLDINGS
COMTECH TELECOMMUNICATIONS CORP
COMVERGE INC
CONCUR TECHNOLOGIES INC
CONSTANT CONTACT INC
CORPORATE EXECUTIVE BOARD COMPANY (THE)
COSTAR GROUP INC
CRA INTERNATIONAL INC (CHARLES RIVER)
CRITICAL CARE SYSTEMS
CROWN CASTLE INTERNATIONAL CORP
CRUM & FORSTER HOLDINGS INC
CUBIST PHARMACEUTICALS INC
CULP INC
CUMULUS MEDIA INC
CYBERONICS INC
DANNON COMPANY INC (THE)
DAWSON GEOPHYSICAL COMPANY
DEI HOLDINGS INC
DELPHI FINANCIAL GROUP INC
DIAMOND ADVISORY SERVICES
DIAMOND FOODS INC
DIGITAL GENERATION INC
DORMAN PRODUCTS INC
DPL INC
DRUGSTORE.COM INC
EATON VANCE CORP
EBIX INC
ECHOSTAR CORP
EDELMAN FINANCIAL GROUP (THE)
EDGAR ONLINE INC
EMCORE CORP
EMS TECHNOLOGIES INC
EMULEX CORP
ENERGY TRANSFER PARTNERS LP
ENERNOC INC
ENVIRONMENTAL TECTONICS CORP
EOG RESOURCES INC
EPAM SYSTEMS
EQT CORPORATION
EQUINIX INC
ERESEARCH TECHNOLOGY INC
EVERCORE PARTNERS INC
EVEREST RE GROUP LTD
EXACTECH INC
F5 NETWORKS INC
FAIR ISAAC CORPORATION
FEDEX SUPPLY CHAIN SERVICES INC
FNB CORP
FORRESTER RESEARCH INC
FORTINET INC
FRESHDIRECT LLC
FROZEN FOOD EXPRESS INDUSTRIES INC
FUEL SYSTEMS SOLUTIONS INC
FUEL TECH INC
GAIAM INC
GALLUP ORGANIZATION (THE)
GENCO SHIPPING & TRADING LIMITED
GENENCOR INTERNATIONAL INC
GENERAL ATOMICS
GEN-PROBE INC
GFI GROUP INC
G-III APPAREL GROUP
GLEACHER & COMPANY INC
GLOBAL PARTNERS LP
GLOBECOMM SYSTEMS INC
GOLFSMITH INTERNATIONAL HOLDINGS INC
GREAT AMERICAN FINANCIAL RESOURCES INC
GREAT LAKES CHEESE COMPANY INC
GREEN MOUNTAIN POWER CORPORATION
GTC BIOTHERAPEUTICS INC
HAEMONETICS CORPORATION
HAHN AUTOMOTIVE WAREHOUSE INC
HANOVER FOODS CORPORATION
HARRIS INTERACTIVE INC
HCC INSURANCE HOLDINGS INC
HEALTH INSURANCE PLAN OF GREATER NEW YORK
HEALTHSTREAM INC
HEARUSA INC
HI-TECH PHARMACAL CO INC
HORACE MANN EDUCATORS CORPORATION
HOSPITALITY PROPERTIES TRUST
HOULIHAN LOKEY HOWARD & ZUKIN INC
HUB GROUP INC
HUDSON CITY BANCORP INC
IBASIS INC
ICONIX BRAND GROUP INC
ICU MEDICAL INC
IDACORP INC
IMG WORLDWIDE INC
IMMUCOR INC
IMPAX LABORATORIES INC
INDEPENDENCE HOLDING CO
INFOSPACE INC
INNOPHOS HOLDINGS INC
INNOSPEC INC
INTEGRAL SYSTEMS INC
INTEGRAMED AMERICA INC
INTERACTIVE DATA CORPORATION
INTERACTIVE INTELLIGENCE GROUP INC
INTERCONTINENTALEXCHANGE INC (ICE)
INTERMEC INC
INTERNAP NETWORK SERVICES CORP
INTERNATIONAL CREATIVE MANAGEMENT INC (ICM)
INTERNATIONAL DAIRY QUEEN INC
INVESTMENT TECHNOLOGY GROUP INC (ITG)
IRIDEX CORP
IRIS INTERNATIONAL INC
IROBOT CORP
IVILLAGE INC
JOE'S JEANS INC
JOHN B SANFILIPPO & SON INC
KAMPGROUNDS OF AMERICA INC
KBW INC
KENNETH COLE PRODUCTIONS INC

KEYNOTE SYSTEMS INC
KIMLEY-HORN AND ASSOCIATES INC
KIRBY CORP
KKR & CO LP (KOHLBERG KRAVIS ROBERTS & CO)
KNIGHT CAPITAL GROUP INC
KORN/FERRY INTERNATIONAL
KRONOS WORLDWIDE INC
LAKELAND INDUSTRIES INC
LB FOSTER COMPANY
LCC INTERNATIONAL INC
LESLIE'S POOLMART INC
LIFECELL CORPORATION
LIVEPERSON INC
LOGISTICARE INC
LOJACK CORPORTATION
LUCOR INC
MAGELLAN MIDSTREAM PARTNERS LP
MANAGEMENT NETWORK GROUP INC (THE)
MAPFRE USA CORP
MARTEK BIOSCIENCES CORP
MARVEL ENTERTAINMENT LLC
MEDICINES CO (THE)
MEDICIS PHARMACEUTICAL CORP
MEDIFAST INC
MEDTOX SCIENTIFIC INC
MERIDIAN BIOSCIENCE INC
MERIT MEDICAL SYSTEMS INC
MESIROW FINANCIAL HOLDINGS INC
MICHELINAS INC
MID-AMERICA APARTMENT COMMUNITIES INC
MIDAS INC
MILLENNIUM PHARMACEUTICALS INC
MOELIS & COMPANY
MOTORCAR PARTS OF AMERICA INC
MTR GAMING GROUP INC
NATIONAL DENTEX CORP
NATUS MEDICAL INC
NETFLIX INC
NETSCOUT SYSTEMS INC
NETSUITE INC
NETWORK ENGINES INC
NEUSTAR INC
NEW JERSEY RESOURCES CORPORATION
NEW YORK MERCANTILE EXCHANGE INC
NIC INC
NOVAMED INC
NOVEN PHARMACEUTICALS INC
NTELOS HOLDING CORP
NUSTAR ENERGY LP
ODYSSEY RE HOLDINGS CORP
OMNOVA SOLUTIONS INC
ONLINE RESOURCES CORP
ONSTREAM MEDIA CORPORATION
ORION MARINE GROUP INC
PAR PHARMACEUTICAL COMPANIES INC
PATAGONIA INC
PC CONNECTION INC
PEAPOD LLC
PEGASYSTEMS INC
PERFICIENT INC
PERRY ELLIS INTERNATIONAL INC
PETROLEUM DEVELOPMENT CORPORATION
PHILADELPHIA CONSOLIDATED HOLDING CORP
PHOENIX COMPANIES INC (THE)
PIEDMONT NATURAL GAS COMPANY INC
PIPER JAFFRAY COMPANIES
PLATO LEARNING INC
PMA COMPANIES INC
POLYPORE INTERNATIONAL INC
POWERSECURE INTERNATIONAL INC
PREMIERE GLOBAL SERVICES INC
PRIMEENERGY CORPORATION
PROASSURANCE CORP
PROTECTIVE LIFE CORP
PURPLE COMMUNICATIONS INC
QUAKER CHEMICAL CORP
QUALITY SYSTEMS INC
QUANTUM CORP
RAYTHEON APPLIED SIGNAL TECHNOLOGY INC
REALNETWORKS INC
RECYCLED ENERGY DEVELOPMENT LLC
REDBOX AUTOMATED RETAIL LLC
REGENERON PHARMACEUTICALS INC
RENTRAK CORP
RIGHTNOW TECHNOLOGIES INC
RIVERBED TECHNOLOGY INC
ROBERT W BAIRD & CO INC
ROGERS CORPORATION
ROSETTA STONE INC
ROVI CORPORATION
RPC INC
RSA SECURITY INC
S1 CORPORATION
SALIX PHARMACEUTICALS
SBA COMMUNICATIONS CORP
SCANSOURCE INC
SCHICK TECHNOLOGIES INC
SCIOS INC
SCOULAR COMPANY (THE)
SEACHANGE INTERNATIONAL INC
SENIOR HOUSING PROPERTIES
SERACARE LIFE SCIENCES INC
SHARED TECHNOLOGIES
SHENANDOAH TELECOMMUNICATIONS CO
SHUTTERFLY INC
SILICON LABORATORIES INC
SL GREEN REALTY CORP
SMART MODULAR TECHNOLOGIES INC
SOTHEBYS
SOUTHERN UNION COMPANY
SOVRAN SELF STORAGE INC
SPARTAN MOTORS INC
SPIRE CORPORATION
SPORT SUPPLY GROUP INC
SS&C TECHNOLOGIES HOLDINGS INC
STATE AUTO FINANCIAL CORP
STEPAN COMPANY
STERLING AUTOBODY CENTERS
STEVEN MADDEN LTD
STIEFEL LABORATORIES INC
SUN COMMUNITIES INC
SUNOCO LOGISTICS PARTNERS LP
SUPERIOR UNIFORM GROUP INC
SUPERTEL HOSPITALITY INC
SUPREME INDUSTRIES INC
SVB FINANCIAL GROUP
TAKE-TWO INTERACTIVE SOFTWARE INC
TARGA RESOURCES PARTNERS LP
TEKELEC
TELIRIS
TERREMARK WORLDWIDE INC
TESSCO TECHNOLOGIES INC
THERAGENICS CORP
THORATEC CORPORATION
TII NETWORK TECHNOLOGIES INC
TOOTSIE ROLL INDUSTRIES INC
TOPPS COMPANY INC (THE)
TRANSAMMONIA INC
TRANSATLANTIC HOLDINGS INC
TRANSCEND SERVICES INC
TRAVELZOO INC
TREX COMPANY INC
TRIZETTO GROUP INC (THE)
TRUE RELIGION APPAREL INC
UDR INC
UIL HOLDINGS CORPORATION
ULTRALIFE CORPORATION
UNITED ONLINE INC
UNITED THERAPEUTICS CORP
UNIVERSAL HOSPITAL SERVICES INC
US PHYSICAL THERAPY INC
VARIAN SEMICONDUCTOR EQUIPMENT ASSOCIATES INC
VASCO DATA SECURITY INTERNATIONAL INC
VERENIUM CORPORATION
VIBRANT MEDIA INC
VIROPHARMA INC
VOLCOM INC
VOX INTERNATIONAL CORPORATION
WABASH NATIONAL CORP
WADDELL & REED FINANCIAL INC
WEBMD HEALTH CORP
WEBMEDIA BRANDS INC
WGL HOLDINGS INC
WHITEWAVE FOODS COMPANY
WIKIMEDIA FOUNDATION
WIND RIVER SYSTEMS INC
XO GROUP INC
XTO ENERGY INC
ZAP JONWAY
ZIEBART INTERNATIONAL CORP

INDEX OF FIRMS WITH INTERNATIONAL OPERATIONS

FORTINET INC
FUEL SYSTEMS SOLUTIONS INC
FUEL TECH INC
GALLUP ORGANIZATION (THE)
GENENCOR INTERNATIONAL INC
GENERAL ATOMICS
GEN-PROBE INC
GFI GROUP INC
G-III APPAREL GROUP
GLOBECOMM SYSTEMS INC
GLU MOBILE INC
GOLFSMITH INTERNATIONAL HOLDINGS INC
GULFMARK OFFSHORE INC
HAEMONETICS CORPORATION
HARRIS INTERACTIVE INC
HCC INSURANCE HOLDINGS INC
HEARUSA INC
HELIX ENERGY SOLUTIONS GROUP INC
HESKA CORP
HOSPITALITY PROPERTIES TRUST
HOULIHAN LOKEY HOWARD & ZUKIN INC
HUB GROUP INC
IBASIS INC
ICONIX BRAND GROUP INC
ICU MEDICAL INC
IDACORP INC
I-FLOW CORPORATION
ILLUMINA INC
IMG WORLDWIDE INC
IMMUCOR INC
INNOPHOS HOLDINGS INC
INNOSPEC INC
INTEGRAL SYSTEMS INC
INTERACTIVE DATA CORPORATION
INTERACTIVE INTELLIGENCE GROUP INC
INTERCONTINENTALEXCHANGE INC (ICE)
INTERMEC INC
INTERNAP NETWORK SERVICES CORP
INTERNATIONAL CREATIVE MANAGEMENT INC (ICM)
INTERNATIONAL DAIRY QUEEN INC
INTUITIVE SURGICAL INC
INVESTMENT TECHNOLOGY GROUP INC (ITG)
IRIDEX CORP
IRIS INTERNATIONAL INC
IROBOT CORP
ISILON SYSTEMS INC
J2 GLOBAL COMMUNICATIONS INC
JOE'S JEANS INC
KAMPGROUNDS OF AMERICA INC
KBW INC
KENDALL-JACKSON WINE ESTATES LTD
KENNETH COLE PRODUCTIONS INC
KEY TRONIC CORP
KEYNOTE SYSTEMS INC
KKR & CO LP (KOHLBERG KRAVIS ROBERTS & CO)
KNIGHT CAPITAL GROUP INC
KORN/FERRY INTERNATIONAL
KRONOS WORLDWIDE INC
LAKELAND INDUSTRIES INC
LCC INTERNATIONAL INC
LIVEPERSON INC
LOJACK CORPORTATION
LUCASFILM LTD
LUMINEX CORPORATION
MANAGEMENT NETWORK GROUP INC (THE)
MANHATTAN ASSOCIATES INC
MARVEL ENTERTAINMENT LLC
MEDICINES CO (THE)
MENTOR CORP
MERIDIAN BIOSCIENCE INC
MERIT MEDICAL SYSTEMS INC
MESIROW FINANCIAL HOLDINGS INC
MICHELINAS INC
MICROTEK MEDICAL HOLDINGS INC
MIDAS INC
MINDSPEED TECHNOLOGIES INC
MOELIS & COMPANY
MONSTER BEVERAGE CORP
MOTORCAR PARTS OF AMERICA INC
NANOMETRICS INC
NATIONAL DENTEX CORP
NATUS MEDICAL INC
NEKTAR THERAPEUTICS
NEOGEN CORPORATION
NETFLIX INC
NETGEAR INC
NETSCOUT SYSTEMS INC
NETSUITE INC
NETWORK ENGINES INC
NEUSTAR INC
NEW YORK MERCANTILE EXCHANGE INC
NUSTAR ENERGY LP
ODYSSEY RE HOLDINGS CORP
OMNOVA SOLUTIONS INC
OPENTV CORP
PATAGONIA INC
PEGASYSTEMS INC
PERFICIENT INC
PERRY ELLIS INTERNATIONAL INC
PHILADELPHIA CONSOLIDATED HOLDING CORP
PIONEER NATURAL RESOURCES COMPANY
PIPER JAFFRAY COMPANIES
POLYPORE INTERNATIONAL INC
PREMIERE GLOBAL SERVICES INC
QUAKER CHEMICAL CORP
QUALCOMM ATHEROS INC
QUANTUM CORP
QUICKSILVER RESOURCES INC
REALNETWORKS INC
REDBOX AUTOMATED RETAIL LLC
REINSURANCE GROUP OF AMERICA INC
RENTRAK CORP
RIGHTNOW TECHNOLOGIES INC
RIVERBED TECHNOLOGY INC
ROBERT W BAIRD & CO INC
ROGERS CORPORATION
ROVI CORPORATION
RSA SECURITY INC
S1 CORPORATION
SBA COMMUNICATIONS CORP
SCANSOURCE INC
SCHIFF NUTRITION INTERNATIONAL INC
SCICLONE PHARMACEUTICALS INC
SCOULAR COMPANY (THE)
SEACHANGE INTERNATIONAL INC
SELECTICA INC
SENIOR HOUSING PROPERTIES
SERACARE LIFE SCIENCES INC
SIGMA DESIGNS INC
SILICON LABORATORIES INC
SMART MODULAR TECHNOLOGIES INC
SOLARRESERVE
SOLFOCUS INC
SOTHEBYS
SPECTRANETICS CORP
SPECTRUM PHARMACEUTICALS INC
SPIRE CORPORATION
SRS LABS INC
SS&C TECHNOLOGIES HOLDINGS INC
STAAR SURGICAL CO
STEPAN COMPANY
STEVEN MADDEN LTD
STIEFEL LABORATORIES INC
SUPER MICRO COMPUTER INC
SVB FINANCIAL GROUP
SYNAPTICS INC
SYNIVERSE TECHNOLOGIES
TAKE-TWO INTERACTIVE SOFTWARE INC
TARGA RESOURCES PARTNERS LP
TECHNE CORP
TEKELEC
TELIRIS
TERREMARK WORLDWIDE INC
TESCO CORPORATION
TESSCO TECHNOLOGIES INC
THORATEC CORPORATION
TOOTSIE ROLL INDUSTRIES INC
TOPPS COMPANY INC (THE)
TRANSAMMONIA INC
TRANSATLANTIC HOLDINGS INC
TRAVELZOO INC
TRUE RELIGION APPAREL INC
ULTIMATE SOFTWARE GROUP INC
ULTRALIFE CORPORATION
UNITED ONLINE INC
UNITED THERAPEUTICS CORP
USANA HEALTH SCIENCES INC
UTAH MEDICAL PRODUCTS INC
VARIAN SEMICONDUCTOR EQUIPMENT ASSOCIATES INC
VASCO DATA SECURITY INTERNATIONAL INC
VENTANA MEDICAL SYSTEMS INC
VIASAT INC
VIBRANT MEDIA INC

Individual Data Profiles On Each Of THE MID-SIZE EMPLOYERS 500

24/7 REAL MEDIA INC

www.247realmedia.com

Industry Group Code: 541810E

Management:		Sales/Marketing:		Liberal Arts:		Information Systems:		Professionals:		Technical/Scientific:	
Mgmt. Trainees:		Mktg. Professionals:	Y	Gen. Writing/Editing:	Y	Info. Management:	Y	Finance/Acct.:	Y	Engineers, Elec.:	
Experienced Mgmt.:	Y	Retail Sales:		Technical Writing:		Software Dev.:	Y	Law:	Y	Engineers, Other:	
Int'l Business:	Y	Commercial/Industrial:	Y	Graphic Arts/Photog.:	Y	Hardware Dev.:		HR/Other:	Y	Health/Lab	
MBA Graduates:	Y	Sales Trainees:	Y	Music:		Consulting/Other:		Training:	Y	Scientists/Research:	
		Advertising Pros.:	Y	Broadcasting:				Health Care:		Petroleum/Chemicals:	
				Other:	Y			Consulting:		Math/Other:	

TYPES OF BUSINESS:

Internet Advertising
Web Design
Software
Direct Marketing
Promotions
Data Analysis

BRANDS/DIVISIONS/AFFILIATES:

WPP PLC
Rich Media Foundry
24/7 Global Web Alliance
Open AdStream
Decide DNA
Dentsu Search & Link
Panache

CONTACTS: *Note: Officers with more than one job title may be intentionally listed here more than once.*

David J. Moore, CEO
Ari Bluman, Pres.
Kris Heinrichs, CFO
Peter Jurew, Sr. VP-Mktg.
Pammy Brooks, VP-Human Resources
Oleg Vishnepolsky, CTO
Ari Bluman, Sr. VP-U.S. Oper.
Rob Schneider, VP-Corp. Strategy & Platform Dev.
Nicolle Pangis, Pres., Europe
David J. Moore, Chmn.
Jae Woo Chung, Pres., Asia

Phone: 212-231-7100 | **Fax:** 212-760-1774
Toll-Free: 877-247-2477
Address: 132 W. 31st St., New York, NY 10001 US

GROWTH PLANS/SPECIAL FEATURES:

24/7 Real Media, Inc. is a global provider of interactive technology and marketing solutions for web publishers, online advertisers, advertising agencies and e-marketers. The firm's services include advertising and direct marketing sales, search engine marketing services, online advertisement serving, web advertising, site representation and web analytics. The company maintains 18 offices and provides its products and services in 12 countries internationally. 24/7 is organized into three solution divisions: Technology, Media and Search. The Technology segment, through its Open AdStream platform, is designed for advertisers/agencies, web publishers and e-commerce merchants. The Media division consists of 24/7 Global Web Alliance, a group of web sites that allow client advertisers to place targeted ad campaigns. The Search division provides search marketing services for the Internet through its Decide DNA technology platform. Decide DNA generates keyword lists, manages bids across multiple engines and supports multiple languages and currencies. Dentsu Search & Link, its Japanese subsidiary, targets search engine marketing in Asia and the Pacific Rim. The firm's Rich Media Foundry creates and traffics rich media advertising. 24/7 is a subsidiary of global communications firm, WPP plc. In December 2011, the company acquired Panache, a provider of digital video advertising fulfillment software and services.

FINANCIALS: **Sales and profits are in thousands of dollars—add 000 to get the full amount. 2011 Note: Financial information for 2011 was not available for all companies at press time.**

2011 Sales: $ | 2011 Profits: $
2010 Sales: $ | 2010 Profits: $
2009 Sales: $ | 2009 Profits: $
2008 Sales: $ | 2008 Profits: $
2007 Sales: $ | 2007 Profits: $

U.S. Stock Ticker: Subsidiary
Int'l Ticker:
Int'l Exchange:
Employees: Fiscal Year Ends: 12/31
Parent Company: WPP PLC

SALARIES/BENEFITS:

Pension Plan: | ESOP Stock Plan: | Profit Sharing: | Top Exec. Salary: $ | Bonus: $
Savings Plan: | Stock Purch. Plan: | | Second Exec. Salary: $ | Bonus: $

OTHER THOUGHTS:

Apparent Women Officers or Directors: 2
Hot Spot for Advancement for Women/Minorities:

LOCATIONS: ("Y" = Yes)

West:	Southwest:	Midwest:	Southeast:	Northeast:	International:
Y		Y		Y	Y

AAMCO TRANSMISSIONS INC

www.aamco.com

Industry Group Code: 8111

Management:		Sales/Marketing:		Liberal Arts:		Information Systems:		Professionals:		Technical/Scientific:	
Mgmt. Trainees:	Y	Mktg. Professionals:	Y	Gen. Writing/Editing:	Y	Info. Management:	Y	Finance/Acct.:	Y	Engineers, Elec.:	
Experienced Mgmt.:	Y	Retail Sales:		Technical Writing:	Y	Software Dev.:	Y	Law:	Y	Engineers, Other:	
Int'l Business:	Y	Commercial/Industrial:		Graphic Arts/Photog.:		Hardware Dev.:		HR/Other:	Y	Health/Lab	
MBA Graduates:	Y	Sales Trainees:		Music:		Consulting/Other:		Training:	Y	Scientists/Research:	
		Advertising Pros.:	Y	Broadcasting:				Health Care:		Petroleum/Chemicals:	
				Other:				Consulting:		Math/Other:	

TYPES OF BUSINESS:

Automotive Repair & Maintenance-Transmissions
Automatic Transmission Fluid
Bioethanol Conversion

BRANDS/DIVISIONS/AFFILIATES:

AAMCO Automatic Transmission Fluid
AAMCO Synthetic Blend ATF
AAMCO ATF D/M
AAMCO Mercon V
Flex-Box Smart Kit
American Driveline Systems
American Capital

CONTACTS: *Note: Officers with more than one job title may be intentionally listed here more than once.*

Marc C. Graham, CEO
Marc C. Graham, Pres.
Mike Sumsky, CFO
Jack Bachinsky, VP-Mktg.
James Goniea, General Counsel/VP-Law
Brian O'Donnell, Sr. VP-Oper.
Bruce Chidsey, VP-East Oper. & Tech. Svcs.
John Baumgartner, VP-West Oper.
Micahel Dacko, VP-Training
Rob Fillman, VP-Equipment

Phone: 215-643-5885	**Fax:** 215-956-0340
Toll-Free: 800-462-2626	
Address: 201 Gibraltar Rd., Horsham, PA 19044 US	

GROWTH PLANS/SPECIAL FEATURES:

AAMCO Transmissions, Inc. is a chain of auto transmission shops with more than 900 independently owned and operated franchise locations in the U.S., Canada and Puerto Rico. AAMCO's services include diagnostic, repair and maintenance services for automatic and standard transmissions in cars and trucks; free towing; external and multi- point inspections; and estimates. The company guarantees its services through a selection of six warranty packages from 90-day limited contracts to lifetime coverage. AAMCO also offers a national fleet program in which more than 500 owners of large fleets of vehicles contract transmission services at discounted prices. Moreover, the firm manufactures a branded automatic transmission fluid, AAMCO Automatic Transmission Fluid (ATF). Additional transmission fluid products include AAMCO Mercon V, AAMCO Synthetic Blend ATF, and AAMCO ATF D/M. Transmission fluids are available through automotive product retailers across North America. The firm offers its Eco-Green Auto Service at approximately 50 locations in the U.S., which meet eco-friendly standards such as solvent and waste fluid recycling. These locations offer, in addition to standard AAMCO services, a bioethanol fuel conversion kit called the Flex-Box Smart Kit, developed in partnership with Flex Fuel U.S. The company is a subsidiary of American Driveline Systems, which is owned by investment company American Capital. In May 2011, the firm announced the opening of five new AAMCO Auto Service Centers based in Horsham, PA. In June 2011, AAMCA announced it would be expanding its operations in Detroit with the construction of eight additional transmission shops.

FINANCIALS: **Sales and profits are in thousands of dollars—add 000 to get the full amount. 2011 Note: Financial information for 2011 was not available for all companies at press time.**

2011 Sales: $	2011 Profits: $	**U.S. Stock Ticker: Private**
2010 Sales: $	2010 Profits: $	**Int'l Ticker:**
2009 Sales: $	2009 Profits: $	Int'l Exchange:
2008 Sales: $	2008 Profits: $	Employees: Fiscal Year Ends: 12/31
2007 Sales: $	2007 Profits: $	Parent Company: AMERICAN CAPITAL

SALARIES/BENEFITS:

Pension Plan:	ESOP Stock Plan:	Profit Sharing:	Top Exec. Salary: $	Bonus: $
Savings Plan:	Stock Purch. Plan:		Second Exec. Salary: $	Bonus: $

OTHER THOUGHTS:

Apparent Women Officers or Directors:
Hot Spot for Advancement for Women/Minorities:

LOCATIONS: ("Y" = Yes)

West:	Southwest:	Midwest:	Southeast:	Northeast:	International:
Y	Y	Y	Y	Y	Y

ABAXIS INC

www.abaxis.com

Industry Group Code: 33911

Management:		**Sales/Marketing:**		**Liberal Arts:**		**Information Systems:**		**Professionals:**		**Technical/Scientific:**	
Mgmt. Trainees:		Mktg. Professionals:	Y	Gen. Writing/Editing:		Info. Management:	Y	Finance/Acct.:	Y	Engineers, Elec.:	Y
Experienced Mgmt.:	Y	Retail Sales:		Technical Writing:	Y	Software Dev.:	Y	Law:	Y	Engineers, Other:	Y
Int'l Business:	Y	Commercial/Industrial:	Y	Graphic Arts/Photog.:		Hardware Dev.:	Y	HR/Other:	Y	Health/Lab	Y
MBA Graduates:	Y	Sales Trainees:	Y	Music:		Consulting/Other:		Training:	Y	Scientists/Research:	Y
		Advertising Pros.:		Broadcasting:				Health Care:	Y	Petroleum/Chemicals:	
				Other:				Consulting:		Math/Other:	

TYPES OF BUSINESS:

Point-of-Care Blood Analyzer Systems Equipment
Veterinary Blood Analyzer Systems
Reagents & Supplies

BRANDS/DIVISIONS/AFFILIATES:

VetScan VS2
Piccolo Classic
VetScan Vspro
Piccolo Xpress
VetScan Rapid Test
Orbos Discrete Lyophilization Process
VetScan HM5
VetScan HM2

CONTACTS: *Note: Officers with more than one job title may be intentionally listed here more than once.*

Clint Severson, CEO
Donald Wood, COO
Clint Severson, Pres.
Alberto Santa Ines, CFO
Martin Mulroy, VP-Mktg. & Sales, North American Animal Health
Kenneth Aron, CTO
Michael Solomon, Dir.-Bus. Dev., Animal Health
Alberto Santa Ines, VP-Finance
Brenton G.A. Hanlon, VP-Medical Sales & Mktg., North America
Valerie Goodwin-Adams, Dir.-Mktg., Animal Health
Rick Betts, Dir.-Mktg. Medical Diagnostics, U.S.
Clint Severson, Chmn.
Vladimir E. Ostoich, VP-Gov't Affairs & Mktg., Pacific Rim
Jeff Sumpter, Mgr.-U.S. Dist.

Phone: 510-675-6500 **Fax:** 510-441-6150
Toll-Free:
Address: 3240 Whipple Rd., Union City, CA 94587 US

GROWTH PLANS/SPECIAL FEATURES:

Abaxis, Inc. develops, manufactures and markets portable blood analysis systems for use in veterinary or human patient-care settings to provide clinicians with rapid blood constituent measurements. The firm operates in two business segments: the veterinary market, which accounted for 75% of 2011 revenues; and the medical market, which accounted for 20%. The firm's analysis systems includes the VetScan VS2, VetScan HM5, VetScan VSpro, Vet Scan Rapid Test, VetScan Profiles, VetScan i-STAT 1 Handheld Analyzer and VetScan HM2 in the veterinary market; and the Piccolo Xpress, Piccolo Panels and the Piccolo Classic in the human medical market. Abaxis' blood analysis systems consist of a compact analyzer and a series of single-use plastic discs, called reagent discs, containing all the chemicals required to perform a panel of up to 29 diagnostic tests. In addition to blood analysis systems, the company sells the VetScan HM5 hematology analyzer that provides a 22-parameter blood count analysis, including a five-part white blood cell differential. To produce the dry reagents used in the reagent disks, Abaxis uses its Orbos Discrete Lyophilization Process (Orbos process), which freeze dries reagents in small quantities, enabling efficient manufacturing of reagents in a convenient and stable format. In October 2011, the company's Abaxis Veterinary Reference Laboratory (AVRL), a commercial laboratory testing center located in Kansas City, Kansas, became fully operational and began accepting and processing samples throughout the U.S. Throughout 2011 to 2012, Abaxis expanded its VetScan Rapid Diagnostics Test line, adding rapid tests for Giardia, a gastrointestinal infection caused by Giardia parasites; feline heartworm applications; and Canine Parvovirus, a highly contagious and potentially deadly virus most common in puppies.

Employees are offered medical, dental and vision insurance; life insurance; disability coverage; a 401(k) plan; flexible spending accounts; and memberships to financial institutions, retail stores and clubs.

FINANCIALS: **Sales and profits are in thousands of dollars—add 000 to get the full amount. 2011 Note: Financial information for 2011 was not available for all companies at press time.**

2011 Sales: $143,676	2011 Profits: $14,537	**U.S. Stock Ticker: ABAX**
2010 Sales: $124,557	2010 Profits: $13,023	**Int'l Ticker:**
2009 Sales: $105,562	2009 Profits: $12,013	Int'l Exchange:
2008 Sales: $100,551	2008 Profits: $12,503	Employees: 388 Fiscal Year Ends: 3/31
2007 Sales: $86,221	2007 Profits: $10,073	Parent Company:

SALARIES/BENEFITS:

Pension Plan:	ESOP Stock Plan:	Profit Sharing:	Top Exec. Salary: $370,385	Bonus: $488,251
Savings Plan: Y	Stock Purch. Plan:		Second Exec. Salary: $215,539	Bonus: $279,000

OTHER THOUGHTS:

Apparent Women Officers or Directors: 3
Hot Spot for Advancement for Women/Minorities: Y

LOCATIONS: ("Y" = Yes)

West:	Southwest:	Midwest:	Southeast:	Northeast:	International:
Y					Y

ACI WORLDWIDE INC

www.aciworldwide.com

Industry Group Code: 511201

Management:		Sales/Marketing:		Liberal Arts:		Information Systems:		Professionals:		Technical/Scientific:	
Mgmt. Trainees:		Mktg. Professionals:	Y	Gen. Writing/Editing:		Info. Management:	Y	Finance/Acct.:	Y	Engineers, Elec.:	Y
Experienced Mgmt.:	Y	Retail Sales:		Technical Writing:	Y	Software Dev.:	Y	Law:	Y	Engineers, Other:	
Int'l Business:	Y	Commercial/Industrial:	Y	Graphic Arts/Photog.:		Hardware Dev.:		HR/Other:	Y	Health/Lab	
MBA Graduates:	Y	Sales Trainees:	Y	Music:		Consulting/Other:		Training:	Y	Scientists/Research:	
		Advertising Pros.:		Broadcasting:				Health Care:		Petroleum/Chemicals:	
				Other:				Consulting:		Math/Other:	

TYPES OF BUSINESS:

Computer Software-Electronic Funds Transfer
Information Management Solutions
Electronic Banking & Smart Card Solutions
International Payments & Message Processing Software

BRANDS/DIVISIONS/AFFILIATES:

ACI Enterprise Banker
ACI Global Banker
ACI Proactive Risk Manager
ACI Case Manager
ISD Corporation
S1 Corporation

CONTACTS: *Note: Officers with more than one job title may be intentionally listed here more than once.*

Philip G. Heasley, CEO
J. Ronald Totaro, COO
Philip G. Heasley, Pres.
Scott Behrens, CFO/Exec. VP
Louis Blatt, Sr. VP-Corp. Mktg. & Strategic Planning
Charles H. Linberg, CTO
Dennis Byrnes, General Counsel/Exec. VP/Sec.
David N. Norem, Exec. VP-Global Customer Oper.
Tony Scotto, Chief Dev. Officer/Exec. VP
Catherine Eyres, Contact-Media Rel.
Tamar Gerber, VP-Investor Rel. & Financial Comm.
Scott Behrens, Chief Acct. Officer
Craig Maki, Sr. VP-Corp. Dev.
Ralph Dangelmaier, Pres., Global Markets & Svcs.
James Farrell, Managing Dir.-Pacific Region
Harlan F. Seymour, Chmn.
Jeremy Wilmot, Pres., ACI Asia Pacific

Phone: 646-348-6700 **Fax:** 212-470-4000
Toll-Free:
Address: 120 Broadway, Ste. 3350, New York, NY 10271 US

GROWTH PLANS/SPECIAL FEATURES:

ACI Worldwide, Inc. develops, markets, installs and supports software products and services focused on facilitating electronic payments. Generally, ACI's products address three primary market segments: retail banking, including debit and credit card issuers; wholesale banking, including corporate cash management and treasury management operations; and retailers. Its product lines are divided into four categories: Initiate, Manage, Secure and Operate. Initiate products are designed around the initiation of payments through online banking systems and include the products ACI Enterprise Banker, which is used as an Internet-based business banking product with electronic payment initiation capability and information reporting; and ACI Global Banker, which serves corporate cash management, trade finance, reporting and data exchange needs. The Manage segment serves retail payment engines, which are designed to route electronic payment transactions from transaction generators to the acquiring institutions so that they can be authorized for payment; back office services, which are card issuing and merchant management services; and wholesale payment engines, which focus on global, super-regional and regional financial institutions that provide treasury management services to large corporations. The products in the Secure division, such as ACI Proactive Risk Manager and ACI Case Manager, work to protect against fraud and money laundering. The Operate products work to support and augment the products in the Initiate, Manage and Secure divisions, and offer services such as legacy product support, automated data streams, protected monitoring and simulation services. In addition to its own products, it also distributes or acts as a sales agent for software developed by third parties. The majority of ACI's products are sold and supported through three distribution networks: the Americas, which represented 53% of 2010 revenues; Europe/Middle East/Africa (EMEA), 36%; and Asia Pacific, 11%. In March 2011, ACI acquired ISD Corporation, a provider of payment management software. In October 2011, it signed a definitive agreement to acquire S1 Corporation.

FINANCIALS: **Sales and profits are in thousands of dollars—add 000 to get the full amount. 2011 Note: Financial information for 2011 was not available for all companies at press time.**

2011 Sales: $465,095 | 2011 Profits: $45,852
2010 Sales: $418,424 | 2010 Profits: $27,195
2009 Sales: $405,755 | 2009 Profits: $19,626
2008 Sales: $417,653 | 2008 Profits: $10,582
2007 Sales: $366,218 | 2007 Profits: $-9,131

U.S. Stock Ticker: ACIW
Int'l Ticker:
Int'l Exchange:
Employees: 2,134 Fiscal Year Ends: 12/31
Parent Company:

SALARIES/BENEFITS:

Pension Plan: | ESOP Stock Plan: | Profit Sharing: | Top Exec. Salary: $575,000 | Bonus: $864,822
Savings Plan: Y | Stock Purch. Plan: Y | | Second Exec. Salary: $275,000 | Bonus: $330,888

OTHER THOUGHTS:

Apparent Women Officers or Directors: 2
Hot Spot for Advancement for Women/Minorities:

LOCATIONS: ("Y" = Yes)

West:	Southwest:	Midwest:	Southeast:	Northeast:	International:
	Y	Y	Y	Y	Y

ACME PACKET INC

www.acmepacket.com

Industry Group Code: 561499

Management:		Sales/Marketing:		Liberal Arts:		Information Systems:		Professionals:		Technical/Scientific:	
Mgmt. Trainees:		Mktg. Professionals:	Y	Gen. Writing/Editing:		Info. Management:	Y	Finance/Acct.:	Y	Engineers, Elec.:	Y
Experienced Mgmt.:	Y	Retail Sales:		Technical Writing:	Y	Software Dev.:	Y	Law:	Y	Engineers, Other:	Y
Int'l Business:	Y	Commercial/Industrial:	Y	Graphic Arts/Photog.:		Hardware Dev.:		HR/Other:	Y	Health/Lab	
MBA Graduates:	Y	Sales Trainees:	Y	Music:		Consulting/Other:		Training:	Y	Scientists/Research:	
		Advertising Pros.:		Broadcasting:				Health Care:		Petroleum/Chemicals:	
				Other:				Consulting:		Math/Other:	

TYPES OF BUSINESS:

Session Border Controllers
Professional Support Services

BRANDS/DIVISIONS/AFFILIATES:

Net-Net OS
Net-Net 3800
Net-Net 4500
Net-Net 9200
Net-Net EMS
Acme Packet Session Aware Networking
Net-Net 2600
Net-Net Policy Director

CONTACTS: *Note: Officers with more than one job title may be intentionally listed here more than once.*

Andy Ory, CEO
Dino Di Palma, COO
Andy Ory, Pres.
Peter Minihane, CFO
Marianne Budnik, Chief Mktg. Officer
Patrick MeLampy, CTO
Steven Aulds, Sr. VP-Eng.
John Shields, VP-Mfg. Oper.
Seamus Hourihan, Sr. VP-Corp. Strategy
Erin Medeiros, Sr. VP-Professional Svcs.

Phone: 781-328-4400 **Fax:** 781-275-8800
Toll-Free:
Address: 100 Crosby Dr., Bedford, MA 01730 US

GROWTH PLANS/SPECIAL FEATURES:

Acme Packet, Inc. provides session border controllers (SBCs) that enable interactive communications service providers to deliver secure and high quality communications. Its technology is used to transmit voice, video and other real-time multimedia sessions across defined border points where Internet protocol (IP) networks connect. SBCs are designed to complement, rather than replace, softswitches, data firewalls and routers. Acme Packet Session Aware Networking, the firm's technology architecture, enables the delivery of secure and high-quality interactive communication sessions across IP network borders. Implemented by the integration of the Net-Net OS software and Net-Net hardware platforms, the technology combines session routing policy; session signaling service; session media control; session monitoring and reporting; and session security service. Acme Packet's Net-Net family of products includes Net-Net OS, 2600, 3800, 4500, 9200, Route Manager Central and EMS. The Net-Net products serve as a central element in unifying the separate IP networks that include wireline, wireless and cable networks. The company also provides a broad range of professional support services through every stage of its products' deployment. The firm sells its products and support services through over 200 distribution partners and a direct sales force. Customers include incumbent and competitive local exchange and long distance providers; international service providers; cable operators; Internet telephony service providers; voice application service providers; and wireless service providers. Over 1,525 customers in 107 countries have deployed more than 14,000 Acme Packet systems. In February 2011, the company introduced Net-Net Policy Director, a policy exchange controller (PEC) that addresses security and operability issues in next-generation IP networks.

The company offers its employees life, disability, medical, dental and vision insurance; a flexible spending account; a 401(k) plan; and a stock purchase plan.

FINANCIALS: **Sales and profits are in thousands of dollars—add 000 to get the full amount. 2011 Note: Financial information for 2011 was not available for all companies at press time.**

2011 Sales: $
2010 Sales: $231,232
2009 Sales: $141,458
2008 Sales: $116,358
2007 Sales: $113,052

2011 Profits: $
2010 Profits: $43,037
2009 Profits: $17,106
2008 Profits: $11,572
2007 Profits: $19,561

U.S. Stock Ticker: APKT
Int'l Ticker:
Int'l Exchange:
Employees: 570 Fiscal Year Ends: 12/31
Parent Company:

SALARIES/BENEFITS:

Pension Plan: ESOP Stock Plan: Profit Sharing: Top Exec. Salary: $460,149 Bonus: $93,855
Savings Plan: Y Stock Purch. Plan: Y Second Exec. Salary: $415,000 Bonus: $441,983

OTHER THOUGHTS:

Apparent Women Officers or Directors: 2
Hot Spot for Advancement for Women/Minorities:

LOCATIONS: ("Y" = Yes)

West:	Southwest:	Midwest:	Southeast:	Northeast:	International:
				Y	Y

ACXIOM DIGITAL INC

www.acxiomdigital.com

Industry Group Code: 541810E

Management:		**Sales/Marketing:**		**Liberal Arts:**		**Information Systems:**		**Professionals:**		**Technical/Scientific:**	
Mgmt. Trainees:		Mktg. Professionals:	Y	Gen. Writing/Editing:	Y	Info. Management:	Y	Finance/Acct.:	Y	Engineers, Elec.:	
Experienced Mgmt.:	Y	Retail Sales:		Technical Writing:		Software Dev.:	Y	Law:	Y	Engineers, Other:	
Int'l Business:	Y	Commercial/Industrial:	Y	Graphic Arts/Photog.:	Y	Hardware Dev.:		HR/Other:	Y	Health/Lab	
MBA Graduates:	Y	Sales Trainees:	Y	Music:		Consulting/Other:		Training:	Y	Scientists/Research:	
		Advertising Pros.:	Y	Broadcasting:				Health Care:		Petroleum/Chemicals:	
				Other:	Y			Consulting:		Math/Other:	

TYPES OF BUSINESS:

Direct Marketing E-Mail Services
Search Engine Marketing Services
Strategy & Analysis Services
Data Management
Web Development & Creative Design

BRANDS/DIVISIONS/AFFILIATES:

Relevance-X Social
Acxiom Corporation
IMPACT-X
Acxiom Impact-X Mobile
Acxiom Impact-X Email
Relevance-X TV
CertifiedEmail
Forrester Wave

CONTACTS:

Note: Officers with more than one job title may be intentionally listed here more than once.

John Meyer, CEO/Pres., Acxiom Corp.

Phone: 650-356-3400	**Fax:** 650-356-3410
Toll-Free: 800-491-9320	
Address: 601 E. 3rd St., Little Rock, AR 72201 US	

GROWTH PLANS/SPECIAL FEATURES:

Acxiom Digital, Inc. is Acxiom Corporation's online direct marketing subsidiary. Acxiom Digital assists clients with the design, analysis, optimization and delivery of marketing communications across multiple channels, including e-mail, web sites, banners and other web display ads, mobile devices, TV, social media and direct mail. The firm's team offers services in 27 languages and manages over 300,000 campaigns annually to clients across120 countries. The company offers services in six areas: e-mail marketing, multi-channel marketing, web site personalization, mobile marketing, targeted advertising and agency services. The firm provides these services primarily through its proprietary technology, such as the IMPACT-X platform, which helps enterprise marketing groups design, send and analyze direct marketing communications through integrated campaign management and analytics. It also provides several tools to develop and enhance e-mail related marketing strategies. The company's technology, Forrester Wave provides customers with e-mail deliverability solutions, which helps customize e-mails to navigate around spam filters; Transactional e-mail, which helps clients up-sell and cross-sell by analyzing previous transactions; and, through a partnership with GoodMail Systems, CertifiedEmail, a premium class of trusted e-mail that allows consumers to identify authentic messages from legitimate senders. Customers can access mobile marketing services using Acxiom Impact-X Mobile or Acxiom Impact-X Email and mobile messaging, which provide SMS, e-mail integration and geographical based advertising applications. The company's multidimensional platforms, Relevance-X Online; Relevance-X Social; and Relevance-X TV, allow customers to target audiences across a variety of channels using real time matching and personalization engines. Acxiom Digital serves clients in the retail, financial services, telecommunications and technology sectors, among others.

FINANCIALS:

Sales and profits are in thousands of dollars—add 000 to get the full amount. 2011 Note: Financial information for 2011 was not available for all companies at press time.

2011 Sales: $	2011 Profits: $	**U.S. Stock Ticker: Subsidiary**
2010 Sales: $	2010 Profits: $	**Int'l Ticker:**
2009 Sales: $	2009 Profits: $	Int'l Exchange:
2008 Sales: $	2008 Profits: $	Employees: Fiscal Year Ends: 3/31
2007 Sales: $	2007 Profits: $	Parent Company: ACXIOM CORP

SALARIES/BENEFITS:

Pension Plan:	ESOP Stock Plan:	Profit Sharing:	Top Exec. Salary: $	Bonus: $79,830
Savings Plan:	Stock Purch. Plan:		Second Exec. Salary: $	Bonus: $

OTHER THOUGHTS:

Apparent Women Officers or Directors:
Hot Spot for Advancement for Women/Minorities:

LOCATIONS: ("Y" = Yes)

West:	Southwest:	Midwest:	Southeast:	Northeast:	International:
Y			Y	Y	Y

ADEPT TECHNOLOGY INC

www.adept.com

Industry Group Code: 334111

Management:		**Sales/Marketing:**		**Liberal Arts:**		**Information Systems:**		**Professionals:**		**Technical/Scientific:**	
Mgmt. Trainees:		Mktg. Professionals:	Y	Gen. Writing/Editing:		Info. Management:	Y	Finance/Acct.:	Y	Engineers, Elec.:	Y
Experienced Mgmt.:	Y	Retail Sales:		Technical Writing:	Y	Software Dev.:	Y	Law:	Y	Engineers, Other:	
Int'l Business:	Y	Commercial/Industrial:	Y	Graphic Arts/Photog.:		Hardware Dev.:	Y	HR/Other:	Y	Health/Lab	
MBA Graduates:	Y	Sales Trainees:	Y	Music:		Consulting/Other:	Y	Training:	Y	Scientists/Research:	
		Advertising Pros.:		Broadcasting:				Health Care:		Petroleum/Chemicals:	
				Other:				Consulting:		Math/Other:	

TYPES OF BUSINESS:

Factory Automation Systems
Factory Automation Software
Industrial Robotics
Machine Vision Systems

BRANDS/DIVISIONS/AFFILIATES:

Cobra
Viper
Quattro
Adept Python
InMoTx Inc
MobileRobots Inc

CONTACTS: *Note: Officers with more than one job title may be intentionally listed here more than once.*

John Dulchinos, CEO
John Dulchinos, Pres.
Lisa Cummins, CFO/Sr. VP
John Boutsikaris, Sr. VP-Global Sales & Mktg.
Jeff Baird, VP-Eng.
Joachim Melis, VP-Bus. & Dev.
Rush LaSelle, VP/Gen. Mgr.-Mobile Robots
Michael P. Kelly, Chmn.
Joachim Melis, Managing Dir.-Adept Europe

Phone: 925-245-3400	**Fax:** 925-960-0452
Toll-Free: 800-292-3378	
Address: 5960 Inglewood Dr, Pleasanton, CA 94588 US	

GROWTH PLANS/SPECIAL FEATURES:

Adept Technology, Inc. designs, manufactures and sells intelligent robotics systems. It produces factory automation components and systems for the fiber optic, telecommunications, industrial tooling, packaging, life science, alternative energy, automotive electronics and semiconductor industries worldwide. The company operates in two business segments: Robotics, accounting for 78% of the firm's 2011 revenue; and Services & Support, 22%. The Robotics segment offers intelligent motion controls systems; production automation software, including vision-guidance and application software; and robot mechanisms. Adept intelligent automation product lines include industrial robots; configurable linear modules; machine controllers for robot mechanisms and other flexible automation equipment; machine vision and systems; and applications software. The company's Automation Control Environment (ACE) software simplifies the integration, programming and operation of robot, vision and flexible feeder applications with a user-friendly interface. This software allows users real-time control of robots with industry-standard computers running operating systems such as Microsoft Windows, enabling the integration of robotic systems into existing computer networks. Its most widely deployed robots are the Cobra family, which are 4-axis SCARA (Selective Compliance Assembly Robot Arm) robot mechanisms, designed for assembly and material handling tasks. Other robots include Quattro parallel robots, Viper 6-axis articulated robots, Modular Adept Python single axis mechanisms and mobile robots. The Services & Support segment provides spare parts for existing systems, consultation, technical support and training courses in the use of Adept's products. The firm markets and sells its products worldwide through more than 200 systems integrators, a direct sales force and original equipment manufacturers (OEMs). In 2010, the firm acquired MobileRobots, Inc., which develops autonomous robot and automated guided vehicle technologies. In January 2011, it acquired InMoTx, Inc., a provider of robotic technology to the food processing market.

FINANCIALS: **Sales and profits are in thousands of dollars—add 000 to get the full amount. 2011 Note: Financial information for 2011 was not available for all companies at press time.**

2011 Sales: $57,505	2011 Profits: $-6,764
2010 Sales: $51,627	2010 Profits: $-1,428
2009 Sales: $41,536	2009 Profits: $-13,068
2008 Sales: $60,783	2008 Profits: $3,636
2007 Sales: $48,688	2007 Profits: $-11,513

U.S. Stock Ticker: ADEP
Int'l Ticker:
Int'l Exchange:
Employees: 183 Fiscal Year Ends: 6/30
Parent Company:

SALARIES/BENEFITS:

Pension Plan:	ESOP Stock Plan:	Profit Sharing:	Top Exec. Salary: $285,000	Bonus: $
Savings Plan:	Stock Purch. Plan: Y		Second Exec. Salary: $231,798	Bonus: $

OTHER THOUGHTS:

Apparent Women Officers or Directors: 1
Hot Spot for Advancement for Women/Minorities:

LOCATIONS: ("Y" = Yes)

West:	Southwest:	Midwest:	Southeast:	Northeast:	International:
Y				Y	Y

ADTRAN INC

www.adtran.com

Industry Group Code: 334210

Management:		Sales/Marketing:		Liberal Arts:		Information Systems:		Professionals:		Technical/Scientific:	
Mgmt. Trainees:		Mktg. Professionals:	Y	Gen. Writing/Editing:		Info. Management:	Y	Finance/Acct.:	Y	Engineers, Elec.:	Y
Experienced Mgmt.:	Y	Retail Sales:		Technical Writing:	Y	Software Dev.:	Y	Law:	Y	Engineers, Other:	
Int'l Business:	Y	Commercial/Industrial:	Y	Graphic Arts/Photog.:		Hardware Dev.:	Y	HR/Other:	Y	Health/Lab	
MBA Graduates:	Y	Sales Trainees:	Y	Music:		Consulting/Other:		Training:	Y	Scientists/Research:	
		Advertising Pros.:		Broadcasting:				Health Care:		Petroleum/Chemicals:	
				Other:				Consulting:		Math/Other:	

TYPES OF BUSINESS:

Carrier Networks
Enterprise Networks

BRANDS/DIVISIONS/AFFILIATES:

Total Access 500
Total Reach
Total Access 300
NetVanta

CONTACTS: *Note: Officers with more than one job title may be intentionally listed here more than once.*

Thomas R. Stanton, CEO
James E. Matthews, CFO
Kevin W. Schneider, CTO
James E. Matthews, Corp. Sec.
Michael Foliano, Sr. VP-Global Oper.
Tammie Dodson, Mgr.-Public Rel.
Gayle Ellis, Contact-Investor Rel.
James E. Matthews, Sr. VP-Finance/Treas.
Jay Wilson, Sr. VP/Gen. Mgr.-Carrier Networks Div.
Rick Schansman, Sr. VP/Gen Mgr.-Enterprise Networks Div.
Thomas R. Stanton, Chmn.

Phone: 256-963-8000 **Fax:** 256-963-8030
Toll-Free: 800-923-8726
Address: 901 Explorer Blvd., Huntsville, AL 35806 US

GROWTH PLANS/SPECIAL FEATURES:

ADTRAN, Inc. designs, manufactures, markets and services network access applications for communications networks for use across IP, Asynchronous Transfer Mode (ATM) and Time Division Multiplexed (TDM) architectures. The company's products are used to enable voice, data, video and Internet communications across copper, fiber and wireless networks; to deploy new broadband networks; and to upgrade slower, established networks. ADTRAN operates in two segments: carrier networks, which accounts for about 78.6% of net sales, and enterprise networks, about 21.4% of sales. The carrier networks division caters to service providers with products that deliver voice, data and video services from their equipment to a customer's premises. The enterprise networks division provides products used by enterprise customers to construct voice, data and video networks within an enterprise customer's site or between distributed sites. ADTRAN sells over 1,800 high-speed network access and communications devices. All of the company's products are used to link end-user subscribers to a local service provider, called last mile access products. Products fall into three categories: carrier systems, business networking and loop access. Carrier systems include broadband access and optical access product lines, as well as the Total Access 5000 multi-service access and aggregation platform. The business networking category includes Integrated Access Devices (IADs), Optical Network Terminals (ONTs) and Internetworking products such as IP Business Gateways and the NetVanta product line, which includes multi-service routers, managed Ethernet switches and IP phone products. The loop access category includes products such as Digital Data Service (DDS), Integrated Services Digital Network (Total Reach) products and High bit-rate Digital Subscriber Line (HDSL) products, including Total Access 3000 HDSL.

Employees are offered medical, dental and vision insurance; life and disability insurance; flexible spending accounts; an employee assistance program; on-site medical services; a 401(k) plan; education assistance; and a computer purchase plan.

FINANCIALS: **Sales and profits are in thousands of dollars—add 000 to get the full amount. 2011 Note: Financial information for 2011 was not available for all companies at press time.**

2011 Sales: $717,000 | 2011 Profits: $138,577
2010 Sales: $605,674 | 2010 Profits: $113,989
2009 Sales: $484,185 | 2009 Profits: $74,221
2008 Sales: $500,676 | 2008 Profits: $78,581
2007 Sales: $476,778 | 2007 Profits: $76,335

U.S. Stock Ticker: ADTN
Int'l Ticker:
Int'l Exchange:
Employees: 1,663 Fiscal Year Ends: 12/31
Parent Company:

SALARIES/BENEFITS:

Pension Plan:	ESOP Stock Plan:	Profit Sharing:	Top Exec. Salary: $510,000	Bonus: $1,310,000
Savings Plan: Y	Stock Purch. Plan:		Second Exec. Salary: $300,000	Bonus: $320,000

OTHER THOUGHTS:

Apparent Women Officers or Directors: 2
Hot Spot for Advancement for Women/Minorities:

LOCATIONS: ("Y" = Yes)

West:	Southwest:	Midwest:	Southeast:	Northeast:	International:
Y	Y	Y	Y		Y

ADVISORY BOARD COMPANY (THE) www.advisoryboardcompany.com

Industry Group Code: 54161

Management:		Sales/Marketing:		Liberal Arts:		Information Systems:		Professionals:		Technical/Scientific:	
Mgmt. Trainees:		Mktg. Professionals:	Y	Gen. Writing/Editing:	Y	Info. Management:	Y	Finance/Acct.:	Y	Engineers, Elec.:	
Experienced Mgmt.:	Y	Retail Sales:		Technical Writing:	Y	Software Dev.:	Y	Law:	Y	Engineers, Other:	
Int'l Business:	Y	Commercial/Industrial:	Y	Graphic Arts/Photog.:		Hardware Dev.:		HR/Other:	Y	Health/Lab	
MBA Graduates:	Y	Sales Trainees:	Y	Music:		Consulting/Other:	Y	Training:	Y	Scientists/Research:	
		Advertising Pros.:		Broadcasting:				Health Care:		Petroleum/Chemicals:	
				Other:	Y			Consulting:	Y	Math/Other:	

TYPES OF BUSINESS:

Consulting-Best Management Practices
Executive Conferences & Seminars
Research Reports & Databases
Health Care Sector Consulting
Education Sector Consulting

BRANDS/DIVISIONS/AFFILIATES:

CONTACTS:

Note: Officers with more than one job title may be intentionally listed here more than once.

Robert W. Musslewhite, CEO
David L. Felsenthal, Pres.
Michael T. Kirshbaum, CFO
Mary D. Van Hoose, Chief Talent Officer
Cormac F. Miller, Exec. Dir.-New Prod. Dev. & Strategic Planning
Evan R. Farber, General Counsel/Corp Sec.
Richard A. Schwartz, Exec. VP-Strategic Planning
Michael T. Kirshbaum, Treas.
Scott A. Schirmeier, Exec. VP
Martin D. Coulter, Exec. Dir.-Business Intelligence & Software
Frank J. Williams, Chmn.

Phone: 202-266-5600	**Fax:** 202-266-5700
Toll-Free:	
Address: 2445 M St. NW, Washington, DC 20037 US	

GROWTH PLANS/SPECIAL FEATURES:

The Advisory Board Company (ABC) is a provider of research and advisory services to the healthcare and education sectors. Its services include best practices research and analysis; executive education; leadership development; business intelligence and software tools; installation support; and advisory services management. The firm serves over 3,200 members including hospitals, health systems, pharmaceutical and biotech companies, health care insurers, medical device companies, universities and other educational institutions. In total, ABC's programs reach more than 6,900 CEOs and COOs and 81,500 senior executives, health care management professionals, department heads and product-line managers. The firm offers roughly 50 distinct membership programs, each targeting the issues of a specific executive constituency or business function. Examples of ABC's membership programs include the heath care advisory board, which monitors, reports and provides support services to members on issues affecting hospitals and health systems; the health care industry committee, which researches clinical, financial, operational and policy changes likely to affect the industry; and the nursing leadership academy, which offers courses on leadership, business and operations skills specific to roles in nursing. Other programs are aimed at maximizing overall hospital profitability and efficiency. Sales to the health care market currently represent the bulk of ABC's sales, while its education clients generate about 5% of its revenues. ABC has domestic offices in Washington, D.C.; Austin, Texas; Chicago, Illinois; Nashville, Tennessee; Ann Arbor, Michigan; Portland, Oregon; and San Francisco, California. The firm also maintains an office in Chennai, India.

Employee are offered medical, dental and vision insurance; life, AD&D and disability coverage; a 401(k) plan; an employee assistance program; gym, computer and retail discounts; and flexible spending accounts.

FINANCIALS:

Sales and profits are in thousands of dollars—add 000 to get the full amount. 2011 Note: Financial information for 2011 was not available for all companies at press time.

2011 Sales: $290,248	2011 Profits: $18,524	**U.S. Stock Ticker: ABCO**
2010 Sales: $239,323	2010 Profits: $11,433	**Int'l Ticker:**
2009 Sales: $230,360	2009 Profits: $21,468	Int'l Exchange:
2008 Sales: $218,971	2008 Profits: $32,062	Employees: 1,600 Fiscal Year Ends: 3/31
2007 Sales: $189,843	2007 Profits: $27,395	Parent Company:

SALARIES/BENEFITS:

Pension Plan:	ESOP Stock Plan:	Profit Sharing:	Top Exec. Salary: $500,000	Bonus: $640,000
Savings Plan: Y	Stock Purch. Plan:		Second Exec. Salary: $425,000	Bonus: $512,000

OTHER THOUGHTS:

Apparent Women Officers or Directors: 2
Hot Spot for Advancement for Women/Minorities:

LOCATIONS: ("Y" = Yes)

West:	Southwest:	Midwest:	Southeast:	Northeast:	International:
Y	Y	Y	Y	Y	Y

AFFILIATED MANAGERS GROUP

www.amg.com

Industry Group Code: 523920

Management:		**Sales/Marketing:**		**Liberal Arts:**		**Information Systems:**		**Professionals:**		**Technical/Scientific:**	
Mgmt. Trainees:		Mktg. Professionals:	Y	Gen. Writing/Editing:		Info. Management:	Y	Finance/Acct.:	Y	Engineers, Elec.:	
Experienced Mgmt.:	Y	Retail Sales:		Technical Writing:		Software Dev.:		Law:	Y	Engineers, Other:	
Int'l Business:	Y	Commercial/Industrial:		Graphic Arts/Photog.:		Hardware Dev.:		HR/Other:	Y	Health/Lab	
MBA Graduates:	Y	Sales Trainees:		Music:		Consulting/Other:		Training:		Scientists/Research:	
		Advertising Pros.:		Broadcasting:				Health Care:		Petroleum/Chemicals:	
				Other:				Consulting:		Math/Other:	Y

TYPES OF BUSINESS:

Investment Management
Mutual Funds

BRANDS/DIVISIONS/AFFILIATES:

AMG Wealth Partners

CONTACTS:

Note: Officers with more than one job title may be intentionally listed here more than once.

Sean M. Healey, CEO
Nathaniel Dalton, COO/Exec. VP
Nathaniel Dalton, Pres.
Jay C. Horgen, CFO
John Kingston, III, General Counsel/Vice Chrm
Peter MacEwen, Sr. VP-Capital Planning
Riz Jamal, Sr. VP-Investor Rel., AMG Affiliates
Dean A. Maines, Chief Acct. Officer/Sr. VP
Jeffrey S. Murphy, Sr. VP-Affiliate Dev.
Lewis Collins, Sr. VP-Legal Compliance
Daniel J. Shea, Sr. VP-Acct., Tax & Financial Reporting
Sean M. Healey, Chmn.
Andrew Dyson, Head-Global Div./Exec. VP

Phone: 617-747-3300 **Fax:** 617-747-3380
Toll-Free:
Address: 600 Hale St., Prides Crossing, MA 01965 US

GROWTH PLANS/SPECIAL FEATURES:

Affiliated Managers Group (AMG) is a global asset management company with equity investments in a diverse group of boutique investment management firms (its affiliates) in three principal distribution channels: mutual fund, institutional and high-net-worth. Through its mutual fund distribution channel, AMG provides advisory or sub-advisory services to more than 100 mutual funds, which are distributed to retail and institutional clients directly and through intermediaries, including independent investment advisors, retirement plan sponsors, broker-dealers, major fund marketplaces and bank trust deposits. Through its institutional distribution channel, AMG offers 200 investment products across approximately 50 different investment styles. In addition, its affiliates offer quantitative, alternative, credit arbitrage and fixed income products. The company's high-net-worth distribution channel is comprised broadly of two client groups. The first group consists principally of high net worth individuals, families and charitable foundations. For these clients, affiliates provide investment management or customized investment counseling and fiduciary services. Within this group, the company is currently distributing around 30 investment products managed by six affiliates. The second group consists of individual managed account client relationships established through intermediaries, generally brokerage firms or other sponsors. AMG operates by acquiring a controlling interest in a firm, but allowing it to retain independence and autonomy of operations and remaining equity interests. Company growth stems from the internal growth of its affiliate companies as well as investments in new affiliates. AMG's affiliated firms manage $306 billion in assets for over 350 investment products across the world. In 2011, AMG expanded its presence and global institutional distribution into the Asian marketplace with the opening of an office in Hong Kong. In June 2011, John Copeland was appointed President of AMG Wealth Partners, a newly formed subsidiary focused on investments in boutique wealth management firms.

FINANCIALS:

Sales and profits are in thousands of dollars—add 000 to get the full amount. 2011 Note: Financial information for 2011 was not available for all companies at press time.

2011 Sales: $	2011 Profits: $
2010 Sales: $1,358,242	2010 Profits: $287,328
2009 Sales: $841,840	2009 Profits: $212,916
2008 Sales: $1,158,217	2008 Profits: $23,170
2007 Sales: $1,369,866	2007 Profits: $181,961

U.S. Stock Ticker: AMG
Int'l Ticker:
Int'l Exchange:
Employees: 1,910 Fiscal Year Ends: 12/31
Parent Company:

SALARIES/BENEFITS:

Pension Plan:	ESOP Stock Plan:	Profit Sharing:	Top Exec. Salary: $750,000	Bonus: $7,000,000
Savings Plan:	Stock Purch. Plan:		Second Exec. Salary: $500,000	Bonus: $3,500,000

OTHER THOUGHTS:

Apparent Women Officers or Directors: 5
Hot Spot for Advancement for Women/Minorities: Y

LOCATIONS: ("Y" = Yes)

West:	Southwest:	Midwest:	Southeast:	Northeast:	International:
				Y	Y

AKAMAI TECHNOLOGIES INC

www.akamai.com

Industry Group Code: 518210

Management:		**Sales/Marketing:**		**Liberal Arts:**		**Information Systems:**		**Professionals:**		**Technical/Scientific:**	
Mgmt. Trainees:		Mktg. Professionals:	Y	Gen. Writing/Editing:	Y	Info. Management:	Y	Finance/Acct.:	Y	Engineers, Elec.:	Y
Experienced Mgmt.:	Y	Retail Sales:		Technical Writing:	Y	Software Dev.:	Y	Law:	Y	Engineers, Other:	
Int'l Business:	Y	Commercial/Industrial:	Y	Graphic Arts/Photog.:		Hardware Dev.:		HR/Other:	Y	Health/Lab	
MBA Graduates:	Y	Sales Trainees:	Y	Music:		Consulting/Other:		Training:	Y	Scientists/Research:	
		Advertising Pros.:		Broadcasting:				Health Care:		Petroleum/Chemicals:	
				Other:				Consulting:		Math/Other:	

TYPES OF BUSINESS:

Online Information Service-Streaming Content
e-Business Software
Web Analytics
Online Content Distribution Support Services

BRANDS/DIVISIONS/AFFILIATES:

CONTACTS:

Note: Officers with more than one job title may be intentionally listed here more than once.

Paul Sagan, CEO
Paul Sagan, Pres.
J. D. Sherman, CFO
Robert W. Hughes, Exec. VP-Global Sales, Mktg & Svcs.
Debra L. Canner, Sr. VP-Human Resources
Tom Leighton, Chief Scientist
Kumud Kalia, CIO
Rick McConnell, Exec. VP-Prod. & Dev.
Melanie Haratunian, General Counsel/Sr. VP/Corp. Sec.
Robert Wood, Chief Dev. Officer/Sr. VP
Michael M. Afergan, Sr. VP/Gen. Mgr.-Site Div.
Robert Blumofe, Sr. VP-Platform Div.
Chris Schoettle, Exec. VP-Bus. Transformation
Willie M. Tejada, Sr. VP/Gen. Mgr.-Enterprise Cloud Div.
George Conrades, Chmn.
David Rich, VP-Asia Pacific

Phone: 617-444-3000 **Fax:** 617-444-3001
Toll-Free: 877-425-2624
Address: 8 Cambridge Ctr., Cambridge, MA 02142 US

GROWTH PLANS/SPECIAL FEATURES:

Akamai Technologies, Inc. is a software and Internet content company that provides enterprise and government clients with e-business infrastructure services, enabling them to deliver web content and applications such as ads, videos and games at higher speeds and with greater reliability. Akamai's cloud-based distribution network is one of the largest in the world, consisting of 95,000 servers within 1,900 networks in 71 countries, handling billions of web interactions each day. Service offerings are broadly grouped into five areas: Application Performance Solutions; Digital Asset Solutions; Advertising Decision Solutions; Dynamic Site Solutions; and Other Solutions. Application Performance Solutions are designed to improve the performance of dynamic applications used by enterprises to connect with their employees, suppliers and customers, with a particular focus on portal applications and other web-based systems. Digital Asset Solutions allow customers to execute large file management and distribution strategies while improving end-user experience and reducing the costs associated with Internet-related infrastructure. Advertising Decision Solutions specialize in helping advertisers reach their target audiences online. Dynamic Site Solutions help to accelerate business-to-consumer web sites that integrate rich, collaborative content and applications within their online architecture, allowing for greater process optimization as well as localization and customization of content. Other Solutions consist of site intelligence, security and custom solutions. Site intelligence offerings encompass network data feeds and web site analytics, giving clients real time site performance data. Security solutions address Internet security issues, including payment security and malicious attack protection. Custom solutions include a range of individualized services, such as facilitating content delivery behind firewalls and supporting mission-critical applications relying on intranets. In December 2011, Akamai agreed to acquire Cotendo, a developer of cloud-based acceleration technologies.

Akamai offers its employees medical, dental and vision coverage; short- and long-term disability; a 401(k) plan; life and AD&D insurance; and an employee stock purchase plan, among other benefits.

FINANCIALS:

Sales and profits are in thousands of dollars—add 000 to get the full amount. 2011 Note: Financial information for 2011 was not available for all companies at press time.

2011 Sales: $1,158,500	2011 Profits: $200,900	**U.S. Stock Ticker: AKAM**
2010 Sales: $1,023,586	2010 Profits: $171,220	**Int'l Ticker:**
2009 Sales: $859,773	2009 Profits: $145,913	Int'l Exchange:
2008 Sales: $790,924	2008 Profits: $212,264	Employees: 2,200 Fiscal Year Ends: 12/31
2007 Sales: $636,406	2007 Profits: $100,967	Parent Company:

SALARIES/BENEFITS:

Pension Plan:	ESOP Stock Plan:	Profit Sharing:	Top Exec. Salary: $602,710	Bonus: $1,375,430
Savings Plan: Y	Stock Purch. Plan: Y		Second Exec. Salary: $430,166	Bonus: $561,958

OTHER THOUGHTS:

Apparent Women Officers or Directors: 5
Hot Spot for Advancement for Women/Minorities: Y

LOCATIONS: ("Y" = Yes)

West:	Southwest:	Midwest:	Southeast:	Northeast:	International:
Y	Y	Y	Y	Y	Y

AKORN INC

Industry Group Code: 325412

www.akorn.com

Management:		Sales/Marketing:		Liberal Arts:		Information Systems:		Professionals:		Technical/Scientific:	
Mgmt. Trainees:		Mktg. Professionals:	Y	Gen. Writing/Editing:		Info. Management:	Y	Finance/Acct.:	Y	Engineers, Elec.:	
Experienced Mgmt.:	Y	Retail Sales:		Technical Writing:	Y	Software Dev.:	Y	Law:	Y	Engineers, Other:	
Int'l Business:		Commercial/Industrial:	Y	Graphic Arts/Photog.:		Hardware Dev.:		HR/Other:	Y	Health/Lab	Y
MBA Graduates:	Y	Sales Trainees:	Y	Music:		Consulting/Other:		Training:	Y	Scientists/Research:	Y
		Advertising Pros.:		Broadcasting:				Health Care:	Y	Petroleum/Chemicals:	Y
				Other:				Consulting:		Math/Other:	Y

TYPES OF BUSINESS:

Ophthalmic & Hospital Drugs & Injectables
Contract Manufacturing Services

BRANDS/DIVISIONS/AFFILIATES:

Akorn (New Jersey), Inc.
Akorn-Strides, LLC
Advanced Vision Research, Inc.
TheraTears
MacuTrition

CONTACTS: *Note: Officers with more than one job title may be intentionally listed here more than once.*

Raj Rai, CEO
Timothy Dick, CFO
John R. Sabat, Sr. VP-Global Sales & Mktg.
Sean Brynjelsen, VP-R&D & New Bus. Dev.
Mark M. Silverberg, Exec. VP-Tech. Svcs.
Joseph Bonaccorsi, General Counsel/Sr. VP/Sec.
Mark M. Silverberg, Exec. VP-Oper. & Global Quality Assurance
Bruce Kutinsky, Sr. VP-Corp. Strategy
John R. Sabat, Sr. VP-National Accounts
Sam Boddapati, Sr. VP-Regulatory Affairs
Michael P. Stehn, Sr. VP-Oper.
John N. Kapoor, Chmn.

Phone: 847-279-6100	**Fax:** 800-943-3694
Toll-Free: 800-932-5676	
Address: 1925 W. Field Ct., Ste. 300, Lake Forest, IL 60045 US	

GROWTH PLANS/SPECIAL FEATURES:

Akorn, Inc. provides diagnostic and therapeutic pharmaceuticals for specialty areas such as ophthalmology, rheumatology, anesthesia and antidotal medicine. The company operates in four segments: ophthalmic, which accounted for 38% of its 2010 revenue; hospital drugs and injectables, 33%; contract services, 23%; and biologics and vaccines, 6%. The ophthalmic division markets a line of diagnostic and therapeutic products for eye health. Diagnostic products, primarily used in the office setting, include mydriatics, cycloplegics, anesthetics, topical stains, gonioscopic solutions and angiography dyes. Therapeutic products, sold primarily to wholesalers and other national account customers, include antibiotics, anti-infectives, steroids, glaucoma medications, decongestants /antihistamines and anti-edema medications. Non-pharmaceutical products include various artificial tear solutions, lubricating ointments and contact lens accessories. Through the hospital drugs and injectables segment, Akorn markets a line of specialty products, including antidotes, anesthesia and treatments for rheumatoid arthritis and pain management. The contract services segment manufactures products for third-party pharmaceutical and biotechnology customers based on their specifications. The biologics and vaccines segment, which the firm discontinued in early 2010, focused on adult Tetanus-Diphtheria vaccines, as well as the production of flu vaccines. Akorn (New Jersey), Inc., a wholly-owned subsidiary, is involved in manufacturing, product development and administrative activities related to the ophthalmic and hospital drugs and injectables segments. Additionally, the firm maintained Akorn-Strides, LLC, a joint venture with Strides Arcolab Limited that focused on developing liquid, lyophilized and dry powder formulations of generic injectable drugs. In December 2010, the company sold the product portfolio controlled by this joint venture to Pfizer, Inc. In May 2011, Akorn agreed to acquire Advanced Vision Research, Inc., a premier OTC ophthalmic company that markets eye care products under the TheraTears and MacuTrition brand names.

Employees are offered medical, dental and vision insurance; flexible spending accounts; life insurance; adoption assistance; an employee assistance program; and educational assistance.

FINANCIALS: **Sales and profits are in thousands of dollars—add 000 to get the full amount. 2011 Note: Financial information for 2011 was not available for all companies at press time.**

2011 Sales: $	2011 Profits: $	**U.S. Stock Ticker: AKRX**
2010 Sales: $86,409	2010 Profits: $21,824	**Int'l Ticker:**
2009 Sales: $75,891	2009 Profits: $-25,306	Int'l Exchange:
2008 Sales: $93,598	2008 Profits: $-7,939	Employees: 410 Fiscal Year Ends: 12/31
2007 Sales: $52,895	2007 Profits: $-19,168	Parent Company:

SALARIES/BENEFITS:

Pension Plan:	ESOP Stock Plan:	Profit Sharing:	Top Exec. Salary: $263,900	Bonus: $118,800
Savings Plan: Y	Stock Purch. Plan: Y		Second Exec. Salary: $260,870	Bonus: $112,752

OTHER THOUGHTS:

Apparent Women Officers or Directors:
Hot Spot for Advancement for Women/Minorities:

LOCATIONS: ("Y" = Yes)

West:	Southwest:	Midwest:	Southeast:	Northeast:	International:
		Y		Y	

AKQA INC

www.akqa.com

Industry Group Code: 541810E

Management:		Sales/Marketing:		Liberal Arts:		Information Systems:		Professionals:		Technical/Scientific:	
Mgmt. Trainees:		Mktg. Professionals:	Y	Gen. Writing/Editing:	Y	Info. Management:	Y	Finance/Acct.:	Y	Engineers, Elec.:	
Experienced Mgmt.:	Y	Retail Sales:		Technical Writing:		Software Dev.:	Y	Law:	Y	Engineers, Other:	
Int'l Business:	Y	Commercial/Industrial:	Y	Graphic Arts/Photog.:	Y	Hardware Dev.:		HR/Other:	Y	Health/Lab	
MBA Graduates:	Y	Sales Trainees:	Y	Music:		Consulting/Other:		Training:	Y	Scientists/Research:	
		Advertising Pros.:	Y	Broadcasting:				Health Care:		Petroleum/Chemicals:	
				Other:				Consulting:		Math/Other:	

TYPES OF BUSINESS:

Online Marketing
E-Mail Marketing
Web Site Design
Web Site Hosting

BRANDS/DIVISIONS/AFFILIATES:

AKQA Film

CONTACTS:

Note: Officers with more than one job title may be intentionally listed here more than once.

Tom Bedecarre, CEO
Jim Rossman, COO
Jim Rossman, Pres.
Ajaz Ahmed, Chmn.

Phone: 415-645-9400	**Fax:** 415-645-9420
Toll-Free:	
Address: 118 King St., 6th Fl., San Francisco, CA 94107 US	

GROWTH PLANS/SPECIAL FEATURES:

A.K.Q.A., Inc. is a digital advertising firm with locations in San Francisco, New York, Washington, D.C., London, Amsterdam and Shanghai. The company creates web sites, conducts e-mail marketing campaigns and produces online interactive advertising. Additionally, the firm offers web site hosting services to clients. A.K.Q.A. has worked with media such as feature films, mobile phones, kiosks, digital organizers, DVDs and interactive TV. A.K.Q.A. Mobile works with clients to create digital products, services and content for the mobile platform. A.K.Q.A. Search provides search engine optimization and marketing. Clients include VolksWagon, Smirnoff, Unilever, X-Box 360, Heineken, Nike, Fiat, Ferrari, The GAP, Warner Brothers, Sprite, Visa; Bethesda; and the United States Postal Service (USPS). Among the company's most notable achievements is the design of Microsoft's X-Box 360 console interface. The firm also offers AKQA Film, a distributor and creator of digital programming, aimed at independent projects.

FINANCIALS:

Sales and profits are in thousands of dollars—add 000 to get the full amount. 2011 Note: Financial information for 2011 was not available for all companies at press time.

2011 Sales: $	2011 Profits: $	**U.S. Stock Ticker: Private**
2010 Sales: $	2010 Profits: $	**Int'l Ticker:**
2009 Sales: $	2009 Profits: $	Int'l Exchange:
2008 Sales: $	2008 Profits: $	Employees: Fiscal Year Ends:
2007 Sales: $	2007 Profits: $	Parent Company:

SALARIES/BENEFITS:

Pension Plan:	ESOP Stock Plan:	Profit Sharing:	Top Exec. Salary: $	Bonus: $
Savings Plan:	Stock Purch. Plan:		Second Exec. Salary: $	Bonus: $

OTHER THOUGHTS:

Apparent Women Officers or Directors:
Hot Spot for Advancement for Women/Minorities:

LOCATIONS: ("Y" = Yes)

West:	Southwest:	Midwest:	Southeast:	Northeast:	International:
Y				Y	Y

Sales, profits and employees may be estimates. Financial information, benefits and other data can change quickly and may vary from those stated here.

ALBANY MOLECULAR RESEARCH INC

www.amriglobal.com

Industry Group Code: 541712

Management:		**Sales/Marketing:**		**Liberal Arts:**		**Information Systems:**		**Professionals:**		**Technical/Scientific:**	
Mgmt. Trainees:		Mktg. Professionals:	Y	Gen. Writing/Editing:		Info. Management:	Y	Finance/Acct.:	Y	Engineers, Elec.:	
Experienced Mgmt.:	Y	Retail Sales:		Technical Writing:	Y	Software Dev.:	Y	Law:	Y	Engineers, Other:	
Int'l Business:	Y	Commercial/Industrial:	Y	Graphic Arts/Photog.:		Hardware Dev.:		HR/Other:	Y	Health/Lab	Y
MBA Graduates:	Y	Sales Trainees:		Music:		Consulting/Other:		Training:	Y	Scientists/Research:	Y
		Advertising Pros.:		Broadcasting:				Health Care:	Y	Petroleum/Chemicals:	
				Other:				Consulting:		Math/Other:	Y

TYPES OF BUSINESS:

Contract Drug Discovery & Development
Custom Biotech & Genomic Research
Chemistry Research
Manufacturing Services
Consulting Services
Analytical Chemistry Services

BRANDS/DIVISIONS/AFFILIATES:

Allegra
Telfast
Proteros Biostructures GmbH
BioPontis Alliance LLC
Revolymer
Rev7
Eli Lilly and Company

CONTACTS:

Note: Officers with more than one job title may be intentionally listed here more than once.

Thomas E. D'Ambra, CEO
Thomas E. D'Ambra, Pres.
Mark T. Frost, CFO
Brian D. Russell, VP-Human Resources
Bruce J. Sargent, Sr. VP-Drug Discovery
Steven R. Hagen, VP-Pharmaceutical Mfg. & Dev.
Mark T. Frost, Sr. VP-Admin.
Lori M. Henderson, General Counsel/VP/Sec.
Mark T. Frost, Treas.
Thomas E. D'Ambra, Chmn.

Phone: 518-464-0279	**Fax:** 518-512-2020
Toll-Free:	
Address: 26 Corporate Cir., Albany, NY 12212 US	

GROWTH PLANS/SPECIAL FEATURES:

Albany Molecular Research, Inc. (AMRI) provides scientific services, technologies and products. Its fee-for-service contract services platform encompasses drug discovery; development and manufacturing services; and a separate technology division. Drug discovery services include medicinal chemistry, drug metabolism and pharmacokinetics (DMPK) and in vitro biology. The development division focuses on small scale manufacturing of products mostly used in clinical trials, as well as provides custom research and analytical discovery services for the pharmaceutical, genomic and biotechnology industries. The separate technology division consists of proprietary technology investments, internal drug discovery and niche generic active pharmaceutical ingredient product development. It derives revenue from discovering then licensing new compounds with commercial potential for service fees, milestone and royalty payments. AMRI's research led to the development of the active ingredient fexofenadine HCl, used in non-sedating antihistamines for brands Allegra and Telfast. The company also provides contract services across the entire product development cycle, from lead discovery to commercial manufacturing. The firm's services allow pharmaceutical companies to outsource their chemistry departments in order to pursue a greater number of drug discovery and development opportunities. An integral part of these contract operations consists of facilities in India, Hungary and Singapore, which were launched as part of a strategic move to globalize its services. Throughout 2011, the firm partnered with a variety of companies, making a preferred provider agreement with BioPontis Alliance LLC to provide molecule and drug research discovery; a supply agreement with Revolymer to become the primary manufacturer and supplier of Rev7; a collaboration agreement with Eli Lilly and Company to produce 40 synthetic chemicals; and a strategic alliance with Proteros Biostructures GmbH.

FINANCIALS:

Sales and profits are in thousands of dollars—add 000 to get the full amount. 2011 Note: Financial information for 2011 was not available for all companies at press time.

2011 Sales: $	2011 Profits: $	**U.S. Stock Ticker: AMRI**
2010 Sales: $198,066	2010 Profits: $-62,871	**Int'l Ticker:**
2009 Sales: $196,417	2009 Profits: $-16,695	Int'l Exchange:
2008 Sales: $229,260	2008 Profits: $20,560	Employees: 1,421 Fiscal Year Ends: 12/31
2007 Sales: $192,511	2007 Profits: $8,936	Parent Company:

SALARIES/BENEFITS:

Pension Plan:	ESOP Stock Plan:	Profit Sharing:	Top Exec. Salary: $438,462	Bonus: $60,000
Savings Plan: Y	Stock Purch. Plan:		Second Exec. Salary: $353,635	Bonus: $

OTHER THOUGHTS:

Apparent Women Officers or Directors: 3
Hot Spot for Advancement for Women/Minorities: Y

LOCATIONS: ("Y" = Yes)

West:	Southwest:	Midwest:	Southeast:	Northeast:	International:
				Y	Y

ALEXANDER & BALDWIN INC

www.alexanderbaldwin.com

Industry Group Code: 483111

Management:		Sales/Marketing:		Liberal Arts:		Information Systems:		Professionals:		Technical/Scientific:	
Mgmt. Trainees:		Mktg. Professionals:	Y	Gen. Writing/Editing:		Info. Management:	Y	Finance/Acct.:	Y	Engineers, Elec.:	
Experienced Mgmt.:	Y	Retail Sales:		Technical Writing:		Software Dev.:		Law:	Y	Engineers, Other:	
Int'l Business:	Y	Commercial/Industrial:	Y	Graphic Arts/Photog.:		Hardware Dev.:		HR/Other:	Y	Health/Lab	
MBA Graduates:	Y	Sales Trainees:	Y	Music:		Consulting/Other:		Training:		Scientists/Research:	
		Advertising Pros.:		Broadcasting:				Health Care:		Petroleum/Chemicals:	
				Other:				Consulting:		Math/Other:	

TYPES OF BUSINESS:

Property Management & Development
Coffee & Sugar Plantations
Logistics
Deep Sea Freight Transportation
Rail & Highway Transportation
Electrical Generation
Port Operations

BRANDS/DIVISIONS/AFFILIATES:

A&B Properties Inc
Hawaiian Commercial & Sugar Company
Kauai Coffee Company
Matson Navigation Company
Matson Integrated Logistics
Kahului Trucking and Storage Co

CONTACTS: *Note: Officers with more than one job title may be intentionally listed here more than once.*

Stanley M. Kuriyama, CEO
Stanley M. Kuriyama, Pres.
Joel M. Wine, CFO/Sr. VP/Treas.
Son-Jai Paik, VP-Human Resources
Nelson N. S. Chun, Chief Legal Officer/Sr. VP
Meredith J. Ching, Sr. VP-Gov't & Community Rel.
Suzy P. Hollinger, Dir.-Investor Rel.
Paul K. Ito, Controller/VP
Alyson J. Nakamura, Sec.
Matthew J. Cox, Pres., Matson Navigation Company, Inc.
Christopher J. Benjamin, Pres., A&B Land Group
Walter A. Dods, Jr., Chmn.

Phone: 808-525-6611 **Fax:** 808-525-6652
Toll-Free:
Address: 822 Bishop St., Honolulu, HI 96813 US

GROWTH PLANS/SPECIAL FEATURES:

Alexander & Baldwin, Inc. (A&B) is a diversified corporation that deals principally in property management and development, sugar and coffee production and ocean transportation. The company, along with its subsidiary, A&B Properties, Inc., owns and manages 88,298 acres of land, consisting of 87,840 acres in Hawaii and 458 acres in California, Texas, Georgia, Utah, Arizona, Nevada and Colorado. Uses of A&B land include master-planned communities, managed watersheds, industrial parks, resort residential developments, agricultural activities, leased commercial properties and others. The company's food production arm, Hawaiian Commercial & Sugar Company (HC&S), grows and mills sugarcane; produces raw sugar, specialty sugar and molasses; and generates and sells electricity. HC&S operates a 36,000-acre Maui plantation that produces approximately 171,800 tons of sugar a year. Sugars are sold under the Maui Brand trademark or repackaged by distributors under their own labels. A&B also operates Kauai Coffee Company, which operates a coffee plantation and sells green bean coffee, as well as packaged coffee under the Kauai Coffee trademark; and Kahului Trucking and Storage, Inc., which provides sugar and molasses hauling and storage. Matson Navigation Company, A&B's largest subsidiary, headquartered in Oakland, California, is a leading U.S. ocean carrier operating in the Pacific. It is a large carrier of containerized freight and automobiles between the U.S. Pacific coast and Hawaii, Guam, China and the mid-Pacific. Matson's fleet consists of 10 containerships, three combination container/trailer ships, one roll-on/roll-off barge, two container barges equipped with cranes that service Hawaii and one container barge equipped with cranes that is available for charter. Matson Integrated Logistics (MIL) provides multimodal transportation services to the North American market. MIL's capabilities include domestic and international intermodal rail service; long-haul and regional highway services; specialized hauling; and international air freight.

FINANCIALS: **Sales and profits are in thousands of dollars—add 000 to get the full amount. 2011 Note: Financial information for 2011 was not available for all companies at press time.**

2011 Sales: $1,722,400 | 2011 Profits: $34,200
2010 Sales: $1,646,200 | 2010 Profits: $92,100
2009 Sales: $1,396,600 | 2009 Profits: $44,200
2008 Sales: $1,871,000 | 2008 Profits: $132,400
2007 Sales: $1,651,000 | 2007 Profits: $142,000

U.S. Stock Ticker: ALEX
Int'l Ticker:
Int'l Exchange:
Employees: 2,300 Fiscal Year Ends: 12/31
Parent Company:

SALARIES/BENEFITS:

Pension Plan: Y | ESOP Stock Plan: | Profit Sharing: Y | Top Exec. Salary: $615,000 | Bonus: $615,000
Savings Plan: Y | Stock Purch. Plan: | | Second Exec. Salary: $414,769 | Bonus: $482,994

OTHER THOUGHTS:

Apparent Women Officers or Directors: 4
Hot Spot for Advancement for Women/Minorities: Y

LOCATIONS: ("Y" = Yes)

West:	Southwest:	Midwest:	Southeast:	Northeast:	International:
Y	Y	Y	Y	Y	Y

ALEXION PHARMACEUTICALS INC

www.alexionpharm.com

Industry Group Code: 325412

Management:		Sales/Marketing:		Liberal Arts:		Information Systems:		Professionals:		Technical/Scientific:	
Mgmt. Trainees:		Mktg. Professionals:	Y	Gen. Writing/Editing:		Info. Management:	Y	Finance/Acct.:	Y	Engineers, Elec.:	
Experienced Mgmt.:	Y	Retail Sales:		Technical Writing:	Y	Software Dev.:	Y	Law:	Y	Engineers, Other:	
Int'l Business:	Y	Commercial/Industrial:	Y	Graphic Arts/Photog.:		Hardware Dev.:		HR/Other:	Y	Health/Lab	Y
MBA Graduates:	Y	Sales Trainees:	Y	Music:		Consulting/Other:		Training:	Y	Scientists/Research:	Y
		Advertising Pros.:		Broadcasting:				Health Care:	Y	Petroleum/Chemicals:	Y
				Other:				Consulting:		Math/Other:	Y

TYPES OF BUSINESS:

Therapeutic Products
Hematologic Diseases
Neurological Diseases
Oncology
Autoimmune Disorders

BRANDS/DIVISIONS/AFFILIATES:

Soliris
Alexion Europe SAS
Taligen Pharmaceuticals Inc
Orphatc Pharmaceuticals GmbH
Enobia Pharma Corp

CONTACTS:

Note: Officers with more than one job title may be intentionally listed here more than once.

Leonard Bell, CEO
Vikas Sinha, CFO/Sr. VP
Clare Carmichael, Chief Human Resources Officer/Sr. VP
Camille Bedrosian, Chief Medical Officer/Sr. VP
James Bilotta, CIO/VP
M. Stacy Hooks, Sr. VP-Tech. Oper.
Claude Nicaise, Sr. VP-Strategic Prod. Dev. & Regulatory Affairs
Daniel Caron, VP-Eng. & Site Oper.
Thomas Dubin, Chief Legal Officer/Sr. VP
David Hallal, Sr. VP-Global Commercial Oper.
Jeremy Springhorn, VP-Corp. Strategy & Bus. Dev.
Heidi Wafner, VP-Global Gov't Affairs
Leonard Bell, Treas./Sec.
Stephen P. Squinto, Head-R&D/Exec. VP
Thomas Bock, Sr. VP-Global Medical Affairs
Max Link, Chmn.
Patrice Coissac, Pres., Alexion Int'l Sarl/Sr. VP

Phone: 203-272-2596 **Fax:** 203-271-8190
Toll-Free:
Address: 352 Knotter Dr., Cheshire, CT 06410 US

GROWTH PLANS/SPECIAL FEATURES:

Alexion Pharmaceuticals, Inc. engages in the discovery, development and commercialization of therapeutic products designed to treat patients with severe illnesses such as hematologic diseases, neurologic disease, cancer and autoimmune disorders. The company devotes substantially all of its resources to drug discovery, research, and product and clinical development. The firm has one marketed product, Soliris (eculizumab), the first therapy approved for the treatment of paroxysmal nocturnal hemoglobinuria (PNH). PNH is a rare genetic deficiency blood disorder in which a patient's own complement system attacks and destroys blood cells. Soliris, a genetically altered antibody known as C5 complement inhibitor, treats PNH by selectively blocking the production of inflammation-causing proteins in the complement cascade. The company's other products are currently in preclinical or phase trial stages. These products include intravenous eculizumab for the treatment of a variety of conditions, including Atypical Hemolytic Uremic Syndrome, Dense Deposit Disease, Acute Humoral Rejection and Myasthenia Gravis; and samalizumab (monoclonal antibody) for the treatment of multiple myeloma and leukemia. The firm's products focus on anti-inflammatory therapeutics for disease in which the complement cascade is activated. Alexion also operates several subsidiaries in Europe, including Alexion Europe SAS, which supports commercial and regulatory international operations. In January 2011, Alexion expanded its portfolio of pre-clinical compounds and translational medicine with the acquisition of Taligen Therapeutics, Inc. The same month the firm also acquired a variety of patents and assets from Germany-based Orphatec Pharmaceuticals GmbH related to investigational therapies for patients with Type A molybdenum cofactor deficiency. In February 2012, the firm acquired Enobia Pharma Corp. and its developmental therapies for patients with life-threatening genetic metabolic disorders.

The firm offers its employees a 401(k) plan; medical, dental, vision, life and disability insurance; a college savings plan; and automobile and homeowners insurance discounts.

FINANCIALS:

Sales and profits are in thousands of dollars—add 000 to get the full amount. 2011 Note: Financial information for 2011 was not available for all companies at press time.

2011 Sales: $783,431 — 2011 Profits: $175,315
2010 Sales: $540,957 — 2010 Profits: $97,030
2009 Sales: $386,800 — 2009 Profits: $295,166
2008 Sales: $259,099 — 2008 Profits: $33,149
2007 Sales: $72,041 — 2007 Profits: $-92,290

U.S. Stock Ticker: ALXN
Int'l Ticker:
Int'l Exchange:
Employees: 792 Fiscal Year Ends: 12/31
Parent Company:

SALARIES/BENEFITS:

Pension Plan: ESOP Stock Plan: Profit Sharing: Top Exec. Salary: $800,000 Bonus: $1,200,000
Savings Plan: Y Stock Purch. Plan: Second Exec. Salary: $464,967 Bonus: $470,000

OTHER THOUGHTS:

Apparent Women Officers or Directors: 6
Hot Spot for Advancement for Women/Minorities: Y

LOCATIONS: ("Y" = Yes)

West:	Southwest:	Midwest:	Southeast:	Northeast:	International:
				Y	Y

ALIEN TECHNOLOGY CORPORATION

www.alientechnology.com

Industry Group Code: 334220

Management:		Sales/Marketing:		Liberal Arts:		Information Systems:		Professionals:		Technical/Scientific:	
Mgmt. Trainees:		Mktg. Professionals:	Y	Gen. Writing/Editing:	Y	Info. Management:	Y	Finance/Acct.:	Y	Engineers, Elec.:	Y
Experienced Mgmt.:	Y	Retail Sales:		Technical Writing:	Y	Software Dev.:	Y	Law:	Y	Engineers, Other:	Y
Int'l Business:	Y	Commercial/Industrial:	Y	Graphic Arts/Photog.:		Hardware Dev.:	Y	HR/Other:	Y	Health/Lab	
MBA Graduates:	Y	Sales Trainees:	Y	Music:		Consulting/Other:	Y	Training:	Y	Scientists/Research:	
		Advertising Pros.:		Broadcasting:				Health Care:		Petroleum/Chemicals:	
				Other:				Consulting:		Math/Other:	

TYPES OF BUSINESS:

RFID Equipment
RFID Training Services

BRANDS/DIVISIONS/AFFILIATES:

Fluidic Self Assembly
RFID Academy
Squiggle
Higgs 3IC
Quatrotec
Higgs 4

CONTACTS:

Note: Officers with more than one job title may be intentionally listed here more than once.

Peter Green, CEO
Glenn R. Haegele, CFO
Patrick Ervin, VP-Worldwide Mktg. & Sales
John Stephen Smith, CTO
Sandeep Gupta, VP-Eng.
David A. Aaron, Chief Legal Officer
David A. Aaron, VP-Bus. Dev.
Mike Frieswyk, Sr. VP-Worldwide Sales & Mktg.
Duane Zitzner, Chmn.

Phone: 408-782-3900 **Fax:** 408-782-3910
Toll-Free:
Address: 18220 Butterfield Blvd., Ste. 150, Morgan Hill, CA 95037 US

GROWTH PLANS/SPECIAL FEATURES:

Alien Technology Corporation is a leading provider of UHF radio frequency identification (RFID) products. Alien's patented Fluidic Self Assembly (FSATM) manufacturing process allows it to manufacture high-volume, low-cost RFID tags. The company manufactures a variety of RFID tags and upgradeable scanners compatible with next-generation technology, including electronic product code (EPC) Class I UHF tags for complex applications such as tagging liquids and metals. In addition, the firm offers battery-assisted passive RFID tags, which support additional features, including increased data memory storage, increased range, secure access systems, tamper detection, shock sensors and time/temperature monitoring. It also supplies RFID readers for specific industry applications including supply chain management, security, vehicle asset tracking, product recall management, logistics and anti-counterfeiting. Alien's products are certified as Qualified Anti-Terrorism Technologies, allowing the products to be used in airport baggage and cargo handling situations. Its Quatrotec subsidiary specializes in the transportation sector. Through the RFID Academy, Alien offers various instructional courses in RFID software, hardware and implementation. The firm's line of 2nd generation tags, called Squiggle, are powered by the industry leading Higgs 3IC tag for LAN (Local Area Network) and WAN (Wide Area Network) computer-based networks. Its key markets are the retail, defense, transportation and life sciences industries. In April 2011, the company introduced Higgs 4, a series of three new RFID products.

Employees of the firm are offered health care options; dental and vision; short- and long-term disability; an employee assistance program; an employee stock purchase plan; flexible spending accounts; voluntary life insurance; and a 401(k).

FINANCIALS:

Sales and profits are in thousands of dollars—add 000 to get the full amount. 2011 Note: Financial information for 2011 was not available for all companies at press time.

2011 Sales: $	2011 Profits: $	**U.S. Stock Ticker: Private**
2010 Sales: $	2010 Profits: $	**Int'l Ticker:**
2009 Sales: $	2009 Profits: $	Int'l Exchange:
2008 Sales: $	2008 Profits: $	Employees: Fiscal Year Ends: 9/30
2007 Sales: $	2007 Profits: $	Parent Company:

SALARIES/BENEFITS:

Pension Plan:	ESOP Stock Plan: Y	Profit Sharing:	Top Exec. Salary: $	Bonus: $
Savings Plan: Y	Stock Purch. Plan:		Second Exec. Salary: $	Bonus: $

OTHER THOUGHTS:

Apparent Women Officers or Directors:
Hot Spot for Advancement for Women/Minorities:

LOCATIONS: ("Y" = Yes)

West:	Southwest:	Midwest:	Southeast:	Northeast:	International:
Y		Y			Y

ALIGN TECHNOLOGY INC

www.aligntech.com

Industry Group Code: 33911

Management:		Sales/Marketing:		Liberal Arts:		Information Systems:		Professionals:		Technical/Scientific:	
Mgmt. Trainees:		Mktg. Professionals:	Y	Gen. Writing/Editing:		Info. Management:	Y	Finance/Acct.:	Y	Engineers, Elec.:	
Experienced Mgmt.:	Y	Retail Sales:		Technical Writing:	Y	Software Dev.:	Y	Law:	Y	Engineers, Other:	Y
Int'l Business:	Y	Commercial/Industrial:	Y	Graphic Arts/Photog.:		Hardware Dev.:	Y	HR/Other:	Y	Health/Lab	Y
MBA Graduates:	Y	Sales Trainees:	Y	Music:		Consulting/Other:		Training:	Y	Scientists/Research:	Y
		Advertising Pros.:		Broadcasting:				Health Care:	Y	Petroleum/Chemicals:	
				Other:				Consulting:		Math/Other:	

TYPES OF BUSINESS:

Orthodontic Equipment

BRANDS/DIVISIONS/AFFILIATES:

Invisalign
ClinCheck
Invisalign Express
Invisalign Teen
Invisalign Assist
Invisalign Lite
Invisalign Anterior
Vivera Retainers

CONTACTS: *Note: Officers with more than one job title may be intentionally listed here more than once.*

Thomas M. Prescott, CEO
Thomas M. Prescott, Pres.
Kenneth B. Arola, CFO
Sheila Tan, Chief Mktg. Officer/VP
Dana C. Cambra, VP-R&D
Dana C. Cambra, VP-IT
Roger E. George, General Counsel/Sec./VP-Legal Affairs
Emory M. Wright, VP-Oper.
Kenneth B. Arola, VP-Finance
Dan S. Ellis, VP-North American Sales
Len Hedge, Sr. VP-Bus. Oper.
C. Raymond Larkin, Jr., Chmn.
Richard M.L. Twomey, VP-Int'l

Phone: 408-470-1000 **Fax:** 408-470-1010
Toll-Free:
Address: 2560 Orchard Pkwy., San Jose, CA 95131 US

GROWTH PLANS/SPECIAL FEATURES:

Align Technology, Inc. (ATI) designs, manufactures and markets Invisalign, a proprietary system for treating malocclusion, or the misalignment of teeth, as an alternative to traditional dental braces. The Invisalign system has two components: ClinCheck and Aligners. ClinCheck is an Internet-based application that allows dental professionals to simulate treatment, in three dimensions, by modeling two-week stages of tooth movement. Aligners are thin, clear plastic, removable dental appliances that are manufactured in a series to correspond to each two-week stage of the ClinCheck simulation. Aligners are customized to perform the treatment prescribed for an individual patient by dental professionals using ClinCheck. Its family of products consists of six treatment options. Invisalign Full, accounting for 75% of sales, is intended to be used as a complete treatment for a broad range of malocclusions and includes as many aligners indicated by ClinCheck in order to achieve treatment goals. Invisalign Express is a lower cost option for less complex orthodontic cases that consist of up to 14 sets of aligners. Invisalign Teen is used for teen-aged patients and features compliance indicators and Power Ridges, which provide extra force. Invisalign Assist is used for minor misalignment cases. Other treatment options include Invisalign Lite and Invisalign Anterior. Upon completion of the Invisalign treatment, either traditional single retainers or Vivera retainers are used for retention of the patient's results. At ATI's facility in Costa Rica, technicians prepare electronic treatment plans, which are transmitted electronically back to the U.S. These files form the basis of ClinCheck and are used in conjunction with stereo lithography technology to manufacture Aligner molds. Manufacturing operations are conducted in Mexico, and completed Aligners are then shipped directly to ATI's customers. In May 2011, ATI acquired 3D digital scanning solutions provider Cadent Holdings, Inc.

FINANCIALS: **Sales and profits are in thousands of dollars—add 000 to get the full amount. 2011 Note: Financial information for 2011 was not available for all companies at press time.**

2011 Sales: $479,700 2011 Profits: $66,700
2010 Sales: $387,126 2010 Profits: $74,253
2009 Sales: $312,333 2009 Profits: $-31,269
2008 Sales: $303,976 2008 Profits: $79,987
2007 Sales: $284,332 2007 Profits: $35,724

U.S. Stock Ticker: ALGN
Int'l Ticker:
Int'l Exchange:
Employees: 2,097 Fiscal Year Ends: 12/31
Parent Company:

SALARIES/BENEFITS:

Pension Plan: ESOP Stock Plan: Profit Sharing: Top Exec. Salary: $537,674 Bonus: $800,000
Savings Plan: Y Stock Purch. Plan: Y Second Exec. Salary: $335,346 Bonus: $327,445

OTHER THOUGHTS:

Apparent Women Officers or Directors: 1
Hot Spot for Advancement for Women/Minorities:

LOCATIONS: ("Y" = Yes)

West:	Southwest:	Midwest:	Southeast:	Northeast:	International:
Y					Y

ALLEGIANT TRAVEL COMPANY

www.allegiantair.com

Industry Group Code: 481111

Management:		**Sales/Marketing:**		**Liberal Arts:**		**Information Systems:**		**Professionals:**		**Technical/Scientific:**	
Mgmt. Trainees:		Mktg. Professionals:	Y	Gen. Writing/Editing:	Y	Info. Management:	Y	Finance/Acct.:	Y	Engineers, Elec.:	
Experienced Mgmt.:	Y	Retail Sales:		Technical Writing:		Software Dev.:	Y	Law:	Y	Engineers, Other:	
Int'l Business:		Commercial/Industrial:	Y	Graphic Arts/Photog.:	Y	Hardware Dev.:		HR/Other:	Y	Health/Lab	
MBA Graduates:	Y	Sales Trainees:	Y	Music:		Consulting/Other:		Training:	Y	Scientists/Research:	
		Advertising Pros.:	Y	Broadcasting:				Health Care:		Petroleum/Chemicals:	
				Other:				Consulting:		Math/Other:	

TYPES OF BUSINESS:

Airline
Packaged Vacations

BRANDS/DIVISIONS/AFFILIATES:

CONTACTS:

Note: Officers with more than one job title may be intentionally listed here more than once.

Maurice J. Gallagher, Jr., CEO
Andrew C. Levy, Pres.
Scott Sheldon, CFO/Sr. VP
Michael Reichartz, Sr. VP-Mktg.
Scott Allard, CIO
Jude Bricker, Corp. Sec.
Kris Bauer, Sr. VP-Oper.
Greg Rehwaldt, VP-Stations
Greg Baden, VP-Flight & System Oper.
Maurice J. Gallagher, Jr., Chmn.

Phone: 702-851-7300	**Fax:**
Toll-Free:	
Address: 8360 S. Durango Dr., Las Vegas, NV 89113 US	

GROWTH PLANS/SPECIAL FEATURES:

Allegiant Travel Company is an airline focused on transporting travelers in small cities to leisure destinations. The company sells air travel both on a stand-alone basis and bundled with hotel rooms, rental cars and other travel-related services. Allegiant provides nonstop air service from 62 small cities on 161 routes in 35 states to primarily Las Vegas, Nevada; Orlando, Tampa/St. Petersburg and Ft. Lauderdale, Florida; Phoenix, Arizona; and Los Angeles, California. Its fleet of 51 aircraft consists of 39 MD-83s, two MD-87s, six MD-88s and four MD-82s. It also owns eight MD-80s in long-term storage. The company maintains full control over its inventory and only distributes its product through its web site, its call center and at its airport ticket counters. The firm markets its services through advertising and promotions in newspapers, magazines, television, radio and targeted public relations and promotional efforts. Allegiant pays a commission for vacation packages sold through travel agencies and has fixed fee flying agreements with various subsidiaries of Caesars Entertainment, Inc. (formerly Harrah's Entertainment, Inc.).

Employees are offered medical, dental and 401(k) plans; paid time off; supplemental life insurance; and long-term disability.

FINANCIALS:

Sales and profits are in thousands of dollars—add 000 to get the full amount. 2011 Note: Financial information for 2011 was not available for all companies at press time.

2011 Sales: $779,117	2011 Profits: $49,398	**U.S. Stock Ticker: ALGT**
2010 Sales: $663,600	2010 Profits: $65,700	**Int'l Ticker:**
2009 Sales: $557,900	2009 Profits: $76,300	Int'l Exchange:
2008 Sales: $504,012	2008 Profits: $35,407	Employees: 1,614 Fiscal Year Ends: 12/31
2007 Sales: $360,573	2007 Profits: $31,509	Parent Company:

SALARIES/BENEFITS:

Pension Plan:	ESOP Stock Plan:	Profit Sharing:	Top Exec. Salary: $285,000	Bonus: $726,750
Savings Plan: Y	Stock Purch. Plan:		Second Exec. Salary: $154,375	Bonus: $354,000

OTHER THOUGHTS:

Apparent Women Officers or Directors:
Hot Spot for Advancement for Women/Minorities:

LOCATIONS: ("Y" = Yes)

West:	Southwest:	Midwest:	Southeast:	Northeast:	International:
Y	Y	Y	Y		

ALLIED HEALTHCARE INTERNATIONAL INC

www.alliedhealthcare.com

Industry Group Code: 561

Management:		Sales/Marketing:		Liberal Arts:		Information Systems:		Professionals:		Technical/Scientific:	
Mgmt. Trainees:	Y	Mktg. Professionals:	Y	Gen. Writing/Editing:	Y	Info. Management:	Y	Finance/Acct.:	Y	Engineers, Elec.:	
Experienced Mgmt.:	Y	Retail Sales:		Technical Writing:	Y	Software Dev.:	Y	Law:	Y	Engineers, Other:	
Int'l Business:	Y	Commercial/Industrial:		Graphic Arts/Photog.:		Hardware Dev.:		HR/Other:	Y	Health/Lab	Y
MBA Graduates:	Y	Sales Trainees:		Music:		Consulting/Other:		Training:	Y	Scientists/Research:	
		Advertising Pros.:		Broadcasting:				Health Care:		Petroleum/Chemicals:	
				Other:				Consulting:		Math/Other:	

TYPES OF BUSINESS:

Home Health Care
Nursing & Para-Professional Services
Home Medical Equipment & Oxygen
Respiration Therapy
Medical Staffing

BRANDS/DIVISIONS/AFFILIATES:

ScotHomecare
Allied Healthcare Group, Ltd.
BiJu Limited
Homecare Independent Living Group

CONTACTS: *Note: Officers with more than one job title may be intentionally listed here more than once.*

Sandy Young, CEO
Paul Weston, CFO
Louise Cherry, Dir.-Human Resources
Mark Stanyer, Dir.-IT
Leslie J. Levinson, Corp. Sec.
Russell Baldwin, Dir.-Oper., South
Stephen Bateman, Dir.-Service, Quality & Compliance
Helen Hodgson, Dir.-Clinical Svcs.
Jayne Tarbuck, Dir.-Bus. Improvement
Jeffrey S. Peris, Chmn.

Phone: 212-750-0064 **Fax:**
Toll-Free:
Address: 245 Park Ave., New York, NY 10167 US

GROWTH PLANS/SPECIAL FEATURES:

Allied Healthcare International, Inc. (AHI) is a leading provider of flexible healthcare staffing to the U.K. healthcare industry. The company operates a network of 115 branches in England, Scotland, and Wales, providing staff including nurses, nurse aides and home health aides. AHI places its staff with hospitals, nursing homes, care homes, private companies, the prison service, the police service, armed services hospitals and private homes on a per diem basis from a pool of roughly 12,000 healthcare professionals. During 2010, the firm performed an average of 8,000 placements each week. The company's mix of staff is roughly 87% homecare aides, 5% nurses and 10% nurses' aides. Approximately 83.3% of the company's revenue comes from customers that are U.K. government entities, primarily local social-services departments and NHS hospitals. The firm's staffing business is provided under the names Allied Healthcare Group and Homecare Independent Living. AHI generally focuses on the per diem staffing market rather than the long-term staffing market, as the per diem market has favorable pricing structure and commands higher service fees. In addition, the company provides staffing services for the National Health Service. In May 2010, AHI acquired a majority stake in the Ireland-based Homecare Independent Living Group, a provider of healthcare support services for elderly, physically disabled and mentally disabled patients. In March 2011, the firm (through Allied Healthcare Group Limited) acquired ScotHomecare, the homecare operations of Health and Lifecare Options Limited. In May 2011, Allied Healthcare Group Limited acquired home services provider BiJu Limited.

AHI offers its employees ongoing training and a pension plan.

FINANCIALS: **Sales and profits are in thousands of dollars—add 000 to get the full amount. 2011 Note: Financial information for 2011 was not available for all companies at press time.**

2011 Sales: $	2011 Profits: $
2010 Sales: $271,079	2010 Profits: $10,056
2009 Sales: $249,810	2009 Profits: $10,303
2008 Sales: $298,577	2008 Profits: $8,786
2007 Sales: $277,795	2007 Profits: $66,353

U.S. Stock Ticker: Subsidiary
Int'l Ticker:
Int'l Exchange:
Employees: 1,160 Fiscal Year Ends: 12/31
Parent Company: SAGA GROUP LIMITED

SALARIES/BENEFITS:

Pension Plan: Y	ESOP Stock Plan:	Profit Sharing:	Top Exec. Salary: $339,784	Bonus: $49,115
Savings Plan:	Stock Purch. Plan: Y		Second Exec. Salary: $250,794	Bonus: $37,733

OTHER THOUGHTS:

Apparent Women Officers or Directors: 3
Hot Spot for Advancement for Women/Minorities: Y

LOCATIONS: ("Y" = Yes)

West:	Southwest:	Midwest:	Southeast:	Northeast:	International:
				Y	Y

ALLSCRIPTS HEALTHCARE SOLUTIONS INC

www.allscripts.com

Industry Group Code: 511210D

Management:		**Sales/Marketing:**		**Liberal Arts:**		**Information Systems:**		**Professionals:**		**Technical/Scientific:**	
Mgmt. Trainees:		Mktg. Professionals:	Y	Gen. Writing/Editing:		Info. Management:	Y	Finance/Acct.:	Y	Engineers, Elec.:	Y
Experienced Mgmt.:	Y	Retail Sales:		Technical Writing:	Y	Software Dev.:	Y	Law:	Y	Engineers, Other:	
Int'l Business:		Commercial/Industrial:	Y	Graphic Arts/Photog.:	Y	Hardware Dev.:		HR/Other:	Y	Health/Lab	
MBA Graduates:	Y	Sales Trainees:	Y	Music:		Consulting/Other:		Training:	Y	Scientists/Research:	
		Advertising Pros.:		Broadcasting:				Health Care:		Petroleum/Chemicals:	
				Other:				Consulting:		Math/Other:	

TYPES OF BUSINESS:

Prescription Management Software
Interactive Education Services
Clinical Software
Electronic Records Systems
Care Management Software

BRANDS/DIVISIONS/AFFILIATES:

Eclipsys Corporation
Allscripts MyWay EHR
Allscripts Professional EHR
Allscripts Enterprise EHR
PeakPractice PM
PeakPractice SC
Sunrise Enterprise

CONTACTS: *Note: Officers with more than one job title may be intentionally listed here more than once.*

Glen E. Tullman, CEO
Eileen McPartland, COO
Lee Shapiro, Pres.
Bill Davis, CFO
Dan Michelson, Chief Mktg. Officer/Exec. VP
Diane Adams, Exec. VP-Culture & Talent
Cliff Meltzer, Exec. VP-Solutions Dev.
Jacqueline Studer, General Counsel/Sr. VP
Dan Michelson, Chief Strategy Officer
Cosmo Battinelli, Sr. VP-Client Support Svcs.
Laurie McGraw, Chief Client Officer
Stephen Lalonde, Exec. VP-Sales Oper.
Joe Carey, VP-Strategic Accounts
Philip Pead, Chmn.

Phone: 312-506-1200 **Fax:** 312-506-1201
Toll-Free: 800-654-0889
Address: 222 Merchandise Mart Plz., Ste. 2024, Chicago, IL 60654 US

GROWTH PLANS/SPECIAL FEATURES:

Allscripts Healthcare Solutions, Inc. provides clinical software, connectivity and information solutions that physicians and healthcare providers use to improve service delivery. Its business groups are designed to deliver timely information connecting physicians to each other and to the broader healthcare community, and to contribute to healthcare by improving both the quality and efficiency of care. The firm provides software solutions in five primary categories: ambulatory, practice management, acute, post-acute and performance management. Its ambulatory solutions include Electronic Health Records (EHR), electronic prescribing and document imaging solutions. Specific tools include Allscripts MyWay EHR, Allscripts Professional EHR and Allscripts Enterprise EHR. The firm's practice management tools combine scheduling, billing and revenue cycle management software in a single package. Allscripts' acute solutions for hospitals and health systems include integrated enterprise solutions that provide clinical, revenue cycle and performance management software. Its acute solutions also provide offerings for hospitals that are seeking stand-alone Emergency Department Information System (EDIS) and care management solutions. The firm's acute software solutions comprise its Sunrise Enterprise family of products. Its post-acute tools help to smooth the patient transition from hospital to post-acute care facilities, including home health providers, hospices and private duty organizations. Lastly, the company's performance management products include such tools as PeakPractice PM and PeakPractice SC, a web-based inventory management application that electronically tracks and orders medical supplies and inventory for physician practices. Additionally, Allscripts offers professional services, such as conversion and integration of historical data into its software, training and support services, as well as consulting, remote hosting and IT outsourcing services related to the implementation of its various software products. In August 2010, the company merged with Eclipsys Corporation.

FINANCIALS: **Sales and profits are in thousands of dollars—add 000 to get the full amount. 2011 Note: Financial information for 2011 was not available for all companies at press time.**

2011 Sales: $1,449,100 — 2011 Profits: $75,500
2010 Sales: $704,502 — 2010 Profits: $62,870
2009 Sales: $548,439 — 2009 Profits: $26,022
2008 Sales: $383,771 — 2008 Profits: $25,399
2007 Sales: $379,693 — 2007 Profits: $3,854

U.S. Stock Ticker: MDRX
Int'l Ticker:
Int'l Exchange:
Employees: 2,428 Fiscal Year Ends: 12/31
Parent Company:

SALARIES/BENEFITS:

Pension Plan: — ESOP Stock Plan: — Profit Sharing: — Top Exec. Salary: $741,667 — Bonus: $1,065,000
Savings Plan: Y — Stock Purch. Plan: Y — Second Exec. Salary: $594,792 — Bonus: $813,750

OTHER THOUGHTS:

Apparent Women Officers or Directors: 3
Hot Spot for Advancement for Women/Minorities: Y

LOCATIONS: ("Y" = Yes)

West:	Southwest:	Midwest:	Southeast:	Northeast:	International:
Y	Y	Y	Y	Y	

AMAG PHARMACEUTICALS INC

www.amagpharma.com

Industry Group Code: 541711

Management:		**Sales/Marketing:**		**Liberal Arts:**		**Information Systems:**		**Professionals:**		**Technical/Scientific:**	
Mgmt. Trainees:		Mktg. Professionals:		Gen. Writing/Editing:		Info. Management:	Y	Finance/Acct.:	Y	Engineers, Elec.:	
Experienced Mgmt.:	Y	Retail Sales:		Technical Writing:	Y	Software Dev.:		Law:	Y	Engineers, Other:	
Int'l Business:		Commercial/Industrial:	Y	Graphic Arts/Photog.:		Hardware Dev.:		HR/Other:	Y	Health/Lab	Y
MBA Graduates:	Y	Sales Trainees:		Music:		Consulting/Other:		Training:	Y	Scientists/Research:	Y
		Advertising Pros.:		Broadcasting:				Health Care:		Petroleum/Chemicals:	
				Other:				Consulting:		Math/Other:	

TYPES OF BUSINESS:

Nanoparticles, Pharmaceutical
MRI Contrast Agents
Iron Replacement Therapeutics

BRANDS/DIVISIONS/AFFILIATES:

GastroMARK
Feraheme
Allos Therapeutics Inc

CONTACTS:

Note: Officers with more than one job title may be intentionally listed here more than once.

Frank Thomas, Interim CEO
Frank Thomas, COO
Lee F. Allen, Chief Medical Officer/Exec. VP
Joseph L. Farmer, Chief Admin. Officer
Joseph L. Farmer, General Counsel/Sr. VP-Legal Affairs
John Tucker, VP-Commercial Oper.
Chris White, Chief Bus. Officer
Amy Sullivan, VP-Corp. Comm.
Amy Sullivan, VP-Investor Rel.
Scott Holmes, Chief Acct. Officer
Alka Batycky, VP-Program & Alliance Mgmt.
Scott Holmes, VP/Controller
Michael Narachi, Chmn.

Phone: 617-498-3300 **Fax:** 617-499-3361
Toll-Free:
Address: 100 Hayden Ave., Cambridge, MA 02141 US

GROWTH PLANS/SPECIAL FEATURES:

AMAG Pharmaceuticals, Inc. (AMAG) is a biomedical company that develops and manufactures therapeutic iron compounds to treat anemia, as well as other novel imaging agents to aid in the diagnosis of cancer and cardiovascular disease. Its products are manufactured with bioavailable iron oxide, which is used to coat nanoparticles. Due to their super-paramagnetic properties, these products can also become strongly polarized in magnetic fields, making nanoparticles ideal candidates for MRI (magnetic resonance imaging) testing and IV iron replacement therapeutics. AMAG currently has two FDA approved products on the market: GastroMARK, an oral contrast agent used for delineating the bowel in MRI; and Feraheme (ferumoxytol injection), an intravenous iron replacement therapeutic agent for the treatment of iron deficiency anemia (IDA) in patients with chronic kidney disease. The firm is actively conducting clinical trials for the efficacy of Feraheme as an IDA treatment in a broader range of patients. The company has a manufacturing facility in Cambridge, Massachusetts that manufactures GastroMARK and Feraheme for commercial sale. AMAG markets and sells its products through its own sales organization, as well as through collaboration agreements with marketing and distribution centers. The firm earns its revenue through licensing fees, product sales and royalties. In July 2011, the company announced plans to merge with Allos Therapeutics, Inc., in which both firms will combine through an all-stock merger with total equity valued at $686 million.

The firm offers its employees medical, dental and vision coverage; flexible spending accounts for healthcare and dependent care; life, disability and AD&D insurance; a 401(k) plan; an employee stock purchase plan; tuition assistance; and credit union membership.

FINANCIALS:

Sales and profits are in thousands of dollars—add 000 to get the full amount. 2011 Note: Financial information for 2011 was not available for all companies at press time.

2011 Sales: $	2011 Profits: $
2010 Sales: $66,245	2010 Profits: $-81,153
2009 Sales: $17,178	2009 Profits: $-93,351
2008 Sales: $1,938	2008 Profits: $-71,647
2007 Sales: $2,552	2007 Profits: $-33,894

U.S. Stock Ticker: AMAG
Int'l Ticker:
Int'l Exchange:
Employees: 226 Fiscal Year Ends: 12/31
Parent Company:

SALARIES/BENEFITS:

Pension Plan:	ESOP Stock Plan:	Profit Sharing:	Top Exec. Salary: $614,615	Bonus: $
Savings Plan: Y	Stock Purch. Plan: Y		Second Exec. Salary: $392,308	Bonus: $

OTHER THOUGHTS:

Apparent Women Officers or Directors: 2
Hot Spot for Advancement for Women/Minorities:

LOCATIONS: ("Y" = Yes)

West:	Southwest:	Midwest:	Southeast:	Northeast:	International:
				Y	

AMCOL INTERNATIONAL CORP

www.amcol.com

Industry Group Code: 327

Management:		Sales/Marketing:		Liberal Arts:		Information Systems:		Professionals:		Technical/Scientific:	
Mgmt. Trainees:		Mktg. Professionals:	Y	Gen. Writing/Editing:		Info. Management:	Y	Finance/Acct.:	Y	Engineers, Elec.:	
Experienced Mgmt.:	Y	Retail Sales:		Technical Writing:	Y	Software Dev.:		Law:	Y	Engineers, Other:	Y
Int'l Business:	Y	Commercial/Industrial:	Y	Graphic Arts/Photog.:		Hardware Dev.:		HR/Other:	Y	Health/Lab	
MBA Graduates:	Y	Sales Trainees:	Y	Music:		Consulting/Other:		Training:	Y	Scientists/Research:	
		Advertising Pros.:		Broadcasting:				Health Care:		Petroleum/Chemicals:	Y
				Other:				Consulting:		Math/Other:	

TYPES OF BUSINESS:

Minerals & Composites
Bentonite
Truck & Freight Services
Nanocomposites
Environmental Products
Mining Services
Environmental Services

BRANDS/DIVISIONS/AFFILIATES:

Nanocor Inc
Volclay
Panther Creek
Premium Gel
Additrol
Volclay International
Amcol Minerals and Materials
American Colloid Company

CONTACTS: *Note: Officers with more than one job title may be intentionally listed here more than once.*

Ryan F. McKendrick, CEO
Ryan F. McKendrick, Pres.
Donald W. Pearson, CFO/Sr. VP
Robert J. Trauger, VP/Pres., CETCO
Gary L. Castagna, Sr. VP/Pres., Global Minerals
Michael Johnson, VP/Pres., CETCO Oilfield Svcs. Co.
John Hughes, Chmn.

Phone: 847-851-1500 **Fax:**
Toll-Free: 800-426-5564
Address: 2870 Forbs Ave., Hoffman Estates, IL 60192 US

GROWTH PLANS/SPECIAL FEATURES:

Amcol International Corp. produces and markets a wide range of specialty minerals to the industrial, environmental and consumer-related industries. The company operates in five segments: minerals and materials, which accounted for 50% of the firm's 2010 sales; environmental, 27%; oilfield services, 18%; transportation, 6%; and corporate, -1%. Amcol's minerals and materials segment mines, processes and distributes clays, bentonite and bentonite-related products. This division serves the metalcasting, pet products, basic minerals and specialty minerals markets. It includes products marketed under the trademark names Volclay, Panther Creek, Premium Gel, Hevi-Sand and Additrol. The environmental segment processes and distributes geosynthetic clays and minerals as moisture barriers for commercial construction, landfill liners and other industrial applications under the Bentomat and Claymax names. The oilfield services segment offers both onshore and offshore water treatment filtration and pipeline separation. The transportation segment provides trucking and freight brokerage services for domestic subsidiaries and third parties. The corporate division includes certain expenses associated with stewardship, management, benefits and IT activities for the company. The company's main subsidiaries include American Colloid Company; Volclay International Corp.; Amcol Health & Beauty Solutions, Inc.; Amcol Minerals and Materials; and CETCO Oilfield Services Ltd. Additionally, through subsidiary Nanocor, Inc., the company manufactures nanocomposites that modify the surface of bentonite minerals in order to improve the physical properties of manufactured polymers. Amcol is located in approximately 25 countries and operates over 60 facilities worldwide. Approximately 67% of revenue is generated in the Americas.

Employees are offered medical and dental insurance; life insurance; AD&D coverage; and a 401(k) plan.

FINANCIALS: **Sales and profits are in thousands of dollars—add 000 to get the full amount. 2011 Note: Financial information for 2011 was not available for all companies at press time.**

2011 Sales: $942,400 | 2011 Profits: $59,100
2010 Sales: $852,538 | 2010 Profits: $29,924
2009 Sales: $703,237 | 2009 Profits: $34,871
2008 Sales: $883,552 | 2008 Profits: $25,331
2007 Sales: $744,334 | 2007 Profits: $56,735

U.S. Stock Ticker: ACO
Int'l Ticker:
Int'l Exchange:
Employees: 2,383 Fiscal Year Ends: 12/31
Parent Company:

SALARIES/BENEFITS:

Pension Plan: | ESOP Stock Plan: | Profit Sharing: | Top Exec. Salary: $670,000 | Bonus: $136,000
Savings Plan: Y | Stock Purch. Plan: | | Second Exec. Salary: $408,333 | Bonus: $65,000

OTHER THOUGHTS:

Apparent Women Officers or Directors: 1
Hot Spot for Advancement for Women/Minorities:

LOCATIONS: ("Y" = Yes)

West:	Southwest:	Midwest:	Southeast:	Northeast:	International:
Y	Y	Y	Y	Y	Y

AMCON DISTRIBUTING CO

Industry Group Code: 4244

www.amcon.com

Management:		Sales/Marketing:		Liberal Arts:		Information Systems:		Professionals:		Technical/Scientific:	
Mgmt. Trainees:	Y	Mktg. Professionals:	Y	Gen. Writing/Editing:		Info. Management:	Y	Finance/Acct.:	Y	Engineers, Elec.:	
Experienced Mgmt.:	Y	Retail Sales:		Technical Writing:		Software Dev.:	Y	Law:	Y	Engineers, Other:	
Int'l Business:		Commercial/Industrial:	Y	Graphic Arts/Photog.:	Y	Hardware Dev.:		HR/Other:	Y	Health/Lab	
MBA Graduates:	Y	Sales Trainees:	Y	Music:		Consulting/Other:		Training:	Y	Scientists/Research:	
		Advertising Pros.:		Broadcasting:				Health Care:		Petroleum/Chemicals:	
				Other:				Consulting:		Math/Other:	

TYPES OF BUSINESS:

Groceries, Distribution
Health Food Products, Retail
Cigarette Sales

BRANDS/DIVISIONS/AFFILIATES:

Chamberlin's Market & Cafe
Akin's Natural Food Market
LP Shanks Copmpany Inc

CONTACTS:

Note: Officers with more than one job title may be intentionally listed here more than once.

Christopher Atayan, CEO
Kathleen Evans, Pres.
Andrew Plummer, CFO/VP
Rick Vance, VP-Mktg.
Andrew C. Plummer, Corp. Sec.
Philip Campbell, Sr. VP-Planning & Compliance
Atom Jones, Mgr.-Corp. Sales
Chuck Schmaderer, Dir.-SEC & Financial Reporting
Bill Bailey, Gen. Mgr.
Clem O'Donnel, VP-Sales
Christopher Atayan, Chmn.

Phone: 402-331-3727 **Fax:** 402-331-4834
Toll-Free:
Address: 7405 Irvington Rd., Omaha, NE 68122 US

GROWTH PLANS/SPECIAL FEATURES:

AMCON Distributing Co. (ADC) is a leading wholesale distributor and specialty retailer of consumer products. The company is divided into two segments: wholesale and retail. The wholesale segment services approximately 5,000 retail outlets, including convenience stores, grocery stores, liquor stores, drug stores and tobacco shops. The segment currently distributes over 14,000 different consumer products, including cigarettes and tobacco products; candy and other confectionery; beverages; groceries; paper products; health and beauty care products; frozen and chilled products; and institutional food service products. Other products include private label lines of snuff, water, candy products, batteries and film. The segment also operates six distribution centers located in Illinois, Missouri, Nebraska, North Dakota, South Dakota and Tennessee. These distribution centers, combined with cross-dock facilities, make up approximately 601,000 square feet of floor space. The retail segment operates the health food stores Chamberlin's Market & Cafe (six stores) in and around Orlando, Florida; and Akin's Natural Foods Market (eight stores) in Oklahoma, Nebraska, Missouri and Kansas. These stores carry more than 30,000 different national and regionally branded and private label products, including natural, organic and specialty foods, consisting of produce, baked goods, frozen foods, nutritional supplements, personal care items and general merchandise. While the company sells a diversified product line, it remains dependent on cigarette sales, which represent 72% of its revenue. ADC's principal suppliers include Philip Morris USA; RJ Reynolds; Commonwealth Brands; Hershey; Mars; Quaker; Lorillard; Proctor & Gamble; and Nabisco. In May 2011, ADC acquired the assets of southeastern U.S. consumer product distributor L.P. Shanks Company, Inc.

Employees are offered medical and life insurance as well as a 401(k) plan.

FINANCIALS:

Sales and profits are in thousands of dollars—add 000 to get the full amount. 2011 Note: Financial information for 2011 was not available for all companies at press time.

2011 Sales: $1,041,632	2011 Profits: $8,064
2010 Sales: $1,010,538	2010 Profits: $8,966
2009 Sales: $907,953	2009 Profits: $12,974
2008 Sales: $860,451	2008 Profits: $5,332
2007 Sales: $853,567	2007 Profits: $4,440

U.S. Stock Ticker: DIT
Int'l Ticker:
Int'l Exchange:
Employees: 792 Fiscal Year Ends: 9/30
Parent Company:

SALARIES/BENEFITS:

Pension Plan:	ESOP Stock Plan:	Profit Sharing:	Top Exec. Salary: $450,000	Bonus: $1,304,203
Savings Plan: Y	Stock Purch. Plan:		Second Exec. Salary: $375,000	Bonus: $130,000

OTHER THOUGHTS:

Apparent Women Officers or Directors: 1
Hot Spot for Advancement for Women/Minorities:

LOCATIONS: ("Y" = Yes)

West:	Southwest:	Midwest:	Southeast:	Northeast:	International:
	Y	Y	Y		

AMERESCO INC

www.ameresco.com

Industry Group Code: 541690

Management:		**Sales/Marketing:**		**Liberal Arts:**		**Information Systems:**		**Professionals:**		**Technical/Scientific:**	
Mgmt. Trainees:		Mktg. Professionals:	Y	Gen. Writing/Editing:		Info. Management:	Y	Finance/Acct.:	Y	Engineers, Elec.:	Y
Experienced Mgmt.:	Y	Retail Sales:		Technical Writing:	Y	Software Dev.:		Law:	Y	Engineers, Other:	
Int'l Business:	Y	Commercial/Industrial:	Y	Graphic Arts/Photog.:		Hardware Dev.:		HR/Other:	Y	Health/Lab	
MBA Graduates:	Y	Sales Trainees:	Y	Music:		Consulting/Other:	Y	Training:	Y	Scientists/Research:	
		Advertising Pros.:		Broadcasting:				Health Care:		Petroleum/Chemicals:	
				Other:				Consulting:	Y	Math/Other:	

TYPES OF BUSINESS:

Energy Consulting
Landfill Gas-to-Energy Generation
Solar Power Technology
Cogeneration

BRANDS/DIVISIONS/AFFILIATES:

Ameresco Canada
Ameresco Enertech
AmerescoSolutions
Quantum Engineering and Development, Inc.
Applied Energy Group
APS Energy Services Company, Inc.

CONTACTS: *Note: Officers with more than one job title may be intentionally listed here more than once.*

George P. Sakellaris, CEO
George P. Sakellaris, Pres.
Andrew B. Spence, CFO/VP
CarolAnn Hibbard, VP-Strategic Mktg.
Kathleen A. Devlin, VP-Human Resources
Joseph P. DeManche, Exec. VP-Eng.
Kathleen A. Devlin, VP-Admin.
David J. Corrsin, General Counsel/Exec. VP/Corp. Sec.
Joseph P. DeManche, Exec. VP-Oper.
David J. Anderson, Exec. VP-Bus. Dev.
CarolAnn Hibbard, VP-Comm.
Michael T. Bakas, Sr. VP-Renewable Energy
Keith A. Derrington, Exec. VP/Gen. Mgr.-Federal Oper.
William J. Cunningham, Sr. VP-Corp. Gov't Rel.
Bruce McLeish, VP-Energy Supply & Risk Mgmt.
George P. Sakellaris, Chmn.
Mario Iusi, Pres., Ameresco Canada

Phone: 508-661-2200	**Fax:** 508-661-2201
Toll-Free: 866-263-7372	
Address: 111 Speen St., Ste. 410, Framingham, MA 01701 US	

GROWTH PLANS/SPECIAL FEATURES:

Ameresco, Inc. is an independent efficiency consulting company that helps corporations decrease operating expenses, upgrade and maintain facilities and stabilize operating costs. From 56 offices in the U.S. and Canada, the firm works with corporate customers to reduce energy consumption, lower operating costs and realize environmental benefits. The company's services address almost all aspects of purchasing and using energy within a facility, including upgrades to a facility's energy infrastructure and the construction and operation of small-scale renewable energy plants. These small-scale plants are typically located near landfills and use landfill gases (LFG) to generate energy. In addition, the company sells and installs photovoltaic (PV) panels and integrated PV systems. It generally retains ownership of these plants, and then sells the generated power to its clients, or sells the entire facility to the customer. Ameresco primary customers include governmental, educational, utility, healthcare and other institutional, commercial and industrial clients. Subsidiaries of the firm include Ameresco Canada, which serves institutional, commercial and industrial energy users in Canada; AmerescoSolutions, which focuses on federal government clients and has national contracts with the U.S. Departments of Defense and Energy; and Ameresco Enertech, which focuses on primary education, higher education and industrial and commercial facilities within Tennessee and Kentucky. In 2010, the firm acquired Quantum Engineering and Development, Inc., an energy service company active in Oregon and Washington. In July 2011, Ameresco purchased Applied Energy Group. In August 2011, it acquired APS Energy Services Company, Inc.

FINANCIALS: **Sales and profits are in thousands of dollars—add 000 to get the full amount. 2011 Note: Financial information for 2011 was not available for all companies at press time.**

2011 Sales: $728,200	2011 Profits: $34,700	**U.S. Stock Ticker: AMRC**
2010 Sales: $618,226	2010 Profits: $28,726	**Int'l Ticker:**
2009 Sales: $428,517	2009 Profits: $19,907	Int'l Exchange:
2008 Sales: $395,854	2008 Profits: $18,273	Employees: 735 Fiscal Year Ends: 12/31
2007 Sales: $	2007 Profits: $	Parent Company:

SALARIES/BENEFITS:

Pension Plan:	ESOP Stock Plan:	Profit Sharing:	Top Exec. Salary: $500,000	Bonus: $200,000
Savings Plan: Y	Stock Purch. Plan:		Second Exec. Salary: $264,750	Bonus: $80,000

OTHER THOUGHTS:

Apparent Women Officers or Directors: 3
Hot Spot for Advancement for Women/Minorities: Y

LOCATIONS: ("Y" = Yes)

West:	Southwest:	Midwest:	Southeast:	Northeast:	International:
Y	Y	Y	Y	Y	Y

AMERICAN CAMPUS COMMUNITIES INC

americancampus.com

Industry Group Code: 5311

Management:		Sales/Marketing:		Liberal Arts:		Information Systems:		Professionals:		Technical/Scientific:	
Mgmt. Trainees:	Y	Mktg. Professionals:		Gen. Writing/Editing:	Y	Info. Management:	Y	Finance/Acct.:	Y	Engineers, Elec.:	
Experienced Mgmt.:	Y	Retail Sales:		Technical Writing:		Software Dev.:		Law:	Y	Engineers, Other:	
Int'l Business:	Y	Commercial/Industrial:		Graphic Arts/Photog.:		Hardware Dev.:		HR/Other:	Y	Health/Lab Scientists/Research:	
MBA Graduates:	Y	Sales Trainees:		Music:		Consulting/Other:		Training:		Petroleum/Chemicals:	
		Advertising Pros.:		Broadcasting:				Health Care:		Math/Other:	
				Other:				Consulting:			

TYPES OF BUSINESS:

Student Housing Development

BRANDS/DIVISIONS/AFFILIATES:

American Campus Communities Operating Partnership
American Campus Equity

CONTACTS: *Note: Officers with more than one job title may be intentionally listed here more than once.*

William C. Bayless, Jr., CEO
Greg A. Dowell, COO/Exec. VP/Treas.
William C. Bayless, Jr., Pres.
Jonathan A. Graf, CFO/Exec. VP/Treas.
Jorge de Cardenas, Sr. VP-IT
Kim K. Voss, Sr. VP/Controller
James C. Hopke, Jr., Exec. VP-Project Mgmt. & Construction
Daniel Perry, Exec. VP-Capital Markets
William Talbot, Exec.VP-Investments
Steve Crawford, Sr. VP-Mgmt. Svcs.
R.D. Burck, Chmn.

Phone: 512-732-1000 **Fax:** 517-732-2450
Toll-Free:
Address: 805 Las Cimas Pkwy., Ste. 400, Austin, TX 78746 US

GROWTH PLANS/SPECIAL FEATURES:

American Campus Communities, Inc. (ACC) is a real estate investment trust (REIT) with expertise in the acquisition, design, financing, development, construction management, leasing and management of student housing properties. The company, operating primarily via subsidiary American Campus Communities Operating Partnership LP, is one of the largest owners, managers and developers of student housing properties in the U.S. in terms of beds owned, developed and under management. ACC's property portfolio consists of 104 student housing properties with approximately 65,000 beds and 20,800 apartment units. The company operates in four segments: wholly-owned properties, on-campus participating properties, development services and property management services. The wholly-owned properties segment consists of all properties in proximity to college campuses; these include 96 wholly-owned complexes in 27 states, as well as four properties operated under a ground/facility lease through American Campus Equity. The on-campus participating properties segment consists of facilities leased from universities that are managed by the company. The development services segment provides consulting services, through the company's subsidiaries, to colleges and universities for all stages of property construction. The property management services segment is conducted primarily through subsidiaries for college or university clients and includes all aspect of facility maintenance and administration. ACC provides property management services to 37 properties. ACC's communities contain modern housing units and are supported by a resident assistant system and other student-oriented programming, with many offering resort-style amenities. In 2011, the company began construction on new housing in locations including Dekalb, Illinois; Normal, Illinois; Laramie, Wyoming; Arlington, Texas; Albuquerque, New Mexico; and Amherst, New York. In February 2012, the company began construction on student housing in Philadelphia, Pennsylvania.

FINANCIALS: **Sales and profits are in thousands of dollars—add 000 to get the full amount. 2011 Note: Financial information for 2011 was not available for all companies at press time.**

2011 Sales: $390,317 | 2011 Profits: $57,972
2010 Sales: $344,991 | 2010 Profits: $16,210
2009 Sales: $304,946 | 2009 Profits: $-12,840
2008 Sales: $233,579 | 2008 Profits: $-13,055
2007 Sales: $147,135 | 2007 Profits: $-1,686

U.S. Stock Ticker: ACC
Int'l Ticker:
Int'l Exchange:
Employees: 2,334 Fiscal Year Ends: 12/31
Parent Company:

SALARIES/BENEFITS:

Pension Plan: ESOP Stock Plan: Profit Sharing: Top Exec. Salary: $459,000 Bonus: $475,000
Savings Plan: Stock Purch. Plan: Second Exec. Salary: $351,900 Bonus: $350,000

OTHER THOUGHTS:

Apparent Women Officers or Directors: 3
Hot Spot for Advancement for Women/Minorities: Y

LOCATIONS: ("Y" = Yes)

West:	Southwest:	Midwest:	Southeast:	Northeast:	International:
Y	Y	Y	Y	Y	Y

AMERICAN FIDELITY ASSURANCE COMPANY

www.afadvantage.com

Industry Group Code: 524113

Management:		Sales/Marketing:		Liberal Arts:		Information Systems:		Professionals:		Technical/Scientific:	
Mgmt. Trainees:	Y	Mktg. Professionals:	Y	Gen. Writing/Editing:	Y	Info. Management:	Y	Finance/Acct.:	Y	Engineers, Elec.:	
Experienced Mgmt.:	Y	Retail Sales:		Technical Writing:	Y	Software Dev.:		Law:	Y	Engineers, Other:	
Int'l Business:	Y	Commercial/Industrial:		Graphic Arts/Photog.:		Hardware Dev.:		HR/Other:	Y	Health/Lab	
MBA Graduates:	Y	Sales Trainees:	Y	Music:		Consulting/Other:		Training:	Y	Scientists/Research:	
		Advertising Pros.:	Y	Broadcasting:				Health Care:	Y	Petroleum/Chemicals:	
				Other:				Consulting:		Math/Other:	Y

TYPES OF BUSINESS:

Life Insurance
Disability Insurance
Annuities
Supplemental Health Insurance
Asset Management

BRANDS/DIVISIONS/AFFILIATES:

American Fidelity Educational Services
Association & Worksite Division (The)
American Public Life Insurance Company (APL)
AFAmeriLife (AFAL)
Latin America Life Insurance

CONTACTS:

Note: Officers with more than one job title may be intentionally listed here more than once.

William M. Cameron, CEO
David R. Carpenter, COO
David R. Carpenter, Pres.
Robert D. Brearton, CFO/Exec. VP
Kim Fisher, CIO
Stephen P. Garrett, Corp. Sec./Sr. VP
Robert Brearton, Treas.
Gary E. Tredway, Pres., American Fidelity Educational Svcs/Exec. VP
Jim Pate, Pres., American Public Life
Rick Summerlin, Pres., Association Worksite Div.
William M. Cameron, Chmn.

Phone: 405-523-2000	**Fax:** 405-523-5963
Toll-Free: 800-654-8489	
Address: 2000 N. Classen Blvd., Oklahoma City, OK 73106 US	

GROWTH PLANS/SPECIAL FEATURES:

American Fidelity Assurance Company (AFA) is a private, family-owned life insurance company. Based in Oklahoma City, it serves more than 1 million customers in 49 U.S. states and 30 countries and manages over $5.6 million in consolidated assets, with more than 1.6 million policies currently in force. AFA focuses on providing insurance products and financial services to education employees, trade association members and companies. The firm's primary businesses include disability income insurance, life insurance, annuities and supplemental health insurance. AFA's specific offerings include accident only protection insurance; health savings accounts (HSAs); 403(b) tax-deferred annuities; after-tax annuities; individual retirement annuities; Roth IRAs; children's life insurance; whole life insurance; group disability income insurance; Section 125 administration; health reimbursement arrangement (HRA) services; cancer protection plans; hospital GAP Plans; and hospital indemnity. Subsidiary American Fidelity Educational Services (AFES) provides supplemental insurance products, investment products and financial services to the educational community. The Association & Worksite Division (AWD) of the company provides employee-paid personal wealth, asset and family protection, including group disability, cancer, life, accident and hospital indemnity insurance. The Life Division was formed as the result of a merger between AFAmeriLife (AFAL) and AFA's Latin America Life Insurance. Subsidiary American Public Life Insurance Company (APL) provides worksite brokers with whole and term life, supplemental, specified disease and dental health insurance products. Through strategic alliances with several firms, the company offers medical stop-loss, mini-medical business and specialty insurance products to companies with large workforces and industries with high turnover or employees with low incomes.

AFA offers its employees on-site fitness centers, training facilities, banking facilities and a deli; discounts on event tickets; off-site fitness and wellness reimbursements; a 401(k) plan and a traditional pension plan; flexible reimbursement accounts for medical and dependent daycare expenses; a holiday bonus; and health, dental and vision insurance.

FINANCIALS:

Sales and profits are in thousands of dollars—add 000 to get the full amount. 2011 Note: Financial information for 2011 was not available for all companies at press time.

2011 Sales: $	2011 Profits: $	**U.S. Stock Ticker: Private**
2010 Sales: $846,000	2010 Profits: $	**Int'l Ticker:**
2009 Sales: $828,000	2009 Profits: $	Int'l Exchange:
2008 Sales: $739,000	2008 Profits: $	Employees: 1,400 Fiscal Year Ends: 12/31
2007 Sales: $752,000	2007 Profits: $	Parent Company:

SALARIES/BENEFITS:

Pension Plan: Y	ESOP Stock Plan:	Profit Sharing:	Top Exec. Salary: $	Bonus: $
Savings Plan: Y	Stock Purch. Plan:		Second Exec. Salary: $	Bonus: $

OTHER THOUGHTS:

Apparent Women Officers or Directors: 1
Hot Spot for Advancement for Women/Minorities: Y

LOCATIONS: ("Y" = Yes)

West:	Southwest:	Midwest:	Southeast:	Northeast:	International:
Y	Y	Y	Y	Y	Y

AMERICAN MEDICAL SYSTEMS HOLDINGS INC

www.americanmedicalsystems.com

Industry Group Code: 33911

Management:		Sales/Marketing:		Liberal Arts:		Information Systems:		Professionals:		Technical/Scientific:	
Mgmt. Trainees:		Mktg. Professionals:	Y	Gen. Writing/Editing:		Info. Management:	Y	Finance/Acct.:	Y	Engineers, Elec.:	
Experienced Mgmt.:	Y	Retail Sales:		Technical Writing:	Y	Software Dev.:	Y	Law:	Y	Engineers, Other:	Y
Int'l Business:	Y	Commercial/Industrial:	Y	Graphic Arts/Photog.:		Hardware Dev.:	Y	HR/Other:	Y	Health/Lab	Y
MBA Graduates:	Y	Sales Trainees:	Y	Music:		Consulting/Other:		Training:	Y	Scientists/Research:	Y
		Advertising Pros.:		Broadcasting:				Health Care:	Y	Petroleum/Chemicals:	
				Other:				Consulting:		Math/Other:	

TYPES OF BUSINESS:

Urological Devices Manufacturing
Erectile Dysfunction Products
Incontinence Products
Prostate Disease Products

BRANDS/DIVISIONS/AFFILIATES:

AMS 700 LGX
AMS 800
MoXy Liquid Cooled Fiber
Endo Pharmaceuticals

CONTACTS: *Note: Officers with more than one job title may be intentionally listed here more than once.*

Anthony P. Bihl, III, CEO
Anthony P. Bihl, III, Pres.
Mark A. Heggestad, CFO/Exec. VP
Randall Ross, Sr. VP-Human Resources
Maximillian D. Fiore, CTO/Sr. VP
Jeanne Forneris, General Counsel/Sr. VP
Thomas K. Rasmussen, VP-Minnetonka Oper.
Whitney D. Erickson, Sr. VP/Gen. Mgr.-Men's Health
Joe W. Martin, Sr. VP/Gen. Mgr.-BPH Therapy
Richard D. Staples, VP-U.S. Sales
Michael E. Ryan, VP/Gen. Mgr.-Asia Pacific/Latin America
Derrill Palidwar, Sr. VP/Gen. Mgr.-EMEA
Thomas K. Rasmussen, VP-Supply Chain

Phone: 952-930-6000 **Fax:** 952-930-6373
Toll-Free: 800-328-3881
Address: 10700 Bren Rd. W., Minnetonka, MN 55343 US

GROWTH PLANS/SPECIAL FEATURES:

American Medical Systems Holdings, Inc. (AMS) supplies medical devices for treating men's and women's pelvic health conditions, including urological and gynecological disorders. The company manufactures and markets a broad and well-established line of proprietary products, focusing on three major urological disorders for men: incontinence, erectile dysfunction and prostate disease, and incontinence and pelvic floor prolapse for women. It primary customers include physicians such as urologists, gynecologists, urogynecologists and colorectal surgeons. AMS offers a range of products designed to treat men and women suffering from urinary and fecal incontinence. Products encompass artificial sphincters, such as the firm's AMS 800; male and female sling systems such as the MiniArc for women; a vaginal vault prolapse system under the Elevate name; and graft materials. AMS provides products for the diagnosis and treatment of erectile dysfunction such as inflatable and malleable penile prostheses and accessories, including its AMS 700 inflatable prostheses. The company sells its products directly through a network of field representatives in the U.S., Canada, Australia, Brazil and a number of Western European countries. Additionally, AMS products are sold through roughly 80 independent international distributors in countries where the firm does not have direct field representation. In September 2010, the company introduced the MoXy Liquid Cooled Fiber, designed to be used in laser treatments for enlarged prostate. In April 2011, AMS agreed to be acquired by Endo Pharmaceuticals for $2.9 billion.

Employees are offered medical, dental and vision insurance; life insurance; short- and long-term disability coverage; health care and dependent care flexible spending accounts; an educational assistance plan; a 401(k) plan; profit sharing; an employee stock purchase plan; group legal plans; auto and home insurance plans; access to an onsite fitness center and wellness programs and access to an onsite cafeteria.

FINANCIALS: **Sales and profits are in thousands of dollars—add 000 to get the full amount. 2011 Note: Financial information for 2011 was not available for all companies at press time.**

2011 Sales: $	2011 Profits: $
2010 Sales: $542,316	2010 Profits: $87,010
2009 Sales: $519,270	2009 Profits: $84,838
2008 Sales: $501,641	2008 Profits: $42,552
2007 Sales: $463,928	2007 Profits: $12,900

U.S. Stock Ticker: Subsidiary
Int'l Ticker:
Int'l Exchange:
Employees: 1,255 Fiscal Year Ends: 12/31
Parent Company: ENDO PHARMACEUTICALS

SALARIES/BENEFITS:

Pension Plan:	ESOP Stock Plan:	Profit Sharing: Y	Top Exec. Salary: $527,692	Bonus: $622,220
Savings Plan: Y	Stock Purch. Plan: Y		Second Exec. Salary: $311,046	Bonus: $182,968

OTHER THOUGHTS:

Apparent Women Officers or Directors: 3
Hot Spot for Advancement for Women/Minorities: Y

LOCATIONS: ("Y" = Yes)

West:	Southwest:	Midwest:	Southeast:	Northeast:	International:
Y	Y	Y			Y

AMERICAN SCIENCE & ENGINEERING INC

www.as-e.com

Industry Group Code: 3345

Management:		Sales/Marketing:		Liberal Arts:		Information Systems:		Professionals:		Technical/Scientific:	
Mgmt. Trainees:		Mktg. Professionals:	Y	Gen. Writing/Editing:		Info. Management:	Y	Finance/Acct.:	Y	Engineers, Elec.:	Y
Experienced Mgmt.:	Y	Retail Sales:		Technical Writing:	Y	Software Dev.:	Y	Law:	Y	Engineers, Other:	Y
Int'l Business:	Y	Commercial/Industrial:	Y	Graphic Arts/Photog.:		Hardware Dev.:	Y	HR/Other:	Y	Health/Lab	
MBA Graduates:	Y	Sales Trainees:	Y	Music:		Consulting/Other:		Training:	Y	Scientists/Research:	
		Advertising Pros.:		Broadcasting:				Health Care:		Petroleum/Chemicals:	
				Other:				Consulting:		Math/Other:	Y

TYPES OF BUSINESS:

X-Ray Inspection Solutions
Security Systems
Radiation Detection Technology
Maintenance, Warranty & Research Services
Engineering & Training Services

BRANDS/DIVISIONS/AFFILIATES:

Z Portal
Z Backscatter Van
Shaped Energy
Radioactive Threat Detection
MobileSearch HE
ParcelSearch
OmniView
Gemini

CONTACTS: *Note: Officers with more than one job title may be intentionally listed here more than once.*

Anthony R. Fabiano, CEO
Anthony R. Fabiano, Pres.
Ken Galaznik, CFO
Robert G. Postle, Sr. VP-Worldwide Mktg. & Sales
George M. Peterman, Sr. VP-Human Resources
Joseph Callerame, Sr. VP-Science
Joseph Callerame, Sr. VP-Tech.
Michael N. Tropeano, Sr. VP-Prod. Mgmt.
Michael Williams, Sr. VP-Eng & Dev.
Patricia A. Gray, General Counsel/Sr. VP
Robert Cline, Sr. VP-Oper.
Paul H. Grazewski, Sr. VP-Strategic Planning
Ken Galaznik, Treas./Sr. VP
Denis R. Brown, Chmn.
Kenneth Breur, Sr. VP-Logistics & Advanced Dev.

Phone: 978-262-8700 **Fax:** 978-262-8804
Toll-Free: 800-225-1608
Address: 829 Middlesex Turnpike, Billerica, MA 01821 US

GROWTH PLANS/SPECIAL FEATURES:

American Science & Engineering, Inc. (ASE) develops, manufactures, markets and sells X-ray inspection and other detection products for homeland security and other targeted markets. The company provides maintenance, warranty, research, engineering and training services related to these products. The firm's X-ray imaging products utilize several technologies, including traditional transmission X-ray technology, its proprietary Z Backscatter technology, Shaped Energy technology and Radioactive Threat Detection (RTD). The Z Backscatter technology creates photo-quality X-ray images that highlight organic threats and contraband such as explosives, plastic weapons and drugs. The Shaped Energy technology allows high X-ray penetration without using a radioactive source. The RTD technology detects radioactive materials in vehicles. ASE technologies are incorporated into systems such as the Sentry Portal, OmniView Gantry, Z Portal, Z Gantry, MobileSearch HE (High-Energy), Gemini and SmartCheck. The Z Backscatter Van (ZBV) is a screening system built into a commercially available delivery van, which allows operators to conduct X-ray imaging of suspect vehicles, highlighting organic materials such as plastic explosives. ASE's products are used to inspect parcels, baggage, vehicles, pallets, cargo containers and people, and are sold in the U.S. and throughout the world to a variety of customers, including port and border security authorities; aviation security agencies; legal enforcement agencies; military organizations; and high threat commercial and government facilities. Customers use ASE's products to help combat terrorism, trade fraud, drug trafficking, weapons smuggling and illegal immigration; and for military force protection and general facility security.

Employees are offered medical, dental, disability and life insurance; a 401(k), tuition reimbursement; travel accident insurance; and flexible spending accounts.

FINANCIALS: **Sales and profits are in thousands of dollars—add 000 to get the full amount. 2011 Note: Financial information for 2011 was not available for all companies at press time.**

2011 Sales: $278,576 | 2011 Profits: $42,817
2010 Sales: $242,093 | 2010 Profits: $36,176
2009 Sales: $218,367 | 2009 Profits: $28,353
2008 Sales: $166,733 | 2008 Profits: $17,478
2007 Sales: $153,186 | 2007 Profits: $24,610

U.S. Stock Ticker: ASEI
Int'l Ticker:
Int'l Exchange:
Employees: 420 Fiscal Year Ends: 3/31
Parent Company:

SALARIES/BENEFITS:

Pension Plan: | ESOP Stock Plan: | Profit Sharing: | Top Exec. Salary: $545,000 | Bonus: $1,194,000
Savings Plan: Y | Stock Purch. Plan: | | Second Exec. Salary: $282,000 | Bonus: $344,000

OTHER THOUGHTS:

Apparent Women Officers or Directors: 2
Hot Spot for Advancement for Women/Minorities:

LOCATIONS: ("Y" = Yes)

West:	Southwest:	Midwest:	Southeast:	Northeast:	International:
				Y	

AMERICAN TIRE DISTRIBUTORS

www.americantiredistributors.com

Industry Group Code: 423120

Management:		Sales/Marketing:		Liberal Arts:		Information Systems:		Professionals:		Technical/Scientific:	
Mgmt. Trainees:	Y	Mktg. Professionals:	Y	Gen. Writing/Editing:		Info. Management:	Y	Finance/Acct.:	Y	Engineers, Elec.:	
Experienced Mgmt.:	Y	Retail Sales:	Y	Technical Writing:	Y	Software Dev.:		Law:	Y	Engineers, Other:	
Int'l Business:		Commercial/Industrial:	Y	Graphic Arts/Photog.:	Y	Hardware Dev.:		HR/Other:	Y	Health/Lab	
MBA Graduates:	Y	Sales Trainees:	Y	Music:		Consulting/Other:		Training:	Y	Scientists/Research:	
		Advertising Pros.:	Y	Broadcasting:				Health Care:		Petroleum/Chemicals:	
				Other:				Consulting:		Math/Other:	

TYPES OF BUSINESS:

Tires & Related Products, Distribution

BRANDS/DIVISIONS/AFFILIATES:

TPG Capital
Monarch
Silver State Tire Company
ATD Service Bay
Samaritan Wholesale Tire Company
Texas Market Tire
ATDOnline
TireBuyer.com

CONTACTS: *Note: Officers with more than one job title may be intentionally listed here more than once.*

William Berry, CEO
William Berry, Pres.
Dave Dyckman, CFO/Exec. VP
Daniel Brown, Sr. VP-Sales
Michael Gaither, General Counsel/Exec. VP
Ron Sinclair, Sr. VP-Mktg.
Phillip Marrett, Sr. VP-Procurement

Phone: 704-992-2000 **Fax:** 704-992-1384
Toll-Free: 800-222-1167
Address: 12200 Herbert Wayne Ct., Ste. 150, Huntersville, NC 28070 US

GROWTH PLANS/SPECIAL FEATURES:

American Tire Distributors (ATD) is one of the nation's largest suppliers of tires and wheels, as well as tools and other automotive service equipment. The company serves the replacement tire market through approximately 82 regional warehouses, two national mixing warehouses, 96 warehouse distribution centers and more than 700 delivery vehicles, delivering products to 39 states, with an extensive independent dealer network. ATD offers its tire retailers and service shop clients various tires for passenger vehicles and light trucks, tractor-trailers, buses, farm machinery and specialty and recreational vehicles. The company carries brands including Michelin, Goodyear, Bridgestone/Firestone, Dunlop and BFGoodrich, as well as its Monarch house brand, which is manufactured by Goodyear. Its wheel selection ranges from 13- to 26-inch rims for passenger vehicles and light trucks. The firm runs ATD Service Bay, which provides programs, services, tools and technologies to dealers. ATD owns Texas Market Tire, which expanded the company's presence through Texas, Oklahoma and New Mexico; Silver State Tire Company, in Nevada; Golden State Tire Distributors, which expanded its presence in northern California; and Samaritan Wholesale Tire Company, which expanded service across Minnesota and in western Wisconsin. Additionally, the firm maintains ATDOnline, which offers dealers access to prices, availability and the ability to place orders 24 hours a day, seven days a week; and TireBuyer.com, where customers can buy tires and wheels, as well as choose a dealer location for installation. TireBuyer.com also allows potential purchasers to view tires and wheels on their particular vehicle, using the web site's 3D visualizer. The company is owned by TPG Capital.

FINANCIALS: **Sales and profits are in thousands of dollars—add 000 to get the full amount. 2011 Note: Financial information for 2011 was not available for all companies at press time.**

2011 Sales: $	2011 Profits: $
2010 Sales: $	2010 Profits: $
2009 Sales: $	2009 Profits: $
2008 Sales: $	2008 Profits: $
2007 Sales: $	2007 Profits: $

U.S. Stock Ticker: Private
Int'l Ticker:
Int'l Exchange:
Employees: 2,400 Fiscal Year Ends: 12/31
Parent Company: TPG CAPITAL

SALARIES/BENEFITS:

Pension Plan:	ESOP Stock Plan:	Profit Sharing:	Top Exec. Salary: $	Bonus: $
Savings Plan:	Stock Purch. Plan:		Second Exec. Salary: $	Bonus: $

OTHER THOUGHTS:

Apparent Women Officers or Directors:
Hot Spot for Advancement for Women/Minorities:

LOCATIONS: ("Y" = Yes)

West:	Southwest:	Midwest:	Southeast:	Northeast:	International:
Y	Y	Y	Y	Y	

AMERICAN TOWER CORP

www.americantower.com

Industry Group Code: 237130

Management:		Sales/Marketing:		Liberal Arts:		Information Systems:		Professionals:		Technical/Scientific:	
Mgmt. Trainees:		Mktg. Professionals:	Y	Gen. Writing/Editing:		Info. Management:	Y	Finance/Acct.:	Y	Engineers, Elec.:	Y
Experienced Mgmt.:	Y	Retail Sales:		Technical Writing:	Y	Software Dev.:		Law:	Y	Engineers, Other:	Y
Int'l Business:	Y	Commercial/Industrial:	Y	Graphic Arts/Photog.:		Hardware Dev.:		HR/Other:	Y	Health/Lab	
MBA Graduates:	Y	Sales Trainees:	Y	Music:		Consulting/Other:		Training:	Y	Scientists/Research:	
		Advertising Pros.:		Broadcasting:				Health Care:		Petroleum/Chemicals:	
				Other:				Consulting:		Math/Other:	

TYPES OF BUSINESS:

Broadcast & Communications Towers
Cellular Telephone Towers
Radio & TV Broadcast Towers
Network Development & Consulting
Antenna Site Leasing

BRANDS/DIVISIONS/AFFILIATES:

American Tower REIT Inc
SpectraSite Communications LLC
American Tower International Inc
Insight Infrastructure Pte Ltd
American Towers Inc

CONTACTS: *Note: Officers with more than one job title may be intentionally listed here more than once.*

James Taiclet, CEO
James Taiclet, COO
James Taiclet, Pres.
Tom Bartlett, CFO
Ed DiSanto, Chief Admin. Officer
Ed DiSanto, General Counsel/Exec. VP
Steven Marshall, Exec. VP/Pres., U.S. Tower Div.
Amit Sharma, Exec. VP/Pres., Asia
James Taiclet, Chmn.
Hal Hess, Exec. VP-Int'l Oper./Pres., EMEA & Latin America

Phone: 617-375-7500 **Fax:** 617-375-7575
Toll-Free: 877-282-7483
Address: 116 Huntington Ave., 11th Fl., Boston, MA 02116 US

GROWTH PLANS/SPECIAL FEATURES:

American Tower Corp. (ATC) is leading wireless and broadcast communications infrastructure company with a portfolio of more than 39,000 communications sites, including wireless communications towers, broadcast communications towers and distributed antenna systems (DAS). Its portfolio consists of about 20,900 tower sites throughout the U.S. and approximately 13,900 internationally, as well as aproximately 200 in-building distributed antenna systems that it operates in malls, casinos and hotel resorts throughout the U.S. and Mexico. The company conducts business in the U.S. primarily through its American Towers, Inc. (ATI) and SpectraSite Communications, LLC subsidiaries, while subsidiary American Tower International, Inc. conducts its international business. ATC operates in three segments: domestic rental and management, international rental and management and network development services. The company derives more than 98% of its total revenues from its rental and management segment, in which it leases antenna sites on multi-tenant towers to wireless service providers and radio and television broadcast companies. The company's major domestic wireless customers include AT&T Mobility; Sprint Nextel; T-Mobile USA; and Verizon Wireless. Its largest international wireless customers include Grupo Iusacell, which controls both Iusacell Cellular and Unefon in Mexico. ATC's network development services, which generate approximately 3% of its revenues, include site acquisition, zoning, permitting services and structural analysis services. In January 2012, the firm expanded its portfolio through a merger with and into wholly owned subsidiary American Tower REIT, Inc., allowing it to restructure its business operations and qualify as a real estate investment trust under the name American Tower Corp. In December 2011, ATC acquired 2,500 additional tower sites from Pagaso PCS, S.A. de C.V., a Mexican subsidiary of Telefonica.

The company offers employees medical, dental and vision health care plans; educational assistance; a 401(k) plan; an employee stock purchase plan; life insurance; disability coverage; adoption assistance; and an employee assistance program.

FINANCIALS: **Sales and profits are in thousands of dollars—add 000 to get the full amount. 2011 Note: Financial information for 2011 was not available for all companies at press time.**

2011 Sales: $2,443,532 | 2011 Profits: $381,840
2010 Sales: $1,985,335 | 2010 Profits: $373,606
2009 Sales: $1,724,114 | 2009 Profits: $247,127
2008 Sales: $1,593,504 | 2008 Profits: $347,246
2007 Sales: $1,456,594 | 2007 Profits: $56,316

U.S. Stock Ticker: AMT
Int'l Ticker:
Int'l Exchange:
Employees: 1,729 Fiscal Year Ends: 12/31
Parent Company:

SALARIES/BENEFITS:

Pension Plan: | ESOP Stock Plan: | Profit Sharing: | Top Exec. Salary: $900,000 | Bonus: $181,250
Savings Plan: Y | Stock Purch. Plan: Y | | Second Exec. Salary: $650,000 | Bonus: $1,000,005

OTHER THOUGHTS:

Apparent Women Officers or Directors: 4
Hot Spot for Advancement for Women/Minorities: Y

LOCATIONS: ("Y" = Yes)

West:	Southwest:	Midwest:	Southeast:	Northeast:	International:
Y	Y	Y	Y	Y	Y

Sales, profits and employees may be estimates. Financial information, benefits and other data can change quickly and may vary from those stated here.

AMERICAN VANGUARD CORP

www.amvac-chemical.com

Industry Group Code: 11511

Management:		Sales/Marketing:		Liberal Arts:		Information Systems:		Professionals:		Technical/Scientific:	
Mgmt. Trainees:		Mktg. Professionals:		Gen. Writing/Editing:		Info. Management:	Y	Finance/Acct.:	Y	Engineers, Elec.:	
Experienced Mgmt.:	Y	Retail Sales:		Technical Writing:		Software Dev.:		Law:	Y	Engineers, Other:	Y
Int'l Business:	Y	Commercial/Industrial:	Y	Graphic Arts/Photog.:		Hardware Dev.:		HR/Other:	Y	Health/Lab	
MBA Graduates:	Y	Sales Trainees:		Music:		Consulting/Other:		Training:	Y	Scientists/Research:	
		Advertising Pros.:	Y	Broadcasting:				Health Care:		Petroleum/Chemicals:	Y
				Other:				Consulting:		Math/Other:	

TYPES OF BUSINESS:

Pesticides
Specialty Chemicals & Agricultural Products
Distribution Services
Environmental Analysis & Consulting Services

BRANDS/DIVISIONS/AFFILIATES:

AMVAC Chemical Corporation
GemChem Inc
Environmental Mediation Inc
AMVAC Chemical UK Ltd
Quimica Amvac de Mexico SA de CV
AMVAC Chemical GmbH
AMVAC do Brasil Representacoes Ltda
2110 Davie Corporation

CONTACTS:

Note: Officers with more than one job title may be intentionally listed here more than once.

Eric Wintemute, CEO
Trevor Thorley, COO/Exec. VP
Eric Wintemute, Pres.
David T. Johnson, CFO/Sr. VP
Bill Feiler, Chief Scientist
John L. Killmer, Head-Prod. Tech.
John E. Orr, Mgr.-Prod. Dev., Northern Region
Doug Ashmore, VP/Dir.-Mfg.
Timothy J. Donnelly, Chief Admin. Officer
Timothy J. Donnelly, General Counsel/Corp. Sec./VP
Glen Johnson, Sr. VP/Dir.-Bus. Dev.
William A. Kuser, Dir.-Corp. Comm.
William A. Kuser, Dir.-Investor Rel.
Ian S. Chart, VP/Dir.-Regulatory Affairs
Ann Manley, Dir.-Toxicology
Jon Wood, Dir.-Registrations
Glenn A. Wintemute, Co-Chmn.
Herbert A. Kraft, Co-Chmn.
Alfredo Pelaez, Dir-Int'l Bus.

Phone: 949-260-1200 **Fax:** 949-260-1201
Toll-Free: 888-462-6822
Address: 4695 MacArthur Ct., Newport Beach, CA 92660 US

GROWTH PLANS/SPECIAL FEATURES:

American Vanguard Corp. (AMVAC) is a holding company that operates through three main subsidiaries: AMVAC Chemical Corporation; GemChem, Inc.; and Environmental Mediation, Inc. (EMI). AMVAC Chemical develops and manufactures chemicals for crops, human and animal health protection. Its chemicals include insecticides, fungicides, herbicides, molluscicides, plant-growth regulators and soil fumigants in liquid, powder and granular forms. Its products are sold in the U.S. and in various foreign countries. AMVAC Chemical also conducts business through international subsidiaries AMVAC Chemical UK Ltd. and Quimica AMVAC de Mexico S.A. de C.V. GemChem is a national chemical distributor. It purchases raw materials for the company and acts as AMVAC's sales force. Its primary markets in the U.S. include the cosmetic, nutritional and pharmaceutical industries. Lastly, EMI provides hazardous waste, air toxin, water quality and other environmental analysis and consulting services. Its services include issue analysis, strategic planning, government relations, regulatory strategy, environmental consulting and public affairs services. AMVAC also owns 2110 Davie Corporation, a subsidiary that owns real estate for corporate use; AMVAC Chemical GmbH; AMVAC do Brasil Representacoes Ltda; and AMVAC de Costa Rica SA. In December 2010, the company acquired three global insecticide product lines from Bayer CropScience AG: one relating to the active ingredient Tebupirimfos, sold under the Aztec, Azteca and Capinda names; a second relating to Fenamiphos, sold as Nemacur; and another relating to Ethoprophos, sold under the name Mocap.

FINANCIALS:

Sales and profits are in thousands of dollars—add 000 to get the full amount. 2011 Note: Financial information for 2011 was not available for all companies at press time.

2011 Sales: $ | 2011 Profits: $
2010 Sales: $229,620 | 2010 Profits: $10,984
2009 Sales: $209,329 | 2009 Profits: $-5,789
2008 Sales: $237,538 | 2008 Profits: $20,019
2007 Sales: $216,662 | 2007 Profits: $18,728

U.S. Stock Ticker: AVD
Int'l Ticker:
Int'l Exchange:
Employees: 350 Fiscal Year Ends: 12/31
Parent Company:

SALARIES/BENEFITS:

Pension Plan: ESOP Stock Plan: Profit Sharing: Top Exec. Salary: $501,481 Bonus: $137,500
Savings Plan: Stock Purch. Plan: Second Exec. Salary: $275,000 Bonus: $85,000

OTHER THOUGHTS:

Apparent Women Officers or Directors: 2
Hot Spot for Advancement for Women/Minorities:

LOCATIONS: ("Y" = Yes)

West:	Southwest:	Midwest:	Southeast:	Northeast:	International:
Y		Y	Y	Y	Y

AMERICA'S CAR-MART INC

www.car-mart.com

Industry Group Code: 441110

Management:		Sales/Marketing:		Liberal Arts:		Information Systems:		Professionals:		Technical/Scientific:	
Mgmt. Trainees:	Y	Mktg. Professionals:	Y	Gen. Writing/Editing:	Y	Info. Management:	Y	Finance/Acct.:	Y	Engineers, Elec.:	
Experienced Mgmt.:	Y	Retail Sales:	Y	Technical Writing:		Software Dev.:	Y	Law:	Y	Engineers, Other:	
Int'l Business:	Y	Commercial/Industrial:		Graphic Arts/Photog.:		Hardware Dev.:		HR/Other:	Y	Health/Lab	
MBA Graduates:	Y	Sales Trainees:	Y	Music:		Consulting/Other:		Training:	Y	Scientists/Research:	
		Advertising Pros.:	Y	Broadcasting:				Health Care:		Petroleum/Chemicals:	
				Other:				Consulting:		Math/Other:	

TYPES OF BUSINESS:

Used Auto Dealers, Retail
Used Car Financing & Servicing

BRANDS/DIVISIONS/AFFILIATES:

America's Car-Mart, Inc.
Car-Mart of Arkansas
Colonial Auto Finance, Inc.

CONTACTS: *Note: Officers with more than one job title may be intentionally listed here more than once.*

William H. Henderson, CEO
Eddie L. Hight, COO
William H. Henderson, Pres.
Jeffrey A. Williams, CFO
Tilman J. Falgout, III, General Counsel
William H. Henderson, Vice Chmn.
Tilman J. Falgout, III, Chmn.

Phone: 479-464-9944 **Fax:** 479-273-7556

Toll-Free:

Address: 802 Southeast Plz. Ave., Ste. 200, Bentonville, AR 72712 US

GROWTH PLANS/SPECIAL FEATURES:

America's Car-Mart, Inc. is one of the largest publicly-held automotive retailers focused exclusively on the buy-here/pay-here segment of the used car market in the U.S. America's Car-Mart operates 107 dealerships located primarily in small cities throughout Alabama, Arkansas, Indiana, Kentucky, Missouri, Oklahoma, Tennessee and Texas, with populations of 50,000 or less. However, the company does have a number of dealerships in larger cities such as Tulsa, Oklahoma; Lexington, Kentucky; Springfield Missouri; and Little Rock, Arkansas. The firm operates primarily through its two subsidiaries, America's Car-Mart, Inc., an Arkansas-based company also known as Car-Mart of Arkansas, and Colonial Auto Finance, Inc. The company targets credit-impaired borrowers living in small to midsize cities and towns who would typically not qualify for conventional financing. Stores are run on a decentralized basis, with each dealership responsible for purchasing (with the help of a corporate buyer), making credit decisions, servicing vehicles and collecting the installment loans it originates. The company operates both regular and satellite stores. Satellite stores tend to be smaller, sell fewer vehicles and have their financing reported with the corresponding regular stores that sponsor them. The majority of the company's vehicles are purchased through wholesalers, new car dealers, individuals and from auctions. Generally, the firm's buyers purchase vehicles between 5-10 years old with 90,000-130,000 miles, paying between $3,000-$6,000 per vehicle.

The company offers employers medical, dental and life insurance; disability coverage; a 401(k) plan; and education assistance.

FINANCIALS: **Sales and profits are in thousands of dollars—add 000 to get the full amount. 2011 Note: Financial information for 2011 was not available for all companies at press time.**

2011 Sales: $379,251 | 2011 Profits: $28,175
2010 Sales: $338,930 | 2010 Profits: $26,799
2009 Sales: $298,966 | 2009 Profits: $17,903
2008 Sales: $274,631 | 2008 Profits: $15,033
2007 Sales: $240,334 | 2007 Profits: $4,232

U.S. Stock Ticker: CRMT
Int'l Ticker:
Int'l Exchange:
Employees: 1,025 Fiscal Year Ends: 4/30
Parent Company:

SALARIES/BENEFITS:

Pension Plan: | ESOP Stock Plan: | Profit Sharing: | Top Exec. Salary: $300,000 | Bonus: $162,523
Savings Plan: Y | Stock Purch. Plan: | | Second Exec. Salary: $210,319 | Bonus: $98,574

OTHER THOUGHTS:

Apparent Women Officers or Directors:
Hot Spot for Advancement for Women/Minorities:

LOCATIONS: ("Y" = Yes)

West:	Southwest:	Midwest:	Southeast:	Northeast:	International:
	Y	Y	Y		

AMTECH SYSTEMS INC

www.amtechsystems.com

Industry Group Code: 333295

Management:		Sales/Marketing:		Liberal Arts:		Information Systems:		Professionals:		Technical/Scientific:	
Mgmt. Trainees:		Mktg. Professionals:	Y	Gen. Writing/Editing:		Info. Management:	Y	Finance/Acct.:	Y	Engineers, Elec.:	Y
Experienced Mgmt.:	Y	Retail Sales:		Technical Writing:	Y	Software Dev.:	Y	Law:	Y	Engineers, Other:	Y
Int'l Business:	Y	Commercial/Industrial:	Y	Graphic Arts/Photog.:		Hardware Dev.:	Y	HR/Other:	Y	Health/Lab	
MBA Graduates:	Y	Sales Trainees:	Y	Music:		Consulting/Other:		Training:	Y	Scientists/Research:	Y
		Advertising Pros.:		Broadcasting:				Health Care:		Petroleum/Chemicals:	
				Other:				Consulting:		Math/Other:	Y

TYPES OF BUSINESS:

Semiconductor Manufacturing Equipment
Diffusion Furnace Systems
Wafer Polishing Systems
Machinery Support & Maintenance Services

BRANDS/DIVISIONS/AFFILIATES:

Bruce Technologies Inc
Tempress Systems Inc
PR Hoffman Machine Products Inc
R2D Automation SAS
Kingstone Technology Hong Kong Limited

CONTACTS: *Note: Officers with more than one job title may be intentionally listed here more than once.*

Jong S. Whang, CEO
Fokko Pentinga, Pres.
Bradley C. Anderson, CFO/VP-Finance/Treas.
Jeong-Mo Hwang, CTO/VP
Bradley C. Anderson, Sec.
Robert T. Hass, Chief Acct. Officer
Jong S. Whang, Exec. Chmn.

Phone: 480-967-5146	**Fax:** 480-968-3763
Toll-Free:	
Address: 131 S. Clark Dr., Tempe, AZ 85281 US	

GROWTH PLANS/SPECIAL FEATURES:

Amtech Systems, Inc. is a supplier of horizontal diffusion furnace systems that are used in photovoltaic and semiconductor manufacturing. The company separates operations into two segments: the solar and semiconductor segment and the polishing supplies segment. The solar and semiconductor segment operates through subsidiaries Bruce Technologies, Inc. and Tempress Systems, Inc. Bruce Technologies produces horizontal batch furnaces under the brand names Bruce Diffusion Furnace, APEX and Amtech Automation. Tempress Systems develops and manufactures horizontal and vertical diffusion furnace systems, in addition to producing and supplying application equipment for the photovoltaic, semiconductor, hybrid and nanotechnology industries. The company conducts its polishing supplies segment through P.R. Hoffman Machine Products, Inc. and R2D Automation SAS. P.R Hoffman develops and sells lapping carriers, polishing templates, gears, double sided lapping and machines to high-tech companies throughout the world. R2D Automation manufactures and sells silicon wafers, as well as selling and producing handling equipment. R2D's products are used by the solar and semiconductor industries for ID readers and solar cell transfer systems. The company's automation products help to reduce the amount of human handling of the silicon wafers, thereby reducing exposure to particle sources during the loading and unloading of the process tubes. Amtech's main market for it products are companies involved in semiconductor wafer manufacturing and semiconductor integrated circuit manufacturing. The company also finds a demand from manufacturers of optical components and solar cells, as well as research and development facilities. Additionally, research institutes and universities make use of the company's products. In February 2011, Amtech acquired 55% ownership of Chinese ion implant technology firm Kingstone Technology Hong Kong Limited.

FINANCIALS: **Sales and profits are in thousands of dollars—add 000 to get the full amount. 2011 Note: Financial information for 2011 was not available for all companies at press time.**

2011 Sales: $246,705	2011 Profits: $22,882	**U.S. Stock Ticker: ASYS**
2010 Sales: $120,019	2010 Profits: $9,563	**Int'l Ticker:**
2009 Sales: $52,973	2009 Profits: $-1,589	Int'l Exchange:
2008 Sales: $80,296	2008 Profits: $2,857	Employees: 340 Fiscal Year Ends: 9/30
2007 Sales: $45,984	2007 Profits: $2,417	Parent Company:

SALARIES/BENEFITS:

Pension Plan:	ESOP Stock Plan:	Profit Sharing:	Top Exec. Salary: $339,231	Bonus: $420,000
Savings Plan:	Stock Purch. Plan:		Second Exec. Salary: $247,509	Bonus: $382,091

OTHER THOUGHTS:

Apparent Women Officers or Directors:
Hot Spot for Advancement for Women/Minorities:

LOCATIONS: ("Y" = Yes)

West:	Southwest:	Midwest:	Southeast:	Northeast:	International:
	Y			Y	Y

AMTRUST FINANCIAL SERVICES INC

www.amtrustgroup.com

Industry Group Code: 524126

Management:		Sales/Marketing:		Liberal Arts:		Information Systems:		Professionals:		Technical/Scientific:	
Mgmt. Trainees:	Y	Mktg. Professionals:	Y	Gen. Writing/Editing:	Y	Info. Management:	Y	Finance/Acct.:	Y	Engineers, Elec.:	
Experienced Mgmt.:	Y	Retail Sales:		Technical Writing:	Y	Software Dev.:		Law:	Y	Engineers, Other:	
Int'l Business:	Y	Commercial/Industrial:	Y	Graphic Arts/Photog.:		Hardware Dev.:		HR/Other:	Y	Health/Lab	Y
MBA Graduates:	Y	Sales Trainees:	Y	Music:		Consulting/Other:		Training:	Y	Scientists/Research:	
		Advertising Pros.:		Broadcasting:				Health Care:	Y	Petroleum/Chemicals:	
				Other:				Consulting:		Math/Other:	Y

TYPES OF BUSINESS:

Specialty Property & Casualty Insurance
Workers' Compensation Insurance
Specialty Risk & Extended Warranty
Reinsurance

BRANDS/DIVISIONS/AFFILIATES:

Technology Insurance Co., Inc.
Rochdale Insurance Co.
Wesco Insurance Co.
AmTrust International Underwriters, Ltd.
AmTrust International Insurance, Ltd.
IGI Group, Ltd.
Associated Industries Insurance Company, Inc.
AmTrust Lloyd's Corporation

CONTACTS: *Note: Officers with more than one job title may be intentionally listed here more than once.*

Barry D. Zyskind, CEO
Michael J. Saxon, COO
Barry D. Zyskind, Pres.
Ronald E. Pipoly, Jr., CFO
Christopher M. Longo, CIO
Stephen B. Ungar, General Counsel/Sec.
Harry Schlacter, Sr. VP-Finance/Treas.
Max G. Caviet, CEO-AmTrust Europe, Ltd.
David H. Sacks, Chief Legal Officer
Michael Karfunkel, Chmn.
Max G. Caviet, Pres., AmTrust International Insurance, Ltd.

Phone: 212-220-7120 **Fax:** 212-220-7130
Toll-Free:
Address: 59 Maiden Ln., 6th Fl., New York, NY 10038 US

GROWTH PLANS/SPECIAL FEATURES:

AmTrust Financial Services, Inc. provides specialty property and casualty insurance for small and mid-size businesses on a multinational level. The company operates in four segments: Small Commercial Business, which represents roughly 30% of gross written premiums; Specialty Risk and Extended Warranty, 48%; Specialty Program Business, 17%; and Personal Lines Reinsurance, 5%. The Small Commercial Business segment provides workers' compensation, commercial package and other commercial lines of coverage for small low- to medium-hazard businesses such as restaurants, retail stores and strip malls, private schools, light manufacturing, small grocery and specialty food stores, building management operations and physician and other professional offices. The Specialty Risk and Extended Warranty segment primarily serves manufacturers, service providers, retailers and third party warranty administrators that provide coverage for accidental damage, mechanical breakdown and related risks for consumer and commercial goods. The Specialty Program Business segment consists of workers' compensation, general liability, commercial auto liability and commercial property coverage for small- and middle-market businesses. Policyholders in this segment primarily include the retail, wholesale, service operations, artisan contracting and light and medium manufacturing industries. Through its Personal Lines Reinsurance segment, the firm provides reinsurance for 10% of the net premiums held by GMAC's U.S. consumer property and casualty insurance business. AmTrust's domestic subsidiaries include: Technology Insurance Co., Inc.; Rochdale Insurance Co.; Wesco Insurance Co.; Associated Industries Insurance Company, Inc.; Milwaukee Casualty Insurance Co.; Security National Insurance Company; AmTrust Insurance Company of Kansas, Inc.; AmTrust Lloyd's Corporation; and Warrantech Corporation. Its international subsidiaries include AmTrust International Underwriters, Ltd.; IGI Group, Ltd.; and AmTrust International Insurance, Ltd.

FINANCIALS: **Sales and profits are in thousands of dollars—add 000 to get the full amount. 2011 Note: Financial information for 2011 was not available for all companies at press time.**

2011 Sales: $
2010 Sales: $1,002,457
2009 Sales: $740,211
2008 Sales: $576,531
2007 Sales: $576,924

2011 Profits: $
2010 Profits: $146,340
2009 Profits: $103,223
2008 Profits: $82,928
2007 Profits: $90,140

U.S. Stock Ticker: AFSI
Int'l Ticker:
Int'l Exchange:
Employees: 1,400 Fiscal Year Ends: 12/31
Parent Company:

SALARIES/BENEFITS:

Pension Plan: Y ESOP Stock Plan: Profit Sharing: Top Exec. Salary: $975,000 Bonus: $2,925,000
Savings Plan: Stock Purch. Plan: Second Exec. Salary: $583,333 Bonus: $800,000

OTHER THOUGHTS:

Apparent Women Officers or Directors: 1
Hot Spot for Advancement for Women/Minorities:

LOCATIONS: ("Y" = Yes)

West:	Southwest:	Midwest:	Southeast:	Northeast:	International:
Y	Y	Y	Y	Y	Y

ANALOGIC CORP

Industry Group Code: 33911

www.analogic.com

Management:		Sales/Marketing:		Liberal Arts:		Information Systems:		Professionals:		Technical/Scientific:	
Mgmt. Trainees:		Mktg. Professionals:	Y	Gen. Writing/Editing:		Info. Management:	Y	Finance/Acct.:	Y	Engineers, Elec.:	Y
Experienced Mgmt.:	Y	Retail Sales:		Technical Writing:	Y	Software Dev.:	Y	Law:	Y	Engineers, Other:	Y
Int'l Business:	Y	Commercial/Industrial:	Y	Graphic Arts/Photog.:		Hardware Dev.:	Y	HR/Other:	Y	Health/Lab	Y
MBA Graduates:	Y	Sales Trainees:	Y	Music:		Consulting/Other:		Training:	Y	Scientists/Research:	Y
		Advertising Pros.:		Broadcasting:				Health Care:	Y	Petroleum/Chemicals:	
				Other:				Consulting:		Math/Other:	

TYPES OF BUSINESS:

Equipment-Medical Image Processing
Signal Processing Equipment
Patient Monitoring Equipment
Computed Tomography Imaging Systems
Explosive Detection Security Systems

BRANDS/DIVISIONS/AFFILIATES:

B-K Medical Systems, Inc.
Sound Technology, Inc.
ANRAD Corporation
eXaminer
OnGuard
Copley Controls

CONTACTS: *Note: Officers with more than one job title may be intentionally listed here more than once.*

James W. Green, CEO
James W. Green, Pres.
Michael L. Levitz, CFO/Treas./VP
Matthew Theiler, VP-Global Sales, Mktg. & Svcs.
Douglas B. Rosenfeld, VP-Global Human Resources
John P. O'Connor, VP-Tech.
John P. O'Connor, VP-Eng.
Douglas B. Rosenfeld, VP-Admin.
John J. Fry, General Counsel/Corp. Sec./VP
Jim Ryan, VP-Global Oper.
Donald B. Melson, Controller/VP
Mervat Faltas, Sr. VP/Gen. Mgr.-OEM Medical Div.
Farley Peechatka, Sr. VP/Gen. Mgr.-Global Ultrasound Bus. Unit
Edward F. Voboril, Chmn.
Shalabh Chandra, VP/Gen. Mgr.-Analogic Asia

Phone: 978-326-4000	**Fax:** 978-977-6809
Toll-Free:	
Address: 8 Centennial Dr., Peabody, MA 01960 US	

GROWTH PLANS/SPECIAL FEATURES:

Analogic Corp. designs, manufactures and sells image-processing-based medical and security systems and subsystems. The company primarily focuses on advanced technology in the areas of automated explosives detection, computed tomography (CT), digital radiography, ultrasound, MRI, patient monitoring and advance signal processing. Its operations are divided into two segments: medical technology, which accounted for 88% of its 2010 revenue; and security technology, 12%. The medical technology segment is itself divided into three sub-segments: CT and MRI; Specialized Ultrasound; and Digital Radiography. The CT and MRI segment consists primarily of electronic systems and subsystems for medical imaging, sold globally to OEM producers of CT, MRI, and Ultrasound equipment. The Specialized Ultrasound segment operates through subsidiaries B-K Medical Systems, Inc. and Sound Technology, Inc. B-K Medical designs and manufactures ultrasound systems and probes for end-user markets in urology, surgery and radiology. Sound Technology is a leading developer of ultrasound transducers. The Digital Radiography division, through ANRAD Corporation, designs and manufactures direct conversion digital, flat-panel X-ray detectors for diagnostic and interventional applications. The security technology segment provides advanced explosives and weapons detection systems for checked luggage and carry-on luggage at airport checkpoints, cruise ship portals and other high-security applications, such as financial, government and military complexes. The segment designs and manufactures the eXaminer family of scanners, capable of generating data for full three-dimensional images of every object contained within passenger baggage. Analogic has also designed a CT-based checkpoint security imaging system, the OnGuard family of products, to detect explosives, guns and other threats. Through the addition of Copley Controls' motion control product line, the firm has expanded into the industrial market of high-technology automation.

Analogic offers its employees tuition reimbursement; medical, dental and vision coverage; life insurance; a 401(k); and an employee stock purchase plan.

FINANCIALS: **Sales and profits are in thousands of dollars—add 000 to get the full amount. 2011 Note: Financial information for 2011 was not available for all companies at press time.**

2011 Sales: $473,595	2011 Profits: $17,833
2010 Sales: $423,597	2010 Profits: $15,555
2009 Sales: $396,506	2009 Profits: $3,705
2008 Sales: $413,509	2008 Profits: $23,486
2007 Sales: $340,782	2007 Profits: $15,380

U.S. Stock Ticker: ALOG
Int'l Ticker:
Int'l Exchange:
Employees: 1,500 Fiscal Year Ends: 7/31
Parent Company:

SALARIES/BENEFITS:

Pension Plan:	ESOP Stock Plan:	Profit Sharing:	Top Exec. Salary: $490,522	Bonus: $591,570
Savings Plan: Y	Stock Purch. Plan: Y		Second Exec. Salary: $295,022	Bonus: $197,665

OTHER THOUGHTS:

Apparent Women Officers or Directors: 2
Hot Spot for Advancement for Women/Minorities:

LOCATIONS: ("Y" = Yes)

West:	Southwest:	Midwest:	Southeast:	Northeast:	International:
				Y	Y

ANAREN INC

www.anaren.com

Industry Group Code: 334210

Management:		Sales/Marketing:		Liberal Arts:		Information Systems:		Professionals:		Technical/Scientific:	
Mgmt. Trainees:		Mktg. Professionals:	Y	Gen. Writing/Editing:	Y	Info. Management:	Y	Finance/Acct.:	Y	Engineers, Elec.:	Y
Experienced Mgmt.:	Y	Retail Sales:		Technical Writing:	Y	Software Dev.:	Y	Law:	Y	Engineers, Other:	Y
Int'l Business:	Y	Commercial/Industrial:	Y	Graphic Arts/Photog.:		Hardware Dev.:	Y	HR/Other:	Y	Health/Lab	
MBA Graduates:	Y	Sales Trainees:	Y	Music:		Consulting/Other:		Training:	Y	Scientists/Research:	
		Advertising Pros.:		Broadcasting:				Health Care:		Petroleum/Chemicals:	
				Other:				Consulting:		Math/Other:	

TYPES OF BUSINESS:

Wireless Telecommunications Components
Satellite Communications Components
Defense Electronics Components
Thick-Film Ceramic Circuits
Microwave Components
Integrated Radio Modules (AIR)
Wireless Resistive Products

BRANDS/DIVISIONS/AFFILIATES:

Anaren Ceramics Inc
MS Kennedy Corp
Unicircuit Inc
Anaren Communications Suzhou Co Ltd
Anaren Microwave Inc

CONTACTS: *Note: Officers with more than one job title may be intentionally listed here more than once.*

Lawrence A. Sala, CEO
Lawrence A. Sala, Pres.
George A. Blanton, CFO/Sr. VP
Amy B. Tewksbury, Sr. VP-Human Resources
Carl W. Gerst, Jr., CTO/Vice Chmn.
David M. Ferrara, General Counsel/Sec.
Timothy P. Ross, Sr. VP-Bus. Dev.
George A. Blanton, Treas.
Gert Thygesen, Sr. VP-Tech.
Mark Burdick, Sr. VP/Gen. Mgr.-Tech.
Lawrence A. Sala, Chmn.

Phone: 315-432-8909	**Fax**: 315-432-9121
Toll-Free: 800-544-2414	
Address: 6635 Kirkville Rd., E. Syracuse, NY 13057 US	

GROWTH PLANS/SPECIAL FEATURES:

Anaren, Inc. provides integrated microwave components, assemblies and subsystems for the wireless infrastructure, satellite communications, medical, optics, automotive, consumer products and defense sectors. The firm operates in two segments: wireless, which accounted for 33% of its 2010 revenue; and space & defense, which accounted for the remaining 67%. The company's wireless products are used primarily in communication systems, both in user equipment, such as wireless local area network (WLAN), cellular handsets and Bluetooth devices, and in network infrastructure equipment, including cellular telephone base stations and television broadcast equipment applications. Its primary customers in this segment include original equipment manufacturers (OEMs) such as Motorola, Nokia Siemens Networks, EG Components and Huawei Technologies Co. The space & defense segment focuses on the design and manufacture of advanced microwave-based hardware used in radar systems, jamming systems, smart munitions, electronic surveillance systems and satellite and ground based communication systems. Its primary space & defense customers include Boeing, Lockheed Martin and Raytheon. Anaren's product lines include passives (couplers, power dividers, baluns and splitter/combiners), actives (vector modulators and mixers), resistive components (resistors, terminations and attenuators), ferrites (circulators and isolators) and complex assemblies (switching, beamformers, antenna feed networks, DRFMs and IMAs). Using its proprietary multi-layer stripline technology, Anaren is able to custom manufacture its components for individual clients. The company operates through several subsidiaries, including Anaren Ceramics; MS Kennedy; and Unicircuit. Anaren Ceramics specializes in fabricating extremely tight-tolerance and high reliability circuits on traditional ceramic substrates and low temperature co-fired ceramic (LTCC) materials. MS Kennedy provides analog microelectronic solutions for the defense, satellite and aerospace markets. Unicircuit specializes in high-frequency and mixed signal printed circuit boards.

Employees are offered medical and dental insurance; tuition assistance; a 401(k); an employee bonus program; and an on-site gym at its Syracuse headquarters.

FINANCIALS: Sales and profits are in thousands of dollars—add 000 to get the full amount. 2011 Note: Financial information for 2011 was not available for all companies at press time.

2011 Sales: $179,170	2011 Profits: $16,401	**U.S. Stock Ticker: ANEN**
2010 Sales: $168,789	2010 Profits: $13,712	**Int'l Ticker:**
2009 Sales: $166,905	2009 Profits: $9,859	Int'l Exchange:
2008 Sales: $131,316	2008 Profits: $9,233	Employees: 1,032 Fiscal Year Ends: 6/30
2007 Sales: $128,987	2007 Profits: $15,350	Parent Company:

SALARIES/BENEFITS:

Pension Plan:	ESOP Stock Plan:	Profit Sharing:	Top Exec. Salary: $470,000	Bonus: $261,181
Savings Plan: Y	Stock Purch. Plan:		Second Exec. Salary: $240,000	Bonus: $80,021

OTHER THOUGHTS:

Apparent Women Officers or Directors: 2
Hot Spot for Advancement for Women/Minorities:

LOCATIONS: ("Y" = Yes)

West:	Southwest:	Midwest:	Southeast:	Northeast:	International:
Y				Y	Y

ANIKA THERAPEUTICS INC

www.anikatherapeutics.com

Industry Group Code: 325414

Management:		Sales/Marketing:		Liberal Arts:		Information Systems:		Professionals:		Technical/Scientific:	
Mgmt. Trainees:		Mktg. Professionals:	Y	Gen. Writing/Editing:		Info. Management:	Y	Finance/Acct.:	Y	Engineers, Elec.:	
Experienced Mgmt.:	Y	Retail Sales:		Technical Writing:	Y	Software Dev.:	Y	Law:	Y	Engineers, Other:	Y
Int'l Business:		Commercial/Industrial:	Y	Graphic Arts/Photog.:		Hardware Dev.:		HR/Other:	Y	Health/Lab	Y
MBA Graduates:	Y	Sales Trainees:	Y	Music:		Consulting/Other:		Training:	Y	Scientists/Research:	Y
		Advertising Pros.:		Broadcasting:				Health Care:	Y	Petroleum/Chemicals:	Y
				Other:				Consulting:		Math/Other:	Y

TYPES OF BUSINESS:

Tissue Protection, Healing & Repair Drugs
Hyaluronic Acid Based Drugs
Tissue Augmentation Products
Osteoarthritis Pain Relief
Post-Surgical Anti-Adhesion

BRANDS/DIVISIONS/AFFILIATES:

Orthovisc
Elevess
Amvisc
Staarvisc-II
ShellGel
Incert
Hyvisc
Fidia Farmaceutici SpA

CONTACTS:

Note: Officers with more than one job title may be intentionally listed here more than once.

Charles H. Sherwood, CEO
Frank J. Luppino, COO
Charles H. Sherwood, Pres.
Kevin W. Quinlan, CFO
Thomas J. Chambers, VP-Mktg. & Sales
William J. Mrachek, VP-Human Resources
Alessandra Pavesio, VP-R&D
Randall W. Wilhoite, VP-Oper.
Irina B. Kulinets, VP-Regulatory & Clinical Affairs

Phone: 781-457-9000	**Fax:** 781-305-9720
Toll-Free:	
Address: 32 Wiggins Ave., Bedford, MA 01730 US	

GROWTH PLANS/SPECIAL FEATURES:

Anika Therapeutics, Inc. develops, manufactures and markets therapeutic products for tissue protection, healing and repair. These products are based on hyaluronic acid (HA), a naturally occurring, biocompatible polymer found throughout the body that is essential to several physiological functions such as the protection and lubrication of soft tissues and joints; the maintenance of the structural integrity of tissues; and the transport of molecules to and within cells. The firm's currently marketed products include Orthovisc, an HA product which provides lubrication for the knee and helps cushion the knee joint; Monovisc, a single-injection drug designed to alleviate arthritis pain; Staarvisc-II, Amvisc, Amvisc Plus and Optivisc, each an injectable ophthalmic viscoelastic HA product; Hyvisc, an HA product used for treatment of joint dysfunction in horses; Incert-S, an HA-based anti-adhesive for surgical applications; and Elevess, an HA-based injectable dermal filler used for cosmetic tissue applications and products associated with joint health. Another osteoarthritis solution, Cingal, is currently in pre-clinical development. Anika is working to produce more Elevess products in the future, as there is a growing demand for soft tissue fillers for facial wrinkles, scar remediation and lip augmentation. Orthovisc is marketed in the U.S. by DePuy Mitek, a subsidiary of Johnson & Johnson, and outside the U.S. by distributors in roughly 20 countries. Hyvisc is marketed in the U.S. through Boehringer Ingelheim Vetmedica, Inc. Through the recent acquisition of Fidia Farmaceutici S.p.A. (FAB), Anika also offers over 20 FAB products, including Hyalofast, a biodegradable support for human bone marrow mesenchymal stem cells; Hyalograft 3D, for the regeneration of skin; Hyalograft C Autograft for cartilage regeneration; Hyalomatrix, for treatment of burns and ulcers; Hyalonect, a woven gauze used as a graft wrap; and Hyaloss, which are fibers used to mix blood/bone grafts to form a paste for bone regeneration.

FINANCIALS:

Sales and profits are in thousands of dollars—add 000 to get the full amount. 2011 Note: Financial information for 2011 was not available for all companies at press time.

2011 Sales: $	2011 Profits: $
2010 Sales: $55,557	2010 Profits: $4,316
2009 Sales: $40,136	2009 Profits: $3,688
2008 Sales: $35,780	2008 Profits: $3,629
2007 Sales: $30,830	2007 Profits: $6,035

U.S. Stock Ticker: ANIK
Int'l Ticker:
Int'l Exchange:
Employees: 114 Fiscal Year Ends: 12/31
Parent Company:

SALARIES/BENEFITS:

Pension Plan:	ESOP Stock Plan:	Profit Sharing:	Top Exec. Salary: $465,978	Bonus: $214,000
Savings Plan: Y	Stock Purch. Plan:		Second Exec. Salary: $285,000	Bonus: $90,000

OTHER THOUGHTS:

Apparent Women Officers or Directors: 2
Hot Spot for Advancement for Women/Minorities:

LOCATIONS: ("Y" = Yes)

West:	Southwest:	Midwest:	Southeast:	Northeast:	International:
				Y	

APP PHARMACEUTICALS INC

www.apppharma.com

Industry Group Code: 325412

Management:		**Sales/Marketing:**		**Liberal Arts:**		**Information Systems:**		**Professionals:**		**Technical/Scientific:**	
Mgmt. Trainees:		Mktg. Professionals:	Y	Gen. Writing/Editing:		Info. Management:	Y	Finance/Acct.:	Y	Engineers, Elec.:	
Experienced Mgmt.:	Y	Retail Sales:		Technical Writing:	Y	Software Dev.:	Y	Law:	Y	Engineers, Other:	
Int'l Business:	Y	Commercial/Industrial:	Y	Graphic Arts/Photog.:		Hardware Dev.:		HR/Other:	Y	Health/Lab	Y
MBA Graduates:	Y	Sales Trainees:	Y	Music:		Consulting/Other:		Training:	Y	Scientists/Research:	Y
		Advertising Pros.:		Broadcasting:				Health Care:	Y	Petroleum/Chemicals:	Y
				Other:				Consulting:		Math/Other:	Y

TYPES OF BUSINESS:

Pharmaceuticals Manufacturing
Injectable Drugs
Anti-Infective Drugs
Critical Care Drugs

BRANDS/DIVISIONS/AFFILIATES:

Fresenius Kabi Pharmaceuticals Holding Inc
Clonidine Hydrochloride Injection
Nafcillin For Injection USP
Gemcitabine HCI For Injection USP
Levothyroxine Sodium For Injection
Imipenem
Cilastatin For Injection USP
Meropenem For Injection USP

CONTACTS: *Note: Officers with more than one job title may be intentionally listed here more than once.*

John Ducker, CEO
J. Frank Harmon, COO/Exec. VP
John Ducker, Pres.
Steven J. Adams, CFO/Exec. VP
James W. Callanan, VP-Human Resources
Christopher Bryant, Chief Scientific Officer/Exec. VP
Jack Silhavy, General Counsel/Exec. VP
Scott W. Meacham, Exec. VP-Commercial Oper.
Debra L. Ross, Dir.-Corp. Comm.
Surendera Tyagi, Exec. VP-Regional Bus. Support
Brent Eck, Exec. VP-Pharma & Clinical Nutrition

Phone: 847-969-2700 **Fax:** 800-743-7082
Toll-Free: 888-391-1300
Address: 1501 E. Woodfield Rd., Ste. 300 E., Schaumburg, IL 60173 US

GROWTH PLANS/SPECIAL FEATURES:

APP Pharmaceuticals, Inc., a subsidiary of Fresenius Kabi Pharmaceuticals Holding, Inc., is a fully integrated biopharmaceutical company that develops, manufactures and markets injectable pharmaceutical products for use in both patient and ambulatory settings, focusing on the anesthetic/analgesic, anti-infective, critical care and oncology markets. The firm offers injectable products in each of the three basic forms: liquid, powder and lyophilized (freeze-dried). APP manufactures and markets more than 120 products in over 400 dosages and formulations, including injectable products, tablets, transfer pins and transfer spikes, jellies, creams, topical solutions, sterilized vials, vented needles, flushing solution, pumping chamber sets, transfer sets, mineral oils, injection concentrate, additive solutions, syringe tip adaptors and sterile water. The firm's newer injectable products include chlorothiazide sodium, a diuretic and antihypertensive; recuronium bromide, a neuromuscular blocking agent; cefepime hydrochloride, an antibiotic; colistimethate sodium and polymyxin B sulfate, anti-infectives; irinotecan hydrochloride, an antineoplastic; and caffeine citrate, a central nervous system stimulant, also offered as an oral solution. APP manufactures a comprehensive range of dosage formulations used in hospitals, long-term care facilities, alternate care sites and clinics. The firm operates manufacturing facilities in Illinois, New York and North Carolina. In 2011, the company received FDA approval for several of its products, including Clonidine Hydrochloride Injection, an analgesic used to treat cancer patients; Nafcillin for Injection USP, for the treatment of infections; Gemcitabine HCl for Injection USP, for the treatment of ovarian cancer; and Levothyroxine Sodium for Injection, for the treatment of myxedema coma. In February 2012, the firm introduced Imipenem and Cilastatin for Injection USP and Meropenem for Injection USP used to treat serious infections.

Employees are offered medical, dental and vision insurance; life and disability insurance; flexible spending accounts; legal insurance; a 401(k) plan and pension plan; tuition assistance; and an employee assistance program.

FINANCIALS: **Sales and profits are in thousands of dollars—add 000 to get the full amount. 2011 Note: Financial information for 2011 was not available for all companies at press time.**

2011 Sales: $ | 2011 Profits: $
2010 Sales: $ | 2010 Profits: $
2009 Sales: $ | 2009 Profits: $
2008 Sales: $ | 2008 Profits: $
2007 Sales: $ | 2007 Profits: $

U.S. Stock Ticker: Subsidiary
Int'l Ticker:
Int'l Exchange:
Employees: Fiscal Year Ends: 12/31
Parent Company: FRESENIUS KABI PHARMACEUTICALS HOLDING INC

SALARIES/BENEFITS:

Pension Plan: Y | ESOP Stock Plan: | Profit Sharing: | Top Exec. Salary: $ | Bonus: $
Savings Plan: Y | Stock Purch. Plan: | | Second Exec. Salary: $ | Bonus: $

OTHER THOUGHTS:

Apparent Women Officers or Directors: 1
Hot Spot for Advancement for Women/Minorities:

LOCATIONS: ("Y" = Yes)

West:	Southwest:	Midwest:	Southeast:	Northeast:	International:
		Y		Y	Y

ARCSIGHT INC

Industry Group Code: 511210E

www.arcsight.com

Management:		Sales/Marketing:		Liberal Arts:		Information Systems:		Professionals:		Technical/Scientific:	
Mgmt. Trainees:		Mktg. Professionals:	Y	Gen. Writing/Editing:		Info. Management:	Y	Finance/Acct.:	Y	Engineers, Elec.:	Y
Experienced Mgmt.:	Y	Retail Sales:		Technical Writing:	Y	Software Dev.:	Y	Law:	Y	Engineers, Other:	
Int'l Business:	Y	Commercial/Industrial:	Y	Graphic Arts/Photog.:	Y	Hardware Dev.:		HR/Other:	Y	Health/Lab	
MBA Graduates:	Y	Sales Trainees:	Y	Music:		Consulting/Other:		Training:	Y	Scientists/Research:	
		Advertising Pros.:		Broadcasting:				Health Care:		Petroleum/Chemicals:	
				Other:				Consulting:		Math/Other:	

TYPES OF BUSINESS:

IT & Network Security Products & Services
IT Support Services
Regulation Compliance

BRANDS/DIVISIONS/AFFILIATES:

ArcSight Security Information and Event Management
ArcSight ESM
ArcSight Identity View
ArcSight Compliance
ArcSight Logger
ArcSight Connectors
ArcSight Express
Hewlett-Packard Co (HP)

CONTACTS: *Note: Officers with more than one job title may be intentionally listed here more than once.*

Tom Reilly, CEO
Tom Reilly, Pres.
Stewart Grierson, CFO
Hugh Njemanze, Exec. VP-R&D
Bruce Burroughs, CIO/VP
Hugh Njemanze, CTO
Bob Pratt, VP-Prod. Mgmt.
Haiyan Song, VP-Eng.
Tram Phi, General Counsel/Corp. Sec.
Kevin Mosher, Sr. VP-Worldwide Field Oper.
Joni Kahn, Sr. VP-Support & Svcs.
Prescott Winter, CTO-Public Sector
Laura Menicucci, VP-Customer Support
Hector Aguilarmacias, VP-Software Dev.

Phone: 408-864-2600 **Fax:** 408-342-1615
Toll-Free: 888-415-2778
Address: 5 Results Way, Cupertino, CA 95014 US

GROWTH PLANS/SPECIAL FEATURES:

ArcSight, Inc., a subsidiary of Hewlett-Packard Co. (HP), provides security management and compliance solutions for businesses and government agencies. The company assists its clients in complying with corporate and government regulatory policies; as well as controlling risk in the form of rapid identification of compliance violations, cyber-security attacks, policy breaches and insider threats. Its primary security platform, the ArcSight Security Information and Event Management (SIEM) Platform, mitigates the potential risks posed by cyber-theft, cyber-warfare, cyber-espionage and cyber-fraud, from both internal and external threat factors. The SIEM platform is able to integrate into the existing IT infrastructure of businesses and government agencies. Once integrated, the principle components of the SIEM platform are the company's event security management products, which provide a centralized delivery system that alerts customers with real-time status updates and activity messages. ArcSight's products collect, analyze and correlate massive numbers of events from security point solutions and provide analytics and reports tailored to specific compliance and security initiatives, as well as appliances that streamline event log collection, storage, analysis and reporting. The company offers several different products, including the ArcSight ESM, ArcSight Identity View, ArcSight Compliance, ArcSight Logger, ArcSight Connectors and the ArcSight Express. Additionally, ArcSight has strategic partnerships with several companies including Deloitte; IBM; Cisco; McAfee; Oracle; and Wipro Technologies. The company has offices located in California, Texas, Georgia and Massachusetts and international locations in Asia, Canada, Europe and the Middle East.

FINANCIALS: **Sales and profits are in thousands of dollars—add 000 to get the full amount. 2011 Note: Financial information for 2011 was not available for all companies at press time.**

2011 Sales: $
2010 Sales: $181,384
2009 Sales: $136,168
2008 Sales: $101,545
2007 Sales: $69,833

2011 Profits: $
2010 Profits: $28,387
2009 Profits: $9,913
2008 Profits: $-2,009
2007 Profits: $- 257

U.S. Stock Ticker: Subsidiary
Int'l Ticker:
Int'l Exchange:
Employees: 512 Fiscal Year Ends: 4/30
Parent Company: HEWLETT-PACKARD CO (HP)

SALARIES/BENEFITS:

Pension Plan: ESOP Stock Plan: Profit Sharing: Top Exec. Salary: $375,000 Bonus: $337,500
Savings Plan: Stock Purch. Plan: Second Exec. Salary: $300,000 Bonus: $225,000

OTHER THOUGHTS:

Apparent Women Officers or Directors: 4
Hot Spot for Advancement for Women/Minorities: Y

LOCATIONS: ("Y" = Yes)

West:	Southwest:	Midwest:	Southeast:	Northeast:	International:
Y	Y		Y	Y	Y

ARDEN GROUP INC

www.ardengroupinc.com

Industry Group Code: 445110

Management:		Sales/Marketing:		Liberal Arts:		Information Systems:		Professionals:		Technical/Scientific:	
Mgmt. Trainees:	Y	Mktg. Professionals:	Y	Gen. Writing/Editing:	Y	Info. Management:	Y	Finance/Acct.:	Y	Engineers, Elec.:	
Experienced Mgmt.:	Y	Retail Sales:	Y	Technical Writing:		Software Dev.:	Y	Law:	Y	Engineers, Other:	
Int'l Business:		Commercial/Industrial:		Graphic Arts/Photog.:	Y	Hardware Dev.:		HR/Other:	Y	Health/Lab	
MBA Graduates:	Y	Sales Trainees:	Y	Music:		Consulting/Other:		Training:	Y	Scientists/Research:	
		Advertising Pros.:	Y	Broadcasting:				Health Care:		Petroleum/Chemicals:	
				Other:				Consulting:		Math/Other:	

TYPES OF BUSINESS:

Grocery Stores, Retail
Real Estate Holdings

BRANDS/DIVISIONS/AFFILIATES:

Gelson's Markets
Arden-Mayfair Inc
Mayfair Realty Inc

CONTACTS: *Note: Officers with more than one job title may be intentionally listed here more than once.*

Bernard Briskin, CEO
Bernard Briskin, Pres.
Laura J. Neumann, CFO
Rob McDougall, Exec. VP-Mktg., Gelson's
Tom Frattali, Sr. VP-Merch., Gelson's
Rob McDougall, Exec. VP-Oper., Gelson's
Robert E. Stiles, Pres., Gelson's
Donna Tyndall, Sr. VP-Store Oper., Gelson's
Bernard Briskin, Chmn.
Tom Frattali, Sr. VP-Grocery Purchasing & Dist., Gelson's

Phone: 310-638-2842	**Fax:** 310-631-0950
Toll-Free:	
Address: 2020 S. Central Ave., Compton, CA 90220 US	

GROWTH PLANS/SPECIAL FEATURES:

Arden Group, Inc. is a holding company that conducts operations through its wholly-owned subsidiary Arden-Mayfair, Inc. and Arden Mayfair's wholly-owned subsidiary Gelson's Markets, which operates 18 supermarkets in southern California under the Gelson's name. The supermarkets, which range in size from approximately 18,000 to 40,000 square feet, are self-service, cash-and-carry markets that offer a selection of local and national brands as well as a limited number of private-label items. Gelson's stores typically carry a wide range of items, including grocery categories such as dry groceries, produce, meat, seafood, bakery, dairy, wine, liquor, floral, sushi, vitamins, natural food products and health and beauty aids. The stores also offer a selection of organic products. Gelson's merchandising emphasizes specialty items such as imported foods and unusual delicatessen products and organic and natural food products. Some stores include additional service departments such as fresh pizza, coffee bars, hot bars, gelato bars, carving carts offering cooked meats and Wolfgang Puck Express casual dining locations. Additionally, selected stores offer banking and pharmacy services through third parties. Gelson's operates a 127,000-square-foot warehouse with a 4,000-square-foot truck service facility in Commerce, California. The single largest supplier for the company is Unified Grocers, Inc., a cooperative wholesaler that accounts for approximately 15% of Gelson's purchases. Arden Group also owns certain real estate properties through its subsidiary Mayfair Realty, Inc.

Employees are offered a medical benefits program as well as a 401(k) plan.

FINANCIALS: **Sales and profits are in thousands of dollars—add 000 to get the full amount. 2011 Note: Financial information for 2011 was not available for all companies at press time.**

2011 Sales: $	2011 Profits: $	**U.S. Stock Ticker: ARDNA**
2010 Sales: $417,065	2010 Profits: $18,085	**Int'l Ticker:**
2009 Sales: $431,170	2009 Profits: $21,624	Int'l Exchange:
2008 Sales: $479,117	2008 Profits: $24,667	Employees: 1,222 Fiscal Year Ends: 12/31
2007 Sales: $485,939	2007 Profits: $29,207	Parent Company:

SALARIES/BENEFITS:

Pension Plan:	ESOP Stock Plan:	Profit Sharing:	Top Exec. Salary: $669,290	Bonus: $530,073
Savings Plan: Y	Stock Purch. Plan:		Second Exec. Salary: $186,705	Bonus: $35,000

OTHER THOUGHTS:

Apparent Women Officers or Directors: 2
Hot Spot for Advancement for Women/Minorities:

LOCATIONS: ("Y" = Yes)

West:	Southwest:	Midwest:	Southeast:	Northeast:	International:
Y					

ARGON ST INC

Industry Group Code: 541513

www.argonst.com

Management:		Sales/Marketing:		Liberal Arts:		Information Systems:		Professionals:		Technical/Scientific:	
Mgmt. Trainees:		Mktg. Professionals:	Y	Gen. Writing/Editing:		Info. Management:	Y	Finance/Acct.:	Y	Engineers, Elec.:	Y
Experienced Mgmt.:	Y	Retail Sales:		Technical Writing:	Y	Software Dev.:	Y	Law:	Y	Engineers, Other:	
Int'l Business:	Y	Commercial/Industrial:	Y	Graphic Arts/Photog.:		Hardware Dev.:		HR/Other:	Y	Health/Lab	
MBA Graduates:	Y	Sales Trainees:	Y	Music:		Consulting/Other:	Y	Training:	Y	Scientists/Research:	
		Advertising Pros.:		Broadcasting:				Health Care:		Petroleum/Chemicals:	
				Other:				Consulting:	Y	Math/Other:	

TYPES OF BUSINESS:

Systems Engineering & Development
Defense & Intelligence Systems
Defense Simulation Tools
Imaging Systems
Communications Technology
Consulting
Engineering

BRANDS/DIVISIONS/AFFILIATES:

Boeing Company (The)

CONTACTS: *Note: Officers with more than one job title may be intentionally listed here more than once.*

Terry L. Collins, CEO
Kerry M. Rowe, COO
Kerry M. Rowe, Pres.
Robert S. Tamaru, VP-Tech.
Stanford K. Harmon, VP-Oper. Support
Robert S. Tamaru, VP-Strategic Dev.
Michael J. Hettmann, VP-Reconnaissance Systems
James Ross, VP-National Programs
Tery L. Collins, Chmn.

Phone: 703-322-0881	**Fax:** 703-322-0885
Toll-Free:	
Address: 12701 Fair Lakes Cir., Ste. 800, Fairfax, VA 22033 US	

GROWTH PLANS/SPECIAL FEATURES:

Argon ST, Inc., a unit of Boeing's Network & Space Systems division, is a systems engineering, development and services company. The firm provides full-service C4ISR systems (command, control, communications, computers, intelligence, surveillance and reconnaissance) and combat systems, which address several markets, including maritime defense; ground systems; airborne reconnaissance; network systems and security; and tactical communications. Argon serves a wide range of defense and intelligence customers as well as commercial enterprises. The company develops and services hardware and software in four areas: sensors, systems, networks and services. Argon designs and produces signals intelligence (SIGNINT) sensors that seek, exploit, identify and locate the environment for radio frequency (RF) energy, underwater sound, light, heat and complex phenomena. Its systems support a range of different applications, including reconnaissance, communication, navigation, geo-location and threat warning, among others. Argon's network capabilities include system-of-systems and network-of-networks engineering that support wireless networks, mobile ad hoc networks, interference-resistant technologies and satellite communications. Through services such as information analysis and fusion, integration, engineering and manufacturing, the firm helps clients complete various tasks. In recent years, Boeing Co. acquired Argon for $782 million and, as a result, Argon became a wholly-owned subsidiary of Boeing.

The firm offers employees medical and dental coverage; life and disability insurance; a 401(k); a discount stock purchase plan; education assistance; an adoption program; and paid time off.

FINANCIALS: **Sales and profits are in thousands of dollars—add 000 to get the full amount. 2011 Note: Financial information for 2011 was not available for all companies at press time.**

2011 Sales: $	2011 Profits: $
2010 Sales: $	2010 Profits: $
2009 Sales: $366,076	2009 Profits: $23,691
2008 Sales: $340,934	2008 Profits: $20,273
2007 Sales: $282,209	2007 Profits: $14,702

U.S. Stock Ticker: Subsidiary
Int'l Ticker:
Int'l Exchange:
Employees: 800 Fiscal Year Ends: 9/30
Parent Company: BOEING COMPANY (THE)

SALARIES/BENEFITS:

Pension Plan:	ESOP Stock Plan:	Profit Sharing:	Top Exec. Salary: $473,722	Bonus: $
Savings Plan: Y	Stock Purch. Plan: Y		Second Exec. Salary: $382,034	Bonus: $

OTHER THOUGHTS:

Apparent Women Officers or Directors:
Hot Spot for Advancement for Women/Minorities:

LOCATIONS: ("Y" = Yes)

West:	Southwest:	Midwest:	Southeast:	Northeast:	International:
Y	Y		Y	Y	Y

ARIBA INC

Industry Group Code: 511210A

www.ariba.com

Management:		Sales/Marketing:		Liberal Arts:		Information Systems:		Professionals:		Technical/Scientific:	
Mgmt. Trainees:		Mktg. Professionals:	Y	Gen. Writing/Editing:		Info. Management:	Y	Finance/Acct.:	Y	Engineers, Elec.:	Y
Experienced Mgmt.:	Y	Retail Sales:		Technical Writing:	Y	Software Dev.:	Y	Law:	Y	Engineers, Other:	
Int'l Business:	Y	Commercial/Industrial:	Y	Graphic Arts/Photog.:		Hardware Dev.:		HR/Other:	Y	Health/Lab	
MBA Graduates:	Y	Sales Trainees:	Y	Music:		Consulting/Other:		Training:	Y	Scientists/Research:	
		Advertising Pros.:		Broadcasting:				Health Care:		Petroleum/Chemicals:	
				Other:				Consulting:		Math/Other:	Y

TYPES OF BUSINESS:

Computer Software-Transaction Processing
Procurement & Logistics Solutions
Business Process Software
Consulting Services

BRANDS/DIVISIONS/AFFILIATES:

b-process

CONTACTS:

Note: Officers with more than one job title may be intentionally listed here more than once.

Robert M. Calderoni, CEO
Kent Parker, COO
Kevin S. Costello, Pres.
Ahmed Rubaie, CFO
Tim Minahan, Chief Mktg. Officer
Matthew Zack, Sr. VP-Human Resources
Bhaskar Himatsingka, CTO
Sanish Mondkar, Sr. VP-Eng. & Hosting Oper.
Matthew Zack, Sr. VP-Corp. Dev.
Charles Jackson, Exec. VP-Customer Mgmt.
Daryl Rolley, Gen. Mgr.-Ariba, North America & Asia/Sr. VP
Greg Spray, Sr. VP-Solutions Mgmt.
Robert M. Calderoni, Chmn.
Michael J. Arenth, Gen. Mgr.-Ariba, Europe/VP

Phone: 650-390-1000	**Fax:**
Toll-Free: 866-772-7422	
Address: 910 Hermosa Ct., Sunnyvale, CA 94085 US	

GROWTH PLANS/SPECIAL FEATURES:

Ariba, Inc. provides its clients with spend management software and solutions that allow for the efficient procurement of all required non-payroll goods and services. Its products and services enhance the visibility of spending activities across a client's suppliers, divisions and purchased goods or services. The company's software applications are provided as Software-as-a-Service (SaaS) and can integrate with all major business applications. Ariba's collaborative business commerce solutions combine SaaS technology with web-based communities and a global network of trading partners. For buyers Ariba provides a wide range of spend analysis solutions, including contract management, procurement analytics and supplier management. Its contract management solutions for buyers allow customers to streamline and automate the entire contract process. For procurement and expense activities, it offers applications and services for requisitioning and procurement across all kinds of spending. Supplier management solutions enable companies to identify and assess new sources of supply. Services for sellers include supplier sales and marketing programs; network catalog, order and invoice collaboration; and supply chain finance and payment management applications. The company currently has office locations in 25 countries, with its primary offices located in Sunnyvale, California; Pittsburgh, Pennsylvania; Atlanta, Georgia; and Bangalore, India. More than 700,000 companies are active on the Ariba Commerce Cloud. In October 2011, the firm acquired France based electronic invoice network, b-process.

The company offers its employees medical, dental and vision; a 401(k) plan; employee stock purchase plan; and flexible spending accounts.

FINANCIALS:

Sales and profits are in thousands of dollars—add 000 to get the full amount. 2011 Note: Financial information for 2011 was not available for all companies at press time.

2011 Sales: $443,845	2011 Profits: $33,257	**U.S. Stock Ticker: ARBA**
2010 Sales: $361,146	2010 Profits: $16,386	**Int'l Ticker:**
2009 Sales: $338,972	2009 Profits: $8,193	Int'l Exchange:
2008 Sales: $328,060	2008 Profits: $-41,062	Employees: 2,432 Fiscal Year Ends: 9/30
2007 Sales: $301,667	2007 Profits: $-14,977	Parent Company:

SALARIES/BENEFITS:

Pension Plan:	ESOP Stock Plan:	Profit Sharing:	Top Exec. Salary: $675,000	Bonus: $1,120,500
Savings Plan: Y	Stock Purch. Plan: Y		Second Exec. Salary: $500,000	Bonus: $622,500

OTHER THOUGHTS:

Apparent Women Officers or Directors: 1
Hot Spot for Advancement for Women/Minorities:

LOCATIONS: ("Y" = Yes)

West:	Southwest:	Midwest:	Southeast:	Northeast:	International:
Y	Y	Y	Y	Y	Y

ARIZONA CHEMICAL COMPANY

www.arizonachemical.com

Industry Group Code: 325

Management:		Sales/Marketing:		Liberal Arts:		Information Systems:		Professionals:		Technical/Scientific:	
Mgmt. Trainees:		Mktg. Professionals:	Y	Gen. Writing/Editing:		Info. Management:	Y	Finance/Acct.:	Y	Engineers, Elec.:	Y
Experienced Mgmt.:	Y	Retail Sales:		Technical Writing:	Y	Software Dev.:		Law:	Y	Engineers, Other:	Y
Int'l Business:	Y	Commercial/Industrial:	Y	Graphic Arts/Photog.:		Hardware Dev.:		HR/Other:	Y	Health/Lab	
MBA Graduates:	Y	Sales Trainees:	Y	Music:		Consulting/Other:		Training:	Y	Scientists/Research:	
		Advertising Pros.:		Broadcasting:				Health Care:		Petroleum/Chemicals:	Y
				Other:				Consulting:		Math/Other:	

TYPES OF BUSINESS:

Pine-Based Chemicals
Crude Tall Oil Fractionation

BRANDS/DIVISIONS/AFFILIATES:

American Securities LLC
SYLVACLEAR
SYLVARES
UNI-REZ
SYLVAGUM
Sylfat TOFA
Rhone Capital LLC

CONTACTS: *Note: Officers with more than one job title may be intentionally listed here more than once.*

Kees Verhaar, CEO
Kees Verhaar, Pres.
Frederic Jung, CFO/VP
Juhani Tuovinen, VP-Commercial
David Cowfer, VP-Human Resources
Carl Bilgrien, CTO/VP
Dick Stuyfzand, General Counsel/VP
Gary Reed, VP-Oper.
David Cowfer, VP-Comm.

Phone: 904-928-8700 **Fax:** 904-928-8779
Toll-Free: 800-526-5294
Address: 4600 Touchton Rd. E., Ste. 1200, Jacksonville, FL 32246 US

GROWTH PLANS/SPECIAL FEATURES:

Arizona Chemical Company is one of the largest manufacturers and suppliers of pine-based chemicals worldwide. With 10 production facilities located in the U.S. and Europe, the firm's operations are based on the refining and upgrading of Crude Tall Oil and Crude Sulphate Turpentine, both of which are derived from the process of wood pulping. Among the many end-products incorporating Arizona Chemical's refined products are adhesives, chemical intermediates, printing inks and consumer products. The firm's adhesives products are used in bookbinding, carpets, contact cements, labels, nonwoven fabrics, caulks, packaging and construction. Specific products include SYLVARES brand alpha methyl styrene (AMS) resins; UNI-REZ brand hot melt polyamides resins; and three brands of rosin tackifiers (used to make things stickier, or tacky), SYLVALITE, SYLVATAC and SYLVAGUM, used in everything from chewing gum to adhesive tape. The chemical intermediates group has one of the firm's most diverse product lines, with product applications including coatings, epoxy curatives, mining ore floatation, metalworking fluids, asphalt modification, tire manufacturing, synthetic lubricants and fuel additives. Specific products include three brands of tall oil products, Sylfat TOFA, Sylvatal and Sylvaros Rosin, used in plastics, alkyd paints, lubricants and fuel. Its printing inks serve various sub-markets within the commercial printing industry, including flexible packaging inks, lithography inks and publication gravure market. Arizona Chemical's SYLVACLEAR resins, manufactured through the firm's patented Immobilized Fragrance Oil technology, can be utilized in several consumer applications, including automotive and home air fresheners. Additionally, the firm's products are incorporated into flavorings and fragrances; bio-fuels; thermoplastic road markings; and tires and rubber. In November 2010, Rhone Capital LLC sold its controlling interest in Arizona Chemical to American Securities LLC, a New York-based private equity firm.

FINANCIALS: **Sales and profits are in thousands of dollars—add 000 to get the full amount. 2011 Note: Financial information for 2011 was not available for all companies at press time.**

2011 Sales: $ | 2011 Profits: $
2010 Sales: $ | 2010 Profits: $
2009 Sales: $ | 2009 Profits: $
2008 Sales: $ | 2008 Profits: $
2007 Sales: $ | 2007 Profits: $

U.S. Stock Ticker: Private
Int'l Ticker:
Int'l Exchange:
Employees: Fiscal Year Ends: 12/31
Parent Company: AMERICAN SECURITIES LLC

SALARIES/BENEFITS:

Pension Plan: ESOP Stock Plan: Profit Sharing: Top Exec. Salary: $ Bonus: $
Savings Plan: Stock Purch. Plan: Second Exec. Salary: $ Bonus: $

OTHER THOUGHTS:

Apparent Women Officers or Directors:
Hot Spot for Advancement for Women/Minorities:

LOCATIONS: ("Y" = Yes)

West:	Southwest:	Midwest:	Southeast:	Northeast:	International:
		Y	Y		Y

AROTECH CORPORATION

www.arotech.com

Industry Group Code: 332

Management:		Sales/Marketing:		Liberal Arts:		Information Systems:		Professionals:		Technical/Scientific:	
Mgmt. Trainees:		Mktg. Professionals:	Y	Gen. Writing/Editing:		Info. Management:	Y	Finance/Acct.:	Y	Engineers, Elec.:	Y
Experienced Mgmt.:	Y	Retail Sales:		Technical Writing:	Y	Software Dev.:	Y	Law:	Y	Engineers, Other:	Y
Int'l Business:	Y	Commercial/Industrial:	Y	Graphic Arts/Photog.:		Hardware Dev.:	Y	HR/Other:	Y	Health/Lab	
MBA Graduates:	Y	Sales Trainees:	Y	Music:		Consulting/Other:		Training:	Y	Scientists/Research:	
		Advertising Pros.:		Broadcasting:				Health Care:		Petroleum/Chemicals:	
				Other:				Consulting:		Math/Other:	Y

TYPES OF BUSINESS:

Mobile Electric Power Technology
Zinc-Air Batteries
Armor & Armored Vehicles
Defense & Safety Products
Training & Simulation Products

BRANDS/DIVISIONS/AFFILIATES:

MDT Protective Industries Ltd
MDT Armor Corporation
Armour of America
Realtime Technologies Inc
FAAC Inc
Epsilor Electronic Industries Ltd
Electric Fuel Battery Corporation
Concord Safety Solutions Pvt Ltd

CONTACTS: *Note: Officers with more than one job title may be intentionally listed here more than once.*

Robert S. Ehrlich, CEO
Steven Esses, COO
Steven Esses, Pres.
Thomas J. Paup, CFO
Jonathan Whartman, Sr. VP-Mktg.
Yaakov Har-Oz, General Counsel/VP/Corp. Sec.
Thomas J. Paup, VP-Finance
William Graham, VP-Gov't Affairs
Robert S. Ehrlich, Chmn.

Phone:	**Fax:** 734-761-5368
Toll-Free: 800-281-0356	
Address: 1229 Oak Valley Dr., Ann Arbor, MI 48108 US	

GROWTH PLANS/SPECIAL FEATURES:

Arotech Corporation is a defense and security products and services company active in three sectors: high-level armoring; interactive simulation and training; and batteries and charging systems. The company's armoring division specializes in manufacturing military armored combat vehicles based on commercial platforms and up-armoring civilian SUVs, buses and vans through its subsidiaries MDT Protective Industries, Ltd., located in Lod, Israel, and MDT Armor Corporation, located in Auburn, Alabama. It also provides ballistic armor kits for rotary and fixed wing aircraft and marine armor under the Armour of America brand. Additionally, the firm holds a 26% interest in Concord Safety Solutions Pvt. Ltd., an Indian company it jointly established with an Indian vehicle manufacturing company and an Indian armor materials company. Arotech's interactive simulation and training division, operating through FAAC, Inc. and Realtime Technologies, Inc., offers simulators, systems engineering and software products to the U.S. military, government and private enterprises. It also provides specialized use-of-force training for police, security personnel and the military under the trade name IES Interactive Training. Arotech's battery and power systems division manufactures and sells lithium and Zinc-Air batteries for defense and security products as well as other military applications. Through Epsilor Electronic Industries, Ltd., the company develops and sells lithium batteries and chargers to the military and private defense industry in the Middle East, Europe and Asia. Through Electric Fuel Battery Corporation, it produces Zinc-Air batteries, rechargeable batteries and battery chargers for the military. Zinc-Air batteries are lighter in weight and possess higher energy density than lithium-based batteries. Moreover, the company produces water-activated lifejacket lights for commercial aviation and marine applications through Electric Fuel, Ltd. Arotech relies heavily on sales to the U.S. military, which accounted for 42% of the company's revenues during 2010.

FINANCIALS: **Sales and profits are in thousands of dollars—add 000 to get the full amount. 2011 Note: Financial information for 2011 was not available for all companies at press time.**

2011 Sales: $	2011 Profits: $	**U.S. Stock Ticker: ARTX**
2010 Sales: $73,741	2010 Profits: $- 917	**Int'l Ticker:**
2009 Sales: $74,534	2009 Profits: $-3,054	Int'l Exchange:
2008 Sales: $68,949	2008 Profits: $-3,838	Employees: 418 Fiscal Year Ends: 12/31
2007 Sales: $57,719	2007 Profits: $-3,501	Parent Company:

SALARIES/BENEFITS:

Pension Plan:	ESOP Stock Plan:	Profit Sharing:	Top Exec. Salary: $400,000	Bonus: $265,000
Savings Plan:	Stock Purch. Plan:		Second Exec. Salary: $179,776	Bonus: $89,900

OTHER THOUGHTS:

Apparent Women Officers or Directors:
Hot Spot for Advancement for Women/Minorities:

LOCATIONS: ("Y" = Yes)

West:	Southwest:	Midwest:	Southeast:	Northeast:	International:
Y		Y	Y	Y	Y

ARRAY BIOPHARMA INC

www.arraybiopharma.com

Industry Group Code: 541712

Management:		Sales/Marketing:		Liberal Arts:		Information Systems:		Professionals:		Technical/Scientific:	
Mgmt. Trainees:		Mktg. Professionals:	Y	Gen. Writing/Editing:		Info. Management:	Y	Finance/Acct.:	Y	Engineers, Elec.:	
Experienced Mgmt.:	Y	Retail Sales:		Technical Writing:	Y	Software Dev.:	Y	Law:	Y	Engineers, Other:	Y
Int'l Business:		Commercial/Industrial:	Y	Graphic Arts/Photog.:		Hardware Dev.:		HR/Other:	Y	Health/Lab	Y
MBA Graduates:	Y	Sales Trainees:	Y	Music:		Consulting/Other:		Training:		Scientists/Research:	Y
		Advertising Pros.:		Broadcasting:				Health Care:	Y	Petroleum/Chemicals:	
				Other:				Consulting:		Math/Other:	Y

TYPES OF BUSINESS:

Drug Development & Research Services
Small-Molecule Drugs
Arrays

BRANDS/DIVISIONS/AFFILIATES:

Array Discovery Platform
MEK
ARRY-614
ARRY-162
RADICAL
Optimer Building Blocks

CONTACTS: *Note: Officers with more than one job title may be intentionally listed here more than once.*

Robert E. Conway, CEO
David L. Snitman, COO
Kevin Koch, Pres.
R. Michael Carruthers, CFO
Kevin Koch, Chief Scientific Officer
John R. Moore, General Counsel/VP
David L. Snitman, VP-Bus. Dev.
John A. Josey, VP-Discovery Chemistry
James D. Winkler, VP-Discovery & Translational Biology
Gary M. Clark, VP-Biostatistics & Data Mgmt.
Kyle A. Lefkoff, Chmn.

Phone: 303-381-6600	**Fax:** 303-449-5376
Toll-Free: 877-633-2436	
Address: 3200 Walnut St., Boulder, CO 80301 US	

GROWTH PLANS/SPECIAL FEATURES:

Array BioPharma, Inc. is a biopharmaceutical company focused on discovering, developing and commercializing targeted small molecule drugs for the treatment of cancer and inflammatory diseases. The firm's scientists use its Array Discovery Platform, an integrated set of drug discovery technologies including predictive informatics, high throughput screening and information databases of existent drugs, to invent novel small-molecule drugs in collaboration with leading pharmaceutical and biotechnology companies, as well as for its own pipeline of proprietary drugs. The company holds collaborative partnerships with AstraZeneca; Genentech; InterMune; Cellgene Corp.; Amgen, Inc.; and Novartis. Array's prime research focuses are cancer and inflammatory diseases. The company has four cancer drugs and one inflammation drugs in its advanced pipeline. The clinical candidate ARRY-162, or MEK for Cancer, is an orally active drug that is currently in Phase I clinical trials for the treatment of cancer. Other cancer products in development consist of inhibitors targeting breast cancer, acute myeloid leukemia, multiple myeloma and solid tumors. The inflammatory and metabolic drugs aim to regulate biological targets that control inflammation. Its primary inflammatory drug candidate is ARRY-614, an inhibitor for myelodysplastic syndrome (MDS). In collaboration with its partner companies, Array is also developing a glucokinase activation drug for the treatment of Type 2 diabetes; and a hepatitis C virus (HCV) protease inhibitor. Under the firm's software program, RADICAL, Array has created Optimer Building Blocks, a retrosynthetic analysis of small molecule compounds for the purpose of manufacturing pharmaceuticals.

Employees are offered medical, dental and vision insurance; life and AD&D insurance; short- and long-term disability coverage; an employee assistance program; a health savings account; a flexible spending account; an educational assistance program; a 401(k) plan; and an employee stock purchase plan.

FINANCIALS: **Sales and profits are in thousands of dollars—add 000 to get the full amount. 2011 Note: Financial information for 2011 was not available for all companies at press time.**

2011 Sales: $71,901	2011 Profits: $-56,324
2010 Sales: $53,880	2010 Profits: $-77,631
2009 Sales: $24,982	2009 Profits: $-127,815
2008 Sales: $28,808	2008 Profits: $-96,288
2007 Sales: $36,970	2007 Profits: $-55,443

U.S. Stock Ticker: ARRY
Int'l Ticker:
Int'l Exchange:
Employees: 259 Fiscal Year Ends: 6/30
Parent Company:

SALARIES/BENEFITS:

Pension Plan:	ESOP Stock Plan:	Profit Sharing:	Top Exec. Salary: $520,000	Bonus: $152,755
Savings Plan: Y	Stock Purch. Plan: Y		Second Exec. Salary: $421,250	Bonus: $67,366

OTHER THOUGHTS:

Apparent Women Officers or Directors:
Hot Spot for Advancement for Women/Minorities:

LOCATIONS: ("Y" = Yes)

West:	Southwest:	Midwest:	Southeast:	Northeast:	International:
Y				Y	

ARRIS GROUP INC

www.arrisi.com

Industry Group Code: 3342

Management:		**Sales/Marketing:**		**Liberal Arts:**		**Information Systems:**		**Professionals:**		**Technical/Scientific:**	
Mgmt. Trainees:		Mktg. Professionals:	Y	Gen. Writing/Editing:	Y	Info. Management:	Y	Finance/Acct.:	Y	Engineers, Elec.:	Y
Experienced Mgmt.:	Y	Retail Sales:		Technical Writing:	Y	Software Dev.:	Y	Law:	Y	Engineers, Other:	Y
Int'l Business:	Y	Commercial/Industrial:	Y	Graphic Arts/Photog.:		Hardware Dev.:	Y	HR/Other:	Y	Health/Lab	
MBA Graduates:	Y	Sales Trainees:	Y	Music:		Consulting/Other:		Training:	Y	Scientists/Research:	
		Advertising Pros.:		Broadcasting:				Health Care:		Petroleum/Chemicals:	
				Other:				Consulting:		Math/Other:	

TYPES OF BUSINESS:

Communications Equipment-Cable Systems
Optical & Radio Frequency Transmission Equipment
Internet Access Products
Support & Testing Products

BRANDS/DIVISIONS/AFFILIATES:

BigBand Networks Inc

CONTACTS:

Note: Officers with more than one job title may be intentionally listed here more than once.

Robert J. Stanzione, CEO
Robert J. Stanzione, Pres.
David B. Potts, CFO/Exec. VP
Ronald M. Coppock, Pres., ARRIS Worldwide Sales
David B. Potts, CIO
James D. Lakin, Pres., Advanced Tech. & Svcs.
Lawrence A. Margolis, Exec. VP-Admin. & Strategic Planning
Lawrence A. Margolis, General Counsel/Corp. Sec.
James A. Bauer, Dir.-Investor Rel.
Bryant K. Isaacs, Pres., Media & Comm. Systems
Bruce McClelland, Pres., Broadband Comm. Systems
Dan Whalen, Sr. VP-Sales
Robert J. Stanzione, Chmn.
Ming Wu, VP-Bus. Dev., China
John Caezza, Pres., Access, Transport & Supplies

Phone: 678-473-2000	**Fax:** 678-622-8750
Toll-Free:	
Address: 3871 Lakefield Dr., Suwanee, GA 30024 US	

GROWTH PLANS/SPECIAL FEATURES:

ARRIS Group, Inc. is a global telecommunications technology company specializing in the design and engineering of broadband network solutions. The firm develops, manufactures and supplies cable telephony, video and high-speed data products, as well as outside plant construction and maintenance equipment for cable system operators. The company provides products and equipment principally to cable system operators, specifically Multiple System Operators (MSOs). Its products enable MSOs and other broadband service providers to deliver integrated voice, video and high-speed data services. ARRIS operates through three segments: Broadband Communications Systems (BCS); Access, Transport and Supplies (ATS); and Media & Communications Systems (MCS). Its BCS product offerings include VoIP (Voice over Internet Protocol) and high speed data products; and video and IP (Internet Protocol) headend products. The company's VoIP and high speed data products include cable modem termination systems (CMTS); two line residential embedded multimedia terminal adapters (EMTAs); multi-line EMTAs for residential and commercial services; wireless gateway EMTAs; and high-speed data cable modems. Video and IP headend products offered by ARRIS include CMTS and Universal EdgeQAM. ATS division's products include Hybrid Fiber-Coaxial (HFC) plant equipment and infrastructure products for fiber optic or coaxial networks built under or above ground. HFC plant products include headend and hub products; optical nodes; radio frequency products; and transport products. Infrastructure products include cables and strands; vaults; conduits; drop materials; tools; connectors; and test equipment. The firm's MCS products include media delivery and monetization platforms, such as video on demand management and distribution and digital advertising; operations management systems; and fixed mobile convergence networks. The company maintains domestic sales offices in Colorado, Connecticut, Georgia, Oregon, Pennsylvania and Washington; and international sales offices in Argentina, Brazil, Chile, Hong Kong, Japan, Korea, the Netherlands and Spain. In November 2011, the firm acquired BigBand Networks, Inc.

FINANCIALS:

Sales and profits are in thousands of dollars—add 000 to get the full amount. 2011 Note: Financial information for 2011 was not available for all companies at press time.

2011 Sales: $1,088,700	2011 Profits: $-12,700	**U.S. Stock Ticker: ARRS**
2010 Sales: $1,087,506	2010 Profits: $64,128	**Int'l Ticker:**
2009 Sales: $1,107,806	2009 Profits: $90,769	Int'l Exchange:
2008 Sales: $1,144,565	2008 Profits: $-129,639	Employees: 1,942 Fiscal Year Ends: 12/31
2007 Sales: $992,194	2007 Profits: $92,347	Parent Company:

SALARIES/BENEFITS:

Pension Plan:	ESOP Stock Plan:	Profit Sharing:	Top Exec. Salary: $746,500	Bonus: $529,000
Savings Plan: Y	Stock Purch. Plan:		Second Exec. Salary: $393,500	Bonus: $167,270

OTHER THOUGHTS:

Apparent Women Officers or Directors: 1
Hot Spot for Advancement for Women/Minorities:

LOCATIONS: ("Y" = Yes)

West:	Southwest:	Midwest:	Southeast:	Northeast:	International:
Y		Y	Y	Y	Y

ARTHROCARE CORP

www.arthrocare.com

Industry Group Code: 33911

Management:		Sales/Marketing:		Liberal Arts:		Information Systems:		Professionals:		Technical/Scientific:	
Mgmt. Trainees:		Mktg. Professionals:	Y	Gen. Writing/Editing:		Info. Management:	Y	Finance/Acct.:	Y	Engineers, Elec.:	Y
Experienced Mgmt.:	Y	Retail Sales:		Technical Writing:	Y	Software Dev.:	Y	Law:	Y	Engineers, Other:	Y
Int'l Business:	Y	Commercial/Industrial:	Y	Graphic Arts/Photog.:		Hardware Dev.:		HR/Other:	Y	Health/Lab	Y
MBA Graduates:	Y	Sales Trainees:	Y	Music:		Consulting/Other:		Training:	Y	Scientists/Research:	Y
		Advertising Pros.:		Broadcasting:				Health Care:	Y	Petroleum/Chemicals:	
				Other:				Consulting:		Math/Other:	Y

TYPES OF BUSINESS:

Equipment-Tissue Removal Systems
Cosmetic & Dermatologic Surgery Products
Advanced Radiofrequency Devices

BRANDS/DIVISIONS/AFFILIATES:

Coblation
Opus Medical, Inc.
Medical Device Alliance, Inc.
Atlantech Collection
ENT Wands
SpineWand
Parallax Medical
ArthroWand Collection

CONTACTS: *Note: Officers with more than one job title may be intentionally listed here more than once.*

David Fitzgerald, CEO
David Fitzgerald, Pres.
Todd Newton, CFO/Sr. VP
James Pacek, Sr. VP-Mktg. & Sales Oper.
Jean Woloszko, Sr. VP-R&D
Jean Woloszko, CTO
Richard W. Rew II, General Counsel/Sr. VP
Bruce Prothro, Chief Regulatory Officer

Phone: 512-391-3900 | **Fax:** 512-391-3901
Toll-Free:
Address: 7500 Rialto Blvd., Bldg. 2, Ste. 100, Austin, TX 78735 US

GROWTH PLANS/SPECIAL FEATURES:

ArthroCare Corp. is a medical device company that develops, manufactures and markets minimally invasive surgical products, many of which are based on its patented Coblation technology. Coblation employs radio frequency energy for soft tissue removal with minimal damage to surrounding tissue. The firm's products operate at lower temperatures than traditional electrosurgical or laser surgery tools and enable surgeons to ablate, shrink, sculpt, cut, aspirate and suction soft tissue and to seal small bleeding vessels. ArthroCare's strategy includes applying its patented technology to a wide range of soft tissue surgical markets, including arthroscopic surgery; spinal surgery; neurosurgery; cosmetic surgery; urologic surgery; various cardiology applications; gynecological surgery and laparoscopic/general surgical procedures; and ear, nose and throat procedures. The company has labeled its Coblation-based systems for use in neurosurgery; arthroscopic surgery of the knee, shoulder, ankle, elbow, wrist and hip; and for general dermatologic procedures. ArthroCare also manufactures disposable devices for spinal surgery, which are designed to improve the ease of use and functionality of the company's Coblation-based spinal surgery system. The company's technology is also applied in its sports medicine market, in particular to the performance of arthroscopic surgery on selected joints. The firm's product lines include the Atlantech Collection, which offers specialty sports medicine tools including hand-held surgical instruments, procedural kits/trays and reusable accessories to facilitate arthroscopic surgery; ENT Wands, which provides suction wands, channeling wands and excision wands for use in general head, neck and oral surgical procedures; and SpineWand, which offers products for the treatment of soft tissue conditions in the spine. Subsidiaries of ArthroCare include Opus Medical, Inc., which manufactures arthroscopic repair products; Medical Device Alliance, Inc., which distributes vertebral compression fracture treatment products; and Parallax Medical, a majority-owned subsidiary of Medical Device Alliance. In September 2010, the firm introduced Ambient ArthroWand Collection, radiofrequency devices which monitor circulating fluids during athroscopic operations.

FINANCIALS: **Sales and profits are in thousands of dollars—add 000 to get the full amount. 2011 Note: Financial information for 2011 was not available for all companies at press time.**

2011 Sales: $354,885	2011 Profits: $- 902
2010 Sales: $355,379	2010 Profits: $37,084
2009 Sales: $324,117	2009 Profits: $-5,777
2008 Sales: $307,283	2008 Profits: $-35,025
2007 Sales: $279,716	2007 Profits: $ 491

U.S. Stock Ticker: ARTC
Int'l Ticker:
Int'l Exchange:
Employees: 1,407 Fiscal Year Ends: 12/31
Parent Company:

SALARIES/BENEFITS:

Pension Plan:	ESOP Stock Plan:	Profit Sharing:	Top Exec. Salary: $	Bonus: $
Savings Plan: Y	Stock Purch. Plan:		Second Exec. Salary: $	Bonus: $

OTHER THOUGHTS:

Apparent Women Officers or Directors:
Hot Spot for Advancement for Women/Minorities:

LOCATIONS: ("Y" = Yes)

West:	Southwest:	Midwest:	Southeast:	Northeast:	International:
Y	Y				Y

ARUBA NETWORKS INC

www.arubanetworks.com

Industry Group Code: 511210C

Management:		Sales/Marketing:		Liberal Arts:		Information Systems:		Professionals:		Technical/Scientific:	
Mgmt. Trainees:		Mktg. Professionals:	Y	Gen. Writing/Editing:		Info. Management:	Y	Finance/Acct.:	Y	Engineers, Elec.:	Y
Experienced Mgmt.:	Y	Retail Sales:		Technical Writing:	Y	Software Dev.:	Y	Law:	Y	Engineers, Other:	
Int'l Business:	Y	Commercial/Industrial:	Y	Graphic Arts/Photog.:		Hardware Dev.:		HR/Other:	Y	Health/Lab	
MBA Graduates:	Y	Sales Trainees:	Y	Music:		Consulting/Other:		Training:	Y	Scientists/Research:	
		Advertising Pros.:		Broadcasting:				Health Care:		Petroleum/Chemicals:	
				Other:				Consulting:		Math/Other:	

TYPES OF BUSINESS:

WLAN Equipment
Wireless Security Systems
Mobility Software
Convergence Software & Systems

BRANDS/DIVISIONS/AFFILIATES:

Aruba Mobile Edge Architecture
ArubaOS Secure Mobility Software
Aruba Mobility Management System
Aruba Mobility Controllers
Aruba Access Points
Azalea Networks, Inc.
Amigopod

CONTACTS: *Note: Officers with more than one job title may be intentionally listed here more than once.*

Dominic P. Orr, CEO
Hitesh Sheth, COO
Dominic P. Orr, Pres.
Steffan Tomlinson, CFO
Ben Gibson, Chief Mktg. Officer
Aaron Bean, VP-Human Resources
Keerti Melkote, CTO
Ankur Singla, VP-Eng.
Alexa King, General Counsel/VP-Legal
Dave Peterson, VP-Oper.
Sriram Ramachandran, VP-Strategic Initiatives
Robert Bruce, VP-Worldwide Channel Sales
Michael Kirby, VP-Sales
Peter Cellarius, VP-Global Partner Dev. & Oper.
Chris Spain, VP-Prod. Line Mgmt. & Tech. Mktg.
Dominic P. Orr, Chmn.

Phone: 408-227-4500 **Fax:** 408-752-0626
Toll-Free: 866-552-7822
Address: 1344 Crossman Ave., Sunnyvale, CA 94089-1113 US

GROWTH PLANS/SPECIAL FEATURES:

Aruba Networks, Inc. manufactures and markets unified mobility technologies and products including Wi-Fi networks, identity-based security, remote access, cellular services and centralized network management. The company provides its high-performance Wi-Fi-based, wireless local area networks (WLANs) and security systems for businesses that are seeking to implement mobile communications systems over existing wired infrastructures. The firm enables the provision of Mobile Edge, a network architecture that addresses mobility, security and convergence. Aruba's WLAN switches and controllers support a range of functions, including virtual private networks (VPNs), Voice over Internet Protocol (VoIP), user-aware firewalling, RF management and intrusion prevention. Aruba's primary platform is its Aruba Mobile Edge Architecture, which allows users secure and consistent access at any remote location within an enterprise campus or office building. IT departments within each location have the capacity to control network access and prioritize application delivery at a central access control site. Products that utilize this technology include ArubaOS Secure Mobility Software for mobility controllers and access points; the Aruba Mobility Management System, which provides applications for planning, monitoring, fault management, reporting and location visualizations; Aruba Mobility Controllers for high-performance wireless LAN; and Aruba Access Points, which sorts wireless user traffic on the enterprise network towards specific Aruba Mobility Controllers. The company has sold its products to over 11,000 end customers worldwide in such industries as finance, retail, hospitality, technology, manufacturing, media, healthcare, education, utilities, telecom, government, transportation, engineering and construction. Significant U.S. customers include Microsoft; the U.S. Air Force; California State University; and Hess Corporation. Internationally, Aruba's customers include Saudi Aramco; NTT Data Corporation; the Norwegian Ministry of Foreign Affairs; and the University of Tokyo. In September 2010, the company acquired Azalea Networks, a developer of wireless mesh networking (WMN) technology, for $27 million. In December 2010, it purchased the assets and technology of Australia-based Amigopod.

FINANCIALS: **Sales and profits are in thousands of dollars—add 000 to get the full amount. 2011 Note: Financial information for 2011 was not available for all companies at press time.**

2011 Sales: $396,514 — 2011 Profits: $70,688
2010 Sales: $266,534 — 2010 Profits: $-33,998
2009 Sales: $199,259 — 2009 Profits: $-23,413
2008 Sales: $178,260 — 2008 Profits: $-17,124
2007 Sales: $127,499 — 2007 Profits: $-24,382

U.S. Stock Ticker: ARUN
Int'l Ticker:
Int'l Exchange:
Employees: 1,137 Fiscal Year Ends: 7/31
Parent Company:

SALARIES/BENEFITS:

Pension Plan: ESOP Stock Plan: Profit Sharing: Top Exec. Salary: $400,000 Bonus: $
Savings Plan: Y Stock Purch. Plan: Y Second Exec. Salary: $325,000 Bonus: $

OTHER THOUGHTS:

Apparent Women Officers or Directors: 1
Hot Spot for Advancement for Women/Minorities:

LOCATIONS: ("Y" = Yes)

West:	Southwest:	Midwest:	Southeast:	Northeast:	International:
Y			Y	Y	Y

ASTEX PHARMACEUTICALS INC

www.astx.com

Industry Group Code: 325412

Management:		Sales/Marketing:		Liberal Arts:		Information Systems:		Professionals:		Technical/Scientific:	
Mgmt. Trainees:		Mktg. Professionals:		Gen. Writing/Editing:		Info. Management:	Y	Finance/Acct.:	Y	Engineers, Elec.:	
Experienced Mgmt.:	Y	Retail Sales:		Technical Writing:	Y	Software Dev.:		Law:	Y	Engineers, Other:	
Int'l Business:		Commercial/Industrial:	Y	Graphic Arts/Photog.:		Hardware Dev.:		HR/Other:	Y	Health/Lab	Y
MBA Graduates:	Y	Sales Trainees:		Music:		Consulting/Other:		Training:	Y	Scientists/Research:	Y
		Advertising Pros.:		Broadcasting:				Health Care:	Y	Petroleum/Chemicals:	Y
				Other:	Y			Consulting:		Math/Other:	Y

TYPES OF BUSINESS:

Pharmaceuticals Acquisition & Development
Oncology Drugs

BRANDS/DIVISIONS/AFFILIATES:

SuperGen, Inc.
Dacogen
Amuvatinib (MP470)
SGI-110
JAK2
Axl
ETK/BMX
CLIMB

CONTACTS: *Note: Officers with more than one job title may be intentionally listed here more than once.*

James S. Manuso, CEO
James S. Manuso, Pres.
Michael Molkentin, CFO/Corp. Sec.
Mohammad Azab, Chief Medical Officer
Sanjeev Redkar, VP-Mfg. & Pre-Clinical Dev.
Shu Lee, VP-Legal Affairs & Intellectual Property
Michael McCullar, VP-Discovery Oper. & Strategy
Timothy L. Enns, Sr. VP-Bus. Dev.
Timothy L. Enns, Sr. VP-Corp. Comm.
Gavin Choy, VP-Clinical Oper.
David S. Smith, VP-Regulatory & Quality Affairs
James S. Manuso, Chmn.

Phone: 925-560-0100	**Fax:** 925-560-0101
Toll-Free:	
Address: 4140 Dublin Blvd., Ste. 200, Dublin, CA 94568 US	

GROWTH PLANS/SPECIAL FEATURES:

Astex Pharmaceuticals, Inc. (formerly SuperGen, Inc.) develops and commercializes pharmaceutical products intended to treat patients with cancer. The firm's development platform is based on its proprietary CLIMB process that merges rapid screening of compound libraries with computational chemistry and systems biology techniques to identify small-molecule drug candidates. Astex currently possesses a portfolio of five oncological drugs candidates that treat a variety of solid tumors and hematological malignancies. The company's leading product, Amuvatinib (MP-470), is a tyrosine kinase inhibitor/rad 51 suppressor, which has completed Phase I clinical trials. Amuvatinib is being tested on both healthy persons and cancer patients. Astex's preclinical stage product, SGI-110, is a compound which targets and blocks the mechanism by which DNA methylation occurs, thus allowing tumor suppressor genes to function. Products in the company's pipeline that have not yet reached preclinical stages include three kinase inhibitors: the JAK2, Axl and ETK/BMX (epithelial and endothelial tyrosine kinase/ bone marrow X kinase). In addition to drug candidates, Astex continues to generate royalties from the 2004 sale of its drug Dacogen to MGI Pharma, Inc. MGI was acquired by Eisai Corporation, which now has worldwide rights to develop, manufacture and distribute Dacogen and pays the firm at specific regulatory and commercialization milestones. Dacogen is a therapeutic product that decreases the degree of methylation, the replacement of hydrogen with methyl, at certain DNA sites to assist patients with myelodysplastic syndrome. In November 2010, the company discontinued its SGI-1776 oral pim kinase inhibitor due to safety reasons. In April 2011, Astex Therapeutics Limited,was merged into SuperGen, Inc., with the surviving company renamed Astex Pharmaceuticals, Inc.

Employees are offered medical, dental and vision insurance; life and AD&D insurance; short-and long-term disability coverage; flexible spending accounts; cancer and accident insurance; a 401(k) plan; and an employee stock purchase plan.

FINANCIALS: **Sales and profits are in thousands of dollars—add 000 to get the full amount. 2011 Note: Financial information for 2011 was not available for all companies at press time.**

2011 Sales: $	2011 Profits: $	**U.S. Stock Ticker: ASTX**
2010 Sales: $52,972	2010 Profits: $16,273	**Int'l Ticker:**
2009 Sales: $41,253	2009 Profits: $4,737	Int'l Exchange:
2008 Sales: $38,422	2008 Profits: $-9,111	Employees: 97 Fiscal Year Ends: 12/31
2007 Sales: $22,954	2007 Profits: $13,081	Parent Company:

SALARIES/BENEFITS:

Pension Plan:	ESOP Stock Plan:	Profit Sharing:	Top Exec. Salary: $574,237	Bonus: $500,000
Savings Plan: Y	Stock Purch. Plan: Y		Second Exec. Salary: $326,375	Bonus: $119,000

OTHER THOUGHTS:

Apparent Women Officers or Directors:
Hot Spot for Advancement for Women/Minorities:

LOCATIONS: ("Y" = Yes)

West:	Southwest:	Midwest:	Southeast:	Northeast:	International:
Y					

ATHENAHEALTH INC

www.athenahealth.com

Industry Group Code: 522320

Management:		**Sales/Marketing:**		**Liberal Arts:**		**Information Systems:**		**Professionals:**		**Technical/Scientific:**	
Mgmt. Trainees:	Y	Mktg. Professionals:	Y	Gen. Writing/Editing:	Y	Info. Management:	Y	Finance/Acct.:	Y	Engineers, Elec.:	
Experienced Mgmt.:	Y	Retail Sales:		Technical Writing:	Y	Software Dev.:	Y	Law:	Y	Engineers, Other:	
Int'l Business:	Y	Commercial/Industrial:	Y	Graphic Arts/Photog.:		Hardware Dev.:		HR/Other:	Y	Health/Lab	
MBA Graduates:	Y	Sales Trainees:	Y	Music:		Consulting/Other:		Training:	Y	Scientists/Research:	
		Advertising Pros.:	Y	Broadcasting:				Health Care:		Petroleum/Chemicals:	
				Other:				Consulting:		Math/Other:	

TYPES OF BUSINESS:

Outsourced Health Reimbursement Services
Patient Information Management
Billing & Collection Services for Health Care Providers
Automated Messaging

BRANDS/DIVISIONS/AFFILIATES:

athenaNet
athenaCollector
athenaClinicals
athenaCommunicator
PayerView
Proxsys, LLC

CONTACTS: *Note: Officers with more than one job title may be intentionally listed here more than once.*

Jonathan Bush, CEO
Ed Park, COO/Exec. VP
Jonathan Bush, Pres.
Timothy M. Adams, CFO/Sr. VP
Rob Cosinuke, Chief Mktg. Officer/Sr. VP
Leslie Locke, Sr. VP-People & Process
Todd Rothenhaus, Chief Medical Info. Officer/VP
Jeremy Delinsky, CTO/Sr. VP
Derek Hedges, Sr. VP-Prod. Strategy
Daniel H. Orenstein, General Counsel/Sr. VP/Sec.
Derek Hedges, Sr. VP-Bus. Dev.
John Hallock, Dir.-Corp. Comm.
Jennifer Heizer, Dir.-Investor Rel.
Stephen N. Kahane, Pres., Enterprise Svcs.
Jonathan Bush, Chmn.

Phone: 617-402-1000 **Fax:** 617-402-1099
Toll-Free: 800-981-5084
Address: 311 Arsenal St., Watertown, MA 02472 US

GROWTH PLANS/SPECIAL FEATURES:

Athenahealth, Inc. is a provider of Internet-based business services to physician practices and one of the largest firms in the health reimbursement field. The company offers its integrated business services over the Internet on a subscription basis. The firm offers medical group office automation subscription services, as well as related services through its integrated platform, athenaNet. This platform is comprised of three principal tools: athenaCollector, athenaClinicals and athenaCommunicator. Athenahealth's flagship product, athenaCollector, is a revenue cycle management service that includes a management platform and automates and manages billing-related functions for physicians' practices. The athenaCollector system tracks, controls and executes claims and billing processes. athenaClinicals, aimed at simplifying electronic medical record (EMR) handling, provides a wholly integrated system for managing the processes of providing and receiving pay for care. athenaCommunicator is an automated message offering that includes automated patient messaging services, live operator services and a patient web portal. In addition, the firm maintains an annual ranking system that evaluates the relationship between payers and providers called PayerView. Athenahealth serves over 27,000 medical providers in 46 states in the U.S., and its offices include operations in Chennai, India. During 2010, the firm processed over 47 million medical claims; handled approximately 119 million charge postings; and delivered 34.4 million automated calls to patients on behalf of practices. In February 2011, Athenahealth and Microsoft formed a strategic partnership to develop electronic communication health solutions based on Microsoft's Amalga enterprise health intelligence platform. In July 2011, the firm agreed to acquire Proxsys, LLC, a provider of cloud-based care coordination services between physicians and hospitals.

Employees are offered medical, dental and vision insurance; life insurance; disability coverage; a 401(k) plan; and an employee stock purchase plan.

FINANCIALS: **Sales and profits are in thousands of dollars—add 000 to get the full amount. 2011 Note: Financial information for 2011 was not available for all companies at press time.**

2011 Sales: $
2010 Sales: $245,538
2009 Sales: $188,527
2008 Sales: $136,282
2007 Sales: $97,618

2011 Profits: $
2010 Profits: $12,704
2009 Profits: $9,276
2008 Profits: $31,602
2007 Profits: $-7,501

U.S. Stock Ticker: ATHN
Int'l Ticker:
Int'l Exchange:
Employees: 1,242 Fiscal Year Ends: 12/31
Parent Company:

SALARIES/BENEFITS:

Pension Plan: ESOP Stock Plan: Profit Sharing: Top Exec. Salary: $466,538 Bonus: $523,000
Savings Plan: Y Stock Purch. Plan: Y Second Exec. Salary: $296,827 Bonus: $232,700

OTHER THOUGHTS:

Apparent Women Officers or Directors: 1
Hot Spot for Advancement for Women/Minorities:

LOCATIONS: ("Y" = Yes)

West:	Southwest:	Midwest:	Southeast:	Northeast:	International:
			Y	Y	Y

ATLANTIC CITY ELECTRIC COMPANY

www.atlanticcityelectric.com

Industry Group Code: 221

Management:		**Sales/Marketing:**		**Liberal Arts:**		**Information Systems:**		**Professionals:**		**Technical/Scientific:**	
Mgmt. Trainees:		Mktg. Professionals:	Y	Gen. Writing/Editing:	Y	Info. Management:	Y	Finance/Acct.:	Y	Engineers, Elec.:	Y
Experienced Mgmt.:	Y	Retail Sales:		Technical Writing:		Software Dev.:		Law:	Y	Engineers, Other:	Y
Int'l Business:		Commercial/Industrial:	Y	Graphic Arts/Photog.:		Hardware Dev.:		HR/Other:	Y	Health/Lab	
MBA Graduates:	Y	Sales Trainees:		Music:		Consulting/Other:		Training:	Y	Scientists/Research:	
		Advertising Pros.:		Broadcasting:				Health Care:		Petroleum/Chemicals:	Y
				Other:				Consulting:		Math/Other:	

TYPES OF BUSINESS:

Utilities-Electricity

BRANDS/DIVISIONS/AFFILIATES:

Pepco Holdings, Inc.

CONTACTS: *Note: Officers with more than one job title may be intentionally listed here more than once.*

Kirk J. Emge, General Counsel
Ronald K. Clark, Controller
Joseph M. Rigby, CEO/Pres., Pepco Holdings, Inc.

Phone:	**Fax:**
Toll-Free: 800-642-3780	
Address: 5100 Harding Hwy., Mays Landing, NJ 08330 US	

GROWTH PLANS/SPECIAL FEATURES:

Atlantic City Electric Company (ACE), a subsidiary of Pepco Holdings, Inc., is an electrical utility firm engaged in the transmission and distribution of electricity. The firm's primary service area consists of Gloucester, Camden, Burlington, Ocean, Atlantic, Cape May, Cumberland and Salem counties in southern New Jersey. This service area provides electrical service to 547,000 customers in a 2,700 square mile region with an approximate population of 1.1 million. ACE maintains a distribution network consisting of more than 11,000 miles of transmission and distribution lines. It delivers approximately 10 million megawatt hours of electricity to its customers per year. Roughly 46% of this energy is delivered to commercial customers, 44% to residential customers and 10% to industrial customers. ACE relies entirely on purchases from third-party electricity-generating sources. The firm also offers basic generation services (BGS) to retail customers that choose not to purchase electricity from a competitive supplier. It offers two types of BGS: BGS-Fixed Price, which is supplied to smaller residential and commercial customers at seasonally-adjusted fixed prices; and BGS-Commercial and Industrial Energy Price, which is offered to larger customers at hourly PJM RTO real-time market prices for a one-year term. In mid 2010, ACE introduced the Energy Wise Rewards Program, which reduces electrical usage through the use of central air conditioner compressor cycling.

Parent company Pepco Holdings Inc. offers employees medical, dental and vision packages; life and disability coverage; healthcare and dependent care reimbursement accounts; transportation reimbursement accounts; a 401(k) retirement savings plan; and tuition reimbursement.

FINANCIALS: **Sales and profits are in thousands of dollars—add 000 to get the full amount. 2011 Note: Financial information for 2011 was not available for all companies at press time.**

2011 Sales: $	2011 Profits: $	**U.S. Stock Ticker: Subsidiary**
2010 Sales: $	2010 Profits: $	**Int'l Ticker:**
2009 Sales: $	2009 Profits: $	Int'l Exchange:
2008 Sales: $	2008 Profits: $	Employees: Fiscal Year Ends: 12/31
2007 Sales: $	2007 Profits: $	Parent Company: PEPCO HOLDINGS INC

SALARIES/BENEFITS:

Pension Plan: Y	ESOP Stock Plan:	Profit Sharing:	Top Exec. Salary: $	Bonus: $
Savings Plan: Y	Stock Purch. Plan:		Second Exec. Salary: $	Bonus: $

OTHER THOUGHTS:

Apparent Women Officers or Directors:
Hot Spot for Advancement for Women/Minorities:

LOCATIONS: ("Y" = Yes)

West:	Southwest:	Midwest:	Southeast:	Northeast:	International:
				Y	

ATLANTIC TELE-NETWORK INC

www.atni.com

Industry Group Code: 517110

Management:		Sales/Marketing:		Liberal Arts:		Information Systems:		Professionals:		Technical/Scientific:	
Mgmt. Trainees:		Mktg. Professionals:	Y	Gen. Writing/Editing:		Info. Management:	Y	Finance/Acct.:	Y	Engineers, Elec.:	Y
Experienced Mgmt.:	Y	Retail Sales:		Technical Writing:		Software Dev.:	Y	Law:	Y	Engineers, Other:	
Int'l Business:	Y	Commercial/Industrial:	Y	Graphic Arts/Photog.:		Hardware Dev.:		HR/Other:	Y	Health/Lab	
MBA Graduates:	Y	Sales Trainees:		Music:		Consulting/Other:		Training:		Scientists/Research:	
		Advertising Pros.:		Broadcasting:				Health Care:		Petroleum/Chemicals:	
				Other:				Consulting:		Math/Other:	

TYPES OF BUSINESS:

Wired & Wireless Telecommunications
Long Distance & International Telecom Services
Local Exchange Telecom Services
Communications Transport Services

BRANDS/DIVISIONS/AFFILIATES:

Guyana Telephone & Telegraph
Commnet Wireless LLC
Choice Communications LLC
Sovernet Inc
CellularOne
Bermuda Digital Communications Ltd
M3 Wireless Ltd

CONTACTS: *Note: Officers with more than one job title may be intentionally listed here more than once.*

Michael T. Prior, CEO
Michael T. Prior, Pres.
Justin D. Benincasa, CFO/Treas.
Leonard Q. Slap, General Counsel/VP
William F. Kreisher, Sr. VP-Corp. Dev.
Douglas J. Minster, VP-Gov't & Regulatory Affairs
Karl D. Noone, Controller/Sr. VP
John P. Audet, VP-Financial Analysis & Planning
Cornelius B. Prior, Jr., Chmn.
Paul R. Bowersock, Pres., Int'l Oper.

Phone: 978-619-1300	**Fax:** 978-744-3951
Toll-Free:	
Address: 600 Cummings Ctr., Beverly, MA 01915 US	

GROWTH PLANS/SPECIAL FEATURES:

Atlantic Tele-Network, Inc. (ATN) provides wireless and wireline telecommunications services in North America and the Caribbean. The company operates in the U.S., Guyana, Bermuda and U.S. Virgin Islands through a variety of operating subsidiaries. Guyana Telephone & Telegraph (GT&T), of which ATN owns 80%, is the exclusive provider of local exchange and international long-distance telecom services in Guyana, as well as one of two wireless service providers in Guyana. Commnet Wireless LLC, a wholly-owned subsidiary, provides wireless voice and data communications roaming services in the U.S. Commnet accounts for 53% of the firm's revenues. Choice Communications LLC, also wholly-owned, provides fixed wireless broadband data services and dial-up Internet services to retail and business customers in the U.S. Virgin Islands. Sovernet, Inc., of which ATN owns 75%, provides integrated voice and broadband data communications services primarily in Vermont, and wholesale high-capacity transport services in New York, through ION Holdco LLC. Bermuda Digital Communications, Ltd. (BDC), 58%-owned by the company, is one of the largest wireless voice and data communications service providers in Bermuda, operating under the CellularOne brand. This subsidiary also provides wireless services in the Turks and Caicos Islands through Islandcom Telecommunications, Ltd. In May 2011, CellularOne acquired M3 Wireless, Ltd., a Bermuda-based wireless group.

FINANCIALS: **Sales and profits are in thousands of dollars—add 000 to get the full amount. 2011 Note: Financial information for 2011 was not available for all companies at press time.**

2011 Sales: $759,200	2011 Profits: $21,800	**U.S. Stock Ticker: ATNI**
2010 Sales: $619,145	2010 Profits: $38,454	**Int'l Ticker:**
2009 Sales: $242,281	2009 Profits: $35,539	Int'l Exchange:
2008 Sales: $207,264	2008 Profits: $34,798	Employees: 1,765 Fiscal Year Ends: 12/31
2007 Sales: $186,741	2007 Profits: $37,940	Parent Company:

SALARIES/BENEFITS:

Pension Plan:	ESOP Stock Plan:	Profit Sharing:	Top Exec. Salary: $525,000	Bonus: $325,000
Savings Plan:	Stock Purch. Plan:		Second Exec. Salary: $265,000	Bonus: $120,000

OTHER THOUGHTS:

Apparent Women Officers or Directors:
Hot Spot for Advancement for Women/Minorities:

LOCATIONS: ("Y" = Yes)

West:	Southwest:	Midwest:	Southeast:	Northeast:	International:
				Y	Y

ATRION CORPORATION

www.atrioncorp.com

Industry Group Code: 33911

Management:		Sales/Marketing:		Liberal Arts:		Information Systems:		Professionals:		Technical/Scientific:	
Mgmt. Trainees:		Mktg. Professionals:	Y	Gen. Writing/Editing:		Info. Management:	Y	Finance/Acct.:	Y	Engineers, Elec.:	Y
Experienced Mgmt.:	Y	Retail Sales:		Technical Writing:	Y	Software Dev.:	Y	Law:	Y	Engineers, Other:	Y
Int'l Business:	Y	Commercial/Industrial:	Y	Graphic Arts/Photog.:		Hardware Dev.:	Y	HR/Other:	Y	Health/Lab	Y
MBA Graduates:	Y	Sales Trainees:	Y	Music:		Consulting/Other:		Training:	Y	Scientists/Research:	Y
		Advertising Pros.:		Broadcasting:				Health Care:	Y	Petroleum/Chemicals:	
				Other:				Consulting:		Math/Other:	

TYPES OF BUSINESS:

Equipment-Ophthalmic, Diagnostic & Cardiovascular
Fluid Delivery Devices
Medical Device Components
Contract Manufacturing

BRANDS/DIVISIONS/AFFILIATES:

Quest Medical, Inc.
Halkey-Roberts Corporation
Atrion Medical Products, Inc.
LacriCATH
MPS2 Myocardial Protection System
ACTester

CONTACTS: *Note: Officers with more than one job title may be intentionally listed here more than once.*

David A. Battat, CEO
David A. Battat, Pres.
Jeffery Strickland, CFO/VP
Jeffery Strickland, Sec.
Jeffery Strickland, Treas.
Emile A. Battat, Chmn.

Phone: 972-390-9800	**Fax:** 972-396-7581
Toll-Free:	
Address: 1 Allentown Pkwy., Allen, TX 75002 US	

GROWTH PLANS/SPECIAL FEATURES:

Atrion Corporation designs, develops, manufactures, markets, sells and distributes products for the medical and health care industries. The company sells components to other equipment manufacturers and finished products to physicians, hospitals, clinics and other treatment centers. The firm's cardiovascular products, which accounted for 29% of its 2010 revenues, are manufactured by subsidiary Quest Medical, Inc. These include cardiac surgery vacuum relief valves and other tools used in cardiac surgery, such as the MPS2 Myocardial Protection System, a proprietary system used for the delivery of solutions to the heart during open-heart surgery, mixing drugs into the bloodstream without diluting the blood. Subsidiary Halkey-Roberts Corporation is responsible for designing, developing, manufacturing and selling Atrion's fluid delivery products (36% of 2010 revenues) such as intravenous fluid delivery lines, medical tubing clamps and various valves. Atrion's ophthalmic products and services (18% of 2010 revenues) include soft contact lens storage and disinfection cases and the LacriCATH line of balloon catheters used in the treatment of nasolacrimal duct obstruction, as well as custom packaging, warehousing and inventory management offered as part of its pharmaceutical reselling business. The company's other medical and non-medical products, many of which are manufactured by subsidiary Atrion Medical Products, Inc., include inflation devices, oral inflation tubes, right angle connectors, valves and closures for life vests, life rafts, inflatable boats, survival equipment and other inflatable structures. Other products include valves for use on electronics or munitions cases, pressure vessels and transportation container cases, as well as Atrion's ACTester line of tests for measuring blood clotting time. These additional medical and non-medical products collectively accounted for 17% of 2010 revenues. Atrion also owns a 22-mile pipeline in northern Alabama that is leased to an industrial gas producer to transport gaseous oxygen.

Employees are offered medical and dental insurance; disability coverage; life insurance; and a 401(k) plan.

FINANCIALS: **Sales and profits are in thousands of dollars—add 000 to get the full amount. 2011 Note: Financial information for 2011 was not available for all companies at press time.**

2011 Sales: $	2011 Profits: $	**U.S. Stock Ticker: ATRI**
2010 Sales: $108,569	2010 Profits: $20,952	**Int'l Ticker:**
2009 Sales: $100,643	2009 Profits: $16,843	Int'l Exchange:
2008 Sales: $95,895	2008 Profits: $15,667	Employees: 437 Fiscal Year Ends: 12/31
2007 Sales: $88,540	2007 Profits: $14,006	Parent Company:

SALARIES/BENEFITS:

Pension Plan:	ESOP Stock Plan:	Profit Sharing:	Top Exec. Salary: $500,000	Bonus: $417,128
Savings Plan: Y	Stock Purch. Plan:		Second Exec. Salary: $275,000	Bonus: $500,000

OTHER THOUGHTS:

Apparent Women Officers or Directors:
Hot Spot for Advancement for Women/Minorities:

LOCATIONS: ("Y" = Yes)

West:	Southwest:	Midwest:	Southeast:	Northeast:	International:
	Y		Y		

AUDIBLE INC

www.audible.com

Industry Group Code: 451220E

Management:		Sales/Marketing:		Liberal Arts:		Information Systems:		Professionals:		Technical/Scientific:	
Mgmt. Trainees:	Y	Mktg. Professionals:	Y	Gen. Writing/Editing:	Y	Info. Management:	Y	Finance/Acct.:	Y	Engineers, Elec.:	
Experienced Mgmt.:	Y	Retail Sales:	Y	Technical Writing:		Software Dev.:	Y	Law:	Y	Engineers, Other:	
Int'l Business:	Y	Commercial/Industrial:		Graphic Arts/Photog.:	Y	Hardware Dev.:		HR/Other:	Y	Health/Lab	
MBA Graduates:	Y	Sales Trainees:	Y	Music:		Consulting/Other:		Training:	Y	Scientists/Research:	
		Advertising Pros.:	Y	Broadcasting:				Health Care:		Petroleum/Chemicals:	
				Other:	Y			Consulting:		Math/Other:	

TYPES OF BUSINESS:

Audio Books-Online Sales
Audio Programming Software
Time-Shifted Radio Programming
Digital Audio Players
Educational Audio Materials

BRANDS/DIVISIONS/AFFILIATES:

Amazon.com Inc
Audible.com
AudibleListener

CONTACTS: *Note: Officers with more than one job title may be intentionally listed here more than once.*

Donald R. Katz, CEO
William H. Mitchell, CFO
Guy A. Story, Jr., Chief Scientist
Guy A. Story, Jr., CTO
Helene Godin, Corp. Counsel
Brian M. Fielding, Exec. VP-Corp. Dev.
Beth Anderson, Sr. VP/Publisher
Will Lopes, VP-Bus. Dev.
Foy C. Sperring, Jr., Exec. VP-Customer Acquisition
Jason Ojalvo, VP-Content Creation
Donald R. Katz, Chmn.

Phone: 973-820-0400 **Fax:**
Toll-Free: 888-283-5051
Address: 1 Washington Park, 16th Fl., Newark, NJ 07102 US

GROWTH PLANS/SPECIAL FEATURES:

Audible, Inc., a subsidiary of Amazon.com, provides Internet-delivered premium spoken audio content for playback on personal computers and mobile devices. The company offers a variety of software systems and audio programming software designed to download, store and play between two and 24 hours of content from its online store, audible.com. Audible sells a wide array of audio content, including educational materials, humor, periodicals, fiction, nonfiction and time-shifted radio programming comprised of 85,000 different programs and 1,000 content providers. For an annual membership fee, the company's AudibleListener membership plans provide up to two free audiobooks per month, a 30% discount on additional purchases, exposure to periodic sales and member-only free content offerings. It also has partnerships with leading audiobook, magazine and newspaper publishers, as well as broadcasters, business information providers and educational and cultural institutions. Audible.com features daily selected audio content from The Wall Street Journal and The New York Times, both available on a subscription basis, in time for the morning drive to work each day. Other publications offered include Fast Company, Forbes, Harvard Business Review and Scientific American. In addition, the site offers a large collection of audiobook bestsellers and classics by authors such as Stephen King, James Patterson, William Shakespeare and Jane Austen, as well as speeches, lectures and on-demand radio programs. Around 85,000 titles are available for purchase on its U.S., U.K., German and French web sites.

Employees are offered health insurance; a 401(k) savings plan; and a stock ownership program.

FINANCIALS: **Sales and profits are in thousands of dollars—add 000 to get the full amount. 2011 Note: Financial information for 2011 was not available for all companies at press time.**

2011 Sales: $ 2011 Profits: $
2010 Sales: $ 2010 Profits: $
2009 Sales: $ 2009 Profits: $
2008 Sales: $ 2008 Profits: $
2007 Sales: $ 2007 Profits: $

U.S. Stock Ticker: Subsidiary
Int'l Ticker:
Int'l Exchange:
Employees: Fiscal Year Ends: 12/31
Parent Company: AMAZON.COM INC

SALARIES/BENEFITS:

Pension Plan: ESOP Stock Plan: Y Profit Sharing: Top Exec. Salary: $ Bonus: $
Savings Plan: Y Stock Purch. Plan: Second Exec. Salary: $ Bonus: $

OTHER THOUGHTS:

Apparent Women Officers or Directors: 3
Hot Spot for Advancement for Women/Minorities: Y

LOCATIONS: ("Y" = Yes)

West:	Southwest:	Midwest:	Southeast:	Northeast:	International:
				Y	Y

AVALONBAY COMMUNITIES INC

www.avalonbay.com

Industry Group Code: 531110

Management:		Sales/Marketing:		Liberal Arts:		Information Systems:		Professionals:		Technical/Scientific:	
Mgmt. Trainees:	Y	Mktg. Professionals:	Y	Gen. Writing/Editing:	Y	Info. Management:	Y	Finance/Acct.:	Y	Engineers, Elec.:	
Experienced Mgmt.:	Y	Retail Sales:		Technical Writing:		Software Dev.:		Law:	Y	Engineers, Other:	
Int'l Business:		Commercial/Industrial:		Graphic Arts/Photog.:		Hardware Dev.:		HR/Other:	Y	Health/Lab	
MBA Graduates:	Y	Sales Trainees:		Music:		Consulting/Other:		Training:		Scientists/Research:	
		Advertising Pros.:	Y	Broadcasting:				Health Care:		Petroleum/Chemicals:	
				Other:				Consulting:		Math/Other:	

TYPES OF BUSINESS:

Real Estate Investment Trust
Apartment Complexes
Residential Construction

BRANDS/DIVISIONS/AFFILIATES:

CONTACTS:

Note: Officers with more than one job title may be intentionally listed here more than once.

Timothy J.Naughton, CEO
Timothy J. Naughton, Pres.
Thomas J. Sargeant, CFO
Kevin Thompson, VP-Mktg.
Suzanne Jakstavich, VP-Human Resources
Karen A. Hollinger, VP-Info. Svcs.
Edward M. Schulman, General Counsel/Sr. VP/Corp. Sec.
Leo S. Horey, Exec. VP-Oper.
Jonathan B. Cox, Sr. VP-Dev.
Kevin P. O'Shea, Sr. VP-Finance & Investment Mgmt.
David W. Bellman, Sr. VP-Construction
Sean J. Breslin, Exec. VP-Investments & Asset Mgmt.
Lyn C. Lansdale, Sr. VP-Strategic Bus. Svcs.
Keri A. Shea, VP-Finance/Treas.
Bryce Blair, Chmn.

Phone: 703-329-6300	**Fax:** 703-329-1459
Toll-Free:	
Address: 671 N. Glebe Rd., Ste. 800, Arlington, VA 22203 US	

GROWTH PLANS/SPECIAL FEATURES:

AvalonBay Communities, Inc. is a real estate investment trust (REIT) engaged in the development, redevelopment, acquisition, ownership and operation of multifamily communities in high barrier-to-entry markets in the U.S. The company owns or operates 173 apartment communities containing over 51,693 apartment units in 10 states and Washington, D.C. AvalonBay also has 14 communities currently under construction and holds development rights for 26 additional communities. Current properties are primarily garden-style apartment communities consisting of two- and three-story buildings in landscaped settings, as well as high-rise and mid-rise apartment communities. The firm's investments are divided into three classes: Established Communities; Other Stabilized Communities; and Development/Redevelopment Communities. Established Communities are generally operating communities that were owned and had stabilized occupancy and operating expenses as of the beginning of the prior year. Other Stabilized Communities are generally all other operating communities that have stabilized occupancy and operating expenses during the current year, but had not achieved stabilization as of the beginning of the prior year. Development/ Redevelopment Communities consist of communities that are under construction, communities where substantial redevelopment is in progress or is planned to begin during the current year and communities under lease-up. AvalonBay's primary markets are Boston, Massachusetts; Chicago, Illinois; San Jose and Los Angeles, California; Shelton, Connecticut; Virginia Beach, Virginia; Seattle, Washington; New York City; and Washington, D.C. In January 2011, the firm acquired three apartment communities: two in California and one in New Jersey.

Employees are offered medical, dental, and vision insurance; disability benefits; accidental death and dismemberment (AD&D) insurance; flexible spending accounts; a health care account; a dependent care account; an employee assistance program; an employee stock purchase plan; relocation assistance; a 401(k) plan; professional development opportunities through AvalonBay University and tuition reimbursement; and a housing discount for employees who live in an AvalonBay community.

FINANCIALS:

Sales and profits are in thousands of dollars—add 000 to get the full amount. 2011 Note: Financial information for 2011 was not available for all companies at press time.

2011 Sales: $970,800	2011 Profits: $441,600
2010 Sales: $895,266	2010 Profits: $175,331
2009 Sales: $851,107	2009 Profits: $155,647
2008 Sales: $813,764	2008 Profits: $411,487
2007 Sales: $727,786	2007 Profits: $358,160

U.S. Stock Ticker: AVB
Int'l Ticker:
Int'l Exchange:
Employees: 1,993 Fiscal Year Ends: 12/31
Parent Company:

SALARIES/BENEFITS:

Pension Plan:	ESOP Stock Plan:	Profit Sharing:	Top Exec. Salary: $823,368	Bonus: $1,268,501
Savings Plan: Y	Stock Purch. Plan: Y		Second Exec. Salary: $750,000	Bonus: $924,375

OTHER THOUGHTS:

Apparent Women Officers or Directors: 15
Hot Spot for Advancement for Women/Minorities: Y

LOCATIONS: ("Y" = Yes)

West:	Southwest:	Midwest:	Southeast:	Northeast:	International:
Y		Y		Y	

Sales, profits and employees may be estimates. Financial information, benefits and other data can change quickly and may vary from those stated here.

AVIALL INC

www.aviall.com

Industry Group Code: 33641

Management:		Sales/Marketing:		Liberal Arts:		Information Systems:		Professionals:		Technical/Scientific:	
Mgmt. Trainees:		Mktg. Professionals:	Y	Gen. Writing/Editing:		Info. Management:	Y	Finance/Acct.:	Y	Engineers, Elec.:	
Experienced Mgmt.:	Y	Retail Sales:		Technical Writing:	Y	Software Dev.:		Law:	Y	Engineers, Other:	Y
Int'l Business:	Y	Commercial/Industrial:	Y	Graphic Arts/Photog.:		Hardware Dev.:		HR/Other:	Y	Health/Lab	
MBA Graduates:	Y	Sales Trainees:	Y	Music:		Consulting/Other:		Training:	Y	Scientists/Research:	
		Advertising Pros.:		Broadcasting:				Health Care:		Petroleum/Chemicals:	
				Other:				Consulting:		Math/Other:	

TYPES OF BUSINESS:

Aerospace Parts Distribution
E-Commerce-Aerospace Parts
E-Business Services-Aerospace, Defense, Marine
Aftermarket Services

BRANDS/DIVISIONS/AFFILIATES:

Aviall Services
Inventory Locator Service LLC
Internet Business Applications Inc
Aerospace Repairable Management System

CONTACTS: *Note: Officers with more than one job title may be intentionally listed here more than once.*

Dan P. Komnenovich, CEO
Ed Dolanski, COO/Exec. VP
Dan P. Komninovich, Pres.
Colin M. Cohen, CFO/Sr. VP
Terry Scott, Sr. VP-Sales & Mktg.
Scott Shadle, CIO/Sr. VP
Robin Everly, VP-Legal & Compliance
Eric Strafel, Sr. VP-Oper.
Jacque Collier, Sr. VP/Chief Acct. Officer/Controller

Phone: 972-586-1000 **Fax:** 972-586-1361
Toll-Free: 800-284-2551
Address: 2750 Regent Blvd., Dallas Fort Worth Airport, TX 75261-9048 US

GROWTH PLANS/SPECIAL FEATURES:

Aviall, Inc., a wholly-owned subsidiary of The Boeing Company, is a provider of aftermarket supply-chain management services for companies in the aerospace, defense and marine industries. The company manages two main business units: Aviall Services and Inventory Locator Service LLC (ILS). Aviall Services is an independent provider of new aerospace parts and aftermarket services. The unit markets and distributes products for more than 235 manufacturers and offers approximately 2 million catalog items from customer service centers in North America, Europe and Asia. The subsidiary's customer service centers are served by an automated central distribution facility in Dallas, Texas. In addition, Aviall Services offers aviation batteries, hoses, wheels, brakes and oxygen. ILS provides information and global e-commerce services through its online marketplace. Through a subscription, users can buy and sell commercial parts, equipment and services through a database containing more than 50 million line items and more than 5 billion parts. In addition, the subsidiary provides e-business services and consulting for the aviation, marine and defense industries. The company owns Internet Business Applications, Inc., including its inventory management software and Aerospace Repairable Management System (ARMS).

FINANCIALS: **Sales and profits are in thousands of dollars—add 000 to get the full amount. 2011 Note: Financial information for 2011 was not available for all companies at press time.**

2011 Sales: $	2011 Profits: $	**U.S. Stock Ticker: Subsidiary**
2010 Sales: $	2010 Profits: $	**Int'l Ticker:**
2009 Sales: $	2009 Profits: $	Int'l Exchange:
2008 Sales: $	2008 Profits: $	Employees: Fiscal Year Ends: 12/31
2007 Sales: $	2007 Profits: $	Parent Company: BOEING COMPANY (THE)

SALARIES/BENEFITS:

Pension Plan:	ESOP Stock Plan:	Profit Sharing:	Top Exec. Salary: $	Bonus: $
Savings Plan:	Stock Purch. Plan:		Second Exec. Salary: $	Bonus: $

OTHER THOUGHTS:

Apparent Women Officers or Directors:
Hot Spot for Advancement for Women/Minorities:

LOCATIONS: ("Y" = Yes)

West:	Southwest:	Midwest:	Southeast:	Northeast:	International:
Y	Y	Y	Y	Y	Y

AVISTA CORPORATION

www.avistacorp.com

Industry Group Code: 221

Management:		Sales/Marketing:		Liberal Arts:		Information Systems:		Professionals:		Technical/Scientific:	
Mgmt. Trainees:		Mktg. Professionals:	Y	Gen. Writing/Editing:	Y	Info. Management:	Y	Finance/Acct.:	Y	Engineers, Elec.:	Y
Experienced Mgmt.:	Y	Retail Sales:		Technical Writing:		Software Dev.:		Law:	Y	Engineers, Other:	Y
Int'l Business:		Commercial/Industrial:	Y	Graphic Arts/Photog.:		Hardware Dev.:		HR/Other:	Y	Health/Lab	
MBA Graduates:	Y	Sales Trainees:		Music:		Consulting/Other:		Training:	Y	Scientists/Research:	
		Advertising Pros.:		Broadcasting:				Health Care:		Petroleum/Chemicals:	Y
				Other:				Consulting:		Math/Other:	

TYPES OF BUSINESS:

Utilities-Electricity & Natural Gas
Fuel Cells
e-Business & Consulting Services
Energy Marketing
Resource Management
Venture Fund Investment
Metal Fabrication
Real Estate Investment

BRANDS/DIVISIONS/AFFILIATES:

Avista Development
Advantage IQ
Avista Energy, Inc.
Avista Utilities

CONTACTS: *Note: Officers with more than one job title may be intentionally listed here more than once.*

Scott L. Morris, CEO
Scott L. Morris, Pres.
Mark Thies, CFO/Sr. VP
Karen S. Feltes, Sr. VP-Human Resources/Corp. Sec.
James M. Kensok, CIO/VP
Marian Durkin, General Counsel/Sr. VP/Chief Compliance Officer
Jason Lang, Mgr.-Investor Rel.
Chirsty Burmeister-Smith, Principal Acct. Officer/Controller/VP
Don Kopczynski, VP-Customer Solutions
Dennis P. Vermillion, VP/Pres., Avista Utilities
David J. Meyer, Chief Counsel for Regulatory & Gov't Affairs/VP
Jason Thackston, VP-Energy Delivery
Scott L. Morris, Chmn.

Phone: 509-489-0500	**Fax:** 509-495-8725
Toll-Free:	
Address: 1411 E. Mission Ave., Spokane, WA 99220-3727 US	

GROWTH PLANS/SPECIAL FEATURES:

Avista Corporation generates, transmits and distributes electricity and natural gas in the U.S. Pacific Northwest to more than 600,000 customers. The firm operates through two business segments: Avista Utilities and Advantage IQ. Avista Utilities manages the regulated utility business operations, which include generating, transmitting and delivering electricity, natural gas and related services to customers in eastern Washington, northern Idaho and parts of southern and eastern Oregon. Avista Utilities also engages in wholesale purchases and sales of electricity and natural gas. Advantage IQ, Avista's indirect subsidiary, partners with multi-site companies across North America to assess sustainable utility expense management solutions. Advantage IQ's services include strategic management and the processing, payment and auditing of water/sewer, telecom, waste, energy and lease bills. The firm engages in other businesses indirectly, including sheet metal fabrication, venture fund investments and real estate investments, as well as certain natural gas storage facilities held by Avista Energy, Inc.

FINANCIALS: **Sales and profits are in thousands of dollars—add 000 to get the full amount. 2011 Note: Financial information for 2011 was not available for all companies at press time.**

2011 Sales: $1,619,780	2011 Profits: $103,539	**U.S. Stock Ticker: AVA**
2010 Sales: $1,558,740	2010 Profits: $92,425	**Int'l Ticker:**
2009 Sales: $1,512,565	2009 Profits: $87,071	Int'l Exchange:
2008 Sales: $1,676,763	2008 Profits: $73,620	Employees: 2,499 Fiscal Year Ends: 12/31
2007 Sales: $1,417,757	2007 Profits: $38,475	Parent Company:

SALARIES/BENEFITS:

Pension Plan: Y	ESOP Stock Plan:	Profit Sharing:	Top Exec. Salary: $630,001	Bonus: $627,669
Savings Plan: Y	Stock Purch. Plan:		Second Exec. Salary: $323,077	Bonus: $215,865

OTHER THOUGHTS:

Apparent Women Officers or Directors: 3
Hot Spot for Advancement for Women/Minorities: Y

LOCATIONS: ("Y" = Yes)

West:	Southwest:	Midwest:	Southeast:	Northeast:	International:
Y					

B&G FOODS INC

www.bgfoods.com

Industry Group Code: 311

Management:		**Sales/Marketing:**		**Liberal Arts:**		**Information Systems:**		**Professionals:**		**Technical/Scientific:**	
Mgmt. Trainees:		Mktg. Professionals:	Y	Gen. Writing/Editing:	Y	Info. Management:	Y	Finance/Acct.:	Y	Engineers, Elec.:	
Experienced Mgmt.:	Y	Retail Sales:		Technical Writing:		Software Dev.:		Law:	Y	Engineers, Other:	Y
Int'l Business:	Y	Commercial/Industrial:	Y	Graphic Arts/Photog.:		Hardware Dev.:		HR/Other:	Y	Health/Lab	
MBA Graduates:	Y	Sales Trainees:	Y	Music:		Consulting/Other:		Training:	Y	Scientists/Research:	
		Advertising Pros.:		Broadcasting:				Health Care:		Petroleum/Chemicals:	
				Other:				Consulting:		Math/Other:	

TYPES OF BUSINESS:

Food Products Manufacturing
Shelf-Stable Products
Seasonings
Processed Meat Products

BRANDS/DIVISIONS/AFFILIATES:

Ortega
Maple Grove Farms of Vermont
Bloch & Guggenheimer
Polaner
Regina
Underwood
Ac'cent
Cream of Wheat

CONTACTS: *Note: Officers with more than one job title may be intentionally listed here more than once.*

David L. Wenner, CEO
David L. Wenner, Pres.
Robert C. Cantwell, CFO
Vanessa E. Maskal, Exec. VP-Sales & Mktg.
William H. Wright, Exec. VP-R&D & Quality Assurance
Scott E. Lerner, General Counsel/Exec. VP/Sec.
William F. Herbes, Exec. VP-Oper.
Robert C. Cantwell, Exec. VP-Finance
Scott E. Lerner, Chief Compliance Officer
Stephen C. Sherrill, Chmn.

Phone: 973-401-6500	**Fax:**
Toll-Free: 866-211-8151	
Address: 4 Gatehall Dr., Ste. 110, Parsippany, NJ 07054 US	

GROWTH PLANS/SPECIAL FEATURES:

B & G Foods, Inc. manufactures, sells and distributes brand-name foods with long shelf lives throughout the U.S, Canada and Puerto Rico. Major brands include Ortega taco shells, seasonings, dinner kits, taco sauce, peppers, refried beans, salsa and related food products; Maple Grove Farms of Vermont salad dressings, marinades, syrups, confections and pancake mixes; Bloch & Guggenheimer shelf-stable pickles, relishes, peppers, olives and other related specialty items; Polaner, manufacturer of Polaner's All Fruit spread; Emeril's seasonings, salad dressings, marinades, pepper sauces, barbecue sauces and pasta sauces; B&M brick-oven baked beans; Underwood deviled ham, chicken, roast beef and liver wurst spreads; Ac'cent, an all-natural flavor enhancer for beef, poultry, fish and vegetables; Regina vinegar and cooking wines; Las Palmas Mexican enchilada sauce, chili sauce and various pepper products; Brer Rabbit Molasses; Vermont Maid maple syrup; Joan of Arc kidney beans; Wright's all-natural seasoning; Cream of Wheat and Cream of Rice products; Don Pepino and Sclafani pizza and spaghetti sauces; and Grandma's molasses. The firm sells its products to supermarket chains, foodservice outlets, mass merchants, warehouse clubs, dollar stores, drug store chains and specialty food distributors. B & G Foods' largest customers are Wal-Mart, which accounts for roughly 16.2% of its 2010 net sales. The company is headquartered in Parsippany, New Jersey, and operates six manufacturing facilities throughout the U.S. In November 2011, the firm acquired the Culver Specialty Brands of: Mrs. Dash; Molly McButter; Sugar Twin; Baker's Joy; Static Guard; and Kleen Guard from Unilever for $325 million.

FINANCIALS: **Sales and profits are in thousands of dollars—add 000 to get the full amount. 2011 Note: Financial information for 2011 was not available for all companies at press time.**

2011 Sales: $543,866	2011 Profits: $50,243	**U.S. Stock Ticker: BGS**
2010 Sales: $513,337	2010 Profits: $32,379	**Int'l Ticker:**
2009 Sales: $501,016	2009 Profits: $17,441	Int'l Exchange:
2008 Sales: $486,896	2008 Profits: $9,733	Employees: 749 Fiscal Year Ends: 12/31
2007 Sales: $471,336	2007 Profits: $17,825	Parent Company:

SALARIES/BENEFITS:

Pension Plan:	ESOP Stock Plan:	Profit Sharing:	Top Exec. Salary: $489,670	Bonus: $493,000
Savings Plan:	Stock Purch. Plan:		Second Exec. Salary: $352,000	Bonus: $246,400

OTHER THOUGHTS:

Apparent Women Officers or Directors: 3
Hot Spot for Advancement for Women/Minorities: Y

LOCATIONS: ("Y" = Yes)

West:	Southwest:	Midwest:	Southeast:	Northeast:	International:
	Y	Y	Y	Y	

BANKRATE INC

www.bankrate.com

Industry Group Code: 519130

Management:		Sales/Marketing:		Liberal Arts:		Information Systems:		Professionals:		Technical/Scientific:	
Mgmt. Trainees:		Mktg. Professionals:	Y	Gen. Writing/Editing:	Y	Info. Management:	Y	Finance/Acct.:	Y	Engineers, Elec.:	
Experienced Mgmt.:	Y	Retail Sales:		Technical Writing:	Y	Software Dev.:	Y	Law:	Y	Engineers, Other:	
Int'l Business:	Y	Commercial/Industrial:	Y	Graphic Arts/Photog.:		Hardware Dev.:		HR/Other:	Y	Health/Lab	
MBA Graduates:	Y	Sales Trainees:	Y	Music:		Consulting/Other:		Training:		Scientists/Research:	
		Advertising Pros.:	Y	Broadcasting:				Health Care:		Petroleum/Chemicals:	
				Other:				Consulting:		Math/Other:	

TYPES OF BUSINESS:

Portal-Financial Services
Financial Information
Banking Information
e-Commerce

BRANDS/DIVISIONS/AFFILIATES:

Bankrate.com
FeeDisclosure.com
Insureme.com
CreditCards.com
Bargaineering.com
Mortgage-Calc.com
Bankrate.com.cn
Bankrate.ca

CONTACTS:

Note: Officers with more than one job title may be intentionally listed here more than once.

Thomas R. Evans, CEO
Thomas R. Evans, Pres.
Edward J. DiMaria, CFO/Sr. VP
Bruce J. Zanca, Chief Mktg. & Comm. Officer/Sr. VP
Daniel P. Hoogterp, CTO/Sr. VP
Michael J. Ricciardelli, Sr. VP-Bus. Dev. & Consumer Mktg.
Kayleen Keneally, Sr. Dir.-Corp. Comm.
Donaldson M. Ross, Chief Revenue Officer/Sr. VP
Peter C. Morse, Chmn.

Phone: 561-630-2400 | **Fax:** 561-625-4540
Toll-Free:
Address: 11760 U.S. Hwy. 1, Ste. 200, North Palm Beach, FL 33408 US

GROWTH PLANS/SPECIAL FEATURES:

Bankrate, Inc. is an Internet-based consumer banking and personal finance network. The company is a leading publisher, aggregator and distributor of personal finance content on the Internet. Its flagship web site, Bankrate.com, is an aggregator of information on over 300 financial products and fees, including mortgages; credit cards; automobile loans; money market accounts; certificates of deposit; checking and ATM fees; home equity loans; and online banking fees. It regularly aggregates data from more than 4,800 financial institutions in all 50 states. In 2010, its online network received over 150 million visits. Besides Bankrate.com, the firm's online network includes numerous other financial information sites. These include: InsureMe.com, which offers consumers insurance rates for auto, home and life; FeeDisclosure.com, providing information on mortgage transaction and closing fees; Mortgage-Calc.com, which provides mortgage and financing calculators; BankAholic.com, providing rate information on savings products; CreditCards.com, which offers a comprehensive selection of information regarding consumer and business credit and prepaid cards; and NetQuote.com, which offers quotes on insurance products. Other sites include CreditCardGuide.com, CD.com and Bargaineering.com. Its network also includes international sites BankRate.ca (Canada) and BankRate.com.cn (China). Additionally, the company provides financial applications and information to a network of online distribution partners and national, regional and local publications. Bankrate licenses editorial content to more than 100 print publications, including leading nationally newspapers such as The Wall Street Journal, USA Today and the New York Times. In June 2011, the firm held an initial public offering of stock on the New York Stock Exchange. In October 2011, it agreed to acquire the assets relating to InsWeb Corporation's insurance lead generation and marketing business for $65 million.

FINANCIALS:

Sales and profits are in thousands of dollars—add 000 to get the full amount. 2011 Note: Financial information for 2011 was not available for all companies at press time.

2011 Sales: $424,200	2011 Profits: $-13,422	**U.S. Stock Ticker: RATE**
2010 Sales: $220,300	2010 Profits: $-38,900	**Int'l Ticker:**
2009 Sales: $131,500	2009 Profits: $-43,000	Int'l Exchange:
2008 Sales: $166,855	2008 Profits: $19,600	Employees: 285 Fiscal Year Ends: 12/31
2007 Sales: $95,592	2007 Profits: $20,100	Parent Company:

SALARIES/BENEFITS:

Pension Plan:	ESOP Stock Plan:	Profit Sharing:	Top Exec. Salary: $450,000	Bonus: $491,250
Savings Plan: Y	Stock Purch. Plan:		Second Exec. Salary: $375,000	Bonus: $393,000

OTHER THOUGHTS:

Apparent Women Officers or Directors: 1
Hot Spot for Advancement for Women/Minorities:

LOCATIONS: ("Y" = Yes)

West:	Southwest:	Midwest:	Southeast:	Northeast:	International:
Y	Y		Y		Y

BERRY PETROLEUM CO

www.bry.com

Industry Group Code: 211111

Management:		Sales/Marketing:		Liberal Arts:		Information Systems:		Professionals:		Technical/Scientific:	
Mgmt. Trainees:		Mktg. Professionals:		Gen. Writing/Editing:		Info. Management:	Y	Finance/Acct.:	Y	Engineers, Elec.:	
Experienced Mgmt.:	Y	Retail Sales:		Technical Writing:		Software Dev.:		Law:	Y	Engineers, Other:	Y
Int'l Business:	Y	Commercial/Industrial:		Graphic Arts/Photog.:		Hardware Dev.:		HR/Other:	Y	Health/Lab	
MBA Graduates:	Y	Sales Trainees:		Music:		Consulting/Other:		Training:	Y	Scientists/Research:	
		Advertising Pros.:		Broadcasting:				Health Care:		Petroleum/Chemicals:	Y
				Other:				Consulting:		Math/Other:	

TYPES OF BUSINESS:

Oil & Gas Exploration & Production

BRANDS/DIVISIONS/AFFILIATES:

CONTACTS: *Note: Officers with more than one job title may be intentionally listed here more than once.*

Robert F. Heinemann, CEO
Michael Duginski, COO/Exec. VP
Robert F. Heinemann, Pres.
David D. Wolf, CFO/Exec. VP
Walter B. Ayers, VP-Human Resources
Bruce S. Kelso, Chief Geoscientist
Kenneth A Olson., Corp. Sec.
George W. Ciotti, VP-Corp. Dev.
Todd Crabtree, Investor Rel.
Shawn M. Canaday, VP-Finance/Treas.
Dan G. Anderson, VP-Rocky Mountain Prod.
G.Timothy Crawford, VP-California Prod.
Jamie L. Wheat, Controller
Martin H. Young, Jr., Chmn.

Phone: 303-999-4400	**Fax:**
Toll-Free:	
Address: 1999 Broadway, Ste. 3700, Denver, CO 80202 US	

GROWTH PLANS/SPECIAL FEATURES:

Berry Petroleum Co. produces, develops, acquires, exploits and explores for crude oil and natural gas. It is headquartered in Denver Colorado and maintains a regional office in Bakersfield, California, as well as production field offices in Taft and Santa Clarita California; Roosevelt, Utah; Parachute, Colorado; and Palestine and Midland, Texas. The company's principal reserves and producing properties are located in California, Texas (E. Texas and the Permian), Utah (Uinta) and Colorado (Piceance). The firm owns three cogeneration facilities which supply steam that Berry uses for thermal recovery of its oil reserves. Berry's Midway-Sunset field facility utilizes cyclic steam recovery methods to reduce oil viscosity, enabling the oil to flow more efficiently to the surface. In 2010, Berry held 271 million barrels of oil equivalent (MMBOE) in proved reserves. Berry markets its crude oil production to competing buyers, including independent marketing, pipeline and oil refining companies. In October 2010, the company agreed to purchase 9,300 acres of Wolfberry Oil assets in West Texas for around $180 million.

Berry offers its employees health and dental insurance; a 529 college savings plan; and a section 125 tax reduction plan.

FINANCIALS: **Sales and profits are in thousands of dollars—add 000 to get the full amount. 2011 Note: Financial information for 2011 was not available for all companies at press time.**

2011 Sales: $919,558	2011 Profits: $-228,063	**U.S. Stock Ticker: BRY**
2010 Sales: $669,955	2010 Profits: $82,524	**Int'l Ticker:**
2009 Sales: $554,283	2009 Profits: $54,030	Int'l Exchange:
2008 Sales: $748,481	2008 Profits: $133,529	Employees: 270 Fiscal Year Ends: 12/31
2007 Sales: $547,427	2007 Profits: $129,928	Parent Company:

SALARIES/BENEFITS:

Pension Plan:	ESOP Stock Plan:	Profit Sharing:	Top Exec. Salary: $620,000	Bonus: $1,326,800
Savings Plan: Y	Stock Purch. Plan:		Second Exec. Salary: $329,600	Bonus: $450,000

OTHER THOUGHTS:

Apparent Women Officers or Directors:
Hot Spot for Advancement for Women/Minorities:

LOCATIONS: ("Y" = Yes)

West:	Southwest:	Midwest:	Southeast:	Northeast:	International:
Y	Y				

BIO REFERENCE LABORATORIES INC

www.bioreference.com

Industry Group Code: 621511

Management:		Sales/Marketing:		Liberal Arts:		Information Systems:		Professionals:		Technical/Scientific:	
Mgmt. Trainees:		Mktg. Professionals:	Y	Gen. Writing/Editing:		Info. Management:	Y	Finance/Acct.:	Y	Engineers, Elec.:	
Experienced Mgmt.:	Y	Retail Sales:		Technical Writing:	Y	Software Dev.:	Y	Law:	Y	Engineers, Other:	
Int'l Business:		Commercial/Industrial:	Y	Graphic Arts/Photog.:		Hardware Dev.:		HR/Other:	Y	Health/Lab	Y
MBA Graduates:	Y	Sales Trainees:	Y	Music:		Consulting/Other:		Training:	Y	Scientists/Research:	Y
		Advertising Pros.:		Broadcasting:				Health Care:	Y	Petroleum/Chemicals:	
				Other:				Consulting:		Math/Other:	

TYPES OF BUSINESS:

Medical Laboratories & Testing
Clinical Laboratory Services
Clinical Knowledge Database
Online Practice Management Services
Drug Testing

BRANDS/DIVISIONS/AFFILIATES:

PSIMedica
CareEvolve
GeneDx

CONTACTS: *Note: Officers with more than one job title may be intentionally listed here more than once.*

Marc D. Grodman, CEO
Howard Dubinett, COO/Exec. VP
Marc D. Grodman, Pres.
Sam Singer, CFO/Sr. VP
Charles T. Todd, Sr. VP-Sales & Mktg.
James Weisberger, Chief Medical Officer/Sr. VP
Richard L. Faherty, CIO/Pres., PsiMedica
Nick Cetani, VP-Tech. Oper.
Warren Erdmann, Sr. VP-Oper.
Cory Fishkin, Pres., CareEvolve
Tara Mackay, Coordinator-Investor Rel.
Nicholas Papazicos, Sr. VP-Financial Oper.
Sherri Bale, Pres./Clinical Dir.-GeneDx
John Compton, CEO/Scientific Dir.-GeneDx
Scott Fein, Sr. VP
Sally Howlett, VP-Accounts Receivable
Marc D. Grodman, Chmn.

Phone: 201-791-2600 | **Fax:** 201-791-1941
Toll-Free:
Address: 481 Edward H. Ross Dr., Elmwood Park, NJ 07407 US

GROWTH PLANS/SPECIAL FEATURES:

Bio-Reference Laboratories, Inc. (BRLI) is a regional clinical laboratory offering services to clients primarily in the greater New York metropolitan area, New Jersey, and other states in the Northeast. Currently, BRLI operates seven laboratories located in Clarksburg, Maryland; Gaithersburg, Maryland; Elmwood Park, New Jersey; Milford, Massachusetts; Poughkeepsie, New York; and Valley Cottage, New York. Serving health care providers in these areas, the firm offers testing services utilized in detection, diagnosis, evaluation, monitoring and treatment of diseases. The company processes nearly 4.6 million requisitions annually for customers including doctors, employers, clinics and governmental units. BRLI operates a network of over 80 patient service centers for the collection of patient specimens. Routine testing accounted for approximately 44% of 2010 revenue. This includes blood cell counts, cholesterol level testing, HIV-related tests, pap smears, pregnancy tests, urinalysis and drug testing. The company also performs specialized esoteric testing, which accounted for approximately 56% of the firm's 2010 revenues, in medical fields such as endocrinology, genetics, immunology, microbiology, oncology, serology and toxicology. In addition to the clinical testing operations, the firm operates a clinical knowledge management service through the PSIMedica business unit. This system uses customer data from laboratory results, pharmaceutical data, claims data and other data sources to provide administrative and clinical decision support systems that enable its customers to provide higher quality and more efficient healthcare to their populations. Subsidiary GeneDx offers diagnostic genetic testing laboratory services (for example, to detect developmental disorders) to customers in the U.S. and abroad. BRLI also operates a web-based connectivity portal solution for laboratories and physicians through its CareEvolve subsidiary. The company uses this portal to provide laboratory ordering and results to its physician customers including secure messaging to patients, payers, vendors and other health care facilities. BRLI markets this connectivity solution to other laboratories throughout the U.S.

FINANCIALS: **Sales and profits are in thousands of dollars—add 000 to get the full amount. 2011 Note: Financial information for 2011 was not available for all companies at press time.**

2011 Sales: $558,600 | 2011 Profits: $36,400
2010 Sales: $458,024 | 2010 Profits: $26,381
2009 Sales: $362,654 | 2009 Profits: $21,850
2008 Sales: $301,071 | 2008 Profits: $15,617
2007 Sales: $250,431 | 2007 Profits: $13,957

U.S. Stock Ticker: BRLI
Int'l Ticker:
Int'l Exchange:
Employees: 2,424 Fiscal Year Ends: 10/31
Parent Company:

SALARIES/BENEFITS:

Pension Plan: | ESOP Stock Plan: | Profit Sharing: | Top Exec. Salary: $1,013,439 | Bonus: $60,806
Savings Plan: Y | Stock Purch. Plan: | | Second Exec. Salary: $594,000 | Bonus: $34,830

OTHER THOUGHTS:

Apparent Women Officers or Directors: 7
Hot Spot for Advancement for Women/Minorities: Y

LOCATIONS: ("Y" = Yes)

West:	Southwest:	Midwest:	Southeast:	Northeast:	International:
				Y	

BIOMARIN PHARMACEUTICAL INC

www.biomarinpharm.com

Industry Group Code: 325412

Management:		Sales/Marketing:		Liberal Arts:		Information Systems:		Professionals:		Technical/Scientific:	
Mgmt. Trainees:		Mktg. Professionals:	Y	Gen. Writing/Editing:		Info. Management:	Y	Finance/Acct.:	Y	Engineers, Elec.:	
Experienced Mgmt.:	Y	Retail Sales:		Technical Writing:	Y	Software Dev.:	Y	Law:	Y	Engineers, Other:	
Int'l Business:	Y	Commercial/Industrial:	Y	Graphic Arts/Photog.:		Hardware Dev.:		HR/Other:	Y	Health/Lab	Y
MBA Graduates:	Y	Sales Trainees:	Y	Music:		Consulting/Other:		Training:	Y	Scientists/Research:	Y
		Advertising Pros.:		Broadcasting:				Health Care:	Y	Petroleum/Chemicals:	Y
				Other:				Consulting:		Math/Other:	Y

TYPES OF BUSINESS:

Biopharmaceutical Product Development
Drugs-Severe Conditions
Pediatric Disease Treatments
Asthma Treatments
Drug Delivery Technologies

BRANDS/DIVISIONS/AFFILIATES:

Naglazyme
Kuvan
Aldurazyme
Firdapse
PEG-PAL
GALNS for MPS IVA
LEAD Therapeutics, Inc.
BMN-701

CONTACTS: *Note: Officers with more than one job title may be intentionally listed here more than once.*

Jean-Jacques Bienaime, CEO
Jeffrey H. Cooper, CFO/Sr. VP
Mark Wood, VP-Human Resources
Henry J. Fuchs, Chief Medical Officer/Sr. VP
Ed Von Pervieux, CIO/VP
Robert A. Baffi, Sr. VP-Tech. Oper.
Daniel P. Maher, VP-Prod. Dev.
G. Eric Davis, General Counsel/VP/Corp. Sec.
Joshua A. Grass, VP-Bus. Dev./VP-Corp. Dev.
Brian Mueller, Chief Acct. Officer/VP/Controller
Stephen Aselage, Chief Bus. Oper./Sr. VP
Philip Lo Scalzo, VP-Corp. Compliance & Ethics
Pierre Lapalme, Chmn.

Phone: 415-506-6700 **Fax:** 415-382-7889
Toll-Free:
Address: 105 Digital Dr., Novato, CA 94949 US

GROWTH PLANS/SPECIAL FEATURES:

BioMarin Pharmaceutical, Inc. develops and commercializes biopharmaceutical products for serious diseases and medical conditions. BioMarin has four approved products: Naglazyme, for the treatment of mucopolysaccharidosis VI (MPS-VI); Kuvan, for the treatment of phenylketonuria (PKU); Aldurazyme, for the treatment of mucopolysaccharidosis I (MPS-I); and Firdapse, for the treatment of Lambert-Eaton Myasthenic Syndrome (LEMS). MPS-VI is a debilitating life-threatening genetic lysosomal storage disorder for which no other drug treatment currently exists. Naglazyme, an enzyme replacement therapy, has been granted orphan drug status in the U.S. and E.U., which confers market exclusivity for the treatment of MPS VI expiring in 2012 and 2016, respectively. BioMarin has been granted orphan drug status in the U.S. for Kuvan, the first drug treatment for PKU, an inherited metabolic disease that affects at least 50,000 diagnosed patients globally under the age of 40. Aldurazyme, developed through a 50/50 joint-venture with Genzyme Corporation, has been approved for marketing in the U.S., European Union (E.U.) and other countries for patients with MPSI. Firdapse is approved for use in the E.U. and is the only drug available for the treatment of LEMS, a autoimmune disease that affects the muscles. BioMarin's PEG-PAL (formerly referred to as Phenylase) is an investigational enzyme substitution therapy being developed as a subcutaneous injection for those who do not respond to Kuvan. It is currently in Phase II clinical trials. Other drugs in clinical development include GALNS for MPS IVA, designed to treat the lysosomal enzyme efficiency disease Morquio A Syndrome, currently in Phase III clinical trials; BMN-701 for the degenerative lysosomal storage disorder Pompe disease, currently in phase I clinical trials; and BMN-673 for a poly ADP-ribose polymerase (PARP) inhibitor for genetically defined cancers, currently in Phase I clinical trials. In 2010, the firm acquired LEAD Therapeutics, Inc., a drug discovery and early stage development company.

FINANCIALS: **Sales and profits are in thousands of dollars—add 000 to get the full amount. 2011 Note: Financial information for 2011 was not available for all companies at press time.**

2011 Sales: $441,358 — 2011 Profits: $-53,836
2010 Sales: $376,267 — 2010 Profits: $205,819
2009 Sales: $324,656 — 2009 Profits: $- 488
2008 Sales: $296,493 — 2008 Profits: $30,831
2007 Sales: $121,581 — 2007 Profits: $-15,803

U.S. Stock Ticker: BMRN
Int'l Ticker:
Int'l Exchange:
Employees: 871 Fiscal Year Ends: 12/31
Parent Company:

SALARIES/BENEFITS:

Pension Plan: ESOP Stock Plan: Profit Sharing: Top Exec. Salary: $746,041 Bonus: $721,536
Savings Plan: Y Stock Purch. Plan: Y Second Exec. Salary: $421,032 Bonus: $162,685

OTHER THOUGHTS:

Apparent Women Officers or Directors: 2
Hot Spot for Advancement for Women/Minorities:

LOCATIONS: ("Y" = Yes)

West:	Southwest:	Midwest:	Southeast:	Northeast:	International:
Y					Y

BIOSCRIP INC

Industry Group Code: 522320A

www.bioscrip.com

Management:		Sales/Marketing:		Liberal Arts:		Information Systems:		Professionals:		Technical/Scientific:	
Mgmt. Trainees:	Y	Mktg. Professionals:	Y	Gen. Writing/Editing:	Y	Info. Management:	Y	Finance/Acct.:	Y	Engineers, Elec.:	
Experienced Mgmt.:	Y	Retail Sales:		Technical Writing:	Y	Software Dev.:	Y	Law:	Y	Engineers, Other:	
Int'l Business:		Commercial/Industrial:	Y	Graphic Arts/Photog.:		Hardware Dev.:		HR/Other:	Y	Health/Lab	
MBA Graduates:	Y	Sales Trainees:	Y	Music:		Consulting/Other:		Training:	Y	Scientists/Research:	
		Advertising Pros.:		Broadcasting:				Health Care:	Y	Petroleum/Chemicals:	
				Other:				Consulting:		Math/Other:	

TYPES OF BUSINESS:

Pharmacy Benefits Management
Retail, Online & Mail-Order Pharmacies
Disease Management
Specialty Pharmacy Services

BRANDS/DIVISIONS/AFFILIATES:

Critical Homecare Solutions Inc
Scott-Wilson Inc
Cedar Creek Home Health Care Agency Inc
BioScrip Pharmacy (Puerto Rico) Inc
Elk Valley Health Services Inc
Knoxville Home Therapies LLC
Natural Living Inc
Wilcox Medical Inc

CONTACTS: *Note: Officers with more than one job title may be intentionally listed here more than once.*

Richard H. Friedman, CEO
Richard M. Smith, Pres.
M.J. Graves, Interim CFO
Stephen B. Cichy, Sr. VP-Mktg.
Vito Ponzio, Jr., Sr. VP-Human Resources
Rick Goldsby, Interim CIO
Stephen B. Cichy, Sr. VP-Prod. Dev.
Kimberlee Seah, General Counsel/Sr. VP/Corp. Sec.
Russel J. Corvese, Sr. VP-Mail & Managed Care Oper.
David J. Evans, Sr. VP-Strategic Oper.
Pat Bogusz, VP-Finance
Jim Melancon, VP-Managed Care
Michael Saracco, Sr. VP-National Sales
Marc Stranz, VP-Clinical Svcs.
Colleen M. Lederer, Sr. VP-Home Health Svcs.
Richard H. Friedman, Chmn.
Robert Roose, Sr. VP-Procurement

Phone: 914-460-1600 **Fax:** 914-460-1670
Toll-Free: 888-818-3939
Address: 100 Clearbrook Rd., Elmsford, NY 10523 US

GROWTH PLANS/SPECIAL FEATURES:

BioScrip, Inc. is a specialty pharmaceutical healthcare organization that works with patients, physicians, healthcare payors and pharmaceutical manufacturers to provide access to medications and management services to optimize outcomes for chronic and other complex healthcare conditions. The firm operates 112 locations in 29 states and Washington, D.C., comprised of 33 home nursing facilities, 31 community pharmacy locations, three mail service facilities and 45 home infusion centers. It operates in two segments: Infusion/Home Health Services (HIS) and Pharmacy Services. The IHS segment offers products and services such as home infusion therapy; respiratory therapy; durable medical equipment; the dispensation and administration of infusion-based drugs; skilled nursing and therapy visits; and private duty nursing, rehabilitation, hospice and medical social services to patients primarily in their home. BioScrip's Pharmacy Services offers pharmacy mail operations, community pharmacies, prescription discount card programs and integrated pharmacy benefit management services. Medicare and Medicaid accounted for approximately 13% of the firm's combined consolidated revenue. The company's subsidiaries include Cedar Creek Home Health Care Agency, Inc.; Chronimed, LLC; BioScrip Pharmacy (Puerto Rico), Inc.; Elk Valley Health Services, Inc.; Knoxville Home Therapies, LLC; Natural Living, Inc.; East Goshen Pharmacy, Inc.; Scott-Wilson, Inc.; Critical Homecare Solutions, Inc.; and Wilcox Medical, Inc. In February 2012, BioScrip agreed to sell certain pharmaceutical operations to Walgreens Co. for roughly $225 million.

Employees are offered medical and dental insurance; short- and long-term disability coverage; life insurance; pharmacy benefits; and a 401(k) plan.

FINANCIALS: **Sales and profits are in thousands of dollars—add 000 to get the full amount. 2011 Note: Financial information for 2011 was not available for all companies at press time.**

2011 Sales: $	2011 Profits: $
2010 Sales: $1,638,623	2010 Profits: $-69,142
2009 Sales: $1,329,525	2009 Profits: $54,099
2008 Sales: $1,401,911	2008 Profits: $-74,032
2007 Sales: $1,197,732	2007 Profits: $3,317

U.S. Stock Ticker: BIOS
Int'l Ticker:
Int'l Exchange:
Employees: 2,281 Fiscal Year Ends: 12/31
Parent Company:

SALARIES/BENEFITS:

Pension Plan:	ESOP Stock Plan:	Profit Sharing:	Top Exec. Salary: $850,000	Bonus: $
Savings Plan: Y	Stock Purch. Plan:		Second Exec. Salary: $530,385	Bonus: $

OTHER THOUGHTS:

Apparent Women Officers or Directors: 5
Hot Spot for Advancement for Women/Minorities: Y

LOCATIONS: ("Y" = Yes)

West:	Southwest:	Midwest:	Southeast:	Northeast:	International:
Y	Y	Y	Y	Y	

BIOSITE INC

www.biosite.com

Industry Group Code: 334510

Management:		Sales/Marketing:		Liberal Arts:		Information Systems:		Professionals:		Technical/Scientific:	
Mgmt. Trainees:		Mktg. Professionals:	Y	Gen. Writing/Editing:		Info. Management:	Y	Finance/Acct.:	Y	Engineers, Elec.:	Y
Experienced Mgmt.:	Y	Retail Sales:		Technical Writing:	Y	Software Dev.:	Y	Law:	Y	Engineers, Other:	Y
Int'l Business:	Y	Commercial/Industrial:	Y	Graphic Arts/Photog.:		Hardware Dev.:	Y	HR/Other:	Y	Health/Lab	Y
MBA Graduates:	Y	Sales Trainees:	Y	Music:		Consulting/Other:		Training:	Y	Scientists/Research:	Y
		Advertising Pros.:		Broadcasting:				Health Care:	Y	Petroleum/Chemicals:	
				Other:				Consulting:		Math/Other:	Y

TYPES OF BUSINESS:

Medical Diagnostics Products
Rapid Immunoassays
Antibody Development Services
Drug Testing

BRANDS/DIVISIONS/AFFILIATES:

Biosite Discovery
Triage Drugs of Abuse Panel
Triage Cardiac Panel
Triage TOX Drug Screen
Triage BNP Test
Triage Profiler Panels
Triage Parasite Panel
Iverness Medica Ilnnovations Inc

CONTACTS: *Note: Officers with more than one job title may be intentionally listed here more than once.*

Cristopher J. Twomey, CFO
Kenneth F. Buechler, Chief Scientific Officer
Christopher J.Twomey, Sec.
Cristopher J. Twomey, VP-Finance

Phone: 858-805-8378 **Fax:** 858-455-4815
Toll-Free: 888-246-7483
Address: 9975 Summers Ridge Rd., San Diego, CA 92121 US

GROWTH PLANS/SPECIAL FEATURES:

Biosite, Inc. is a global diagnostics company dedicated to utilizing biotechnology in the development of diagnostic products. The firm, a wholly-owned subsidiary of Inverness Medical Innovations, validates and patents novel protein biomarkers and panels of biomarkers; develops and markets products; conducts strategic research on its products; and educates healthcare providers about its products. Biosite markets immunoassay diagnostics in the areas of cardiovascular disease, drug overdose and infectious disease. Cardiovascular products include the Triage BNP Test, Triage Cardiac Panel, Triage Profiler Panels and Triage Stroke Panel. The Triage BNP test is used in thousands of hospitals and doctor's offices, and helps in the diagnosis, and severity assessment, of heart failure. The Triage Drugs of Abuse Panel and Triage TOX Drug Screen are rapid, qualitative urine screens that test for up to nine different illicit and prescription drugs, or drug classes, and provide results in less than 15 minutes. The firm's Biosite Discovery research business seeks to identify new protein markers of diseases that lack effective diagnostic tests. Additionally, with Biosite Discovery, the company has the capacity to offer antibody development services to companies seeking high-affinity antibodies for use in drug research. In return, Biosite seeks diagnostic licenses. The firm's Encompass program provides comprehensive education and consultation programs in support of Biosite customers. These programs include training and education; evaluation support; product training; clinical training; outcomes tracking; POC (purchase of care) reimbursement; CLIA (Clinical Laboratory Improvement Amendments) audit reports, audits on request; and consulting services. In all, Biosite's products are used in about half of all U.S. hospitals, as well as in approximately 50 international markets.

Biosite offers employees a benefits package including medical, dental, vision and life insurance; flexible spending accounts; an employee assistance program; educational assistance; a 401(k) plan; and an employee stock purchase plan.

FINANCIALS: **Sales and profits are in thousands of dollars—add 000 to get the full amount. 2011 Note: Financial information for 2011 was not available for all companies at press time.**

2011 Sales: $	2011 Profits: $	**U.S. Stock Ticker: Subsidiary**
2010 Sales: $	2010 Profits: $	**Int'l Ticker:**
2009 Sales: $	2009 Profits: $	Int'l Exchange:
2008 Sales: $	2008 Profits: $	Employees: Fiscal Year Ends: 12/31
2007 Sales: $	2007 Profits: $	Parent Company: ALERE INC

SALARIES/BENEFITS:

Pension Plan:	ESOP Stock Plan:	Profit Sharing:	Top Exec. Salary: $	Bonus: $
Savings Plan: Y	Stock Purch. Plan: Y		Second Exec. Salary: $	Bonus: $

OTHER THOUGHTS:

Apparent Women Officers or Directors:
Hot Spot for Advancement for Women/Minorities:

LOCATIONS: ("Y" = Yes)

West:	Southwest:	Midwest:	Southeast:	Northeast:	International:
Y					Y

BLACK HILLS CORP

www.blackhillscorp.com

Industry Group Code: 2211

Management:		Sales/Marketing:		Liberal Arts:		Information Systems:		Professionals:		Technical/Scientific:	
Mgmt. Trainees:		Mktg. Professionals:	Y	Gen. Writing/Editing:	Y	Info. Management:	Y	Finance/Acct.:	Y	Engineers, Elec.:	Y
Experienced Mgmt.:	Y	Retail Sales:		Technical Writing:		Software Dev.:		Law:	Y	Engineers, Other:	Y
Int'l Business:		Commercial/Industrial:	Y	Graphic Arts/Photog.:		Hardware Dev.:		HR/Other:	Y	Health/Lab	
MBA Graduates:	Y	Sales Trainees:	Y	Music:		Consulting/Other:		Training:	Y	Scientists/Research:	
		Advertising Pros.:		Broadcasting:				Health Care:		Petroleum/Chemicals:	Y
				Other:				Consulting:		Math/Other:	

TYPES OF BUSINESS:

Utilities-Electricity & Natural Gas
Coal Production
Oil & Natural Gas Exploration & Production

BRANDS/DIVISIONS/AFFILIATES:

Black Hills Energy
Black Hills Power
Cheyenne Light, Fuel & Power
Colorado Natural Gas
Kansas Natural Gas
Nebraska Natural Gas
Mallon Oil Company
Enserco

CONTACTS: *Note: Officers with more than one job title may be intentionally listed here more than once.*

David R. Emery, CEO
David R. Emery, Pres.
Anthony S. Cleberg, CFO/Exec. VP
Robert A. Myers, Sr. VP-Human Resources
Scott A. Buchholz, CIO/Sr. VP
Steven J. Helmers, General Counsel/Sr. VP/Chief Compliance Officer
Richard W. Kinzley, Sr. VP-Strategic Planning & Dev.
Lynnette K. Wilson, Sr. VP-Comm.
Lynnette K. Wilson, Sr. VP-Investor Rel.
Brian G. Iverson, Treas./VP
Linden R. Evans, COO-Utilities
Roxann R. Basham, VP-Governance/Corp. Sec.
Jeffrey B. Berzina, VP-Corp. Controller
Garner M. Anderson, VP-Chief Risk Officer
David R. Emery, Chmn.

Phone: 605-721-1700 **Fax:** 605-348-4748
Toll-Free:
Address: 625 9th St., Rapid City, SD 57701 US

GROWTH PLANS/SPECIAL FEATURES:

Black Hills Corp. is an energy company operating in the west and mid-west regions of the U.S. The firm divides its business into two segments: utilities and non-regulated energy. The utilities group conducts business in two divisions: electric utilities and gas utilities. Through Black Hills Power, the group engages in the generation, transmission and distribution of electricity to customers in South Dakota, Wyoming and Montana. Through Cheyenne Light, Fuel & Power, the group engages in the distribution of electric and natural gas. Other gas utilities operated by the company and doing business as Black Hills Energy are Colorado Natural Gas, Kansas Natural Gas, Nebraska Natural Gas and Iowa Natural Gas. The non-regulated energy group conducts business in four divisions: oil and gas, which develops and produces natural gas and crude oil; power generation, which engages in the production and sale of electric capacity and energy through a diversified portfolio of generating plants; coal mining, which mines and sells coal; and energy marketing, which, through Enserco, engages in the marketing of coal, natural gas and crude oil primarily in the Western portion of the U.S. and in Canada. In September 2011, subsidiary Enserco acquired exclusive rights to market all coal acquired or produced by Dorchester in eastern Kentucky. In June 2011, Black Hills Corp. announced that its subsidiary, Mallon Oil Company, is working with the Costa Rican Government to obtain execution of an oil and gas lease concession contract to begin exploring 2.3 million acres of land in northern Costa Rica.

Employees are offered medical, dental and vision insurance; flexible spending accounts; a 401(k) plan; pension plans; annual incentive bonus plans; disability coverage; life insurance; travel and accident insurance; an employee assistance plan; tuition reimbursement; a computer purchase program; and scholarships for employees' children.

FINANCIALS: **Sales and profits are in thousands of dollars—add 000 to get the full amount. 2011 Note: Financial information for 2011 was not available for all companies at press time.**

2011 Sales: $1,272,200	2011 Profits: $49,700	**U.S. Stock Ticker: BKH**
2010 Sales: $1,307,251	2010 Profits: $68,685	**Int'l Ticker:**
2009 Sales: $1,269,578	2009 Profits: $81,555	Int'l Exchange:
2008 Sales: $1,005,790	2008 Profits: $105,080	Employees: 2,124 Fiscal Year Ends: 12/31
2007 Sales: $574,838	2007 Profits: $98,772	Parent Company:

SALARIES/BENEFITS:

Pension Plan: Y	ESOP Stock Plan:	Profit Sharing:	Top Exec. Salary: $588,924	Bonus: $672,000
Savings Plan: Y	Stock Purch. Plan:		Second Exec. Salary: $353,769	Bonus: $284,000

OTHER THOUGHTS:

Apparent Women Officers or Directors: 3
Hot Spot for Advancement for Women/Minorities: Y

LOCATIONS: ("Y" = Yes)

West:	Southwest:	Midwest:	Southeast:	Northeast:	International:
Y	Y	Y	Y		

BLACKBOARD INC

www.blackboard.com

Industry Group Code: 611410

Management:		**Sales/Marketing:**		**Liberal Arts:**		**Information Systems:**		**Professionals:**		**Technical/Scientific:**	
Mgmt. Trainees:	Y	Mktg. Professionals:	Y	Gen. Writing/Editing:	Y	Info. Management:	Y	Finance/Acct.:	Y	Engineers, Elec.:	
Experienced Mgmt.:	Y	Retail Sales:		Technical Writing:	Y	Software Dev.:	Y	Law:	Y	Engineers, Other:	
Int'l Business:	Y	Commercial/Industrial:	Y	Graphic Arts/Photog.:	Y	Hardware Dev.:		HR/Other:	Y	Health/Lab	
MBA Graduates:	Y	Sales Trainees:	Y	Music:		Consulting/Other:		Training:	Y	Scientists/Research:	
		Advertising Pros.:	Y	Broadcasting:				Health Care:		Petroleum/Chemicals:	
				Other:	Y			Consulting:		Math/Other:	

TYPES OF BUSINESS:

Online Educational Software
e-Learning Software
Content Management Software

BRANDS/DIVISIONS/AFFILIATES:

Providence Equity Partners
Blackboard Learn
Blackboard Transact
Blackboard Connect
SafeAssign
Presidium Inc
ANGEL Learning Management Suite
Blackboard Mobile

CONTACTS: *Note: Officers with more than one job title may be intentionally listed here more than once.*

Michael L. Chasen, CEO
Michael L. Chasen, Pres.
John Kinzer, CFO
Matthew Small, Chief Legal Officer/Sec.
Matthew Small, Chief Bus. Officer
Maurice Heiblum, Pres., Blackboard Collaborate
David Marr, Pres., BlackBoard Transact
Edward Miller, Pres., Blackboard Connect
Ray Henderson, Pres., Blackboard Learn
Matthew Serbin Pittinsky, Chmn.

Phone: 202-463-4860 **Fax:** 202-463-4863
Toll-Free: 800-424-9299
Address: 650 Massachusetts Ave. NW, 6th Fl., Washington, DC 20001 US

GROWTH PLANS/SPECIAL FEATURES:

Blackboard, Inc. is a provider of enterprise software applications and related services to the education industry. Its product line consists of various software applications delivered in six platforms: Blackboard Learn, Blackboard Transact, Blackboard Connect, Blackboard Mobile, Blackboard Collaborate and Blackboard Analytics. Blackboard Learn provides a scalable technology platform for delivering education online, managing digital content and aggregating access to tools and information through an integrated web portal environment. Its portfolio consists of the following modules: Course Delivery, Community Engagement, Content Management, Portfolio Management and Outcomes Assessment. Its products also include SafeAssign, a plagiarism prevention service; and the ANGEL Learning Management Suite, acquired from ANGEL Learning, Inc. Blackboard Transact can be used for on- and off-campus commerce, e-commerce, meal plan administration, vending, laundry services, copy and print management and student and staff identification. Blackboard Connect provides communication systems that enable rapid dissemination of information via voice and text devices. Its product portfolio includes the Connect-ED, Connect-CTY, Connect-GOV and Connect-MIL brands. Blackboard Mobile includes MobileCentral, which provides a set of applications for the transmission of messages and content to mobile devices, acquired from Terriblyclever Design. Blackboard Collaborate provides the collaborative tools to determine educational and administrative needs through voice authorizing, web conferencing and enterprise instant messaging. Blackboard Analytics provides metrics and analytics, data reporting and business intelligence for higher education. In January 2011, the firm acquired Presidium, Inc., and through the acquisition, it launched a new line of student lifecycle services. In October 2011, the company was acquired by Providence Equity Partners for approximately $1.64 billion.

Employees are offered medical, dental, vision and life insurance; disability coverage; and employee discounts.

FINANCIALS: **Sales and profits are in thousands of dollars—add 000 to get the full amount. 2011 Note: Financial information for 2011 was not available for all companies at press time.**

2011 Sales: $ | 2011 Profits: $
2010 Sales: $447,318 | 2010 Profits: $16,644
2009 Sales: $377,000 | 2009 Profits: $7,912
2008 Sales: $312,134 | 2008 Profits: $2,820
2007 Sales: $239,448 | 2007 Profits: $12,865

U.S. Stock Ticker: BBBB
Int'l Ticker:
Int'l Exchange:
Employees: 1,780 Fiscal Year Ends: 12/31
Parent Company: PROVIDENCE EQUITY PARTNERS

SALARIES/BENEFITS:

Pension Plan: | ESOP Stock Plan: | Profit Sharing: | Top Exec. Salary: $572,917 | Bonus: $679,500
Savings Plan: Y | Stock Purch. Plan: | | Second Exec. Salary: $388,750 | Bonus: $288,053

OTHER THOUGHTS:

Apparent Women Officers or Directors:
Hot Spot for Advancement for Women/Minorities:

LOCATIONS: ("Y" = Yes)

West:	Southwest:	Midwest:	Southeast:	Northeast:	International:
Y	Y	Y		Y	Y

BLUE COAT SYSTEMS INC

www.bluecoat.com

Industry Group Code: 511210E

Management:		**Sales/Marketing:**		**Liberal Arts:**		**Information Systems:**		**Professionals:**		**Technical/Scientific:**	
Mgmt. Trainees:		Mktg. Professionals:	Y	Gen. Writing/Editing:		Info. Management:	Y	Finance/Acct.:	Y	Engineers, Elec.:	Y
Experienced Mgmt.:	Y	Retail Sales:		Technical Writing:	Y	Software Dev.:	Y	Law:	Y	Engineers, Other:	
Int'l Business:	Y	Commercial/Industrial:	Y	Graphic Arts/Photog.:		Hardware Dev.:		HR/Other:	Y	Health/Lab	
MBA Graduates:	Y	Sales Trainees:	Y	Music:		Consulting/Other:		Training:	Y	Scientists/Research:	
		Advertising Pros.:		Broadcasting:				Health Care:		Petroleum/Chemicals:	
				Other:				Consulting:		Math/Other:	

TYPES OF BUSINESS:

WAN & Internet Security Applications
WAN Acceleration & Optimization Technology

BRANDS/DIVISIONS/AFFILIATES:

ProxySG Appliances
ProxyClient
ProxyAV Appliances
CacheFlow 5000
Blue Coat WebFilter
WebPulse

CONTACTS:

Note: Officers with more than one job title may be intentionally listed here more than once.

Mike Borman, CEO
Mike Borman, Pres.
Gordon Brooks, CFO/Sr. VP
Steve Daheb, Chief Mktg. Offer/Sr. VP
Sharon Jordan, VP-Human Resources
Jim Haar, CIO
James Whitchurch, VP-Tech.
Dave de Simon, Sr. VP-Products & Tech.
James Whitchurch, VP-Eng.
Betsy E. Bayha, General Counsel/Sec./Sr. VP
Jim Vogt, Sr. VP/Gen. Mgr.-Cloud Prod. Group
Darrell Long, VP/Gen. Mgr.-Security Prod. Group
Tom Shea, VP/Gen. Mgr.-WAN Op Prod. Group
Kevin Biggs, Sr. VP-Worldwide Sales & Field Oper.
David Hanna, Chmn.

Phone: 408-220-2200 **Fax:** 408-220-2250
Toll-Free: 866-302-2628
Address: 420 N. Mary Ave., Sunnyvale, CA 94085 US

GROWTH PLANS/SPECIAL FEATURES:

Blue Coat Systems, Inc. offers business applications that secure and optimize WAN- (Wide Area Network) and Internet-based operations. It specializes in internally and externally hosted network applications with users spread across multiple locations. Blue Coat primarily serves medium and large enterprises in fields such as finance, government and healthcare. In general, the firm's technology has three applications: Web Security, which provide protection from malware, spyware or other malicious threats; WAN Optimization Products, which deal with WAN acceleration and optimization for the delivery of internal, external, real-time and customized applications across distributed enterprises' networks; and Cloud Service, which is a subscription based service that utilizes company-owned equipment located in geographically dispersed data centers to deliver functions through the internet on demand. The company's products include the following. ProxySG Appliances serve as the hardware basis of both the Web Security and WAN Optimization products. They are installed in directly at Internet gateways or at WAN entry or exit points. ProxyClient is a software application installed on desktops or laptops at remote locations that do not have a ProxySG Appliance and on computers used by mobile employees. It offers WAN optimization and security. The CacheFlow 5000 appliance focuses on the reduction of bandwidth consumption. ProxyAV Appliances offer inline threat protection and malware scanning designed to complement the ProxySG appliance. Blue Coat WebFilter works with the ProxySG appliance to block harmful or inappropriate content. WebPulse is a real-time cloud computing security service.

The company offers U.S. employees medical, dental and vision insurance; disability coverage; life and accident insurance; flexible spending accounts; a profit sharing plan; an employee stock purchase plan; a 401(k) plan; business travel accident insurance; an employee assistance program; and educational assistance.

FINANCIALS:

Sales and profits are in thousands of dollars—add 000 to get the full amount. 2011 Note: Financial information for 2011 was not available for all companies at press time.

2011 Sales: $487,113	2011 Profits: $47,024
2010 Sales: $496,137	2010 Profits: $42,879
2009 Sales: $444,745	2009 Profits: $-8,508
2008 Sales: $305,439	2008 Profits: $32,568
2007 Sales: $177,700	2007 Profits: $-7,198

U.S. Stock Ticker: BCSI
Int'l Ticker:
Int'l Exchange:
Employees: 1,331 Fiscal Year Ends: 4/30
Parent Company:

SALARIES/BENEFITS:

Pension Plan:	ESOP Stock Plan:	Profit Sharing: Y	Top Exec. Salary: $350,000	Bonus: $69,563
Savings Plan: Y	Stock Purch. Plan: Y		Second Exec. Salary: $325,000	Bonus: $64,594

OTHER THOUGHTS:

Apparent Women Officers or Directors: 3
Hot Spot for Advancement for Women/Minorities: Y

LOCATIONS: ("Y" = Yes)

West:	Southwest:	Midwest:	Southeast:	Northeast:	International:
Y	Y			Y	Y

BLUE NILE INC

www.bluenile.com

Industry Group Code: 448310E

Management:		Sales/Marketing:		Liberal Arts:		Information Systems:		Professionals:		Technical/Scientific:	
Mgmt. Trainees:	Y	Mktg. Professionals:	Y	Gen. Writing/Editing:	Y	Info. Management:	Y	Finance/Acct.:	Y	Engineers, Elec.:	
Experienced Mgmt.:	Y	Retail Sales:	Y	Technical Writing:		Software Dev.:	Y	Law:	Y	Engineers, Other:	
Int'l Business:	Y	Commercial/Industrial:		Graphic Arts/Photog.:	Y	Hardware Dev.:		HR/Other:	Y	Health/Lab	
MBA Graduates:	Y	Sales Trainees:	Y	Music:		Consulting/Other:		Training:	Y	Scientists/Research:	
		Advertising Pros.:	Y	Broadcasting:				Health Care:		Petroleum/Chemicals:	
				Other:	Y			Consulting:		Math/Other:	

TYPES OF BUSINESS:

Jewelry, Online Retail

BRANDS/DIVISIONS/AFFILIATES:

BlueNile.com
BlueNile.co.uk
BlueNile.ca
Build Your Own Charm Bracelet
Blue Nile LLC
Blue Nile Worldwide Inc
Blue Nile Jewellery Ltd

CONTACTS: *Note: Officers with more than one job title may be intentionally listed here more than once.*

Vijay Talwar, CEO
David Binder, CFO
Jon Sainsbury, VP-Mktg.
Lauren Neiswender, General Counsel/Corp. Sec.
John Baird, Dir.-Corp. Comm.
Nancy Shipp, Dir.-Investor Rel.
Terri Maupin, Chief Acct. Officer
Marianne Marck, Sr. VP
Dwight Gaston, Sr. VP
Susan Bell, Sr. VP
Mark Vadon, Chmn.
Vijay Talwar, Gen. Mgr.-Int'l/Sr. VP

Phone: 206-336-6700 **Fax:** 206-336-6750
Toll-Free: 800-242-2728
Address: 705 5th Ave. S., Ste. 900, Seattle, WA 98104 US

GROWTH PLANS/SPECIAL FEATURES:

Blue Nile, Inc. is a U.S.-based Internet retailer of jewelry. The firm offers a broad selection of diamonds and other fine jewelry through its web site, BlueNile.com. The web site features interactive search functionality; the ability to purchase products in 24 currencies; detailed product information; over 70,000 independently certified diamonds; and over 1,000 styles of jewelry, including rings, wedding bands, necklaces, charms, earrings and bracelets. In addition to loose diamonds and settings, the company offers gold, platinum and silver jewelry with pearls, emeralds, rubies and sapphires. Customers can create their own jewelry by selecting a diamond and a favorite ring, pendant or earring design. Over half of the firm's revenue is derived from engagement jewelry sales. Blue Nile has developed an online cost structure and a unique supply solution that eliminates traditional layers of diamond wholesalers and brokers, which allows the company to purchase most of its products at lower prices by avoiding mark-ups imposed by those intermediaries. This in turn allows the company to offer its products to the consumer at reduced prices. The firm also maintains web sites in the U.K. (BlueNile.co.uk) and Canada (BlueNile.ca). Blue Nile ships its products to over 40 countries, including Greece, Australia, Belgium, France, Germany, Hong Kong, Japan, the Netherlands, New Zealand, Singapore, Spain, Switzerland and Taiwan. The firm's subsidiaries are Blue Nile, LLC, Blue Nile Worldwide, Inc. and Blue Nile Jewellery, Ltd. In October 2011, Blue Nile released new custom online platform Build Your Own Charm Bracelet.

Blue Nile offers its employees life, disability, AD&D, medical, dental and vision insurance; domestic partner coverage; a stock option plan; a 401(k) plan; flexible spending accounts; an employee assistance program; paid time off; a referral bonus program; transportation allowance; an employee discount program; and fitness programs.

FINANCIALS: **Sales and profits are in thousands of dollars—add 000 to get the full amount. 2011 Note: Financial information for 2011 was not available for all companies at press time.**

2011 Sales: $348,013 | 2011 Profits: $11,350
2010 Sales: $332,889 | 2010 Profits: $14,142
2009 Sales: $302,134 | 2009 Profits: $12,800
2008 Sales: $295,329 | 2008 Profits: $11,630
2007 Sales: $319,264 | 2007 Profits: $17,459

U.S. Stock Ticker: NILE
Int'l Ticker:
Int'l Exchange:
Employees: 191 Fiscal Year Ends: 12/31
Parent Company:

SALARIES/BENEFITS:

Pension Plan: | ESOP Stock Plan: | Profit Sharing: | Top Exec. Salary: $471,875 | Bonus: $199,360
Savings Plan: Y | Stock Purch. Plan: | | Second Exec. Salary: $288,621 | Bonus: $

OTHER THOUGHTS:

Apparent Women Officers or Directors: 6
Hot Spot for Advancement for Women/Minorities: Y

LOCATIONS: ("Y" = Yes)

West:	Southwest:	Midwest:	Southeast:	Northeast:	International:
Y					

BOSTON BEER COMPANY INC (THE)

www.bostonbeer.com

Industry Group Code: 312120

Management:		Sales/Marketing:		Liberal Arts:		Information Systems:		Professionals:		Technical/Scientific:	
Mgmt. Trainees:	Y	Mktg. Professionals:	Y	Gen. Writing/Editing:	Y	Info. Management:	Y	Finance/Acct.:	Y	Engineers, Elec.:	
Experienced Mgmt.:	Y	Retail Sales:		Technical Writing:		Software Dev.:		Law:	Y	Engineers, Other:	Y
Int'l Business:		Commercial/Industrial:	Y	Graphic Arts/Photog.:	Y	Hardware Dev.:		HR/Other:	Y	Health/Lab	
MBA Graduates:	Y	Sales Trainees:	Y	Music:		Consulting/Other:		Training:	Y	Scientists/Research:	
		Advertising Pros.:	Y	Broadcasting:				Health Care:		Petroleum/Chemicals:	
				Other:	Y			Consulting:		Math/Other:	

TYPES OF BUSINESS:

Beverages-Breweries
Hard Cider, Tea & Lemonade
Beer

BRANDS/DIVISIONS/AFFILIATES:

Samuel Adams
Twisted Tea
HardCore
Sam Adams
Sam Adams Light
Octoberfest
Summer Ale
Alchemy & Science

CONTACTS: *Note: Officers with more than one job title may be intentionally listed here more than once.*

Martin F. Roper, CEO
Martin F. Roper, Pres.
William F. Urich, CFO
John C. Geist, VP-Sales
Robert P. Pagano, VP-Brand Dev.
Frederick H. Grein, Jr., General Counsel
Thomas W. Lance, VP-Oper.
William F. Urich, Treas.
David L. Grinnell, VP-Brewing
C. James Koch, Chmn.

Phone: 617-368-5000	**Fax:**
Toll-Free: 888-661-2337	
Address: 1 Design Ctr., Ste. 850, Boston, MA 02210 US	

GROWTH PLANS/SPECIAL FEATURES:

The Boston Beer Company, Inc. is a specialty brewer and one of the largest brewers in the U.S. It currently sells a total of 25 beers under the Samuel Adams or Sam Adams brand names, eight flavored malt beverages under the Twisted Tea brand and one hard cider product under the HardCore brand. The firm produces these beverages at its three company-owned breweries in Breinigsville, Pennsylvania; Boston, Massachusetts; and Cincinnati, Ohio, as well as under contract. It maintains a supply of proprietary strains of yeasts for use in its brews. Boston Beer's products are primarily positioned in the better beer category of the beer industry, which includes craft or specialty beers and most imports, and is distinguished by higher price, quality, image and taste compared with regular beers. In most markets, the company focuses its advertising and promotional efforts on Samuel Adams Boston Lager, Sam Adams Light and Samuel Adams Seasonal Beers. Seasonal beers include Octoberfest, Winter Lager, Summer Ale and Noble Pils. Boston Beer also offers the Brewmaster's Collection (including Samuel Adams Boston Ale, Cream Stout and Pale Ale); the Imperial Series (featuring Samuel Adams Double Bock and Imperial White); the Barrel Room Collection (offering Samuel Adams American Kriek and New World Tripel); and limited-edition beers (including Samuel Adams Triple Bock and Infinium). The firm sells its products to a network of approximately 400 wholesale distributors, who then sell to retailers such as pubs, restaurants, grocery chains, package stores, stadiums and other outlets. Products are sold primarily in the U.S., but are also available in Canada, Europe, Israel, the Caribbean, the Pacific Rim and Mexico. In October 2011, the company formed a joint venture partnership with Magic Hat Brewing in the launch of Alchemy & Science, a craft brew incubator.

FINANCIALS: **Sales and profits are in thousands of dollars—add 000 to get the full amount. 2011 Note: Financial information for 2011 was not available for all companies at press time.**

2011 Sales: $513,000	2011 Profits: $66,059
2010 Sales: $505,870	2010 Profits: $50,142
2009 Sales: $453,446	2009 Profits: $31,118
2008 Sales: $449,554	2008 Profits: $8,088
2007 Sales: $380,575	2007 Profits: $22,491

U.S. Stock Ticker: SAM
Int'l Ticker:
Int'l Exchange:
Employees: 780 Fiscal Year Ends: 12/31
Parent Company:

SALARIES/BENEFITS:

Pension Plan:	ESOP Stock Plan:	Profit Sharing:	Top Exec. Salary: $686,750	Bonus: $398,315
Savings Plan:	Stock Purch. Plan:		Second Exec. Salary: $375,000	Bonus: $262,500

OTHER THOUGHTS:

Apparent Women Officers or Directors:
Hot Spot for Advancement for Women/Minorities:

LOCATIONS: ("Y" = Yes)

West:	Southwest:	Midwest:	Southeast:	Northeast:	International:
		Y		Y	

BOTTOMLINE TECHNOLOGIES INC

www.bottomline.com

Industry Group Code: 511210

Management:		**Sales/Marketing:**		**Liberal Arts:**		**Information Systems:**		**Professionals:**		**Technical/Scientific:**	
Mgmt. Trainees:		Mktg. Professionals:	Y	Gen. Writing/Editing:	Y	Info. Management:	Y	Finance/Acct.:	Y	Engineers, Elec.:	Y
Experienced Mgmt.:	Y	Retail Sales:		Technical Writing:	Y	Software Dev.:	Y	Law:	Y	Engineers, Other:	
Int'l Business:	Y	Commercial/Industrial:	Y	Graphic Arts/Photog.:		Hardware Dev.:		HR/Other:	Y	Health/Lab	
MBA Graduates:	Y	Sales Trainees:	Y	Music:		Consulting/Other:		Training:	Y	Scientists/Research:	
		Advertising Pros.:		Broadcasting:				Health Care:		Petroleum/Chemicals:	
				Other:				Consulting:		Math/Other:	

TYPES OF BUSINESS:

Software-Electronic Banking
Online Billing, Payment & Invoicing Software
Software-as-a-Service (SaaS)

BRANDS/DIVISIONS/AFFILIATES:

Legal eXchange
WebSeries
Paymode-X
Inprotica
QuickRecord
SMA Financial Ltd.
Direct Debit Limited
Allegient Systems, Inc.

CONTACTS: *Note: Officers with more than one job title may be intentionally listed here more than once.*

Robert A. Eberle, CEO
Robert A. Eberle, Pres.
Kevin M. Donovan, CFO
Paul Fannon, Group Dir.-Sales, Europe
John Mason, CIO
Eric Campbell, CTO
Andrew Mintzer, Sr. VP-Prod. Strategy & Delivery
Eric Morgan, Controller/VP
Rick Bell, Sr. VP/Gen Mgr.-Financial Process Solutions
Tom Gaillard, Sr. VP/Gen. Mgr.-Transactional Svcs., N. America
Chris Peck, Managing Dir.-Transaction Banking
John Kelly, Gen. Mgr.-Legal Solutions
Joseph L. Mullen, Chmn.
Nigel Savory, Managing Dir.-Europe

Phone: 603-436-0700 **Fax:** 603-436-0300
Toll-Free: 800-243-2528
Address: 325 Corporate Dr., Portsmouth, NH 03801 US

GROWTH PLANS/SPECIAL FEATURES:

Bottomline Technologies, Inc. provides electronic payment and invoice services to corporations, financial institutions and banks around the world. Its services are used to streamline, automate and manage processes and transactions involving global payments, invoice approval, collections, cash management, risk mitigation, reporting and document archiving. Historically, its software has been sold predominantly on a perpetual license basis; however, the company is shifting a large part of its focus to selling subscription and transaction-based product offerings. The company's comprehensive Paymode-X offerings allow businesses to automate the almost entirely paper-based processes central to purchasing requisition and invoice management, as well as to facilitate the ultimate payment. The company-hosted spend management application, Legal eXchange, integrates with claims management and time and billing systems to automate legal invoice management processes. Its WebSeries Electronic Banking platform allows banks and financial institutions to deploy Internet-based cash management services for corporate clients. The company has also developed several electronic healthcare records automation tools, including Inprotica, QuickRecord and MedForms. The firm supports more than 9,000 customers, including 3,000 that access its payment and invoice automation capabilities through convenient subscription and transaction-based services. The company's customers are in industries such as financial services, insurance, health care, technology, communications, education, media, manufacturing and government. In October 2010, the firm acquired SMA Financial Ltd., a London-based provider of Software-as-a-Service (SaaS) technologies. In February 2011, it acquired Direct Debit Limited, a London-based provider of payments automation software. In March 2011, it acquired Allegient Systems, Inc., a provider of legal e-billing, bill review and analytics solutions.

Employees are offered medical and dental insurance; a 401(k) plan; an employee stock purchase plan; tuition reimbursement; health club membership reimbursement; life insurance; disability coverage; and discount home and auto insurance.

FINANCIALS: **Sales and profits are in thousands of dollars—add 000 to get the full amount. 2011 Note: Financial information for 2011 was not available for all companies at press time.**

2011 Sales: $189,381	2011 Profits: $35,893
2010 Sales: $157,990	2010 Profits: $3,954
2009 Sales: $138,014	2009 Profits: $-12,288
2008 Sales: $131,241	2008 Profits: $-5,261
2007 Sales: $118,335	2007 Profits: $-7,030

U.S. Stock Ticker: EPAY
Int'l Ticker:
Int'l Exchange:
Employees: 880 Fiscal Year Ends: 6/30
Parent Company:

SALARIES/BENEFITS:

Pension Plan:	ESOP Stock Plan:	Profit Sharing:	Top Exec. Salary: $325,000	Bonus: $343,000
Savings Plan: Y	Stock Purch. Plan: Y		Second Exec. Salary: $242,382	Bonus: $114,624

OTHER THOUGHTS:

Apparent Women Officers or Directors:
Hot Spot for Advancement for Women/Minorities:

LOCATIONS: ("Y" = Yes)

West:	Southwest:	Midwest:	Southeast:	Northeast:	International:
			Y	Y	Y

BRIGHTSTAR CORPORATION

www.brightstarcorp.com

Industry Group Code: 4236

Management:		**Sales/Marketing:**		**Liberal Arts:**		**Information Systems:**		**Professionals:**		**Technical/Scientific:**	
Mgmt. Trainees:		Mktg. Professionals:	Y	Gen. Writing/Editing:		Info. Management:	Y	Finance/Acct.:	Y	Engineers, Elec.:	
Experienced Mgmt.:	Y	Retail Sales:		Technical Writing:	Y	Software Dev.:	Y	Law:	Y	Engineers, Other:	
Int'l Business:	Y	Commercial/Industrial:	Y	Graphic Arts/Photog.:		Hardware Dev.:		HR/Other:	Y	Health/Lab	
MBA Graduates:	Y	Sales Trainees:	Y	Music:		Consulting/Other:		Training:	Y	Scientists/Research:	
		Advertising Pros.:		Broadcasting:				Health Care:		Petroleum/Chemicals:	
				Other:				Consulting:		Math/Other:	

TYPES OF BUSINESS:

Telecommunication Supply Chain & Distribution Services
Wireless Device & Accessories Distribution
Wireless Device Manufacturing
Supply Chain, Marketing and Retail Consultation

BRANDS/DIVISIONS/AFFILIATES:

Narbitec LLC
Brightstar Accessories
Brightstar Europe
ActiveIT

CONTACTS:

Note: Officers with more than one job title may be intentionally listed here more than once.

R. Marcelo Claure, CEO
Mike Cost, COO
Dennis J. Strand, CFO/Exec. VP
Rafael de Guzman Sr., Chief Mktg. Officer/Sr. VP
Toby Mannheimer, Sr. VP-Global Human Resources
Rafael A. Sanchez, CIO
Rafael M. de Guzman III, VP-Strategy
Oscar Fumagali, Chief Treasury Officer
Brian Corey, Head-Enterprise & Consumer Svcs.
Rod J. Millar, Pres., Brightstar Europe
Arturo Osorio, Pres., Brightstar APAC
Sally Lange Witkowski, Head-Retail Svcs.
R. Marcelo Claure, Chmn.
Oscar A. Rojas, Pres., Brightstar Latin America
Jeff Gower, Head-Supply Chain Services

Phone: 305-421-6000 **Fax:**
Toll-Free:
Address: 9725 N.W. 117th Ave., Ste. 300, Miami, FL 33178 US

GROWTH PLANS/SPECIAL FEATURES:

Brightstar Corporation is a global distributor and provider of value added supply chain services to the wireless and telecommunications industry. It also designs and manufactures products under licensing agreements with leading manufacturers. The company's supply chain services include inventory management, supply chain management logistics, fulfillment, customized packaging and assembly services. The firm distributes handsets, accessories, wireless data, fixed wireless, wireless broadband and prepaid wireless products. Brightstar's wireless data and telecom solutions division addresses vertical market needs through products and services within cellular infrastructure, broadband infrastructure, 2.5G and 3G modems, modules and PCMCIA cards, content applications and wireless PDAs. It also consults and invests in new business ventures. The firm operates facilities in over 50 countries worldwide, with the majority located in Central and South America. Brightstar's customer base includes several network operators, distributors, agents, resellers and retailers around the world, serving more than 90,000 points of sale. Through a joint venture with Narbitec LLC, the company designs, manufactures and distributes a complete line of fixed wireless products with a focus on rural markets. The firm also operates Brightstar Accessories, an accessories company focused on the marketing, sales, procurement and distribution of mobile devices to customers worldwide. In August 2010, the firm opened a Brightstar Miami Operations Center in Beacon Lakes, Florida. In September 2010, the company agreed to acquire OTBT Inc., a provider of wireless devices, activation and service software. In April 2011, the firm agreed to acquire eSecuritel, a cell phone insurance company. Also in April 2011, the company partnered with Tech Data Corporation to establish the U.S. joint venture ActivateIT, which will offer data services, hardware accessories, technical support, software and billing management among other services.

FINANCIALS:

Sales and profits are in thousands of dollars—add 000 to get the full amount. 2011 Note: Financial information for 2011 was not available for all companies at press time.

2011 Sales: $	2011 Profits: $	**U.S. Stock Ticker: Private**
2010 Sales: $	2010 Profits: $	**Int'l Ticker:**
2009 Sales: $	2009 Profits: $	Int'l Exchange:
2008 Sales: $	2008 Profits: $	Employees: Fiscal Year Ends: 12/31
2007 Sales: $	2007 Profits: $	Parent Company:

SALARIES/BENEFITS:

Pension Plan:	ESOP Stock Plan:	Profit Sharing:	Top Exec. Salary: $	Bonus: $
Savings Plan:	Stock Purch. Plan:		Second Exec. Salary: $	Bonus: $

OTHER THOUGHTS:

Apparent Women Officers or Directors: 2
Hot Spot for Advancement for Women/Minorities:

LOCATIONS: ("Y" = Yes)

West:	Southwest:	Midwest:	Southeast:	Northeast:	International:
		Y	Y		Y

CABOT OIL & GAS CORP

www.cabotog.com

Industry Group Code: 211111

Management:		Sales/Marketing:		Liberal Arts:		Information Systems:		Professionals:		Technical/Scientific:	
Mgmt. Trainees:		Mktg. Professionals:		Gen. Writing/Editing:		Info. Management:	Y	Finance/Acct.:	Y	Engineers, Elec.:	
Experienced Mgmt.:	Y	Retail Sales:		Technical Writing:		Software Dev.:		Law:	Y	Engineers, Other:	Y
Int'l Business:		Commercial/Industrial:		Graphic Arts/Photog.:		Hardware Dev.:		HR/Other:	Y	Health/Lab	
MBA Graduates:	Y	Sales Trainees:		Music:		Consulting/Other:		Training:	Y	Scientists/Research:	
		Advertising Pros.:		Broadcasting:				Health Care:		Petroleum/Chemicals:	Y
				Other:				Consulting:		Math/Other:	

TYPES OF BUSINESS:

Oil & Gas Exploration & Production
Gas Gathering & Storage
Gas Pipelines

BRANDS/DIVISIONS/AFFILIATES:

GROWTH PLANS/SPECIAL FEATURES:

Cabot Oil & Gas Corp. (Cabot) is engaged in the development, exploitation and exploration of oil and gas properties in the U.S. The company primarily operates in the Appalachian Basin; the onshore Gulf Coast region, including south and east Texas and north Louisiana; the Rocky Mountains; and the Anadarko Basin. In total, the firm has approximately 2.7 trillion feet of natural gas equivalent in reserves. The firm divides its operations into two regions: north, which accounts for approximately 75% of its reserves; and south, which accounts for the remaining 25%. The north region's operations include activities in Pennsylvania and West Virginia, as well as Cabot's Rocky Mountain activities, concentrated in the Green River and Washakie Basins in Wyoming and the Paradox Basin in Colorado. The south region includes the firm's operations in Louisiana and Texas and its mid-continent operations, concentrated in the Anadarko Basin in southwest Kansas, Oklahoma and the Texas panhandle. In addition to its exploration activities, Cabot operates a number of gas gathering and transmission pipeline systems that consist of 5,069 wells and the production of 126 billion cubic feet of natural gas.

CONTACTS: *Note: Officers with more than one job title may be intentionally listed here more than once.*

Dan O. Dinges, CEO
Dan O. Dinges, Pres.
Scott C. Schroeder, CFO/VP
Jeffrey W. Hutton, VP-Mktg.
Abraham D. Garza, VP-Human Resources
Robert G. Drake, VP-Info. Svcs.
Steven W. Lindeman, VP-Tech.
Steven W. Lindeman, VP-Eng.
G. Kevin Cunningham, General Counsel/VP
Robert G. Drake, VP-Operational Acct.
Lisa A. Machesney, Managing Counsel/VP/Corp. Sec.
Todd M. Roemer, Controller
James M. Reid, VP/Regional Mgr.-South Region
Phil Stalnaker, VP/Regional Mgr.-North Region
Dan O. Dinges, Chmn.

Phone: 281-589-4600	**Fax:** 281-589-4912
Toll-Free:	
Address: 1200 Enclave Pkwy., Houston, TX 77077 US	

FINANCIALS: **Sales and profits are in thousands of dollars—add 000 to get the full amount. 2011 Note: Financial information for 2011 was not available for all companies at press time.**

2011 Sales: $973,700	2011 Profits: $122,400	**U.S. Stock Ticker: COG**
2010 Sales: $884,035	2010 Profits: $103,386	**Int'l Ticker:**
2009 Sales: $879,276	2009 Profits: $148,343	Int'l Exchange:
2008 Sales: $945,791	2008 Profits: $211,290	Employees: 409 Fiscal Year Ends: 12/31
2007 Sales: $732,170	2007 Profits: $167,423	Parent Company:

SALARIES/BENEFITS:

Pension Plan: Y	ESOP Stock Plan:	Profit Sharing:	Top Exec. Salary: $595,833	Bonus: $1,200,000
Savings Plan:	Stock Purch. Plan:		Second Exec. Salary: $362,500	Bonus: $6,205,000

OTHER THOUGHTS:

Apparent Women Officers or Directors: 1
Hot Spot for Advancement for Women/Minorities:

LOCATIONS: ("Y" = Yes)

West:	Southwest:	Midwest:	Southeast:	Northeast:	International:
Y	Y	Y	Y	Y	

CACTUS FEEDERS INC

www.cactusfeeders.com

Industry Group Code: 311612

Management:		**Sales/Marketing:**		**Liberal Arts:**		**Information Systems:**		**Professionals:**		**Technical/Scientific:**	
Mgmt. Trainees:		Mktg. Professionals:		Gen. Writing/Editing:		Info. Management:	Y	Finance/Acct.:	Y	Engineers, Elec.:	
Experienced Mgmt.:	Y	Retail Sales:		Technical Writing:		Software Dev.:		Law:	Y	Engineers, Other:	
Int'l Business:	Y	Commercial/Industrial:	Y	Graphic Arts/Photog.:		Hardware Dev.:		HR/Other:	Y	Health/Lab	
MBA Graduates:	Y	Sales Trainees:		Music:		Consulting/Other:		Training:		Scientists/Research:	
		Advertising Pros.:		Broadcasting:				Health Care:		Petroleum/Chemicals:	
				Other:				Consulting:		Math/Other:	

TYPES OF BUSINESS:

Meat Production-Feed Lots
Cattle Marketing Services

BRANDS/DIVISIONS/AFFILIATES:

Spike Box
Cactus Argentina

CONTACTS:

Note: Officers with more than one job title may be intentionally listed here more than once.

Michael Engler, CEO
Jack Rhoades, COO/Sr. VP
Michael Engler, Pres.
Brad Hastings, CFO/Sr. VP
Monty Koller, VP-Mktg. & Cattle Procurement
Kevin Hazelwood, Dir.-Employee Dev./VP
Spencer Swingle, Dir.-Research & Nutrition/VP
Wayne Craig, Dir.-IT
Steve Johnson, Dir.-Feedyard Oper.
Paul Defoor, Dir.-Strategy & Bus. Dev./Sr. VP
Ronny Hargis, Controller/VP
Mark Engler, Sr. VP/Dir.-Risk Mgmt.
Surcy Peoples, Dir.-Customer Service
Cliff Adams, Dir.-Feed Milling
Sam Ives, Dir.-Veterinary Svcs.
Paul F. Engler, Chmn.
Mutt Schuman, Dir.-Commodity Procurement/VP

Phone: 806-373-2333	**Fax:** 806-371-4767
Toll-Free: 800-698-7355	
Address: 2209 W. 7th Ave., Amarillo, TX 79106 US	

GROWTH PLANS/SPECIAL FEATURES:

Cactus Feeders, Inc., founded in 1975, is one of the largest cattle feedyard operators in the U.S. With 10 feed yards across Texas and Kansas, Cactus has the capacity to support 520,000 head of cattle. At each of its feed lots, the company maintains a cattle to employee ratio of 1,000 to one. Cactus provides its clients and partners with detailed information about cattle genetics, successful ranch practices, health and nutrition. Its in-house research efforts include developing new feeding techniques and animal health regimens, as well as creating new marketing strategies. Cactus is considered to be the first company to initiate a formula-run, value-based marketing program to link producers with packers in the most profitable way possible. Additionally, the company owns ranches in Texas and New Mexico, where it raises stocker and cow-calf pairs under the Spike Box brand, and runs a feedyard and processing operation called Cactus Argentina located in the Pampas region of Argentina. This operation is a co-venture with Tyson and Cresud.

Cactus aggressively promotes from within its own ranks and offers its employees family health coverage, a 401(k) and a significant employee stock ownership program. Employees currently own approximately 40% of the company.

FINANCIALS:

Sales and profits are in thousands of dollars—add 000 to get the full amount. 2011 Note: Financial information for 2011 was not available for all companies at press time.

2011 Sales: $	2011 Profits: $	**U.S. Stock Ticker: Private**
2010 Sales: $750,000	2010 Profits: $	**Int'l Ticker:**
2009 Sales: $750,000	2009 Profits: $	Int'l Exchange:
2008 Sales: $650,000	2008 Profits: $	Employees: 500 Fiscal Year Ends: 10/31
2007 Sales: $678,100	2007 Profits: $	Parent Company:

SALARIES/BENEFITS:

Pension Plan: Y	ESOP Stock Plan: Y	Profit Sharing:	Top Exec. Salary: $	Bonus: $
Savings Plan:	Stock Purch. Plan:		Second Exec. Salary: $	Bonus: $

OTHER THOUGHTS:

Apparent Women Officers or Directors:
Hot Spot for Advancement for Women/Minorities:

LOCATIONS: ("Y" = Yes)

West:	Southwest:	Midwest:	Southeast:	Northeast:	International:
	Y	Y			Y

CAGLE'S INC

www.cagles.net

Industry Group Code: 311615

Management:		Sales/Marketing:		Liberal Arts:		Information Systems:		Professionals:		Technical/Scientific:	
Mgmt. Trainees:		Mktg. Professionals:	Y	Gen. Writing/Editing:		Info. Management:	Y	Finance/Acct.:	Y	Engineers, Elec.:	
Experienced Mgmt.:	Y	Retail Sales:		Technical Writing:		Software Dev.:		Law:	Y	Engineers, Other:	
Int'l Business:		Commercial/Industrial:	Y	Graphic Arts/Photog.:		Hardware Dev.:		HR/Other:	Y	Health/Lab	
MBA Graduates:	Y	Sales Trainees:	Y	Music:		Consulting/Other:		Training:	Y	Scientists/Research:	
		Advertising Pros.:		Broadcasting:				Health Care:		Petroleum/Chemicals:	
				Other:				Consulting:		Math/Other:	

TYPES OF BUSINESS:

Poultry Production
Poultry Processing
Poultry Marketing & Distribution
Feed Mills

BRANDS/DIVISIONS/AFFILIATES:

Cagle's Farms Inc

CONTACTS:

Note: Officers with more than one job title may be intentionally listed here more than once.

J. Douglas Cagle, CEO
J. Douglas Cagle, Pres.
Harry C. Woodring, CFO
Harry C. Woodring, Corp. Sec.
Alvin B. Harp, VP-Live Oper.
Harry C. Woodring, Controller/Treas.
G. Doug Cagle, VP
J. David Cagle, VP
J. Douglas Cagle, Chmn.

Phone: 404-355-2820 **Fax:** 404-350-9605
Toll-Free:
Address: 1385 Collier Rd. NW, Atlanta, GA 30318 US

GROWTH PLANS/SPECIAL FEATURES:

Cagle's, Inc. and its wholly-owned subsidiary Cagle's Farms, Inc. produce, market and distribute a variety of fresh and frozen poultry products. The vertically integrated operations of the company consist of breeding, hatching and growing chickens; feed milling; processing; and marketing operations. Cagle's products are sold to national and regional independent and chain supermarkets; food distributors; food processing companies; national fast-food chains; and institutional users, such as restaurants, schools and distributors. The firm processes 1.93 million birds per week in its two processing plants, one in Georgia, the other in Alabama. Cagle's owns a hatchery located in Dalton, Georgia, with an aggregate capacity of 2.9 million eggs per week. After the chicks are hatched, the company places them with one of approximately 150 contract grower farms located in Georgia and Tennessee. The contract growers provide the housing, equipment, utilities and labor to grow the baby chicks to market age, while Cagle's supplies the baby chicks, the feed and all veterinary and technical services. To supply the needs of the growing birds, the company owns a feed mill in Rockmart, Georgia, with a production capacity of up to 15,000 tons a week. In addition to basic chicken products, the company offers value-added products, such as seasoned deli meats, deboned breast and thigh meat, cut-up marinated raw breaded chicken, fast-food cuts and IQF (individually quick frozen) products. Local distribution of chicken products is operated from warehouse facilities in Atlanta, Georgia and Collinsville, Alabama. In June 2011, the company disclosed plans to cut approximately 300 jobs at its processing facility in Georgia. In October 2011, Cagle's filed for Chapter 11 bankruptcy protection.

FINANCIALS:

Sales and profits are in thousands of dollars—add 000 to get the full amount. 2011 Note: Financial information for 2011 was not available for all companies at press time.

2011 Sales: $310,098 | 2011 Profits: $- 566
2010 Sales: $307,091 | 2010 Profits: $2,537
2009 Sales: $292,585 | 2009 Profits: $-11,494
2008 Sales: $283,649 | 2008 Profits: $- 773
2007 Sales: $233,936 | 2007 Profits: $ 559

U.S. Stock Ticker: CGL
Int'l Ticker:
Int'l Exchange:
Employees: 1,911 Fiscal Year Ends: 3/31
Parent Company:

SALARIES/BENEFITS:

Pension Plan: ESOP Stock Plan: Profit Sharing: Top Exec. Salary: $395,604 Bonus: $
Savings Plan: Stock Purch. Plan: Second Exec. Salary: $246,616 Bonus: $

OTHER THOUGHTS:

Apparent Women Officers or Directors:
Hot Spot for Advancement for Women/Minorities:

LOCATIONS: ("Y" = Yes)

West:	Southwest:	Midwest:	Southeast:	Northeast:	International:
			Y	Y	

CALAVO GROWERS INC

www.calavo.com

Industry Group Code: 1113

Management:		Sales/Marketing:		Liberal Arts:		Information Systems:		Professionals:		Technical/Scientific:	
Mgmt. Trainees:	Y	Mktg. Professionals:	Y	Gen. Writing/Editing:		Info. Management:	Y	Finance/Acct.:	Y	Engineers, Elec.:	
Experienced Mgmt.:	Y	Retail Sales:		Technical Writing:		Software Dev.:		Law:	Y	Engineers, Other:	
Int'l Business:	Y	Commercial/Industrial:	Y	Graphic Arts/Photog.:	Y	Hardware Dev.:		HR/Other:	Y	Health/Lab	
MBA Graduates:	Y	Sales Trainees:	Y	Music:		Consulting/Other:		Training:	Y	Scientists/Research:	
		Advertising Pros.:	Y	Broadcasting:				Health Care:		Petroleum/Chemicals:	
				Other:				Consulting:		Math/Other:	

TYPES OF BUSINESS:

Avocado Growing & Processing
Exotic Fruit
Fresh Produce
Processed & Frozen Avocado Products
Distribution

BRANDS/DIVISIONS/AFFILIATES:

El Dorado
Calavo Gold
Fresh Ripe
Maui Fresh International Inc
Hawaiian Sweet Inc
Hawaii Pride LLC
Calavo Salsa Lisa LLC
Renaissance Food Group LLC

CONTACTS: *Note: Officers with more than one job title may be intentionally listed here more than once.*

Lecil Cole, CEO
Art Bruno, COO
Lecil E. Cole, Pres.
Art Bruno, CFO
Robert Wedin, VP-Fresh Mktg. & Sales
Art Bruno, Corp. Sec.
Mike Browne, VP-Fresh Oper.
James Snyder, Corp. Controller
Al Ahmer, VP-Processed Oper. & Sales
Lecil Cole, Chmn.
Dionisio Ortiz, Dir.-Oper., Calavo de Mexico

Phone: 805-525-1245	**Fax:**
Toll-Free:	
Address: 1141-A Cummings Rd., Santa Paula, CA 93060 US	

GROWTH PLANS/SPECIAL FEATURES:

Calavo Growers, Inc. is engaged in the procurement and marketing of avocados and other perishable foods, as well as the preparation and distribution of processed avocado products. The firm delivers a wide array of fresh and processed food products to food distributors, produce wholesalers, supermarkets and restaurants internationally. It procures avocados primarily from California, Mexico and Chile, with additional imports from Peru, New Zealand and the Dominican Republic. The company operates in two business segments, fresh products and CalavoFoods. The fresh products business involves the distribution of fresh avocados, as well as other produce, such as papayas, pineapples and tomatoes, through its subsidiary Maui Fresh International. The CalavoFoods processed products segment processes avocados into a wide variety of guacamole products, including frozen and cold pasteurized fresh guacamole, as well as packaged pico de gallo recipes, salsas and avocado dips. Calavo's brand names include Avo Fresco, Bueno, Calavo Gold, Salsa Lisa, El Dorado, Fresh Ripe, Select, Taste of Paradise, Tico, Mfresh and Triggered Avocados. Additionally, the firm offers the ProRipeVIP program, which uses sonic technology to test avocados so that they may be delivered at a customer's specified state of ripeness. The company owns operating facilities in California, Texas, Hawaii, New Jersey, Arizona and Mexico. Additional subsidiaries include Calavo de Mexico S.A. de C.V.; Calavo Inversiones (Chile) Limitada; Calavo Salsa Lisa, LLC; Hawaiian Sweet, Inc.; and Hawaiian Pride, LLC. In June 2011, Calavo acquired Renaissance Food Group, LLC, a fresh-food company that produces, markets and distributes fresh produce, prepared salads and sandwiches and other food items.

Employees are offered medical, dental and vision insurance; life insurance; long-term disability coverage; a pension plan; and an employee assistance program.

FINANCIALS: **Sales and profits are in thousands of dollars—add 000 to get the full amount. 2011 Note: Financial information for 2011 was not available for all companies at press time.**

2011 Sales: $522,500	2011 Profits: $11,100	**U.S. Stock Ticker: CVGW**
2010 Sales: $398,351	2010 Profits: $17,764	**Int'l Ticker:**
2009 Sales: $344,765	2009 Profits: $13,611	Int'l Exchange:
2008 Sales: $361,474	2008 Profits: $7,725	Employees: 1,157 Fiscal Year Ends: 10/31
2007 Sales: $302,984	2007 Profits: $7,330	Parent Company:

SALARIES/BENEFITS:

Pension Plan: Y	ESOP Stock Plan:	Profit Sharing:	Top Exec. Salary: $496,012	Bonus: $492,792
Savings Plan:	Stock Purch. Plan:		Second Exec. Salary: $275,127	Bonus: $637,094

OTHER THOUGHTS:

Apparent Women Officers or Directors: 1
Hot Spot for Advancement for Women/Minorities:

LOCATIONS: ("Y" = Yes)

West:	Southwest:	Midwest:	Southeast:	Northeast:	International:
Y	Y	Y	Y	Y	Y

CALGON CARBON CORPORATION

www.calgoncarbon.com

Industry Group Code: 335991

Management:		Sales/Marketing:		Liberal Arts:		Information Systems:		Professionals:		Technical/Scientific:	
Mgmt. Trainees:		Mktg. Professionals:		Gen. Writing/Editing:		Info. Management:	Y	Finance/Acct.:	Y	Engineers, Elec.:	
Experienced Mgmt.:	Y	Retail Sales:		Technical Writing:	Y	Software Dev.:		Law:	Y	Engineers, Other:	
Int'l Business:	Y	Commercial/Industrial:	Y	Graphic Arts/Photog.:		Hardware Dev.:		HR/Other:	Y	Health/Lab	
MBA Graduates:	Y	Sales Trainees:		Music:		Consulting/Other:		Training:		Scientists/Research:	
		Advertising Pros.:		Broadcasting:				Health Care:		Petroleum/Chemicals:	
				Other:				Consulting:		Math/Other:	

TYPES OF BUSINESS:

Manufacturing-Activated Carbons
Purification & Treatment Systems
Reactivation Services
Consumer Products

BRANDS/DIVISIONS/AFFILIATES:

Calgon Sentinel
Calgon C3 Series
Calgon Rayox UV
AllGone
Hyde Marine, Inc.
Zwicky Sweden
Zwicky Denmark
Calgon Carbon Japan KK

CONTACTS: *Note: Officers with more than one job title may be intentionally listed here more than once.*

John S. Stanik, CEO
John S. Stanik, Pres.
Stevan R. Schott, CFO/VP
Gail A. Gerono, VP-Human Resources
Richard D. Rose, General Counsel/Sr. VP/Corp. Sec.
James A. Sullivan, VP-Oper., Americas
Gail A. Gerono, VP-Corp. Comm.
Gail A. Gerono, VP-Investor Rel.
Robert P. O'Brien, Exec. VP-Americas
John S. Stanik, Chmn.
C.H.S. Majoor, Exec. VP-Europe & Asia

Phone: 412-787-6700	**Fax:** 412-787-6676
Toll-Free: 800-422-7266	
Address: 400 Calgon Carbon Dr., Pittsburgh, PA 15205 US	

GROWTH PLANS/SPECIAL FEATURES:

Calgon Carbon Corporation is a global manufacturer and supplier of granular activated carbon and treatment systems for the purification, separation and concentration of liquids and gases. Calgon operates through three business segments: Activated Carbon and Service; Equipment; and Consumer. The Activated Carbon and Service business segment primarily sells activated carbon, which is capable of removing organic compounds from liquids and gases through a process of adsorption. Additionally, Calgon offers various related services, such as the reactivation of spent carbon, and the leasing, monitoring and maintenance of carbon fills at customer sites. The Equipment segment includes adsorption systems that are delivered and installed at treatment sites and used for vapor phase applications such as volatile organic compound control, air stripper off-gases, and landfill gas emissions. Calgon uses an advanced UV oxidation process to purify surface water. Liquid phase equipment systems are used for water purification, wastewater treatment, groundwater remediation and de-chlorination. Its product lines include the Sentinel line, designed to treat drinking water; the C3 Series wastewater disinfection product line; and Rayox UV advanced oxidation equipment for groundwater, process water and industrial wastewater. The Consumer segment's sells activated carbon in three product lines: PreZerve storage products, used to protect jewelry and keepsakes from deterioration; Purrfectly Fresh, a pet odor eliminator; and AllGone, an odor elimination system that utilizes activated carbon discs. In early 2010, the company acquired Zwicky Denmark and Sweden, distributors of its activated carbon products, and Hyde Marine, Inc., a water treatment systems producer. In March 2011, the firm acquired the remaining stake in its Japanese joint venture, Calgon Carbon Japan KK, previously jointly held by Mitsubishi Chemical Corporation.

The company offers its employees medical, dental and disability coverage; tuition reimbursement; a 401(k); and a discount stock purchase plan.

FINANCIALS: **Sales and profits are in thousands of dollars—add 000 to get the full amount. 2011 Note: Financial information for 2011 was not available for all companies at press time.**

2011 Sales: $541,472	2011 Profits: $39,224	**U.S. Stock Ticker: CCC**
2010 Sales: $482,341	2010 Profits: $34,850	**Int'l Ticker:**
2009 Sales: $411,910	2009 Profits: $39,159	Int'l Exchange:
2008 Sales: $400,270	2008 Profits: $28,840	Employees: 1,070 Fiscal Year Ends: 12/31
2007 Sales: $351,124	2007 Profits: $13,597	Parent Company:

SALARIES/BENEFITS:

Pension Plan:	ESOP Stock Plan:	Profit Sharing:	Top Exec. Salary: $527,909	Bonus: $372,000
Savings Plan: Y	Stock Purch. Plan: Y		Second Exec. Salary: $376,669	Bonus: $94,586

OTHER THOUGHTS:

Apparent Women Officers or Directors: 2
Hot Spot for Advancement for Women/Minorities:

LOCATIONS: ("Y" = Yes)

West:	Southwest:	Midwest:	Southeast:	Northeast:	International:
Y	Y	Y	Y	Y	Y

CALIBER HOLDINGS CORP

www.calibernet.com

Industry Group Code: 8111

Management:		**Sales/Marketing:**		**Liberal Arts:**		**Information Systems:**		**Professionals:**		**Technical/Scientific:**	
Mgmt. Trainees:	Y	Mktg. Professionals:	Y	Gen. Writing/Editing:	Y	Info. Management:	Y	Finance/Acct.:	Y	Engineers, Elec.:	
Experienced Mgmt.:	Y	Retail Sales:		Technical Writing:	Y	Software Dev.:	Y	Law:	Y	Engineers, Other:	
Int'l Business:		Commercial/Industrial:		Graphic Arts/Photog.:		Hardware Dev.:		HR/Other:	Y	Health/Lab	
MBA Graduates:	Y	Sales Trainees:		Music:		Consulting/Other:		Training:	Y	Scientists/Research:	
		Advertising Pros.:	Y	Broadcasting:				Health Care:		Petroleum/Chemicals:	
				Other:				Consulting:		Math/Other:	

TYPES OF BUSINESS:

Automotive Repair & Maintenance
Body Shops

BRANDS/DIVISIONS/AFFILIATES:

Caliber Collision Centers
CaliberCare Limited Lifetime Warranty

CONTACTS: *Note: Officers with more than one job title may be intentionally listed here more than once.*

Steve Grimshaw, CEO
Mark Sanders, COO
Steve Grimshaw, Pres.
Robert Kliewe, CFO
Anie Chinarian, Sr. VP-Human Resources & Training
Anie Chinarian, Sr. VP-Admin.
Rusty Barsanti, VP-Oper., Texas
Robert Tavarez, VP-Client Support
Todd Dillender, VP-Oper., Houston & North Texas
David Goldstein, VP-Oper., California
Matthew Ohrnstein, Chmn.
Dan Mossman, VP-Procurement

Phone: 949-224-0300	**Fax:** 949-224-0313
Toll-Free: 888-225-4237	
Address: 17771 Cowan Ave., Ste. 100, Irvine, CA 92614 US	

GROWTH PLANS/SPECIAL FEATURES:

Caliber Holdings Corp., one of the largest independent body shop companies in the U.S., operates a chain of 75 automotive repair shops located throughout southern California and Texas, including a large-scale, 90,000-square-foot collision repair center in Santa Monica, California. The company offers comprehensive collision repair, which includes the equipment necessary to repair composites, high-strength steel, aluminum, safety systems, on-board computers and complex finishes. Caliber Collision Centers work with 24-hour-a-day towing services, as well as rental car networks, with many of its locations featuring on-site Enterprise Rent-A-Car offices. In addition, the firm has partnered with most insurance companies in order to expedite and simplify repair. Caliber warrantees repair work against defects in materials and workmanship with its CaliberCare Limited Lifetime Warranty for as long as the customer owns the vehicle. The company also keeps its service centers open year-round, 24-hours-a-day.

Caliber offers its employees a benefits package including a cafeteria plan with medical and dental enrollment options, a 401(k) plan, flexible spending accounts, life insurance, an employee credit union, technical training and paid educational opportunities for continued advancement.

FINANCIALS: **Sales and profits are in thousands of dollars—add 000 to get the full amount. 2011 Note: Financial information for 2011 was not available for all companies at press time.**

2011 Sales: $	2011 Profits: $	**U.S. Stock Ticker: Private**
2010 Sales: $	2010 Profits: $	**Int'l Ticker:**
2009 Sales: $	2009 Profits: $	Int'l Exchange:
2008 Sales: $	2008 Profits: $	Employees: Fiscal Year Ends: 12/31
2007 Sales: $	2007 Profits: $	Parent Company:

SALARIES/BENEFITS:

Pension Plan:	ESOP Stock Plan:	Profit Sharing:	Top Exec. Salary: $	Bonus: $
Savings Plan: Y	Stock Purch. Plan:		Second Exec. Salary: $	Bonus: $

OTHER THOUGHTS:

Apparent Women Officers or Directors: 1
Hot Spot for Advancement for Women/Minorities:

LOCATIONS: ("Y" = Yes)

West:	Southwest:	Midwest:	Southeast:	Northeast:	International:
Y	Y				

CALIPER LIFE SCIENCES INC

www.caliperls.com

Industry Group Code: 334510

Management:		Sales/Marketing:		Liberal Arts:		Information Systems:		Professionals:		Technical/Scientific:	
Mgmt. Trainees:		Mktg. Professionals:	Y	Gen. Writing/Editing:		Info. Management:	Y	Finance/Acct.:	Y	Engineers, Elec.:	Y
Experienced Mgmt.:	Y	Retail Sales:		Technical Writing:	Y	Software Dev.:	Y	Law:	Y	Engineers, Other:	Y
Int'l Business:	Y	Commercial/Industrial:	Y	Graphic Arts/Photog.:		Hardware Dev.:	Y	HR/Other:	Y	Health/Lab	Y
MBA Graduates:	Y	Sales Trainees:	Y	Music:		Consulting/Other:		Training:	Y	Scientists/Research:	Y
		Advertising Pros.:		Broadcasting:				Health Care:	Y	Petroleum/Chemicals:	
				Other:				Consulting:		Math/Other:	Y

TYPES OF BUSINESS:

Bioanalysis Equipment
Microfluidic Systems
High-Throughput Screening Machines
Liquid Handling Systems
Drug Discovery Platforms
Laboratory Automation Solutions
Software
Contract Research

BRANDS/DIVISIONS/AFFILIATES:

Caliper Discovery Alliances & Services
IVIS
LabChip
PerkinElmer Inc

CONTACTS: *Note: Officers with more than one job title may be intentionally listed here more than once.*

E. Kevin Hrusovsky, CEO
E. Kevin Hrusovsky, Pres.
Robert F. Friel, CEO/Chmn.-PerkinElmer, Inc.

Phone: 508-435-9500 **Fax:** 508-435-3439
Toll-Free: 877-522-2447
Address: 68 Elm St., Hopkinton, MA 01748 US

GROWTH PLANS/SPECIAL FEATURES:

Caliper Life Sciences, Inc. provides products and services to the life sciences research community, including pharmaceutical and biotechnology companies, government institutions and other not-for-profit research organizations. The company produces integrated systems, consisting of instruments, software, reagents, laboratory automation tools and assay and discovery services. These technologies are designed to enable researchers not only to discover new drugs but to conduct environmental-related, agricultural and forensic testing as well as possible in vitro and in vivo diagnostic applications. The firm's product offerings are organized into three core business areas: optical molecular imaging (imaging), discovery research (research) and Caliper Discovery Alliances and Services (CDAS). The imaging business focuses on preclinical imaging and its activities include the expansion of its IVIS imaging instrument product lines, development of new therapeutic area applications and facilitating additional imaging modalities. The research segment is responsible for developing Caliper's core automation and microfluidic technologies, including its flagship product LabChip, for applications such as molecular biology sample preparation for genomics, protomics, cellular screening and forensics. CDAS, operated by subsidiary NovaScreen Biosciences, is responsible for expanding drug discovery collaborations and alliances and increasing sales of drug discovery services by providing outsourcing services and securing contracts with the Environmental Protection Agency under its ToxCast screening program. In November 2011, Caliper Life Sciences was acquired by PerkinElmer, Inc. and became a wholly-owned subsidiary.

The firm offers its employees medical, dental, vision, life and AD&D insurance; short- and long-term disability coverage; a 401(k); a discount stock purchase plan; tuition reimbursement; and an employee assistance plan.

FINANCIALS: **Sales and profits are in thousands of dollars—add 000 to get the full amount. 2011 Note: Financial information for 2011 was not available for all companies at press time.**

2011 Sales: $
2010 Sales: $123,696
2009 Sales: $130,412
2008 Sales: $134,054
2007 Sales: $140,707

2011 Profits: $
2010 Profits: $4,276
2009 Profits: $-8,225
2008 Profits: $-68,292
2007 Profits: $-24,080

U.S. Stock Ticker: Subsidiary
Int'l Ticker:
Int'l Exchange:
Employees: 469 Fiscal Year Ends: 12/31
Parent Company: PERKINELMER INC

SALARIES/BENEFITS:

Pension Plan: ESOP Stock Plan: Profit Sharing: Top Exec. Salary: $454,480 Bonus: $599,914
Savings Plan: Y Stock Purch. Plan: Y Second Exec. Salary: $280,485 Bonus: $129,584

OTHER THOUGHTS:

Apparent Women Officers or Directors: 2
Hot Spot for Advancement for Women/Minorities:

LOCATIONS: ("Y" = Yes)

West:	Southwest:	Midwest:	Southeast:	Northeast:	International:
Y				Y	Y

CAL-MAINE FOODS INC

www.calmainefoods.com

Industry Group Code: 112310

Management:		**Sales/Marketing:**		**Liberal Arts:**		**Information Systems:**		**Professionals:**		**Technical/Scientific:**	
Mgmt. Trainees:	Y	Mktg. Professionals:	Y	Gen. Writing/Editing:		Info. Management:	Y	Finance/Acct.:	Y	Engineers, Elec.:	
Experienced Mgmt.:	Y	Retail Sales:		Technical Writing:		Software Dev.:		Law:	Y	Engineers, Other:	
Int'l Business:		Commercial/Industrial:	Y	Graphic Arts/Photog.:	Y	Hardware Dev.:		HR/Other:	Y	Health/Lab	
MBA Graduates:	Y	Sales Trainees:	Y	Music:		Consulting/Other:		Training:	Y	Scientists/Research:	
		Advertising Pros.:	Y	Broadcasting:				Health Care:		Petroleum/Chemicals:	
				Other:				Consulting:		Math/Other:	

TYPES OF BUSINESS:

Egg Production
Shell Egg Production & Distribution

BRANDS/DIVISIONS/AFFILIATES:

Egg-Land's Best
Farmhouse
Rio Grande
Sunups
4-Grain
Cal-Maine

CONTACTS:

Note: Officers with more than one job title may be intentionally listed here more than once.

Adolphus B. Baker, CEO
Sherman Miller, COO/VP
Adolphus B. Baker, Pres.
Timothy A. Dawson, CFO/VP/Treas./Sec.
Jeff Hardin, VP-Sales
Jack B. Self, VP-Oper., Prod.
James Neeld, III, General Counsel
Bob Scott, VP-Oper.
Charles F. Collins, Controller/VP
Steve Storm, VP-Oper.
Matthew Arrowsmith, VP-Egg Sales
Joe M. Wyatt, VP-Feed Mill Div.
Jim Hull, VP-Egg Prod.
Fred R. Adams, Jr., Chmn.

Phone: 601-948-6813	**Fax:** 601-969-0905
Toll-Free:	
Address: 3320 Woodrow Wilson Dr., Jackson, MS 39209 US	

GROWTH PLANS/SPECIAL FEATURES:

Cal-Maine Foods, Inc. produces, grades, packages and markets fresh shell eggs to retailers in approximately 29 states in the Southeastern, Southwestern, Midwestern and Mid-Atlantic regions of the U.S. In 2011, Cal-Maine sold 821.4 million dozen shell eggs. Company owned facilities produce roughly 92% of the shell eggs the firm distributes. Customers include national and regional grocery store chains; club stores; egg product manufacturers; and food service distributors. The company's flock is comprised of 33.5 million layers (mature female chickens), pullets (young female chickens) and breeders (male or female chickens used to produce fertile eggs). Brands under which the company's eggs are marketed include Cal-Maine, Rio Grande and Sunups. Feed for the laying flocks is produced by company-owned and -operated mills located throughout the country, which have the capability of producing 700 tons of feed per hour. Cal-Maine also produces specialty shell eggs, such as reduced-cholesterol, cage-free and organic eggs, which are marketed under the Farmhouse, 4-Grain and Egg-Land's Best brands. Specialty shell eggs accounted for approximately 24% of 2011 sales. The firm is headquartered in Jackson, Mississippi and maintains additional facilities in Florida, Alabama, Arkansas, Georgia, Louisiana, Kansas, Kentucky, North Carolina, New Mexico, Ohio, Oklahoma, Tennessee, South Carolina, Utah and Texas.

FINANCIALS:

Sales and profits are in thousands of dollars—add 000 to get the full amount. 2011 Note: Financial information for 2011 was not available for all companies at press time.

2011 Sales: $941,981 — 2011 Profits: $60,839
2010 Sales: $910,143 — 2010 Profits: $67,823
2009 Sales: $928,812 — 2009 Profits: $79,500
2008 Sales: $915,939 — 2008 Profits: $151,861
2007 Sales: $598,128 — 2007 Profits: $36,656

U.S. Stock Ticker: CALM
Int'l Ticker:
Int'l Exchange:
Employees: 2,037 Fiscal Year Ends: 5/31
Parent Company:

SALARIES/BENEFITS:

Pension Plan: ESOP Stock Plan: Profit Sharing: Top Exec. Salary: $279,808 Bonus: $280,000
Savings Plan: Stock Purch. Plan: Second Exec. Salary: $250,000 Bonus: $250,000

OTHER THOUGHTS:

Apparent Women Officers or Directors:
Hot Spot for Advancement for Women/Minorities:

LOCATIONS: ("Y" = Yes)

West:	Southwest:	Midwest:	Southeast:	Northeast:	International:
Y	Y	Y	Y	Y	

CAMBREX CORP

www.cambrex.com

Industry Group Code: 325412

Management:		Sales/Marketing:		Liberal Arts:		Information Systems:		Professionals:		Technical/Scientific:	
Mgmt. Trainees:		Mktg. Professionals:	Y	Gen. Writing/Editing:		Info. Management:	Y	Finance/Acct.:	Y	Engineers, Elec.:	
Experienced Mgmt.:	Y	Retail Sales:		Technical Writing:	Y	Software Dev.:	Y	Law:	Y	Engineers, Other:	
Int'l Business:	Y	Commercial/Industrial:	Y	Graphic Arts/Photog.:		Hardware Dev.:		HR/Other:	Y	Health/Lab	Y
MBA Graduates:	Y	Sales Trainees:	Y	Music:		Consulting/Other:		Training:	Y	Scientists/Research:	Y
		Advertising Pros.:		Broadcasting:				Health Care:	Y	Petroleum/Chemicals:	Y
				Other:				Consulting:		Math/Other:	Y

TYPES OF BUSINESS:

Contract Pharmaceutical Manufacturing
Contract Research
Pharmaceutical Ingredients
Testing Products & Services

BRANDS/DIVISIONS/AFFILIATES:

Cambrex Charles City, Inc.
Cambrex Kariskoga AB
Cambrex Profarmaco Milano Srl
Cambrex Tallinn AS
Cambrex Zenara

CONTACTS: *Note: Officers with more than one job title may be intentionally listed here more than once.*

Steven M. Klosk, CEO
Shawn P. Cavanagh, COO/Exec. VP
Steven M. Klosk, Pres.
Gregory P. Sargen, CFO/VP
William M. Haskel, General Counsel/Sr. VP/Sec.
John Miller, Chmn.
Paolo Russolo, Pres., Cambrex Profarmaco Milano

Phone: 201-804-3000	**Fax:** 201-804-9852
Toll-Free: 866-286-9133	
Address: 1 Meadowlands Plz., East Rutherford, NJ 07073 US	

GROWTH PLANS/SPECIAL FEATURES:

Cambrex Corp. provides products and services to aid and enhance the discovery and commercialization of therapeutics. The firm manufactures products, which are sold to research organizations, pharmaceutical, biopharmaceutical and generic drug companies. It also provides testing services and safety assessments. Products include Cambrex Camouflage, a polymer resin-based drug delivery technology, which masks the bitter taste of certain drugs, as well as advanced pharmaceutical intermediates, enzyme-catalyzed biotransformers, controlled substances and fine chemicals. The firm also manufactures over 70 generic active pharmaceutical ingredients (APIs) for respiratory, pain management, cardiovascular, gastrointestinal, central nervous system and endocrine purposes. These APIs are developed by Italian subsidiary Cambrex Profarmaco Milano Srl and serve the pharmaceutical market in Italy, the U.S., Germany, Japan, France, Belgium, England and countries in Eastern Europe. Other subsidiaries of the firm include Cambrex Charles City, Inc. in Iowa; Cambrex Karlskoga AB in Sweden; and Cambrex Tallinn AS in Estonia. The firm also owns a 51% interest in Cambrex Zenara (formerly Zenara Pharma), an India-based pharmaceutical company. Cambrex Corp. currently owns 15 issued patents and has 13 patent applications pending in the U.S., and owns 139 patents and has 96 patent applications pending in other countries.

Cambrex offers its employees medical, dental, vision and prescription drug coverage; short- and long-term disability; a 401(k) plan; life and AD&D insurance; flexible spending accounts; education assistance; an employee assistance program; tuition reimbursement; scholarship awards; employee training courses; and business travel accident insurance.

FINANCIALS: **Sales and profits are in thousands of dollars—add 000 to get the full amount. 2011 Note: Financial information for 2011 was not available for all companies at press time.**

2011 Sales: $	2011 Profits: $	**U.S. Stock Ticker: CBM**
2010 Sales: $226,236	2010 Profits: $9,647	**Int'l Ticker:**
2009 Sales: $236,277	2009 Profits: $10,392	Int'l Exchange:
2008 Sales: $249,618	2008 Profits: $7,929	Employees: 829 Fiscal Year Ends: 12/31
2007 Sales: $252,574	2007 Profits: $209,248	Parent Company:

SALARIES/BENEFITS:

Pension Plan:	ESOP Stock Plan:	Profit Sharing:	Top Exec. Salary: $450,000	Bonus: $237,354
Savings Plan: Y	Stock Purch. Plan:		Second Exec. Salary: $344,968	Bonus: $181,955

OTHER THOUGHTS:

Apparent Women Officers or Directors: 2
Hot Spot for Advancement for Women/Minorities:

LOCATIONS: ("Y" = Yes)

West:	Southwest:	Midwest:	Southeast:	Northeast:	International:
		Y		Y	Y

CANTEL MEDICAL CORP

www.cantelmedical.com

Industry Group Code: 33911

Management:		Sales/Marketing:		Liberal Arts:		Information Systems:		Professionals:		Technical/Scientific:	
Mgmt. Trainees:		Mktg. Professionals:	Y	Gen. Writing/Editing:		Info. Management:	Y	Finance/Acct.:	Y	Engineers, Elec.:	
Experienced Mgmt.:	Y	Retail Sales:		Technical Writing:	Y	Software Dev.:		Law:	Y	Engineers, Other:	Y
Int'l Business:	Y	Commercial/Industrial:	Y	Graphic Arts/Photog.:		Hardware Dev.:		HR/Other:	Y	Health/Lab	Y
MBA Graduates:	Y	Sales Trainees:	Y	Music:		Consulting/Other:		Training:	Y	Scientists/Research:	Y
		Advertising Pros.:		Broadcasting:				Health Care:	Y	Petroleum/Chemicals:	
				Other:				Consulting:		Math/Other:	

TYPES OF BUSINESS:

Equipment-Disinfection & Disposable Equipment
Infection Control Products
Diagnostic Medical Equipment
Precision Instruments
Industrial Equipment
Water Treatment Equipment & Services
Maintenance Services
Dental Care Products

BRANDS/DIVISIONS/AFFILIATES:

Minntech Corp
Mar Cor Purification
Crosstex International Inc.
Saf-T-Pak

CONTACTS: *Note: Officers with more than one job title may be intentionally listed here more than once.*

Andrew Krakauer, CEO
Andrew Krakauer, Pres.
Craig A. Sheldon, CFO/Sr. VP/Treas.
Eric Nodiff, General Counsel/Sr. VP/Corp. Sec.
Steven Anaya, Controller/VP
Seth Segel, Exec. VP
Roy Malkin, CEO/Pres., Minntech Corporation
Charles Diker, Chmn.

Phone: 973-890-7220	**Fax:** 973-890-7270
Toll-Free:	
Address: 150 Clove Rd., 9th Fl., Little Falls, NJ 07424 US	

GROWTH PLANS/SPECIAL FEATURES:

Cantel Medical Corp. provides products and services for the control and prevention of infection. It operates through a diverse circle of subsidiaries. The dialysis, therapeutic filtration and endoscope reprocessing segments are operated through the Minntech Corporation, which develops, manufactures and markets disinfection and reprocessing systems and dialysate concentrates for renal dialysis; hollow fiber membrane filtration and separation technologies for medical applications; and medical device reprocessing systems, disinfectants, detergents and other supplies used to clean flexible endoscopes. The water purification and filtration segment, operated through Mar Cor Purification, offers water purification equipment and services, filtration and separation products and disinfectants to the medical, pharmaceutical, biotech, beverage and commercial industrial industries. The healthcare disposables segment, operated through Crosstex International, Inc., produces single-use infection control products primarily for the dental market, such as face masks, towels and bibs, tray covers, saliva ejectors, germicidal wipes, plastic cups, sterilization pouches and disinfectants. The specialty packaging segment is operated by Saf-T-Pak and provides specialty packaging and thermal control products, as well as compliance training for the transport of biological specimens and temperature-sensitive pharmaceutical, medical and other materials.

FINANCIALS: **Sales and profits are in thousands of dollars—add 000 to get the full amount. 2011 Note: Financial information for 2011 was not available for all companies at press time.**

2011 Sales: $321,651	2011 Profits: $20,425	**U.S. Stock Ticker: CMN**
2010 Sales: $273,952	2010 Profits: $19,941	**Int'l Ticker:**
2009 Sales: $260,050	2009 Profits: $15,569	Int'l Exchange:
2008 Sales: $249,374	2008 Profits: $8,693	Employees: 1,177 Fiscal Year Ends: 7/31
2007 Sales: $219,044	2007 Profits: $8,446	Parent Company:

SALARIES/BENEFITS:

Pension Plan:	ESOP Stock Plan:	Profit Sharing:	Top Exec. Salary: $437,500	Bonus: $441,000
Savings Plan:	Stock Purch. Plan:		Second Exec. Salary: $408,689	Bonus: $286,000

OTHER THOUGHTS:

Apparent Women Officers or Directors: 1
Hot Spot for Advancement for Women/Minorities:

LOCATIONS: ("Y" = Yes)

West:	Southwest:	Midwest:	Southeast:	Northeast:	International:
Y		Y	Y	Y	Y

CANTOR FITZGERALD LP

www.cantor.com

Industry Group Code: 523110

Management:		Sales/Marketing:		Liberal Arts:		Information Systems:		Professionals:		Technical/Scientific:	
Mgmt. Trainees:	Y	Mktg. Professionals:		Gen. Writing/Editing:	Y	Info. Management:	Y	Finance/Acct.:	Y	Engineers, Elec.:	
Experienced Mgmt.:	Y	Retail Sales:		Technical Writing:		Software Dev.:	Y	Law:	Y	Engineers, Other:	
Int'l Business:	Y	Commercial/Industrial:		Graphic Arts/Photog.:		Hardware Dev.:		HR/Other:	Y	Health/Lab	
MBA Graduates:	Y	Sales Trainees:		Music:		Consulting/Other:		Training:	Y	Scientists/Research:	
		Advertising Pros.:		Broadcasting:				Health Care:		Petroleum/Chemicals:	
				Other:				Consulting:		Math/Other:	

TYPES OF BUSINESS:

Stock Brokerage
Bond Trading
Financial Market Data
Risk Arbitrage
Asset Management
Investment Banking
Electronic Exchanges & Related Trading Technology
Online Casinos/Gaming

BRANDS/DIVISIONS/AFFILIATES:

Cantor Fitzgerald & Co
CantorCO2e
Cantor Insurance Group
LexNet
Cantor Spectrum & Tower Exchange
Cantor Prime Services
Cantor Gaming
Cantor Private Markets Group

CONTACTS: *Note: Officers with more than one job title may be intentionally listed here more than once.*

Howard W. Lutnick, CEO
Douglas R. Barnard, CFO
Paul M. Pion, Chief Admin. Officer/Sr. Managing Dir.
Stephen Merkel, General Counsel/Corp. Sec./Exec. Managing Dir.
Thomas Anzalone, Dir.-Global Oper./Exec. VP
Nneoma Njoku, Contact-Media
Steve Kantor, Exec. Managing Dir./Global Head-Investment Banking
Shawn Matthews, CEO-Cantor Fitzgerald & Co.
Michael Lehrman, Exec. Managing Dir./Deputy Head-Investment Banking
Howard W. Lutnick, Chmn.
Laurence Rose, Pres., Cantor Fitzgerald Canada/Sr. Managing Dir.

Phone: 212-938-5000	**Fax:** 212-829-5280
Toll-Free:	
Address: 110 E. 59th St., New York, NY 10022 US	

GROWTH PLANS/SPECIAL FEATURES:

Cantor Fitzgerald L.P. is a leading financial services provider to the institutional equity and fixed income markets, with products and services including sales and trading, investment banking, asset management, market data and market commentary. The company's sales and trading services include Debt Capital Markets (DCM) and Equity Capital Markets. DCM offers such services as repo and securities lending; credit securities; mortgage securities; structured products; small business administration (SBA) securities; interest rate products; and agency structures. Cantor's Equity Capital Markets includes its Domestic Equities desk; International Equities group; Equity Derivatives desk; Convertibles and Structured Products group; Portfolio Trading group; Risk Arbitrage and Relative Value Transactions desk; Stock Loan group; Cantor CFDs, a leading wholesale provider of Contracts for Difference (CFDs); and Cantor U.S. Equity Research. Subsidiary Cantor Fitzgerald & Co. provides investment banking services, as well as asset management, market data and market commentary. The company's brokerage services consist of Cantor Prime Services, a leading securities clearing intermediary; CantorCO2e, a leading provider of transaction, financing, technology and consultancy in the global environmental and alternative energy markets; Cantor Insurance Group, which focuses on the life settlement industry and operates the online marketplace, LexNet; and Cantor Spectrum & Tower Exchange, one of the first online, market-based exchanges for radio frequency spectrum rights, digital sub-channel distribution capacity, radio tower sales and rooftop assets. In June 2011, Cantor Gaming and Las Vegas Sands Corp. announced the signing of a long-term agreement for Cantor Gaming to operate the Race & Sports Books at The Venetian and Palazzo. In August 2011, the firm announced that it is expanding its exchange traded funds operations by launching an ETF arbitrage business in New York. In October 2011, Cantor announced the expansion of its private securities business with the formation of Cantor Private Markets Group.

FINANCIALS: **Sales and profits are in thousands of dollars—add 000 to get the full amount. 2011 Note: Financial information for 2011 was not available for all companies at press time.**

2011 Sales: $	2011 Profits: $	**U.S. Stock Ticker: Private**
2010 Sales: $	2010 Profits: $	**Int'l Ticker:**
2009 Sales: $	2009 Profits: $	Int'l Exchange:
2008 Sales: $	2008 Profits: $	Employees: 1,400 Fiscal Year Ends: 12/31
2007 Sales: $	2007 Profits: $	Parent Company:

SALARIES/BENEFITS:

Pension Plan:	ESOP Stock Plan:	Profit Sharing:	Top Exec. Salary: $	Bonus: $
Savings Plan:	Stock Purch. Plan:		Second Exec. Salary: $	Bonus: $

OTHER THOUGHTS:

Apparent Women Officers or Directors:
Hot Spot for Advancement for Women/Minorities:

LOCATIONS: ("Y" = Yes)

West:	Southwest:	Midwest:	Southeast:	Northeast:	International:
Y	Y	Y	Y	Y	Y

CAPITOL FEDERAL FINANCIAL INC

www.capfed.com

Industry Group Code: 522110

Management:		**Sales/Marketing:**		**Liberal Arts:**		**Information Systems:**		**Professionals:**		**Technical/Scientific:**	
Mgmt. Trainees:	Y	Mktg. Professionals:	Y	Gen. Writing/Editing:	Y	Info. Management:	Y	Finance/Acct.:	Y	Engineers, Elec.:	
Experienced Mgmt.:	Y	Retail Sales:		Technical Writing:		Software Dev.:		Law:	Y	Engineers, Other:	
Int'l Business:		Commercial/Industrial:		Graphic Arts/Photog.:		Hardware Dev.:		HR/Other:	Y	Health/Lab	
MBA Graduates:	Y	Sales Trainees:		Music:		Consulting/Other:		Training:	Y	Scientists/Research:	
		Advertising Pros.:	Y	Broadcasting:				Health Care:		Petroleum/Chemicals:	
				Other:				Consulting:		Math/Other:	

TYPES OF BUSINESS:

Banking
Mortgages
Consumer Lending
Construction Loans
Multi-Family Real Estate Loans

BRANDS/DIVISIONS/AFFILIATES:

Capitol Federal Savings Bank

CONTACTS:

Note: Officers with more than one job title may be intentionally listed here more than once.

John B. Dicus, CEO
John B. Dicus, Pres.
Kent G. Townsend, CFO/Exec. VP/Treas.
Richard J. Aleshire, Exec. VP-Retail Oper.
James D. Wempe, VP-Investor Rel.
Tara D. Van Houweling, Principal Acct. Officer/VP/Dir.-Reporting
Larry K. Brubaker, Exec. VP-Corp. Svcs.
Rick C. Jackson, Chief Lending Officer/Exec. VP
John C. Dicus, Chmn.

Phone: 785-235-1341 **Fax:** 785-231-6264
Toll-Free: 888-822-7333
Address: 700 S. Kansas Ave., Topeka, KS 66603 US

GROWTH PLANS/SPECIAL FEATURES:

Capitol Federal Financial, Inc. (CapFed) is the stock holding company for subsidiary Capitol Federal Savings Bank, which operates in Kansas. CapFed has total assets of $9.6 billion, a loan portfolio of $5.16 billion and deposits of $4.55 billion. The bank serves the metropolitan areas of Kansas City, Topeka, Wichita, Lawrence, Manhattan, Emporia and Salina, Kansas through 35 traditional and 11 in-store banking offices. The bank is the only operating subsidiary of CapFed. The company attracts retail deposits from the general public and invests those funds primarily in loans secured by mortgages on owner-occupied, single- or multi-family residences. It also originates consumer loans, construction loans secured by commercial real estate, multi-family real estate loans and a limited number of loans outside its market area. The company purchases residential mortgage loans from correspondent lenders located within its market areas and select market areas in Missouri as well as nationwide lenders. It also invests in certain investment and mortgage-related securities funded through retail deposits, advances from Federal Home Loan Bank Topeka and other borrowings. Mortgage loans originated by CapFed carry either a fixed or adjustable rate of interest and are generally long-term loans that amortize monthly. The firm offers a variety of deposit accounts, including passbook and passcard savings accounts, money market accounts, interest-bearing and non-interest-bearing checking accounts and certificates of deposit with terms that range from 91 days to 96 months. In December 2010, CapFed completed a restructuring and reorganization plan whereby the firm was converted to a stock holding company.

FINANCIALS:

Sales and profits are in thousands of dollars—add 000 to get the full amount. 2011 Note: Financial information for 2011 was not available for all companies at press time.

2011 Sales: $346,865 | 2011 Profits: $38,403
2010 Sales: $408,462 | 2010 Profits: $67,840
2009 Sales: $441,380 | 2009 Profits: $66,298
2008 Sales: $440,833 | 2008 Profits: $50,954
2007 Sales: $435,563 | 2007 Profits: $32,296

U.S. Stock Ticker: CFFN
Int'l Ticker:
Int'l Exchange:
Employees: 593 Fiscal Year Ends: 9/30
Parent Company:

SALARIES/BENEFITS:

Pension Plan: ESOP Stock Plan: Y Profit Sharing: Y Top Exec. Salary: $530,414 Bonus: $264,394
Savings Plan: Stock Purch. Plan: Second Exec. Salary: $232,916 Bonus: $85,534

OTHER THOUGHTS:

Apparent Women Officers or Directors: 1
Hot Spot for Advancement for Women/Minorities:

LOCATIONS: ("Y" = Yes)

West:	Southwest:	Midwest:	Southeast:	Northeast:	International:
		Y			

CARACO PHARMACEUTICAL LABORATORIES LTD

www.caraco.com

Industry Group Code: 325412

Management:		Sales/Marketing:		Liberal Arts:		Information Systems:		Professionals:		Technical/Scientific:	
Mgmt. Trainees:		Mktg. Professionals:	Y	Gen. Writing/Editing:		Info. Management:	Y	Finance/Acct.:	Y	Engineers, Elec.:	
Experienced Mgmt.:	Y	Retail Sales:		Technical Writing:	Y	Software Dev.:	Y	Law:	Y	Engineers, Other:	
Int'l Business:		Commercial/Industrial:	Y	Graphic Arts/Photog.:		Hardware Dev.:		HR/Other:	Y	Health/Lab	Y
MBA Graduates:	Y	Sales Trainees:	Y	Music:		Consulting/Other:		Training:	Y	Scientists/Research:	Y
		Advertising Pros.:		Broadcasting:				Health Care:	Y	Petroleum/Chemicals:	Y
				Other:				Consulting:		Math/Other:	Y

TYPES OF BUSINESS:

Drugs-Generic

BRANDS/DIVISIONS/AFFILIATES:

Sun Pharmaceutical Industries
Flumadine
Nicardipine HCl
Theophylline
Synalgos-DC

CONTACTS: *Note: Officers with more than one job title may be intentionally listed here more than once.*

Singh Sachdeva, CEO
Mukul Rathi, Interim CFO
Thomas Versosky, Dir.-Bus. Strategies
Robert Kurkiewicz, Sr. VP-Regulatory Affairs
Jayesh Shah, Dir.-Commercial
Dilip S. Shanghvi, Chmn.

Phone: 313-871-8400 **Fax:** 313-871-8314
Toll-Free: 800-818-4555
Address: 1150 Elijah McCoy Dr., Detroit, MI 48202 US

GROWTH PLANS/SPECIAL FEATURES:

Caraco Pharmaceutical Laboratories, Ltd. develops, manufactures and markets generic and private-label drugs for prescription and over-the-counter markets. The company's product portfolio includes 42 products in 93 strengths and various package sizes. These drugs relate to a variety of therapeutic segments, including arthritis, pain control, epilepsy, diabetes, antipsychotic and neurological disorders. Pharmaceutical products that the company produces include Flumadine, an influenza A virus medication; Nicardipine HCl, a calcium ion influx inhibitor for the short-term treatment of hypertension; Theophylline, which is used to treat the symptoms of chronic asthma and other chronic lung diseases, and Synalgos-DC, a prescription pain killer. The company also has several drugs awaiting FDA approval. The company has collaborative agreements with several companies, with the most prominent being Sun Pharmaceutical Industries (Sun Pharma), the majority stock holder of Caraco. Under these agreements, Caraco develops generic drugs for each company to market as its own brand. The firm distributes its products through wholesalers, chain drug stores, retail pharmacies, mail-order companies, managed care organizations, hospital groups and nursing homes. Some of the wholesalers that distribute Caraco's products include Amerisource-Bergen Corporation; McKesson Corporation; and Cardinal Health. In July 2010, the company started marketing generic Flomax, Wellbutrin, Optivar and Exelon. In June 2011, the company merged with its majority stock holder, Sun Pharmaceutical Industries, with Caraco being the surviving entity. Subsequent to the merger, Caraco delisted from the New York Stock Exchange.

The company offered employees medical, dental and vision insurance; a 401(k) plan; life insurance; short- and long-term disability coverage; and health and dependent care accounts.

FINANCIALS: **Sales and profits are in thousands of dollars—add 000 to get the full amount. 2011 Note: Financial information for 2011 was not available for all companies at press time.**

2011 Sales: $	2011 Profits: $	**U.S. Stock Ticker: Private**
2010 Sales: $233,674	2010 Profits: $-8,660	**Int'l Ticker:**
2009 Sales: $337,177	2009 Profits: $20,537	Int'l Exchange:
2008 Sales: $350,367	2008 Profits: $35,388	Employees: 535 Fiscal Year Ends: 3/31
2007 Sales: $117,027	2007 Profits: $26,858	Parent Company:

SALARIES/BENEFITS:

Pension Plan:	ESOP Stock Plan:	Profit Sharing:	Top Exec. Salary: $243,104	Bonus: $
Savings Plan: Y	Stock Purch. Plan:		Second Exec. Salary: $177,692	Bonus: $

OTHER THOUGHTS:

Apparent Women Officers or Directors:
Hot Spot for Advancement for Women/Minorities:

LOCATIONS: ("Y" = Yes)

West:	Southwest:	Midwest:	Southeast:	Northeast:	International:
		Y			

CARBO CERAMICS INC

www.carboceramics.com

Industry Group Code: 213112

Management:		**Sales/Marketing:**		**Liberal Arts:**		**Information Systems:**		**Professionals:**		**Technical/Scientific:**	
Mgmt. Trainees:		Mktg. Professionals:	Y	Gen. Writing/Editing:		Info. Management:	Y	Finance/Acct.:	Y	Engineers, Elec.:	Y
Experienced Mgmt.:	Y	Retail Sales:		Technical Writing:	Y	Software Dev.:		Law:	Y	Engineers, Other:	Y
Int'l Business:	Y	Commercial/Industrial:	Y	Graphic Arts/Photog.:		Hardware Dev.:		HR/Other:	Y	Health/Lab	
MBA Graduates:	Y	Sales Trainees:	Y	Music:		Consulting/Other:		Training:	Y	Scientists/Research:	
		Advertising Pros.:		Broadcasting:				Health Care:		Petroleum/Chemicals:	Y
				Other:				Consulting:		Math/Other:	

TYPES OF BUSINESS:

Drilling Supplies
Hydraulic Fracturing Proppants
Hydraulic Fracture Diagnostic & Design Services
Reservoir Diagnostics
Fracture Simulation Software

BRANDS/DIVISIONS/AFFILIATES:

CARBOHSP
CARBOPROP
CARBOLITE
CARBOECONOPROP
CARBOTAG
StrataGen Engineering
FracproPT

CONTACTS: *Note: Officers with more than one job title may be intentionally listed here more than once.*

Gary Kolstad, CEO
Gary Kolstad, Pres.
Ernesto Bautista, III, CFO/VP
David G. Gallagher, VP-Mktg. & Sales
R. Sean Elliott, General Counsel/Sec./Chief Compliance Officer
Mark L. Edmunds, VP-Oper.
William Morris, Chmn.

Phone: 281-921-6400 **Fax:** 281-921-6401
Toll-Free:
Address: 575 N. Dairy Ashford, Ste. 300, Houston, TX 77079 US

GROWTH PLANS/SPECIAL FEATURES:

Carbo Ceramics, Inc. is a leading worldwide provider of ceramic proppants, which are materials used in hydraulic fracturing of oil and natural gas wells. The firm is one of the largest suppliers of this specialized product in the world. Proppants are granular structures, such as ceramic or sand, contained in the liquids that companies use to fracture the inside of an oil or natural gas well in order to increase the flow of hydrocarbons. The proppant slips into the fractures in order to hold them open after the high-pressure pumping stops, keeping the cracks wide enough for natural gas or oil to slip through. Ceramic proppants are usually on the higher-end of the cost range due to greater strength and more uniform size and shape. The firm's Proppant unit has five main products: CARBOHSP and CARBOPROP, high-strength products designed for use in deep gas wells; and CARBOLITE, CARBOHYDROPROP and CARBOECONOPROP, lighter-weight products designed for use in gas wells of moderate depth and oil wells. The company also offers CARBOTAG, a patent pending process of adding over 20 chemical markers to proppants during production that allow an operator to identify the precise well or fracture stage that is failing and allowing the flow of proppant back to the surface. Other well products include the firm's FracproPT fracture simulation software, which aids in the design and modeling of fractures. The firm provides consulting services to drilling and exploration companies through StrataGen Engineering.

FINANCIALS: **Sales and profits are in thousands of dollars—add 000 to get the full amount. 2011 Note: Financial information for 2011 was not available for all companies at press time.**

2011 Sales: $625,700	2011 Profits: $130,100	**U.S. Stock Ticker: CRR**
2010 Sales: $473,082	2010 Profits: $78,716	**Int'l Ticker:**
2009 Sales: $341,872	2009 Profits: $52,810	Int'l Exchange:
2008 Sales: $387,828	2008 Profits: $110,316	Employees: 806 Fiscal Year Ends: 12/31
2007 Sales: $299,996	2007 Profits: $53,870	Parent Company:

SALARIES/BENEFITS:

Pension Plan:	ESOP Stock Plan:	Profit Sharing: Y	Top Exec. Salary: $600,000	Bonus: $816,710
Savings Plan: Y	Stock Purch. Plan:		Second Exec. Salary: $272,500	Bonus: $363,472

OTHER THOUGHTS:

Apparent Women Officers or Directors:
Hot Spot for Advancement for Women/Minorities:

LOCATIONS: ("Y" = Yes)

West:	Southwest:	Midwest:	Southeast:	Northeast:	International:
Y	Y		Y		Y

CARDIONET INC

www.cardionet.com

Industry Group Code: 33911

Management:		Sales/Marketing:		Liberal Arts:		Information Systems:		Professionals:		Technical/Scientific:	
Mgmt. Trainees:		Mktg. Professionals:	Y	Gen. Writing/Editing:		Info. Management:	Y	Finance/Acct.:	Y	Engineers, Elec.:	Y
Experienced Mgmt.:	Y	Retail Sales:		Technical Writing:	Y	Software Dev.:		Law:	Y	Engineers, Other:	
Int'l Business:		Commercial/Industrial:	Y	Graphic Arts/Photog.:		Hardware Dev.:	Y	HR/Other:	Y	Health/Lab	Y
MBA Graduates:	Y	Sales Trainees:	Y	Music:		Consulting/Other:		Training:	Y	Scientists/Research:	Y
		Advertising Pros.:		Broadcasting:				Health Care:	Y	Petroleum/Chemicals:	
				Other:				Consulting:		Math/Other:	

TYPES OF BUSINESS:

Mobile Cardiac Monitoring Equipment
Mobile Cardiac Monitoring Services

BRANDS/DIVISIONS/AFFILIATES:

Mobile Cardiac Outpatient Telemetry (MCOT)
CardioNet Monitoring Center
Biotel, Inc.

CONTACTS: *Note: Officers with more than one job title may be intentionally listed here more than once.*

Joseph H. Capper, CEO
Joseph H. Capper, Pres.
Heather Getz, CFO/Sr. VP
Andy Broadway, VP-Mktg.
George Hrenko, Sr. VP-Human Resources & Organizational Excellence
Charles Gropper, Sr. VP-R&D
Bill Swavely, VP-IT
Peter Ferola, General Counsel
Anna McNamara, Sr. VP-Clinical Oper.
Peter Ferola, Sr. VP-Corp. Dev.
Anthony Schuler, Sr. VP-Sales
Daniel Wisniewski, Sr. VP-Bus. Oper.
Jareer Kasrawi, Sr. VP-Strategic Contracting
Randy H. Thurman, Chmn.

Phone: 610-729-7000 **Fax:** 610-828-8048
Toll-Free: 888-312-2328
Address: 227 Washington St., Conshohocken, PA 19428 US

GROWTH PLANS/SPECIAL FEATURES:

CardioNet, Inc. offers cardiac monitoring equipment to medical professionals in 49 states. Its primary product is the Mobile Cardiac Outpatient Telemetry (MCOT) device. MCOT automatically detects a patient's cardiac rhythm irregularities and transmits this electrocardiogram (ECG or EKG) data to the continuously staffed CardioNet Monitoring Center in Conshohocken, Pennsylvania. CardioNet's MCOT service incorporates a lightweight patient-worn sensor attached to electrodes that capture two-channel ECG data, measuring electrical activity of the heart and communicating wirelessly with a compact, handheld monitor. At the CardioNet Monitoring Center, certified cardiac monitoring specialists analyze the sent data, respond to urgent events and report results in the manner prescribed by the physician. The MCOT devices currently store 21 days of ECG data. MCOT employs two-way wireless communications, permitting physicians to remotely adjust monitoring parameters and request previous ECG data from the memory stored in the monitor. Since its initial FDA approval, CardioNet has released five generations of MCOT monitoring devices (C5), offering expanded wireless transmitting capabilities and improved user interface characteristics. To date, physicians have enrolled over 400,000 patients in the company's MCOT services. Besides MCOT, CardioNet also offers conventional heart monitors: Holter monitors and event monitors. Holter monitors cover a generic class of patient-worn ECG equipment that records heart arrhythmias over a 1-2 day period on a tape or other storage medium, which must be delivered by hand, mail or Internet to be analyzed. Event monitors, typically worn for 30 days, store up to 10 minutes of ECG data that is typically transmitted to the physician via a home or cellular telephone. CardioNet packages and repairs its equipment, while third-party Jabil Circuit, Inc. manufactures the original equipment in Tempe, Arizona. In December 2010, the firm acquired Biotel, Inc. for roughly $11.6 million.

Employees are offered medical, dental and vision insurance; flexible spending accounts; disability insurance; life insurance; and a transportation allowance.

FINANCIALS: **Sales and profits are in thousands of dollars—add 000 to get the full amount. 2011 Note: Financial information for 2011 was not available for all companies at press time.**

2011 Sales: $	2011 Profits: $
2010 Sales: $119,924	2010 Profits: $-19,860
2009 Sales: $140,621	2009 Profits: $-20,476
2008 Sales: $120,454	2008 Profits: $9,205
2007 Sales: $72,992	2007 Profits: $- 358

U.S. Stock Ticker: BEAT
Int'l Ticker:
Int'l Exchange:
Employees: 754 Fiscal Year Ends: 12/31
Parent Company:

SALARIES/BENEFITS:

Pension Plan:	ESOP Stock Plan:	Profit Sharing:	Top Exec. Salary: $308,868	Bonus: $
Savings Plan: Y	Stock Purch. Plan: Y		Second Exec. Salary: $307,846	Bonus: $89,700

OTHER THOUGHTS:

Apparent Women Officers or Directors: 3
Hot Spot for Advancement for Women/Minorities: Y

LOCATIONS: ("Y" = Yes)

West:	Southwest:	Midwest:	Southeast:	Northeast:	International:
Y			Y	Y	

CARDTRONICS INC

www.cardtronics.com

Industry Group Code: 522320

Management:		Sales/Marketing:		Liberal Arts:		Information Systems:		Professionals:		Technical/Scientific:	
Mgmt. Trainees:	Y	Mktg. Professionals:	Y	Gen. Writing/Editing:	Y	Info. Management:	Y	Finance/Acct.:	Y	Engineers, Elec.:	
Experienced Mgmt.:	Y	Retail Sales:		Technical Writing:	Y	Software Dev.:	Y	Law:	Y	Engineers, Other:	
Int'l Business:	Y	Commercial/Industrial:	Y	Graphic Arts/Photog.:		Hardware Dev.:		HR/Other:	Y	Health/Lab	
MBA Graduates:	Y	Sales Trainees:	Y	Music:		Consulting/Other:		Training:	Y	Scientists/Research:	
		Advertising Pros.:	Y	Broadcasting:				Health Care:		Petroleum/Chemicals:	
				Other:				Consulting:		Math/Other:	

TYPES OF BUSINESS:

ATM Network Management
ATM Process Outsourcing
Primary Branding Programs

BRANDS/DIVISIONS/AFFILIATES:

Allpoint Network
EDC ATM Subsidiary LLC
Efmark Deployment I Inc
LocatorSearch LLC
Access to Money Inc
Mr. Cash ATM Network Inc

CONTACTS: *Note: Officers with more than one job title may be intentionally listed here more than once.*

Steven Rathgaber, CEO
J. Chris Brewster, CFO
Tom Pierce, Chief Mktg. Officer
Debra Bonder, Exec. VP-Human Resources
Jerry Garcia, CIO
Bill Knoll, Exec. VP-Prod. Mgmt.
Michael E. Keller, General Counsel/Corp. Sec.
Jeffery B. Keith, Exec. VP-Global Oper.
Todd Ruden, Sr. VP-Planning/Treas.
Brad Conrad, Chief Acct. Officer
Rick Updyke, Pres., U.S. Bus. Group
Michael Clinard, Pres., Global Svcs.
Tres Thompson, Exec. VP-Domestic ATM Svcs.
Ben Psillas, Exec. VP-Network/Financial Svcs.
Dennis Lynch, Chmn.
Ron Delnevo, Managing Dir.-U.K. & Europe

Phone: 832-308-4000 **Fax:** 832-308-4001
Toll-Free: 800-786-9666
Address: 3250 Briarpark Dr., Ste. 400, Houston, TX 77042 US

GROWTH PLANS/SPECIAL FEATURES:

Cardtronics, Inc. is a single-source provider of automated teller machines (ATMs), ATM management and equipment related services. Its clients include large, national retailers, as well as smaller retailers and operators of facilities such as shopping malls and airports. Cardtronics operates 52,900 devices throughout the U.S. and worldwide. Approximately 15,400 of the company's ATMs have a branding arrangement with one of 53 domestic financial institutions. The company operates the Allpoint Network, one of the largest surcharge-free ATM networks in the U.S. based on the number of participating ATMs. Cardtronics deploys and operates its ATMs under two types of arrangements with its merchant customers: company-owned and merchant-owned. Under company-owned arrangements, which represent roughly 64% of its ATM network, Cardtronics provides the ATM and is typically responsible for all aspects of its operation, including transaction processing, procuring cash, supplies and telecommunications as well as routine and technical maintenance. Under merchant-owned arrangements, which represent roughly 36% of its ATM network, the merchant owns the ATM and is usually responsible for providing cash and performing simple maintenance tasks, while Cardtronics provides more complex maintenance services, transaction processing and connection to electronic funds transfer networks. The company's revenues are recurring in nature and are primarily derived from ATM surcharge fees, which are paid by the cardholders, and interchange fees, which are paid by the cardholder's financial institution. Additional revenue is generated by branding company ATMs with signage from banks and other financial institutions, resulting in surcharge-free access to its ATMs. In January 2011, the Allpoint Network was extended into Mexico. In 2011, Cardtronics acquired EDC ATM Subsidiary, LLC; Efmark Deployment I, Inc.; LocatorSearch, LLC; Access to Money, Inc.; and Mr. Cash ATM Network, Inc.

Employees are offered medical, dental and vision insurance; health care and dependent care spending accounts; life and disability coverage; and a 401(k).

FINANCIALS: **Sales and profits are in thousands of dollars—add 000 to get the full amount. 2011 Note: Financial information for 2011 was not available for all companies at press time.**

2011 Sales: $624,576 — 2011 Profits: $70,233
2010 Sales: $532,078 — 2010 Profits: $41,133
2009 Sales: $493,353 — 2009 Profits: $5,771
2008 Sales: $493,014 — 2008 Profits: $-72,937
2007 Sales: $378,298 — 2007 Profits: $-27,090

U.S. Stock Ticker: CATM
Int'l Ticker:
Int'l Exchange:
Employees: 535 Fiscal Year Ends: 12/31
Parent Company:

SALARIES/BENEFITS:

Pension Plan:	ESOP Stock Plan:	Profit Sharing:	Top Exec. Salary: $481,250	Bonus: $615,075
Savings Plan: Y	Stock Purch. Plan:		Second Exec. Salary: $385,632	Bonus: $332,923

OTHER THOUGHTS:

Apparent Women Officers or Directors: 3
Hot Spot for Advancement for Women/Minorities:

LOCATIONS: ("Y" = Yes)

West:	Southwest:	Midwest:	Southeast:	Northeast:	International:
	Y			Y	Y

CARRIZO OIL & GAS INC

www.crzo.net

Industry Group Code: 211111

Management:		Sales/Marketing:		Liberal Arts:		Information Systems:		Professionals:		Technical/Scientific:	
Mgmt. Trainees:		Mktg. Professionals:		Gen. Writing/Editing:		Info. Management:	Y	Finance/Acct.:	Y	Engineers, Elec.:	
Experienced Mgmt.:	Y	Retail Sales:		Technical Writing:		Software Dev.:		Law:	Y	Engineers, Other:	Y
Int'l Business:	Y	Commercial/Industrial:		Graphic Arts/Photog.:		Hardware Dev.:		HR/Other:	Y	Health/Lab	
MBA Graduates:	Y	Sales Trainees:		Music:		Consulting/Other:		Training:	Y	Scientists/Research:	
		Advertising Pros.:		Broadcasting:				Health Care:		Petroleum/Chemicals:	Y
				Other:				Consulting:		Math/Other:	

TYPES OF BUSINESS:

Oil & Gas Exploration & Production

BRANDS/DIVISIONS/AFFILIATES:

CONTACTS: *Note: Officers with more than one job title may be intentionally listed here more than once.*

S.P. Johnson, IV, CEO
Brad Fisher, COO/VP
S.P. Johnson, IV, Pres.
Paul F. Boling, CFO/VP/Corp. Sec.
Gregory E. Evans, VP-Exploration & Dev.
Gerry Morton, General Counsel
Gerry Morton, VP-Bus. Dev.
Richard Hunter, VP-Investor Rel.
David Pitts, Chief Acct. Officer
Jim Pritts, VP-Bus. Dev.
Richard H. Smith, VP-Land
Andrew R. Agosto, VP-Bus. Dev.
Steven A. Webster, Chmn.

Phone: 713-328-1000	**Fax:** 713-328-1035
Toll-Free:	
Address: 1000 Louisiana St., Ste. 1500, Houston, TX 77002 US	

GROWTH PLANS/SPECIAL FEATURES:

Carrizo Oil & Gas, Inc. is engaged in the exploration, development, production and transportation of natural gas and oil. The company operates onshore in proven oil- and gas-producing zones along the Gulf Coast, primarily in the Barnett Shale area in north Texas; and the Marcellus Shale play in Pennsylvania, New York, West Virginia and Virginia. The firm also explores for, develops and produces natural gas and oil in onshore Gulf Coast areas in Texas, Louisiana and Alabama, primarily in the Miocene, Wilcox, Frio and Vicksburg trends. Carrizo utilizes 3-D seismic-driven exploratory and development drilling and horizontal drilling and hydraulic-fracturing technologies to evaluate resource prospects. The company currently has licenses for over 13,784 square miles of 3-D seismic data for processing and evaluation. In 2010, Carrizo participated in the drilling of 88 gross (44.6 net) wells, with an apparent success rate of 97% overall and 100% in the Barnett Shale. The firm leases approximately 44,810 acres in the Barnett Shale and over 117,921 acres in the Marcellus Shale. It also has licenses to explore in the U.K. North Sea. Other shale plays the firm has interests in include Fayetteville in Arkansas; Camp Hill Field in Texas; Floyd/Neal in Mississippi; and the New Albany in Kentucky and Illinois. The firm has approximately 670 billion cubic feet of natural gas equivalent in proved reserves.

Carrizo offers its employees health, dental and vision insurance; life and long-term disability insurance; flexible spending accounts; parking and public transportation subsidies; and a 401(k) plan.

FINANCIALS: **Sales and profits are in thousands of dollars—add 000 to get the full amount. 2011 Note: Financial information for 2011 was not available for all companies at press time.**

2011 Sales: $	2011 Profits: $	**U.S. Stock Ticker: CRZO**
2010 Sales: $139,462	2010 Profits: $9,950	**Int'l Ticker:**
2009 Sales: $114,079	2009 Profits: $-204,845	Int'l Exchange:
2008 Sales: $216,677	2008 Profits: $-45,047	Employees: 132 Fiscal Year Ends: 12/31
2007 Sales: $125,789	2007 Profits: $15,469	Parent Company:

SALARIES/BENEFITS:

Pension Plan:	ESOP Stock Plan:	Profit Sharing:	Top Exec. Salary: $448,000	Bonus: $
Savings Plan: Y	Stock Purch. Plan:		Second Exec. Salary: $312,000	Bonus: $

OTHER THOUGHTS:

Apparent Women Officers or Directors:
Hot Spot for Advancement for Women/Minorities:

LOCATIONS: ("Y" = Yes)

West:	Southwest:	Midwest:	Southeast:	Northeast:	International:
	Y		Y	Y	Y

CATALYST HEALTH SOLUTIONS INC www.catalysthealthsolutions.com

Industry Group Code: 522320A

Management:		Sales/Marketing:		Liberal Arts:		Information Systems:		Professionals:		Technical/Scientific:	
Mgmt. Trainees:	Y	Mktg. Professionals:	Y	Gen. Writing/Editing:	Y	Info. Management:	Y	Finance/Acct.:	Y	Engineers, Elec.:	
Experienced Mgmt.:	Y	Retail Sales:		Technical Writing:	Y	Software Dev.:	Y	Law:	Y	Engineers, Other:	
Int'l Business:	Y	Commercial/Industrial:	Y	Graphic Arts/Photog.:		Hardware Dev.:		HR/Other:	Y	Health/Lab	
MBA Graduates:	Y	Sales Trainees:		Music:		Consulting/Other:		Training:	Y	Scientists/Research:	
		Advertising Pros.:		Broadcasting:				Health Care:	Y	Petroleum/Chemicals:	
				Other:				Consulting:		Math/Other:	

TYPES OF BUSINESS:

Pharmacy Benefits Management
Prescription Mail Service

BRANDS/DIVISIONS/AFFILIATES:

Catalyst Rx
HospiScript Services LLC
Immediate Pharmaceutical Services, Inc.
FutureScripts, LLC
FutureScripts Secure, LLC
Walgreens Health Initiatives, Inc.

CONTACTS: *Note: Officers with more than one job title may be intentionally listed here more than once.*

David T. Blair, CEO
Richard Bates, COO
Richard Bates, Pres.
Timothy R. Pearson, CFO/Exec. VP
Bruce Metge, General Counsel/Corp. Sec.
Wayne Dix, Sr. VP-Oper. & Bus. Transformation
Babette Edgar, Pres., Gov't Svcs.
Richard Keane, Pres., Employer Segment
Chris Myers, Sr. VP-Member Svcs.
Andrew Brynes, CFO-Bus. Transformation
Edward S. Civera, Chmn.

Phone: 301-548-2900	**Fax:**
Toll-Free: 800-323-6640	
Address: 800 King Farm Blvd., 4th Fl., Rockville, MD 20850 US	

GROWTH PLANS/SPECIAL FEATURES:

Catalyst Health Solutions, Inc. (Catalyst) is a full-service Pharmacy Benefit Management (PBM) company, providing benefits to more than 7 million members throughout the U.S. and Puerto Rico. Catalyst's services include the development and implementation of pharmacy benefit programs through customized plan designs, clinical programs, physician orientation programs and member education. Clients include self-insured employers, including state and local governments; managed care organizations (MCOs); unions; third-party administrators; hospices; and individuals. The company provides clients with access to a contracted, non-exclusive national network of approximately 63,000 pharmacies. Catalyst is based in Maryland, but also has satellite offices in 18 U.S. states and Puerto Rico. The firm operates primarily under the brand name Catalyst Rx, also the name of its largest operating subsidiary. Other subsidiaries include HospiScript Services LLC, a provider of pharmacy medication therapy management services to the hospice industry; and Immediate Pharmaceutical Services, Inc., a prescription mail service facility based in Ohio. In 2010, Catalyst's largest customers, Wellmark Blue Cross Blue Shield of Iowa and the State of Maryland, accounted for 14% and 10% of its consolidated revenue, respectively. In September 2010, the firm acquired PBM subsidiaries FutureScripts, LLC and FutureScripts Secure, LLC from insurance company Independence Blue Cross. In June 2011, it completed the acquisition of Walgreens' PBM subsidiary, Walgreens Health Initiatives, Inc.

The company offers its employees medical, dental and vision insurance; a 401(k) plan; life insurance; disability benefits; a 529 college savings plan; flexible spending accounts; an employee stock purchase plan; an employee assistance program; educational assistance; health club benefits; and transportation benefits.

FINANCIALS: **Sales and profits are in thousands of dollars—add 000 to get the full amount. 2011 Note: Financial information for 2011 was not available for all companies at press time.**

2011 Sales: $5,329,594	2011 Profits: $66,988	**U.S. Stock Ticker: CHSI**
2010 Sales: $3,764,092	2010 Profits: $80,957	**Int'l Ticker:**
2009 Sales: $2,894,380	2009 Profits: $65,165	Int'l Exchange:
2008 Sales: $2,543,379	2008 Profits: $50,394	Employees: 1,036 Fiscal Year Ends: 12/31
2007 Sales: $1,857,697	2007 Profits: $39,268	Parent Company:

SALARIES/BENEFITS:

Pension Plan:	ESOP Stock Plan:	Profit Sharing:	Top Exec. Salary: $760,385	Bonus: $1,275,000
Savings Plan: Y	Stock Purch. Plan: Y		Second Exec. Salary: $523,103	Bonus: $

OTHER THOUGHTS:

Apparent Women Officers or Directors: 1
Hot Spot for Advancement for Women/Minorities:

LOCATIONS: ("Y" = Yes)

West:	Southwest:	Midwest:	Southeast:	Northeast:	International:
Y	Y	Y	Y	Y	Y

CELLDEX THERAPEUTICS INC

www.celldextherapeutics.com

Industry Group Code: 325412

Management:		Sales/Marketing:		Liberal Arts:		Information Systems:		Professionals:		Technical/Scientific:	
Mgmt. Trainees:		Mktg. Professionals:		Gen. Writing/Editing:		Info. Management:	Y	Finance/Acct.:	Y	Engineers, Elec.:	
Experienced Mgmt.:	Y	Retail Sales:		Technical Writing:	Y	Software Dev.:	Y	Law:	Y	Engineers, Other:	
Int'l Business:		Commercial/Industrial:	Y	Graphic Arts/Photog.:		Hardware Dev.:		HR/Other:	Y	Health/Lab	Y
MBA Graduates:	Y	Sales Trainees:		Music:		Consulting/Other:		Training:		Scientists/Research:	Y
		Advertising Pros.:		Broadcasting:				Health Care:	Y	Petroleum/Chemicals:	Y
				Other:	Y			Consulting:		Math/Other:	Y

TYPES OF BUSINESS:

Drugs - Vaccines & Immunotherapeutics
Drugs - Oncology, Inflammatory Disease & Infectious Disease

BRANDS/DIVISIONS/AFFILIATES:

CDX-1135
CholeraGarde
Rotarix
CholeraGarde
CDX-110
CDX-1307
APC Targeting Technology

CONTACTS: *Note: Officers with more than one job title may be intentionally listed here more than once.*

Anthony S. Marucci, CEO
Anthony S. Marucci, Pres.
Avery W. (Chip) Catlin, CFO/Sr. VP
Tibor Keler, Chief Scientific Officer/Sr. VP
Ronald A. Pepin, Chief Business Officer/Sr. VP
Thomas Davis, Chief Medical Officer/Sr. VP
Larry Ellberger, Chmn.

Phone: 781-433-0771	**Fax:** 781-433-0262
Toll-Free:	
Address: 119 4th Ave., Needham, MA 02494 US	

GROWTH PLANS/SPECIAL FEATURES:

Celldex Therapeutics, Inc. is a biopharmaceutical company that applies its Precision Targeted Immunotherapy Platform to generate a pipeline of candidates to treat cancer and other difficult-to-treat diseases. The company's APC Targeting Technology uses human monoclonal antibodies linked to disease associated antigens to efficiently deliver the attached antigens to immune cells known as antigen presenting cells (APC). The firm's immunotherapy platform includes a complementary portfolio of monoclonal antibodies, antibody-targeted vaccines and immunomodulators to create novel disease-specific drug candidates. Celldex currently has one product on the market, five products in clinical development and four products in preclinical development. Its marketed product, Rotarix, is a rotavirus vaccine. In Phase II trials are its CDX-110 vaccine for the tumor specific molecule EGFRvIII and CDX-011, which targets glycoprotein NMB that is expressed in a variety of human cancers, including breast cancer and melanoma. In Phase I is CDX-1307, its primary ACP Targeting Technology product candidate, for the treatment of colorectal, pancreatic, bladder, ovarian and breast cancers. Its Phase I/2 candidates are CDX-1401 for multiple solid tumors; and CDX-1135 for renal disease. In pre-clinical development are its CDX-1127 for immuno-modulation and solid tumors; CDX-1189 for renal disease; CDX-301 for cancer, autoimmune disease and transplants; and CDX-014 for renal and ovarian cancer. The company's bacterial vaccines are the CholeraGarde cholera vaccine, the Ty800 typhoid vaccine and the ETEC E. coli vaccine.

Employees are offered medical, dental and vision coverage; flexible spending accounts; life and AD&D insurance; disability coverage; a 401(k) plan; an employee assistance program; educational assistance; and an employee stock purchase plan.

FINANCIALS: **Sales and profits are in thousands of dollars—add 000 to get the full amount. 2011 Note: Financial information for 2011 was not available for all companies at press time.**

2011 Sales: $	2011 Profits: $	**U.S. Stock Ticker: CLDX**
2010 Sales: $46,793	2010 Profits: $-2,533	**Int'l Ticker:**
2009 Sales: $15,180	2009 Profits: $-36,525	Int'l Exchange:
2008 Sales: $7,456	2008 Profits: $-47,501	Employees: 94 Fiscal Year Ends: 12/31
2007 Sales: $1,406	2007 Profits: $-15,073	Parent Company:

SALARIES/BENEFITS:

Pension Plan:	ESOP Stock Plan:	Profit Sharing:	Top Exec. Salary: $464,945	Bonus: $126,146
Savings Plan: Y	Stock Purch. Plan: Y		Second Exec. Salary: $367,573	Bonus: $83,179

OTHER THOUGHTS:

Apparent Women Officers or Directors: 1
Hot Spot for Advancement for Women/Minorities:

LOCATIONS: ("Y" = Yes)

West:	Southwest:	Midwest:	Southeast:	Northeast:	International:
				Y	

CELSIS INTERNATIONAL PLC

www.celsis.com

Industry Group Code: 621511

Management:		Sales/Marketing:		Liberal Arts:		Information Systems:		Professionals:		Technical/Scientific:	
Mgmt. Trainees:		Mktg. Professionals:		Gen. Writing/Editing:		Info. Management:	Y	Finance/Acct.:	Y	Engineers, Elec.:	
Experienced Mgmt.:	Y	Retail Sales:		Technical Writing:	Y	Software Dev.:	Y	Law:	Y	Engineers, Other:	
Int'l Business:	Y	Commercial/Industrial:	Y	Graphic Arts/Photog.:		Hardware Dev.:		HR/Other:	Y	Health/Lab	Y
MBA Graduates:	Y	Sales Trainees:		Music:		Consulting/Other:		Training:		Scientists/Research:	Y
		Advertising Pros.:		Broadcasting:				Health Care:	Y	Petroleum/Chemicals:	Y
				Other:				Consulting:		Math/Other:	Y

TYPES OF BUSINESS:

Microbial Contamination Detection Instruments
Laboratory Services Outsourcing
Microbiotics Detection

BRANDS/DIVISIONS/AFFILIATES:

Celsis Rapid Detection
Celsis In Vitro Technologies
Celsis Analytical Services
RapiScreen
AKuScreen
ReACT
Nastor Investment Limited

CONTACTS:

Note: Officers with more than one job title may be intentionally listed here more than once.

Jay LeCoque, CEO
Jack Rowell, Chmn.

Phone: 312-476-1200	**Fax:** 312-476-1201
Toll-Free:	
Address: 600 W. Chicago Ave., Ste. 625, Chicago, IL 60654-2822 US	

GROWTH PLANS/SPECIAL FEATURES:

Celsis International plc is a global provider of life sciences products and laboratory services to the pharmaceutical and consumer products industries. Its core technology involves bioluminescence-based technology, in which ATP (adenosine triphosphate), a nucleotide present in all biological matter, is catalyzed to produce light (as in the abdomen of a firefly). The firm operates through three divisions: Celsis Rapid Detection, Celsis In Vitro Technologies and Celsis Analytical Services. Celsis Rapid Detection uses proprietary enzyme technology to develop and supply screening systems, including instruments, software and reagents, for the rapid detection of microbial contamination in pharmaceutical and consumer products. Celsis' detection product lines include RapiScreen and AKuScreen assays. Celsis In Vitro Technologies uses proprietary hepatocyte (liver cell) and cryopreservation technologies to provide in vitro testing products for pharmaceutical and biotechnological companies, and is a leading provider of ADME-Tox products for drug discovery and development. Celsis Analytical Services provides outsourced laboratory testing services, including analytical chemistry and microbiological laboratory services and stability testing and storage programs, to pharmaceutical, biopharmaceutical, medical device and consumer products companies. The firm has offices in the U.K., the U.S., France, the Netherlands, Germany and Belgium. Celsis serves the pharmaceuticals, personal care, home care, consumer products and food and beverage industries. It is owned by Nastor Investment Limited.

FINANCIALS:

Sales and profits are in thousands of dollars—add 000 to get the full amount. 2011 Note: Financial information for 2011 was not available for all companies at press time.

2011 Sales: $	2011 Profits: $	**U.S. Stock Ticker: Private**
2010 Sales: $	2010 Profits: $	**Int'l Ticker:**
2009 Sales: $52,500	2009 Profits: $6,800	Int'l Exchange:
2008 Sales: $52,900	2008 Profits: $6,700	Employees: 262 Fiscal Year Ends: 3/31
2007 Sales: $47,441	2007 Profits: $5,921	Parent Company: NASTOR INVESTMENT LIMITED

SALARIES/BENEFITS:

Pension Plan:	ESOP Stock Plan:	Profit Sharing:	Top Exec. Salary: $451,523	Bonus: $151,235
Savings Plan: Y	Stock Purch. Plan:		Second Exec. Salary: $394,485	Bonus: $142,078

OTHER THOUGHTS:

Apparent Women Officers or Directors:
Hot Spot for Advancement for Women/Minorities:

LOCATIONS: ("Y" = Yes)

West:	Southwest:	Midwest:	Southeast:	Northeast:	International:
		Y		Y	Y

CENTRAL VERMONT PUBLIC SERVICE CORP

www.cvps.com

Industry Group Code: 2211

Management:		Sales/Marketing:		Liberal Arts:		Information Systems:		Professionals:		Technical/Scientific:	
Mgmt. Trainees:		Mktg. Professionals:	Y	Gen. Writing/Editing:	Y	Info. Management:	Y	Finance/Acct.:	Y	Engineers, Elec.:	Y
Experienced Mgmt.:	Y	Retail Sales:		Technical Writing:		Software Dev.:		Law:	Y	Engineers, Other:	Y
Int'l Business:	Y	Commercial/Industrial:	Y	Graphic Arts/Photog.:		Hardware Dev.:		HR/Other:	Y	Health/Lab	
MBA Graduates:	Y	Sales Trainees:	Y	Music:		Consulting/Other:		Training:	Y	Scientists/Research:	
		Advertising Pros.:		Broadcasting:				Health Care:		Petroleum/Chemicals:	Y
				Other:				Consulting:		Math/Other:	

TYPES OF BUSINESS:

Utilities-Electric
Real Estate Services
Wind, Biomass & Hydroelectric Power
Nuclear Power
Bovine Methane Power

BRANDS/DIVISIONS/AFFILIATES:

C.V. Realty, Inc
East Barnet
Custom
CRC
SmartEnergy Water Heating Services, Inc
Vermont Marble Power Division
Gaz Metro Limited Partnership
Green Mountain Power Corp

CONTACTS: *Note: Officers with more than one job title may be intentionally listed here more than once.*

Lawrence J. Reilly, CEO
Lawrence J. Reilly, Pres.
Pamela J. Keefe, CFO/Sr. VP
Joseph M. Kraus, Sr. VP-Eng.
Dale A. Rocheleau, General Counsel/Sr. VP/Corp. Sec.
Joseph M. Kraus, Sr. VP-Oper./Customer Svcs.
Joan F. Gamble, VP-Strategic Change & Bus. Svcs.
Brian P. Keefe, VP-Gov't & Public Affairs
Pamela J. Keefe, Treas.
William J. Deehan, VP-Power Planning & Regulatory Affairs

Phone: 802-773-2711 **Fax:** 802-747-2199
Toll-Free: 800-649-2877
Address: 77 Grove St., Rutland, VT 05701 US

GROWTH PLANS/SPECIAL FEATURES:

Central Vermont Public Service Corp. (CVPS) is one of the largest energy and utility businesses in Vermont, engaging in the purchase, production, transmission, distribution and sale of electricity. The firm's primary source of revenue is from retail electricity sales, with lesser revenues produced from the sale of power to third parties in New England and to ISO-NE, the operator of the region's bulk power system. CVPS serves 159,000 customers in 163 communities, with 2010 earnings of $21 million. The firms 23 generating stations are operated as a single system, interconnecting the transmission lines of Transco, New England Power and PSNH to produce a nameplate capability of 74.3 megawatts (MW). These include: 20 hydroelectric facilities, two oil-fired gas turbines and one diesel plant. Joint investment is owned in three generating facilities and one transmission facility. CVPS operates 616 miles of overhead transmission lines; 8,486 miles of overhead distribution lines; and 478 miles of underground distribution lines, all predominantly within Vermont, with some coverage throughout New Hampshire and New York. The firm's properties include 722 miles of high-voltage overhead and underground transmission lines and related substations. The firm's wholly-owned subsidiaries include: C.V. Realty, Inc; East Barnet, created to finance and construct a Vermont hydroelectric facility; Custom, a passive investment holding company; and CRC, an unregulated business investment holding company. CRC wholly owns SmartEnergy Water Heating Svcs., Inc., a water heater sales and rental company operating throughout Vermont and New Hampshire. In March 2011, CVPS purchased Vermont Marble Power Division and their subsequent operating territory for $29 million. In July 2011, the company announced the sale of CVPS to Gaz Metro Limited Partnership. CVPS will be combined with Gaz Metro subsidiary Green Mountain Power Corporation. The deal was expected to close during the second quarter of 2012.

Employment benefits include: health insurance; 401(k) with a 4.25% match; and wellness offerings.

FINANCIALS: **Sales and profits are in thousands of dollars—add 000 to get the full amount. 2011 Note: Financial information for 2011 was not available for all companies at press time.**

2011 Sales: $ | 2011 Profits: $
2010 Sales: $341,925 | 2010 Profits: $20,954
2009 Sales: $342,098 | 2009 Profits: $20,749
2008 Sales: $342,162 | 2008 Profits: $16,385
2007 Sales: $329,107 | 2007 Profits: $15,804

U.S. Stock Ticker: CV
Int'l Ticker:
Int'l Exchange:
Employees: 517 Fiscal Year Ends: 12/31
Parent Company: GAZ METRO LTD PARTNERSHIP

SALARIES/BENEFITS:

Pension Plan: Y | ESOP Stock Plan: | Profit Sharing: | Top Exec. Salary: $410,000 | Bonus: $16,191
Savings Plan: Y | Stock Purch. Plan: | | Second Exec. Salary: $228,000 | Bonus: $16,370

OTHER THOUGHTS:

Apparent Women Officers or Directors: 4
Hot Spot for Advancement for Women/Minorities: Y

LOCATIONS: ("Y" = Yes)

West:	Southwest:	Midwest:	Southeast:	Northeast:	International:
				Y	Y

CEPHEID

Industry Group Code: 334510

www.cepheid.com

Management:		Sales/Marketing:		Liberal Arts:		Information Systems:		Professionals:		Technical/Scientific:	
Mgmt. Trainees:		Mktg. Professionals:	Y	Gen. Writing/Editing:		Info. Management:	Y	Finance/Acct.:	Y	Engineers, Elec.:	Y
Experienced Mgmt.:	Y	Retail Sales:		Technical Writing:	Y	Software Dev.:	Y	Law:	Y	Engineers, Other:	Y
Int'l Business:	Y	Commercial/Industrial:	Y	Graphic Arts/Photog.:		Hardware Dev.:	Y	HR/Other:	Y	Health/Lab	Y
MBA Graduates:	Y	Sales Trainees:	Y	Music:		Consulting/Other:		Training:	Y	Scientists/Research:	Y
		Advertising Pros.:		Broadcasting:				Health Care:	Y	Petroleum/Chemicals:	
				Other:				Consulting:		Math/Other:	Y

TYPES OF BUSINESS:

Equipment-Biological Testing
Genetic Profiling
DNA Analysis Systems
Molecular Diagnostics

BRANDS/DIVISIONS/AFFILIATES:

Smart Cycler
GeneXpert
GeneXpert Infinity

CONTACTS:

Note: Officers with more than one job title may be intentionally listed here more than once.

John L. Bishop, CEO
Humberto Reyes, COO/Exec. VP
Andrew D. Miller, CFO/Sr. VP
Mike Fitzgerald, Sr. VP-Human Resources
Michael Bates, VP-Oncology R&D
David H. Persing, CTO/Chief Medical Officer/Exec. VP
Joseph H. Smith, Sr. VP-Legal/Corp. Sec.
Nicolaas Arnold, Exec. VP-Worldwide Commercial Oper.
Joseph H. Smith, Sr. VP-Bus. Dev.
Jared Tipton, Dir.-Corp. Comm.
Kerry Flom, Sr. VP-Clinical Affairs & Regulatory Submissions
Robert Kwiatkowski, VP-Infectious Disease R&D
Thomas L. Gutshall, Chmn.
Paul Steuperaert, Pres., Cepheid SAS

Phone: 408-541-4191 **Fax:** 408-541-4192
Toll-Free: 888-838-3222
Address: 904 Caribbean Dr., Sunnyvale, CA 94089 US

GROWTH PLANS/SPECIAL FEATURES:

Cepheid is a molecular diagnostics company that develops, manufactures and markets fully integrated systems for the clinical genetic assessment, life sciences, industrial and biothreat markets. Cepheid systems enable rapid molecular testing for organisms and genetic-based diseases by implementing automated technology to reduce the complicated and time-intensive steps that are usually involved in molecular testing, such as sample preparation, DNA amplification and detection of targeted genes. The company's two principal system platforms are the GeneXpert and the SmartCycler systems. The GeneXpert system integrates sample preparation and nucleic acid extraction and purification with DNA amplification and detection, while the SmartCycler integrates DNA amplification and detection in order to rapidly analyze samples. One of the latest additions to the GeneXpert product line, the GeneXpert Infinity System, is capable of performing up to 1,300 different molecular tests in a 24 hour period with Xpert tests that typically require less than two minutes of hands-on time per test. Both systems are designed for a variety of user types ranging from reference laboratories and hospital central laboratories to satellite testing locations, such as hospital intensive care units and doctors' offices. In addition, the GeneXpert is suitable for applications in the biothreat market. Other products include tests designed for use with both the GeneXpert and SmartCycler systems such as in vitro diagnostics (IVD) medical devices, Analyte Specific Reagents (ASRs) and Research Use Only (RUO) tests with applications in the healthcare industry. In February 2011, the firm announced plans to collaborate with the Foundation for Innovative New Diagnostics (FIND) on the development of a rapid molecular test for HIV.

Cepheid offers full and part-time employees medical, dental and vision coverage; flexible spending accounts; an employee assistance plan; an income protection plan; an employee stock purchase plan; and a 401(k).

FINANCIALS:

Sales and profits are in thousands of dollars—add 000 to get the full amount. 2011 Note: Financial information for 2011 was not available for all companies at press time.

2011 Sales: $ — 2011 Profits: $
2010 Sales: $212,468 — 2010 Profits: $-5,917
2009 Sales: $170,627 — 2009 Profits: $-22,502
2008 Sales: $169,627 — 2008 Profits: $-22,387
2007 Sales: $129,473 — 2007 Profits: $-21,423

U.S. Stock Ticker: CPHD
Int'l Ticker:
Int'l Exchange:
Employees: 576 Fiscal Year Ends: 12/31
Parent Company:

SALARIES/BENEFITS:

Pension Plan: ESOP Stock Plan: Profit Sharing:
Savings Plan: Y Stock Purch. Plan: Y
Top Exec. Salary: $537,500 Bonus: $330,000
Second Exec. Salary: $397,785 Bonus: $159,440

OTHER THOUGHTS:

Apparent Women Officers or Directors: 1
Hot Spot for Advancement for Women/Minorities:

LOCATIONS: ("Y" = Yes)

West:	Southwest:	Midwest:	Southeast:	Northeast:	International:
Y		Y		Y	Y

CERUS CORPORATION

www.cerus.com

Industry Group Code: 325412

Management:		**Sales/Marketing:**		**Liberal Arts:**		**Information Systems:**		**Professionals:**		**Technical/Scientific:**	
Mgmt. Trainees:		Mktg. Professionals:		Gen. Writing/Editing:		Info. Management:	Y	Finance/Acct.:	Y	Engineers, Elec.:	
Experienced Mgmt.:	Y	Retail Sales:		Technical Writing:	Y	Software Dev.:	Y	Law:	Y	Engineers, Other:	
Int'l Business:	Y	Commercial/Industrial:	Y	Graphic Arts/Photog.:		Hardware Dev.:		HR/Other:	Y	Health/Lab	Y
MBA Graduates:	Y	Sales Trainees:		Music:		Consulting/Other:		Training:	Y	Scientists/Research:	Y
		Advertising Pros.:		Broadcasting:				Health Care:	Y	Petroleum/Chemicals:	Y
				Other:	Y			Consulting:		Math/Other:	Y

TYPES OF BUSINESS:

Pharmaceutical Development
Cancer Vaccines
Blood Treatment Systems

BRANDS/DIVISIONS/AFFILIATES:

INTERCEPT
Helinx
Cerus Europe BV

CONTACTS: *Note: Officers with more than one job title may be intentionally listed here more than once.*

William M. Greenman, CEO
William M. Greenman, Pres.
Laurence M. Corash, Chief Medical Officer/Sr. VP
Lori L. Roll, VP-Admin./Corp. Sec.
Howard G. Ervin, VP-Legal Affairs/Chief Legal Officer
Lainie Corten, Dir.- Global Comm.
Kevin D. Green, VP-Finance/Chief Acct. Officer
B. J. Cassin, Chmn.
Caspar Hogeboom, Gen. Mgr.-Europe

Phone: 925-288-6000	**Fax:** 925-288-6001
Toll-Free:	
Address: 2550 Stanwell Dr., Concord, CA 94520 US	

GROWTH PLANS/SPECIAL FEATURES:

Cerus Corporation develops and commercializes novel, proprietary products and technologies within the field of blood safety. Cerus is developing and commercializing the INTERCEPT Blood System for platelets, plasma and red blood cells, which is based on the company's proprietary Helinx technology for controlling biological replication. INTERCEPT is designed to enhance the safety of donated blood components by inactivating viruses, bacteria, parasites and other pathogens, as well as potentially harmful white blood cells. Cerus' Helinx technology prevents the replication of the DNA or RNA of susceptible pathogens, such as hepatitis B, hepatitis C and HIV. INTERCEPT for platelets and plasma is marketed in the European Union and undergoing clinical trials in the US. Trials for INTERCEPT for red blood cells were temporarily halted due to unsatisfactory results in 2003, but a new round of testing has begun. The firm licenses its technology to other companies for international distribution, including subsidiary Cerus Europe B.V., for Europe and BioOne Corporation for select Asian countries. A number of distribution agreements exist for partners in various other countries, including some in Europe, South America and the Middle East. The company owns about 25 US and 74 foreign patents relating to INTERCEPT. In August 2010, the firm agreed to acquire BioOne Corporation's Asian distribution rights to INTERCEPT.

Employees of the firm are offered medical, dental, and vision coverage; life insurance; tuition reimbursement; flexible spending accounts; stock options; and an employee stock purchase plan.

FINANCIALS: **Sales and profits are in thousands of dollars—add 000 to get the full amount. 2011 Note: Financial information for 2011 was not available for all companies at press time.**

2011 Sales: $	2011 Profits: $	**U.S. Stock Ticker: CERS**
2010 Sales: $23,109	2010 Profits: $-16,911	**Int'l Ticker:**
2009 Sales: $17,982	2009 Profits: $-24,135	Int'l Exchange:
2008 Sales: $16,507	2008 Profits: $-29,181	Employees: 79 Fiscal Year Ends: 12/31
2007 Sales: $11,044	2007 Profits: $-45,304	Parent Company:

SALARIES/BENEFITS:

Pension Plan:	ESOP Stock Plan:	Profit Sharing:	Top Exec. Salary: $490,000	Bonus: $194,040
Savings Plan: Y	Stock Purch. Plan: Y		Second Exec. Salary: $353,125	Bonus: $86,625

OTHER THOUGHTS:

Apparent Women Officers or Directors: 3
Hot Spot for Advancement for Women/Minorities: Y

LOCATIONS: ("Y" = Yes)

West:	Southwest:	Midwest:	Southeast:	Northeast:	International:
Y					Y

CF INDUSTRIES HOLDINGS INC

www.cfindustries.com

Industry Group Code: 11511

Management:		Sales/Marketing:		Liberal Arts:		Information Systems:		Professionals:		Technical/Scientific:	
Mgmt. Trainees:		Mktg. Professionals:		Gen. Writing/Editing:		Info. Management:	Y	Finance/Acct.:	Y	Engineers, Elec.:	
Experienced Mgmt.:	Y	Retail Sales:		Technical Writing:		Software Dev.:		Law:	Y	Engineers, Other:	
Int'l Business:	Y	Commercial/Industrial:	Y	Graphic Arts/Photog.:		Hardware Dev.:		HR/Other:	Y	Health/Lab	
MBA Graduates:	Y	Sales Trainees:		Music:		Consulting/Other:		Training:		Scientists/Research:	
		Advertising Pros.:		Broadcasting:				Health Care:		Petroleum/Chemicals:	
				Other:				Consulting:		Math/Other:	

TYPES OF BUSINESS:

Phosphate & Nitrogen Fertilizers

BRANDS/DIVISIONS/AFFILIATES:

CF Industries, Inc.
Terra Industries Inc

CONTACTS:

Note: Officers with more than one job title may be intentionally listed here more than once.

Stephen R. Wilson, CEO
Stephen R. Wilson, Pres.
Bert Frost, VP-Sales & Market Dev.
Wendy Jablow Spertus, VP-Human Resources
Frank N. Buzzanca, VP-Eng.
W. Anthony Will, VP-Mfg. & Dist.
Doug Barnard, General Counsel/VP/Sec.
Lynn F. White, VP-Corp. Dev.
Rosemary L. O'Brien, VP-Public Affairs
Terry Hulch, Sr. Dir.-Investor Rel.
Richard A. Hoker, Corp. Controller/VP
Herschel E. Morris, VP-Phosphate Oper.
Randall W. Selgrad, Treas./VP
Louis M. Frey, III, VP/Gen. Mgr.-Donaldsonville Nitrogen Complex
Russell A. Holowachuk, VP/Gen. Mgr.-Medicine Hat Nitrogen Complex
Stephen R. Wilson, Chmn.
Phillipp P. Koch, VP-Supply Chain

Phone: 847-405-2400 **Fax:** 847-405-2711
Toll-Free:
Address: 4 Parkway N., Ste. 400, Deerfield, IL 60015 US

GROWTH PLANS/SPECIAL FEATURES:

CF Industries Holdings, Inc. (CF) is a global manufacturer and distributor of fertilizer products, operating primarily through its subsidiary CF Industries, Inc. The company's operations are organized into two business segments: nitrogen and phosphate. The nitrogen business' principal products are ammonia, urea, urea ammonium nitrate solution (UAN), ammonium nitrate (AN), diesel exhaust fluid (DEF) and aqua ammonia Principal products in the phosphate fertilizer business are diammonium phosphate (DAP) and monoammonium phosphate (MAP). Through its operating segments, the firm owns or maintains an ownership interest in facilities in Donaldsonville, Louisiana; Medicine Hat, Alberta; and Tampa, Plant City and Hardee County, Florida. CF also owns and rents facilities at 85 in-market storage terminals and warehouses in 20 states across the U.S. The company's largest production facility is the Donaldsonville Nitrogen Complex, which contains five ammonia plants, five urea plants and two UAN plants. The plant has the capacity to produce over 4.5 million tons of ammonia, liquid urea and UAN a year. The company's largest manufacturing plant in Canada is the Medicine Hat Nitrogen Complex, which has the capacity to produce approximately 1.1 million tons of ammonia and 800,000 tons of urea per year. The company's main phosphate fertilizer manufacturer, Plant City Phosphate Complex, produces 2.1 million tons of fertilizer a year, receiving its phosphate rock supply from CF's Hardee County mine. The firm also owns a 50% interest in KEYTRADE AG, a fertilizer trading company in Switzerland. In 2010, the company acquired Terra Industries, Inc., a nitrogen products producer. In January 2011, the firm agreed to sell four of its dry product warehouses to GROWMARK, Inc.

Employers are offered medical and dental insurance; disability coverage; a 401(k) plan; educational assistance; flexible spending accounts; automobile and home insurance; long-term care insurance; and life insurance.

FINANCIALS:

Sales and profits are in thousands of dollars—add 000 to get the full amount. 2011 Note: Financial information for 2011 was not available for all companies at press time.

2011 Sales: $6,097,900	2011 Profits: $1,761,000
2010 Sales: $3,965,000	2010 Profits: $440,700
2009 Sales: $2,608,400	2009 Profits: $448,500
2008 Sales: $3,921,100	2008 Profits: $684,600
2007 Sales: $2,756,700	2007 Profits: $372,700

U.S. Stock Ticker: CF
Int'l Ticker:
Int'l Exchange:
Employees: 2,500 Fiscal Year Ends: 12/31
Parent Company:

SALARIES/BENEFITS:

Pension Plan:	ESOP Stock Plan:	Profit Sharing:	Top Exec. Salary: $925,000	Bonus: $1,378,300
Savings Plan: Y	Stock Purch. Plan:		Second Exec. Salary: $360,000	Bonus: $321,800

OTHER THOUGHTS:

Apparent Women Officers or Directors: 3
Hot Spot for Advancement for Women/Minorities: Y

LOCATIONS: ("Y" = Yes)

West:	Southwest:	Midwest:	Southeast:	Northeast:	International:
Y	Y	Y	Y	Y	Y

CHANNELL COMMERCIAL CORP

www.channellcomm.com

Industry Group Code: 334210

Management:		Sales/Marketing:		Liberal Arts:		Information Systems:		Professionals:		Technical/Scientific:	
Mgmt. Trainees:		Mktg. Professionals:	Y	Gen. Writing/Editing:	Y	Info. Management:	Y	Finance/Acct.:	Y	Engineers, Elec.:	Y
Experienced Mgmt.:	Y	Retail Sales:		Technical Writing:	Y	Software Dev.:	Y	Law:	Y	Engineers, Other:	Y
Int'l Business:	Y	Commercial/Industrial:	Y	Graphic Arts/Photog.:		Hardware Dev.:	Y	HR/Other:	Y	Health/Lab	
MBA Graduates:	Y	Sales Trainees:	Y	Music:		Consulting/Other:	Y	Training:	Y	Scientists/Research:	
		Advertising Pros.:		Broadcasting:				Health Care:		Petroleum/Chemicals:	
				Other:				Consulting:		Math/Other:	

TYPES OF BUSINESS:

Telecommunications Infrastructure Hardware
Thermoplastic & Metal Enclosures
Fiber-Optic Cable Management Systems
Termination & Connection Products
Heat Shrink Products
Water Storage Tanks

BRANDS/DIVISIONS/AFFILIATES:

Bushman Tanks
MAH Series
Mini-Rocker
DSLink
Rhino

CONTACTS: *Note: Officers with more than one job title may be intentionally listed here more than once.*

William H. Channell, Jr., CEO
Guy Marge, COO
Guy Marge, Pres.
Edward Burke, CTO
Jacqueline M. Channell, Sec.
Robert Swelgin, VP-Americas Oper.
Jacqueline M. Channell, Chmn.
Christopher Glenn, Managing Dir.-Australia Oper.

Phone: 951-719-2600 **Fax:** 951-296-2322
Toll-Free:
Address: 26040 Ynez Rd., Temecula, CA 92592 US

GROWTH PLANS/SPECIAL FEATURES:

Channell Commercial Corp., founded in 1922, designs, manufactures and supplies telecommunications equipment to broadband and telephone network providers worldwide. The company's major product lines include thermoplastic and metal fabricated enclosures; advanced copper termination and connection products; fiber optic cable management systems for fiber to the premises (FTTP) networks; and heat shrink products. In addition to serving customers in the global telecommunications industry, Channell also operates in the Australian water storage tank industry through its subsidiary, Bushman Tanks. Channell's enclosure products provide protection against weather and vandalism, include both above- and below-ground versions, and provide advanced heat dissipation properties. Channell designs thermo-molded application-specific thermoplastic and metal fabricated enclosures for advanced telecommunications hardware such as radio frequency (RF) electronics and photonics and transmission media. Products include the MAH Series free breathing telephony enclosures, Grade Level Box (GLB) subsurface enclosures and a range of Rhino metal fabricated enclosures. The company's copper connectivity products include the Mini-Rocker line of copper connectivity modules and the DSLink modular terminal block. Channell's fiber optic products include electronic enclosures, fiber optic splice cases and fiber optic cable assemblies. The company sells its telecommunications products directly to broadband operators and telephones companies principally within developed nations around the world, and sells its water storage products in Australia directly to end users as well as to retailers, wholesalers, distributors and agents.

FINANCIALS: **Sales and profits are in thousands of dollars—add 000 to get the full amount. 2011 Note: Financial information for 2011 was not available for all companies at press time.**

2011 Sales: $ 2011 Profits: $
2010 Sales: $ 2010 Profits: $
2009 Sales: $ 2009 Profits: $
2008 Sales: $ 2008 Profits: $
2007 Sales: $ 2007 Profits: $

U.S. Stock Ticker: CHNL.PK
Int'l Ticker:
Int'l Exchange:
Employees: Fiscal Year Ends: 12/31
Parent Company:

SALARIES/BENEFITS:

Pension Plan: ESOP Stock Plan: Profit Sharing: Top Exec. Salary: $ Bonus: $
Savings Plan: Stock Purch. Plan: Second Exec. Salary: $ Bonus: $

OTHER THOUGHTS:

Apparent Women Officers or Directors: 1
Hot Spot for Advancement for Women/Minorities:

LOCATIONS: ("Y" = Yes)

West:	Southwest:	Midwest:	Southeast:	Northeast:	International:
Y					Y

CHATTEM INC

www.chattem.com

Industry Group Code: 325411

Management:		Sales/Marketing:		Liberal Arts:		Information Systems:		Professionals:		Technical/Scientific:	
Mgmt. Trainees:		Mktg. Professionals:	Y	Gen. Writing/Editing:	Y	Info. Management:	Y	Finance/Acct.:	Y	Engineers, Elec.:	
Experienced Mgmt.:	Y	Retail Sales:		Technical Writing:	Y	Software Dev.:		Law:	Y	Engineers, Other:	
Int'l Business:	Y	Commercial/Industrial:	Y	Graphic Arts/Photog.:		Hardware Dev.:		HR/Other:	Y	Health/Lab	Y
MBA Graduates:	Y	Sales Trainees:	Y	Music:		Consulting/Other:		Training:	Y	Scientists/Research:	Y
		Advertising Pros.:	Y	Broadcasting:				Health Care:	Y	Petroleum/Chemicals:	Y
				Other:	Y			Consulting:		Math/Other:	Y

TYPES OF BUSINESS:

Branded Consumer Products - Medicinal
Over-the-Counter Drugs
Toiletries
Skin Care Products
Dietary Supplements

BRANDS/DIVISIONS/AFFILIATES:

Sanofi-aventis SA
Chattem (UK), Ltd.
Chattem Canada
Chattem Global Consumer Products Ltd
Gold Bond
Icy Hot
Selsun Blue
Cortizone

CONTACTS: *Note: Officers with more than one job title may be intentionally listed here more than once.*

Serge Weinberg, Chmn.

Phone: 423-821-4571	**Fax:** 423-821-0395
Toll-Free:	
Address: 1715 W. 38th St., Chattanooga, TN 37409 US	

GROWTH PLANS/SPECIAL FEATURES:

Chattem, Inc., a subsidiary of Sanofi-aventis SA, is a leading marketer and manufacturer of a broad portfolio of branded over-the-counter (OTC) healthcare products, toiletries and dietary supplements in such categories as pain relief, skin and hair care and health and wellness. Pain relief products include arthritis pain relief cream, pain relieving gel, itch relief cream, topical analgesic, muscle pain and menstrual pain relief products. Skin and hair care products include diaper rash cream, sunblock, medicated skin care, body lotion, dandruff and chlorine removal shampoo and hair lightener. Health and wellness products include fluoride rinse, mouthwash, dental pain relieving cream, dietary supplements, indigestion relief products and sleep aids. The company's products target niche market segments, which are often overlooked by larger companies. Chattem's brands are some of the most widely recognized brands on the market and include Icy Hot, Aspercreme, Flexall, Capzasin, Gold Bond, Cortizone, Balmex, Selsun Blue, Melatonex, Pamprin, Bullfrog and more. The company also operates an international division, which is concentrated in Canada and Europe. In Canada, its products are marketed through subsidiary Chattem Canada. European business is conducted through Chattem Global Consumer Products, Ltd., an Irish subsidiary of Chattem's, as well as Chattem (U.K.) Limited, a subsidiary located in England. The company also exports products to distributors in the Caribbean and Latin America. The firm's customers consist of mass merchandisers and drug and food retailers such as Wal-Mart, Walgreens and Kroger.

FINANCIALS: **Sales and profits are in thousands of dollars—add 000 to get the full amount. 2011 Note: Financial information for 2011 was not available for all companies at press time.**

2011 Sales: $	2011 Profits: $	**U.S. Stock Ticker: Subsidiary**
2010 Sales: $	2010 Profits: $	**Int'l Ticker:**
2009 Sales: $463,342	2009 Profits: $63,171	Int'l Exchange:
2008 Sales: $454,879	2008 Profits: $66,286	Employees: Fiscal Year Ends: 11/30
2007 Sales: $423,378	2007 Profits: $59,690	Parent Company: SANOFI-AVENTIS SA

SALARIES/BENEFITS:

Pension Plan:	ESOP Stock Plan:	Profit Sharing:	Top Exec. Salary: $	Bonus: $
Savings Plan:	Stock Purch. Plan:		Second Exec. Salary: $	Bonus: $

OTHER THOUGHTS:

Apparent Women Officers or Directors:
Hot Spot for Advancement for Women/Minorities:

LOCATIONS: ("Y" = Yes)

West:	Southwest:	Midwest:	Southeast:	Northeast:	International:
			Y		Y

CHINDEX INTERNATIONAL INC

www.chindex.com

Industry Group Code: 423450

Management:		Sales/Marketing:		Liberal Arts:		Information Systems:		Professionals:		Technical/Scientific:	
Mgmt. Trainees:		Mktg. Professionals:	Y	Gen. Writing/Editing:		Info. Management:	Y	Finance/Acct.:	Y	Engineers, Elec.:	
Experienced Mgmt.:	Y	Retail Sales:		Technical Writing:	Y	Software Dev.:	Y	Law:	Y	Engineers, Other:	
Int'l Business:	Y	Commercial/Industrial:	Y	Graphic Arts/Photog.:		Hardware Dev.:		HR/Other:	Y	Health/Lab	
MBA Graduates:	Y	Sales Trainees:	Y	Music:		Consulting/Other:	Y	Training:	Y	Scientists/Research:	
		Advertising Pros.:		Broadcasting:				Health Care:	Y	Petroleum/Chemicals:	
				Other:				Consulting:		Math/Other:	

TYPES OF BUSINESS:

Health Care Products Distribution
Hospitals
Healthcare Services

BRANDS/DIVISIONS/AFFILIATES:

United Family Healthcare
Beijing United Family Hospital
Shanghai United Family Hospital
Chindex Medical Ltd.

CONTACTS: *Note: Officers with more than one job title may be intentionally listed here more than once.*

Roberta Lipson, CEO
Roberta Lipson, Pres.
Lawrence Pemble, CFO/Exec. VP
Daniel Fulton, VP-IT Svcs.
Elyse Beth Silverberg, Sec.
Robert Low, Chief Acct. Officer/VP-Finance/Corp. Controller
Elyse Beth Silverberg, Exec. VP
Walter Xue, Sr. VP-Finance/Controller-China
Judy Zakreski, VP-U.S. Oper., Chindex Medical Ltd.
Wai Ho Leung, VP-Medical Diagnostic & Imaging Prod.
Kenneth A. Nilsson, Chmn.
Walter Stryker, Sr. VP-China Admin.

Phone: 301-215-7777 **Fax:** 301-215-7719
Toll-Free:
Address: 4340 E. W. Highway, Ste. 1100, Bethesda, MD 20814 US

GROWTH PLANS/SPECIAL FEATURES:

Chindex International, Inc., an American company operating in several healthcare markets in China, including Hong Kong, provides healthcare services and sells medical equipment, instruments and products. The firm operates in two segments: healthcare services and medical products. The healthcare services division operates the United Family Healthcare (UFH) network of private hospitals and clinics, the Beijing United Family Hospital, the Shanghai United Family Hospital and a managed clinic in the city of Wuxi. The United Family Healthcare facilities offer a wide range of family healthcare services, including 24-hours-a-day, seven-days-a-week emergency rooms; intensive care units; neonatal intensive care units; operating rooms; and clinical laboratory, radiology and blood baking services for men, women and children. The medical products division, operated through recently established joint venture Chindex Medical Ltd., distributes select medical capital equipment, instrumentation and other medical products for use in hospitals in China and Hong Kong. Products sold include diagnostic color ultrasound imaging devices; robotic surgical systems and instrumentation; chemistry analyzers; sterilization systems; bone densitometers; mammography; and breast biopsy devices and lasers for cosmetic surgery. In December 2010, Chindex International and Shanghai Fosun Pharmaceutical (Group) Co., Ltd., a manufacturer and distributor of western and Chinese medicine and devices, officially established Chindex Medical Ltd., a joint venture that combines Chindex International's former medical products distribution segment with some of Shanghai Fosun's medical device operations. The company controls 49% of the newly formed venture, while Shanghai Fosun controls the remaining 51%.

FINANCIALS: **Sales and profits are in thousands of dollars—add 000 to get the full amount. 2011 Note: Financial information for 2011 was not available for all companies at press time.**

2011 Sales: $	2011 Profits: $
2010 Sales: $171,191	2010 Profits: $8,204
2009 Sales: $171,442	2009 Profits: $4,964
2008 Sales: $130,058	2008 Profits: $3,655
2007 Sales: $105,921	2007 Profits: $2,982

U.S. Stock Ticker: CHDX
Int'l Ticker:
Int'l Exchange:
Employees: 1,328 Fiscal Year Ends: 12/31
Parent Company:

SALARIES/BENEFITS:

Pension Plan:	ESOP Stock Plan:	Profit Sharing:	Top Exec. Salary: $618,454	Bonus: $306,268
Savings Plan:	Stock Purch. Plan:		Second Exec. Salary: $556,608	Bonus: $234,866

OTHER THOUGHTS:

Apparent Women Officers or Directors: 5
Hot Spot for Advancement for Women/Minorities: Y

LOCATIONS: ("Y" = Yes)

West:	Southwest:	Midwest:	Southeast:	Northeast:	International:
				Y	Y

CHOICESTREAM INC

www.choicestream.com

Industry Group Code: 541810E

Management:		Sales/Marketing:		Liberal Arts:		Information Systems:		Professionals:		Technical/Scientific:	
Mgmt. Trainees:		Mktg. Professionals:	Y	Gen. Writing/Editing:	Y	Info. Management:	Y	Finance/Acct.:	Y	Engineers, Elec.:	
Experienced Mgmt.:	Y	Retail Sales:		Technical Writing:		Software Dev.:	Y	Law:	Y	Engineers, Other:	
Int'l Business:		Commercial/Industrial:	Y	Graphic Arts/Photog.:	Y	Hardware Dev.:		HR/Other:	Y	Health/Lab	
MBA Graduates:	Y	Sales Trainees:	Y	Music:		Consulting/Other:		Training:	Y	Scientists/Research:	
		Advertising Pros.:	Y	Broadcasting:				Health Care:		Petroleum/Chemicals:	
				Other:	Y			Consulting:		Math/Other:	

TYPES OF BUSINESS:

Online Personalized Display Ads & Product Information

BRANDS/DIVISIONS/AFFILIATES:

RealRelevance Advertising
RealRelevance eMail
RealRelevance Recommendations
Crunch

CONTACTS:

Note: Officers with more than one job title may be intentionally listed here more than once.

Steve Johnson, CEO
Eric Bosco, COO
Mark Gallagher, CFO
Daniel McDermott, Dir.-Mktg
Jerry Harris, Dir.-Eng.
Daniel McDermott, Dir.-Comm.
Lori Trahan, Chief Revenue Officer
Glenn Pagan, Mgr.-Regional Sales, New England Territory
Shawn Burroughs, Mgr.-Regional Sales, Mid-West Territory

Phone: 617-498-7800 **Fax:**
Toll-Free:
Address: 1 Charles Park, 6th Fl., Cambridge, MA 02142 US

GROWTH PLANS/SPECIAL FEATURES:

ChoiceStream, Inc. is a provider of personalization services such as online display ads and product recommendation advertising for entertainment, e-commerce, television and mobile phone companies. The firm's RealRelevance Advertising product features a landing page and ad format combination and predicts consumer demand for future products by utilizing actual consumer shopping data. The product allows the automatic generation of thousands of different ads through a single tag and produces individually target messages and product recommendation for a wide range of audience categories. RealRelevance provides an online store and personalized call center for retail stores and a customer rating system for recommendations, as well as promotions and editorial content for media and entertainment businesses. The firm also offers RealRelevance Recommendations, a technology which generates personalized product recommendations, and RealRelevance eMail, which delivers personalized product recommendations in e-mail campaigns and transaction e-mails. The company's aim is to streamline data, allowing consumers to find products more efficiently and to increase clients' revenue by driving consumption. ChoiceStream serves companies such as Zappos.com; Blockbuster; BBC; Yahoo!; Overstock.com; and Ticketmaster. In June 2011, the firm introduced Crunch, a custom audience targeting platform.

FINANCIALS:

Sales and profits are in thousands of dollars—add 000 to get the full amount. 2011 Note: Financial information for 2011 was not available for all companies at press time.

2011 Sales: $ — 2011 Profits: $
2010 Sales: $ — 2010 Profits: $
2009 Sales: $ — 2009 Profits: $
2008 Sales: $ — 2008 Profits: $
2007 Sales: $ — 2007 Profits: $

U.S. Stock Ticker: Private
Int'l Ticker:
Int'l Exchange:
Employees: Fiscal Year Ends:
Parent Company:

SALARIES/BENEFITS:

Pension Plan: ESOP Stock Plan: Profit Sharing: Top Exec. Salary: $ Bonus: $
Savings Plan: Stock Purch. Plan: Second Exec. Salary: $ Bonus: $

OTHER THOUGHTS:

Apparent Women Officers or Directors: 1
Hot Spot for Advancement for Women/Minorities:

LOCATIONS: ("Y" = Yes)

West:	Southwest:	Midwest:	Southeast:	Northeast:	International:
Y				Y	

CHOLESTECH CORP

www.cholestech.com

Industry Group Code: 325413

Management:		Sales/Marketing:		Liberal Arts:		Information Systems:		Professionals:		Technical/Scientific:	
Mgmt. Trainees:		Mktg. Professionals:	Y	Gen. Writing/Editing:		Info. Management:	Y	Finance/Acct.:	Y	Engineers, Elec.:	Y
Experienced Mgmt.:	Y	Retail Sales:		Technical Writing:	Y	Software Dev.:	Y	Law:	Y	Engineers, Other:	Y
Int'l Business:	Y	Commercial/Industrial:	Y	Graphic Arts/Photog.:		Hardware Dev.:	Y	HR/Other:	Y	Health/Lab	Y
MBA Graduates:	Y	Sales Trainees:	Y	Music:		Consulting/Other:		Training:	Y	Scientists/Research:	Y
		Advertising Pros.:	Y	Broadcasting:				Health Care:	Y	Petroleum/Chemicals:	
				Other:				Consulting:		Math/Other:	Y

TYPES OF BUSINESS:

Equipment-Blood Diagnostic Test Systems
Cholesterol Tests

BRANDS/DIVISIONS/AFFILIATES:

LDX System
GDX System
LDX Analyzer
Aspartate Aminotransferase (AST) Test
Alere Inc

CONTACTS:

Note: Officers with more than one job title may be intentionally listed here more than once.

Warren E. Pinckert, II, CEO
Warren E. Pinckert, II, Pres.
Terry Wassmann, VP-Human Resources
Gregory L. Bennett, VP-R&D
Barbara McAleer, VP-Quality Assurance & Regulatory Affairs

Phone: 510-732-7200 **Fax:** 510-732-7227
Toll-Free: 877-441-7440
Address: 3347 Investment Blvd., Hayward, CA 94545-3808 US

GROWTH PLANS/SPECIAL FEATURES:

Cholestech Corp., a subsidiary of Alere, Inc. (formerly Inverness Medical Innovations, Inc.), provides diagnostic tools for immediate risk assessment and monitoring of heart disease, inflammatory disorders and diabetes. The company manufactures the LDX System, which includes the LDX Analyzer and a variety of single-use test cassettes. Cholestech markets the LDX System in the U.S., Europe, Asia, Australia and South America. The LDX System allows health care providers to perform individual tests or combinations of tests for blood cholesterol, related lipids, glucose, liver enzymes and high sensitivity C-reactive protein using a single drop of blood within five minutes. Cholestech also markets and distributes the GDX System, which measures hemoglobin A1C, an indicator of a patient's long-term glycemic control. Cholestech distributes the GDX under a multi-year global agreement with Provalis Diagnostics, Ltd. Unlike daily glucose monitoring, which only measures a patient's glucose level at the time of testing, A1C provides an average glucose level over the previous 90 days, which indicates the long-term progress of a patient's diabetes and therapy management. Cholestech specifically targets its products for markets outside of traditional hospital or clinical laboratories. The firm's primary market is the physician office laboratory market. In addition, Cholestech has a development and product distribution agreement with Itamar Medical Limited, involving a system for assessing vascular endothelial dysfunction, which is recognized as an early stage in the development of atherosclerosis. The company also provides an Aspartate Aminotransferase (AST) Test for monitoring the effects of various drugs on the liver.

FINANCIALS:

Sales and profits are in thousands of dollars—add 000 to get the full amount. 2011 Note: Financial information for 2011 was not available for all companies at press time.

2011 Sales: $	2011 Profits: $	**U.S. Stock Ticker: Subsidiary**
2010 Sales: $	2010 Profits: $	**Int'l Ticker:**
2009 Sales: $	2009 Profits: $	Int'l Exchange:
2008 Sales: $	2008 Profits: $	Employees: Fiscal Year Ends: 3/31
2007 Sales: $	2007 Profits: $	Parent Company: ALERE INC

SALARIES/BENEFITS:

Pension Plan:	ESOP Stock Plan:	Profit Sharing:	Top Exec. Salary: $	Bonus: $
Savings Plan:	Stock Purch. Plan:		Second Exec. Salary: $	Bonus: $

OTHER THOUGHTS:

Apparent Women Officers or Directors: 1
Hot Spot for Advancement for Women/Minorities:

LOCATIONS: ("Y" = Yes)

West:	Southwest:	Midwest:	Southeast:	Northeast:	International:
Y					

CIRRUS LOGIC INC

www.cirrus.com

Industry Group Code: 33441

Management:		Sales/Marketing:		Liberal Arts:		Information Systems:		Professionals:		Technical/Scientific:	
Mgmt. Trainees:		Mktg. Professionals:	Y	Gen. Writing/Editing:		Info. Management:	Y	Finance/Acct.:	Y	Engineers, Elec.:	Y
Experienced Mgmt.:	Y	Retail Sales:		Technical Writing:	Y	Software Dev.:	Y	Law:	Y	Engineers, Other:	Y
Int'l Business:	Y	Commercial/Industrial:	Y	Graphic Arts/Photog.:		Hardware Dev.:	Y	HR/Other:	Y	Health/Lab	
MBA Graduates:	Y	Sales Trainees:		Music:		Consulting/Other:		Training:		Scientists/Research:	
		Advertising Pros.:		Broadcasting:				Health Care:		Petroleum/Chemicals:	
				Other:				Consulting:		Math/Other:	Y

TYPES OF BUSINESS:

Integrated Circuits-Analog & Digital
DSP Chips
Audio Chips

BRANDS/DIVISIONS/AFFILIATES:

Cirrus
CobraNet
Apex Precision Power

CONTACTS: *Note: Officers with more than one job title may be intentionally listed here more than once.*

Jason Rhode, CEO
Jason Rhode, Pres.
Thurman K. Case, CFO
Timothy R. Turk, VP-Worldwide Sales
Jo-Dee M. Benson, Chief Culture Officer/VP
Gregory Scott Thomas, General Counsel/VP/Corp. Sec.
Thurman K. Case, VP-Finance/Treas.
Greg Brennan, VP/Gen. Mgr.-Apex Precision Power Bus. Unit
Scott Anderson, Sr. VP/Gen. Mgr.-Mixed Signal Audio Div.
Lewis Venters, VP-Corp. Quality
Tom Stein, VP/Gen. Mgr.-Energy, Exploration & Lighting Div.
Michael L. Hackworth, Chmn.
Randy Carlson, VP-Supply Chain Mgmt.

Phone: 512-851-4000 **Fax:** 512-851-4977
Toll-Free: 800-888-5016
Address: 2901 Via Fortuna, Austin, TX 78746 US

GROWTH PLANS/SPECIAL FEATURES:

Cirrus Logic, Inc. is a developer of analog, high-precision and mixed-signal integrated circuits (ICs) for a broad range of audio and energy industries. The company also produces audio chips for high-volume audio, storage and communications applications providers. With regard to audio products, Cirrus Logic offers high-precision analog components, mixed-signal components and audio digital signal processor (DSP) products for consumer, professional and automotive entertainment markets. The company offers a broad line of products under the Cirrus Logic name as well as the Cirrus, Apex Precision Power and CobraNet brands. These brands allow system-level applications in mass storage (magnetic and optical), audio (professional, consumer and PC) and precision data conversion (16 bits and higher). These products include DSPs and CODECs for A/V receivers, DVD receivers, DVD recorders and portable players; analog-to-digital and digital-to-analog converters, CODECs and other components optimized for professional audio applications; embedded processor solutions; and automotive electronics components. Cirrus Logic's energy products include high-precision analog and mixed-signal components for energy-related applications, such as energy measurement, energy exploration and energy control systems; and board-level modules, ICs and hybrids for high-power pulse width modulation and power amplifier applications. The firm owns roughly 1,100 U.S. patents and has 100 U.S. patents pending. It offers more than 700 products that serve over 3,000 end customers worldwide through both direct and distributor-based sales.

The firm offers its employees benefits including health, dental, vision, life and disability insurance; a 401(k) plan; health and dependent care reimbursement accounts; an employee stock option plan; paid time off and holidays; tuition reimbursement; and an employee assistance program.

FINANCIALS: **Sales and profits are in thousands of dollars—add 000 to get the full amount. 2011 Note: Financial information for 2011 was not available for all companies at press time.**

2011 Sales: $369,571 | 2011 Profits: $203,503
2010 Sales: $220,989 | 2010 Profits: $38,398
2009 Sales: $174,642 | 2009 Profits: $3,475
2008 Sales: $181,885 | 2008 Profits: $-5,846
2007 Sales: $182,304 | 2007 Profits: $27,895

U.S. Stock Ticker: CRUS
Int'l Ticker:
Int'l Exchange:
Employees: 570 Fiscal Year Ends: 3/31
Parent Company:

SALARIES/BENEFITS:

Pension Plan: | ESOP Stock Plan: | Profit Sharing: | Top Exec. Salary: $408,616 | Bonus: $736,500
Savings Plan: Y | Stock Purch. Plan: Y | | Second Exec. Salary: $277,560 | Bonus: $341,913

OTHER THOUGHTS:

Apparent Women Officers or Directors: 2
Hot Spot for Advancement for Women/Minorities:

LOCATIONS: ("Y" = Yes)

West:	Southwest:	Midwest:	Southeast:	Northeast:	International:
Y	Y				Y

CKX INC

www.ckx.com

Industry Group Code: 711410

Management:		Sales/Marketing:		Liberal Arts:		Information Systems:		Professionals:		Technical/Scientific:	
Mgmt. Trainees:		Mktg. Professionals:	Y	Gen. Writing/Editing:	Y	Info. Management:	Y	Finance/Acct.:	Y	Engineers, Elec.:	
Experienced Mgmt.:	Y	Retail Sales:		Technical Writing:		Software Dev.:		Law:	Y	Engineers, Other:	
Int'l Business:	Y	Commercial/Industrial:	Y	Graphic Arts/Photog.:		Hardware Dev.:		HR/Other:	Y	Health/Lab	
MBA Graduates:	Y	Sales Trainees:	Y	Music:		Consulting/Other:		Training:	Y	Scientists/Research:	
		Advertising Pros.:		Broadcasting:				Health Care:		Petroleum/Chemicals:	
				Other:				Consulting:		Math/Other:	

TYPES OF BUSINESS:

Name, Image & Likeness Licensing
Television Content
Artist Management

BRANDS/DIVISIONS/AFFILIATES:

19 Entertainment Limited
Elvis Presley
CKX Entertainment Inc
Apollo Global Managemet LLC
American Idol
Elvis Presley Enterprises, Inc.
Muhammad Ali Enterprises
Beckham Brand Limited

CONTACTS: *Note: Officers with more than one job title may be intentionally listed here more than once.*

Michael G. Ferrel, CEO
Kraig G. Fox, COO
Thomas P. Benson, CFO/Exec. VP
Chris Gannett, Chief Mktg. Officer
Howard J. Tytel, Dir.-Legal Affairs/Sr. Exec. VP
Howard J. Tytel, Dir.-Gov't Affairs
Thomas P. Benson, Treas.
Jack Soden, CEO-Elvis Presley Enterprises, Inc.
Michael G. Ferrel, Chmn.

Phone: 212-838-3100 **Fax:**
Toll-Free:
Address: 650 Madison Ave., New York, NY 10022 US

GROWTH PLANS/SPECIAL FEATURES:

CKX, Inc. operates as an indirect wholly-owned subsidiary of the company CKX Entertainment, Inc., which is controlled by the global investment funds and asset manager; Apollo Global Management, LLC. CKX is engaged in the ownership, development and commercial utilization of entertainment content. Its primary assets and operations include an 85% interest in Elvis Prelsey Enterprises, an 80% interest Muhammad Ali Enterprises and proprietary rights to the So You Think You Can Dance and IDOLS television brand. The firm's Elvis Presley business consists of two components: intellectual property, including the licensing of the name, image, likeness and trademarks associated with Elvis Presley, as well as other intellectual property and the collection of royalties from certain motion pictures, television specials and recorded musical works and music compositions; and the operation of the Graceland museum and related attractions, including Elvis Presley's Heartbreak Hotel. Through subsidiary 19 Entertainment Limited, CKX owns proprietary rights to the So You Think You Can Dance IDOLS television brand, including the American Idol series in the United States along with various local adaptations of the IDOLS television show format worldwide, as well as related music, sponsorship, touring and artist management activities. 19 Entertainment also manages the merchandising activities of Victoria and David Beckham, through joint venture, Beckham Brand Limited. The business has also entered into an exclusive arrangement with Cirque du Soleil for the development and promotion of touring and permanent shows, as well as multimedia interactive shows throughout the world that incorporate the image, likeness and music of Elvis Presley.

FINANCIALS: **Sales and profits are in thousands of dollars—add 000 to get the full amount. 2011 Note: Financial information for 2011 was not available for all companies at press time.**

2011 Sales: $
2010 Sales: $273,724
2009 Sales: $328,353
2008 Sales: $288,128
2007 Sales: $266,777

2011 Profits: $
2010 Profits: $-12,526
2009 Profits: $26,368
2008 Profits: $17,127
2007 Profits: $10,320

U.S. Stock Ticker: Private
Int'l Ticker:
Int'l Exchange:
Employees: 458 Fiscal Year Ends: 12/31
Parent Company: APOLLO GLOBAL MANAGEMENT LLC

SALARIES/BENEFITS:

Pension Plan: ESOP Stock Plan: Profit Sharing: Top Exec. Salary: $828,198 Bonus: $1,173,750
Savings Plan: Stock Purch. Plan: Second Exec. Salary: $786,944 Bonus: $102,781

OTHER THOUGHTS:

Apparent Women Officers or Directors: 2
Hot Spot for Advancement for Women/Minorities:

LOCATIONS: ("Y" = Yes)

West:	Southwest:	Midwest:	Southeast:	Northeast:	International:
				Y	Y

CLAYTON WILLIAMS ENERGY INC

www.claytonwilliams.com

Industry Group Code: 211111

Management:		Sales/Marketing:		Liberal Arts:		Information Systems:		Professionals:		Technical/Scientific:	
Mgmt. Trainees:		Mktg. Professionals:		Gen. Writing/Editing:		Info. Management:	Y	Finance/Acct.:	Y	Engineers, Elec.:	
Experienced Mgmt.:	Y	Retail Sales:		Technical Writing:		Software Dev.:		Law:	Y	Engineers, Other:	Y
Int'l Business:		Commercial/Industrial:		Graphic Arts/Photog.:		Hardware Dev.:		HR/Other:	Y	Health/Lab	
MBA Graduates:	Y	Sales Trainees:		Music:		Consulting/Other:		Training:	Y	Scientists/Research:	
		Advertising Pros.:		Broadcasting:				Health Care:		Petroleum/Chemicals:	Y
				Other:				Consulting:		Math/Other:	

TYPES OF BUSINESS:

Oil & Gas Exploration & Production
Pipelines
Treatment Plants
Drilling Rigs

BRANDS/DIVISIONS/AFFILIATES:

Clayton Williams Pipeline Corp.
Desta Drilling GP LLC

CONTACTS:

Note: Officers with more than one job title may be intentionally listed here more than once.

Clayton W. Williams, CEO
Mel G. Riggs, COO/Exec. VP
Clayton W. Williams, Pres.
Michael L. Pollard, CFO/Sr. VP-Finance/Treas.
Robert C. Lyon, VP-Gas Gathering & Mktg.
T. Mark Tisdale, General Counsel/VP
Patrick C. Reesby, VP-Acquisitions & New Ventures
Patti Hollums, Dir.-Investor Rel.
Robert L. Thomas, VP-Acct.
Greg S. Welborn, VP-Land
Clayton W. Williams, Chmn.

Phone: 432-682-6324	**Fax:** 432-688-3247
Toll-Free:	
Address: 6 Desta Dr., Ste. 6500, Midland, TX 79705 US	

GROWTH PLANS/SPECIAL FEATURES:

Clayton Williams Energy, Inc. (CWE) is an independent oil and gas company engaged in the exploration and production of oil and natural gas. The company operates primarily in Texas, Louisiana and New Mexico. Its key production areas are located in the Permian Basin in West Texas and Southeastern New Mexico, which represents 73.5% of its total proved reserves; the Giddings area, including the Austin Chalk and Eagle Ford Shale formations in east Texas; and South Louisiana. Before drilling an exploratory well, the company uses geophysical technology to attempt to make a picture of the underlying geography of an area. The factors considered include the field recording parameters of the data, type of processing, extent of attribute analyses, availability of subsurface geological data and the depth and complexity of the subsurface. The company will only attempt an exploratory well if the reserve potential is higher than an ordinary development prospect. CWE has proved reserves of 51.1 million barrels of oil equivalent (MMBOE), of which 74% is oil and natural gas liquids and 26% is natural gas. Additional assets of the company include interests in 108 miles of gas pipeline, four treating plants, one dehydration facility and seven wellhead type treating/compression stations. CWE also owns the contract drilling company Desta Drilling GP, LLC, which has a fleet of 12 operating drill rigs. In 2010, the firm's production totaled 3.37 million barrels of oil, 10.75 billion cubic feet of natural gas and 292,000 barrels of natural gas liquids, for a combined total of 5.45 MMBOE.

FINANCIALS:

Sales and profits are in thousands of dollars—add 000 to get the full amount. 2011 Note: Financial information for 2011 was not available for all companies at press time.

2011 Sales: $410,700	2011 Profits: $93,800	**U.S. Stock Ticker: CWEI**
2010 Sales: $331,631	2010 Profits: $36,938	**Int'l Ticker:**
2009 Sales: $255,961	2009 Profits: $-117,415	Int'l Exchange:
2008 Sales: $565,517	2008 Profits: $140,534	Employees: 437 Fiscal Year Ends: 12/31
2007 Sales: $393,895	2007 Profits: $5,900	Parent Company:

SALARIES/BENEFITS:

Pension Plan:	ESOP Stock Plan:	Profit Sharing:	Top Exec. Salary: $608,121	Bonus: $279,845
Savings Plan:	Stock Purch. Plan:		Second Exec. Salary: $336,686	Bonus: $227,728

OTHER THOUGHTS:

Apparent Women Officers or Directors: 1
Hot Spot for Advancement for Women/Minorities:

LOCATIONS: ("Y" = Yes)

West:	Southwest:	Midwest:	Southeast:	Northeast:	International:
Y	Y		Y		

CLEAN ENERGY FUELS CORP

www.cleanenergyfuels.com

Industry Group Code: 454319

Management:		Sales/Marketing:		Liberal Arts:		Information Systems:		Professionals:		Technical/Scientific:	
Mgmt. Trainees:	Y	Mktg. Professionals:		Gen. Writing/Editing:		Info. Management:	Y	Finance/Acct.:	Y	Engineers, Elec.:	
Experienced Mgmt.:	Y	Retail Sales:		Technical Writing:		Software Dev.:		Law:	Y	Engineers, Other:	
Int'l Business:	Y	Commercial/Industrial:		Graphic Arts/Photog.:		Hardware Dev.:		HR/Other:	Y	Health/Lab	
MBA Graduates:	Y	Sales Trainees:		Music:		Consulting/Other:		Training:		Scientists/Research:	
		Advertising Pros.:		Broadcasting:				Health Care:		Petroleum/Chemicals:	
				Other:				Consulting:		Math/Other:	

TYPES OF BUSINESS:

Automotive Natural Gas Retailing
LNG, Liquefied Natural Gas Production & Sales
CNG, Compressed Natural Gas Production & Sales

BRANDS/DIVISIONS/AFFILIATES:

Dallas Clean Energy LLC
BAF Technologies Inc
IMW Industries Ltd
Wyoming Northstar Inc
Southstar LLC
M&S Rental LLC
Clean Energy del Peru

CONTACTS: *Note: Officers with more than one job title may be intentionally listed here more than once.*

Andrew J. Littlefair, CEO
Mitchell Pratt, COO
Andrew J. Littlefair, Pres.
Richard R. Wheeler, CFO
Peter Grace, Sr. VP-Sales
Dennis C.K. Ding, VP-Eng. & Construction
Nate Jensen, General Counsel/VP
Brian Powers, VP-Oper.
Raymond P. Burke, VP-Bus. Dev., Solid Waste
James L. Hooley, VP-Gov't. Rel.
Peter Grace, Sr. VP-Finance
Barclay F. Corbus, Sr. VP-Strategic Dev.
Harrison Clay, VP-Renewable Fuels
Todd Campbell, VP-Public Policy & Regulatory Affairs

Phone: 562-493-2804	**Fax:** 562-493-4532
Toll-Free:	
Address: 3020 Old Ranch Pkwy., Ste. 400, Seal Beach, CA 90740 US	

GROWTH PLANS/SPECIAL FEATURES:

Clean Energy Fuels Corp. is a leading supplier of natural gas vehicle fuel, which includes both compressed natural gas (CNG) and liquefied natural gas (LNG). Additionally, the company builds CNG and LNG fueling stations; sells renewable biomethane; converts natural gas vehicles; sells natural gas vehicle compression equipment; and finances vehicle acquisitions by customers. Clean Energy serves fleet vehicle operators in markets, such as public transit, waste transport, airports, taxis, seaports and regional trucking. Clean Energy supplies LNG and CNG to approximately 480 customers, operating over 21,270 vehicles. The firm owns, operates or supplies natural gas to 224 fueling stations throughout the U.S. and Canada. Through a joint venture with Clean Energy del Peru, the firm operates one CNG gas station in Lima, Peru. The firm's first LNG plant, located in Willis, Texas, produces up to 35 million gallons of vehicle-grade LNG per year and is equipped with both loading facilities and a 1 million gallon storage tank. The company's LNG plant located in Boron, California has a 1.8 million gallon storage tank and is built to produce up to 60 million gallons of LNG per year. Substantial contract agreements to build and operate CNG and LNG fueling facilities or to buy the exclusive fuel supplier exist with agencies, such as the Los Angeles International Airport, the Metropolitan Tulsa Transit Authority, UPS and major contract freight carrier Dillon Transport. Clean Energy's subsidiaries include Dallas Clean Energy, LLC; BAF Technologies, Inc.; I.M.W. Industries Ltd.; Wyoming Northstar Inc., Southstar LLC and M&S Rental LLC.

FINANCIALS: Sales and profits are in thousands of dollars—add 000 to get the full amount. 2011 Note: Financial information for 2011 was not available for all companies at press time.

2011 Sales: $	2011 Profits: $	**U.S. Stock Ticker: CLNE**
2010 Sales: $211,834	2010 Profits: $-44,568	**Int'l Ticker:**
2009 Sales: $131,503	2009 Profits: $-33,688	Int'l Exchange:
2008 Sales: $129,473	2008 Profits: $-40,857	Employees: 710 Fiscal Year Ends: 12/31
2007 Sales: $117,716	2007 Profits: $-8,894	Parent Company:

SALARIES/BENEFITS:

Pension Plan:	ESOP Stock Plan:	Profit Sharing:	Top Exec. Salary: $520,000	Bonus: $212,888
Savings Plan:	Stock Purch. Plan:		Second Exec. Salary: $345,000	Bonus: $111,519

OTHER THOUGHTS:

Apparent Women Officers or Directors:
Hot Spot for Advancement for Women/Minorities:

LOCATIONS: ("Y" = Yes)

West:	Southwest:	Midwest:	Southeast:	Northeast:	International:
Y	Y	Y	Y	Y	Y

CLEARONE COMMUNICATIONS INC

www.clearone.com

Industry Group Code: 334220

Management:		Sales/Marketing:		Liberal Arts:		Information Systems:		Professionals:		Technical/Scientific:	
Mgmt. Trainees:		Mktg. Professionals:	Y	Gen. Writing/Editing:	Y	Info. Management:	Y	Finance/Acct.:	Y	Engineers, Elec.:	Y
Experienced Mgmt.:	Y	Retail Sales:		Technical Writing:	Y	Software Dev.:	Y	Law:	Y	Engineers, Other:	
Int'l Business:	Y	Commercial/Industrial:	Y	Graphic Arts/Photog.:		Hardware Dev.:	Y	HR/Other:	Y	Health/Lab	
MBA Graduates:	Y	Sales Trainees:	Y	Music:		Consulting/Other:		Training:	Y	Scientists/Research:	
		Advertising Pros.:		Broadcasting:				Health Care:		Petroleum/Chemicals:	
				Other:	Y			Consulting:		Math/Other:	

TYPES OF BUSINESS:

Teleconferencing Products & Services
Tabletop Conferencing Phones
Installed Audio Systems
Microphones
Conference Furniture
Streaming A/V Equipment
Digital Signage

BRANDS/DIVISIONS/AFFILIATES:

Distributed Echo Cancellation
XAP
Converge Pro SR1212
CHAT 50
MAX
ClearOneExpress
NetStreams, Inc.
StreamNet

CONTACTS:

Note: Officers with more than one job title may be intentionally listed here more than once.

Zee Hakimoglu, CEO
Zee Hakimoglu, Pres.
Stephen R. DiEugenio, VP-Unified Comm. Sales, Americas
Narsi Narayanan, Corp. Sec.
Michael E. Braithwaite, Chief Strategy Officer
Mary Evans, Dir.-Mktg. Comm.
Narsi Narayanan, VP-Finance
Zee Hakimoglu, Chmn.

Phone: 801-975-7200 **Fax:** 801-977-0087
Toll-Free: 800-945-7730
Address: 5225 Wiley Post Way, Ste. 500, Salt Lake City, UT 84116 US

GROWTH PLANS/SPECIAL FEATURES:

ClearOne Communications, Inc. develops, manufactures and markets a comprehensive line of audio conferencing systems and related products for streaming audio and video applications. The company's conferencing products range from tabletop conferencing phones to installed audio systems, which are utilized in large group conferencing venues, boardrooms, training centers, courtrooms and auditoriums. The firm splits its conferencing products into four groups: professional audio conferencing products, which include the Converge Pro SR1212 and XAP products; premium conferencing products, which are complete, out-of-the-box systems that include an audio mixer, Bose loudspeakers, microphones and a control device that can be either wired or wireless; tabletop conferencing phones through the MAX product line; and personal conferencing devices, including the CHAT 50 personal speaker phone, which can be used in conjunction with cell phones, telephones, PCs, Macs and other electronic tools. Products throughout these lines incorporate the firm's proprietary Distributed Echo Cancellation technology, which eliminates acoustical echoes and background noise. In addition to its audio conferencing products, ClearOne markets microphones and conferencing furniture, such as audiovisual carts, plasma screen carts and video conferencing carts. The firm also offers streaming media products, which it acquired through a recent merger with NetStreams, Inc., including Musica, a NetStreams branded residential audio streaming system; Quartet, a simplified, less expensive option than Musica; and Panorama, a point to multi-point high definition multimedia distribution and control system. In June 2011, the firm introduced IMPRESS, a streaming digital signage tool capable of delivering high definition media messages over a network of displays.

ClearOne offers its employees cash compensation; a stock purchase plan and stock options; a 401(k) plan; flexible spending accounts; medical, dental and vision insurance; insurance protection; and an employee referral program.

FINANCIALS:

Sales and profits are in thousands of dollars—add 000 to get the full amount. 2011 Note: Financial information for 2011 was not available for all companies at press time.

2011 Sales: $	2011 Profits: $
2010 Sales: $41,284	2010 Profits: $2,374
2009 Sales: $35,700	2009 Profits: $2,227
2008 Sales: $38,758	2008 Profits: $5,259
2007 Sales: $39,861	2007 Profits: $5,209

U.S. Stock Ticker: CLRO
Int'l Ticker:
Int'l Exchange:
Employees: 122 Fiscal Year Ends: 12/31
Parent Company:

SALARIES/BENEFITS:

Pension Plan:	ESOP Stock Plan:	Profit Sharing:	Top Exec. Salary: $225,000	Bonus: $73,523
Savings Plan: Y	Stock Purch. Plan: Y		Second Exec. Salary: $152,500	Bonus: $49,548

OTHER THOUGHTS:

Apparent Women Officers or Directors: 2
Hot Spot for Advancement for Women/Minorities:

LOCATIONS: ("Y" = Yes)

West:	Southwest:	Midwest:	Southeast:	Northeast:	International:
Y	Y				Y

COGENT COMMUNICATIONS

www.cogentco.com

Industry Group Code: 517110

Management:		Sales/Marketing:		Liberal Arts:		Information Systems:		Professionals:		Technical/Scientific:	
Mgmt. Trainees:		Mktg. Professionals:	Y	Gen. Writing/Editing:		Info. Management:	Y	Finance/Acct.:	Y	Engineers, Elec.:	Y
Experienced Mgmt.:	Y	Retail Sales:		Technical Writing:		Software Dev.:	Y	Law:	Y	Engineers, Other:	
Int'l Business:	Y	Commercial/Industrial:	Y	Graphic Arts/Photog.:		Hardware Dev.:		HR/Other:	Y	Health/Lab	
MBA Graduates:	Y	Sales Trainees:	Y	Music:		Consulting/Other:		Training:	Y	Scientists/Research:	
		Advertising Pros.:		Broadcasting:				Health Care:		Petroleum/Chemicals:	
				Other:				Consulting:		Math/Other:	

TYPES OF BUSINESS:

Facilities-Based Internet Service Provider
VOIP Service

BRANDS/DIVISIONS/AFFILIATES:

CONTACTS:

Note: Officers with more than one job title may be intentionally listed here more than once.

Dave Schaeffer, CEO
Tad Weed, CFO
Travis Wachter, Mgr.-Mktg. Comm.
Dave Schaeffer, Chmn.

Phone: 202-295-4200	**Fax:** 202-295-9061
Toll-Free: 877-875-4432	
Address: 1015 31st St., NW, Washington, DC 20007 US	

GROWTH PLANS/SPECIAL FEATURES:

Cogent Communications is a facilities-based provider of Internet access and Internet Protocol (IP) communications services. Its network is specifically designed and optimized to transmit data using IP. Cogent delivers its services through approximately 25,000 customer connections in North America and Europe. The firm's primary on-net service is Internet access at a speed of 100 megabits per second. It offers this on-net service exclusively through its own facilities, which run all the way to its customers' premises. Because of its integrated network architecture, the firm is not dependent on local telephone companies to serve its on-net customers. Cogent's typical customers in multi-tenant office buildings are law firms, financial services firms, advertising and marketing firms and other professional services businesses. It also provides on-net Internet access to certain bandwidth-intensive users such as universities, other Internet service providers (ISPs), telephone companies, cable television companies and commercial content providers at speeds of up to 10 gigabits per second. The company also provides on-net services in carrier-neutral collocation facilities and in single-tenant office buildings. It has 41 data centers that are located throughout North American and Europe. Cogent's on-net customers generate approximately 77.8% of its total net service revenue. The firm also provides Internet connectivity to customers that are not located in buildings directly connected to its network. It serves these off-net customers using other carriers' facilities to provide the last mile portion of the link from its customers' premises to its network. Cogent's off-net customers generate approximately 21.0% of net its service revenue. The firm's non-core services, which generate approximately 1.2% of its net service revenue, are those services it acquired but does not actively sell, including managed modem services, dial-up Internet access services and voice services.

FINANCIALS:

Sales and profits are in thousands of dollars—add 000 to get the full amount. 2011 Note: Financial information for 2011 was not available for all companies at press time.

2011 Sales: $305,500	2011 Profits: $7,542	**U.S. Stock Ticker: CCOI**
2010 Sales: $263,416	2010 Profits: $ 669	**Int'l Ticker:**
2009 Sales: $235,807	2009 Profits: $-17,151	Int'l Exchange:
2008 Sales: $215,489	2008 Profits: $26,779	Employees: 568 Fiscal Year Ends: 12/31
2007 Sales: $185,663	2007 Profits: $-31,025	Parent Company:

SALARIES/BENEFITS:

Pension Plan:	ESOP Stock Plan:	Profit Sharing:	Top Exec. Salary: $323,122	Bonus: $
Savings Plan:	Stock Purch. Plan:		Second Exec. Salary: $249,920	Bonus: $

OTHER THOUGHTS:

Apparent Women Officers or Directors:
Hot Spot for Advancement for Women/Minorities:

LOCATIONS: ("Y" = Yes)

West:	Southwest:	Midwest:	Southeast:	Northeast:	International:
				Y	Y

COHERENT INC

www.coherent.com

Industry Group Code: 33911

Management:		Sales/Marketing:		Liberal Arts:		Information Systems:		Professionals:		Technical/Scientific:	
Mgmt. Trainees:		Mktg. Professionals:	Y	Gen. Writing/Editing:		Info. Management:	Y	Finance/Acct.:	Y	Engineers, Elec.:	Y
Experienced Mgmt.:	Y	Retail Sales:		Technical Writing:	Y	Software Dev.:	Y	Law:	Y	Engineers, Other:	Y
Int'l Business:	Y	Commercial/Industrial:	Y	Graphic Arts/Photog.:		Hardware Dev.:	Y	HR/Other:	Y	Health/Lab	Y
MBA Graduates:	Y	Sales Trainees:	Y	Music:		Consulting/Other:		Training:	Y	Scientists/Research:	Y
		Advertising Pros.:		Broadcasting:				Health Care:	Y	Petroleum/Chemicals:	
				Other:				Consulting:		Math/Other:	Y

TYPES OF BUSINESS:

Equipment-Lasers & Laser Systems
Precision Optics
Laser Accessories

BRANDS/DIVISIONS/AFFILIATES:

Specialty Lasers and Systems
Commercial Lasers and Components
Beam Dynamics Inc
SiOnyx Inc

CONTACTS:

Note: Officers with more than one job title may be intentionally listed here more than once.

John R. Ambroseo, CEO
John R. Ambroseo, Pres.
Helene Simonet, CFO/Exec. VP
Luis Spinelli, CTO/Exec. VP
Bret M. DiMarco, General Counsel/Exec. VP
Mark S. Sobey, Exec. VP/Gen. Mgr.-Specialty Laser Systems Bus.
Garry W. Rogerson, Chmn.

Phone: 408-764-4000 **Fax:** 408-764-4800
Toll-Free: 800-527-3786
Address: 5100 Patrick Henry Dr., Santa Clara, CA 95054 US

GROWTH PLANS/SPECIAL FEATURES:

Coherent, Inc. designs, manufactures and markets lasers, precision optics and related accessories to customers in over 80 countries. The company operates in two segments: Specialty Lasers and Systems (SLS) and Commercial Lasers and Components (CLC). SLS develops and manufactures configurable, advanced-performance products and serves the microelectronics and scientific research markets. CLC offers OEMs (original equipment manufacturers) components and instrumentation and materials processing. The firm groups its products into four categories based on target application: microelectronics, which accounted for 38% of net sales in 2010; materials processing, 14%; OEM components and instrumentation, 25%; and scientific research and government programs, 23%. The microelectronics segment has four main operations: semiconductor front-end manufacturing; advanced packaging and interconnects; flat panel display manufacturing; and solar cell production and other emerging processes. The material processing segment's products include high-power lasers for metal processing, as well as low-to-medium power lasers for nonmetals processing, precision micromachining and laser marking. Products for the OEM components and instrumentation segment include bio-instrumentation lasers, with applications in confocal microscopy, DNA sequencing, flow cytometry and drug discovery. Products in the scientific research and government programs segment include ultrafast lasers, diode-pumped solid-state lasers, continuous-wave systems, excimer lasers and water-cooled gas lasers, with applications in biology, physics, chemistry and engineering. The firm holds nearly 400 U.S. and foreign patents for its products and technologies. In April 2010, Coherent opened a carbon dioxide laser applications laboratory in Beijing. In May 2010, it acquired Beam Dynamics, Inc. In the same month, it entered a joint development agreement with SiOnyx, Inc. for solar cell capital equipment manufacturing using SiOnyx's Black Silicon processing technology.

Employees are offered medical, dental and vision insurance; disability coverage; life and AD&D insurance; travel insurance; educational assistance; healthcare and dependent day care reimbursement accounts; commuter flexible spending accounts; an employee assistance program; credit union membership; and discounts on entertainment tickets.

FINANCIALS:

Sales and profits are in thousands of dollars—add 000 to get the full amount. 2011 Note: Financial information for 2011 was not available for all companies at press time.

2011 Sales: $802,834 — 2011 Profits: $93,238
2010 Sales: $605,067 — 2010 Profits: $36,916
2009 Sales: $435,882 — 2009 Profits: $-35,319
2008 Sales: $599,262 — 2008 Profits: $23,403
2007 Sales: $601,153 — 2007 Profits: $15,951

U.S. Stock Ticker: COHR
Int'l Ticker:
Int'l Exchange:
Employees: 2,309 Fiscal Year Ends: 9/30
Parent Company:

SALARIES/BENEFITS:

Pension Plan: ESOP Stock Plan: Profit Sharing: Y Top Exec. Salary: $580,008 Bonus: $870,012
Savings Plan: Y Stock Purch. Plan: Y Second Exec. Salary: $369,990 Bonus: $388,490

OTHER THOUGHTS:

Apparent Women Officers or Directors: 2
Hot Spot for Advancement for Women/Minorities:

LOCATIONS: ("Y" = Yes)

West:	Southwest:	Midwest:	Southeast:	Northeast:	International:
Y	Y	Y	Y	Y	Y

COMDATA CORP

www.comdata.com

Industry Group Code: 522320

Management:		Sales/Marketing:		Liberal Arts:		Information Systems:		Professionals:		Technical/Scientific:	
Mgmt. Trainees:	Y	Mktg. Professionals:	Y	Gen. Writing/Editing:	Y	Info. Management:	Y	Finance/Acct.:	Y	Engineers, Elec.:	
Experienced Mgmt.:	Y	Retail Sales:		Technical Writing:	Y	Software Dev.:	Y	Law:	Y	Engineers, Other:	
Int'l Business:		Commercial/Industrial:	Y	Graphic Arts/Photog.:		Hardware Dev.:		HR/Other:	Y	Health/Lab	
MBA Graduates:	Y	Sales Trainees:	Y	Music:		Consulting/Other:		Training:	Y	Scientists/Research:	
		Advertising Pros.:	Y	Broadcasting:				Health Care:		Petroleum/Chemicals:	
				Other:				Consulting:		Math/Other:	

TYPES OF BUSINESS:

Electronic Funds Transfers
Transaction Processing
Stored-Value Cards
Regulatory Compliance Services

BRANDS/DIVISIONS/AFFILIATES:

Ceridian Corp
Comdata Card
Comdata Smart Solutions

CONTACTS:

Note: Officers with more than one job title may be intentionally listed here more than once.

Melinda Stickley, COO/Sr. VP
Steve Stevenson, Pres.
Randy Morgan, Exec. VP-Sales & Mktg.
Tracey Power, Sr. VP-Human Resources
Todd Joseph, Sr. VP-IT
Lisa Peerman, General Counsel/Sr. VP/Corp. Sec.
Gilbert Niwa, Sr. VP-Finance
Walt Hannabass, Sr. VP-Credit & Collections
Kurt Schusterman, Sr. VP-Regulatory Compliance Solutions

Phone: 615-370-7000 **Fax:** 615-370-7209
Toll-Free: 800-266-3282
Address: 5301 Maryland Way, Brentwood, TN 37027 US

GROWTH PLANS/SPECIAL FEATURES:

Comdata Corp., a subsidiary of the Ceridian Corp., processes financial data transactions. It specializes in trust-enabled payment transactions, based on an individual company's business rules, which include controlled spending, purchasing, payroll, cash card and other similar transactions. Based in Brentwood, Tennessee, the company is credited with the 1981 introduction of the first electronic fund distribution system for the transportation industry. Comdata is currently separated into five divisions: Corporate Spending, Prepaid Solutions, Merchant Solutions, Receivables Financing and Regulatory Compliance. The Corporate Spending division offers corporate expense management solutions through the Comdata card, which allows trucking companies to deliver corporate purchase, fuel and payroll money to professional truck drivers on the road; and other companies to control and establish parameters for employee spending on company cards. This segment also provides maintenance management and roadside assistance services. The Prepaid Solutions segment provides prepaid offshoots of Comdata Card services, including expense reimbursement and employee incentives. The Merchant Solutions segment is a provider of point-of-sale (POS) and payment terminal solutions for truck stops and convenience stores. The Receivables Financing segment provides receivables collection and purchasing solutions. Finally, the Regulatory Compliance segment provides solutions related to permits, fuel tax filing, annual licensing and driver log auditing to transportation companies. The firm serves customers in the fleet, retail, hospitality, aviation, construction, healthcare and government sectors. Comdata recently launched Comdata Smart Solutions, a POS platform that consolidates all retail and fuel purchases. In August 2011, the company introduced a cardless fueling solution for transportation companies and travel centers.

The company offers its employees medical, dental and vision insurance; a 401(k) plan; tuition assistance; short- and long-term disability; life insurance; adoption assistance; a scholarship program for employees' children; long-term care insurance; an employee assistance program; a day care cost-sharing program; discounted auto, homeowners and renters insurance; and subsidized business travel.

FINANCIALS:

Sales and profits are in thousands of dollars—add 000 to get the full amount. 2011 Note: Financial information for 2011 was not available for all companies at press time.

2011 Sales: $	2011 Profits: $	**U.S. Stock Ticker: Subsidiary**
2010 Sales: $	2010 Profits: $	**Int'l Ticker:**
2009 Sales: $	2009 Profits: $	Int'l Exchange:
2008 Sales: $	2008 Profits: $	Employees: Fiscal Year Ends: 12/31
2007 Sales: $	2007 Profits: $	Parent Company: CERIDIAN CORP

SALARIES/BENEFITS:

Pension Plan:	ESOP Stock Plan:	Profit Sharing:	Top Exec. Salary: $	Bonus: $
Savings Plan: Y	Stock Purch. Plan:		Second Exec. Salary: $	Bonus: $

OTHER THOUGHTS:

Apparent Women Officers or Directors: 3
Hot Spot for Advancement for Women/Minorities: Y

LOCATIONS: ("Y" = Yes)

West:	Southwest:	Midwest:	Southeast:	Northeast:	International:
Y	Y	Y	Y	Y	

COMPASS DIVERSIFIED HOLDINGS

codi.client.shareholder.com

Industry Group Code: 523910

Management:		**Sales/Marketing:**		**Liberal Arts:**		**Information Systems:**		**Professionals:**		**Technical/Scientific:**	
Mgmt. Trainees:		Mktg. Professionals:		Gen. Writing/Editing:		Info. Management:	Y	Finance/Acct.:	Y	Engineers, Elec.:	
Experienced Mgmt.:	Y	Retail Sales:		Technical Writing:		Software Dev.:		Law:	Y	Engineers, Other:	
Int'l Business:		Commercial/Industrial:		Graphic Arts/Photog.:		Hardware Dev.:		HR/Other:	Y	Health/Lab	
MBA Graduates:	Y	Sales Trainees:		Music:		Consulting/Other:		Training:		Scientists/Research:	
		Advertising Pros.:		Broadcasting:				Health Care:		Petroleum/Chemicals:	
				Other:				Consulting:		Math/Other:	Y

TYPES OF BUSINESS:

Private Equity Investments

BRANDS/DIVISIONS/AFFILIATES:

Advanced Circuits
Tridien Medical
HALO Lee Wayne LLC
American Furniture Manufacturing Inc
Fox Factory Inc
CamelBak Products LLC
ERGObaby Carrier Inc
Liberty Safe

CONTACTS: *Note: Officers with more than one job title may be intentionally listed here more than once.*

I. Joseph Massoud, CEO
James J. Bottiglieri, CFO
Carrie W. Ryan, Sec.
C. Sean Day, Chmn.

Phone: 203-221-1703	**Fax:**
Toll-Free:	
Address: 61 Wilton Rd., 2nd Fl., Westport, CT 06880 US	

GROWTH PLANS/SPECIAL FEATURES:

Compass Diversified Holdings acquires and manages U.S.-based small and medium-sized companies. The company acquires controlling interests in businesses operating in industries with long-term macroeconomic growth opportunities, stable cash flow, diversified customer and supplier bases, minimal threats of technological or product obsolescence and strong management teams. The firm offers its investors diversified portfolio risk and ownership of companies traditionally owned by private equity firms, wealthy individuals and families. For the companies it purchases, Compass provides strategic and financial support. The firm owns controlling interests in the following companies: Advanced Circuits, a rigid printed circuit boards (PCBs) manufacturer; Tridien Medical, a manufacturer of medical support surfaces; HALO Lee Wayne LLC, a customized promotional products distributor; American Furniture Manufacturing, Inc., a manufacturer of upholstered furniture; Fox Factory, Inc., a manufacturer of mountain bike suspension products; CamelBak Products, a manufacturer of hydration products for outdoor, recreation and military use; ERGObaby, a baby carrier and associated products design and marketing firm; and Liberty Safe, a designer of home and gun safes. These companies, in turn, actively acquire complementary companies in their fields. In August 2011, Compass acquired a controlling interest in CamelBak Products, LLC for $257.5 million. In October 2011, the company sold Staffmark Holdings, Inc. for $295 million. In November 2011, subsidiary ERGObaby Carrier, Inc. acquired Orbit Baby, Inc. for $17.5 million.

FINANCIALS: **Sales and profits are in thousands of dollars—add 000 to get the full amount. 2011 Note: Financial information for 2011 was not available for all companies at press time.**

2011 Sales: $	2011 Profits: $	**U.S. Stock Ticker: CODI**
2010 Sales: $1,657,609	2010 Profits: $-44,770	**Int'l Ticker:**
2009 Sales: $1,248,740	2009 Profits: $-39,645	Int'l Exchange:
2008 Sales: $1,538,473	2008 Profits: $78,294	Employees: 399 Fiscal Year Ends: 12/31
2007 Sales: $841,791	2007 Profits: $40,368	Parent Company:

SALARIES/BENEFITS:

Pension Plan:	ESOP Stock Plan:	Profit Sharing:	Top Exec. Salary: $390,000	Bonus: $300,000
Savings Plan:	Stock Purch. Plan:		Second Exec. Salary: $	Bonus: $

OTHER THOUGHTS:

Apparent Women Officers or Directors: 1
Hot Spot for Advancement for Women/Minorities:

LOCATIONS: ("Y" = Yes)

West:	Southwest:	Midwest:	Southeast:	Northeast:	International:
				Y	

COMTECH TELECOMMUNICATIONS CORP

www.comtechtel.com

Industry Group Code: 3342

Management:		**Sales/Marketing:**		**Liberal Arts:**		**Information Systems:**		**Professionals:**		**Technical/Scientific:**	
Mgmt. Trainees:		Mktg. Professionals:	Y	Gen. Writing/Editing:	Y	Info. Management:	Y	Finance/Acct.:	Y	Engineers, Elec.:	Y
Experienced Mgmt.:	Y	Retail Sales:		Technical Writing:	Y	Software Dev.:	Y	Law:	Y	Engineers, Other:	Y
Int'l Business:	Y	Commercial/Industrial:	Y	Graphic Arts/Photog.:		Hardware Dev.:	Y	HR/Other:	Y	Health/Lab	
MBA Graduates:	Y	Sales Trainees:	Y	Music:		Consulting/Other:		Training:	Y	Scientists/Research:	
		Advertising Pros.:		Broadcasting:				Health Care:		Petroleum/Chemicals:	
				Other:				Consulting:		Math/Other:	

TYPES OF BUSINESS:

Communications Equipment-Microwave & RF
Satellite Equipment & Services

BRANDS/DIVISIONS/AFFILIATES:

Comtech EF Data Corp.
Comtech Systems, Inc.
Comtech Mobile Datacom Corporation
Comtech AeroAstro, Inc.
Comtech PST Corp.
Comtech Xicom Technology, Inc.

CONTACTS: *Note: Officers with more than one job title may be intentionally listed here more than once.*

Fred Kornberg, CEO
Fred Kornberg, Pres.
Michael Porcelain, CFO/Sr. VP
Robert Rause, Sr. VP-Strategy & Mergers & Acquisitions
Robert McCollom, Sr. VP/Pres., Comtech EF Data Corp.
Richard Burt, Sr. VP/Pres., Comtech Systems, Inc.
Dan Wood, Sr. VP/Pres., Comtech Mobile Datacom Corp.
Larry Konopelko, Sr. VP/Pres., Comtech PST Corp.
Fred Kornberg, Chmn.

Phone: 631-962-7000 **Fax:**
Toll-Free:
Address: 68 S. Service Rd., Ste. 230, Melville, NY 11747 US

GROWTH PLANS/SPECIAL FEATURES:

Comtech Telecommunications Corp. is a communications equipment manufacturer specializing in microwave and radio frequency (RF) applications. The company operates in three segments: telecommunications transmission, mobile data communications and RF microwave amplifiers. Comtech's telecommunications transmission segment provides advanced equipment and systems that are used to enhance satellite transmission efficiency and enable wireless communications in environments where terrestrial communications are unavailable, inefficient or too expensive. Its main telecommunications transmission products include satellite earth station equipment and systems, such as modems, frequency converters, power amplifiers, transceivers, access devices and over-the-horizon microwave equipment capable of transmitting signals over unfriendly or inaccessible terrain from 20-600 miles. Subsidiaries in this segment include Comtech EF Data Corp. and Comtech Systems, Inc. The mobile data communications segment develops products enabling global satellite-based communications for mobile, real-time, secure transmission. Products and systems in this segment include mobile satellite transceivers, satellite packet data networks, ruggedized computers and satellite earth station network gateways, as well as associated installation, training and maintenance. Significant subsidiaries in this segment are Comtech Mobile Datacom Corporation and Comtech AeroAstro, Inc. Comtech's RF microwave amplifiers segment provides solid-state broadband amplifiers in the microwave and RF spectrums. Its amplifiers are used in defense applications by U.S. and foreign military customers, as well as commercial customers, who use Comtech's products in oncology treatment systems; the provision of e-mail, Internet access and video conferencing through an aircraft satellite communication system; and testing electronic systems for electromagnetic compatibility and susceptibility to interference. Subsidiaries in this segment include Comtech PST Corp. and Comtech Xicom Technology, Inc.

FINANCIALS: **Sales and profits are in thousands of dollars—add 000 to get the full amount. 2011 Note: Financial information for 2011 was not available for all companies at press time.**

2011 Sales: $612,379	2011 Profits: $67,895
2010 Sales: $778,205	2010 Profits: $60,630
2009 Sales: $586,372	2009 Profits: $47,525
2008 Sales: $531,627	2008 Profits: $73,650
2007 Sales: $445,684	2007 Profits: $65,213

U.S. Stock Ticker: CMTL
Int'l Ticker:
Int'l Exchange:
Employees: 1,268 Fiscal Year Ends: 7/31
Parent Company:

SALARIES/BENEFITS:

Pension Plan:	ESOP Stock Plan:	Profit Sharing:	Top Exec. Salary: $695,000	Bonus: $3,475,000
Savings Plan:	Stock Purch. Plan: Y		Second Exec. Salary: $375,000	Bonus: $520,000

OTHER THOUGHTS:

Apparent Women Officers or Directors:
Hot Spot for Advancement for Women/Minorities:

LOCATIONS: ("Y" = Yes)

West:	Southwest:	Midwest:	Southeast:	Northeast:	International:
Y	Y		Y	Y	Y

COMVERGE INC

www.comverge.com

Industry Group Code: 33411

Management:		**Sales/Marketing:**		**Liberal Arts:**		**Information Systems:**		**Professionals:**		**Technical/Scientific:**	
Mgmt. Trainees:		Mktg. Professionals:		Gen. Writing/Editing:		Info. Management:	Y	Finance/Acct.:	Y	Engineers, Elec.:	Y
Experienced Mgmt.:	Y	Retail Sales:		Technical Writing:	Y	Software Dev.:	Y	Law:	Y	Engineers, Other:	
Int'l Business:		Commercial/Industrial:		Graphic Arts/Photog.:		Hardware Dev.:	Y	HR/Other:	Y	Health/Lab	
MBA Graduates:	Y	Sales Trainees:		Music:		Consulting/Other:	Y	Training:		Scientists/Research:	
		Advertising Pros.:		Broadcasting:				Health Care:		Petroleum/Chemicals:	
				Other:				Consulting:		Math/Other:	Y

TYPES OF BUSINESS:

Smart Grid Technology

BRANDS/DIVISIONS/AFFILIATES:

IntelliSOURCE

CONTACTS:

Note: Officers with more than one job title may be intentionally listed here more than once.

R. Blake Young, CEO
Steve Moffitt, COO/Exec. VP
R. Blake Young, Pres.
David Mathieson, CFO/Exec. VP
Christopher Camino, Chief Mktg. Officer/Exec. VP-Sales
Teresa Naylor, Sr. VP-Human Resources
Arthur Vos, IV, CTO/Sr. VP-Utility Sales
Matthew H. Smith, General Counsel/Sr. VP/Sec.
Jason Cigarran, VP-Investor Rel.
John A. Waterworth, Controller/VP
George Hunt, Sr. VP-Commercial & Industrial Sales
Jason Cigarran, VP-Mktg.
Alec G. Dreyer, Chmn.
Michael D. Picchi, Pres., Comverge Int'l

Phone:	**Fax:** 770-696-7665
Toll-Free: 888-565-5525	
Address: 5390 Triangle Pkwy., Ste. 300, Norcross, GA 30092 US	

GROWTH PLANS/SPECIAL FEATURES:

Comverge, Inc. is a clean energy company and a leading provider of intelligent energy management (IEM) solutions. Its products are designed to improve the smart grid, a system of multiple suppliers and operators delivering power to consumers with the ability to control and adjust power according to usage and demand for the purpose of cutting costs and saving energy. The company operates in two segments: Residential Business and Commercial & Industrial (C&I). The Residential Business segment offers IEM networks to utility customers for use in programs with residential and small commercial end-use participants. Its solutions include a broad range of hardware products, from basic one-way load control switches to more sophisticated smart thermostats, in-home displays and comprehensive two-way data and control systems; its IntelliSOURCE software and various services such as installation and marketing. The segment offers programs that address both peak and base load demands for residential and small commercial end consumers. Such programs include the Virtual Peaking Capacity (VPC) Program, which provides additional capacity through long-term contracts with utilities. The C&I segment provides IEM solutions to utilities and independent system operators, enabling them to reduce energy use and costs. This segment contracts with utilities to provide available capacity to utility customers through pay-for-performance VPC programs. The C&I segment also performs upgrades and maintenance of power systems.

FINANCIALS:

Sales and profits are in thousands of dollars—add 000 to get the full amount. 2011 Note: Financial information for 2011 was not available for all companies at press time.

2011 Sales: $	2011 Profits: $	**U.S. Stock Ticker: COMV**
2010 Sales: $119,389	2010 Profits: $-31,351	**Int'l Ticker:**
2009 Sales: $98,844	2009 Profits: $-31,666	Int'l Exchange:
2008 Sales: $77,238	2008 Profits: $-94,106	Employees: 562 Fiscal Year Ends: 12/31
2007 Sales: $	2007 Profits: $	Parent Company:

SALARIES/BENEFITS:

Pension Plan:	ESOP Stock Plan:	Profit Sharing:	Top Exec. Salary: $372,115	Bonus: $350,000
Savings Plan: Y	Stock Purch. Plan:		Second Exec. Salary: $300,000	Bonus: $146,100

OTHER THOUGHTS:

Apparent Women Officers or Directors: 1
Hot Spot for Advancement for Women/Minorities:

LOCATIONS: ("Y" = Yes)

West:	Southwest:	Midwest:	Southeast:	Northeast:	International:
Y			Y	Y	

CONCUR TECHNOLOGIES INC

www.concur.com

Industry Group Code: 511210

Management:		Sales/Marketing:		Liberal Arts:		Information Systems:		Professionals:		Technical/Scientific:	
Mgmt. Trainees:		Mktg. Professionals:	Y	Gen. Writing/Editing:		Info. Management:	Y	Finance/Acct.:	Y	Engineers, Elec.:	Y
Experienced Mgmt.:	Y	Retail Sales:		Technical Writing:	Y	Software Dev.:	Y	Law:	Y	Engineers, Other:	
Int'l Business:	Y	Commercial/Industrial:	Y	Graphic Arts/Photog.:		Hardware Dev.:		HR/Other:	Y	Health/Lab	
MBA Graduates:	Y	Sales Trainees:	Y	Music:		Consulting/Other:		Training:	Y	Scientists/Research:	
		Advertising Pros.:		Broadcasting:				Health Care:		Petroleum/Chemicals:	
				Other:				Consulting:		Math/Other:	

TYPES OF BUSINESS:

Software Manufacturer-Expense Reporting
Corporate Expense Management Solutions
Professional Services
Travel and Entertainment Expense Reporting Software
Meeting Expense Reporting Software

BRANDS/DIVISIONS/AFFILIATES:

Concur Expense
Ulysse Travel & Expense
Concur Invoice Management
Concur Travel
GlobalExpense
GlobalExpense.
TripIt
Concur Japan

CONTACTS: *Note: Officers with more than one job title may be intentionally listed here more than once.*

S. Steven Singh, CEO
Rajeev Singh, COO
Rajeev Singh, Pres.
Frank Pelzer, CFO
Michael Hilton, Exec. VP-Worldwide Mktg.
John Love, Exec. VP-Tech.
Kyle R. Sugamele, Chief Legal Officer/Corp. Sec.
Scott Torrey, Gen. Mgr.-Oper. & Public Sector/Exec. VP
John Torrey, Exec. VP-Corp. Dev.
Robert Cavanaugh, Exec. VP/Gen. Mgr.-North America
Elena Donio, Exec. VP/Gen. Mgr.-Small & Mid-Sized Bus.
Mike Koetting, Exec. VP-Supplier Mgmt. & Advertising
Bob Robison, Exec. VP-Client Svcs.
S. Steven Singh, Chmn.
Michael Eberhard, Gen. Mgr.-Asia Pacific/Exec. VP

Phone: 425-702-8808 **Fax:** 425-702-8828
Toll-Free: 800-401-8412
Address: 18400 N.E. Union Hill Rd., Redmond, WA 98052 US

GROWTH PLANS/SPECIAL FEATURES:

Concur Technologies, Inc. provides business automation process services and software products for the management of travel- and meeting-related corporate expenses. Its products are designed to automate and streamline corporate expense reimbursement processes, reduce operating costs and improve internal controls. The firm's portfolio includes six flagship products. Concur Travel & Expense integrates online travel booking with automated expense reporting to provide unified end-to-end corporate travel procurement and expense reporting. Concur Expense provides report preparation, report routing and approval, report processing and data capture. Concur Travel is a corporate travel management software product that combines travel booking and expense reporting into an automated on-demand service. Concur Breeze is an online expense reporting suite designed specifically for small businesses. Concur Invoice Management is designed to automate and reduce the costs associated with the management of the payment of vendor invoices. Lastly, Ulysse Travel & Expense is an on-demand service that allows users to manage expenses in stages. Its features include integration to existing back office systems and multicurrency and multilingual support. The company also offers value-added services and software that integrate with the company's primary products. These include Concur Pay, Concur Audit, Concur Intelligence, Concur Meeting, Concur Mobile, SmartExpense, Concur Advantage and Concur Connect. The company provides its solutions as a subscription service on an outsourced basis over the Internet or through a dedicated telecommunications connection. Additionally, Concur offers professional services including consulting, customer support and training. The company has more than 100,000 customers in over 100 countries. In early 2011, Concur acquired TripIt, a developer of mobile trip management software; and established Concur Japan, a joint venture with SunBridge Corporation,to serve the Japanese market. In July 2011, the firm acquired U.K.-based expense management group GlobalExpense.

Employees are offered life, disability, medical, dental and vision insurance; flexible spending accounts; a 401(k); and discounted hardware and software.

FINANCIALS: **Sales and profits are in thousands of dollars—add 000 to get the full amount. 2011 Note: Financial information for 2011 was not available for all companies at press time.**

2011 Sales: $349,488	2011 Profits: $-10,743	**U.S. Stock Ticker: CNQR**
2010 Sales: $292,936	2010 Profits: $20,581	**Int'l Ticker:**
2009 Sales: $247,596	2009 Profits: $25,677	Int'l Exchange:
2008 Sales: $215,491	2008 Profits: $17,184	Employees: 1,600 Fiscal Year Ends: 9/30
2007 Sales: $129,107	2007 Profits: $8,225	Parent Company:

SALARIES/BENEFITS:

Pension Plan:	ESOP Stock Plan:	Profit Sharing:	Top Exec. Salary: $500,000	Bonus: $623,801
Savings Plan: Y	Stock Purch. Plan: Y		Second Exec. Salary: $450,000	Bonus: $571,818

OTHER THOUGHTS:

Apparent Women Officers or Directors: 1
Hot Spot for Advancement for Women/Minorities:

LOCATIONS: ("Y" = Yes)

West:	Southwest:	Midwest:	Southeast:	Northeast:	International:
Y	Y	Y	Y	Y	Y

CONSTANT CONTACT INC

www.constantcontact.com

Industry Group Code: 541810E

Management:		Sales/Marketing:		Liberal Arts:		Information Systems:		Professionals:		Technical/Scientific:	
Mgmt. Trainees:		Mktg. Professionals:		Gen. Writing/Editing:	Y	Info. Management:	Y	Finance/Acct.:	Y	Engineers, Elec.:	
Experienced Mgmt.:	Y	Retail Sales:		Technical Writing:		Software Dev.:	Y	Law:	Y	Engineers, Other:	
Int'l Business:		Commercial/Industrial:	Y	Graphic Arts/Photog.:	Y	Hardware Dev.:		HR/Other:	Y	Health/Lab	
MBA Graduates:	Y	Sales Trainees:	Y	Music:		Consulting/Other:		Training:		Scientists/Research:	
		Advertising Pros.:		Broadcasting:				Health Care:		Petroleum/Chemicals:	
				Other:				Consulting:		Math/Other:	

TYPES OF BUSINESS:

E-mail Marketing Services
Event Promotion
Online Surveys
Social Media Marketing

BRANDS/DIVISIONS/AFFILIATES:

Experts Program
Social Campaigns

CONTACTS: *Note: Officers with more than one job title may be intentionally listed here more than once.*

Gail F. Goodman, CEO
Gail F. Goodman, Pres.
Harpreet Grewal, CFO
Rick Jensen, Chief Mktg. & Sales Officer/Sr. VP
Bob Nicoson, Chief Human Resources Officer/VP
Ellen M. Brezniak, Sr. VP-Prod. Strategy
John J. Walsh, Sr. VP-Eng.
Robert P. Nault, General Counsel/VP
John J. Walsh, Sr. VP-Oper.
Joel Hughes, Sr. VP-Corp. Dev. & Strategy
Mark Schmulen, Gen. Mgr.-Social Media
Harpreet Grewal, Treas./Exec. VP
Christopher M. Litster, VP/Gen. Mgr.-Event Mktg. Bus.
Thomas C. Howd, Sr. VP-Customer Oper.
Gail F. Goodman, Chmn.

Phone: 781-472-8100	**Fax:** 781-472-8101
Toll-Free:	
Address: 1601 Trapelo Rd., 3rd Fl., Waltham, MA 02451 US	

GROWTH PLANS/SPECIAL FEATURES:

Constant Contact, Inc. provides on-demand email marketing, event marketing and online survey solutions, primarily for small organizations such as small businesses and non-profit agencies. The company's email marketing products and services enable clients to develop, implement and analyze email marketing campaigns. Its services feature a campaign creation wizard; more than 450 customizable templates for newsletters, business letters, promotions and announcements; contact list growth and management; email tracking and reporting statistics; image hosting and archive services; and security and privacy solutions. Its event marketing service allows customers to promote and manage events, invite guests, capture and track registrations, collect online payments and communicate with registrants. Its services include the creation of event homepages, email invitations, pre-designed registration forms and online tracking of registration, payment and attendance figures, as well as an event creation wizard that features over 130 preformatted and customizable event theme templates. For online surveys, the firm provides over 80 customizable survey templates for clients to edit and adapt to their needs. It also offers analytic services that allow customers to segment results based on survey responses, apply filters for quick analysis and view results in graphical and detailed data formats. Additionally, the firm offers various professional services and an Experts Program, an online training program covering the email marketing business. Constant Contact has roughly 435,000 customers in over 160 countries. In December 2011, the firm opened a new office in the U.K. In January 2012, the company released Social Campaigns, a new social marketing platform for nonprofits and small businesses.

FINANCIALS: **Sales and profits are in thousands of dollars—add 000 to get the full amount. 2011 Note: Financial information for 2011 was not available for all companies at press time.**

2011 Sales: $	2011 Profits: $	**U.S. Stock Ticker: CTCT**
2010 Sales: $174,231	2010 Profits: $2,914	**Int'l Ticker:**
2009 Sales: $129,061	2009 Profits: $-1,260	Int'l Exchange:
2008 Sales: $87,268	2008 Profits: $-2,056	Employees: 734 Fiscal Year Ends: 12/31
2007 Sales: $	2007 Profits: $	Parent Company:

SALARIES/BENEFITS:

Pension Plan:	ESOP Stock Plan:	Profit Sharing:	Top Exec. Salary: $370,000	Bonus: $285,455
Savings Plan:	Stock Purch. Plan:		Second Exec. Salary: $235,000	Bonus: $111,588

OTHER THOUGHTS:

Apparent Women Officers or Directors: 3
Hot Spot for Advancement for Women/Minorities: Y

LOCATIONS: ("Y" = Yes)

West:	Southwest:	Midwest:	Southeast:	Northeast:	International:
Y			Y	Y	

CONTINENTAL RESOURCES INC

www.contres.com

Industry Group Code: 211111

Management:		Sales/Marketing:		Liberal Arts:		Information Systems:		Professionals:		Technical/Scientific:	
Mgmt. Trainees:		Mktg. Professionals:		Gen. Writing/Editing:		Info. Management:	Y	Finance/Acct.:	Y	Engineers, Elec.:	
Experienced Mgmt.:	Y	Retail Sales:		Technical Writing:		Software Dev.:		Law:	Y	Engineers, Other:	Y
Int'l Business:		Commercial/Industrial:		Graphic Arts/Photog.:		Hardware Dev.:		HR/Other:	Y	Health/Lab	
MBA Graduates:	Y	Sales Trainees:		Music:		Consulting/Other:		Training:	Y	Scientists/Research:	
		Advertising Pros.:		Broadcasting:				Health Care:		Petroleum/Chemicals:	Y
				Other:				Consulting:		Math/Other:	

TYPES OF BUSINESS:

Oil & Gas Exploration & Production
Shale Oil

BRANDS/DIVISIONS/AFFILIATES:

CONTACTS: *Note: Officers with more than one job title may be intentionally listed here more than once.*

Harold G. Hamm, CEO
Jeffery B. Hume, COO
Jeffery B.Hume, Pres.
John D. Hart, CFO/Sr. VP
Jack Stark, Sr. VP-Exploration
Eric S. Eissenstat, General Counsel/Sr. VP
Richard E. Muncrief, Sr. VP-Oper.
Brian Engel, VP-Public Affairs
Warren Henry, VP-Investor Rel.
John D. Hart, Treas.
Steven K. Owen, Sr. VP-Land
Richard H. Straeter, VP-Eastern Div.
Gene R. Carlson, Sr. VP-Resource Dev.
Harold G. Hamm, Chmn.

Phone: 580-233-8955 **Fax:** 580-548-5253
Toll-Free: 800-256-8955
Address: 302 N. Independence, Enid, OK 73702 US

GROWTH PLANS/SPECIAL FEATURES:

Continental Resources, Inc. is an independent oil and natural gas exploration and production company with primary operations in the North, South and East regions of the United States. Continental has estimated proved reserves of 364.7 million barrels of oil equivalent (MMBoe), with estimated proved developed reserves of 140.4 MMBoe, or 38% of its total proved reserves. Approximately 62% of the company's proved reserves consist of crude oil. The company targets large repeatable resource plays where it uses horizontal drilling, advanced fracture stimulation and enhanced recovery technologies to develop and produce oil and natural gas reserves with unconventional formations. The company's North Region operations produces approximately 37,623 barrels (Bbls) equivalent per day, with the principal producing properties in the Red River units, representing approximately 28.9% of total production; and the Bakken shale fields in Montana and North Dakota, representing roughly 46.9%. Continental's average production from its South Region operations was 9,097 Bbls equivalent per day, with the principal producing properties located in the Anadarko Shelf of western Oklahoma and the Arkoma Shale in southeastern Oklahoma. Other minor operations are located in the Haynesville Shale in the East Texas and North Louisiana Salt Basin, the Illinois Basin and the Trenton-Black River properties in Michigan.

Employees are offered health, dental and vision insurance; life insurance; disability coverage; flexible spending accounts; a 401(k) plan; an incentive bonus plan; an employee assistance program; and an education assistance program.

FINANCIALS: **Sales and profits are in thousands of dollars—add 000 to get the full amount. 2011 Note: Financial information for 2011 was not available for all companies at press time.**

2011 Sales: $1,679,838 | 2011 Profits: $429,072
2010 Sales: $839,065 | 2010 Profits: $168,255
2009 Sales: $626,211 | 2009 Profits: $71,338
2008 Sales: $960,490 | 2008 Profits: $320,950
2007 Sales: $582,215 | 2007 Profits: $28,580

U.S. Stock Ticker: CLR
Int'l Ticker:
Int'l Exchange:
Employees: 493 Fiscal Year Ends: 12/31
Parent Company:

SALARIES/BENEFITS:

Pension Plan: | ESOP Stock Plan: | Profit Sharing: | Top Exec. Salary: $807,692 | Bonus: $750,000
Savings Plan: Y | Stock Purch. Plan: Y | | Second Exec. Salary: $361,539 | Bonus: $400,000

OTHER THOUGHTS:

Apparent Women Officers or Directors:
Hot Spot for Advancement for Women/Minorities:

LOCATIONS: ("Y" = Yes)

West:	Southwest:	Midwest:	Southeast:	Northeast:	International:
	Y	Y	Y		

CONTINUCARE CORP

Industry Group Code: 6211

www.continucare.com

Management:		Sales/Marketing:		Liberal Arts:		Information Systems:		Professionals:		Technical/Scientific:	
Mgmt. Trainees:	Y	Mktg. Professionals:	Y	Gen. Writing/Editing:	Y	Info. Management:	Y	Finance/Acct.:	Y	Engineers, Elec.:	
Experienced Mgmt.:	Y	Retail Sales:		Technical Writing:	Y	Software Dev.:	Y	Law:	Y	Engineers, Other:	
Int'l Business:		Commercial/Industrial:	Y	Graphic Arts/Photog.:		Hardware Dev.:		HR/Other:	Y	Health/Lab	Y
MBA Graduates:	Y	Sales Trainees:	Y	Music:		Consulting/Other:		Training:	Y	Scientists/Research:	
		Advertising Pros.:	Y	Broadcasting:				Health Care:	Y	Petroleum/Chemicals:	
				Other:				Consulting:		Math/Other:	

TYPES OF BUSINESS:

Outpatient Health Care
Managed Health Care
Practice Management Services
Sleep Diagnostic Centers

BRANDS/DIVISIONS/AFFILIATES:

Professional Sleep Diagnostics, Inc.
Sleep Disorder Solutions, Inc.

CONTACTS:

Note: Officers with more than one job title may be intentionally listed here more than once.

Richard C. Pfenniger, Jr., CEO
Richard C. Pfenniger, Jr., Pres.
Fernando Fernandez, CFO
Luis H. Izquierdo, Sr. VP-Mktg.
Alfredo Ginory, Chief Medical Officer
Gemma Rosello, Exec. VP-Oper.
Luis H. Izquierdo, Sr. VP-Bus. Dev.
Tom Aponte, VP-Center Oper.
Holly Lopez, VP-Support Svcs.
Dora Rodriguez-Duran, Sr. VP-Support Svcs.
Sonia Michael, Dir.-Medical
Richard C. Pfenniger, Jr., Chmn.

Phone: 305-500-2000 **Fax:** 305-500-2080
Toll-Free:
Address: 7200 Corporate Center Dr., Ste. 600, Miami, FL 33126 US

GROWTH PLANS/SPECIAL FEATURES:

Continucare Corp. is a provider of primary care physician services. Through a network of 18 medical centers, the company provides primary health care services on an outpatient basis. Continucare also provides practice management services to independent physician affiliates (IPAs). All of Continucare's medical centers and IPAs are located in Miami-Dade, Broward and Hillsborough Counties, Florida. These facilities provide services for approximately 25,700 patients on a risk basis and 9,000 patients on a limited or non-risk basis. Additionally, over 6,000 patients are served on a non-risk fee-for-services basis. Medicare eligible patients, under risk arrangements with Continucare, accounted for approximately 90% of the firm's revenue in 2010. The firm's medical centers provide facilities for physicians practicing in the areas of general, family and internal medicine. Services provided to independent physician associate clinics enrolled in Humana health plans include assistance with medical utilization management; pharmacy management; specialist network development; and financial reports. The company has managed care agreements with a number of HMOs, most notably with Humana, accounting for approximately 72% of 2010 revenues; Vista, accounting for 20%; and with Wellcare, generating approximately 6% of revenues. Under these agreements, Continucare receives monthly payments per patient (at a rate established by the contract) in return for providing all medical care required by patients. Subsidiary Seredor Corporation conducts sleep service facilities and operates sleep diagnostic centers in Florida, South Carolina, North Carolina, West Virginia, Virginia, Colorado and Ohio. In 2010, Seredor acquired Precision Diagnostic Services, Inc., an operator of 47 sleep diagnostic centers in eight states; and SleepEasy Therapeutics, Inc., a producer of continuous airway pressure devices and supplies. The same year, the subsidiary also acquired sleep diagnostic center operator United Sleep Diagnostics, Inc.

The company offers employees a 401(k) plan, as well as medical benefits.

FINANCIALS:

Sales and profits are in thousands of dollars—add 000 to get the full amount. 2011 Note: Financial information for 2011 was not available for all companies at press time.

2011 Sales: $333,458	2011 Profits: $23,911	**U.S. Stock Ticker: CNU**
2010 Sales: $310,791	2010 Profits: $22,176	**Int'l Ticker:**
2009 Sales: $281,270	2009 Profits: $15,281	Int'l Exchange:
2008 Sales: $254,440	2008 Profits: $11,270	Employees: 870 Fiscal Year Ends: 6/30
2007 Sales: $217,146	2007 Profits: $6,303	Parent Company:

SALARIES/BENEFITS:

Pension Plan:	ESOP Stock Plan:	Profit Sharing:	Top Exec. Salary: $444,462	Bonus: $400,000
Savings Plan: Y	Stock Purch. Plan:		Second Exec. Salary: $255,888	Bonus: $100,000

OTHER THOUGHTS:

Apparent Women Officers or Directors: 5
Hot Spot for Advancement for Women/Minorities: Y

LOCATIONS: ("Y" = Yes)

West:	Southwest:	Midwest:	Southeast:	Northeast:	International:
			Y		

CORPORATE EXECUTIVE BOARD COMPANY (THE)

www.executiveboard.com

Industry Group Code: 54161

Management:		Sales/Marketing:		Liberal Arts:		Information Systems:		Professionals:		Technical/Scientific:	
Mgmt. Trainees:		Mktg. Professionals:	Y	Gen. Writing/Editing:	Y	Info. Management:	Y	Finance/Acct.:	Y	Engineers, Elec.:	
Experienced Mgmt.:	Y	Retail Sales:		Technical Writing:	Y	Software Dev.:		Law:	Y	Engineers, Other:	
Int'l Business:	Y	Commercial/Industrial:	Y	Graphic Arts/Photog.:		Hardware Dev.:		HR/Other:	Y	Health/Lab	
MBA Graduates:	Y	Sales Trainees:	Y	Music:		Consulting/Other:	Y	Training:	Y	Scientists/Research:	
		Advertising Pros.:		Broadcasting:				Health Care:		Petroleum/Chemicals:	
				Other:	Y			Consulting:	Y	Math/Other:	

TYPES OF BUSINESS:

Consulting-Best Management Practices
Executive Conferences & Seminars
Research Reports & Databases

BRANDS/DIVISIONS/AFFILIATES:

Toolbox.com
Valtera
Baumgartner & Partner Unternehmensberatung GmbH

CONTACTS: *Note: Officers with more than one job title may be intentionally listed here more than once.*

Thomas L. Monahan, III, CEO
Richard S. Lindahl, CFO
Haniel Lynn, Gen. Mgr.-Mktg. & Sales
Melody L. Jones, Chief Human Resources Officer
Warren Thune, Exec. Dir.-IT & Human Resources
Anthony Parslow, Exec. Dir.-Corp. Strategy
Haniel Lynn, Gen. Mgr.-Corp. Comm.
Kurt Reisenberg, Exec. Dir.-Corp. Finance & Corp. Strategy
Steve Meyer, Chief Commercial Officer/Gen. Mgr.
Thomas L. Monahan, III, Chmn.
Anthony Parslow, Exec. Dir.-Global Dev.

Phone: 571-303-3000	**Fax:** 571-303-3100
Toll-Free:	
Address: 1919 N. Lynn St., Arlington, VA 22209 US	

GROWTH PLANS/SPECIAL FEATURES:

The Corporate Executive Board Company (CEB) provides products and services that enable executives and professionals to improve business outcomes. It focuses its offerings on five key areas: finance, strategy and operations; human resources; information technology; legal and compliance; and sales, marketing and communications. It serves executives and professionals at some 5,200 institutions in over 50 countries, providing best practices research and analysis; peer information sharing through web and e-mail networks; performance benchmarking; diagnostics and other workflow enhancement tools; decision support and advice on urgent issues; and executive education focusing on corporate strategy, operations and general management issues. The company's client network includes approximately 94% of Fortune 100 companies and 85% of Fortune 500 companies. CEB's membership-based model offers its executive clients access to function-specific resources; a vice president of finance or IT, for instance, could receive information and support services tailored to their own particular needs. The firm's services are typically purchased through annual subscriptions (averaging about $28,685), and include hosted member meetings; member teleconferences; executive education seminars; customized research briefs; web-based access to various content databases and decision support tools; and best practice research studies. Additionally, the firm offers clients an online professional networking community through subsidiary ToolBox.com. CEB operates through offices in Virginia, Massachusetts, Pennsylvania, Minnesota, Illinois, Arizona, the U.K., Canada, Singapore, Australia and India. In October 2011, the firm acquired German transformation and optimization consultancy firm Baumgartner & Partner Unternehmensberatung GmbH. In February 2012, it acquired talent management group Valtera.

The firm offers its employees medical, dental and vision coverage; life and disability insurance; flexible spending accounts; an employee assistance program; group legal benefits; fitness club discounts; and discounts on other products and services, including home and auto insurance and wireless phone service plans.

FINANCIALS: **Sales and profits are in thousands of dollars—add 000 to get the full amount. 2011 Note: Financial information for 2011 was not available for all companies at press time.**

2011 Sales: $484,700	2011 Profits: $52,700	**U.S. Stock Ticker: EXBD**
2010 Sales: $438,907	2010 Profits: $40,363	**Int'l Ticker:**
2009 Sales: $442,906	2009 Profits: $45,629	Int'l Exchange:
2008 Sales: $558,352	2008 Profits: $44,797	Employees: 1,879 Fiscal Year Ends: 12/31
2007 Sales: $532,716	2007 Profits: $80,587	Parent Company:

SALARIES/BENEFITS:

Pension Plan:	ESOP Stock Plan:	Profit Sharing:	Top Exec. Salary: $641,250	Bonus: $850,000
Savings Plan: Y	Stock Purch. Plan: Y		Second Exec. Salary: $457,500	Bonus: $375,000

OTHER THOUGHTS:

Apparent Women Officers or Directors: 2
Hot Spot for Advancement for Women/Minorities: Y

LOCATIONS: ("Y" = Yes)

West:	Southwest:	Midwest:	Southeast:	Northeast:	International:
Y	Y	Y		Y	Y

COSTAR GROUP INC

www.costar.com

Industry Group Code: 519130

Management:		Sales/Marketing:		Liberal Arts:		Information Systems:		Professionals:		Technical/Scientific:	
Mgmt. Trainees:		Mktg. Professionals:	Y	Gen. Writing/Editing:	Y	Info. Management:	Y	Finance/Acct.:	Y	Engineers, Elec.:	
Experienced Mgmt.:	Y	Retail Sales:		Technical Writing:	Y	Software Dev.:	Y	Law:	Y	Engineers, Other:	
Int'l Business:	Y	Commercial/Industrial:	Y	Graphic Arts/Photog.:		Hardware Dev.:		HR/Other:	Y	Health/Lab	
MBA Graduates:	Y	Sales Trainees:	Y	Music:		Consulting/Other:		Training:		Scientists/Research:	
		Advertising Pros.:		Broadcasting:				Health Care:		Petroleum/Chemicals:	
				Other:				Consulting:		Math/Other:	

TYPES OF BUSINESS:

Online Commercial Real Estate Information
Data Hosting Services
Advertising Services

BRANDS/DIVISIONS/AFFILIATES:

CoStar Property Professional
CoStar Tenant
CoStar COMPS Professional
FOCUS
CoStar U.K. Limited
Resolve Technology Inc
Loopnet Inc
Virtual Premise Inc

CONTACTS: *Note: Officers with more than one job title may be intentionally listed here more than once.*

Andrew C. Florance, CEO
Andrew C. Florance, Pres.
Brian Radecki, CFO
John Stanfill, Sr. VP-Sales & Customer Service
Jennifer Kitchen, Sr. VP-Research
Frank Simuro, CIO
Jonathan Coleman, General Counsel/Corp. Sec.
Michael R. Klein, Chmn.
Paul Marples, Managing Dir.-FOCUS Information Limited

Phone: 202-346-6500	**Fax:** 202-346-6370
Toll-Free: 800-204-5960	
Address: 1331 L St., NW, Washington, DC 20005 US	

GROWTH PLANS/SPECIAL FEATURES:

CoStar Group, Inc. is a leading national provider of commercial real estate sales information. The company offers customers online access to a comprehensive, verified database of commercial real estate information in U.S. markets, as well as in London, other U.K. markets and France. CoStar has a highly developed data collection system that includes sales prices, income and expenses, capitalization rates, loan data, property photographs, buyers, sellers, brokers and other key details. The firm provides commercial real estate professionals with critical knowledge that enables them to complete transactions by offering the most up-to-date, consolidated and standardized information on U.S. commercial real estate. CoStar's subscription-based information services consist primarily of CoStar Property Professional, the firm's flagship service, which provides a comprehensive inventory of office, industrial, retail, multifamily properties and land in markets throughout the U.S., including for-lease and for-sales listings, historical data, building photographs, maps and floor plans; CoStar Tenant, an online business-to-business prospecting and analytical tool providing commercial real estate professionals with commercial U.S. tenant information; CoStar COMPS Professional, a provider of comprehensive coverage of comparable sales information in the U.S. commercial real estate industry; and FOCUS (offered by CoStar U.K. Limited, the firm's U.K. subsidiary), a digital online service offering information on the U.K. real estate market. A diverse portfolio of customers consists of asset managers, mortgage lenders, investors, security analysts and property managers. Other subsidiaries of the company include Resolve Technology, Inc., a real estate investment management software provider; Property and Portfolio Research, Inc., a commercial real estate market forecaster; and Grecam S.A.S., a commercial property information provider. In 2011, the firm acquired Loopnet, Inc., an online commercial real estate market, and Virtual Premise, Inc., a Software-as-a-Service (SaaS)-based real estate information management provider.

The firm offers employees medical, dental and vision insurance; a 401(k); an employee assistance program; tuition reimbursement; life insurance; and disability coverage.

FINANCIALS: **Sales and profits are in thousands of dollars—add 000 to get the full amount. 2011 Note: Financial information for 2011 was not available for all companies at press time.**

2011 Sales: $	2011 Profits: $	**U.S. Stock Ticker: CSGP**
2010 Sales: $226,260	2010 Profits: $13,289	**Int'l Ticker:**
2009 Sales: $209,659	2009 Profits: $18,693	Int'l Exchange:
2008 Sales: $212,428	2008 Profits: $24,623	Employees: 1,389 Fiscal Year Ends: 12/31
2007 Sales: $192,805	2007 Profits: $15,951	Parent Company:

SALARIES/BENEFITS:

Pension Plan:	ESOP Stock Plan:	Profit Sharing:	Top Exec. Salary: $456,560	Bonus: $350,559
Savings Plan: Y	Stock Purch. Plan:		Second Exec. Salary: $249,600	Bonus: $136,487

OTHER THOUGHTS:

Apparent Women Officers or Directors: 1
Hot Spot for Advancement for Women/Minorities:

LOCATIONS: ("Y" = Yes)

West:	Southwest:	Midwest:	Southeast:	Northeast:	International:
Y	Y	Y	Y	Y	Y

COUPONS INC

Industry Group Code: 541810E

www.couponsinc.com

Management:		Sales/Marketing:		Liberal Arts:		Information Systems:		Professionals:		Technical/Scientific:	
Mgmt. Trainees:		Mktg. Professionals:	Y	Gen. Writing/Editing:	Y	Info. Management:	Y	Finance/Acct.:	Y	Engineers, Elec.:	
Experienced Mgmt.:	Y	Retail Sales:		Technical Writing:		Software Dev.:	Y	Law:	Y	Engineers, Other:	
Int'l Business:	Y	Commercial/Industrial:	Y	Graphic Arts/Photog.:	Y	Hardware Dev.:		HR/Other:	Y	Health/Lab	
MBA Graduates:	Y	Sales Trainees:	Y	Music:		Consulting/Other:		Training:	Y	Scientists/Research:	
		Advertising Pros.:	Y	Broadcasting:				Health Care:		Petroleum/Chemicals:	
				Other:	Y			Consulting:		Math/Other:	

TYPES OF BUSINESS:

Online Coupon Advertising & Distribution

BRANDS/DIVISIONS/AFFILIATES:

Coupons.com
Grocery iQ
Surecaster
SuperSaver Newsletter
Couponstar
Save to Card

CONTACTS:

Note: Officers with more than one job title may be intentionally listed here more than once.

Steven R. Boal, CEO
Brian Weisfeld, COO
Steven R. Boal, Pres.
Richard Hornstein, CFO
Gary Calega, VP-Mktg.
Michael R. Walsh, Head-R&D/Chief Security Officer
Steve Horowitz, CTO
Bruce Sattley, VP-Prod. Mgmt.
Sunil Bopardikar, VP-Eng.
Richard Hornstein, General Counsel
Anthony Espiritu, VP-Oper.
Daniel Callaghan, Corp. Controller/VP
Shachar Torem, VP-Sales

Phone: 650-605-4600	**Fax:** 650-605-4700
Toll-Free:	
Address: 400 Logue Ave., Mountain View, CA 94043 US	

GROWTH PLANS/SPECIAL FEATURES:

Coupons, Inc. is an online promotion company that provides marketing technology solutions and printable coupon promotional opportunities. The firm's goal is to provide coupons through digital networks and increase the number of new consumers using coupons through the use of portals such as social media, internet and mobile phone applications. Currently, the company offers its coupons through in store kiosks, web pages, e-mail campaigns, shopping carts, consumer electronics, social media initiatives and mobile devices. The firm's network of sites includes thousands of retailer sites that include more than 46,000 store locations. The company distributes its coupons through its Digital FSI network of thousands of coupon content sites, which enable consumers to find coupons on retail store web sites, radio station/TV sites and lifestyle sites. The network provides value-added features and services, including offers of the week; Surecaster, which targets coupons to high volume audience segments; and the SuperSaver Newsletter, which advertises the most popular coupons in a weekly subscription only e-mail newsletter. The company markets its products to consumers through Coupons.com and Grocery iQ as well as mobile applications. Grocery iQ allows customers to add items through barcode scanning and includes real-time lost synchronization and integrated coupons. The firm's Save to Card solution allows consumers the ability to download electronic coupons from their mobile phones or online directly onto the savings cards. To the publishing market, the company's offerings include branded microsites and Brandcaster, aimed at monetizing website traffic. The firm's clients include Clorox; CVS; General Mills; HEB; Johnson & Johnson; Kellogg's Kmart; Kroger; Walgreens; Kraft Foods; and Safeway. The company is headquartered in Mountain View, California and maintains its European headquarters in Hammersmith, U.K. In October 2011, the company acquired UK-based firm Couponstar.

FINANCIALS:

Sales and profits are in thousands of dollars—add 000 to get the full amount. 2011 Note: Financial information for 2011 was not available for all companies at press time.

2011 Sales: $	2011 Profits: $	**U.S. Stock Ticker: Private**
2010 Sales: $	2010 Profits: $	**Int'l Ticker:**
2009 Sales: $	2009 Profits: $	Int'l Exchange:
2008 Sales: $	2008 Profits: $	Employees: Fiscal Year Ends:
2007 Sales: $	2007 Profits: $	Parent Company:

SALARIES/BENEFITS:

Pension Plan:	ESOP Stock Plan:	Profit Sharing:	Top Exec. Salary: $	Bonus: $
Savings Plan:	Stock Purch. Plan:		Second Exec. Salary: $	Bonus: $

OTHER THOUGHTS:

Apparent Women Officers or Directors:
Hot Spot for Advancement for Women/Minorities:

LOCATIONS: ("Y" = Yes)

West:	Southwest:	Midwest:	Southeast:	Northeast:	International:
Y					Y

CRA INTERNATIONAL INC (CHARLES RIVER)

www.crai.com

Industry Group Code: 54161

Management:		Sales/Marketing:		Liberal Arts:		Information Systems:		Professionals:		Technical/Scientific:	
Mgmt. Trainees:		Mktg. Professionals:		Gen. Writing/Editing:	Y	Info. Management:	Y	Finance/Acct.:	Y	Engineers, Elec.:	
Experienced Mgmt.:	Y	Retail Sales:		Technical Writing:		Software Dev.:		Law:	Y	Engineers, Other:	
Int'l Business:	Y	Commercial/Industrial:	Y	Graphic Arts/Photog.:		Hardware Dev.:		HR/Other:	Y	Health/Lab	
MBA Graduates:	Y	Sales Trainees:		Music:		Consulting/Other:	Y	Training:		Scientists/Research:	
		Advertising Pros.:		Broadcasting:				Health Care:		Petroleum/Chemicals:	
				Other:				Consulting:	Y	Math/Other:	

TYPES OF BUSINESS:

Consulting
Litigation/Finance Consulting
Software

BRANDS/DIVISIONS/AFFILIATES:

NeuCo Inc
CRA International (Saudi Arabia) LLC

CONTACTS:

Note: Officers with more than one job title may be intentionally listed here more than once.

Paul A. Maleh, CEO
Monica G. Noether, COO/Exec. VP
Paul A. Maleh, Pres.
Wayne D. Mackie, CFO/Exec. VP
Elizabeth Ramos, VP-Human Resources
Steven J. Anthony, CIO
Jonathan D. Yellin, General Counsel/VP
Arnold J. Lowenstein, Chief Strategy Officer/Exec. VP
Andrea Goodman, Dir.-Comm.
Wayne D. Mackie, Treas.
Rhett Johnson, VP-Life Sciences & Healthcare
Chad Holmes, VP-Corp. Dev
Scott Niemann, VP-Energy & Environment
Peter Schwechheimer, VP-Intellectual Property
Rowland T. Moriarty, Chmn.
Andrew Macpherson, VP-Value Management

Phone: 617-425-3000 **Fax:** 617-425-3132
Toll-Free:
Address: 200 Clarendon St, John Hancock Tower, T-33, Boston, MA 02116-5092 US

GROWTH PLANS/SPECIAL FEATURES:

CRA International, Inc., operating as Charles River Associates (CRA), is an economic, financial and management consulting firm serving a range of clients, including businesses, law firms, accounting firms and government agencies. CRA operates in 20 offices around the world with areas of expertise across 17 vertical industries, including aerospace and defense; banking and capital markets; chemicals; energy and utilities; financial services; healthcare; insurance; manufacturing; media; mining; metals and materials; oil and gas; pharmaceuticals; real estate; retail; sports; telecommunications; and transportation. CRA offers consulting services in two broad areas: litigation, regulatory and financial consulting; and management consulting. Through its litigation, regulatory and financial platform, the firm provides consulting services to corporate clients and attorneys in a wide range of litigation and regulatory proceedings, providing research and analysis; expert testimony; and comprehensive support in litigation and regulatory proceedings in all areas of finance, accounting, financial economics, risk management, insurance and forensic accounting and investigations. It also applies its expertise in economics, finance and business to offer its clients management consulting services such as strategy development, performance improvement, corporate portfolio analysis, estimation of market demand, new product pricing strategies, valuation of intellectual property, assessment of competitors' actions and analysis of new sources of supply. The firm also develops and markets a family of neutral software tools and application consulting services through its subsidiary, NeuCo, Inc. CRA's consulting business accounts for approximately 98% of total revenues, with the remaining 2% attributed to NeuCo, Inc. In April 2010, the company established CRA International (Saudi Arabia) LLC and opened an office in Riyadh, Saudi Arabia.

Employees are offered medical, dental and vision insurance; life insurance; short- and long-term disability coverage; flexible spending accounts; counseling services; and identity theft protection.

FINANCIALS:

Sales and profits are in thousands of dollars—add 000 to get the full amount. 2011 Note: Financial information for 2011 was not available for all companies at press time.

2011 Sales: $305,200 — 2011 Profits: $16,900
2010 Sales: $287,424 — 2010 Profits: $1,960
2009 Sales: $301,639 — 2009 Profits: $5,691
2008 Sales: $376,751 — 2008 Profits: $6,150
2007 Sales: $394,645 — 2007 Profits: $31,132

U.S. Stock Ticker: CRAI
Int'l Ticker:
Int'l Exchange:
Employees: 710 Fiscal Year Ends: 12/31
Parent Company:

SALARIES/BENEFITS:

Pension Plan: ESOP Stock Plan: Profit Sharing: Y Top Exec. Salary: $548,077 Bonus: $450,000
Savings Plan: Y Stock Purch. Plan: Second Exec. Salary: $493,269 Bonus: $350,000

OTHER THOUGHTS:

Apparent Women Officers or Directors: 3
Hot Spot for Advancement for Women/Minorities: Y

LOCATIONS: ("Y" = Yes)

West:	Southwest:	Midwest:	Southeast:	Northeast:	International:
Y	Y	Y	Y	Y	Y

CRAY INC

www.cray.com

Industry Group Code: 334111

Management:		Sales/Marketing:		Liberal Arts:		Information Systems:		Professionals:		Technical/Scientific:	
Mgmt. Trainees:		Mktg. Professionals:	Y	Gen. Writing/Editing:		Info. Management:	Y	Finance/Acct.:	Y	Engineers, Elec.:	Y
Experienced Mgmt.:	Y	Retail Sales:		Technical Writing:	Y	Software Dev.:	Y	Law:	Y	Engineers, Other:	
Int'l Business:	Y	Commercial/Industrial:	Y	Graphic Arts/Photog.:		Hardware Dev.:	Y	HR/Other:	Y	Health/Lab	
MBA Graduates:	Y	Sales Trainees:		Music:		Consulting/Other:	Y	Training:	Y	Scientists/Research:	
		Advertising Pros.:		Broadcasting:				Health Care:		Petroleum/Chemicals:	
				Other:				Consulting:		Math/Other:	

TYPES OF BUSINESS:

Computer Hardware-Supercomputers
Custom Computers
Software Design

BRANDS/DIVISIONS/AFFILIATES:

Cray XE6
Cray XE6m
Cray XMT
Cray CX1000
Cray CX1
Cray Threadstorm
Cray XK6
Cray Sonexion 1300

CONTACTS: *Note: Officers with more than one job title may be intentionally listed here more than once.*

Peter J. Ungaro, CEO
Peter J. Ungaro, Pres.
Brian C. Henry, CFO/Exec. VP
Barry C. Bolding, VP-Mktg., Storage & Data Mktg.
Michael C. Piraino, VP-Admin.
Michael C. Piraino, General Counsel/VP/Corp. Sec.
Charles A. Morreale, VP-Field Oper.
Margaret A. Williams, Sr. VP-High Performance Computing Systems
Robert Pencek, Dir.-Intelligence Accounts
Ulla Thiel, VP-Europe
Andrew Wyatt, VP-Asia-Pacific South
Stephen C. Kiely, Chmn.
Mamoru Nakano, Pres., Cray Japan

Phone: 206-701-2000 **Fax:** 206-701-2500
Toll-Free: 877-272-9462
Address: 901 5th Ave., Ste. 1000, Seattle, WA 98164 US

GROWTH PLANS/SPECIAL FEATURES:

Cray, Inc. is a global leader in the design, development, marketing and servicing of high-performance computer (HPC) systems, more commonly known as supercomputers, for government, industry and academic institutions. The company manufactures a standard supercomputer product line, as well as designing and manufacturing customized computers. Its key product lines include the XE6, XE6m, XMT, CX1000 and CX1 supercomputers, all sold under the Cray brand name. Cray supercomputers feature an interconnection system that allows users to network dozens of processors with multiple cores. The Cray XE6 and XE6m lines are designed to support up to 192 AMD Opteron 6100 Series processors per cabinet. The Cray XMT utilizes a Cray Threadstorm processor and is compatible with up to 96 AMD Opteron CPUs per cabinet. The company's CX1000 technology line supports Intel Xeon 5600 processors and NVIDIA Tesla graphics processing units (GPUs). Offered in two configurations, the CX1 line is a personal workstation that can operate using Microsoft Windows software and does not require machine room configurations. The firm sells its products primarily through a direct sales force that operates throughout the U.S., Canada, Europe, Japan and Asia-Pacific. In May 2011, Cray introduced Cray XK6, a new production hybrid supercomputing program. In November 2011, the company released integrated file system, software and storage solution Cray Sonexion 1300.

FINANCIALS: **Sales and profits are in thousands of dollars—add 000 to get the full amount. 2011 Note: Financial information for 2011 was not available for all companies at press time.**

2011 Sales: $236,046
2010 Sales: $319,388
2009 Sales: $284,047
2008 Sales: $282,853
2007 Sales: $186,153

2011 Profits: $14,329
2010 Profits: $15,062
2009 Profits: $- 604
2008 Profits: $-40,359
2007 Profits: $-10,635

U.S. Stock Ticker: CRAY
Int'l Ticker:
Int'l Exchange:
Employees: 885 Fiscal Year Ends: 12/31
Parent Company:

SALARIES/BENEFITS:

Pension Plan:
Savings Plan: Y
ESOP Stock Plan:
Stock Purch. Plan: Y
Profit Sharing:
Top Exec. Salary: $450,000 Bonus: $603,450
Second Exec. Salary: $340,000 Bonus: $180,336

OTHER THOUGHTS:

Apparent Women Officers or Directors: 2
Hot Spot for Advancement for Women/Minorities: Y

LOCATIONS: ("Y" = Yes)

West:	Southwest:	Midwest:	Southeast:	Northeast:	International:
Y		Y			Y

CRITICAL CARE SYSTEMS

www.criticalcaresystems.com

Industry Group Code: 6214

Management:		Sales/Marketing:		Liberal Arts:		Information Systems:		Professionals:		Technical/Scientific:	
Mgmt. Trainees:	Y	Mktg. Professionals:	Y	Gen. Writing/Editing:	Y	Info. Management:	Y	Finance/Acct.:	Y	Engineers, Elec.:	
Experienced Mgmt.:	Y	Retail Sales:		Technical Writing:	Y	Software Dev.:	Y	Law:	Y	Engineers, Other:	
Int'l Business:		Commercial/Industrial:	Y	Graphic Arts/Photog.:		Hardware Dev.:		HR/Other:	Y	Health/Lab	Y
MBA Graduates:	Y	Sales Trainees:	Y	Music:		Consulting/Other:		Training:	Y	Scientists/Research:	
		Advertising Pros.:	Y	Broadcasting:				Health Care:	Y	Petroleum/Chemicals:	
				Other:				Consulting:		Math/Other:	

TYPES OF BUSINESS:

Pharmacy Services

BRANDS/DIVISIONS/AFFILIATES:

Medco Health Solutions
Acredo Health Group Inc

CONTACTS:

Note: Officers with more than one job title may be intentionally listed here more than once.

Bruce Scott, Pres.
David B. Snow, Jr., CEO/Chmn.-Medco Health Solutions

Phone: 603-888-1500 **Fax:** 603-888-0990
Toll-Free:
Address: 61 Spit Brook Rd., Executive Tower, Nashua, NH 03060 US

GROWTH PLANS/SPECIAL FEATURES:

Critical Care Systems (CCS) provides health care products, services and support to patients with chronic medical conditions. It is a wholly-owned subsidiary of the Acredo Health Group, Inc., which constitutes the Specialty Pharmacy segment of Medco Health Solutions. CCS primarily operates a specialty infusion business unit. The specialty infusion unit provides intravenous and injectable biopharmaceutical and compounded pharmaceutical products and comprehensive infusion services to patients in chronic and critical disease states. All such patient care services are delivered through a coast to coast network of over 40 community-based branch offices in approximately 29 states, each including a multidisciplinary team of pharmacists, nurses, reimbursement specialists and patient service representatives.

Employees of the firm receive benefits including medical, dental and short- and long-term disability coverage; life and AD&D insurance; flexible spending accounts; an employee assistance program; a 401(k) plan; and paid vacations, holidays, sick days and personal time.

FINANCIALS:

Sales and profits are in thousands of dollars—add 000 to get the full amount. 2011 Note: Financial information for 2011 was not available for all companies at press time.

2011 Sales: $ | 2011 Profits: $
2010 Sales: $ | 2010 Profits: $
2009 Sales: $ | 2009 Profits: $
2008 Sales: $ | 2008 Profits: $
2007 Sales: $ | 2007 Profits: $

U.S. Stock Ticker: Subsidiary
Int'l Ticker:
Int'l Exchange:
Employees: Fiscal Year Ends: 12/31
Parent Company: MEDCO HEALTH SOLUTIONS

SALARIES/BENEFITS:

Pension Plan: | ESOP Stock Plan: | Profit Sharing: | Top Exec. Salary: $ | Bonus: $
Savings Plan: Y | Stock Purch. Plan: | | Second Exec. Salary: $ | Bonus: $

OTHER THOUGHTS:

Apparent Women Officers or Directors:
Hot Spot for Advancement for Women/Minorities:

LOCATIONS: ("Y" = Yes)

West:	Southwest:	Midwest:	Southeast:	Northeast:	International:
Y	Y	Y	Y	Y	

CROWN CASTLE INTERNATIONAL CORP

www.crowncastle.com

Industry Group Code: 237130

Management:		Sales/Marketing:		Liberal Arts:		Information Systems:		Professionals:		Technical/Scientific:	
Mgmt. Trainees:		Mktg. Professionals:	Y	Gen. Writing/Editing:		Info. Management:	Y	Finance/Acct.:	Y	Engineers, Elec.:	Y
Experienced Mgmt.:	Y	Retail Sales:		Technical Writing:	Y	Software Dev.:	Y	Law:	Y	Engineers, Other:	Y
Int'l Business:	Y	Commercial/Industrial:	Y	Graphic Arts/Photog.:		Hardware Dev.:		HR/Other:	Y	Health/Lab	
MBA Graduates:	Y	Sales Trainees:	Y	Music:		Consulting/Other:		Training:	Y	Scientists/Research:	
		Advertising Pros.:		Broadcasting:				Health Care:		Petroleum/Chemicals:	
				Other:				Consulting:		Math/Other:	

TYPES OF BUSINESS:

Wireless Communications Towers
Broadcast Infrastructure Services
Site Management Services
Construction & Engineering Services
Radio & Television Broadcast Towers

BRANDS/DIVISIONS/AFFILIATES:

Crown Castle USA Inc
Crown Castle Australia Pty Ltd
NewPath Networks Inc

CONTACTS:

Note: Officers with more than one job title may be intentionally listed here more than once.

W. Benjamin Moreland, CEO
James D. Young, COO/Sr. VP
W. Benjamin Moreland, Pres.
Jay A. Brown, CFO/Sr. VP
Patrick Slowey, Sr. VP-Sales & Customer Rel.
E. Blake Hawk, General Counsel/Exec. VP
Phil Kelley, Sr. VP-Corp. Dev.
J. Landis Martin, Chmn.

Phone: 713-570-3000 **Fax:** 713-570-3100
Toll-Free: 877-486-9377
Address: 1220 Augusta Dr., Ste. 500, Houston, TX 77057 US

GROWTH PLANS/SPECIAL FEATURES:

Crown Castle International Corp. owns, operates and leases towers and other communications structures for wireless communications. Crown Castle leases antenna space on wireless and broadcast towers; operates analog and digital audio and television broadcast transmission networks; operates wireless networks; and also offers construction, engineering and management services for telecommunications towers. The company has a significant presence in 92 of the 100 largest basic trading areas (BTAs) in the U.S. and Puerto Rico and has a strategic presence in Australia's major metropolitan areas, including Sydney, Melbourne, Brisbane, Adelaide and Perth. In total, the company owns, leases or manages approximately 22,300 towers in the U.S., including Puerto Rico; and approximately 1,600 towers in Australia. The company has operations in a variety of wireless communications industries, including cellular, personal communications services (PCS), enhanced specialized mobile radio (ESMR), 3G and 4G, wireless data, paging, fixed point-to-point radio and point to multipoint broadcasting (such as radio and television broadcasting). Crown Castle operates through two primary segments: CCUSA and CCAL. Crown Castle's domestic operations are run by Crown Castle USA, Inc. (CCUSA), while Crown Castle Australia Pty. (CCAL) conducts operations in Australia. The company's major U.S. clients include Sprint; Verizon Wireless; AT&T; and T-Mobile. Major foreign clients include Optus; Telstra; and VHA in Australia. In September 2010, the firm acquired NewPath Networks, Inc.

Crown Castle offers its employees a 401(k) plan; comprehensive medical, dental and vision insurance; prescription drug coverage; flexible spending accounts; short- and long-term disability insurance; tuition reimbursement; an employee assistance program; and a 529 college savings program.

FINANCIALS:

Sales and profits are in thousands of dollars—add 000 to get the full amount. 2011 Note: Financial information for 2011 was not available for all companies at press time.

2011 Sales: $2,032,729	2011 Profits: $171,077
2010 Sales: $1,878,658	2010 Profits: $-311,259
2009 Sales: $1,685,407	2009 Profits: $-114,123
2008 Sales: $1,526,504	2008 Profits: $-48,858
2007 Sales: $1,385,486	2007 Profits: $-222,813

U.S. Stock Ticker: CCI
Int'l Ticker:
Int'l Exchange:
Employees: 1,200 Fiscal Year Ends: 12/31
Parent Company:

SALARIES/BENEFITS:

Pension Plan:	ESOP Stock Plan:	Profit Sharing:	Top Exec. Salary: $578,702	Bonus: $1,012,500
Savings Plan: Y	Stock Purch. Plan:		Second Exec. Salary: $410,291	Bonus: $444,006

OTHER THOUGHTS:

Apparent Women Officers or Directors: 2
Hot Spot for Advancement for Women/Minorities:

LOCATIONS: ("Y" = Yes)

West:	Southwest:	Midwest:	Southeast:	Northeast:	International:
Y	Y	Y	Y	Y	Y

CRUM & FORSTER HOLDINGS INC

www.cfins.com

Industry Group Code: 524126

Management:		Sales/Marketing:		Liberal Arts:		Information Systems:		Professionals:		Technical/Scientific:	
Mgmt. Trainees:	Y	Mktg. Professionals:	Y	Gen. Writing/Editing:	Y	Info. Management:	Y	Finance/Acct.:	Y	Engineers, Elec.:	
Experienced Mgmt.:	Y	Retail Sales:		Technical Writing:	Y	Software Dev.:		Law:	Y	Engineers, Other:	
Int'l Business:		Commercial/Industrial:	Y	Graphic Arts/Photog.:		Hardware Dev.:		HR/Other:	Y	Health/Lab	Y
MBA Graduates:	Y	Sales Trainees:	Y	Music:		Consulting/Other:		Training:	Y	Scientists/Research:	
		Advertising Pros.:		Broadcasting:				Health Care:	Y	Petroleum/Chemicals:	
				Other:				Consulting:		Math/Other:	Y

TYPES OF BUSINESS:

Insurance, Direct Property & Casualty
Workers' Compensation
Commercial Automobile Insurance
Loss & Risk Control Services
Surety
Online Claims Services
Safety Consulting

BRANDS/DIVISIONS/AFFILIATES:

Fairfax Financial Holdings Ltd
United States Fire Insurance Company
North River Insurance Company (The)
Crum & Forster Insurance Company
Crum & Forster Indemnity Company
Crum & Forster Specialty Insurance Company
Seneca Specialty Insurance Company
Seneca Insurance Company Inc

CONTACTS: *Note: Officers with more than one job title may be intentionally listed here more than once.*

Douglas M. Libby, CEO
Mary Jane Robertson, CFO/Exec. VP/Treas.
Jorge A. Echemendia, Chief Mktg. Officer
Martha Van Hise, VP-Human Resources
Nicole Bennett, CIO/Sr. VP
Richard Yien, CTO
James V. Kraus, General Counsel/Sr. VP/Sec.
Chris I. Stormo, Sr. VP-Corp. Oper.
David J. Ghezzi, Sr. VP-Financial Oper.
Mark L. Owens, Sr. VP-Field Oper.
Mark Brown, Sr. VP-Environmental Div.
Stephen A. Eisenmann, Sr. VP-Claims
Dennis J. Hammer, Controller/Sr. VP
Douglas M. Libby, Chmn.

Phone: 973-490-6600	**Fax:** 973-490-6940
Toll-Free:	
Address: 305 Madison Ave., Morristown, NJ 07962 US	

GROWTH PLANS/SPECIAL FEATURES:

Crum & Forster Holdings, Inc. (C&F), a subsidiary of Canadian firm Fairfax Financial Holdings, Ltd., is a national commercial property and casualty insurance company in the U.S. Founded in 1896, C&F provides its insurance products and services through seven companies: United States Fire Insurance Company; The North River Insurance Company; Crum & Forster Insurance Company; Crum & Forster Indemnity Company; Crum & Forster Specialty Insurance Company; Seneca Specialty Insurance Company; and Seneca Insurance Company, Inc. The company writes a broad range of commercial coverage, including workers' compensation, general liability, commercial automobile, property, commercial multi-peril, accident and health and an umbrella policy. The company generally conducts business on a brokerage basis through its home office and a regional branch network, allowing it to control centrally the underwriting process, respond to local market conditions and build close relationships with producers and policyholders. Other lines of business include bail bonds, personal automobile, homeowners' and surety coverage. In addition, the company provides a range of specialized preventative loss control and risk mitigation services to the manufacturing, wholesale, healthcare, transportation and logistics, printing and publishing, retail, distribution and service industries. The firm also provides its clients with online claims reporting and an anti-fraud protection program. C&F has over 1,400 producers located throughout the U.S., including wholesale brokers, independent regional retail firms and national brokers. In 2011, the firm acquired Valiant Insurance, First Mercury Financial Corporation and American Management Corporation.

C&F offers its employees health and dependent care flexible spending accounts; educational assistance; a qualified transportation expense plan; a legal services plan; adoption assistance; a matching gifts program; business travel accident insurance; a retirement plan; an employee stock ownership plan; and medical, vision and dental insurance.

FINANCIALS: **Sales and profits are in thousands of dollars—add 000 to get the full amount. 2011 Note: Financial information for 2011 was not available for all companies at press time.**

2011 Sales: $
2010 Sales: $
2009 Sales: $836,827
2008 Sales: $1,019,569
2007 Sales: $1,563,647

2011 Profits: $
2010 Profits: $
2009 Profits: $201,981
2008 Profits: $332,806
2007 Profits: $293,182

U.S. Stock Ticker: Subsidiary
Int'l Ticker:
Int'l Exchange:
Employees: Fiscal Year Ends: 12/31
Parent Company: FAIRFAX FINANCIAL HOLDINGS LTD

SALARIES/BENEFITS:

Pension Plan:	ESOP Stock Plan: Y	Profit Sharing:	Top Exec. Salary: $	Bonus: $
Savings Plan: Y	Stock Purch. Plan:		Second Exec. Salary: $	Bonus: $

OTHER THOUGHTS:

Apparent Women Officers or Directors: 3
Hot Spot for Advancement for Women/Minorities: Y

LOCATIONS: ("Y" = Yes)

West:	Southwest:	Midwest:	Southeast:	Northeast:	International:
Y	Y	Y	Y	Y	

CRYOLIFE INC

www.cryolife.com

Industry Group Code: 621511

Management:		**Sales/Marketing:**		**Liberal Arts:**		**Information Systems:**		**Professionals:**		**Technical/Scientific:**	
Mgmt. Trainees:		Mktg. Professionals:	Y	Gen. Writing/Editing:		Info. Management:	Y	Finance/Acct.:	Y	Engineers, Elec.:	
Experienced Mgmt.:	Y	Retail Sales:		Technical Writing:	Y	Software Dev.:		Law:	Y	Engineers, Other:	
Int'l Business:	Y	Commercial/Industrial:	Y	Graphic Arts/Photog.:		Hardware Dev.:		HR/Other:	Y	Health/Lab	Y
MBA Graduates:	Y	Sales Trainees:	Y	Music:		Consulting/Other:		Training:	Y	Scientists/Research:	Y
		Advertising Pros.:		Broadcasting:				Health Care:	Y	Petroleum/Chemicals:	
				Other:				Consulting:		Math/Other:	

TYPES OF BUSINESS:

Transplant Tissue Preservation & Distribution
Surgical Adhesives
Heart Valves
Medical Implants
Biomedical Research

BRANDS/DIVISIONS/AFFILIATES:

CryoValve SG
BioGlue
Hemostase
BioFoam
CryoPatch SG
Cardiogenesis Corporation
SynerGraft

CONTACTS: *Note: Officers with more than one job title may be intentionally listed here more than once.*

Steven G. Anderson, CEO
D. Ashley Lee, COO/Exec. VP
Steven G. Anderson, Pres.
D. Ashley Lee, CFO/Treas.
Gerald B. Seery, Sr. VP-Sales & Mktg.
Albert E. Heacox, Sr. VP-R&D
Jeffrey W. Burris, General Counsel/VP
Timothy M. Neja, VP-Laboratory Oper.
Amy D. Horton, Chief Acct. Officer
David M. Fronk, VP-Regulatory Affairs & Quality Assurance
Scott B. Capps, VP-Clinical Research
Bruce G. Anderson, VP-U.S. Sales & Mktg.
William F. Northrup, III, VP-Physician Rel. & Education
Steven G. Anderson, Chmn.
David Hollinworth, VP/Gen. Mgr.-CryoLife Europa Ltd.

Phone: 770-419-3355 **Fax:** 770-426-0031
Toll-Free: 800-438-8285
Address: 1655 Roberts Blvd. NW, Kennesaw, GA 30144 US

GROWTH PLANS/SPECIAL FEATURES:

CryoLife, Inc. develops and commercializes medical devices and preserves and distributes human tissue for cardiac and vascular transplant applications. The human tissue distributed by the company includes the CryoValve SG pulmonary human heart valve, processed using its proprietary SynerGraft technology. The firm distributes preserved human cardiac and vascular tissue to implanting institutions throughout the U.S., Canada and Europe. CryoLife's medical devices include BioGlue Surgical Adhesive, BioFoam Surgical Matrix and Hemostase, which it distributes for Medafor, Inc BioGlue, designed for cardiac, vascular, pulmonary and general surgical applications, is a polymer based on bovine blood protein and an agent for cross-linking proteins. The company distributes BioGlue throughout the U.S. and in more than 75 other countries. In the U.S., BioGlue is approved by the Food and Drug Administration (FDA) as an adjunct to sutures and staples for use in adult patients in open surgical repair of large vessels. BioFoam is a mixed-cell adhesive foam, delivered as a liquid, designed to stop bleeding. BioFoam is particularly effective in the post-operative stage of abdominal surgical procedures. Hemostase is a plant-based, flowable powder engineered to rapidly dehydrate blood, enhancing clotting on contact. CryoLife currently distributes the product in the U.S., the U.K., Germany, France and other markets in Europe. The firm's products are often sold in international markets several years before they can be marketed in the U.S. International revenue generates approximately 17% of the company's total revenue. In Augusto 2010, the company was granted 510(k) clearance from the FDA for shelf life of five years for the CryoPatch SG pulmonary cardiac patch tissue. In April 2011, CryoLife released BioGlue in Japan. In May 2011, the firm acquired Cardiogenesis Corporation.

The firm offers its employees medical and dental coverage; life insurance; a 401(k) plan; an employee stock purchase plan; and tuition reimbursement.

FINANCIALS: **Sales and profits are in thousands of dollars—add 000 to get the full amount. 2011 Note: Financial information for 2011 was not available for all companies at press time.**

2011 Sales: $ | 2011 Profits: $
2010 Sales: $116,645 | 2010 Profits: $3,744
2009 Sales: $111,685 | 2009 Profits: $8,679
2008 Sales: $105,059 | 2008 Profits: $32,908
2007 Sales: $94,763 | 2007 Profits: $7,201

U.S. Stock Ticker: CRY
Int'l Ticker:
Int'l Exchange:
Employees: 393 Fiscal Year Ends: 12/31
Parent Company:

SALARIES/BENEFITS:

Pension Plan: | ESOP Stock Plan: | Profit Sharing: | Top Exec. Salary: $619,229 | Bonus: $283,907
Savings Plan: Y | Stock Purch. Plan: Y | | Second Exec. Salary: $350,897 | Bonus: $158,249

OTHER THOUGHTS:

Apparent Women Officers or Directors: 2
Hot Spot for Advancement for Women/Minorities:

LOCATIONS: ("Y" = Yes)

West:	Southwest:	Midwest:	Southeast:	Northeast:	International:
			Y		Y

CUBIST PHARMACEUTICALS INC

www.cubist.com

Industry Group Code: 325412

Management:		Sales/Marketing:		Liberal Arts:		Information Systems:		Professionals:		Technical/Scientific:	
Mgmt. Trainees:		Mktg. Professionals:	Y	Gen. Writing/Editing:		Info. Management:	Y	Finance/Acct.:	Y	Engineers, Elec.:	
Experienced Mgmt.:	Y	Retail Sales:		Technical Writing:	Y	Software Dev.:	Y	Law:	Y	Engineers, Other:	
Int'l Business:	Y	Commercial/Industrial:	Y	Graphic Arts/Photog.:		Hardware Dev.:		HR/Other:	Y	Health/Lab	Y
MBA Graduates:	Y	Sales Trainees:	Y	Music:		Consulting/Other:		Training:	Y	Scientists/Research:	Y
		Advertising Pros.:		Broadcasting:				Health Care:	Y	Petroleum/Chemicals:	Y
				Other:				Consulting:		Math/Other:	Y

TYPES OF BUSINESS:

Drugs-Infectious Disease
Antimicrobial Drugs
Antiviral Drugs

BRANDS/DIVISIONS/AFFILIATES:

CUBICIN
Calixa Therapeutics Inc.

CONTACTS: *Note: Officers with more than one job title may be intentionally listed here more than once.*

Michael W. Bonney, CEO
Robert J. Perez, COO/Exec. VP
Michael W. Bonney, Pres.
David W.J. McGirr, CFO/Sr. VP
Maureen H. Powers, VP-Human Resources
Steven C. Gilman, Chief Scientific Officer/Exec. VP-R&D
Tamara L. Joseph, General Counsel/Sr. VP/Corp. Sec.
Ed Campanaro, VP-Clinical Oper.
Santosh Vetticaden, Chief Dev. & Medical Officer/Sr. VP
Timothy D. Hunt, Sr. VP-Public Affairs
Mary C. Stack, VP-Finance
Gregory Stea, Sr. VP-Commercial Oper.

Phone: 781-860-8660	**Fax:** 781-240-0256
Toll-Free:	
Address: 65 Hayden Ave., Lexington, MA 02421 US	

GROWTH PLANS/SPECIAL FEATURES:

Cubist Pharmaceuticals, Inc. is a biopharmaceutical company focused on the research, development and commercialization of pharmaceutical products for the acute care environment. Cubist derives substantially all of its revenues from CUBICIN, a once-daily, bactericidal, intravenous antibiotic with activity against methicillin-resistant Staphylococcus aureus (MRSA). CUBICIN is approved in the U.S. for the treatment of complicated skin and skin structure infections caused by MRSA and certain other Gram-positive bacteria, as well as for MRSA bloodstream infections. Cubist markets CUBICIN to over 2,500 U.S. hospitals and outpatient acute care settings. CUBICIN has received regulatory approval in 71 countries and is marketed in 45 countries; in the U.S., it has been used by roughly 1.1 million patients. Novartis AG, through a subsidiary, is responsible for regulatory filings, sales, marketing and distribution costs of CUBICIN in Europe, Australia, New Zealand, India and certain Central American, South American and Middle Eastern countries. Merck & Co. subsidiary Banyu Pharmaceutical is responsible for the development and commercialization of CUBICIN in Japan. AstraZeneca develops and commercializes CUBICIN in China and over 100 additional countries. Other international partners for CUBICIN include Medison Pharma for Israel; Sunovion for Canada; TTY BioPharm for Taiwan; and Kuhnil Pharma for Korea. Under an agreement with AstraZeneca, Cubist promotes MERREM I.V., an antibiotic used for intra-abdominal infections and bacterial meningitis in pediatric patients. From its recent acquisition of Calixa Therapeutics Inc., Cubist also attained the rights to CXA-201, an I.V. combination of a novel anti-pseudomonal cephalosporin.

Employees are offered tuition reimbursement; medical, life, disability and dental insurance; supplemental vision care; flexible spending accounts; domestic partner coverage; a 401(k); a discounted stock purchase plan; an adoption assistance program; daily fitness classes; an onsite workout center, massage therapist and meditation room; an annual childcare and eldercare subsidy; an assistance program; and free weekly summer ice cream truck visits.

FINANCIALS: **Sales and profits are in thousands of dollars—add 000 to get the full amount. 2011 Note: Financial information for 2011 was not available for all companies at press time.**

2011 Sales: $753,972	2011 Profits: $33,023	**U.S. Stock Ticker: CBST**
2010 Sales: $636,458	2010 Profits: $94,325	**Int'l Ticker:**
2009 Sales: $562,144	2009 Profits: $79,600	Int'l Exchange:
2008 Sales: $433,641	2008 Profits: $127,892	Employees: 638 Fiscal Year Ends: 12/31
2007 Sales: $294,620	2007 Profits: $48,147	Parent Company:

SALARIES/BENEFITS:

Pension Plan:	ESOP Stock Plan:	Profit Sharing:	Top Exec. Salary: $500,000	Bonus: $420,000
Savings Plan: Y	Stock Purch. Plan: Y		Second Exec. Salary: $430,011	Bonus: $207,265

OTHER THOUGHTS:

Apparent Women Officers or Directors: 3
Hot Spot for Advancement for Women/Minorities: Y

LOCATIONS: ("Y" = Yes)

West:	Southwest:	Midwest:	Southeast:	Northeast:	International:
Y		Y	Y	Y	

CULP INC

www.culpinc.com

Industry Group Code: 313

Management:		Sales/Marketing:		Liberal Arts:		Information Systems:		Professionals:		Technical/Scientific:	
Mgmt. Trainees:		Mktg. Professionals:	Y	Gen. Writing/Editing:	Y	Info. Management:	Y	Finance/Acct.:	Y	Engineers, Elec.:	
Experienced Mgmt.:	Y	Retail Sales:		Technical Writing:		Software Dev.:		Law:	Y	Engineers, Other:	
Int'l Business:	Y	Commercial/Industrial:	Y	Graphic Arts/Photog.:	Y	Hardware Dev.:		HR/Other:	Y	Health/Lab	
MBA Graduates:	Y	Sales Trainees:	Y	Music:		Consulting/Other:		Training:		Scientists/Research:	
		Advertising Pros.:		Broadcasting:				Health Care:		Petroleum/Chemicals:	
				Other:	Y			Consulting:		Math/Other:	

TYPES OF BUSINESS:

Upholstery Fabrics
Mattress Fabrics
Yarn

BRANDS/DIVISIONS/AFFILIATES:

Culp Home Fashions
Culp Decorative Fabrics
Culp Velvet Prints

CONTACTS: *Note: Officers with more than one job title may be intentionally listed here more than once.*

Franklin N. Saxon, CEO
Franklin N. Saxon, Pres.
Kenneth R. Bowling, CFO/Treas.
Kenneth R. Bowling, Corp. Sec.
Thomas B. Gallagher, Jr., Controller
Robert G. Culp, IV, Pres., Culp Home Fashions
Robert G. Culp, III, Chmn.

Phone: 336-889-5161	**Fax:** 336-889-7246
Toll-Free:	
Address: 1823 Eastchester Dr., High Point, NC 27265 US	

GROWTH PLANS/SPECIAL FEATURES:

Culp, Inc. is a leading manufacturer of mattress fabrics used for covering mattresses and box springs, and upholstery fabrics primarily for use in the production of residential and commercial upholstered furniture. Culp's fabrics go into sofas, recliners, chairs, love seats, sectionals, sofa-beds and office seating manufactured by companies and brands like La-Z-Boy, Lane, Broyhill, Basset and Flexsteel; and into mattress sets by Sealy, Serta and Simmons. The company is divided into two segments: mattress fabrics, representing 56% of sales and upholstery fabrics, which accounts for 44%. Subsidiary Culp Home Fashions produces the company's mattress fabrics, which encompass woven jacquards (floral and other intricate designs woven on complex looms), knitted ticking (designs produced on special-width circular machines utilizing a variety of synthetic and natural yarns) and prints. The upholstery fabrics division includes Culp Decorative Fabrics which consists of upholstery fabrics such as jacquard woven fabrics, woven dobbies (fabrics that use straight lines to produce geometric designs such as plaids, stripes and solids), knitted fabrics and piece-dyed woven products. It also produces yarn, primarily for internal use by the company. Culp Velvet Prints is focused on the marketing of velvet, suede and printed fabrics used in the production of residential furniture. The company has manufacturing facilities located in North and South Carolina; Poznan, Poland; Quebec, Canada; and Shanghai, China. Culp also sources fabrics from other manufacturers, located primarily in China and Turkey, with almost all of such fabrics being produced specifically for Culp and created by Culp designers. In recent years, the portion of the company's sales represented by fabrics produced outside of the U.S. and Canada has increased significantly, especially in the company's upholstery fabrics segment, where more than half of its sales consist of fabrics produced in Asia.

FINANCIALS: **Sales and profits are in thousands of dollars—add 000 to get the full amount. 2011 Note: Financial information for 2011 was not available for all companies at press time.**

2011 Sales: $216,806	2011 Profits: $16,164	**U.S. Stock Ticker: CFI**
2010 Sales: $206,416	2010 Profits: $13,188	**Int'l Ticker:**
2009 Sales: $203,938	2009 Profits: $-38,842	Int'l Exchange:
2008 Sales: $254,046	2008 Profits: $5,385	Employees: 1,143 Fiscal Year Ends: 4/30
2007 Sales: $250,533	2007 Profits: $-1,316	Parent Company:

SALARIES/BENEFITS:

Pension Plan:	ESOP Stock Plan:	Profit Sharing:	Top Exec. Salary: $350,000	Bonus: $258,667
Savings Plan:	Stock Purch. Plan:		Second Exec. Salary: $270,833	Bonus: $203,238

OTHER THOUGHTS:

Apparent Women Officers or Directors:
Hot Spot for Advancement for Women/Minorities:

LOCATIONS: ("Y" = Yes)

West:	Southwest:	Midwest:	Southeast:	Northeast:	International:
				Y	Y

CUMULUS MEDIA INC

www.cumulus.com

Industry Group Code: 515111

Management:		Sales/Marketing:		Liberal Arts:		Information Systems:		Professionals:		Technical/Scientific:	
Mgmt. Trainees:		Mktg. Professionals:		Gen. Writing/Editing:	Y	Info. Management:	Y	Finance/Acct.:	Y	Engineers, Elec.:	
Experienced Mgmt.:	Y	Retail Sales:		Technical Writing:		Software Dev.:		Law:	Y	Engineers, Other:	
Int'l Business:		Commercial/Industrial:	Y	Graphic Arts/Photog.:		Hardware Dev.:		HR/Other:	Y	Health/Lab	
MBA Graduates:	Y	Sales Trainees:	Y	Music:	Y	Consulting/Other:		Training:		Scientists/Research:	
		Advertising Pros.:		Broadcasting:	Y			Health Care:		Petroleum/Chemicals:	
				Other:	Y			Consulting:		Math/Other:	

TYPES OF BUSINESS:

Radio Station Operator
Sales & Marketing Services
Media Operations Software

BRANDS/DIVISIONS/AFFILIATES:

Cumulus Media Partners LLC
Broadcast Software International Inc
Citadel Broadcasting Corp

CONTACTS: *Note: Officers with more than one job title may be intentionally listed here more than once.*

Lewis W. Dickey, Jr., CEO
Jonathan G. Pinch, Co-COO/Exec. VP
Lewis W. Dickey, Jr., Pres.
Joseph P. Hannan, CFO/Sr. VP/Treas.
Richard Denning, General Counsel/Sr. VP/Sec.
John W. Dickey, Co-COO/Exec. VP
Linda A. Hill, Chief Acct. Officer/Controller/VP
Mike McVay, Sr. VP-Programming
Jan Jeffries, Sr. VP-Programming
Lewis W. Dickey, Jr., Chmn.

Phone: 404-949-0700 **Fax:** 404-949-0740
Toll-Free:
Address: 3280 Peachtree Rd. NW, Ste. 2300, Atlanta, GA 30305 US

GROWTH PLANS/SPECIAL FEATURES:

Cumulus Media, Inc. is one of the leading pure-play radio broadcasters in the U.S. The firm primarily owns, operates, acquires and develops radio stations and clusters serving regional mid-size markets throughout the U.S. It currently owns 570 radio stations in 120 U.S. markets and a nationwide radio network serving over 4,000 stations. Cumulus maintains diversified radio formats and target audiences within each market to attract larger and broader listener audiences and thereby interest a wider range of advertisers. Stations within each market share infrastructure in terms of office space, support personnel and certain senior management. However, each station is developed and marketed as an individual brand with its own identity, programming, inventory of time slots and sales force. Approximately 85% of the firm's net broadcasting revenue is generated from the sale of local and regional advertising. Through subsidiary Cumulus Media Partners LLC, the company owns and operates 32 radio stations in nine large-sized U.S. markets, including San Francisco, Dallas, Houston, Atlanta, Cincinnati, Indianapolis and Kansas City. Additionally, it owns Broadcast Software International, Inc., a media operations software and systems company. Cumulus uses Internet-based software applications to monitor daily sales performance by station and market compared with each station's respective budget. This system also allows stations to exchange ideas and views regarding station operations and ways to increase advertising revenues. In August 2011, Cumulus acquired the remaining outstanding interest in Cumulus Media Partners LLC that it did not already own. In September 2011, the company acquired Citadel Broadcasting Corp., extending the firm's operations to 570 radio stations and doubling its market presence to 120 U.S. markets. In December of the same year, it agreed to make its radio stations available on Clear Channel's digital radio platform, iHeartRadio.

FINANCIALS: **Sales and profits are in thousands of dollars—add 000 to get the full amount. 2011 Note: Financial information for 2011 was not available for all companies at press time.**

2011 Sales: $
2010 Sales: $263,333
2009 Sales: $256,048
2008 Sales: $311,538
2007 Sales: $328,327

2011 Profits: $
2010 Profits: $29,402
2009 Profits: $-126,702
2008 Profits: $-361,669
2007 Profits: $-223,804

U.S. Stock Ticker: CMLS
Int'l Ticker:
Int'l Exchange:
Employees: 2,318 Fiscal Year Ends: 12/31
Parent Company:

SALARIES/BENEFITS:

Pension Plan: ESOP Stock Plan: Profit Sharing: Top Exec. Salary: $940,000 Bonus: $939,960
Savings Plan: Y Stock Purch. Plan: Second Exec. Salary: $597,400 Bonus: $290,000

OTHER THOUGHTS:

Apparent Women Officers or Directors: 2
Hot Spot for Advancement for Women/Minorities:

LOCATIONS: ("Y" = Yes)

West:	Southwest:	Midwest:	Southeast:	Northeast:	International:
Y	Y	Y	Y	Y	

CYBERONICS INC

www.cyberonics.com

Industry Group Code: 33911

Management:		Sales/Marketing:		Liberal Arts:		Information Systems:		Professionals:		Technical/Scientific:	
Mgmt. Trainees:		Mktg. Professionals:	Y	Gen. Writing/Editing:		Info. Management:	Y	Finance/Acct.:	Y	Engineers, Elec.:	Y
Experienced Mgmt.:	Y	Retail Sales:		Technical Writing:	Y	Software Dev.:	Y	Law:	Y	Engineers, Other:	Y
Int'l Business:	Y	Commercial/Industrial:	Y	Graphic Arts/Photog.:		Hardware Dev.:	Y	HR/Other:	Y	Health/Lab	Y
MBA Graduates:	Y	Sales Trainees:	Y	Music:		Consulting/Other:		Training:	Y	Scientists/Research:	Y
		Advertising Pros.:		Broadcasting:				Health Care:	Y	Petroleum/Chemicals:	
				Other:				Consulting:		Math/Other:	

TYPES OF BUSINESS:

Equipment-Epilepsy Therapy
Vagus Nerve Stimulation Devices

BRANDS/DIVISIONS/AFFILIATES:

Vagus Nerve Stimulation Therapy System

CONTACTS: *Note: Officers with more than one job title may be intentionally listed here more than once.*

Daniel J. Moore, CEO
Daniel J. Moore, Pres.
Gregory H. Browne, CFO
Mark Verratti, VP-Sales, Americas
Milton M. Morris, VP-R&D
David S. Wise, Chief Admin. Officer/Sr. VP/Sec.
Darren Alch, General Counsel/VP-Compliance
Randal L. Simpson, VP-Oper.
Gregory H. Browne, VP-Finance
Bryan D. Olin, VP-Clinical Affairs & Quality
James A. Reinstein, Sr. VP/Chief Commercial Officer
Hugh M. Morrison, Chmn.
Mark Verratti, VP-Sales, EMEA & Asia

Phone: 281-228-7200 **Fax:** 281-218-9332
Toll-Free: 800-332-1375
Address: 100 Cyberonics Blvd., Houston, TX 77058-2072 US

GROWTH PLANS/SPECIAL FEATURES:

Cyberonics, Inc. is the designer, developer, manufacturer and marketer of the Vagus Nerve Stimulation (VNS) Therapy System, an implantable medical device for the treatment of epilepsy, depression and other debilitating chronic disorders. The product delivers an electrical signal through an implantable lead to the left cervical vagus nerve in the patient's neck on a chronic, intermittent basis. The patient or caregiver may also initiate stimulation with a hand-held magnet. A study performed by physicians at New York University (published in 2011) involving 436 patients with refractory epilepsy treated with VNS Therapy reported that 63.7% of patients experienced at least a 50% reduction in seizure frequency. Other studies suggest that efficacy is maintained or improved over time when the VNS Therapy System is used with drugs as part of a patient's long-term treatment regimen. To date, an estimated 68,000 patients worldwide have been treated with the system for epilepsy and an estimated 4,000 patients worldwide have been treated with the VNS Therapy System for depression. Cyberonics also uses VNS to treat depression in patients who have not responded to other treatments, but is not currently marketing VNS for that use. In addition, the company has conducted pilot studies for the treatment of Alzheimer's disease, anxiety, bulimia, fibromyalgia, obesity, obsessive-compulsive disorder, multiple sclerosis and traumatic brain injury. The FDA has approved the VNS Therapy system for both treatment-resistant epilepsy and depression.

The company offers its employees medical, dental, vision, life and worker's compensation insurance; short- and long-term disability; and flexible spending accounts

FINANCIALS: **Sales and profits are in thousands of dollars—add 000 to get the full amount. 2011 Note: Financial information for 2011 was not available for all companies at press time.**

2011 Sales: $190,464	2011 Profits: $46,726	**U.S. Stock Ticker: CYBX**
2010 Sales: $167,776	2010 Profits: $78,449	**Int'l Ticker:**
2009 Sales: $143,601	2009 Profits: $26,721	Int'l Exchange:
2008 Sales: $121,230	2008 Profits: $-10,335	Employees: 484 Fiscal Year Ends: 4/30
2007 Sales: $130,968	2007 Profits: $-51,180	Parent Company:

SALARIES/BENEFITS:

Pension Plan:	ESOP Stock Plan:	Profit Sharing:	Top Exec. Salary: $500,673	Bonus: $525,566
Savings Plan: Y	Stock Purch. Plan:		Second Exec. Salary: $310,073	Bonus: $220,493

OTHER THOUGHTS:

Apparent Women Officers or Directors:
Hot Spot for Advancement for Women/Minorities:

LOCATIONS: ("Y" = Yes)

West:	Southwest:	Midwest:	Southeast:	Northeast:	International:
Y	Y	Y	Y	Y	Y

CYBERSOURCE CORP

www.cybersource.com

Industry Group Code: 511210

Management:		Sales/Marketing:		Liberal Arts:		Information Systems:		Professionals:		Technical/Scientific:	
Mgmt. Trainees:		Mktg. Professionals:	Y	Gen. Writing/Editing:		Info. Management:	Y	Finance/Acct.:	Y	Engineers, Elec.:	Y
Experienced Mgmt.:	Y	Retail Sales:		Technical Writing:	Y	Software Dev.:	Y	Law:	Y	Engineers, Other:	
Int'l Business:	Y	Commercial/Industrial:	Y	Graphic Arts/Photog.:		Hardware Dev.:		HR/Other:	Y	Health/Lab	
MBA Graduates:	Y	Sales Trainees:	Y	Music:		Consulting/Other:		Training:	Y	Scientists/Research:	
		Advertising Pros.:		Broadcasting:				Health Care:		Petroleum/Chemicals:	
				Other:				Consulting:		Math/Other:	Y

TYPES OF BUSINESS:

E-Commerce Processing Services & Systems
Risk Management Solutions
Credit Card Processing
Tax Calculation
Fraud Screening
Compliance Services
Consulting Services

BRANDS/DIVISIONS/AFFILIATES:

Authorize.Net
Visa, Inc.
eCheck.Net

CONTACTS: *Note: Officers with more than one job title may be intentionally listed here more than once.*

Michael Walsh, CEO
Scott Cruickshank, COO
Michael Walsh, Pres.
Steven D. Pellizzer, CFO
Perry Dembner, Chief Mktg. Officer/Sr. VP
Neil Buckley, VP-Prod. Dev.
David J. Kim, General Counsel/VP
George Barby, VP-Worldwide Oper.
John McDonnell, VP-Bus. Dev.
Steven D. Pellizzer, VP-Finance
Carolyn Brackett, VP-Channels & Alliances
David A. Glaser, VP-Professional Svcs.
Trish Martin, VP-Customer Support
Michael Orlando, Sr. VP-Global Sales & Svcs.
William S. McKiernan, Chmn.

Phone: 650-965-6000 **Fax:** 650-625-9145
Toll-Free: 888-330-2300
Address: 1295 Charleston Rd., Mountain View, CA 94043 US

GROWTH PLANS/SPECIAL FEATURES:

CyberSource Corp., a subsidiary of Visa Corp., provides secure electronic payment and risk management services to organizations that sell products and services over the Internet. The company's payment systems allow e-commerce merchants to accept a range of online payment options, including credit cards, electronic checks and global payment options. CyberSource Payment Solutions offers four product lines: Global Payment Processing, Fraud Management, Payment Security Management and Professional Services. Global Payment Processing allows business customers to provide a variety of different payment options through CyberSource. The Fraud Management service screens orders to detect illegitimate claims. The Payment Security Management business limits risk by hosting data in secure storage schemes. CyberSource's Professional Services provides business and technical consulting services that include technology selection and systems installation; integration of CyberSource products and services into the merchants' existing internal systems; devising merchant-specific risk management strategies and building custom reporting tools; analyzing the impact of online business on internal processes; disaster recovery planning; and security consulting. The company also offers Authorize.Net, which allows merchants to authorize, settle, and manage credit card and electronic check payments via web sites, retail stores, mail orders, telephone order call centers and mobile devices. Services offered by Authorize.Net include card code verification, address verification, virtual terminals, verified merchant seals, virtual points of sale, eCheck.Net, automated billing and advanced fraud detection. In mid 2010, the company was acquired by Visa, Inc. for $2 billion.

The company offers employees medical, dental and vision coverage; short- and long-term disability; life insurance; a 401(k) plan; flexible spending accounts; educational assistance; a cafeteria plan; and an on-site fitness center.

FINANCIALS: **Sales and profits are in thousands of dollars—add 000 to get the full amount. 2011 Note: Financial information for 2011 was not available for all companies at press time.**

2011 Sales: $ | 2011 Profits: $
2010 Sales: $ | 2010 Profits: $
2009 Sales: $265,136 | 2009 Profits: $10,965
2008 Sales: $229,026 | 2008 Profits: $10,729
2007 Sales: $116,999 | 2007 Profits: $2,429

U.S. Stock Ticker: Subsidiary
Int'l Ticker:
Int'l Exchange:
Employees: Fiscal Year Ends: 12/31
Parent Company: VISA INC

SALARIES/BENEFITS:

Pension Plan: | ESOP Stock Plan: | Profit Sharing: | Top Exec. Salary: $375,000 | Bonus: $
Savings Plan: Y | Stock Purch. Plan: | | Second Exec. Salary: $322,500 | Bonus: $

OTHER THOUGHTS:

Apparent Women Officers or Directors: 2
Hot Spot for Advancement for Women/Minorities: Y

LOCATIONS: ("Y" = Yes)

West:	Southwest:	Midwest:	Southeast:	Northeast:	International:
Y					Y

DANNON COMPANY INC (THE)

www.dannon.com

Industry Group Code: 3115

Management:		Sales/Marketing:		Liberal Arts:		Information Systems:		Professionals:		Technical/Scientific:	
Mgmt. Trainees:		Mktg. Professionals:	Y	Gen. Writing/Editing:	Y	Info. Management:	Y	Finance/Acct.:	Y	Engineers, Elec.:	
Experienced Mgmt.:	Y	Retail Sales:		Technical Writing:		Software Dev.:		Law:	Y	Engineers, Other:	Y
Int'l Business:		Commercial/Industrial:	Y	Graphic Arts/Photog.:		Hardware Dev.:		HR/Other:	Y	Health/Lab	
MBA Graduates:	Y	Sales Trainees:	Y	Music:		Consulting/Other:		Training:	Y	Scientists/Research:	
		Advertising Pros.:	Y	Broadcasting:				Health Care:		Petroleum/Chemicals:	
				Other:				Consulting:		Math/Other:	

TYPES OF BUSINESS:

Dairy Products, Manufacturing
Yogurt Products
Nutrition Education Programs
Nutrition Professionals Training Program

BRANDS/DIVISIONS/AFFILIATES:

DanActive
All-Natural
Danimals
Fruit on the Bottom
Dan-o-nino
Oikos
Activia
Light & Fit

CONTACTS: *Note: Officers with more than one job title may be intentionally listed here more than once.*

Gustavo Valle, CEO
Gustavo Valle, Pres.
Antoine Remy, CFO
Mark Jove Gesti, Sr. VP-Mktg.
Tony Cicio, VP-Human Resources
Albe Wendt, VP-R&D, North America
Tracy Feehan, VP-Bus. Dev., North America
Antoine Remy, VP-Finance
Christian Maisonneuve, VP-Quality
Philippe Caradec, VP-Regulatory & Corp. Affairs, North America
Philippe Domenge, VP-Industrial
Diane Preston, VP-Supply Chain

Phone: 914-872-8400 **Fax:** 914-872-1565
Toll-Free: 877-326-6668
Address: 100 Hillside Ave., White Plains, NY 10603 US

GROWTH PLANS/SPECIAL FEATURES:

The Dannon Company, Inc., a subsidiary of French company Danone S.A., produces and distributes yogurt products throughout the U.S. and Puerto Rico. The company is headquartered in White Plains, New York and operates manufacturing facilities in Minster, Ohio; Fort Worth, Texas; and West Jordan, Utah. The company's Ohio facility is one of the world's largest yogurt manufacturing plants, producing 3 million yogurt cups per day. The firm's products include DanActive, an immune system booster containing beneficial live cultures; Danimals, calcium-fortified yogurt and Dan-o-nino, calcium, protein and Vitamin D-fortified yogurt for children; Activia, a probiotic yogurt for help with digestive system regulation; Light & Fit, a low-fat yogurt; Fruit on the Bottom, a low-fat yogurt made with real fruit; All-Natural, a yogurt made using only all natural ingredients; Pure, a yogurt made using only 7-9 natural ingredients; and Oikos, the firm's Greek yogurt brand. The firm has a product line of almost 100 different flavors and styles, and in addition to its production operations, the company founded the Dannon Institute in 1997 to support programs that address the relationship between health and good nutrition. The firm's website, Dannon.com, offers sections to address ways to live a healthy lifestyle; tips and information for parents to raise and develop healthy lifestyle habits in their children; and healthy recipe ideas. In September 2011, the company opened the new Dannon Discovery and Innovation Center within its corporate headquarters, featuring labs for quality analysis, fruit & flavor and sensory & consumer insights.

Employee benefits include medical and prescription drug, vision and dental insurance; health care flexible spending accounts; short- and long-term disability coverage; a 401(k) and pension plan; an employee assistance program; gym incentive program; travel insurance; a legal plan; and tuition reimbursement.

FINANCIALS: **Sales and profits are in thousands of dollars—add 000 to get the full amount. 2011 Note: Financial information for 2011 was not available for all companies at press time.**

2011 Sales: $ 2011 Profits: $
2010 Sales: $ 2010 Profits: $
2009 Sales: $ 2009 Profits: $
2008 Sales: $ 2008 Profits: $
2007 Sales: $ 2007 Profits: $

U.S. Stock Ticker: Subsidiary
Int'l Ticker:
Int'l Exchange:
Employees: Fiscal Year Ends: 12/31
Parent Company: DANONE SA

SALARIES/BENEFITS:

Pension Plan: Y ESOP Stock Plan: Profit Sharing: Top Exec. Salary: $ Bonus: $
Savings Plan: Y Stock Purch. Plan: Second Exec. Salary: $ Bonus: $

OTHER THOUGHTS:

Apparent Women Officers or Directors: 2
Hot Spot for Advancement for Women/Minorities:

LOCATIONS: ("Y" = Yes)

West:	Southwest:	Midwest:	Southeast:	Northeast:	International:
Y	Y	Y		Y	

DAWSON GEOPHYSICAL COMPANY

www.dawson3d.com

Industry Group Code: 541360

Management:		Sales/Marketing:		Liberal Arts:		Information Systems:		Professionals:		Technical/Scientific:	
Mgmt. Trainees:		Mktg. Professionals:	Y	Gen. Writing/Editing:		Info. Management:	Y	Finance/Acct.:	Y	Engineers, Elec.:	Y
Experienced Mgmt.:	Y	Retail Sales:		Technical Writing:	Y	Software Dev.:	Y	Law:	Y	Engineers, Other:	Y
Int'l Business:	Y	Commercial/Industrial:	Y	Graphic Arts/Photog.:		Hardware Dev.:		HR/Other:	Y	Health/Lab	
MBA Graduates:	Y	Sales Trainees:		Music:		Consulting/Other:		Training:	Y	Scientists/Research:	Y
		Advertising Pros.:		Broadcasting:				Health Care:		Petroleum/Chemicals:	Y
				Other:				Consulting:		Math/Other:	Y

TYPES OF BUSINESS:

Seismic Data Acquisition
Geophysical Services
3-D Seismic Interpretation

BRANDS/DIVISIONS/AFFILIATES:

ARAM ARIES
I/O System II RSR Radio Telemetry
I/O System II MRX

CONTACTS:

Note: Officers with more than one job title may be intentionally listed here more than once.

Stephen C. Jumper, CEO
C. Ray Tobias, COO/Exec. VP
Stephen C. Jumper, Pres.
Christina W. Hagan, CFO/Exec. VP
Mark Pruitt, VP-Mktg.
James Walter (Tom) Thomas, Chief Geophysicist/VP
Howell (Hal) W. Pardue, Exec. VP-Data Processing
Robert C. Chandler, Dir.-Tech Support
Robert C. Chandler, Dir.-Eng.
Christina W. Hagan, Corp. Sec.
George E. McDonald, VP-Field Oper.
Melody Y. Crowl, Controller/Treas.
Sam Dobbs, VP-Data Processing
K.S. Forsdick, Sr. VP
Dave Wisniewski, VP
Stuart A. Wright, VP-Applied Geophysics
L. Decker Dawson, Chmn.

Phone: 915-684-3000 **Fax:** 915-684-3030
Toll-Free: 800-332-9766
Address: 508 W. Wall St., Ste. 800, Midland, TX 79701 US

GROWTH PLANS/SPECIAL FEATURES:

Dawson Geophysical Company, headquartered in Midland, Texas, is a leading provider of onshore seismic data acquisition services in the U.S. The company acquires and processes 2-D, 3-D and multi-component seismic data used to analyze subsurface geologic conditions to identify favorable areas for potential oil and natural gas accumulation. In-house services include seismic survey design, permitting, surveying, data acquisition and processing functions for each seismic program. Dawson, with 12 3-D seismic data acquisition crews operating in the continental U.S. and a seismic data processing center, serves major and intermediate-sized oil and gas companies, independent oil operators and providers of multi-client data libraries. Of its 12 active crews, seven are equipped with ARAM ARIES precise data, four with I/O System II RSR Radio Telemetry and one with I/O System II MRX cable-based recording systems. The survey personnel uses dynamite charges or vibrator energy sources mounted on vehicles, the majority of which weigh over 62,000 pounds, to generate seismic energy. The crew utilizes its seismic recording devices, or geophones, to detect and record shear wave data, before rendering the information visually. The company's data processing center is operated in Midland, Texas and includes processes such as the enhancement of seismic data by improving signal resolution, removing ambient noise and applying proper spatial relationships of geologic features. It provides additional data processing services from its offices in Houston and Oklahoma City. To avoid potential conflicts, Dawson does not acquire data for its own account nor does it participate in oil and gas ventures.

FINANCIALS:

Sales and profits are in thousands of dollars—add 000 to get the full amount. 2011 Note: Financial information for 2011 was not available for all companies at press time.

2011 Sales: $333,279	2011 Profits: $-3,246
2010 Sales: $205,272	2010 Profits: $-9,352
2009 Sales: $243,995	2009 Profits: $10,222
2008 Sales: $324,926	2008 Profits: $35,007
2007 Sales: $257,763	2007 Profits: $27,158

U.S. Stock Ticker: DWSN
Int'l Ticker:
Int'l Exchange:
Employees: 1,507 Fiscal Year Ends: 9/30
Parent Company:

SALARIES/BENEFITS:

Pension Plan:	ESOP Stock Plan:	Profit Sharing:	Top Exec. Salary: $350,000	Bonus: $
Savings Plan: Y	Stock Purch. Plan:		Second Exec. Salary: $230,000	Bonus: $

OTHER THOUGHTS:

Apparent Women Officers or Directors: 2
Hot Spot for Advancement for Women/Minorities: Y

LOCATIONS: ("Y" = Yes)

West:	Southwest:	Midwest:	Southeast:	Northeast:	International:
Y	Y	Y		Y	

DEI HOLDINGS INC

www.deiholdings.com

Industry Group Code: 334290

Management:		Sales/Marketing:		Liberal Arts:		Information Systems:		Professionals:		Technical/Scientific:	
Mgmt. Trainees:		Mktg. Professionals:	Y	Gen. Writing/Editing:	Y	Info. Management:	Y	Finance/Acct.:	Y	Engineers, Elec.:	Y
Experienced Mgmt.:	Y	Retail Sales:		Technical Writing:	Y	Software Dev.:	Y	Law:	Y	Engineers, Other:	Y
Int'l Business:	Y	Commercial/Industrial:	Y	Graphic Arts/Photog.:		Hardware Dev.:	Y	HR/Other:	Y	Health/Lab	
MBA Graduates:	Y	Sales Trainees:	Y	Music:		Consulting/Other:		Training:	Y	Scientists/Research:	
		Advertising Pros.:	Y	Broadcasting:				Health Care:		Petroleum/Chemicals:	
				Other:				Consulting:		Math/Other:	

TYPES OF BUSINESS:

Electronic Equipment-Stolen Vehicle Recovery
Remote Start Systems
Car Audio Equipment
Amplifiers
Speakers
Signal Processors
Mobile Video Systems

BRANDS/DIVISIONS/AFFILIATES:

Directed Electronics Inc
Directed Canada
Definitive Technology
Polk Audio
Charlesbank Capital Partners
Clifford
Orion
Viper

CONTACTS: *Note: Officers with more than one job title may be intentionally listed here more than once.*

James E. Minarik, CEO
James E. Minarik, Pres.
Kevin Duffy, CFO/Exec. VP
Paul DiComo, Sr. VP-Mktg.
David Peet, Exec. VP-Definitive Tech.
Paul DiComo, Sr. VP-Prod. Dev.
Michael N. Smith, VP-Oper.
Mike Simmons, Exec. VP
Joe Tristani, COO-Polk Audio
Ben Newhall, VP-Sales, Polk Audio
Jeffrey Nemec, VP-Prod. Dev., Polk Audio
Julien Joly, Pres., Direct Electronics Canada

Phone: 760-598-6200 **Fax:** 760-598-6400
Toll-Free: 800-876-0800
Address: 1 Viper Way, Vista, CA 92081 US

GROWTH PLANS/SPECIAL FEATURES:

DEI Holdings, Inc. (DEI) is a holding company for several consumer electronics firms. Formerly Directed Electronics, Inc., the firm was restructured in recent years to align its corporate structure with its daily operations. DEI is the now the parent of the following companies: Directed Electronics, Inc., Directed Canada, Polk Audio and Definitive Technology. Directed Electronics and Directed Canada design and market vehicle security and remote start systems; product brand names include XPressKit, Viper, Clifford, Python, Orion, Astroflex and Autostart. Polk Audio and Definitive Technology design and market premium home audio equipment such as floor, bookshelf, in-wall/in-ceiling and surround speakers. In addition, Polk Audio offers car and marine audio equipment; iPod and HD radio systems; and self-powered speaker bars for computer and video games. DEI operates out of offices in Maryland, California, Europe, Asia and Canada. All of the firm's manufacturing activities are outsourced to third party developers, most of which operate out of locations in Asia. In June 2011, the company was acquired by Charlesbank Capital Partners in a transaction worth roughly $305 million.

FINANCIALS: **Sales and profits are in thousands of dollars—add 000 to get the full amount. 2011 Note: Financial information for 2011 was not available for all companies at press time.**

2011 Sales: $	2011 Profits: $
2010 Sales: $	2010 Profits: $
2009 Sales: $	2009 Profits: $
2008 Sales: $	2008 Profits: $
2007 Sales: $	2007 Profits: $

U.S. Stock Ticker: Private
Int'l Ticker:
Int'l Exchange:
Employees: Fiscal Year Ends: 12/31
Parent Company: CHARLESBANK CAPITAL PARTNERS

SALARIES/BENEFITS:

Pension Plan:	ESOP Stock Plan:	Profit Sharing:	Top Exec. Salary: $	Bonus: $
Savings Plan: Y	Stock Purch. Plan:		Second Exec. Salary: $	Bonus: $

OTHER THOUGHTS:

Apparent Women Officers or Directors:
Hot Spot for Advancement for Women/Minorities:

LOCATIONS: ("Y" = Yes)

West:	Southwest:	Midwest:	Southeast:	Northeast:	International:
Y				Y	Y

DELPHI FINANCIAL GROUP INC

www.delphifin.com

Industry Group Code: 524114

Management:		Sales/Marketing:		Liberal Arts:		Information Systems:		Professionals:		Technical/Scientific:	
Mgmt. Trainees:	Y	Mktg. Professionals:	Y	Gen. Writing/Editing:	Y	Info. Management:	Y	Finance/Acct.:	Y	Engineers, Elec.:	
Experienced Mgmt.:	Y	Retail Sales:		Technical Writing:	Y	Software Dev.:		Law:	Y	Engineers, Other:	
Int'l Business:	Y	Commercial/Industrial:	Y	Graphic Arts/Photog.:		Hardware Dev.:		HR/Other:	Y	Health/Lab	Y
MBA Graduates:	Y	Sales Trainees:	Y	Music:		Consulting/Other:		Training:	Y	Scientists/Research:	
		Advertising Pros.:		Broadcasting:				Health Care:	Y	Petroleum/Chemicals:	
				Other:				Consulting:		Math/Other:	Y

TYPES OF BUSINESS:

Insurance-Supplemental & Specialty Health
Employee Absence Management
Workers' Compensation
Life, Disability & Accident Insurance
Annuities

BRANDS/DIVISIONS/AFFILIATES:

Reliance Standard Life Insurance Company
First Reliance Standard Life Insurance Company
Safety National Casualty Corporation
Matrix Absence Management, Inc.
Delphi Capital Management, Inc.

CONTACTS: *Note: Officers with more than one job title may be intentionally listed here more than once.*

Robert Rosenkranz, CEO
Donald A. Sherman, COO
Donald A. Sherman, Pres.
Stephan A. Kiratsous, CFO/Exec. VP
Chad W. Coulter, General Counsel/Sr. VP/Corp. Sec.
Harold F. Ilg, Exec. VP-Bus. Dev.
Bernard J. Kilkelly, VP-Investor Rel.
Thomas W. Burghart, Treas./Sr. VP
Lawrence E. Daurelle, CEO/Pres., Reliance Standard Life Insurance Co.
Mark A. Wilhelm, CEO-Safety National Casualty Corp.
Robert Rosenkranz, Chmn.

Phone: 302-478-5142	**Fax:** 302-427-7663
Toll-Free:	
Address: 1105 N. Market St., Ste. 1230, Wilmington, DE 19899 US	

GROWTH PLANS/SPECIAL FEATURES:

Delphi Financial Group, Inc. is a holding company whose subsidiaries provide integrated employee benefit services primarily to small- to mid-sized employers. The firm provides the following related insurance coverages: long- and short-term disability; excess and primary workers' compensation; group life; travel accident; and dental. Delphi's asset accumulation business emphasizes individual fixed annuity products. The company offers its products and services in all 50 states and Washington, D.C. Delphi's group employee benefits products are sold to employer groups primarily through independent brokers and agents. The company's product offerings include the Integrated Employee Benefit program; a suite of elective benefits chosen by individual employees; and an employee paid coverage for hourly and part-time members. One of the group's primary operating subsidiaries is Reliance Standard Life Insurance Company and its subsidiary, First Reliance Standard Life Insurance Company. These companies underwrite a portfolio of group life, disability and accident insurance products targeted to the employee benefits market, as well as marketing fixed annuities to individuals and groups. Delphi also operates Safety National Casualty Corporation, which provides excess workers' compensation insurance, self-insurance bonds, alternative risk services to the self-insured market; and Matrix Absence Management, Inc., which offers integrated disability and absence management services to the employee benefits market across the U.S. Additionally, the firm manages certain of its investment management activities through its wholly-owned subsidiary, Delphi Capital Management, Inc. In 2010, disability income represented 40% of the firm's written premiums; life insurance premiums were 29%; excess workers' compensation, 21%; assumed workers' compensation and casualty reinsurance, 4%; limited benefit health insurance, 3%; and accident and dental, 3%.

FINANCIALS: **Sales and profits are in thousands of dollars—add 000 to get the full amount. 2011 Note: Financial information for 2011 was not available for all companies at press time.**

2011 Sales: $	2011 Profits: $	**U.S. Stock Ticker: DFG**
2010 Sales: $1,737,248	2010 Profits: $173,147	**Int'l Ticker:**
2009 Sales: $1,571,685	2009 Profits: $99,104	Int'l Exchange:
2008 Sales: $1,430,965	2008 Profits: $36,683	Employees: 1,885 Fiscal Year Ends: 12/31
2007 Sales: $1,570,619	2007 Profits: $164,512	Parent Company:

SALARIES/BENEFITS:

Pension Plan: Y	ESOP Stock Plan:	Profit Sharing:	Top Exec. Salary: $865,000	Bonus: $1,750,000
Savings Plan:	Stock Purch. Plan: Y		Second Exec. Salary: $865,000	Bonus: $1,400,000

OTHER THOUGHTS:

Apparent Women Officers or Directors:
Hot Spot for Advancement for Women/Minorities:

LOCATIONS: ("Y" = Yes)

West:	Southwest:	Midwest:	Southeast:	Northeast:	International:
Y	Y	Y	Y	Y	

DENBURY RESOURCES INC

www.denbury.com

Industry Group Code: 211111

Management:		**Sales/Marketing:**		**Liberal Arts:**		**Information Systems:**		**Professionals:**		**Technical/Scientific:**	
Mgmt. Trainees:		Mktg. Professionals:		Gen. Writing/Editing:		Info. Management:	Y	Finance/Acct.:	Y	Engineers, Elec.:	
Experienced Mgmt.:	Y	Retail Sales:		Technical Writing:		Software Dev.:		Law:	Y	Engineers, Other:	Y
Int'l Business:	Y	Commercial/Industrial:		Graphic Arts/Photog.:		Hardware Dev.:		HR/Other:	Y	Health/Lab	
MBA Graduates:	Y	Sales Trainees:		Music:		Consulting/Other:		Training:	Y	Scientists/Research:	
		Advertising Pros.:		Broadcasting:				Health Care:		Petroleum/Chemicals:	Y
				Other:				Consulting:		Math/Other:	

TYPES OF BUSINESS:

Oil & Gas Exploration & Production
CO2 Reserves
CO2 Pipeline

BRANDS/DIVISIONS/AFFILIATES:

Encore Acquisition Company

CONTACTS:

Note: Officers with more than one job title may be intentionally listed here more than once.

Phil Rykhoek, CEO
Phil Rykhoek, Pres.
Mark C. Allen, CFO/Sr. VP
Dan E. Cole, VP-Mktg.
Whitney Shelley, VP-Human Resources
Steve McLaurin, CIO/VP
Ray Dubuisson, VP-Legal
Craig McPherson, Sr. VP-Prod. Oper.
Bradley A. Cox, VP-Bus. Dev.
Laurie Burkes, Mgr.-Public Rel.
Laurie Burkes, Mgr.-Investor Rel.
Alan Rhoades, VP-Acct.
Robert Cornelius, Sr. VP- Carbon Dioxide Oper.
John Filiatrault, VP-Carbon Dioxide Supply & Pipeline Oper.
Jeff Marcel, VP-Drilling
Greg Dover, VP-North Region
Wieland F. Wettstein, Chmn.

Phone: 972-673-2000	**Fax:** 972-673-2150
Toll-Free:	
Address: 5320 Legacy Dr., Plano, TX 75024 US	

GROWTH PLANS/SPECIAL FEATURES:

Denbury Resources, Inc. is an independent oil and gas exploration and production company with over 397 million barrels of oil equivalent (MMBOE) in proved reserves. The company is one of the largest oil and natural gas operators in Mississippi, and owns some of the leading reserves of sequestered carbon dioxide (CO2), used for tertiary oil recovery east of the Mississippi river. CO2 injection is one of the most efficient ways of extracting crude oil, although, due to limited supplies of CO2, the technique is not widely practiced. The firm utilizes its reserves at the Jackson Dome field to supply CO2 to its planned projects through a network of pipelines. Denbury Resources divides its production areas into two regions: the Gulf Coast Region and the Rocky Mountain Region. Its Gulf Coast Region is sub-divided into nine phases. Phase 1 includes several fields along its 183-mile CO2 pipeline, running through southwest Mississippi and into Louisiana. Phase 2 includes Eucutta, Soso, Martinville and Heidelberg Fields in Eastern Mississippi. Its Phase 3 operations are located at Tinsley Field in Mississippi. Phase 4 includes the Cranfield and Lake St. John Fields, located, respectively, in Mississippi and Louisiana. Phase 5 is Delhi Field, located in Louisiana. Phase 6 consists of the Citronelle Field in Southwest Alabama. Phases 7 and 8 include the Hastings Field and Seabreeze Complex, both in Houston. Phase 9 consists of the Conroe Field located north of Houston. The Rocky Mountain Region consists of land assets gained through the acquisition of Encore Acquisition Company in 2010. Significant holdings in this area include the Riley Ridge Federal Unit located in southwestern Wyoming and properties in Ball Creek Field and the Bakken play.

The company offers employees medical, dental and vision insurance; life insurance; educational assistance; an employee assistance program; and flexible spending accounts.

FINANCIALS:

Sales and profits are in thousands of dollars—add 000 to get the full amount. 2011 Note: Financial information for 2011 was not available for all companies at press time.

2011 Sales: $2,291,900	2011 Profits: $573,300	**U.S. Stock Ticker: DNR**
2010 Sales: $1,921,791	2010 Profits: $285,527	**Int'l Ticker:**
2009 Sales: $889,150	2009 Profits: $-75,156	Int'l Exchange:
2008 Sales: $1,371,056	2008 Profits: $388,396	Employees: 1,195 Fiscal Year Ends: 12/31
2007 Sales: $971,950	2007 Profits: $253,147	Parent Company:

SALARIES/BENEFITS:

Pension Plan:	ESOP Stock Plan:	Profit Sharing:	Top Exec. Salary: $495,000	Bonus: $1,487,396
Savings Plan: Y	Stock Purch. Plan: Y		Second Exec. Salary: $495,000	Bonus: $1,487,396

OTHER THOUGHTS:

Apparent Women Officers or Directors: 2
Hot Spot for Advancement for Women/Minorities:

LOCATIONS: ("Y" = Yes)

West:	Southwest:	Midwest:	Southeast:	Northeast:	International:
Y	Y		Y		

DIAMOND ADVISORY SERVICES

www.diamondconsultants.com

Industry Group Code: 541512

Management:		Sales/Marketing:		Liberal Arts:		Information Systems:		Professionals:		Technical/Scientific:	
Mgmt. Trainees:		Mktg. Professionals:		Gen. Writing/Editing:	Y	Info. Management:	Y	Finance/Acct.:	Y	Engineers, Elec.:	
Experienced Mgmt.:	Y	Retail Sales:		Technical Writing:		Software Dev.:		Law:	Y	Engineers, Other:	
Int'l Business:	Y	Commercial/Industrial:		Graphic Arts/Photog.:		Hardware Dev.:		HR/Other:	Y	Health/Lab	
MBA Graduates:	Y	Sales Trainees:		Music:		Consulting/Other:	Y	Training:		Scientists/Research:	
		Advertising Pros.:		Broadcasting:				Health Care:		Petroleum/Chemicals:	
				Other:				Consulting:	Y	Math/Other:	

TYPES OF BUSINESS:

Consulting Services
Strategic Consulting

BRANDS/DIVISIONS/AFFILIATES:

PricewaterhouseCoopers
Diamond Management & Technology Consultants Inc

CONTACTS:

Note: Officers with more than one job title may be intentionally listed here more than once.

Adam J. Gutstein, Head-Diamond Advisory Svcs.

Phone: 312-255-5000 **Fax:** 312-255-6000
Toll-Free:
Address: 875 N. Michigan Ave., John Hancock Ctr., Ste. 3000, Chicago, IL 60611 US

GROWTH PLANS/SPECIAL FEATURES:

Diamond Advisory Services, formerly Diamond Management & Technology Consultants, Inc., is a management and technology consulting company operating as a subsidiary of PricewaterhouseCoopers. Diamond Advisory offers consulting services to clients in industries where technological development has made a significant impact. These include consumer packaged goods; financial services; healthcare; insurance; logistics; manufacturing; public sector; retail and distribution; telecommunications and high-tech; and transportation and travel services. Its consultations typically revolve around technology, strategy, operations and program management. The firm's services are divided across four board categories: business design and performance improvement, which involves the design of broad-based business models, detailed organizational plans and implementation strategies; information advantage services are intended to help clients extract and analyze complex operational data and make informed decisions; customer impact services aid clients in attracting and retaining customers; and execution, which includes strategy implementation and results analysis services. The firm tends to take a multidisciplinary approach to its work, and strives to include its clients' own employees as much as possible. It maintains a group of external advisors, named the Diamond Fellows, consisting of university professors and industry leaders. In November 2010, the firm was acquired by PricewaterhouseCoopers.

FINANCIALS:

Sales and profits are in thousands of dollars—add 000 to get the full amount. 2011 Note: Financial information for 2011 was not available for all companies at press time.

2011 Sales: $ | 2011 Profits: $
2010 Sales: $209,944 | 2010 Profits: $12,373
2009 Sales: $174,978 | 2009 Profits: $-8,398
2008 Sales: $205,056 | 2008 Profits: $21,094
2007 Sales: $190,273 | 2007 Profits: $31,401

U.S. Stock Ticker: Subsidiary
Int'l Ticker:
Int'l Exchange:
Employees: 643 Fiscal Year Ends: 3/31
Parent Company: PRICEWATERHOUSECOOPERS

SALARIES/BENEFITS:

Pension Plan: ESOP Stock Plan: Profit Sharing: Top Exec. Salary: $625,000 Bonus: $
Savings Plan: Stock Purch. Plan: Second Exec. Salary: $475,000 Bonus: $89,063

OTHER THOUGHTS:

Apparent Women Officers or Directors:
Hot Spot for Advancement for Women/Minorities:

LOCATIONS: ("Y" = Yes)

West:	Southwest:	Midwest:	Southeast:	Northeast:	International:
		Y		Y	Y

DIAMOND FOODS INC

www.diamondfoods.com

Industry Group Code: 1113

Management:		Sales/Marketing:		Liberal Arts:		Information Systems:		Professionals:		Technical/Scientific:	
Mgmt. Trainees:	Y	Mktg. Professionals:	Y	Gen. Writing/Editing:		Info. Management:	Y	Finance/Acct.:	Y	Engineers, Elec.:	
Experienced Mgmt.:	Y	Retail Sales:		Technical Writing:		Software Dev.:		Law:	Y	Engineers, Other:	
Int'l Business:	Y	Commercial/Industrial:	Y	Graphic Arts/Photog.:	Y	Hardware Dev.:		HR/Other:	Y	Health/Lab	
MBA Graduates:	Y	Sales Trainees:	Y	Music:		Consulting/Other:		Training:	Y	Scientists/Research:	
		Advertising Pros.:	Y	Broadcasting:				Health Care:		Petroleum/Chemicals:	
				Other:				Consulting:		Math/Other:	

TYPES OF BUSINESS:

Nut Processing
Almond-Related Products
International Distribution
Popcorn Production

BRANDS/DIVISIONS/AFFILIATES:

Emerald
Diamond of California
Pop Secret
Diamond International
Kettle Brands
Pringles
Emerald/Harmony

CONTACTS: *Note: Officers with more than one job title may be intentionally listed here more than once.*

Rick Wolford, Acting CEO
Rick Wolford, Acting Pres.
Michael Murphy, Acting CFO
Andrew Burke, Chief Mktg. Officer/Exec. VP
Stephen Kim, Sr. VP-Human Resources
Steven M. Neil, Chief Admin. Officer
Stephen Kim, General Counsel/Sr. VP
Linda Segre, Sr. VP-Corp. Strategy
Stephen Sibert, VP-Corp. Comm. & Affairs
Lloyd J. Johnson, Chief Sales Officer/Exec. VP
Robert J. Zollars, Chmn.

Phone: 209-467-6000	**Fax:**
Toll-Free:	
Address: 1050 S. Diamond St., Stockton, CA 95205 US	

GROWTH PLANS/SPECIAL FEATURES:

Diamond Foods, Inc. is a branded food company specializing in processing, marketing and distributing nuts and snack products. The company has three product lines: snack, which accounted for 57% of its 2011 revenues; culinary and retail in-shell, 27%; and non-retail, 16%. Snack products are sold under the Emerald and Emerald/Harmony brands. These products, which include roasted, glazed and flavored nuts, trail mixes, seeds, chips and similar offerings packaged in re-sealable containers, are typically available in grocery store snack and produce aisles, mass merchandisers, club stores, convenience stores, drug stores and other places where snacks are sold. The snack division also includes the Pop Secret brand of popcorn and the recently acquired Kettle Brands potato chips. The firm sells culinary and retail in-shell nuts under the Diamond of California brand in grocery stores, mass merchandisers and club stores. Culinary nuts are used to prepare meals or baked goods at home, while in-shell nuts are typically only available during the holiday season. Its non-retail product division sells ingredient nuts; unshelled nuts; shelled and processed nuts; and custom-processed nuts to customers around the globe. The company markets ingredient and food service nuts under the Diamond of California brand to food processors, restaurants, bakeries, food service companies and their suppliers. Diamond Foods obtains all of its walnuts directly from growers in California and the majority of the company's nuts come from the U.S. It purchases other nuts from importers and domestic processors. The company imports Brazil nuts from the Amazon basin; cashew nuts from India, Africa, Brazil and Southeast Asia; hazelnuts from Turkey; pecans from Mexico; and pine nuts from China and Turkey.

FINANCIALS: **Sales and profits are in thousands of dollars—add 000 to get the full amount. 2011 Note: Financial information for 2011 was not available for all companies at press time.**

2011 Sales: $965,922	2011 Profits: $50,211	**U.S. Stock Ticker: DMND**
2010 Sales: $680,162	2010 Profits: $26,211	**Int'l Ticker:**
2009 Sales: $570,940	2009 Profits: $23,743	Int'l Exchange:
2008 Sales: $531,492	2008 Profits: $14,756	Employees: 1,797 Fiscal Year Ends: 7/31
2007 Sales: $522,585	2007 Profits: $8,433	Parent Company:

SALARIES/BENEFITS:

Pension Plan: Y	ESOP Stock Plan:	Profit Sharing:	Top Exec. Salary: $721,985	Bonus: $1,789,122
Savings Plan:	Stock Purch. Plan:		Second Exec. Salary: $448,596	Bonus: $746,917

OTHER THOUGHTS:

Apparent Women Officers or Directors: 1
Hot Spot for Advancement for Women/Minorities:

LOCATIONS: ("Y" = Yes)

West:	Southwest:	Midwest:	Southeast:	Northeast:	International:
Y		Y	Y	Y	Y

DIGITAL GENERATION INC

www.dgit.com

Industry Group Code: 541870

Management:		**Sales/Marketing:**		**Liberal Arts:**		**Information Systems:**		**Professionals:**		**Technical/Scientific:**	
Mgmt. Trainees:		Mktg. Professionals:	Y	Gen. Writing/Editing:	Y	Info. Management:	Y	Finance/Acct.:	Y	Engineers, Elec.:	
Experienced Mgmt.:	Y	Retail Sales:		Technical Writing:		Software Dev.:	Y	Law:	Y	Engineers, Other:	
Int'l Business:	Y	Commercial/Industrial:	Y	Graphic Arts/Photog.:		Hardware Dev.:		HR/Other:	Y	Health/Lab	
MBA Graduates:	Y	Sales Trainees:	Y	Music:		Consulting/Other:		Training:	Y	Scientists/Research:	
		Advertising Pros.:	Y	Broadcasting:				Health Care:		Petroleum/Chemicals:	
				Other:	Y			Consulting:		Math/Other:	

TYPES OF BUSINESS:

Advertising Distribution Services
Digital Content Distribution
Online Database-TV Commercials
Digital Transmission Equipment
Editing & Media Production Services

BRANDS/DIVISIONS/AFFILIATES:

SourceEcreative
Springbox Ltd
Unicast Communications Corp
Match Point Media LLC
Treehouse Media Services Inc
Voltage Video Inc
MIJO Corporation
MediaMind Technologies Inc

CONTACTS: *Note: Officers with more than one job title may be intentionally listed here more than once.*

Neil Nguyen, CEO
Neil Nguyen, Pres.
Omar A. Choucair, CFO
Omar A. Choucair, Sec.
Carlos Alegria, Sr. VP-Corp. Planning & Dev.
Gal Trifon, Chief Digital Officer/Gen. Mgr.-MediaMind
Scott K. Ginsberg, Exec. Chmn.

Phone: 972-581-2000 **Fax:** 972-581-2001
Toll-Free: 800-324-5672
Address: 750 W. John Carpenter Freeway., Ste. 700, Irving, TX 75039 US

GROWTH PLANS/SPECIAL FEATURES:

Digital Generation, Inc. (DG), formerly DG FastChannel, Inc., is a provider of digital technology services to the global media production industry. The firm operates a nationwide digital network linking more than 5,000 advertisers and advertising agencies to diverse media destinations across the U.S., Europe and Canada. Its services include online creative research, media production, digital advertising distribution and management. Online creative research is provided through the SourceEcreative searchable database, containing content and credits for over 400,000 U.S. television commercials, 80,000 professionals and 16,000 companies, allowing advertisers to contact directors, composers and other talent for new commercials. Its media productions services include editing, duplication and dubbing services, as well as storage of client masters or storyboards. The firm's digital advertising distribution services connect its advertisers with 4,800 TV, cable and network broadcast destinations; over 5,000 online publishers; 11,000 radio stations; and 8,400 print publishing destinations, allowing advertisers to have content distributed to radio and television stations in as little as one hour. The company operates through several subsidiaries, including Unicast Communications Corp., an online advertising campaign management product provider, and Springbox Ltd., a web-based marketing company. In late 2010, DG acquired Direct Response (DR) advertising distributor, Match Point Media LLC, along with its divisions, Treehouse Media Services, Inc. and Voltage Video, Inc. In 2011, it acquired Canadian digital media services firm MIJO Corporation; MediaMind Technologies, Inc. for $499 million; and the EyeWonder advertising unit of Limelight Networks, Inc. for $56 million.

DG offers employees health and dental insurance; life insurance; disability coverage; and a 401(k) plan.

FINANCIALS: **Sales and profits are in thousands of dollars—add 000 to get the full amount. 2011 Note: Financial information for 2011 was not available for all companies at press time.**

2011 Sales: $	2011 Profits: $
2010 Sales: $247,528	2010 Profits: $41,569
2009 Sales: $190,886	2009 Profits: $20,501
2008 Sales: $157,081	2008 Profits: $15,079
2007 Sales: $97,687	2007 Profits: $10,413

U.S. Stock Ticker: DGIT
Int'l Ticker:
Int'l Exchange:
Employees: 897 Fiscal Year Ends: 12/31
Parent Company:

SALARIES/BENEFITS:

Pension Plan: ESOP Stock Plan: Profit Sharing: Top Exec. Salary: $475,560 Bonus: $1,865,040
Savings Plan: Y Stock Purch. Plan: Second Exec. Salary: $394,077 Bonus: $1,311,250

OTHER THOUGHTS:

Apparent Women Officers or Directors:
Hot Spot for Advancement for Women/Minorities:

LOCATIONS: ("Y" = Yes)

West:	Southwest:	Midwest:	Southeast:	Northeast:	International:
Y	Y	Y	Y	Y	Y

DJO GLOBAL INC

www.djoglobal.com

Industry Group Code: 33911

Management:		**Sales/Marketing:**		**Liberal Arts:**		**Information Systems:**		**Professionals:**		**Technical/Scientific:**	
Mgmt. Trainees:		Mktg. Professionals:	Y	Gen. Writing/Editing:		Info. Management:	Y	Finance/Acct.:	Y	Engineers, Elec.:	Y
Experienced Mgmt.:	Y	Retail Sales:		Technical Writing:	Y	Software Dev.:		Law:	Y	Engineers, Other:	Y
Int'l Business:	Y	Commercial/Industrial:	Y	Graphic Arts/Photog.:		Hardware Dev.:		HR/Other:	Y	Health/Lab	Y
MBA Graduates:	Y	Sales Trainees:	Y	Music:		Consulting/Other:		Training:	Y	Scientists/Research:	Y
		Advertising Pros.:		Broadcasting:				Health Care:	Y	Petroleum/Chemicals:	
				Other:				Consulting:		Math/Other:	

TYPES OF BUSINESS:

Clinical Orthopedic Rehabilitation Products & Devices
Electrotherapy Products
Rehabilitation Products

BRANDS/DIVISIONS/AFFILIATES:

DJO Incorporated
Blackstone Capital Partners
DonJoy
Empi
Chattanooga Group
ProCare
Aircast
Turon Modular Shoulder System

CONTACTS: *Note: Officers with more than one job title may be intentionally listed here more than once.*

Michael P. Mogul, CEO
Luke T. Faulstick, COO/Exec. VP
Michael P. Mogul, Pres.
Vickie L. Capps, CFO/Exec. VP
Thomas A. Capizzi, Exec. VP-Global Human Resources
Donald M. Roberts, General Counsel/Sec./Exec. VP
Vickie L. Capps, Treas.
Andrew Holman, Exec. VP-Sales & Mktg., U.S. Commercial Bus.
Kenneth W. Davidson, Chmn.
Stephen Murphy, Exec. VP-Sales & Mktg., Int'l Commercial Bus.

Phone: 760-727-1280	**Fax:** 800-936-6569
Toll-Free:	
Address: 1430 Decision St., Vista, CA 92081 US	

GROWTH PLANS/SPECIAL FEATURES:

DJO Global, Inc. (formerly DJO Incorporated) designs, manufactures, markets and distributes orthopedic devices, sports medicine equipment and other related products for the orthopedic industry worldwide. A private firm primarily owned by affiliates of Blackstone Capital Partners, its products are used to treat patients with musculoskeletal conditions resulting from degenerative diseases, deformities and acute injuries. These products serve the needs of physical therapists, orthopedic surgeons and other health care professionals. The firm operates in three segments: Domestic Rehabilitation, International Rehabilitation and Surgical Implant. The Domestic Rehabilitation division is subdivided into three divisions: DonJoy, ProCare and Aircast; Empi; and Chattanooga. The DonJoy, ProCare and Aircast division manufactures products including rigid knee bracing, cold therapy products and orthopedic soft goods, which include products that offer immobilization from head to toe. Empi's offerings include transcutaneous electrical nerve stimulation (TENS) devices that block pain messages through electrical stimulation; combined magnetic field (CMF) devices that encourage bone healing; and iontophoresis transdermal medical delivery devices. The Chattanooga Group manufactures clinical rehabilitation equipment for treating skeletal, muscular, neurological and soft tissue disorders. Its offerings include electrotherapy products, traction devices and dry heat therapy products. The International Rehabilitation division, operating mainly in Europe, distributes DonJoy, ProCare and Aircast products internationally; offers Ormed brand products, including electrotherapy and bracing products, primarily in Germany; and provides Cefar-Compex electrotherapy and rehabilitation products. The Surgical Implant division, operating under the name DJO Surgical, manufactures orthopedic reconstructive joint implants, including those for the hip, knee and shoulder. In February 2011, the company changed its name to DJO Global, Inc. July 2011, the firm introduced the Turon Modular Shoulder System for shoulder joint replacement surgery.

Employee benefits include medical, dental and vision insurance; a 401(k) savings plan; paid vacation; life, auto, home, pet and AD&D insurance; an employee assistance program; and paid vacation.

FINANCIALS: **Sales and profits are in thousands of dollars—add 000 to get the full amount. 2011 Note: Financial information for 2011 was not available for all companies at press time.**

2011 Sales: $	2011 Profits: $	**U.S. Stock Ticker: Private**
2010 Sales: $965,973	2010 Profits: $-50,750	**Int'l Ticker:**
2009 Sales: $946,126	2009 Profits: $-50,433	Int'l Exchange:
2008 Sales: $948,469	2008 Profits: $-97,786	Employees: Fiscal Year Ends: 12/31
2007 Sales: $464,811	2007 Profits: $-82,422	Parent Company:

SALARIES/BENEFITS:

Pension Plan:	ESOP Stock Plan:	Profit Sharing:	Top Exec. Salary: $	Bonus: $
Savings Plan: Y	Stock Purch. Plan:		Second Exec. Salary: $	Bonus: $

OTHER THOUGHTS:

Apparent Women Officers or Directors: 2
Hot Spot for Advancement for Women/Minorities:

LOCATIONS: ("Y" = Yes)

West:	Southwest:	Midwest:	Southeast:	Northeast:	International:
Y					

DOLBY LABORATORIES INC

www.dolby.com

Industry Group Code: 334310

Management:		**Sales/Marketing:**		**Liberal Arts:**		**Information Systems:**		**Professionals:**		**Technical/Scientific:**	
Mgmt. Trainees:		Mktg. Professionals:	Y	Gen. Writing/Editing:		Info. Management:	Y	Finance/Acct.:	Y	Engineers, Elec.:	Y
Experienced Mgmt.:	Y	Retail Sales:		Technical Writing:	Y	Software Dev.:	Y	Law:	Y	Engineers, Other:	Y
Int'l Business:	Y	Commercial/Industrial:	Y	Graphic Arts/Photog.:		Hardware Dev.:	Y	HR/Other:	Y	Health/Lab	
MBA Graduates:	Y	Sales Trainees:		Music:		Consulting/Other:		Training:	Y	Scientists/Research:	
		Advertising Pros.:		Broadcasting:				Health Care:		Petroleum/Chemicals:	
				Other:	Y			Consulting:		Math/Other:	

TYPES OF BUSINESS:

Audio Technology

BRANDS/DIVISIONS/AFFILIATES:

Dolby
Dolby Digital
Dolby Digital Plus
Dolby Home Theater
Dolby Mobile
Dolby TrueHD
Dolby Digital Cinema
Dolby Headphone

CONTACTS: *Note: Officers with more than one job title may be intentionally listed here more than once.*

Kevin Yeaman, CEO
Kevin Yeaman, Pres.
Murray J. Demo, CFO/Exec. VP
Ramzi Haidamus, Exec. VP-Mktg. & Sales
Andrew Dahlkemper, Sr. VP-Human Resources
Steve E. Forshay, Sr. VP-Research
Craig Todd, CTO/Sr. VP
Michael Rockwell, Exec. VP-Prod. & Tech.
Andy Sherman, General Counsel/Exec. VP/Sec.
Eric Cohen, Sr. VP-Corp. Dev.
J. Stuart Mitchell, Sr. VP-Sales
Ioan Allen, Sr. VP
Robin Selden, Sr. VP-Mktg.
Ray Dolby, Chmn.

Phone: 415-558-0200	**Fax:** 415-863-1373
Toll-Free:	
Address: 100 Potrero Ave., San Francisco, CA 94103 US	

GROWTH PLANS/SPECIAL FEATURES:

Dolby Laboratories, Inc. designs, manufactures and sells audio products for the motion picture, broadcast and music industries. The firm's products are used in content creation, distribution and playback to provide surround sound, improve sound quality and increase the efficiency of sound storage and distribution. The majority of Dolby's product sales are derived from traditional cinema processors, which movie theatres use to process film soundtracks; and, to a lesser extent, broadcast products used to encode and distribute content to viewers. The firm also offers related digital cinema processors and media adapters to decode digital cinema soundtracks, and digital cinema accessories to interface its digital cinema servers with theaters' existing automation systems. These products represent roughly 14% of the firm's revenue. The company licenses its technologies to manufacturers of consumer electronics products and media software vendors. Licensing accounts for approximately 83% of Dolby's revenues. Dolby also offers a variety of audio engineering services to support production of motion picture, broadcast, music and video game content, which accounts for approximately 3% of revenue. The firm's technologies are used in virtually all entertainment platforms, including DVD players, computer software, digital televisions, set top boxes, portable media devices and in a wide array of consumer electronic products such as gaming systems and audio/video receivers. Dolby has licensed its technologies to manufacturers around the world and sells its products and services in over 60 countries. The firm derives 68% of its revenue from outside the US.

Dolby offers its employees medical, dental and vision coverage; a 401(k) plan; an employee assistance program; flexible spending accounts; life and AD&D insurance; short- and long-term disability; educational assistance; Dolby equipment discounts; company movies; and the company ski cabin at discounted rates. U.K.-based employees receive a pension plan.

FINANCIALS: **Sales and profits are in thousands of dollars—add 000 to get the full amount. 2011 Note: Financial information for 2011 was not available for all companies at press time.**

2011 Sales: $955,505	2011 Profits: $309,267	**U.S. Stock Ticker: DLB**
2010 Sales: $922,713	2010 Profits: $283,447	**Int'l Ticker:**
2009 Sales: $719,503	2009 Profits: $242,991	Int'l Exchange:
2008 Sales: $640,231	2008 Profits: $199,458	Employees: 1,369 Fiscal Year Ends: 9/30
2007 Sales: $482,028	2007 Profits: $142,831	Parent Company:

SALARIES/BENEFITS:

Pension Plan:	ESOP Stock Plan:	Profit Sharing:	Top Exec. Salary: $625,039	Bonus: $451,140
Savings Plan: Y	Stock Purch. Plan:		Second Exec. Salary: $450,027	Bonus: $211,134

OTHER THOUGHTS:

Apparent Women Officers or Directors: 1
Hot Spot for Advancement for Women/Minorities:

LOCATIONS: ("Y" = Yes)

West:	Southwest:	Midwest:	Southeast:	Northeast:	International:
Y					Y

DORMAN PRODUCTS INC

www.dormanproducts.com

Industry Group Code: 3363

Management:		Sales/Marketing:		Liberal Arts:		Information Systems:		Professionals:		Technical/Scientific:	
Mgmt. Trainees:		Mktg. Professionals:	Y	Gen. Writing/Editing:		Info. Management:	Y	Finance/Acct.:	Y	Engineers, Elec.:	Y
Experienced Mgmt.:	Y	Retail Sales:		Technical Writing:	Y	Software Dev.:	Y	Law:	Y	Engineers, Other:	Y
Int'l Business:	Y	Commercial/Industrial:	Y	Graphic Arts/Photog.:		Hardware Dev.:		HR/Other:	Y	Health/Lab	
MBA Graduates:	Y	Sales Trainees:		Music:		Consulting/Other:		Training:	Y	Scientists/Research:	
		Advertising Pros.:		Broadcasting:				Health Care:		Petroleum/Chemicals:	
				Other:				Consulting:		Math/Other:	

TYPES OF BUSINESS:

Automobile Parts Manufacturer
Replacement & Aftermarket Parts

BRANDS/DIVISIONS/AFFILIATES:

Scan-Tech
Dorman Canada
AutoGrade
First Stop
Conduct-Tite
Pik-A-Nut
OE Solutions
HELP!

CONTACTS: *Note: Officers with more than one job title may be intentionally listed here more than once.*

Steven L. Berman, CEO
Steven L. Berman, COO
Steven L. Berman, Pres.
Mathias J. Barton, CFO/Sr. VP
Joseph M. Beretta, Sr. VP-Prod.
Steven L. Berman, Corp. Sec.
Fred Frigo, Sr. VP-Oper.
Steven L. Berman, Treas.
Richard N. Berman, Chmn.

Phone: 215-997-1800	**Fax:** 215-997-7968
Toll-Free:	
Address: 3400 E. Walnut St., Colmar, PA 18915 US	

GROWTH PLANS/SPECIAL FEATURES:

Dorman Products, Inc. is a leading supplier of original equipment automotive replacement parts, fasteners and service line products for the automotive aftermarket. The company designs, packages and markets over 122,000 different automotive replacement parts that are sold primarily in the U.S. to automotive aftermarket retailers (such as AutoZone, Advance Auto Parts and O'Reilly), which accounted for 44% of the firm's 2010 revenue; national, regional and local warehouse dealers (such as NAPA and Carquest), 42%; and international entities, specialty markets, mass merchants and salvage yards, 14%. The automotive replacements parts market is divided into two components: parts for passenger cars and light trucks; and parts for heavy-duty trucks, with most of the firm's parts designed for passenger cars and light trucks. Dorman categorizes its products into four classes: automotive body, which accounted for 28% of its 2010 sales; power-train, 32%; chassis, 25%; and hardware, 15%. The majority of the company's sales consist of original equipment dealer parts that include intake manifolds, exhaust manifolds, oil cooler lines, window regulators, radiator fan assemblies, power steering pulleys and harmonic balancers. Dorman currently sells its products under a number of proprietary brand names, including OE Solutions, AutoGrade, First Stop, HELP!, Conduct-Tite, Scan-Tech and Pik-A-Nut. Approximately 85% of the company's products are sold under its proprietary brand names, with the remainder sold for resale under customers' private labels or in bulk. Through its Scan-Tech subsidiary and Dorman Canada unit, the company has increased its international distribution of automotive replacement parts through sales in Canada, Europe, the Middle East and Asia.

Dorman offers its employees medical, dental and vision coverage; flexible spending accounts; a 401(k) plan; a 529 college savings plan; life and disability insurance; tuition reimbursement; credit union membership; a company-sponsored health club membership; personal protection programs; and auto insurance.

FINANCIALS: **Sales and profits are in thousands of dollars—add 000 to get the full amount. 2011 Note: Financial information for 2011 was not available for all companies at press time.**

2011 Sales: $529,300	2011 Profits: $53,300	**U.S. Stock Ticker: DORM**
2010 Sales: $455,716	2010 Profits: $46,138	**Int'l Ticker:**
2009 Sales: $377,378	2009 Profits: $26,495	Int'l Exchange:
2008 Sales: $342,325	2008 Profits: $17,813	Employees: 1,185 Fiscal Year Ends: 12/31
2007 Sales: $327,725	2007 Profits: $19,193	Parent Company:

SALARIES/BENEFITS:

Pension Plan:	ESOP Stock Plan:	Profit Sharing: Y	Top Exec. Salary: $545,872	Bonus: $970,273
Savings Plan: Y	Stock Purch. Plan:		Second Exec. Salary: $545,872	Bonus: $970,273

OTHER THOUGHTS:

Apparent Women Officers or Directors:
Hot Spot for Advancement for Women/Minorities:

LOCATIONS: ("Y" = Yes)

West:	Southwest:	Midwest:	Southeast:	Northeast:	International:
		Y	Y	Y	Y

DPL INC

www.dplinc.com

Industry Group Code: 2211

Management:		Sales/Marketing:		Liberal Arts:		Information Systems:		Professionals:		Technical/Scientific:	
Mgmt. Trainees:		Mktg. Professionals:	Y	Gen. Writing/Editing:	Y	Info. Management:	Y	Finance/Acct.:	Y	Engineers, Elec.:	Y
Experienced Mgmt.:	Y	Retail Sales:		Technical Writing:		Software Dev.:		Law:	Y	Engineers, Other:	Y
Int'l Business:		Commercial/Industrial:	Y	Graphic Arts/Photog.:		Hardware Dev.:		HR/Other:	Y	Health/Lab	
MBA Graduates:	Y	Sales Trainees:	Y	Music:		Consulting/Other:		Training:	Y	Scientists/Research:	
		Advertising Pros.:		Broadcasting:				Health Care:		Petroleum/Chemicals:	Y
				Other:				Consulting:		Math/Other:	

TYPES OF BUSINESS:

Utilities-Electricity & Natural Gas
Power Generation
Real Estate
Equipment Leasing
Financial Services

BRANDS/DIVISIONS/AFFILIATES:

Dayton Power and Light Company
DPL Energy, LLC
DPL Energy Resources, Inc.
MVE, Inc.
Miami Valley Insurance Company
MC Squared Energy Services LLC
AES Corporation (The)

CONTACTS: *Note: Officers with more than one job title may be intentionally listed here more than once.*

Paul M. Barbas, CEO
Paul M. Barbas, Pres.
Frederick J. Boyle, CFO/Sr. VP
Daniel J. McCabe, Chief Admin. Officer/Sr. VP
Arthur G. Meyer, General Counsel/Sr. VP
Gary G. Stephenson, Exec. VP-Oper.
Teresa F. Marrinan, Sr. VP-Bus. Planning & Dev.
Joseph Mulpas, Chief Acct. Officer/VP/Controller
Kevin W. Crawford, VP-Generation
Bryce Nickel, VP-Service Oper.
Scott J. Kelly, Sr. VP-Retail Oper.
Craig L. Jackson, Treas./VP
Glenn E. Harder, Chmn.

Phone: 937-224-6000	**Fax:** 937-259-7147
Toll-Free:	
Address: 1065 Woodman Dr., Dayton, OH 45432 US	

GROWTH PLANS/SPECIAL FEATURES:

DPL, Inc. is a diversified regional energy company operating primarily through its subsidiary Dayton Power and Light Company (DP&L). Providing approximately 98% of DPL's total consolidated revenue and approximately 95% of DPL's total consolidated asset base, DP&L is a public utility selling electricity to residential, commercial, industrial and governmental customers in a 6,000-square-mile area of west central Ohio. Electricity for DP&L's 24 county service area is primarily generated at eight coal-fired power plants and is distributed to more than 500,000 retail customers. DP&L also purchases retail peak load requirements from another of DPL's subsidiaries, DPL Energy, LLC. Other significant subsidiaries of DPL include DPL Energy Resources, Inc., which sells retail electric energy under contract to major industrial and commercial customers in west central Ohio; MVE, Inc., which is primarily responsible for the management of its financial asset portfolio; and Miami Valley Insurance Company, a captive insurance company that provides DPL and its subsidiaries with coverage. In 2010, DP&L opened a 1.1 megawatt solar power facility in Washington Township, Montgomery County, Ohio. In March 2011, the company acquired Chicago-based MC Squared Energy Services LLC, a retail electricity supplier serving approximately 2,000 customers in northern Illinois. In April 2011, The AES Corporation agreed to acquire DPL for $4.7 billion.

The company offers employees medical benefits, flexible spending accounts, a bonus incentive program, educational assistance, a 401(k) savings plan and life insurance.

FINANCIALS: **Sales and profits are in thousands of dollars—add 000 to get the full amount. 2011 Note: Financial information for 2011 was not available for all companies at press time.**

2011 Sales: $	2011 Profits: $	**U.S. Stock Ticker: DPL**
2010 Sales: $1,883,100	2010 Profits: $290,300	**Int'l Ticker:**
2009 Sales: $1,588,900	2009 Profits: $229,100	Int'l Exchange:
2008 Sales: $1,601,600	2008 Profits: $244,500	Employees: 1,535 Fiscal Year Ends: 12/31
2007 Sales: $1,515,700	2007 Profits: $221,800	Parent Company:

SALARIES/BENEFITS:

Pension Plan:	ESOP Stock Plan:	Profit Sharing:	Top Exec. Salary: $675,000	Bonus: $668,024
Savings Plan: Y	Stock Purch. Plan:		Second Exec. Salary: $357,985	Bonus: $286,487

OTHER THOUGHTS:

Apparent Women Officers or Directors: 3
Hot Spot for Advancement for Women/Minorities: Y

LOCATIONS: ("Y" = Yes)

West:	Southwest:	Midwest:	Southeast:	Northeast:	International:
		Y		Y	

DREAMWORKS ANIMATION SKG INC www.dreamworksanimation.com

Industry Group Code: 512110

Management:		Sales/Marketing:		Liberal Arts:		Information Systems:		Professionals:		Technical/Scientific:	
Mgmt. Trainees:		Mktg. Professionals:	Y	Gen. Writing/Editing:	Y	Info. Management:	Y	Finance/Acct.:	Y	Engineers, Elec.:	
Experienced Mgmt.:	Y	Retail Sales:		Technical Writing:		Software Dev.:	Y	Law:	Y	Engineers, Other:	
Int'l Business:		Commercial/Industrial:	Y	Graphic Arts/Photog.:	Y	Hardware Dev.:		HR/Other:	Y	Health/Lab	
MBA Graduates:	Y	Sales Trainees:	Y	Music:	Y	Consulting/Other:		Training:	Y	Scientists/Research:	
		Advertising Pros.:	Y	Broadcasting:				Health Care:		Petroleum/Chemicals:	
				Other:	Y			Consulting:		Math/Other:	

TYPES OF BUSINESS:

Animated Film Production
Animation Software

BRANDS/DIVISIONS/AFFILIATES:

DreamWorks Studios
Wallace & Gromit: Curse of the Were-Rabbit
Shrek
Paramount Pictures Corp
Shrek the Musical
Madagascar
Monsters vs. Aliens
Kung Fu Panda

CONTACTS: *Note: Officers with more than one job title may be intentionally listed here more than once.*

Jeffrey Katzenberg, CEO
Ann Daly, COO
Lew Coleman, Pres.
Lew Coleman, CFO
Anne Globe, Head-Worldwide Mktg. & Consumer Products
Daniel Satterthwaite, Head-Human Resources
Andrew Chang, General Counsel/Corp. Sec.
Heather O'Connor, Chief Acct. Officer
Richard Sullivan, Head-Corp. Finance
Richard Sherman, Dir.
Roger A. Enrico, Chmn.

Phone: 818-695-3900 **Fax:** 818-695-6123
Toll-Free:
Address: 1000 Flower St., Glendale, CA 91201 US

GROWTH PLANS/SPECIAL FEATURES:

DreamWorks Animation SKG, Inc. creates family entertainment, such as animated computer-generated (CG) feature films, as well as non feature films, such as television specials and series, live entertainment properties, an online virtual world and other related consumer products. Animated feature films are advertized, promoted, distributed and marketed by Paramount. The firm uses proprietary software to produce its films, and its operations take place at two facilities in Glendale and Redwood City, California. The company has released a total of 21 animated feature films, including 12 that were CG-only. It aims to release five CG films every two years. Past releases include such box office hits as Antz, Shrek, Shrek 2 (the highest-grossing animated film in U.S. box office history and fifth highest of any release), Madagascar and Shrek the Third. DreamWorks Animation has also collaborated with Aardman Animations to release Chicken Run and Wallace & Gromit: Curse of the Were-Rabbit. Beyond film, the company also produces a TV series, the Penguins of Madagascar; made-for-TV specials; direct-to-video specials; and a live-action Broadway musical, Shrek the Musical. The company has a multi-year deal with THQ, Inc. to develop video games based on DreamWorks Animation's characters, including those of Kung Fu Panda, Shrek and Madagascar. In July 2011, the company produced half-hour television specials based on its films, Shrek, Kung Fu Panda, Madagascar and Monsters vs. Aliens. In addition, the firm launched a nationwide touring production of a play based on Shrek. In December 2011, the company partnered with Nickelodean Studios to produce an animated television series based on Kung Fu Panda. Throughout the year, Dream Works has also been working on producing additional live shows based on How To Train Your Dragon and Kung Fu Panda.

FINANCIALS: **Sales and profits are in thousands of dollars—add 000 to get the full amount. 2011 Note: Financial information for 2011 was not available for all companies at press time.**

2011 Sales: $706,023 | 2011 Profits: $86,801
2010 Sales: $784,791 | 2010 Profits: $170,639
2009 Sales: $725,179 | 2009 Profits: $151,035
2008 Sales: $650,052 | 2008 Profits: $142,498
2007 Sales: $767,178 | 2007 Profits: $218,364

U.S. Stock Ticker: DWA
Int'l Ticker:
Int'l Exchange:
Employees: 2,100 Fiscal Year Ends: 12/31
Parent Company:

SALARIES/BENEFITS:

Pension Plan: | ESOP Stock Plan: | Profit Sharing: | Top Exec. Salary: $1,262,000 | Bonus: $750,000
Savings Plan: Y | Stock Purch. Plan: | Second Exec. Salary: $1,012,000 | Bonus: $562,500

OTHER THOUGHTS:

Apparent Women Officers or Directors: 3
Hot Spot for Advancement for Women/Minorities: Y

LOCATIONS: ("Y" = Yes)

West:	Southwest:	Midwest:	Southeast:	Northeast:	International:
Y					

DRUGSTORE.COM INC

www.drugstore.com

Industry Group Code: 446110E

Management:		Sales/Marketing:		Liberal Arts:		Information Systems:		Professionals:		Technical/Scientific:	
Mgmt. Trainees:	Y	Mktg. Professionals:	Y	Gen. Writing/Editing:	Y	Info. Management:	Y	Finance/Acct.:	Y	Engineers, Elec.:	
Experienced Mgmt.:	Y	Retail Sales:	Y	Technical Writing:		Software Dev.:	Y	Law:	Y	Engineers, Other:	
Int'l Business:	Y	Commercial/Industrial:		Graphic Arts/Photog.:	Y	Hardware Dev.:		HR/Other:	Y	Health/Lab	
MBA Graduates:	Y	Sales Trainees:	Y	Music:		Consulting/Other:		Training:	Y	Scientists/Research:	
		Advertising Pros.:	Y	Broadcasting:				Health Care:		Petroleum/Chemicals:	
				Other:				Consulting:		Math/Other:	

TYPES OF BUSINESS:

Retail-Online Drug Store
Over-the-Counter & Prescription Drugs
Health & Beauty Products
Vision Products
Nutritional Supplements

BRANDS/DIVISIONS/AFFILIATES:

Walgreen Co
Beauty.com
Walgreens.com
VisionDirect.com
SkinStore.com

CONTACTS:

Note: Officers with more than one job title may be intentionally listed here more than once.

Phone: 425-372-3200	**Fax:** 425-372-3800
Toll-Free: 800-378-4786	
Address: 411 108th Ave. NE, Ste. 1400, Bellevue, WA 98004 US	

GROWTH PLANS/SPECIAL FEATURES:

Drugstore.com, Inc., a wholly-owned subsidiary of Walgreen Co., is an online drugstore, offering an array of health, beauty, wellness, personal care, household goods and pharmaceutical products. The firm operates drugstore.com; Beauty.com; VisionDirect.com; SkinStore.com; and Walgreens.com. Drugstore.com offers more than 60,000 name brand and private label health, beauty, pharmaceutical and vision products. Through a partnership with GNC Corporation, the firm offers GNC vitamins and wellness products through its website. Beauty.com offers beauty products from 300 top brand names, and allows customers to purchase products as well as receive beauty tips and advice. VisionDirect.com offers customers the ability to order contact lenses and related products and solutions, and features the Acuvue, Air Optix and Freshlook brands. SkinStore.com offers over 200 premium label skin care brands that are usually only available through outlets such as doctors' offices, spas and fine retail stores. These brands include Alterna, Belli, D'Arcy and DermaNew.. Additionally, the website offers hair care, cosmetic and fragrance products. Walgreens.com is an online pharmacy that allows customers to schedule appointments for flu shots, reorder prescriptions, print photos and shop for products such as home medical supplies, fitness products, gifts and grocery items. In March 2011, the firm was acquired by Walgreen Co. for $409 million.

Employee benefits include: medical, dental and vision insurance; flexible spending accounts; an employee assistance program; life and accidental death insurance; short and long-term disability; gym access; tuition reimbursement; and a 20% employee discount.

FINANCIALS:

Sales and profits are in thousands of dollars—add 000 to get the full amount. 2011 Note: Financial information for 2011 was not available for all companies at press time.

2011 Sales: $	2011 Profits: $
2010 Sales: $456,507	2010 Profits: $-3,550
2009 Sales: $375,574	2009 Profits: $-1,377
2008 Sales: $366,579	2008 Profits: $-8,287
2007 Sales: $339,331	2007 Profits: $-11,511

U.S. Stock Ticker: Subsidiary
Int'l Ticker:
Int'l Exchange:
Employees: 945 Fiscal Year Ends: 12/31
Parent Company: WALGREEN CO

SALARIES/BENEFITS:

Pension Plan:	ESOP Stock Plan:	Profit Sharing:	Top Exec. Salary: $538,594	Bonus: $1,400,000
Savings Plan: Y	Stock Purch. Plan: Y		Second Exec. Salary: $271,495	Bonus: $129,103

OTHER THOUGHTS:

Apparent Women Officers or Directors: 5
Hot Spot for Advancement for Women/Minorities: Y

LOCATIONS: ("Y" = Yes)

West:	Southwest:	Midwest:	Southeast:	Northeast:	International:
Y				Y	Y

EATON VANCE CORP

www.eatonvance.com

Industry Group Code: 523920

Management:		Sales/Marketing:		Liberal Arts:		Information Systems:		Professionals:		Technical/Scientific:	
Mgmt. Trainees:		Mktg. Professionals:	Y	Gen. Writing/Editing:	Y	Info. Management:	Y	Finance/Acct.:	Y	Engineers, Elec.:	
Experienced Mgmt.:	Y	Retail Sales:		Technical Writing:	Y	Software Dev.:		Law:	Y	Engineers, Other:	
Int'l Business:	Y	Commercial/Industrial:		Graphic Arts/Photog.:		Hardware Dev.:		HR/Other:	Y	Health/Lab	
MBA Graduates:	Y	Sales Trainees:		Music:		Consulting/Other:		Training:		Scientists/Research:	
		Advertising Pros.:		Broadcasting:				Health Care:		Petroleum/Chemicals:	
				Other:				Consulting:		Math/Other:	Y

TYPES OF BUSINESS:

Investment Management/Mutual Funds
Fund Advising
Broker/Dealer

BRANDS/DIVISIONS/AFFILIATES:

Eaton Vance Management
Boston Management & Research
Eaton Vance Investment Counsel
Eaton Vance Trust Co
Eaton Vance (Ireland) Ltd
Navigate Fund Solutions LLC
Pelican Investment Management Inc
Eaton Vance Distributors Inc

CONTACTS: *Note: Officers with more than one job title may be intentionally listed here more than once.*

Thomas E. Faust, Jr., CEO
Thomas E. Faust, Jr., Pres.
Robert J. Whelan, CFO/VP/Treas.
Jeffrey P. Beale, Chief Admin. Officer/VP
Frederick S. Marius, Chief Legal Officer/VP/Sec.
Laurie G. Hylton, Chief Acct. Officer/VP
Duncan W. Richardson, Chief Equity Investment Officer/Exec. VP
Matthew J. Witkos, Pres., Eaton Vance Distributors, Inc.
Thomas E. Faust, Jr., Chmn.

Phone: 617-482-8260 **Fax:**
Toll-Free: 800-225-6265
Address: 2 International Place, Boston, MA 02110 US

GROWTH PLANS/SPECIAL FEATURES:

Eaton Vance Corp., with over $188.2 billion in assets under management, operates primarily as a manager of investment funds and an adviser to high-net-worth individuals and institutions. The company operates in one business segment, as an investment adviser to funds and separate accounts, and competes in a variety of investment areas, including tax-managed and emerging market equity; equity income; floating-rate bank loan; and municipal bond, investment grade and high-yield bond investing. The company's products and services include company-sponsored open-end funds (40% of total 2010 assets), closed-end funds (13%), private funds (9%), retail managed accounts (13%) and high-net-worth and institutional separate accounts (25%). The company conducts its investment management business through five wholly-owned subsidiaries: Eaton Vance Management (EVM); Boston Management and Research (BMR); Eaton Vance Investment Counsel (EVIC); Eaton Vance Trust Company (EVTC); and Eaton Vance (Ireland) Limited (EVAI). The firm also offers investment management through four consolidated subsidiaries: Atlanta Capital Management Company, LLC; Fox Asset Management LLC; Parametric Portfolio Associates LLC; and Parametric Risk Advisors LLC. Eaton Vance Distributors, Inc., a wholly-owned broker/dealer, markets and sells the Eaton Vance funds and retail managed accounts. In April 2011, the company acquired Pelican Investment Management, Inc., including $500 million in client assets. In October 2011, Eaton Vance established Navigate Fund Solutions LLC to commercialize net asset value-based trading of exchange-traded funds and to develop exchange-traded managed funds.

FINANCIALS: **Sales and profits are in thousands of dollars—add 000 to get the full amount. 2011 Note: Financial information for 2011 was not available for all companies at press time.**

2011 Sales: $1,212,804 | 2011 Profits: $643,505
2010 Sales: $1,121,661 | 2010 Profits: $174,298
2009 Sales: $890,371 | 2009 Profits: $130,107
2008 Sales: $1,095,800 | 2008 Profits: $195,663
2007 Sales: $1,084,100 | 2007 Profits: $142,811

U.S. Stock Ticker: EV
Int'l Ticker:
Int'l Exchange:
Employees: 1,155 Fiscal Year Ends: 10/31
Parent Company:

SALARIES/BENEFITS:

Pension Plan: | ESOP Stock Plan: | Profit Sharing: | Top Exec. Salary: $512,500 | Bonus: $3,850,371
Savings Plan: | Stock Purch. Plan: | | Second Exec. Salary: $384,000 | Bonus: $2,286,953

OTHER THOUGHTS:

Apparent Women Officers or Directors: 1
Hot Spot for Advancement for Women/Minorities:

LOCATIONS: ("Y" = Yes)

West:	Southwest:	Midwest:	Southeast:	Northeast:	International:
Y			Y	Y	Y

EBIX INC

www.ebix.com

Industry Group Code: 511201

Management:		Sales/Marketing:		Liberal Arts:		Information Systems:		Professionals:		Technical/Scientific:	
Mgmt. Trainees:		Mktg. Professionals:	Y	Gen. Writing/Editing:	Y	Info. Management:	Y	Finance/Acct.:	Y	Engineers, Elec.:	Y
Experienced Mgmt.:	Y	Retail Sales:		Technical Writing:	Y	Software Dev.:	Y	Law:	Y	Engineers, Other:	
Int'l Business:	Y	Commercial/Industrial:	Y	Graphic Arts/Photog.:		Hardware Dev.:		HR/Other:	Y	Health/Lab	
MBA Graduates:	Y	Sales Trainees:		Music:		Consulting/Other:		Training:	Y	Scientists/Research:	
		Advertising Pros.:		Broadcasting:				Health Care:		Petroleum/Chemicals:	
				Other:				Consulting:		Math/Other:	

TYPES OF BUSINESS:

Insurance Computer Software
BPO Services

BRANDS/DIVISIONS/AFFILIATES:

Winbeat
EbixASP
eGlobal
EbixExchange
Ebix New Zealand
Ebix Singapore Pte Ltd
A.D.A.M., Inc.
Ebix Software India Private Limited

CONTACTS: *Note: Officers with more than one job title may be intentionally listed here more than once.*

Robin Raina, CEO
Robin Raina, Pres.
Robert F. Kerris, CFO
Robert F. Kerris, Corp. Sec.
Steven N. Barlow, VP-Investor Rel.
Robert F. Kerris, Principal Acct. Officer
Andy Wakefield, Managing Dir.-Ebix Singapore
Leon d'Apice, Managing Dir.-Ebix Australia
Dan Delity, Sr. VP-EbixExchange (Life & Annuity)
Jim Senge, Sr. VP-EbixExchange (Health & Employee Benefits)
Robin Raina, Chmn.
Graham Prior, Sr. VP-Int'l Bus. & Intellectual Property

Phone: 678-281-2020	**Fax:** 678-281-2019
Toll-Free:	
Address: 5 Concourse Pkwy., Ste. 3200, Atlanta, GA 30328 US	

GROWTH PLANS/SPECIAL FEATURES:

Ebix, Inc. is a worldwide supplier of software and e-commerce products and services to the insurance industry. The firm offers a range of application software products, including carrier systems, agency systems, exchanges and custom software development, for all entities involved in the insurance and financial industries. The company's product and service offerings are divided into four groups: insurance carrier systems, broker systems, exchanges and business process outsourcing (BPO). The company's carrier system's offerings include Ebix Advantage, which targets property and casualty carriers in the U.S.; and Ebix Advantageweb, designed for personal and casualty carriers in both U.S. and international markets. Ebix sells and supports several broker systems, including EbixASP, eGlobal and Winbeat. In the exchanges group, the company offers EbixExchange, a life, health, annuity and property/casualty product suite aimed at improving connectivity between consumers, agents, carriers and third party providers. Life insurance exchanges include LifeSpeed and Winflex. In this group, employee benefits services are also offered through two platforms: Facts and LuminX. The firm's BPO services include certificate tracking and origination; and call center and back office support. Ebix derives the majority of its revenues from the following services: ASP services; transaction based exchanges; transaction based BPO services; and professional and support services to insurance companies, large corporate clients, distributors and brokers. The company's wholly-owned subsidiaries include Ebix International, Inc.; Ebix Australia Pty, Ltd.; EbixExchange Pty, Ltd.; Ebix Software India Private Limited; Ebix Insurance Agency, Inc.; EbixLife, Inc.; Ebix Singapore Pte Ltd.; and Ebix New Zealand. In February 2011, Ebix acquired health information and benefits technology services provider A.D.A.M., Inc.

FINANCIALS: **Sales and profits are in thousands of dollars—add 000 to get the full amount. 2011 Note: Financial information for 2011 was not available for all companies at press time.**

2011 Sales: $	2011 Profits: $
2010 Sales: $132,188	2010 Profits: $59,019
2009 Sales: $97,685	2009 Profits: $38,822
2008 Sales: $74,752	2008 Profits: $27,314
2007 Sales: $42,841	2007 Profits: $12,666

U.S. Stock Ticker: EBIX
Int'l Ticker:
Int'l Exchange:
Employees: 1,179 Fiscal Year Ends: 12/31
Parent Company:

SALARIES/BENEFITS:

Pension Plan:	ESOP Stock Plan:	Profit Sharing:	Top Exec. Salary: $800,000	Bonus: $1,600,000
Savings Plan:	Stock Purch. Plan:		Second Exec. Salary: $146,481	Bonus: $81,564

OTHER THOUGHTS:

Apparent Women Officers or Directors: 1
Hot Spot for Advancement for Women/Minorities:

LOCATIONS: ("Y" = Yes)

West:	Southwest:	Midwest:	Southeast:	Northeast:	International:
Y	Y	Y	Y	Y	Y

ECHO GLOBAL LOGISTICS INC

www.echo.com

Industry Group Code: 484

Management:		Sales/Marketing:		Liberal Arts:		Information Systems:		Professionals:		Technical/Scientific:	
Mgmt. Trainees:		Mktg. Professionals:	Y	Gen. Writing/Editing:	Y	Info. Management:	Y	Finance/Acct.:	Y	Engineers, Elec.:	
Experienced Mgmt.:	Y	Retail Sales:		Technical Writing:		Software Dev.:		Law:	Y	Engineers, Other:	
Int'l Business:		Commercial/Industrial:	Y	Graphic Arts/Photog.:		Hardware Dev.:		HR/Other:	Y	Health/Lab	
MBA Graduates:	Y	Sales Trainees:		Music:		Consulting/Other:		Training:		Scientists/Research:	
		Advertising Pros.:		Broadcasting:				Health Care:		Petroleum/Chemicals:	
				Other:				Consulting:		Math/Other:	

TYPES OF BUSINESS:

Transportation & Logistic Services
Shipment Tracking
Freight Analysis
Web-based Logistics Tools

BRANDS/DIVISIONS/AFFILIATES:

FlexTMS
Trailer Transport Systems
Advantage Transport

CONTACTS:

Note: Officers with more than one job title may be intentionally listed here more than once.

Douglas R. Waggoner, CEO
David B. Menzel, CFO
Scott Boyer, Sr. VP-Sales
David C. Rowe, CTO
Michael Mobley, Sr. VP-Oper.
Marty Sinicrope, Sr. VP-Station Sales
Samuel K. Skinner, Chmn.

Phone: **Fax:** 888-796-4445
Toll-Free: 800-354-7993
Address: 600 W. Chicago Ave., Ste. 725, Chicago, IL 60654 US

GROWTH PLANS/SPECIAL FEATURES:

Echo Global Logistics, Inc. is a provider of technology-supported transportation and supply chain management services, delivered on a proprietary technology platform serving the transportation and logistics needs of its clients. Echo's web-based technology platform compiles and analyzes data from a network of more than 24,000 transportation providers in order to serve clients' shipping and freight management needs. The platform, composed of web-based software applications and a proprietary database, enables the firm to identify excess transportation capacity, obtain competitive rates and execute thousands of shipments each day on behalf of its clients. The company focuses primarily on arranging transportation across the major modes, including truckload (TL), less than truckload (LTL) and small parcel. Echo also offers inter-modal (involving moving a shipment by both rail and truck), domestic air, expedited and international transportation services. Core logistics services include rate negotiation; shipment execution and tracking; carrier management; routing compliance; freight bill audit; and payment and performance management and reporting, including web-based dashboard tools available to client companies. Echo serves more than 22,800 clients across a range of industries, including manufacturing, construction, consumer products and retail. The company's clients fall into two main categories, enterprise and transactional. Enterprise clients typically enter into multi-year contracts, which can be on an exclusive basis for a specific transportation mode or point of origin. Meanwhile, transactional clients are those who arrange for transportation and logistics services on a shipment-by-shipment basis. In 2011, the firm's acquisitions included Trailer Transport Systems and Advantage Transport. In February 2011, the company launched FlexTMS, a self service transportation management system.

Echo offers its employees benefits that include medical, dental and vision coverage; an employee assistance program; paid continuous training; referral bonuses; discounted gym memberships; short-term disability coverage; a 401(k) plan; and free shuttle service to and from public transportation stops.

FINANCIALS:

Sales and profits are in thousands of dollars—add 000 to get the full amount. 2011 Note: Financial information for 2011 was not available for all companies at press time.

2011 Sales: $602,800	2011 Profits: $12,000	**U.S. Stock Ticker: ECHO**
2010 Sales: $426,400	2010 Profits: $8,400	**Int'l Ticker:**
2009 Sales: $259,600	2009 Profits: $5,200	Int'l Exchange:
2008 Sales: $202,800	2008 Profits: $2,900	Employees: 908 Fiscal Year Ends: 12/31
2007 Sales: $	2007 Profits: $	Parent Company:

SALARIES/BENEFITS:

Pension Plan:	ESOP Stock Plan:	Profit Sharing:	Top Exec. Salary: $393,750	Bonus: $125,000
Savings Plan: Y	Stock Purch. Plan:		Second Exec. Salary: $330,000	Bonus: $125,000

OTHER THOUGHTS:

Apparent Women Officers or Directors:
Hot Spot for Advancement for Women/Minorities:

LOCATIONS: ("Y" = Yes)

West:	Southwest:	Midwest:	Southeast:	Northeast:	International:
		Y			

ECHOSTAR CORP

Industry Group Code: 517110

www.echostar.com

Management:		Sales/Marketing:		Liberal Arts:		Information Systems:		Professionals:		Technical/Scientific:	
Mgmt. Trainees:		Mktg. Professionals:	Y	Gen. Writing/Editing:	Y	Info. Management:	Y	Finance/Acct.:	Y	Engineers, Elec.:	Y
Experienced Mgmt.:	Y	Retail Sales:		Technical Writing:	Y	Software Dev.:	Y	Law:	Y	Engineers, Other:	
Int'l Business:	Y	Commercial/Industrial:	Y	Graphic Arts/Photog.:		Hardware Dev.:		HR/Other:	Y	Health/Lab	
MBA Graduates:	Y	Sales Trainees:		Music:		Consulting/Other:		Training:		Scientists/Research:	
		Advertising Pros.:		Broadcasting:				Health Care:		Petroleum/Chemicals:	
				Other:				Consulting:		Math/Other:	

TYPES OF BUSINESS:

Digital Set-Top Boxes & Related Products
Fixed Satellite Services

BRANDS/DIVISIONS/AFFILIATES:

DISH Network Corp.
EchoStar Satellite Services LLC
Sling Media Inc
Hughes Communications, Inc.
EchoStar International Corporation

CONTACTS: *Note: Officers with more than one job title may be intentionally listed here more than once.*

Michael T. Dugan, CEO
Michael T. Dugan, Pres.
David Rayner, CFO
Roger Lynch, Exec. VP-Advanced Tech.
R. Stanton Dodge, General Counsel/Exec. VP/Corp. Sec.
Marc Lumpkin, Media Rel.
Mark W. Jackson, Pres., EchoStar Technologies, LLC
Charles W. Ergen, Chmn.
Steven B. Schaver, Pres., EchoStar Int'l Corp.

Phone: 303-706-4000 **Fax:**
Toll-Free:
Address: 100 Inverness Terrace E., Englewood, CO 80112-5308 US

GROWTH PLANS/SPECIAL FEATURES:

EchoStar Corp. is a provider of digital set-top box and satellite services. The set-top box business designs, develops and distributes set-top boxes and related products for direct-to-home satellite service providers. While the majority of EchoStar's set-top boxes are sold to DISH Network and DISH Mexico, the firm also provides a significant number to Canadian company Bell TV and other international clients. The company's satellite services business lease capacity on a full time and occasional-use basis to enterprise, broadcast news and government organizations using its eight owned and leased in-orbit satellites and related Federal Communication Commission (FCC) licenses. As with its digital set-top boxes segment, the fixed satellite services division's primary customer is DISH Network; however, it also leases to Internet service providers, government entities, broadcast news organizations and private enterprise customers. As part of the company's spin-off from DISH Network, EchoStar acquired Sling Media, Inc., manufacturer of the Slingbox, a technology that allows consumers to watch and control their home digital video and audio content anywhere in the world via a broadband Internet connection. Slingbox products have been incorporated into EchoStar Corp.'s digital set-top boxes division. The firm and MVS Comunicaciones, a Mexican media and telecommunications conglomerate, operate joint venture Dish Mexico, which offers affordable satellite service to Mexico. In June 2010, subsidiary EchoStar International Corporation began offering pay-service DishHD in Taiwan. In February 2011, the firm agreed to acquire Hughes Communications, Inc., a broadband satellite technology provider, for $1.35 billion.

FINANCIALS: **Sales and profits are in thousands of dollars—add 000 to get the full amount. 2011 Note: Financial information for 2011 was not available for all companies at press time.**

2011 Sales: $2,761,431 — 2011 Profits: $25,775
2010 Sales: $2,350,369 — 2010 Profits: $204,358
2009 Sales: $1,903,559 — 2009 Profits: $364,704
2008 Sales: $2,150,520 — 2008 Profits: $-944,001
2007 Sales: $1,544,065 — 2007 Profits: $-85,300

U.S. Stock Ticker: SATS
Int'l Ticker:
Int'l Exchange:
Employees: 2,300 Fiscal Year Ends: 12/31
Parent Company:

SALARIES/BENEFITS:

Pension Plan: ESOP Stock Plan: Profit Sharing: Top Exec. Salary: $750,000 Bonus: $
Savings Plan: Stock Purch. Plan: Second Exec. Salary: $471,346 Bonus: $

OTHER THOUGHTS:

Apparent Women Officers or Directors:
Hot Spot for Advancement for Women/Minorities:

LOCATIONS: ("Y" = Yes)

West:	Southwest:	Midwest:	Southeast:	Northeast:	International:
Y	Y	Y	Y	Y	Y

ECOLLEGE.COM

www.ecollege.com

Industry Group Code: 611410

Management:		Sales/Marketing:		Liberal Arts:		Information Systems:		Professionals:		Technical/Scientific:	
Mgmt. Trainees:	Y	Mktg. Professionals:	Y	Gen. Writing/Editing:	Y	Info. Management:	Y	Finance/Acct.:	Y	Engineers, Elec.:	
Experienced Mgmt.:	Y	Retail Sales:		Technical Writing:	Y	Software Dev.:	Y	Law:	Y	Engineers, Other:	
Int'l Business:	Y	Commercial/Industrial:	Y	Graphic Arts/Photog.:	Y	Hardware Dev.:		HR/Other:	Y	Health/Lab	
MBA Graduates:	Y	Sales Trainees:	Y	Music:		Consulting/Other:		Training:	Y	Scientists/Research:	
		Advertising Pros.:	Y	Broadcasting:				Health Care:		Petroleum/Chemicals:	
				Other:	Y			Consulting:		Math/Other:	

TYPES OF BUSINESS:

Online Education Software
e-Learning Solutions
Enrollment Marketing Services

BRANDS/DIVISIONS/AFFILIATES:

Pearson eLearningStudio
eCollege System
eCollege Teaching Solutions
eCollege Program Administration Solutions
Pearson PLC

CONTACTS: *Note: Officers with more than one job title may be intentionally listed here more than once.*

Matthew Leavy, CEO
Kendrick H. McLish, VP-Mktg.
Vance Allen, CTO
Kendrick H. McLish, VP-Prod.
Kendrick H. McLish, VP-Strategy

Phone: 303-658-100 **Fax:** 303-873-7449
Toll-Free: 888-884-7325
Address: 2154 E. Commons Ave., Centennial, CO 80122 US

GROWTH PLANS/SPECIAL FEATURES:

ECollege.com, a subsidiary of Pearson PLC, builds and supports online learning communities for colleges, universities, K-12 school districts and corporate training organizations. It provides these services through the Pearson eLearningStudio platform, which enables colleges, universities and high schools to offer online and hybrid educational programs as well as on-campus courses. Selected products include the eCollege System, which uses software and services to support customers' online programs. The eCollege System includes eCollege Teaching Solutions, eCollege Program Administration Solutions and technology infrastructure. Its outsourced product incorporates a course management system, designed toward maximum efficiency and interaction; a program administration system, which helps administrators manage the online community; and a secure hosted environment, with all the hardware, security and ancillary software necessary to function well. eLearning solutions and services offered include, but are not limited to, hosting and infrastructure; a course management system; a program administration system; content manager; operational support; academic training and consulting; course development; enterprise reporting; a course evaluation system; and 24/7 user support. The firm has international offices in Australia, India, the U.K. and Mexico.

FINANCIALS: **Sales and profits are in thousands of dollars—add 000 to get the full amount. 2011 Note: Financial information for 2011 was not available for all companies at press time.**

2011 Sales: $	2011 Profits: $	**U.S. Stock Ticker: Subsidiary**
2010 Sales: $	2010 Profits: $	**Int'l Ticker:**
2009 Sales: $	2009 Profits: $	Int'l Exchange:
2008 Sales: $	2008 Profits: $	Employees: Fiscal Year Ends: 12/31
2007 Sales: $	2007 Profits: $	Parent Company: PEARSON PLC

SALARIES/BENEFITS:

Pension Plan:	ESOP Stock Plan:	Profit Sharing:	Top Exec. Salary: $	Bonus: $
Savings Plan:	Stock Purch. Plan:		Second Exec. Salary: $	Bonus: $

OTHER THOUGHTS:

Apparent Women Officers or Directors:
Hot Spot for Advancement for Women/Minorities:

LOCATIONS: ("Y" = Yes)

West:	Southwest:	Midwest:	Southeast:	Northeast:	International:
Y					Y

EDELMAN FINANCIAL GROUP (THE)

www.smhgroup.com

Industry Group Code: 523110

Management:		Sales/Marketing:		Liberal Arts:		Information Systems:		Professionals:		Technical/Scientific:	
Mgmt. Trainees:	Y	Mktg. Professionals:	Y	Gen. Writing/Editing:	Y	Info. Management:	Y	Finance/Acct.:	Y	Engineers, Elec.:	
Experienced Mgmt.:	Y	Retail Sales:		Technical Writing:		Software Dev.:	Y	Law:	Y	Engineers, Other:	
Int'l Business:		Commercial/Industrial:		Graphic Arts/Photog.:		Hardware Dev.:		HR/Other:	Y	Health/Lab	
MBA Graduates:	Y	Sales Trainees:		Music:		Consulting/Other:		Training:		Scientists/Research:	
		Advertising Pros.:		Broadcasting:				Health Care:		Petroleum/Chemicals:	
				Other:				Consulting:		Math/Other:	

TYPES OF BUSINESS:

Stock Brokerage
Investment Banking
Merchant Banking
Loan Servicing
Asset Management
Trust-Related Services
Financial Planning
Sports Representation & Management

BRANDS/DIVISIONS/AFFILIATES:

Edelman Financial Center LLC
Edelman Managed Asset Program
Sanders Morris Harris Inc
Kissinger Financial Services
Sanders Morris Harris Group
The Rikoon Group LLC
Leonetti & Associates LLC

CONTACTS: *Note: Officers with more than one job title may be intentionally listed here more than once.*

George L. Ball, Co-CEO
Ric Edelman, Pres.
Rick Berry, CFO
Lesley V. Roberts, Chief of Staff
Bill Coquelin, CIO
Ric Edelman, Co-CEO
Ed Moore, Exec. VP-Wealth Mgmt.
George L. Ball, Chmn.

Phone: 713-993-4610	**Fax:**
Toll-Free: 888-752-6742	
Address: 600 Travis, Ste. 5800, Houston, TX 77002 US	

GROWTH PLANS/SPECIAL FEATURES:

The Edelman Financial Group, formerly Sanders Morris Harris Group, is a wealth management holding company. Through its subsidiaries, the company offers investment advice; wealth management; tax efficient estate and financial planning; and institutional services to both individual and corporate clientele. The firm is organized by its three major client sectors: Mass Affluent, High Net Worth and Institutional Services. The Mass Affluent sector is managed by the firm's largest subsidiary Edelman Financial Center, LLC, and provides financial planning to households with investable assets ranging from $50,000-$1 million. Investments are handled by the Edelman Managed Asset Program (EMAP), which creates professional portfolios and offers clients an array of security selections. EMAP has 12,000 investors and manages $5.5 billion in assets. The High Net Worth sector provides clients with assets of over $1 million with investment advice, investment and asset management and financial planning. The sector is divided into units based on a particular facet of wealth management. Each unit operates as its own individual business. Significant subsidiaries include Sanders Morris Harris, Inc.; Kissinger Financial Services; The Rikoon Group, LLC; and Leonetti & Associates LLC. Combined, the sector's subsidiaries manage $11.2 billion in assets. The Institutional Services sector provides worldwide institutions, such as banks, retirement funds, mutual funds, endowments, investment advisors and insurance companies with institutional brokerage, fixed income brokerage and prime brokerage services. In May 2011, the company name was officially changed from Sanders Morris Harris Group to The Edelman Financial Group. In October 2011, the firm announced plans to exit the independent representative business by the year's end.

FINANCIALS: **Sales and profits are in thousands of dollars—add 000 to get the full amount. 2011 Note: Financial information for 2011 was not available for all companies at press time.**

2011 Sales: $	2011 Profits: $	**U.S. Stock Ticker: EF**
2010 Sales: $168,843	2010 Profits: $9,696	**Int'l Ticker:**
2009 Sales: $167,240	2009 Profits: $-5,482	Int'l Exchange:
2008 Sales: $171,941	2008 Profits: $-25,293	Employees: 529 Fiscal Year Ends: 12/31
2007 Sales: $185,812	2007 Profits: $5,093	Parent Company:

SALARIES/BENEFITS:

Pension Plan:	ESOP Stock Plan:	Profit Sharing:	Top Exec. Salary: $750,000	Bonus: $400,000
Savings Plan:	Stock Purch. Plan:		Second Exec. Salary: $425,000	Bonus: $627,124

OTHER THOUGHTS:

Apparent Women Officers or Directors: 1
Hot Spot for Advancement for Women/Minorities:

LOCATIONS: ("Y" = Yes)

West:	Southwest:	Midwest:	Southeast:	Northeast:	International:
Y	Y	Y	Y	Y	

EDGAR ONLINE INC

www.edgar-online.com

Industry Group Code: 519130

Management:		**Sales/Marketing:**		**Liberal Arts:**		**Information Systems:**		**Professionals:**		**Technical/Scientific:**	
Mgmt. Trainees:		Mktg. Professionals:	Y	Gen. Writing/Editing:	Y	Info. Management:	Y	Finance/Acct.:	Y	Engineers, Elec.:	
Experienced Mgmt.:	Y	Retail Sales:		Technical Writing:	Y	Software Dev.:	Y	Law:	Y	Engineers, Other:	
Int'l Business:		Commercial/Industrial:	Y	Graphic Arts/Photog.:		Hardware Dev.:		HR/Other:	Y	Health/Lab	
MBA Graduates:	Y	Sales Trainees:		Music:		Consulting/Other:		Training:		Scientists/Research:	
		Advertising Pros.:	Y	Broadcasting:				Health Care:		Petroleum/Chemicals:	
				Other:				Consulting:		Math/Other:	

TYPES OF BUSINESS:

Online Financial Data
Data Mining

BRANDS/DIVISIONS/AFFILIATES:

EDGAR Pro
EDGAR Access
I-Metrix Professional
I-Metrix
Pro.Edgar-Online.com
Access.Edgar-Online.com
Ubmatrix

CONTACTS: *Note: Officers with more than one job title may be intentionally listed here more than once.*

Robert J. Farrell, CEO
David J. Price, COO
Robert J. Farrell, Pres.
David J. Price, CFO
David A. Frankel, Chief Mktg. Officer
Gregory A. Carter, CTO
Darren Peterson, VP-Prod. Mgmt.
Steven E. Friedman, General Counsel
Richard Jones, Sr. VP-Oper.
Jeannie Tshontikidis, VP-Data Oper.
Mark Maged, Chmn.

Phone: 301-287-0300 **Fax:** 301-287-0390
Toll-Free: 888-870-2316
Address: 11200 Rockville Pike, Ste. 310, Rockville, MD 20852 US

GROWTH PLANS/SPECIAL FEATURES:

EDGAR Online, Inc. creates and distributes financial data and public filings for equities, mutual funds and a variety of other publically traded assets. The company delivers information in the financial reporting standard XBRL (Extensible Business Reporting Language); this information is then used in the analysis of an investment's financial, business and ownership conditions. The firm also provides tools to assist organizations in the creation, management and distribution of XBRL financial reports; and tools and web sites for easy viewing and analysis of XBRL data. EDGAR delivers its information products in the form of online end-user subscriptions, as well as through data licenses and bulk data feeds. Its data products include fundamental financial data, annual and quarterly financial statements, insider trades, institutional holdings, initial and secondary public offerings, Form 8-K disclosures, electronic prospectuses and other investment instrument disclosure information. EDGAR's subscription services include I-Metrix and I-Metrix Professional, web-based subscription services; EDGAR Pro, a professional research subscription service that offers access to financial data, stock ownership, public offering data sets and advanced search tools via Pro.Edgar-Online.com; and EDGAR Access, which offers limited access via Access.Edgar-Online.com. In addition to its revenue-generating services, EDGAR operates a general database of SEC filings with restricted navigation tools. Consumers of the firm's information products are generally financial, corporate and advisory professionals who work in investment funds, asset management firms, insurance companies and banks, stock exchanges and government agencies, as well as accounting firms, law firms, corporations and individual investors. In recent years, the company merged with UBmatrix, a leader in XBRL content. UBmatrix will operate as a subsidiary of EDGAR.

FINANCIALS: **Sales and profits are in thousands of dollars—add 000 to get the full amount. 2011 Note: Financial information for 2011 was not available for all companies at press time.**

2011 Sales: $ | 2011 Profits: $
2010 Sales: $19,468 | 2010 Profits: $-8,649
2009 Sales: $19,174 | 2009 Profits: $- 950
2008 Sales: $19,463 | 2008 Profits: $-2,659
2007 Sales: $17,908 | 2007 Profits: $-7,363

U.S. Stock Ticker: EDGR
Int'l Ticker:
Int'l Exchange:
Employees: 143 Fiscal Year Ends: 12/31
Parent Company:

SALARIES/BENEFITS:

Pension Plan: | ESOP Stock Plan: | Profit Sharing: | Top Exec. Salary: $262,800 | Bonus: $50,000
Savings Plan: | Stock Purch. Plan: | | Second Exec. Salary: $205,957 | Bonus: $110,000

OTHER THOUGHTS:

Apparent Women Officers or Directors: 1
Hot Spot for Advancement for Women/Minorities:

LOCATIONS: ("Y" = Yes)

West:	Southwest:	Midwest:	Southeast:	Northeast:	International:
Y				Y	

EDUCATIONAL DEVELOPMENT CORP

www.edcpub.com

Industry Group Code: 511130

Management:		**Sales/Marketing:**		**Liberal Arts:**		**Information Systems:**		**Professionals:**		**Technical/Scientific:**	
Mgmt. Trainees:		Mktg. Professionals:	Y	Gen. Writing/Editing:	Y	Info. Management:	Y	Finance/Acct.:	Y	Engineers, Elec.:	
Experienced Mgmt.:	Y	Retail Sales:		Technical Writing:		Software Dev.:	Y	Law:	Y	Engineers, Other:	
Int'l Business:		Commercial/Industrial:	Y	Graphic Arts/Photog.:	Y	Hardware Dev.:		HR/Other:	Y	Health/Lab	
MBA Graduates:	Y	Sales Trainees:		Music:		Consulting/Other:		Training:		Scientists/Research:	
		Advertising Pros.:	Y	Broadcasting:				Health Care:		Petroleum/Chemicals:	
				Other:	Y			Consulting:		Math/Other:	

TYPES OF BUSINESS:

Children's Book Publishing
Book Distribution

BRANDS/DIVISIONS/AFFILIATES:

Usborne Publishing Limited
Usborne Books and More
Kane/Miller Book Publishers

CONTACTS: *Note: Officers with more than one job title may be intentionally listed here more than once.*

Randall W. White, CEO
Randall W. White, Pres.
Randall W. White, Treas.
Randall W. White, Chmn.

Phone: 918-622-4522 **Fax:** 918-665-7919
Toll-Free: 800-743-5660
Address: 10302 E. 55th Pl., Tulsa, OK 74146 US

GROWTH PLANS/SPECIAL FEATURES:

Educational Development Corp. (EDC) is the sole U.S. trade publisher and distributor of a line of children's books produced in the U.K. by Usborne Publishing Limited. With over 1,500 titles available, many of the company's products are interactive in nature and include Touchy-Feely board books; jigsaw puzzles; activity and flashcards; adventure and search books; art books; sticker books and foreign language books. The company operates two divisions, Usborne Books and More (UBAM), representing 67% of the firm's revenue and the publishing division, accounting for 33%. UBAM is a mutli-level direct selling organization that markets its products through independent sales representatives. Independent consultants hold book showings in individual homes, as well as through book fairs, direct sales and Internet sales. The consumer base of UBAM is primarily comprised of individual purchases, but also includes schools and public libraries. The publishing division operates in wholesale markets, selling books to various retail accounts that include approximately 5,000 bookstores, toy stores, specialty stores and other retail outlets, including museums and schools, as well as over the Internet. The firm also owns Kane/Miller Book Publishers, a California-based children's book publisher. The company operates out of its 105,000-square-foot office and warehouse facilities in Tulsa, Oklahoma.

FINANCIALS: **Sales and profits are in thousands of dollars—add 000 to get the full amount. 2011 Note: Financial information for 2011 was not available for all companies at press time.**

2011 Sales: $27,243 — 2011 Profits: $1,168
2010 Sales: $28,671 — 2010 Profits: $1,914
2009 Sales: $29,398 — 2009 Profits: $1,912
2008 Sales: $30,521 — 2008 Profits: $2,324
2007 Sales: $31,404 — 2007 Profits: $2,407

U.S. Stock Ticker: EDUC
Int'l Ticker:
Int'l Exchange:
Employees: 70 Fiscal Year Ends: 2/28
Parent Company:

SALARIES/BENEFITS:

Pension Plan: | ESOP Stock Plan: | Profit Sharing: | Top Exec. Salary: $150,000 | Bonus: $28,000
Savings Plan: Y | Stock Purch. Plan: | | Second Exec. Salary: $ | Bonus: $

OTHER THOUGHTS:

Apparent Women Officers or Directors: 1
Hot Spot for Advancement for Women/Minorities:

LOCATIONS: ("Y" = Yes)

West:	Southwest:	Midwest:	Southeast:	Northeast:	International:
Y	Y				

EHEALTH INC

www.ehealthinsurance.com

Industry Group Code: 524210A

Management:		**Sales/Marketing:**		**Liberal Arts:**		**Information Systems:**		**Professionals:**		**Technical/Scientific:**	
Mgmt. Trainees:	Y	Mktg. Professionals:	Y	Gen. Writing/Editing:	Y	Info. Management:	Y	Finance/Acct.:	Y	Engineers, Elec.:	
Experienced Mgmt.:	Y	Retail Sales:		Technical Writing:	Y	Software Dev.:	Y	Law:	Y	Engineers, Other:	
Int'l Business:		Commercial/Industrial:		Graphic Arts/Photog.:		Hardware Dev.:		HR/Other:	Y	Health/Lab	Y
MBA Graduates:	Y	Sales Trainees:		Music:		Consulting/Other:		Training:	Y	Scientists/Research:	
		Advertising Pros.:	Y	Broadcasting:				Health Care:	Y	Petroleum/Chemicals:	
				Other:				Consulting:		Math/Other:	Y

TYPES OF BUSINESS:

Health Insurance Brokerage-Online
Health Insurance
Student Health Insurance
Short-term Health Insurance
Health Savings Accounts
Dental Insurance
Term Life Insurance
Dental Discount Cards

BRANDS/DIVISIONS/AFFILIATES:

PlanPrescriber.com

CONTACTS: *Note: Officers with more than one job title may be intentionally listed here more than once.*

Gary L. Lauer, CEO
Gary L. Lauer, Pres.
Stuart M. Huizinga, CFO/Sr. VP
Robert S. Hurley, Sr. VP-Sales
Sheldon X. Wang, CTO/Exec. VP-Tech.
Robert S. Hurley, Sr. VP-Oper.
Bruce Telkamp, Exec. VP-Bus. & Corp. Dev.
Brian Mast, VP-Corp. Comm.
Samuel C. Gibbs, III, Pres., EHealth Gov't Systems
Gary L. Lauer, Chmn.

Phone: 650-584-2700 **Fax:** 650-961-2153
Toll-Free: 800-977-8860
Address: 440 E. Middlefield Rd., Mountain View, CA 94043 US

GROWTH PLANS/SPECIAL FEATURES:

EHealth, Inc. is a leading online provider of health insurance for individuals, families and small businesses. The company is licensed to market and sell health insurance in all 50 states and Washington, D.C. It has developed partnerships with over 180 health insurance carriers in the U.S., enabling it to offer thousands of health insurance products online. EHealth organizes and presents health insurance online in a user-friendly format enabling its customers to choose from a variety of health insurance products. The firm generates revenue primarily from commissions it receives from health insurance carriers, generally based on a percentage of the premium its members have paid to the carrier. It also, in some instances, receives commission override payments for achieving certain sales volume thresholds. In addition to the revenue the company derives from the sale of health insurance products, it derives revenue from its online sponsorship advertising program and from licensing the use if its ecommerce technology. Products offered by eHealth include preferred provider organization (PPO), health maintenance organization (HMO), indemnity plans, short-term medical insurance, student health insurance, health savings account (HSA) eligible health insurance plans and ancillary products such as dental, vision and life insurance. Elements of its platform include online rate quoting, comprehensive plan information, plan comparison, recommendations and online application and enrollment forms. The platform also uses Electronic Processing Interchange (EPI) technology to integrate its online application process with health insurance carriers' technology systems. The company has approximately 778,300 members. Members are able to enroll in select plans online through the firm's wholly-owned subsidiary, PlanPrescriber.com, which was acquired by eHealth in mid 2010. Revenue derived from carriers owned by Aetna, Wellpoint and UnitedHealthcare represent approximately 14%, 16% and 17% of eHealth's revenue, respectively.

FINANCIALS: **Sales and profits are in thousands of dollars—add 000 to get the full amount. 2011 Note: Financial information for 2011 was not available for all companies at press time.**

2011 Sales: $	2011 Profits: $	**U.S. Stock Ticker: EHTH**
2010 Sales: $160,404	2010 Profits: $17,482	**Int'l Ticker:**
2009 Sales: $134,890	2009 Profits: $15,347	Int'l Exchange:
2008 Sales: $111,711	2008 Profits: $14,168	Employees: 213 Fiscal Year Ends: 12/31
2007 Sales: $87,791	2007 Profits: $31,595	Parent Company:

SALARIES/BENEFITS:

Pension Plan:	ESOP Stock Plan:	Profit Sharing:	Top Exec. Salary: $586,058	Bonus: $422,107
Savings Plan: Y	Stock Purch. Plan:		Second Exec. Salary: $399,108	Bonus: $240,593

OTHER THOUGHTS:

Apparent Women Officers or Directors:
Hot Spot for Advancement for Women/Minorities:

LOCATIONS: ("Y" = Yes)

West:	Southwest:	Midwest:	Southeast:	Northeast:	International:
Y					

EMBARCADERO TECHNOLOGIES INC

www.embarcadero.com

Industry Group Code: 511210J

Management:		Sales/Marketing:		Liberal Arts:		Information Systems:		Professionals:		Technical/Scientific:	
Mgmt. Trainees:		Mktg. Professionals:	Y	Gen. Writing/Editing:		Info. Management:	Y	Finance/Acct.:	Y	Engineers, Elec.:	Y
Experienced Mgmt.:	Y	Retail Sales:		Technical Writing:	Y	Software Dev.:	Y	Law:	Y	Engineers, Other:	
Int'l Business:	Y	Commercial/Industrial:	Y	Graphic Arts/Photog.:		Hardware Dev.:		HR/Other:	Y	Health/Lab	
MBA Graduates:	Y	Sales Trainees:	Y	Music:		Consulting/Other:		Training:	Y	Scientists/Research:	
		Advertising Pros.:		Broadcasting:				Health Care:		Petroleum/Chemicals:	
				Other:				Consulting:		Math/Other:	

TYPES OF BUSINESS:

Software-Application & Database Management

BRANDS/DIVISIONS/AFFILIATES:

JBuilder
TurboRuby
Studio Software Architect
Schema Examiner
DB Optimizer XE
Blackfish SQL
AppWave

CONTACTS: *Note: Officers with more than one job title may be intentionally listed here more than once.*

Wayne D. Williams, CEO
Jim Lines, CFO
Bob Couch, VP-Mktg.
Lorraine C. Gnecco, VP-Human Resources
Tony de la Lama, Sr. VP-Worldwide R&D
James Pitts, CTO
Michael Swindell, Sr. VP-Prod. Mgmt.
Michelle Chase, Contact-Media Rel.
Allen Lovett, VP-Sales, Americas
David Intersimone, VP-Developer Rel./Chief Evangelist
Nigel Brown, Gen. Mgr.-Int'l/VP

Phone: 415-834-3131 **Fax:** 415-434-1721
Toll-Free: 877-783-5332
Address: 100 California St., 12th Fl., San Francisco, CA 94111 US

GROWTH PLANS/SPECIAL FEATURES:

Embarcadero Technologies, Inc. is a technology company that addresses application and database lifecycle operations for corporate clients. Embarcadero designs and develops products for information transmission across databases. The products compress time frames and increase database performance and availability, allowing companies to more efficiently build, optimize and manage their databases and applications. The firm offers its products to more than 3 million users in 80 countries, with a client list that includes roughly 90 of the Fortune 100 companies. Products are offered in subgroups such as design and architecture tools; application development; database management and development; performance optimization; and embedded and workgroup database management systems. Examples of Embarcadero software include JBuilder, an application development tool for Java; TurboRuby, a development tool for Ruby environments; Studio Software Architect, a design tool and visualization program for use on the UML 2.0 specification; Schema Examiner, an automated error checking application for database developers; DB Optimizer XE, for SQL database profiling, monitoring and tuning; and Blackfish SQL, a managed, SQL-compliant embedded database management system. Major industry sectors served by Embarcadero include government, health care, financial services, food services, insurance, pharmaceuticals, education, research and technology, travel and utilities. International sales account for roughly a quarter of annual revenues, and the group maintains sales offices in North and South America, Europe and Asia. The firm also markets products through independent distributors in various countries worldwide. In December 2011, Embarcadero launched new free self-service platform AppWave.

FINANCIALS: **Sales and profits are in thousands of dollars—add 000 to get the full amount. 2011 Note: Financial information for 2011 was not available for all companies at press time.**

2011 Sales: $	2011 Profits: $	**U.S. Stock Ticker: Private**
2010 Sales: $	2010 Profits: $	**Int'l Ticker:**
2009 Sales: $	2009 Profits: $	Int'l Exchange:
2008 Sales: $	2008 Profits: $	Employees: 500 Fiscal Year Ends: 12/31
2007 Sales: $	2007 Profits: $	Parent Company: THOMA BRAVO LLC

SALARIES/BENEFITS:

Pension Plan:	ESOP Stock Plan:	Profit Sharing:	Top Exec. Salary: $	Bonus: $
Savings Plan: Y	Stock Purch. Plan:		Second Exec. Salary: $	Bonus: $

OTHER THOUGHTS:

Apparent Women Officers or Directors: 2
Hot Spot for Advancement for Women/Minorities:

LOCATIONS: ("Y" = Yes)

West:	Southwest:	Midwest:	Southeast:	Northeast:	International:
Y					Y

EMCORE CORP

www.emcore.com

Industry Group Code: 33441

Management:		Sales/Marketing:		Liberal Arts:		Information Systems:		Professionals:		Technical/Scientific:	
Mgmt. Trainees:		Mktg. Professionals:	Y	Gen. Writing/Editing:		Info. Management:	Y	Finance/Acct.:	Y	Engineers, Elec.:	Y
Experienced Mgmt.:	Y	Retail Sales:		Technical Writing:	Y	Software Dev.:	Y	Law:	Y	Engineers, Other:	Y
Int'l Business:	Y	Commercial/Industrial:	Y	Graphic Arts/Photog.:	Y	Hardware Dev.:	Y	HR/Other:	Y	Health/Lab	
MBA Graduates:	Y	Sales Trainees:	Y	Music:		Consulting/Other:		Training:	Y	Scientists/Research:	Y
		Advertising Pros.:		Broadcasting:				Health Care:		Petroleum/Chemicals:	
				Other:				Consulting:		Math/Other:	Y

TYPES OF BUSINESS:

Nanotechnology-Semiconductors
Telecommunications Equipment Components
Lasers
Photovoltaic (PV) Cells
Fiber Optics
Concentrating Photovoltaics (CPVs)

BRANDS/DIVISIONS/AFFILIATES:

EMCORE Photovoltaics
Suncore Photovoltaics Co Ltd

CONTACTS: *Note: Officers with more than one job title may be intentionally listed here more than once.*

Hong Q. Hou, CEO
Christopher Larocca, COO
Mark Weinswig, CFO
Monica Van Berkel, Chief Admin. Officer
Alfredo Gomez, General Counsel/Corp. Sec.
Reuben F. Richards, Jr., Chmn.
Charlie Wang, Exec. VP/Gen. Mgr.-Emcore China

Phone: 505-332-5000	**Fax:** 505-332-5038
Toll-Free:	
Address: 10420 Research Rd. SE, Albuquerque, NM 87123 US	

GROWTH PLANS/SPECIAL FEATURES:

EMCORE Corp. is a provider of compound semiconductor-based components and subsystems for the broadband, fiber optic, satellite and terrestrial solar power markets. The company operates in two segments: fiber optics and photovoltaics (PV). The fiber optics segment provides optical components, subsystems and systems that enable the transmission of video, voice and data over high-capacity fiber optic cable for the high-speed data and telecommunications, cable television and fiber-to-the-premises networks. The segment also serves satellite communications networks, storage area networks, video transport and defense and homeland security markets. The PV segment provides solar products for satellite and terrestrial applications. Unlike most other PV manufacturers, the company uses non-silicon-based materials, which are more efficient and less prone to material shortages. For satellite applications, EMCORE offers high-efficiency compound semiconductor-based gallium arsenide (GaAs) solar cells, covered interconnect cells and fully integrated solar panels. These panels are designed to withstand high levels of heat and radiation while adhering to efficiency and size requirements. For terrestrial applications, the company offers its high-efficiency GaAs solar cells for use in solar power concentrator systems. EMCORE supplies both government and private industries, including the NASA Jet Propulsion Laboratory; Lockheed Martin; Northrop Grumman; Boeing; and Dutch Space. The firm has four manufacturing facilities, located in New Mexico, California, Pennsylvania and China. In 2010, the company established Suncore Photovoltaics Co., Ltd., a joint venture with San'an Optoelectronics Co., Ltd. for the development, marketing and distribution of concentrating PV (CPV) receivers and systems for terrestrial solar power applications. In March 2011, EMCORE acquired the assets of Soliant Energy, Inc.'s rooftop solar energy product line.

The company offers its employees medical, dental and vision insurance; life and AD&D insurance; a 401(k); an employee assistance program; tuition reimbursement; flexible spending accounts; prepaid legal services; employee referral bonuses; and an employee stock purchase plan.

FINANCIALS: **Sales and profits are in thousands of dollars—add 000 to get the full amount. 2011 Note: Financial information for 2011 was not available for all companies at press time.**

2011 Sales: $200,928	2011 Profits: $-34,219	**U.S. Stock Ticker: EMKR**
2010 Sales: $191,278	2010 Profits: $-23,694	**Int'l Ticker:**
2009 Sales: $176,356	2009 Profits: $-136,069	Int'l Exchange:
2008 Sales: $239,303	2008 Profits: $-80,860	Employees: 1,000 Fiscal Year Ends: 9/30
2007 Sales: $169,606	2007 Profits: $-58,722	Parent Company:

SALARIES/BENEFITS:

Pension Plan:	ESOP Stock Plan:	Profit Sharing:	Top Exec. Salary: $434,129	Bonus: $95,000
Savings Plan: Y	Stock Purch. Plan: Y		Second Exec. Salary: $425,167	Bonus: $85,000

OTHER THOUGHTS:

Apparent Women Officers or Directors: 1
Hot Spot for Advancement for Women/Minorities:

LOCATIONS: ("Y" = Yes)

West:	Southwest:	Midwest:	Southeast:	Northeast:	International:
Y	Y			Y	Y

EMS TECHNOLOGIES INC

www.ems-t.com

Industry Group Code: 3342

Management:		Sales/Marketing:		Liberal Arts:		Information Systems:		Professionals:		Technical/Scientific:	
Mgmt. Trainees:		Mktg. Professionals:	Y	Gen. Writing/Editing:	Y	Info. Management:	Y	Finance/Acct.:	Y	Engineers, Elec.:	Y
Experienced Mgmt.:	Y	Retail Sales:		Technical Writing:	Y	Software Dev.:	Y	Law:	Y	Engineers, Other:	Y
Int'l Business:	Y	Commercial/Industrial:	Y	Graphic Arts/Photog.:		Hardware Dev.:	Y	HR/Other:	Y	Health/Lab	
MBA Graduates:	Y	Sales Trainees:	Y	Music:		Consulting/Other:		Training:	Y	Scientists/Research:	
		Advertising Pros.:		Broadcasting:				Health Care:		Petroleum/Chemicals:	
				Other:				Consulting:		Math/Other:	

TYPES OF BUSINESS:

Wireless Communications Equipment
Space & Technology Products
Satellite Equipment
Antennas
Wireless LAN Products
Mobile Computers
Military Communications Equipment

BRANDS/DIVISIONS/AFFILIATES:

EMS Aviation Inc
EMS Defense Technologies Inc
EMS Global Tracking Inc
LXE Inc

CONTACTS: *Note: Officers with more than one job title may be intentionally listed here more than once.*

Neilson A. Mackay, CEO
Neilson A. Mackay, Pres.
Gary Shell, CFO/Sr. VP/Treas.
Matthew Carlomagno, Chief Human Resources Officer/VP
Timothy C. Reis, General Counsel/VP
Gary M. Hebb, VP-Innovation & Strategy
David Sheffield, Chief Acct. Officer/VP-Finance
Nils Helle, Chief of Staff/VP
Marion Van Fosson, VP/Gen. Mgr.-EMS Defense & Space
Constandino Koutrouki, VP/Gen. Mgr.-EMS Global Resource Management
John Jarrell, VP/Gen. Mgr.-EMS Aviation
John B. Mowell, Chmn.

Phone: 770-263-9200	**Fax:** 770-263-9207
Toll-Free:	
Address: 660 Engineering Dr., Norcross, GA 30092 US	

GROWTH PLANS/SPECIAL FEATURES:

EMS Technologies, Inc. designs, manufactures and markets advanced wireless communications products. Its services are primarily used in supply chain management networks, satellite-based voice and data communications and defense and space applications for communications surveillance and electronic countermeasures. The company operates through four units: aviation, which accounted for 30% of the firm's 2010 revenue; defense & space systems (D&S), 19%; global tracking, 11%; and LXE, 40%. The aviation division develops satellite-based communications solutions such as in-cabin connection devices and computers to process data on board aircraft for the jet, air-transport, general aviation and military aviation markets. The D&S unit, operating as EMS Defense Technologies, Inc., manufactures highly engineered, microwave-based hardware for satellites and defense electronics applications primarily for space and defense prime contractors or commercial communications systems integrators. Its products and solutions include subsystems and components for terrestrial, airborne and space-based communication; for radar and electronic warfare systems; and supports advanced surveillance, electronic counter-measure and secure communications capabilities. Additionally, it performs research and development services directly for the U.S. Department of Defense. The global tracking division provides satellite-based communication products and services for telematics and micro telemetry applications. Its tracking products enable customers to locate, track, communicate, and safeguard mobile assets, fleets, cargo and personnel, as well as to monitor fixed assets in hostile and remote terrains. The LXE segment designs, manufactures and installs rugged mobile terminals for use in wireless local area networks (WLANs). Designed to operate in harsh environments and in settings with difficult radio-connectivity characteristics, its products consist of hand-held and vehicle-mounted terminals, wireless networks and host connectivity software and accessories. During 2010, sales to various customers for U.S. government end use collectively amounted to roughly 24% of the company's total revenue.

FINANCIALS: **Sales and profits are in thousands of dollars—add 000 to get the full amount. 2011 Note: Financial information for 2011 was not available for all companies at press time.**

2011 Sales: $	2011 Profits: $	**U.S. Stock Ticker: Subsidiary**
2010 Sales: $355,225	2010 Profits: $14,065	**Int'l Ticker:**
2009 Sales: $359,972	2009 Profits: $-20,065	Int'l Exchange:
2008 Sales: $335,045	2008 Profits: $20,471	Employees: 1,160 Fiscal Year Ends: 12/31
2007 Sales: $287,879	2007 Profits: $18,744	Parent Company: HONEYWELL INTERNATIONAL

SALARIES/BENEFITS:

Pension Plan:	ESOP Stock Plan:	Profit Sharing:	Top Exec. Salary: $426,933	Bonus: $408,771
Savings Plan:	Stock Purch. Plan:		Second Exec. Salary: $264,482	Bonus: $69,206

OTHER THOUGHTS:

Apparent Women Officers or Directors:
Hot Spot for Advancement for Women/Minorities:

LOCATIONS: ("Y" = Yes)

West:	Southwest:	Midwest:	Southeast:	Northeast:	International:
			Y	Y	Y

EMULEX CORP

www.emulex.com

Industry Group Code: 33411

Management:		Sales/Marketing:		Liberal Arts:		Information Systems:		Professionals:		Technical/Scientific:	
Mgmt. Trainees:		Mktg. Professionals:	Y	Gen. Writing/Editing:		Info. Management:	Y	Finance/Acct.:	Y	Engineers, Elec.:	Y
Experienced Mgmt.:	Y	Retail Sales:		Technical Writing:	Y	Software Dev.:	Y	Law:	Y	Engineers, Other:	
Int'l Business:	Y	Commercial/Industrial:	Y	Graphic Arts/Photog.:		Hardware Dev.:	Y	HR/Other:	Y	Health/Lab	
MBA Graduates:	Y	Sales Trainees:	Y	Music:		Consulting/Other:	Y	Training:	Y	Scientists/Research:	Y
		Advertising Pros.:		Broadcasting:				Health Care:		Petroleum/Chemicals:	
				Other:				Consulting:		Math/Other:	Y

TYPES OF BUSINESS:

Networking Equipment-High-Performance Interfaces
High-Speed Fiber-Channel Products
Networking Software

BRANDS/DIVISIONS/AFFILIATES:

LightPulse
InSpeed
FibreSpy
ServerEngines Corp

CONTACTS: *Note: Officers with more than one job title may be intentionally listed here more than once.*

Jim McCluney, CEO
Jeff Benck, COO
Jeff Benck, Pres.
Michael J. Rockenbach, CFO/Exec. VP
Jeff Hoogenboom, Sr. VP-Worldwide Sales
Susan Bowman, Sr. VP-Human Resources & Facilities
Dave Goff, CIO/VP
Randall Wick, General Counsel/Sr. VP
John Warwick, Sr. VP-Oper.
Margie Evashenk, Chief Dev. Exec.
Katherine Lane, Dir.-Corp. Comm.
Fred B. Cox, Chmn.
Adam Winkelmann, VP-Intl. Oper.

Phone: 714-662-5600	**Fax:** 714-241-0792
Toll-Free: 800-368-5391	
Address: 3333 Susan St., Costa Mesa, CA 92626 US	

GROWTH PLANS/SPECIAL FEATURES:

Emulex Corp. manufactures network convergence solutions that intelligently connect servers, storage and networks within data centers. The firm is a global supplier of storage networking host bus adapters (HBAs); converged network adapters (CNAs); network interface cards (NICs); mezzanine cards for blade servers; application specific integrated circuits (ASICs); embedded storage bridges, routers and switches; and input/output (I/O) controllers. These products are electronic component parts assembled on internally designed printed circuit boards (PCBs), which are sold as board-level products. Host server products include LightPulse HBAs, which connect servers and storage to networks using a variety of industry standard protocols. Embedded storage products include InSpeed and FibreSpy switches, which work to intelligently connect storage controllers to networks. Emulex's products are used by many different companies, including original equipment manufacturers (OEMs) such as Cisco, Fujitsu, Hitachi, Dell, Hewlett-Packard, Oracle and IBM. During fiscal 2011, the firm's host server products accounted for 78% of its revenue, with embedded storage products accounting for the remaining 22%. In 2010, the company acquired ServerEngines Corp., a semiconductor design company, for about $78 million.

Emulex offers its employees medical and dental benefits; life insurance; short- and long-term disability; flexible spending accounts; a 401(k) plan; an employee stock purchase plan; education assistance; health club memberships; computer purchase discounts; and access to a credit union.

FINANCIALS: **Sales and profits are in thousands of dollars—add 000 to get the full amount. 2011 Note: Financial information for 2011 was not available for all companies at press time.**

2011 Sales: $452,543	2011 Profits: $-83,160	**U.S. Stock Ticker: ELX**
2010 Sales: $399,150	2010 Profits: $23,620	**Int'l Ticker:**
2009 Sales: $378,222	2009 Profits: $7,544	Int'l Exchange:
2008 Sales: $488,301	2008 Profits: $-7,071	Employees: 972 Fiscal Year Ends: 6/30
2007 Sales: $470,187	2007 Profits: $29,434	Parent Company:

SALARIES/BENEFITS:

Pension Plan:	ESOP Stock Plan:	Profit Sharing:	Top Exec. Salary: $607,806	Bonus: $535,963
Savings Plan: Y	Stock Purch. Plan: Y		Second Exec. Salary: $585,750	Bonus: $577,772

OTHER THOUGHTS:

Apparent Women Officers or Directors: 3
Hot Spot for Advancement for Women/Minorities: Y

LOCATIONS: ("Y" = Yes)

West:	Southwest:	Midwest:	Southeast:	Northeast:	International:
Y	Y			Y	Y

ENCORE CAPITAL GROUP INC

www.encorecapitalgroup.com

Industry Group Code: 522291

Management:		Sales/Marketing:		Liberal Arts:		Information Systems:		Professionals:		Technical/Scientific:	
Mgmt. Trainees:	Y	Mktg. Professionals:	Y	Gen. Writing/Editing:	Y	Info. Management:	Y	Finance/Acct.:	Y	Engineers, Elec.:	
Experienced Mgmt.:	Y	Retail Sales:		Technical Writing:		Software Dev.:	Y	Law:	Y	Engineers, Other:	
Int'l Business:		Commercial/Industrial:		Graphic Arts/Photog.:		Hardware Dev.:		HR/Other:	Y	Health/Lab	
MBA Graduates:	Y	Sales Trainees:		Music:		Consulting/Other:		Training:	Y	Scientists/Research:	
		Advertising Pros.:		Broadcasting:				Health Care:		Petroleum/Chemicals:	
				Other:				Consulting:		Math/Other:	

TYPES OF BUSINESS:

Credit Card Receivables
Collections

BRANDS/DIVISIONS/AFFILIATES:

Ascension Capital Group, Inc.
Midland Credit Management, Inc.

CONTACTS: *Note: Officers with more than one job title may be intentionally listed here more than once.*

J. Brandon Black, CEO
J. Brandon Black, Pres.
Paul J. Grinberg, CFO/Exec. VP
Jim Syran, Chief Mktg. Officer
Steve Gonabe, Sr. VP-Human Resources
Christopher Trepel, Chief Scientific Officer
Olivier Baudoux, CIO/Sr. VP-IT
Gregory L. Call, General Counsel/Sr. VP/Corp. Sec.
Jim Syran, Sr. VP-Oper.
Christopher Trepel, Sr. VP-Corp. Affairs
Paul J. Grinberg, Treas.
Ashish Masih, Sr. VP-Legal Collections Oper.
Brandon Homuth, Gen. Mgr.-Ascension Capital Group
George Lund, Exec. Chmn.
Manu Rikhye, Sr. VP-Indian Oper.

Phone: 858-560-2600	**Fax:** 800-306-4443
Toll-Free: 877-445-4581	
Address: 8875 Aero Dr., Ste. 200, San Diego, CA 92123 US	

GROWTH PLANS/SPECIAL FEATURES:

Encore Capital Group, Inc. is a systems-driven purchaser and manager of charged-off consumer receivable portfolios. Additionally, through wholly-owned subsidiary Ascension Capital Group, Inc., it provides bankruptcy services to the finance industry. The firm acquires receivable portfolios at large discounts from face value using its proprietary valuation process, which analyzes the underlying accounts through individual consumer attributes. The firm's receivable portfolios consist primarily of unsecured, charged-off domestic consumer credit card, auto loan deficiency and telecom receivables purchased from national financial institutions, major retail credit corporations, telecom companies and resellers of such portfolios. Encore determines the purchase price of a portfolio by evaluating many different variables, including stratification and analysis of critical portfolio attributes, such as the number of agencies previously attempting to collect the receivables in the portfolio, the average balance of the receivables, number of days since charge off, payments since charge off and locations of the debtors. Unlike collection agencies that typically have only a specified period of time to recover a debt, the company's collection time horizon is much longer, allowing for more flexibility in establishing payment programs. Encore's collection strategies include the use of a nationwide network of collection attorneys to pursue legal action and outbound calling, driven by proprietary predictive software and its own collection workforce located at three domestic call centers and an international call center in India. Subsidiary Midland Credit Management, Inc. receives and processes the payments from consumers. The firm also utilizes multiple third party collection agencies, direct mail campaigns coordinated by its in-house marketing group, the transfer of accounts to a credit card provider and the sale of accounts.

Encore offers its employees discounted fitness center memberships; an employee assistance program; flexible spending accounts; medical, dental, vision and life insurance; and a 401(k) plan.

FINANCIALS: **Sales and profits are in thousands of dollars—add 000 to get the full amount. 2011 Note: Financial information for 2011 was not available for all companies at press time.**

2011 Sales: $466,977	2011 Profits: $60,958	**U.S. Stock Ticker: ECPG**
2010 Sales: $381,308	2010 Profits: $49,052	**Int'l Ticker:**
2009 Sales: $316,419	2009 Profits: $33,047	Int'l Exchange:
2008 Sales: $255,889	2008 Profits: $18,834	Employees: 1,900 Fiscal Year Ends: 12/31
2007 Sales: $254,011	2007 Profits: $15,042	Parent Company:

SALARIES/BENEFITS:

Pension Plan:	ESOP Stock Plan:	Profit Sharing:	Top Exec. Salary: $500,000	Bonus: $
Savings Plan: Y	Stock Purch. Plan:		Second Exec. Salary: $424,298	Bonus: $770,000

OTHER THOUGHTS:

Apparent Women Officers or Directors: 1
Hot Spot for Advancement for Women/Minorities:

LOCATIONS: ("Y" = Yes)

West:	Southwest:	Midwest:	Southeast:	Northeast:	International:
Y	Y	Y			

ENERGY TRANSFER PARTNERS LP

www.energytransfer.com

Industry Group Code: 486

Management:		Sales/Marketing:		Liberal Arts:		Information Systems:		Professionals:		Technical/Scientific:	
Mgmt. Trainees:		Mktg. Professionals:		Gen. Writing/Editing:		Info. Management:	Y	Finance/Acct.:	Y	Engineers, Elec.:	
Experienced Mgmt.:	Y	Retail Sales:		Technical Writing:		Software Dev.:		Law:	Y	Engineers, Other:	Y
Int'l Business:		Commercial/Industrial:		Graphic Arts/Photog.:		Hardware Dev.:		HR/Other:	Y	Health/Lab Scientists/Research:	
MBA Graduates:	Y	Sales Trainees:		Music:		Consulting/Other:		Training:		Petroleum/Chemicals:	Y
		Advertising Pros.:		Broadcasting:				Health Care:		Math/Other:	
				Other:				Consulting:			

TYPES OF BUSINESS:

Pipelines
Natural Gas Midstream Services
Propane, Retail
Natural Gas Treatment & Processing

BRANDS/DIVISIONS/AFFILIATES:

La Grange Acquisition LP
Energy Transfer Company
Transwestern Pipeline Company
Midcontinent Express Pipeline LLC
Energy Transfer Partners GP, LP
Energy Transfer Partners, LLC
Energy Transfer Equity, LP
Heritage Operating, LP

CONTACTS: *Note: Officers with more than one job title may be intentionally listed here more than once.*

Kelcy L. Warren, CEO
Mackie McCrea, COO
Mackie McCrea, Pres.
Martin Salinas, Jr., CFO
Jerry J. Langdon, Chief Admin. & Compliance Officer
Thomas P. Mason, General Counsel/VP/Sec.
Brent Ratliff, Contact-Investor Rel.
William G. Powers, Jr., Pres., Propane
Kelcy L. Warren, Chmn.

Phone: 214-981-0700	**Fax:** 214-981-0703
Toll-Free:	
Address: 3738 Oak Lawn Ave., Dallas, TX 75219 US	

GROWTH PLANS/SPECIAL FEATURES:

Energy Transfer Partners, LP (ETP) is a company mainly engaged in the natural gas transportation business and U.S. propane retail marketing. The company's natural gas operations consist of intrastate/interstate transportation and storage services provided by La Grange Acquisition LP, which does business as Energy Transfer Company; and interstate transportation services provided by Transwestern Pipeline Company and ETC Midcontinent Express Pipeline LLC, subsidiaries of Energy Transfer Interstate Holdings, LLC. In total, ETP operates roughly 7,700 miles of intrastate and 2,895 miles of interstate pipelines. Through joint ventures, the firm has an additional 500 miles of interstate natural gas pipeline and 185 miles under construction. The firm's midstream operations are concentrated in the Austin Chalk trend of southeast Texas; the Permian Basin of New Mexico and west Texas; the Bossier Sands in east Texas; the Barnett Shale in north Texas; the Uinta Basin in Utah; and the Piceance Basin in Colorado. Besides 7,000 miles of pipelines, the segment operates three natural gas processing plants; 17 treating facilities, which remove carbon dioxide and hydrogen sulfide before the gas is introduced into the pipelines; and 10 conditioning facilities, which remove heavy hydrocarbons. The retail propane division markets propane through subsidiaries Heritage Operating, LP and Titan Energy Partners, LP to over 1 million customers through over 440 locations in 41 states. The company is managed by its general partner, Energy Transfer Partners GP, LP, which is in turn managed by Energy Transfer Partners, LLC, which is owned by Energy Transfer Equity, LP, another publicly traded master limited partnership. In June 2011, Energy Transfer Equity LP agreed to acquire natural gas company Southern Union Co. for $7.9 billion. In July 2011, the company agreed to acquire 50% of Citrus Corp.

FINANCIALS: **Sales and profits are in thousands of dollars—add 000 to get the full amount. 2011 Note: Financial information for 2011 was not available for all companies at press time.**

2011 Sales: $6,850,440	2011 Profits: $235,826	**U.S. Stock Ticker: ETP**
2010 Sales: $5,884,827	2010 Profits: $617,222	**Int'l Ticker:**
2009 Sales: $5,417,295	2009 Profits: $791,542	Int'l Exchange:
2008 Sales: $9,293,868	2008 Profits: $866,023	Employees: 1,946 Fiscal Year Ends: 12/31
2007 Sales: $6,792,037	2007 Profits: $676,139	Parent Company:

SALARIES/BENEFITS:

Pension Plan:	ESOP Stock Plan:	Profit Sharing:	Top Exec. Salary: $538,077	Bonus: $729,500
Savings Plan: Y	Stock Purch. Plan:		Second Exec. Salary: $427,513	Bonus: $482,530

OTHER THOUGHTS:

Apparent Women Officers or Directors:
Hot Spot for Advancement for Women/Minorities:

LOCATIONS: ("Y" = Yes)

West:	Southwest:	Midwest:	Southeast:	Northeast:	International:
Y	Y	Y		Y	

ENERNOC INC

www.enernoc.com

Industry Group Code: 541690

Management:		Sales/Marketing:		Liberal Arts:		Information Systems:		Professionals:		Technical/Scientific:	
Mgmt. Trainees:		Mktg. Professionals:	Y	Gen. Writing/Editing:		Info. Management:	Y	Finance/Acct.:	Y	Engineers, Elec.:	Y
Experienced Mgmt.:	Y	Retail Sales:		Technical Writing:	Y	Software Dev.:	Y	Law:	Y	Engineers, Other:	
Int'l Business:	Y	Commercial/Industrial:	Y	Graphic Arts/Photog.:		Hardware Dev.:		HR/Other:	Y	Health/Lab	
MBA Graduates:	Y	Sales Trainees:	Y	Music:		Consulting/Other:	Y	Training:	Y	Scientists/Research:	Y
		Advertising Pros.:		Broadcasting:				Health Care:		Petroleum/Chemicals:	
				Other:				Consulting:		Math/Other:	

TYPES OF BUSINESS:

Energy Efficiency Technology & Services

BRANDS/DIVISIONS/AFFILIATES:

M2M Communications Corp
Global Energy Partners LLC
PowerTrak
ENERBLOG
PowerTalk
EnergySMART
SiteSMART
SupplySMART

CONTACTS: *Note: Officers with more than one job title may be intentionally listed here more than once.*

Tim Healy, CEO
David Brewster, Pres.
Timothy Weller, CFO
Gregg Dixon, Sr. VP-Mktg. & Sales
Hugh Scandrett, VP-Eng.
Timothy Weller, Treas.
David Samuels, Exec. VP
Tim Healy, Chmn.

Phone: 617-224-9900 **Fax:** 617-224-9910
Toll-Free:
Address: 101 Federal St., Ste. 1100, Boston, MA 02110 US

GROWTH PLANS/SPECIAL FEATURES:

EnerNOC, Inc. is a developer and provider of clean energy solutions. The firm uses its network operations center (NOC) to remotely manage and reduce electricity consumption across a network of commercial, institutional and industrial customer sites to enable a more information-based and responsive electric power grid. Its customers are electric power grid operators and utilities, as well as large end-users of electricity. The company has developed a proprietary suite of technology applications and operational processes that enables the ability to make capacity and energy available to grid operators and utilities on demand and remotely manage electricity consumption at commercial and industrial customer sites. These services offer several benefits including reduced environmental impact, value proposition to grid operators and utilities and energy management solutions for end-use customers. Additionally, the firm provides several technology-enabled energy management services to its customers. Advanced metering applications offer meter data gathering and storage services for advanced meters. Building management and energy analytics offer technology-based energy services designed to optimize the way buildings operate, measure the impact of key energy and environmental decisions and enhance the comfort of occupants. The firm's PowerTrak application integrates data from disparate energy management systems with utility metering to gather data on a customer's overall energy usage. Its analysts then use tools, filters and applications to monitor and review this data and provide distilled information and recommendations for performance optimization; energy and carbon emissions reduction; and maintenance prioritizing. The firm's brands include ENERBLOG, PowerTalk, EnergySMART, SiteSMART, SupplySMART and CarbonTrak. In 2011, the firm acquired M2M Communications, a wireless technology solutions provider; and Global Energy, an energy efficiency and demand response program and technology provider.

FINANCIALS: **Sales and profits are in thousands of dollars—add 000 to get the full amount. 2011 Note: Financial information for 2011 was not available for all companies at press time.**

2011 Sales: $286,600	2011 Profits: $-13,400
2010 Sales: $280,157	2010 Profits: $9,577
2009 Sales: $190,675	2009 Profits: $-6,829
2008 Sales: $106,115	2008 Profits: $-36,662
2007 Sales: $70,242	2007 Profits: $-23,582

U.S. Stock Ticker: ENOC
Int'l Ticker:
Int'l Exchange:
Employees: 484 Fiscal Year Ends: 12/31
Parent Company:

SALARIES/BENEFITS:

Pension Plan:	ESOP Stock Plan:	Profit Sharing:	Top Exec. Salary: $401,538	Bonus: $440,000
Savings Plan:	Stock Purch. Plan:		Second Exec. Salary: $326,250	Bonus: $275,000

OTHER THOUGHTS:

Apparent Women Officers or Directors:
Hot Spot for Advancement for Women/Minorities:

LOCATIONS: ("Y" = Yes)

West:	Southwest:	Midwest:	Southeast:	Northeast:	International:
Y				Y	Y

ENVIRONMENTAL TECTONICS CORP

www.etcusa.com

Industry Group Code: 33911

Management:		Sales/Marketing:		Liberal Arts:		Information Systems:		Professionals:		Technical/Scientific:	
Mgmt. Trainees:		Mktg. Professionals:	Y	Gen. Writing/Editing:		Info. Management:	Y	Finance/Acct.:	Y	Engineers, Elec.:	Y
Experienced Mgmt.:	Y	Retail Sales:		Technical Writing:	Y	Software Dev.:	Y	Law:	Y	Engineers, Other:	Y
Int'l Business:	Y	Commercial/Industrial:	Y	Graphic Arts/Photog.:		Hardware Dev.:	Y	HR/Other:	Y	Health/Lab	Y
MBA Graduates:	Y	Sales Trainees:		Music:		Consulting/Other:		Training:	Y	Scientists/Research:	Y
		Advertising Pros.:		Broadcasting:				Health Care:	Y	Petroleum/Chemicals:	
				Other:				Consulting:		Math/Other:	

TYPES OF BUSINESS:

Medical Equipment & Supplies Manufacturing
Flight Simulators
Decompression Chambers
Hyperbaric Chambers
Human Centrifuges
Motion-Based Simulation Amusement Rides
Steam & Gas Sterilizers
Environmental Simulation Systems

BRANDS/DIVISIONS/AFFILIATES:

Entertainment Technology Corporation
ETC-PZL Aerospace Industries
ETC-Europe
NASTAR Center LLC
ETC Biomedical Systems
O.S.C.A.R.

CONTACTS: *Note: Officers with more than one job title may be intentionally listed here more than once.*

William F. Mitchell, CEO
William F. Mitchell, Pres.
Robert L. Laurent, Jr., CFO
James D. Cashel, General Counsel/Corp. Sec.
Steve Wood, Pres., Biomedical Div.
William F. Mitchell, Chmn.
David Kong, Gen. Mgr.-ETC, China

Phone: 215-355-9100	**Fax:** 215-357-4000
Toll-Free:	
Address: 125 James Way, Southampton, PA 18966 US	

GROWTH PLANS/SPECIAL FEATURES:

Environmental Tectonics Corp. (ETC) designs, manufactures and sells testing, motion-simulation and medical products. Its products and services include flight simulation systems; high-performance jet tactical flight simulation systems; steam and gas sterilization; testing and simulation devices for the automotive industry; hyperbaric and hypobaric chambers; and driving and disaster simulation systems. The company operates in two segments: the Training Services Group (TSG) and the Control Systems Group (CSG). Product categories in TSG are pilot training and flight simulators; disaster management systems; and entertainment applications. CSG product categories include sterilizers, environmental control devices and hyperbaric chambers, along with parts and service support. The sterilization division of CSG manufactures medium to large sized steam and gas sterilization chambers designed in sections that are easily transportable. The hyperbaric chamber manufacturing division, operating as ETC Biomedical Systems, recently obtained market approval from the FDA for its O.S.C.A.R. (Operating System for Control and Recordkeeping) computerized system. O.S.C.A.R. can operate, control and record whole-body hyperbaric oxygen therapy treatments. ETC has four operating subsidiaries: Entertainment Technology Corporation; ETC-PZL Aerospace Industries; ETC-Europe; and NASTAR Center LLC. Entertainment Technology Corporation, a wholly-owned subsidiary, develops, manufactures and distributes entertainment products. ETC-PZL, a 95%-owned subsidiary, is a Polish corporation that manufactures simulators. ETC-Europe, a 99%-owned subsidiary, manages international sales. NASTAR, a wholly-owned subsidiary, operates the NASTAR (National AeroSpace Training and Research) Center, which provides training to prospective astronauts and research support for the aerospace industry. The firm has international branch offices in the U.K., Turkey, India, Singapore, China, Egypt, the U.A.E. and Malaysia.

FINANCIALS: **Sales and profits are in thousands of dollars—add 000 to get the full amount. 2011 Note: Financial information for 2011 was not available for all companies at press time.**

2011 Sales: $55,451	2011 Profits: $12,256	**U.S. Stock Ticker: ETCC.PK**
2010 Sales: $42,271	2010 Profits: $6,453	**Int'l Ticker:**
2009 Sales: $36,687	2009 Profits: $-1,974	Int'l Exchange:
2008 Sales: $22,730	2008 Profits: $-13,895	Employees: 321 Fiscal Year Ends: 2/28
2007 Sales: $17,419	2007 Profits: $-8,940	Parent Company:

SALARIES/BENEFITS:

Pension Plan:	ESOP Stock Plan:	Profit Sharing:	Top Exec. Salary: $330,000	Bonus: $247,500
Savings Plan: Y	Stock Purch. Plan:		Second Exec. Salary: $158,000	Bonus: $119,445

OTHER THOUGHTS:

Apparent Women Officers or Directors:
Hot Spot for Advancement for Women/Minorities:

LOCATIONS: ("Y" = Yes)

West:	Southwest:	Midwest:	Southeast:	Northeast:	International:
			Y	Y	Y

EOG RESOURCES INC

Industry Group Code: 211111

www.eogresources.com

Management:		Sales/Marketing:		Liberal Arts:		Information Systems:		Professionals:		Technical/Scientific:	
Mgmt. Trainees:		Mktg. Professionals:		Gen. Writing/Editing:		Info. Management:	Y	Finance/Acct.:	Y	Engineers, Elec.:	
Experienced Mgmt.:	Y	Retail Sales:		Technical Writing:		Software Dev.:		Law:	Y	Engineers, Other:	Y
Int'l Business:	Y	Commercial/Industrial:		Graphic Arts/Photog.:		Hardware Dev.:		HR/Other:	Y	Health/Lab Scientists/Research:	
MBA Graduates:	Y	Sales Trainees:		Music:		Consulting/Other:		Training:	Y		
		Advertising Pros.:		Broadcasting:				Health Care:		Petroleum/Chemicals:	Y
				Other:				Consulting:		Math/Other:	

TYPES OF BUSINESS:

Oil & Gas Exploration & Production
Energy Marketing

BRANDS/DIVISIONS/AFFILIATES:

Enron Oil and Gas Company
EOG Resources Canada, Inc.
Galveston LNG, Inc.

CONTACTS: *Note: Officers with more than one job title may be intentionally listed here more than once.*

Mark G. Papa, CEO
Gary L. Thomas, COO
William R. Thomas, Pres.
Timothy K. Driggers, CFO/VP
Marc R. Eschenburg, VP-Mktg. & Regulatory Affairs
Patricia L. Edwards, VP-Human Resources
Sandeep Bhakhri, CIO/VP
Patricia L. Edwards, VP-Admin.
Frederick J. Plaeger, II, General Counsel/Sr. VP
Maire A. Baldwin, VP-Investor Rel.
Ann D. Jansen, VP-Acct.
Kevin S. Hanzel, VP- Audit
Kurt D. Doerr, Exec. VP/Gen. Mgr.-Denver
Micheal P. Donaldson, Corp. Sec.
Robert C. Smith, VP-Drilling
Mark G. Papa, Chmn.
Lindell L. Looger, VP/Gen. Mgr.-Int'l Pres., EOG Resources Int'l Inc.

Phone: 713-651-7000 **Fax:** 713-651-6995
Toll-Free: 877-363-3647
Address: 1111 Bagby, Sky Lobby 2, Houston, TX 77002-7361 US

GROWTH PLANS/SPECIAL FEATURES:

EOG Resources, Inc. (EOG), formerly Enron Oil and Gas Company, is one of the largest independent oil and gas companies in the U.S. Together with its subsidiaries, EOG explores for, develops, produces and markets natural gas and crude oil in the U.S., Canada, Trinidad, the U.K. and other international areas. EOG's total estimated net proved reserves are 8,470 billion cubic feet (Bcf) for a total of 1,950 million barrels of oil equivalent (MMBoe), of which 386 million barrels are crude oil and condensate reserves, 152 million barrels are natural gas liquids reserves and 8,470 Bcf are natural gas reserves. Approximately 81% of EOG's reserves on a crude oil equivalent basis are located in the United States, 11% in Canada, 7% in Trinidad and less than 1% in the United Kingdom, North Sea and China. In the U.S., EOG produces 1,588 MMBoe of crude oil, condensate and NGL with an average of 7.8 thousand barrels per day. Key producing areas in the U.S. include the Fort Worth Basin Barnett Shale play, the Upper Gulf Coast, the Permian Basin, the Rocky Mountains area, the Mid-Continent area, South Texas, the Gulf of Mexico and the Appalachian Basin. In Canada, the firm produces 216 MMBoe of crude oil, condensate and NGL through its subsidiary, EOG Resources Canada, Inc. Key producing areas in Canada are the Southeast Alberta/Southwest Saskatchewan shallow natural gas trends including the Drumheller, Twining and Halkirk areas, the Pembina/Highvale area of Central Alberta, the grand Prairie/Wapiti area of Northwest Alberta and the Waskada area in Southwest Manitoba.

EOG offers employees comprehensive benefits including retirement plans; flex dollars; flexible work schedules; life, medical, dental and vision insurance; long-term disability, accidental death and dismemberment insurance; healthcare and dependent daycare spending accounts; and retirement health plans.

FINANCIALS: **Sales and profits are in thousands of dollars—add 000 to get the full amount. 2011 Note: Financial information for 2011 was not available for all companies at press time.**

2011 Sales: $10,126,115 | 2011 Profits: $1,091,123
2010 Sales: $6,099,896 | 2010 Profits: $160,654
2009 Sales: $4,786,959 | 2009 Profits: $546,627
2008 Sales: $7,127,143 | 2008 Profits: $2,436,476
2007 Sales: $4,239,303 | 2007 Profits: $1,083,255

U.S. Stock Ticker: EOG
Int'l Ticker:
Int'l Exchange:
Employees: 2,290 Fiscal Year Ends: 12/31
Parent Company:

SALARIES/BENEFITS:

Pension Plan: Y | ESOP Stock Plan: | Profit Sharing: | Top Exec. Salary: $940,000 | Bonus: $975,000
Savings Plan: Y | Stock Purch. Plan: Y | | Second Exec. Salary: $601,269 | Bonus: $720,000

OTHER THOUGHTS:

Apparent Women Officers or Directors: 4
Hot Spot for Advancement for Women/Minorities: Y

LOCATIONS: ("Y" = Yes)

West:	Southwest:	Midwest:	Southeast:	Northeast:	International:
Y	Y	Y	Y	Y	Y

EPAM SYSTEMS

www.epam.com

Industry Group Code: 541511

Management:		Sales/Marketing:		Liberal Arts:		Information Systems:		Professionals:		Technical/Scientific:	
Mgmt. Trainees:		Mktg. Professionals:	Y	Gen. Writing/Editing:	Y	Info. Management:	Y	Finance/Acct.:	Y	Engineers, Elec.:	
Experienced Mgmt.:	Y	Retail Sales:		Technical Writing:	Y	Software Dev.:	Y	Law:	Y	Engineers, Other:	
Int'l Business:	Y	Commercial/Industrial:	Y	Graphic Arts/Photog.:		Hardware Dev.:		HR/Other:	Y	Health/Lab	
MBA Graduates:	Y	Sales Trainees:	Y	Music:		Consulting/Other:	Y	Training:	Y	Scientists/Research:	
		Advertising Pros.:		Broadcasting:				Health Care:		Petroleum/Chemicals:	
				Other:	Y			Consulting:	Y	Math/Other:	Y

TYPES OF BUSINESS:

IT Support Services
Customer Relationship Management
Consulting
Technical Writing

BRANDS/DIVISIONS/AFFILIATES:

B2BITS Corp.

CONTACTS:

Note: Officers with more than one job title may be intentionally listed here more than once.

Arkadiy Dobkin, CEO
Arkadiy Dobkin, Pres.
Ilya Cantor, CFO
Balazs Fejes, CTO
Isaak Karaev, Sr. VP-Bus. Info.
Karl Robb, Pres., Europe Oper./Exec. VP
Max Bogretsov, Sr. VP-Global Delivery

Phone: 267-759-9000	**Fax:** 267-759-8989
Toll-Free:	
Address: 41 University Dr., Ste. 202, Newtown, PA 18940 US	

GROWTH PLANS/SPECIAL FEATURES:

EPAM Systems is an IT outsourcing company that provides software services through 18 offices located across Europe, Asia and North America. The company has deployed projects in over 30 countries and 13 languages, with a business focus on Central and Eastern Europe and Russia. EPAM offers software development and related services, including technology consulting, custom software development, software product development, embedded software development and low-level programming, technical writing and documentation, application testing, application maintenance, application reengineering and offshore development center (ODC) setup services. The firm's technology consulting expertise includes IT strategy development; Enterprise Application Integration strategy; business and technical analysis; and technology-specific support. EPAM's software development services include product research; prototyping; development; quality assurance and testing; deployment; performance tuning; maintenance and support; customization; porting and cross-platform migration; and component design and integration. The company's mobile application development services include development for iPhone, Android, Blackberry, Windows Mobile and other mobile platforms. The firm's technical writing and documentation services cover software documentation, online help, product specifications, proofreading, software localization and translation. The company's application testing services include functional testing, automated testing and continuous integration for distributed software project implementation. The company serves clients in various industries, including software and technology; healthcare and insurance; travel and hospitality; financial services; media, entertainment, research, publishing and online learning; energy, oil, metal, manufacturing and construction; retail and consumer goods; telecommunications; and high tech. EPAM's clients have included Microsoft, Oracle, Reuters, Colgate-Palmolive, Philips, the London Stock Exchange and Lufthansa Systems. The firm has one subsidiary, B2BITS Corp, a provider of solutions and consulting services to capital markets organizations. In May 2011, the firm opened a new development facility in Krakow, Poland. In February 2012, the company launched its initial public offering.

FINANCIALS:

Sales and profits are in thousands of dollars—add 000 to get the full amount. 2011 Note: Financial information for 2011 was not available for all companies at press time.

2011 Sales: $	2011 Profits: $	**U.S. Stock Ticker: EPAM**
2010 Sales: $	2010 Profits: $	**Int'l Ticker:**
2009 Sales: $	2009 Profits: $	Int'l Exchange:
2008 Sales: $	2008 Profits: $	Employees: Fiscal Year Ends: 12/31
2007 Sales: $	2007 Profits: $	Parent Company:

SALARIES/BENEFITS:

Pension Plan:	ESOP Stock Plan:	Profit Sharing:	Top Exec. Salary: $	Bonus: $
Savings Plan:	Stock Purch. Plan:		Second Exec. Salary: $	Bonus: $

OTHER THOUGHTS:

Apparent Women Officers or Directors:
Hot Spot for Advancement for Women/Minorities:

LOCATIONS: ("Y" = Yes)

West:	Southwest:	Midwest:	Southeast:	Northeast:	International:
				Y	Y

EQT CORPORATION

www.eqt.com

Industry Group Code: 221210

Management:		Sales/Marketing:		Liberal Arts:		Information Systems:		Professionals:		Technical/Scientific:	
Mgmt. Trainees:		Mktg. Professionals:	Y	Gen. Writing/Editing:	Y	Info. Management:	Y	Finance/Acct.:	Y	Engineers, Elec.:	Y
Experienced Mgmt.:	Y	Retail Sales:		Technical Writing:		Software Dev.:		Law:	Y	Engineers, Other:	Y
Int'l Business:	Y	Commercial/Industrial:	Y	Graphic Arts/Photog.:		Hardware Dev.:		HR/Other:	Y	Health/Lab	
MBA Graduates:	Y	Sales Trainees:	Y	Music:		Consulting/Other:		Training:	Y	Scientists/Research:	
		Advertising Pros.:		Broadcasting:				Health Care:		Petroleum/Chemicals:	Y
				Other:				Consulting:		Math/Other:	

TYPES OF BUSINESS:

Utilities-Natural Gas
Pipelines
Well Operations
Gas Production
Energy Marketing

BRANDS/DIVISIONS/AFFILIATES:

Equitable Resources, Inc.
EQT Production
EQT Midstream
Equitable Gas Company LLC
EQT Energy LLC

CONTACTS:

Note: Officers with more than one job title may be intentionally listed here more than once.

David L. Porges, CEO
David L. Porges, Pres.
Philip P. Conti, CFO/Sr. VP
M. Elise Hyland, Pres., Commercial Oper./VP
Charlene G. Petrelli, Chief Human Resources Officer/VP
Lewis B. Gardner, General Counsel/VP
Martin A. Fritz, Pres., Midstream Oper./VP
Steven T. Schlotterbeck, Pres., Prod. & Exploration/Sr. VP
David L. Porges, Chmn.
Randall L. Crawford, Pres., Distribution, Midsteam & Commercial/Sr. VP

Phone: 412-553-5700 **Fax:** 412-553-5757
Toll-Free:
Address: 625 Liberty Ave., Ste. 1700, Pittsburgh, PA 15222 US

GROWTH PLANS/SPECIAL FEATURES:

EQT Corporation (EQT), formerly Equitable Resources, Inc., is a fully integrated energy exploration, production, transmission, distribution and marketing company, focusing on the Appalachian Basin's natural gas resources. It currently operates in three divisions: EQT Production, EQT Midstream and Distribution. The EQT Production segment includes the company's natural gas exploration, development and production operations in the Appalachian Basin. Across its 3.5 million acres of land holdings, in major plays such as the Marcellus Shale and Huron Shale, the firm has total proved reserves in excess of 5.2 trillion cubic feet. In 2010, it produced over 139 billion cubic feet of natural gas equivalent (bcfe). EQT Midstream's operations include the natural gas gathering, transportation and storage activities of the firm; sales of natural gas liquids from 10,900 miles of gathering lines; and 770 miles of transmission lines. EQT has 14 natural gas storage reservoirs, with the capacity to 63 billion cubic feet (bcf) of gas. The Distribution segment, through Equitable Gas Company LLC, distributes and sells natural gas to commercial, industrial and residential costumers in southwestern Pennsylvania, eastern Kentucky and West Virginia. Additionally, through EQT's gas marketing subsidiary, EQT Energy LLC, the company provides optimization of capacity and storage assets; and natural gas liquid (NGL) sales and gas sales to commercial and industrial customers. In February 2011, EQT Midstream sold its Kentucky Hydrocarbon gas processing facility to MarkWest Energy Partners, LP for $230 million. In July 2011, EQT sold the Big Sandy Pipeline to Spectra Energy Partners, LP for $390 million.

EQT's employee benefits include medical, dental and vision coverage; life and AD&D insurance; a wellness program; short- and long-term disability; employee assistance and education assistance programs; credit union membership; savings bonds; a discount stock purchase plan; and commuter reimbursement accounts.

FINANCIALS:

Sales and profits are in thousands of dollars—add 000 to get the full amount. 2011 Note: Financial information for 2011 was not available for all companies at press time.

2011 Sales: $1,639,934 — 2011 Profits: $479,769
2010 Sales: $1,322,708 — 2010 Profits: $227,700
2009 Sales: $1,269,827 — 2009 Profits: $156,929
2008 Sales: $1,576,488 — 2008 Profits: $255,604
2007 Sales: $1,361,406 — 2007 Profits: $257,483

U.S. Stock Ticker: EQT
Int'l Ticker:
Int'l Exchange:
Employees: 1,815 Fiscal Year Ends: 12/31
Parent Company:

SALARIES/BENEFITS:

Pension Plan: ESOP Stock Plan: Profit Sharing: Top Exec. Salary: $750,000 Bonus: $500,000
Savings Plan: Y Stock Purch. Plan: Y Second Exec. Salary: $587,291 Bonus: $1,500,000

OTHER THOUGHTS:

Apparent Women Officers or Directors: 2
Hot Spot for Advancement for Women/Minorities:

LOCATIONS: ("Y" = Yes)

West:	Southwest:	Midwest:	Southeast:	Northeast:	International:
		Y	Y	Y	

EQUINIX INC

www.equinix.com

Industry Group Code: 518210

Management:		Sales/Marketing:		Liberal Arts:		Information Systems:		Professionals:		Technical/Scientific:	
Mgmt. Trainees:		Mktg. Professionals:	Y	Gen. Writing/Editing:		Info. Management:	Y	Finance/Acct.:	Y	Engineers, Elec.:	Y
Experienced Mgmt.:	Y	Retail Sales:		Technical Writing:	Y	Software Dev.:	Y	Law:	Y	Engineers, Other:	
Int'l Business:	Y	Commercial/Industrial:	Y	Graphic Arts/Photog.:		Hardware Dev.:		HR/Other:	Y	Health/Lab	
MBA Graduates:	Y	Sales Trainees:	Y	Music:		Consulting/Other:		Training:	Y	Scientists/Research:	
		Advertising Pros.:		Broadcasting:				Health Care:		Petroleum/Chemicals:	
				Other:				Consulting:		Math/Other:	

TYPES OF BUSINESS:

Data Networks
Internet Exchange Services

BRANDS/DIVISIONS/AFFILIATES:

Smart Hands
ALOG Data Centers of Brazil S.A.

CONTACTS:

Note: Officers with more than one job title may be intentionally listed here more than once.

Stephen M. Smith, CEO
Stephen M. Smith, Pres.
Keith D. Taylor, CFO
Jarrett Appleby, Chief Mktg. Officer
Gary Ronco, Sr. VP-Global Human Resources
Brian Lillie, CIO
Lane Patterson, CTO
Brandi Galvin Morandi, General Counsel/Corp. Sec.
Mark Adams, Chief Dev. Officer
Jason Starr, Sr. Dir.-Investor Rel.
Howard Horowitz, Sr. VP-Global Real Estate
Peter Ferris, Chief Sales Officer
Samuel Lee, Pres., Equinix APAC
Charles J. Meyers, Pres., Equinix U.S.
Peter F. Van Camp, Exec. Chmn.
Eric Schwartz, Pres., Equinix Europe

Phone: 650-598-6000 **Fax:** 650-598-6900
Toll-Free:
Address: 1 Lagoon Dr., 4th Fl., Redwood City, CA 94065 US

GROWTH PLANS/SPECIAL FEATURES:

Equinix, Inc. provides network neutral co-location, interconnection and managed services to enterprises, content companies, systems integrators and some of the world's largest network providers. The company operates 95 data centers in 37 markets in 12 countries from which customers can interconnect with the providers that serve over 90% of the world's Internet networks. These hubs are located in cities such as Ashburn, Virginia; Newark and Secaucus, New Jersey; Sunnyvale, San Jose, Santa Clara and Los Angeles, California; Chicago, Illinois; Dallas, Texas; Tokyo, Japan; Hong Kong, China; London, U.K.; Paris, France; Zurich and Geneva, Switzerland; Frankfurt, Munich and Dusseldorf, Germany; Enschede, Zwolle and Amsterdam, Netherlands; Sydney, Australia; and Singapore. Because Equinix does not operate its own network, it can connect users to whichever network has the most available bandwidth. The company's products and services include co-location services, such as cabinets, AC and DC power, operations personnel and equipment; direct connection between business partners, which allows customers to easily trade network traffic without purchasing circuits, and managed IT infrastructure services, which uses the company's IBX hubs to optimize customers' infrastructure and resources. The firm's Smart Hands service provides access to IBX technical staff when a customer's own staff is unavailable. Equinix has roughly 3,916 customers including Amazon.com, Yahoo!, Microsoft, The McGraw-Hill Companies, IBM, Barnes & Noble and Bloomberg. In April 2011, Equinix and Riverwood Capital jointly acquired ALOG Data Centers of Brazil S.A. Equinix recently opened several new data centers in locations such as Dallas, Texas; San Jose, California; and Tambore, Brazil. Equinix hopes to build revenues to $3 billion by 2015, and it is investing heavily in new data centers and equipment.

Employees are offered life, disability, medical, dental, vision and AD&D insurance; paid time off; a 401(k); flexible spending accounts; a stock purchase plan; and tuition reimbursement.

FINANCIALS:

Sales and profits are in thousands of dollars—add 000 to get the full amount. 2011 Note: Financial information for 2011 was not available for all companies at press time.

2011 Sales: $1,606,842	2011 Profits: $94,004	**U.S. Stock Ticker: EQIX**
2010 Sales: $1,220,334	2010 Profits: $36,881	**Int'l Ticker:**
2009 Sales: $882,509	2009 Profits: $69,431	Int'l Exchange:
2008 Sales: $704,680	2008 Profits: $131,538	Employees: 1,921 Fiscal Year Ends: 12/31
2007 Sales: $419,442	2007 Profits: $-5,188	Parent Company:

SALARIES/BENEFITS:

Pension Plan:	ESOP Stock Plan:	Profit Sharing:	Top Exec. Salary: $490,000	Bonus: $490,000
Savings Plan: Y	Stock Purch. Plan: Y		Second Exec. Salary: $342,500	Bonus: $222,625

OTHER THOUGHTS:

Apparent Women Officers or Directors: 2
Hot Spot for Advancement for Women/Minorities:

LOCATIONS: ("Y" = Yes)

West:	Southwest:	Midwest:	Southeast:	Northeast:	International:
Y		Y		Y	Y

ERESEARCH TECHNOLOGY INC

www.ert.com

Industry Group Code: 511210D

Management:		**Sales/Marketing:**		**Liberal Arts:**		**Information Systems:**		**Professionals:**		**Technical/Scientific:**	
Mgmt. Trainees:		Mktg. Professionals:	Y	Gen. Writing/Editing:		Info. Management:	Y	Finance/Acct.:	Y	Engineers, Elec.:	Y
Experienced Mgmt.:	Y	Retail Sales:		Technical Writing:	Y	Software Dev.:	Y	Law:	Y	Engineers, Other:	
Int'l Business:	Y	Commercial/Industrial:	Y	Graphic Arts/Photog.:		Hardware Dev.:		HR/Other:	Y	Health/Lab	
MBA Graduates:	Y	Sales Trainees:	Y	Music:		Consulting/Other:		Training:	Y	Scientists/Research:	Y
		Advertising Pros.:		Broadcasting:				Health Care:		Petroleum/Chemicals:	
				Other:				Consulting:		Math/Other:	

TYPES OF BUSINESS:

Software-Clinical Research Technology
Technology Consulting Services
Cardiac Safety Services
Service-Business Services, NEC
Service-Testing Laboratories

BRANDS/DIVISIONS/AFFILIATES:

EXPeRT
ePRO Solutions
My Study Portal

CONTACTS: *Note: Officers with more than one job title may be intentionally listed here more than once.*

Jeffrey Litwin, CEO
Amy Furlong, COO/Exec. VP
Jeffrey Litwin, Pres.
Keith D. Schneck, CFO/Exec. VP
John Blakeley, Exec. VP-Mktg. & Sales
Valerie Mattern, VP-Human Resources
Joel Morganroth, Chief Scientific Officer
Tom Devine, CIO/Exec. VP
Achim Schulke, CTO/Exec. VP
Thomas P. Devine, Chief Dev. Officer/Exec. VP
Amy Furlong, Exec. VP-Cardiac Safety Oper.
John B. Sory, Chief Dev. Officer/Exec. VP
John Blakeley, Contact-Investor Rel.
Robert Brown, Sr. VP-Strategic Mktg., Planning, & Partnerships
John Blakeley, Exec. VP/Chief Commerical Officer
Joel Morganroth, Chmn.
George Tiger, Sr. VP-Global Sales

Phone: 215-972-0420	**Fax:** 215-972-0414
Toll-Free:	
Address: 1818 Market St., Ste. 1000, Philadelphia, PA 19103 US	

GROWTH PLANS/SPECIAL FEATURES:

eResearch Technology, Inc. (ERT) is a provider of technology and service solutions that enable the pharmaceutical, biotechnology and medical device companies to collect, interpret and distribute cardiac safety and clinical data more efficiently. The company also provides centralized electrocardiograph (ECG) services (through its EXPeRT Cardiac Safety Intelligent Data Management system) and clinical research technology and services, which include the development, marketing and support of clinical research technology. Clinical trial sponsors and clinical research organizations use the cardiac safety services during clinical trials. ERT's clinical research technology and services include the licensing of its proprietary software products and the provision of maintenance and consulting services supporting its proprietary software products. The service's My Study Portal supports access to data without a software footprint, as it utilizes the web rather than installed programs. The company's electronic patient reported outcomes (ePRO) business allows users to collect, monitor and store patient information in a centralized database and utilize expert consultants to extrapolate strategies.

eResearch Technology's benefits include medical, vision and dental coverage; spending accounts; short- and long-term disability coverage; tuition reimbursement; and transit credits.

FINANCIALS: **Sales and profits are in thousands of dollars—add 000 to get the full amount. 2011 Note: Financial information for 2011 was not available for all companies at press time.**

2011 Sales: $	2011 Profits: $	**U.S. Stock Ticker: ERT**
2010 Sales: $140,992	2010 Profits: $9,871	**Int'l Ticker:**
2009 Sales: $93,823	2009 Profits: $10,687	Int'l Exchange:
2008 Sales: $133,140	2008 Profits: $25,002	Employees: 647 Fiscal Year Ends: 12/31
2007 Sales: $98,698	2007 Profits: $15,252	Parent Company:

SALARIES/BENEFITS:

Pension Plan:	ESOP Stock Plan:	Profit Sharing:	Top Exec. Salary: $500,890	Bonus: $
Savings Plan: Y	Stock Purch. Plan: Y		Second Exec. Salary: $475,000	Bonus: $237,500

OTHER THOUGHTS:

Apparent Women Officers or Directors: 2
Hot Spot for Advancement for Women/Minorities: Y

LOCATIONS: ("Y" = Yes)

West:	Southwest:	Midwest:	Southeast:	Northeast:	International:
				Y	Y

ESSEX PROPERTY TRUST INC

www.essexpropertytrust.com

Industry Group Code: 531110

Management:		Sales/Marketing:		Liberal Arts:		Information Systems:		Professionals:		Technical/Scientific:	
Mgmt. Trainees:		Mktg. Professionals:	Y	Gen. Writing/Editing:		Info. Management:	Y	Finance/Acct.:	Y	Engineers, Elec.:	
Experienced Mgmt.:	Y	Retail Sales:		Technical Writing:		Software Dev.:		Law:	Y	Engineers, Other:	
Int'l Business:		Commercial/Industrial:		Graphic Arts/Photog.:		Hardware Dev.:		HR/Other:	Y	Health/Lab	
MBA Graduates:	Y	Sales Trainees:		Music:		Consulting/Other:		Training:		Scientists/Research:	
		Advertising Pros.:		Broadcasting:				Health Care:		Petroleum/Chemicals:	
				Other:				Consulting:		Math/Other:	

TYPES OF BUSINESS:

Real Estate Investment Trust
Apartments
Residential Brokerage
Property Management

BRANDS/DIVISIONS/AFFILIATES:

Essex Portfolio LP
Arbors At Parc Rose

CONTACTS: *Note: Officers with more than one job title may be intentionally listed here more than once.*

Michael J. Schall, CEO
Michael J. Schall, Pres.
Michael T. Dance, CFO/Exec. VP
Darcey Forbes, Dir.-Mktg.
Suzanne M. Golden, VP-Human Resources
Jordan E. Ritter, General Counsel/Sr. VP
John D. Eudy, Exec. VP-Dev.
Bryan G. Hunt, Chief Acct. Officer/VP
Craig K. Zimmerman, Exec. VP-Acquisitions
John F. Burkart, Exec. VP-Asset Mgmt.
Mark J. Mikl, Sr. VP-Capital Markets & Strategic Planning
Jeff Lambert, VP-Construction
George M. Marcus, Chmn.

Phone: 650-494-3700 **Fax:** 650-494-8743
Toll-Free:
Address: 925 E. Meadow Dr., Palo Alto, CA 94303 US

GROWTH PLANS/SPECIAL FEATURES:

Essex Property Trust, Inc. (EPT) is a self-administered and self-managed real estate investment trust (REIT) that acquires, develops, redevelops and manages multifamily residential properties in West Coast communities. The firm owns all of its interest in properties either directly or through Essex Portfolio, L.P., in which EPT owns about 93% general partnership interest and is the sole general partner. The company's holdings encompass 147 apartment communities, aggregating approximately 30,072 units; five office buildings, totaling roughly 215,840 square feet; and two active development projects, with 436 units in various stages of completion. Most of the firm's holdings are concentrated in coastal markets in Southern California, the San Francisco Bay area and the Seattle, Washington, metropolitan area. EPT's apartment communities are primarily suburban garden-style apartment communities and town homes comprising multiple clusters of two and three-story buildings situated on three to fifteen acres of land. The property portfolio currently includes 110 garden-style, 33 mid-rise and four high-rise apartment communities averaging approximately 205 units each. These communities contain a mixture of studio, one, two and some three-bedroom units. EPT's investment strategy has various components, including monitoring of current markets as well as the evaluation of new metropolitan markets in search of areas with relatively high rental growth potential. The company typically targets properties with over 100 units with a total value greater than $10 million. In May 2011, the firm acquired Arbors at Parc Rose, located in Oxnard, California, for approximately $92 million.

EPT offers its employees medical, dental and vision coverage; flexible spending accounts; life and disability insurance, including dependent insurance coverage; a 401(k) plan with company match; educational assistance; and a company-paid employee assistance plan, among other benefits.

FINANCIALS: **Sales and profits are in thousands of dollars—add 000 to get the full amount. 2011 Note: Financial information for 2011 was not available for all companies at press time.**

2011 Sales: $475,100 | 2011 Profits: $47,100
2010 Sales: $415,732 | 2010 Profits: $50,782
2009 Sales: $411,389 | 2009 Profits: $53,739
2008 Sales: $408,434 | 2008 Profits: $84,395
2007 Sales: $374,749 | 2007 Profits: $203,061

U.S. Stock Ticker: ESS
Int'l Ticker:
Int'l Exchange:
Employees: 1,039 Fiscal Year Ends: 12/31
Parent Company:

SALARIES/BENEFITS:

Pension Plan: | ESOP Stock Plan: | Profit Sharing: | Top Exec. Salary: $350,000 | Bonus: $400,000
Savings Plan: Y | Stock Purch. Plan: | | Second Exec. Salary: $300,000 | Bonus: $300,000

OTHER THOUGHTS:

Apparent Women Officers or Directors: 6
Hot Spot for Advancement for Women/Minorities: Y

LOCATIONS: ("Y" = Yes)

West:	Southwest:	Midwest:	Southeast:	Northeast:	International:
Y					

EVERCORE PARTNERS INC

www.evercore.com

Industry Group Code: 523110

Management:		Sales/Marketing:		Liberal Arts:		Information Systems:		Professionals:		Technical/Scientific:	
Mgmt. Trainees:		Mktg. Professionals:		Gen. Writing/Editing:	Y	Info. Management:	Y	Finance/Acct.:	Y	Engineers, Elec.:	
Experienced Mgmt.:	Y	Retail Sales:		Technical Writing:		Software Dev.:	Y	Law:	Y	Engineers, Other:	
Int'l Business:	Y	Commercial/Industrial:		Graphic Arts/Photog.:		Hardware Dev.:		HR/Other:	Y	Health/Lab	
MBA Graduates:	Y	Sales Trainees:		Music:		Consulting/Other:		Training:	Y	Scientists/Research:	
		Advertising Pros.:		Broadcasting:				Health Care:		Petroleum/Chemicals:	
				Other:				Consulting:		Math/Other:	

TYPES OF BUSINESS:

Investment Banking
Merger, Acquisition & Divestiture Advisory Services
Financing & Restructuring Advisory
Asset Management

BRANDS/DIVISIONS/AFFILIATES:

Trilantic Capital Partners
Evercore Mexico Capital Partners
Evercore Capital Partners
Evercore Trust NA
Atalanta Sosnoff Capital LLC
Evercore Protego
Evercore Asset Management
Lexicon Partners Inc

CONTACTS: *Note: Officers with more than one job title may be intentionally listed here more than once.*

Ralph Schlosstein, CEO
Ralph Schlosstein, Pres.
Robert B. Walsh, CFO
Liz Lynch, Head-Human Resources
Adam Frankel, General Counsel
Ciara Burnham, Head-Strategy & Bus. Dev.
Eduardo G. Mestre, Head-US Investment Banking
Bernard Taylor, Chmn.-Europe Investment Banking
Timothy G. LaLonde, Global COO-Investment Banking
Jeffrey Maurer, CEO-Wealth Mgmt.
Roger C. Altman, Co-Chmn.
Andrew Sibbald, CEO-Europe Investment Banking

Phone: 212-857-3100 **Fax:** 212-857-3101
Toll-Free:
Address: 55 E. 52nd St., 38th Floor, New York, NY 10055 US

GROWTH PLANS/SPECIAL FEATURES:

Evercore Partners, Inc. is an investment banking firm providing advisory services to multinational corporations on significant mergers, acquisitions, divestitures, restructurings and other strategic corporate transactions. The company's operations consist of two business segments: investment banking (accounting for 80% of total revenues) and investment management. The investment banking segment provides strategic and tactical advice primarily to large, multinational corporations. The segment generates revenue from fees for providing advice on matters of strategic importance to its clients, including mergers, acquisitions, restructurings and divestitures. The segment also includes institutional equities services, which offer equity research and agency-only equity securities trading. The investment management segment is comprised of three sectors: private equity, institutional asset management and wealth management. The private equity sector is composed of Trilantic Capital Partners, Evercore Mexico Capital Partners and Evercore Capital Partners. The asset management activities are conducted by Evercore Trust, N.A., Atalanta Sosnoff Capital LLC, Evercore Protego and Evercore Asset Management. Wealth management operations are conducted by Evercore Wealth Management in the U.S. and Pan-Asset Capital Management in the U.K. The firm maintains a 50% interest in the Brazilian firm G5. In August 2011, the firm acquired Lexicon Partners Inc. for $134 million. In November 2011, Evercore purchased a 45% interest in ABS Investment Management LLC for $45 million.

FINANCIALS: **Sales and profits are in thousands of dollars—add 000 to get the full amount. 2011 Note: Financial information for 2011 was not available for all companies at press time.**

2011 Sales: $524,300 | 2011 Profits: $7,000
2010 Sales: $378,897 | 2010 Profits: $8,954
2009 Sales: $314,545 | 2009 Profits: $-1,570
2008 Sales: $194,655 | 2008 Profits: $-9,563
2007 Sales: $321,599 | 2007 Profits: $-34,495

U.S. Stock Ticker: EVR
Int'l Ticker:
Int'l Exchange:
Employees: 610 Fiscal Year Ends: 12/31
Parent Company:

SALARIES/BENEFITS:

Pension Plan: ESOP Stock Plan: Profit Sharing: Top Exec. Salary: $500,000 Bonus: $2,050,000
Savings Plan: Y Stock Purch. Plan: Second Exec. Salary: $500,000 Bonus: $540,000

OTHER THOUGHTS:

Apparent Women Officers or Directors: 2
Hot Spot for Advancement for Women/Minorities:

LOCATIONS: ("Y" = Yes)

West:	Southwest:	Midwest:	Southeast:	Northeast:	International:
Y	Y	Y		Y	Y

EVEREST RE GROUP LTD

www.everestre.com

Industry Group Code: 524130

Management:		Sales/Marketing:		Liberal Arts:		Information Systems:		Professionals:		Technical/Scientific:	
Mgmt. Trainees:		Mktg. Professionals:	Y	Gen. Writing/Editing:	Y	Info. Management:	Y	Finance/Acct.:	Y	Engineers, Elec.:	
Experienced Mgmt.:	Y	Retail Sales:		Technical Writing:	Y	Software Dev.:		Law:	Y	Engineers, Other:	
Int'l Business:	Y	Commercial/Industrial:	Y	Graphic Arts/Photog.:		Hardware Dev.:		HR/Other:	Y	Health/Lab	
MBA Graduates:	Y	Sales Trainees:		Music:		Consulting/Other:		Training:	Y	Scientists/Research:	
		Advertising Pros.:		Broadcasting:				Health Care:		Petroleum/Chemicals:	
				Other:				Consulting:		Math/Other:	Y

TYPES OF BUSINESS:

Insurance-Reinsurance
Property & Casualty Insurance
Health Reinsurance
Excess & Surplus Lines

BRANDS/DIVISIONS/AFFILIATES:

Everest Reinsurance (Bermuda), Ltd.
Everest Security Insurance Company
Everest International Reinsurance, Ltd.
Everest National Insurance Company
Everst Indemnity Insurance Company
Everest Reinsurance Company
Heartland Crop Insurance, Inc.
Premiere Underwriting Services

CONTACTS: *Note: Officers with more than one job title may be intentionally listed here more than once.*

Joseph V. Taranto, CEO
Dominic J. Addresso, Pres.
Dominic J. Addresso, CFO/Exec. VP
Barry H. Smith, Chief Admin. Officer/Exec. VP
Sanjoy Mukherjee, General Counsel/Corp. Sec./Sr. VP
Daryl Bradley, Pres., U.S. Insurance Oper.
Elizabeth B. Farrell, VP-Investor Rel.
Frank N. Lopapa, Treas./Sr. VP
Mark de Saram, CEO-Everest Reinsurance Bermuda Ltd.
Jack Nelson, Chief Investment Officer/Sr. VP
Keith Shoemaker, VP/Controller
Barry H. Smith, Chief Underwriting Officer/Exec. VP
Joseph V. Taranto, Chmn.
Jean-Luc Gourgeon, Gen. Mgr.-Europe/Sr. VP

Phone: 908-604-3000	**Fax:** 908-604-3322
Toll-Free: 800-269-6660	
Address: 477 Martinsville Rd., Liberty Corner, NJ 07938 US	

GROWTH PLANS/SPECIAL FEATURES:

Everest Re Group, Ltd. (Everest), a Bermuda-based company, is engaged, through its operating subsidiaries, in the underwriting of reinsurance and insurance in the U.S., Bermuda and international markets. It operates in five segments: U.S. Reinsurance, U.S. Insurance, Specialty Underwriting, International and Bermuda. The U.S. Reinsurance operation writes property and casualty reinsurance on both treaty and facultative bases, while the U.S. Insurance segment, through general agents and surplus lines brokers, writes property and casualty insurance. Through the Specialty Underwriting operation, Everest writes accident and health (A&H), marine, aviation and surety business within the U.S. and globally. The A&H unit offers health reinsurance for traditional indemnity plans, self-insured health plans, accident coverage and specialty medical plans. The marine and aviation business underwrites a significant number of international claims, originating primarily in London. The surety business consists of reinsurance of contract surety bonds. The International segment writes non-U.S. property and casualty reinsurance through branches in Canada, Brazil and Singapore, with offices in Florida and New Jersey. The Bermuda segment provides reinsurance and insurance to worldwide property and casualty markets and reinsurance to life insurers, as well as property and casualty reinsurance to U.K. and European markets. Everest's main operating subsidiaries are Everest International Reinsurance, Ltd.; Everest Global Services, Inc.; Everest National Insurance Company; Everest Indemnity Insurance Company; Everest Security Insurance Company; and Everest Reinsurance (Bermuda), Ltd. In 2010, Everest had gross written premiums of $4.2 billion, with approximately 80% representing reinsurance and 20% representing insurance. In January 2011, the firm acquired the business and operations of Heartland Crop Insurance, Inc., a specialty underwriter of crop insurance. In February 2011, Everest subsidiary, Everest Reinsurance Company, acquired Premiere Underwriting Services, a managing general agent headquartered in Toronto, Canada that specializes in Entertainment, Sports and Leisure related risks.

FINANCIALS: **Sales and profits are in thousands of dollars—add 000 to get the full amount. 2011 Note: Financial information for 2011 was not available for all companies at press time.**

2011 Sales: $4,717,100	2011 Profits: $-80,500	**U.S. Stock Ticker: RE**
2010 Sales: $4,705,807	2010 Profits: $610,754	**Int'l Ticker:**
2009 Sales: $4,498,578	2009 Profits: $806,989	Int'l Exchange:
2008 Sales: $3,527,579	2008 Profits: $-18,758	Employees: 973 Fiscal Year Ends: 12/31
2007 Sales: $4,780,000	2007 Profits: $840,000	Parent Company:

SALARIES/BENEFITS:

Pension Plan: Y	ESOP Stock Plan:	Profit Sharing:	Top Exec. Salary: $1,000,000	Bonus: $1,400,000
Savings Plan: Y	Stock Purch. Plan:		Second Exec. Salary: $538,461	Bonus: $500,000

OTHER THOUGHTS:

Apparent Women Officers or Directors: 2
Hot Spot for Advancement for Women/Minorities:

LOCATIONS: ("Y" = Yes)

West:	Southwest:	Midwest:	Southeast:	Northeast:	International:
Y		Y	Y	Y	Y

EXACTECH INC

Industry Group Code: 33911

www.exac.com

Management:		Sales/Marketing:		Liberal Arts:		Information Systems:		Professionals:		Technical/Scientific:	
Mgmt. Trainees:		Mktg. Professionals:	Y	Gen. Writing/Editing:		Info. Management:	Y	Finance/Acct.:	Y	Engineers, Elec.:	
Experienced Mgmt.:	Y	Retail Sales:		Technical Writing:	Y	Software Dev.:		Law:	Y	Engineers, Other:	Y
Int'l Business:	Y	Commercial/Industrial:	Y	Graphic Arts/Photog.:		Hardware Dev.:		HR/Other:	Y	Health/Lab	Y
MBA Graduates:	Y	Sales Trainees:	Y	Music:		Consulting/Other:		Training:	Y	Scientists/Research:	Y
		Advertising Pros.:		Broadcasting:				Health Care:	Y	Petroleum/Chemicals:	
				Other:				Consulting:		Math/Other:	

TYPES OF BUSINESS:

Equipment-Joint Replacement
Orthopedic Implant Devices
Surgical Instruments
Biologic Products
Bone Fusion Materials

BRANDS/DIVISIONS/AFFILIATES:

Optetrak
AcuMatch Integrated Hip System
Opteform
Optefil
Regenaform
Regenafil
Equinoxe
Silverbolt Percutaneous Pedicle Screw System

CONTACTS: *Note: Officers with more than one job title may be intentionally listed here more than once.*

William Petty, CEO
David W. Petty, Pres.
Joel C. Phillips, CFO
Betty B. Petty, VP-Human Resources
Gary J. Miller, Exec. VP-R&D
Betty B. Petty, VP-Admin.
Betty B. Petty, Corp. Sec.
Bruce Thompson, Sr. VP/Gen. Mgr.-Biologics Div.
William Petty, Chmn.

Phone: 352-377-1140	**Fax:** 352-378-2617
Toll-Free: 800-266-7883	
Address: 2320 NW 66th Ct., Gainesville, FL 32653 US	

GROWTH PLANS/SPECIAL FEATURES:

Exactech, Inc. develops, manufactures, distributes and sells orthopedic implant devices, surgical instrumentation and biologic services to hospitals and physicians in the U.S. and internationally. The company's revenues are principally derived from sales and distribution of its joint replacement systems, including knee (40.1%), hip (15.1%) and extremity implant systems (15.8%), as well as the distribution of biologics and spine products (14.7%) and other products (14.3%). Knee implant products include the Optetrak knee system, designed to address the issues of contact stress, patellar tracking, polyethylene wear, joint stability and bone preservation. Its hip implant and instrumentation products include the AcuMatch Integrated Hip System, which is used in total hip replacement procedures. Exactech's biologics and spine products include the Opteform and Optefil lines of demineralized bone matrix, as well as Regenaform and Regenafil allograft tissue implants for oral and dental applications. Other products include the AcuDriver Automated Osteotome System and the Cemex bone cement system. Exactech manufactures some components of its joint replacement systems at its facility in Gainesville, Florida, utilizing automated computer-aided manufacturing equipment. The firm has also formed strategic alliances with suppliers and business partners to externally manufacture some components. Additionally, the company acquires and distributes other products and services through exclusive agreements, such as its agreement with Tecres S.p.A., and non-exclusive agreements, such as with RTI Biologics, Inc. and Biomatlante SARL. In August 2010, the company acquired assets from VertiFlex Inc., including the Silverbolt Percutaneous Pedicle Screw System.

Exactech offers its employees medical, dental and life insurance; short- and long-term disability; flexible spending accounts; an employee assistance program; a 401(k) program; an employee stock purchase program; profit sharing; employee discounts; tuition reimbursement; wellness services; and access to a company gym.

FINANCIALS: **Sales and profits are in thousands of dollars—add 000 to get the full amount. 2011 Note: Financial information for 2011 was not available for all companies at press time.**

2011 Sales: $	2011 Profits: $	**U.S. Stock Ticker: EXAC**
2010 Sales: $190,483	2010 Profits: $10,465	**Int'l Ticker:**
2009 Sales: $177,310	2009 Profits: $8,327	Int'l Exchange:
2008 Sales: $161,730	2008 Profits: $11,093	Employees: 553 Fiscal Year Ends: 12/31
2007 Sales: $124,209	2007 Profits: $8,483	Parent Company:

SALARIES/BENEFITS:

Pension Plan:	ESOP Stock Plan:	Profit Sharing: Y	Top Exec. Salary: $526,762	Bonus: $279,125
Savings Plan: Y	Stock Purch. Plan: Y		Second Exec. Salary: $347,733	Bonus: $190,759

OTHER THOUGHTS:

Apparent Women Officers or Directors: 1
Hot Spot for Advancement for Women/Minorities:

LOCATIONS: ("Y" = Yes)

West:	Southwest:	Midwest:	Southeast:	Northeast:	International:
		Y	Y	Y	Y

F5 NETWORKS INC

www.f5.com

Industry Group Code: 511210B

Management:		Sales/Marketing:		Liberal Arts:		Information Systems:		Professionals:		Technical/Scientific:	
Mgmt. Trainees:		Mktg. Professionals:	Y	Gen. Writing/Editing:		Info. Management:	Y	Finance/Acct.:	Y	Engineers, Elec.:	Y
Experienced Mgmt.:	Y	Retail Sales:		Technical Writing:	Y	Software Dev.:	Y	Law:	Y	Engineers, Other:	
Int'l Business:	Y	Commercial/Industrial:	Y	Graphic Arts/Photog.:		Hardware Dev.:		HR/Other:	Y	Health/Lab	
MBA Graduates:	Y	Sales Trainees:	Y	Music:		Consulting/Other:		Training:	Y	Scientists/Research:	
		Advertising Pros.:		Broadcasting:				Health Care:		Petroleum/Chemicals:	
				Other:				Consulting:		Math/Other:	

TYPES OF BUSINESS:

Server Software
Internet Traffic Management Solutions
Firewall Software
File Virtualization

BRANDS/DIVISIONS/AFFILIATES:

Application Security Manager
BIG-IP Controller
FirePass Controller
iControl Software
ARX
VIPRION
Enterprise Manager

CONTACTS: *Note: Officers with more than one job title may be intentionally listed here more than once.*

John McAdam, CEO
John McAdam, Pres.
Andy Reinland, CFO/Sr. VP
Dan Matte, Sr. VP-Mktg.
Karl Triebes, CTO
Karl Triebes, Sr. VP-Prod. Dev.
Jeffrey A. Christianson, General Counsel/Sr. VP
Edward J. Eames, Sr. VP-Bus. Oper.
Dan Matte, Sr. VP-Bus. Dev.
Alane Moran, Contact-Investor Rel.
John Rodriguez, Chief Acct. Officer/Sr. VP
Alan J. Higginson, Chmn.
Mark Anderson, Sr. VP-Worldwide Sales

Phone: 206-272-5555 **Fax:** 206-272-5556
Toll-Free: 888-882-4447
Address: 401 Elliott Ave. W., Seattle, WA 98119 US

GROWTH PLANS/SPECIAL FEATURES:

F5 Networks, Inc. provides application delivery networking products that improve the security, availability and performance of network applications. Its core products, the BIG-IP controller, FirePass controller data manager, Application Security Manager firewall and iControl, help manage traffic to servers and network devices in a way that maximizes availability and throughput. BIG-IP products share a common full-proxy operating system that enables them to inspect and modify traffic flow to and from servers and has built-in functionality to secure, optimize and ensure the availability of application traffic. F5 Data Manager provides customers with expanded visibility into their file storage environments, allowing them to see statistics and graphical reporting relating to their data. The company's FirePass product provides Secure Socket Layer-Virtual Private Network (SSL-VPN) that allows enterprises to provide authorized users connected to the Internet with secure remote access to corporate networks and applications by leveraging standard Web browser technology. The Application Security Manager firewall provides content-based, application-level security against attacks. The iControl software interface products enable communication with one another and allow integration with third party products, including custom and commercial enterprise applications. Intelligent file virtualization manages file storage infrastructure through non-disruptive data migration, automated storage tiering, dynamic load balancing, and efficient data replication though the ARX product family. The company sells its products and services to large enterprise customers and service providers through a variety of channels, including distributors, value-added resellers and systems integrators.

F5 Networks offers employees medical, dental and vision insurance as well as life and disability insurance; flexible spending accounts; and tuition assistance.

FINANCIALS: **Sales and profits are in thousands of dollars—add 000 to get the full amount. 2011 Note: Financial information for 2011 was not available for all companies at press time.**

2011 Sales: $1,151,834	2011 Profits: $241,397	**U.S. Stock Ticker: FFIV**
2010 Sales: $881,972	2010 Profits: $151,153	**Int'l Ticker:**
2009 Sales: $653,079	2009 Profits: $91,535	Int'l Exchange:
2008 Sales: $650,173	2008 Profits: $74,331	Employees: 2,488 Fiscal Year Ends: 9/30
2007 Sales: $525,667	2007 Profits: $77,000	Parent Company:

SALARIES/BENEFITS:

Pension Plan:	ESOP Stock Plan:	Profit Sharing:	Top Exec. Salary: $626,916	Bonus: $733,576
Savings Plan: Y	Stock Purch. Plan: Y		Second Exec. Salary: $409,597	Bonus: $299,789

OTHER THOUGHTS:

Apparent Women Officers or Directors: 2
Hot Spot for Advancement for Women/Minorities:

LOCATIONS: ("Y" = Yes)

West:	Southwest:	Midwest:	Southeast:	Northeast:	International:
Y	Y	Y		Y	Y

FAIR ISAAC CORPORATION

www.fico.com

Industry Group Code: 561450

Management:		**Sales/Marketing:**		**Liberal Arts:**		**Information Systems:**		**Professionals:**		**Technical/Scientific:**	
Mgmt. Trainees:		Mktg. Professionals:	Y	Gen. Writing/Editing:	Y	Info. Management:	Y	Finance/Acct.:	Y	Engineers, Elec.:	
Experienced Mgmt.:	Y	Retail Sales:		Technical Writing:	Y	Software Dev.:	Y	Law:	Y	Engineers, Other:	
Int'l Business:	Y	Commercial/Industrial:	Y	Graphic Arts/Photog.:		Hardware Dev.:		HR/Other:	Y	Health/Lab	
MBA Graduates:	Y	Sales Trainees:	Y	Music:		Consulting/Other:		Training:	Y	Scientists/Research:	
		Advertising Pros.:		Broadcasting:				Health Care:		Petroleum/Chemicals:	
				Other:				Consulting:		Math/Other:	

TYPES OF BUSINESS:

Credit Scoring Systems
Data Management Systems & Services
Marketing Services & Support
Personal Lines Insurance Industry Services
Financial Risk Management
Computer-Related Services
Strategic Application Processing Systems
Customer Relationship Management

BRANDS/DIVISIONS/AFFILIATES:

FICO Model Builder
Precision Marketing Manager
Capstone Decision Accelerator
LiquidCredit
FICO Revenue Scores
myFICO
FICO Blaze Advisor
FICO Xpress Optimization Suite

CONTACTS:

Note: Officers with more than one job title may be intentionally listed here more than once.

Mark N. Greene, CEO
Michael J. Pung, CFO/Sr. VP
Charles L. III, Exec. VP-Mktg., Sales & Svcs.
Richard S. Deal, Chief Human Resources Officer/Sr. VP
Deborah Kerr, CTO/Exec. VP
Mark R. Scadina, General Counsel/Exec. VP/Corp. Sec.
Michael J. Pung, Sr. VP-Investor Rel.
Steven P. Weber, Treas.
Andrew N. Jennings, Chief Analytics Officer/Sr. VP
Jordan Graham, Pres., FICO Consumer Svcs. Div./Exec. VP-Scores
Amber Minson, VP/Gen. Mgr.-Consumer Scores Bus.
A. George Battle, Chmn.

Phone: 612-758-5200 **Fax:** 612-758-5201
Toll-Free: 800-999-2955
Address: 901 Marquette Ave., Ste. 3200, Minneapolis, MN 55402 US

GROWTH PLANS/SPECIAL FEATURES:

Fair Isaac Corporation (FICO) is a leading developer of credit scoring systems and related products for the consumer credit industry. Several thousand companies in approximately 80 countries use FICO technology to help them acquire customers more efficiently; increase customer retention; reduce fraud and credit losses; lower operating costs; and enter new markets more profitably. Its principal products are statistically derived, rule-based analytic tools designed to help businesses manage decision-making processes related to targeting and acquiring customers, account origination, customer management, claims processing, fraud, collections and recovery. The firm divides its products and services along three primary categories: Applications, which accounted for 61% of its 2010 revenue; Scores, 28%; and Tools, 11%. Its Applications products are pre-configured decision management applications designed for a specific type of business problem or process, such as marketing, account origination, customer management, fraud and insurance claims management. Key products in this segment include Precision Marketing Manager, Capstone Decision Accelerator and its LiquidCredit solution. The Scores segment includes business-to-business scoring solutions and services, such as FICO Revenue Scores, Bankruptcy Scores and Insurance Scores, as well as the myFICO solution for consumers, which allows consumers to purchase their FICO scores and credit reports. The Tools category is composed of software tools that clients can use to create their own custom decision management applications. This segment's main products include FICO Blaze Advisor, FICO Xpress Optimization Suite and FICO Model Builder. FICO's products are used by clients in industries such as banking, mortgage and credit cards; insurance; retail; telecommunications; and healthcare and pharmaceuticals, as well as by various government agencies. During 2010, the firm derived 76% of its revenue within the banking and insurance industries.

FICO's employees receive health insurance, retirement savings plans, tuition reimbursement, flexible scheduling, a discount stock purchase plan and commuter benefits.

FINANCIALS:

Sales and profits are in thousands of dollars—add 000 to get the full amount. 2011 Note: Financial information for 2011 was not available for all companies at press time.

2011 Sales: $619,683	2011 Profits: $71,562	**U.S. Stock Ticker: FICO**
2010 Sales: $605,643	2010 Profits: $64,457	**Int'l Ticker:**
2009 Sales: $630,735	2009 Profits: $65,102	Int'l Exchange:
2008 Sales: $744,842	2008 Profits: $83,952	Employees: 2,023 Fiscal Year Ends: 9/30
2007 Sales: $784,188	2007 Profits: $104,650	Parent Company:

SALARIES/BENEFITS:

Pension Plan:	ESOP Stock Plan:	Profit Sharing:	Top Exec. Salary: $625,000	Bonus: $161,800
Savings Plan: Y	Stock Purch. Plan: Y		Second Exec. Salary: $450,961	Bonus: $100,000

OTHER THOUGHTS:

Apparent Women Officers or Directors: 3
Hot Spot for Advancement for Women/Minorities: Y

LOCATIONS: ("Y" = Yes)

West:	Southwest:	Midwest:	Southeast:	Northeast:	International:
Y	Y	Y	Y	Y	Y

FEDEX SUPPLY CHAIN SERVICES INC

www.fedex.com

Industry Group Code: 4885

Management:		Sales/Marketing:		Liberal Arts:		Information Systems:		Professionals:		Technical/Scientific:	
Mgmt. Trainees:		Mktg. Professionals:	Y	Gen. Writing/Editing:	Y	Info. Management:	Y	Finance/Acct.:	Y	Engineers, Elec.:	
Experienced Mgmt.:	Y	Retail Sales:		Technical Writing:	Y	Software Dev.:		Law:	Y	Engineers, Other:	
Int'l Business:	Y	Commercial/Industrial:	Y	Graphic Arts/Photog.:		Hardware Dev.:		HR/Other:	Y	Health/Lab	
MBA Graduates:	Y	Sales Trainees:	Y	Music:		Consulting/Other:		Training:	Y	Scientists/Research:	
		Advertising Pros.:		Broadcasting:				Health Care:		Petroleum/Chemicals:	
				Other:				Consulting:		Math/Other:	

TYPES OF BUSINESS:

Supply Chain Management
Transportation Management
Warehousing
Consulting
Inventory Visibility Services

BRANDS/DIVISIONS/AFFILIATES:

FedEx Corporation
FedEx Services

CONTACTS:

Note: Officers with more than one job title may be intentionally listed here more than once.

Craig M. Simon, CEO
Craig M. Simon, Pres.

Phone: 330-342-3000	**Fax:**
Toll-Free: 800-543-7657	
Address: 5455 Darrow Rd., Hudson, OH 44236 US	

GROWTH PLANS/SPECIAL FEATURES:

FedEx Supply Chain Services, Inc., a division of FedEx Services, which in turn is a subsidiary of FedEx Corporation, offers an extensive range of supply chain management services. The firm's portfolio of services includes transportation management, order fulfillment, orchestrated delivery and returns programs. These services are generally tailored to the apparel, automotive, healthcare, high-tech, industrial machinery and retail industries. FedEx Supply Chain's transportation management programs use advanced electronic data interchange to speed communications between customers and their suppliers, which results in more cost-effective solutions and enhanced levels of customer service. Its fulfillment program provides order administration, configuring services, comprehensive visibility of inventory (including inbound, outbound and static inventory), order execution and emergency delivery (completed in 2-4 hours). Return management services include billable stamps, a package returns program and other electronically produced return labels.

FedEx Supply Chain employee benefits include: medical, dental and vision insurance; life insurance; accidental death and dismemberment insurance; flexible spending accounts; business travel accident insurance; and educational assistance.

FINANCIALS:

Sales and profits are in thousands of dollars—add 000 to get the full amount. 2011 Note: Financial information for 2011 was not available for all companies at press time.

2011 Sales: $	2011 Profits: $	**U.S. Stock Ticker: Subsidiary**
2010 Sales: $	2010 Profits: $	**Int'l Ticker:**
2009 Sales: $	2009 Profits: $	Int'l Exchange:
2008 Sales: $	2008 Profits: $	Employees: Fiscal Year Ends: 12/31
2007 Sales: $	2007 Profits: $	Parent Company: FEDEX CORPORATION

SALARIES/BENEFITS:

Pension Plan: Y	ESOP Stock Plan:	Profit Sharing:	Top Exec. Salary: $	Bonus: $
Savings Plan: Y	Stock Purch. Plan: Y		Second Exec. Salary: $	Bonus: $

OTHER THOUGHTS:

Apparent Women Officers or Directors:
Hot Spot for Advancement for Women/Minorities:

LOCATIONS: ("Y" = Yes)

West:	Southwest:	Midwest:	Southeast:	Northeast:	International:
Y	Y	Y	Y	Y	Y

FIRST FINANCIAL BANCORP (OH)

www.bankatfirst.com

Industry Group Code: 522110

Management:		Sales/Marketing:		Liberal Arts:		Information Systems:		Professionals:		Technical/Scientific:	
Mgmt. Trainees:	Y	Mktg. Professionals:	Y	Gen. Writing/Editing:	Y	Info. Management:	Y	Finance/Acct.:	Y	Engineers, Elec.:	
Experienced Mgmt.:	Y	Retail Sales:		Technical Writing:		Software Dev.:		Law:	Y	Engineers, Other:	
Int'l Business:		Commercial/Industrial:		Graphic Arts/Photog.:		Hardware Dev.:		HR/Other:	Y	Health/Lab	
MBA Graduates:	Y	Sales Trainees:		Music:		Consulting/Other:		Training:	Y	Scientists/Research:	
		Advertising Pros.:	Y	Broadcasting:				Health Care:		Petroleum/Chemicals:	
				Other:				Consulting:		Math/Other:	

TYPES OF BUSINESS:

Banking
Investment Management
Commercial & Consumer Lending
Trust Services

BRANDS/DIVISIONS/AFFILIATES:

First Financial Bank, National Association
First Financial Capital Advisors, LLC
First Financial (OH) Statutory Trust II
First Funds Group

CONTACTS: *Note: Officers with more than one job title may be intentionally listed here more than once.*

Claude E. Davis, CEO
J. Franklin Hall, COO/Exec. VP
Claude E. Davis, Pres.
J. Franklin Hall, CFO
Alisa E. Poe, Chief Talent Officer/Exec. VP
Kevin T. Langford, Chief Admin. Officer/Exec. VP
Gregory A. Gehlmann, General Counsel/Exec. VP
Kenneth Lovik, VP-Corp. Dev.
Cheryl Lipp, Dir.-Comm./First VP
Kenneth Lovik, VP-Investor Rel.
Richard S. Barbercheck, Chief Credit Officer/Exec. VP
Samuel J. Munafo, Chief Commercial Banking Officer/Exec. VP
Michael J. Cassani, Exec. VP-First Financial Wealth Mgmt.
Anthony M. Stollings, Chief Risk Officer/Exec. VP
Murph Knapfe, Chmn.

Phone: 513-979-5782 **Fax:**
Toll-Free: 877-322-9530
Address: 201 E. 4th St., Ste. 1900, Cincinnati, OH 45202 US

GROWTH PLANS/SPECIAL FEATURES:

First Financial Bancorp (OH) is a bank holding company for subsidiary First Financial Bank, National Association. The bank operates more than 102 banking centers in Ohio, Indiana and northern Kentucky, with total assets of $6 billion, deposits of $5 billion and loans of $4 billion. First Financial Capital Advisors, LLC is the company's investment advisory subsidiary, which serves as investment advisor to the First Funds Group, the firm's proprietary mutual funds. The firm also owns First Financial (OH) Statutory Trust II, which facilitates raising Tier I capital in the form of Trust Preferred Securities. The range of banking services provided by the firm's subsidiaries includes commercial lending; real estate lending; consumer credit; credit cards; checking and savings accounts; treasury management services; merchant services; mutual funds; retirement planning; deposit services; online cash management services for commercial customers; and trust and asset management services, provided through the Wealth Management division. Loan interest and fees make up the majority of First Financial's income. The firm principally offers commercial real estate and consumer loans. Commercial loans are offered to businesses for a variety of needs. Real estate loans are offered for both residential and commercial properties and are secured by a mortgage lien on the real property of the borrower. Consumer loans are primarily made to individuals and include new and used vehicle loans; second mortgages on residential real estate; and unsecured loans. In December 2010, First Financial agreed to close five branches: four in Michigan and one in Kentucky. In June 2011, the firm agreed to acquire Liberty Savings Bank, FSB's 16 Ohio branches. In August 2011, the company agreed to acquire Flagstar Bank, FSB's 22 bank branches in Indiana.

FINANCIALS: **Sales and profits are in thousands of dollars—add 000 to get the full amount. 2011 Note: Financial information for 2011 was not available for all companies at press time.**

2011 Sales: $451,348	2011 Profits: $66,739
2010 Sales: $490,333	2010 Profits: $57,386
2009 Sales: $674,535	2009 Profits: $246,546
2008 Sales: $238,792	2008 Profits: $22,962
2007 Sales: $270,030	2007 Profits: $35,681

U.S. Stock Ticker: FFBC
Int'l Ticker:
Int'l Exchange:
Employees: 1,664 Fiscal Year Ends: 12/31
Parent Company:

SALARIES/BENEFITS:

Pension Plan:	ESOP Stock Plan:	Profit Sharing:	Top Exec. Salary: $643,654	Bonus: $583,332
Savings Plan:	Stock Purch. Plan: Y		Second Exec. Salary: $315,962	Bonus: $257,340

OTHER THOUGHTS:

Apparent Women Officers or Directors: 7
Hot Spot for Advancement for Women/Minorities: Y

LOCATIONS: ("Y" = Yes)

West:	Southwest:	Midwest:	Southeast:	Northeast:	International:
		Y			

FNB CORP

www.fnbcorporation.com

Industry Group Code: 522110

Management:		Sales/Marketing:		Liberal Arts:		Information Systems:		Professionals:		Technical/Scientific:	
Mgmt. Trainees:	Y	Mktg. Professionals:	Y	Gen. Writing/Editing:	Y	Info. Management:	Y	Finance/Acct.:	Y	Engineers, Elec.:	
Experienced Mgmt.:	Y	Retail Sales:		Technical Writing:		Software Dev.:		Law:	Y	Engineers, Other:	
Int'l Business:		Commercial/Industrial:		Graphic Arts/Photog.:		Hardware Dev.:		HR/Other:	Y	Health/Lab	
MBA Graduates:	Y	Sales Trainees:		Music:		Consulting/Other:		Training:	Y	Scientists/Research:	
		Advertising Pros.:	Y	Broadcasting:				Health Care:		Petroleum/Chemicals:	
				Other:				Consulting:		Math/Other:	

TYPES OF BUSINESS:

Banking
Mortgages & Consumer Loans
Insurance & Reinsurance
Trust Services
Investment Services

BRANDS/DIVISIONS/AFFILIATES:

First National Bank of Pennsylvania
First National Trust Company
First National Investment Services Company, LLC.
F.N.B. Investment Advisors, Inc.
First National Insurance Agency, LLC.
Regency Finance Company
F.N.B. Capital Corp.
Comm Bancorp, Inc.

CONTACTS: *Note: Officers with more than one job title may be intentionally listed here more than once.*

Steven J. Gurgovits, CEO
Brian F. Lilly, COO/Vice Chmn.
Vincent J. Delie, Jr., Pres.
Vincent J. Calabrese, CFO
James G. Orie, Chief Legal Officer/VP
Scott D. Free, Treas./VP
Vincent J. Delie, Jr., CEO-First National Bank
Gary L. Guerrieri, Chief Credit Officer
David B. Mogle, Corp. Sec./VP
John C. Williams, Pres., First National Bank
William B. Campbell, Chmn.

Phone: 724-981-6000 **Fax:** 724-983-4873
Toll-Free: 800-555-5455
Address: 1 F.N.B. Blvd., Hermitage, PA 16148 US

GROWTH PLANS/SPECIAL FEATURES:

F.N.B. Corp. is a financial services holding company with total assets of approximately $9.95 billion. In total, the company has over 220 banking offices located in Pennsylvania and Ohio; 62 consumer finance offices located throughout Pennsylvania, Ohio, Kentucky and Tennessee; and 4 loan production offices located in Pennsylvania and Florida. It manages and conducts operations through four segments: community banking, wealth management, insurance and consumer finance. The community banking segment consists of the First National Bank of Pennsylvania, which offers traditional commercial banking products and loan products through its various offices. The wealth management segment, which operates primarily through the First National Trust Company, offers estate planning, trusts production and investment programs such as mutual funds, annuities, stocks and bonds through registered investment advisor, F.N.B. Investment Advisors, Inc. The firm also offers investment products and services through First National Investment Services Company, LLC. The consumer finance segment provides personal installment loans to individuals through the Regency Finance Company. The company's insurance segment operates primarily through its full service insurance broker subsidiary, First National Insurance Agency, LLC. Additionally, through subsidiary F.N.B. Capital Corp., the firm provides financing products for small and middle market customers. In January 2011, F.N.B. completed the acquisition of Comm Bancorp, Inc., a bank holding company based in Pennsylvania. In June 2011, it agreed to acquire Parkvale Financial Corporation, the holding company for Parkvale Savings Bank.

The company offers employees medical, dental and vision benefits; disability coverage; a 401(k) plan; flexible spending accounts; an employee assistance program; a stock purchase program; discounted banking services; and education assistance.

FINANCIALS: **Sales and profits are in thousands of dollars—add 000 to get the full amount. 2011 Note: Financial information for 2011 was not available for all companies at press time.**

2011 Sales: $402,800	2011 Profits: $87,000	**U.S. Stock Ticker: FNB**
2010 Sales: $489,693	2010 Profits: $74,652	**Int'l Ticker:**
2009 Sales: $493,700	2009 Profits: $41,111	Int'l Exchange:
2008 Sales: $513,085	2008 Profits: $35,595	Employees: 2,241 Fiscal Year Ends: 12/31
2007 Sales: $450,617	2007 Profits: $69,678	Parent Company:

SALARIES/BENEFITS:

Pension Plan:	ESOP Stock Plan:	Profit Sharing:	Top Exec. Salary: $766,875	Bonus: $690,188
Savings Plan: Y	Stock Purch. Plan: Y		Second Exec. Salary: $368,100	Bonus: $276,075

OTHER THOUGHTS:

Apparent Women Officers or Directors:
Hot Spot for Advancement for Women/Minorities:

LOCATIONS: ("Y" = Yes)

West:	Southwest:	Midwest:	Southeast:	Northeast:	International:
		Y	Y	Y	

FORRESTER RESEARCH INC

www.forrester.com

Industry Group Code: 541910

Management:		Sales/Marketing:		Liberal Arts:		Information Systems:		Professionals:		Technical/Scientific:	
Mgmt. Trainees:		Mktg. Professionals:	Y	Gen. Writing/Editing:	Y	Info. Management:	Y	Finance/Acct.:	Y	Engineers, Elec.:	
Experienced Mgmt.:	Y	Retail Sales:		Technical Writing:	Y	Software Dev.:	Y	Law:	Y	Engineers, Other:	
Int'l Business:	Y	Commercial/Industrial:	Y	Graphic Arts/Photog.:		Hardware Dev.:		HR/Other:	Y	Health/Lab	
MBA Graduates:	Y	Sales Trainees:		Music:		Consulting/Other:	Y	Training:	Y	Scientists/Research:	
		Advertising Pros.:		Broadcasting:				Health Care:		Petroleum/Chemicals:	
				Other:	Y			Consulting:	Y	Math/Other:	

TYPES OF BUSINESS:

Market Research
Consulting & Advisory
Workshops & Events

BRANDS/DIVISIONS/AFFILIATES:

RoleView
Forrester Wave (The)
Consumer Technographics Data & Services
Strategic Oxygen LLC
Forrester Leadership Boards
Forrester's Forrsights
Community Speaks
Data Explorer

CONTACTS: *Note: Officers with more than one job title may be intentionally listed here more than once.*

George F. Colony, CEO
Charles Rutstein, COO
Michael A. Doyle, CFO
Dwight Griesman, Chief Mktg. Officer
Elizabeth Lemons, Chief People Officer
Tom Pohlmann, Managing Dir.-IT Client Group
Steven Peltzman, Chief Bus. Tech. Officer
Gail S. Mann, Chief Legal Officer/Sec.
Michael A. Doyle, Treas.
Greg Nelson, Chief Sales Officer
Mark R. Nemec, Managing Dir.-Tech. Industry Client Group
Dennis van Lingen, Managing Dir.-Mktg. & Strategy Client Group
George F. Colony, Chmn.
Dennis van Lingen, Chief EMEA Officer

Phone: 617-613-6000 **Fax:** 617-613-5200
Toll-Free: 866-367-7378
Address: 400 Technology Square, Cambridge, MA 02139 US

GROWTH PLANS/SPECIAL FEATURES:

Forrester Research, Inc., an independent research firm, provides research, analysis and advisory services related to technology change and its impact on changing business models, best practices, technology investments, implementation and customer trends. Forrester's primary research product, RoleView, includes The Forrester Wave, which provides detailed analyses of vendors' technologies and services, in addition to a library of cross-linked documents that interconnects reports, data, product rankings, best practices, evaluation tools and research archives. Forrester Leadership Boards provides clients with membership-directed research, industry-specific benchmark data, industry trends and best practices coverage and networking through event meetings and group audio-conferences. The firm's data products and services focus on consumers' and business users' attitudes and behavior toward technology, including ownership, future purchases and adoption trends. Data products include Consumer Technographics, which deliver survey-based data and quantitative research; Forrester's Forrsights, which provides assessments of what motivates businesses to choose certain technologies and vendors; and Forrester's Strategic Oxygen, a decision support tool that measures and reports on the current information consumption patterns of key influences effecting large technology purchases. Forrester Consulting services leverages RoleView research in order to deliver customized information that assists clients in the development and execution of technology and business strategies; critical decision making; and reduction of business risk. In July 2011, the firm launched two new data offerings that include the Community Speaks, which provides qualitative consumer insights on topics such as media and internet behaviors and attitudes, customer loyalty and experience, as well as consumer technology adoption; in addition to Data Explorer, a customizable data technology that allows clients freedom to choose how to view survey data.

Forrester offers its employees medical, dental and vision insurance; a 401(k); a discount stock purchase plan; employee assistance programs; flexible spending accounts; performance bonuses; travel assistance; backup childcare; and on-site massages, gyms and piano lessons.

FINANCIALS: **Sales and profits are in thousands of dollars—add 000 to get the full amount. 2011 Note: Financial information for 2011 was not available for all companies at press time.**

2011 Sales: $283,616	2011 Profits: $23,010
2010 Sales: $250,726	2010 Profits: $20,507
2009 Sales: $233,352	2009 Profits: $18,866
2008 Sales: $240,875	2008 Profits: $29,215
2007 Sales: $212,056	2007 Profits: $18,943

U.S. Stock Ticker: FORR
Int'l Ticker:
Int'l Exchange:
Employees: 1,078 Fiscal Year Ends: 12/31
Parent Company:

SALARIES/BENEFITS:

Pension Plan:	ESOP Stock Plan:	Profit Sharing:	Top Exec. Salary: $350,000	Bonus: $232,050
Savings Plan: Y	Stock Purch. Plan: Y		Second Exec. Salary: $336,000	Bonus: $175,968

OTHER THOUGHTS:

Apparent Women Officers or Directors: 2
Hot Spot for Advancement for Women/Minorities: Y

LOCATIONS: ("Y" = Yes)

West:	Southwest:	Midwest:	Southeast:	Northeast:	International:
Y	Y			Y	Y

FORTINET INC

www.fortinet.com

Industry Group Code: 33411

Management:		Sales/Marketing:		Liberal Arts:		Information Systems:		Professionals:		Technical/Scientific:	
Mgmt. Trainees:		Mktg. Professionals:	Y	Gen. Writing/Editing:		Info. Management:	Y	Finance/Acct.:	Y	Engineers, Elec.:	Y
Experienced Mgmt.:	Y	Retail Sales:		Technical Writing:	Y	Software Dev.:	Y	Law:	Y	Engineers, Other:	
Int'l Business:	Y	Commercial/Industrial:	Y	Graphic Arts/Photog.:		Hardware Dev.:	Y	HR/Other:	Y	Health/Lab	
MBA Graduates:	Y	Sales Trainees:	Y	Music:		Consulting/Other:		Training:		Scientists/Research:	
		Advertising Pros.:		Broadcasting:				Health Care:		Petroleum/Chemicals:	
				Other:				Consulting:		Math/Other:	

TYPES OF BUSINESS:

Software-Network Security
ASIC Network Security Appliances
Security Subscription Services

BRANDS/DIVISIONS/AFFILIATES:

FortiGate
FortiManager
FortiGuard
FortiMail
FortiDB
FortiWeb

CONTACTS: *Note: Officers with more than one job title may be intentionally listed here more than once.*

Ken Xie, CEO
Ken Xie, Pres.
Ken Goldman, CFO
Michael Valentine, VP-Americas Sales & Support
Sherry Pulvers, VP-Human Resources
Michael Xie, CTO
Michael Xie, VP-Eng.
John Whittle, VP-Legal Dept.
John Wittle, VP-Corp. Dev.
Michelle Spolver, VP-Corp. Comm.
Michael Andeson, VP-Svcs.
Charles Weonshik Choi, Mgr.-Korea
John Walecka, Chmn.
Patrice Perche, VP-Int'l Sales & Support

Phone: 408-235-7700 **Fax:** 408-235-7737
Toll-Free: 866-868-3678
Address: 1090 Kifer Rd., Sunnyvale, CA 94086 US

GROWTH PLANS/SPECIAL FEATURES:

Fortinet, Inc., with a presence in more than 30 countries, is a worldwide market leader in unified threat management security systems. The company specializes in protecting computers from web-based threats, such as viruses, worms, intrusions and inappropriate web content, among others, while ensuring that network performance is undisturbed. The company offers two brands of hardware products, FortiGate and FortiManager. FortiGate systems are network-based, application-specific integrated circuit (ASIC)-accelerated appliances. These are external modules that contain all the software and hardware necessary to protect the networks and consoles to which they are connected. Defensive tactics involve firewalls, the establishment of secure virtual private networks (VPNs), antivirus, antispam and antispyware applications, intrusion prevention systems (IPS), web filtering and traffic shaping. The FortiGate units are designed for a wide variety of customers with a variety of needs and therefore come with different capacities. The larger FortiGate-5000 series modules are marketed to service providers and large enterprises, while smaller versions, such as the Fortigate-50 series, are more suitable for smaller businesses or individual telecommuters. The company's FortiManager systems are external modules that centralize the management and updating of multiple FortiGate products. Fortinet's software offerings include FortiGuard, a suite of security software that includes antivirus, intrusion prevention and firewall capabilities; FortiMail, an e-mail antispam and security application; FortiWeb, an Internet application; and FortiDB, a database security suite. Typical Fortinet customers are educational and healthcare institutions, financial services enterprises, government agencies, IT firms, wireless service providers and VoIP companies. The firm has shipped more than 675,000 appliances to over 5,000 channel partners and 100,000 end-customers worldwide.

Employees are offered medical, dental and vision insurance; life insurance; disability coverage; flexible spending accounts; a 401(k) plan; and discounted network security products.

FINANCIALS: **Sales and profits are in thousands of dollars—add 000 to get the full amount. 2011 Note: Financial information for 2011 was not available for all companies at press time.**

2011 Sales: $433,576 2011 Profits: $62,492
2010 Sales: $324,696 2010 Profits: $41,245
2009 Sales: $252,115 2009 Profits: $60,179
2008 Sales: $211,791 2008 Profits: $7,363
2007 Sales: $ 2007 Profits: $

U.S. Stock Ticker: FTNT
Int'l Ticker:
Int'l Exchange:
Employees: 1,336 Fiscal Year Ends: 12/31
Parent Company:

SALARIES/BENEFITS:

Pension Plan: ESOP Stock Plan: Profit Sharing: Top Exec. Salary: $328,879 Bonus: $98,614
Savings Plan: Y Stock Purch. Plan: Second Exec. Salary: $318,270 Bonus: $96,499

OTHER THOUGHTS:

Apparent Women Officers or Directors: 3
Hot Spot for Advancement for Women/Minorities: Y

LOCATIONS: ("Y" = Yes)

West:	Southwest:	Midwest:	Southeast:	Northeast:	International:
Y	Y	Y	Y	Y	Y

FRESHDIRECT LLC

www.freshdirect.com

Industry Group Code: 445110E

Management:		Sales/Marketing:		Liberal Arts:		Information Systems:		Professionals:		Technical/Scientific:	
Mgmt. Trainees:	Y	Mktg. Professionals:	Y	Gen. Writing/Editing:	Y	Info. Management:	Y	Finance/Acct.:	Y	Engineers, Elec.:	
Experienced Mgmt.:	Y	Retail Sales:	Y	Technical Writing:		Software Dev.:	Y	Law:	Y	Engineers, Other:	
Int'l Business:		Commercial/Industrial:		Graphic Arts/Photog.:	Y	Hardware Dev.:		HR/Other:	Y	Health/Lab	
MBA Graduates:	Y	Sales Trainees:	Y	Music:		Consulting/Other:		Training:	Y	Scientists/Research:	
		Advertising Pros.:	Y	Broadcasting:				Health Care:		Petroleum/Chemicals:	
				Other:				Consulting:		Math/Other:	

TYPES OF BUSINESS:

Online Grocery Sales
Home Grocery Delivery
Catering

BRANDS/DIVISIONS/AFFILIATES:

CONTACTS: *Note: Officers with more than one job title may be intentionally listed here more than once.*

Jason Ackerman, CEO
Dean Marano, CIO
Jim Manzi, Chmn.

Phone: 718-928-1000	**Fax:** 718-433-0648
Toll-Free:	
Address: 23-30 Borden Ave., Long Island, NY 11101 US	

GROWTH PLANS/SPECIAL FEATURES:

FreshDirect LLC is an online retail grocery business serving approximately 650,000 customers in New York City and the surrounding areas. It offers more than 3,000 fresh food and grocery items, including fruits and vegetables, meat, seafood, deli items, cheese, dairy, coffee, tea, bakery goods, pasta and frozen food, as well as kosher and organic produce, health and beauty items and wine. It also provides catering services and a full line of ready-to-heat meals prepared by its on-staff chef. FreshDirect owns and operates a 300,000-square-foot state-of-the-art processing facility, which enables the company to process and ship fresh meats, produce and dairy products quickly and efficiently. The company is also able to offer lower prices, on average 25% lower than traditional retail grocers, due to the lack of intermediary distribution channels. Products may be delivered in the mornings if the order is placed by 7 p.m. the previous day and in the evenings if placed by 11 p.m. Deliveries are made from 6:30 a.m.-11:30 p.m. Monday through Friday; from 7 a.m.-5 p.m. on Saturday; and from 6:30 a.m. to 11:30 p.m. on Sunday. Minimum order amounts for home deliveries are $30, and each order is charged a $5.49-$6.79 delivery fee depending on location. For offices, the minimum order amount is $50 and delivery costs are $9.99 Tuesday-Friday and $14.99 on Monday. Customers can also pick up their orders at the facility. The firm also serves Westchester County, New York, as well as Connecticut, New Jersey and Long Island.

FINANCIALS: **Sales and profits are in thousands of dollars—add 000 to get the full amount. 2011 Note: Financial information for 2011 was not available for all companies at press time.**

2011 Sales: $310,000	2011 Profits: $	**U.S. Stock Ticker: Private**
2010 Sales: $300,000	2010 Profits: $	**Int'l Ticker:**
2009 Sales: $250,000	2009 Profits: $	Int'l Exchange:
2008 Sales: $215,000	2008 Profits: $	Employees: Fiscal Year Ends: 9/30
2007 Sales: $200,000	2007 Profits: $	Parent Company:

SALARIES/BENEFITS:

Pension Plan:	ESOP Stock Plan:	Profit Sharing:	Top Exec. Salary: $	Bonus: $
Savings Plan:	Stock Purch. Plan:		Second Exec. Salary: $	Bonus: $

OTHER THOUGHTS:

Apparent Women Officers or Directors:
Hot Spot for Advancement for Women/Minorities:

LOCATIONS: ("Y" = Yes)

West:	Southwest:	Midwest:	Southeast:	Northeast:	International:
				Y	

FROZEN FOOD EXPRESS INDUSTRIES INC

www.ffeinc.com

Industry Group Code: 4842

Management:		**Sales/Marketing:**		**Liberal Arts:**	**Information Systems:**		**Professionals:**		**Technical/Scientific:**
Mgmt. Trainees:		Mktg. Professionals:	Y	Gen. Writing/Editing:	Info. Management:	Y	Finance/Acct.:	Y	Engineers, Elec.:
Experienced Mgmt.:	Y	Retail Sales:		Technical Writing:	Software Dev.:		Law:	Y	Engineers, Other:
Int'l Business:		Commercial/Industrial:	Y	Graphic Arts/Photog.:	Hardware Dev.:		HR/Other:	Y	Health/Lab
MBA Graduates:	Y	Sales Trainees:		Music:	Consulting/Other:		Training:	Y	Scientists/Research:
		Advertising Pros.:		Broadcasting:			Health Care:		Petroleum/Chemicals:
				Other:			Consulting:		Math/Other:

TYPES OF BUSINESS:

Trucking
Temperature-Controlled Trucking
Medical Supply Delivery
Dedicated Fleets
Freight Brokerage

BRANDS/DIVISIONS/AFFILIATES:

FFE Logistics Inc
FFE Transportation Services
Lisa Motor Lines Inc

CONTACTS: *Note: Officers with more than one job title may be intentionally listed here more than once.*

Stoney M. Stubbs, Jr., CEO
John T. Hickerson, COO/Exec. VP
Stoney R. Stubbs, Pres.
John McManama, CFO/Sr. VP
Leonard W. Bartholomew, Corp. Sec.
David Hedgpeth, VP-Risk Mgmt., Compliance & Safety
Stoney M. Stubbs, Jr., Chmn.

Phone: 214-630-8090 **Fax:** 214-819-5625
Toll-Free: 800-569-9200
Address: 1145 Empire Central Place, Dallas, TX 75247 US

GROWTH PLANS/SPECIAL FEATURES:

Frozen Food Express Industries, Inc. (FFE) is one of the largest publicly owned temperature-controlled trucking companies in North America. The firm's temperature-controlled trucks transport a variety of products across the 48 contiguous U.S. states, as well as into Mexico and Canada. FFE conducts business primarily through order-based services, through which the firm bills companies for specific shipments of food products, pharmaceuticals and/or medical supplies. The firm also provides asset-based services, whereby a company may utilize FFE's trucks and/or trailers for a specified amount of time. FFE's shipping and hauling options include full-truckload linehaul services, which manage load sizes between 20,000 and 40,000 pounds; dedicated fleets, which provide dedicated contract services to specific customers; and less-than-truckload (LTL) linehaul services, which move loads between 50 and 20,000 pounds. Additionally, the firm's freight brokerage service outsources shipments to other carriers. Temperature controlled shipments account for about 83% of FFE's total freight revenue. Subsidiaries of the company include FFE Transportation Services (its primary operating subsidiary); Lisa Motor Lines, Inc; and FFE Logistics, Inc. Typical products the company hauls include meat; ice; candy and other confectionaries; poultry; seafood; pharmaceuticals; processed foods; dairy products; medical supplies; fresh and frozen fruits and vegetables; cosmetics; film; and Christmas trees. Depending on specific needs, FFE's trailers have the ability to keep freight frozen, as with ice; to keep freight cool, as with candy; or to keep freight from freezing, for example, when delivering fresh produce or flowers during the winter months. The company's refrigerated and non-refrigerated (dry) truck operations serve nearly 4,400 customers in the U.S., Mexico and Canada. In October 2011, the firm agreed to sell its 435 dry van trailers; FFE will continue to offer some dry freight options through its temperature-controlled trailers.

FFE offers its employees a 401(k) plan, tuition reimbursement and an employee assistance program.

FINANCIALS: **Sales and profits are in thousands of dollars—add 000 to get the full amount. 2011 Note: Financial information for 2011 was not available for all companies at press time.**

2011 Sales: $	2011 Profits: $	**U.S. Stock Ticker: FFEX**
2010 Sales: $368,822	2010 Profits: $-11,930	**Int'l Ticker:**
2009 Sales: $373,051	2009 Profits: $-16,415	Int'l Exchange:
2008 Sales: $490,536	2008 Profits: $ 605	Employees: 2,286 Fiscal Year Ends: 12/31
2007 Sales: $452,214	2007 Profits: $-7,670	Parent Company:

SALARIES/BENEFITS:

Pension Plan:	ESOP Stock Plan:	Profit Sharing:	Top Exec. Salary: $408,766	Bonus: $3,930
Savings Plan: Y	Stock Purch. Plan:		Second Exec. Salary: $291,344	Bonus: $3,029

OTHER THOUGHTS:

Apparent Women Officers or Directors:
Hot Spot for Advancement for Women/Minorities:

LOCATIONS: ("Y" = Yes)

West:	Southwest:	Midwest:	Southeast:	Northeast:	International:
Y	Y	Y	Y	Y	

FUEL SYSTEMS SOLUTIONS INC

www.fuelsystemssolutions.com

Industry Group Code: 3363

Management:		Sales/Marketing:		Liberal Arts:		Information Systems:		Professionals:		Technical/Scientific:	
Mgmt. Trainees:		Mktg. Professionals:	Y	Gen. Writing/Editing:		Info. Management:	Y	Finance/Acct.:	Y	Engineers, Elec.:	Y
Experienced Mgmt.:	Y	Retail Sales:		Technical Writing:	Y	Software Dev.:		Law:	Y	Engineers, Other:	Y
Int'l Business:	Y	Commercial/Industrial:	Y	Graphic Arts/Photog.:		Hardware Dev.:	Y	HR/Other:	Y	Health/Lab	
MBA Graduates:	Y	Sales Trainees:	Y	Music:		Consulting/Other:		Training:	Y	Scientists/Research:	
		Advertising Pros.:		Broadcasting:				Health Care:		Petroleum/Chemicals:	
				Other:				Consulting:		Math/Other:	

TYPES OF BUSINESS:

Automobile Parts Manufacturer
Fuel Components & Systems

BRANDS/DIVISIONS/AFFILIATES:

IMPCO Technologies, Inc.
B.R.C. Società a Responsabilità Limitata
EvoTek, LLC
BRC FuelMaker
Alternative Fuel Systems, Inc
NaturalDrive Partners LLC
MTE S.r.L.

CONTACTS: *Note: Officers with more than one job title may be intentionally listed here more than once.*

Mariano Costamagna, CEO
Pietro Bersani, CFO
Matthew Beale, Corp. Sec.
Roberto Olivo, Head-BRC Oper.
Michael Helfand, Chief Acct. Officer/Sr. VP-Finance
Pier Antonio Costamagna, Managing Dir.-BRC
Matthew Beale, Co-Pres., Fuel Systems/Head-IMPCO
Roberto Olivo, Co-Pres., Fuel Systems
Mariano Costamagna, Chmn.

Phone: 646-502-7170 **Fax:** 646-502-7171
Toll-Free:
Address: 780 3rd Ave., 25th Fl., New York, NY 10017 US

GROWTH PLANS/SPECIAL FEATURES:

Fuel Systems Solutions, Inc. designs, manufactures, installs and supplies alternative fuel components and systems for use in the transportation, industrial and power generation industries. Its components and systems control the pressure and flow of gaseous alternative fuels, such as propane and natural gas used in internal combustion engines, and improve efficiency, enhance power output and reduce emissions by electronically sensing and regulating the proper proportion of fuel and air required by the engine. The company operates in three main segments, organized around its subsidiaries: the industrial segment, including mobile and power generation equipment, consists of IMPCO Technologies, Inc.; the infrastructure segment includes BRC FuelMaker; and the transportation segment consists of BRC S.r.L., based in Italy. The company's products include those for natural gas compressors; for fuel delivery, such as pressure regulators, fuel injectors and flow control valves; electronic controls, including solid-state components and proprietary software to monitor and optimize fuel pressure and flow; gaseous fuel internal combustion engines; systems integration; and auxiliary power systems. The company also designs, assembles and markets ancillary components required for complete systems operation on alternative fuels. The firm markets its products through a global network of 850 distributors and dealers in over 65 countries, and more than 175 original equipment manufacturers (OEMs). In September 2010, the company acquired the alternative fuel vehicle operations of Productive Concepts International, LLC; and acquired EvoTek, LLC. In April 2011, IMPCO Technologies acquired NaturalDrive Partners LLC. In May 2011, through two transactions, Fuel Systems Solutions acquired 91.85% of Alternative Fuel Systems, Inc. In June 2011, the firm acquired the remaining 50% interest in MTE S.r.L., making it a wholly-owned subsidiary.

FINANCIALS: **Sales and profits are in thousands of dollars—add 000 to get the full amount. 2011 Note: Financial information for 2011 was not available for all companies at press time.**

2011 Sales: $	2011 Profits: $	**U.S. Stock Ticker: FSYS**
2010 Sales: $430,632	2010 Profits: $40,284	**Int'l Ticker:**
2009 Sales: $452,325	2009 Profits: $49,841	Int'l Exchange:
2008 Sales: $382,697	2008 Profits: $23,342	Employees: 1,600 Fiscal Year Ends: 12/31
2007 Sales: $265,331	2007 Profits: $5,883	Parent Company:

SALARIES/BENEFITS:

Pension Plan:	ESOP Stock Plan:	Profit Sharing:	Top Exec. Salary: $589,344	Bonus: $149,395
Savings Plan:	Stock Purch. Plan:		Second Exec. Salary: $397,920	Bonus: $74,000

OTHER THOUGHTS:

Apparent Women Officers or Directors:
Hot Spot for Advancement for Women/Minorities:

LOCATIONS: ("Y" = Yes)

West:	Southwest:	Midwest:	Southeast:	Northeast:	International:
Y		Y		Y	Y

FUEL TECH INC

www.fuel-tech.com

Industry Group Code: 541712

Management:		Sales/Marketing:		Liberal Arts:		Information Systems:		Professionals:		Technical/Scientific:	
Mgmt. Trainees:		Mktg. Professionals:	Y	Gen. Writing/Editing:		Info. Management:	Y	Finance/Acct.:	Y	Engineers, Elec.:	
Experienced Mgmt.:	Y	Retail Sales:		Technical Writing:	Y	Software Dev.:	Y	Law:	Y	Engineers, Other:	
Int'l Business:	Y	Commercial/Industrial:	Y	Graphic Arts/Photog.:		Hardware Dev.:		HR/Other:	Y	Health/Lab	
MBA Graduates:	Y	Sales Trainees:		Music:		Consulting/Other:		Training:	Y	Scientists/Research:	Y
		Advertising Pros.:		Broadcasting:				Health Care:		Petroleum/Chemicals:	
				Other:				Consulting:		Math/Other:	

TYPES OF BUSINESS:

Nitrogen Oxide Reduction Technology
Combustion Unit Efficiency Technology
Air Pollution Control (APC)
Boiler Optimization Technology
Efficiency Improvement Technology
Carbon Emission Reduction Technologies

BRANDS/DIVISIONS/AFFILIATES:

FUEL CHEM
NOxOUT
NOxOUT ULTRA
NOxOUT-SCR
TIFI Targeted In-Furnace Injection
NOxOUT CASCADE
Fuel Tech Environmenal Technologies Co., Ltd.

CONTACTS: *Note: Officers with more than one job title may be intentionally listed here more than once.*

Douglas G. Bailey, CEO
Douglas G. Bailey, Pres.
David S. Collins, CFO/Sr. VP
Robert E. Puissant, Exec. VP-Mktg. & Sales
Albert G. Grigonis, General Counsel/Sec./Sr. VP
Vincent J. Arnone, Exec. VP-Worldwide Oper.
David S. Collins, Treas.
William E. Cummings, Jr., Sr. VP-Air Pollution Control Sales
Vincent M. Albanese, Sr. VP-Regulatory Affairs
Timothy J. Eibes, Sr. VP-Project Execution
Stephen P. Brady, Sr. VP-Fuel Chem. Sales
Douglas G. Bailey, Chmn.

Phone: 630-845-4433 **Fax:** 630-845-4502
Toll-Free: 800-666-9688
Address: 27601 Bella Vista Pkwy., Warrenville, IL 60555 US

GROWTH PLANS/SPECIAL FEATURES:

Fuel Tech, Inc. develops and commercializes state-of-the-art proprietary technologies to control air pollution, process optimization and optimize combustion efficiency for utility and industrial customer worldwide. It owns exceptional technologies that aid coal-fired electric generating plants in reducing carbon emissions. Fuel Tech's special focus is the worldwide marketing of its nitrogen oxide (NOx) reduction and FUEL CHEM processes. NOx reduction technology includes the NOxOUT, NOxOUT ULTRA and NOxOUT-SCR processes, which can reduce NOx emissions from 65% to 85% in fuel gas from boilers, incinerators, furnaces and other stationary combustion sources. The NOx reduction business is primarily driven by the U.S. air pollution control market, which depends on air pollution regulations and regulation enforcement. Outside the U.S., Fuel Tech sells NOx control systems in Europe, providing technology that enables waste incinerators and cement plants to comply with specified NOx regulation standards. FUEL CHEM improves the efficiency, reliability and environmental status of plants in the electric utility, pulp and paper, industrial and waste-to-energy markets. It controls slagging, fouling, corrosion, loss on ignition, opacity and acid plume, and controls sulfur trioxide, ammonium bisulfate, particulate matter, carbon dioxide and NOx formation by adding chemicals into the fuel or via TIFI Targeted In-Furnace Injection programs. FUEL CHEM programs currently operate in over 95 combustion units, treating various solid and liquid fuels, including coal, heavy oil, biomass and municipal waste.

FINANCIALS: Sales and profits are in thousands of dollars—add 000 to get the full amount. 2011 Note: Financial information for 2011 was not available for all companies at press time.

2011 Sales: $
2010 Sales: $81,795
2009 Sales: $71,397
2008 Sales: $81,074
2007 Sales: $80,297

2011 Profits: $
2010 Profits: $1,735
2009 Profits: $-2,306
2008 Profits: $3,602
2007 Profits: $7,243

U.S. Stock Ticker: FTEK
Int'l Ticker:
Int'l Exchange:
Employees: 161 Fiscal Year Ends: 12/31
Parent Company:

SALARIES/BENEFITS:

Pension Plan: ESOP Stock Plan: Profit Sharing: Top Exec. Salary: $300,000 Bonus: $65,000
Savings Plan: Stock Purch. Plan: Second Exec. Salary: $292,500 Bonus: $73,000

OTHER THOUGHTS:

Apparent Women Officers or Directors:
Hot Spot for Advancement for Women/Minorities:

LOCATIONS: ("Y" = Yes)

West:	Southwest:	Midwest:	Southeast:	Northeast:	International:
		Y		Y	Y

GAIAM INC

www.gaiam.com

Industry Group Code: 45399

Management:		Sales/Marketing:		Liberal Arts:		Information Systems:		Professionals:		Technical/Scientific:	
Mgmt. Trainees:	Y	Mktg. Professionals:	Y	Gen. Writing/Editing:	Y	Info. Management:	Y	Finance/Acct.:	Y	Engineers, Elec.:	
Experienced Mgmt.:	Y	Retail Sales:	Y	Technical Writing:		Software Dev.:	Y	Law:	Y	Engineers, Other:	
Int'l Business:		Commercial/Industrial:		Graphic Arts/Photog.:	Y	Hardware Dev.:		HR/Other:	Y	Health/Lab	
MBA Graduates:	Y	Sales Trainees:	Y	Music:		Consulting/Other:		Training:		Scientists/Research:	
		Advertising Pros.:	Y	Broadcasting:				Health Care:		Petroleum/Chemicals:	
				Other:				Consulting:		Math/Other:	

TYPES OF BUSINESS:

Environmental Products, Retail
Solar & Renewable Energy Products
Healthy Living Products
Design & Consulting Services
Catalog & Online Retail
Movie & DVD Distribution
Movie & DVD Production

BRANDS/DIVISIONS/AFFILIATES:

Kettlenetics
Real Goods Solar, Inc.
Spiritual Cinema Circle
GaiamTV.com

CONTACTS: *Note: Officers with more than one job title may be intentionally listed here more than once.*

Lynn Powers, CEO
Bill Sondheim, Pres.
Steve Thomas, CFO
John Jackson, Sec.
John Jackson, VP-Corp. Dev.
Jirka Rysavy, Chmn.

Phone: 303-222-3600	**Fax:** 303-222-3700
Toll-Free:	
Address: 360 Interlocken Blvd., Broomfield, CO 80021 US	

GROWTH PLANS/SPECIAL FEATURES:

Gaiam, Inc. is a lifestyle media company providing information and services related to the firm's mission: Lifestyles of Health and Sustainability (LOHAS). The name Gaiam was created with the fusion of the word Gaia, meaning mother earth, with the clause I am. Gaiam connects with customers through the following venues: Media channels including Discovery Channel, Fine Living and Lifetime; almost 67,000 retail stores; catalogues; the Internet; and community programs. The firm is divided into three segments: Business, which sells to media and retail partners and generates roughly 35.5% of revenues; Direct-To-Consumer Operations (36.3% of revenues), which provides products and services in the fitness/wellness market directly to consumers; and the Solar Segment (28.2% of revenues), which designs and installs solar systems and related products. Retailers of the firm's products include Barnes & Noble, Borders, Whole Foods, REI and Wal-Mart. The company currently has 10 million direct customers. The firm offers community and subscription clubs such as the Spiritual Cinema Circle and Kettlenetics. The firm's bestselling products include fitness products, organic cotton apparel, home textiles, children's DVDs and renewable energy solutions. The solar segment sells renewable energy products through the firm's subsidiary Real Goods Solar, Inc., products include solar panels and long-lasting rechargeable lithium batteries. Environmental products consist of a full spectrum of energy-efficient lighting equipment; high-efficiency appliances; water-saving devices such as low-flow showerheads, low-flush toilets and faucet aerators; recycled paper products including toilet paper, paper towels and facial tissue; bed and bath products; organic cotton apparel; and household products including a wide variety of non-toxic cleaners.

FINANCIALS: **Sales and profits are in thousands of dollars—add 000 to get the full amount. 2011 Note: Financial information for 2011 was not available for all companies at press time.**

2011 Sales: $	2011 Profits: $	**U.S. Stock Ticker: GAIA**
2010 Sales: $274,268	2010 Profits: $4,275	**Int'l Ticker:**
2009 Sales: $278,473	2009 Profits: $ 296	Int'l Exchange:
2008 Sales: $257,172	2008 Profits: $-35,623	Employees: 557 Fiscal Year Ends: 12/31
2007 Sales: $262,943	2007 Profits: $8,524	Parent Company:

SALARIES/BENEFITS:

Pension Plan:	ESOP Stock Plan:	Profit Sharing:	Top Exec. Salary: $330,000	Bonus: $
Savings Plan: Y	Stock Purch. Plan: Y		Second Exec. Salary: $330,000	Bonus: $

OTHER THOUGHTS:

Apparent Women Officers or Directors: 2
Hot Spot for Advancement for Women/Minorities:

LOCATIONS: ("Y" = Yes)

West:	Southwest:	Midwest:	Southeast:	Northeast:	International:
Y		Y		Y	

GALLUP ORGANIZATION (THE)

www.gallup.com

Industry Group Code: 541613

Management:		Sales/Marketing:		Liberal Arts:		Information Systems:		Professionals:		Technical/Scientific:	
Mgmt. Trainees:		Mktg. Professionals:	Y	Gen. Writing/Editing:	Y	Info. Management:	Y	Finance/Acct.:	Y	Engineers, Elec.:	
Experienced Mgmt.:	Y	Retail Sales:		Technical Writing:	Y	Software Dev.:	Y	Law:	Y	Engineers, Other:	
Int'l Business:	Y	Commercial/Industrial:	Y	Graphic Arts/Photog.:		Hardware Dev.:		HR/Other:	Y	Health/Lab	
MBA Graduates:	Y	Sales Trainees:		Music:		Consulting/Other:	Y	Training:	Y	Scientists/Research:	
		Advertising Pros.:		Broadcasting:				Health Care:		Petroleum/Chemicals:	
				Other:	Y			Consulting:	Y	Math/Other:	Y

TYPES OF BUSINESS:

Research & Surveys
Management Consulting
Customer Loyalty Surveys
Brand & Advertising Research
Performance Improvement Programs

BRANDS/DIVISIONS/AFFILIATES:

Gallup Poll (The)
Gallup Path
Gallup Press
Gallup University

CONTACTS:

Note: Officers with more than one job title may be intentionally listed here more than once.

James K. Clifton, CEO
Jane E. Miller, COO/Exec. VP
James K. Clifton, Chmn.

Phone: 202-715-3030	**Fax:** 202-715-3041
Toll-Free: 877-242-5587	
Address: 901 F St. NW, Washington, DC 20004 US	

GROWTH PLANS/SPECIAL FEATURES:

The Gallup Organization has been recognized for its Gallup Poll surveys since Dr. George Gallup founded the company in 1935. Since its beginning, the firm has diversified its business operations to include a variety of advisory services. It currently offers corporate services such as management consulting; customer loyalty surveys; brand and advertising research; and performance improvement programs. Advising committees harness a variety of research-based measurement tools, development programs and strategic advisory services that help individuals and organizations maximize performance. The model that Gallup employs is known as the Gallup Path, and its step-by-step methodology is designed to leave companies with stock and profit increases. The approach is centered on effective leadership, engaged employees and the capitalization of the strength of all team members. The firm uses its vast research sources concerning human behavior to achieve these ends. The scientists and consultants at Gallup are trained to measure and improve customer and employee engagement, create performance review systems, design performance-based compensation systems and design and implement an organizational performance strategy. Gallup serves companies within a number of industries, including automotive, business services, health care, hospitality and retail, as well as education, government and nonprofit organizations. The company's expertise, whether concerning public opinion polling, societal issues, education, management or human talent, is shared with the public through the company's publishing venture, Gallup Press. Gallup University offers specialized business degree programs that center on the company's core strategies. The firm operates through over 40 international offices.

FINANCIALS:

Sales and profits are in thousands of dollars—add 000 to get the full amount. 2011 Note: Financial information for 2011 was not available for all companies at press time.

2011 Sales: $	2011 Profits: $	**U.S. Stock Ticker: Private**
2010 Sales: $	2010 Profits: $	**Int'l Ticker:**
2009 Sales: $	2009 Profits: $	Int'l Exchange:
2008 Sales: $	2008 Profits: $	Employees: Fiscal Year Ends: 12/31
2007 Sales: $	2007 Profits: $	Parent Company:

SALARIES/BENEFITS:

Pension Plan:	ESOP Stock Plan:	Profit Sharing:	Top Exec. Salary: $	Bonus: $
Savings Plan:	Stock Purch. Plan:		Second Exec. Salary: $	Bonus: $

OTHER THOUGHTS:

Apparent Women Officers or Directors: 1
Hot Spot for Advancement for Women/Minorities:

LOCATIONS: ("Y" = Yes)

West:	Southwest:	Midwest:	Southeast:	Northeast:	International:
Y	Y	Y	Y	Y	Y

GENCO SHIPPING & TRADING LIMITED

www.gencoshipping.com

Industry Group Code: 483111

Management:		Sales/Marketing:		Liberal Arts:		Information Systems:		Professionals:		Technical/Scientific:	
Mgmt. Trainees:		Mktg. Professionals:	Y	Gen. Writing/Editing:		Info. Management:	Y	Finance/Acct.:	Y	Engineers, Elec.:	
Experienced Mgmt.:	Y	Retail Sales:		Technical Writing:		Software Dev.:	Y	Law:	Y	Engineers, Other:	
Int'l Business:	Y	Commercial/Industrial:	Y	Graphic Arts/Photog.:		Hardware Dev.:		HR/Other:	Y	Health/Lab	
MBA Graduates:	Y	Sales Trainees:		Music:		Consulting/Other:		Training:		Scientists/Research:	
		Advertising Pros.:		Broadcasting:				Health Care:		Petroleum/Chemicals:	
				Other:				Consulting:		Math/Other:	

TYPES OF BUSINESS:

Deep Sea Shipping
Dry Bulk Shipping

BRANDS/DIVISIONS/AFFILIATES:

Wallem Shipmanagement Limited
V. Ships Limited
Anglo-Eastern Group

CONTACTS:

Note: Officers with more than one job title may be intentionally listed here more than once.

Robert G. Buchanan, Pres.
John C. Wobensmith, CFO
John C. Wobensmith, Corp. Sec.
John C. Wobensmith, Principal Acct. Officer/Treas.
Peter C. Georgiopoulos, Chmn.

Phone: 646-443-8550	**Fax**: 646-443-8551
Toll-Free:	
Address: 299 Park Ave., 20th Fl., New York, NY 10171 US	

GROWTH PLANS/SPECIAL FEATURES:

Genco Shipping & Trading Limited owns a fleet of dry bulk sea carriers for transporting large volumes of basic commodities and finished products along worldwide shipping routes. The company's vessels transport iron ore, coal, grain, steel products and other drybulk cargoes. V. Ships Limited, Wallem Shipmanagement Limited and Anglo-Eastern Group, international vessel management companies, provide Genco with the technical management for its vessels, including individual ship management, shipping agency, ship broking and IT services. Genco's fleet consists of 53 drybulk carriers, including 17 Supramax, nine Capesize, eight Panamax, six Handymax and 13 Handysize drybulk carriers with an aggregate carrying capacity of approximately 3.81 million dwt (deadweight tonnage). The average age of the vessels is approximately 6.3 years, and all of its ships were built in Japanese, Korean, Philippine or Chinese shipyards. The firm's fleet contains six groups of sister ships, which are vessels of virtually identical sizes and specifications, allowing for greater operational and scheduling flexibility. Genco employs its drybulk carriers under time charters. This arrangement involves the hiring of a vessel from its owner for a period of time, with the charterer paying a fixed daily charterhire rate and bearing all costs associated with the voyage, including fuel, port expenses, agent fees and canal dues. Genco's customers include national, regional and international companies. In March 2011, the firm acquired 13 Supramax vessels from Setaf SAS. In November 2011, the firm acquired five Handysize vessels from Metrostar Group.

FINANCIALS:

Sales and profits are in thousands of dollars—add 000 to get the full amount. 2011 Note: Financial information for 2011 was not available for all companies at press time.

2011 Sales: $392,214	2011 Profits: $25,386	**U.S. Stock Ticker: GNK**
2010 Sales: $448,687	2010 Profits: $147,409	**Int'l Ticker:**
2009 Sales: $379,531	2009 Profits: $148,624	Int'l Exchange:
2008 Sales: $405,370	2008 Profits: $86,580	Employees: 1,313 Fiscal Year Ends: 12/31
2007 Sales: $185,387	2007 Profits: $106,809	Parent Company:

SALARIES/BENEFITS:

Pension Plan:	ESOP Stock Plan:	Profit Sharing:	Top Exec. Salary: $450,000	Bonus: $1,500,000
Savings Plan:	Stock Purch. Plan:		Second Exec. Salary: $450,000	Bonus: $700,000

OTHER THOUGHTS:

Apparent Women Officers or Directors:
Hot Spot for Advancement for Women/Minorities:

LOCATIONS: ("Y" = Yes)

West:	Southwest:	Midwest:	Southeast:	Northeast:	International:
				Y	

GENENCOR INTERNATIONAL INC

www.genencor.com

Industry Group Code: 325414

Management:		Sales/Marketing:		Liberal Arts:		Information Systems:		Professionals:		Technical/Scientific:	
Mgmt. Trainees:		Mktg. Professionals:	Y	Gen. Writing/Editing:		Info. Management:	Y	Finance/Acct.:	Y	Engineers, Elec.:	
Experienced Mgmt.:	Y	Retail Sales:		Technical Writing:	Y	Software Dev.:	Y	Law:	Y	Engineers, Other:	Y
Int'l Business:	Y	Commercial/Industrial:	Y	Graphic Arts/Photog.:		Hardware Dev.:		HR/Other:	Y	Health/Lab	Y
MBA Graduates:	Y	Sales Trainees:	Y	Music:		Consulting/Other:		Training:	Y	Scientists/Research:	Y
		Advertising Pros.:		Broadcasting:				Health Care:	Y	Petroleum/Chemicals:	Y
				Other:				Consulting:		Math/Other:	Y

TYPES OF BUSINESS:

Biological Manufacturing
Biotech Research & Discovery
Enzyme-Based Products
Protein-Based Products
Bioethanol Technology Research & Development
Enzymes for Ethanol Production

BRANDS/DIVISIONS/AFFILIATES:

Danisco A/S
Gentle Power Bleach
Accellerase DUET
PuraFast
SPEZYME
Accellerace TRIO

CONTACTS: *Note: Officers with more than one job title may be intentionally listed here more than once.*

Tjerk de Ruiter, CEO
Jim Sjoerdsma, Exec. VP-Human Resources
Michael V. Arbige, Exec. VP-Tech.
Soonhee Jang, Chief IP Counsel/VP-Intellectual Property
Philippe Lavielle, Exec. VP-Bus. Dev.
Wendy B. Rosen, Contact-Media Rel.
James Laughton, Exec. VP-Animal Nutrition/Food & Beverage Enzymes
Ken Herfert, Sr. VP-Supply

Phone: 650-846-7500 **Fax:** 650-845-6500
Toll-Free:
Address: 925 Page Mill Rd., Palo Alto, CA 94304 US

GROWTH PLANS/SPECIAL FEATURES:

Genencor International, Inc., the biotechnology division of Danish firm Danisco A/S, manufactures, develops and sells biocatalysts and other biochemicals. It delivers 250 products to customers in 80 countries throughout the world. The firm operates three research and development centers, located in the U.S and Europe, and 10 manufacturing centers worldwide. The company divides its products into five categories: agri processing, industrial processing, consumer products, food and beverages and animal nutrition. Agri processing products serve customers who process agricultural raw materials to produce animal feeds, food ingredients and renewable fuels. Industrial processing products include enzyme-based solutions for use in the textiles; pulp and paper processing; wastewater treatment; oil and gas production; and medical instrument cleaning industries. These products are also used as decontamination agents in chemical and biological warfare attack situations, or for removing environmental contaminants. Consumer products applications include laundry and dishwashing detergent, fabric and household care products, diabetic test kits, contact lens solution, toothpaste and mouthwash. Food and beverages and animal nutrition applications also consist of enzyme-based processing products. The firm maintains strategic alliances with several companies, including Procter and Gamble; DuPont; Cargill Dow; and Eastman Chemical. The company's recently introduced products include: Gentle Power Bleach, a low temperature peroxide bleach system for textiles; Accellerase DUET, an improved biomass-to-sugar conversion application enzyme with higher sugar and biofuel yields; PuraFast, a performance ingredient for laundry detergents, which improves cleaning power in shorter cycles and lower temperatures; and SPEZYME Robust Starch Liquefaction, an enzyme for the efficient liquefaction of dry ground corn and increasing ethanol production yields. In June 2011, the firm introduced Accellerase TRIO, which will enable biofuel producers to manufacture cellulosic ethanol more cost effectively.

FINANCIALS: Sales and profits are in thousands of dollars—add 000 to get the full amount. 2011 Note: Financial information for 2011 was not available for all companies at press time.

2011 Sales: $ | 2011 Profits: $
2010 Sales: $ | 2010 Profits: $
2009 Sales: $ | 2009 Profits: $
2008 Sales: $ | 2008 Profits: $
2007 Sales: $ | 2007 Profits: $

U.S. Stock Ticker: Subsidiary
Int'l Ticker:
Int'l Exchange:
Employees: Fiscal Year Ends: 12/31
Parent Company: DANISCO A/S

SALARIES/BENEFITS:

Pension Plan: ESOP Stock Plan: Profit Sharing: Top Exec. Salary: $ Bonus: $
Savings Plan: Stock Purch. Plan: Second Exec. Salary: $ Bonus: $

OTHER THOUGHTS:

Apparent Women Officers or Directors: 2
Hot Spot for Advancement for Women/Minorities:

LOCATIONS: ("Y" = Yes)

West:	Southwest:	Midwest:	Southeast:	Northeast:	International:
Y		Y		Y	Y

GENERAL ATOMICS

www.ga.com

Industry Group Code: 332410

Management:		Sales/Marketing:		Liberal Arts:		Information Systems:		Professionals:		Technical/Scientific:	
Mgmt. Trainees:		Mktg. Professionals:		Gen. Writing/Editing:		Info. Management:	Y	Finance/Acct.:	Y	Engineers, Elec.:	Y
Experienced Mgmt.:	Y	Retail Sales:		Technical Writing:	Y	Software Dev.:	Y	Law:	Y	Engineers, Other:	Y
Int'l Business:	Y	Commercial/Industrial:	Y	Graphic Arts/Photog.:		Hardware Dev.:	Y	HR/Other:	Y	Health/Lab	
MBA Graduates:	Y	Sales Trainees:		Music:		Consulting/Other:		Training:		Scientists/Research:	Y
		Advertising Pros.:		Broadcasting:				Health Care:		Petroleum/Chemicals:	
				Other:				Consulting:		Math/Other:	Y

TYPES OF BUSINESS:

Nuclear Power Reactor Systems
Electromagnetic Systems
Nuclear Waste Disposal
Remotely Operated Aircraft
Sensor Networks

BRANDS/DIVISIONS/AFFILIATES:

TRIGA
General Atomics Aeronautical Systems Inc
General Atomics Electronic Systems Inc
General Atomics Systems Integration LLC

CONTACTS: *Note: Officers with more than one job title may be intentionally listed here more than once.*

James N. Blue, CEO
Carl Fisher, Dir.-Bus. Dev., Advanced Tech. Group
David E. Baldwin, Sr. VP
Sam Gurol, Dir.-Maglev Systems
Constantin Scheder, Chief Architect/Dir.-Nirvana Div.
James N. Blue, Chmn.

Phone: 858-455-3000	**Fax:** 858-455-3621
Toll-Free:	
Address: 3550 General Atomics Ct., San Diego, CA 92121 US	

GROWTH PLANS/SPECIAL FEATURES:

General Atomics (GA) is a government contractor and facilities operator that researches and produces high-technology systems related to the nuclear fuel cycle; electromagnetic systems; remotely operated surveillance aircraft; airborne sensors; and advanced wireless, electronic and laser technologies. GA operates through three segments: the Advanced Technologies Group, the Energy Group and the Nuclear Fuels group. The Advanced Technologies Group is further divided into four divisions: the Advanced Process Systems division, which develops destruction systems for organic waste and conventional and chemical munitions; the Electromagnetic Systems division, which develops advanced electromagnetic technologies for military and commercial applications; the Systems, Space and Materials division, which develops sensor networks, logistics technology, information systems, signature control and space power technologies; and the Nuclear Waste Management division, which focuses on the design, fabrication, testing, licensing and operation of nuclear material transportation and storage systems. The Energy Operating Group conducts nuclear research and development, focusing on nuclear power, magnetic fusion and inertial fusion applications. The Nuclear Fuels Group is the developer of TRIGA (Training, Research, Isotopes, General Atomics), one of the most widely used research nuclear reactor in the world. GA's affiliated companies include, among others: General Atomics Aeronautical Systems, Inc., a manufacturer of unmanned aircraft and surveillance and radar imaging systems; General Atomics Electronic Systems, Inc., an energy products company; and General Atomics Systems Integration, LLC, a military and commercial engineering services company. The firm operates as a facilities operator and government contractor to the U.S. Department of Defense, Department of Energy and the National Science Foundation. In November 2011, the company opened an electric motor facility in Tupelo, Mississippi.

The company offers employees medical, dental and vision insurance; life and AD&D insurance; long-term disability coverage; a 401(k); a pension plan; tuition reimbursement; insurance for legal services; and an employee assistance program.

FINANCIALS: **Sales and profits are in thousands of dollars—add 000 to get the full amount. 2011 Note: Financial information for 2011 was not available for all companies at press time.**

2011 Sales: $	2011 Profits: $	**U.S. Stock Ticker: Private**
2010 Sales: $	2010 Profits: $	**Int'l Ticker:**
2009 Sales: $	2009 Profits: $	Int'l Exchange:
2008 Sales: $	2008 Profits: $	Employees: Fiscal Year Ends: 12/31
2007 Sales: $	2007 Profits: $	Parent Company:

SALARIES/BENEFITS:

Pension Plan: Y	ESOP Stock Plan:	Profit Sharing:	Top Exec. Salary: $	Bonus: $
Savings Plan: Y	Stock Purch. Plan:		Second Exec. Salary: $	Bonus: $

OTHER THOUGHTS:

Apparent Women Officers or Directors:
Hot Spot for Advancement for Women/Minorities:

LOCATIONS: ("Y" = Yes)

West:	Southwest:	Midwest:	Southeast:	Northeast:	International:
Y	Y	Y	Y	Y	Y

GENERAL COMMUNICATION INC (GCI)

www.gci.com

Industry Group Code: 517110

Management:		Sales/Marketing:		Liberal Arts:		Information Systems:		Professionals:		Technical/Scientific:	
Mgmt. Trainees:		Mktg. Professionals:	Y	Gen. Writing/Editing:	Y	Info. Management:	Y	Finance/Acct.:	Y	Engineers, Elec.:	Y
Experienced Mgmt.:	Y	Retail Sales:		Technical Writing:		Software Dev.:	Y	Law:	Y	Engineers, Other:	
Int'l Business:		Commercial/Industrial:	Y	Graphic Arts/Photog.:		Hardware Dev.:		HR/Other:	Y	Health/Lab	
MBA Graduates:	Y	Sales Trainees:	Y	Music:		Consulting/Other:		Training:	Y	Scientists/Research:	
		Advertising Pros.:		Broadcasting:				Health Care:		Petroleum/Chemicals:	
				Other:				Consulting:		Math/Other:	

TYPES OF BUSINESS:

Local Telephone Service
Long-Distance Services
Cable Television Services
Wireless Communications Services
Video-on-Demand Services
Network Management
Satellite-Based Services
Internet Services

BRANDS/DIVISIONS/AFFILIATES:

Alaska DigiTel
SchoolAccess
ConnectMD
Cycle30, Inc.

CONTACTS: *Note: Officers with more than one job title may be intentionally listed here more than once.*

Ronald A. Duncan, CEO
Ronald A. Duncan, Pres.
John M. Lowber, CFO/Sr. VP
Tina Pidgeon, Sr. Counsel
Richard P. Dowling, Sr. VP-Corp. Dev.
Tina Pidgeon, Sr. VP-Gov't Affairs
Bruce Broquet, VP-Finance
G. Wilson Hughes, Exec. VP/Gen. Mgr.
Gregory F. Chapados, Sr. VP
William C. Behnke, Sr. VP-Strategic Initiatives
Stephen M. Brett, Chmn.

Phone: 907-868-5600	**Fax:** 907-868-5676
Toll-Free: 800-770-7886	
Address: 2550 Denali St., Ste. 1000, Anchorage, AK 99503 US	

GROWTH PLANS/SPECIAL FEATURES:

General Communication, Inc. (GCI) is a leading diversified communications company in Alaska. The firm provides facilities-based local and long distance voice, cable video, Internet and data communication services under the GCI brand and reselling wireless telephone services under the Alaska DigiTel brand. The company has approximately 97,500 long-distance subscribers; 144,800 local access lines; 147,100 basic cable subscribers; 138,700 wireless customers; and 116,900 cable modem subscribers. Many of GCI's customers subscribe to product bundles that include two or more of its services. Through its SchoolAccess program, GCI provides satellite-delivered voice, video and data services to many of Alaska's rural communities, serving 25 school districts in rural Alaska and 13 schools in Montana and New Mexico. SchoolAccess enables students, teachers and administrators to access information, curriculum and distance-learning courses. Additionally, the firm offers ConnectMD, allowing rural health care providers to obtain affordable access to telecommunication services. ConnectMD currently serves customers in Alaska, Montana and Washington. Wholly-owned subsidiary Cycle30, Inc. offers order-to-cash systems and hosted billing services to cable, telecom and utility providers.

The company offers employees benefits including medical, dental, vision, life, and disability insurance; a 401(k); educational reimbursement; a health and wellness program; an assistance program; and paid time off.

FINANCIALS: **Sales and profits are in thousands of dollars—add 000 to get the full amount. 2011 Note: Financial information for 2011 was not available for all companies at press time.**

2011 Sales: $	2011 Profits: $	**U.S. Stock Ticker: GNCMA**
2010 Sales: $651,250	2010 Profits: $8,955	**Int'l Ticker:**
2009 Sales: $595,811	2009 Profits: $3,516	Int'l Exchange:
2008 Sales: $575,442	2008 Profits: $-3,372	Employees: 1,655 Fiscal Year Ends: 12/31
2007 Sales: $520,311	2007 Profits: $13,733	Parent Company:

SALARIES/BENEFITS:

Pension Plan:	ESOP Stock Plan:	Profit Sharing:	Top Exec. Salary: $600,000	Bonus: $750,000
Savings Plan: Y	Stock Purch. Plan:		Second Exec. Salary: $486,459	Bonus: $134,453

OTHER THOUGHTS:

Apparent Women Officers or Directors: 1
Hot Spot for Advancement for Women/Minorities:

LOCATIONS: ("Y" = Yes)

West:	Southwest:	Midwest:	Southeast:	Northeast:	International:
Y					

GENESIS ENERGY LP

www.genlp.com

Industry Group Code: 486

Management:		Sales/Marketing:		Liberal Arts:		Information Systems:		Professionals:		Technical/Scientific:	
Mgmt. Trainees:		Mktg. Professionals:	Y	Gen. Writing/Editing:		Info. Management:	Y	Finance/Acct.:	Y	Engineers, Elec.:	
Experienced Mgmt.:	Y	Retail Sales:		Technical Writing:		Software Dev.:		Law:	Y	Engineers, Other:	
Int'l Business:		Commercial/Industrial:	Y	Graphic Arts/Photog.:		Hardware Dev.:		HR/Other:	Y	Health/Lab	
MBA Graduates:	Y	Sales Trainees:	Y	Music:		Consulting/Other:		Training:	Y	Scientists/Research:	
		Advertising Pros.:		Broadcasting:				Health Care:		Petroleum/Chemicals:	Y
				Other:				Consulting:		Math/Other:	

TYPES OF BUSINESS:

Crude Oil Distribution
Crude Oil Gathering & Marketing
Carbon Dioxide Marketing
Pipelines
Synthetic Fuel
Road Transportation
Carbon Dioxide Processing

BRANDS/DIVISIONS/AFFILIATES:

Cameron Highway Oil Pipeline Company
T&P Syngas
Sandhill Group LLC
DG Marine Transportation LLC

CONTACTS: *Note: Officers with more than one job title may be intentionally listed here more than once.*

Grant E. Sims, CEO
Steven R. Nathanson, COO
Steven R. Nathanson, Pres.
Robert V. Deere, CFO
Karen N. Pape, Controller/Sr. VP
Stephen M. Smith, VP
Robert C. Sturdivant, Chmn.

Phone: 713-860-2500	**Fax:** 713-860-2640
Toll-Free:	
Address: 919 Milam, Ste. 2100, Houston, TX 77002 US	

GROWTH PLANS/SPECIAL FEATURES:

Genesis Energy, LP is a limited partnership energy firm active in the midstream sector of the oil and gas industry. Its operations, which are concentrated in the U.S. Gulf Coast region, are divided into four segments: pipeline transportation; refinery services; supply and logistics; and industrial gases. In the pipeline transportation segment, the company transports crude oil and CO_2 through approximately 930 miles of pipeline. The firm operates three onshore crude oil pipelines and two CO_2 pipelines and holds a 50% interest in Cameron Highway Oil Pipeline Company, which operates one of the largest crude oil pipeline systems in the Gulf of Mexico. The refinery services segment provides services to ten refining operations located predominantly in Texas, Louisiana, Arkansas and Utah. Its activities involve processing refiners' high sulfur (or sour) gas streams to remove the sulfur. Using a logistical portfolio that consists of trucks, terminals, pipelines and barges, the supply and logistics segment serves oil and gas producers and refineries through a combination of purchasing, transporting, storing, blending and marketing of crude oil and refined products. The industrial gases segment supplies CO_2 and certain other industrial gases to industrial and commercial enterprises. This segment includes the company's 50% interests in T&P Syngas and Sandhill Group LLC. Through its wholly-owned subsidiary, DG Marine Transportation LLC, the firm owns 30 marine vessels that serve refineries and storage terminals in the Gulf Coast, Intracoastal Canal and western U.S. river systems. In August 2011, Genesis acquired the black oil barge transportation business of Florida Marine Transporters, Inc., including 30 barges and 14 push/tow boats. In October 2011, it agreed to acquire interests in several Gulf of Mexico crude oil pipeline systems from Marathon Oil Company.

Genesis Energy offers employees a 401(k) and medical, dental, life and disability insurance.

FINANCIALS: **Sales and profits are in thousands of dollars—add 000 to get the full amount. 2011 Note: Financial information for 2011 was not available for all companies at press time.**

2011 Sales: $3,089,699	2011 Profits: $51,249
2010 Sales: $2,101,324	2010 Profits: $-48,459
2009 Sales: $1,435,360	2009 Profits: $8,063
2008 Sales: $2,141,684	2008 Profits: $26,089
2007 Sales: $1,199,653	2007 Profits: $-13,550

U.S. Stock Ticker: GEL
Int'l Ticker:
Int'l Exchange:
Employees: 690 Fiscal Year Ends: 12/31
Parent Company:

SALARIES/BENEFITS:

Pension Plan:	ESOP Stock Plan:	Profit Sharing:	Top Exec. Salary: $440,000	Bonus: $446,200
Savings Plan: Y	Stock Purch. Plan:		Second Exec. Salary: $413,167	Bonus: $101,850

OTHER THOUGHTS:

Apparent Women Officers or Directors: 2
Hot Spot for Advancement for Women/Minorities:

LOCATIONS: ("Y" = Yes)

West:	Southwest:	Midwest:	Southeast:	Northeast:	International:
Y	Y		Y		

GENOMIC HEALTH INC

www.genomichealth.com

Industry Group Code: 621511

Management:		Sales/Marketing:		Liberal Arts:		Information Systems:		Professionals:		Technical/Scientific:	
Mgmt. Trainees:		Mktg. Professionals:	Y	Gen. Writing/Editing:		Info. Management:	Y	Finance/Acct.:	Y	Engineers, Elec.:	
Experienced Mgmt.:	Y	Retail Sales:		Technical Writing:	Y	Software Dev.:	Y	Law:	Y	Engineers, Other:	
Int'l Business:		Commercial/Industrial:	Y	Graphic Arts/Photog.:		Hardware Dev.:	Y	HR/Other:	Y	Health/Lab	Y
MBA Graduates:	Y	Sales Trainees:	Y	Music:		Consulting/Other:		Training:	Y	Scientists/Research:	Y
		Advertising Pros.:		Broadcasting:				Health Care:	Y	Petroleum/Chemicals:	
				Other:				Consulting:		Math/Other:	Y

TYPES OF BUSINESS:

Genomic-Based Cancer Diagnostic Test Development

BRANDS/DIVISIONS/AFFILIATES:

Oncotype DX

CONTACTS: *Note: Officers with more than one job title may be intentionally listed here more than once.*

Kimberly J. Popovits, CEO
G. Bradley Cole, COO
Kim Popovits, Pres.
Dean L. Schorno, CFO
Tricia Tomlinson, Sr. VP-Human Resources
Joffre B. Baker, Chief Scientific Officer
Paul Aldridge, CIO
Kathy Hibbs, General Counsel/Sr. VP
Laura Leber, Sr. VP-Corp. Comm.
Dean Schorno, Sr. VP-Finance
Steven Shak, Chief Medical Officer
Randal W. Scott, Exec. Chmn.
David Logan, Exec. VP-Worldwide Commercialization

Phone: 650-556-9300 **Fax:** 650-556-1132
Toll-Free: 866-662-6897
Address: 301 Penobscot Dr., Redwood City, CA 94063 US

GROWTH PLANS/SPECIAL FEATURES:

Genomic Health, Inc. focuses on the development and commercialization of genomic-based clinical diagnostic tests for cancer. Oncotype DX is designed to help physicians determine the most effective treatment type for patients with node-negative, estrogen-receptor positive early stage breast cancer. Unlike comparable test assay systems that use fresh or frozen samples, Oncotype DX uses tissue samples that are chemically preserved and sealed in paraffin wax, thus allowing for easier handling and transportation. Hence, unlike other tests that may require a frozen sample shipped on dry ice, the Oncotype DX sample can be sent via regular overnight mail. All samples are processed at the firm's laboratory in Redwood City, California, and most physicians receive the results of their test within 10-14 days. Oncotype DX is offered as a laboratory service that tests 21 specific genes in a tumor sample to provide tumor-specific information (or the oncotype of the tumor), mainly to calculate the probability of recurrence and the potential efficacy of chemotherapy. This technology compares the genetic makeup of the tissue sample with archived information from other cancer patients, in order to facilitate a correlation between the patient's condition and known clinical outcomes. It expresses the resulting profile as a single quantitative score, called the Recurrence Score, which ranges from 0-100. Higher Recurrence Scores indicate a more aggressive tumor, lower scores indicate less aggressive tumors. The company's second product, the Oncotype DX colon cancer test, multigene expression test developed to assess the risk of recurrence in patients with stage II colon cancer.

Genomic employees receive medical, dental, vision and disability coverage; a 401(k) plan; reimbursement accounts; employee assistance plans; and discounted gym memberships.

FINANCIALS: **Sales and profits are in thousands of dollars—add 000 to get the full amount. 2011 Note: Financial information for 2011 was not available for all companies at press time.**

2011 Sales: $	2011 Profits: $	**U.S. Stock Ticker: GHDX**
2010 Sales: $178,101	2010 Profits: $4,288	**Int'l Ticker:**
2009 Sales: $149,548	2009 Profits: $-9,411	Int'l Exchange:
2008 Sales: $110,579	2008 Profits: $-16,089	Employees: 472 Fiscal Year Ends: 12/31
2007 Sales: $64,027	2007 Profits: $-27,292	Parent Company:

SALARIES/BENEFITS:

Pension Plan:	ESOP Stock Plan:	Profit Sharing:	Top Exec. Salary: $465,000	Bonus: $38,585
Savings Plan: Y	Stock Purch. Plan: Y		Second Exec. Salary: $380,000	Bonus: $32,620

OTHER THOUGHTS:

Apparent Women Officers or Directors: 5
Hot Spot for Advancement for Women/Minorities: Y

LOCATIONS: ("Y" = Yes)

West:	Southwest:	Midwest:	Southeast:	Northeast:	International:
Y					

GEN-PROBE INC

www.gen-probe.com

Industry Group Code: 334510

Management:		Sales/Marketing:		Liberal Arts:		Information Systems:		Professionals:		Technical/Scientific:	
Mgmt. Trainees:		Mktg. Professionals:	Y	Gen. Writing/Editing:		Info. Management:	Y	Finance/Acct.:	Y	Engineers, Elec.:	Y
Experienced Mgmt.:	Y	Retail Sales:		Technical Writing:	Y	Software Dev.:	Y	Law:	Y	Engineers, Other:	Y
Int'l Business:	Y	Commercial/Industrial:	Y	Graphic Arts/Photog.:		Hardware Dev.:	Y	HR/Other:	Y	Health/Lab	Y
MBA Graduates:	Y	Sales Trainees:	Y	Music:		Consulting/Other:		Training:	Y	Scientists/Research:	Y
		Advertising Pros.:		Broadcasting:				Health Care:	Y	Petroleum/Chemicals:	
				Other:				Consulting:		Math/Other:	Y

TYPES OF BUSINESS:

Medical Diagnostics Products
Diagnostic Tests
Blood Screening Assays
Services-Commercial Physical Research
Services-Commercial Biological Research

BRANDS/DIVISIONS/AFFILIATES:

TIGRIS
PANTHER
Procleix
ELUCIGENETM KRAS.BRAF
GTI Diagnostics

CONTACTS:

Note: Officers with more than one job title may be intentionally listed here more than once.

Carl W. Hull, CEO
Carl W. Hull, Pres.
Herm Rosenman, CFO/Sr. VP-Finance
Diana De Walt, Sr. VP-Human Resources
Eric Lai, Sr. VP-R&D
Brad Phillips, CIO/VP
R. William Bowen, General Counsel/Sr. VP/Sec.
Jorgine Ellerbrock, Sr. VP-Oper.
Paul Gargan, Sr. VP-Bus. Dev.
Michael Watts, VP-Corp. Comm.
Michael Watts, VP-Investor Rel.
Kevin Herde, VP-Finance/Corp. Controller
Robert B.Blake, VP-Instrument Systems
Tammy J. Brach, VP-Program Mgmt.
Christina Yang, Sr. VP-Clinical, Regulatory & Quality
Cristina Giachetti, VP-Dev.
Henry L. Nordhoff, Chmn.
Michael H. Barrendorf, VP-Europe

Phone: 858-410-8000	**Fax:** 800-288-3141
Toll-Free: 800-523-5001	
Address: 10210 Genetic Center Dr., San Diego, CA 92121 US	

GROWTH PLANS/SPECIAL FEATURES:

Gen-Probe, Inc. develops, manufactures and markets nucleic acid testing (NAT) products for clinical diagnosis of human diseases and screening of human blood donations. Gen-Probe has received U.S. Food and Drug Administration (FDA) approval for over 60 products to detect infectious microorganisms causing sexually transmitted diseases, tuberculosis, strep throat, pneumonia and fungal infections. It has developed and commercialized one of the first fully automated, integrated, high-throughput NAT instrument systems, the TIGRIS instrument. The company also developed, and now manufactures, the Procleix assay, the only FDA-approved blood screening assay for the simultaneous detection of HIV-1 and HCV (hepatitis C virus); and the Procleix Ultrio assay, which is used to detect the hepatitis B virus in addition to HIV-1 and HCV. The firm also designs and develops, often with outside vendors, a range of clinical diagnostics instruments for use with its assays. The company is currently developing NAT assays and instruments for the detection of human papillomavirus (HPV), gene-based markers for prostate cancer, Trichomonas, different types of influenza virus and human leukocyte antigens. In June 2010, the company announced a $50 million strategic investment in Pacific Biosciences, a private sequencing company. In November 2010, the firm introduced PANTHER, a molecular testing system. Also in November 2010, the company launched the ELUCIGENETM KRAS.BRAF kit which focuses on the prevention of colorectal cancer through the detection of genetic mutation. In December 2010, the firm acquired GTI Diagnostics for $53 million.

Gen-Probe offers its employees medical, dental and vision insurance, flexible spending accounts, an employee assistance program, tuition reimbursement, wellness programs and on-site car wash, gym and cafeteria facilities.

FINANCIALS:

Sales and profits are in thousands of dollars—add 000 to get the full amount. 2011 Note: Financial information for 2011 was not available for all companies at press time.

2011 Sales: $576,234	2011 Profits: $50,124
2010 Sales: $543,327	2010 Profits: $106,937
2009 Sales: $489,302	2009 Profits: $91,783
2008 Sales: $472,695	2008 Profits: $106,954
2007 Sales: $403,014	2007 Profits: $86,140

U.S. Stock Ticker: GPRO
Int'l Ticker:
Int'l Exchange:
Employees: 1,363   Fiscal Year Ends: 12/31
Parent Company:

SALARIES/BENEFITS:

Pension Plan:	ESOP Stock Plan:	Profit Sharing:	Top Exec. Salary: $611,507	Bonus: $150,000
Savings Plan: Y	Stock Purch. Plan: Y		Second Exec. Salary: $586,700	Bonus: $465,773

OTHER THOUGHTS:

Apparent Women Officers or Directors: 5
Hot Spot for Advancement for Women/Minorities: Y

LOCATIONS: ("Y" = Yes)

West:	Southwest:	Midwest:	Southeast:	Northeast:	International:
Y				Y	Y

GFI GROUP INC

www.gfigroup.com

Industry Group Code: 523120

Management:		**Sales/Marketing:**		**Liberal Arts:**		**Information Systems:**		**Professionals:**		**Technical/Scientific:**	
Mgmt. Trainees:		Mktg. Professionals:		Gen. Writing/Editing:		Info. Management:	Y	Finance/Acct.:	Y	Engineers, Elec.:	
Experienced Mgmt.:	Y	Retail Sales:		Technical Writing:		Software Dev.:	Y	Law:	Y	Engineers, Other:	
Int'l Business:	Y	Commercial/Industrial:		Graphic Arts/Photog.:		Hardware Dev.:		HR/Other:	Y	Health/Lab	
MBA Graduates:	Y	Sales Trainees:		Music:		Consulting/Other:		Training:		Scientists/Research:	
		Advertising Pros.:		Broadcasting:				Health Care:		Petroleum/Chemicals:	
				Other:				Consulting:		Math/Other:	Y

TYPES OF BUSINESS:

Specialty Stock Broker, Derivatives
Securities Trading
Stock Data & Analytics Products
Electronic Trading Systems
Energy Derivatives

BRANDS/DIVISIONS/AFFILIATES:

Trayport Ltd
GlobalVision
Amerex Brokers LLC
EnergyMatch
CreditMatch
ForexMatch
FENICS
RatesMatch

CONTACTS: *Note: Officers with more than one job title may be intentionally listed here more than once.*

Michael A. Gooch, CEO
Ron Levi, COO
Colin Heffron, Pres.
James A. Peers, CFO
Richard Brunt, Head-Global Sales, FENICS Analytics & Data
Sheena Griffiths, Dir.-Global Human Resources
Jerry Dobner, CTO
Scott Pintoff, General Counsel/Corp. Sec.
Prash Naik, Managing Dir.-European Oper. & Finance
J. Christopher Giancarlo, Exec. VP-Corp. Dev.
Chris Ann Casaburri, Mgr.-Investor Rel.
Tom Cancro, Controller
Nick Brown, Managing Dir.-Financial Prod. Brokerage, N America
Jim Higgins, Managing Dir.-North America Credit Brokerage
Mark Souffir, Managing Dir.-Paris
Julian Swain, Managing Dir.-London
Michael A. Gooch, Chmn.
Scott Tatham, Managing Dir.-Asia

Phone: 212-968-4100	**Fax:** 212-968-4124
Toll-Free:	
Address: 55 Water St., New York, NY 10041 US	

GROWTH PLANS/SPECIAL FEATURES:

GFI Group, Inc. is an inter-dealer broker specializing in over-the-counter derivatives products and related securities. The firm provides brokerage services and data and analytics products to institutional clients, functioning as an intermediary on behalf of its clients by matching their trading needs with counterparties having reciprocal interests. GFI has offices in North America, Europe, the U.K., Asia, Africa, the Middle East and Australia. The company focuses on the relatively complex and often less liquid markets for sophisticated financial instruments, primarily over-the-counter derivatives, that offer an opportunity for strong growth and higher commissions per transaction than the markets for more standardized financial instruments. GFI has approximately 963 brokers serving over 2,600 brokerage and data and analytics clients, including leading commercial and investment banks. The firm's primary offering is credit derivatives. GFI also offers investment grade, crossover, high-yield and distressed bonds; asset-backed securities; mortgages; bank capital, floating rate notes, loans and preferred shares; emerging market bond options; FX options; interest rate derivatives; repurchase agreements; various equity products; energy and commodity trading; and property derivatives. It owns Trayport Ltd., a supplier of multi-asset class electronic trading systems such as the GlobalVision platform; and Amerex Brokers LLC, an over-the-counter energy derivatives broker. The company has electronic trading systems to support its voice brokerage operations in a number of energy markets, including EnergyMatch, enabling efficient price discovery and trade input, displaying firm and tradable prices; CreditMatch, a platform for credit derivatives and bonds; and ForexMatch, for use with FX option trading. The firm provides data and analysis services to most of these markets using its FENICS technology. In 2011, GFI introduced several new products, including foreign exchange options solution FENICS Trader and cleared interest rate swap electronic trading system RatesMatch. In October 2011, the company opened an office in Switzerland.

FINANCIALS: **Sales and profits are in thousands of dollars—add 000 to get the full amount. 2011 Note: Financial information for 2011 was not available for all companies at press time.**

2011 Sales: $1,015,473	2011 Profits: $-3,181	**U.S. Stock Ticker: GFIG**
2010 Sales: $862,113	2010 Profits: $25,615	**Int'l Ticker:**
2009 Sales: $818,707	2009 Profits: $16,288	Int'l Exchange:
2008 Sales: $1,015,503	2008 Profits: $53,106	Employees: 1,990 Fiscal Year Ends: 12/31
2007 Sales: $970,541	2007 Profits: $94,858	Parent Company:

SALARIES/BENEFITS:

Pension Plan:	ESOP Stock Plan:	Profit Sharing:	Top Exec. Salary: $850,000	Bonus: $
Savings Plan:	Stock Purch. Plan:		Second Exec. Salary: $700,000	Bonus: $

OTHER THOUGHTS:

Apparent Women Officers or Directors: 2
Hot Spot for Advancement for Women/Minorities:

LOCATIONS: ("Y" = Yes)

West:	Southwest:	Midwest:	Southeast:	Northeast:	International:
				Y	Y

G-III APPAREL GROUP

Industry Group Code: 315

www.g-iii.com

Management:		Sales/Marketing:		Liberal Arts:		Information Systems:		Professionals:		Technical/Scientific:	
Mgmt. Trainees:	Y	Mktg. Professionals:	Y	Gen. Writing/Editing:	Y	Info. Management:	Y	Finance/Acct.:	Y	Engineers, Elec.:	
Experienced Mgmt.:	Y	Retail Sales:		Technical Writing:		Software Dev.:		Law:	Y	Engineers, Other:	
Int'l Business:	Y	Commercial/Industrial:	Y	Graphic Arts/Photog.:	Y	Hardware Dev.:		HR/Other:	Y	Health/Lab	
MBA Graduates:	Y	Sales Trainees:	Y	Music:		Consulting/Other:		Training:		Scientists/Research:	
		Advertising Pros.:	Y	Broadcasting:				Health Care:		Petroleum/Chemicals:	
				Other:	Y			Consulting:		Math/Other:	

TYPES OF BUSINESS:

Apparel Importing & Manufacturing
Outerwear & Sportswear
Handbags & Luggage
Leather Accessories

BRANDS/DIVISIONS/AFFILIATES:

Andrew Marc
G-III
Black Rivet
Jessica Howard
Vince Camuto
Winlit
Wilson
AM Retail Group Inc

CONTACTS: *Note: Officers with more than one job title may be intentionally listed here more than once.*

Morris Goldfarb, CEO
Wayne S. Miller, COO
Jeanette Nostra, Pres.
Neal Nackman, CFO
Sammy Aaron, Vice Chmn.
Morris Goldfarb, Chmn.

Phone: 212-403-0500 | **Fax:** 212-403-0551
Toll-Free:
Address: 512 7th Ave., New York, NY 10018 US

GROWTH PLANS/SPECIAL FEATURES:

G-III Apparel Group designs, manufactures, imports and markets an extensive range of licensed and private-label branded outerwear and sportswear, including coats, jackets, pants, dresses and other sportswear items, as well as handbags and luggage. G-III operates in three segments: licensed apparel, which accounted for roughly 65% of its net sales in 2010; non-licensed apparel, 22%; and retail, 13%. Licensed brands include Calvin Klein, Guess?, Kenneth Cole, Cole Haan, Tommy Hilfiger, Levi's, Dockers, Jessica Simpson, Sean John, Jones New York, Nine West and Ellen Tracy labels, as well as products containing trademarks for the National Football League, National Basketball Association, Major League Baseball, National Hockey League and over 100 U.S. colleges and universities. The company-owned labels sold by the unlicensed apparel segment include G-III, Black Rivet, Marc New York, Andrew Marc, G-III by Carl Banks, Winlit, Jessica Howard and Eliza J, among others. The retail segment operates through subsidiary AM Retail Group, Inc., which owns 130 Wilson retail outlet stores. This segment also includes a recently established joint venture with the Camuto Group that operates about 12 footwear and accessory retail outlet stores under the Vince Camuto banner. G-III's products are generally sold by department, specialty and mass merchant retail stores, such as Macy's, Bloomingdale's, Nordstrom, Lord & Taylor, JC Penney and Kohl's. The firm imports its products from independent manufacturers located primarily in China and, to a lesser extent, in Vietnam, India, Indonesia, Thailand, Sri Lanka, Taiwan and Central and South America. A small portion of G-III's wool garments are manufactured in the U.S. Approximately 97% of the firm's sales are derived in the U.S. In November 2011, it signed a licensing agreement to develop apparel under the Kensie brand.

FINANCIALS: **Sales and profits are in thousands of dollars—add 000 to get the full amount. 2011 Note: Financial information for 2011 was not available for all companies at press time.**

2011 Sales: $1,063,404 | 2011 Profits: $56,682
2010 Sales: $800,864 | 2010 Profits: $31,718
2009 Sales: $711,146 | 2009 Profits: $-14,029
2008 Sales: $518,868 | 2008 Profits: $17,490
2007 Sales: $427,017 | 2007 Profits: $13,189

U.S. Stock Ticker: GIII
Int'l Ticker:
Int'l Exchange:
Employees: 2,154 Fiscal Year Ends: 1/31
Parent Company:

SALARIES/BENEFITS:

Pension Plan: ESOP Stock Plan: Profit Sharing: Top Exec. Salary: $1,000,000 Bonus: $5,802,444
Savings Plan: Stock Purch. Plan: Second Exec. Salary: $750,000 Bonus: $3,787,708

OTHER THOUGHTS:

Apparent Women Officers or Directors: 1
Hot Spot for Advancement for Women/Minorities:

LOCATIONS: ("Y" = Yes)

West:	Southwest:	Midwest:	Southeast:	Northeast:	International:
Y	Y	Y	Y	Y	Y

GLEACHER & COMPANY INC

www.gleacher.com

Industry Group Code: 523110

Management:		**Sales/Marketing:**		**Liberal Arts:**		**Information Systems:**		**Professionals:**		**Technical/Scientific:**	
Mgmt. Trainees:		Mktg. Professionals:	Y	Gen. Writing/Editing:	Y	Info. Management:	Y	Finance/Acct.:	Y	Engineers, Elec.:	
Experienced Mgmt.:	Y	Retail Sales:		Technical Writing:		Software Dev.:	Y	Law:	Y	Engineers, Other:	
Int'l Business:	Y	Commercial/Industrial:		Graphic Arts/Photog.:		Hardware Dev.:		HR/Other:	Y	Health/Lab	
MBA Graduates:	Y	Sales Trainees:		Music:		Consulting/Other:		Training:		Scientists/Research:	
		Advertising Pros.:		Broadcasting:				Health Care:		Petroleum/Chemicals:	
				Other:				Consulting:		Math/Other:	

TYPES OF BUSINESS:

Stock Brokerage/Investment Banking
Municipal & Government Securities
Asset Management
Venture Capital
Fixed Income Securities
Emerging Companies Securities

BRANDS/DIVISIONS/AFFILIATES:

Broadpoint Gleacher Securities Group Inc
FA Technology Ventures LP
Descap Mortgage Funding LLC
ClearPoint Funding Inc

CONTACTS: *Note: Officers with more than one job title may be intentionally listed here more than once.*

Thomas Hughes, CEO
John Griff, COO
Patricia Arciero-Craig, General Counsel/Sec.
Jeffrey Tepper, Managing Dir./Head-Investment Banking
Robert Fine, Pres., Gleacher Descap
Robert Tirschwell, Head-Gleacher Descap Trading
Joseph Mannello, Head-Corp. Credit
Eric Gleacher, Chmn.

Phone: 212-273-7178	**Fax:**
Toll-Free:	
Address: 1290 Ave. of the Americas, New York, NY 10104 US	

GROWTH PLANS/SPECIAL FEATURES:

Gleacher & Company, Inc., formerly Broadpoint Gleacher Securities Group, Inc., is an independent investment group that provides value-added advice and capital raising services in connection with mergers, acquisitions and other strategic matters to corporations and over 1,000 institutional investors. The company operates in five segments: Corporate Credit; MBS/ABS & Rates; Investment Banking; Equities; and Other. The company's Corporate Credit segment provides sales and trading of corporate debt securities, including bank debt, investment grade and high-yield debt, convertibles, treasuries, distressed debt, preferred debt and reorganization equities to corporate and institutional investors. With approximately $1 billion in inventory, the MBS/ABS & Rates division provides sales and trading on a wide range of mortgage and asset-backed securities; U.S. treasury and government agency securities; structured products such as CLOs and CDOs; whole loans; swaps; and other securities. The Investment Banking division offers advice on mergers, divestitures, acquisitions, joint ventures, equity investments, fairness opinion and other elements of corporate strategy. The Equities segment assists corporate clients with debt and equity capital raising solutions using proprietary research to identify value-added investment ideas in differing sectors and individual securities. Its research coverage is focused on the aerospace & defense, industrials, technology, healthcare and real estate invesment trust (REIT) sectors. The Other division consists of the management and investment in FA Technology Ventures L.P., a venture capital limited partnership that provides early stage growth capital to companies in the information and new energy technology sectors. In January 2011, after completing the acquisition of ClearPoint Funding, Inc., the company established a new subsidiary, Descap Mortgage Funding, LLC, to support its residential mortgage baking initiative.

FINANCIALS: **Sales and profits are in thousands of dollars—add 000 to get the full amount. 2011 Note: Financial information for 2011 was not available for all companies at press time.**

2011 Sales: $259,400	2011 Profits: $-82,300	**U.S. Stock Ticker: GLCH**
2010 Sales: $282,227	2010 Profits: $-20,621	**Int'l Ticker:**
2009 Sales: $354,368	2009 Profits: $54,920	Int'l Exchange:
2008 Sales: $145,013	2008 Profits: $-17,362	Employees: 368 Fiscal Year Ends: 12/31
2007 Sales: $47,111	2007 Profits: $-19,462	Parent Company:

SALARIES/BENEFITS:

Pension Plan:	ESOP Stock Plan:	Profit Sharing:	Top Exec. Salary: $350,000	Bonus: $3,150,000
Savings Plan:	Stock Purch. Plan:		Second Exec. Salary: $300,000	Bonus: $1,250,000

OTHER THOUGHTS:

Apparent Women Officers or Directors: 1
Hot Spot for Advancement for Women/Minorities:

LOCATIONS: ("Y" = Yes)

West:	Southwest:	Midwest:	Southeast:	Northeast:	International:
Y		Y	Y	Y	

GLOBAL PARTNERS LP

www.globalp.com

Industry Group Code: 424710

Management:		Sales/Marketing:		Liberal Arts:		Information Systems:		Professionals:		Technical/Scientific:	
Mgmt. Trainees:		Mktg. Professionals:	Y	Gen. Writing/Editing:		Info. Management:	Y	Finance/Acct.:	Y	Engineers, Elec.:	
Experienced Mgmt.:	Y	Retail Sales:		Technical Writing:		Software Dev.:		Law:	Y	Engineers, Other:	
Int'l Business:	Y	Commercial/Industrial:	Y	Graphic Arts/Photog.:		Hardware Dev.:		HR/Other:	Y	Health/Lab	
MBA Graduates:	Y	Sales Trainees:	Y	Music:		Consulting/Other:		Training:	Y	Scientists/Research:	
		Advertising Pros.:		Broadcasting:				Health Care:		Petroleum/Chemicals:	
				Other:				Consulting:		Math/Other:	

TYPES OF BUSINESS:

Energy Marketing
Wholesale Distillates & Gasoline
Fuel Distribution

BRANDS/DIVISIONS/AFFILIATES:

Global Companies, LLC
Glen Hes Corp.
SubZero
Chelsea Sandwich, LLC
Global Operating, LLC
Heating Oil Plus
DieselOne
Global Energy Marketing, LLC

CONTACTS: *Note: Officers with more than one job title may be intentionally listed here more than once.*

Eric Slifka, CEO
Thomas J. Hollister, COO
Eric Slifka, Pres.
Thomas J. Hollister, CFO
Edward J. Faneuil, General Counsel/Exec. VP/Corp. Sec.
Charles A. Rudinsky, Chief Acct. Officer/Exec. VP
Alfred A. Slifka, Chmn.

Phone: 781-894-8800 **Fax:**
Toll-Free:
Address: 800 South St., Ste. 200, Waltham, MA 02454-9161 US

GROWTH PLANS/SPECIAL FEATURES:

Global Partners, LP is an energy limited partnership. The firm is a wholesale and commercial distributor of gasoline, distillates (such as home heating oil, diesel and kerosene) and residual oil to wholesalers, retailers and commercial customers. The company is organized within two operating segments: wholesale and commercial. Within these segments, the company divides its products into three categories: distillates, gasoline and residual oil. Gasoline accounts for 60% of the company's total volume sold, with distillates accounting for 34% and residual oil accounting for the remaining 6%. The firm is one of the leading wholesalers of distillates and gasoline throughout the northeastern U.S. Global Partners, through wholly-owned subsidiary Global Operating, LLC, owns five operating subsidiaries: Global Companies LLC; Global Energy Marketing, LLC; Glen Hes Corp.; Global Montello Group Corp.; and Chelsea Sandwich LLC. Through a network of deepwater and inland terminals, the firm wholesales premium heating oil under the name Heating Oil Plus; generic diesel under the name Diesel One; and kerosene and pour point depressant under the name SubZero to unbranded retail gasoline stations and other resellers. Global Partners also wholesales distillates and gasoline through 24 bulk terminals each with a storage capacity of more than 50,000 barrels. In addition, the company has throughput or exchange agreements at over 50 bulk terminals and inland storage facilities. The commercial segment sells unbranded gasoline, home heating oil, diesel, kerosene and residual oil to customers in the public sector and to large commercial and industrial customers, such as federal and state agencies; municipalities; large industrial companies; transportation and water resource authorities; colleges and universities; and small utilities. In late 2010, Global Partners acquired 148 dealer-operated and 42 Exxon Mobil-operated Mobil stations from Exxon Mobil Corporation.

FINANCIALS: **Sales and profits are in thousands of dollars—add 000 to get the full amount. 2011 Note: Financial information for 2011 was not available for all companies at press time.**

2011 Sales: $	2011 Profits: $
2010 Sales: $7,801,559	2010 Profits: $27,038
2009 Sales: $5,818,411	2009 Profits: $34,134
2008 Sales: $9,019,123	2008 Profits: $21,055
2007 Sales: $6,757,834	2007 Profits: $47,013

U.S. Stock Ticker: GLP
Int'l Ticker:
Int'l Exchange:
Employees: 286 Fiscal Year Ends: 12/31
Parent Company:

SALARIES/BENEFITS:

Pension Plan:	ESOP Stock Plan:	Profit Sharing:	Top Exec. Salary: $800,000	Bonus: $480,000
Savings Plan:	Stock Purch. Plan:		Second Exec. Salary: $578,000	Bonus: $202,500

OTHER THOUGHTS:

Apparent Women Officers or Directors:
Hot Spot for Advancement for Women/Minorities:

LOCATIONS: ("Y" = Yes)

West:	Southwest:	Midwest:	Southeast:	Northeast:	International:
				Y	

GLOBECOMM SYSTEMS INC

www.globecommsystems.com

Industry Group Code: 334220

Management:		**Sales/Marketing:**		**Liberal Arts:**		**Information Systems:**		**Professionals:**		**Technical/Scientific:**	
Mgmt. Trainees:		Mktg. Professionals:	Y	Gen. Writing/Editing:	Y	Info. Management:	Y	Finance/Acct.:	Y	Engineers, Elec.:	Y
Experienced Mgmt.:	Y	Retail Sales:		Technical Writing:	Y	Software Dev.:	Y	Law:	Y	Engineers, Other:	Y
Int'l Business:	Y	Commercial/Industrial:	Y	Graphic Arts/Photog.:		Hardware Dev.:	Y	HR/Other:	Y	Health/Lab	
MBA Graduates:	Y	Sales Trainees:	Y	Music:		Consulting/Other:	Y	Training:	Y	Scientists/Research:	
		Advertising Pros.:		Broadcasting:				Health Care:		Petroleum/Chemicals:	
				Other:				Consulting:		Math/Other:	Y

TYPES OF BUSINESS:

Satellite Ground Systems & Networks
Satellite Data Transmission

BRANDS/DIVISIONS/AFFILIATES:

Globecomm Network Services Corp
Globecomm Services Maryland LLC
Globecomm Maritime
Telaurus Communications LLC
Mach 6
Cachendo LLC
Carrier to Carrier Telecom BV
ComSource, Inc.

CONTACTS: *Note: Officers with more than one job title may be intentionally listed here more than once.*

David E. Hershberg, CEO
Keith A. Hall, COO
Keith A. Hall, Pres.
Andrew C. Melfi, CFO/Sr. VP
Paul Scardino, VP-Mktg. & Sales
Paul Eterno, VP-Human Resources
Stephen C. Yablonski, CTO/Sr. VP
Andrew C. Melfi, Treas.
Matthew Byron, Sr. VP-Corp. Office
Paul J. Johnson, Sr. VP-Customer Rel. & Contracts
Andrew Silberstein, VP/Gen. Mgr.
Thomas C. Coyle, Sr. VP/Gen. Mgr.
David E. Hershberg, Chmn.

Phone: 631-231-9800 **Fax:** 631-231-1557
Toll-Free:
Address: 45 Oser Ave., Hauppauge, NY 11788 US

GROWTH PLANS/SPECIAL FEATURES:

Globecomm Systems, Inc. (GSI) provides end-to-end value-added satellite-based communications products, services and solutions. GSI combines its core satellite ground segment systems and network capabilities with the satellite communication services capabilities that are provided by its wholly-owned subsidiaries Globecomm Network Service Corp. and Globecomm Services Maryland, LLC. The products and services that the company offers are pre-engineered systems (through its Orion, AxxSys, Summit and Explorer brands); systems design and integration services; managed network services; content distribution; and Internet/IP telephony support. Through wholly-owned subsidiary Cachendo, LLC, the company's engineers provide all the necessary satellite and terrestrial facilities, as well as the integration services required to implement those facilities. GSI also operates and maintains managed networks and provides life cycle support service on an ongoing basis. The firm designs, engineers, integrates and installs satellite-based ground systems and network solutions, which typically consist of earth stations (integrated systems consisting of antennas, radio signal transmitting and receiving equipment, modulation/demodulation equipment, monitor and control systems, as well as voice, data and video network interface equipment) and ancillary subsystems. GSI's business is global, and it derives most of its revenue from developing countries. Recent GSI acquisitions include Mach 6, Telaurus Communications, LLC, Carrier to Carrier Telecom BV and Evolution Communication Ltd. In March 2011, the firm introduced Globecomm Maritime, a suite of solutions that offer maritime communication services to the maritime, fishing, commercial, leisure and government sectors. In April 2011, the company acquired telecommunications equipment testing specialist ComSource, Inc. for roughly $20 million.

FINANCIALS: **Sales and profits are in thousands of dollars—add 000 to get the full amount. 2011 Note: Financial information for 2011 was not available for all companies at press time.**

2011 Sales: $274,191 | 2011 Profits: $8,988
2010 Sales: $227,817 | 2010 Profits: $7,902
2009 Sales: $170,161 | 2009 Profits: $3,299
2008 Sales: $196,525 | 2008 Profits: $27,019
2007 Sales: $150,745 | 2007 Profits: $8,326

U.S. Stock Ticker: GCOM
Int'l Ticker:
Int'l Exchange:
Employees: 475 Fiscal Year Ends: 6/30
Parent Company:

SALARIES/BENEFITS:

Pension Plan: | ESOP Stock Plan: | Profit Sharing: | Top Exec. Salary: $506,971 | Bonus: $125,000
Savings Plan: Y | Stock Purch. Plan: | | Second Exec. Salary: $333,231 | Bonus: $112,500

OTHER THOUGHTS:

Apparent Women Officers or Directors:
Hot Spot for Advancement for Women/Minorities:

LOCATIONS: ("Y" = Yes)

West:	Southwest:	Midwest:	Southeast:	Northeast:	International:
				Y	Y

GLU MOBILE INC

www.glu.com

Industry Group Code: 511210G

Management:		**Sales/Marketing:**		**Liberal Arts:**		**Information Systems:**		**Professionals:**		**Technical/Scientific:**	
Mgmt. Trainees:		Mktg. Professionals:	Y	Gen. Writing/Editing:		Info. Management:	Y	Finance/Acct.:	Y	Engineers, Elec.:	Y
Experienced Mgmt.:	Y	Retail Sales:		Technical Writing:	Y	Software Dev.:	Y	Law:	Y	Engineers, Other:	
Int'l Business:	Y	Commercial/Industrial:	Y	Graphic Arts/Photog.:	Y	Hardware Dev.:		HR/Other:	Y	Health/Lab	
MBA Graduates:	Y	Sales Trainees:	Y	Music:	Y	Consulting/Other:		Training:	Y	Scientists/Research:	
		Advertising Pros.:		Broadcasting:				Health Care:		Petroleum/Chemicals:	
				Other:	Y			Consulting:		Math/Other:	

TYPES OF BUSINESS:

Mobile Entertainment Applications
Mobile Phone Games

BRANDS/DIVISIONS/AFFILIATES:

Space Monkey
Super K.O. Boxing
Beat It!
Brain Genius
Gun Bros
Glyder
Circus City
Rogue Racing

CONTACTS: *Note: Officers with more than one job title may be intentionally listed here more than once.*

Niccolo de Masi, CEO
Niccolo de Masi, Pres.
Eric Ludwig, CFO/Exec. VP
Adam Flanders, Sr. VP-Sales & Mktg.
Kal Iyer, Sr. VP-R&D
Daren Chencinski, VP-Prod.
Scott Leichtner, General Counsel/VP
Nicolas Beraudo, VP-Bus. Dev.
Greg Cannon, VP-Finance/Corp. Controller
Ray Cheng, Pres., China Region
Mike DeLaet, VP-Sales & Mktg.
Jesse Taylor, VP-Studios
William J. Miller, Chmn.
Oliver Bernard, Gen. Mgr.-EMEA & Asia Pacific

Phone: 415-800-6100 **Fax:** 415-800-6087
Toll-Free:
Address: 45 Fremont St., Ste. 2800, San Francisco, CA 94105 US

GROWTH PLANS/SPECIAL FEATURES:

Glu Mobile, Inc. is a global developer and publisher of mobile games for cell phones, smartphones and social networking web sites. The company has developed and published an extensive portfolio of casual and traditional games across a number of genres, including action, board game, card/casino, puzzle, sports, strategy/role playing and television/movie. Glu Mobile has offices in the U.S., Brazil, China, Canada, Russia and the U.K. The firm creates games and related applications based on third-party licensed brands and other intellectual property, as well as on its own original brands and intellectual property. Glu Mobile's business leverages the marketing resources and distribution infrastructure of wireless carriers and the brands and other intellectual property of third-party content owners, allowing it to focus its efforts on developing and publishing mobile games. Original Glu Mobile games include Space Monkey; Stranded; Bonsai Blast; Glyder; Super K.O. Boxing; Brain Genius; Gun Bros.; Hero Project; Magic Life; Jump O'Clock; Zombie Isle; Toyshop Adventures; and Beat It! The company's marketed third-party licensed games include The Price Is Right; Deer Hunter; Call of Duty; World Series of Poker; Build-a-lot; DJ Hero; Diner Dash; Guitar Hero; Lord of the Rings; Family Guy; Wedding Dash; Paperboy; Who Wants to be a Millionaire?; Family Feud; Transformers; and Zuma. In 2011, the firm launched new games including: Big Time Gangsta; Circus City; Eternal Warriors; and Blood & Glory. In February 2012, the company released Rogue Racing.

FINANCIALS: **Sales and profits are in thousands of dollars—add 000 to get the full amount. 2011 Note: Financial information for 2011 was not available for all companies at press time.**

2011 Sales: $ | 2011 Profits: $
2010 Sales: $64,345 | 2010 Profits: $-13,423
2009 Sales: $79,344 | 2009 Profits: $-18,194
2008 Sales: $89,767 | 2008 Profits: $-107,312
2007 Sales: $66,867 | 2007 Profits: $-3,591

U.S. Stock Ticker: GLUU
Int'l Ticker:
Int'l Exchange:
Employees: 384 Fiscal Year Ends: 12/31
Parent Company:

SALARIES/BENEFITS:

Pension Plan: | ESOP Stock Plan: | Profit Sharing: | Top Exec. Salary: $350,000 | Bonus: $357,000
Savings Plan: | Stock Purch. Plan: | | Second Exec. Salary: $293,405 | Bonus: $122,400

OTHER THOUGHTS:

Apparent Women Officers or Directors: 2
Hot Spot for Advancement for Women/Minorities: Y

LOCATIONS: ("Y" = Yes)

West:	Southwest:	Midwest:	Southeast:	Northeast:	International:
Y					Y

GOLDEN ENTERPRISES INC

www.goldenflake.com

Industry Group Code: 31191

Management:		Sales/Marketing:		Liberal Arts:		Information Systems:		Professionals:		Technical/Scientific:	
Mgmt. Trainees:		Mktg. Professionals:	Y	Gen. Writing/Editing:	Y	Info. Management:	Y	Finance/Acct.:	Y	Engineers, Elec.:	
Experienced Mgmt.:	Y	Retail Sales:		Technical Writing:		Software Dev.:		Law:	Y	Engineers, Other:	
Int'l Business:		Commercial/Industrial:	Y	Graphic Arts/Photog.:	Y	Hardware Dev.:		HR/Other:	Y	Health/Lab	
MBA Graduates:	Y	Sales Trainees:	Y	Music:		Consulting/Other:		Training:	Y	Scientists/Research:	
		Advertising Pros.:	Y	Broadcasting:				Health Care:		Petroleum/Chemicals:	
				Other:	Y			Consulting:		Math/Other:	

TYPES OF BUSINESS:

Snack Products, Manufacturing

BRANDS/DIVISIONS/AFFILIATES:

Golden Flake Snack Foods Inc

CONTACTS: *Note: Officers with more than one job title may be intentionally listed here more than once.*

Mark W. McCutcheon, CEO
Mark W. McCutcheon, Pres.
Patty Townsend, CFO
Paul Bates, Exec. VP-Mktg., Sales & Transportation
David Jones, Exec. VP-Human Resources
Patty Townsend, Sec./VP
David Jones, Exec. VP-Oper. & Quality Control
Mark W. McCutcheon, Chmn.

Phone: 205-458-7316 **Fax:** 205-458-7327
Toll-Free: 800-239-2447
Address: 1 Golden Flake Dr., Birmingham, AL 35205 US

GROWTH PLANS/SPECIAL FEATURES:

Golden Enterprises, Inc. is the holding company for Golden Flake Snack Foods, Inc., based in Birmingham, Alabama. Golden Flake manufactures and distributes a full line of salted snack items, such as potato chips, tortilla chips, corn chips, fried pork skins, baked and fried cheese curls, onion rings and puff corn. Golden Flake also sells lines of canned dips, pretzels, peanut butter crackers, cheese crackers, dried meat products and nuts packaged by other manufacturers using the Golden Flake label. The company sells its products through its own sales organization and independent distributors, as well as direct sales through its web site. The firm primarily serves commercial and retail customers in parts of Alabama, Tennessee, Kentucky, Georgia, Florida, Mississippi, Louisiana, North Carolina, South Carolina, Arkansas, Missouri and Texas. Golden Flake operates manufacturing plants in Ocala, Florida and Birmingham, Alabama. It also owns branch warehouses throughout the Southeastern U.S. During 2011, company-manufactured products accounted for 77% of the firm's total sales, while resale products represented the remaining 23%. Golden Flake Potato Chips are the official chip of the Talladega Superspeedway, home of NASCAR car racing, and the firm is an official corporate partner of the NCAA's Southeastern Conference (SEC).

The company offers employees medical and dental insurance; life and disability insurance; health care and dependent care flexible spending accounts; an employee stock ownership plan; and a 401(k) plan.

FINANCIALS: **Sales and profits are in thousands of dollars—add 000 to get the full amount. 2011 Note: Financial information for 2011 was not available for all companies at press time.**

2011 Sales: $131,048
2010 Sales: $128,441
2009 Sales: $122,169
2008 Sales: $113,380
2007 Sales: $110,827

2011 Profits: $3,015
2010 Profits: $4,209
2009 Profits: $1,990
2008 Profits: $1,128
2007 Profits: $1,213

U.S. Stock Ticker: GLDC
Int'l Ticker:
Int'l Exchange:
Employees: 767 Fiscal Year Ends: 5/31
Parent Company:

SALARIES/BENEFITS:

Pension Plan: ESOP Stock Plan: Y Profit Sharing: Top Exec. Salary: $282,083 Bonus: $55,124
Savings Plan: Y Stock Purch. Plan: Second Exec. Salary: $190,000 Bonus: $41,343

OTHER THOUGHTS:

Apparent Women Officers or Directors: 1
Hot Spot for Advancement for Women/Minorities:

LOCATIONS: ("Y" = Yes)

West:	Southwest:	Midwest:	Southeast:	Northeast:	International:
		Y	Y		

GOLFSMITH INTERNATIONAL HOLDINGS INC www.golfsmith.com

Industry Group Code: 451110E

Management:		Sales/Marketing:		Liberal Arts:		Information Systems:		Professionals:		Technical/Scientific:	
Mgmt. Trainees:	Y	Mktg. Professionals:	Y	Gen. Writing/Editing:	Y	Info. Management:	Y	Finance/Acct.:	Y	Engineers, Elec.:	
Experienced Mgmt.:	Y	Retail Sales:	Y	Technical Writing:		Software Dev.:	Y	Law:	Y	Engineers, Other:	
Int'l Business:	Y	Commercial/Industrial:	Y	Graphic Arts/Photog.:	Y	Hardware Dev.:		HR/Other:	Y	Health/Lab	
MBA Graduates:	Y	Sales Trainees:	Y	Music:		Consulting/Other:		Training:	Y	Scientists/Research:	
		Advertising Pros.:	Y	Broadcasting:				Health Care:		Petroleum/Chemicals:	
				Other:				Consulting:		Math/Other:	

TYPES OF BUSINESS:

Golf Equipment Manufacturing
Retail Sales
Catalog Publication
Tennis Equipment
Used Golf and Tennis Equipment

BRANDS/DIVISIONS/AFFILIATES:

Golfsmith International, Inc.
Lynx
Zevo
Snake Eyes
Golfsmith
Killer Bee
Clubmaker Magazine
Golfsmith Xtreme

CONTACTS: *Note: Officers with more than one job title may be intentionally listed here more than once.*

Martin E. Hanaka, CEO
Sue E. Grove, COO/Exec. VP
Sue E. Grove, CFO
Matthew Corey, Sr. VP-Mktg. & Brand
Ron Ivanitch, VP-Human Resources
Andrew Spratt, VP-Info. Svcs.
David Lowe, VP-Prod. Dev.
Joseph J. Kester, Sr. VP-Store Oper.
Anna Jobe, Controller/VP
Adrian Gonzalez, VP-Retail Growth & Dev.
Steve Larkin, Sr. VP-Direct
Martin E. Hanaka, Chmn.
David Lowe, VP-Int'l Bus.

Phone: 512-837-8810 **Fax:** 512-821-1245
Toll-Free: 800-813-6897
Address: 11000 N. IH-35, Austin, TX 78753 US

GROWTH PLANS/SPECIAL FEATURES:

Golfsmith International Holdings, Inc., operating through Golfsmith International, Inc., is a specialty retailer of golf and tennis equipment, apparel and accessories. The firm is also a catalog retailer, principally publishing Golfsmith Consumer Catalog, which targets the avid golfer, and Golfsmith Clubmaking Catalog, a specialty catalog for people who build their own clubs. Originally founded as a club components and custom club making company, Golfsmith continues to design and manufacture under brand names such as Lynx, Zevo, Snake Eyes, Golfsmith and Killer Bee. The company founded the Golf Clubmakers Association (GCA), the largest such organization in the golf industry. Golfsmith operates as an integrated multi-channel retailer and has 75 stores in 21 U.S. states in 33 markets. These stores range in size from 8,000 to 60,000 square feet (20,000 average). In the U.K., the firm sells its equipment through a commissioned sales force directly to retailers. Through most of Europe and parts of Asia, it sells its products through a network of agents, distributors and through its web site. The company's website, GolfSmith.com, sells over 36,000 products. In 57 stores, the firm has an activity-based shopping environment, GolfTEC Learning Centers, where customers can test the performance of golf clubs, obtain precision club-fitting through its SmartFit program and benefit from PGA-certified golf instruction. Golfsmith Xtreme, a 30,000 to 40,000 square foot store format, features indoor driving ranges with launch monitors, indoor putting greens and virtual reality custom fitting studios that match club types to a person's particular swing. The firm's stores generate 82.3% of the company's revenues. In February 2011, the company agreed to enter the markets of New Zealand and Australia through new licensing agreements. In March 2011, the firm opened a new store in Missouri.

Employees are offered life, medical and dental insurance; educational assistance; a 401(k) plan; and employee discounts.

FINANCIALS: **Sales and profits are in thousands of dollars—add 000 to get the full amount. 2011 Note: Financial information for 2011 was not available for all companies at press time.**

2011 Sales: $387,266	2011 Profits: $ 909	**U.S. Stock Ticker: GOLF**
2010 Sales: $351,851	2010 Profits: $-5,493	**Int'l Ticker:**
2009 Sales: $338,026	2009 Profits: $-3,545	Int'l Exchange:
2008 Sales: $378,772	2008 Profits: $- 516	Employees: 1,621 Fiscal Year Ends: 12/31
2007 Sales: $388,157	2007 Profits: $-40,820	Parent Company:

SALARIES/BENEFITS:

Pension Plan:	ESOP Stock Plan:	Profit Sharing:	Top Exec. Salary: $696,539	Bonus: $
Savings Plan: Y	Stock Purch. Plan:		Second Exec. Salary: $513,000	Bonus: $

OTHER THOUGHTS:

Apparent Women Officers or Directors: 3
Hot Spot for Advancement for Women/Minorities: Y

LOCATIONS: ("Y" = Yes)

West:	Southwest:	Midwest:	Southeast:	Northeast:	International:
Y	Y	Y	Y	Y	Y

GREAT AMERICAN FINANCIAL RESOURCES INC www.gafri.com

Industry Group Code: 524113

Management:		Sales/Marketing:		Liberal Arts:		Information Systems:		Professionals:		Technical/Scientific:	
Mgmt. Trainees:	Y	Mktg. Professionals:	Y	Gen. Writing/Editing:	Y	Info. Management:	Y	Finance/Acct.:	Y	Engineers, Elec.:	
Experienced Mgmt.:	Y	Retail Sales:		Technical Writing:	Y	Software Dev.:	Y	Law:	Y	Engineers, Other:	
Int'l Business:		Commercial/Industrial:		Graphic Arts/Photog.:		Hardware Dev.:		HR/Other:	Y	Health/Lab	
MBA Graduates:	Y	Sales Trainees:	Y	Music:		Consulting/Other:		Training:	Y	Scientists/Research:	
		Advertising Pros.:	Y	Broadcasting:				Health Care:	Y	Petroleum/Chemicals:	
				Other:				Consulting:		Math/Other:	Y

TYPES OF BUSINESS:

Retirement Insurance
Health Insurance
Supplemental Health Insurance
Short & Long Term Disability Insurance
Life Insurance

BRANDS/DIVISIONS/AFFILIATES:

United Teacher Associates Insurance Co
Loyal American Life Insurance Co
American Retirement Life Insurance Company
Annuity Investors Life Insurance Company
Manhattan National Life Insurance Company
Great American Life Insurance Company of New York
Old West Annuity and Life Insurance Company
American Financial Group Inc

CONTACTS: *Note: Officers with more than one job title may be intentionally listed here more than once.*

S. Craig Lindner, CEO
Charles R. Scheper, COO
S. Craig Lindner, Pres.
Paul Severt, CFO/Exec. VP
Jim Niehaus, CIO
Mark F. Muething, General Counsel/Exec. VP/Sec.
James E. Moffett, Exec. VP-Oper.
Jeffrey G. Hester, Controller
Mathew T. Dutkiewicz, Exec. VP
John B. Berding, Exec. VP-Investments
Michael J. Prager, Chief Actuary/Exec. VP
Tom Maxey, Exec. VP

Phone: 513-333-5300	**Fax:** 513-412-3777
Toll-Free: 888-497-8556	
Address: 525 Vine St., Cincinnati, OH 45202 US	

GROWTH PLANS/SPECIAL FEATURES:

Great American Financial Resources, Inc. (GAFRI), a wholly-owned subsidiary of American Financial Group, Inc., markets retirement products, primarily fixed, indexed and variable annuities, and various forms of supplemental insurances. The company's principal annuities products are flexible premium deferred annuities and single premium deferred annuities. Annuities are long-term retirement savings instruments that benefit from income accruing on a tax-deferred basis. In addition to traditional fixed rate annuities and indexed-annuities, the firm offers variable annuities, in which the earnings credited to the policy vary based on the investment results of the underlying investment options chosen by the policyholder, generally without any guarantee of principal except in the case of death of the insured. The firm maintains nine subsidiaries and one affiliate. Subsidiaries include United Teacher Associates Insurance Co. (UTA), which offers a variety of supplemental insurance products and annuities through independent agents; and Loyal American Life Insurance Co., which offers a variety of supplemental health and life products including cancer, accidental injury, short-term disability and hospital indemnity coverage. Other subsidiaries include Annuity Investors Life Insurance Company; Manhattan National Life Insurance Company; Old West Annuity and Life Insurance Company; Great American Life Assurance Company; Great American Life Insurance Company of New York; and American Retirement Life Insurance Company.

The company offers its employees medical, dental and vision insurance; flexible spending accounts; short- and long-term disability insurance; life insurance; a retirement and savings plan; an employee stock purchase plan; an education financial assistance program; an employee assistance program; and a wellness program.

FINANCIALS: **Sales and profits are in thousands of dollars—add 000 to get the full amount. 2011 Note: Financial information for 2011 was not available for all companies at press time.**

2011 Sales: $	2011 Profits: $	**U.S. Stock Ticker: Subsidiary**
2010 Sales: $	2010 Profits: $	**Int'l Ticker:**
2009 Sales: $	2009 Profits: $	Int'l Exchange:
2008 Sales: $	2008 Profits: $	Employees: Fiscal Year Ends:
2007 Sales: $	2007 Profits: $	Parent Company: AMERICAN FINANCIAL GROUP INC

SALARIES/BENEFITS:

Pension Plan: Y	ESOP Stock Plan:	Profit Sharing:	Top Exec. Salary: $	Bonus: $
Savings Plan: Y	Stock Purch. Plan: Y		Second Exec. Salary: $	Bonus: $

OTHER THOUGHTS:

Apparent Women Officers or Directors:
Hot Spot for Advancement for Women/Minorities:

LOCATIONS: ("Y" = Yes)

West:	Southwest:	Midwest:	Southeast:	Northeast:	International:
	Y	Y	Y	Y	

GREAT LAKES CHEESE COMPANY INC

www.greatlakescheese.com

Industry Group Code: 3115

Management:		Sales/Marketing:		Liberal Arts:		Information Systems:		Professionals:		Technical/Scientific:	
Mgmt. Trainees:		Mktg. Professionals:	Y	Gen. Writing/Editing:	Y	Info. Management:	Y	Finance/Acct.:	Y	Engineers, Elec.:	
Experienced Mgmt.:	Y	Retail Sales:		Technical Writing:		Software Dev.:		Law:	Y	Engineers, Other:	Y
Int'l Business:		Commercial/Industrial:	Y	Graphic Arts/Photog.:		Hardware Dev.:		HR/Other:	Y	Health/Lab	
MBA Graduates:	Y	Sales Trainees:	Y	Music:		Consulting/Other:		Training:	Y	Scientists/Research:	
		Advertising Pros.:	Y	Broadcasting:				Health Care:		Petroleum/Chemicals:	
				Other:				Consulting:		Math/Other:	

TYPES OF BUSINESS:

Dairy Products, Manufacturing
Deli
Dairy
Food Service

BRANDS/DIVISIONS/AFFILIATES:

Empire Cheese
Great Lakes
Adams Reserve

CONTACTS: *Note: Officers with more than one job title may be intentionally listed here more than once.*

Gary Vanic, CEO
Gary Vanic, Pres.
Russell (Russ) Mullins, CFO
Hans Epprecht, Chmn.

Phone: 440-834-2500	**Fax:** 440-834-1002
Toll-Free:	
Address: 17825 Great Lakes Pkwy., Hiram, OH 44234 US	

GROWTH PLANS/SPECIAL FEATURES:

Great Lakes Cheese Company, Inc. is a privately owned cheese producer and distributor. The company consists of cheese processing and manufacturing plants in Wisconsin and New York, as well as packaging plants in Utah and its 220,000-square-foot headquarters facility in Ohio. The firm also operates a facility in Cuba, New York that operates under the Empire Cheese brand name. In total, there are seven plants, including the company's three super plants, which are located Ohio, Utah and Wisconsin. Great Lakes Cheese offers a wide variety of cheese, including natural, processed and imported cheese such as provolone, mozzarellas, cheddars, colby's, swiss and Jack, as well as popular imported cheeses such as Danish havarti and Blue, Holland gouda, Switzerland gruyere, Jarlsberg; and Boursin garlic and herb. All products are available to dairy (store brand), deli or foodservice specifications. Cheeses manufactured by the company are available under a wide variety of private label store brands plus the Great Lakes and Adams Reserve names. Primary customers include supermarket chains, club stores, national foodservice accounts and foodservice distributors.

Great Lakes Cheese provides its employees with medical, dental and life insurance; long-term disability insurance; a profit sharing and 401(k) plan; an employee stock ownership plan; and an employee assistance program.

FINANCIALS: **Sales and profits are in thousands of dollars—add 000 to get the full amount. 2011 Note: Financial information for 2011 was not available for all companies at press time.**

2011 Sales: $	2011 Profits: $	**U.S. Stock Ticker: Private**
2010 Sales: $	2010 Profits: $	**Int'l Ticker:**
2009 Sales: $	2009 Profits: $	Int'l Exchange:
2008 Sales: $	2008 Profits: $	Employees: Fiscal Year Ends: 12/31
2007 Sales: $	2007 Profits: $	Parent Company:

SALARIES/BENEFITS:

Pension Plan:	ESOP Stock Plan: Y	Profit Sharing: Y	Top Exec. Salary: $	Bonus: $
Savings Plan: Y	Stock Purch. Plan:		Second Exec. Salary: $	Bonus: $

OTHER THOUGHTS:

Apparent Women Officers or Directors:
Hot Spot for Advancement for Women/Minorities:

LOCATIONS: ("Y" = Yes)

West:	Southwest:	Midwest:	Southeast:	Northeast:	International:
Y		Y		Y	

GREEN MOUNTAIN POWER CORPORATION

www.gmpvt.com

Industry Group Code: 221113

Management:		Sales/Marketing:		Liberal Arts:		Information Systems:		Professionals:		Technical/Scientific:	
Mgmt. Trainees:		Mktg. Professionals:	Y	Gen. Writing/Editing:	Y	Info. Management:	Y	Finance/Acct.:	Y	Engineers, Elec.:	Y
Experienced Mgmt.:	Y	Retail Sales:		Technical Writing:		Software Dev.:		Law:	Y	Engineers, Other:	Y
Int'l Business:		Commercial/Industrial:	Y	Graphic Arts/Photog.:		Hardware Dev.:		HR/Other:	Y	Health/Lab	
MBA Graduates:	Y	Sales Trainees:	Y	Music:		Consulting/Other:		Training:	Y	Scientists/Research:	
		Advertising Pros.:		Broadcasting:				Health Care:		Petroleum/Chemicals:	Y
				Other:				Consulting:		Math/Other:	

TYPES OF BUSINESS:

Utilities-Electric & Natural Gas
Hydroelectric Power Generation
Nuclear Power Generation
Wind Power Generation
Biomass Power Generation

BRANDS/DIVISIONS/AFFILIATES:

Gaz Metro Limited Partnership
Vermont Electric Power Company
Entergy Vermont Yankee Nuclear LLC
Central Vermont Public Service Corporation

CONTACTS: *Note: Officers with more than one job title may be intentionally listed here more than once.*

Mary G. Powell, CEO
Mary G. Powell, Pres.
Dawn D. Bugbee, CFO/VP
Donald J. Rendall, Jr., General Counsel/Corp. Sec./VP
Brian Otley, VP-Oper.
Robert J. Griffin, VP-Power Supply & Risk Mgmt.
Robert Tessier, Chmn.

Phone: 802-864-5731	**Fax:** 802-655-8419
Toll-Free: 888-835-4672	
Address: 163 Acorn Ln., Colchester, VT 05446 US	

GROWTH PLANS/SPECIAL FEATURES:

Green Mountain Power Corporation (GMP), a wholly-owned subsidiary of Gaz Metro Limited Partnership, is a utility company that provides electricity and energy services and products based primarily on renewable fuels to approximately 90,000 retail electricity customers in Vermont, with a service area covering about a quarter of Vermont's population with 4,723 miles of wire. The company also sells wholesale electricity throughout New England and markets operation services to other utility companies in Vermont. GMP's major power source comes from a 620-megawatt nuclear generating plant, owned and operated by Entergy Vermont Yankee Nuclear LLC. Its transmission system is owned by Vermont Electric Power Company, a high-volt transmission operator that is minority-owned by GMP. GMP is known as one of the few environmentally progressive utility companies, owning a total of eight hydroelectric generating stations and a wind generating facility. The firm is one of the nation's leading utilities for low sulfur dioxide and carbon dioxide emissions, low nitrogen oxide emissions and for the percentage of renewable energy with respect to the total mix of energy sources. In late 2010, the firm initiated production at three new solar power plants in Vermont. In July 2011, the company announced plans to acquire Central Vermont Public Service Corporation. The deal was expected to close during the second quarter of 2012.

FINANCIALS: **Sales and profits are in thousands of dollars—add 000 to get the full amount. 2011 Note: Financial information for 2011 was not available for all companies at press time.**

2011 Sales: $	2011 Profits: $	**U.S. Stock Ticker: Subsidiary**
2010 Sales: $	2010 Profits: $	**Int'l Ticker:**
2009 Sales: $	2009 Profits: $	Int'l Exchange:
2008 Sales: $	2008 Profits: $	Employees: Fiscal Year Ends: 12/31
2007 Sales: $	2007 Profits: $	Parent Company: GAZ METRO LIMITED PARTNERSHIP

SALARIES/BENEFITS:

Pension Plan:	ESOP Stock Plan:	Profit Sharing:	Top Exec. Salary: $	Bonus: $
Savings Plan:	Stock Purch. Plan:		Second Exec. Salary: $	Bonus: $

OTHER THOUGHTS:

Apparent Women Officers or Directors: 5
Hot Spot for Advancement for Women/Minorities: Y

LOCATIONS: ("Y" = Yes)

West:	Southwest:	Midwest:	Southeast:	Northeast:	International:
				Y	

GTC BIOTHERAPEUTICS INC

www.gtc-bio.com

Industry Group Code: 325414

Management:		Sales/Marketing:		Liberal Arts:		Information Systems:		Professionals:		Technical/Scientific:	
Mgmt. Trainees:		Mktg. Professionals:	Y	Gen. Writing/Editing:		Info. Management:	Y	Finance/Acct.:	Y	Engineers, Elec.:	
Experienced Mgmt.:	Y	Retail Sales:		Technical Writing:	Y	Software Dev.:	Y	Law:	Y	Engineers, Other:	
Int'l Business:	Y	Commercial/Industrial:	Y	Graphic Arts/Photog.:		Hardware Dev.:		HR/Other:	Y	Health/Lab	Y
MBA Graduates:	Y	Sales Trainees:	Y	Music:		Consulting/Other:		Training:	Y	Scientists/Research:	Y
		Advertising Pros.:		Broadcasting:				Health Care:	Y	Petroleum/Chemicals:	Y
				Other:				Consulting:		Math/Other:	Y

TYPES OF BUSINESS:

Recombinant Proteins
Drugs-Anticoagulants
Transgenic Animals

BRANDS/DIVISIONS/AFFILIATES:

Atryn
LFB Biotechnologies S.A.S.

CONTACTS:

Note: Officers with more than one job title may be intentionally listed here more than once.

William Heiden, CEO
William Heiden, Pres.
Harry M. Meade, Sr. VP-R&D
Richard A. Scotland, Sr. VP-Regulatory Affairs
William Heiden, Chmn.

Phone: 508-620-9700 **Fax:** 508-370-3797
Toll-Free:
Address: 175 Crossing Blvd., Framingham, MA 01702 US

GROWTH PLANS/SPECIAL FEATURES:

GTC Biotherapeutics, Inc. (GTC), a wholly-owned subsidiary of LFB Biotechnologies S.A.S. applies transgenic technology to develop recombinant proteins and monoclonal antibodies for human therapeutic uses. The company uses transgenic animals that express specific recombinant proteins in their milk. The firm generates transgenic animals through microinjection and nuclear transfer. GTC uses goats in most of its commercial development programs due to the relatively short gestation times and relatively high milk production volume of the animals. The company's leading product is ATryn for patients with hereditary antithrombin deficiency undergoing surgical procedures. Antithrombin is an important protein found in the bloodstream with anticoagulant and anti-inflammatory properties. The drug is in clinical trials for disseminated intravascular coagulation, which is an acquired deficiency of antithrombin that occurs in sepsis. The company is also using transgenic methods to produce monoclonal antibodies (MAbs), including potential therapeutic and follow-on biologics. This line of research could lead to treatments for cancer and autoimmune diseases. Other transgenic projects currently under development include a recombinant human coagulation factor for the treatment of hemophilia; a second recombinant human coagulation factor for type B hemophilia; another to treat autoimmune disorders; and an elastase inhibitor to treat emphysema and several other respiratory disorders. In December 2010, the firm was acquired by LFB Biotechnologies S.A.S.

FINANCIALS:

Sales and profits are in thousands of dollars—add 000 to get the full amount. 2011 Note: Financial information for 2011 was not available for all companies at press time.

2011 Sales: $
2010 Sales: $7,226
2009 Sales: $2,826
2008 Sales: $16,656
2007 Sales: $13,896

2011 Profits: $
2010 Profits: $-31,053
2009 Profits: $-26,953
2008 Profits: $-22,665
2007 Profits: $-36,321

U.S. Stock Ticker: Subsidiary
Int'l Ticker:
Int'l Exchange:
Employees: 109 Fiscal Year Ends: 12/31
Parent Company: LFB BIOTECHNOLOGIES SAS

SALARIES/BENEFITS:

Pension Plan: ESOP Stock Plan: Profit Sharing: Top Exec. Salary: $452,308 Bonus: $137,904
Savings Plan: Y Stock Purch. Plan: Y Second Exec. Salary: $288,668 Bonus: $65,435

OTHER THOUGHTS:

Apparent Women Officers or Directors: 2
Hot Spot for Advancement for Women/Minorities:

LOCATIONS: ("Y" = Yes)

West:	Southwest:	Midwest:	Southeast:	Northeast:	International:
				Y	

GULFMARK OFFSHORE INC

www.gulfmark.com

Industry Group Code: 483111

Management:		Sales/Marketing:		Liberal Arts:		Information Systems:		Professionals:		Technical/Scientific:	
Mgmt. Trainees:		Mktg. Professionals:	Y	Gen. Writing/Editing:		Info. Management:	Y	Finance/Acct.:	Y	Engineers, Elec.:	
Experienced Mgmt.:	Y	Retail Sales:		Technical Writing:		Software Dev.:		Law:	Y	Engineers, Other:	
Int'l Business:	Y	Commercial/Industrial:	Y	Graphic Arts/Photog.:		Hardware Dev.:		HR/Other:	Y	Health/Lab	
MBA Graduates:	Y	Sales Trainees:	Y	Music:		Consulting/Other:		Training:	Y	Scientists/Research:	
		Advertising Pros.:		Broadcasting:				Health Care:		Petroleum/Chemicals:	Y
				Other:				Consulting:		Math/Other:	

TYPES OF BUSINESS:

Oil & Gas Drilling Support Services
Offshore Services

BRANDS/DIVISIONS/AFFILIATES:

Gulf Offshore North Sea, Ltd.
Gulf Marine Far East Pte., Ltd.
Gulf Offshore Norge AS
Gulf Marine Do Brasil, Ltda.
GulfMark Servicios de Mexico
GulfMark Americas, Inc.
GM Offshore, Inc.

CONTACTS: *Note: Officers with more than one job title may be intentionally listed here more than once.*

Bruce A. Streeter, CEO
Bruce A. Streeter, Pres.
Quintin V. Kneen, CFO/Exec. VP
John E. Leech, Exec. VP-Oper.
David J. Butters, Chmn.

Phone: 713-963-9522	**Fax:** 713-664-5057
Toll-Free:	
Address: 10111 Richmond Ave., Ste. 340, Houston, TX 77042 US	

GROWTH PLANS/SPECIAL FEATURES:

GulfMark Offshore, Inc. provides offshore marine support and transportation services primarily to companies involved in offshore oil and natural gas exploration and production. Its fleet of 88 vessels is used to transport drilling materials, supplies and personnel to offshore facilities, as well as moving and positioning drilling structures. The firm is organized into three geographically defined operating segments: the North Sea, offshore Southeast Asia and the Americas. The North Sea market includes offshore operations in Norway, Denmark, the Netherlands, Great Britain, Ireland, the Norwegian Sea and the area west of Shetlands. The Southeast Asia market includes offshore operations in Brunei, Cambodia, Indonesia, Malaysia, Myanmar, the Philippines, Vietnam, Thailand, Australia and Singapore. The Americas market is comprised of offshore presence in the Gulf of Mexico, Brazil, Mexico and Trinidad. GulfMark also operates in other international markets, including offshore India, the Persian Gulf and the Mediterranean Sea. Its fleet includes anchor handling, towing and support vessels; platform support vessels; fast supply and crew vessels; specialty vessels; standby rescue vessels; construction support vessels; and utility vessels. The firm's customers are major integrated oil companies and large independent oil and natural gas exploration and production companies working in international markets, as well as foreign government-owned oil companies and companies that provide logistics, construction and other services to such organizations. GulfMark subsidiaries include GulfMark North Sea Ltd.; GulfMark Servicios de Mexico; Gulf Offshore Norge AS; GulfMark Americas, Inc.; GM Offshore, Inc.; Gulf Marine Do Brasil, Ltda.; and Gulf Marine Far East PTE Ltd. In October 2011, the company added three new vessels to its fleet.

GulfMark offers its employees health, dental, prescription drug and vision coverage, life insurance, short- and long-term disability insurance, flexible spending accounts and a 401(k) plan.

FINANCIALS: **Sales and profits are in thousands of dollars—add 000 to get the full amount. 2011 Note: Financial information for 2011 was not available for all companies at press time.**

2011 Sales: $381,870 — 2011 Profits: $49,934
2010 Sales: $359,766 — 2010 Profits: $-34,745
2009 Sales: $388,871 — 2009 Profits: $50,583
2008 Sales: $411,740 — 2008 Profits: $183,784
2007 Sales: $306,026 — 2007 Profits: $98,975

U.S. Stock Ticker: GLF
Int'l Ticker:
Int'l Exchange:
Employees: 1,700 Fiscal Year Ends: 12/31
Parent Company:

SALARIES/BENEFITS:

Pension Plan:	ESOP Stock Plan:	Profit Sharing:	Top Exec. Salary: $610,275	Bonus: $427,195
Savings Plan: Y	Stock Purch. Plan:		Second Exec. Salary: $323,935	Bonus: $272,125

OTHER THOUGHTS:

Apparent Women Officers or Directors:
Hot Spot for Advancement for Women/Minorities:

LOCATIONS: ("Y" = Yes)

West:	Southwest:	Midwest:	Southeast:	Northeast:	International:
	Y		Y		Y

HAEMONETICS CORPORATION

www.haemonetics.com

Industry Group Code: 33911

Management:		Sales/Marketing:		Liberal Arts:		Information Systems:		Professionals:		Technical/Scientific:	
Mgmt. Trainees:		Mktg. Professionals:	Y	Gen. Writing/Editing:		Info. Management:	Y	Finance/Acct.:	Y	Engineers, Elec.:	Y
Experienced Mgmt.:	Y	Retail Sales:		Technical Writing:	Y	Software Dev.:	Y	Law:	Y	Engineers, Other:	Y
Int'l Business:	Y	Commercial/Industrial:	Y	Graphic Arts/Photog.:		Hardware Dev.:	Y	HR/Other:	Y	Health/Lab	Y
MBA Graduates:	Y	Sales Trainees:	Y	Music:		Consulting/Other:		Training:	Y	Scientists/Research:	Y
		Advertising Pros.:		Broadcasting:				Health Care:	Y	Petroleum/Chemicals:	
				Other:				Consulting:		Math/Other:	

TYPES OF BUSINESS:

Equipment-Blood-Recovery Systems
Surgical Blood Salvage Equipment
Blood Component Therapy Equipment
Automated Blood Collection Equipment

BRANDS/DIVISIONS/AFFILIATES:

PCS
MCS
Global Med Technologies
Cell Saver
OrthoPAT
cardioPAT
SmartSuction
Arryx, Inc.

CONTACTS: *Note: Officers with more than one job title may be intentionally listed here more than once.*

Brian Concannon, CEO
Brian Concannon, Pres.
Christopher Lindop, CFO
Peter Allen, Chief Mktg. Officer
Joseph Forish, VP-Human Resources
Jonathan White, VP-R&D
James O'Shaughnessy, General Counsel/VP
Christopher Lindop, VP-Bus. Dev.
Bryanne Salmon, Contact-Media Rel.
Gerry Gould, VP-Investor Rel.
Susan Hanlon, VP-Finance
Sandra Jesse, Chief Legal Officer/VP
Mike Kelly, Pres., North America & Global Plasma
Remi Corlin, Pres., Asia Pacific
Mikael Gordon, Pres., Global Markets
Richard Meelia, Chmn.
Lionel Hadjadjeba, Pres., Europe
Dottie Barr, VP-Supply Chain Mgmt.

Phone: 781-848-7100 **Fax:** 781-848-5106
Toll-Free: 800-225-5242
Address: 400 Wood Rd., Braintree, MA 02184 US

GROWTH PLANS/SPECIAL FEATURES:

Haemonetics Corporation manufactures automated systems for the collection, processing and surgical salvage of blood. Haemonetics' customers include hospitals, commercial plasma fractionators and national health organizations in over 50 countries. The firm divides its products into four categories: Plasma, blood bank, hospital and software solutions. Plasma products comprise all the necessary equipment for the collection of donor plasma and consumables such as, PCS plasma systems, automating the collection of plasma from donors and SEBRA shakers and sealers. The company's blood bank products include: MCS brand blood bank systems, automating the collection of platelets from volunteer donors; ACP, which controls the freezing, thawing and washing of red blood cells; and Cymbal mobile blood bank systems, automating the red cell collection process. Haemonetics' hospital products consist of the Cell Saver, OrthoPAT and cardioPAT brand blood salvage systems, which collect blood lost during or after surgery for transfusion; and the SmartSuction family of products used to clear the surgical field. The firm's software solutions family of products includes integrated software applications to manage the blood and plasma collection, management and storage processes, as well as consulting services. All of Haemonetics' products are designed to integrate with its information technology solutions. The company's subsidiary Arryx, Inc.'s proprietary technology uses light to move and manipulate microscopic objects using technologies such as holographic optical trapping. Other subsidiaries include Altivation; Global Med Technologies; Inlog; Wyndgate Technologies; and Haemoscope. Nearly half of the Haemonetics' sales are derived from the Americas, while Europe and Asia each account for roughly 25%. The firm has offices in 16 countries.

Haemonetics offers its employees life, disability, medical, dental and vision insurance; on-site child care; a flexible spending program; an employee stock purchase plan; a 401(k) plan; and tuition reimbursement.

FINANCIALS: **Sales and profits are in thousands of dollars—add 000 to get the full amount. 2011 Note: Financial information for 2011 was not available for all companies at press time.**

2011 Sales: $676,694	2011 Profits: $79,980
2010 Sales: $645,430	2010 Profits: $58,370
2009 Sales: $597,879	2009 Profits: $59,304
2008 Sales: $516,440	2008 Profits: $51,080
2007 Sales: $449,607	2007 Profits: $49,109

U.S. Stock Ticker: HAE
Int'l Ticker:
Int'l Exchange:
Employees: 2,201 Fiscal Year Ends: 3/31
Parent Company:

SALARIES/BENEFITS:

Pension Plan:	ESOP Stock Plan:	Profit Sharing:	Top Exec. Salary: $546,197	Bonus: $550,708
Savings Plan: Y	Stock Purch. Plan: Y		Second Exec. Salary: $420,251	Bonus: $160,279

OTHER THOUGHTS:

Apparent Women Officers or Directors: 5
Hot Spot for Advancement for Women/Minorities: Y

LOCATIONS: ("Y" = Yes)

West:	Southwest:	Midwest:	Southeast:	Northeast:	International:
Y		Y		Y	Y

HAHN AUTOMOTIVE WAREHOUSE INC

www.hahnauto.com

Industry Group Code: 423120

Management:		Sales/Marketing:		Liberal Arts:		Information Systems:		Professionals:		Technical/Scientific:	
Mgmt. Trainees:	Y	Mktg. Professionals:	Y	Gen. Writing/Editing:		Info. Management:	Y	Finance/Acct.:	Y	Engineers, Elec.:	
Experienced Mgmt.:	Y	Retail Sales:	Y	Technical Writing:		Software Dev.:	Y	Law:	Y	Engineers, Other:	
Int'l Business:		Commercial/Industrial:		Graphic Arts/Photog.:	Y	Hardware Dev.:		HR/Other:	Y	Health/Lab	
MBA Graduates:	Y	Sales Trainees:	Y	Music:		Consulting/Other:		Training:	Y	Scientists/Research:	
		Advertising Pros.:	Y	Broadcasting:				Health Care:		Petroleum/Chemicals:	
				Other:				Consulting:		Math/Other:	

TYPES OF BUSINESS:

Auto Parts, Retail Stores
Auto Parts, Wholesale Distribution
Auto Repair Instruction & Publications

BRANDS/DIVISIONS/AFFILIATES:

Advantage Auto Stores
Genuine Auto Parts
University of Auto Value Installer Training Guide
Auto Value Service Center Program
Auto Value Group

CONTACTS:

Note: Officers with more than one job title may be intentionally listed here more than once.

Eli N. Futerman, Co-CEO/Co-Pres.
Daniel J. Chessin, Co-Pres./Co-CEO
Albert J. Van Erp, CFO
Mike Piccolo, VP-Oper.
Albert J. Van Erp, VP-Finance

Phone: 585-235-1595 **Fax:** 585-235-8615
Toll-Free:
Address: 415 W. Main St., Rochester, NY 14608 US

GROWTH PLANS/SPECIAL FEATURES:

Hahn Automotive Warehouse, Inc. sells automotive aftermarket products to commercial service establishments. Its business is conducted through nine full-service distribution centers and 22 pick-up warehouses in 15 states in the Northeastern and Midwestern U.S. The company also operates an accessory warehouse in New York under the RAAC brand. To complement its distribution centers, Hahn Automotive operates 80 retail locations under the Advantage Auto Stores and Genuine Auto Parts brands; these locations sell to both professional dealers and do-it-yourself individuals. The company's inventory is comprised of 150,000 automotive aftermarket stock keeping units (SKUs), consisting predominately of nationally branded automotive hard parts, as well as maintenance items, accessories and private-label products. Hahn Automotive is a member of the Auto Value group, a collection of aftermarket automotive companies, for marketing and support. As a member of the Auto Value group, the stores are affiliated with over 100 distribution centers and more than 1,700 stores throughout North America, including Canada and Mexico. Advantage Auto stores also supply customers with the University of Auto Value Installer Training Guide, which has information on hundreds of publications, clinics, videos and workshops across the country. In addition, the group offers customized marketing assistance, as well as its Auto Value Service Center Program, which provides Auto Value signage, on-hold messaging, installer uniforms, the 1-800 Service Center Locator Service and equipment leasing programs.

FINANCIALS:

Sales and profits are in thousands of dollars—add 000 to get the full amount. 2011 Note: Financial information for 2011 was not available for all companies at press time.

2011 Sales: $ | 2011 Profits: $
2010 Sales: $ | 2010 Profits: $
2009 Sales: $ | 2009 Profits: $
2008 Sales: $ | 2008 Profits: $
2007 Sales: $ | 2007 Profits: $

U.S. Stock Ticker: Private
Int'l Ticker:
Int'l Exchange:
Employees: Fiscal Year Ends: 9/30
Parent Company:

SALARIES/BENEFITS:

Pension Plan: ESOP Stock Plan: Profit Sharing: Top Exec. Salary: $ Bonus: $
Savings Plan: Stock Purch. Plan: Second Exec. Salary: $ Bonus: $

OTHER THOUGHTS:

Apparent Women Officers or Directors:
Hot Spot for Advancement for Women/Minorities:

LOCATIONS: ("Y" = Yes)

West:	Southwest:	Midwest:	Southeast:	Northeast:	International:
		Y		Y	

HANCOCK HOLDING COMPANY

www.hancockbank.com

Industry Group Code: 522110

Management:		Sales/Marketing:		Liberal Arts:		Information Systems:		Professionals:		Technical/Scientific:	
Mgmt. Trainees:	Y	Mktg. Professionals:		Gen. Writing/Editing:	Y	Info. Management:	Y	Finance/Acct.:	Y	Engineers, Elec.:	
Experienced Mgmt.:	Y	Retail Sales:		Technical Writing:		Software Dev.:		Law:	Y	Engineers, Other:	
Int'l Business:		Commercial/Industrial:		Graphic Arts/Photog.:		Hardware Dev.:		HR/Other:	Y	Health/Lab	
MBA Graduates:	Y	Sales Trainees:		Music:		Consulting/Other:		Training:	Y	Scientists/Research:	
		Advertising Pros.:	Y	Broadcasting:				Health Care:		Petroleum/Chemicals:	
				Other:				Consulting:		Math/Other:	

TYPES OF BUSINESS:

Banking
Mortgages
Insurance
Investment Services
Trust Services
Credit Cards
Wealth Management
Loans

BRANDS/DIVISIONS/AFFILIATES:

Hancock Bank
Hancock Bank of Louisiana
Harrison Finance Company
Hancock Investment Services, Inc.
Hancock Insurance Agency, Inc.
Whitney Holding Corporation
Whitney Bank
Hancock Bank of Alabama

CONTACTS: *Note: Officers with more than one job title may be intentionally listed here more than once.*

Carl J. Chaney, Co-CEO
John M. Hairston, COO/Co-CEO
Carl J. Chaney, Pres.
Michael M. Achary, CFO/Exec. VP
Robert A. Seals, Dir.-Mktg./Sr. VP
D. Shane Loper, Chief Admin & Risk Officer/Exec. VP
Joy L. Phillips, General Counsel/Exec. VP
Paul D. Guichet, Contact-Investor Rel.
Gerald S. Dugal, Treas./Sr. VP
Samuel B. Kendricks, Chief Credit Officer/Exec. VP
Clifton J. Saik, Chief Wealth Mgmt. Officer/Exec. VP
Richard T. Hill, Chief Retail Banking Officer/Exec. VP
Edward G. Francis, Chief Commercial Banking Officer/Exec. VP
James B. Estabrook, Jr., Chmn.

Phone: 228-868-4000	**Fax:**
Toll-Free: 800-522-6542	
Address: 1 Hancock Plz., Gulfport, MS 39501 US	

GROWTH PLANS/SPECIAL FEATURES:

Hancock Holding Company (HHC) is a holding company with four wholly-owned bank subsidiaries: Hancock Bank, based in Mississippi; Whitney Bank, headquartered in New Orleans; Hancock Bank of Louisiana; and Hancock Bank of Alabama. These subsidiaries combined operate nearly 300 full-service offices and over 350 ATMs throughout south Mississippi, Louisiana, Alabama and Florida. Other company subsidiaries include Hancock Investment Services, Inc.; Hancock Insurance Agency, Inc.; Harrison Finance Company; Magna Insurance Company; and three real estate corporations owning land and buildings that house bank branches and other facilities. The company has approximately $20 billion in total assets. HHC's branch locations offer commercial, consumer and mortgage loans and deposit services to individuals and small to middle market businesses in their respective market areas. Its loan products also include consumer, nonresidential real estate, home equity and business and industry loans. Other services include wealth management, private banking, retirement plan services, cash management, brokerage and insurance products. In June 2011, HHC acquired Whitney Holding Corporation.

The company offers employees medical, dental and vision insurance; life and disability insurance benefits; an associate assistance program; a 401(k) plan; a retirement plan; a discount stock purchase plan; and other supplemental policies, such as auto and home insurance. HHC also offers educational opportunities through Hancock University to associates interested in leadership development, front line skills, managerial and supervisory skills, regulatory and compliance and personal and professional development.

FINANCIALS: **Sales and profits are in thousands of dollars—add 000 to get the full amount. 2011 Note: Financial information for 2011 was not available for all companies at press time.**

2011 Sales: $798,540	2011 Profits: $76,759	**U.S. Stock Ticker: HBHC**
2010 Sales: $489,507	2010 Profits: $52,206	**Int'l Ticker:**
2009 Sales: $481,054	2009 Profits: $74,775	Int'l Exchange:
2008 Sales: $463,215	2008 Profits: $65,366	Employees: 2,299 Fiscal Year Ends: 12/31
2007 Sales: $463,994	2007 Profits: $73,892	Parent Company:

SALARIES/BENEFITS:

Pension Plan: Y	ESOP Stock Plan:	Profit Sharing:	Top Exec. Salary: $432,073	Bonus: $258,194
Savings Plan: Y	Stock Purch. Plan: Y		Second Exec. Salary: $432,073	Bonus: $258,194

OTHER THOUGHTS:

Apparent Women Officers or Directors: 4
Hot Spot for Advancement for Women/Minorities: Y

LOCATIONS: ("Y" = Yes)

West:	Southwest:	Midwest:	Southeast:	Northeast:	International:
			Y		

HANOVER FOODS CORPORATION

www.hanoverfoods.com

Industry Group Code: 311

Management:		**Sales/Marketing:**		**Liberal Arts:**		**Information Systems:**		**Professionals:**		**Technical/Scientific:**	
Mgmt. Trainees:		Mktg. Professionals:	Y	Gen. Writing/Editing:	Y	Info. Management:	Y	Finance/Acct.:	Y	Engineers, Elec.:	
Experienced Mgmt.:	Y	Retail Sales:		Technical Writing:		Software Dev.:		Law:	Y	Engineers, Other:	Y
Int'l Business:	Y	Commercial/Industrial:	Y	Graphic Arts/Photog.:		Hardware Dev.:		HR/Other:	Y	Health/Lab	
MBA Graduates:	Y	Sales Trainees:	Y	Music:		Consulting/Other:		Training:	Y	Scientists/Research:	
		Advertising Pros.:	Y	Broadcasting:				Health Care:		Petroleum/Chemicals:	
				Other:				Consulting:		Math/Other:	

TYPES OF BUSINESS:

Food Products-Manufacturing
Frozen Foods
Canned Vegetables
Snack Products
Agriculture

BRANDS/DIVISIONS/AFFILIATES:

Hanover
Bickle's
Aunt Kitty's
Spring Glen
Wege

GROWTH PLANS/SPECIAL FEATURES:

Hanover Foods Corporation, founded in 1924, is a leading independent food processor. The company's products include canned and frozen vegetables; soups; broth; frozen soft pretzels, frozen entrees and salads. The firm distributes these items in the Eastern U.S. Hanover cultivates, processes and packages all of its products from start to finish, producing over 40 million cases of food per year. At the company's canning plant, located in Hanover, Pennsylvania, vegetable, bean and pasta items are produced in 7-10 ounce sizes and are stored in cans and glass jars. Hanover produces its frozen soft pretzels and shelf-stable hard pretzels at its nearby sales building. The company operates a tomato plant in California to stabilize its tomato paste costs. It markets its products under several brand names including Hanover; Spring Glen; Aunt Kitty's; Bickel's; and Wege.

CONTACTS: *Note: Officers with more than one job title may be intentionally listed here more than once.*

John A. Warehime, CEO
John A. Warehime, Pres.
Gary T. Knisely, CFO/Exec. VP
Gary T. Knisely, General Counsel/Corp. Sec.
John A. Warehime, Chmn.

Phone: 717-632-6000	**Fax:** 717-637-2890
Toll-Free:	
Address: 1486 York Rd., Hanover, PA 17331 US	

FINANCIALS: **Sales and profits are in thousands of dollars—add 000 to get the full amount. 2011 Note: Financial information for 2011 was not available for all companies at press time.**

2011 Sales: $	2011 Profits: $	**U.S. Stock Ticker: Private**
2010 Sales: $	2010 Profits: $	**Int'l Ticker:**
2009 Sales: $	2009 Profits: $	Int'l Exchange:
2008 Sales: $	2008 Profits: $	Employees: Fiscal Year Ends: 5/31
2007 Sales: $	2007 Profits: $	Parent Company:

SALARIES/BENEFITS:

Pension Plan:	ESOP Stock Plan:	Profit Sharing:	Top Exec. Salary: $	Bonus: $
Savings Plan:	Stock Purch. Plan:		Second Exec. Salary: $	Bonus: $

OTHER THOUGHTS:

Apparent Women Officers or Directors:
Hot Spot for Advancement for Women/Minorities:

LOCATIONS: ("Y" = Yes)

West:	Southwest:	Midwest:	Southeast:	Northeast:	International:
Y				Y	

HARRIS INTERACTIVE INC

www.harrisinteractive.com

Industry Group Code: 541910

Management:		Sales/Marketing:		Liberal Arts:		Information Systems:		Professionals:		Technical/Scientific:	
Mgmt. Trainees:		Mktg. Professionals:	Y	Gen. Writing/Editing:	Y	Info. Management:	Y	Finance/Acct.:	Y	Engineers, Elec.:	
Experienced Mgmt.:	Y	Retail Sales:		Technical Writing:	Y	Software Dev.:	Y	Law:	Y	Engineers, Other:	
Int'l Business:	Y	Commercial/Industrial:	Y	Graphic Arts/Photog.:		Hardware Dev.:		HR/Other:	Y	Health/Lab	
MBA Graduates:	Y	Sales Trainees:	Y	Music:		Consulting/Other:	Y	Training:	Y	Scientists/Research:	
		Advertising Pros.:		Broadcasting:				Health Care:		Petroleum/Chemicals:	
				Other:	Y			Consulting:	Y	Math/Other:	Y

TYPES OF BUSINESS:

Market Research
Internet-Based Research
Consulting Services

BRANDS/DIVISIONS/AFFILIATES:

Harris Poll
Harris Interactive Service Bureau
Harris Interactive Text Analytics

CONTACTS:

Note: Officers with more than one job title may be intentionally listed here more than once.

Al Angrisani, Interim CEO
Eric W. Narowski, Interim CFO
Todd Myers, Interim Head-Tech./Sr. VP
Marc H. Levin, Chief Admin. Officer
Marc H. Levin, General Counsel/Exec. VP/Corp. Sec.
Todd Myers, Interim Head-Oper. & Panel/Sr. VP
Michael T. Burns, VP-Investor Rel. & External Reporting
Eric W. Narowski, Principal Acct. Officer/Sr. VP/Global Controller
Michael de Vere, Pres., U.S. Bus. Groups
Nathalie Perrio-Combeaux, Co-CEO-France & U.K. Oper.
Howard L. Shecter, Chmn.
Patrick Van Bloeme, Co-CEO-France & U.K. Oper.

Phone: 212-539-9600 **Fax:**
Toll-Free: 800-866-7655
Address: 161 6th Ave., New York, NY 10013 US

GROWTH PLANS/SPECIAL FEATURES:

Harris Interactive, Inc. is a worldwide market research and consulting firm. The firm is one of the largest Internet-based research and polling firms in the world, based on the size of its Internet panel, number of online surveys completed and the amount of revenue it derives from online research. The company is best known for the Harris Poll and for pioneering an accurate method for Internet market research. It has made significant expenditures to drive the transformation of the market research and polling industry to an Internet-based platform. Harris conducts research mainly for companies in the travel, energy, public policy, automotive/transportation, financial services, consumer goods, health care, pharmaceuticals, retail, product development, reputation management, brand consulting, technology and telecommunications industries. Harris also conducts international research through its various U.S. offices and its foreign offices in Hong Kong, the U.K., China, Germany, France, Singapore and Canada, as well as its global network of local market and opinion research firms. Harris has three main product and service categories: custom research, including Internet-based and traditional market research studies and polling conducted on specific issues for specific customers; tracking study research, including Internet-based studies conducted on general-interest issues and sold to numerous clients; and service bureau research, which consists of Internet-based data collection conducted for other market research firms by the company's Harris Interactive Service Bureau subsidiary. Harris recently launched Harris Interactive Text Analytics, a program developed to integrate several sources of information about a company's industry in order to optimize investment in market research dollars and produce better trend forecasting. In August 2011, Harris disposed of its telephone data collection center in the U.K.

The company offers employee benefits including medical, dental, vision, AD&D, disability and life insurance; tuition assistance; a 401(k); domestic partner benefits; an assistance plan; a stock purchase plan; eight paid holidays and two floater holidays; flexible spending accounts; and paid vacation.

FINANCIALS:

Sales and profits are in thousands of dollars—add 000 to get the full amount. 2011 Note: Financial information for 2011 was not available for all companies at press time.

2011 Sales: $165,264	2011 Profits: $-8,453
2010 Sales: $138,415	2010 Profits: $-2,166
2009 Sales: $184,334	2009 Profits: $-75,331
2008 Sales: $238,723	2008 Profits: $-84,618
2007 Sales: $211,803	2007 Profits: $9,076

U.S. Stock Ticker: HPOL
Int'l Ticker:
Int'l Exchange:
Employees: 920 Fiscal Year Ends: 6/30
Parent Company:

SALARIES/BENEFITS:

Pension Plan:	ESOP Stock Plan:	Profit Sharing:	Top Exec. Salary: $593,077	Bonus: $
Savings Plan: Y	Stock Purch. Plan: Y		Second Exec. Salary: $306,346	Bonus: $

OTHER THOUGHTS:

Apparent Women Officers or Directors: 1
Hot Spot for Advancement for Women/Minorities:

LOCATIONS: ("Y" = Yes)

West:	Southwest:	Midwest:	Southeast:	Northeast:	International:
Y		Y		Y	Y

HCC INSURANCE HOLDINGS INC

www.hcc.com

Industry Group Code: 524126

Management:		Sales/Marketing:		Liberal Arts:		Information Systems:		Professionals:		Technical/Scientific:	
Mgmt. Trainees:	Y	Mktg. Professionals:	Y	Gen. Writing/Editing:	Y	Info. Management:	Y	Finance/Acct.:	Y	Engineers, Elec.:	
Experienced Mgmt.:	Y	Retail Sales:		Technical Writing:	Y	Software Dev.:		Law:	Y	Engineers, Other:	
Int'l Business:	Y	Commercial/Industrial:	Y	Graphic Arts/Photog.:		Hardware Dev.:		HR/Other:	Y	Health/Lab	Y
MBA Graduates:	Y	Sales Trainees:	Y	Music:		Consulting/Other:		Training:	Y	Scientists/Research:	
		Advertising Pros.:		Broadcasting:				Health Care:	Y	Petroleum/Chemicals:	
				Other:				Consulting:		Math/Other:	Y

TYPES OF BUSINESS:

Insurance, Direct Property & Casualty
Health Insurance
Offshore Energy Insurance
Aviation & Marine Insurance
Accident Insurance
Reinsurance
Consulting Services

BRANDS/DIVISIONS/AFFILIATES:

CONTACTS:

Note: Officers with more than one job title may be intentionally listed here more than once.

John N. Molbeck, Jr., CEO
W. Tobin Whamond, COO/Exec. VP
Christopher J.B. Williams, Pres.
Brad T. Irick, CFO/Exec. VP
Susan L. Howie, VP-Human Resources
William W. Lukefahr, CIO/VP
Deborah L. Riffe, VP-Admin.
Randy D. Rinicella, General Counsel/Sr. VP
Pamela J. Penny, Chief Acct. Officer/Exec. VP
Frank H. Ahlborn, VP/Treas.
Michael J. Schell, Chief Property & Casualty Insurance Officer
Brenda K. Bull, VP/Controller
Mark W. Callahan, Chief Actuary/Exec. VP
Robert A. Rosholt, Chmn.
Barry J. Cook, Exec. VP-Int'l Oper.

Phone: 713-690-7300	**Fax:** 713-462-2401
Toll-Free:	
Address: 13403 NW Fwy., Houston, TX 77040 US	

GROWTH PLANS/SPECIAL FEATURES:

HCC Insurance Holdings, Inc. provides insurance coverages and related agency and reinsurance brokerage services to commercial customers and individuals. Its products include specialized property and casualty; surety; and group life, accident and health insurance coverages. The company operates primarily in the U.S., the U.K., Spain, Bermuda and Ireland. HCC's lines of business include five underwriting segments: U.S. Property & Casualty, which accounted for 21% of gross written premiums in 2010; Professional Liability, 23%; Accident & Health, 30%; U.S. Surety & Credit, 9%; and International, 17%. In its U.S. Property & Casualty business, the company writes specialty lines of insurance such as aviation, small account errors and omissions liability (E&O), public risk, employment practices liability, title, residual value, disability, contingency, kidnap and ransom, difference in conditions, occupational accident and brown water marine. The Professional Liability segment offers directors' and officers' (D&O) liability, large account E&O liability, fiduciary liability, fidelity and bankers' blanket bonds. The firm's Accident & Health business line includes medical stop-loss, short-term domestic and international medical, HMO reinsurance and medical excess coverages. The U.S. Surety & Credit segment includes surety products written in the U.S. and credit insurance managed in the U.S. The International segment includes energy, property treaty, liability, surety, credit, property (direct and facultative), ocean marine, accident and health and other smaller product lines written outside the U.S.

FINANCIALS:

Sales and profits are in thousands of dollars—add 000 to get the full amount. 2011 Note: Financial information for 2011 was not available for all companies at press time.

2011 Sales: $	2011 Profits: $	**U.S. Stock Ticker: HCC**
2010 Sales: $2,303,254	2010 Profits: $345,096	**Int'l Ticker:**
2009 Sales: $2,318,516	2009 Profits: $353,868	Int'l Exchange:
2008 Sales: $2,206,569	2008 Profits: $302,120	Employees: 1,883 Fiscal Year Ends: 12/31
2007 Sales: $2,388,373	2007 Profits: $395,429	Parent Company:

SALARIES/BENEFITS:

Pension Plan:	ESOP Stock Plan:	Profit Sharing:	Top Exec. Salary: $1,950,000	Bonus: $3,250,000
Savings Plan:	Stock Purch. Plan:		Second Exec. Salary: $810,929	Bonus: $978,000

OTHER THOUGHTS:

Apparent Women Officers or Directors: 10
Hot Spot for Advancement for Women/Minorities: Y

LOCATIONS: ("Y" = Yes)

West:	Southwest:	Midwest:	Southeast:	Northeast:	International:
Y	Y	Y	Y	Y	Y

HEALTH GRADES INC

www.healthgrades.com

Industry Group Code: 519130

Management:		Sales/Marketing:		Liberal Arts:		Information Systems:		Professionals:		Technical/Scientific:	
Mgmt. Trainees:		Mktg. Professionals:	Y	Gen. Writing/Editing:	Y	Info. Management:	Y	Finance/Acct.:	Y	Engineers, Elec.:	
Experienced Mgmt.:	Y	Retail Sales:		Technical Writing:	Y	Software Dev.:	Y	Law:	Y	Engineers, Other:	
Int'l Business:		Commercial/Industrial:	Y	Graphic Arts/Photog.:	Y	Hardware Dev.:		HR/Other:	Y	Health/Lab	
MBA Graduates:	Y	Sales Trainees:	Y	Music:		Consulting/Other:		Training:	Y	Scientists/Research:	
		Advertising Pros.:	Y	Broadcasting:				Health Care:		Petroleum/Chemicals:	
				Other:				Consulting:		Math/Other:	

TYPES OF BUSINESS:

Online Health Information
Health Providers Ratings Data
Consulting Services
Marketing Assistance Services

BRANDS/DIVISIONS/AFFILIATES:

Vestar Capital Partners V LP
Hospital Quality Guide
Physician Quality Guide
Nursing Home Quality Guide
Home Health Quality
Connecting Point
Mountain Merger Sub Corp.
Mountain Acquisition Corp.

CONTACTS: *Note: Officers with more than one job title may be intentionally listed here more than once.*

Kerry R. Hicks, CEO
Wes Crews, COO/Exec. VP
Kerry R. Hicks, Pres.
Allen Dodge, CFO/Exec. VP
Mark Bartling, Sr. VP-IT
Andrea Pearson, Exec. VP-Oper.
M. John Neal, Exec. VP-Bus. Dev. & Corp. Strategy
Andrea Pearson, Exec. VP-Internet Strategy
Scott Shapiro, Sr. VP-Corp. Comm.
Tod Baker, Sr. VP-Professional Svcs.
David G. Hicks, Exec. VP
Mike Shanks, Sr. VP
Kerry R. Hicks, Chmn.

Phone: 303-716-0041 **Fax:** 303-716-1298
Toll-Free:
Address: 500 Golden Ridge Rd., Ste. 100, Golden, CO 80401 US

GROWTH PLANS/SPECIAL FEATURES:

Health Grades, Inc. is a health care ratings and consulting company that provides the means to assess and compare the quality or qualifications of health care providers, including hospitals, nursing homes, home health agencies, hospice programs and fertility clinics. It currently provides ratings or profile information on roughly 5,000 hospitals; 750,000 physicians in over 100 specialties; and 16,000 nursing homes. This information is available on the firm's web site free of charge to consumers, employers and health plans, with more detailed reports available for a fee. Over 100 million users utilize Health Grades services each year. Health Grades offers hospitals with high ratings the opportunity to license its ratings and trademarks. The company also provides marketing assistance. Through HealthGrades Clinical Excellence Research & Consulting, the company also offers consulting services to hospitals that either want to build a reputation based on quality of care or are working to identify areas to improve quality. The firm's Health Management Suite of products is available to organizations to license under the Hospital Quality Guide, Physician Quality Guide, Nursing Home Quality Guide and Home Health Quality Guide brands. For physicians, Health Grades offers its Connecting Point program, allowing physicians to sponsor their own profile, as an alternative form of marketing. The company has an ongoing collaboration with the Leapfrog Group to analyze and report the findings of hospital patient safety surveys. Leapfrog's survey assesses the extent to which hospitals strive to implement patient safety practices. In October 2010, Health Grades was acquired by Vestar Capital Partners V, L.P. affiliates Mountain Acquisition Corp. and Mountain Merger Sub Corp.

The firm offers employee benefits including life, medical, dental, vision and AD&D insurance; a 401(k) plan; and a discount stock purchase plan.

FINANCIALS: **Sales and profits are in thousands of dollars—add 000 to get the full amount. 2011 Note: Financial information for 2011 was not available for all companies at press time.**

2011 Sales: $	2011 Profits: $	**U.S. Stock Ticker: Private**
2010 Sales: $	2010 Profits: $	**Int'l Ticker:**
2009 Sales: $52,498	2009 Profits: $1,784	Int'l Exchange:
2008 Sales: $39,663	2008 Profits: $4,691	Employees: 200 Fiscal Year Ends: 12/31
2007 Sales: $32,742	2007 Profits: $6,748	Parent Company: VESTAR CAPITAL PARTNERS

SALARIES/BENEFITS:

Pension Plan:	ESOP Stock Plan:	Profit Sharing:	Top Exec. Salary: $400,038	Bonus: $353,000
Savings Plan: Y	Stock Purch. Plan: Y		Second Exec. Salary: $240,000	Bonus: $126,223

OTHER THOUGHTS:

Apparent Women Officers or Directors: 4
Hot Spot for Advancement for Women/Minorities: Y

LOCATIONS: ("Y" = Yes)

West:	Southwest:	Midwest:	Southeast:	Northeast:	International:
Y					

HEALTH INSURANCE PLAN OF GREATER NEW YORK

www.hipusa.com

Industry Group Code: 524114

Management:		Sales/Marketing:		Liberal Arts:		Information Systems:		Professionals:		Technical/Scientific:	
Mgmt. Trainees:	Y	Mktg. Professionals:	Y	Gen. Writing/Editing:	Y	Info. Management:	Y	Finance/Acct.:	Y	Engineers, Elec.:	
Experienced Mgmt.:	Y	Retail Sales:		Technical Writing:	Y	Software Dev.:		Law:	Y	Engineers, Other:	
Int'l Business:		Commercial/Industrial:	Y	Graphic Arts/Photog.:		Hardware Dev.:		HR/Other:	Y	Health/Lab	Y
MBA Graduates:	Y	Sales Trainees:	Y	Music:		Consulting/Other:		Training:	Y	Scientists/Research:	
		Advertising Pros.:		Broadcasting:				Health Care:	Y	Petroleum/Chemicals:	
				Other:				Consulting:		Math/Other:	Y

TYPES OF BUSINESS:

Insurance-Medical & Health, HMOs & PPOs

BRANDS/DIVISIONS/AFFILIATES:

ConnectiCare Holding Company
Vera Health Plans
HIP Integrative Wellness
Group Health, Inc. (GHI)
PerfectHealth
EmblemHealth Inc

CONTACTS:

Note: Officers with more than one job title may be intentionally listed here more than once.

Anthony L. Watson, CEO
Frank J. Branchini, COO
Frank J. Branchini, Pres.
Michael D. Fullwood, CFO/Exec. VP
Charlene Maher, Sr. VP-Mktg. & Sales
Thomas A. Nemeth, Sr. VP-Human Resources
William A. Gillespie,, Chief Medical Officer/Sr. VP
John H. Steber, CIO/Exec. VP
Pedro J. Villalba, CTO/Sr. VP-IT
Michael D. Fullwood, General Counsel
Thomas K. Dwyer, Sr. VP-Oper.
Ilene D. Margolin, Sr. VP-Corp. Comm. & Public Affairs
Michael Palmateer, Sr. VP-Finance
Daniel P. Finke, Exec. VP-Healthcare Oper.
George Babitsch, Sr. VP-Sales & Acct. Mgmt.
David S. Abernethy, Sr. VP-Gov't Rel.
William Mastro, Sr. VP/Corp. Sec.
Anthony L. Watson, Chmn.

Phone: 212-421-0473	**Fax:**
Toll-Free: 800-447-8255	
Address: 240 E. 59th St., New York, NY 10022 US	

GROWTH PLANS/SPECIAL FEATURES:

Health Insurance Plan of Greater New York (HIP), owned by EmblemHealth, Inc., is a New York City based HMO. HIP maintains contracts with 160 hospitals, including acute care institutions, to provide services to members. HIP's total network, including subsidiaries, comprises roughly 43,000 physicians and other providers in over 72,000 locations in New York, Connecticut and Massachusetts. The company has acquired several businesses in its history including Vera Health Plans, ConnectiCare and PerfectHealth, bringing its total combined membership to approximately 1.2 million. The company supplements its traditional heath insurance options with a range of programs and discounts for alternative medical practices such as acupuncture, massage therapy and nutritional counseling; mental health services and chemical dependency treatments; pharmacy services; dental plans; and women's wellness programs. HIP Integrative Wellness is an initiative that promotes the importance of spiritual, emotional and mental care along with physical care. The company was one of the first health insurance firms in the nation to translate its web site into Chinese and Korean in addition to Spanish. HIP is affiliated with Group Health, Inc. (GHI) through shared parent company EmblemHealth. The companies have a combined total of 3.4 million members and 106,000 providers in more than 142,000 northeastern locations.

HIP offers its employees reduced-cost medical, dental, optical and life insurance; short- and long-term disability; a pension plan; a 401(k) plan; commuter benefits; college savings plans; discounted health club memberships; flexible spending accounts; and tuition assistance.

FINANCIALS:

Sales and profits are in thousands of dollars—add 000 to get the full amount. 2011 Note: Financial information for 2011 was not available for all companies at press time.

2011 Sales: $	2011 Profits: $	**U.S. Stock Ticker: Nonprofit**
2010 Sales: $	2010 Profits: $	**Int'l Ticker:**
2009 Sales: $	2009 Profits: $	Int'l Exchange:
2008 Sales: $	2008 Profits: $	Employees: Fiscal Year Ends: 12/31
2007 Sales: $	2007 Profits: $	Parent Company: EMBLEMHEALTH INC

SALARIES/BENEFITS:

Pension Plan: Y	ESOP Stock Plan:	Profit Sharing:	Top Exec. Salary: $	Bonus: $
Savings Plan: Y	Stock Purch. Plan:		Second Exec. Salary: $	Bonus: $

OTHER THOUGHTS:

Apparent Women Officers or Directors: 4
Hot Spot for Advancement for Women/Minorities: Y

LOCATIONS: ("Y" = Yes)

West:	Southwest:	Midwest:	Southeast:	Northeast:	International:
				Y	

HEALTHSTREAM INC

www.healthstream.com

Industry Group Code: 611410

Management:		Sales/Marketing:		Liberal Arts:		Information Systems:		Professionals:		Technical/Scientific:	
Mgmt. Trainees:	Y	Mktg. Professionals:	Y	Gen. Writing/Editing:	Y	Info. Management:	Y	Finance/Acct.:	Y	Engineers, Elec.:	
Experienced Mgmt.:	Y	Retail Sales:		Technical Writing:	Y	Software Dev.:	Y	Law:	Y	Engineers, Other:	
Int'l Business:		Commercial/Industrial:	Y	Graphic Arts/Photog.:	Y	Hardware Dev.:		HR/Other:	Y	Health/Lab	
MBA Graduates:	Y	Sales Trainees:	Y	Music:		Consulting/Other:		Training:	Y	Scientists/Research:	
		Advertising Pros.:	Y	Broadcasting:				Health Care:		Petroleum/Chemicals:	
				Other:				Consulting:		Math/Other:	

TYPES OF BUSINESS:

Educational & Training Content
Internet-based Educational Programs

BRANDS/DIVISIONS/AFFILIATES:

HealthStream Learning Center
Authoring Pro
HCAHPS Preparation and Improvement Library
HealthStream Express
HealthStream Research
SimVentures
HealthStream Improvement Center

CONTACTS: *Note: Officers with more than one job title may be intentionally listed here more than once.*

Robert A. Frist, Jr., CEO
Robert A. Frist, Jr., Pres.
Gerard M. Hayden, Jr., CFO/Sr. VP
Jeffrey Doster, CTO/Sr. VP
Kevin P. O'Hara, General Counsel/Sec./Sr. VP
Arthur E. Newman, Exec. VP
J. Edward Pearson, Sr. VP/Pres., HealthStream Research
Michael J. Sousa, Sr. VP
Robert A. Frist, Jr., Chmn.

Phone: 615-301-3100 **Fax:** 615-301-3200
Toll-Free: 800-933-9293
Address: 209 10th Ave. S., Ste. 450, Nashville, TN 37203 US

GROWTH PLANS/SPECIAL FEATURES:

HealthStream, Inc. provides Internet-based training, information and services for the health care industry. The firm provides services to healthcare organizations (HCOs) throughout the U.S. for acute-care facilities and pharmaceutical and medical device (PMD) companies. Within its HCO business unit, HealthStream focuses on expanding its web-based application service provider and its e-learning and installed learning management products. The company's flagship HealthStream Learning Center (HLC) platform provides organizations with Internet-based training and continuing education services. Training material is hosted on a central data center, eliminating the need for on-site installations. HLC enables administrators to configure and modify materials, track completion and predict training expenses. HealthStream has provided training to over 2,500 healthcare organizations, and has approximately 2.45 million hospital-based subscribers currently enrolled in HLC. In addition to its standard HLC subscription, the firm offers the Authoring Pro upgrade, with an industry leading image library, owned by A.D.A.M., Inc. The company also offers HealthStream Express, a streamlined version of HLC. HealthStream Research (HSR) is the newest branch of the company with approximately 1,100 customer hospitals. HSR provides hospital-based customers with patient, physician, employee and community surveys; data analyses of survey results; and other research-based measurement tools to compliment the HLC platform. Its services include HCAHPS Preparation and Improvement Library, an online courseware to address the findings of patient survey research; and HealthStream Improvement Center, a web-based system that allows hospital heads to optimize and accelerate the execution of improvement plans, including those based on results from employee, physician, community and HCAHPS surveys. Software-as-a-service (SOS) web site Insights Online offers actionable HSR data solicited information to healthcare providers. SimVentures, a joint venture between HealthStream and Laerdal Medical, provides products and services that increase the worldwide use of simulation-based learning programs by healthcare providers.

FINANCIALS: **Sales and profits are in thousands of dollars—add 000 to get the full amount. 2011 Note: Financial information for 2011 was not available for all companies at press time.**

2011 Sales: $
2010 Sales: $65,754
2009 Sales: $57,398
2008 Sales: $51,600
2007 Sales: $43,949

2011 Profits: $
2010 Profits: $4,154
2009 Profits: $13,972
2008 Profits: $2,855
2007 Profits: $4,087

U.S. Stock Ticker: HSTM
Int'l Ticker:
Int'l Exchange:
Employees: 432 Fiscal Year Ends: 12/31
Parent Company:

SALARIES/BENEFITS:

Pension Plan: ESOP Stock Plan: Profit Sharing: Top Exec. Salary: $223,333 Bonus: $80,500
Savings Plan: Y Stock Purch. Plan: Second Exec. Salary: $220,000 Bonus: $77,875

OTHER THOUGHTS:

Apparent Women Officers or Directors: 1
Hot Spot for Advancement for Women/Minorities:

LOCATIONS: ("Y" = Yes)

West:	Southwest:	Midwest:	Southeast:	Northeast:	International:
			Y	Y	

HEALTHTRONICS INC

www.healthtronics.com

Industry Group Code: 6214

Management:		Sales/Marketing:		Liberal Arts:		Information Systems:		Professionals:		Technical/Scientific:	
Mgmt. Trainees:		Mktg. Professionals:	Y	Gen. Writing/Editing:		Info. Management:	Y	Finance/Acct.:	Y	Engineers, Elec.:	
Experienced Mgmt.:	Y	Retail Sales:		Technical Writing:	Y	Software Dev.:	Y	Law:	Y	Engineers, Other:	
Int'l Business:	Y	Commercial/Industrial:	Y	Graphic Arts/Photog.:		Hardware Dev.:		HR/Other:	Y	Health/Lab	Y
MBA Graduates:	Y	Sales Trainees:	Y	Music:		Consulting/Other:		Training:	Y	Scientists/Research:	
		Advertising Pros.:	Y	Broadcasting:				Health Care:	Y	Petroleum/Chemicals:	
				Other:				Consulting:		Math/Other:	

TYPES OF BUSINESS:

Lithotripsy Services
Prostate Cancer Treatment
Urologic Staffing

BRANDS/DIVISIONS/AFFILIATES:

RevoLix
Endocare
Endo Pharmaceuticals Holdings Inc

CONTACTS: *Note: Officers with more than one job title may be intentionally listed here more than once.*

Roger H. Kimmel, Chmn.-Endo Pharmaceuticals

Phone: 512-328-2892 **Fax:** 512-328-8303
Toll-Free: 888-252-6575
Address: 9825 Spectrum Dr., Bldg. 3, Austin, TX 78717 US

GROWTH PLANS/SPECIAL FEATURES:

HealthTronics, Inc. is a health care service provider and medical device manufacturer, primarily operating in the urology sector. HealthTronics is the leading provider of urological and lithotripsy services and products in the U.S., serving a network of over 3,000 physicians. Lithotripsy is the non-invasive treatment of kidney stones using shockwaves to break up the stones and allow them to pass painlessly from the body with a short recovery period, usually a matter of hours. The company's lithotripsy services include scheduling, staffing, training, quality assurance, regulatory compliance and contracting with payors, hospitals and surgery centers. HealthTronics provides benign and cancerous prostate disease treatment services. In treating benign prostate disease, the company uses three technologies: photo-selective vaporization of the prostate; trans-urethral needle ablation; and trans-urethral microwave therapy. For treating cancerous conditions, the firm uses cryosurgery, a process that uses a double freeze thaw cycle to destroy cancers cells. HealthTronics also provides related services such as equipment operation, scheduling, training, quality assurance, regulatory compliance and contracting. Additional company operations include providing image-guided radiation therapy (IGRT) technical services for cancer treatment centers; and providing anatomical pathology services, such as laboratory detection and diagnosis services, to urologists. HealthTronics also sells and maintains lithotripters and related spare parts and consumables, and is the sole U.S. distributer of the RevoLix minimally invasive line of laser products for urological procedures. In mid 2010, the firm acquired Endocare, a subsidiary of Endo Pharmaceuticals. Healthtronics Inc. was then acquired by Endo Pharmaceuticals Holdings Corp., making it a wholly-owned subsidiary.

FINANCIALS: **Sales and profits are in thousands of dollars—add 000 to get the full amount. 2011 Note: Financial information for 2011 was not available for all companies at press time.**

2011 Sales: $
2010 Sales: $197,005
2009 Sales: $185,330
2008 Sales: $165,942
2007 Sales: $140,418

2011 Profits: $
2010 Profits: $55,008
2009 Profits: $-3,916
2008 Profits: $-128,693
2007 Profits: $-14,632

U.S. Stock Ticker: Subsidiary
Int'l Ticker:
Int'l Exchange:
Employees: 658 Fiscal Year Ends: 12/31
Parent Company: ENDO PHARMACEUTICALS HOLDINGS INC

SALARIES/BENEFITS:

Pension Plan: ESOP Stock Plan: Profit Sharing: Top Exec. Salary: $390,000 Bonus: $175,000
Savings Plan: Stock Purch. Plan: Second Exec. Salary: $218,400 Bonus: $90,000

OTHER THOUGHTS:

Apparent Women Officers or Directors:
Hot Spot for Advancement for Women/Minorities:

LOCATIONS: ("Y" = Yes)

West:	Southwest:	Midwest:	Southeast:	Northeast:	International:
	Y		Y		

HEARUSA INC

Industry Group Code: 6214

www.hearusa.com

Management:		Sales/Marketing:		Liberal Arts:		Information Systems:		Professionals:		Technical/Scientific:	
Mgmt. Trainees:	Y	Mktg. Professionals:	Y	Gen. Writing/Editing:	Y	Info. Management:	Y	Finance/Acct.:	Y	Engineers, Elec.:	
Experienced Mgmt.:	Y	Retail Sales:	Y	Technical Writing:	Y	Software Dev.:	Y	Law:	Y	Engineers, Other:	
Int'l Business:	Y	Commercial/Industrial:		Graphic Arts/Photog.:		Hardware Dev.:		HR/Other:	Y	Health/Lab	Y
MBA Graduates:	Y	Sales Trainees:	Y	Music:		Consulting/Other:		Training:	Y	Scientists/Research:	
		Advertising Pros.:	Y	Broadcasting:				Health Care:	Y	Petroleum/Chemicals:	
				Other:				Consulting:		Math/Other:	

TYPES OF BUSINESS:

Hearing Care Centers
Hearing Benefits Management
Hearing Aids
Hearing Care Devices

BRANDS/DIVISIONS/AFFILIATES:

Audiology Distribution, LLC
Siemens Hearing Instruments, Inc.

CONTACTS: *Note: Officers with more than one job title may be intentionally listed here more than once.*

Gino Chouinard, Interim CEO
Gino Chouinard, COO
Gino Chouinard, Pres.
Francisco Punal, CFO/Sr. VP
David J. McLachlan, Chmn.

Phone: 561-478-8770 **Fax:** 561-478-9603
Toll-Free: 800-323-3277
Address: 1250 Northpoint Pkwy., West Palm Beach, FL 33407 US

GROWTH PLANS/SPECIAL FEATURES:

HearUSA, Inc. owns and manages a network of approximately 175 HearUSA hearing care centers in 11 states that provide a full range of audiological products and services for the hearing impaired. The company serves customers in Florida, New York, New Jersey, Massachusetts, Ohio, Michigan, Missouri, Pennsylvania, North Carolina, South Carolina and California. HearUSA also sponsors a network of approximately 2,000 credentialed audiologist providers that participate in selected hearing benefit programs contracted by the company with employer groups, health insurers and benefit sponsors in 49 states. Through the network, the company can pursue national hearing care contracts and offer managed hearing benefits in areas outside its center markets. HearUSA services over 400 benefit programs for hearing care with various health maintenance organizations, preferred provider organizations, insurers, benefit administrators and health care providers. Each HearUSA center is staffed by a licensed audiologist or hearing instrument specialist, and most are located in shopping or medical centers. The centers offer a complete range of high quality hearing aids, with emphasis on the latest digital technology along with assessment and evaluation of hearing. In addition, HearUSA offers other products related to hearing care, such as telephone and television amplifiers, telecaptioners and decoders, pocket talkers, specially adapted telephones, alarm clocks, doorbells and fire alarms. HearUSA also offers online information about hearing loss, hearing aids, assistive listening devices and the services offered by hearing health care professionals. In May 2011, the firm filed for Chapter 11 bankruptcy protection. In August 2011, the company agreed to sell all of its assets to Audiology Distribution, LLC, a wholly-owned subsidiary of Siemens Hearing Instruments, Inc.

Employees are offered medical benefits; a 401(k) plan; access to rehabilitation programs; and continuing education programs.

FINANCIALS: **Sales and profits are in thousands of dollars—add 000 to get the full amount. 2011 Note: Financial information for 2011 was not available for all companies at press time.**

2011 Sales: $
2010 Sales: $83,502
2009 Sales: $88,934
2008 Sales: $95,297
2007 Sales: $102,804

2011 Profits: $
2010 Profits: $-7,737
2009 Profits: $1,514
2008 Profits: $-3,201
2007 Profits: $-3,282

U.S. Stock Ticker: EAR
Int'l Ticker:
Int'l Exchange:
Employees: 427 Fiscal Year Ends: 12/31
Parent Company:

SALARIES/BENEFITS:

Pension Plan: ESOP Stock Plan: Profit Sharing: Top Exec. Salary: $406,000 Bonus: $99,408
Savings Plan: Y Stock Purch. Plan: Second Exec. Salary: $333,000 Bonus: $82,840

OTHER THOUGHTS:

Apparent Women Officers or Directors: 1
Hot Spot for Advancement for Women/Minorities:

LOCATIONS: ("Y" = Yes)

West:	Southwest:	Midwest:	Southeast:	Northeast:	International:
Y		Y	Y	Y	Y

HELIOVOLT CORP

www.heliovolt.net

Industry Group Code: 334413

Management:		**Sales/Marketing:**		**Liberal Arts:**		**Information Systems:**		**Professionals:**		**Technical/Scientific:**	
Mgmt. Trainees:		Mktg. Professionals:	Y	Gen. Writing/Editing:		Info. Management:	Y	Finance/Acct.:	Y	Engineers, Elec.:	Y
Experienced Mgmt.:	Y	Retail Sales:		Technical Writing:	Y	Software Dev.:	Y	Law:	Y	Engineers, Other:	Y
Int'l Business:		Commercial/Industrial:	Y	Graphic Arts/Photog.:	Y	Hardware Dev.:	Y	HR/Other:	Y	Health/Lab	
MBA Graduates:	Y	Sales Trainees:	Y	Music:		Consulting/Other:		Training:	Y	Scientists/Research:	Y
		Advertising Pros.:		Broadcasting:				Health Care:		Petroleum/Chemicals:	
				Other:				Consulting:		Math/Other:	Y

TYPES OF BUSINESS:

Architectural Solar Cells
Thin-Film Photovoltaic Technology

BRANDS/DIVISIONS/AFFILIATES:

FASST Technology
SK Group

CONTACTS:

Note: Officers with more than one job title may be intentionally listed here more than once.

Jim Flanary, CEO
Jim Flanary, Pres.
Steve Darnell, CFO
B.J. Stanberry, Chief Strategy Officer
B.J. Stanberry, Chmn.
John Prater, Dir.-Supply Chain

Phone: 512-767-6000 **Fax:**

Toll-Free:

Address: 6301-8 E. Stassney Ln., Bldg. 8, Austin, TX 78744-3055 US

GROWTH PLANS/SPECIAL FEATURES:

Heliovolt Corp. is a producer of high-efficiency thin-film solar energy products, which develops and markets technology for applying thin-film photovoltaic coatings to conventional construction materials. The company's primary solution is its proprietary FASST process, a low-cost, flexible manufacturing process for high-performance solar thin-film photovoltaics that prints copper indium gallium selenide (CIGS), a reliable and high-performing thin film compound, directly onto a variety of substrates, such as glass, steel, metal, composites and some polymers. The firm's products can be adapted for use in architectural modules, such as sunshades, sun louvers and curtains, skylights, curtain walls, spandrels, windows and atria; and can also be used in building-integrated photovoltaic (BIPV) systems by being embedded directly into roofing materials, glass and cladding, sunshades, canopies, skylights and modules. Heliovolt also offers customized printing services for a variety of materials. The firm operates a 122,400 square foot sustainable thin-film factory, located in Austin, Texas. In September 2011, Heliovolt announced that the Korean energy group SK Group had invested $50 million to help develop HelioVolt's global capabilities.

FINANCIALS:

Sales and profits are in thousands of dollars—add 000 to get the full amount. 2011 Note: Financial information for 2011 was not available for all companies at press time.

2011 Sales: $ 2011 Profits: $
2010 Sales: $ 2010 Profits: $
2009 Sales: $ 2009 Profits: $
2008 Sales: $ 2008 Profits: $
2007 Sales: $ 2007 Profits: $

U.S. Stock Ticker: Private
Int'l Ticker:
Int'l Exchange:
Employees: Fiscal Year Ends:
Parent Company:

SALARIES/BENEFITS:

Pension Plan: ESOP Stock Plan: Profit Sharing: Top Exec. Salary: $ Bonus: $
Savings Plan: Stock Purch. Plan: Second Exec. Salary: $ Bonus: $

OTHER THOUGHTS:

Apparent Women Officers or Directors:
Hot Spot for Advancement for Women/Minorities:

LOCATIONS: ("Y" = Yes)

West:	Southwest:	Midwest:	Southeast:	Northeast:	International:
	Y				

HELIX ENERGY SOLUTIONS GROUP INC

www.helixesg.com

Industry Group Code: 213112

Management:		Sales/Marketing:		Liberal Arts:		Information Systems:		Professionals:		Technical/Scientific:	
Mgmt. Trainees:		Mktg. Professionals:	Y	Gen. Writing/Editing:		Info. Management:	Y	Finance/Acct.:	Y	Engineers, Elec.:	
Experienced Mgmt.:	Y	Retail Sales:		Technical Writing:	Y	Software Dev.:		Law:	Y	Engineers, Other:	Y
Int'l Business:	Y	Commercial/Industrial:	Y	Graphic Arts/Photog.:		Hardware Dev.:		HR/Other:	Y	Health/Lab	
MBA Graduates:	Y	Sales Trainees:		Music:		Consulting/Other:		Training:	Y	Scientists/Research:	
		Advertising Pros.:		Broadcasting:				Health Care:		Petroleum/Chemicals:	Y
				Other:				Consulting:		Math/Other:	

TYPES OF BUSINESS:

Subsea Drilling Support Contractor
Subsea Construction, Maintenance & Salvage Services
Remotely Operated Vehicles & Equipment
Oil & Gas Production
Subsea Cable Burial
Oil Spill Response & Containment

BRANDS/DIVISIONS/AFFILIATES:

Kommandor LLC
Deepwater Gateway L.L.C.
Independence Hub LLC
Helix Fast Response System
CloughHelix Pty. Ltd.

CONTACTS: *Note: Officers with more than one job title may be intentionally listed here more than once.*

Owen Kratz, CEO
Bart H. Heijermans, COO/Exec. VP
Owen Kratz, Pres.
Tony Tripodo, CFO/Exec. VP
Alisa B. Johnson, General Counsel/Exec. VP/Corp. Sec.
Jeremy Woulds, VP-Bus. & Commercial Dev.
Lloyd A. Hajdik, Chief Acct. Officer/Sr. VP-Finance
Johnny Edwards, Exec. VP-Oil & Gas
Cliff Chamblee, Exec. VP-Contracting Svcs.
Kimberly Seitz, VP-Internal Audit
Sharon Adams, VP-Global Contracts & Risk
William L. Transier, Chmn.

Phone: 281-618-0400 **Fax:** 281-618-0500
Toll-Free:
Address: 400 N. Sam Houston Pkwy. E., Houston, TX 77060 US

GROWTH PLANS/SPECIAL FEATURES:

Helix Energy Solutions Group, Inc. (Helix) is an international offshore energy company that provides development services and contracting service operations to the open energy market as well as to its own reservoirs. Helix operates in three principal divisions: Contracting Services; Production Facilities; and Oil and Gas. The Contracting Services division, encompassing services for the entire life cycle of a field, utilizes vessels, offshore equipment and methodologies to provide services to reduce the costs associated with offshore hydrocarbon exploration and development activities. The operations of this division consist of three sub-segments: subsea construction, which includes services such as pipelay and robotics in water depths exceeding 1,000 feet; well operations, which engineers, manages and conducts well construction, intervention and decommissioning operations in water depths ranging from 200 to 10,000 feet; and robotics, which comprises Helix's 39 remote operated vehicles (ROVs), five trenchers and two ROVDrills designed for offshore construction. The Production Facilities segment includes the company's ownership in production facilities in the Gulf of Mexico in hub locations where there is potential for significant subsea tieback activity. These include an 81% interest in Kommandor LLC; a 50% interest in Deepwater Gateway L.L.C., which owns the Marco Polo facility; and a 20% interest in Independence Hub LLC, which owns the Independence Hub platform. Helix's Oil and Gas operations include 227 billion cubic feet of natural gas and 25 million barrels of oil in proved reserves located in the Gulf of Mexico. Additionally, the firm has developed the Helix Fast Response System, an oil spill containment resource for the Gulf of Mexico. In 2010, the company established CloughHelix Pty. Ltd., a joint venture with Clough Limited, to provide subsea services in the Asia-Pacific region.

The firm offers employees medical, dental and vision insurance; life insurance; disability coverage; and a 401(k) plan.

FINANCIALS: **Sales and profits are in thousands of dollars—add 000 to get the full amount. 2011 Note: Financial information for 2011 was not available for all companies at press time.**

2011 Sales: $1,398,607 — 2011 Profits: $129,979
2010 Sales: $1,199,838 — 2010 Profits: $-126,988
2009 Sales: $1,461,687 — 2009 Profits: $156,054
2008 Sales: $2,114,074 — 2008 Profits: $-635,930
2007 Sales: $1,767,445 — 2007 Profits: $316,762

U.S. Stock Ticker: HLX
Int'l Ticker:
Int'l Exchange:
Employees: 1,590 Fiscal Year Ends: 12/31
Parent Company:

SALARIES/BENEFITS:

Pension Plan: ESOP Stock Plan: Profit Sharing: Top Exec. Salary: $700,000 Bonus: $2,108,100
Savings Plan: Y Stock Purch. Plan: Second Exec. Salary: $450,000 Bonus: $1,506,549

OTHER THOUGHTS:

Apparent Women Officers or Directors: 4
Hot Spot for Advancement for Women/Minorities: Y

LOCATIONS: ("Y" = Yes)

West:	Southwest:	Midwest:	Southeast:	Northeast:	International:
	Y		Y		Y

HESKA CORP

www.heska.com

Industry Group Code: 325412B

Management:		Sales/Marketing:		Liberal Arts:		Information Systems:		Professionals:		Technical/Scientific:	
Mgmt. Trainees:		Mktg. Professionals:	Y	Gen. Writing/Editing:		Info. Management:	Y	Finance/Acct.:	Y	Engineers, Elec.:	
Experienced Mgmt.:	Y	Retail Sales:		Technical Writing:	Y	Software Dev.:	Y	Law:	Y	Engineers, Other:	
Int'l Business:	Y	Commercial/Industrial:	Y	Graphic Arts/Photog.:		Hardware Dev.:		HR/Other:	Y	Health/Lab	Y
MBA Graduates:	Y	Sales Trainees:	Y	Music:		Consulting/Other:		Training:	Y	Scientists/Research:	Y
		Advertising Pros.:		Broadcasting:				Health Care:	Y	Petroleum/Chemicals:	Y
				Other:				Consulting:		Math/Other:	Y

TYPES OF BUSINESS:

Drugs-Animal Health & Pet Care
Veterinary Diagnostics Products & Services
Animal Dietary Supplements
Veterinary Vaccines

BRANDS/DIVISIONS/AFFILIATES:

Core Companion Animal Health
HESKA Feline UltraNasal FVRCP Vaccine
VitalPath Blood Gas and Electrolyte Analyzer
DRI-CHEM Veterinary Chemistry Analyzer
HEMATRUE Veterinary Hematology Analyzer
VET/IV 2.2 Infusion Pump
ALLERCEPT
Roche Diagnostics Corp.

CONTACTS: *Note: Officers with more than one job title may be intentionally listed here more than once.*

Robert B. Grieve, CEO
Michael J. McGinley, COO
Michael J. McGinley, Pres.
Jason A. Napolitano, CFO/Exec. VP
Claudine Zachara, VP-Mktg.
Nancy Wisnewski, VP-Prod. Dev.
Jason A. Napolitano, Corp. Sec.
Claudine Zachara, VP-Comm.
Michael A. Bent, Controller/Principle Acct. Officer/VP
Laurie Peterson, Gen. Mgr.-Heska Des Moines
Nancy Wisnewski, VP-Tech. Customer Service
Robert B. Grieve, Chmn.
Donald L. Wassom, Managing Dir.-Heska Fribourg/Dir.-Global Allergy

Phone: 970-493-7272	**Fax:** 970-619-3003
Toll-Free: 800-464-3752	
Address: 3760 Rocky Mountain Ave., Loveland, CO 80538 US	

GROWTH PLANS/SPECIAL FEATURES:

Heska Corp. focuses on the discovery, development, manufacture, marketing and support of animal health care products. The company uses biotechnology to create a broad range of diagnostic, therapeutic and vaccine products for dogs, cats and other animals. The business is divided into two segments: Core Companion Animal Health (CCA); and Other Vaccines, Pharmaceuticals and Products (OVP). The CCA segment includes diagnostic instruments and supplies, single-use diagnostic tests, vaccines and pharmaceuticals, primarily for canine and feline use. Its line of veterinary diagnostic instruments includes the DRI-CHEM 4000 Veterinary Chemistry Analyzer, which analyzes blood chemistry and electrolytes; the HEMATRUE Veterinary Hematology Analyzer, a blood analyzer focused on white blood cell count, red blood cell count, platelet count and hemoglobin levels; the VitalPath Blood Gas and Electrolyte Analyzer, which analyzes blood gases, electrolytes and hemocrit; and the VET/IV 2.2 infusion pump for regulated infusion of fluids, drugs or nutritional products. Heska's point-of-care diagnostic tests include tests for heartworms and early renal damage detection products. The E.R.D.-Healthscreen Urine Tests can identify dogs and cats at risk for kidney disease before the majority of kidney function is lost. The company also sells a variety of laboratory diagnostics products, including the ALLERCEPT Definitive Allergy Panels for the determination of specific allergies in dogs, cats and horses. This business segment also markets heartworm prevention pharmaceuticals, hypothyroid treatment supplements and nutritional supplements, immunotherapy treatments for allergies and the Feline Ultranasal FVRCP Vaccine for the prevention of disease caused by respiratory viruses in cats. The OVP business manufactures private-label vaccines and pharmaceutical products that are marketed and distributed by third parties primarily for cattle, although some products are also manufactured for small mammals and fish.

FINANCIALS: **Sales and profits are in thousands of dollars—add 000 to get the full amount. 2011 Note: Financial information for 2011 was not available for all companies at press time.**

2011 Sales: $	2011 Profits: $	**U.S. Stock Ticker: HSKA**
2010 Sales: $55,655	2010 Profits: $ 18	**Int'l Ticker:**
2009 Sales: $75,678	2009 Profits: $2,242	Int'l Exchange:
2008 Sales: $81,653	2008 Profits: $- 850	Employees: 276 Fiscal Year Ends: 12/31
2007 Sales: $82,335	2007 Profits: $34,808	Parent Company:

SALARIES/BENEFITS:

Pension Plan:	ESOP Stock Plan:	Profit Sharing:	Top Exec. Salary: $440,000	Bonus: $
Savings Plan:	Stock Purch. Plan:		Second Exec. Salary: $260,000	Bonus: $

OTHER THOUGHTS:

Apparent Women Officers or Directors: 3
Hot Spot for Advancement for Women/Minorities: Y

LOCATIONS: ("Y" = Yes)

West:	Southwest:	Midwest:	Southeast:	Northeast:	International:
Y		Y			Y

HICKORY TECH CORPORATION

www.hickorytech.com

Industry Group Code: 517110

Management:		Sales/Marketing:		Liberal Arts:		Information Systems:		Professionals:		Technical/Scientific:	
Mgmt. Trainees:		Mktg. Professionals:	Y	Gen. Writing/Editing:	Y	Info. Management:	Y	Finance/Acct.:	Y	Engineers, Elec.:	Y
Experienced Mgmt.:	Y	Retail Sales:		Technical Writing:		Software Dev.:	Y	Law:	Y	Engineers, Other:	
Int'l Business:		Commercial/Industrial:	Y	Graphic Arts/Photog.:		Hardware Dev.:		HR/Other:	Y	Health/Lab	
MBA Graduates:	Y	Sales Trainees:	Y	Music:		Consulting/Other:		Training:	Y	Scientists/Research:	
		Advertising Pros.:		Broadcasting:				Health Care:		Petroleum/Chemicals:	
				Other:				Consulting:		Math/Other:	

TYPES OF BUSINESS:

Local Exchange Carrier
Computer Data Processing
Local Telephone Service
Internet Access
Billing Services
Digital TV

BRANDS/DIVISIONS/AFFILIATES:

National Independent Billing Inc
Crystal Communications Inc
Enventis Telecom Inc
Mankato Citizens Telephone Company
Mid-Communications Inc
Heartland Telecommunications Company of Iowa Inc
Cable Network Inc
CP Telecom

CONTACTS: *Note: Officers with more than one job title may be intentionally listed here more than once.*

John W. Finke, CEO
Carol Wirsbinski, COO/Corp. VP
John W. Finke, Pres.
David A. Christensen, CFO/Sr. VP
Jennifer M. Spaude, Dir.-Mktg.
Mary T. Jacobs, VP-Human Resources
Lane C. Nordquist, CIO
David A. Christensen, Sec.
Walt A. Prahl, VP-Bus. Dev.
Jennifer M. Spaude, Dir.-Public Rel.
Jennifer M. Spaude, Dir.-Investor Rel.
David A. Christensen, Treas.
Lane C. Nordquist, VP/Pres., Info. Solutions Div.
Walt A. Prahl, Corp. VP/Pres., Wholesale Solutions
Damon D. Dutz, VP/Pres., Consumer & Network Solutions Div.
Dale Parker, Chmn.

Phone: 507-387-1151	**Fax:** 507-625-9191
Toll-Free: 800-326-5789	
Address: 221 E. Hickory St., Mankato, MN 56002-3248 US	

GROWTH PLANS/SPECIAL FEATURES:

Hickory Tech Corporation is a telecommunications company. The firm operates in two business segments: telecom and business. Hickory Tech's core business is conducted through its telecom sector, which consists of the operations of six subsidiaries: incumbent local telephone companies Mankato Citizens Telephone Company, Mid-Communications, Inc. and Heartland Telecommunications Company of Iowa, Inc.; one competitive local exchange carrier Crystal Communications, Inc.; unregulated carrier firm Cable Network, Inc.; and data processing subsidiary National Independent Billing, Inc. (NIBI). Crystal Communications provides local telephone service, long-distance, DSL and digital TV, and also connects communications networks of interexchange carriers and wireless carriers with the equipment and facilities of end users. Cable Network administers part of Hickory Tech's southern Minnesota fiber network. NIBI provides data processing and related services to the company and other telecommunications firms. NIBI services include processing of long-distance telephone calls, preparation of subscriber telephone bills, customer record keeping and carrier access bills. In addition to these companies, the telecom sector operates fiber-optic cable facilities. Hickory Tech's business segment, which operates primarily through subsidiary Enventis Telecom, Inc., provides integrated fiber network, IP (Internet protocol) telephony and data services. Enventis own or leases roughly 1,850 route miles of fiber optic table that directly connects clients to the Enventis Network. Enventis specializes in providing integrated unified communication solutions for businesses of all sizes, primarily in the upper Midwest. This segment also includes subsidiary Computer Pro, Inc. (which does business as CP Telecom). In September 2010, Hickory Tech made NFL Network available in the southern Minnesota region.

Employees are offered life, disability, health, dental and vision insurance; flexible spending accounts; an employee stock purchase plan; paid time off; tuition reimbursement; and a 401(k) plan.

FINANCIALS: **Sales and profits are in thousands of dollars—add 000 to get the full amount. 2011 Note: Financial information for 2011 was not available for all companies at press time.**

2011 Sales: $	2011 Profits: $	**U.S. Stock Ticker: HTCO**
2010 Sales: $162,247	2010 Profits: $12,094	**Int'l Ticker:**
2009 Sales: $139,102	2009 Profits: $11,273	Int'l Exchange:
2008 Sales: $153,175	2008 Profits: $8,029	Employees: 463 Fiscal Year Ends: 12/31
2007 Sales: $156,649	2007 Profits: $8,611	Parent Company:

SALARIES/BENEFITS:

Pension Plan:	ESOP Stock Plan:	Profit Sharing:	Top Exec. Salary: $300,000	Bonus: $207,945
Savings Plan: Y	Stock Purch. Plan: Y		Second Exec. Salary: $175,000	Bonus: $106,139

OTHER THOUGHTS:

Apparent Women Officers or Directors: 5
Hot Spot for Advancement for Women/Minorities: Y

LOCATIONS: ("Y" = Yes)

West:	Southwest:	Midwest:	Southeast:	Northeast:	International:
		Y			

HI-TECH PHARMACAL CO INC

www.hitechpharm.com

Industry Group Code: 325412

Management:		**Sales/Marketing:**		**Liberal Arts:**		**Information Systems:**		**Professionals:**		**Technical/Scientific:**	
Mgmt. Trainees:		Mktg. Professionals:	Y	Gen. Writing/Editing:		Info. Management:	Y	Finance/Acct.:	Y	Engineers, Elec.:	
Experienced Mgmt.:	Y	Retail Sales:		Technical Writing:	Y	Software Dev.:	Y	Law:	Y	Engineers, Other:	
Int'l Business:	Y	Commercial/Industrial:	Y	Graphic Arts/Photog.:		Hardware Dev.:		HR/Other:	Y	Health/Lab	Y
MBA Graduates:	Y	Sales Trainees:	Y	Music:		Consulting/Other:		Training:	Y	Scientists/Research:	Y
		Advertising Pros.:		Broadcasting:				Health Care:	Y	Petroleum/Chemicals:	Y
				Other:				Consulting:		Math/Other:	Y

TYPES OF BUSINESS:

Drugs-Generic
Nutritional Products
Over-the-Counter Products
Ophthalmic Products
Manufacturing Contract Services
Inhalation Products
Diabetes Products
Generic Drugs

BRANDS/DIVISIONS/AFFILIATES:

Diabetic Tussin
DiabetiSweet
DiabetDerm
Multi-Betic
Zostrix
Levaquin
Midlothian Laboratories
Xylocaine

CONTACTS: *Note: Officers with more than one job title may be intentionally listed here more than once.*

David S. Seltzer, CEO
David S. Seltzer, Pres.
William Peters, CFO/VP
Kamel Egbaria, Chief Scientific Officer/Exec. VP
David S. Seltzer, Sec.
David S. Seltzer, Treas.
Gary M. April, Pres., Health Care Prod. Div.
Bryce M. Harvey, Pres., Midlothian Laboratories Div.
David S. Caskey, VP-Pharmaceutical Oper., ECR Pharmaceuticals, Inc.
David S. Seltzer, Chmn.

Phone: 631-789-8228	**Fax:** 631-789-8429
Toll-Free:	
Address: 369 Bayview Ave., Amityville, NY 11701-2802 US	

GROWTH PLANS/SPECIAL FEATURES:

Hi-Tech Pharmacal Co., Inc. is a manufacturer and marketer of prescription, over-the-counter (OTC) and nutritional products available in various forms. The firm's products are produced for various disease states, including asthma, bronchial disorders, dermatological disorders, allergies, pain, stomach, oral care, neurological disorders and other conditions. The firm divides its products into three divisions: generic, branded prescription and OTC brands. The generic products division, which formerly operated as Midlothian Laboratories, primarily includes prescription items such as oral solutions and suspensions, topical creams and ointments as well as nasal sprays. This division also manufactures ophthalmic, optic and inhalation products and provides sterile manufacturing contract services. The company's branded prescription products include antihistamines, corticosteroids and analgesic tablets. The firm's OTC brands division, also named the Health Care Products Division, develops and markets a line of branded products primarily for people with diabetes, including Diabetic Tussin, a line of cough medications; DiabetiSweet, sugar substitutes that can be used for baking and cooking; Multi-betic, a daily multi-vitamin; and DiabetiDerm, a diabetic skin care line. This division also sells Zostrix, a brand of capsaisin products for pain and arthritis. In 2010, sales of generic pharmaceuticals represented 82% of total sales, prescriptions accounted for 11% and the health care products line of over-the-counter products accounted for 7%. The company's customers consist of generic distributors, drug wholesalers, chain drug stores, mass merchandise chains, certain government agencies and mail-order pharmacies. In early 2010, the firm acquired the magnesium supplement Mag-Ox product line from Blaine Company, Inc. In early 2011, the firm received FDA approval for the generic form of Xylocaine, a sterile lidocaine HCI jelly developed by APP Pharmaceuticals LLC; the generic form Zantac syrup, developed by GlaxoSmithKline; and the generic form of Levaquin oral solution, a levofloxacin oral solution developed by McNeil Pharmaceutical. In May 2011, the firm divested its Midlothian Laboratories division.

FINANCIALS: **Sales and profits are in thousands of dollars—add 000 to get the full amount. 2011 Note: Financial information for 2011 was not available for all companies at press time.**

2011 Sales: $190,848	2011 Profits: $41,454	**U.S. Stock Ticker: HITK**
2010 Sales: $163,691	2010 Profits: $31,121	**Int'l Ticker:**
2009 Sales: $108,651	2009 Profits: $9,817	Int'l Exchange:
2008 Sales: $62,017	2008 Profits: $-5,098	Employees: 406 Fiscal Year Ends: 4/30
2007 Sales: $58,898	2007 Profits: $-2,036	Parent Company:

SALARIES/BENEFITS:

Pension Plan:	ESOP Stock Plan:	Profit Sharing:	Top Exec. Salary: $451,000	Bonus: $225,000
Savings Plan: Y	Stock Purch. Plan:		Second Exec. Salary: $278,000	Bonus: $1,000,000

OTHER THOUGHTS:

Apparent Women Officers or Directors: 2
Hot Spot for Advancement for Women/Minorities: Y

LOCATIONS: ("Y" = Yes)

West:	Southwest:	Midwest:	Southeast:	Northeast:	International:
				Y	

HOLLYFRONTIER CORPORATION

www.hollyfrontier.com

Industry Group Code: 324110

Management:		Sales/Marketing:		Liberal Arts:		Information Systems:		Professionals:		Technical/Scientific:	
Mgmt. Trainees:		Mktg. Professionals:	Y	Gen. Writing/Editing:		Info. Management:	Y	Finance/Acct.:	Y	Engineers, Elec.:	Y
Experienced Mgmt.:	Y	Retail Sales:		Technical Writing:	Y	Software Dev.:		Law:	Y	Engineers, Other:	Y
Int'l Business:	Y	Commercial/Industrial:	Y	Graphic Arts/Photog.:		Hardware Dev.:		HR/Other:	Y	Health/Lab	
MBA Graduates:	Y	Sales Trainees:		Music:		Consulting/Other:		Training:	Y	Scientists/Research:	
		Advertising Pros.:		Broadcasting:				Health Care:		Petroleum/Chemicals:	Y
				Other:				Consulting:		Math/Other:	

TYPES OF BUSINESS:

Petroleum Refining
Petroleum Distribution
Pipelines & Terminals
Asphalt
Ethanol Blending
Biodiesel Production

BRANDS/DIVISIONS/AFFILIATES:

Holly Corporation
Frontier Oil Corporation
Holly Energy Partners LP
Navajo Refining Co., L.P.
NK Asphalt Partners
Holly Asphalt Co.
Ethanol Management Company
Sabine Biofuels II, LLC

CONTACTS: *Note: Officers with more than one job title may be intentionally listed here more than once.*

Michael C. Jennings, CEO
David L. Lamp, COO/Exec. VP
Michael C. Jennings, Pres.
Doug S. Aron, CFO/Exec. VP
George J. Damiris, Sr. VP-Mktg.
Denise C. McWatters, General Counsel/VP/Sec.
James M. Stump, Sr. VP-Refining Oper.
Bruce R. Shaw, Sr. VP-Corp. Dev. & Strategy
M. Neale Hickerson, VP-Investor Rel.
Scott C. Surplus, Controller/VP
Matthew P. Clifton, Chmn.
George J. Damiris, Sr. VP-Supply

Phone: 214-871-3555	**Fax:** 214-871-3560
Toll-Free:	
Address: 2828 Harwood, Ste. 1300, Dallas, TX 75201 US	

GROWTH PLANS/SPECIAL FEATURES:

HollyFrontier Corporation (the result of a merger between Holly Corporation and Frontier Oil Corporation) is an independent petroleum refiner. The company produces high-value light products such as diesel fuel, gasoline and jet fuel; specialty lubricant products; and specialty and modified asphalt. The firm operates five refineries in Kansas, New Mexico, Oklahoma, Utah and Wyoming with a combined crude oil processing capacity of 443,000 barrels per day (bbl/d), and oversees 900 miles of crude oil pipelines located primarily in west Texas and New Mexico. The El Dorado Refinery, located in El Dorado, Kansas, has a crude oil capacity of 135,000 bbl/d. HollyFrontier's wholly-owned subsidiary Navajo Refining Co., L.P. owns the Navajo refinery located in New Mexico, which has a crude oil capacity of 100,000 bbl/d. In Oklahoma, the firm operates a 125,000-bbl/d capacity refinery in Tulsa. In Utah, HollyFrontier operates the 31,000-bbl/d capacity Woods Cross facility near Salt Lake City, which specializes in high processing regional sweet and Canadian sour crude oils. In Cheyenne, Wyoming, the firm owns a 52,000-bbl/d refinery. The company's operations also include NK Asphalt Partners (operating as Holly Asphalt Co.), which manufactures and markets asphalt products from various terminals in New Mexico, Texas, Arizona and northern Mexico; and HollyFrontier Lubricants. Additionally, HollyFrontier owns Ethanol Management Company, a products terminal and blending facility near Denver; a 50% interest in Sabine Biofuels II, LLC, a biodiesel production facility in Texas; and a 34% interest in Holly Energy Partners, L.P. (HEP), a limited partnership with various logistics assets, including a jet fuel terminal, 10 refined product terminals and four refinery truck rack facilities. In July 2011, Holly Corporation completed a merger with Frontier Oil Corporation. In November 2011, HollyFrontier sold certain pipeline, tankage, loading rack and crude receiving assets at its Kansas and Wyoming facilities to HEP.

FINANCIALS: **Sales and profits are in thousands of dollars—add 000 to get the full amount. 2011 Note: Financial information for 2011 was not available for all companies at press time.**

2011 Sales: $15,439,528	2011 Profits: $1,059,704
2010 Sales: $8,322,929	2010 Profits: $133,051
2009 Sales: $4,834,268	2009 Profits: $53,269
2008 Sales: $5,867,668	2008 Profits: $120,558
2007 Sales: $4,791,742	2007 Profits: $334,128

U.S. Stock Ticker: HFC
Int'l Ticker:
Int'l Exchange:
Employees: 1,661 Fiscal Year Ends: 12/31
Parent Company:

SALARIES/BENEFITS:

Pension Plan:	ESOP Stock Plan:	Profit Sharing:	Top Exec. Salary: $922,500	Bonus: $2,269,000
Savings Plan:	Stock Purch. Plan:		Second Exec. Salary: $553,500	Bonus: $1,000,000

OTHER THOUGHTS:

Apparent Women Officers or Directors: 1
Hot Spot for Advancement for Women/Minorities:

LOCATIONS: ("Y" = Yes)

West:	Southwest:	Midwest:	Southeast:	Northeast:	International:
Y	Y	Y			

HORACE MANN EDUCATORS CORPORATION www.horacemann.com

Industry Group Code: 524126

Management:		Sales/Marketing:		Liberal Arts:		Information Systems:		Professionals:		Technical/Scientific:	
Mgmt. Trainees:	Y	Mktg. Professionals:	Y	Gen. Writing/Editing:	Y	Info. Management:	Y	Finance/Acct.:	Y	Engineers, Elec.:	
Experienced Mgmt.:	Y	Retail Sales:		Technical Writing:	Y	Software Dev.:		Law:	Y	Engineers, Other:	
Int'l Business:		Commercial/Industrial:	Y	Graphic Arts/Photog.:		Hardware Dev.:		HR/Other:	Y	Health/Lab	
MBA Graduates:	Y	Sales Trainees:	Y	Music:		Consulting/Other:		Training:	Y	Scientists/Research:	
		Advertising Pros.:		Broadcasting:				Health Care:		Petroleum/Chemicals:	
				Other:				Consulting:		Math/Other:	Y

TYPES OF BUSINESS:

Insurance, Direct Property & Casualty
Annuities
Life Insurance
Investment Products

BRANDS/DIVISIONS/AFFILIATES:

Horace Mann Insurance Company
Teachers Insurance Company
Horace Mann Life Insurance Company
Horace Mann Property & Casualty Insurance Company
Horace Mann Lloyds
Life by Design

CONTACTS: *Note: Officers with more than one job title may be intentionally listed here more than once.*

Peter H. Heckman, CEO
Peter H. Heckman, Pres.
Dwayne D. Hallman, CFO/Exec. VP
Stephen P. Cardinal, Chief Mktg. Officer/Exec. VP
Paul D. Andrews, Sr. VP-Human Resources
Paul D. Andrews, Sr. VP-Admin. Oper.
Ann M. Caparros, General Counsel/Corp Sec.
Todd Nelson, VP-Finance
Thomas C. Wilkinson, Exec. VP-Property & Casualty
Brent H. Hamann, Sr. VP-Life & Annuity
Ann M. Caparros, Chief Compliance Officer
Bret A. Conklin, Sr. VP/Controller
Gabriel L. Shaheen, Chmn.

Phone: 217-789-2500	**Fax:** 217-788-5161
Toll-Free:	
Address: 1 Horace Mann Plz., Springfield, IL 62715 US	

GROWTH PLANS/SPECIAL FEATURES:

Horace Mann Educators Corporation (HMEC), with $7 billion in assets, underwrites and markets personal lines of property, casualty and life insurance and retirement annuities in the U.S. Its products, including those underwritten by third-parties, are marketed primarily to K-12 teachers, administrators and other employees of public schools and their families. HMEC is one of the largest national, multi-line insurance corporations to focus on the needs of educators, with nearly 1 million customers, typically in households with two sources of income that focus their financial planning needs on retirement, security, savings and primary insurance. The company primarily employs its own insurance agents, many of whom are former teachers or other individuals who have strong ties to the educational community. It operates in three divisions: Property and casualty insurance, annuities and life insurance. The property and casualty division represented 53% of the company's total insurance premiums written and contract deposits in 2010. Private passenger automobile insurance generated approximately 67% of the division's 2010 premiums written, with homeowners insurance generating 32%. The annuities division has approved pay-roll reduction for its 403(b) tax-qualified annuity products for approximately one-third of the 15,400 school districts in the U.S. Approximately 71% of accumulated annuity value in 2010 was 403(b) tax-qualified. Lastly, the life insurance segment primarily offers the Life by Design portfolio of life insurance products, including term, whole and group life insurance policies. The segment has approximately 142,000 life insurance policies in force. The firm's principal insurance subsidiaries located in Illinois are Horace Mann Insurance Company; Teachers Insurance Company; and Horace Mann Life Insurance Company. Other subsidiaries include Horace Mann Property & Casualty Insurance Company, headquartered in California; and Horace Mann Lloyds, which operates out of Texas. Collectively, its principle subsidiaries are licensed to write business in 48 states and Washington, D.C.

FINANCIALS: Sales and profits are in thousands of dollars—add 000 to get the full amount. 2011 Note: Financial information for 2011 was not available for all companies at press time.

2011 Sales: $998,300	2011 Profits: $70,500	**U.S. Stock Ticker: HMN**
2010 Sales: $974,800	2010 Profits: $80,900	**Int'l Ticker:**
2009 Sales: $937,400	2009 Profits: $73,500	Int'l Exchange:
2008 Sales: $834,800	2008 Profits: $10,900	Employees: 1,400 Fiscal Year Ends: 12/31
2007 Sales: $887,005	2007 Profits: $82,788	Parent Company:

SALARIES/BENEFITS:

Pension Plan: Y	ESOP Stock Plan:	Profit Sharing:	Top Exec. Salary: $472,392	Bonus: $364,264
Savings Plan: Y	Stock Purch. Plan:		Second Exec. Salary: $441,441	Bonus: $401,711

OTHER THOUGHTS:

Apparent Women Officers or Directors: 2
Hot Spot for Advancement for Women/Minorities:

LOCATIONS: ("Y" = Yes)

West:	Southwest:	Midwest:	Southeast:	Northeast:	International:
Y	Y	Y	Y	Y	

HOSPITALITY PROPERTIES TRUST

www.hptreit.com

Industry Group Code: 531120

Management:		Sales/Marketing:		Liberal Arts:		Information Systems:		Professionals:		Technical/Scientific:	
Mgmt. Trainees:		Mktg. Professionals:	Y	Gen. Writing/Editing:	Y	Info. Management:	Y	Finance/Acct.:	Y	Engineers, Elec.:	
Experienced Mgmt.:	Y	Retail Sales:		Technical Writing:		Software Dev.:		Law:	Y	Engineers, Other:	
Int'l Business:	Y	Commercial/Industrial:		Graphic Arts/Photog.:		Hardware Dev.:		HR/Other:	Y	Health/Lab Scientists/Research:	
MBA Graduates:	Y	Sales Trainees:		Music:		Consulting/Other:		Training:		Petroleum/Chemicals:	
		Advertising Pros.:	Y	Broadcasting:				Health Care:		Math/Other:	
				Other:				Consulting:			

TYPES OF BUSINESS:

Real Estate Investment Trust
Hotels
Travel Centers

BRANDS/DIVISIONS/AFFILIATES:

REIT Management & Research LLC
Courtyard by Marriott
Candlewood Suites
Staybridge Suites
Residence Inn by Marriott
Crowne Plaza Hotels & Resorts
Hyatt Place
Royal Sonesta Hotels

CONTACTS: *Note: Officers with more than one job title may be intentionally listed here more than once.*

John G. Murray, COO
John G. Murray, Pres.
Mark L. Kleifges, CFO
Jennifer B. Clark, Sec.
Timothy A. Bonang, VP-Investor Rel.
Mark L. Kleifges, Treas.
William J. Sheehan, Dir.-Internal Audit & Compliance
Ethan S.Bornstein, Sr. VP

Phone: 617-964-8389 | **Fax:** 617-969-5730
Toll-Free:
Address: 255 Washington St., 2 Newton Pl., Ste. 300, Newton, MA 02458 US

GROWTH PLANS/SPECIAL FEATURES:

Hospitality Properties Trust (HPT) is a real estate investment trust (REIT) that owns 288 hotels with 42,880 rooms or suites, as well as 185 travel centers, located in 44 U.S. states, Puerto Rico and Canada. All of its properties are operated by unaffiliated hospitality management companies as part of 13 combination management or lease agreements. HPT's hotel properties currently include the following brands: Courtyard by Marriott, Candlewood Suites, Staybridge Suites, Residence Inn by Marriott, Crowne Plaza Hotels & Resorts, Hyatt Place, InterContinental Hotels & Resorts, Marriott Hotels and Resorts, Radisson Hotels & Resorts, TownePlace Suites by Marriott, Country Inns & Suites by Carlson, Holiday Inn Hotels & Resorts, SpringHill Suites by Marriott and Park Plaza Hotels & Resorts. The company's 185 travel centers include 145 operated under the TravelCenters of America brand and 40 operated under the Petro Stopping Centers brand name. All of HPT's management agreements or leases share eight points: first, managers are required to pay a fixed minimum rent; second, operators must pay percentage returns on gross hotel revenues exceeding a certain threshold; third, all agreements are long-term (15 years or more); fourth, each hotel is a part of a combination of hotels and is subject to cross-default obligations with respect to all other hotels in the same combination; fifth, each combination of hotels is geographically diverse; sixth, contract renewals may only be pursued for a combination of hotels, not for each hotel individually; seventh, the firm's agreements require the deposit of 5% to 6% of gross hotel revenues into escrows to fund periodic renovations; finally, each management agreement or lease includes security terms to ensure payments to HPT. In January 2012, the firm acquired Royal Sonesta Hotels in Cambridge Massachusetts.

FINANCIALS: **Sales and profits are in thousands of dollars—add 000 to get the full amount. 2011 Note: Financial information for 2011 was not available for all companies at press time.**

2011 Sales: $1,210,333	2011 Profits: $190,440
2010 Sales: $1,085,488	2010 Profits: $21,351
2009 Sales: $1,037,033	2009 Profits: $193,341
2008 Sales: $1,251,362	2008 Profits: $133,995
2007 Sales: $1,285,479	2007 Profits: $330,968

U.S. Stock Ticker: HPT
Int'l Ticker:
Int'l Exchange:
Employees: 650 Fiscal Year Ends: 12/31
Parent Company:

SALARIES/BENEFITS:

Pension Plan:	ESOP Stock Plan:	Profit Sharing:	Top Exec. Salary: $132,060	Bonus: $
Savings Plan:	Stock Purch. Plan:		Second Exec. Salary: $132,060	Bonus: $

OTHER THOUGHTS:

Apparent Women Officers or Directors: 1
Hot Spot for Advancement for Women/Minorities:

LOCATIONS: ("Y" = Yes)

West:	Southwest:	Midwest:	Southeast:	Northeast:	International:
Y	Y	Y	Y	Y	Y

HOULIHAN LOKEY HOWARD & ZUKIN INC

www.hlhz.com

Industry Group Code: 523110

Management:		Sales/Marketing:		Liberal Arts:		Information Systems:		Professionals:		Technical/Scientific:	
Mgmt. Trainees:		Mktg. Professionals:		Gen. Writing/Editing:	Y	Info. Management:	Y	Finance/Acct.:	Y	Engineers, Elec.:	
Experienced Mgmt.:	Y	Retail Sales:		Technical Writing:		Software Dev.:	Y	Law:	Y	Engineers, Other:	
Int'l Business:	Y	Commercial/Industrial:		Graphic Arts/Photog.:		Hardware Dev.:		HR/Other:	Y	Health/Lab	
MBA Graduates:	Y	Sales Trainees:		Music:		Consulting/Other:		Training:	Y	Scientists/Research:	
		Advertising Pros.:		Broadcasting:				Health Care:		Petroleum/Chemicals:	
				Other:				Consulting:		Math/Other:	

TYPES OF BUSINESS:

Investment Banking
Mergers & Acquisitions
Financing
Financial Advisory Services
Financial Restructuring

BRANDS/DIVISIONS/AFFILIATES:

Orix Corporation
Orix USA Corp.
Business Forum
BusinessForum.hlhz.com

CONTACTS: *Note: Officers with more than one job title may be intentionally listed here more than once.*

Scott Beiser, Co-CEO
Jeff Werbalowsky, Co-CEO/Sr. Managing Dir.
Scott Adelson, Sr. Managing Dir.
Anita Antenucci, Sr. Managing Dir.
Steven Tishman, Global Head-Mergers & Acquisition Group

Phone: 310-553-8871	**Fax:** 310-553-2173
Toll-Free: 800-788-5300	
Address: 1930 Century Park W., Los Angeles, CA 90067 US	

GROWTH PLANS/SPECIAL FEATURES:

Houlihan, Lokey, Howard & Zukin, Inc. (Houlihan Lokey) is an investment banking firm that constitutes the investment banking arm of Orix USA Corp., which in turn is a subsidiary of Orix Corporation. The company's services fall into four categories: mergers and acquisitions (M&A); financing; financial opinions and advisory services; and financial restructuring. With regard to mergers and acquisitions, Houlihan Lokey initializes purchases or divestitures; offers transaction negotiation; coordinates financial closures; and acquires financial assistance for buyers. It also works with firms seeking to set up equity or joint venture partnerships. For financing, the company offers financial products and services targeting mid-sized corporations, including creating employee stock ownership plans (ESOPs). It also raises public and private equity for corporate clients. For financial opinions and advisory services, Houlihan Lokey analyzes everything from transactions and financial reporting to corporate benefits such as equity incentive plans and ESOPs. Lastly, the firm's financial restructuring services focus on helping companies facing bankruptcy or other special situations. In the past 10 years, the firm has handled over 900 restructuring transactions, valued in excess of $1.5 trillion. It has also worked extensively with M&A transactions for distressed companies, completing over 150 such transactions. Besides the above-mentioned services, the company also hosts Business Forum, available at BusinessForum.hlhz.com, an online community for business professionals that allows members, who must meet strict requirements (including minimum salary requirements), to meet and form networks with other members, promote their businesses and discover the services offered by other members.

FINANCIALS: **Sales and profits are in thousands of dollars—add 000 to get the full amount. 2011 Note: Financial information for 2011 was not available for all companies at press time.**

2011 Sales: $	2011 Profits: $	**U.S. Stock Ticker: Subsidiary**
2010 Sales: $	2010 Profits: $	**Int'l Ticker:**
2009 Sales: $	2009 Profits: $	Int'l Exchange:
2008 Sales: $	2008 Profits: $	Employees: Fiscal Year Ends:
2007 Sales: $	2007 Profits: $	Parent Company: ORIX CORPORATION

SALARIES/BENEFITS:

Pension Plan:	ESOP Stock Plan:	Profit Sharing:	Top Exec. Salary: $	Bonus: $
Savings Plan:	Stock Purch. Plan:		Second Exec. Salary: $	Bonus: $

OTHER THOUGHTS:

Apparent Women Officers or Directors: 1
Hot Spot for Advancement for Women/Minorities:

LOCATIONS: ("Y" = Yes)

West:	Southwest:	Midwest:	Southeast:	Northeast:	International:
Y	Y	Y	Y	Y	Y

HUB GROUP INC

www.hubgroup.com

Industry Group Code: 4885

Management:		Sales/Marketing:		Liberal Arts:		Information Systems:		Professionals:		Technical/Scientific:	
Mgmt. Trainees:		Mktg. Professionals:	Y	Gen. Writing/Editing:		Info. Management:	Y	Finance/Acct.:	Y	Engineers, Elec.:	
Experienced Mgmt.:	Y	Retail Sales:		Technical Writing:		Software Dev.:	Y	Law:	Y	Engineers, Other:	
Int'l Business:	Y	Commercial/Industrial:	Y	Graphic Arts/Photog.:		Hardware Dev.:		HR/Other:	Y	Health/Lab	
MBA Graduates:	Y	Sales Trainees:	Y	Music:		Consulting/Other:		Training:		Scientists/Research:	
		Advertising Pros.:		Broadcasting:				Health Care:		Petroleum/Chemicals:	
				Other:				Consulting:		Math/Other:	

TYPES OF BUSINESS:

Freight Transportation Arrangement
Trucking & Drayage Services
Warehousing
Supply Chain Management
Store Displays & Fixtures Installation
Pharmaceutical Distribution
Logistics Consulting

BRANDS/DIVISIONS/AFFILIATES:

Unyson Logistics
Comtrak Logistics Inc
Vendor Interface
Trucker Advantage
Customer Advantage
Exel Transportation Services

CONTACTS: *Note: Officers with more than one job title may be intentionally listed here more than once.*

David P. Yeager, CEO
Mark A. Yeager, COO
Mark A. Yeager, Pres.
Terri A. Pizzuto, CFO/Exec. VP
David L. Marsh, Chief Mktg. Officer
Dennis R. Polsen, Exec. VP-Info. Svcs.
David C. Zeilstra, General Counsel/VP/Sec.
Terri A. Pizzuto, Treas.
David C. Porter, Exec. VP-Supply Chian Solutions
Christopher R. Kravas, Chief Intermodal Officer
James B. Gaw, Exec. VP-Sales
James J. Damman, Pres., Mode Transportation
David P. Yeager, Chmn.
Donald G. Maltby, Chief Supply Chain Officer

Phone: 630-271-3600 **Fax:** 630-964-6475
Toll-Free:
Address: 3050 Highland Pkwy., Ste. 100, Downers Grove, IL 60515 US

GROWTH PLANS/SPECIAL FEATURES:

Hub Group, Inc. is a leading North American asset-light freight transportation company. Hub's services include comprehensive intermodal, truck brokerage and logistics services, which it offers through a network of operating centers throughout the U.S., Canada and Mexico. As an intermodal marketing company, Hub arranges for the movement of freight in containers and trailers, typically over long distances of 750 miles or more. The firm contracts with railroads to provide transportation for the long-haul portion of the shipment and with local trucking companies for pickup and delivery. Hub is one of the largest truck brokers in the U.S., matching its customers' needs with carriers' capacity to provide the most effective service and price combinations. The company's logistics business operates under the name of Unyson Logistics, and offers such services as shipment optimization, load consolidation, mode selection, carrier management, load planning and web-based shipment visibility, with multi-modal transportation capabilities including small parcel, heavyweight expedited, less-than-truckload, truckload, intermodal and railcar. Subsidiary Comtrak Logistics, Inc. provides hub's drayage services (i.e. unloading goods hauled by rail onto trucks and transporting them to another location). Comtrak owns 283 tractors, leases or owns 502 trailers, employs 283 drivers and contracts 1,414 owner-operators. Hub Group provides several online services through its website, such as Vendor Interface, which tenders loads to drayage partners and captures event status information; Trucker Advantage; an information exchange for available hub loads and carrier capacity; and Customer Advantage, which offers customers immediate pricing as well as the ability to place orders, track shipments and review historical shipping data. In April 2011, the firm acquired agent-based intermodal and truck brokerage services specialist Exel Transportation Services for roughly $83 million. Also in 2011, Comtrak acquired certain assets of intermodal drayage carriers Domestic Transport, Inc. and Challenge Transportation.

FINANCIALS: **Sales and profits are in thousands of dollars—add 000 to get the full amount. 2011 Note: Financial information for 2011 was not available for all companies at press time.**

2011 Sales: $2,751,534	2011 Profits: $58,178
2010 Sales: $1,833,737	2010 Profits: $43,458
2009 Sales: $1,510,970	2009 Profits: $34,265
2008 Sales: $1,860,608	2008 Profits: $59,245
2007 Sales: $1,658,168	2007 Profits: $59,799

U.S. Stock Ticker: HUBG
Int'l Ticker:
Int'l Exchange:
Employees: 1,392 Fiscal Year Ends: 12/31
Parent Company:

SALARIES/BENEFITS:

Pension Plan:	ESOP Stock Plan:	Profit Sharing:	Top Exec. Salary: $574,867	Bonus: $517,380
Savings Plan: Y	Stock Purch. Plan:		Second Exec. Salary: $460,000	Bonus: $414,000

OTHER THOUGHTS:

Apparent Women Officers or Directors: 1
Hot Spot for Advancement for Women/Minorities:

LOCATIONS: ("Y" = Yes)

West:	Southwest:	Midwest:	Southeast:	Northeast:	International:
Y	Y	Y	Y	Y	Y

HUDSON CITY BANCORP INC

www.hcbk.com

Industry Group Code: 522110

Management:		Sales/Marketing:		Liberal Arts:		Information Systems:		Professionals:		Technical/Scientific:	
Mgmt. Trainees:	Y	Mktg. Professionals:	Y	Gen. Writing/Editing:	Y	Info. Management:	Y	Finance/Acct.:	Y	Engineers, Elec.:	
Experienced Mgmt.:	Y	Retail Sales:		Technical Writing:		Software Dev.:		Law:	Y	Engineers, Other:	
Int'l Business:		Commercial/Industrial:		Graphic Arts/Photog.:		Hardware Dev.:		HR/Other:	Y	Health/Lab	
MBA Graduates:	Y	Sales Trainees:		Music:		Consulting/Other:		Training:	Y	Scientists/Research:	
		Advertising Pros.:	Y	Broadcasting:				Health Care:		Petroleum/Chemicals:	
				Other:				Consulting:		Math/Other:	

TYPES OF BUSINESS:

Banking
Consumer Lending
Mortgages

BRANDS/DIVISIONS/AFFILIATES:

Hudson City Savings Bank

CONTACTS:

Note: Officers with more than one job title may be intentionally listed here more than once.

Ronald E. Hermance, Jr., CEO
Denis J. Salamone, COO
Denis J. Salamone, Pres.
James C. Kranz, CFO/Exec. VP
Steven Schlesinger, Sr. VP-Info. Svcs.
Veronica Olszewski, Corp. Sec./Sr. VP/Treas.
Susan K. Munhall, Dir.-Investor Rel.
Anthony J. Fabiano, Sr. VP-Finance
Thomas E. Laird, Chief Lending Officer/Exec. VP
V. Barry Corridon, Sr. VP-Mortgage Servicing
Louis J. Beierle, Sr. VP
Ronald J. Butkovich, Sr. VP
Ronald E. Hermance, Jr., Chmn.

Phone: 201-967-1900 **Fax:**
Toll-Free:
Address: W. 80 Century Rd., Paramus, NJ 07652 US

GROWTH PLANS/SPECIAL FEATURES:

Hudson City Bancorp, Inc. serves as the holding company of its only subsidiary Hudson City Savings Bank (HCS). HCS is a federally chartered stock savings bank with over $60 billion in assets, operating 135 branch locations throughout the New York Metropolitan area and New Jersey, as well as nine branches in Connecticut. Of the branches, 97 are dispersed in 17 counties throughout New Jersey. As a retail savings bank, HCS offers traditional deposit products such as savings and club accounts, CDs, retirement accounts and personal checking accounts. HCS loan portfolio consists of one-to-four family residential first mortgage loans. HCS offers multi-family and commercial mortgage loans; construction loans; and consumer loans, which primarily consist of fixed-rate second mortgage loans and home equity credit lines. The company's primary lending emphasis is the origination and purchase of first mortgage loans secured by family properties that serve as the primary or secondary residence of the owner. Approximately 78.4% of the firm's mortgage loan portfolio was secured by real estate located in the states of New Jersey, New York and Connecticut. Multi-family mortgage loans generally are secured by multi-family rental properties and are normally offered with both fixed and adjustable interest rates. Most commonly, these loans are originated for terms of up to 30 years. The bank also originates construction loans to local builders and to individuals who have a contract with a builder for the construction of their residence. The company's construction loans are disbursed as certain portions of the project are completed. The bank's consumer and other loans typically offer fixed-rate second mortgage loans and home equity credit lines. The company also serves customers across the U.S. through online savings accounts.

Hudson City Bancorp offers health, dental and life insurance; a profit incentive bonus; and an employee stock ownership program.

FINANCIALS:

Sales and profits are in thousands of dollars—add 000 to get the full amount. 2011 Note: Financial information for 2011 was not available for all companies at press time.

2011 Sales: $2,281,554	2011 Profits: $-735,989
2010 Sales: $2,947,490	2010 Profits: $537,206
2009 Sales: $2,975,370	2009 Profits: $527,244
2008 Sales: $2,661,710	2008 Profits: $445,558
2007 Sales: $2,134,778	2007 Profits: $295,858

U.S. Stock Ticker: HCBK
Int'l Ticker:
Int'l Exchange:
Employees: 1,569 Fiscal Year Ends: 12/31
Parent Company:

SALARIES/BENEFITS:

Pension Plan:	ESOP Stock Plan: Y	Profit Sharing: Y	Top Exec. Salary: $1,621,538	Bonus: $2,000,000
Savings Plan:	Stock Purch. Plan:		Second Exec. Salary: $985,385	Bonus: $1,000,000

OTHER THOUGHTS:

Apparent Women Officers or Directors: 2
Hot Spot for Advancement for Women/Minorities:

LOCATIONS: ("Y" = Yes)

West:	Southwest:	Midwest:	Southeast:	Northeast:	International:
				Y	

IBASIS INC

www.ibasis.com

Industry Group Code: 517110

Management:		Sales/Marketing:		Liberal Arts:		Information Systems:		Professionals:		Technical/Scientific:	
Mgmt. Trainees:		Mktg. Professionals:	Y	Gen. Writing/Editing:	Y	Info. Management:	Y	Finance/Acct.:	Y	Engineers, Elec.:	Y
Experienced Mgmt.:	Y	Retail Sales:		Technical Writing:		Software Dev.:	Y	Law:	Y	Engineers, Other:	
Int'l Business:	Y	Commercial/Industrial:	Y	Graphic Arts/Photog.:		Hardware Dev.:		HR/Other:	Y	Health/Lab	
MBA Graduates:	Y	Sales Trainees:	Y	Music:		Consulting/Other:		Training:	Y	Scientists/Research:	
		Advertising Pros.:	Y	Broadcasting:				Health Care:		Petroleum/Chemicals:	
				Other:				Consulting:		Math/Other:	

TYPES OF BUSINESS:

International Long Distance Service
Wholesale Voice Services
Prepaid Calling Cards
VoIP Service

BRANDS/DIVISIONS/AFFILIATES:

Mobile Matrix
DirectSIP
Pingo
KPN B.V.
Royal KPN NV

CONTACTS: *Note: Officers with more than one job title may be intentionally listed here more than once.*

Willem Offerhaus, CEO
Paul Floyd, COO
Roelant Lyppens, CFO
Gert-Jan Huizer, Sr. VP-Mktg.
Tamah Solomon Rosker, VP-Human Resources
Ajay T. Joseph, CTO
Gert-Jan Huizer, Sr. VP-Prod. Mgmt.
Ellen W. Schmidt, General Counsel/VP/Corp. Sec.
Brad Guth, Sr. VP-Oper.
Kristin Bynoe, Contact-Media & Analyst Rel.
Eelco Blok, Chmn.
Edwin van Ierland, Global Sales Officer

Phone: 781-505-7500 **Fax:** 781-505-7300
Toll-Free:
Address: 20 2nd Ave., Burlington, MA 01803 US

GROWTH PLANS/SPECIAL FEATURES:

IBasis, Inc. is a carrier of international telephone calls over a global Voice over IP (VoIP) infrastructure as well as over a Time-division multiplexing (TDM) infrastructure. In addition to its international voice services, the company also offers mobile data services and prepaid calling services. The company operates a wholesale trading business, in which it connects buyers and sellers of international telecommunications services and a retail business. In its trading business, iBasis receives voice traffic from buyers, local service providers and telecommunications carriers. The firm uses proprietary technology to automate the selection of routes and termination partners based on a variety of performance, quality and business metrics. It offers its trading service on a wholesale basis to carriers, mobile operators, consumer VoIP companies, telephony resellers and other service providers worldwide. iBasis has call termination agreements with local service providers in more than 100 countries in North America, Europe, Asia, the Middle East, Latin America, Africa and Australia. In the mobile market, the company offers its Mobile Matrix portfolio of mobile data services, which includes mobile messaging and roaming. In targeting the emerging consumer VoIP providers, iBasis has expanded its DirectVoIP IP interconnection offering with DirectSIP, which supports Session Initiation Protocol interconnection. The firm's retail business consists of retail prepaid calling cards that are marketed through distributors primarily to ethnic communities within major metropolitan markets in the U.S. and Pingo, an online international prepaid calling service. Both offerings can be private-labeled for other service providers. IBasis is a subsidiary Royal KPN N.V., a Dutch incumbent telecommunications company.

Employees are offered health and dental insurance; life insurance; and disability coverage.

FINANCIALS: **Sales and profits are in thousands of dollars—add 000 to get the full amount. 2011 Note: Financial information for 2011 was not available for all companies at press time.**

2011 Sales: $ | 2011 Profits: $
2010 Sales: $ | 2010 Profits: $
2009 Sales: $ | 2009 Profits: $
2008 Sales: $ | 2008 Profits: $
2007 Sales: $ | 2007 Profits: $

U.S. Stock Ticker: Subsidiary
Int'l Ticker:
Int'l Exchange:
Employees: Fiscal Year Ends: 12/31
Parent Company: ROYAL KPN NV

SALARIES/BENEFITS:

Pension Plan: | ESOP Stock Plan: | Profit Sharing: | Top Exec. Salary: $490,000 | Bonus: $281,750
Savings Plan: Y | Stock Purch. Plan: | | Second Exec. Salary: $360,000 | Bonus: $207,000

OTHER THOUGHTS:

Apparent Women Officers or Directors: 2
Hot Spot for Advancement for Women/Minorities:

LOCATIONS: ("Y" = Yes)

West:	Southwest:	Midwest:	Southeast:	Northeast:	International:
Y			Y	Y	Y

ICONIX BRAND GROUP INC

www.iconixbrand.com

Industry Group Code: 3162

Management:		Sales/Marketing:		Liberal Arts:		Information Systems:		Professionals:		Technical/Scientific:	
Mgmt. Trainees:		Mktg. Professionals:	Y	Gen. Writing/Editing:	Y	Info. Management:	Y	Finance/Acct.:	Y	Engineers, Elec.:	
Experienced Mgmt.:	Y	Retail Sales:		Technical Writing:		Software Dev.:		Law:	Y	Engineers, Other:	
Int'l Business:	Y	Commercial/Industrial:	Y	Graphic Arts/Photog.:		Hardware Dev.:		HR/Other:	Y	Health/Lab	
MBA Graduates:	Y	Sales Trainees:	Y	Music:		Consulting/Other:		Training:		Scientists/Research:	
		Advertising Pros.:		Broadcasting:				Health Care:		Petroleum/Chemicals:	
				Other:	Y			Consulting:		Math/Other:	

TYPES OF BUSINESS:

Brand Management

BRANDS/DIVISIONS/AFFILIATES:

Candie's
Joe Boxer
Mudd
London Fog
Mossimo
Ocean Pacific
Danskin
The Sharper Image

CONTACTS: *Note: Officers with more than one job title may be intentionally listed here more than once.*

Neil Cole, CEO
Yehuda Shmidman, COO
Neil Cole, Pres.
Warren Clamen, CFO/Exec. VP
Dari Marder, Chief Mktg. Officer
Lanie List, Chief Merch. Officer
Andrew Tarshis, General Counsel/Exec. VP
David Blumberg, Head-Strategic Dev./Exec. VP
Tara Levy, Dir.-Public Rel.
Neil Cole, Chmn.

Phone: 212-730-0030 **Fax:** 212-391-2057
Toll-Free:
Address: 1450 Broadway, 3rd Fl., New York, NY 10018 US

GROWTH PLANS/SPECIAL FEATURES:

Iconix Brand Group, Inc. is a brand management company engaged in the licensing, marketing and trend direction of its owned consumer brands. These brands include Mossimo, Badgley Mischka, Candie's, Bongo, Joe Boxer, Rampage, Mudd, London Fog, Ocean Pacific/OP, Danskin, Rocawear, Fieldcrest, Cannon, Royal Velvet, Charisma, Starter and Waverly. Mossimo is a contemporary lifestyle brand; it is licensed in the U.S. exclusively by Target for casual sportswear, denim, swimwear, body wear, watches, handbags and other fashion accessories. Badgley Mischka is a premier couture eveningwear brand. Candie's is a junior lifestyle brand in the footwear, apparel and accessories categories. Bongo offers a range of women's and children's casual apparel and accessories. Joe Boxer is an underwear, sleepwear and loungewear brand. Rampage is a contemporary women's and junior's sportswear brand. Mudd is a junior apparel brand, with a primary presence in the denim and footwear categories. London Fog is a classic brand for outerwear, cold weather accessories, umbrellas, luggage and travel products. Ocean Pacific and OP are global action-sports lifestyle brands that have roots as a 1960's surfboard label. Danskin is a brand of women's active wear and fitness equipment. Rocawear is an urban lifestyle apparel brand. Fieldcrest, Cannon, Royal Velvet and Charisma manufacture home textiles. Starter is a brand of athletic apparel and footwear. The Waverly brand focuses on home furnishings and lifestyle products. Additionally, the firm owns interests in Hardy Way LLC, the owner of the Ed Hardy brands; and the Ecko portfolio of brands, including Zoo York and Mark Ecko. In October 2011, the firm agreed to acquire The Sharper Image brand and certain assets from Sharper Image Acquisition, LLC for approximately $65.6 million.

FINANCIALS: **Sales and profits are in thousands of dollars—add 000 to get the full amount. 2011 Note: Financial information for 2011 was not available for all companies at press time.**

2011 Sales: $369,800 — 2011 Profits: $126,100
2010 Sales: $332,559 — 2010 Profits: $110,480
2009 Sales: $232,058 — 2009 Profits: $76,031
2008 Sales: $216,761 — 2008 Profits: $62,908
2007 Sales: $160,004 — 2007 Profits: $63,755

U.S. Stock Ticker: ICON
Int'l Ticker:
Int'l Exchange:
Employees: 133 Fiscal Year Ends: 12/31
Parent Company:

SALARIES/BENEFITS:

Pension Plan: ESOP Stock Plan: Profit Sharing:
Savings Plan: Y Stock Purch. Plan:
Top Exec. Salary: $1,000,000 Bonus: $1,000,000
Second Exec. Salary: $600,000 Bonus: $649,000

OTHER THOUGHTS:

Apparent Women Officers or Directors: 3
Hot Spot for Advancement for Women/Minorities: Y

LOCATIONS: ("Y" = Yes)

West:	Southwest:	Midwest:	Southeast:	Northeast:	International:
				Y	Y

ICU MEDICAL INC

www.icumed.com

Industry Group Code: 33911

Management:		Sales/Marketing:		Liberal Arts:		Information Systems:		Professionals:		Technical/Scientific:	
Mgmt. Trainees:		Mktg. Professionals:	Y	Gen. Writing/Editing:		Info. Management:	Y	Finance/Acct.:	Y	Engineers, Elec.:	
Experienced Mgmt.:	Y	Retail Sales:		Technical Writing:	Y	Software Dev.:	Y	Law:	Y	Engineers, Other:	Y
Int'l Business:	Y	Commercial/Industrial:	Y	Graphic Arts/Photog.:		Hardware Dev.:		HR/Other:	Y	Health/Lab	Y
MBA Graduates:	Y	Sales Trainees:	Y	Music:		Consulting/Other:		Training:	Y	Scientists/Research:	Y
		Advertising Pros.:		Broadcasting:				Health Care:	Y	Petroleum/Chemicals:	
				Other:				Consulting:		Math/Other:	

TYPES OF BUSINESS:

Equipment-Intravenous Connection Devices
Custom IV Systems

BRANDS/DIVISIONS/AFFILIATES:

CLAVE
CLC2000 Positive Pressure Connector
Lopez Valve
TEGO Connector
SetSource
Neutron Neutral-Pressure Needleless Connector

CONTACTS:

Note: Officers with more than one job title may be intentionally listed here more than once.

George A. Lopez, CEO
George A. Lopez, Pres.
Scott E. Lamb, CFO
Richard A. Costello, VP-Mktg. & Sales
Alison D. Burcar, VP-Prod. Dev.
Scott E. Lamb, Corp. Sec.
Steven C. Riggs, VP-Oper.
Scott E. Lamb, Treas.
George A. Lopez, Chmn.

Phone: 949-366-2183	**Fax:** 949-366-8368
Toll-Free: 800-824-7890	
Address: 951 Calle Amanecer, San Clemente, CA 92673 US	

GROWTH PLANS/SPECIAL FEATURES:

ICU Medical, Inc. develops, manufactures and sells disposable medical connection systems for use in intravenous (I.V.) therapy applications. These products are designed to protect health care workers and their patients from exposure to infectious diseases such as hepatitis B and C and HIV by accidental needle sticks. The firm also produces custom I.V. systems and low-cost generic I.V. systems. The company's main product, the CLAVE, is a one-piece, needleless I.V. connection device that represents about 35% of the company's revenue. The CLAVE allows protected, secure and sterile I.V. connections without needles. Other products include the CLC2000 Positive Pressure Connector, which prevents the back-flow of blood into the catheter; the TEGO Connector, an infection control connector for use with dialysis catheters; and Lopez Valve, which allows the user to access enteral systems without breaking open the lines, protecting the user from exposure to bodily fluids. ICU focuses on the development and implementation of proprietary software for custom product design, customer orders and order tracking, combined with an innovative system to coordinate the manufacture of components in the U.S., assembly of components into sets in Mexico and Italy and international distribution of finished products. ICU has a contract with specialty pharmaceutical and medication delivery firm Hospira, Inc., wherein ICU manufactures all custom I.V. sets for Hospira, and the two companies jointly promote the products under the SetSource name. Approximately 40% of the firm's revenues are derived from sales to Hospira. In August 2010, ICU Medical received FDA clearance for its Neutron Neutral-Pressure Needleless Connector.

FINANCIALS:

Sales and profits are in thousands of dollars—add 000 to get the full amount. 2011 Note: Financial information for 2011 was not available for all companies at press time.

2011 Sales: $302,200	2011 Profits: $44,700	**U.S. Stock Ticker: ICUI**
2010 Sales: $284,582	2010 Profits: $30,929	**Int'l Ticker:**
2009 Sales: $231,513	2009 Profits: $26,557	Int'l Exchange:
2008 Sales: $204,726	2008 Profits: $24,300	Employees: 2,216 Fiscal Year Ends: 12/31
2007 Sales: $188,138	2007 Profits: $23,079	Parent Company:

SALARIES/BENEFITS:

Pension Plan:	ESOP Stock Plan:	Profit Sharing:	Top Exec. Salary: $670,000	Bonus: $1,137,500
Savings Plan: Y	Stock Purch. Plan:		Second Exec. Salary: $341,000	Bonus: $304,600

OTHER THOUGHTS:

Apparent Women Officers or Directors:
Hot Spot for Advancement for Women/Minorities:

LOCATIONS: ("Y" = Yes)

West:	Southwest:	Midwest:	Southeast:	Northeast:	International:
Y				Y	Y

IDACORP INC

www.idacorpinc.com

Industry Group Code: 2211

Management:		Sales/Marketing:		Liberal Arts:		Information Systems:		Professionals:		Technical/Scientific:	
Mgmt. Trainees:		Mktg. Professionals:	Y	Gen. Writing/Editing:	Y	Info. Management:	Y	Finance/Acct.:	Y	Engineers, Elec.:	Y
Experienced Mgmt.:	Y	Retail Sales:		Technical Writing:		Software Dev.:		Law:	Y	Engineers, Other:	Y
Int'l Business:	Y	Commercial/Industrial:	Y	Graphic Arts/Photog.:		Hardware Dev.:		HR/Other:	Y	Health/Lab	
MBA Graduates:	Y	Sales Trainees:	Y	Music:		Consulting/Other:		Training:	Y	Scientists/Research:	
		Advertising Pros.:		Broadcasting:				Health Care:		Petroleum/Chemicals:	Y
				Other:				Consulting:		Math/Other:	

TYPES OF BUSINESS:

Utility-Electric
Hydroelectric Generation
Energy Solutions & Marketing
Housing & Real Estate Investments

BRANDS/DIVISIONS/AFFILIATES:

Idaho Power Company
IDACORP Financial Services Inc
Ida-West Energy Company
Idaho Energy Resources Co

CONTACTS: *Note: Officers with more than one job title may be intentionally listed here more than once.*

J. LaMont Keen, CEO
J. LaMont Keen, Pres.
Darrel T. Anderson, CFO
Luci K. McDonald, VP-Human Resources & Corp. Svcs.
Dennis C. Gribble, CIO/VP
Darrel T. Anderson, Exec. VP-Admin. Svcs.
Rex Blackburn, General Counsel/Sr. VP
Daniel B. Minor, Exec. VP-Oper.
Lori D. Smith, VP-Corp. Dev.
Jeffery L. Malmen, VP-Public Affairs
Ken Petersen, Chief Acct. Officer/Corp. Controller
Lori D. Smith, Chief Risk Officer/VP
Steve R. Keen, VP-Finance/Treas.
Patrick A. Harrington, Corp. Sec.
Lisa Grow, VP-Power Supply
Gary J. Michael, Chmn.
Naomi C. Shankel, VP-Supply Chain

Phone: 208-388-2200	**Fax:**
Toll-Free:	
Address: 1221 W. Idaho St., Boise, ID 83702-5627 US	

GROWTH PLANS/SPECIAL FEATURES:

IDACORP, Inc. is a holding company whose principal operating subsidiary is Idaho Power Company (IPC). IPC, which accounted for 98.5% of the company's 2010 net income, is an investor-owned utility company involved in the generation, purchase, transmission, distribution and sale of electricity. Its service area covers a 24,000-square-mile region that includes 71 cities in Idaho and nine in Oregon, serving 492,000 customers. IPC owns and operates 17 hydroelectric power plants, two natural gas-fired plants and shares ownership in three coal-fired generating plants. It is the parent company of Idaho Energy Resources Co., a joint venture with Bridger Coal Co., which supplies coal to the Jim Bridger generating plant operated by IPC. Other subsidiaries of IDACORP include Ida-West Energy (Ida-West), which has a 50% interest in nine hydroelectric plants in Idaho and California; and IDACORP Financial Services, Inc. (IFS), which owns and manages tax-advantaged real estate investments, historic real estate properties and other multi-family apartment style homes. IFS invests primarily in affordable housing developments, which provide a return principally by reducing federal and state income taxes through tax credits and accelerated tax depreciation benefits. As of 2010, IFS investments cover 49 states, Puerto Rico and the U.S. Virgin Islands and include over 700 properties.

FINANCIALS: **Sales and profits are in thousands of dollars—add 000 to get the full amount. 2011 Note: Financial information for 2011 was not available for all companies at press time.**

2011 Sales: $1,026,756	2011 Profits: $166,693	**U.S. Stock Ticker: IDA**
2010 Sales: $1,036,029	2010 Profits: $142,798	**Int'l Ticker:**
2009 Sales: $1,049,800	2009 Profits: $124,350	Int'l Exchange:
2008 Sales: $960,414	2008 Profits: $98,414	Employees: 2,032 Fiscal Year Ends: 12/31
2007 Sales: $879,394	2007 Profits: $82,339	Parent Company:

SALARIES/BENEFITS:

Pension Plan:	ESOP Stock Plan:	Profit Sharing:	Top Exec. Salary: $619,231	Bonus: $10,052
Savings Plan:	Stock Purch. Plan:		Second Exec. Salary: $364,038	Bonus: $10,368

OTHER THOUGHTS:

Apparent Women Officers or Directors: 9
Hot Spot for Advancement for Women/Minorities: Y

LOCATIONS: ("Y" = Yes)

West:	Southwest:	Midwest:	Southeast:	Northeast:	International:
Y	Y	Y	Y	Y	Y

I-FLOW CORPORATION

www.iflo.com

Industry Group Code: 33911

Management:		**Sales/Marketing:**		**Liberal Arts:**		**Information Systems:**		**Professionals:**		**Technical/Scientific:**	
Mgmt. Trainees:		Mktg. Professionals:	Y	Gen. Writing/Editing:		Info. Management:	Y	Finance/Acct.:	Y	Engineers, Elec.:	Y
Experienced Mgmt.:	Y	Retail Sales:		Technical Writing:	Y	Software Dev.:	Y	Law:	Y	Engineers, Other:	Y
Int'l Business:	Y	Commercial/Industrial:	Y	Graphic Arts/Photog.:		Hardware Dev.:	Y	HR/Other:	Y	Health/Lab	Y
MBA Graduates:	Y	Sales Trainees:	Y	Music:		Consulting/Other:		Training:	Y	Scientists/Research:	Y
		Advertising Pros.:		Broadcasting:				Health Care:	Y	Petroleum/Chemicals:	
				Other:				Consulting:		Math/Other:	

TYPES OF BUSINESS:

Medical Equipment-Mobile Infusion Systems
Anesthesia Kits
Elastomeric Products
Antimicrobial Products

BRANDS/DIVISIONS/AFFILIATES:

On-Q PainBuster Post-Operative Pain Relief System
ON-Q SilverSoaker Catheter
SilvaGard
On-Q C-bloc Continuous Nerve Block System
Kimberly-Clark Corp
OxyGenesys
On-Q SilverDressing
On-Q E epidural

CONTACTS: *Note: Officers with more than one job title may be intentionally listed here more than once.*

Joanne Bauer, CEO
Joanne Bauer, Pres.
Mark Buthman, CFO
Chris Smith, VP-Strategic Accts.
Thomas Mielke, Exec. VP

Phone: 929-206-2700 **Fax:** 949-206-2600
Toll-Free: 800-448-3569
Address: 20202 Windrow Dr., Lake Forest, CA 92630 US

GROWTH PLANS/SPECIAL FEATURES:

I-Flow Corporation, a subsidiary of Kimberly-Clark Corp., designs, develops and markets technically-advanced, low-cost drug delivery systems and innovative products, principally used for post-surgical pain relief and surgical site care. Its products are used in hospitals, homes and freestanding surgery centers. The firm focuses on two market segments: regional anesthesia and IV infusion therapy. I-Flow's regional anesthesia products include a line of portable infusion pumps, catheters and acute pain relief systems, including the On-Q PainBuster Post-Operative Pain Relief System, the On-Q SilverSoaker Catheter with SilvaGard, the On-Q C-bloc Continuous Nerve Block System and the On-Q E epidural. The IV infusion therapy product line of elastomeric pumps delivers medication from an elastic balloon that does not rely on gravity for proper delivery, making it safe and simple enough self-administration. The company's elastomeric line of products, including its Homepump Eclipse and Homepump Eclipse C Series, can be used for antibiotic therapy, pain management medications, chemotherapy and other medications. I-Flow's non-electric IV bag delivery systems, including its Paragon ambulatory infusion pumps, consist of a reusable mechanical infuser and specially designed administration sets. The firm also offers infection reduction and wound healing dressing products, such as OxyGenesys, containing dissolved oxygen; and On-Q SilverDressing, containing an added antimicrobial barrier.

FINANCIALS: **Sales and profits are in thousands of dollars—add 000 to get the full amount. 2011 Note: Financial information for 2011 was not available for all companies at press time.**

2011 Sales: $	2011 Profits: $
2010 Sales: $	2010 Profits: $
2009 Sales: $	2009 Profits: $
2008 Sales: $	2008 Profits: $
2007 Sales: $	2007 Profits: $

U.S. Stock Ticker: Subsidiary
Int'l Ticker:
Int'l Exchange:
Employees: Fiscal Year Ends: 12/31
Parent Company: KIMBERLY-CLARK CORP

SALARIES/BENEFITS:

Pension Plan:	ESOP Stock Plan:	Profit Sharing:	Top Exec. Salary: $468,791	Bonus: $162,853
Savings Plan:	Stock Purch. Plan:		Second Exec. Salary: $296,156	Bonus: $108,569

OTHER THOUGHTS:

Apparent Women Officers or Directors: 1
Hot Spot for Advancement for Women/Minorities:

LOCATIONS: ("Y" = Yes)

West:	Southwest:	Midwest:	Southeast:	Northeast:	International:
Y	Y				Y

ILLUMINA INC

www.illumina.com

Industry Group Code: 3345

Management:		**Sales/Marketing:**		**Liberal Arts:**		**Information Systems:**		**Professionals:**		**Technical/Scientific:**	
Mgmt. Trainees:		Mktg. Professionals:	Y	Gen. Writing/Editing:		Info. Management:	Y	Finance/Acct.:	Y	Engineers, Elec.:	Y
Experienced Mgmt.:	Y	Retail Sales:		Technical Writing:	Y	Software Dev.:	Y	Law:	Y	Engineers, Other:	Y
Int'l Business:	Y	Commercial/Industrial:	Y	Graphic Arts/Photog.:		Hardware Dev.:	Y	HR/Other:	Y	Health/Lab	Y
MBA Graduates:	Y	Sales Trainees:	Y	Music:		Consulting/Other:		Training:	Y	Scientists/Research:	Y
		Advertising Pros.:		Broadcasting:				Health Care:	Y	Petroleum/Chemicals:	
				Other:				Consulting:		Math/Other:	Y

TYPES OF BUSINESS:

Instruments-Genetic Variation Measurement
Array Technology
Digital Microbead Technology
Software
Genotyping Services

BRANDS/DIVISIONS/AFFILIATES:

BeadArray Technology
Genome Analyzer
iScan System
Oligator
VeraCode
Illumina Sequencing
BeadXpress Reader
Epicentre Technologies Corporation

CONTACTS: *Note: Officers with more than one job title may be intentionally listed here more than once.*

Jay T. Flatley, CEO
Jay T. Flatley, Pres.
Christian Henry, CFO/Sr. VP
Mostafa Ronaghi, CTO/Sr. VP
Christian G. Cabou, General Counsel/Sr. VP
Nicholas J. Naclerio, VP-Corp. Dev.
Peter J. Fromen, Sr. Dir.-Investor Rel.
Christian Henry, Gen. Mgr.-Life Sciences
Gregory F. Heath, Sr. VP/Gen. Mgr.-Diagnostics Bus. Unit
Tristan Orpin, Sr. VP/Chief Commercial Officer
William H. Rastetter, Chmn.
Elizabeth Brady, VP-Global Supply Chain

Phone: 858-202-4500 **Fax:** 858-202-4766
Toll-Free: 800-809-4566
Address: 9885 Towne Centre Dr., San Diego, CA 92121 US

GROWTH PLANS/SPECIAL FEATURES:

Illumina, Inc. develops tools for the large-scale analysis of genetic variation and function. The firm's tools provide genomic information that can be used to improve drugs and therapies, customize diagnoses and treatments and cure disease. The company deploys three primary systems for analyzing genetic variation and function: the Genome Analyzer, based on Illumina Sequencing technology, provides DNA sequencing services; the iScan System, based on BeadArray technology, performs multiple assays simultaneously; and the BeadXpress Reader, based on VeraCode technology acquired from the CyVera Corporation, is similar to the BeadArray but is used in lower multiplex projects. These use fiber optics to achieve a level of array miniaturization that allows experimentation to be easily scaled up. The firm also markets a series of sequencing kits and BeadChips for use in their instrumentation. Illumina arranges its arrays in patterns that match the wells of industry-standard microtiter plates, allowing higher throughput than other technologies. The company's other, complementary technology, Oligator, permits parallel synthesis of the millions of pieces of DNA necessary to perform large-scale genetic analysis. Illumina additionally provides genotyping services for other companies, as well as software, benchtop and production systems, installation and certain warranty services for its products. Illumina is one of six U.S. research groups participating in the International HapMap Project, a global consortium aimed at creating a detailed map of genetic variation. The firm is also one of three participating in the 1000 Genomes Project, which will build on HapMap. In January 2011, Illumina acquired nucleic acid sample preparation specialist Epicentre Technologies Corporation. In February 2011, the firm opened a new office in Sao Paulo, Brazil.

Illumina offers its employees medical, disability, dental, vision and prescription drug plans; flexible spending accounts; and a stock purchase plan.

FINANCIALS: **Sales and profits are in thousands of dollars—add 000 to get the full amount. 2011 Note: Financial information for 2011 was not available for all companies at press time.**

2011 Sales: $1,055,500	2011 Profits: $86,600	**U.S. Stock Ticker: ILMN**
2010 Sales: $902,741	2010 Profits: $124,891	**Int'l Ticker:**
2009 Sales: $666,324	2009 Profits: $72,281	Int'l Exchange:
2008 Sales: $573,225	2008 Profits: $50,477	Employees: 2,100 Fiscal Year Ends: 12/31
2007 Sales: $366,799	2007 Profits: $-278,359	Parent Company:

SALARIES/BENEFITS:

Pension Plan:	ESOP Stock Plan:	Profit Sharing:	Top Exec. Salary: $749,162	Bonus: $498,731
Savings Plan: Y	Stock Purch. Plan: Y		Second Exec. Salary: $390,203	Bonus: $159,600

OTHER THOUGHTS:

Apparent Women Officers or Directors:
Hot Spot for Advancement for Women/Minorities:

LOCATIONS: ("Y" = Yes)

West:	Southwest:	Midwest:	Southeast:	Northeast:	International:
Y					Y

IMG WORLDWIDE INC

www.imgworld.com

Industry Group Code: 711410

Management:		**Sales/Marketing:**		**Liberal Arts:**		**Information Systems:**		**Professionals:**		**Technical/Scientific:**	
Mgmt. Trainees:		Mktg. Professionals:	Y	Gen. Writing/Editing:		Info. Management:	Y	Finance/Acct.:	Y	Engineers, Elec.:	
Experienced Mgmt.:	Y	Retail Sales:		Technical Writing:		Software Dev.:		Law:	Y	Engineers, Other:	
Int'l Business:	Y	Commercial/Industrial:	Y	Graphic Arts/Photog.:		Hardware Dev.:		HR/Other:	Y	Health/Lab	
MBA Graduates:	Y	Sales Trainees:	Y	Music:		Consulting/Other:		Training:	Y	Scientists/Research:	
		Advertising Pros.:		Broadcasting:				Health Care:		Petroleum/Chemicals:	
				Other:				Consulting:		Math/Other:	

TYPES OF BUSINESS:

Agents-Athletes
Agents-Models
Agents-Writers, Artists & Musicians
Event Marketing
Corporate Marketing Consulting Services
Sports Television Programming
Sports Schools & Training

BRANDS/DIVISIONS/AFFILIATES:

TWI
CSI Sports
Tigress Productions Limited
Nunet AG
Darlow Smithson Productions

CONTACTS:

Note: Officers with more than one job title may be intentionally listed here more than once.

Michael J. Dolan, CEO
Michel Masquelier, Pres., IMG Media
George Pyne, Pres., IMG Sports & Entertainment
Michael J. Dolan, Chmn.

Phone: 212-355-5656	**Fax:** 212-759-9059
Toll-Free:	
Address: 767 5th Ave., New York, NY 10153 US	

GROWTH PLANS/SPECIAL FEATURES:

IMG Worldwide, Inc. is one of largest sports and lifestyle marketing and management agencies in the world. The company represents some of the world's top athletes, broadcasters, models, classical musicians, authors and newsmakers from offices in 30 countries. The agency operates in a number of industries, including professional sports, college sports, entertainment, fashion, media and other various entertainment categories. Its sports operations handle everything from events and sponsorships to client representation and training. The company owns, produces and manages several prestigious sporting events including events at Wimbledon and Nobel Prize functions. Sports clients include pro golfer Tiger Woods; tennis player Venus Williams; baseball player Derek Jeter; basketball player Charles Barkley; and hockey player Jaromir Jagr. Fashion and entertainment operations handle a multitude of events and personalities, including models Gisele Bundchen and Cindy Crawford. Media operations create, distribute, sell and represent content across every medium. IMG's Media division, along with the firm's subsidiaries TWI, Darlow Smithson Productions, CSI Sports, Tiger Aspect Productions, Tigress Productions Limited and Nunet AG, is one of the world's largest independent producers and distributors of televised sports programming. It annually produces and distributes original programming to over 200 countries. IMG is owned by private equity firm Forstmann Little & Co.

FINANCIALS:

Sales and profits are in thousands of dollars—add 000 to get the full amount. 2011 Note: Financial information for 2011 was not available for all companies at press time.

2011 Sales: $	2011 Profits: $	**U.S. Stock Ticker: Private**
2010 Sales: $	2010 Profits: $	**Int'l Ticker:**
2009 Sales: $	2009 Profits: $	Int'l Exchange:
2008 Sales: $	2008 Profits: $	Employees: Fiscal Year Ends: 12/31
2007 Sales: $	2007 Profits: $	Parent Company: FORSTMANN LITTLE & CO

SALARIES/BENEFITS:

Pension Plan:	ESOP Stock Plan:	Profit Sharing:	Top Exec. Salary: $	Bonus: $
Savings Plan:	Stock Purch. Plan:		Second Exec. Salary: $	Bonus: $

OTHER THOUGHTS:

Apparent Women Officers or Directors:
Hot Spot for Advancement for Women/Minorities:

LOCATIONS: ("Y" = Yes)

West:	Southwest:	Midwest:	Southeast:	Northeast:	International:
Y	Y	Y	Y	Y	Y

IMMUCOR INC

www.immucor.com

Industry Group Code: 325413

Management:		Sales/Marketing:		Liberal Arts:		Information Systems:		Professionals:		Technical/Scientific:	
Mgmt. Trainees:		Mktg. Professionals:	Y	Gen. Writing/Editing:		Info. Management:	Y	Finance/Acct.:	Y	Engineers, Elec.:	
Experienced Mgmt.:	Y	Retail Sales:		Technical Writing:	Y	Software Dev.:	Y	Law:	Y	Engineers, Other:	Y
Int'l Business:	Y	Commercial/Industrial:	Y	Graphic Arts/Photog.:		Hardware Dev.:	Y	HR/Other:	Y	Health/Lab	Y
MBA Graduates:	Y	Sales Trainees:	Y	Music:		Consulting/Other:		Training:	Y	Scientists/Research:	Y
		Advertising Pros.:	Y	Broadcasting:				Health Care:	Y	Petroleum/Chemicals:	
				Other:				Consulting:		Math/Other:	Y

TYPES OF BUSINESS:

Diagnostic Products
Automated Blood Bank Instruments
Blood Reagents

BRANDS/DIVISIONS/AFFILIATES:

NEO
Echo
Capture
Array Imaging System
BeadChip
BASIS
TPG Capital

CONTACTS: *Note: Officers with more than one job title may be intentionally listed here more than once.*

Joshua H. Levine, CEO
Joshua H. Levine, Pres.
Richard A. Flynt, CFO/Exec. VP
Philip H. Moise, General Counsel/Sec./Exec. VP
Michele Howard, VP-External Comm.
Michele Howard, VP-Investor Rel.
Joseph E. Rosen, Chmn.

Phone: 770-441-2051	**Fax:** 770-441-3807
Toll-Free: 800-829-2553	
Address: 3130 Gateway Dr., Norcross, GA 30091 US	

GROWTH PLANS/SPECIAL FEATURES:

Immucor, Inc. develops, manufactures and markets immunological diagnostic medical products, primarily reagents and automated systems used by hospitals, clinical laboratories and blood banks in tests performed to detect and identify certain properties of human blood prior to blood transfusions. The company has manufacturing facilities in the U.S. and Canada and sells products from these facilities and through its affiliates in Europe and Japan. Transfusion blood potentially contains antigens, which can cause a recipient's body to produce antibodies. The interaction between antigens and antibodies can cause severe complications. To protect against these potential complications, the firm produces an automated blood testing instrument, NEO, which allows technicians to analyze samples for potentially life-threatening foreign agents. The NEO is capable of performing all routine blood bank tests, including blood grouping, antibody screening, crossmatch, direct antiglobulin test (DAT) and antibody identification. A high-volume output instrument, NEO processes up to 224 different samples at once and can perform approximately 60 type-and-screen tests an hour. The system, which was launched in 2010, is a replacement for its legacy Galileo instrument. Other products include the Capture, a semi-automated device marketed as a back-up system for the NEO or a stand-alone system for small laboratories; the Echo, a device geared toward the small- to medium-sized hospital market that is able to perform up to 14 type-and-screen tests an hour; and the molecular Array Imaging System, which uses the firm's BeadChip technology and its BASIS database to automate test result interpretation. In August 2011, Immucor was acquired by an affiliate of private equity firm TPG Capital.

FINANCIALS: Sales and profits are in thousands of dollars—add 000 to get the full amount. 2011 Note: Financial information for 2011 was not available for all companies at press time.

2011 Sales: $333,091	2011 Profits: $89,327	**U.S. Stock Ticker: Private**
2010 Sales: $329,073	2010 Profits: $82,583	**Int'l Ticker:**
2009 Sales: $300,547	2009 Profits: $76,183	Int'l Exchange:
2008 Sales: $261,199	2008 Profits: $71,454	Employees: 757 Fiscal Year Ends: 5/31
2007 Sales: $223,678	2007 Profits: $60,068	Parent Company: TPG CAPITAL

SALARIES/BENEFITS:

Pension Plan: Y	ESOP Stock Plan:	Profit Sharing:	Top Exec. Salary: $571,304	Bonus: $50,264
Savings Plan: Y	Stock Purch. Plan:		Second Exec. Salary: $488,973	Bonus: $49,207

OTHER THOUGHTS:

Apparent Women Officers or Directors: 1
Hot Spot for Advancement for Women/Minorities:

LOCATIONS: ("Y" = Yes)

West:	Southwest:	Midwest:	Southeast:	Northeast:	International:
			Y	Y	Y

IMPAX LABORATORIES INC

www.impaxlabs.com

Industry Group Code: 325412A

Management:		Sales/Marketing:		Liberal Arts:		Information Systems:		Professionals:		Technical/Scientific:	
Mgmt. Trainees:		Mktg. Professionals:	Y	Gen. Writing/Editing:		Info. Management:	Y	Finance/Acct.:	Y	Engineers, Elec.:	
Experienced Mgmt.:	Y	Retail Sales:		Technical Writing:	Y	Software Dev.:	Y	Law:	Y	Engineers, Other:	
Int'l Business:		Commercial/Industrial:	Y	Graphic Arts/Photog.:		Hardware Dev.:		HR/Other:	Y	Health/Lab	Y
MBA Graduates:	Y	Sales Trainees:		Music:		Consulting/Other:		Training:	Y	Scientists/Research:	Y
		Advertising Pros.:		Broadcasting:				Health Care:	Y	Petroleum/Chemicals:	
				Other:				Consulting:		Math/Other:	Y

TYPES OF BUSINESS:

Drug Delivery Systems
Drugs-Generic
Pharmaceutical Discovery & Development
Drugs-Central Nervous System

BRANDS/DIVISIONS/AFFILIATES:

Global Pharmaceuticals
IMPAX Pharmaceuticals

CONTACTS: *Note: Officers with more than one job title may be intentionally listed here more than once.*

Larry Hsu, CEO
Larry Hsu, Pres.
Arthur A. Koch, Jr., CFO
Mark A. Schlossberg, General Counsel/Sr. VP
Mark Fitch, Sr. VP-Global Oper.
Arthur A. Koch, Jr., Sr. VP-Finance
Michael J. Nestor, Pres., IMPAX Pharmaceuticals
Robert L. Burr, Chmn.
Jeff Nornhold, Sr. VP-Global Quality Affairs

Phone: 510-476-2000	**Fax:** 510-471-3200
Toll-Free:	
Address: 30831 Huntwood Ave., Hayward, CA 94544 US	

GROWTH PLANS/SPECIAL FEATURES:

IMPAX Laboratories, Inc. is a technology-based, specialty pharmaceutical company focused on the development and commercialization of generic and brand-name pharmaceuticals. In the generic pharmaceuticals market, the firm focuses on controlled-release generic versions of brand-name pharmaceuticals covering a range of therapeutic areas with technically challenging drug-delivery mechanisms or limited competition. The company also develops specialty generic pharmaceuticals that present barriers to entry by competitors, such as special handling requirements, difficulty in raw materials sourcing or complex formulation or development characteristics. In the brand-name pharmaceuticals market, IMPAX develops products for the treatment of central nervous system disorders. The company markets generic products through its Global Pharmaceuticals division and intends to market branded products through its IMPAX Pharmaceuticals division. The firm markets 99 generic pharmaceuticals representing dosage variations of 29 different pharmaceutical compounds through its Global Pharmaceuticals division; and another 10 products representing dosage variations of four different pharmaceutical compounds through its alliance agreements' partners. It has 62 abbreviated new drug applications (ANDAs) approved by the U.S. Food and Drug Administration (FDA), including generic versions of Brethine, Ditropan XL, Depakote ER, Florinef, Minocine, Claritin-D 12-hour, Claritin-D 24-hour, Wellbutrin SR and Prilosec; 38 applications pending at the FDA, including two tentatively approved; and 61 products in various stages of development. IMPAX also has one branded pharmaceutical product for which it has completed two Phase II clinical studies and other programs in the early exploratory phase. In December 2010, the FDA approved the firm's ANDA for the generic form of Doryx.

IMPAX offers its employees flexible spending accounts; an employee assistance program; medical, dental, life and long-term disability insurance; supplemental insurance options; a 401(k) plan; and an employee stock purchase plan.

FINANCIALS: **Sales and profits are in thousands of dollars—add 000 to get the full amount. 2011 Note: Financial information for 2011 was not available for all companies at press time.**

2011 Sales: $512,900	2011 Profits: $65,500	**U.S. Stock Ticker: IPXL**
2010 Sales: $879,509	2010 Profits: $250,418	**Int'l Ticker:**
2009 Sales: $358,409	2009 Profits: $50,061	Int'l Exchange:
2008 Sales: $210,071	2008 Profits: $15,987	Employees: 918 Fiscal Year Ends: 12/31
2007 Sales: $273,753	2007 Profits: $125,410	Parent Company:

SALARIES/BENEFITS:

Pension Plan:	ESOP Stock Plan:	Profit Sharing:	Top Exec. Salary: $682,043	Bonus: $546,000
Savings Plan: Y	Stock Purch. Plan: Y		Second Exec. Salary: $456,081	Bonus: $264,697

OTHER THOUGHTS:

Apparent Women Officers or Directors:
Hot Spot for Advancement for Women/Minorities:

LOCATIONS: ("Y" = Yes)

West:	Southwest:	Midwest:	Southeast:	Northeast:	International:
Y				Y	

INDEPENDENCE HOLDING CO

www.ihcgroup.com

Industry Group Code: 524113

Management:		Sales/Marketing:		Liberal Arts:		Information Systems:		Professionals:		Technical/Scientific:	
Mgmt. Trainees:	Y	Mktg. Professionals:	Y	Gen. Writing/Editing:	Y	Info. Management:	Y	Finance/Acct.:	Y	Engineers, Elec.:	
Experienced Mgmt.:	Y	Retail Sales:		Technical Writing:	Y	Software Dev.:		Law:	Y	Engineers, Other:	
Int'l Business:		Commercial/Industrial:		Graphic Arts/Photog.:		Hardware Dev.:		HR/Other:	Y	Health/Lab	
MBA Graduates:	Y	Sales Trainees:	Y	Music:		Consulting/Other:		Training:	Y	Scientists/Research:	
		Advertising Pros.:	Y	Broadcasting:				Health Care:	Y	Petroleum/Chemicals:	
				Other:				Consulting:		Math/Other:	Y

TYPES OF BUSINESS:

Insurance Underwriting
Medical Stop-Loss
Group Disability & Life Insurance
Individual Life Insurance

BRANDS/DIVISIONS/AFFILIATES:

Standard Security Life Insurance Company
Madison National Life Insurance Company Inc
Insurers Administrative Corporation
Majestic Underwriters LLC
Alliance Underwriters LLC
IHC Health Solutions Inc
Actuarial Management Corporation
Independent Producers of America

CONTACTS: *Note: Officers with more than one job title may be intentionally listed here more than once.*

Roy T. K. Thung, CEO
David Kettig, COO/Sr. VP
Roy T. K. Thung, Pres.
Teresa A. Herbert, CFO/Sr. VP
Jeffrey C. Smedsrud, Chief Mktg. Officer/Sr. VP
Adam C. Vandervoort, General Counsel/VP/Sec.
Jeffrey C. Smedsrud, Chief Strategy Officer
Larry R. Graber, Sr. VP-Life & Annuities
Bernon R. Erickson, Jr., Chief Health Actuary/Sr. VP
Henry B. Spencer, VP-Investments
Roy T. K. Thung, Chmn.

Phone: 203-358-8000 **Fax:** 203-348-3103
Toll-Free: 877-442-4467
Address: 96 Cummings Point Rd., Stamford, CT 06902 US

GROWTH PLANS/SPECIAL FEATURES:

Independence Holding Co. (IHC) is a holding company principally engaged in the life and health insurance business. The company operates predominately through two of its wholly-owned insurance companies, Standard Security Insurance Company and Madison National Life Insurance Company, Inc. but the firm also has many other subsidiaries including; IHC Health Solutions; Independent Producers of America; Majestic Underwriters LLC; MedWatch, LLC; Alliance Underwriters; and Actuarial Management Corporation. Additionally, the firm owns a 50.1% equity interest in American Independence Corp., which owns Independence American Insurance Company and several managing general underwriters. The company's employer medical stop-loss is its largest product line. Medical stop-loss insurance allows self-insured employers to manage the risk of excessive health insurance exposures by limiting aggregate and specific losses to a predetermined amount. Standard Security Life markets major medical stop-loss in all 50 states, Washington D.C., the Virgin Islands and Puerto Rico. It also sells short-term statutory disability benefit product in New York and certain life, annuity and blanket accident coverage sold primarily in New York to volunteer emergency personnel. Madison National Life sells group life and disability insurance, credit life, and disability insurance in 49 states, Washington D.C., the U.S. Virgin Islands and Guam. The types of insurance that the firm sells is short-term medical; individual medical; dental plans for individual or group; disability; group life insurance; limited medical benefits; and plans for government, students and military personnel. The firm also acquires block of life policies from other insurance companies. Independence American reinsures a significant portion of the medical stop-loss business written by Standard Security Life and Madison National Life.

FINANCIALS: **Sales and profits are in thousands of dollars—add 000 to get the full amount. 2011 Note: Financial information for 2011 was not available for all companies at press time.**

2011 Sales: $ — 2011 Profits: $
2010 Sales: $435,368 — 2010 Profits: $23,413
2009 Sales: $354,838 — 2009 Profits: $-7,132
2008 Sales: $353,687 — 2008 Profits: $-23,840
2007 Sales: $402,322 — 2007 Profits: $-2,328

U.S. Stock Ticker: IHC
Int'l Ticker:
Int'l Exchange:
Employees: 650 Fiscal Year Ends: 12/31
Parent Company:

SALARIES/BENEFITS:

Pension Plan: ESOP Stock Plan: Profit Sharing: Top Exec. Salary: $421,601 Bonus: $228,000
Savings Plan: Stock Purch. Plan: Second Exec. Salary: $319,712 Bonus: $89,744

OTHER THOUGHTS:

Apparent Women Officers or Directors: 1
Hot Spot for Advancement for Women/Minorities:

LOCATIONS: ("Y" = Yes)

West:	Southwest:	Midwest:	Southeast:	Northeast:	International:
Y	Y	Y	Y	Y	

INFOSPACE INC

www.infospaceinc.com

Industry Group Code: 519130

Management:		Sales/Marketing:		Liberal Arts:		Information Systems:		Professionals:		Technical/Scientific:	
Mgmt. Trainees:		Mktg. Professionals:	Y	Gen. Writing/Editing:	Y	Info. Management:	Y	Finance/Acct.:	Y	Engineers, Elec.:	
Experienced Mgmt.:	Y	Retail Sales:		Technical Writing:		Software Dev.:	Y	Law:	Y	Engineers, Other:	
Int'l Business:	Y	Commercial/Industrial:	Y	Graphic Arts/Photog.:	Y	Hardware Dev.:		HR/Other:	Y	Health/Lab	
MBA Graduates:	Y	Sales Trainees:	Y	Music:		Consulting/Other:		Training:		Scientists/Research:	
		Advertising Pros.:	Y	Broadcasting:				Health Care:		Petroleum/Chemicals:	
				Other:				Consulting:		Math/Other:	

TYPES OF BUSINESS:

Internet Search Engines
Online Retail

BRANDS/DIVISIONS/AFFILIATES:

DogPile.com
WebCrawler.com
MetaCrawler.com
WebFetch.com
Mercantila
Mercantila.com
TaxACT

CONTACTS:

Note: Officers with more than one job title may be intentionally listed here more than once.

William J. Ruckelshaus, CEO
William J. Ruckelshaus, Pres.
Eric Emans, CFO
Travis McElfresh, CTO
Linda Schoemaker, General Counsel/Sec.
Mike Glover, VP-Bus. Dev.
Stacy Ybarra, Head-Public Rel.
Stacy Ybarra, Head-Investor Rel.
Stephen P. Hawthornthwaite, VP-Corp. Dev.
John Rodkin, Gen. Mgr.-Search
John E. Cunningham, IV, Chmn.

Phone: 425-201-6100	**Fax:** 425-201-6150
Toll-Free:	
Address: 601 108th Ave. NE, Ste. 1200, Bellevue, WA 98004 US	

GROWTH PLANS/SPECIAL FEATURES:

InfoSpace, Inc. is a developer of search tools and technologies designed to assist consumers in finding content and information on the Internet. The firm operates its business in two primary segments: E-Commerce and Core. The E-Commerce segment includes a collection of more than 200 specialty online retail stores under the Mercantila brand. Mercantila's online stores offer specialty items that are typically niche and difficult to find, fulfill a specific customer need, require a significant amount of research before the purchase decision, and are more expensive than the average online purchase. The company's Core segment offers search services that enable Internet users to locate and view content information, merchants, individuals and products online through its web sites DogPile.com; WebCrawler.com; MetaCrawler.com; and WebFetch.com, as well as through the web properties of distribution partners. DogPile is the firm's basic metasearch engine. WebCrawler is InfoSpace's full text metasearch engine. MetaCrawler is a metasearch engine with search options for images, audio, video, news, yellow pages and white pages. WebFetch is a metasearch engine catering to English-speaking Internet users in Europe. Partner versions of its web offerings are generally private-labeled and delivered with each distribution partner's unique requirements. InfoSpace's customers are primarily search content providers, from whom it receives revenues when an end user of its search services clicks on a customer's paid search link that is either displayed on an InfoSpace web site or displayed on the web property of a distribution partner. In January 2012, InfoSpace acquired TaxACT, a provider of online tax products, for $287.5 million.

Employees are offered medical, dental and vision insurance; health club subsidies; and a 401(k) plan.

FINANCIALS:

Sales and profits are in thousands of dollars—add 000 to get the full amount. 2011 Note: Financial information for 2011 was not available for all companies at press time.

2011 Sales: $	2011 Profits: $
2010 Sales: $246,835	2010 Profits: $13,703
2009 Sales: $207,646	2009 Profits: $7,403
2008 Sales: $156,727	2008 Profits: $-18,699
2007 Sales: $140,537	2007 Profits: $21,733

U.S. Stock Ticker: INSP
Int'l Ticker:
Int'l Exchange:
Employees: 174 Fiscal Year Ends: 12/31
Parent Company:

SALARIES/BENEFITS:

Pension Plan:	ESOP Stock Plan:	Profit Sharing:	Top Exec. Salary: $354,808	Bonus: $
Savings Plan: Y	Stock Purch. Plan:		Second Exec. Salary: $236,193	Bonus: $89,958

OTHER THOUGHTS:

Apparent Women Officers or Directors: 2
Hot Spot for Advancement for Women/Minorities:

LOCATIONS: ("Y" = Yes)

West:	Southwest:	Midwest:	Southeast:	Northeast:	International:
Y				Y	

INNOPHOS HOLDINGS INC

www.innophos.com

Industry Group Code: 325

Management:		Sales/Marketing:		Liberal Arts:		Information Systems:		Professionals:		Technical/Scientific:	
Mgmt. Trainees:		Mktg. Professionals:	Y	Gen. Writing/Editing:		Info. Management:	Y	Finance/Acct.:	Y	Engineers, Elec.:	
Experienced Mgmt.:	Y	Retail Sales:		Technical Writing:	Y	Software Dev.:		Law:	Y	Engineers, Other:	
Int'l Business:	Y	Commercial/Industrial:	Y	Graphic Arts/Photog.:		Hardware Dev.:		HR/Other:	Y	Health/Lab Scientists/Research:	
MBA Graduates:	Y	Sales Trainees:		Music:		Consulting/Other:		Training:			
		Advertising Pros.:		Broadcasting:				Health Care:		Petroleum/Chemicals:	Y
				Other:				Consulting:		Math/Other:	

TYPES OF BUSINESS:

Specialty Phosphates
Specialty Acids & Salts
Purified Phosphoric Acid
Technical Sodium Tripolyphosphate
Fertilizers

BRANDS/DIVISIONS/AFFILIATES:

CONTACTS:

Note: Officers with more than one job title may be intentionally listed here more than once.

Randolph Gress, CEO
Randolph Gress, Pres.
Neil Salmon, CFO/VP
Gail Holler, VP-Human Resources
Russell Kemp, VP-R&D/Chief Risk Officer
William Farran, General Counsel/VP
Louis Calvarin, VP-Oper.
Mark Thurston, VP-Strategy & Worldwide Bus. Dev.
Mark Feuerbach, VP-Treasury, Financial Planning & Analysis
Joseph Golowski, VP-Specialty Phosphate Bus.
Charles Brodheim, Corp. Controller
Randolph Gress, Chmn.
Abraham Shabot, VP/Dir. Gen.-Latin America
Michael Lovrich, VP-Supply Chain

Phone: 609-495-2495	**Fax:** 609-860-0138
Toll-Free:	
Address: 259 Prospect Plains Rd., Cranbury, NJ 08512 US	

GROWTH PLANS/SPECIAL FEATURES:

Innophos Holdings, Inc. produces specialty phosphates for marketing in the food, beverage and pharmaceutical industries. The company has three product lines: food and technical grade purified phosphoric acid (PPA); specialty ingredients; and technical grade sodium tripolyphosphate (STTP) and detergent grade PPA. Food and technical grade PPA is used as an input to specialty salts and acids and as a flavor enhancer in soft drinks, as well as being used in water treatment applications. Specialty ingredients include salts are used as flavor enhancers in beverages; electrolytes in sports drinks; texture additives in cheeses; leavening agents in baked goods; calcium and phosphorus sources for nutritional supplements; cleaning agents in toothpaste; pharmaceutical excipients; and lead control additives in water treatment. Specialty acids are used in industrial applications such as asphalt modification and petrochemical catalysis. STTP is an ingredient in cleaning products such as automatic dishwashing, commercial/industrial detergent and home laundry detergents. Other products provided by Innophos include fertilizers produced in Mexico primarily as co-products of manufacturing purified phosphoric acid. The firm's customers include consumer goods manufacturers, distributors and specialty chemical manufacturers. The company derives approximately 50% of sales from the food/beverage, pharmaceutical and oral care markets. As part of its research and development work, Innophos has created a line of clear, tasteless calcium phosphates that allow its clients to make a calcium label claim. The company's manufacturing facilities are located strategically throughout the U.S., Canada and Mexico.

Innophos offers its employees benefits including medical coverage; a 401(k) plan with company contributions; life and disability insurance; a stock options incentive plan; various wellness programs; and an employee assistance program.

FINANCIALS:

Sales and profits are in thousands of dollars—add 000 to get the full amount. 2011 Note: Financial information for 2011 was not available for all companies at press time.

2011 Sales: $810,500 | 2011 Profits: $86,500
2010 Sales: $714,231 | 2010 Profits: $45,155
2009 Sales: $666,759 | 2009 Profits: $63,144
2008 Sales: $934,758 | 2008 Profits: $207,183
2007 Sales: $578,982 | 2007 Profits: $-5,487

U.S. Stock Ticker: IPHS
Int'l Ticker:
Int'l Exchange:
Employees: 1,087 Fiscal Year Ends: 12/31
Parent Company:

SALARIES/BENEFITS:

Pension Plan: | ESOP Stock Plan: | Profit Sharing: | Top Exec. Salary: $680,000 | Bonus: $1,038,244
Savings Plan: Y | Stock Purch. Plan: | | Second Exec. Salary: $281,875 | Bonus: $281,029

OTHER THOUGHTS:

Apparent Women Officers or Directors: 3
Hot Spot for Advancement for Women/Minorities: Y

LOCATIONS: ("Y" = Yes)

West:	Southwest:	Midwest:	Southeast:	Northeast:	International:
		Y	Y	Y	Y

Sales, profits and employees may be estimates. Financial information, benefits and other data can change quickly and may vary from those stated here.

INNOSPEC INC

www.innospecinc.com

Industry Group Code: 325

Management:		Sales/Marketing:		Liberal Arts:		Information Systems:		Professionals:		Technical/Scientific:	
Mgmt. Trainees:		Mktg. Professionals:	Y	Gen. Writing/Editing:		Info. Management:	Y	Finance/Acct.:	Y	Engineers, Elec.:	
Experienced Mgmt.:	Y	Retail Sales:		Technical Writing:	Y	Software Dev.:		Law:	Y	Engineers, Other:	
Int'l Business:	Y	Commercial/Industrial:		Graphic Arts/Photog.:		Hardware Dev.:		HR/Other:	Y	Health/Lab	
MBA Graduates:	Y	Sales Trainees:		Music:		Consulting/Other:		Training:		Scientists/Research:	
		Advertising Pros.:		Broadcasting:				Health Care:		Petroleum/Chemicals:	Y
				Other:				Consulting:		Math/Other:	

TYPES OF BUSINESS:

Fuel Additives
Fuel Additives
Octane Additives
Tetra Ethyl Lead Production
Personal Care Chemicals

BRANDS/DIVISIONS/AFFILIATES:

Finsolv
Iselux
Natrlquest
Enviomet

CONTACTS: *Note: Officers with more than one job title may be intentionally listed here more than once.*

Patrick Williams, CEO
Patrick Williams, Pres.
Ian Cleminson, CFO/Exec. VP
Cathy Hessner, Sr. VP-Human Resources
Ian McRobble, Sr. VP-R&D
David Williams, General Counsel/VP/Chief Compliance Officer
Phil Boon, Exec. VP-Bus. Oper.
Brian Watt, VP-Strategic Planning & Regulatory Affairs
Kate Davison, Head-Investor Rel.
Mark A. Bracewell, Controller
Patrick McDuff, Pres., Fuel Specialties Americas
Robert E. Bew, Chmn.
Andrew Hartley, VP/General Counsel-EMEA & APAC

Phone: 303-792-5554	**Fax:**
Toll-Free:	
Address: 8375 S. Willow St., Littleton, CO 80124 US	

GROWTH PLANS/SPECIAL FEATURES:

Innospec, Inc., develops, manufactures, blends and delivers fuel additives and other specialty chemicals. The company operates in three segments: fuel specialties, active chemicals and octane additives. The fuel specialties segment manufactures and delivers various specialty chemicals used as additives in a wide range of fuels. The additives help improve fuel efficiency, boost engine performance and reduce harmful emissions. The business's products are used in the operation of automotive, marine and aviation engines; power station generators; and heating and diesel particulate filter systems. The active chemicals segment manufactures chemicals used in the personal care, pulp/paper, household, institutional and fragrance ingredients industries. Products include Natrlquest and Enviomet biodegradable chelating agents; Iselux, a series of sulfate-free surfactants for personal care; and Finsolv, a line of benzoate esters for cosmetic products. These products are used in the manufacture of such items as laundry detergent, sunscreens, moisturizers and rubber shoe soles. In addition, this segment produces ethylene-based EVA and PE waxes for industrial processes. The octane additives segment is a producer of tetra ethyl lead (TEL), an octane booster for gasoline. TEL, a primary ingredient in aviation fuel, also acts as a lubricant and reduces engine wear. Innospec's products are sold primarily to oil refineries and other chemical and industrial companies.

FINANCIALS: **Sales and profits are in thousands of dollars—add 000 to get the full amount. 2011 Note: Financial information for 2011 was not available for all companies at press time.**

2011 Sales: $774,400	2011 Profits: $48,900	**U.S. Stock Ticker: IOSP**
2010 Sales: $683,200	2010 Profits: $73,700	**Int'l Ticker:**
2009 Sales: $598,500	2009 Profits: $6,400	Int'l Exchange:
2008 Sales: $640,500	2008 Profits: $12,500	Employees: 850 Fiscal Year Ends: 12/31
2007 Sales: $602,400	2007 Profits: $29,500	Parent Company:

SALARIES/BENEFITS:

Pension Plan:	ESOP Stock Plan:	Profit Sharing:	Top Exec. Salary: $763,461	Bonus: $1,421,250
Savings Plan:	Stock Purch. Plan: Y		Second Exec. Salary: $281,844	Bonus: $514,188

OTHER THOUGHTS:

Apparent Women Officers or Directors: 2
Hot Spot for Advancement for Women/Minorities:

LOCATIONS: ("Y" = Yes)

West:	Southwest:	Midwest:	Southeast:	Northeast:	International:
Y				Y	Y

INTEGRAL SYSTEMS INC

www.integ.com

Industry Group Code: 511210C

Management:		Sales/Marketing:		Liberal Arts:		Information Systems:		Professionals:		Technical/Scientific:	
Mgmt. Trainees:		Mktg. Professionals:	Y	Gen. Writing/Editing:		Info. Management:	Y	Finance/Acct.:	Y	Engineers, Elec.:	Y
Experienced Mgmt.:	Y	Retail Sales:		Technical Writing:	Y	Software Dev.:	Y	Law:	Y	Engineers, Other:	
Int'l Business:	Y	Commercial/Industrial:	Y	Graphic Arts/Photog.:		Hardware Dev.:		HR/Other:	Y	Health/Lab	
MBA Graduates:	Y	Sales Trainees:	Y	Music:		Consulting/Other:		Training:	Y	Scientists/Research:	
		Advertising Pros.:		Broadcasting:				Health Care:		Petroleum/Chemicals:	
				Other:				Consulting:		Math/Other:	

TYPES OF BUSINESS:

Satellite Systems & Software
Signal Monitoring Systems & Software
Telemetry Processing Systems
Systems Integration Services

BRANDS/DIVISIONS/AFFILIATES:

Real Time Logic, Inc.
SAT Corporation
Newpoint Technologies, Inc.
EPOCH Integrated Product Suite
SATCOM Solutions
EPOCH Web Server
Task Initiator
EPOCH Triggers

CONTACTS:

Note: Officers with more than one job title may be intentionally listed here more than once.

Paul G. Casner, Jr., CEO
Paul G. Casner, Jr., Pres.
Christopher Roberts, CFO
R. Miller Adams, General Counsel
Andrew Miller, VP-External Comm.
Christopher Roberts, Treas.
Stuart C. Daughtridge, Exec. VP/Gen. Mgr.-Prod. Grouop
James B. Kramer, Sr. VP/Gen Mgr.-Civil & Commercial Group
Robert Wright, Jr., Sr. VP/Gen. Mgr.-Military & Intelligence Group
R. Miller Adams, Exec. VP-Corp. Affairs
John M. Albertine, Chmn.
Bruno Dupas, Pres., Integral Systems Europe

Phone: 443-539-5008 **Fax:** 410-312-2705
Toll-Free:
Address: 6721 Columbia Gateway Dr., Columbia, MD 21046 US

GROWTH PLANS/SPECIAL FEATURES:

Integral Systems, Inc. is a Maryland-based company that builds satellite ground systems and equipment for command and control; integration and test; data processing; and simulation. The company's products are designed to reduce the cost and minimize the development risk associated with traditional, custom-built satellite ground systems. Integral Systems was the first company to offer a comprehensive commercial off-the-shelf (COTS) software product line for command and control. As a systems integrator, it configures its products to provide turnkey satellite control facilities that can operate multiple satellites from most manufacturers. Subsidiary Real Time Logic, Inc. designs and builds the company's satellite communications equipment and systems, which are used principally for satellite tracking stations, control centers, spacecraft factories and range facilities. Subsidiaries SAT Corporation and Newpoint Technologies, Inc. provide complimentary ground system components and systems. Most of the company's sales involve a combination of COTS software and hardware products together with development services for mission-specific requirements and system integration. SATCOM Solutions provides secure, satellite-based communication solutions to government and commercial markets and offers integrated ground systems infrastructure solutions. SATCOM was formed from the early 2010 acquisitions of CVG, Incorporated and its subsidiary, Avtec Systems, Inc.; and certain assets of Sophia Wireless, Inc. The EPOCH Integrated Product Suite is designed to operate a variety of satellites with minimum personnel and features a distributed architecture consisting of a series of servers and user workstations interconnected by an ethernet local area network (LAN). Included in the product suite are the EPOCH T&C Server and EPOCH Client, its real-time satellite data processing and control software products; OASYS, its mission-planning software; and Archive Manager, which performs archive data generation, storage, storage management and retrieval. Additional products include EPOCH Web Server and EPOCH Triggers.

Employees are offered medical, dental and vision insurance; a 401(k); a stock purchase program; and tuition reimbursement.

FINANCIALS:

Sales and profits are in thousands of dollars—add 000 to get the full amount. 2011 Note: Financial information for 2011 was not available for all companies at press time.

2011 Sales: $	2011 Profits: $
2010 Sales: $177,895	2010 Profits: $-2,396
2009 Sales: $159,933	2009 Profits: $1,105
2008 Sales: $160,170	2008 Profits: $18,174
2007 Sales: $128,654	2007 Profits: $12,826

U.S. Stock Ticker: ISYS
Int'l Ticker:
Int'l Exchange:
Employees: 690 Fiscal Year Ends: 9/30
Parent Company:

SALARIES/BENEFITS:

Pension Plan:	ESOP Stock Plan:	Profit Sharing: Y	Top Exec. Salary: $387,000	Bonus: $
Savings Plan: Y	Stock Purch. Plan: Y		Second Exec. Salary: $300,000	Bonus: $

OTHER THOUGHTS:

Apparent Women Officers or Directors: 2
Hot Spot for Advancement for Women/Minorities:

LOCATIONS: ("Y" = Yes)

West:	Southwest:	Midwest:	Southeast:	Northeast:	International:
Y				Y	Y

INTEGRAMED AMERICA INC

www.integramed.com

Industry Group Code: 621410

Management:		Sales/Marketing:		Liberal Arts:		Information Systems:		Professionals:		Technical/Scientific:	
Mgmt. Trainees:	Y	Mktg. Professionals:	Y	Gen. Writing/Editing:		Info. Management:	Y	Finance/Acct.:	Y	Engineers, Elec.:	
Experienced Mgmt.:	Y	Retail Sales:		Technical Writing:	Y	Software Dev.:	Y	Law:	Y	Engineers, Other:	
Int'l Business:		Commercial/Industrial:		Graphic Arts/Photog.:		Hardware Dev.:		HR/Other:	Y	Health/Lab	Y
MBA Graduates:	Y	Sales Trainees:	Y	Music:		Consulting/Other:		Training:	Y	Scientists/Research:	
		Advertising Pros.:		Broadcasting:				Health Care:	Y	Petroleum/Chemicals:	
				Other:				Consulting:		Math/Other:	

TYPES OF BUSINESS:

Fertility Treatments
Physician Practice Management-Reproductive Services
Treatment Financing Programs
Fertility-Related Pharmaceutical Distribution

BRANDS/DIVISIONS/AFFILIATES:

Attain IVF Program
AttainFertility.com
Vein Clinics of America, Inc.
VeinClinics.com
Northwest Center for Reproductive Sciences.
Attain Fertility Centers
Vein Clinics

CONTACTS:

Note: Officers with more than one job title may be intentionally listed here more than once.

Jay Higham, CEO
Jay Higham, Pres.
Timothy Sheehan, Interim CFO
Doug Weiss, Dir.-Mktg.
Lori Falcone, VP-Human Resources
Jeffrey C. Futterman, CIO/VP-IT/Chief Security Officer
Scott Soifer, Chief Admin. Officer/Exec. VP
Claude E. White, General Counsel/VP/Sec.
Timothy Sheehan, VP-Finance
Andrew Mintz, Pres., Attain Fertility Centers/Exec. VP
Daniel P. Doman, Pres., Vein Clinics of America, Inc./Exec. VP
Pamela Schumann, Exec. VP-Attain Fertility Centers
Jay Higham, Chmn.

Phone: 914-253-8000	**Fax:** 914-253-8008
Toll-Free: 800-458-0044	
Address: 2 Manhattanville Rd., 3rd Fl., Purchase, NY 10577 US	

GROWTH PLANS/SPECIAL FEATURES:

IntegraMed America, Inc. offers products and services to patients and providers in the fertility and vein segments of the healthcare industry. The company provides services to a network of 86 clinics, which provide conventional fertility and assisted reproductive technology services. The firm operates in two segments: Attain Fertility Centers and Vein Clinics. Attain Fertility Centers has partner contract agreements for the operation of 14 fertility centers, in which the company owns clinic assets and provides turnkey business infrastructure services, marketing services and consumer product offerings. The segment operates the Attain IVF Program, which offers patients up to six assisted reproductive technology treatments for a fixed price and a refund if treatment is unsuccessful. This division maintains a network of 28 independent fertility clinics through its affiliate program. IntegraMed America also operates AttainFertility.com, a web site offering fertility information, as well as treatment options and planning information. The Vein Care division, operated by subsidiary Vein Clinics of America, Inc., provides business and management services to a network of 44 clinics in 14 states specializing in the treatment of vein disease and disorders. This division also offers VeinClinics.com, a website offering information regarding vein care. IntegraMed America supports its operating divisions and their clinics with business infrastructure services, including clinical and financial information systems, revenue cycle management, patient recruitment, sales and marketing, legal services, human resources and group purchasing. In January 2011, the firm acquired Washington-based Northwest Center for Reproductive Sciences.

FINANCIALS:

Sales and profits are in thousands of dollars—add 000 to get the full amount. 2011 Note: Financial information for 2011 was not available for all companies at press time.

2011 Sales: $	2011 Profits: $
2010 Sales: $243,169	2010 Profits: $4,725
2009 Sales: $216,760	2009 Profits: $4,494
2008 Sales: $198,153	2008 Profits: $3,915
2007 Sales: $151,998	2007 Profits: $3,257

U.S. Stock Ticker: INMD
Int'l Ticker:
Int'l Exchange:
Employees: 1,428 Fiscal Year Ends: 12/31
Parent Company:

SALARIES/BENEFITS:

Pension Plan:	ESOP Stock Plan:	Profit Sharing:	Top Exec. Salary: $400,000	Bonus: $94,000
Savings Plan:	Stock Purch. Plan: Y		Second Exec. Salary: $275,500	Bonus: $27,500

OTHER THOUGHTS:

Apparent Women Officers or Directors: 4
Hot Spot for Advancement for Women/Minorities: Y

LOCATIONS: ("Y" = Yes)

West:	Southwest:	Midwest:	Southeast:	Northeast:	International:
Y	Y	Y	Y	Y	

INTERACTIVE DATA CORPORATION

www.interactivedata.com

Industry Group Code: 519130

Management:		Sales/Marketing:		Liberal Arts:		Information Systems:		Professionals:		Technical/Scientific:	
Mgmt. Trainees:		Mktg. Professionals:	Y	Gen. Writing/Editing:	Y	Info. Management:	Y	Finance/Acct.:	Y	Engineers, Elec.:	
Experienced Mgmt.:	Y	Retail Sales:		Technical Writing:	Y	Software Dev.:	Y	Law:	Y	Engineers, Other:	
Int'l Business:	Y	Commercial/Industrial:	Y	Graphic Arts/Photog.:		Hardware Dev.:		HR/Other:	Y	Health/Lab	
MBA Graduates:	Y	Sales Trainees:	Y	Music:		Consulting/Other:		Training:		Scientists/Research:	
		Advertising Pros.:		Broadcasting:				Health Care:		Petroleum/Chemicals:	
				Other:				Consulting:		Math/Other:	

TYPES OF BUSINESS:

Financial Information
Stock Market & Equities Information
Portfolio Management Software
Consulting & Valuation Services
Online Information Service

BRANDS/DIVISIONS/AFFILIATES:

Warburg Pincus LLC
Data Canada Inc
Interactive Data Desktop Solutions
Silver Lake Partners

CONTACTS: *Note: Officers with more than one job title may be intentionally listed here more than once.*

Mason Slaine, CEO
Jay Nadler, COO
Mason Slaine, Pres.
Vincent A. Chippari, CFO/Sr. VP
Bob Skea, Exec. VP-Sales, North America
Lori Hannay, Chief Human Resources Officer/VP
Alex Goor, CIO
Carol Sweeney, General Counsel/Sr. VP
Brendan Beith, Head-EMEA Bus.
Emmanuel Doe, Pres., Trading Solutions Group
Mark Hepsworth, Pres., Institutional Bus.
Mason Slaine, Chmn.
Roger Sargeant, Managing Dir.-Int'l

Phone: 781-687-8500	**Fax:** 781-687-8005
Toll-Free:	
Address: 32 Crosby Dr., Bedford, MA 01730 US	

GROWTH PLANS/SPECIAL FEATURES:

Interactive Data Corporation (IDC), controlled by private equity companies Silver Lake Partners and Warburg Pincus LLC, provides financial market data, analytics and related services to financial institutions, active traders and individual investors. IDC distributes real-time, end-of-day and archived data to customers through a variety of products featuring Internet, dedicated line, satellite and dialup delivery protocols. It also provides links to financial service and software companies, offering trading, analysis, portfolio management and valuation services. The company's Institutional Services segment targets financial institutions, such as banks, brokerage firms, mutual fund companies, insurance companies and money management firms through three businesses. The Interactive Data Pricing and Reference Data business (64.5% of 2010 revenue) provides historical, intraday and end-of-day pricing, evaluations and reference data for a range of securities, commodities and derivative instruments. The Real-Time Data Services business (21.2% of revenue) provides global real-time and delayed financial market information covering equities, derivative instruments, futures, fixed income securities and foreign exchange. IDC's Active Trader Services segment (10%) targets active traders, individual investors and investment community professionals with the Interactive Data Desktop Solutions product, which provides real-time financial market information and access to decision-support tools, assisting in the analysis of securities traded on all major world markets. The Fixed Income Analytics business (4.4%) provides fixed income data and portfolio analytics for risk management. In January 2011, the firm announced its further expansion throughout Canada, including the opening of Data Canada, Inc. in Toronto.

FINANCIALS: **Sales and profits are in thousands of dollars—add 000 to get the full amount. 2011 Note: Financial information for 2011 was not available for all companies at press time.**

2011 Sales: $	2011 Profits: $	**U.S. Stock Ticker: Private**
2010 Sales: $796,645	2010 Profits: $-71,789	**Int'l Ticker:**
2009 Sales: $757,218	2009 Profits: $141,406	Int'l Exchange:
2008 Sales: $750,541	2008 Profits: $142,648	Employees: 2,450 Fiscal Year Ends: 12/31
2007 Sales: $689,610	2007 Profits: $125,983	Parent Company: SILVER LAKE PARTNERS

SALARIES/BENEFITS:

Pension Plan:	ESOP Stock Plan:	Profit Sharing:	Top Exec. Salary: $591,750	Bonus: $697,414
Savings Plan:	Stock Purch. Plan:		Second Exec. Salary: $362,000	Bonus: $254,925

OTHER THOUGHTS:

Apparent Women Officers or Directors: 2
Hot Spot for Advancement for Women/Minorities:

LOCATIONS: ("Y" = Yes)

West:	Southwest:	Midwest:	Southeast:	Northeast:	International:
Y		Y		Y	Y

INTERACTIVE INTELLIGENCE GROUP INC

www.inin.com

Industry Group Code: 33411

Management:		Sales/Marketing:		Liberal Arts:		Information Systems:		Professionals:		Technical/Scientific:	
Mgmt. Trainees:		Mktg. Professionals:	Y	Gen. Writing/Editing:		Info. Management:	Y	Finance/Acct.:	Y	Engineers, Elec.:	Y
Experienced Mgmt.:	Y	Retail Sales:		Technical Writing:	Y	Software Dev.:	Y	Law:	Y	Engineers, Other:	
Int'l Business:	Y	Commercial/Industrial:	Y	Graphic Arts/Photog.:		Hardware Dev.:		HR/Other:	Y	Health/Lab	
MBA Graduates:	Y	Sales Trainees:	Y	Music:		Consulting/Other:	Y	Training:	Y	Scientists/Research:	
		Advertising Pros.:		Broadcasting:				Health Care:		Petroleum/Chemicals:	
				Other:				Consulting:		Math/Other:	

TYPES OF BUSINESS:

Business Communication Software
Accounts Receivable Management Software
Business Process Automation

BRANDS/DIVISIONS/AFFILIATES:

Interactive Intelligence Inc
Global Software Services Inc
Latitude Software
Agori Communications GmbH
CallTime Solutions

CONTACTS: *Note: Officers with more than one job title may be intentionally listed here more than once.*

Donald E. Brown, CEO
Donald E. Brown, Pres.
Stephen R. Head, CFO
Joseph A. Staples, Chief Mktg. Officer/Sr. VP
Michael D. Gagle, Chief Scientist
Stephen R. Head, Sr. VP-Admin.
Stephen R. Head, Corp. Sec.
William J. Gildea, III, Sr. VP-Bus. Dev.
Stephen R. Head, Sr. VP-Finance/Treas.
Pamela J. Hynes, VP-Worldwide Comm.-as-a-Service & Education
Hans W. Heltzel, VP-Support & Professional Svcs.
Gary R. Blough, Exec. VP-Worldwide Sales
Donald E. Brown, Chmn.

Phone: 317-872-3000	**Fax:** 317-872-3000
Toll-Free: 800-267-1364	
Address: 7601 Interactive Way, Indianapolis, IN 46278 US	

GROWTH PLANS/SPECIAL FEATURES:

Interactive Intelligence Group, Inc. (ININ Group) is a holding company for Interactive Intelligence, Inc. (ININ), which develops software applications for various business communication services. With more than 3,500 customers, the firm's primary markets are contact centers, enterprise IP telephony and enterprise messaging. For contact centers, the firm's products allow clients to intelligently route, monitor, record, track and report on phone calls, as well as fax, e-mail and web interactions, whether in a single center or across multi-site contact center operations. Contact center applications also provide clients with services including predictive dialing, workforce management and screen recording. The company's enterprise IP telephony solutions build off its contact center platform. It offers software solutions for various IP telephony applications, including multimedia queuing, mobile access and messaging, targeting enterprises with 100 to 5,000 users, especially those that rely on the Microsoft platform. The business process automation platform allows users to automate and unify phone calls, faxes, e-mails and web interactions. Additionally, through subsidiary Global Software Services, Inc. (operating as Latitude Software), ININ Group provides accounts receivable management software to collection agencies, credit departments, debt buyers, creditors and attorneys to manage all aspects of the debt collection and recovery process. In March 2011, the firm acquired Agori Communications GmbH. In July 2011, it acquired Sydney-based CallTime Solutions. Also in July, the firm completed a holding company reorganization, with ININ becoming a wholly-owned subsidiary of publicly-held ININ Group. In January 2012, the company acquired the contact center assets of its South African-based reseller, ATIO Corp. Pty Ltd.

Employees are offered health insurance; life insurance; disability coverage; flexible spending accounts; health savings accounts; an employee assistance program; tuition reimbursement; and adoption assistance.

FINANCIALS: **Sales and profits are in thousands of dollars—add 000 to get the full amount. 2011 Note: Financial information for 2011 was not available for all companies at press time.**

2011 Sales: $	2011 Profits: $	**U.S. Stock Ticker: ININ**
2010 Sales: $166,315	2010 Profits: $14,901	**Int'l Ticker:**
2009 Sales: $131,418	2009 Profits: $8,640	Int'l Exchange:
2008 Sales: $121,406	2008 Profits: $4,338	Employees: 849 Fiscal Year Ends: 12/31
2007 Sales: $109,901	2007 Profits: $17,456	Parent Company:

SALARIES/BENEFITS:

Pension Plan:	ESOP Stock Plan:	Profit Sharing:	Top Exec. Salary: $361,500	Bonus: $463,308
Savings Plan: Y	Stock Purch. Plan: Y		Second Exec. Salary: $242,500	Bonus: $324,316

OTHER THOUGHTS:

Apparent Women Officers or Directors: 1
Hot Spot for Advancement for Women/Minorities:

LOCATIONS: ("Y" = Yes)

West:	Southwest:	Midwest:	Southeast:	Northeast:	International:
Y		Y	Y	Y	Y

INTERCONTINENTALEXCHANGE INC (ICE)

www.theice.com

Industry Group Code: 523210

Management:		Sales/Marketing:		Liberal Arts:		Information Systems:		Professionals:		Technical/Scientific:	
Mgmt. Trainees:		Mktg. Professionals:	Y	Gen. Writing/Editing:	Y	Info. Management:	Y	Finance/Acct.:	Y	Engineers, Elec.:	
Experienced Mgmt.:	Y	Retail Sales:		Technical Writing:	Y	Software Dev.:	Y	Law:	Y	Engineers, Other:	
Int'l Business:	Y	Commercial/Industrial:		Graphic Arts/Photog.:		Hardware Dev.:		HR/Other:	Y	Health/Lab	
MBA Graduates:	Y	Sales Trainees:		Music:		Consulting/Other:		Training:	Y	Scientists/Research:	
		Advertising Pros.:	Y	Broadcasting:				Health Care:		Petroleum/Chemicals:	
				Other:				Consulting:		Math/Other:	Y

TYPES OF BUSINESS:

Commodity Futures Exchange
Energy Futures
Real-Time Market Data
OTC Clearing
Options Trading
Electronic Trade Confirmations

BRANDS/DIVISIONS/AFFILIATES:

ICE Futures US
ICE Futures Canada
ICE Trust
ICE Clear Europe
Chicago Climate Futures Exchange
ICE Link
ICE Data

CONTACTS: *Note: Officers with more than one job title may be intentionally listed here more than once.*

Jeffrey C. Sprecher, CEO
Charles A. Vice, COO
Charles A. Vice, Pres.
David S. Goone, CFO/Sr. VP
Edwin Marcial, CTO/Sr. VP
Johnathan H. Short, General Counsel/Sr. VP/Corp. Sec.
David S. Goone, Chief Strategic Officer/Sr. VP
Thomas W. Farley, Pres., ICE Futures U.S.
E. Bradley Vannan, Pres./COO-ICE Futures Canada
Christopher S. Edmonds, Pres., ICE Trust
Thomas J. Hammond, Pres./COO-ICE Clear U.S.
Jeffrey C. Sprecher, Chmn.
David J. Peniket, Pres./COO-ICE Futures Europe

Phone: 770-857-4700 **Fax:** 770-857-4755
Toll-Free:
Address: 2100 RiverEdge Pkwy., Ste. 500, Atlanta, GA 30328 US

GROWTH PLANS/SPECIAL FEATURES:

InterContinentalExchange, Inc. (ICE) is an operator of global futures exchanges, Over-The-Counter (OTC) markets and derivatives clearing houses. The company operates through three business segments: futures, global OTC and market data. The futures division has four businesses that operate in regulated exchanges throughout the U.S., the U.K., and Canada and include Chicago Climate Futures Exchange (CCFE), ICE Futures U.S., ICE Futures Canada and ICE Clear Europe. The OTC business manages energy and credit default swaps (CDS) markets through the IntercontinentalExchange online platform where trading and clearing of hundreds of contracts is offered on products such as natural gas and power through clear and bilateral agreements. Clearing services for the OTC energy and European CDS markets are offered through ICE Clear Europe, and clearing for North American CDS is managed by ICE Trust, a limited New York trust. Market data services for futures and OTC markets operate through subsidiary ICE Data, which services energy futures, OTC markets, agricultural commodities, equity indexes and currency pairs by compiling, formatting, and offering packages of market data to customers throughout 24 countries using an online platform. ICE operates on an electronic platform knows as ICE Link that automates post-trade processing for the dealer-to-client and dealer-to-dealer segments of the CDS market.

FINANCIALS: **Sales and profits are in thousands of dollars—add 000 to get the full amount. 2011 Note: Financial information for 2011 was not available for all companies at press time.**

2011 Sales: $1,327,491	2011 Profits: $509,673
2010 Sales: $1,149,944	2010 Profits: $407,767
2009 Sales: $994,788	2009 Profits: $314,154
2008 Sales: $813,078	2008 Profits: $300,972
2007 Sales: $574,293	2007 Profits: $240,612

U.S. Stock Ticker: ICE
Int'l Ticker:
Int'l Exchange:
Employees: 933 Fiscal Year Ends: 12/31
Parent Company:

SALARIES/BENEFITS:

Pension Plan:	ESOP Stock Plan:	Profit Sharing:	Top Exec. Salary: $908,333	Bonus: $2,250,000
Savings Plan: Y	Stock Purch. Plan:		Second Exec. Salary: $600,000	Bonus: $1,000,000

OTHER THOUGHTS:

Apparent Women Officers or Directors: 1
Hot Spot for Advancement for Women/Minorities:

LOCATIONS: ("Y" = Yes)

West:	Southwest:	Midwest:	Southeast:	Northeast:	International:
	Y	Y	Y	Y	Y

INTERMEC INC

www.intermec.com

Industry Group Code: 334119

Management:		Sales/Marketing:		Liberal Arts:		Information Systems:		Professionals:		Technical/Scientific:	
Mgmt. Trainees:		Mktg. Professionals:	Y	Gen. Writing/Editing:	Y	Info. Management:	Y	Finance/Acct.:	Y	Engineers, Elec.:	Y
Experienced Mgmt.:	Y	Retail Sales:		Technical Writing:	Y	Software Dev.:	Y	Law:	Y	Engineers, Other:	Y
Int'l Business:	Y	Commercial/Industrial:	Y	Graphic Arts/Photog.:	Y	Hardware Dev.:	Y	HR/Other:	Y	Health/Lab	
MBA Graduates:	Y	Sales Trainees:	Y	Music:		Consulting/Other:		Training:	Y	Scientists/Research:	
		Advertising Pros.:		Broadcasting:				Health Care:		Petroleum/Chemicals:	
				Other:				Consulting:		Math/Other:	

TYPES OF BUSINESS:

Computer Hardware-Bar Code Systems
Supply Chain Software & Services
RFID Products
Software
Mobile Computing Products

BRANDS/DIVISIONS/AFFILIATES:

CONTACTS:

Note: Officers with more than one job title may be intentionally listed here more than once.

Patrick J. Byrne, CEO
Patrick J. Byrne, Pres.
Robert J. Driessnack, CFO/Sr. VP
James McDonnell, Sr. VP-Global Sales & Mktg.
Jeanne Lyon, VP-Human Resources
Arvin Danielson, CTO
Yukio Morikubo, General Counsel/Sr. VP/Corp. Sec.
Geoffrey Buscher, Dir.-Investor Rel.
Earl Thompson, Sr. VP-Mobile Solutions Bus. Unit
Larry Klimczyk, VP-Intermec Global Solutions
Allen J. Lauer, Chmn.
Dennis Faerber, Sr. VP-Global Supply Chain Oper.

Phone: 425-348-2600 **Fax:** 425-267-2983
Toll-Free: 800-755-5505
Address: 6001 36th Ave. W., Everett, WA 98203-1264 US

GROWTH PLANS/SPECIAL FEATURES:

Intermec, Inc. designs, develops, integrates, sells and offers repair services for fixed and portable automated identification and data collection (AIDC) products used to manage, identify and track supply chain information and assets. Its operations are divided into two segments: products and services. The products segment consists of four primary products lines: mobile computers, including handheld computers and forklift-mounted computers, often with barcode scanning, GPS and RFID (radio frequency identification) features; printers and label media, which includes fixed, desktop and portable barcode and RFID printers, as well as pressure-sensitive bar code labels, thermal transfer ribbons and RFID smart labels; bar code scanners, including fixed and portable devices; and RFID products, such as readers tags and high value inserts for RFID tags. Its services include repair services, providing customers with post-warranty repair or replacement of defective or damaged devices and components; advanced services, which consist of wireless site surveys and assessments, project management, truck and forklift installations and software consulting services, among others; education services, which primarily consist of product training programs; support services; and managed services that wirelessly connect to customers mobile devices and manage operations using real time tracking.

Intermec offers its employees medical, dental and vision coverage; life and AD&D insurance; a 401(k) plan; and more.

FINANCIALS:

Sales and profits are in thousands of dollars—add 000 to get the full amount. 2011 Note: Financial information for 2011 was not available for all companies at press time.

2011 Sales: $848,200	2011 Profits: $-30,800
2010 Sales: $679,111	2010 Profits: $-5,325
2009 Sales: $658,205	2009 Profits: $-11,843
2008 Sales: $890,883	2008 Profits: $35,462
2007 Sales: $849,200	2007 Profits: $23,100

U.S. Stock Ticker: IN
Int'l Ticker:
Int'l Exchange:
Employees: 1,745 Fiscal Year Ends: 12/31
Parent Company:

SALARIES/BENEFITS:

Pension Plan:	ESOP Stock Plan:	Profit Sharing:	Top Exec. Salary: $698,508	Bonus: $
Savings Plan: Y	Stock Purch. Plan: Y		Second Exec. Salary: $349,315	Bonus: $

OTHER THOUGHTS:

Apparent Women Officers or Directors: 2
Hot Spot for Advancement for Women/Minorities: Y

LOCATIONS: ("Y" = Yes)

West:	Southwest:	Midwest:	Southeast:	Northeast:	International:
Y	Y	Y	Y	Y	Y

INTERNAP NETWORK SERVICES CORP

www.internap.com

Industry Group Code: 517110

Management:		Sales/Marketing:		Liberal Arts:		Information Systems:		Professionals:		Technical/Scientific:	
Mgmt. Trainees:		Mktg. Professionals:	Y	Gen. Writing/Editing:	Y	Info. Management:	Y	Finance/Acct.:	Y	Engineers, Elec.:	Y
Experienced Mgmt.:	Y	Retail Sales:		Technical Writing:	Y	Software Dev.:	Y	Law:	Y	Engineers, Other:	
Int'l Business:	Y	Commercial/Industrial:	Y	Graphic Arts/Photog.:		Hardware Dev.:		HR/Other:	Y	Health/Lab	
MBA Graduates:	Y	Sales Trainees:	Y	Music:		Consulting/Other:		Training:	Y	Scientists/Research:	
		Advertising Pros.:		Broadcasting:				Health Care:		Petroleum/Chemicals:	
				Other:				Consulting:		Math/Other:	

TYPES OF BUSINESS:

Internet Access Provider
Voice-Over-Internet Protocol
Multimedia Streaming
Virtual Private Networking
Value-Added Services

BRANDS/DIVISIONS/AFFILIATES:

Internap Japan Co Ltd
Flow Control Platform

CONTACTS: *Note: Officers with more than one job title may be intentionally listed here more than once.*

Eric Cooney, CEO
Eric Cooney, Pres.
George E. Kilguss, III, CFO
Mandira Mehra, Sr. VP-Mktg.
Bruce Meyer, Sr. VP-Human Resources
Paul Carmody, Sr. VP-Prod. Mgmt.
Tashia L. Rivard, Sr. VP-Legal Svcs./Corp. Sec.
Steven Orchard, Sr. VP-Oper. & Support
Paul Carmody, Sr. VP-Bus. Dev.
Drew Miale, Contact-Press
Andrew McBath, Contact-Investor Rel.
Michael Higgins, Sr. VP-Data Center Svcs.
Daniel C. Stanzione, Chmn.
Randal Thompson, Sr. VP-Global Sales

Phone: 404-302-9700	**Fax:** 404-475-0520
Toll-Free: 877-843-7627	
Address: 250 Williams St., Atlanta, GA 30303 US	

GROWTH PLANS/SPECIAL FEATURES:

Internap Network Services Corp. markets products and services that optimize the performance and reliability of strategic business Internet applications and provides Internet access. Applications served include e-commerce, customer relationship management, multimedia streaming, VoIP (Voice over Internet Protocol), virtual private networks and supply chain management. The company operates in two segments: IP services and data center services. The IP services segment offers appropriate network solutions to each customer's individual business needs. The Flow Control Platform is included in this segment and is a premise-based intelligent routing hardware product for customers who run their own multiple network architectures. IP services are offered at 76 service points across Europe, North America and Asia-Pacific. This segment also offers CDN services that allow customers to quickly and securely stream and distribute video, audio and software to audiences across the globe; and provides capacity-on-demand to handle large events and traffic spikes and the delivery of high quality content. Internap Network's data center services segment consists of data centers where customers can host their applications directly on the network to eliminate issues associated with the quality of local connections. The facilities are a combination of company-owned centers as well as facilities managed by third parties or partner sites. Internap Network currently operates 37 data centers in North America, Europe and Asia-Pacific. Comprehensive solutions are provided at 28 partner sites and nine company-controlled facilities. The company offers its services to roughly 2,700 customers in 28 markets worldwide. Internap Japan Co., Ltd., a joint venture with Japanese telecom giants Nippon Telegraph & Telephone Corp. and NTT-ME Corporation, provides Internet connectivity for Japanese businesses. In 2010, Internap Network Services opened a new company-controlled data center in Santa Clara, California. It also expanded its data centers in Houston, Texas; Boston, Massachusetts; and Seattle, Washington.

Employees are offered medical, dental, and vision insurance; discounted auto, legal, home and renter's insurance; an employee assistance program; and paid time off.

FINANCIALS: **Sales and profits are in thousands of dollars—add 000 to get the full amount. 2011 Note: Financial information for 2011 was not available for all companies at press time.**

2011 Sales: $	2011 Profits: $
2010 Sales: $244,164	2010 Profits: $-3,622
2009 Sales: $256,259	2009 Profits: $-69,725
2008 Sales: $253,989	2008 Profits: $-104,813
2007 Sales: $234,090	2007 Profits: $-5,555

U.S. Stock Ticker: INAP
Int'l Ticker:
Int'l Exchange:
Employees: 416 Fiscal Year Ends: 12/31
Parent Company:

SALARIES/BENEFITS:

Pension Plan:	ESOP Stock Plan:	Profit Sharing:	Top Exec. Salary: $475,000	Bonus: $500,000
Savings Plan: Y	Stock Purch. Plan: Y		Second Exec. Salary: $275,000	Bonus: $97,103

OTHER THOUGHTS:

Apparent Women Officers or Directors: 4
Hot Spot for Advancement for Women/Minorities: Y

LOCATIONS: ("Y" = Yes)

West:	Southwest:	Midwest:	Southeast:	Northeast:	International:
Y	Y	Y	Y	Y	Y

INTERNATIONAL CREATIVE MANAGEMENT INC (ICM)

www.icmtalent.com

Industry Group Code: 711410

Management:		Sales/Marketing:		Liberal Arts:		Information Systems:		Professionals:		Technical/Scientific:	
Mgmt. Trainees:		Mktg. Professionals:	Y	Gen. Writing/Editing:		Info. Management:	Y	Finance/Acct.:	Y	Engineers, Elec.:	
Experienced Mgmt.:	Y	Retail Sales:		Technical Writing:		Software Dev.:		Law:	Y	Engineers, Other:	
Int'l Business:	Y	Commercial/Industrial:	Y	Graphic Arts/Photog.:		Hardware Dev.:		HR/Other:	Y	Health/Lab	
MBA Graduates:	Y	Sales Trainees:	Y	Music:		Consulting/Other:		Training:	Y	Scientists/Research:	
		Advertising Pros.:		Broadcasting:				Health Care:		Petroleum/Chemicals:	
				Other:				Consulting:		Math/Other:	

TYPES OF BUSINESS:

Agents-Actors & Directors
Agents-Writers & Musicians
Agents-Literary
Agents-Lecture

BRANDS/DIVISIONS/AFFILIATES:

ICM Artists
ICM Foreign Rights

CONTACTS: *Note: Officers with more than one job title may be intentionally listed here more than once.*

Jeffrey Berg, CEO
Dan Donahue, COO
Chris Silbermann, Pres.
Richard B. Levy, General Counsel
Richard Levy, Chief Bus. Dev. Officer
Joe Friedman, Controller/Sr. VP
Esther Newberg, Sr. VP
Jeffrey Berg, Chmn.

Phone: 310-550-4000	**Fax:** 310-550-4100
Toll-Free:	
Address: 10250 Constellation Blvd., Los Angeles, CA 90067 US	

GROWTH PLANS/SPECIAL FEATURES:

International Creative Management, Inc. (ICM) is one of the world's largest talent and literary agencies, with offices in Los Angeles, New York and London. The company represents actors, directors, musicians and writers, as well as creative talent in theater, commercials, public speaking and new media. ICM's clients include actors Christopher Walken, Alan Alda, Al Pacino, Jon Stewart, Sigourney Weaver, Ellen DeGeneres, Robert Duvall and Samuel L. Jackson; musicians Courtney Love, Beyonce Knowles and Nadia Turner; authors E. L. Doctorow, Tom Bodett and Toni Morrison; and film directors Roman Polanski and Woody Allen, among others. The firm's branded entertainment division uses its assets to form alliances with major corporations for a range of activities, including celebrity endorsements, product integrations and tour sponsorships. Its music and performance subsidiary, ICM Artists, represents classical instrumentalists, vocalists and conductors, chamber ensembles, choirs and dance and opera companies, as well as other performing groups. ICM's Foreign Rights department, based in London, sells ICM book and magazine products in the U.K. and other foreign countries.

FINANCIALS: **Sales and profits are in thousands of dollars—add 000 to get the full amount. 2011 Note: Financial information for 2011 was not available for all companies at press time.**

2011 Sales: $	2011 Profits: $	**U.S. Stock Ticker: Private**
2010 Sales: $	2010 Profits: $	**Int'l Ticker:**
2009 Sales: $	2009 Profits: $	Int'l Exchange:
2008 Sales: $	2008 Profits: $	Employees: Fiscal Year Ends: 6/30
2007 Sales: $	2007 Profits: $	Parent Company:

SALARIES/BENEFITS:

Pension Plan:	ESOP Stock Plan:	Profit Sharing:	Top Exec. Salary: $	Bonus: $
Savings Plan:	Stock Purch. Plan:		Second Exec. Salary: $	Bonus: $

OTHER THOUGHTS:

Apparent Women Officers or Directors: 1
Hot Spot for Advancement for Women/Minorities:

LOCATIONS: ("Y" = Yes)

West:	Southwest:	Midwest:	Southeast:	Northeast:	International:
Y				Y	Y

INTERNATIONAL DAIRY QUEEN INC

www.dairyqueen.com

Industry Group Code: 722110

Management:		Sales/Marketing:		Liberal Arts:		Information Systems:		Professionals:		Technical/Scientific:	
Mgmt. Trainees:	Y	Mktg. Professionals:	Y	Gen. Writing/Editing:	Y	Info. Management:	Y	Finance/Acct.:	Y	Engineers, Elec.:	
Experienced Mgmt.:	Y	Retail Sales:		Technical Writing:		Software Dev.:	Y	Law:	Y	Engineers, Other:	
Int'l Business:	Y	Commercial/Industrial:		Graphic Arts/Photog.:	Y	Hardware Dev.:		HR/Other:	Y	Health/Lab	
MBA Graduates:	Y	Sales Trainees:		Music:		Consulting/Other:		Training:	Y	Scientists/Research:	
		Advertising Pros.:	Y	Broadcasting:				Health Care:		Petroleum/Chemicals:	
				Other:				Consulting:		Math/Other:	

TYPES OF BUSINESS:

Restaurants
Fast Food Chains
Frozen Desserts

BRANDS/DIVISIONS/AFFILIATES:

Dairy Queen
Karmelkorn Shoppe
Orange Julius
BLIZZARD
Berkshire Hathaway Inc

CONTACTS: *Note: Officers with more than one job title may be intentionally listed here more than once.*

John Gainor, CEO
John Gainor, Pres.
Charles J. Chapman, COO-U.S.
Eric D. Lavanger, VP-Dev.
Dean Peters, Dir.-Comm.
Eric D. Lavanger, VP-Design & Architecture

Phone: 952-830-8696 **Fax:** 952-830-0273
Toll-Free:
Address: 7505 Metro Blvd., Minneapolis, MN 55439 US

GROWTH PLANS/SPECIAL FEATURES:

International Dairy Queen, Inc., owned by Berkshire Hathaway, Inc., develops and services a system of Dairy Queen restaurants, Karmelkorn Shoppes and Orange Julius stores. There are more than 5,900 Dairy Queens located in 20 countries. Restaurant locations include the U.S., Canada, Europe, Asia, Mexico, and the Middle East. Dairy Queen's dairy dessert product line includes soft-serve ice cream cones, BLIZZARD flavor treats, shakes, malts, sundaes and specialty frozen confections. The restaurants also offer a menu of fast food items including hamburgers, hot dogs, chicken strips, barbecue and chicken sandwiches, French fries and onion rings. International Dairy Queen operates over 700 Orange Julius stores, featuring blended drinks made from orange juice, fruits and fruit flavors; and over 20 Karmelkorn Shoppes featuring popcorn and other treat items. In 2011, the firm opened several new stores in locations including Allen, Texas; Lansing, Michigan; Cameron, North Carolina; and West Palm Beach, Florida. In January 2012, the company opened several new stores in locations including Peoria, Arizona; Tempe, Arizona; Bridgeport, West Virginia; and Memphis, Tennessee. In February 2012, the company opened a new store in China.

The company offers its employees a benefits package including medical and dental insurance; short- and long-term disability; life insurance; and a global medical assistance program.

FINANCIALS: **Sales and profits are in thousands of dollars—add 000 to get the full amount. 2011 Note: Financial information for 2011 was not available for all companies at press time.**

2011 Sales: $	2011 Profits: $	**U.S. Stock Ticker: Subsidiary**
2010 Sales: $	2010 Profits: $	**Int'l Ticker:**
2009 Sales: $	2009 Profits: $	Int'l Exchange:
2008 Sales: $	2008 Profits: $	Employees: Fiscal Year Ends: 12/31
2007 Sales: $	2007 Profits: $	Parent Company: BERKSHIRE HATHAWAY INC

SALARIES/BENEFITS:

Pension Plan:	ESOP Stock Plan:	Profit Sharing:	Top Exec. Salary: $	Bonus: $
Savings Plan:	Stock Purch. Plan:		Second Exec. Salary: $	Bonus: $

OTHER THOUGHTS:

Apparent Women Officers or Directors:
Hot Spot for Advancement for Women/Minorities:

LOCATIONS: ("Y" = Yes)

West:	Southwest:	Midwest:	Southeast:	Northeast:	International:
Y	Y	Y	Y	Y	Y

INTUITIVE SURGICAL INC

www.intuitivesurgical.com

Industry Group Code: 33911

Management:		**Sales/Marketing:**		**Liberal Arts:**		**Information Systems:**		**Professionals:**		**Technical/Scientific:**	
Mgmt. Trainees:		Mktg. Professionals:	Y	Gen. Writing/Editing:		Info. Management:	Y	Finance/Acct.:	Y	Engineers, Elec.:	Y
Experienced Mgmt.:	Y	Retail Sales:		Technical Writing:	Y	Software Dev.:	Y	Law:	Y	Engineers, Other:	Y
Int'l Business:	Y	Commercial/Industrial:	Y	Graphic Arts/Photog.:		Hardware Dev.:	Y	HR/Other:	Y	Health/Lab	Y
MBA Graduates:	Y	Sales Trainees:	Y	Music:		Consulting/Other:		Training:	Y	Scientists/Research:	Y
		Advertising Pros.:		Broadcasting:				Health Care:	Y	Petroleum/Chemicals:	
				Other:				Consulting:		Math/Other:	

TYPES OF BUSINESS:

Endoscopic Surgery Products
Operative Surgical Robots

BRANDS/DIVISIONS/AFFILIATES:

da Vinci Surgical System
EndoWrist
da Vinci HD Surgical System
da Vinci Si Surgical System

CONTACTS:

Note: Officers with more than one job title may be intentionally listed here more than once.

Gary S. Guthart, CEO
Gary S. Guthart, Pres.
Marshall L. Mohr, CFO/Sr. VP
Jerry J. McNamara, Exec. VP-Worldwide Sales & Mktg.
Nancy L. Hill, VP-Human Resources
William C. Nowlin, VP-Research & Prod. Quality
Dave J. Rosa, Sr. VP-Prod. Dev.
Salvatore J. Brogna, Sr. VP-Eng.
Mark J. Meltzer, General Counsel/Sr. VP
Augusto V. Castello, Sr. VP-Prod. Oper.
Frank Grillo, VP-Bus. & Mktg. Dev.
Nora Distefano, Contact-Media
Benjamin Gong, VP-Finance
Colin Morales, Sr. VP-Customer Support Group
Aleks Cukic, VP-Strategy
Lonnie M. Smith, Chmn.
Pierre Rivaux, VP-Sales & Mktg., Int'l

Phone: 408-523-2100 **Fax:** 408-523-1390
Toll-Free: 888-868-4647
Address: 1266 Kifer Rd., Sunnyvale, CA 94086 US

GROWTH PLANS/SPECIAL FEATURES:

Intuitive Surgical, Inc. manufactures operative surgical robotics, including the da Vinci Surgical System, which consists of a surgeon's console, a patient-side cart, a high-performance vision system and Intuitive's proprietary wristed instruments. The system provides the surgeon with the control, range of motion, fine tissue manipulation capability and 3-D visualization characteristics of open surgery, but utilizes the small ports of minimally invasive surgery (MIS). The da Vinci Surgical System controls Intuitive's endoscopic instruments. Surgeons operate while seated at a console viewing a 3-D high definition (HD) vision system, which enhances visualization of tissue planes and critical anatomy, and has a digital zoom feature, allowing surgeons to magnify the surgical field of view without adjusting endoscope position. The system also includes a motorized patient cart. Intuitive also manufactures a variety of EndoWrist instruments; each incorporates a wrist joint with tips customized for various surgical procedures. The firm's da Vinci HD Surgical System offers, in addition to 3-D high-definition vision, better resolution and 20% more viewing area than the original design. Recently, the company released the da Vinci Si Surgical System, a more efficient, higher resolution version of the da Vinci HD Surgical System. Intuitive has sold over 1,752 da Vinci systems, covering approximately 278,000 procedures in hospitals worldwide. The firm recently began marketing the da Vinci line in Japan, and so far has sold 13 units in the country.

Intuitive offers its employees a dependent care plan; a medical expenses reimbursement plan; a commuter check program; an employee assistance program; an employee recognition program; a patent bonus program; on-site dental services; on-site dry cleaning and oil change services; entertainment discounts; company events; a 401(k) plan; a discount stock purchase plan; and prescription, dental and vision coverage.

FINANCIALS:

Sales and profits are in thousands of dollars—add 000 to get the full amount. 2011 Note: Financial information for 2011 was not available for all companies at press time.

2011 Sales: $1,757,300	2011 Profits: $495,100
2010 Sales: $1,413,000	2010 Profits: $381,800
2009 Sales: $1,052,168	2009 Profits: $232,606
2008 Sales: $874,919	2008 Profits: $204,315
2007 Sales: $600,828	2007 Profits: $144,537

U.S. Stock Ticker: ISRG
Int'l Ticker:
Int'l Exchange:
Employees: 700 Fiscal Year Ends: 12/31
Parent Company:

SALARIES/BENEFITS:

Pension Plan:	ESOP Stock Plan:	Profit Sharing:	Top Exec. Salary: $504,167	Bonus: $361,463
Savings Plan: Y	Stock Purch. Plan: Y		Second Exec. Salary: $365,000	Bonus: $571,938

OTHER THOUGHTS:

Apparent Women Officers or Directors: 2
Hot Spot for Advancement for Women/Minorities: Y

LOCATIONS: ("Y" = Yes)

West:	Southwest:	Midwest:	Southeast:	Northeast:	International:
Y					Y

INVESTMENT TECHNOLOGY GROUP INC (ITG) www.itg.com

Industry Group Code: 518210

Management:		Sales/Marketing:		Liberal Arts:		Information Systems:		Professionals:		Technical/Scientific:	
Mgmt. Trainees:	Y	Mktg. Professionals:	Y	Gen. Writing/Editing:	Y	Info. Management:	Y	Finance/Acct.:	Y	Engineers, Elec.:	Y
Experienced Mgmt.:	Y	Retail Sales:		Technical Writing:	Y	Software Dev.:	Y	Law:	Y	Engineers, Other:	
Int'l Business:	Y	Commercial/Industrial:	Y	Graphic Arts/Photog.:		Hardware Dev.:		HR/Other:	Y	Health/Lab	
MBA Graduates:	Y	Sales Trainees:	Y	Music:		Consulting/Other:		Training:	Y	Scientists/Research:	
		Advertising Pros.:		Broadcasting:				Health Care:		Petroleum/Chemicals:	
				Other:				Consulting:		Math/Other:	

TYPES OF BUSINESS:

Online Trading Systems
Transaction Research
Data Processing Services

BRANDS/DIVISIONS/AFFILIATES:

ITG Inc
POSIT
AlterNet Securities Inc
Radical
Triton
ITG Derivatives LLC
POSIT Alert LLC
Smart Liquidity

CONTACTS: *Note: Officers with more than one job title may be intentionally listed here more than once.*

Robert Gasser, CEO
Robert Gasser, Pres.
Steven Vigliotti, CFO/Managing Dir.
Peter Goldstein, Head-Human Resources/Managing Dir.
Ian Domowitz, Managing Dir.-Research, Networking & Analytical
David L. Meitz, Managing. Dir.-Software Tech. & Dev.
Mats Goebels, General Counsel/Corp. Sec./Managing Dir.
Jamie Selway, Managing Dir.- Bus. Strategy & Liquidity
Angelo Bulone, Controller/Managing Dir.
Andrew Larkin, Managing Dir.-Int'l Sales & Portfolio Trading Bus.
Rob Boardman, Managing Dir./CEO-EMEA
Frank Nebbeling, Managing Dir.-Global Client & Tech. Svcs.
Lorelei Skillman, Managing Dir.-Products & Svcs.
Maureen O'Hara, Chmn.
David Stevens, CEO-Asia Pacific

Phone: 212-588-4000	**Fax:** 212-444-6353
Toll-Free: 800-991-4484	
Address: 380 Madison Ave., New York, NY 10017 US	

GROWTH PLANS/SPECIAL FEATURES:

Investment Technology Group, Inc. (ITG) is an independent agency research broker that partners with asset managers globally, using a consultative approach in delivering high quality liquidity, execution services, analytical tools and proprietary research grounded in data. ITG offers asset managers with brokerage and financial technology that combines pre-trade analysis, portfolio management, trade execution and post-trade evaluation. The firm operates in four segments: U.S. Operations, Canada Operations, European Operations and Asia Pacific Operations. The company's primary services include pre-trade solutions, such as portfolio management, optimization and compliance and pre-trade analytics products; trade offerings, including execution, management and connectivity, POSIT equity securities crossing and algorithmic trading products; and post-trade solutions, such as measurement and analytics and post-trade processing products. Trade is executed using global execution management systems (EMS) such as Triton, a multi-asset EMS for global equity & equity derivatives; Radical, an active single-stock and options EMS; Macgregor XIP, a multi-asset order management system (OMS); ITG Channel, a POSIT liquidity sweeper; ITG Net, a global network service and Trading Services, a global agency for trading & hedge fund services. ITG's principal subsidiaries include ITG, Inc.; AlterNet Securities, Inc.; ITG Derivatives LLC; and POSIT Alert LLC. International subsidiaries include Investment Technology Group Limited (ITG Europe), an institutional broker-dealer in Europe; ITG Australia Limited; ITG Canada Corp.; ITG Hong Kong Limited and ITG Japan, Ltd. In April 2011, ITG launched Smart Liquidity, a multimedia microsite offering strategies for finding and capitalizing on quality liquidity in today's fragmented markets. In September 2011, ITG expanded their global liquidity aggregation platform with the launch of POSIT Marketplace for Japanese equities.

FINANCIALS: **Sales and profits are in thousands of dollars—add 000 to get the full amount. 2011 Note: Financial information for 2011 was not available for all companies at press time.**

2011 Sales: $570,000 | 2011 Profits: $-179,800
2010 Sales: $570,754 | 2010 Profits: $23,980
2009 Sales: $633,069 | 2009 Profits: $42,834
2008 Sales: $762,983 | 2008 Profits: $114,642
2007 Sales: $730,999 | 2007 Profits: $111,107

U.S. Stock Ticker: ITG
Int'l Ticker:
Int'l Exchange:
Employees: 1,186 Fiscal Year Ends: 12/31
Parent Company:

SALARIES/BENEFITS:

Pension Plan: ESOP Stock Plan: Profit Sharing: Top Exec. Salary: $750,000 Bonus: $1,375,000
Savings Plan: Stock Purch. Plan: Second Exec. Salary: $500,000 Bonus: $450,000

OTHER THOUGHTS:

Apparent Women Officers or Directors: 2
Hot Spot for Advancement for Women/Minorities:

LOCATIONS: ("Y" = Yes)

West:	Southwest:	Midwest:	Southeast:	Northeast:	International:
Y		Y		Y	Y

INVESTORS REAL ESTATE TRUST

www.iret.com

Industry Group Code: 531110

Management:		Sales/Marketing:		Liberal Arts:		Information Systems:		Professionals:		Technical/Scientific:	
Mgmt. Trainees:		Mktg. Professionals:		Gen. Writing/Editing:	Y	Info. Management:	Y	Finance/Acct.:	Y	Engineers, Elec.:	
Experienced Mgmt.:	Y	Retail Sales:		Technical Writing:		Software Dev.:		Law:	Y	Engineers, Other:	
Int'l Business:		Commercial/Industrial:		Graphic Arts/Photog.:		Hardware Dev.:		HR/Other:	Y	Health/Lab	
MBA Graduates:	Y	Sales Trainees:		Music:		Consulting/Other:		Training:		Scientists/Research:	
		Advertising Pros.:	Y	Broadcasting:				Health Care:		Petroleum/Chemicals:	
				Other:				Consulting:		Math/Other:	

TYPES OF BUSINESS:

Real Estate Investment Trust
Apartment Communities
Retail, Office & Industrial Properties
Medical Properties

BRANDS/DIVISIONS/AFFILIATES:

IRET Properties

CONTACTS:

Note: Officers with more than one job title may be intentionally listed here more than once.

Timothy P. Mihalick, CEO
Thomas A. Wentz, Jr., COO/Sr. VP
Timothy P. Mihalick, Pres.
Diane K. Bryantt, CFO/Sr. VP
Thomas A. Wentz, Sr., CIO/Sr. VP
Michael Bosh, General Counsel/Sr. VP/Assistant Sec.
Ted E. Holmes, Sr. VP-Finance
Karin M. Wentz, Chief Compliance Officer/Sr. VP/Sec.
Charles A. Greenberg, Sr. VP-Asset Management Group
Andrew Martin, Sr. VP-Residential Property Mgmt.
Jeffrey L. Miller, Chmn.

Phone: 701-837-4738 **Fax:** 701-838-7785
Toll-Free: 888-478-4738
Address: 1400 31st Ave. SW, Ste. 60, Minot, ND 58702 US

GROWTH PLANS/SPECIAL FEATURES:

Investors Real Estate Trust is a self-advised real estate investment trust (REIT) involved in the ownership and operation of multi-family residential, commercial office, medical, industrial and retail properties. The firm conducts its business operations through its operating partnership, IRET Properties. Its portfolio contains approximately 78 multi-family residential properties, with a total of 8,661 apartment units; 68 office properties containing 5.1 million square feet of leasable space; 56 medical properties, including senior housing properties, for a total of approximately 2.7 million square feet of leasable space; 19 industrial properties, with a total of 3 million square feet of leasable space; and 33 retail properties, containing approximately 1.4 million square feet of leasable space. The day-to-day management activities of many of the firm's properties are either maintained through the company's employees or by third party property management firms. The trust's main geographical area of concentration is in the upper Midwest, primarily Minnesota and North Dakota, with these two states together representing approximately 68.6% of 2011 revenue. The firm also owns properties in Colorado, Kansas, Nebraska, South Dakota, Wyoming, Montana, Idaho, Missouri, Iowa, Wisconsin and Michigan.

FINANCIALS:

Sales and profits are in thousands of dollars—add 000 to get the full amount. 2011 Note: Financial information for 2011 was not available for all companies at press time.

2011 Sales: $237,407	2011 Profits: $17,710
2010 Sales: $242,775	2010 Profits: $4,585
2009 Sales: $240,005	2009 Profits: $8,526
2008 Sales: $221,170	2008 Profits: $12,088
2007 Sales: $197,817	2007 Profits: $14,110

U.S. Stock Ticker: IRET
Int'l Ticker:
Int'l Exchange:
Employees: 383 Fiscal Year Ends: 4/30
Parent Company:

SALARIES/BENEFITS:

Pension Plan:	ESOP Stock Plan:	Profit Sharing:	Top Exec. Salary: $386,772	Bonus: $103,826
Savings Plan:	Stock Purch. Plan:		Second Exec. Salary: $330,792	Bonus: $88,798

OTHER THOUGHTS:

Apparent Women Officers or Directors: 3
Hot Spot for Advancement for Women/Minorities:

LOCATIONS: ("Y" = Yes)

West:	Southwest:	Midwest:	Southeast:	Northeast:	International:
Y		Y			

IRIDEX CORP

www.iridex.com

Industry Group Code: 33911

Management:		Sales/Marketing:		Liberal Arts:		Information Systems:		Professionals:		Technical/Scientific:	
Mgmt. Trainees:		Mktg. Professionals:	Y	Gen. Writing/Editing:		Info. Management:	Y	Finance/Acct.:	Y	Engineers, Elec.:	Y
Experienced Mgmt.:	Y	Retail Sales:		Technical Writing:	Y	Software Dev.:	Y	Law:	Y	Engineers, Other:	Y
Int'l Business:	Y	Commercial/Industrial:	Y	Graphic Arts/Photog.:		Hardware Dev.:	Y	HR/Other:	Y	Health/Lab	Y
MBA Graduates:	Y	Sales Trainees:	Y	Music:		Consulting/Other:		Training:	Y	Scientists/Research:	Y
		Advertising Pros.:		Broadcasting:				Health Care:	Y	Petroleum/Chemicals:	
				Other:				Consulting:		Math/Other:	

TYPES OF BUSINESS:

Equipment-Laser Systems
Ophthalmological & Dermatological Laser Systems

BRANDS/DIVISIONS/AFFILIATES:

DioLite XP
VariLite Dual Wavelength Laser
OcuLight TX
IRIS Medical IQ810
OcuLight Symphony
OcuLight SL
OcuLight SLx
DioVet

CONTACTS: *Note: Officers with more than one job title may be intentionally listed here more than once.*

Theodore A. Boutacoff, CEO
Theodore A. Boutacoff, Pres.
James H. Mackaness, CFO
Eduardo Arias, Sr. VP-Bus. Dev.
William M. Moore, Chmn.
Eduardo Arias, Sr. VP-Int'l Sales

Phone: 650-940-4700 **Fax:** 650-940-4710
Toll-Free: 800-388-4747
Address: 1212 Terra Bella Ave., Mountain View, CA 94043-1824 US

GROWTH PLANS/SPECIAL FEATURES:

IRIDEX Corp. provides therapeutic based laser systems and delivery devices used in aesthetic medicine, ophthalmology and otolaryngology. IRIDEX markets its products through a direct sales force in the U.S. and a network of approximately 100 distributors that sells in 107 countries. In the aesthetic medicine division, the company's products treat skin conditions, primarily vascular and pigmented lesions. IRIDEX also has two European subsidiaries in the aesthetics division, in the U.K. and France. The company's dermatology laser systems include the DioLite XP and the VariLite Dual Wavelength Laser systems. IRIDEX's ophthalmologic division includes the company's family of OcuLight laser systems, which accounts for the majority of its revenues. These systems are used for ophthalmic applications primarily in operating rooms. The OcuLight product family includes the OcuLight TX; the IRIS Medical IQ810 laser system; OcuLight Symphony; OcuLight SL; OcuLight SLx; and the OcuLight GL and OcuLight GLx laser photocoagulation systems. The firm also offers products for veterinary ophthalmology, including the DioVet laser system for the treatment of glaucoma, pigmented tumors and retinal disorders. IRIDEX's ophthalmology products are used in the treatment of serious eye diseases, including the three leading causes of irreversible blindness: age-related macular degeneration, diabetic retinopathy and glaucoma. The company's ophthalmic and dermatology laser system consists of small, portable laser consoles and delivery devices. Ophthalmologists use the company's laser with either an indirect laser ophthalmoscope or a disposable single-use EndoProbe. IRIDEX's consoles include 532 nanometer laser systems, such as the OcuLight TX, OcuLight GLx and OcuProbe, which perform certain hearing loss correction procedures as well.

FINANCIALS: **Sales and profits are in thousands of dollars—add 000 to get the full amount. 2011 Note: Financial information for 2011 was not available for all companies at press time.**

2011 Sales: $
2010 Sales: $43,694
2009 Sales: $43,212
2008 Sales: $48,528
2007 Sales: $55,532

2011 Profits: $
2010 Profits: $3,046
2009 Profits: $2,585
2008 Profits: $-7,370
2007 Profits: $-22,272

U.S. Stock Ticker: IRIX
Int'l Ticker:
Int'l Exchange:
Employees: 145 Fiscal Year Ends: 12/31
Parent Company:

SALARIES/BENEFITS:

Pension Plan: ESOP Stock Plan: Profit Sharing: Top Exec. Salary: $267,539 Bonus: $15,815
Savings Plan: Y Stock Purch. Plan: Second Exec. Salary: $252,135 Bonus: $10,312

OTHER THOUGHTS:

Apparent Women Officers or Directors:
Hot Spot for Advancement for Women/Minorities:

LOCATIONS: ("Y" = Yes)

West:	Southwest:	Midwest:	Southeast:	Northeast:	International:
Y	Y	Y	Y	Y	Y

IRIS INTERNATIONAL INC

www.proiris.com

Industry Group Code: 33911

Management:		Sales/Marketing:		Liberal Arts:		Information Systems:		Professionals:		Technical/Scientific:	
Mgmt. Trainees:		Mktg. Professionals:	Y	Gen. Writing/Editing:		Info. Management:	Y	Finance/Acct.:	Y	Engineers, Elec.:	Y
Experienced Mgmt.:	Y	Retail Sales:		Technical Writing:	Y	Software Dev.:	Y	Law:	Y	Engineers, Other:	Y
Int'l Business:	Y	Commercial/Industrial:	Y	Graphic Arts/Photog.:		Hardware Dev.:	Y	HR/Other:	Y	Health/Lab	Y
MBA Graduates:	Y	Sales Trainees:	Y	Music:		Consulting/Other:		Training:	Y	Scientists/Research:	Y
		Advertising Pros.:		Broadcasting:				Health Care:	Y	Petroleum/Chemicals:	
				Other:				Consulting:		Math/Other:	

TYPES OF BUSINESS:

Equipment-Body Fluid Analysis
Automated Urinalysis Workstations
Digital Imaging Software, Research & Development
Molecular Pathology Testing Services

BRANDS/DIVISIONS/AFFILIATES:

iQ
iChem VELOCITY
iRICELL
IRIS Sample Processing
IRIS Molecular Diagnostics
Arista Molecular
OvaTube
NADiA ProsVue

CONTACTS: *Note: Officers with more than one job title may be intentionally listed here more than once.*

Cesar M. Garcia, CEO
Cesar M. Garcia, Pres.
Amin I. Khalifa, CFO
Richard O'Leary, VP-Human Resources
Philip J. Ginsburg, Chief Medical Officer/VP
Thomas H. Adams, CTO/VP/Head-Iris Molecular Diagnostics
Richard O'Leary, VP-Admin.
Peter L. Donato, Sec.
John U. Yi, VP-Oper.
Amin I. Khalifa, VP-Finance
Thomas E. Warekois, VP/Pres., Iris Diagnostics
Robert A. Mello, VP/Pres., Iris Sample Processing
Vance R. White, VP/Pres., Arista Molecular
Cesar M. Garcia, Chmn.
Alain Richard, Dir.-Direct Sales, Europe

Phone: 818-709-1244	**Fax:** 818-700-9661
Toll-Free: 800-776-4747	
Address: 9172 Eton Ave., Chatsworth, CA 91311 US	

GROWTH PLANS/SPECIAL FEATURES:

IRIS International, Inc. is a global in vitro diagnostics (IVD) company focused on products that analyze particles and living cell morphologies of various body fluids. The initial applications for IRIS's technology have been in the urinalysis market, where it is a leading worldwide provider of urine microscopy systems, with an installed base of over 3,000 systems in more than 50 countries. In this market, the company also provides integrated solutions comprising urine microscopy and urine chemistry products as well as consumable supplies, system support services and sample preparation products. The firm's iQ analyzers are a family of fully automated, image-based bench-top analyzers for fluid microscopy. The iQ analyzer can be integrated with its proprietary fluid chemistry analyzer, the iChem VELOCITY, to simultaneously perform fluid microscopy and chemistry testing. Through its IRIS Sample Processing division, the company offers a line of small centrifuge products and DNA workstations. The division also markets the OvaTube for parasite testing in veterinarian procedures. IRIS additionally has an active Personalized Medicine division that is currently developing diagnostics solutions based on its Nucleic Acid Detection Immunoassay (NADiA) platform for various applications in oncology and infectious diseases. This division operates primarily through Iris Molecular Diagnostics and Arista Molecular, a CLIA-certified laboratory focused on oncology and molecular diagnostics. In November 2010, the firm acquired the technological assets of a bench-top instrument platform used for automating highly repetitive, manual laboratory protocols for FISH (fluorescence in-situ hybridization) testing and other slide-based cytogenetic applications. In March 2011, it received U.S. FDA clearance to begin marketing its iChem VELOCITY Automated Urine Chemistry Analyzer and iRICELL Urinalysis Workstation. In September 2011, IRIS received FDA approval for its NADiA ProsVue prognostic cancer test.

IRIS offers its employees education reimbursement; a 401(k) plan; and medical, dental, vision, life and disability insurance.

FINANCIALS: **Sales and profits are in thousands of dollars—add 000 to get the full amount. 2011 Note: Financial information for 2011 was not available for all companies at press time.**

2011 Sales: $	2011 Profits: $	**U.S. Stock Ticker: IRIS**
2010 Sales: $107,672	2010 Profits: $3,042	**Int'l Ticker:**
2009 Sales: $92,566	2009 Profits: $6,251	Int'l Exchange:
2008 Sales: $95,502	2008 Profits: $9,013	Employees: 377 Fiscal Year Ends: 12/31
2007 Sales: $84,306	2007 Profits: $7,549	Parent Company:

SALARIES/BENEFITS:

Pension Plan:	ESOP Stock Plan:	Profit Sharing:	Top Exec. Salary: $424,820	Bonus: $90,000
Savings Plan: Y	Stock Purch. Plan:		Second Exec. Salary: $309,846	Bonus: $

OTHER THOUGHTS:

Apparent Women Officers or Directors: 1
Hot Spot for Advancement for Women/Minorities:

LOCATIONS: ("Y" = Yes)

West:	Southwest:	Midwest:	Southeast:	Northeast:	International:
Y				Y	Y

IROBOT CORP

www.irobot.com

Industry Group Code: 335

Management:		Sales/Marketing:		Liberal Arts:		Information Systems:		Professionals:		Technical/Scientific:	
Mgmt. Trainees:		Mktg. Professionals:	Y	Gen. Writing/Editing:		Info. Management:	Y	Finance/Acct.:	Y	Engineers, Elec.:	Y
Experienced Mgmt.:	Y	Retail Sales:		Technical Writing:	Y	Software Dev.:	Y	Law:	Y	Engineers, Other:	Y
Int'l Business:	Y	Commercial/Industrial:	Y	Graphic Arts/Photog.:		Hardware Dev.:	Y	HR/Other:	Y	Health/Lab	
MBA Graduates:	Y	Sales Trainees:		Music:		Consulting/Other:		Training:	Y	Scientists/Research:	Y
		Advertising Pros.:		Broadcasting:				Health Care:		Petroleum/Chemicals:	
				Other:				Consulting:		Math/Other:	Y

TYPES OF BUSINESS:

Robotics

BRANDS/DIVISIONS/AFFILIATES:

Roomba
Scooba
Looj
Dirt Dog
Negotiator
Seaglider
PackBot
AWARE

CONTACTS: *Note: Officers with more than one job title may be intentionally listed here more than once.*

Colin Angle, CEO
Joseph Dyer, COO
John L. Leahy, CFO/Treas./Exec. VP
Russ Campanello, Sr. VP-Human Resources
Jay Leader, CIO/Sr. VP-IT
Tom Wagner, CTO
Glen Weinstein, General Counsel/Sr. VP
Alison Dean, Principal Acct. Officer/Sr. VP-Corp. Finance
Robert L. Moses, Pres., Gov't & Industrial Robot Div.
Jeffery A. Beck, Pres., Home Robots Div.
Tod Loofbourrow, Pres., Healthcare Bus.
Colin Angle, Chmn.

Phone: 781-430-3000	**Fax:** 781-430-3001
Toll-Free:	
Address: 8 Crosby Dr., Bedford, MA 01730 US	

GROWTH PLANS/SPECIAL FEATURES:

iRobot Corp. develops and manufactures robots that incorporate navigation, mobility and artificial intelligence concepts for both the consumer and defense markets. Based on its proprietary robot intelligence system, AWARE, the firm's robots are capable of accomplishing complex tasks while avoiding obstacles. Among the company's consumer products are the Roomba, Scooba, Dirt Dog, Verro and Looj. The Roomba is an automated vacuum for home use that continuously cleans a designated area; it utilizes Virtual Wall technology that allows the consumer to set off limit areas. Roomba models include the pet series, which is specifically designed for pet owners. The Scooba preps, washes, scrubs and dries hard surface flooring. The Dirt Dog model is a high capacity vacuum designed for workshop, basement and patio cleaning. The Verro is a self-contained vacuum, filter system and pump that is designed to clean in-ground pools, and Looj is used to automate home gutter system cleaning. The company has developed robots for defense purposes used by U.S. and foreign government agencies, including the PackBot, Small Unmanned Ground Vehicle (SUGV), Seaglider and Negotiator. The SUGV and the PackBot are utilized by the U.S. military and perform battlefield reconnaissance and bomb disposal. The Seaglider is an unmanned robot that performs endurance oceanic missions, while the Negotiator is a ground robot that is utilized by first responders and local police forces. The company is under contract with several government agencies and is currently working with the U.S. military to develop Future Combat Systems (FCS), including the remote controlled Warrior vehicles. It has sold over 6 million consumer use robots and over 3,500 PackBots to the U.S. military.

The company offers its employees medical, dental and vision insurance; flexible spending accounts; tuition assistance; short- and long-term disability coverage; a 529 savings plan; supplemental life insurance; a smoking cessation reimbursement program; and employee discounts on home and auto insurance.

FINANCIALS: **Sales and profits are in thousands of dollars—add 000 to get the full amount. 2011 Note: Financial information for 2011 was not available for all companies at press time.**

2011 Sales: $465,500	2011 Profits: $40,191	**U.S. Stock Ticker: IRBT**
2010 Sales: $400,952	2010 Profits: $25,514	**Int'l Ticker:**
2009 Sales: $298,617	2009 Profits: $3,300	Int'l Exchange:
2008 Sales: $307,621	2008 Profits: $ 756	Employees: 657 Fiscal Year Ends: 12/31
2007 Sales: $249,081	2007 Profits: $9,060	Parent Company:

SALARIES/BENEFITS:

Pension Plan:	ESOP Stock Plan:	Profit Sharing:	Top Exec. Salary: $463,897	Bonus: $578,926
Savings Plan: Y	Stock Purch. Plan:		Second Exec. Salary: $360,849	Bonus: $346,683

OTHER THOUGHTS:

Apparent Women Officers or Directors: 4
Hot Spot for Advancement for Women/Minorities: Y

LOCATIONS: ("Y" = Yes)

West:	Southwest:	Midwest:	Southeast:	Northeast:	International:
Y				Y	Y

ISILON SYSTEMS INC

www.isilon.com

Industry Group Code: 334112

Management:		Sales/Marketing:		Liberal Arts:		Information Systems:		Professionals:		Technical/Scientific:	
Mgmt. Trainees:		Mktg. Professionals:	Y	Gen. Writing/Editing:		Info. Management:	Y	Finance/Acct.:	Y	Engineers, Elec.:	Y
Experienced Mgmt.:	Y	Retail Sales:		Technical Writing:	Y	Software Dev.:	Y	Law:	Y	Engineers, Other:	Y
Int'l Business:	Y	Commercial/Industrial:	Y	Graphic Arts/Photog.:		Hardware Dev.:	Y	HR/Other:	Y	Health/Lab	
MBA Graduates:	Y	Sales Trainees:		Music:		Consulting/Other:	Y	Training:	Y	Scientists/Research:	
		Advertising Pros.:		Broadcasting:				Health Care:		Petroleum/Chemicals:	
				Other:				Consulting:		Math/Other:	

TYPES OF BUSINESS:

Clustered Storage Systems

BRANDS/DIVISIONS/AFFILIATES:

Isilon IQ
OneFS
Isilon IQ Accelerator-x
Isilon EX 6000
SyncIQ
SmartConnect
SnapshotIQ
SmartQuotas

CONTACTS: *Note: Officers with more than one job title may be intentionally listed here more than once.*

Sujal M. Patel, Pres.
Bill Richter, CFO
Eric Broderson, Sr. VP-Mktg.
Gwen E. Weld, VP-Human Resources & Organizational Dev.
Paul Rutherford, CTO
Brett Helsel, Sr. VP-Eng.
Keenan M. Conder, General Counsel/VP/Corp. Sec.
Mary Godwin, VP-Oper.
Eric Broderson, Sr. VP-Bus. Dev.
Bill Richter, VP-Finance
George Bennett, Sr. VP-Worldwide Field Oper.

Phone: 206-315-7500 **Fax:** 206-315-7501
Toll-Free: 877-247-4566
Address: 505 1st Ave. S., Seattle, WA 98104 US

GROWTH PLANS/SPECIAL FEATURES:

Isilon Systems, Inc., a subsidiary of EMC Corporation, is a provider of scale-out network attached storage (NAS) systems for digital content. The company's Isilon IQ storage systems comprise three or more nodes, each of which is a self-contained, rack-mountable device that contains industry standard hardware, including disk drives, a central processing unit (CPU), memory chips and network interfaces. Isilon IQ is integrated with its proprietary OneFS operating system software, which unifies a cluster of nodes into a single shared resource. OneFS combines the three distinct layers of traditional storage architecture, which consist of a file system, a volume manager and a redundant array of independent disks (RAID), into a single unified software layer. Consequently, Isilon IQ nodes automatically work together to aggregate their collective computing power into a single, unified storage system that is designed to withstand the failure of any piece of hardware, including disks, switches or even entire nodes. The company's Isilon IQ Accelerator-x and Isilon EX 6000, EX 9000 and EX 12000 platform extension nodes optimize system performance. Isilon Systems also carries four related software applications that extend the capabilities and functionality of its systems: SyncIQ replication software; SmartQuotas provisioning and management software; SmartConnect load-balancing software; and SnapshotIQ protection software. The company has sold its clustered storage systems to over 1,200 customers across a wide range of industries. The firm sells its products both directly through its field sales force and indirectly through a channel partner program that includes over 210 resellers and distributors.

FINANCIALS: **Sales and profits are in thousands of dollars—add 000 to get the full amount. 2011 Note: Financial information for 2011 was not available for all companies at press time.**

2011 Sales: $ | 2011 Profits: $
2010 Sales: $ | 2010 Profits: $
2009 Sales: $123,911 | 2009 Profits: $-18,873
2008 Sales: $114,422 | 2008 Profits: $-25,078
2007 Sales: $88,998 | 2007 Profits: $-26,932

U.S. Stock Ticker: Subsidiary
Int'l Ticker:
Int'l Exchange:
Employees: 356 Fiscal Year Ends: 12/31
Parent Company: EMC CORP

SALARIES/BENEFITS:

Pension Plan: | ESOP Stock Plan: | Profit Sharing: | Top Exec. Salary: $250,865 | Bonus: $160,161
Savings Plan: | Stock Purch. Plan: | | Second Exec. Salary: $230,796 | Bonus: $120,121

OTHER THOUGHTS:

Apparent Women Officers or Directors: 2
Hot Spot for Advancement for Women/Minorities: Y

LOCATIONS: ("Y" = Yes)

West:	Southwest:	Midwest:	Southeast:	Northeast:	International:
Y					Y

IVILLAGE INC

www.ivillage.com

Industry Group Code: 519130

Management:		**Sales/Marketing:**		**Liberal Arts:**		**Information Systems:**		**Professionals:**		**Technical/Scientific:**	
Mgmt. Trainees:		Mktg. Professionals:	Y	Gen. Writing/Editing:	Y	Info. Management:	Y	Finance/Acct.:	Y	Engineers, Elec.:	
Experienced Mgmt.:	Y	Retail Sales:		Technical Writing:		Software Dev.:	Y	Law:	Y	Engineers, Other:	
Int'l Business:		Commercial/Industrial:	Y	Graphic Arts/Photog.:	Y	Hardware Dev.:		HR/Other:	Y	Health/Lab	
MBA Graduates:	Y	Sales Trainees:	Y	Music:		Consulting/Other:		Training:	Y	Scientists/Research:	
		Advertising Pros.:	Y	Broadcasting:				Health Care:		Petroleum/Chemicals:	
				Other:	Y			Consulting:		Math/Other:	

TYPES OF BUSINESS:

Online Women's Network
Educational Publishing
Online Promotions & Direct Marketing
Consulting Services

BRANDS/DIVISIONS/AFFILIATES:

NBC Universal LLC
iVillage.com
iVillage UK
iVillage Turkey
Astrology.com
GardenWeb
PetSide.com
TravelSkoot.com

CONTACTS: *Note: Officers with more than one job title may be intentionally listed here more than once.*

Jodi Khan, Pres.
Mark Graham, Sr. VP-Tech.
John Curbishley, Sr. VP-Bus. Dev.

Phone: 212-664-4444	**Fax:** 212-664-4085
Toll-Free:	
Address: 500 7th Ave., 14th Fl., New York, NY 10018 US	

GROWTH PLANS/SPECIAL FEATURES:

iVillage, Inc., a subsidiary of NBC Universal LLC, is a leading women's media company consisting of several online and offline properties, offering unique content, community applications, tools and interactive features. The company's iVillage.com web site, with 34 million unique visitors, provides information on such topics as health, parenting, pregnancy, beauty, style, fitness, relationships, food and entertainment. The web site contains thousands of message boards and a variety of social networking tools. iVillage's portfolio includes iVillage UK, its U.K.-oriented online information network; iVillage Turkey; iVillage Total Health, providing information on women's health issues; iVillage Weddings, a web site offering wedding-oriented information and support; NeverSayDiet, a health and nutrition web site that offers weight loss advice; and Momtourage.com., a web site offering tips and ideas for mothers. The firm also owns the web sites Astrology.com, a horoscope web site; DinnerTool.com, featuring meal planning, recipes and instructional videos; TravelSkoot.com, which provides travel tips and information; GardenWeb, a gardening network; and PetSide.com, a web site focused on pet health information.

FINANCIALS: **Sales and profits are in thousands of dollars—add 000 to get the full amount. 2011 Note: Financial information for 2011 was not available for all companies at press time.**

2011 Sales: $ | 2011 Profits: $
2010 Sales: $ | 2010 Profits: $
2009 Sales: $ | 2009 Profits: $
2008 Sales: $ | 2008 Profits: $
2007 Sales: $ | 2007 Profits: $

U.S. Stock Ticker: Subsidiary
Int'l Ticker:
Int'l Exchange:
Employees: Fiscal Year Ends: 12/31
Parent Company: NBC UNIVERSAL

SALARIES/BENEFITS:

Pension Plan: ESOP Stock Plan: Profit Sharing: Top Exec. Salary: $ Bonus: $
Savings Plan: Stock Purch. Plan: Second Exec. Salary: $ Bonus: $

OTHER THOUGHTS:

Apparent Women Officers or Directors: 1
Hot Spot for Advancement for Women/Minorities:

LOCATIONS: ("Y" = Yes)

West:	Southwest:	Midwest:	Southeast:	Northeast:	International:
				Y	

J2 GLOBAL COMMUNICATIONS INC

www.j2global.com

Industry Group Code: 518210

Management:		Sales/Marketing:		Liberal Arts:		Information Systems:		Professionals:		Technical/Scientific:	
Mgmt. Trainees:		Mktg. Professionals:	Y	Gen. Writing/Editing:	Y	Info. Management:	Y	Finance/Acct.:	Y	Engineers, Elec.:	Y
Experienced Mgmt.:	Y	Retail Sales:		Technical Writing:	Y	Software Dev.:	Y	Law:	Y	Engineers, Other:	
Int'l Business:	Y	Commercial/Industrial:	Y	Graphic Arts/Photog.:		Hardware Dev.:		HR/Other:	Y	Health/Lab	
MBA Graduates:	Y	Sales Trainees:	Y	Music:		Consulting/Other:		Training:	Y	Scientists/Research:	
		Advertising Pros.:		Broadcasting:				Health Care:		Petroleum/Chemicals:	
				Other:				Consulting:		Math/Other:	

TYPES OF BUSINESS:

Unified Messaging & Communication Services
Internet-Based Faxing
Internet Conferencing
Web-base Voicemail

BRANDS/DIVISIONS/AFFILIATES:

eFax
jBlast
OneBox
eVoice
Alban Telecom Limited
Venali, Inc.
keepITsafe Data Solutions, Ltd.
Protus IP Solutions, Inc.

CONTACTS:

Note: Officers with more than one job title may be intentionally listed here more than once.

Hemi Zucker, CEO
Scott Turicchi, Pres.
Kathy Griggs, CFO
Mike Pugh, VP-Mktg.
Patty Brunton, VP-Human Resources
Vince Niedielski, VP-Eng.
Jeff Adelman, General Counsel/VP/Sec.
Alan Alters, VP-Network Oper.
Zohar Loshitzer, Exec. VP-Corp. Strategy
Paul Kinsella, VP/Gen. Mgr.-Europe
Ken Truesdale, VP-Corp. Dev.
Richard S. Ressler, Chmn.
Tim McLean, VP-Int'l

Phone: 323-860-9200	**Fax:** 323-860-9201
Toll-Free:	
Address: 6922 Hollywood Blvd., Los Angeles, CA 90028 US	

GROWTH PLANS/SPECIAL FEATURES:

j2 Global Communications, Inc. is a provider of messaging and communications services to individuals and businesses to 11 million subscribers in over 4,300 cities in 49 countries. The company provides faxing and voicemail services, document management services, web-initiated conference calling and unified-messaging and communications services. The company's faxing services enable customers to fax documents over the Internet. Brands include eFax, eFax Corporate, eFax Broadcast, fax.com and jBlast, which are offered to individuals and small businesses. The firm's voice services provide small-to-medium business clients a suite of virtual voice services that enable these clients to utilize the features of professional phone systems, such as automatic attendants and menu trees, at a lower cost. Voice services brands include eVoice, eReceptionist, Phone People and Onebox. E-mail services provide customized e-mail services to any size business. Services include e-mail hosting, security, archiving, as well as e-mail marketing campaigns. Brands include Electric Mail, FuseMail and WebMail. The firm recently acquired Alban Telecom Limited, a U.K.-based provider of enhanced voice services; Venali, Inc.; which offers Internet fax messaging services; keepITsafe Data Solutions, Ltd., an Irish company which provides cloud-based, online backup applications; Protus IP Solutions, Inc., a Software-as-a-Service (SaaS) provider based in Canada.

j2 offers employees medical, dental and vision insurance; life insurance; a 401(k) plan; an employee stock purchase plan; flexible spending accounts; and tuition reimbursement.

FINANCIALS:

Sales and profits are in thousands of dollars—add 000 to get the full amount. 2011 Note: Financial information for 2011 was not available for all companies at press time.

2011 Sales: $330,159	2011 Profits: $114,766
2010 Sales: $255,394	2010 Profits: $83,047
2009 Sales: $245,571	2009 Profits: $66,827
2008 Sales: $241,513	2008 Profits: $72,562
2007 Sales: $220,697	2007 Profits: $68,461

U.S. Stock Ticker: JCOM
Int'l Ticker:
Int'l Exchange:
Employees: 600 Fiscal Year Ends: 12/31
Parent Company:

SALARIES/BENEFITS:

Pension Plan:	ESOP Stock Plan:	Profit Sharing:	Top Exec. Salary: $459,000	Bonus: $541,125
Savings Plan: Y	Stock Purch. Plan: Y		Second Exec. Salary: $377,885	Bonus: $187,050

OTHER THOUGHTS:

Apparent Women Officers or Directors: 2
Hot Spot for Advancement for Women/Minorities:

LOCATIONS: ("Y" = Yes)

West:	Southwest:	Midwest:	Southeast:	Northeast:	International:
Y					Y

JAZZ PHARMACEUTICALS INC

www.jazzpharmaceuticals.com

Industry Group Code: 325412

Management:		Sales/Marketing:		Liberal Arts:		Information Systems:		Professionals:		Technical/Scientific:	
Mgmt. Trainees:		Mktg. Professionals:	Y	Gen. Writing/Editing:		Info. Management:	Y	Finance/Acct.:	Y	Engineers, Elec.:	
Experienced Mgmt.:	Y	Retail Sales:		Technical Writing:	Y	Software Dev.:	Y	Law:	Y	Engineers, Other:	
Int'l Business:		Commercial/Industrial:	Y	Graphic Arts/Photog.:		Hardware Dev.:		HR/Other:	Y	Health/Lab	Y
MBA Graduates:	Y	Sales Trainees:	Y	Music:		Consulting/Other:		Training:	Y	Scientists/Research:	Y
		Advertising Pros.:		Broadcasting:				Health Care:	Y	Petroleum/Chemicals:	Y
				Other:				Consulting:		Math/Other:	Y

TYPES OF BUSINESS:

Pharmaceuticals Discovery & Development
Neurological & Psychiatric Therapeutics

BRANDS/DIVISIONS/AFFILIATES:

Xyrem
Luvox CR
JZP-6
JZP-8

CONTACTS:

Note: Officers with more than one job title may be intentionally listed here more than once.

Bruce C. Cozadd, CEO
Robert M. Myers, Pres.
Kathryn E. Falberg, CFO/Sr. VP
Russell J. Cox, VP-Mktg. & Sales
Heather McGaughey, VP-Human Resources
Mark G. Eller, Sr. VP-Research & Clinical Dev.
Michael DesJardin, Sr. VP-Prod. Dev.
Carol A. Gamble, General Counsel/Sr. VP/Corp. Sec.
Joel M. Rothman, VP-Dev. Oper.
P. J. Honerkamp, VP-Corp. Dev.
Karen J. Wilson, VP-Finance
Diane R. Guinta, VP-Clinical Dev. & Scientific Affairs
Janne L. T. Wissel, Chief Regulatory & Compliance Officer/Sr. VP
Edwin W. Luker, VP-Sales
Bruce C. Cozadd, Chmn.

Phone: 650-496-3777	**Fax:** 650-496-3781
Toll-Free:	
Address: 3180 Porter Dr., Palo Alto, CA 94304 US	

GROWTH PLANS/SPECIAL FEATURES:

Jazz Pharmaceuticals, Inc. develops and commercializes products that address unmet medical needs in neurology and psychiatry. The firm's portfolio includes two marketed products and several product candidates in various stages of clinical development. Its marketed products are Xyrem and Luvox CR. Xyrem is one of the only products approved by the U.S. Food and Drug Administration (FDA) for the treatment of both excessive daytime sleepiness and cataplexy in patients with narcolepsy. Luvox CR, a once-daily extended-release formulation of selective serotonin reuptake inhibitor fluvoxamine, was recently approved by the FDA for the treatment of both obsessive-compulsive disorder and social anxiety disorder. Jazz is also developing sodium oxybate (JZP-6), the active pharmaceutical ingredient in Xyrem, for the treatment of fibromyalgia. The firm's other product candidates include oral tablet forms of sodium oxybate; and JZP-8 (intranasal clonazepam) for the treatment of recurrent acute repetitive seizures in epilepsy patients who continue to have seizures while on stable anti-epileptic regimens.

Jazz offers its employees medical and dependent care flexible spending accounts; a choice of Preferred Provider Organization (PPO) and Health Maintenance Organization (HMO) plans; a 401(k) plan; dental and vision insurance; and life, AD&D and disability insurance.

FINANCIALS:

Sales and profits are in thousands of dollars—add 000 to get the full amount. 2011 Note: Financial information for 2011 was not available for all companies at press time.

2011 Sales: $	2011 Profits: $	**U.S. Stock Ticker: JAZZ**
2010 Sales: $173,781	2010 Profits: $32,778	**Int'l Ticker:**
2009 Sales: $128,449	2009 Profits: $-6,836	Int'l Exchange:
2008 Sales: $67,514	2008 Profits: $-184,339	Employees: 242 Fiscal Year Ends: 12/31
2007 Sales: $65,303	2007 Profits: $-138,778	Parent Company:

SALARIES/BENEFITS:

Pension Plan:	ESOP Stock Plan:	Profit Sharing:	Top Exec. Salary: $496,877	Bonus: $267,300
Savings Plan: Y	Stock Purch. Plan:		Second Exec. Salary: $449,092	Bonus: $224,000

OTHER THOUGHTS:

Apparent Women Officers or Directors: 6
Hot Spot for Advancement for Women/Minorities: Y

LOCATIONS: ("Y" = Yes)

West:	Southwest:	Midwest:	Southeast:	Northeast:	International:
Y					

JOE'S JEANS INC

www.joesjeans.com

Industry Group Code: 315

Management:		Sales/Marketing:		Liberal Arts:		Information Systems:		Professionals:		Technical/Scientific:	
Mgmt. Trainees:		Mktg. Professionals:	Y	Gen. Writing/Editing:		Info. Management:	Y	Finance/Acct.:	Y	Engineers, Elec.:	
Experienced Mgmt.:	Y	Retail Sales:		Technical Writing:		Software Dev.:		Law:	Y	Engineers, Other:	
Int'l Business:	Y	Commercial/Industrial:	Y	Graphic Arts/Photog.:	Y	Hardware Dev.:		HR/Other:	Y	Health/Lab	
MBA Graduates:	Y	Sales Trainees:	Y	Music:		Consulting/Other:		Training:		Scientists/Research:	
		Advertising Pros.:		Broadcasting:				Health Care:		Petroleum/Chemicals:	
				Other:	Y			Consulting:		Math/Other:	

TYPES OF BUSINESS:

Apparel Design-Jeans & Denim

BRANDS/DIVISIONS/AFFILIATES:

Rocker
The Shirt
Joe's
Chelsea
Cigarette
Honey
Ex-Lover
Twiggy

CONTACTS:

Note: Officers with more than one job title may be intentionally listed here more than once.

Marc B. Crossman, CEO
Marc B. Crossman, Pres.
Hamish S. Sandhu, CFO
Joseph Dahan, Dir.-Creative
Samuel J. (Sam) Furrow, Chmn.

Phone: 323-837-3700	**Fax:** 323-837-3790
Toll-Free: 877-528-5637	
Address: 2340 S. Eastern Ave., Commerce, CA 90040 US	

GROWTH PLANS/SPECIAL FEATURES:

Joe's Jeans, Inc. designs, develops and markets Joe's brand denim jeans, casual wear and accessories. The company was formed through the merger of Innovo, Inc. and JD Holdings. Joe's Jeans relies on third parties in Mexico, the U.S., Morocco, Hong Kong, India, Portugal, Peru, Korea and China to manufacture its apparel products. The firm's products include women's, men's and children's denim jeans, pants, sweaters and jackets. Its women's product line accounts for the largest source of revenue and consists primarily of denim jeans in a variety of different fits, fabrics, washes and detailing. Joe's Jeans has branded its different women's fit styles, which include Chelsea (ultra slim), Cigarette (straight and narrow), Visionaire (high waist bootcut), Stardust (super flare), Honey (curvy), Ex-Lover (relaxed), Icon Muse (high waist), Provocateur (petit), Rocker (lean flare), Socialite (classic bootcut), Starlet (slim bootcut) and Twiggy (tall). The company has also branded its men's fit styles, which include the Rebel, the Brixton, The Outsider, the Classic and the Rocker. Children's product offerings include basic denim bottoms, tops, t-shirts and jackets for infants', toddlers', girls' and boys' sizes. Additionally, the company offers a line of unisex woven shirts marketed under The Shirt brand name. Product development for the Joe's brand is managed internally by a team of designers led by Joe Dahan. Joe's Jeans sells its products to retailers such as Bloomingdale's, Macy's, Neiman Marcus, Nordstrom, Saks Fifth Avenue, Dillard's, American Rag, Anthropologie, Bergdorf Goodman, Scoop NYC, Galleries Lafayette, Le Bon Marche, Barney's Japan, Harvey Nichols, Selfridges & Co. and Gio Moretti. In 2011, the company formed an agreement with MultiTrend International allowing it to open at least seven branded stores within the Middle East. In 2011, the firm opened a location in Dubai, United Arab Emirates, and in Safat, Kuwait.

FINANCIALS:

Sales and profits are in thousands of dollars—add 000 to get the full amount. 2011 Note: Financial information for 2011 was not available for all companies at press time.

2011 Sales: $	2011 Profits: $
2010 Sales: $98,176	2010 Profits: $2,601
2009 Sales: $80,116	2009 Profits: $24,520
2008 Sales: $69,174	2008 Profits: $4,902
2007 Sales: $62,767	2007 Profits: $2,254

U.S. Stock Ticker: JOEZ
Int'l Ticker:
Int'l Exchange:
Employees: 281 Fiscal Year Ends: 11/30
Parent Company:

SALARIES/BENEFITS:

Pension Plan:	ESOP Stock Plan:	Profit Sharing:	Top Exec. Salary: $429,300	Bonus: $328,125
Savings Plan:	Stock Purch. Plan:		Second Exec. Salary: $300,000	Bonus: $250,000

OTHER THOUGHTS:

Apparent Women Officers or Directors:
Hot Spot for Advancement for Women/Minorities:

LOCATIONS: ("Y" = Yes)

West:	Southwest:	Midwest:	Southeast:	Northeast:	International:
Y	Y	Y	Y	Y	Y

JOHN B SANFILIPPO & SON INC

www.jbssinc.com

Industry Group Code: 31191

Management:		**Sales/Marketing:**		**Liberal Arts:**		**Information Systems:**		**Professionals:**		**Technical/Scientific:**	
Mgmt. Trainees:		Mktg. Professionals:	Y	Gen. Writing/Editing:	Y	Info. Management:	Y	Finance/Acct.:	Y	Engineers, Elec.:	
Experienced Mgmt.:	Y	Retail Sales:		Technical Writing:		Software Dev.:		Law:	Y	Engineers, Other:	
Int'l Business:		Commercial/Industrial:	Y	Graphic Arts/Photog.:	Y	Hardware Dev.:		HR/Other:	Y	Health/Lab	
MBA Graduates:	Y	Sales Trainees:	Y	Music:		Consulting/Other:		Training:	Y	Scientists/Research:	
		Advertising Pros.:	Y	Broadcasting:				Health Care:		Petroleum/Chemicals:	
				Other:				Consulting:		Math/Other:	

TYPES OF BUSINESS:

Nut Processing
Snack Products
Candy

BRANDS/DIVISIONS/AFFILIATES:

Fisher
Sunshine Country
Orchid Valley Harvest

CONTACTS: *Note: Officers with more than one job title may be intentionally listed here more than once.*

Jeffrey T. Sanfilippo, CEO
Jasper B. Sanfilippo, Jr., COO
Jasper B. Sanfilippo, Jr., Pres.
Michael J. Valentine, CFO/Group Pres.
Howard Brandeisky, VP-Mktg., Innovation & Customer Solutions
Thomas Fordonski, Sr. VP-Human Resources
James A. Valentine, CIO
Michael J. Valentine, Sec.
Everardo Soria, Sr. VP-Pecan Oper. & Procurement
Robert J. Sarlls, Sr. VP-Bus. Dev. & Strategy
William R. Pokrajac, VP-Investor Rel.& Risk Mgmt./Treas.
Frank S. Pellegrino, VP-Finance/Controller
Walter R. Tankersley, Jr., Sr. VP-Industrial Sales
Christopher Gardier, VP-Consumer Sales
Herbert J. Marros, Dir.-Financial Reporting & Taxation
Michael G. Cannon, Sr. VP-Corp. Oper.
Jeffrey T. Sanfilippo, Chmn.
Jose Cabanin, VP-Intl. Sales
Walter Tankersley, Jr., Sr. VP-Procurement & Commodity Risk Mgmt.

Phone: 847-289-1800	**Fax:** 847-289-1843
Toll-Free:	
Address: 1703 N. Randall Rd., Elgin, IL 60123 US	

GROWTH PLANS/SPECIAL FEATURES:

John B. Sanfilippo & Son, Inc. (JBSS) processes and markets tree nuts and peanuts in the U.S. Nuts are sold under a variety of private labels and under the company's Fisher, Orchard Valley Harvest and Sunshine Country brand names. JBSS also produces other snack products, including peanut butter, candy and confections, natural snacks and trail mixes, sunflower seeds, corn snacks, sesame sticks and other sesame snack products. The company's vertically integrated nut processing operation includes procurement from growers, shelling, processing, packing and marketing. Products are sold through a network of approximately 100 independent brokers and various independent distributors and suppliers to approximately 825 customers. Retailers of the company's products include grocery chains, mass merchandisers, drug store chains, convenience stores and membership clubs. Its largest customers are Wal-Mart (20% of sales) and Target (12% of sales). The firm's nut product line includes peanuts, almonds, Brazil nuts, pecans, pistachios, filberts, cashews, English walnuts, black walnuts, pine nuts and macadamia nuts. Products are sold in numerous package styles and sizes, from poly-cellophane packages, composite cans, vacuum-packed tins, plastic jars and glass jars for retail sales, to large cases and sacks for bulk sales to industrial, food service and government customers. In addition, the company offers its nut products in a variety of different styles and seasonings, including natural (with skins), blanched (without skins), oil-roasted, dry-roasted, unsalted, honey-roasted, butter toffee, praline and cinnamon-toasted. JBSS distributes its products from its Georgia, Illinois, California, North Carolina and Texas production facilities, and from public warehouse and distribution facilities located in various other states.

Employees are offered life, medical, dental and vision insurance; flexible spending accounts; disability coverage; a 401(K) plan; and education reimbursement.

FINANCIALS: **Sales and profits are in thousands of dollars—add 000 to get the full amount. 2011 Note: Financial information for 2011 was not available for all companies at press time.**

2011 Sales: $674,212	2011 Profits: $2,835	**U.S. Stock Ticker: JBSS**
2010 Sales: $561,633	2010 Profits: $14,425	**Int'l Ticker:**
2009 Sales: $553,846	2009 Profits: $6,917	Int'l Exchange:
2008 Sales: $541,771	2008 Profits: $-5,957	Employees: 1,400 Fiscal Year Ends: 6/30
2007 Sales: $540,858	2007 Profits: $-13,577	Parent Company:

SALARIES/BENEFITS:

Pension Plan:	ESOP Stock Plan:	Profit Sharing:	Top Exec. Salary: $364,867	Bonus: $
Savings Plan: Y	Stock Purch. Plan:		Second Exec. Salary: $364,867	Bonus: $

OTHER THOUGHTS:

Apparent Women Officers or Directors: 2
Hot Spot for Advancement for Women/Minorities:

LOCATIONS: ("Y" = Yes)

West:	Southwest:	Midwest:	Southeast:	Northeast:	International:
Y	Y	Y	Y	Y	

KAMPGROUNDS OF AMERICA INC

www.koapressroom.com

Industry Group Code: 721211

Management:		**Sales/Marketing:**		**Liberal Arts:**		**Information Systems:**		**Professionals:**		**Technical/Scientific:**	
Mgmt. Trainees:	Y	Mktg. Professionals:	Y	Gen. Writing/Editing:	Y	Info. Management:	Y	Finance/Acct.:	Y	Engineers, Elec.:	
Experienced Mgmt.:	Y	Retail Sales:		Technical Writing:		Software Dev.:		Law:	Y	Engineers, Other:	
Int'l Business:	Y	Commercial/Industrial:		Graphic Arts/Photog.:	Y	Hardware Dev.:		HR/Other:	Y	Health/Lab	
MBA Graduates:	Y	Sales Trainees:		Music:		Consulting/Other:		Training:	Y	Scientists/Research:	
		Advertising Pros.:	Y	Broadcasting:				Health Care:		Petroleum/Chemicals:	
				Other:				Consulting:		Math/Other:	

TYPES OF BUSINESS:

Campgrounds
RV Camping Services
Rental Cabins

BRANDS/DIVISIONS/AFFILIATES:

KOA
Kamping Kabins
Kamping Kottages
Kamping Lodges
Care Camps

CONTACTS:

Note: Officers with more than one job title may be intentionally listed here more than once.

Jim Rogers, CEO
Pat Hittmeier, Pres.
John J. Burke, CFO/VP
Lorne Armer, VP-Mktg.
Lora Burrowes, VP-Human Resources
Mike Zimmerman, General Counsel/VP
Jef Sutherland, VP-Franchise Oper.
Mike Gast, VP-Comm.
John J. Burke, Treas.
Terry Shade, VP-Company Owned Properties
Jim Rogers, Chmn.

Phone: 406-248-7444	**Fax:** 406-248-7414
Toll-Free:	
Address: 550 N. 31st St., Billings, MT 59101 US	

GROWTH PLANS/SPECIAL FEATURES:

Kampgrounds of America, Inc. (KOA), founded in 1962, operates and franchises one of the largest networks of commercial campsites in North America, with over 475 established KOA campgrounds. These campgrounds offer toll-free reservations, restrooms, showers, laundry facilities, playgrounds and pools, as well as RV sites and cabins, which come in three basic varieties: 144- or 232-square-foot Kamping Kabins; 230- or 280-square-foot Kamping Kottages; and Kamping Lodges of up to 400 square feet. Kottages and Lodges offer full bathrooms with showers. The company also offers tent camping, which offers a kamp store, kamping kitchens and tent sites with electricity. Additionally, the firm offers free high-speed wireless Internet access, available in the campsite itself, in over 350 locations and chargeable wireless access in 30 additional sites. KOA has a scout program that is open to Boy Scouts, Girl Scouts and Girl Guides throughout the U.S., which gives special discounts to troops interested in using KOA facilities for camping and earning badges. The firm also runs 43 Care Camps, specifically for children with cancer, and hosts annual fundraising events to sponsor it.

KOA employees who have completed one season in the Work Kamper program receive benefits including entrance into various cash drawings, discounted camping and free camping for 2-5 days while traveling to their next assignment.

FINANCIALS:

Sales and profits are in thousands of dollars—add 000 to get the full amount. 2011 Note: Financial information for 2011 was not available for all companies at press time.

2011 Sales: $	2011 Profits: $	**U.S. Stock Ticker: Private**
2010 Sales: $	2010 Profits: $	**Int'l Ticker:**
2009 Sales: $	2009 Profits: $	Int'l Exchange:
2008 Sales: $	2008 Profits: $	Employees: Fiscal Year Ends: 12/31
2007 Sales: $	2007 Profits: $	Parent Company:

SALARIES/BENEFITS:

Pension Plan:	ESOP Stock Plan:	Profit Sharing:	Top Exec. Salary: $	Bonus: $
Savings Plan:	Stock Purch. Plan:		Second Exec. Salary: $	Bonus: $

OTHER THOUGHTS:

Apparent Women Officers or Directors: 1
Hot Spot for Advancement for Women/Minorities:

LOCATIONS: ("Y" = Yes)

West:	Southwest:	Midwest:	Southeast:	Northeast:	International:
Y	Y	Y	Y	Y	Y

KBW INC

www.kbw.com

Industry Group Code: 523110

Management:		Sales/Marketing:		Liberal Arts:		Information Systems:		Professionals:		Technical/Scientific:	
Mgmt. Trainees:		Mktg. Professionals:		Gen. Writing/Editing:	Y	Info. Management:	Y	Finance/Acct.:	Y	Engineers, Elec.:	
Experienced Mgmt.:	Y	Retail Sales:		Technical Writing:		Software Dev.:	Y	Law:	Y	Engineers, Other:	
Int'l Business:	Y	Commercial/Industrial:		Graphic Arts/Photog.:		Hardware Dev.:		HR/Other:	Y	Health/Lab	
MBA Graduates:	Y	Sales Trainees:		Music:		Consulting/Other:		Training:		Scientists/Research:	
		Advertising Pros.:		Broadcasting:				Health Care:		Petroleum/Chemicals:	
				Other:				Consulting:		Math/Other:	

TYPES OF BUSINESS:

Investment Banking
Equity & Fixed Income Sales & Trading
Equity & Fixed Income Research
Asset Management

BRANDS/DIVISIONS/AFFILIATES:

Keefe, Bruyette & Woods Inc
Keefe, Bruyette & Woods Limited
Keefe Bruyette & Woods Asia Limited

CONTACTS: *Note: Officers with more than one job title may be intentionally listed here more than once.*

Thomas B. Michaud, CEO
Thomas B. Michaud, Pres.
Alan Oshiki, Head-Investor Rel.
Fred Cannon, Dir.-Research-Keefe, Bruyette & Woods, Inc.
Scott Studwell, Co-Head-U.S. Capital Markets
Dennis O'Rourke, Co-Head-U.S. Capital Markets
Andrew M. Senchak, Chmn.
John Spence, Managing Dir.-Investment Banking, Asia Pacific

Phone: 212-887-7777 **Fax:**
Toll-Free:
Address: 787 Seventh Ave., The Equitable Bldg., 4th Fl., New York, NY 10019 US

GROWTH PLANS/SPECIAL FEATURES:

KBW, Inc. is a full-service investment bank specializing in the financial services industry. The firm's business is organized into four principal segments: investment banking; equity and fixed income; research; and asset management. KBW's investment banking offerings include mergers and acquisitions services, strategic advisory services, equity and fixed income securities offerings, structured finance and mutual thrift conversions. The equity and fixed income offerings include sales and trading. The firm's research products offer analysis to identify investment opportunities and help customers make investment decisions. KBW's asset management services include investment management and other advisory services to institutional clients and other high net worth clients and investment vehicles. The firm's focus includes bank and thrift holding companies, banking companies, thrift institutions, insurance companies, broker-dealers, mortgage banks, asset management companies, mortgage and equity real estate investment trusts, consumer and specialty finance firms, financial processing companies and securities exchanges. Business is conducted throughout the U.S, Europe, and Asia through the company's three wholly-owned subsidiaries: Keefe, Bruyette & Woods, Inc., a U.S. broker dealer located in New York; Keefe, Bruyette & Woods Limited, a U.K. investment firm located in London; and Keefe, Bruyette & Woods Asia Limited, an investment firm located in Hong Kong. KBW is headquartered in New York and has regional offices worldwide in cities such as Boston, San Francisco, Chicago, Houston, Richmond, Atlanta and Tokyo.

FINANCIALS: **Sales and profits are in thousands of dollars—add 000 to get the full amount. 2011 Note: Financial information for 2011 was not available for all companies at press time.**

2011 Sales: $263,500 — 2011 Profits: $-31,700
2010 Sales: $425,857 — 2010 Profits: $26,628
2009 Sales: $387,154 — 2009 Profits: $23,607
2008 Sales: $242,217 — 2008 Profits: $-62,349
2007 Sales: $427,528 — 2007 Profits: $27,292

U.S. Stock Ticker: KBW
Int'l Ticker:
Int'l Exchange:
Employees: 585 Fiscal Year Ends: 12/31
Parent Company:

SALARIES/BENEFITS:

Pension Plan: ESOP Stock Plan: Profit Sharing: Y Top Exec. Salary: $400,000 Bonus: $1,580,000
Savings Plan: Y Stock Purch. Plan: Second Exec. Salary: $400,000 Bonus: $1,580,000

OTHER THOUGHTS:

Apparent Women Officers or Directors:
Hot Spot for Advancement for Women/Minorities:

LOCATIONS: ("Y" = Yes)

West:	Southwest:	Midwest:	Southeast:	Northeast:	International:
Y	Y	Y	Y	Y	Y

KENDALL-JACKSON WINE ESTATES LTD

www.kj.com

Industry Group Code: 312130

Management:		**Sales/Marketing:**		**Liberal Arts:**		**Information Systems:**		**Professionals:**		**Technical/Scientific:**	
Mgmt. Trainees:	Y	Mktg. Professionals:	Y	Gen. Writing/Editing:	Y	Info. Management:	Y	Finance/Acct.:	Y	Engineers, Elec.:	
Experienced Mgmt.:	Y	Retail Sales:		Technical Writing:		Software Dev.:		Law:	Y	Engineers, Other:	Y
Int'l Business:	Y	Commercial/Industrial:	Y	Graphic Arts/Photog.:	Y	Hardware Dev.:		HR/Other:	Y	Health/Lab	
MBA Graduates:	Y	Sales Trainees:	Y	Music:		Consulting/Other:		Training:	Y	Scientists/Research:	
		Advertising Pros.:	Y	Broadcasting:				Health Care:		Petroleum/Chemicals:	
				Other:	Y			Consulting:		Math/Other:	

TYPES OF BUSINESS:

Beverages-Wineries
Barrel Manufacturing
Wine Distribution
Online Sales
Wine Club

BRANDS/DIVISIONS/AFFILIATES:

Napa Mountain
Stature
Highland Estates
Grand Reserve
Vintner's Reserve
World Cooperage
Kendall-Jackson Wine Center
Healdsburg Tasting Room

CONTACTS: *Note: Officers with more than one job title may be intentionally listed here more than once.*

Barbara Banke, CEO
Susan Cagann, Counsel/VP
Mark Osmun, Dir.-Public Rel.
Randy Ullom, Winemaster
Matt Smith, Winemaker-Bordeaux
Mark Theis, Winemaker-Whites
Robert Boller, VP-Sustainability
Barbara Banke, Chmn.

Phone: 707-544-4000	**Fax**:
Toll-Free: 800-769-3649	
Address: 421 Aviation Blvd., Santa Rosa, CA 95403 US	

GROWTH PLANS/SPECIAL FEATURES:

Kendall-Jackson Wine Estates, Ltd., a family-owned and -operated company, is one of California's largest wineries. The company's vineyards include approximately 10,545 acres predominately located in Sonoma County, as well as Mendocino, Napa, Monterey and Santa Barbara counties in both Northern and Southern California. Kendall-Jackson also had two tasting rooms, one located in Fulton, California and the other located in Healdsburg, California. Kendall-Jackson centers on what are known as the eight grape varietals: Sauvignon blanc, chardonnay, Riesling, pinot noir, syrah, merlot, cabernet sauvignon and zinfandel. The company's wine is bottled with the labels Napa Mountain, Stature, Highland Estates, Grand Reserve and Vintner's Reserve. Together with partner World Cooperage, the company runs one of the only American-owned stave mills in France, which is where all of its white oak barrels are manufactured. Kendall-Jackson distributes its wines to grocery chains and retail liquor stores nationwide. Its products are available at many fine restaurants and other food service operations, as well as through the company's web site. Finally, Kendall-Jackson wine clubs offer discounts; VIP access at events and seminars; free tasting at the Kendall-Jackson Wine Center in Fulton and the Healdsburg Tasting Room in Healdsburg, both in California; newsletters; online customized boxed gift sets, wine glasses and other gifts and accessories, including cookbooks; as well as other benefits. Recently the firm began implementing a new water conservation system at its Sonoma County, California Winery , which is expected to reduce water usage by 600,000 gallons and conserve approximately 133,000 kilowatt hour (kWh) of electricity.

Employees of the firm are offered health insurance, short- and long-term disability, vacation pay and a 401(k) plan.

FINANCIALS: **Sales and profits are in thousands of dollars—add 000 to get the full amount. 2011 Note: Financial information for 2011 was not available for all companies at press time.**

2011 Sales: $	2011 Profits: $	**U.S. Stock Ticker: Private**
2010 Sales: $	2010 Profits: $	**Int'l Ticker:**
2009 Sales: $	2009 Profits: $	Int'l Exchange:
2008 Sales: $	2008 Profits: $	Employees: Fiscal Year Ends: 6/30
2007 Sales: $	2007 Profits: $	Parent Company:

SALARIES/BENEFITS:

Pension Plan:	ESOP Stock Plan:	Profit Sharing:	Top Exec. Salary: $	Bonus: $
Savings Plan: Y	Stock Purch. Plan:		Second Exec. Salary: $	Bonus: $

OTHER THOUGHTS:

Apparent Women Officers or Directors: 2
Hot Spot for Advancement for Women/Minorities:

LOCATIONS: ("Y" = Yes)

West:	Southwest:	Midwest:	Southeast:	Northeast:	International:
Y					Y

KENNETH COLE PRODUCTIONS INC

www.kennethcole.com

Industry Group Code: 3162

Management:		Sales/Marketing:		Liberal Arts:		Information Systems:		Professionals:		Technical/Scientific:	
Mgmt. Trainees:	Y	Mktg. Professionals:	Y	Gen. Writing/Editing:	Y	Info. Management:	Y	Finance/Acct.:	Y	Engineers, Elec.:	
Experienced Mgmt.:	Y	Retail Sales:		Technical Writing:		Software Dev.:		Law:	Y	Engineers, Other:	
Int'l Business:	Y	Commercial/Industrial:	Y	Graphic Arts/Photog.:	Y	Hardware Dev.:		HR/Other:	Y	Health/Lab	
MBA Graduates:	Y	Sales Trainees:	Y	Music:		Consulting/Other:		Training:	Y	Scientists/Research:	
		Advertising Pros.:	Y	Broadcasting:				Health Care:		Petroleum/Chemicals:	
				Other:	Y			Consulting:		Math/Other:	

TYPES OF BUSINESS:

Shoes, Manufacturing
Footwear & Handbags
Men's & Women's Apparel
Retail Stores
Catalog & Online Sales

BRANDS/DIVISIONS/AFFILIATES:

Kenneth Cole New York
Kenneth Cole Reaction
Unlisted
Le Tigre
Gentle Souls

CONTACTS: *Note: Officers with more than one job title may be intentionally listed here more than once.*

Paul Blum, CEO
David P. Edelman, CFO
Kristen Dykstra, Chief Mktg. Officer/Sr. VP
Danesha Dixon Smith, Sr. VP-Human Resources
Michael F. Colosi, General Counsel/Sr. VP/Sec.
David P. Edelman, Treas.
Kenneth D. Cole, Chief Creative Officer
Chris Nakatani, Pres., Wholesale Div.
Carol Massoni, Pres., Consumer Direct
Ingo Wilts, Sr. VP/Dir.-Creative
Kenneth D. Cole, Chmn.
Michael DeVirgilio, Pres., Licensing & Int'l
Peter J. Charles, Chief Supply Chain Officer

Phone: 212-265-1500 **Fax:** 866-741-5753
Toll-Free: 800-536-2653
Address: 603 W. 50th St., New York, NY 10019 US

GROWTH PLANS/SPECIAL FEATURES:

Kenneth Cole Productions, Inc. (KCP) designs, sources, markets and licenses a broad range of fashion footwear, handbags, apparel and accessories under the Kenneth Cole New York, Kenneth Cole Reaction, Unlisted, Le Tigre and Gentle Souls brand names. The firm's products are targeted to appeal to modern, fashion-conscious consumers who seek accessible designer fashion that reflects a metropolitan lifestyle. Its operations are divided into three segments: wholesale, which accounted for 48% of its 2010 revenue; consumer direct, 42%; and licensing, 10%. The wholesale segment includes sales to department stores, independent specialty stores, national chains and mass market retailers. Its products are currently distributed to over 4,700 U.S. retail shops, as well as select locations in Canada, Europe, Australia, Malaysia and the Middle East. This segment also designs, develops and sources private label footwear and handbags for selected retailers. The consumer direct segment is responsible for the firm's full-priced retail stores and outlets, as well as its e-commerce operations. It currently operates 105 retail locations, which includes 33 Kenneth Cole full-priced retail stores and 72 outlet stores under the Kenneth Cole name. The licensing segment handles the firm's relationships with its licensing partners. Though KCP maintains in-house design teams for the development of footwear, handbags and men's sportswear collections, all other product categories sold under its various brands are produced by licensee partners. Licensed product categories include men's tailored clothing, neckwear, belts, socks and jewelry; women's apparel, outerwear, jewelry and swimwear; children's apparel; and men's and women's watches, optical frames, sunglasses and fragrances. In November 2011, the company made its first steps into the Indian market through a licensing agreement with Reliance Brands Limited for retail and premium wholesale distribution.

FINANCIALS: **Sales and profits are in thousands of dollars—add 000 to get the full amount. 2011 Note: Financial information for 2011 was not available for all companies at press time.**

2011 Sales: $478,900 — 2011 Profits: $-2,900
2010 Sales: $411,652 — 2010 Profits: $2,084
2009 Sales: $370,955 — 2009 Profits: $-63,238
2008 Sales: $448,578 — 2008 Profits: $-14,800
2007 Sales: $466,405 — 2007 Profits: $7,083

U.S. Stock Ticker: KCP
Int'l Ticker:
Int'l Exchange:
Employees: 1,800 Fiscal Year Ends: 12/31
Parent Company:

SALARIES/BENEFITS:

Pension Plan: ESOP Stock Plan: Profit Sharing: Top Exec. Salary: $1,000,000 Bonus: $670,000
Savings Plan: Y Stock Purch. Plan: Y Second Exec. Salary: $1,000,000 Bonus: $670,000

OTHER THOUGHTS:

Apparent Women Officers or Directors: 3
Hot Spot for Advancement for Women/Minorities: Y

LOCATIONS: ("Y" = Yes)

West:	Southwest:	Midwest:	Southeast:	Northeast:	International:
Y	Y	Y	Y	Y	Y

KEY TRONIC CORP

www.keytronic.com

Industry Group Code: 334419

Management:		Sales/Marketing:		Liberal Arts:		Information Systems:		Professionals:		Technical/Scientific:	
Mgmt. Trainees:		Mktg. Professionals:	Y	Gen. Writing/Editing:		Info. Management:	Y	Finance/Acct.:	Y	Engineers, Elec.:	Y
Experienced Mgmt.:	Y	Retail Sales:		Technical Writing:	Y	Software Dev.:	Y	Law:	Y	Engineers, Other:	Y
Int'l Business:	Y	Commercial/Industrial:	Y	Graphic Arts/Photog.:	Y	Hardware Dev.:	Y	HR/Other:	Y	Health/Lab	
MBA Graduates:	Y	Sales Trainees:	Y	Music:		Consulting/Other:		Training:	Y	Scientists/Research:	
		Advertising Pros.:		Broadcasting:				Health Care:		Petroleum/Chemicals:	
				Other:				Consulting:		Math/Other:	

TYPES OF BUSINESS:

Contract Electronics Manufacturing
Keyboard & Mouse Manufacturing

BRANDS/DIVISIONS/AFFILIATES:

KeyTronicEMS Co

CONTACTS:

Note: Officers with more than one job title may be intentionally listed here more than once.

Craig D. Gates, CEO
Craig D. Gates, Pres.
Ronald F. Klawitter, CFO/Treas.
Lawrence J. Bostwick, VP-Eng. & Quality
Ronald F. Klawitter, Exec. VP-Admin.
Kathleen L. Nemeth, Sec.
Douglas G. Burkhardt, VP-Worldwide Oper.
Philip S. Hochberg, VP-Bus. Dev.
Michael Newman, Investor Rel.
Brett R. Larsen, VP-Finance/Controller
Frank Crispigna, III, VP-Materials
Dale F. Pilz, Chmn.

Phone: 509-928-8000 **Fax:** 509-927-5555
Toll-Free: 877-941-8609
Address: N. 4424 Sullivan Rd., Spokane Valley, WA 99216 US

GROWTH PLANS/SPECIAL FEATURES:

Key Tronic Corp., doing business as KeyTronicEMS Co., is an electronics manufacturing services (EMS) provider. The firm manufactures keyboards and mice for personal computers, terminals and workstations for distributors and resellers. Its production capabilities include tool making, product design, liquid injection molding, printed screened silver flexible circuit membranes, automated tape winding and box build, or pre-built products. The firm's automated manufacturing processes enable it to work closely with its customers during design and prototype stages of production for new custom products and to jointly increase productivity and reduce response time to the marketplace. It uses computer-aided design (CAD) techniques and unique software to assist in preparation of the tool design layout and fabrications; reduce costs; improve component and product quality; and accelerate turnaround time during product development. Key Tronic's current customer production programs include consumer electronics and plastics; specialty printers and sub-assemblies; household products; gaming devices; telecommunication satellite units; multimedia touch panels; digital control panels; computer accessories; medical devices; exercise equipment; educational toys; industrial tools; networking equipment; scientific instruments; and security surveillance devices. The firm's largest customers include Kaz, Inc.; Lexmark International, Inc.; and International Gaming Technology, Inc. Key Tronic operates facilities totaling nearly 700,000 square feet in the U.S., China and Mexico engaged in production, testing, engineering and distribution.

Key Tronic offers its employees life, disability, medical, dental and vision insurance, as well as tuition reimbursement and a 401(k) plan.

FINANCIALS:

Sales and profits are in thousands of dollars—add 000 to get the full amount. 2011 Note: Financial information for 2011 was not available for all companies at press time.

2011 Sales: $253,846	2011 Profits: $5,736
2010 Sales: $199,620	2010 Profits: $8,690
2009 Sales: $184,924	2009 Profits: $1,063
2008 Sales: $204,122	2008 Profits: $5,584
2007 Sales: $201,712	2007 Profits: $5,230

U.S. Stock Ticker: KTCC
Int'l Ticker:
Int'l Exchange:
Employees: 1,997 Fiscal Year Ends: 6/30
Parent Company:

SALARIES/BENEFITS:

Pension Plan:	ESOP Stock Plan:	Profit Sharing:	Top Exec. Salary: $437,000	Bonus: $409,885
Savings Plan: Y	Stock Purch. Plan:		Second Exec. Salary: $301,029	Bonus: $269,006

OTHER THOUGHTS:

Apparent Women Officers or Directors: 1
Hot Spot for Advancement for Women/Minorities:

LOCATIONS: ("Y" = Yes)

West:	Southwest:	Midwest:	Southeast:	Northeast:	International:
Y	Y				Y

KEYNOTE SYSTEMS INC

www.keynote.com

Industry Group Code: 541512

Management:		Sales/Marketing:		Liberal Arts:		Information Systems:		Professionals:		Technical/Scientific:	
Mgmt. Trainees:		Mktg. Professionals:	Y	Gen. Writing/Editing:		Info. Management:	Y	Finance/Acct.:	Y	Engineers, Elec.:	Y
Experienced Mgmt.:	Y	Retail Sales:		Technical Writing:	Y	Software Dev.:	Y	Law:	Y	Engineers, Other:	Y
Int'l Business:	Y	Commercial/Industrial:	Y	Graphic Arts/Photog.:		Hardware Dev.:		HR/Other:	Y	Health/Lab	
MBA Graduates:	Y	Sales Trainees:		Music:		Consulting/Other:	Y	Training:	Y	Scientists/Research:	
		Advertising Pros.:		Broadcasting:				Health Care:		Petroleum/Chemicals:	
				Other:	Y			Consulting:	Y	Math/Other:	Y

TYPES OF BUSINESS:

Consulting-Internet Performance Management
e-Commerce Transactions Measurement
Benchmarking & Testing Services

BRANDS/DIVISIONS/AFFILIATES:

Global Roamer
SIGOS System Integrated Test Environment (SITE)
Mobile Complete Inc

CONTACTS: *Note: Officers with more than one job title may be intentionally listed here more than once.*

Umang Gupta, CEO
Curtis Smith, CFO
Anshu Agarwal, VP-Mktg.
Vik Chaudhary, VP-Prod. Mgmt.
Krishna Khadloya, VP-Eng.
Shawn White, VP-Oper.
Vik Chaudhary, VP-Corp. Dev.
Dan Berkowitz, Sr. Dir.-Corp. Comm.
David Peterson, Chief Acct. Officer
Don Aoki, Sr. VP-Professional Svcs.
Umang Gupta, Chmn.
Jeff Kraatz, Sr. VP-Worldwide Sales & Svcs.

Phone: 650-403-2400 | **Fax:** 650-403-5500
Toll-Free: 888-539-7978
Address: 777 Mariners Island Blvd., San Mateo, CA 94404 US

GROWTH PLANS/SPECIAL FEATURES:

Keynote Systems, Inc. develops and sells technology solutions to measure, test, assure and improve the quality of service for Internet and mobile cloud communications. The firm also offers licensed solutions. Keynote's Internet services are based upon an extensive network of strategically-located measurement and testing computers, running its proprietary software that measures online business performance. Keynote operates over 3,000 measurement computers in over 300 locations around the world. Internet Cloud services include web site and transaction/application monitoring and measurement services; Voice over Internet Protocol (VoIP) and streaming measurement services; load testing services; customer experience management services; competitive research and industry scorecard services; and custom professional services focused on load and capacity problems, online customer satisfaction and usability issues. Keynote's Mobile Cloud services are based on a worldwide infrastructure of distributed mobile devices, both simulated and real, to benchmark, monitor and test the performance quality of those services from multiple regional markets. In addition, this segment includes the firm's Global Roamer services and its System Integrated Test Environment (SITE) system, which allows mobile and telecommunications providers to test and monitor their mobile roaming partners' voice and data networks. The company markets its products through its field sales and telesales organization, as well as through its web site. Keynote maintains offices internationally in the U.K., France, Germany and Sweden and sells indirectly through reseller partners throughout the rest of Europe, the Middle East, Africa and Asia. In October 2011, the firm acquired the cloud-based testing platform provider Mobile Complete, Inc. for approximately $60 million.

The company offers employees medical, dental and vision insurance; a 401(k) plan; an educational assistance program; life insurance; flexible spending accounts; a travel assistance program; and an employee assistance program.

FINANCIALS: **Sales and profits are in thousands of dollars—add 000 to get the full amount. 2011 Note: Financial information for 2011 was not available for all companies at press time.**

2011 Sales: $103,000 — 2011 Profits: $50,900
2010 Sales: $79,851 — 2010 Profits: $1,686
2009 Sales: $80,107 — 2009 Profits: $3,257
2008 Sales: $76,908 — 2008 Profits: $-2,764
2007 Sales: $67,754 — 2007 Profits: $-4,691

U.S. Stock Ticker: KEYN
Int'l Ticker:
Int'l Exchange:
Employees: 323 — Fiscal Year Ends: 9/30
Parent Company:

SALARIES/BENEFITS:

Pension Plan: — ESOP Stock Plan: — Profit Sharing: — Top Exec. Salary: $297,000 — Bonus: $158,400
Savings Plan: Y — Stock Purch. Plan: — Second Exec. Salary: $254,371 — Bonus: $216,728

OTHER THOUGHTS:

Apparent Women Officers or Directors: 2
Hot Spot for Advancement for Women/Minorities:

LOCATIONS: ("Y" = Yes)

West:	Southwest:	Midwest:	Southeast:	Northeast:	International:
Y	Y	Y	Y	Y	Y

KIMLEY-HORN AND ASSOCIATES INC

www.kimley-horn.com

Industry Group Code: 541330

Management:		**Sales/Marketing:**		**Liberal Arts:**		**Information Systems:**		**Professionals:**		**Technical/Scientific:**	
Mgmt. Trainees:		Mktg. Professionals:	Y	Gen. Writing/Editing:		Info. Management:	Y	Finance/Acct.:	Y	Engineers, Elec.:	Y
Experienced Mgmt.:	Y	Retail Sales:		Technical Writing:	Y	Software Dev.:		Law:	Y	Engineers, Other:	Y
Int'l Business:		Commercial/Industrial:	Y	Graphic Arts/Photog.:		Hardware Dev.:		HR/Other:	Y	Health/Lab	
MBA Graduates:	Y	Sales Trainees:		Music:		Consulting/Other:	Y	Training:	Y	Scientists/Research:	
		Advertising Pros.:		Broadcasting:				Health Care:		Petroleum/Chemicals:	
				Other:				Consulting:		Math/Other:	

TYPES OF BUSINESS:

Engineering
Project Consulting

BRANDS/DIVISIONS/AFFILIATES:

CONTACTS:

Note: Officers with more than one job title may be intentionally listed here more than once.

John C. Atz, Pres.
Nicholas L. Ellis, CFO
Julie Beauvais, Dir.-Corp. Comm.
Peter A. Bishop, Principal
Ed Vick, Co-Founder
Charles A. Nickols, Sr. VP
Patrick B. Hart, VP
Mark S. Wilson, Chmn.

Phone: 919-677-2000 **Fax:** 919-677-2050
Toll-Free:
Address: 3001 Weston Pkwy., Cary, NC 27513 US

GROWTH PLANS/SPECIAL FEATURES:

Kimley-Horn and Associates, Inc. is an engineering and land-planning firm, operating from over 60 offices throughout the U.S. The company offers a variety of design and planning services to clients in the private and public sectors in a wide range of industries. For the aviation industry, Kimley-Horn is able to plan, design and administer various construction projects. In the environmental sector, it offers a variety of services, such as planning and feasibility studies; environmental documentation; and environmental restoration. The company provides engineering and consulting services to clients in the biomass, solar, wind energy and fossil fuel-based power industries. Solutions for the intelligent transportation segment include intelligent transportation system (ITS) architectures; systems engineering analyses; ITS master planning; deployment plans and feasibility studies. Other transit sector services include bus system planning, regional operations studies, modeling and simulation, as well as financial feasibility and cost studies for mass transit systems. For the urban planning/landscape architecture industry, it provides clients with design, redevelopment, architecture and construction services. In the wireless communications market, Kimley-Horn offers wireless systems inventory and assessment; network development; wireless camouflage applications; and distributed antenna systems. For clients in the water resources and utilities segment, the company offers alternative supplies; flood control; storm water management; wastewater collection; treatment and disposal; water resources permitting; and water supply, treatment and distribution.

Employee benefits include medical, prescription, dental and vision coverage; a health savings account; a flexible spending account; short- and long-term disability insurance; life insurance; an employee assistance program; tuition reimbursement; and a 401(k) plan with company match.

FINANCIALS:

Sales and profits are in thousands of dollars—add 000 to get the full amount. 2011 Note: Financial information for 2011 was not available for all companies at press time.

2011 Sales: $	2011 Profits: $	**U.S. Stock Ticker: Private**
2010 Sales: $	2010 Profits: $	**Int'l Ticker:**
2009 Sales: $	2009 Profits: $	Int'l Exchange:
2008 Sales: $	2008 Profits: $	Employees: Fiscal Year Ends: 12/31
2007 Sales: $	2007 Profits: $	Parent Company:

SALARIES/BENEFITS:

Pension Plan:	ESOP Stock Plan:	Profit Sharing:	Top Exec. Salary: $	Bonus: $
Savings Plan: Y	Stock Purch. Plan:		Second Exec. Salary: $	Bonus: $

OTHER THOUGHTS:

Apparent Women Officers or Directors: 1
Hot Spot for Advancement for Women/Minorities:

LOCATIONS: ("Y" = Yes)

West:	Southwest:	Midwest:	Southeast:	Northeast:	International:
Y	Y	Y	Y	Y	

KIRBY CORP

www.kirbycorp.com

Industry Group Code: 48321

Management:		Sales/Marketing:		Liberal Arts:		Information Systems:		Professionals:		Technical/Scientific:	
Mgmt. Trainees:		Mktg. Professionals:	Y	Gen. Writing/Editing:		Info. Management:	Y	Finance/Acct.:	Y	Engineers, Elec.:	
Experienced Mgmt.:	Y	Retail Sales:		Technical Writing:		Software Dev.:	Y	Law:	Y	Engineers, Other:	
Int'l Business:	Y	Commercial/Industrial:	Y	Graphic Arts/Photog.:		Hardware Dev.:		HR/Other:	Y	Health/Lab	
MBA Graduates:	Y	Sales Trainees:	Y	Music:		Consulting/Other:		Training:		Scientists/Research:	
		Advertising Pros.:		Broadcasting:				Health Care:		Petroleum/Chemicals:	
				Other:				Consulting:		Math/Other:	

TYPES OF BUSINESS:

Inland Water Transportation
Barges & Tugs
Diesel Engine Services

BRANDS/DIVISIONS/AFFILIATES:

Kirby Inland Marine LP
Kirby Engine Systems Inc

CONTACTS: *Note: Officers with more than one job title may be intentionally listed here more than once.*

Joseph H. Pyne, CEO
Joseph H. Pyne, Pres.
David W. Grzebinski, CFO/Exec. VP
Joseph H. Reniers, VP-Human Resources
David R. Mosley, CIO/VP
Amy D. Husted, VP-Legal
G. Stephen Holcomb, VP-Investor Rel.
Ronald A. Dragg, Controller/VP
Thomas G. Adler, Corp. Sec.
Greg R. Binion, Pres., Kirby Inland Marine
Dorman Lynn Strahan, Pres., Kirby Engine Systems
Renato A. Castro, Treas.
Joseph H. Pyne, Chmn.

Phone: 713-435-1000	**Fax:** 713-435-1010
Toll-Free:	
Address: 55 Waugh Dr., Ste. 1000, Houston, TX 77007 US	

GROWTH PLANS/SPECIAL FEATURES:

Kirby Corp. is one of the largest inland barge operators in the U.S. It primarily transports bulk liquid products across the Mississippi River System, the Gulf Intracoastal Waterway, the Ohio River and the Illinois River. The company operates in two segments: marine transportation and diesel engine services. The marine transportation segment, through subsidiary Kirby Inland Marine, LP, is engaged in the inland transportation of petrochemicals, black oil products, refined petroleum products and agricultural chemicals by tank barges and, to a lesser extent, the offshore transportation of dry-bulk cargoes by barge. The division is a provider of transportation services for its customers but does not assume ownership of the products it transports. The equipment owned or operated by the segment is comprised of 825 active inland tank barges, 222 active inland towboats, four offshore dry-cargo barges, four offshore tugboats and one offshore shifting tugboat. The diesel engine services segment, through subsidiary Kirby Engine Systems, Inc., is engaged in the overhaul and repair of medium-speed and high-speed diesel engines and reduction gears and related parts sales in three distinct markets: the marine market, providing aftermarket service for vessels powered by diesel engines utilized in the various inland and offshore marine industries; the power generation market, providing aftermarket service for diesel engines that provide standby, peak and base load power generation, for users of industrial reduction gears and for standby generation components of the nuclear industry; and the railroad market, providing aftermarket service and parts for shortline, industrial, class II and certain transit railroads. In February 2011, the firm acquired 21 inland and offshore tank barges and 15 inland towboats and offshore tugboats from Enterprise Marine Services. Additionally, the company purchased a 51% interest in Kinder Morgan's fleeting facility and shifting operation for dry tank and cargo barges on the Houston Ship Channel.

FINANCIALS: **Sales and profits are in thousands of dollars—add 000 to get the full amount. 2011 Note: Financial information for 2011 was not available for all companies at press time.**

2011 Sales: $1,850,417	2011 Profits: $183,026
2010 Sales: $1,109,557	2010 Profits: $116,249
2009 Sales: $1,082,158	2009 Profits: $125,941
2008 Sales: $1,360,154	2008 Profits: $157,168
2007 Sales: $1,172,625	2007 Profits: $123,341

U.S. Stock Ticker: KEX
Int'l Ticker:
Int'l Exchange:
Employees: 2,010 Fiscal Year Ends: 12/31
Parent Company:

SALARIES/BENEFITS:

Pension Plan: Y	ESOP Stock Plan:	Profit Sharing:	Top Exec. Salary: $680,000	Bonus: $2,446,392
Savings Plan: Y	Stock Purch. Plan:		Second Exec. Salary: $338,750	Bonus: $397,659

OTHER THOUGHTS:

Apparent Women Officers or Directors: 1
Hot Spot for Advancement for Women/Minorities:

LOCATIONS: ("Y" = Yes)

West:	Southwest:	Midwest:	Southeast:	Northeast:	International:
		Y	Y	Y	

KKR & CO LP (KOHLBERG KRAVIS ROBERTS & CO) www.kkr.com

Industry Group Code: 523910

Management:		Sales/Marketing:		Liberal Arts:		Information Systems:		Professionals:		Technical/Scientific:	
Mgmt. Trainees:		Mktg. Professionals:	Y	Gen. Writing/Editing:	Y	Info. Management:	Y	Finance/Acct.:	Y	Engineers, Elec.:	
Experienced Mgmt.:	Y	Retail Sales:		Technical Writing:		Software Dev.:		Law:	Y	Engineers, Other:	
Int'l Business:	Y	Commercial/Industrial:		Graphic Arts/Photog.:		Hardware Dev.:		HR/Other:	Y	Health/Lab	
MBA Graduates:	Y	Sales Trainees:		Music:		Consulting/Other:		Training:		Scientists/Research:	
		Advertising Pros.:		Broadcasting:				Health Care:		Petroleum/Chemicals:	
				Other:				Consulting:		Math/Other:	Y

TYPES OF BUSINESS:

Private Equity Investments
Asset Management
Fixed Income Investments

BRANDS/DIVISIONS/AFFILIATES:

Kohlberg Kravis Roberts & Co
KKR Private Equity Investors
KKR Financial Holdings LLC
KKR Capstone
Samson Investment Company
Ipreo Holdings LLC
Academy Sports & Outdoors Ltd
Go Daddy Group Inc

CONTACTS:

Note: Officers with more than one job title may be intentionally listed here more than once.

Henry R. Kravis, Co-CEO/Co-Chmn.
William J. Janetschek, CFO
Robert D. Gottlieb, Chief Human Resources Officer
Edward Brandman, CIO
Todd Fisher, Chief Admin. Officer
David J. Sorkin, General Counsel
Kenneth B. Mehlman, Global Head-Public Affairs
Edward Law, Managing Dir.-KKR Capital Markets
Robert Howard, Managing Dir.-KKR Equity Strategies
Ralph Rosenberg, Managing Dir.-Real Estate
Kaveh Samie, Managing Dir.-Middle East & North Africa
George R. Roberts, Co-Chmn./Co-CEO
Clifford Chiu, Managing Dir.-Asia

Phone: 212-750-8300	**Fax:** 212-750-0003
Toll-Free:	
Address: 9 W. 57th St., Ste. 4200, New York, NY 10019 US	

GROWTH PLANS/SPECIAL FEATURES:

KKR & Co. L.P. (Kohlberg Kravis Roberts & Co.), with over $61 billion in assets under management, is an alternative asset management firm specializing in large, complex buyouts. KKR organizes its business into three segments: private markets; public markets; and capital market and principal activities. The private markets segment is comprised of private equity funds with finite life and investment periods. KKR's private equity business includes acquisitions of companies it believes it can help to make more profitable. It specializes in large, complex industries as well as global infrastructure investments. The public markets business includes fixed income and other investments managed by KKR Asset Management (KAM) and KKR Financial Holdings LLC. KAM is the company's asset management platform that provides return profiles and products that satisfy a range of fixed-income investment mandates. KKR Financial Holdings is a specialty finance company that focuses on investing in corporate debt and other public and private equity securities. Its capital market activities are chiefly conducted through KKR Capital Markets, a broker-dealer. The firm's investment managers help identify which companies to invest in and form strategies to improve those companies. An internal consulting group, KKR Capstone, supports the investment managers. The company currently has interests in industries including financial services, health care, pharmaceuticals, communications, hospitality, energy, chemicals, retail, consumer products and technology. In April 2011, KKR acquired Pfizer's Capsugel business. In August 2011, it acquired sporting goods retailer Academy Sports & Outdoors Ltd.; and Ipreo Holdings LLC, a provider of data and market research. In November 2011, KKR, together with several investment partners, agreed to acquire Samson Investment Company, a private oil and gas exploration and production company. In December 2011, the firm, along with Silver Lake Partners and Technology Crossover Ventures, acquired Internet address registration firm Go Daddy Group, Inc.

FINANCIALS:

Sales and profits are in thousands of dollars—add 000 to get the full amount. 2011 Note: Financial information for 2011 was not available for all companies at press time.

2011 Sales: $650,862	2011 Profits: $1,921	**U.S. Stock Ticker: KKR**
2010 Sales: $382,287	2010 Profits: $333,178	**Int'l Ticker:**
2009 Sales: $251,600	2009 Profits: $849,700	Int'l Exchange:
2008 Sales: $109,600	2008 Profits: $-1,204,500	Employees: 698 Fiscal Year Ends: 12/31
2007 Sales: $	2007 Profits: $	Parent Company:

SALARIES/BENEFITS:

Pension Plan:	ESOP Stock Plan:	Profit Sharing:	Top Exec. Salary: $300,000	Bonus: $4,750,000
Savings Plan:	Stock Purch. Plan:		Second Exec. Salary: $300,000	Bonus: $2,045,000

OTHER THOUGHTS:

Apparent Women Officers or Directors: 1
Hot Spot for Advancement for Women/Minorities:

LOCATIONS: ("Y" = Yes)

West:	Southwest:	Midwest:	Southeast:	Northeast:	International:
Y	Y			Y	Y

KNIGHT CAPITAL GROUP INC

www.knight.com

Industry Group Code: 523120

Management:		Sales/Marketing:		Liberal Arts:		Information Systems:		Professionals:		Technical/Scientific:	
Mgmt. Trainees:		Mktg. Professionals:	Y	Gen. Writing/Editing:	Y	Info. Management:	Y	Finance/Acct.:	Y	Engineers, Elec.:	
Experienced Mgmt.:	Y	Retail Sales:		Technical Writing:		Software Dev.:	Y	Law:	Y	Engineers, Other:	
Int'l Business:	Y	Commercial/Industrial:		Graphic Arts/Photog.:		Hardware Dev.:		HR/Other:	Y	Health/Lab	
MBA Graduates:	Y	Sales Trainees:		Music:		Consulting/Other:		Training:	Y	Scientists/Research:	
		Advertising Pros.:		Broadcasting:				Health Care:		Petroleum/Chemicals:	
				Other:				Consulting:		Math/Other:	Y

TYPES OF BUSINESS:

Equities Trade Execution
Equities Research
Fixed Income Trading

BRANDS/DIVISIONS/AFFILIATES:

Knight Capital Markets LLC
Knight Equity Markets LP
Knight Capital Europe Limited
Knight Direct LLC
Hotspot FX Holdings Inc
Knight Bondpoint Inc
Knight Libertas Holdings LLC
Knight Capital Asia Limited

CONTACTS: *Note: Officers with more than one job title may be intentionally listed here more than once.*

Thomas M. Joyce, CEO
Steven Bisgay, CFO/Sr. Managing Dir.
Margaret E. Wyrwas, Sr. Managing Dir.-Mktg.
Bronwen Bastone, Sr. Managing Dir.-Human Resources
Steven J. Sadoff, Exec. VP-Global Tech. & Svcs.
Leonard J. Amoruso, General Counsel/Sr. Managing Dir.
Steven J. Sadoff, Exec. VP-Oper.
Margaret E. Wyrwas, Sr. Managing Dir.-Comm.
Margaret Wyrwas, Sr. Managing Dir.-Investor Rel.
Alan Lhota, Sr. Managing Dir.-Institutional Fixed Income
Robert N. Stein, Head-Global Asset Mgmt.
David S. Lehmann, Managing Dir./Head-Electronic Execution Svcs.
Thomas M. Merritt, Corp. Sec.
Thomas M. Joyce, Chmn.

Phone: 201-222-9400	**Fax:** 201-557-6853
Toll-Free: 800-544-7508	
Address: 545 Washington Blvd., Jersey City, NJ 07310 US	

GROWTH PLANS/SPECIAL FEATURES:

Knight Capital Group, Inc. is a financial services firm that provides market access and trade execution services. The firm's clients include global, national and regional broker-dealers; online brokers; mutual funds; pension plans; plan sponsors; hedge funds; trusts; and endowments. The company operates in four segments: Market Making; Institutional Sales and Trading (IST); Electronic Execution Services (EES); and Corporate and Other. The Market Making segment consists of market making in global equities and listed domestic options. The division includes client and non-client electronic market making operations in which Knight Capital acts as a market maker in equity securities quoted and traded on the NASDAQ Stock Market; the over-the-counter market for New York Stock Exchange (NYSE); NYSE Arca listed securities; NYSE Amex Equities; and several European exchanges. The IST division offers global voice equity and fixed income sales, reverse mortgage origination and securitization, capital markets and asset management activities. Knight Capital's EES division offers access to markets and self-directed trading through several electronic agency-based platforms, including customizable execution management program Knight Direct; electronic foreign exchange trading system Hotspot FX; and Knight BondPoint platform, an electronic fixed income trading platform for sell-side companies. The Corporate and Other segment invests in strategic financial services-oriented opportunities; allocates, deploys and monitors the firm's capital; and maintains corporate overhead expenses and other expenses that are not attributable to the company's other segments. Subsidiaries of Knight Capital Group include Knight Equity Markets L.P.; Knight Capital Markets LLC; Knight Capital Europe Limited; Knight Direct LLC; Hotspot FX Holdings, Inc.; Knight Capital Asia Limited; Knight BondPoint, Inc; and Knight Libertas Holdings LLC. The firm recently acquired Urban Financial Group and Astor Asset Management, LLC. In 2011, the firm introduced several new offerings, including Knight Match Europe and Knight Global Program Trading.

The firm offers its employees health benefits and a 401(k) plan.

FINANCIALS: **Sales and profits are in thousands of dollars—add 000 to get the full amount. 2011 Note: Financial information for 2011 was not available for all companies at press time.**

2011 Sales: $1,362,500	2011 Profits: $115,200	**U.S. Stock Ticker: KCG**
2010 Sales: $1,149,056	2010 Profits: $91,638	**Int'l Ticker:**
2009 Sales: $1,162,431	2009 Profits: $117,102	Int'l Exchange:
2008 Sales: $938,857	2008 Profits: $177,911	Employees: 1,326 Fiscal Year Ends: 12/31
2007 Sales: $896,749	2007 Profits: $122,240	Parent Company:

SALARIES/BENEFITS:

Pension Plan:	ESOP Stock Plan:	Profit Sharing:	Top Exec. Salary: $750,000	Bonus: $2,699,390
Savings Plan: Y	Stock Purch. Plan:		Second Exec. Salary: $250,000	Bonus: $2,520,000

OTHER THOUGHTS:

Apparent Women Officers or Directors: 2
Hot Spot for Advancement for Women/Minorities:

LOCATIONS: ("Y" = Yes)

West:	Southwest:	Midwest:	Southeast:	Northeast:	International:
Y	Y	Y	Y	Y	Y

KNOLOGY INC

www.knology.com

Industry Group Code: 517110

Management:		Sales/Marketing:		Liberal Arts:		Information Systems:		Professionals:		Technical/Scientific:	
Mgmt. Trainees:		Mktg. Professionals:	Y	Gen. Writing/Editing:	Y	Info. Management:	Y	Finance/Acct.:	Y	Engineers, Elec.:	Y
Experienced Mgmt.:	Y	Retail Sales:		Technical Writing:		Software Dev.:	Y	Law:	Y	Engineers, Other:	
Int'l Business:		Commercial/Industrial:		Graphic Arts/Photog.:		Hardware Dev.:		HR/Other:	Y	Health/Lab	
MBA Graduates:	Y	Sales Trainees:		Music:		Consulting/Other:		Training:		Scientists/Research:	
		Advertising Pros.:		Broadcasting:				Health Care:		Petroleum/Chemicals:	
				Other:				Consulting:		Math/Other:	

TYPES OF BUSINESS:

Cable TV Service
Internet Service Provider
Local & Long-Distance Telephone Service
Passive Optical Network
Managed Integrated Network Solutions
Subscriber Video-on-Video Demand
Interactive Television
High-Definition Television

BRANDS/DIVISIONS/AFFILIATES:

Passive Optical Network
MATRIX

CONTACTS: *Note: Officers with more than one job title may be intentionally listed here more than once.*

Rodger L. Johnson, CEO
M. Todd Holt, Pres.
Rob Mills, CFO
Ron Johnson, VP-Sales
Brad M. Vanacore, VP-Human Resources
Marcus R. Luke, Chief Scientist/VP
Richard D. Perkins, VP-IT & Billing
John Treece, CTO
Chad S. Wachter, General Counsel/VP/Sec.
Bret T. McCants, Exec. VP-Oper.
Tony Palermo, VP-Mktg.
Weldon Feightner, VP-Regional Oper.
Andrew M. Sivell, VP-Network Oper.
Felix L. Boccucci, VP-Regulatory Affairs
Rodger L. Johnson, Chmn.

Phone: 706-645-8553	**Fax:**
Toll-Free:	
Address: 1241 O.G. Skinner Dr., West Point, GA 31833 US	

GROWTH PLANS/SPECIAL FEATURES:

Knology, Inc. is a provider of video, voice, data and advanced communications services throughout the southeastern and midwestern U.S. Knology's services are offered over its wholly-owned 750 MHz broadband network, including over 200 channels of digital cable TV, high-speed Internet access, digital telephone service with voice messaging features, subscriber video-on-video demand (SVOD), digital video recorders (DVR), interactive television (iTV), and High-Definition Television (HDTV). Knology operates in Alabama, Georgia, Florida, Iowa, Minnesota, South Carolina, South Dakota and Tennessee. In addition to separate video, voice and data services, Knology provides a broad range of service bundles. The firm's interactive broadband network is designed using redundant fiber-optic cables, and its fiber rings provide for rapid, automatic redirection of network traffic. The self-correcting properties of the fiber rings allow service to continue even during single-point failures. Knology's fiber-based business voice and data services include Passive Optical Network (PON), which supplies IP architecture with segmented voice and data bandwidth, and Managed Integrated Network Solutions (MATRIX), an integrated IP-based technology, which combines data and voice. Knology's network passes through approximately 1,045,355 residential and business units.

The company offers its employees a 401(k) plan; tuition reimbursement; free or discounted Knology Services; an employee assistance program; and medical, prescription, dental and vision benefits.

FINANCIALS: **Sales and profits are in thousands of dollars—add 000 to get the full amount. 2011 Note: Financial information for 2011 was not available for all companies at press time.**

2011 Sales: $518,600	2011 Profits: $48,300	**U.S. Stock Ticker: KNOL**
2010 Sales: $459,546	2010 Profits: $- 281	**Int'l Ticker:**
2009 Sales: $425,565	2009 Profits: $-3,407	Int'l Exchange:
2008 Sales: $410,230	2008 Profits: $-12,125	Employees: 1,846 Fiscal Year Ends: 12/31
2007 Sales: $347,652	2007 Profits: $-43,918	Parent Company:

SALARIES/BENEFITS:

Pension Plan: Y	ESOP Stock Plan:	Profit Sharing:	Top Exec. Salary: $503,130	Bonus: $285,778
Savings Plan: Y	Stock Purch. Plan:		Second Exec. Salary: $300,000	Bonus: $160,000

OTHER THOUGHTS:

Apparent Women Officers or Directors:
Hot Spot for Advancement for Women/Minorities:

LOCATIONS: ("Y" = Yes)

West:	Southwest:	Midwest:	Southeast:	Northeast:	International:
		Y	Y		

Sales, profits and employees may be estimates. Financial information, benefits and other data can change quickly and may vary from those stated here.

KORN/FERRY INTERNATIONAL

www.kornferry.com

Industry Group Code: 541612

Management:		**Sales/Marketing:**		**Liberal Arts:**		**Information Systems:**		**Professionals:**		**Technical/Scientific:**	
Mgmt. Trainees:		Mktg. Professionals:	Y	Gen. Writing/Editing:		Info. Management:	Y	Finance/Acct.:	Y	Engineers, Elec.:	
Experienced Mgmt.:	Y	Retail Sales:		Technical Writing:		Software Dev.:	Y	Law:	Y	Engineers, Other:	
Int'l Business:	Y	Commercial/Industrial:	Y	Graphic Arts/Photog.:		Hardware Dev.:		HR/Other:	Y	Health/Lab	
MBA Graduates:	Y	Sales Trainees:	Y	Music:		Consulting/Other:		Training:	Y	Scientists/Research:	
		Advertising Pros.:		Broadcasting:				Health Care:		Petroleum/Chemicals:	
				Other:				Consulting:	Y	Math/Other:	

TYPES OF BUSINESS:

Personnel Recruitment
Executive Search
Middle Management Recruitment
Leadership Development

BRANDS/DIVISIONS/AFFILIATES:

Futurestep
Executive Compensation Advisors
Lore International Institute, Inc.
SENSA Solutions

CONTACTS: *Note: Officers with more than one job title may be intentionally listed here more than once.*

Gary D. Burnison, CEO
Mike DiGregorio, CFO/Exec. VP
Michael Distefano, Chief Mktg. Officer
Linda Hyman, Exec. VP-Global Human Resources
Dan Demeter, CIO
Peter Dunn, General Counsel
Brian Suh, Sr. VP-Corp. Dev.
Don Spetner, Exec. VP-Corp. Affairs
Ana Dutra, CEO-Leadership & Talent Consulting
Byrne Mulrooney, CEO-Futurestep
Robert A. Damon, Pres., North America
Charles Tseng, Pres., APAC
Kenneth Whipple, Chmn.
Bernard S. Zen-Ruffinen, Pres., Europe, Middle East & Africa

Phone: 310-552-1834	**Fax:** 310-553-6452
Toll-Free:	
Address: 1900 Ave. of the Stars, Ste. 2600, Los Angeles, CA 90067 US	

GROWTH PLANS/SPECIAL FEATURES:

Korn/Ferry International is a provider of executive search, outsourced recruiting and leadership development solutions with a broad global presence in the recruitment industry, conducting over 10,000 executive searches yearly. Korn/Ferry operates in 76 offices across 36 countries in North America, Europe, Asia/Pacific, Latin America, the Middle East and Africa. The firm's offerings are divided into three segments: executive recruitment; talent acquisition solutions, which operates through Futurestep; and leadership and talent consulting (LTC). The executive recruitment segment focuses on board-level, chief executive and other senior executive positions for clients predominately in the consumer, financial services, industrial, life sciences and technology industries. Futurestep, the firm's outsourced recruiting subsidiary, creates customized recruitment solutions based on a client's individual workforce needs. The subsidiary serves as a recruitment process outsourcing (RPO) provider and offers mid-level search, project recruitment and interim solutions. The LTC segment helps assist clients with the ongoing assessment and development of their leadership teams. This segment's services address three leadership and talent management needs: strategic and organizational alignment; leadership and executive development; and talent and performance management. The majority of Korn/Ferry's revenue is generated through executive recruitment. In April 2010, Korn/Ferry established an alliance partnership with Woodburn Mann, a South African recruitment, leadership and talent management firm. Woodburn Mann will extend the firm's search and talent management services in Angola, Botswana, Lesotho, Malawi, South Africa, Zambia and Zimbabwe. In December 2010, the firm began operations at its facility in Houston, Texas.

FINANCIALS: **Sales and profits are in thousands of dollars—add 000 to get the full amount. 2011 Note: Financial information for 2011 was not available for all companies at press time.**

2011 Sales: $776,251	2011 Profits: $58,874	**U.S. Stock Ticker: KFY**
2010 Sales: $599,649	2010 Profits: $5,298	**Int'l Ticker:**
2009 Sales: $676,128	2009 Profits: $-10,092	Int'l Exchange:
2008 Sales: $835,642	2008 Profits: $66,211	Employees: 2,463 Fiscal Year Ends: 4/30
2007 Sales: $689,201	2007 Profits: $55,498	Parent Company:

SALARIES/BENEFITS:

Pension Plan:	ESOP Stock Plan:	Profit Sharing:	Top Exec. Salary: $589,424	Bonus: $650,000
Savings Plan:	Stock Purch. Plan:		Second Exec. Salary: $432,693	Bonus: $550,000

OTHER THOUGHTS:

Apparent Women Officers or Directors: 4
Hot Spot for Advancement for Women/Minorities: Y

LOCATIONS: ("Y" = Yes)

West:	Southwest:	Midwest:	Southeast:	Northeast:	International:
Y	Y	Y	Y	Y	Y

KRONOS WORLDWIDE INC

www.kronosww.com

Industry Group Code: 325

Management:		Sales/Marketing:		Liberal Arts:		Information Systems:		Professionals:		Technical/Scientific:	
Mgmt. Trainees:		Mktg. Professionals:	Y	Gen. Writing/Editing:		Info. Management:	Y	Finance/Acct.:	Y	Engineers, Elec.:	
Experienced Mgmt.:	Y	Retail Sales:		Technical Writing:	Y	Software Dev.:		Law:	Y	Engineers, Other:	Y
Int'l Business:	Y	Commercial/Industrial:	Y	Graphic Arts/Photog.:		Hardware Dev.:		HR/Other:	Y	Health/Lab	
MBA Graduates:	Y	Sales Trainees:		Music:		Consulting/Other:		Training:	Y	Scientists/Research:	
		Advertising Pros.:		Broadcasting:				Health Care:		Petroleum/Chemicals:	Y
				Other:				Consulting:		Math/Other:	

TYPES OF BUSINESS:

Titanium Dioxide Manufacturer & Distributor
Ilmenite Mining
Iron-Based Chemicals

BRANDS/DIVISIONS/AFFILIATES:

NL Industries Inc
Valhi Inc
Kronos International Inc
Huntsman Holding LLC
Kronos Ecochem
Louisiana Pigment Company, LP

CONTACTS: *Note: Officers with more than one job title may be intentionally listed here more than once.*

Steven L. Watson, CEO
Gregory M. Swalwell, CFO/Exec. VP
H. Joseph Maas, Pres., Sales & Mktg.
Ulfert Fiand, CTO
Klemens Schlueter, Pres., Mfg.
Robert D. Graham, General Counsel/Exec. VP
Douglas C. Weaver, Sr. VP-Dev.
Timothy C. Hafer, Controller/VP
Steven L. Watson, Vice Chmn.
John A. St. Wrba, VP/Treas.
Kelly C. Luttmer, VP/Dir.-Tax
Harold C. Simmons, Chmn.

Phone: 972-233-1700 **Fax:**
Toll-Free:
Address: 5430 LBJ Freeway, Ste. 1700, Dallas, TX 75240 US

GROWTH PLANS/SPECIAL FEATURES:

Kronos Worldwide, Inc. is a global producer and marketer of titanium dioxide, or TiO2, pigments, used for products such as coatings, plastics, paper, inks, food and cosmetics. TiO2, an inorganic whitening pigment imparting durability, opacity and brightness, is manufactured with chloride and sulfate processes. The company offers over 40 different grades of TiO2, which it produces in two crystalline forms: rutile and anatase. Sales of TiO2 account for approximately 90% of the company's total revenue, and are made primarily to domestic and international paint, plastics and paper manufacturers. In addition, Kronos provides product lines that are complementary to TiO2, including ilmenite, a raw material used directly as a feedstock by some sulfate-process TiO2 plants; iron-based chemicals, which are co-products of the TiO2 pigment production process; and titanium oxychloride and titanyl sulfate, which are side-stream products from the production of TiO2. The firm's iron-based chemicals, marketed through its Ecochem division, are used to treat industrial and municipal wastewater; and in the manufacture of iron pigments, cement and agricultural products. Titanium oxychloride is used in the production of electroceramic capacitors for cell phones and other electronic devices, while titanyl sulfate products are used in pearlescent pigments and natural gas pipe applications. The company sells and provides technical services for its products to over 4,000 customers in over 100 countries, with the majority of sales in Europe and North America. Kronos manufactures its products through seven international facilities in Fredrikstad and Hauge, Norway; Leverkusen and Norderham, Germany; Langerbrugge, Belgium; Varennes, Canada; and Lake Charles, Louisiana. The firm holds a 50% interest in, Louisiana Pigment Company, L.P., a manufacturing joint venture with Huntsman Corporation. The joint venture owns and operates the chloride process TiO2 facility in Louisiana. Valhi, Inc. owns approximately 50% of the Kronos Worldwide stock; NL Industries, Inc. owns about 30%.

FINANCIALS: **Sales and profits are in thousands of dollars—add 000 to get the full amount. 2011 Note: Financial information for 2011 was not available for all companies at press time.**

2011 Sales: $
2010 Sales: $1,499,700
2009 Sales: $1,142,000
2008 Sales: $1,316,900
2007 Sales: $1,310,300

2011 Profits: $
2010 Profits: $130,600
2009 Profits: $-34,700
2008 Profits: $9,000
2007 Profits: $-66,700

U.S. Stock Ticker: KRO
Int'l Ticker:
Int'l Exchange:
Employees: 2,440 Fiscal Year Ends: 12/31
Parent Company:

SALARIES/BENEFITS:

Pension Plan: ESOP Stock Plan: Profit Sharing: Top Exec. Salary: $1,024,000 Bonus: $
Savings Plan: Y Stock Purch. Plan: Second Exec. Salary: $1,016,500 Bonus: $

OTHER THOUGHTS:

Apparent Women Officers or Directors: 1
Hot Spot for Advancement for Women/Minorities:

LOCATIONS: ("Y" = Yes)

West:	Southwest:	Midwest:	Southeast:	Northeast:	International:
Y	Y	Y	Y	Y	Y

LACLEDE GROUP INC (THE)

www.thelaclede group.com

Industry Group Code: 221210

Management:		Sales/Marketing:		Liberal Arts:		Information Systems:		Professionals:		Technical/Scientific:	
Mgmt. Trainees:		Mktg. Professionals:	Y	Gen. Writing/Editing:	Y	Info. Management:	Y	Finance/Acct.:	Y	Engineers, Elec.:	Y
Experienced Mgmt.:	Y	Retail Sales:		Technical Writing:		Software Dev.:		Law:	Y	Engineers, Other:	Y
Int'l Business:		Commercial/Industrial:	Y	Graphic Arts/Photog.:		Hardware Dev.:		HR/Other:	Y	Health/Lab	
MBA Graduates:	Y	Sales Trainees:		Music:		Consulting/Other:		Training:	Y	Scientists/Research:	
		Advertising Pros.:		Broadcasting:				Health Care:		Petroleum/Chemicals:	Y
				Other:				Consulting:		Math/Other:	

TYPES OF BUSINESS:

Utilities-Natural Gas
Underground Natural Gas Storage Fields
Transportation & Storage of Liquid Propane
Underground Locating & Marking Services
Insurance Services
Real Estate Development
Natural Gas Marketing

BRANDS/DIVISIONS/AFFILIATES:

Laclede Gas Company
Laclede Gas Family Services, Inc.
Laclede Development Company
Laclede Venture Corp.
Laclede Investment, LLC
Laclede Pipeline Company
Laclede Energy Resources, Inc.

CONTACTS: *Note: Officers with more than one job title may be intentionally listed here more than once.*

Douglas H. Yaeger, CEO
Suzanne Sitherwood, Pres.
Mark D. Waltermire, CFO
Mark C. Darrell, General Counsel
Michael C. Geiselhart, VP-Strategic Dev. & Planning
Mary C. Kullman, Contact-Investor Rel.
Lynn D. Rawlings, Treas.
Mary C. Kullman, Chief Governance Officer/Corp. Sec.
Michael R. Spotanski, Sr. VP-Oper. & Mktg., Laclede Gas Company
James A. Fallert, Controller-Laclede Gas Company
Scott E. Jaskowiak, Pres., Laclede Energy Resources
Douglas H. Yaeger, Chmn.

Phone: 314-342-0500	**Fax:** 314-421-1979
Toll-Free:	
Address: 720 Olive St., St. Louis, MO 63101 US	

GROWTH PLANS/SPECIAL FEATURES:

The Laclede Group, Inc. is a public utility holding company that operates primarily in two divisions, regulated core utility operations and non-regulated activities. It provides natural gas service through its regulated core utility operations. The regulated gas distribution segment includes Laclede Gas Company, Laclede Group's largest subsidiary and core business unit. Laclede Gas is a public utility engaged in the retail distribution and sale of natural gas. It is one of the largest natural gas distribution utility firms in Missouri, serving roughly 630,000 residential, commercial, and industrial customers in St. Louis and parts of 10 other counties in eastern Missouri. Laclede Group's non-regulated services segment includes Laclede Energy Resources, Inc. (LER), a subsidiary engaged in the non-regulated marketing of natural gas and related activities. Other non-regulated subsidiaries of the Laclede Group include Laclede Pipeline Company, which operates a propane pipeline to third-party facilities in Illinois; Laclede Investment, LLC, which invests in other enterprises; Laclede Gas Family Services, Inc., a registered insurance agency in Missouri; Laclede Development Company, which participates in real estate development; and Laclede Venture Corp., which offers services for the compression of natural gas.

FINANCIALS: **Sales and profits are in thousands of dollars—add 000 to get the full amount. 2011 Note: Financial information for 2011 was not available for all companies at press time.**

2011 Sales: $1,603,307	2011 Profits: $63,825	**U.S. Stock Ticker: LG**
2010 Sales: $1,735,029	2010 Profits: $54,040	**Int'l Ticker:**
2009 Sales: $1,895,198	2009 Profits: $64,247	Int'l Exchange:
2008 Sales: $2,208,973	2008 Profits: $77,922	Employees: 1,624 Fiscal Year Ends: 9/30
2007 Sales: $1,855,861	2007 Profits: $49,771	Parent Company:

SALARIES/BENEFITS:

Pension Plan:	ESOP Stock Plan:	Profit Sharing:	Top Exec. Salary: $643,333	Bonus: $421,445
Savings Plan: Y	Stock Purch. Plan:		Second Exec. Salary: $367,333	Bonus: $184,538

OTHER THOUGHTS:

Apparent Women Officers or Directors: 6
Hot Spot for Advancement for Women/Minorities: Y

LOCATIONS: ("Y" = Yes)

West:	Southwest:	Midwest:	Southeast:	Northeast:	International:
	Y	Y			

LAKELAND INDUSTRIES INC

www.lakeland.com

Industry Group Code: 33911

Management:		Sales/Marketing:		Liberal Arts:		Information Systems:		Professionals:		Technical/Scientific:	
Mgmt. Trainees:		Mktg. Professionals:	Y	Gen. Writing/Editing:		Info. Management:	Y	Finance/Acct.:	Y	Engineers, Elec.:	
Experienced Mgmt.:	Y	Retail Sales:		Technical Writing:	Y	Software Dev.:		Law:	Y	Engineers, Other:	Y
Int'l Business:	Y	Commercial/Industrial:	Y	Graphic Arts/Photog.:		Hardware Dev.:		HR/Other:	Y	Health/Lab	Y
MBA Graduates:	Y	Sales Trainees:	Y	Music:		Consulting/Other:		Training:	Y	Scientists/Research:	Y
		Advertising Pros.:		Broadcasting:				Health Care:		Petroleum/Chemicals:	
				Other:				Consulting:		Math/Other:	

TYPES OF BUSINESS:

Safety Clothing
Reusable Industrial & Medical Apparel
Chemical Protection Clothing
Specialty Safety Gloves
Heat Resistant Clothing
Disposable Protective Garments

BRANDS/DIVISIONS/AFFILIATES:

TyChem
Fyrepel
Kevlar
Tyvek

CONTACTS: *Note: Officers with more than one job title may be intentionally listed here more than once.*

Christopher J. Ryan, CEO
Christopher J. Ryan, Pres.
Gary Pokrassa, CFO
Paul C. Smith, VP-Sales
Gregory D. Pontes, VP-Mfg.
Christopher J. Ryan, Corp. Sec.
Stephen M. Bachelder, Chmn.
Charles D. Robseron, VP-Int'l Sales

Phone: 631-981-9700	**Fax:** 631-981-9751
Toll-Free: 800-645-9291	
Address: 701 Koehler Ave., Ste. 7, Ronkonkoma, NY 11779 US	

GROWTH PLANS/SPECIAL FEATURES:

Lakeland Industries, Inc. manufactures and sells a comprehensive line of safety garments and accessories for roughly 1,000 customers in the industrial safety and protective clothing industries in the U.S. The company's major product areas include disposable and limited-use protective clothing; chemical protective suits; fire fighting and heat protective apparel; gloves and arm guards for the food service market; reusable woven garments; and high visibility clothing for traffic and public safety officials. The firm's disposable and reusable garments protect the wearer from contaminants or irritants, such as chemicals, pesticides, fertilizers, paint, grease and dust; from viruses and bacteria; and from limited exposure to hazardous waste and toxic chemicals including acids, asbestos, lead and hydro-carbons (PCBs). Lakeland's products are also used to prevent human contamination of manufacturing processes in clean-room environments. Disposable clothing products include coveralls, lab coats, hoods, aprons, sleeves and smocks. Lakeland's heat protective gear is used by firefighters (under the Fyrepel brand), as well as for maintenance of extreme high-temperature industrial equipment (up to 1,500 degrees Fahrenheit ambient) and for crash and rescue operations. The company's high-end chemical protective suits protect wearers from highly concentrated and powerful chemical and biological toxins such as toxic wastes at Super Fund sites, accidental toxic chemical spills or biological discharges, the handling of chemical or biological warfare weapons and the cleaning and maintenance of chemical, petrochemical and nuclear facilities. Lakeland buys most of its raw materials for manufacturing from DuPont, including those required for the TyChem, Kevlar and Tyvek brands.

FINANCIALS: **Sales and profits are in thousands of dollars—add 000 to get the full amount. 2011 Note: Financial information for 2011 was not available for all companies at press time.**

2011 Sales: $101,236	2011 Profits: $ 972
2010 Sales: $94,141	2010 Profits: $1,030
2009 Sales: $102,268	2009 Profits: $4,549
2008 Sales: $95,740	2008 Profits: $3,291
2007 Sales: $100,171	2007 Profits: $5,104

U.S. Stock Ticker: LAKE
Int'l Ticker:
Int'l Exchange:
Employees: 1,840 Fiscal Year Ends: 1/31
Parent Company:

SALARIES/BENEFITS:

Pension Plan: Y	ESOP Stock Plan:	Profit Sharing:	Top Exec. Salary: $327,504	Bonus: $
Savings Plan: Y	Stock Purch. Plan:		Second Exec. Salary: $207,036	Bonus: $

OTHER THOUGHTS:

Apparent Women Officers or Directors:
Hot Spot for Advancement for Women/Minorities:

LOCATIONS: ("Y" = Yes)

West:	Southwest:	Midwest:	Southeast:	Northeast:	International:
		Y	Y	Y	Y

LB FOSTER COMPANY

www.lbfoster.com

Industry Group Code: 4233

Management:		Sales/Marketing:		Liberal Arts:		Information Systems:		Professionals:		Technical/Scientific:	
Mgmt. Trainees:		Mktg. Professionals:	Y	Gen. Writing/Editing:		Info. Management:	Y	Finance/Acct.:	Y	Engineers, Elec.:	
Experienced Mgmt.:	Y	Retail Sales:		Technical Writing:	Y	Software Dev.:		Law:	Y	Engineers, Other:	
Int'l Business:		Commercial/Industrial:	Y	Graphic Arts/Photog.:		Hardware Dev.:		HR/Other:	Y	Health/Lab	
MBA Graduates:	Y	Sales Trainees:		Music:		Consulting/Other:		Training:		Scientists/Research:	
		Advertising Pros.:		Broadcasting:				Health Care:		Petroleum/Chemicals:	
				Other:				Consulting:		Math/Other:	

TYPES OF BUSINESS:

Engineered Building Materials
Railroad Materials

BRANDS/DIVISIONS/AFFILIATES:

LB Pipe & Coupling Products LLC
CXT Inc

CONTACTS:

Note: Officers with more than one job title may be intentionally listed here more than once.

Robert P. Bauer, CEO
Robert P. Bauer, Pres.
David J. Russo, CFO/Sr. VP/Treas.
Gregory W. Lippard, VP-Rail Prod. Sales
Brian H. Kelly, VP-Human Resources
John F. Kasel, Sr. VP-Mfg.
David L. Voltz, General Counsel/VP/Corp. Sec.
John F. Kasel, Sr. VP-Oper.
David R. Sauder, VP-Global Bus. Dev.
Linda K. Patterson, Controller
Samuel K. Fisher, VP-Rail Prod.
Donald L. Foster, Sr. VP-Construction Prod.
Kevin R. Haugh, Pres., CXT, Inc.
Merry L. Brumbaugh, VP-Tubular Prod.
Lee B. Foster, II, Chmn.

Phone: 412-928-3417	**Fax:** 412-928-7891
Toll-Free:	
Address: 415 Holiday Dr., Pittsburgh, PA 15220 US	

GROWTH PLANS/SPECIAL FEATURES:

L.B. Foster Company, founded in 1902, manufactures, fabricates and distributes products and services for the rail, construction, energy and utility industries. The company operates in three business segments: rail products, construction products and tubular products. The rail products segment, serving the railroad industry, provides a full line of new and used rail, trackwork and related accessories to the railroad, mining and industrial markets. L.B. Foster also designs and produces insulated rail joints, power rail, concrete railroad ties, track fasteners, coverboards and special accessories for mass transit and other rail systems worldwide. The construction products division manufactures and sells steel sheet piling, H-bearing piling and pipe piling, as well as providing rental sheet piling for foundation requirements. In addition, the segment supplies fabricated structural steel, bridge decking, bridge railing, expansion joints and other products for highway construction and repair. L.B. Foster's tubular products segment supplies pipe coatings for natural gas pipelines and utilities. The firm also produces threaded pipe products for industrial water well and irrigation markets and sells micropiles for construction foundation repair and slope stabilization. Joint venture, L.B. Pipe & Coupling Products, LLC (with L.B. Industries, Inc.) manufactures couplings. The company maintains 15 sales offices, as well as 22 warehouses and plants located throughout the U.S. In February 2011, the firm agreed to close its Grand Island manufacturing facility (operated by subsidiary CXT, Inc.).

L.B. Foster offers its employees benefits such as life, AD&D, disability, medical, dental and vision insurance; flexible spending accounts; profit sharing; a 401(k) plan; and an employee assistance plan.

FINANCIALS:

Sales and profits are in thousands of dollars—add 000 to get the full amount. 2011 Note: Financial information for 2011 was not available for all companies at press time.

2011 Sales: $590,900 | 2011 Profits: $22,900
2010 Sales: $475,050 | 2010 Profits: $20,492
2009 Sales: $404,020 | 2009 Profits: $15,727
2008 Sales: $539,236 | 2008 Profits: $27,746
2007 Sales: $508,981 | 2007 Profits: $110,724

U.S. Stock Ticker: FSTR
Int'l Ticker:
Int'l Exchange:
Employees: 866 Fiscal Year Ends: 12/31
Parent Company:

SALARIES/BENEFITS:

Pension Plan: | ESOP Stock Plan: | Profit Sharing: Y | Top Exec. Salary: $498,834 | Bonus: $537,496
Savings Plan: Y | Stock Purch. Plan: | | Second Exec. Salary: $254,583 | Bonus: $192,464

OTHER THOUGHTS:

Apparent Women Officers or Directors: 4
Hot Spot for Advancement for Women/Minorities: Y

LOCATIONS: ("Y" = Yes)

West:	Southwest:	Midwest:	Southeast:	Northeast:	International:
Y	Y	Y	Y	Y	

LCC INTERNATIONAL INC

www.lcc.com

Industry Group Code: 541512

Management:		Sales/Marketing:		Liberal Arts:		Information Systems:		Professionals:		Technical/Scientific:	
Mgmt. Trainees:		Mktg. Professionals:	Y	Gen. Writing/Editing:		Info. Management:	Y	Finance/Acct.:	Y	Engineers, Elec.:	Y
Experienced Mgmt.:	Y	Retail Sales:		Technical Writing:	Y	Software Dev.:	Y	Law:	Y	Engineers, Other:	Y
Int'l Business:	Y	Commercial/Industrial:	Y	Graphic Arts/Photog.:		Hardware Dev.:		HR/Other:	Y	Health/Lab	
MBA Graduates:	Y	Sales Trainees:	Y	Music:		Consulting/Other:	Y	Training:	Y	Scientists/Research:	
		Advertising Pros.:		Broadcasting:				Health Care:		Petroleum/Chemicals:	
				Other:				Consulting:	Y	Math/Other:	Y

TYPES OF BUSINESS:

Radio-Frequency Engineering & Consulting
Network Design
Deployment Services
Network Operations Maintenance
Training Services
Telecommunications Consulting

BRANDS/DIVISIONS/AFFILIATES:

Wireless Institute
TotalView

CONTACTS:

Note: Officers with more than one job title may be intentionally listed here more than once.

Kenneth Young, CEO
Kenneth Young, Pres.
Rebecca (Becky) Stahl, Interim CFO
Brian J. Dunn, General Counsel/VP
Nancy O. Feeney, VP-Corp. Oper.
Antonio Harnecker, Sr. VP-Latin America Region
Ananth Veluppillai, Sr. VP-Americas Region
Stan Schreuder, Sr. VP-Europe & Middle Eeast

Phone: 703-873-2000 **Fax:** 703-873-2100

Toll-Free:

Address: 4800 Westfields Blvd., Ste. 200, Chantilly, VA 20151 US

GROWTH PLANS/SPECIAL FEATURES:

LCC International, Inc. is an independent provider of RF (radio-frequency) engineering and consulting services to the wireless telecommunications industry. LCC has serviced hundreds of cellular, paging and other two-way mobile systems worldwide. The firm helps wireless operators meet their network deployment objectives and improve financial performance by using LCC's resources and capital. The company's services are broken down into four groups. LCC's technology and business consulting group solves engineering, deployment, operational and business challenges that have not been addressed before; the design and optimization group develops networks in locations spanning the globe; the deployment and turnkey group utilizes interdisciplinary teams to deploy its networks; and the operations and maintenance group provides 24-hours-a-day, seven-days-a-week management and maintenance of its outsourced wireless network operations. The company's service offerings also include the TotalView platform, which offers tools-based solutions to increase the performance and value of network and wireless operators, mobile virtual network operators and content providers. LCC operates its own Wireless Institute (WI-LCC), which provides multilingual premier wireless industry training to engineers and other professionals.

LCC offers employees medical, dental and vision insurance; short- and long-term disability; life and AD&D insurance; an employee assistance program; flexible spending accounts; a 401(k); legal services; an adoption assistance program; a 529 college savings plan; credit union membership; tuition assistance; career development programs; and auto and home insurance.

FINANCIALS:

Sales and profits are in thousands of dollars—add 000 to get the full amount. 2011 Note: Financial information for 2011 was not available for all companies at press time.

2011 Sales: $	2011 Profits: $
2010 Sales: $	2010 Profits: $
2009 Sales: $	2009 Profits: $
2008 Sales: $	2008 Profits: $
2007 Sales: $	2007 Profits: $

U.S. Stock Ticker: Private
Int'l Ticker:
Int'l Exchange:
Employees: Fiscal Year Ends: 12/31
Parent Company:

SALARIES/BENEFITS:

Pension Plan:	ESOP Stock Plan:	Profit Sharing:	Top Exec. Salary: $	Bonus: $
Savings Plan: Y	Stock Purch. Plan:		Second Exec. Salary: $	Bonus: $

OTHER THOUGHTS:

Apparent Women Officers or Directors: 2
Hot Spot for Advancement for Women/Minorities:

LOCATIONS: ("Y" = Yes)

West:	Southwest:	Midwest:	Southeast:	Northeast:	International:
Y	Y	Y	Y	Y	Y

LESLIE'S POOLMART INC

www.lesliespool.com

Industry Group Code: 45399

Management:		Sales/Marketing:		Liberal Arts:		Information Systems:		Professionals:		Technical/Scientific:	
Mgmt. Trainees:	Y	Mktg. Professionals:	Y	Gen. Writing/Editing:	Y	Info. Management:	Y	Finance/Acct.:	Y	Engineers, Elec.:	
Experienced Mgmt.:	Y	Retail Sales:	Y	Technical Writing:		Software Dev.:	Y	Law:	Y	Engineers, Other:	
Int'l Business:		Commercial/Industrial:		Graphic Arts/Photog.:	Y	Hardware Dev.:		HR/Other:	Y	Health/Lab	
MBA Graduates:	Y	Sales Trainees:	Y	Music:		Consulting/Other:		Training:	Y	Scientists/Research:	
		Advertising Pros.:	Y	Broadcasting:				Health Care:		Petroleum/Chemicals:	
				Other:				Consulting:		Math/Other:	

TYPES OF BUSINESS:

Swimming Pool Supplies, Retail
Catalog & Online Sales
Installation, Repair & Maintenance Services

BRANDS/DIVISIONS/AFFILIATES:

Leslie's Swimming Pool Supplies
Leslie's Holdings Inc

CONTACTS: *Note: Officers with more than one job title may be intentionally listed here more than once.*

Lawrence H. Hayward, CEO
Michael L. Hatch, COO
Michael L. Hatch, Pres.
Steven L. Ortega, CFO/Exec. VP
Bill Hicks, Sr. VP-Sales
Craig A. Wright, CIO/Sr. VP
Bill Hicks, Sr. VP-Merch.
Kory Klecker, General Counsel/Sr. VP
Christian Shaffer, Sr. VP-Retail Oper.
Brian Agnew, Sr. VP-Commercial & Service
Lawrence H. Hayward, Chmn.
Bradley S. Smith, Sr. VP-Supply Chain

Phone: 602-366-3999 **Fax:** 602-366-3934
Toll-Free: 800-537-5437
Address: 3925 E. Broadway Rd., Ste. 100, Phoenix, AZ 85040 US

GROWTH PLANS/SPECIAL FEATURES:

Leslie's Poolmart, Inc. is a leading national specialty retailer of swimming pool supplies and related products. The firm is a wholly-owned subsidiary of Leslie's Holdings, Inc. The company currently markets its products through over 600 Leslie's Swimming Pool Supplies retail stores in 35 states, a mail-order catalog and an e-commerce site. Leslie's major product categories are pool chemicals; major equipment; cleaning and testing equipment; spas and sauna; pool covers, lighting and liners; above-ground pools in certain stores; and recreational items, including floats, games, lounges, masks, fins and snorkels. Leslie's also manufactures chlorine tablets and repackages a variety of bulk chemicals into various containers suitable for retail sales. Additionally, the firm formulates a variety of specialty liquids, including water clarifiers, tile cleaners, algaecides and stain preventives. Leslie's focuses on customer service, with most stores supported by a service department that offers poolside equipment installation and repair; leak detection and repair; and seasonal opening and closing services. The company's commercial clients, which include apartments, hotels, resorts, water parks and golf courses, are offered free delivery within 25 miles, certified pool operator training, on-site inspections and chemical automation programs. The company has expanded its line of recreational accessories and now offers a free water analysis service. Leslie's is a sponsor of the NBA's Phoenix Suns, Arizona State University Athletics and the WNBA's Phoenix Mercury.

The company offers its employee's medical, vision, dental and prescription drug coverage; life and disability insurance; a 401(k); paid time off; and an employee assistance program.

FINANCIALS: **Sales and profits are in thousands of dollars—add 000 to get the full amount. 2011 Note: Financial information for 2011 was not available for all companies at press time.**

2011 Sales: $	2011 Profits: $	**U.S. Stock Ticker: Subsidiary**
2010 Sales: $	2010 Profits: $	**Int'l Ticker:**
2009 Sales: $509,642	2009 Profits: $46,234	Int'l Exchange:
2008 Sales: $488,818	2008 Profits: $40,476	Employees: Fiscal Year Ends: 9/30
2007 Sales: $468,882	2007 Profits: $32,226	Parent Company: LESLIE'S HOLDINGS INC

SALARIES/BENEFITS:

Pension Plan:	ESOP Stock Plan:	Profit Sharing:	Top Exec. Salary: $517,000	Bonus: $373,480
Savings Plan: Y	Stock Purch. Plan:		Second Exec. Salary: $330,750	Bonus: $204,800

OTHER THOUGHTS:

Apparent Women Officers or Directors:
Hot Spot for Advancement for Women/Minorities:

LOCATIONS: ("Y" = Yes)

West:	Southwest:	Midwest:	Southeast:	Northeast:	International:
Y	Y	Y	Y	Y	

LIFECELL CORPORATION

www.lifecell.com

Industry Group Code: 325414

Management:		Sales/Marketing:		Liberal Arts:		Information Systems:		Professionals:		Technical/Scientific:	
Mgmt. Trainees:		Mktg. Professionals:	Y	Gen. Writing/Editing:		Info. Management:	Y	Finance/Acct.:	Y	Engineers, Elec.:	
Experienced Mgmt.:	Y	Retail Sales:		Technical Writing:	Y	Software Dev.:	Y	Law:	Y	Engineers, Other:	Y
Int'l Business:	Y	Commercial/Industrial:	Y	Graphic Arts/Photog.:		Hardware Dev.:		HR/Other:	Y	Health/Lab	Y
MBA Graduates:	Y	Sales Trainees:	Y	Music:		Consulting/Other:		Training:	Y	Scientists/Research:	Y
		Advertising Pros.:		Broadcasting:				Health Care:	Y	Petroleum/Chemicals:	
				Other:				Consulting:		Math/Other:	Y

TYPES OF BUSINESS:

Tissue Replacement Products
Skin Replacement Technology
Regenerative Medicine

BRANDS/DIVISIONS/AFFILIATES:

Kinetic Concepts Inc
AlloDerm
Strattice
Cymetra

CONTACTS: *Note: Officers with more than one job title may be intentionally listed here more than once.*

Lisa Colleran, Pres.
Steven T. Sobieski, CFO
Steven T. Sobieski, VP-Admin.
Steven T. Sobieski, VP-Finance

Phone: 908-947-1100	**Fax:**
Toll-Free:	
Address: 1 Millennium Way, Branchburg, NJ 08876 US	

GROWTH PLANS/SPECIAL FEATURES:

LifeCell Corporation, a wholly-owned subsidiary of Kinetic Concepts, Inc. (KCI), specializes in regenerative medicine, developing and manufacturing products geared toward the repair, replacement and preservation of human tissues. The firm's products are used in a variety of reconstructive, orthopedic and urogynecologic surgical procedures. Of the company's products, AlloDerm is the flagship. AlloDerm is a tissue matrix derived from human skin. Originally used as a skin graft for deep second and third degree burns, it is now commonly used as a soft tissue replacement in a variety of procedures, including plastic, reconstructive, general surgical, burn and periodontal. Additional applications include abdominal wall reconstruction, post-mastectomy breast reconstruction, ENT/head and neck plastic reconstruction and grafting. The firm also offers its AlloDerm tissue in an injectable form. Marketed as Cymetra Micronized AlloDerm, this product offers a minimally invasive alternative for soft tissue defect correction. Additionally, LifeCell offers Strattice Reconstructive Tissue Matrix, a sterile reconstructive tissue matrix that supports tissue regeneration. Strattice is used for soft tissue reinforcement in reconstructive and general surgical procedures, including hernia repair and breast reconstruction or plastic surgery. LifeCell also maintains an interest in the researching of new biologics for multiple therapeutic areas, including reconstructive surgery, orthopedics and cardiovascular applications.

Employee benefits include: medical, dental and vision insurance; life/AD&D insurance; short- and long-term disability; paid holidays; tuition reimbursement; 401(k) and stock purchase plans; and alternative summer working hours.

FINANCIALS: **Sales and profits are in thousands of dollars—add 000 to get the full amount. 2011 Note: Financial information for 2011 was not available for all companies at press time.**

2011 Sales: $	2011 Profits: $	**U.S. Stock Ticker: Subsidiary**
2010 Sales: $	2010 Profits: $	**Int'l Ticker:**
2009 Sales: $	2009 Profits: $	Int'l Exchange:
2008 Sales: $	2008 Profits: $	Employees: Fiscal Year Ends: 12/31
2007 Sales: $	2007 Profits: $	Parent Company: KINETIC CONCEPTS INC

SALARIES/BENEFITS:

Pension Plan:	ESOP Stock Plan:	Profit Sharing:	Top Exec. Salary: $	Bonus: $
Savings Plan: Y	Stock Purch. Plan:		Second Exec. Salary: $	Bonus: $

OTHER THOUGHTS:

Apparent Women Officers or Directors: 1
Hot Spot for Advancement for Women/Minorities:

LOCATIONS: ("Y" = Yes)

West:	Southwest:	Midwest:	Southeast:	Northeast:	International:
				Y	

LIFECORE BIOMEDICAL INC

www.lifecore.com

Industry Group Code: 325414

Management:		Sales/Marketing:		Liberal Arts:		Information Systems:		Professionals:		Technical/Scientific:	
Mgmt. Trainees:		Mktg. Professionals:	Y	Gen. Writing/Editing:		Info. Management:	Y	Finance/Acct.:	Y	Engineers, Elec.:	
Experienced Mgmt.:	Y	Retail Sales:		Technical Writing:	Y	Software Dev.:	Y	Law:	Y	Engineers, Other:	Y
Int'l Business:	Y	Commercial/Industrial:	Y	Graphic Arts/Photog.:		Hardware Dev.:	Y	HR/Other:	Y	Health/Lab	Y
MBA Graduates:	Y	Sales Trainees:	Y	Music:		Consulting/Other:		Training:	Y	Scientists/Research:	Y
		Advertising Pros.:		Broadcasting:				Health Care:	Y	Petroleum/Chemicals:	
				Other:				Consulting:		Math/Other:	Y

TYPES OF BUSINESS:

Biomaterials Manufacturing

BRANDS/DIVISIONS/AFFILIATES:

Landec Corporation
Lurocoat Ophthalmic Viscoelastic
Corgel BioHydrogel
Ortholure Orthopedic Viscosupplement

CONTACTS: *Note: Officers with more than one job title may be intentionally listed here more than once.*

Dennis J. Allingham, CEO
Dennis J. Allingham, Pres.
Kipling Thacker, Chief Scientific Officer/VP
James G. Hall, VP-Oper.
Kipling Thacker, VP-New Bus. Dev.
David M. Noel, VP-Finance
Larry D. Hiebert, VP/Gen. Mgr.-Hyaluronan Div.

Phone: 952-368-4300	**Fax:** 952-368-3411
Toll-Free:	
Address: 3515 Lyman Blvd., Chaska, MN 55318 US	

GROWTH PLANS/SPECIAL FEATURES:

Lifecore Biomedical, Inc. develops and manufactures biomaterials and medical devices with applications in various surgical markets. The firm has two divisions, hyaluronan and hyaluronan finished products. The company's hyaluronan division is principally involved in the development and manufacture of products utilizing hyaluronan, a naturally occurring polysaccharide that is widely distributed in the extra-cellular matrix of connective tissues in both animals and humans. This division sells primarily to three medical segments: ophthalmic, orthopedic and veterinary. Lifecore also supplies hyaluronan to customers pursuing other medical applications, such as wound care, aesthetic surgery, medical device coatings, tissue engineering, drug delivery and pharmaceuticals. In the hyaluronan finished products division, the company manufactures Hyaluronan into several finished products for various medical applications. These applications are Lurocoat Ophthalmic Viscoelastic, for use in ophthalmic surgical procedures such as, cataract extraction and intraocular lens implantation; and Ortholure Orthopedic Viscosupplement used for pain relief of degenerative and traumatic changes in synovial joints. In mid 2010, private equity firm Warburg Pincus sold the company to the Landec Corporation for approximately $40 million.

Employees of the firm are offered medical and dental coverage; life insurance; paid time off; short- and long-term disability; an employee assistance program; exercise room; flexible spending accounts and a 401(k) program.

FINANCIALS: **Sales and profits are in thousands of dollars—add 000 to get the full amount. 2011 Note: Financial information for 2011 was not available for all companies at press time.**

2011 Sales: $	2011 Profits: $	**U.S. Stock Ticker: Private**
2010 Sales: $	2010 Profits: $	**Int'l Ticker:**
2009 Sales: $	2009 Profits: $	Int'l Exchange:
2008 Sales: $	2008 Profits: $	Employees: Fiscal Year Ends: 6/30
2007 Sales: $	2007 Profits: $	Parent Company: LANDEC CORPORATION

SALARIES/BENEFITS:

Pension Plan:	ESOP Stock Plan:	Profit Sharing:	Top Exec. Salary: $	Bonus: $
Savings Plan: Y	Stock Purch. Plan: Y		Second Exec. Salary: $	Bonus: $

OTHER THOUGHTS:

Apparent Women Officers or Directors:
Hot Spot for Advancement for Women/Minorities:

LOCATIONS: ("Y" = Yes)

West:	Southwest:	Midwest:	Southeast:	Northeast:	International:
		Y			

LIVEPERSON INC

www.liveperson.com

Industry Group Code: 511210K

Management:		Sales/Marketing:		Liberal Arts:		Information Systems:		Professionals:		Technical/Scientific:	
Mgmt. Trainees:		Mktg. Professionals:	Y	Gen. Writing/Editing:	Y	Info. Management:	Y	Finance/Acct.:	Y	Engineers, Elec.:	Y
Experienced Mgmt.:	Y	Retail Sales:		Technical Writing:	Y	Software Dev.:	Y	Law:	Y	Engineers, Other:	
Int'l Business:	Y	Commercial/Industrial:	Y	Graphic Arts/Photog.:		Hardware Dev.:		HR/Other:	Y	Health/Lab	
MBA Graduates:	Y	Sales Trainees:	Y	Music:		Consulting/Other:		Training:	Y	Scientists/Research:	
		Advertising Pros.:	Y	Broadcasting:				Health Care:		Petroleum/Chemicals:	
				Other:	Y			Consulting:		Math/Other:	

TYPES OF BUSINESS:

E-Commerce Software
Customer Service Software
Sales & Marketing Service Software
Live Chat Applications

BRANDS/DIVISIONS/AFFILIATES:

LivePerson Enterprise for Sales
LivePerson Enterprise for Service
LivePerson Enterprise Platinum
LivePerson Pro
LivePerson Premier
LivePerson Expert Platform

CONTACTS:

Note: Officers with more than one job title may be intentionally listed here more than once.

Robert P. LoCascio, CEO
Daniel Murphy, CFO
Yaron Zeidman, VP-R&D
Yaron Zeidman, CTO
Monica Greenberg, General Counsel
Monica Greenberg, Sr. VP-Bus. Affairs
Michael I. Kovach, Controller/Sr. VP
Robert P. LoCascio, Chmn.
Eli Campo, Exec. VP/Gen. Mgr.-Tech. Oper., Israel

Phone: 212-609-4200	**Fax:**
Toll-Free:	
Address: 462 7th Ave., 3rd Fl., New York, NY 10018 US	

GROWTH PLANS/SPECIAL FEATURES:

LivePerson, Inc. is a facilitator of online e-commerce interaction, enhancing real-time sales, customer support and personalized expert advice through more than 1 billion chat interactions annually. The company offers real-time sales, marketing and customer service to online businesses with the aim of improving customer relationships. LivePerson's integrated multi-channel communication software platform combines a variety of features that help companies manage online customer sales and support. The firm divides its products into two categories: small and midsize business services and enterprise services. Small and midsize business services include LivePerson Pro, which enables small business clients to economically increase online sales; and LivePerson Premier, an all-in-one platform encompassing live chat, e-mail, self-service and telephone logs. Enterprise products include LivePerson Enterprise for Sales, which combines online site traffic monitoring software with a sophisticated rules engine to enable LivePerson clients to proactively engage web site visitors; LivePerson Enterprise for Service, which utilizes a proactive customer care center to reduce attrition rates; and LivePerson Enterprise Platinum, combining the functionality of its sales and service tools. These services are offered to a number of different industries, such as the financial services, retail, telecom, high tech, travel and automotive industries. Currently, LivePerson's client base includes more than 8,500 companies, including Cisco, Hewlett-Packard, IBM, Microsoft, Qwest and Verizon. The firm's professional services team provides consulting to enterprise clients, helping to analyze their needs and implement appropriate strategies. In addition to its business services, LivePerson also hosts an online marketplace platform, LivePerson Expert Platform, that allows experts and individual service providers to sell their information and knowledge via real-time chat with consumers. Users of LivePerson Expert Platform can seek advice in various categories including personal counseling; computers and programming; health and medicine; education; shopping; professional development; spirituality; legal services; and other topics.

FINANCIALS:

Sales and profits are in thousands of dollars—add 000 to get the full amount. 2011 Note: Financial information for 2011 was not available for all companies at press time.

2011 Sales: $	2011 Profits: $	**U.S. Stock Ticker: LPSN**
2010 Sales: $109,862	2010 Profits: $9,259	**Int'l Ticker:**
2009 Sales: $87,490	2009 Profits: $7,763	Int'l Exchange:
2008 Sales: $74,655	2008 Profits: $-23,837	Employees: 481 Fiscal Year Ends: 12/31
2007 Sales: $52,228	2007 Profits: $5,821	Parent Company:

SALARIES/BENEFITS:

Pension Plan:	ESOP Stock Plan:	Profit Sharing:	Top Exec. Salary: $325,000	Bonus: $161,000
Savings Plan: Y	Stock Purch. Plan: Y		Second Exec. Salary: $325,000	Bonus: $161,000

OTHER THOUGHTS:

Apparent Women Officers or Directors: 1
Hot Spot for Advancement for Women/Minorities:

LOCATIONS: ("Y" = Yes)

West:	Southwest:	Midwest:	Southeast:	Northeast:	International:
Y			Y	Y	Y

LOGISTICARE INC

www.logisticare.com

Industry Group Code: 541614

Management:		Sales/Marketing:		Liberal Arts:		Information Systems:		Professionals:		Technical/Scientific:	
Mgmt. Trainees:		Mktg. Professionals:	Y	Gen. Writing/Editing:		Info. Management:	Y	Finance/Acct.:	Y	Engineers, Elec.:	
Experienced Mgmt.:	Y	Retail Sales:		Technical Writing:	Y	Software Dev.:	Y	Law:	Y	Engineers, Other:	
Int'l Business:		Commercial/Industrial:	Y	Graphic Arts/Photog.:		Hardware Dev.:		HR/Other:	Y	Health/Lab	
MBA Graduates:	Y	Sales Trainees:	Y	Music:		Consulting/Other:	Y	Training:	Y	Scientists/Research:	
		Advertising Pros.:		Broadcasting:				Health Care:		Petroleum/Chemicals:	
				Other:				Consulting:	Y	Math/Other:	

TYPES OF BUSINESS:

Medical Transportation Management Services
Outsourced Logistics Services

BRANDS/DIVISIONS/AFFILIATES:

LogistiCAD
EMTrack
Providence Service Corporation

CONTACTS: *Note: Officers with more than one job title may be intentionally listed here more than once.*

Herman M. Schwarz, CEO
Rob Cornell, CIO
Albert Cortina, Chief Admin. Officer
Chinta Gaston, General Counsel
Gregg Bryars, Sr. VP-Oper.
Ken Piehl, Exec. VP-Bus. Dev.
Windy Brooks, Controller/VP
Sandy Reifel, VP-Managed Care Accounts

Phone: 770-907-7596 **Fax:** 770-907-7598
Toll-Free: 800-486-7647
Address: 1275 Peachtree St., NE 6th Fl., Atlanta, GA 30349 US

GROWTH PLANS/SPECIAL FEATURES:

LogistiCare, Inc., a subsidiary of Providence Service Corporation, is an outsourced scheduler of non-emergency patient transport services for insurance companies, managed care organizations and government health agencies. Instead of owning its own vehicles, the firm manages call centers, patient eligibility screening, scheduling, dispatch, billing and quality assurance. It also manages local transportation provider networks of local, commercial, non-profit and public transportation companies. LogistiCare recruits and accredits local firms for its network of providers. In sum, the company has contracts with 1,300 transportation providers and roughly 9,000 vehicles, coordinating about 18 million trips per year. LogistiCare operates 18 call centers, which handle a call volume of approximately 4.1 million per year. All calls are recorded digitally and archived in the system database. The firm developed its integrated software system, known as LogistiCAD, in order to automatically coordinate all of its data and to and generate scheduling, routing, quality assurance reporting, transportation cost estimates and billing verification. It processes transportation requests and dispatches drivers through its network of carriers using its proprietary EMTrack system, which tracks all of the company's vehicles. LogistiCare is able to use its LogistiCAD system in conjunction with sophisticated GPS navigation to gain improved transportation access and service delivery in rural and remote areas. Additionally, the firm provides finance and consulting services, including billing management, customer reimbursement, medical services billing, fraud detection and risk management. The company's government clients include state Medicaid agencies, school boards and Americans with Disabilities Act (ADA) paratransit authorities. Healthcare sector clients include hospital systems and many of the nations largest managed care organizations.

FINANCIALS: **Sales and profits are in thousands of dollars—add 000 to get the full amount. 2011 Note: Financial information for 2011 was not available for all companies at press time.**

2011 Sales: $ 2011 Profits: $
2010 Sales: $ 2010 Profits: $
2009 Sales: $ 2009 Profits: $
2008 Sales: $ 2008 Profits: $
2007 Sales: $ 2007 Profits: $

U.S. Stock Ticker: Subsidiary
Int'l Ticker:
Int'l Exchange:
Employees: Fiscal Year Ends: 12/31
Parent Company: PROVIDENCE SERVICE CORPORATION

SALARIES/BENEFITS:

Pension Plan: ESOP Stock Plan: Profit Sharing: Top Exec. Salary: $ Bonus: $
Savings Plan: Stock Purch. Plan: Y Second Exec. Salary: $ Bonus: $

OTHER THOUGHTS:

Apparent Women Officers or Directors: 2
Hot Spot for Advancement for Women/Minorities: Y

LOCATIONS: ("Y" = Yes)

West:	Southwest:	Midwest:	Southeast:	Northeast:	International:
Y	Y	Y	Y	Y	

LOJACK CORPORATION

www.lojack.com

Industry Group Code: 334290

Management:		Sales/Marketing:		Liberal Arts:		Information Systems:		Professionals:		Technical/Scientific:	
Mgmt. Trainees:		Mktg. Professionals:	Y	Gen. Writing/Editing:	Y	Info. Management:	Y	Finance/Acct.:	Y	Engineers, Elec.:	Y
Experienced Mgmt.:	Y	Retail Sales:		Technical Writing:	Y	Software Dev.:	Y	Law:	Y	Engineers, Other:	Y
Int'l Business:	Y	Commercial/Industrial:	Y	Graphic Arts/Photog.:		Hardware Dev.:	Y	HR/Other:	Y	Health/Lab	
MBA Graduates:	Y	Sales Trainees:	Y	Music:		Consulting/Other:		Training:	Y	Scientists/Research:	
		Advertising Pros.:	Y	Broadcasting:				Health Care:		Petroleum/Chemicals:	
				Other:				Consulting:		Math/Other:	

TYPES OF BUSINESS:

Electronic Equipment-Stolen Vehicle Recovery
Asset Monitoring & Recovery

BRANDS/DIVISIONS/AFFILIATES:

LoJack Stolen Vehicle Recovery System
LoJack Early Warning Recovery System
Boomerang Tracking
LoJack for Laptops
LoJack SafetyNet
SC-Integrity

CONTACTS: *Note: Officers with more than one job title may be intentionally listed here more than once.*

Richard T. Riley, CEO
Richard T. Riley, Pres.
John Barrett, Interim CFO
Kathleen Lundy, General Counsel/Exec. VP
Casey Delaney, Chief Acct. Officer/VP/Controller
Paul Weichselbaum, Exec. VP
Kevin M. Mullins, Gen. Mgr.-U.S. Automotive/Sr. VP
Steven Schlerf, Sr. VP-Order Fulfillment
Richard T. Riley, Chmn.
Thomas M. Camp, Gen. Mgr.-Int'l/Sr. VP

Phone: 781-251-4700	**Fax:**
Toll-Free: 800-445-6522	
Address: 200 Lowder Brook Dr., Ste. 1000, Westwood, MA 02090 US	

GROWTH PLANS/SPECIAL FEATURES:

LoJack Corporation creates and markets technology products and services for the tracking and recovery of valuable mobile assets. The company operates in three segments: The North America segment, accounting for 66% of revenues in 2010, involves U.S. domestic operations and Boomerang in Canada; the International segment, 32% of revenue, involves the sale of licenses and branded products; and the All Other segment, 2%, involves LoJack SafetyNet and SC-Integrity. The LoJack System, based on radio frequency (RF) technology, is comprised of a Registration System, maintained and operated by LoJack; a Sector Activation System and Vehicle Tracking Units, both operated by law enforcement officials; and a LoJack Unit, a VHF transponder. If a car equipped with a LoJack unit is stolen, its owner reports the theft and a radio signal is transmitted automatically to the unit in the stolen vehicle, activating its tracking signal. The Boomerang System is based on RF and cellular technology and uses internally developed tracking devices and a wireless telecommunications network for locating and tracking stolen assets. The coverage area for Boomerang's tracking includes most of North America; however, it primarily operates in Canada. LoJack SafetyNet is designed to monitor the location and aid in the discovery and rescue of people who could potentially wander off, such as individuals with Alzheimer's. LoJack Supply Chain Integrity (SCI), through its InTransit system, covertly monitors shipped cargo and aid in recovery if it is stolen. LoJack operates in 28 U.S. states and Washington, D.C. and in 32 countries internationally. LoJack licenses its name to Absolute Software, which markets LoJack for Laptops, a computer theft recovery product.

Employees are offered medical and dental insurance; life insurance; short- and long-term disability coverage; a 401(k) plan; flexible spending accounts; a college fund plan; discounted home and auto insurance; discounts on company products; adoption assistance; and tuition reimbursement.

FINANCIALS: **Sales and profits are in thousands of dollars—add 000 to get the full amount. 2011 Note: Financial information for 2011 was not available for all companies at press time.**

2011 Sales: $	2011 Profits: $	**U.S. Stock Ticker: LOJN**
2010 Sales: $146,600	2010 Profits: $-18,600	**Int'l Ticker:**
2009 Sales: $135,013	2009 Profits: $-35,282	Int'l Exchange:
2008 Sales: $198,679	2008 Profits: $-32,530	Employees: 624 Fiscal Year Ends: 12/31
2007 Sales: $222,749	2007 Profits: $21,405	Parent Company:

SALARIES/BENEFITS:

Pension Plan:	ESOP Stock Plan:	Profit Sharing:	Top Exec. Salary: $555,274	Bonus: $79,293
Savings Plan: Y	Stock Purch. Plan:		Second Exec. Salary: $311,193	Bonus: $141,697

OTHER THOUGHTS:

Apparent Women Officers or Directors: 3
Hot Spot for Advancement for Women/Minorities: Y

LOCATIONS: ("Y" = Yes)

West:	Southwest:	Midwest:	Southeast:	Northeast:	International:
Y	Y	Y	Y	Y	Y

LUCASFILM LTD

www.lucasfilm.com

Industry Group Code: 512110

Management:		Sales/Marketing:		Liberal Arts:		Information Systems:		Professionals:		Technical/Scientific:	
Mgmt. Trainees:		Mktg. Professionals:	Y	Gen. Writing/Editing:	Y	Info. Management:	Y	Finance/Acct.:	Y	Engineers, Elec.:	
Experienced Mgmt.:	Y	Retail Sales:		Technical Writing:	Y	Software Dev.:	Y	Law:	Y	Engineers, Other:	
Int'l Business:	Y	Commercial/Industrial:	Y	Graphic Arts/Photog.:	Y	Hardware Dev.:		HR/Other:	Y	Health/Lab	
MBA Graduates:	Y	Sales Trainees:	Y	Music:	Y	Consulting/Other:		Training:	Y	Scientists/Research:	
		Advertising Pros.:	Y	Broadcasting:				Health Care:		Petroleum/Chemicals:	
				Other:	Y			Consulting:		Math/Other:	

TYPES OF BUSINESS:

Film Production
Special Effects
Sound Effects
Digital Animation
Software & Video Games
Online Publishing
Merchandising

BRANDS/DIVISIONS/AFFILIATES:

Industrial Light & Magic
Skywalker Sound
Lucas Digital
LucasArts
Lucas Online
Indiana Jones
Star Wars
Lucasfilm Animation Singapore

CONTACTS: *Note: Officers with more than one job title may be intentionally listed here more than once.*

Micheline Chau, COO
Micheline Chau, Pres.
Richard Kerris, CTO
Jan van der Voort, Chief Admin. Officer
Steve Condiotti, VP-Finance/Chief Acct. Officer
Lynwen Brennan, Pres., Industrial Light & Magic
Phil Benson, Head-Skywalker Sound
Howard Roffman, Pres., Lucas Licensing
George Lucas, Chmn.

Phone: 415-662-1800 **Fax:**
Toll-Free:
Address: 1110 Gorgas Ave., San Francisco, CA 94129 US

GROWTH PLANS/SPECIAL FEATURES:

Lucasfilm Ltd., created by filmmaker George Lucas in 1971, is one of the most successful independent film production companies. The firm has produced some of the most popular films in history, including the original Star Wars franchise and the Indiana Jones films. The company operates through seven divisions. Lucasfilm is responsible for production, promotion and strategic management of theatrical, television and entertainment properties. Industrial Light & Magic (ILM) creates digital and visual special effects for the entertainment industry and has received 15 Academy Award nominations and 19 Scientific and Technical Achievement Awards. Skywalker Sound produces post-production digital sound effects, for which it has won 18 Academy Awards. LucasArts is a software company that develops video games based on Lucas's movies. The firm's licensing division is responsible for licensing and merchandising Lucasfilm properties. Animation and Lucasfilm Animation Singapore are the firm's digital animation studios. Finally, Lucasfilm's online division produces entertainment, education, reference and e-commerce sites for Lucasfilm properties. The company is headquartered at the Letterman Digital Arts Center in San Francisco, California and maintains two other offices in Marin County, California and one in Singapore. The Letterman Digital Arts Center brings the entire organization together and enables units producing games and films to collaborate more closely and share technologies.

The firm's Letterman Digital Arts Center campus contains a 300-seat theater, a childcare center, a fitness center and an ultra-fast 1-gigabyte network hookup at every desktop.

FINANCIALS: **Sales and profits are in thousands of dollars—add 000 to get the full amount. 2011 Note: Financial information for 2011 was not available for all companies at press time.**

2011 Sales: $	2011 Profits: $	**U.S. Stock Ticker: Private**
2010 Sales: $	2010 Profits: $	**Int'l Ticker:**
2009 Sales: $	2009 Profits: $	Int'l Exchange:
2008 Sales: $	2008 Profits: $	Employees: Fiscal Year Ends: 3/31
2007 Sales: $	2007 Profits: $	Parent Company:

SALARIES/BENEFITS:

Pension Plan:	ESOP Stock Plan:	Profit Sharing:	Top Exec. Salary: $	Bonus: $
Savings Plan: Y	Stock Purch. Plan:		Second Exec. Salary: $	Bonus: $

OTHER THOUGHTS:

Apparent Women Officers or Directors: 2
Hot Spot for Advancement for Women/Minorities:

LOCATIONS: ("Y" = Yes)

West:	Southwest:	Midwest:	Southeast:	Northeast:	International:
Y					Y

LUCOR INC

Industry Group Code: 811191

www.jiffylube.com

Management:		Sales/Marketing:		Liberal Arts:		Information Systems:		Professionals:		Technical/Scientific:	
Mgmt. Trainees:	Y	Mktg. Professionals:	Y	Gen. Writing/Editing:	Y	Info. Management:	Y	Finance/Acct.:	Y	Engineers, Elec.:	
Experienced Mgmt.:	Y	Retail Sales:		Technical Writing:	Y	Software Dev.:		Law:	Y	Engineers, Other:	
Int'l Business:		Commercial/Industrial:		Graphic Arts/Photog.:		Hardware Dev.:		HR/Other:	Y	Health/Lab	
MBA Graduates:	Y	Sales Trainees:		Music:		Consulting/Other:		Training:	Y	Scientists/Research:	
		Advertising Pros.:	Y	Broadcasting:				Health Care:		Petroleum/Chemicals:	
				Other:				Consulting:		Math/Other:	

TYPES OF BUSINESS:

Automotive Oil Change & Lubrication Shops

BRANDS/DIVISIONS/AFFILIATES:

Jiffy Lube International

CONTACTS:

Note: Officers with more than one job title may be intentionally listed here more than once.

Stephen P. Conway, CEO
Jerry B. Conway, COO
Jerry B. Conway, Pres.
Kendall A. Carr, CFO
Kendall A. Carr, VP-Finance
Stephen P. Conway, Chmn.

Phone: 919-828-9511	**Fax:** 919-828-4847
Toll-Free:	
Address: 790 Pershing Rd., Raleigh, NC 27608 US	

GROWTH PLANS/SPECIAL FEATURES:

Lucor, Inc. is one of largest franchisers of Jiffy Lube International in the U.S. Jiffy Lube is known for its fast oil changes, which it provides across North America with more than 2,000 locations. Jiffy Lube is one of the largest systems of franchised service centers in the fast lube industry. Lucor operates a chain of about 175 of these automotive service shops, with locations in North Carolina, Tennessee, Virginia, Pennsylvania, Kentucky, Ohio, Michigan and Georgia. Lucor's service centers offer basic maintenance services including oil and oil filter changes, chassis lubrication, battery checks, air filter replacement, tire inflation, vacuuming and window washing, as well as preventative maintenance services such as emissions inspections. The shops also check lights and wiper blades and replenish fluids, among other services. The private company is partially owned by Stephen and Jerry Conway, brothers who co-founded the company in 1986.

FINANCIALS:

Sales and profits are in thousands of dollars—add 000 to get the full amount. 2011 Note: Financial information for 2011 was not available for all companies at press time.

2011 Sales: $	2011 Profits: $	**U.S. Stock Ticker: Private**
2010 Sales: $2,027,000	2010 Profits: $	**Int'l Ticker:**
2009 Sales: $	2009 Profits: $	Int'l Exchange:
2008 Sales: $	2008 Profits: $	Employees: 2,011 Fiscal Year Ends: 12/31
2007 Sales: $	2007 Profits: $	Parent Company:

SALARIES/BENEFITS:

Pension Plan:	ESOP Stock Plan:	Profit Sharing:	Top Exec. Salary: $	Bonus: $
Savings Plan:	Stock Purch. Plan:		Second Exec. Salary: $	Bonus: $

OTHER THOUGHTS:

Apparent Women Officers or Directors:
Hot Spot for Advancement for Women/Minorities:

LOCATIONS: ("Y" = Yes)

West:	Southwest:	Midwest:	Southeast:	Northeast:	International:
				Y	

LUMINEX CORPORATION

www.luminexcorp.com

Industry Group Code: 334510

Management:		**Sales/Marketing:**		**Liberal Arts:**		**Information Systems:**		**Professionals:**		**Technical/Scientific:**	
Mgmt. Trainees:	Y	Mktg. Professionals:	Y	Gen. Writing/Editing:		Info. Management:	Y	Finance/Acct.:	Y	Engineers, Elec.:	Y
Experienced Mgmt.:	Y	Retail Sales:		Technical Writing:	Y	Software Dev.:	Y	Law:	Y	Engineers, Other:	Y
Int'l Business:	Y	Commercial/Industrial:	Y	Graphic Arts/Photog.:		Hardware Dev.:	Y	HR/Other:	Y	Health/Lab	Y
MBA Graduates:	Y	Sales Trainees:	Y	Music:		Consulting/Other:		Training:	Y	Scientists/Research:	Y
		Advertising Pros.:		Broadcasting:				Health Care:	Y	Petroleum/Chemicals:	
				Other:				Consulting:		Math/Other:	Y

TYPES OF BUSINESS:

Medical Diagnostics
Bioassays
Software
xMAP Testing

BRANDS/DIVISIONS/AFFILIATES:

xMAP
Luminex 100 System
Luminex 200 System
FLEXMAP 3D
xPONENT
MagPlex Magnetic Microspheres
Luminex Molecular Diagnostics
EraGen Biosciences Inc

CONTACTS: *Note: Officers with more than one job title may be intentionally listed here more than once.*

Patrick J. Balthrop, Sr., CEO
Patrick J. Balthrop, Sr., Pres.
Harriss T. Currie, CFO
Timothy R. Dehne, VP-Systems R&D
Steven Back, VP-Mfg. & Quality Surveillance
David S. Reiter, General Counsel/VP/Corp. Sec.
Michael F. Pintek, Sr. VP-Oper.
Russell W. Bradley, VP-Bus. Dev. & Strategic Planning
Harriss T. Currie, VP-Finance/Treas.
Nancy Krunic, VP-Luminex Molecular Diagnostics
Gregory J. Gosch, VP-Immunodiagnostics
Jeremy Bridge-Cook, Sr. VP-Assay Group
Amy L. Altman, VP-Biodefense
G. Walter Loewenbaum, Chmn.

Phone: 512-219-8020	**Fax:** 512-219-5195
Toll-Free: 888-219-8020	
Address: 12212 Technology Blvd., Austin, TX 78727 US	

GROWTH PLANS/SPECIAL FEATURES:

Luminex Corporation develops, manufactures and markets biological testing technologies for the life science and diagnostic industries. The company operates in two segments: technology and assays. Through the technology segment, the firm has established 64 strategic partnerships to develop diagnostics tests based on its xMap technology. The xMAP system makes use of microspheres (microscopic polystyrene beads), lasers, digital signal processing and proprietary software in order to run various diagnostic tests. It can perform up to 500 bioassays on a single drop of fluid. Luminex licenses this technology to its partners, who then develop reagent-based products utilizing the xMAP technology. Luminex also manufactures and sells xMAP instrumentation and microspheres to its partners. These include the Luminex 100 and 200 systems, which are compact analyzers that integrate fluidics, optics and digital signal processing to perform up to 100 bioassays simultaneously; and the FLEXMAP 3D, a general use laboratory instrument capable of measuring 500 analytes from a one sample simultaneously. The assays segment consists of Luminex Bioscience Group (LLBG) and Luminex Molecular Diagnostics (LMD). This segment is primarily involved in the development and sale of assays utilizing the firm's proprietary xMAP technology. Additional products include xPONENT software and MagPlex magnetic microspheres, which enhance ease-of-use and automation capabilities in the xMAP technologies. The firm's xTAG Respiratory Viral Panel, developed by LMD, is an assay cleared by the FDA to simultaneously detect and identify 12 viruses and viral subtypes that together are responsible for more than 85% of respiratory infections. xMAP technology is used within various segments of the life sciences industry, including drug discovery and development; clinical diagostics; genetic analysis; bio-defense; protein analysis; and biomedical research. In June 2011, Luminex acquired molecular diagnostic testing technology firm EraGen Biosciences, Inc.

The firm offers its employees a 401(k); and health, dental and life insurance.

FINANCIALS: **Sales and profits are in thousands of dollars—add 000 to get the full amount. 2011 Note: Financial information for 2011 was not available for all companies at press time.**

2011 Sales: $	2011 Profits: $	**U.S. Stock Ticker: LMNX**
2010 Sales: $141,557	2010 Profits: $5,231	**Int'l Ticker:**
2009 Sales: $120,643	2009 Profits: $17,729	Int'l Exchange:
2008 Sales: $104,447	2008 Profits: $3,057	Employees: 525 Fiscal Year Ends: 12/31
2007 Sales: $75,010	2007 Profits: $-2,711	Parent Company:

SALARIES/BENEFITS:

Pension Plan:	ESOP Stock Plan:	Profit Sharing:	Top Exec. Salary: $506,138	Bonus: $440,340
Savings Plan: Y	Stock Purch. Plan:		Second Exec. Salary: $345,861	Bonus: $148,720

OTHER THOUGHTS:

Apparent Women Officers or Directors: 2
Hot Spot for Advancement for Women/Minorities:

LOCATIONS: ("Y" = Yes)

West:	Southwest:	Midwest:	Southeast:	Northeast:	International:
	Y				Y

MAGELLAN MIDSTREAM PARTNERS LP

www.magellanlp.com

Industry Group Code: 486

Management:		Sales/Marketing:		Liberal Arts:		Information Systems:		Professionals:		Technical/Scientific:	
Mgmt. Trainees:		Mktg. Professionals:	Y	Gen. Writing/Editing:		Info. Management:	Y	Finance/Acct.:	Y	Engineers, Elec.:	Y
Experienced Mgmt.:	Y	Retail Sales:		Technical Writing:		Software Dev.:		Law:	Y	Engineers, Other:	Y
Int'l Business:		Commercial/Industrial:	Y	Graphic Arts/Photog.:		Hardware Dev.:		HR/Other:	Y	Health/Lab	
MBA Graduates:	Y	Sales Trainees:	Y	Music:		Consulting/Other:		Training:	Y	Scientists/Research:	
		Advertising Pros.:		Broadcasting:				Health Care:		Petroleum/Chemicals:	Y
				Other:				Consulting:		Math/Other:	

TYPES OF BUSINESS:

Pipelines-Petroleum Storage & Distribution Services
Petroleum Pipelines
Petroleum Products Terminal Facilities
Ammonia Pipelines

BRANDS/DIVISIONS/AFFILIATES:

CONTACTS:

Note: Officers with more than one job title may be intentionally listed here more than once.

Michael N. Mears, CEO
Michael N. Mears, Pres.
John D. Chandler, CFO/Sr. VP
Lisa J. Korner, Sr. VP-Human Resources
Larry J. Davied, Sr. VP-Tech. Svcs.
Lisa J. Korner, Sr. VP-Admin.
Lonny E. Townsend, General Counsel/Compliance & Ethics Officer/Sr. VP
Larry J. Davied, Sr. VP-Oper.
Brett C. Riley, Sr. VP-Bus. Dev.
Jeff R. Selvidge, Sr. VP-Trans. and Terminals
Michael N. Mears, Chmn.

Phone: 918-574-7000	**Fax:**
Toll-Free: 800-574-6671	
Address: 1 Williams Ctr., Tulsa, OK 74172 US	

GROWTH PLANS/SPECIAL FEATURES:

Magellan Midstream Partners, L.P. transports, stores and distributes refined petroleum products and crude oil, and holds interests in both pipeline and terminal facilities. Magellan owns and operates a petroleum products pipeline system of 9,600 miles over a 13-state area and 85 petroleum terminals, with 70 million barrels of storage. The pipeline system transports primarily transportation fuels (i.e. gasoline, aviation fuels/LPG and crude oil), which produced 85% of 2010's profits. Magellan operates six marine storage terminal facilities and 27 inland terminals. The company's ammonia pipeline system provides ammonia, used as an agricultural fertilizer, for distribution to end-users throughout the Midwest. With six associated terminals, the system extends 1,100 miles from production facilities located in Texas and Oklahoma to the end point facilities. Magellan customers include petroleum retailers, wholesalers, exchange transaction customers and traders. In February 2011, Magellan acquired the remaining interest in a joint venture project to construct 4.25 million barrels of crude oil storage in Cushing, Oklahoma. As of March 2011, the company, along with M3 Midstream LLC, will begin to construct a 180 mile pipeline to extend from LaSalle and Live Oak County, Texas to Corpus Christi, Texas, carrying crude oil from the Eagle Ford Shale formation to Magellan's current terminal. The pipeline will have the potential to supply 180,000 barrels of crude oil per day to gulf coast markets. In November 2011, Magellan started a project to build a six mile pipeline between the Genoa and Speed Junction interchanges to connect to the Houston Ship Channel pipeline, furthering its ability to supply to Houston area refineries.

Employee benefits include: life, AD&D, medical and dental insurance, paid time off, flexible spending accounts, retirement benefits, and an education assistance program.

FINANCIALS:

Sales and profits are in thousands of dollars—add 000 to get the full amount. 2011 Note: Financial information for 2011 was not available for all companies at press time.

2011 Sales: $1,748,700	2011 Profits: $413,600
2010 Sales: $1,557,447	2010 Profits: $311,580
2009 Sales: $1,014,171	2009 Profits: $226,205
2008 Sales: $1,212,786	2008 Profits: $346,613
2007 Sales: $1,318,121	2007 Profits: $242,790

U.S. Stock Ticker: MMP
Int'l Ticker:
Int'l Exchange:
Employees: 1,271 Fiscal Year Ends: 12/31
Parent Company:

SALARIES/BENEFITS:

Pension Plan:	ESOP Stock Plan:	Profit Sharing:	Top Exec. Salary: $476,331	Bonus: $14,700
Savings Plan: Y	Stock Purch. Plan:		Second Exec. Salary: $349,315	Bonus: $14,700

OTHER THOUGHTS:

Apparent Women Officers or Directors: 3
Hot Spot for Advancement for Women/Minorities: Y

LOCATIONS: ("Y" = Yes)

West:	Southwest:	Midwest:	Southeast:	Northeast:	International:
Y	Y	Y	Y	Y	

MAKO SURGICAL CORP

www.makosurgical.com

Industry Group Code: 33911

Management:		**Sales/Marketing:**		**Liberal Arts:**		**Information Systems:**		**Professionals:**		**Technical/Scientific:**	
Mgmt. Trainees:		Mktg. Professionals:		Gen. Writing/Editing:		Info. Management:	Y	Finance/Acct.:	Y	Engineers, Elec.:	
Experienced Mgmt.:	Y	Retail Sales:		Technical Writing:	Y	Software Dev.:		Law:	Y	Engineers, Other:	
Int'l Business:		Commercial/Industrial:	Y	Graphic Arts/Photog.:		Hardware Dev.:		HR/Other:	Y	Health/Lab	Y
MBA Graduates:	Y	Sales Trainees:		Music:		Consulting/Other:		Training:	Y	Scientists/Research:	Y
		Advertising Pros.:		Broadcasting:				Health Care:	Y	Petroleum/Chemicals:	
				Other:				Consulting:		Math/Other:	

TYPES OF BUSINESS:

Surgical Equipment-Robotics
Implants

BRANDS/DIVISIONS/AFFILIATES:

MAKO Tactile Guidance System
MAKOplasty
RESTORIS
Z-KAT Inc
RIO (Robotic Arm Interactive Orthopedic)
RESTORIS MCK

CONTACTS: *Note: Officers with more than one job title may be intentionally listed here more than once.*

Maurice R. Ferre, CEO
Maurice R. Ferre, Pres.
Fritz L. LaPorte, CFO
Steven J. Nunes, Sr. VP-Sales & Mktg.
Samantha C. Brodsky, Dir.-Human Resources
Richard Leparmentier, Sr. VP-Eng.
Fritz L. LaPorte, Sr. VP-Admin.
Menashe R. Frank, General Counsel/Sr. VP/Sec.
Duncan H. Moffat, Sr. VP-Oper.
Ivan Delevic, Sr. VP-Strategic Mktg. & Bus. Dev.
Fritz L. LaPorte, Sr. VP-Finance/Treas.
Rony A. Abovitz, Chief Visionary Officer
James E. Keller, Sr. VP-Regulatory Affairs & Quality Assurance
Maurice R. Ferre, Chmn.

Phone: 954-927-2044	**Fax:** 954-927-0446
Toll-Free:	
Address: 2555 Davie Rd., Ft. Lauderdale, FL 33317 US	

GROWTH PLANS/SPECIAL FEATURES:

MAKO Surgical Corp. is a medical device company that develops and markets its MAKO brand advanced robotic arm solution and RESTORIS brand implants for minimally invasive orthopedic knee procedures. The second generation MAKO Tactile Guidance System (TGS), RIO (Robotic Arm Interactive Orthopedic), includes a surgeon-interactive tactile robotic arm platform that utilizes a robotic arm and patient-specific visualization to prepare the knee joint for the insertion and alignment of resurfacing implants through a minimal incision. This Food and Drug Administration (FDA)-cleared platform allows surgeons to provide a tissue-sparing, bone resurfacing procedure called MAKOplasty to a large, yet underserved population suffering from early to mid-stage osteoarthritic knee disease. The firm has FDA approval for two types of RESTORIS knee implants in both inlay and onlay versions; a multi-compartmental knee implant system, RESTORIS MCK, and RESTORIS uni-compartmental implants. MAKO contractually requires purchasers of its RIO systems to use only its manufactured implants in procedures using RIO. The company has installed 67 TGS units for commercial use. Approximately 5,869 MAKOplasty procedures have been performed by these units. Most of the components of the TGS platform are manufactured by third-parties and are then assembled at the firm's Fort Lauderdale plant. MAKO has an intellectual property portfolio of over 300 licensed or owned patent applications and patents relating to the areas of computer assisted surgery, haptics, robotics and implants. The company was originally formed as a spin-off by Z-KAT, Inc., a computer-assisted surgery applications firm, and many of its current patents and patent applications are licensed from Z-KAT.

FINANCIALS: **Sales and profits are in thousands of dollars—add 000 to get the full amount. 2011 Note: Financial information for 2011 was not available for all companies at press time.**

2011 Sales: $	2011 Profits: $	**U.S. Stock Ticker: MAKO**
2010 Sales: $44,296	2010 Profits: $-38,687	**Int'l Ticker:**
2009 Sales: $34,208	2009 Profits: $-34,023	Int'l Exchange:
2008 Sales: $2,944	2008 Profits: $-37,082	Employees: 315 Fiscal Year Ends: 12/31
2007 Sales: $ 771	2007 Profits: $-20,658	Parent Company:

SALARIES/BENEFITS:

Pension Plan:	ESOP Stock Plan:	Profit Sharing:	Top Exec. Salary: $391,796	Bonus: $240,149
Savings Plan: Y	Stock Purch. Plan:		Second Exec. Salary: $262,724	Bonus: $103,346

OTHER THOUGHTS:

Apparent Women Officers or Directors: 1
Hot Spot for Advancement for Women/Minorities:

LOCATIONS: ("Y" = Yes)

West:	Southwest:	Midwest:	Southeast:	Northeast:	International:
			Y		

MALT-O-MEAL COMPANY

www.malt-o-meal.com

Industry Group Code: 311230

Management:		**Sales/Marketing:**		**Liberal Arts:**		**Information Systems:**		**Professionals:**		**Technical/Scientific:**	
Mgmt. Trainees:		Mktg. Professionals:	Y	Gen. Writing/Editing:	Y	Info. Management:	Y	Finance/Acct.:	Y	Engineers, Elec.:	
Experienced Mgmt.:	Y	Retail Sales:		Technical Writing:		Software Dev.:		Law:	Y	Engineers, Other:	Y
Int'l Business:		Commercial/Industrial:	Y	Graphic Arts/Photog.:		Hardware Dev.:		HR/Other:	Y	Health/Lab	
MBA Graduates:	Y	Sales Trainees:	Y	Music:		Consulting/Other:		Training:	Y	Scientists/Research:	
		Advertising Pros.:	Y	Broadcasting:				Health Care:		Petroleum/Chemicals:	
				Other:	Y			Consulting:		Math/Other:	

TYPES OF BUSINESS:

Breakfast Cereal Manufacturing
Hot Wheat Cereals
Instant Oatmeal

BRANDS/DIVISIONS/AFFILIATES:

Tootie Fruities
Golden Puffs
Crispy Rice
Coco Roos
Raisin Bran
Cinnamon Toasters
Frosted Flakes
Frosted Mini Spooners

CONTACTS:

Note: Officers with more than one job title may be intentionally listed here more than once.

Chris Neugent, CEO
Chris Neugent, Pres.
John Gappa, CFO
Gene Pagel, CIO
Linda Fisher, Mgr.-Consumer Promotion

Phone: 612-338-8551	**Fax:** 612-339-5710
Toll-Free: 800-743-3029	
Address: 80 S. 8th St., Ste. 2700, Minneapolis, MN 55402 US	

GROWTH PLANS/SPECIAL FEATURES:

Malt-O-Meal Company, founded in 1919, manufactures a line of hot and cold breakfast cereals sold nationwide. Malt-O-Meal currently operates three production facilities and three distribution centers in the U.S. The company's original business was cream of wheat cereal, but it has expanded to produce a line of nearly 20 bagged and boxed cereals that imitate popular box brands. These cereals use similar naming and color schemes but less advertising and packaging than their counterparts. For example, Malt-O-Meal's Tootie Fruities are similar to Fruit Loops, a more recognized Kellogg's brand. Other Malt-O-Meal cold cereal offerings include Coco Roos, Raisin Bran, Honey Buzzers, Frosted Flakes, Golden Puffs, Crispy Rice, Frosted Mini Spooners and Cinnamon Toasters. The firm also offers natural cereals with no artificial preservatives, colors or flavors, no hydrogenated oils and no high fructose corn syrup under the Mom's Best brand. Malt-O-Meal offers hot wheat cereal in original, chocolate, maple and brown sugar and creamy varieties. Through its foodservice division, the company provides cereal to schools, universities and the hospitality, healthcare and corrections markets. The company's web site includes nutritional and product information in both English and Spanish. Additionally, the site offers links to several blogs including a recipe blog, a news blog and the M-O-M blog. The firm is currently expanding its production plant in Asheboro, North Carolina, which will expand its production space by 200,000 square feet and include the construction of an 80,000 square foot warehouse.

Employees are of the firm are offered a 401(k) plan; retirement plans; bonus programs; health care programs; flexible spending accounts; 100% tuition payment, including books; life and disability insurance; and an employee assistance program.

FINANCIALS:

Sales and profits are in thousands of dollars—add 000 to get the full amount. 2011 Note: Financial information for 2011 was not available for all companies at press time.

2011 Sales: $	2011 Profits: $	**U.S. Stock Ticker: Private**
2010 Sales: $	2010 Profits: $	**Int'l Ticker:**
2009 Sales: $	2009 Profits: $	Int'l Exchange:
2008 Sales: $	2008 Profits: $	Employees: Fiscal Year Ends: 12/31
2007 Sales: $	2007 Profits: $	Parent Company:

SALARIES/BENEFITS:

Pension Plan: Y	ESOP Stock Plan:	Profit Sharing:	Top Exec. Salary: $	Bonus: $
Savings Plan: Y	Stock Purch. Plan:		Second Exec. Salary: $	Bonus: $

OTHER THOUGHTS:

Apparent Women Officers or Directors: 1
Hot Spot for Advancement for Women/Minorities:

LOCATIONS: ("Y" = Yes)

West:	Southwest:	Midwest:	Southeast:	Northeast:	International:
Y		Y			

MANAGEMENT NETWORK GROUP INC (THE)

www.tmng.com

Industry Group Code: 54161

Management:		Sales/Marketing:		Liberal Arts:		Information Systems:		Professionals:		Technical/Scientific:	
Mgmt. Trainees:		Mktg. Professionals:	Y	Gen. Writing/Editing:	Y	Info. Management:	Y	Finance/Acct.:	Y	Engineers, Elec.:	
Experienced Mgmt.:	Y	Retail Sales:		Technical Writing:	Y	Software Dev.:		Law:	Y	Engineers, Other:	
Int'l Business:	Y	Commercial/Industrial:	Y	Graphic Arts/Photog.:		Hardware Dev.:		HR/Other:	Y	Health/Lab	
MBA Graduates:	Y	Sales Trainees:	Y	Music:		Consulting/Other:	Y	Training:		Scientists/Research:	
		Advertising Pros.:		Broadcasting:				Health Care:		Petroleum/Chemicals:	
				Other:				Consulting:	Y	Math/Other:	

TYPES OF BUSINESS:

Consulting Services
Management Consulting
Strategic Consulting
Technology Consulting
Marketing Consulting

BRANDS/DIVISIONS/AFFILIATES:

TMNG
CSMG
Cartesian
Strategic Planning Management
Ascertain
Ascertain Inter Operator Provisioning Platform
SmartXchange

CONTACTS: *Note: Officers with more than one job title may be intentionally listed here more than once.*

Richard P. Nespola, CEO
Micky K. Woo, COO
Micky K. Woo, Pres.
Donald E. Klumb, CFO/VP
Debby Brannon, VP-Corp. Mktg.
Nancy Morrow, VP-Human Resources
Jim Baker, CIO
Jim Baker, CTO
Thurston Cromwell, General Counsel
Ronald Angner, Sr. VP-Oper.
William Opet, Sr. VP-North American Bus. Dev.
Susan Simmons, Sr. VP/Managing Dir.-CSMG
Howard Watson, Managing Dir.-Cartesian
Richard P. Nespola, Chmn.

Phone: 913-345-9315	**Fax:** 913-451-1845
Toll-Free: 888-480-8664	
Address: 7300 College Blvd., Ste. 302, Overland Park, KS 66210 US	

GROWTH PLANS/SPECIAL FEATURES:

The Management Network Group, Inc. (TMNG Global) is a consulting firm that provides strategy, management, marketing, operational and technology consulting to communications service providers, technology companies and financial services firms. TMNG Global clients are located principally in the U.S., the U.K. and Western Europe. TMNG Global specializes in strategic and business case development for media/entertainment companies; equipment manufacturers and financial investors in the communications industry; product development and management; customer acquisition and retention; revenue and cost management; business redesigning/ reengineering; and corporate investment services. The company operates through three groups: TMNG, Cartesian and CSMG. The TMNG sector is the core of the firm's business, offering management consulting. Cartesian is the developer of Ascertain, a modular software suite which features advanced revenue management and data integrity tools to assist customers with fixed, wireless, Internet service provider (ISP), data and content environments. Cartesian's client list includes Tier 1 companies in the U.K. and Europe. CSMG, the firm's strategy consulting division, offers services such as opportunity analysis; business case development; and strategic and tactical assistance through its Strategic Planning Management program. In May 2010, the firm introduced SmartXchange, a solution that allows wireless phone companies to locate unused phones so that they may be reused and not thrown out by customers. In October 2010, TMNG Global agreed to partner with Scientia Advisors to jointly offer strategic consulting to the home healthcare industry.

FINANCIALS: **Sales and profits are in thousands of dollars—add 000 to get the full amount. 2011 Note: Financial information for 2011 was not available for all companies at press time.**

2011 Sales: $	2011 Profits: $	**U.S. Stock Ticker: TMNG**
2010 Sales: $67,243	2010 Profits: $-2,903	**Int'l Ticker:**
2009 Sales: $64,953	2009 Profits: $-3,016	Int'l Exchange:
2008 Sales: $74,042	2008 Profits: $-14,825	Employees: 514 Fiscal Year Ends: 12/31
2007 Sales: $71,875	2007 Profits: $-2,337	Parent Company:

SALARIES/BENEFITS:

Pension Plan:	ESOP Stock Plan:	Profit Sharing:	Top Exec. Salary: $624,250	Bonus: $125,000
Savings Plan:	Stock Purch. Plan:		Second Exec. Salary: $460,562	Bonus: $75,000

OTHER THOUGHTS:

Apparent Women Officers or Directors: 2
Hot Spot for Advancement for Women/Minorities: Y

LOCATIONS: ("Y" = Yes)

West:	Southwest:	Midwest:	Southeast:	Northeast:	International:
		Y		Y	Y

MANHATTAN ASSOCIATES INC

www.manh.com

Industry Group Code: 511210A

Management:		Sales/Marketing:		Liberal Arts:		Information Systems:		Professionals:		Technical/Scientific:	
Mgmt. Trainees:		Mktg. Professionals:	Y	Gen. Writing/Editing:		Info. Management:	Y	Finance/Acct.:	Y	Engineers, Elec.:	Y
Experienced Mgmt.:	Y	Retail Sales:		Technical Writing:	Y	Software Dev.:	Y	Law:	Y	Engineers, Other:	
Int'l Business:	Y	Commercial/Industrial:	Y	Graphic Arts/Photog.:		Hardware Dev.:		HR/Other:	Y	Health/Lab	
MBA Graduates:	Y	Sales Trainees:	Y	Music:		Consulting/Other:		Training:	Y	Scientists/Research:	
		Advertising Pros.:		Broadcasting:				Health Care:		Petroleum/Chemicals:	
				Other:				Consulting:		Math/Other:	

TYPES OF BUSINESS:

Software-Supply Chain
Consulting & Support
RFID System Integration

BRANDS/DIVISIONS/AFFILIATES:

Manhattan SCOPE

CONTACTS: *Note: Officers with more than one job title may be intentionally listed here more than once.*

Peter Sinisgalli, CEO
Eddie Capel, COO/Exec. VP
Peter Sinisgalli, Pres.
Dennis Story, CFO/Exec. VP
Jonathan Colehower, VP-Global Mktg.
Terry Geraghty, Sr. VP-Global Human Resources
Bruce Richards, Chief Legal Officer/Sr. VP
Jeff Cashman, Sr. VP-Bus. Dev.
Jeff Mitchell, Exec. VP-Americas
Steve Smith, Sr. VP-EMEA
Terrie O'Hanlon, Sr. VP-Global Brand Strategy
John J. Huntz, Jr., Chmn.
Jeff Baum, Sr. VP-Asia-Pacific

Phone: 770-955-7070 **Fax:** 770-955-0302
Toll-Free:
Address: 2300 Windy Ridge Pkwy., Ste. 1000, Atlanta, GA 30339 US

GROWTH PLANS/SPECIAL FEATURES:

Manhattan Associates, Inc. develops and provides technology-based supply chain software services. Its products consist of software, services and hardware and are used for both the planning and execution of supply chain activities. The company's services include design, configuration, implementation, product assessment and training, as well as customer support and software enhancement subscriptions. The firm specializes in demand forecasting and inventory replenishment; warehouse and labor management; performance analysis; and event planning. Manhattan Associates' software includes Manhattan SCOPE (Supply Chain Optimization, Planning through Execution), designed to reduce implementation cost and risk. Through several vendor partnerships, the company offers many hardware systems including bar code scanners, data collection terminals and document printers. The company's professional services provide clients with a team of consultants who offer training programs concerning the use of the firm's equipment, as well as 24-hour customer support and software enhancement subscriptions. The firm serves various industries including consumer goods, food, government, high-tech/electronics, industrial/wholesale, life science, logistics service providers, retail and transportation. Manhattan Associates operates in geographical segments covering the Americas; EMEA; and the Asia-Pacific Region. International sources typically account for about 27% of the company's revenues. Outside of the U.S., the firm has offices in Australia, China, France, India, Japan, the Netherlands, Singapore and the U.K., as well as representatives in Mexico and reseller partnerships in Latin America, Eastern Europe, the Middle East, South Africa and Asia.

Manhattan Associates offers its employees medical, dental, vision and prescription drug coverage; flexible spending accounts; life and AD&D insurance; short- and long-term disability; a 401(k) plan; access to a credit union; discounted health club membership; and educational assistance.

FINANCIALS: **Sales and profits are in thousands of dollars—add 000 to get the full amount. 2011 Note: Financial information for 2011 was not available for all companies at press time.**

2011 Sales: $329,253 — 2011 Profits: $44,907
2010 Sales: $297,117 — 2010 Profits: $28,061
2009 Sales: $246,667 — 2009 Profits: $16,562
2008 Sales: $337,201 — 2008 Profits: $22,798
2007 Sales: $337,401 — 2007 Profits: $30,751

U.S. Stock Ticker: MANH
Int'l Ticker:
Int'l Exchange:
Employees: 1,925 Fiscal Year Ends: 12/31
Parent Company:

SALARIES/BENEFITS:

Pension Plan: | ESOP Stock Plan: | Profit Sharing: | Top Exec. Salary: $474,000 | Bonus: $677,820
Savings Plan: Y | Stock Purch. Plan: | | Second Exec. Salary: $350,000 | Bonus: $500,500

OTHER THOUGHTS:

Apparent Women Officers or Directors: 1
Hot Spot for Advancement for Women/Minorities:

LOCATIONS: ("Y" = Yes)

West:	Southwest:	Midwest:	Southeast:	Northeast:	International:
		Y	Y		Y

MAPFRE USA CORP

www.mapfreusa.com

Industry Group Code: 524126

Management:		Sales/Marketing:		Liberal Arts:		Information Systems:		Professionals:		Technical/Scientific:	
Mgmt. Trainees:	Y	Mktg. Professionals:	Y	Gen. Writing/Editing:	Y	Info. Management:	Y	Finance/Acct.:	Y	Engineers, Elec.:	
Experienced Mgmt.:	Y	Retail Sales:		Technical Writing:	Y	Software Dev.:		Law:	Y	Engineers, Other:	
Int'l Business:		Commercial/Industrial:	Y	Graphic Arts/Photog.:		Hardware Dev.:		HR/Other:	Y	Health/Lab	
MBA Graduates:	Y	Sales Trainees:	Y	Music:		Consulting/Other:		Training:	Y	Scientists/Research:	
		Advertising Pros.:		Broadcasting:				Health Care:		Petroleum/Chemicals:	
				Other:				Consulting:		Math/Other:	Y

TYPES OF BUSINESS:

Insurance, Direct Property & Casualty
Commercial Automobile Insurance
Homeowners' Insurance
Inland Marine Insurance
Fire Insurance
General Liability Insurance
Mortgages

BRANDS/DIVISIONS/AFFILIATES:

MAPFRE S.A.
Commerce Group, Inc. (The)
Commerce West Insurance Co.
MAPFRE Florida
State Wide Insurance Company
Citation Insurance Company (The)
Commerce Insurance Co.
American Commerce Insurance Co.

CONTACTS:

Note: Officers with more than one job title may be intentionally listed here more than once.

Jaime Tamayo, CEO
Randall V. Becker, CFO

Phone: 508-943-9000	**Fax:** 508-949-4921
Toll-Free: 800-922-8276	
Address: 211 Main St., Webster, MA 01570 US	

GROWTH PLANS/SPECIAL FEATURES:

MAPFRE U.S.A. Corp., formerly The Commerce Group, Inc., through its subsidiaries, writes personal and commercial property, casualty, auto and homeowners' insurance policies in 15 states. The company services its customers with personal and commercial property and casualty insurance primarily in Massachusetts and, to a lesser extent, in other states. MAPFRE U.S.A. consists of six companies: Commerce Insurance Co.; The Citation Insurance Company; American Commerce Insurance Co.; Commerce West Insurance Co.; MAPFRE Florida; and State-Wide Insurance Company. With its primary offices in Massachusetts and New Hampshire, Commerce Insurance Co. offers private passenger auto, homeowners', personal liability, earthquake, flood and business insurance. It is one of the largest writers of private passenger auto insurance in Massachusetts. The Citation Insurance Company provides property and casualty insurance in Massachusetts. American Commerce, based in Columbus, Ohio, provides auto and homeowners' insurance. Commerce West, formerly Western Pioneer Insurance Co., provides similar insurance services to customers in California. MAPFRE Florida is a property and casualty insurance company with headquarters in Miami, Florida and branches in Orlando, Jacksonville and Tampa. State Wide Insurance Company provides property and casualty insurance. The group markets its products primarily through a network of independent agents. MAPFRE U.S.A. is owned by the international insurance company MAPFRE S.A., based in Spain.

The company offers its employees medical, dental and vision insurance; life insurance; a 401(k) plan; profit sharing; domestic partner benefits; a dependent care reimbursement account; a health care reimbursement account; an employee assistance program; and tuition assistance.

FINANCIALS:

Sales and profits are in thousands of dollars—add 000 to get the full amount. 2011 Note: Financial information for 2011 was not available for all companies at press time.

2011 Sales: $	2011 Profits: $	**U.S. Stock Ticker: Subsidiary**
2010 Sales: $	2010 Profits: $	**Int'l Ticker:**
2009 Sales: $	2009 Profits: $	Int'l Exchange:
2008 Sales: $	2008 Profits: $	Employees: 2,400 Fiscal Year Ends: 12/31
2007 Sales: $	2007 Profits: $	Parent Company: MAPFRE SA

SALARIES/BENEFITS:

Pension Plan:	ESOP Stock Plan:	Profit Sharing: Y	Top Exec. Salary: $	Bonus: $
Savings Plan: Y	Stock Purch. Plan:		Second Exec. Salary: $	Bonus: $

OTHER THOUGHTS:

Apparent Women Officers or Directors:
Hot Spot for Advancement for Women/Minorities:

LOCATIONS: ("Y" = Yes)

West:	Southwest:	Midwest:	Southeast:	Northeast:	International:
Y		Y		Y	

MARTEK BIOSCIENCES CORP

www.martekbio.com

Industry Group Code: 325411

Management:		**Sales/Marketing:**		**Liberal Arts:**		**Information Systems:**		**Professionals:**		**Technical/Scientific:**	
Mgmt. Trainees:		Mktg. Professionals:	Y	Gen. Writing/Editing:	Y	Info. Management:	Y	Finance/Acct.:	Y	Engineers, Elec.:	
Experienced Mgmt.:	Y	Retail Sales:		Technical Writing:	Y	Software Dev.:		Law:	Y	Engineers, Other:	
Int'l Business:	Y	Commercial/Industrial:	Y	Graphic Arts/Photog.:		Hardware Dev.:		HR/Other:	Y	Health/Lab	Y
MBA Graduates:	Y	Sales Trainees:	Y	Music:		Consulting/Other:		Training:	Y	Scientists/Research:	Y
		Advertising Pros.:	Y	Broadcasting:				Health Care:	Y	Petroleum/Chemicals:	Y
				Other:				Consulting:		Math/Other:	Y

TYPES OF BUSINESS:

Microalgae-Based Product Manufacturing
Drugs-Nutritional Oils
Dietary Supplements
Contract Manufacturing

BRANDS/DIVISIONS/AFFILIATES:

Neuromins
ARASCO
DHASCO
life'sDHA
life'sARA
DSM NV
Brain Armor

CONTACTS:

Note: Officers with more than one job title may be intentionally listed here more than once.

Steve Dubin, CEO
Peter A. Nitze, COO/Exec. VP
David Abramson, Pres.
Peter L. Buzy, CFO
Barney Easterling, Sr. VP-Mfg.
Peter L. Buzy, Exec. VP-Admin.
David M. Feitel, General Counsel/Sr. VP/Corp. Sec.
Cassie France-Kelly, Sr. Mgr.-Public Rel.
Peter L. Buzy, Exec. VP-Finance/Treas.
Robert Flanagan, Chmn.

Phone: 410-740-0081	**Fax:** 410-740-2985
Toll-Free:	
Address: 6480 Dobbin Rd., Columbia, MD 21045 US	

GROWTH PLANS/SPECIAL FEATURES:

Martek Biosciences Corp., a subsidiary of DSM NV, commercially develops nutritional supplements and diagnostic aids from microbial sources including algae, fungi and other microbes. The company's nutritional products group currently manufactures and sells two patented nutritional fatty acids: DHA (docosahexaenoic acid), under the DHASCO, Neuromins and life'sDHA brand names; and ARA (arachidonic acid), under the ARASCO and life'sARA brand names. Life'sDHA is a vegetarian source of the omega-3 fatty acid DHA and is used in infant formula, perinatal products, animal feed, foods and beverages and dietary supplements. Life'sARA is a vegetarian source of the omega-6 fatty acid ARA that is primarily used in infant formula. These fatty acids assist in the development of the optic and central nervous systems in newborns and also promote adult mental, optical and cardiovascular health, which lowers the risk of developing cardiovascular disease, Alzheimer's disease and dementia. The company's licensees and clients for DHA and ARA include Abbott Laboratories under the Similac ADVANCE brand; Mead Johnson Nutritionals, under the Enfamil LIPIL brand; PBM Products, Inc., under the Bright Beginnings brand; Nestle under the Good Start Supreme brand; Hain Celestial, under the Earth's Best brand; Nutricia North America, under the Neocate brand; and under private label brands, including Wal-Mart Parent's Choice. Martek supplies over 40 infant formula customers with its nutritional oils, and its customers sell infant formula products containing its oils collectively in over 75 countries. Martek's customers include Mead Johnson Nutritionals; Nestle; Abbott Nutrition; Pfizer; and Danone. In September 2010, the company introduced an algal DHA supplement for athletes called Brain Armor. In February 2011, the firm was acquired by DSM NV, a developer of industrial chemicals, as well as pharmaceutical and nutritional ingredients.

FINANCIALS:

Sales and profits are in thousands of dollars—add 000 to get the full amount. 2011 Note: Financial information for 2011 was not available for all companies at press time.

2011 Sales: $	2011 Profits: $
2010 Sales: $434,752	2010 Profits: $27,900
2009 Sales: $345,197	2009 Profits: $40,590
2008 Sales: $352,362	2008 Profits: $37,667
2007 Sales: $306,813	2007 Profits: $32,013

U.S. Stock Ticker: Subsidiary
Int'l Ticker:
Int'l Exchange:
Employees: 592 Fiscal Year Ends: 10/31
Parent Company: DSM NV

SALARIES/BENEFITS:

Pension Plan:	ESOP Stock Plan:	Profit Sharing:	Top Exec. Salary: $589,160	Bonus: $100,157
Savings Plan:	Stock Purch. Plan:		Second Exec. Salary: $456,331	Bonus: $77,576

OTHER THOUGHTS:

Apparent Women Officers or Directors: 1
Hot Spot for Advancement for Women/Minorities:

LOCATIONS: ("Y" = Yes)

West:	Southwest:	Midwest:	Southeast:	Northeast:	International:
Y		Y		Y	

MARVEL ENTERTAINMENT LLC

www.marvel.com

Industry Group Code: 511130

Management:		Sales/Marketing:		Liberal Arts:		Information Systems:		Professionals:		Technical/Scientific:	
Mgmt. Trainees:		Mktg. Professionals:	Y	Gen. Writing/Editing:	Y	Info. Management:	Y	Finance/Acct.:	Y	Engineers, Elec.:	
Experienced Mgmt.:	Y	Retail Sales:		Technical Writing:		Software Dev.:	Y	Law:	Y	Engineers, Other:	
Int'l Business:	Y	Commercial/Industrial:		Graphic Arts/Photog.:	Y	Hardware Dev.:		HR/Other:	Y	Health/Lab	
MBA Graduates:	Y	Sales Trainees:		Music:		Consulting/Other:		Training:	Y	Scientists/Research:	
		Advertising Pros.:	Y	Broadcasting:				Health Care:		Petroleum/Chemicals:	
				Other:	Y			Consulting:		Math/Other:	

TYPES OF BUSINESS:

Comic Book Publishing
Toys
Licensing & Merchandising
Movie Production
Online Services

BRANDS/DIVISIONS/AFFILIATES:

Spiderman
Marvel Comics
Walt Disney Company (The)
X-Men
Incredible Hulk
Fantastic Four
Daredevil
Thor

CONTACTS: *Note: Officers with more than one job title may be intentionally listed here more than once.*

Isaac Perlmutter, CEO
Kenneth P. West, CFO/Exec. VP
Simon Philips, Pres., Worldwide Consumer Prod.
Jeff Klein, Exec. VP-Comm.
Kevin Feige, CEO-Marvel Studios
Morton E. Handel, Chmn.

Phone: 212-576-4000	**Fax:**
Toll-Free:	
Address: 135 W. 50th St., 7th Fl., New York, NY 10016 US	

GROWTH PLANS/SPECIAL FEATURES:

Marvel Entertainment, LLC, a subsidiary of The Walt Disney Company, is one of the world's most prominent character-based entertainment companies, with a proprietary library of over 8,000 characters. Some of its most recognizable properties include Spider-Man, Iron Man, The Incredible Hulk, Captain America, X-Men, The Punisher, The Avengers and Silver Surfer. The company's business is divided into three divisions: licensing, publishing and film production. The licensing division licenses the company's characters for use in a wide variety of products and media, including toys, games, apparel, accessories and collectibles. This division also receives fees from the sale of licenses to a variety of media, including feature films, television and video games. The publishing segment creates and publishes comic books and trade paperbacks principally in North America. Aside from traditional printed retail sales and subscriptions, the company also sells subscription virtual access to Marvel Digital Comics Unlimited, which allows users to browse through over 9,000 comics in the firm's online catalog, with more being added all the time. The film production segment develops, produces and distributes films based on its character properties, which are financed by a company-owned $525 million film facility. The company also operates a kids' web site, MarvelKids.com, featuring Marvel characters and content for children ages 6-11.

FINANCIALS: **Sales and profits are in thousands of dollars—add 000 to get the full amount. 2011 Note: Financial information for 2011 was not available for all companies at press time.**

2011 Sales: $	2011 Profits: $	**U.S. Stock Ticker: Subsidiary**
2010 Sales: $	2010 Profits: $	**Int'l Ticker:**
2009 Sales: $	2009 Profits: $	Int'l Exchange:
2008 Sales: $	2008 Profits: $	Employees: Fiscal Year Ends: 12/31
2007 Sales: $	2007 Profits: $	Parent Company: WALT DISNEY COMPANY (THE)

SALARIES/BENEFITS:

Pension Plan:	ESOP Stock Plan:	Profit Sharing:	Top Exec. Salary: $	Bonus: $
Savings Plan:	Stock Purch. Plan:		Second Exec. Salary: $	Bonus: $

OTHER THOUGHTS:

Apparent Women Officers or Directors:
Hot Spot for Advancement for Women/Minorities:

LOCATIONS: ("Y" = Yes)

West:	Southwest:	Midwest:	Southeast:	Northeast:	International:
Y			Y	Y	Y

MEDICINES CO (THE)

www.themedicinescompany.com

Industry Group Code: 325412

Management:		Sales/Marketing:		Liberal Arts:		Information Systems:		Professionals:		Technical/Scientific:	
Mgmt. Trainees:		Mktg. Professionals:	Y	Gen. Writing/Editing:		Info. Management:	Y	Finance/Acct.:	Y	Engineers, Elec.:	
Experienced Mgmt.:	Y	Retail Sales:		Technical Writing:	Y	Software Dev.:	Y	Law:	Y	Engineers, Other:	
Int'l Business:	Y	Commercial/Industrial:	Y	Graphic Arts/Photog.:		Hardware Dev.:		HR/Other:	Y	Health/Lab	Y
MBA Graduates:	Y	Sales Trainees:	Y	Music:		Consulting/Other:		Training:	Y	Scientists/Research:	Y
		Advertising Pros.:		Broadcasting:				Health Care:	Y	Petroleum/Chemicals:	Y
				Other:				Consulting:		Math/Other:	Y

TYPES OF BUSINESS:

Pharmaceuticals Acquisition & Development
Acute Care Hospital Products
Anticoagulants
Blood Pressure Control

BRANDS/DIVISIONS/AFFILIATES:

Angiomax
Cleviprex (Clevidine)
Cangrelor
Oritavancin

CONTACTS: *Note: Officers with more than one job title may be intentionally listed here more than once.*

Clive A. Meanwell, CEO
John P. Kelley, COO
John P. Kelley, Pres.
Glenn Sblendorio, CFO/Exec. VP
Leslie C. Rohrbacker, Chief Human Strategy Officer/VP
Paul M. Antinori, General Counsel/Sr. VP
Bill O'Connor, Chief Acct. Officer
Clive A. Meanwell, Chmn.

Phone: 973-290-6000 | **Fax:** 973-656-9898
Toll-Free: 800-388-1183
Address: 8 Sylvan Way, Parsippany, NJ 07054 US

GROWTH PLANS/SPECIAL FEATURES:

The Medicines Co. (TMC) is a global pharmaceutical company specializing in acute care hospital products. The firm acquires, develops and commercializes pharmaceutical products in late stages of development. The company has two marketed products: Angiomax and Cleviprex. Angiomax is an intravenous direct thrombin inhibitor approved for use in patients undergoing percutaneous coronary intervention and, in Europe, for adult patients with acute coronary syndrome. Cleviprex is an intravenous drug intended for the control of blood pressure in anesthesiology and surgery, critical care and emergency conditions. The firm currently has two products in the Phase III stage of development: Cangrelor, an intravenous antiplatelet agent that prevents platelet activation and aggregation, which is believed to have potential advantages in the treatment of vascular disease; and Oritavancin, an intravenous antibiotic being developed for the treatment of gram-positive bacterial infections.

TMC offers its employees medical, dental, prescription and vision insurance; an employee assistance plan; tuition reimbursement; an employee stock purchase plan and associate stock options; and credit union membership.

FINANCIALS: **Sales and profits are in thousands of dollars—add 000 to get the full amount. 2011 Note: Financial information for 2011 was not available for all companies at press time.**

2011 Sales: $484,732 — 2011 Profits: $127,877
2010 Sales: $437,645 — 2010 Profits: $104,635
2009 Sales: $404,241 — 2009 Profits: $-76,229
2008 Sales: $348,157 — 2008 Profits: $-8,504
2007 Sales: $257,534 — 2007 Profits: $-18,272

U.S. Stock Ticker: MDCO
Int'l Ticker:
Int'l Exchange:
Employees: 420 Fiscal Year Ends: 12/31
Parent Company:

SALARIES/BENEFITS:

Pension Plan: ESOP Stock Plan: Profit Sharing: Top Exec. Salary: $702,000 Bonus: $620,217
Savings Plan: Y Stock Purch. Plan: Y Second Exec. Salary: $486,675 Bonus: $294,439

OTHER THOUGHTS:

Apparent Women Officers or Directors: 2
Hot Spot for Advancement for Women/Minorities:

LOCATIONS: ("Y" = Yes)

West:	Southwest:	Midwest:	Southeast:	Northeast:	International:
				Y	Y

MEDICIS PHARMACEUTICAL CORP

www.medicis.com

Industry Group Code: 325412

Management:		**Sales/Marketing:**		**Liberal Arts:**		**Information Systems:**		**Professionals:**		**Technical/Scientific:**	
Mgmt. Trainees:		Mktg. Professionals:	Y	Gen. Writing/Editing:		Info. Management:	Y	Finance/Acct.:	Y	Engineers, Elec.:	
Experienced Mgmt.:	Y	Retail Sales:		Technical Writing:	Y	Software Dev.:	Y	Law:	Y	Engineers, Other:	
Int'l Business:	Y	Commercial/Industrial:	Y	Graphic Arts/Photog.:		Hardware Dev.:		HR/Other:	Y	Health/Lab	Y
MBA Graduates:	Y	Sales Trainees:	Y	Music:		Consulting/Other:		Training:	Y	Scientists/Research:	Y
		Advertising Pros.:		Broadcasting:				Health Care:	Y	Petroleum/Chemicals:	Y
				Other:				Consulting:		Math/Other:	Y

TYPES OF BUSINESS:

Dermatological, Aesthetic & Podiatric Conditions Drugs
Acne Treatment
Topical Creams
Wrinkle Treatment

BRANDS/DIVISIONS/AFFILIATES:

Perlane
Restylane
Solodyn
Buphenyl
Vanos
Ziana
LipoSonix
Dysport

CONTACTS:

Note: Officers with more than one job title may be intentionally listed here more than once.

Jonah Shacknai, CEO
Jason D. Hanson, COO/Exec. VP
Mark A. Prygocki, Sr., Pres.
Richard D. Peterson, CFO/Exec. VP
Vincent Ippolito, Exec. VP-Sales & Mktg.
Mitchell S. Wortzman, Chief Scientific Officer/Exec. VP
Richard D. Peterson, Treas.
Jonah Shacknai, Chmn.

Phone: 602-808-8800 **Fax:** 602-808-0822
Toll-Free:
Address: 7720 North Dobson Rd., Scottsdale, AZ 85256 US

GROWTH PLANS/SPECIAL FEATURES:

Medicis Pharmaceutical Corp. is a specialty pharmaceutical company that develops and markets products for treatment of dermatological and aesthetic conditions. The company offers a range of products addressing various conditions or aesthetic improvement, including facial wrinkles; acne; fungal infections; rosacea; hyperpigmentation; photoaging; psoriasis; seborrheic dermatitis; and cosmesis (improvement in the texture and appearance of skin). The firm offers 13 branded products. Its primary brands include Dysport, an injection used to temporarily remove the look of moderate to severe frown lines between the eyebrows; the Liposonix system, a nonsurgical, non-invasive fat reduction technology that is used to permanently remove abdominal fat; Perlane, an injectable gel for implantation into the deep dermis to superficial subcutis for the correction of facial wrinkles and folds; Restylane, an injectable gel that is indicated for mid-to-deep implantation for treatment of moderate to severe facial wrinkles and folds such as nasolabial folds; Solodyn, an extended-release oral antibiotic for moderate to severe acne; Buphenyl, an oral medication which aids in the management of hyperammonemia in patients with urea cycle disorders; Vanos, a corticosteroid to relieve inflammation and itching caused by certain skin conditions; and Ziana, a topical treatment for mild, moderate and severe acne vulgaris. Medicis customers include wholesale pharmaceutical distributors such as Cardinal Health, Inc.; McKesson Corp.; and other major drug chains. McKesson is the company's sole distributor of Restylane, Perlane and Dysport products in the U.S.

The firm offers employees medical, dental and vision coverage; a prescription plan; educational assistance; a 401(k) plan; and flexible spending accounts.

FINANCIALS:

Sales and profits are in thousands of dollars—add 000 to get the full amount. 2011 Note: Financial information for 2011 was not available for all companies at press time.

2011 Sales: $721,126	2011 Profits: $126,540
2010 Sales: $699,968	2010 Profits: $123,335
2009 Sales: $571,915	2009 Profits: $75,951
2008 Sales: $517,750	2008 Profits: $10,276
2007 Sales: $457,394	2007 Profits: $70,436

U.S. Stock Ticker: MRX
Int'l Ticker:
Int'l Exchange:
Employees: 679 Fiscal Year Ends: 12/31
Parent Company:

SALARIES/BENEFITS:

Pension Plan: ESOP Stock Plan: Profit Sharing: Top Exec. Salary: $1,135,000 Bonus: $1,149,188
Savings Plan: Y Stock Purch. Plan: Second Exec. Salary: $575,000 Bonus: $692,344

OTHER THOUGHTS:

Apparent Women Officers or Directors: 1
Hot Spot for Advancement for Women/Minorities:

LOCATIONS: ("Y" = Yes)

West:	Southwest:	Midwest:	Southeast:	Northeast:	International:
Y	Y	Y	Y	Y	

MEDIFAST INC

www.medifast1.com

Industry Group Code: 446191

Management:		Sales/Marketing:		Liberal Arts:		Information Systems:		Professionals:		Technical/Scientific:	
Mgmt. Trainees:	Y	Mktg. Professionals:	Y	Gen. Writing/Editing:	Y	Info. Management:	Y	Finance/Acct.:	Y	Engineers, Elec.:	
Experienced Mgmt.:	Y	Retail Sales:	Y	Technical Writing:		Software Dev.:	Y	Law:	Y	Engineers, Other:	
Int'l Business:		Commercial/Industrial:		Graphic Arts/Photog.:	Y	Hardware Dev.:		HR/Other:	Y	Health/Lab	
MBA Graduates:	Y	Sales Trainees:	Y	Music:		Consulting/Other:		Training:	Y	Scientists/Research:	
		Advertising Pros.:	Y	Broadcasting:				Health Care:		Petroleum/Chemicals:	
				Other:				Consulting:		Math/Other:	

TYPES OF BUSINESS:

Nutritional Supplements, Retail
Diet Products
Online Retail
Direct Marketing

BRANDS/DIVISIONS/AFFILIATES:

Jason Pharmaceuticals Inc
Take Shape for Life Inc
Jason Properties LLC
Jason Enterprises Inc
Seven Crondall LLC
Hi-Energy Weight Control Centers
Medifast Weight Control Centers
Medifast 5 & 1

CONTACTS:

Note: Officers with more than one job title may be intentionally listed here more than once.

Michael S. McDevitt, CEO
Margaret MacDonald-Sheetz, COO
Margaret MacDonald-Sheetz, Pres.
Brendan Connors, CFO
Leo V. Williams, Exec. VP
Bradley T. MacDonald, Chmn.

Phone: 732-764-0619	**Fax:**
Toll-Free: 800-209-0878	
Address: 11445 Cronhill Dr., Owings Mills, MD 21117 US	

GROWTH PLANS/SPECIAL FEATURES:

Medifast, Inc. produces, distributes and sells weight management and disease management products and other consumable health and diet products. The firm's product lines include weight and disease management, meal replacements and vitamins. Medifast conducts the majority of its business through five wholly-owned subsidiaries: Jason Pharmaceuticals, Inc.; Take Shape for Life, Inc.; Jason Properties LLC; Jason Enterprises, Inc.; and Seven Crondall, LLC. Jason Pharmaceuticals produces over 55% of the Medifast products at its facility in Maryland. The Medifast brand is distributed through physician recommendation, the Medifast Direct and Take Shape for Life channels and through 39 Medifast Weight Control Centers, operating under the names Medifast and Hi-Energy. Through Medifast Direct, products ordered through the firm's web site or in-house call center are shipped directly to customers' home. Medifast's web site offers an online community and library for support, information and meal planning for weight loss and weight maintenance. Take Shape for Life is a physician-led network of independent health coaches that provide coaching and support for Medifast programs. The Weight Control Centers offer Medifast programs, patient counseling and Inbody composition analysis. The company also offers Medifast Weight Control Center franchise opportunities, and operates locations in Alabama, Arizona, California, Pennsylvania and Minnesota. Its central weight loss plan, called Medifast 5 & 1, prescribes five daily Medifast meals, one consisting of meat and vegetables. The firm offers more than 70 meal options, including shakes, soups, stew, chili, oatmeal, eggs, fruit drinks, brownies, pancakes and crunch bars. The firm has programs specially designed for men, women, different age groups and for those with specific medical and dietary needs (such as diabetes, gout, bariatric, celiac disease or vegetarian). June 2011, Medifast opened three Weight Control Centers in the Metro DC area, increasing the area's total to 12 locations.

FINANCIALS:

Sales and profits are in thousands of dollars—add 000 to get the full amount. 2011 Note: Financial information for 2011 was not available for all companies at press time.

2011 Sales: $	2011 Profits: $
2010 Sales: $257,552	2010 Profits: $19,611
2009 Sales: $169,743	2009 Profits: $11,357
2008 Sales: $110,076	2008 Profits: $4,311
2007 Sales: $83,779	2007 Profits: $3,837

U.S. Stock Ticker: MED
Int'l Ticker:
Int'l Exchange:
Employees: 507 Fiscal Year Ends: 12/31
Parent Company:

SALARIES/BENEFITS:

Pension Plan:	ESOP Stock Plan:	Profit Sharing:	Top Exec. Salary: $225,000	Bonus: $758,400
Savings Plan:	Stock Purch. Plan:		Second Exec. Salary: $185,000	Bonus: $644,550

OTHER THOUGHTS:

Apparent Women Officers or Directors: 3
Hot Spot for Advancement for Women/Minorities: Y

LOCATIONS: ("Y" = Yes)

West:	Southwest:	Midwest:	Southeast:	Northeast:	International:
Y	Y	Y	Y	Y	

MEDTOX SCIENTIFIC INC

www.medtox.com

Industry Group Code: 6215

Management:		Sales/Marketing:		Liberal Arts:		Information Systems:		Professionals:		Technical/Scientific:	
Mgmt. Trainees:		Mktg. Professionals:	Y	Gen. Writing/Editing:		Info. Management:	Y	Finance/Acct.:	Y	Engineers, Elec.:	
Experienced Mgmt.:	Y	Retail Sales:		Technical Writing:	Y	Software Dev.:	Y	Law:	Y	Engineers, Other:	
Int'l Business:		Commercial/Industrial:	Y	Graphic Arts/Photog.:		Hardware Dev.:		HR/Other:	Y	Health/Lab	Y
MBA Graduates:	Y	Sales Trainees:	Y	Music:		Consulting/Other:		Training:	Y	Scientists/Research:	Y
		Advertising Pros.:		Broadcasting:				Health Care:	Y	Petroleum/Chemicals:	
				Other:				Consulting:		Math/Other:	

TYPES OF BUSINESS:

Diagnostic Device Manufacturing
Forensic & Clinical Lab Services
Diagnostic Drug Screening Devices

BRANDS/DIVISIONS/AFFILIATES:

MEDTOX Diagnostics, Inc.
MEDTOX Laboratories, Inc.
PROFILE-II
VERDICT-II
ClearCourse
SURE-SCREEN
Drug Abuse Recognition System (DARS)

CONTACTS:

Note: Officers with more than one job title may be intentionally listed here more than once.

Richard J. Braun, CEO
Richard J. Braun, Pres.
Kevin J. Wiersma, CFO
James A. Schoonover, Chief Mktg. Officer/VP-Sales & Mktg.
Kevin J. Wiersma, VP/COO-Forensic Laboratory Oper.
Kevin J. Wiersma, Chief Admin. Officer
Susan E. Puskas, VP-Quality & Regulatory/COO-Clinical Lab Oper.
Steven J. Schmidt, VP-Finance
Kevin J. Wiersma, CFO-Medtox Scientific/COO-Forensic Lab Oper.
B. Mitchell Owens, VP/COO-Diagnostics Div.
Susan E. Puskas, VP-Quality Assurance & Regulatory Affairs
Richard J. Braun, Chmn.

Phone: 651-636-7466 **Fax:** 651-636-5351
Toll-Free: 800-832-3244
Address: 402 W. County Rd. D, St. Paul, MN 55112 US

GROWTH PLANS/SPECIAL FEATURES:

MEDTOX Scientific, Inc. manufactures and distributes diagnostic devices and provides forensic and clinical laboratory services. The firm operates through two divisions, laboratory services and product sales. The laboratory services division is operated by the company's subsidiary MEDTOX Laboratories, Inc., which provides laboratory drug testing services for corporations, medical facilities and the federal government. MEDTOX Laboratories derives the majority of its revenues, 51% in 2010, from workplace drugs-of-abuse testing. It also offers clinical and other laboratory services accounting for 39% of revenues, including clinical toxicology; medical diagnostics; general clinical testing for the pharmaceutical industry; heavy metal, trace element and solvent analysis; it also offers logistics, data and program management services through its WEBTOX and eChain online services. The firm's other subsidiary, MEDTOX Diagnostics, Inc., which operates the product sales division, is based in Burlington, North Carolina and manufactures on-site drug screening products for the corporate, health care, criminal justice, temporary service and drug rehabilitation markets. MEDTOX Diagnostics' point-of-collection testing (POCT) products, which account for 89% of its sales, include the PROFILE line and MEDTOXScan, which are sold to hospitals, and the VERDICT-II and SURE-SCREEN lines, which are sold within the criminal justice and drug rehabilitation markets. These products test for a variety of drugs including amphetamines, marijuana, cocaine, opiates, phencyclidine (PCP), benzoylecgonine, morphine and methamphetamine. The company also offers its ClearCourse comprehensive drug testing program, which consists of Drug Abuse Recognition System (DARS) training; SURE-SCREEN drug testing devices; WEBTOX online data management; and MEDTOX's own laboratory assistance for confirmation testing. This division also offers contract manufacturing services.

MEDTOX offers its employees medical, dental and life insurance; tuition reimbursement; and flexible spending accounts.

FINANCIALS:

Sales and profits are in thousands of dollars—add 000 to get the full amount. 2011 Note: Financial information for 2011 was not available for all companies at press time.

2011 Sales: $	2011 Profits: $
2010 Sales: $97,101	2010 Profits: $3,017
2009 Sales: $84,108	2009 Profits: $1,299
2008 Sales: $85,813	2008 Profits: $5,572
2007 Sales: $80,285	2007 Profits: $6,690

U.S. Stock Ticker: MTOX
Int'l Ticker:
Int'l Exchange:
Employees: 633 Fiscal Year Ends: 12/31
Parent Company:

SALARIES/BENEFITS:

Pension Plan:	ESOP Stock Plan:	Profit Sharing:	Top Exec. Salary: $390,000	Bonus: $1,036,616
Savings Plan: Y	Stock Purch. Plan:		Second Exec. Salary: $235,800	Bonus: $423,060

OTHER THOUGHTS:

Apparent Women Officers or Directors: 1
Hot Spot for Advancement for Women/Minorities:

LOCATIONS: ("Y" = Yes)

West:	Southwest:	Midwest:	Southeast:	Northeast:	International:
		Y		Y	

MENTOR CORP

www.mentorwwllc.com

Industry Group Code: 33911

Management:		Sales/Marketing:		Liberal Arts:		Information Systems:		Professionals:		Technical/Scientific:	
Mgmt. Trainees:		Mktg. Professionals:	Y	Gen. Writing/Editing:		Info. Management:	Y	Finance/Acct.:	Y	Engineers, Elec.:	
Experienced Mgmt.:	Y	Retail Sales:		Technical Writing:	Y	Software Dev.:		Law:	Y	Engineers, Other:	Y
Int'l Business:	Y	Commercial/Industrial:	Y	Graphic Arts/Photog.:		Hardware Dev.:		HR/Other:	Y	Health/Lab	Y
MBA Graduates:	Y	Sales Trainees:	Y	Music:		Consulting/Other:		Training:	Y	Scientists/Research:	Y
		Advertising Pros.:		Broadcasting:				Health Care:	Y	Petroleum/Chemicals:	
				Other:				Consulting:		Math/Other:	

TYPES OF BUSINESS:

Supplies-Plastic Surgery Products
Breast Implants
Liposuction

BRANDS/DIVISIONS/AFFILIATES:

Contour Profile Tissue Expander
Johnson & Johnson
Puragen
Prevell
ETHICON Inc
Mentor Worldwide, LLC
MemoryGel
PDS Flexible

CONTACTS: *Note: Officers with more than one job title may be intentionally listed here more than once.*

Edward S. Northup, COO/VP
David Wilson, Pres.
Brian E. Luedtke, VP-Global Mktg. & Sales
AnnaMarie Daniels, VP-Mentor Biologics

Phone: 805-879-6000	**Fax:** 805-964-2712
Toll-Free: 800-525-0245	
Address: 201 Mentor Dr., Santa Barbara, CA 93111 US	

GROWTH PLANS/SPECIAL FEATURES:

Mentor Corp., which operates as Mentor Worldwide, LLC, develops, manufactures, licenses and markets a broad range of products serving the plastic and reconstructive surgical markets worldwide. The company's aesthetic products fall into three general categories: surgical breast implants; soft tissue aspiration or body contouring (liposuction); and facial rejuvenation products for skin restoration. Mentor's line of breast implant products includes Contour Profile, its saline-filled implant brand, and MemoryGel, its silicone gel-filled implant brand. The company also markets the Contour Profile Tissue Expander lines of breast expanders, which prepare the tissue to hold the implant. All of these mammary prostheses are used in augmentation procedures to enhance breast size and shape, correct breast asymmetries, help restore fullness after breast-feeding and reconstruct breasts following a mastectomy. Mentor's body contouring segment markets a line of liposuction products and disposable supplies, including its Mentor UltraSculpt technology, which is more accurate and less physically traumatic than conventional liposuction. The company also offers a line of extremity tissue expanders used in growing tissue for reconstruction and skin graft procedures. Finally, Mentor supplies dermal filters, such as Puragen and Prevell, and cosmeceutical products that help plastic surgeons and dermatologists correct for wrinkles and various other skin conditions. The firm is owned by Johnson & Johnson and operates as a stand alone business unit of Johnson & Johnson subsidiary ETHICON, Inc. In November 2010, the firm released new absorbable implant PDS Flexible, which offers structural support during nasal reconstruction procedures.

FINANCIALS: **Sales and profits are in thousands of dollars—add 000 to get the full amount. 2011 Note: Financial information for 2011 was not available for all companies at press time.**

2011 Sales: $	2011 Profits: $	**U.S. Stock Ticker: Subsidiary**
2010 Sales: $	2010 Profits: $	**Int'l Ticker:**
2009 Sales: $	2009 Profits: $	Int'l Exchange:
2008 Sales: $	2008 Profits: $	Employees: Fiscal Year Ends: 12/31
2007 Sales: $	2007 Profits: $	Parent Company: JOHNSON & JOHNSON

SALARIES/BENEFITS:

Pension Plan:	ESOP Stock Plan:	Profit Sharing:	Top Exec. Salary: $	Bonus: $
Savings Plan: Y	Stock Purch. Plan: Y		Second Exec. Salary: $	Bonus: $

OTHER THOUGHTS:

Apparent Women Officers or Directors: 1
Hot Spot for Advancement for Women/Minorities: Y

LOCATIONS: ("Y" = Yes)

West:	Southwest:	Midwest:	Southeast:	Northeast:	International:
Y	Y	Y			Y

MERIDIAN BIOSCIENCE INC

www.meridianbioscience.com

Industry Group Code: 325413

Management:		**Sales/Marketing:**		**Liberal Arts:**		**Information Systems:**		**Professionals:**		**Technical/Scientific:**	
Mgmt. Trainees:		Mktg. Professionals:	Y	Gen. Writing/Editing:		Info. Management:	Y	Finance/Acct.:	Y	Engineers, Elec.:	
Experienced Mgmt.:	Y	Retail Sales:		Technical Writing:	Y	Software Dev.:	Y	Law:	Y	Engineers, Other:	Y
Int'l Business:	Y	Commercial/Industrial:	Y	Graphic Arts/Photog.:		Hardware Dev.:	Y	HR/Other:	Y	Health/Lab	Y
MBA Graduates:	Y	Sales Trainees:	Y	Music:		Consulting/Other:		Training:	Y	Scientists/Research:	Y
		Advertising Pros.:	Y	Broadcasting:				Health Care:	Y	Petroleum/Chemicals:	
				Other:				Consulting:		Math/Other:	Y

TYPES OF BUSINESS:

Diagnostic Test Kits
Contract Manufacturing
Bulk Antigens, Antibodies & Reagents

BRANDS/DIVISIONS/AFFILIATES:

Biodesign
OEM Concepts
Viral Antigens

CONTACTS: *Note: Officers with more than one job title may be intentionally listed here more than once.*

John A. Kraeutler, CEO
John A. Kraeutler, COO
John A. Kraeutler, Pres.
Melissa A. Lueke, CFO/VP
Marviette Johnson, VP-Human Resources
Slava A.Elagin, VP-Research
Lawrence J. Baldini, Exec. VP-Info. Systems
Slava A. Elagin, VP-Prod. Dev.
Lawrence J. Baldini, Exec. VP-Oper.
Todd W. Motto, VP-Bus. Dev.
Richard L. Eberly, Chief Commercial Officer
Marco Calzavara, Pres., Meridian Bioscience Europe
Susan D. Rolih, Sr. VP-Regulatory Affairs & Quality Assurance
William J. Motto, Chmn.

Phone: 513-271-3700	**Fax:** 513-271-3762
Toll-Free: 800-543-1980	
Address: 3471 River Hills Dr., Cincinnati, OH 45244 US	

GROWTH PLANS/SPECIAL FEATURES:

Meridian Bioscience, Inc. is a life science company that develops, manufactures, sells and distributes diagnostic test kits, primarily for respiratory, gastrointestinal, viral and parasitic infectious diseases. It also manufactures and distributes bulk antigens, antibodies and reagents; and contract manufactures proteins and other biologicals. The company operates in three segments: U.S. diagnostics, European diagnostics and life science. The U.S. diagnostics segment focuses on the development, manufacture, sale and distribution of diagnostic test kits, which utilize immunodiagnostic technologies that test samples of body fluids or tissue for the presence of antigens and antibodies of specific infectious diseases. Products also include transport media that store and preserve specimen samples from patient collection to laboratory testing. The European diagnostics segment focuses on the sale and distribution of diagnostic test kits. Its sales and distribution network consists of direct sales forces in Belgium, France, Holland and Italy, and independent distributors in other European, African and Middle Eastern countries. The life sciences segment focuses on the development, manufacture, sale and distribution of bulk antigens, antibodies and reagents, as well as contract development and manufacturing services. The segment is represented by four product-line brands: Biodesign, which represents monoclonal and polyclonal antibodies and assay reagents; OEM (original equipment manufacturer) Concepts, which represents contract ascites and antibody production services; and Viral Antigens, which represents viral proteins.

Meridian offers its employees medical, dental and life insurance; short- and long-term disability; stock options; a 401(k) plan; profit sharing; and tuition reimbursement.

FINANCIALS: **Sales and profits are in thousands of dollars—add 000 to get the full amount. 2011 Note: Financial information for 2011 was not available for all companies at press time.**

2011 Sales: $159,723	2011 Profits: $26,831	**U.S. Stock Ticker: VIVO**
2010 Sales: $143,000	2010 Profits: $26,647	**Int'l Ticker:**
2009 Sales: $148,274	2009 Profits: $32,759	Int'l Exchange:
2008 Sales: $139,639	2008 Profits: $30,202	Employees: 525 Fiscal Year Ends: 9/30
2007 Sales: $122,963	2007 Profits: $26,721	Parent Company:

SALARIES/BENEFITS:

Pension Plan:	ESOP Stock Plan:	Profit Sharing: Y	Top Exec. Salary: $511,538	Bonus: $
Savings Plan: Y	Stock Purch. Plan: Y		Second Exec. Salary: $524,999	Bonus: $

OTHER THOUGHTS:

Apparent Women Officers or Directors: 3
Hot Spot for Advancement for Women/Minorities: Y

LOCATIONS: ("Y" = Yes)

West:	Southwest:	Midwest:	Southeast:	Northeast:	International:
		Y	Y	Y	Y

MERIT MEDICAL SYSTEMS INC

www.merit.com

Industry Group Code: 33911

Management:		Sales/Marketing:		Liberal Arts:		Information Systems:		Professionals:		Technical/Scientific:	
Mgmt. Trainees:		Mktg. Professionals:	Y	Gen. Writing/Editing:		Info. Management:	Y	Finance/Acct.:	Y	Engineers, Elec.:	
Experienced Mgmt.:	Y	Retail Sales:		Technical Writing:	Y	Software Dev.:		Law:	Y	Engineers, Other:	Y
Int'l Business:	Y	Commercial/Industrial:	Y	Graphic Arts/Photog.:		Hardware Dev.:		HR/Other:	Y	Health/Lab	Y
MBA Graduates:	Y	Sales Trainees:	Y	Music:		Consulting/Other:		Training:	Y	Scientists/Research:	Y
		Advertising Pros.:		Broadcasting:				Health Care:	Y	Petroleum/Chemicals:	
				Other:				Consulting:		Math/Other:	

TYPES OF BUSINESS:

Disposable Products-Cardiology & Radiology

BRANDS/DIVISIONS/AFFILIATES:

Merit Endotek
Merit Sensor Systems
BioSphere Medical, Inc.
QuadraSphere
HepaShere
EmboGold
Emboshere

CONTACTS:

Note: Officers with more than one job title may be intentionally listed here more than once.

Fred P. Lampropoulos, CEO
Arlin D. Nelson, COO
Fred P. Lampropoulos, Pres.
Kent W. Stanger, CFO/Corp. Sec.
Martin R. Stephens, Exec. VP-Sales & Mktg.
Rashelle Perry, Chief Legal Officer
Anne-Marie Wright, VP-Corp. Comm.
Kent W. Stanger, Treas.
Fred P. Lampropoulos, Chmn.

Phone: 801-253-1600	**Fax:** 801-253-1652
Toll-Free: 800-356-3748	
Address: 1600 W. Merit Pkwy., South Jordan, UT 84095 US	

GROWTH PLANS/SPECIAL FEATURES:

Merit Medical Systems, Inc. manufactures and markets proprietary disposable devices with a focus on five core markets: cardiology, radiology, gastroenterology, pulmonary and vascular surgery. The firm's cardiology products, such as catheters, inflation devices, hemostasis valves and vascular access products, are used to assist in diagnosing and treating coronary artery disease, peripheral vascular disease and other non-vascular diseases. Radiology products include a range of catheters and products for dialysis and interventional nephrology. Gastroenterology and pulmonary products manufactured by the company include non-vascular stents and bi-polar probes. The gastroenterology and pulmonary products are distributed by Merit Endotek. Merit's vascular surgery products are comprised of embolic microspheres, which are precisely calibrated, spherical, hydrophilic, micro-porous beads made with acrylic co-polymer cross-linked with gelatin, are sold under the QuadraSphere, HepaShere, EmboGold and Emboshere brands. Approximately 46% of Merit's sales are made directly to U.S. hospitals; 32% to international markets; 12% to domestic secondary distributors such as U.S. custom packagers and distributors; and 10% to original equipment manufacturers (OEMs). The firm's products are designed to enable physicians and other health care professionals to perform interventional and diagnostic procedures safely and effectively. The company owns over 200 U.S. and international patents. The firm's subsidiary, Merit Sensor Systems, designs and manufactures pressure sensor devices with a wide range of applicability, including automotive, medical, industrial, defense and consumer applications. In September 2010, the company acquired embolotherapeutic product developer BioSphere Medical, Inc.

Employees of the firm are offered medical and dental coverage; a 125 Cafeteria (flexible spending) plan; a 401(k) plan; an employee stock purchase plan; an employee assistance program; free flue shots; employee wellness initiatives; an annual employee golf tournament; and family activities.

FINANCIALS:

Sales and profits are in thousands of dollars—add 000 to get the full amount. 2011 Note: Financial information for 2011 was not available for all companies at press time.

2011 Sales: $359,400	2011 Profits: $23,000
2010 Sales: $296,755	2010 Profits: $12,460
2009 Sales: $257,462	2009 Profits: $22,530
2008 Sales: $227,143	2008 Profits: $20,727
2007 Sales: $207,768	2007 Profits: $15,588

U.S. Stock Ticker: MMSI
Int'l Ticker:
Int'l Exchange:
Employees: 2,178 Fiscal Year Ends: 12/31
Parent Company:

SALARIES/BENEFITS:

Pension Plan:	ESOP Stock Plan:	Profit Sharing:	Top Exec. Salary: $658,462	Bonus: $158,000
Savings Plan: Y	Stock Purch. Plan: Y		Second Exec. Salary: $350,000	Bonus: $100,200

OTHER THOUGHTS:

Apparent Women Officers or Directors: 2
Hot Spot for Advancement for Women/Minorities:

LOCATIONS: ("Y" = Yes)

West:	Southwest:	Midwest:	Southeast:	Northeast:	International:
Y	Y			Y	Y

MESIROW FINANCIAL HOLDINGS INC www.mesirowfinancial.com

Industry Group Code: 523110

Management:		Sales/Marketing:		Liberal Arts:		Information Systems:		Professionals:		Technical/Scientific:	
Mgmt. Trainees:		Mktg. Professionals:	Y	Gen. Writing/Editing:	Y	Info. Management:	Y	Finance/Acct.:	Y	Engineers, Elec.:	
Experienced Mgmt.:	Y	Retail Sales:		Technical Writing:	Y	Software Dev.:	Y	Law:	Y	Engineers, Other:	
Int'l Business:	Y	Commercial/Industrial:		Graphic Arts/Photog.:		Hardware Dev.:		HR/Other:	Y	Health/Lab	
MBA Graduates:	Y	Sales Trainees:		Music:		Consulting/Other:		Training:		Scientists/Research:	
		Advertising Pros.:		Broadcasting:				Health Care:		Petroleum/Chemicals:	
				Other:				Consulting:		Math/Other:	

TYPES OF BUSINESS:

Investment Banking
Financial Consulting
Real Estate Development
Financial Advisory
Insurance Services
Investment Management

BRANDS/DIVISIONS/AFFILIATES:

Mesirow Financial Consulting LLC
Mesirow Financial Real Estate Consulting
Mesirow Compensation & Exec. Benefit Strategies
Mesirow Advanced Strategies

CONTACTS: *Note: Officers with more than one job title may be intentionally listed here more than once.*

Richard S. Price, CEO
Kristie P. Paskvan, CFO
Dominick J. Mondi, Sr. Managing Dir.-Institutional Sales & Trading
Dennis B. Black, General Counsel/Sr. Managing Dir.
Martin B. Kaplan, CEO-Advanced Strategies
Ralph S. Tuliano, Pres., Mesirow Financial Consulting
Marc E. Sacks, Sr. Managing Dir.-Private Equity
Gary C. Klopfenstein, Sr. Managing Dir.-Currency Mgmt.
Julie E. Vander Weele, Sr. Managing Dir.-Investment Advisory
Richard S. Price, Chmn.
Lucy Chen Kruse, Sr. VP-China Financial Market Dev.

Phone: 312-595-6000 **Fax:** 321-595-4246
Toll-Free: 800-453-0600
Address: 353 N. Clark St., Chicago, IL 60654 US

GROWTH PLANS/SPECIAL FEATURES:

Mesirow Financial Holdings, Inc. is a Chicago based financial services company with approximately $59 billion in assets under management. The company offers its services in four divisions: investment management, insurance services, consulting and global markets. The investment management division offers currency management for institutional clients; private equity, which offers direct and fund of funds programs; commodity services for institutions attempting to garner real assets; U.S. and international equity, which covers emerging markets; fixed income management; direct and multi-management real estate; and investment advisory. The firm's insurance services segment offers structured settlements and employee benefits services, as well as life, disability, property, casualty and private client insurance. The company's consulting division is comprised of Mesirow Financial Consulting, LLC, which provides compensation and executive benefits strategies, as well as advisory services to organizations and corporate stakeholders; Mesirow Financial Real Estate Consulting, which constructs commercial and institutional structures, such as university facilities, convention centers and hotels; and Mesirow Compensation and Executive Benefit Strategies, which offers custom employee benefits packages suited to the needs and abilities of employers. The company's global markets segment offers clearing services, public finance, investment banking, institutional sales/trading, credit tenant lease financing, investment brokerage, options strategies and sale-leaseback capital. The company has offices in 18 U.S. cities and an office in London. Subsidiary Mesirow Advanced Strategies is an alternative assets manager that focuses on portfolio construction and risk management.

FINANCIALS: **Sales and profits are in thousands of dollars—add 000 to get the full amount. 2011 Note: Financial information for 2011 was not available for all companies at press time.**

2011 Sales: $510,000 2011 Profits: $
2010 Sales: $526,403 2010 Profits: $
2009 Sales: $467,000 2009 Profits: $
2008 Sales: $492,000 2008 Profits: $
2007 Sales: $ 2007 Profits: $

U.S. Stock Ticker: Private
Int'l Ticker:
Int'l Exchange:
Employees: 1,200 Fiscal Year Ends: 3/31
Parent Company:

SALARIES/BENEFITS:

Pension Plan: ESOP Stock Plan: Profit Sharing: Top Exec. Salary: $ Bonus: $
Savings Plan: Stock Purch. Plan: Second Exec. Salary: $ Bonus: $

OTHER THOUGHTS:

Apparent Women Officers or Directors: 3
Hot Spot for Advancement for Women/Minorities: Y

LOCATIONS: ("Y" = Yes)

West:	Southwest:	Midwest:	Southeast:	Northeast:	International:
Y	Y	Y	Y	Y	Y

METROPOLITAN HEALTH NETWORKS INC

www.metcare.com

Industry Group Code: 524114

Management:		Sales/Marketing:		Liberal Arts:		Information Systems:		Professionals:		Technical/Scientific:	
Mgmt. Trainees:	Y	Mktg. Professionals:	Y	Gen. Writing/Editing:	Y	Info. Management:	Y	Finance/Acct.:	Y	Engineers, Elec.:	
Experienced Mgmt.:	Y	Retail Sales:		Technical Writing:	Y	Software Dev.:	Y	Law:	Y	Engineers, Other:	
Int'l Business:		Commercial/Industrial:	Y	Graphic Arts/Photog.:		Hardware Dev.:		HR/Other:	Y	Health/Lab	Y
MBA Graduates:	Y	Sales Trainees:		Music:		Consulting/Other:		Training:	Y	Scientists/Research:	
		Advertising Pros.:		Broadcasting:				Health Care:	Y	Petroleum/Chemicals:	
				Other:				Consulting:		Math/Other:	Y

TYPES OF BUSINESS:

Provider Service Network
Disease Management

BRANDS/DIVISIONS/AFFILIATES:

Metcare of Florida, Inc.
Humana Inc.

CONTACTS: *Note: Officers with more than one job title may be intentionally listed here more than once.*

Michael M. Earley, CEO
Jose A. Guethon, COO
Jose A. Guethon, Pres.
Robert J. Sabo, CFO
Sharon Munroe, VP-Human Resources
Hymin Zucker, Chief Medical Officer
Frank M. Richter, Sr. VP-Info Svcs.
Roberto L. Palenzuela, General Counsel/Sec.
Albert Palombo, Sr. VP-Corp. Comm.
Nicholas Buscemi, III, Chief Acct. Officer/Sr. VP
Mark Sprangers, Medical Dir.-Central Florida
William H. McCoy, III, Chief Medical Info. Officer
Lucille Soltesz, VP-Quality Mgmt.
Maria A. Xirau, Sr. VP-Medical Oper., South Florida
Michael M. Earley, Chmn.

Phone: 561-805-8500	**Fax:** 561-805-8501
Toll-Free: 888-663-8227	
Address: 777 Yamato Rd., Ste. 510, Boca Raton, FL 33431 US	

GROWTH PLANS/SPECIAL FEATURES:

Metropolitan Health Networks, Inc. (MHN) provides and arranges for medical care for approximately 34,800 Medicare Advantage patients in 16 counties in Florida. The company's services are offered through its provider service network (PSN), operated through wholly-owned subsidiary Metcare of Florida, Inc. Medicare covers the costs of hospitalization, medical care and other related health services for U.S. citizens that are 65 years or older, qualified disabled persons and persons suffering from end-staged renal disease. In addition to its primary care practices, the PSN holds network contracts with Humana, Inc. and independent primary care physician practices. The PSN currently holds three agreements with Humana, in which it provides healthcare services to Medicare beneficiaries in certain Florida counties who have elected to receive benefits under a Humana Medicare Advantage HMO Plan. In 2010, the PSN provided healthcare benefits to approximately 34,800 Medicare Advantage beneficiaries. The PSN also owns and operates 13 primary care centers and an oncology practice. These centers provide and arrange for medical care to about 31% of the PSN's customers.

Employees are offered medical, dental and vision insurance; short- and long-term disability coverage; life insurance; a 401(k) plan; education assistance; credit union membership; and Costco membership.

FINANCIALS: **Sales and profits are in thousands of dollars—add 000 to get the full amount. 2011 Note: Financial information for 2011 was not available for all companies at press time.**

2011 Sales: $	2011 Profits: $	**U.S. Stock Ticker: MDF**
2010 Sales: $368,186	2010 Profits: $25,700	**Int'l Ticker:**
2009 Sales: $354,407	2009 Profits: $14,449	Int'l Exchange:
2008 Sales: $317,212	2008 Profits: $10,204	Employees: 226 Fiscal Year Ends: 12/31
2007 Sales: $277,577	2007 Profits: $5,914	Parent Company:

SALARIES/BENEFITS:

Pension Plan:	ESOP Stock Plan:	Profit Sharing:	Top Exec. Salary: $386,250	Bonus: $675,938
Savings Plan: Y	Stock Purch. Plan:		Second Exec. Salary: $346,080	Bonus: $432,600

OTHER THOUGHTS:

Apparent Women Officers or Directors: 5
Hot Spot for Advancement for Women/Minorities: Y

LOCATIONS: ("Y" = Yes)

West:	Southwest:	Midwest:	Southeast:	Northeast:	International:
			Y		

MICHELINAS INC

www.michelinas.com

Industry Group Code: 31141

Management:		Sales/Marketing:		Liberal Arts:		Information Systems:		Professionals:		Technical/Scientific:	
Mgmt. Trainees:		Mktg. Professionals:	Y	Gen. Writing/Editing:	Y	Info. Management:	Y	Finance/Acct.:	Y	Engineers, Elec.:	
Experienced Mgmt.:	Y	Retail Sales:		Technical Writing:		Software Dev.:		Law:	Y	Engineers, Other:	Y
Int'l Business:	Y	Commercial/Industrial:	Y	Graphic Arts/Photog.:		Hardware Dev.:		HR/Other:	Y	Health/Lab	
MBA Graduates:	Y	Sales Trainees:	Y	Music:		Consulting/Other:		Training:	Y	Scientists/Research:	
		Advertising Pros.:	Y	Broadcasting:				Health Care:		Petroleum/Chemicals:	
				Other:				Consulting:		Math/Other:	

TYPES OF BUSINESS:

Frozen Foods

BRANDS/DIVISIONS/AFFILIATES:

Michelina's Lean Gourmet
Michelina's Authentico
Michelina's Budget Gourmet
Anytime Snackers
Michelina's Traditional Recipes

CONTACTS: *Note: Officers with more than one job title may be intentionally listed here more than once.*

Joel Conner, CEO
Joel Conner, Pres.
Danette Bucsko, CFO
Charlie Pountney, Sr. Exec. VP-Mktg. & Sales
Jeff Wilson, Sr. VP-Oper.
Jeff Tuttle, Sr. VP-Mktg.
Joel Conner, Chmn.

Phone: 218-723-5555 **Fax:** 218-624-7019
Toll-Free: 800-521-1281
Address: 525 S. Lake Ave., Duluth, MN 55802 US

GROWTH PLANS/SPECIAL FEATURES:

Michelina's, Inc. is a leading manufacturer of frozen entrees. The firm offers over 200 products under the Michelina's, Authentico, Michelina's Lean Gourmet, Michelina's Traditional Recipes, Anytime Snackers and Michelina's Budget Gourmet brands. The company's products include ready-to-microwave pasta, meat and sauce dishes, kids' entrees, Mexican dishes, Oriental dishes and frozen pizzas. Some examples include Signature Shrimp Alfredo, Authentico Sweet & Sour Chicken, Authentico Four Cheese Lasagna and Lean Gourmet Roasted Sirloin Supreme. Michelina's founder, Jeno Paulucci, also invented Jeno's Pizza Rolls (now owned by General Mills). Michelina's products are shipped from its Jackson, Ohio, production facility to the mass retail, wholesale club, supermarket, food service and drug store channels. The company's products are distributed all over the U.S., as well as internationally. Michelina's is part of Bellisio Foods, Inc., another frozen entree manufacturer founded by Jeno Paulucci.

FINANCIALS: **Sales and profits are in thousands of dollars—add 000 to get the full amount. 2011 Note: Financial information for 2011 was not available for all companies at press time.**

2011 Sales: $ 2011 Profits: $
2010 Sales: $ 2010 Profits: $
2009 Sales: $ 2009 Profits: $
2008 Sales: $ 2008 Profits: $
2007 Sales: $ 2007 Profits: $

U.S. Stock Ticker: Subsidiary
Int'l Ticker:
Int'l Exchange:
Employees: Fiscal Year Ends: 12/31
Parent Company: BELLISIO FOODS INC

SALARIES/BENEFITS:

Pension Plan: ESOP Stock Plan: Profit Sharing: Top Exec. Salary: $ Bonus: $
Savings Plan: Stock Purch. Plan: Second Exec. Salary: $ Bonus: $

OTHER THOUGHTS:

Apparent Women Officers or Directors: 1
Hot Spot for Advancement for Women/Minorities:

LOCATIONS: ("Y" = Yes)

West:	Southwest:	Midwest:	Southeast:	Northeast:	International:
		Y		Y	Y

MICROTEK MEDICAL HOLDINGS INC

www.microtekmed.com

Industry Group Code: 33911

Management:		Sales/Marketing:		Liberal Arts:		Information Systems:		Professionals:		Technical/Scientific:	
Mgmt. Trainees:		Mktg. Professionals:	Y	Gen. Writing/Editing:		Info. Management:	Y	Finance/Acct.:	Y	Engineers, Elec.:	
Experienced Mgmt.:	Y	Retail Sales:		Technical Writing:	Y	Software Dev.:		Law:	Y	Engineers, Other:	Y
Int'l Business:	Y	Commercial/Industrial:	Y	Graphic Arts/Photog.:		Hardware Dev.:		HR/Other:	Y	Health/Lab	Y
MBA Graduates:	Y	Sales Trainees:	Y	Music:		Consulting/Other:		Training:	Y	Scientists/Research:	Y
		Advertising Pros.:		Broadcasting:				Health Care:	Y	Petroleum/Chemicals:	
				Other:				Consulting:		Math/Other:	

TYPES OF BUSINESS:

Supplies-Assorted Health Care Products
Disposable Products
Biohazard Disposal Products
Safety & Protection Products
Fluid Management Products

BRANDS/DIVISIONS/AFFILIATES:

Microtek Medical, Inc.
CleanOp
Venodyne
OrthoPrep
ISOSORB
LTS-PLUS
Medi-Plast
Ecolab Inc

CONTACTS:

Note: Officers with more than one job title may be intentionally listed here more than once.

Dan R. Lee, CEO
Dan R. Lee, Pres.
Dan R. Lee, Chmn.

Phone: 662-327-1863 | **Fax:** 662-327-5921
Toll-Free: 800-936-9248
Address: 512 Lehmberg Rd., Columbus, MS 39704 US

GROWTH PLANS/SPECIAL FEATURES:

Microtek Medical Holdings, Inc. (MMHI), a wholly-owned subsidiary of Ecolab, Inc., is a leading manufacturer and marketer of infection control products, fluid control products and safety products to healthcare professionals. The firm has locations around the world, including facilities in Germany, France, the Dominican Republic, China, Mexico, Malta and the Netherlands. It conducts virtually all operations through Microtek Medical, Inc. (MMI), a subsidiary that develops, manufactures and sells infection control, fluid control and safety products to health care professionals for use in environments such as operating rooms and outpatient surgical centers. These consist primarily of disposable equipment drapes, specialty patient drapes, CleanOp cleaning kits, Venodyne pneumatic pumps, OrthoPrep orthopedic products, ISOSORB and LTS-PLUS medical waste solidifiers, decanters and wound evacuation products. MMI also offers the Medi-Plast line of fluid management products and ChillBuster portable patient warming system. MMHI, through its Innovative Services Division, engages in contract manufacturing, private labeling and tech support for specialty medical devices.

FINANCIALS:

Sales and profits are in thousands of dollars—add 000 to get the full amount. 2011 Note: Financial information for 2011 was not available for all companies at press time.

2011 Sales: $ | 2011 Profits: $
2010 Sales: $ | 2010 Profits: $
2009 Sales: $ | 2009 Profits: $
2008 Sales: $ | 2008 Profits: $
2007 Sales: $ | 2007 Profits: $

U.S. Stock Ticker: Subsidiary
Int'l Ticker:
Int'l Exchange:
Employees: Fiscal Year Ends: 12/31
Parent Company: ECOLAB INC

SALARIES/BENEFITS:

Pension Plan: ESOP Stock Plan: Profit Sharing: Top Exec. Salary: $ Bonus: $
Savings Plan: Stock Purch. Plan: Second Exec. Salary: $ Bonus: $

OTHER THOUGHTS:

Apparent Women Officers or Directors:
Hot Spot for Advancement for Women/Minorities:

LOCATIONS: ("Y" = Yes)

West:	Southwest:	Midwest:	Southeast:	Northeast:	International:
	Y		Y		Y

MID-AMERICA APARTMENT COMMUNITIES INC www.maac.net

Industry Group Code: 531110

Management:		Sales/Marketing:		Liberal Arts:		Information Systems:		Professionals:		Technical/Scientific:	
Mgmt. Trainees:	Y	Mktg. Professionals:	Y	Gen. Writing/Editing:	Y	Info. Management:	Y	Finance/Acct.:	Y	Engineers, Elec.:	
Experienced Mgmt.:	Y	Retail Sales:		Technical Writing:		Software Dev.:		Law:	Y	Engineers, Other:	
Int'l Business:		Commercial/Industrial:		Graphic Arts/Photog.:		Hardware Dev.:		HR/Other:	Y	Health/Lab	
MBA Graduates:	Y	Sales Trainees:		Music:		Consulting/Other:		Training:		Scientists/Research:	
		Advertising Pros.:	Y	Broadcasting:				Health Care:		Petroleum/Chemicals:	
				Other:				Consulting:		Math/Other:	

TYPES OF BUSINESS:

Real Estate Investment Trust
Apartment Communities

BRANDS/DIVISIONS/AFFILIATES:

Mid-America Apartments LP
MAC II of Delaware Inc
Mid-America Multifamily Fund I LLC
Mid-America Multifamily Fund II LLC

CONTACTS:

Note: Officers with more than one job title may be intentionally listed here more than once.

H. Eric Bolton, Jr., CEO
Albert M. Campbell, III, CFO/Exec. VP
Melintha Ogle, VP/Dir.-Mktg.
Melanie Carpenter, VP/Dir.-Human Resources
Shelton Barron, VP/Dir.-MIS
Leslie Wolfgang, Corp. Sec.
Thomas L. Grimes, Jr., Exec. VP/Dir.-Property Mgmt. Oper.
Ginny Doane, Sr. VP/Dir.-Dev. & Training
Leslie Wolfgang, Dir.-Investor Rel.
Rick Barton, Controller/Sr. VP
James Maclin, Sr. VP/Dir.-Corp. Support
Kevin P. Perkins, Sr. VP/Dir.-Physical Assets
Andrew Schaeffer, VP/Treas.
Doug Clark, VP/Dir.-Risk Mgmt.
H. Eric Bolton, Jr., Chmn.

Phone: 901-682-6600 **Fax:** 901-682-6667
Toll-Free:
Address: 6584 Poplar Ave., Memphis, TN 38138 US

GROWTH PLANS/SPECIAL FEATURES:

Mid-America Apartment Communities, Inc. (MAAC) is a self-administered and self-managed real estate investment trust (REIT) that acquires, owns and operates apartment communities in the south-east and south-central U.S. The firm manages approximately 49,175 apartment homes in 159 communities, conducting business primarily through its subsidiary and sole general partner, Mid-America Apartments LP. MAAC also has a wholly-owned REIT subsidiary, MAC II of Delaware, Inc., as well as a 33.33% equity stake in Mid-America Multifamily Fund I LLC and Mid-America Multifamily Fund II LLC, which own six properties with a total of 1,961 units. The firm's current investment focus involves acquiring relatively new properties (7-15 years old) within its present geographic area with the potential for above-average growth. MAAC also provides on-site property management, through which the firm handles matters concerning rent, occupancy limits and regulations. MAAC maintains an 18 month management training program for property managers, and a large majority of its property managers are Certified Apartment Managers, a designation established by the National Apartment Association. MAAC maintains each property's physical condition through regular landscaping and exterior improvements. In 2011, the firm acquired nine communities (2,425 units) located in Texas, Virginia, Florida, Georgia and Alabama.

MAAC offers its employees life, disability, medical and dental insurance; a 401(k); a stock ownership plan; bonuses; apartment discounts; scholarships; and an employee assistance program. In addition, as employees stay with the firm over time, benefit packages are enhanced with higher bonuses, higher company contribution to retirement savings plans, decreased healthcare costs and additional vacation and leave time.

FINANCIALS:

Sales and profits are in thousands of dollars—add 000 to get the full amount. 2011 Note: Financial information for 2011 was not available for all companies at press time.

2011 Sales: $448,992	2011 Profits: $48,821	**U.S. Stock Ticker: MAA**
2010 Sales: $401,549	2010 Profits: $29,761	**Int'l Ticker:**
2009 Sales: $378,251	2009 Profits: $37,211	Int'l Exchange:
2008 Sales: $370,011	2008 Profits: $30,249	Employees: 1,389 Fiscal Year Ends: 12/31
2007 Sales: $347,444	2007 Profits: $39,946	Parent Company:

SALARIES/BENEFITS:

Pension Plan:	ESOP Stock Plan: Y	Profit Sharing:	Top Exec. Salary: $429,801	Bonus: $705,953
Savings Plan: Y	Stock Purch. Plan:		Second Exec. Salary: $206,416	Bonus: $156,570

OTHER THOUGHTS:

Apparent Women Officers or Directors: 8
Hot Spot for Advancement for Women/Minorities: Y

LOCATIONS: ("Y" = Yes)

West:	Southwest:	Midwest:	Southeast:	Northeast:	International:
	Y	Y	Y	Y	

MIDAS INC

Industry Group Code: 8111

www.midasinc.com

Management:		Sales/Marketing:		Liberal Arts:		Information Systems:		Professionals:		Technical/Scientific:	
Mgmt. Trainees:	Y	Mktg. Professionals:	Y	Gen. Writing/Editing:	Y	Info. Management:	Y	Finance/Acct.:	Y	Engineers, Elec.:	
Experienced Mgmt.:	Y	Retail Sales:		Technical Writing:	Y	Software Dev.:	Y	Law:	Y	Engineers, Other:	
Int'l Business:	Y	Commercial/Industrial:		Graphic Arts/Photog.:		Hardware Dev.:		HR/Other:	Y	Health/Lab	
MBA Graduates:	Y	Sales Trainees:		Music:		Consulting/Other:		Training:	Y	Scientists/Research:	
		Advertising Pros.:	Y	Broadcasting:				Health Care:		Petroleum/Chemicals:	
				Other:				Consulting:		Math/Other:	

TYPES OF BUSINESS:

Automotive Repair & Maintenance
Real Estate Operations

BRANDS/DIVISIONS/AFFILIATES:

Midas International Corporation
Midas
SpeeDee

CONTACTS:

Note: Officers with more than one job title may be intentionally listed here more than once.

Alan D. Feldman, CEO
Alan D. Feldman, Pres.
William M. Guzik, CFO/Exec. VP
Rick Dow, Chief Mktg. Officer/Sr. VP
Ben Parma, VP-Human Resources
Alvin K. Marr, General Counsel/Sr. VP/Corp. Sec.
Mike Gould, Sr. VP-Retail Oper.
John A. Warzecha, Sr. VP-Franchise Bus. Dev.
James M. Haeger, Controller/VP
Alan D. Feldman, Chmn.

Phone: 630-438-3000 **Fax:** 630-438-3880
Toll-Free: 800-621-8545
Address: 1300 Arlington Heights Rd., Itasca, IL 60143 US

GROWTH PLANS/SPECIAL FEATURES:

Midas, Inc. provides auto repair and maintenance services in the U.S., Canada, Europe, Australia, the Middle East, Latin America and the Caribbean through company-operated and franchised shops. The firm operates under numerous subsidiaries including Midas International Corporation. Under the Midas brand, the company offers exhaust, brake, suspension, air conditioning and maintenance services. Midas farms out its wholesale parts distribution and quick-delivery operations through companies such as Uni-Select, Inc.; National Automotive Parts Association; and CarQuest Corporation. Subsidiary Midas Realty Corporation selects, leases and acquires sites and constructs facilities for company-operated and franchised shops throughout North America. It also enters into contingent operating lease agreements in order to ensure control of the real estate used by Midas shops. There are roughly 2,319 Midas shops in 14 countries around the world. North American operations account for approximately 1,538 of these shops, with company-owned shops accounting for nearly 98 locations and franchises for approximately 1,576 locations. The firm also operates the SpeeDee brand of oil change and tune-up shops; there are roughly 106 SpeeDee locations in 10 states and 65 in Mexico. Approximately 11% of Midas' retail business is generated by exhaust; 32% by brakes; 10% by suspension, shocks and struts; and 47% from new Midas categories, which include tires and related services, fleet maintenance services and general maintenance.

FINANCIALS:

Sales and profits are in thousands of dollars—add 000 to get the full amount. 2011 Note: Financial information for 2011 was not available for all companies at press time.

2011 Sales: $	2011 Profits: $
2010 Sales: $192,400	2010 Profits: $-13,400
2009 Sales: $182,800	2009 Profits: $2,600
2008 Sales: $187,400	2008 Profits: $7,800
2007 Sales: $178,200	2007 Profits: $13,000

U.S. Stock Ticker: MDS
Int'l Ticker:
Int'l Exchange:
Employees: 940 Fiscal Year Ends: 12/31
Parent Company:

SALARIES/BENEFITS:

Pension Plan:	ESOP Stock Plan:	Profit Sharing:	Top Exec. Salary: $725,000	Bonus: $157,637
Savings Plan:	Stock Purch. Plan:		Second Exec. Salary: $295,000	Bonus: $45,135

OTHER THOUGHTS:

Apparent Women Officers or Directors: 2
Hot Spot for Advancement for Women/Minorities:

LOCATIONS: ("Y" = Yes)

West:	Southwest:	Midwest:	Southeast:	Northeast:	International:
Y	Y	Y	Y	Y	Y

MILLENNIUM PHARMACEUTICALS INC

www.mlnm.com

Industry Group Code: 325412

Management:		**Sales/Marketing:**		**Liberal Arts:**		**Information Systems:**		**Professionals:**		**Technical/Scientific:**	
Mgmt. Trainees:		Mktg. Professionals:	Y	Gen. Writing/Editing:		Info. Management:	Y	Finance/Acct.:	Y	Engineers, Elec.:	
Experienced Mgmt.:	Y	Retail Sales:		Technical Writing:	Y	Software Dev.:	Y	Law:	Y	Engineers, Other:	
Int'l Business:	Y	Commercial/Industrial:	Y	Graphic Arts/Photog.:		Hardware Dev.:		HR/Other:	Y	Health/Lab	Y
MBA Graduates:	Y	Sales Trainees:	Y	Music:		Consulting/Other:		Training:	Y	Scientists/Research:	Y
		Advertising Pros.:		Broadcasting:				Health Care:	Y	Petroleum/Chemicals:	Y
				Other:				Consulting:		Math/Other:	Y

TYPES OF BUSINESS:

Pharmaceuticals Discovery & Development
Gene-Based Drug Discovery Platform
Small-Molecule Drugs

BRANDS/DIVISIONS/AFFILIATES:

Takeda Pharmaceutical Company Ltd
VELCADE

CONTACTS: *Note: Officers with more than one job title may be intentionally listed here more than once.*

Deborah Dunsire, CEO
Deborah Dunsire, Pres.
Todd Shegog, CFO
Stephen M. Gansler, Sr. VP-Human Resources
Joseph B. Bolen, Chief Scientific Officer
Laurie B. Keating, General Counsel/Sr. VP
Anna Protopapas, Sr. VP-Corp. Dev.
Lisa Adler, VP-Corp. Comm.
Todd Shegog, Sr. VP-Finance/Treas.
Christophe Bianchi, Exec. VP
Peter F. Smith, Sr. VP-Non-Clinical Dev. Sciences
Nancy Simonian, Chief Medical Officer

Phone: 617-679-7000 **Fax:** 617-374-7788
Toll-Free: 800-390-5663
Address: 40 Landsdowne St., Cambridge, MA 02139 US

GROWTH PLANS/SPECIAL FEATURES:

Millennium Pharmaceuticals, Inc., a subsidiary of Takeda Pharmaceuticals Company, Ltd., researches and manufactures therapeutic products for the treatment of patients with cancer and inflammatory diseases. The company's development platform focuses on combing knowledge of genomics and protein homeostasis, a set of particular molecular pathways that affect the establishment and progression of diseases, in order to produce drug candidates. The firm currently has one marketed product called VELCADE. VELCADE is an oncology drug that is injected into patients for the treatment of multiple myeloma, a cancer of the blood, and mantle cell lymphoma. VELCADE is also being tested in Phase II and III trials for the treatment of follicular B-cell non-Hodgkin's lymphoma, hematologic malignancies and solid tumors including lung, breast, prostate and ovarian cancers.

Millennium offers employees medical, dental and vision coverage; a 401(k); flexible spending accounts; life and disability insurance; and education and transportation assistance.

FINANCIALS: **Sales and profits are in thousands of dollars—add 000 to get the full amount. 2011 Note: Financial information for 2011 was not available for all companies at press time.**

2011 Sales: $ — 2011 Profits: $
2010 Sales: $ — 2010 Profits: $
2009 Sales: $ — 2009 Profits: $
2008 Sales: $ — 2008 Profits: $
2007 Sales: $ — 2007 Profits: $

U.S. Stock Ticker: Subsidiary
Int'l Ticker:
Int'l Exchange:
Employees: Fiscal Year Ends: 12/31
Parent Company: TAKEDA PHARMACEUTICAL COMPANY LTD

SALARIES/BENEFITS:

Pension Plan: — ESOP Stock Plan: — Profit Sharing: — Top Exec. Salary: $ — Bonus: $
Savings Plan: Y — Stock Purch. Plan: Y — Second Exec. Salary: $ — Bonus: $

OTHER THOUGHTS:

Apparent Women Officers or Directors: 4
Hot Spot for Advancement for Women/Minorities: Y

LOCATIONS: ("Y" = Yes)

West:	Southwest:	Midwest:	Southeast:	Northeast:	International:
				Y	

MINDSPEED TECHNOLOGIES INC

www.mindspeed.com

Industry Group Code: 33441

Management:		Sales/Marketing:		Liberal Arts:		Information Systems:		Professionals:		Technical/Scientific:	
Mgmt. Trainees:		Mktg. Professionals:	Y	Gen. Writing/Editing:		Info. Management:	Y	Finance/Acct.:	Y	Engineers, Elec.:	Y
Experienced Mgmt.:	Y	Retail Sales:		Technical Writing:	Y	Software Dev.:	Y	Law:	Y	Engineers, Other:	Y
Int'l Business:	Y	Commercial/Industrial:	Y	Graphic Arts/Photog.:		Hardware Dev.:	Y	HR/Other:	Y	Health/Lab	
MBA Graduates:	Y	Sales Trainees:		Music:		Consulting/Other:		Training:		Scientists/Research:	
		Advertising Pros.:		Broadcasting:				Health Care:		Petroleum/Chemicals:	
				Other:				Consulting:		Math/Other:	Y

TYPES OF BUSINESS:

Semiconductors-Communications
Networking Products
Software
Routers & Switches
VoIP Equipment

BRANDS/DIVISIONS/AFFILIATES:

Comcerto
Conexant Systems Inc
Picochip Limited

CONTACTS: *Note: Officers with more than one job title may be intentionally listed here more than once.*

Raouf Y. Halim, CEO
Stephen N. Ananias, CFO/Sr. VP
Gerald J. Hamilton, Sr. VP-Worldwide Sales
Allison K. Garcia, Sr. VP-Human Resources
Brandi Steege, General Counsel/VP
Najabat H. (Hasnain) Bajwa, Sr. VP/Gen. Mgr.-High Performance Analog
Thomas J. Medrek, Sr. VP/Gen. Mgr.-Comm. Convergence Processing
Abdelnaser (Naser) M. Adas, VP/Gen. Mgr.-CPE & Wireless
Dwight W. Decker, Chmn.

Phone: 949-579-3000	**Fax:**
Toll-Free:	
Address: 4000 MacArthur Blvd., E. Tower, Newport Beach, CA 92660 US	

GROWTH PLANS/SPECIAL FEATURES:

Mindspeed Technologies, Inc., a spin-off of Conexant Systems, Inc., designs, develops and sells semiconductor networking products for communications applications in enterprise, access, metropolitan and wide area networks. The firm offers three product families: Communications Convergence Processing (CCP), High-Performance Analog (HPA) and wide area networking (WAN) communications. CCP products include low-power multi-core digital signal processor (DSP) system-on-a-chip (SoC) products for carrier-class triple-play edge gateways, metro trunking gateways and other VoIP platforms. The Comcerto family of packet processors includes a full range of software-compatible solutions that enable original equipment manufacturers (OEMs) to provide scalable systems with customized features for carrier, enterprise and customer premise applications. HPA products include transmission devices and switching products. Transmission devices include laser drivers, transimpedance amplifiers, post amplifiers, clock and data recovery circuits and line equalizers. Switching products include a family of high-speed crosspoint switches, as well as crosspoint switches optimized for standard and high-definition broadcast video routing and production switching applications. WAN communications products include T1/E1, T3/E3 and SONET carrier devices; high-performance ATM/MPLS network processors, which are designed to offer advanced protocol translation and traffic management capabilities; and Ethernet products such as Ethernet media access controllers and oversubscription aggregators. The company sells its products to OEMs for use in a variety of network infrastructure equipment designed to process, transmit and switch voice, data and video traffic between and within the different segments of the communications network. Its network infrastructure equipment includes voice and media gateways, high-speed routers, switches, access multiplexers, cross-connect systems and add-drop multiplexers, digital loop carrier equipment and Internet protocol private branch exchanges. In January 2012, the firm acquired U.K.-based Picochip Limited.

Employees are offered health and life insurance; disability coverage; flexible spending accounts; adoption assistance; educational assistance; and an employee assistance program.

FINANCIALS: **Sales and profits are in thousands of dollars—add 000 to get the full amount. 2011 Note: Financial information for 2011 was not available for all companies at press time.**

2011 Sales: $162,089	2011 Profits: $-755	**U.S. Stock Ticker: MSPD**
2010 Sales: $178,179	2010 Profits: $21,070	**Int'l Ticker:**
2009 Sales: $126,552	2009 Profits: $-25,114	Int'l Exchange:
2008 Sales: $160,699	2008 Profits: $4,285	Employees: 541 Fiscal Year Ends: 9/30
2007 Sales: $127,805	2007 Profits: $-21,914	Parent Company:

SALARIES/BENEFITS:

Pension Plan:	ESOP Stock Plan:	Profit Sharing:	Top Exec. Salary: $559,375	Bonus: $500,000
Savings Plan: Y	Stock Purch. Plan: Y		Second Exec. Salary: $352,755	Bonus: $25,000

OTHER THOUGHTS:

Apparent Women Officers or Directors: 2
Hot Spot for Advancement for Women/Minorities: Y

LOCATIONS: ("Y" = Yes)

West:	Southwest:	Midwest:	Southeast:	Northeast:	International:
Y					Y

MOELIS & COMPANY

www.moelis.com

Industry Group Code: 523110

Management:		Sales/Marketing:		Liberal Arts:		Information Systems:		Professionals:		Technical/Scientific:	
Mgmt. Trainees:		Mktg. Professionals:		Gen. Writing/Editing:	Y	Info. Management:	Y	Finance/Acct.:	Y	Engineers, Elec.:	
Experienced Mgmt.:	Y	Retail Sales:		Technical Writing:		Software Dev.:	Y	Law:	Y	Engineers, Other:	
Int'l Business:	Y	Commercial/Industrial:		Graphic Arts/Photog.:		Hardware Dev.:		HR/Other:	Y	Health/Lab	
MBA Graduates:	Y	Sales Trainees:		Music:		Consulting/Other:		Training:	Y	Scientists/Research:	
		Advertising Pros.:		Broadcasting:				Health Care:		Petroleum/Chemicals:	
				Other:				Consulting:		Math/Other:	

TYPES OF BUSINESS:

Investment Banking
Private Equity
Investment Advisory Services

BRANDS/DIVISIONS/AFFILIATES:

Moelis Capital Partners
Flightstar Aircraft Services
Asia Pacific Advisers
Gracie Asset Management

CONTACTS: *Note: Officers with more than one job title may be intentionally listed here more than once.*

Kenneth D. Moelis, CEO
Elizabeth Crain, COO
Peter Vogelsang, General Counsel/Chief Compliance Officer
Andrea Hurst, Head-Media Rel.
Kate Pilcher, Head-Investor Rel.
Michele Miyakawa, Managing Dir.
John Momtazee, Managing Dir.
Charles Noel-Johnson, Managing Dir.
Richard Orders, Managing Dir.
Mark Aedy, Head-Investment Banking, EMEA/Managing Dir.

Phone: 212-883-3800 **Fax:** 212-880-4260
Toll-Free:
Address: 399 Park Ave., 5th Fl., New York, NY 10022 US

GROWTH PLANS/SPECIAL FEATURES:

Moelis & Company is an investment bank that offers advisory and investment fund management services. With offices in New York, Hong Kong, Dubai, Boston, Chicago, Beijing, Los Angeles, Sydney and London, the firm operates in two business divisions: advisory and Moelis Capital Partners. The advisory segment focuses on providing strategic and financial alternatives involving buy-side and sell-side mergers and acquisitions; accessing potential buyers; negotiating transactions relating to exclusive sales; and offering advice on capital raising and restructuring (particularly on transactions, structuring, pricing, timing, and financing). Select transactions within this division include Hilton Hotels Corporation, Anheuser Busch, WCI Steel and Evergreen International Aviation, Inc. Moelis Capital Partners is a middle market private equity company that manages more than $700 million of committed private equity capital and a $1.2 billion private equity co-investment program. Moelis Capital Partners usually invests between $25 and $100 million in select middle market firms. Its investment portfolio includes RecoverCare, LLC; Ryerson, Inc.; Opportunity Bank, N.A.; MidCap Financial, LLC; Women's Integrated Network, Inc.; Wyle, Inc.; and Kinsale Insurance. Subsidiary Gracie Asset Management, acquired in 2010, manages a family of multi-strategy credit hedge funds with over $2 billion in assets under management. In April 2011, the firm acquired Chinese financial advisory firm Asia Pacific Advisers. In December 2011, Moelis Capital Partners acquired Flightstar Aircraft Services. Also in 2011, Moelis & Company opened new offices in Dubai and Beijing.

FINANCIALS: **Sales and profits are in thousands of dollars—add 000 to get the full amount. 2011 Note: Financial information for 2011 was not available for all companies at press time.**

2011 Sales: $ 2011 Profits: $
2010 Sales: $ 2010 Profits: $
2009 Sales: $ 2009 Profits: $
2008 Sales: $ 2008 Profits: $
2007 Sales: $ 2007 Profits: $

U.S. Stock Ticker: Private
Int'l Ticker:
Int'l Exchange:
Employees: Fiscal Year Ends:
Parent Company:

SALARIES/BENEFITS:

Pension Plan: ESOP Stock Plan: Profit Sharing: Top Exec. Salary: $ Bonus: $
Savings Plan: Stock Purch. Plan: Second Exec. Salary: $ Bonus: $

OTHER THOUGHTS:

Apparent Women Officers or Directors: 12
Hot Spot for Advancement for Women/Minorities: Y

LOCATIONS: ("Y" = Yes)

West:	Southwest:	Midwest:	Southeast:	Northeast:	International:
Y		Y		Y	Y

MONSTER BEVERAGE CORP

monsterbevcorp.com

Industry Group Code: 3121

Management:		Sales/Marketing:		Liberal Arts:		Information Systems:		Professionals:		Technical/Scientific:	
Mgmt. Trainees:	Y	Mktg. Professionals:	Y	Gen. Writing/Editing:	Y	Info. Management:	Y	Finance/Acct.:	Y	Engineers, Elec.:	
Experienced Mgmt.:	Y	Retail Sales:		Technical Writing:		Software Dev.:		Law:	Y	Engineers, Other:	
Int'l Business:	Y	Commercial/Industrial:	Y	Graphic Arts/Photog.:	Y	Hardware Dev.:		HR/Other:	Y	Health/Lab	
MBA Graduates:	Y	Sales Trainees:	Y	Music:		Consulting/Other:		Training:	Y	Scientists/Research:	
		Advertising Pros.:	Y	Broadcasting:				Health Care:		Petroleum/Chemicals:	
				Other:				Consulting:		Math/Other:	

TYPES OF BUSINESS:

Beverages-Natural Sodas
Energy Drinks
Fruit Juice

BRANDS/DIVISIONS/AFFILIATES:

Hansen's
Hansen Natural Corp
Blue Sky
Monster Energy
Primal Energy
Fizzit
Junior Juice
Rumba

CONTACTS: *Note: Officers with more than one job title may be intentionally listed here more than once.*

Rodney C. Sacks, CEO
Hilton H. Schlosberg, COO/Vice Chmn.
Hilton H. Schlosberg, Pres.
Hilton H. Schlosberg, CFO
Hilton H. Schlosberg, Corp. Sec.
Thomas J. Kelly, VP-Finance/Controller
Mark Hall, Pres., Monster Beverage Div.
Rodney C. Sacks, Chmn.

Phone: 951-739-6200 **Fax:** 951-739-6210
Toll-Free: 800-426-7367
Address: 550 Monica Cir., Ste. 201, Corona, CA 92880 US

GROWTH PLANS/SPECIAL FEATURES:

Monster Beverage Corp., formerly Hansen Natural Corp., markets and distributes a range of energy drinks and alternative beverages. Its products include natural sodas, fruit juices, juice drinks, energy drinks, dairy based coffee drinks, fruit juice smoothies, functional drinks, iced teas, juice cocktails, children's multi-vitamin juice drinks, lightly flavored sparkling waters and powdered drink mixes. The company maintains several brands, including Hansen's Natural Sodas; Junior Juice; Monster Energy; Blue Sky; Fizzit; Hansen's Energy Pro; Primal Energy Tea; Hansen's Energy Diet Red; Hansen's Juice Slam Organic; Hansen's Organic Junior Water; and Rumba. The firm outsources its manufacturing needs to third party bottlers and contract packers, whom Monster Beverage supplies with juices, flavors, vitamins, minerals, nutrients, herbs, supplements, caps, labels, trays and ingredients. Distribution levels vary from state to state and a limited range of products are marketed abroad. Domestic customers are usually retail and specialty chains, club stores, mass merchandisers, convenience chains, food service and full service beverage distributors and health food distributors. Major customers include Costco, Trader Joe's, Sam's Club, Wal-Mart, The Kroger Co. and Safeway. In January 2012, the company changed its name from Hansen Natural Corp. to Monster Beverage Corp.

The company offers employees medical and dental insurance; life insurance; disability coverage; and a 401(k) plan.

FINANCIALS: **Sales and profits are in thousands of dollars—add 000 to get the full amount. 2011 Note: Financial information for 2011 was not available for all companies at press time.**

2011 Sales: $1,430,000 | 2011 Profits: $190,800
2010 Sales: $1,303,942 | 2010 Profits: $212,029
2009 Sales: $1,143,299 | 2009 Profits: $208,716
2008 Sales: $1,033,780 | 2008 Profits: $108,032
2007 Sales: $904,465 | 2007 Profits: $149,406

U.S. Stock Ticker: MNST
Int'l Ticker:
Int'l Exchange:
Employees: 1,497 Fiscal Year Ends: 12/31
Parent Company:

SALARIES/BENEFITS:

Pension Plan: | ESOP Stock Plan: | Profit Sharing: | Top Exec. Salary: $410,192 | Bonus: $225,000
Savings Plan: Y | Stock Purch. Plan: | | Second Exec. Salary: $410,192 | Bonus: $225,000

OTHER THOUGHTS:

Apparent Women Officers or Directors:
Hot Spot for Advancement for Women/Minorities:

LOCATIONS: ("Y" = Yes)

West:	Southwest:	Midwest:	Southeast:	Northeast:	International:
Y					Y

MOTORCAR PARTS OF AMERICA INC

www.motorcarparts.com

Industry Group Code: 3363

Management:		Sales/Marketing:		Liberal Arts:		Information Systems:		Professionals:		Technical/Scientific:	
Mgmt. Trainees:		Mktg. Professionals:	Y	Gen. Writing/Editing:		Info. Management:	Y	Finance/Acct.:	Y	Engineers, Elec.:	Y
Experienced Mgmt.:	Y	Retail Sales:		Technical Writing:	Y	Software Dev.:		Law:	Y	Engineers, Other:	Y
Int'l Business:	Y	Commercial/Industrial:	Y	Graphic Arts/Photog.:		Hardware Dev.:		HR/Other:	Y	Health/Lab	
MBA Graduates:	Y	Sales Trainees:	Y	Music:		Consulting/Other:		Training:	Y	Scientists/Research:	
		Advertising Pros.:		Broadcasting:				Health Care:		Petroleum/Chemicals:	
				Other:				Consulting:		Math/Other:	

TYPES OF BUSINESS:

Replacement Alternators & Starters

BRANDS/DIVISIONS/AFFILIATES:

Quality-Built
Talon
Xtreme
Reliance

CONTACTS: *Note: Officers with more than one job title may be intentionally listed here more than once.*

Selwyn Joffe, CEO
Steve Kratz, COO
Selwyn Joffe, Pres.
David Lee, CFO
Rick Mochulsky, VP-Sales
Michael Umansky, General Counsel/VP/Corp. Sec.
Tom Stricker, VP-Bus. Dev.
Kevin Daly, Chief Acct. Officer
Ron Lacombe, VP-Traditional Sales
Selwyn Joffe, Chmn.

Phone: 310-212-7910 **Fax:** 310-212-6315
Toll-Free: 800-890-9988
Address: 2929 California St., Torrance, CA 90503 US

GROWTH PLANS/SPECIAL FEATURES:

Motorcar Parts of America, Inc. (MPA) remanufactures and distributes replacement alternators and starters for import and domestic cars and light trucks. MPA's product line features over 1,600 alternator models and more than 900 starter models; the company also manufactures starter ignition wire sets. The firm's products are sold throughout the U.S. to more than 7,700 automotive parts stores, including some of the largest chains of retail automotive stores such as AutoZone, Pep Boys, CSK Automotive and O'Reilly Automotive. MPA also gears its marketing and sales efforts toward traditional warehouse distributors and supplies remanufactured alternators and starters to General Motors. Approximately 89% of the firm's products are sold for resale under customer private labels, with the remaining 11% sold under brand names such as Quality-Built, Reliance, Talon, and Xtreme. The company has remanufacturing, warehousing and shipping operations in Oregon, Tennessee, North Carolina and New Jersey; a logistics facility in Singapore; an alternator manufacturing facility in Malaysia; and a manufacturing facility in Mexico.

FINANCIALS: **Sales and profits are in thousands of dollars—add 000 to get the full amount. 2011 Note: Financial information for 2011 was not available for all companies at press time.**

2011 Sales: $161,285 | 2011 Profits: $12,220
2010 Sales: $142,250 | 2010 Profits: $9,646
2009 Sales: $134,866 | 2009 Profits: $3,857
2008 Sales: $133,337 | 2008 Profits: $4,607
2007 Sales: $136,323 | 2007 Profits: $-2,475

U.S. Stock Ticker: MPAA
Int'l Ticker:
Int'l Exchange:
Employees: 243 Fiscal Year Ends: 3/31
Parent Company:

SALARIES/BENEFITS:

Pension Plan: ESOP Stock Plan: Profit Sharing: Top Exec. Salary: $500,000 Bonus: $500,100
Savings Plan: Stock Purch. Plan: Second Exec. Salary: $406,000 Bonus: $40,100

OTHER THOUGHTS:

Apparent Women Officers or Directors:
Hot Spot for Advancement for Women/Minorities:

LOCATIONS: ("Y" = Yes)

West:	Southwest:	Midwest:	Southeast:	Northeast:	International:
Y				Y	Y

MTR GAMING GROUP INC

Industry Group Code: 713210

www.mtrgaming.com

Management:		Sales/Marketing:		Liberal Arts:		Information Systems:		Professionals:		Technical/Scientific:	
Mgmt. Trainees:		Mktg. Professionals:	Y	Gen. Writing/Editing:	Y	Info. Management:	Y	Finance/Acct.:	Y	Engineers, Elec.:	
Experienced Mgmt.:	Y	Retail Sales:		Technical Writing:		Software Dev.:		Law:	Y	Engineers, Other:	
Int'l Business:		Commercial/Industrial:		Graphic Arts/Photog.:	Y	Hardware Dev.:		HR/Other:	Y	Health/Lab	
MBA Graduates:	Y	Sales Trainees:		Music:		Consulting/Other:		Training:		Scientists/Research:	
		Advertising Pros.:	Y	Broadcasting:				Health Care:		Petroleum/Chemicals:	
				Other:				Consulting:		Math/Other:	

TYPES OF BUSINESS:

Gaming Facilities
Horse Racing Venues
Casinos
Hotels

BRANDS/DIVISIONS/AFFILIATES:

Mountaineer Casino, Racetrack & Resort (The)
Scotio Downs
Presque Isle Downs & Casino

CONTACTS:

Note: Officers with more than one job title may be intentionally listed here more than once.

Jeffrey J. Dahl, CEO
Jeffrey J. Dahl, Pres.
John W. Bittner, Jr., CFO/Exec. VP
Narciso A. Rodriguez-Cayro, General Counsel/Sec.
Joseph L. Billhimer, Jr., Sr. VP-Oper.
Joseph L. Billhimer, Jr., Sr. VP-Bus. Dev.
Narciso A. Rodriguez-Cayro, VP-Regulatory Affairs
Steven M. Billick, Chmn.

Phone: 304-387-8000 **Fax:** 304-387-2167
Toll-Free: 800-804-0468
Address: State Rte. 2 S., P.O. Box 356, Chester, WV 26034 US

GROWTH PLANS/SPECIAL FEATURES:

MTR Gaming Group, Inc. owns and operates several gaming facilities through its wholly-owned subsidiaries. Its flagship property, The Mountaineer Casino, Racetrack & Resort in Chester, West Virginia, encompasses 122,000 square feet of gaming space that houses 2,500 slot machines, 48 table games and 24 poker tables. It also hosts a thoroughbred racetrack; 357 hotel rooms; a spa; a 12,000 square foot fitness center; a 69,000 square foot theater and events center; dining and entertainment; a golf course; and a 13,500 square foot convention center. MTR also owns the Scioto Downs, a 208-acre harness horse racing facility in Columbus, Ohio; and operates the Presque Isle Downs & Casino in Erie, Pennsylvania. Presque Isle hosts a horse racing facility with a one-mile track, grandstand, barns and a paddock, as well as a 140,000 square foot clubhouse with 2,030 slot machines and 48 table games. MTR's revenues are generated primarily from gaming, which accounts for approximately 87.9% of its total revenue. Pari-mutuel commissions, the wagering system used for the horse-racing, account for 2.6%, while food, beverage and lodging provided 7.4% (other operations account for the remaining 2%).

Employees of the firm receive medical, dental, vision and prescription drug benefits; paid vacations and holidays; and life insurance.

FINANCIALS:

Sales and profits are in thousands of dollars—add 000 to get the full amount. 2011 Note: Financial information for 2011 was not available for all companies at press time.

2011 Sales: $	2011 Profits: $
2010 Sales: $434,697	2010 Profits: $-5,116
2009 Sales: $454,155	2009 Profits: $-22,538
2008 Sales: $478,772	2008 Profits: $-17,711
2007 Sales: $421,814	2007 Profits: $-11,359

U.S. Stock Ticker: MNTG
Int'l Ticker:
Int'l Exchange:
Employees: 2,500 Fiscal Year Ends: 12/31
Parent Company:

SALARIES/BENEFITS:

Pension Plan: Y | ESOP Stock Plan: | Profit Sharing: | Top Exec. Salary: $460,063 | Bonus: $
Savings Plan: | Stock Purch. Plan: | Second Exec. Salary: $331,154 | Bonus: $

OTHER THOUGHTS:

Apparent Women Officers or Directors:
Hot Spot for Advancement for Women/Minorities:

LOCATIONS: ("Y" = Yes)

West:	Southwest:	Midwest:	Southeast:	Northeast:	International:
		Y		Y	

MYRIAD GENETICS INC

www.myriad.com

Industry Group Code: 325412

Management:		Sales/Marketing:		Liberal Arts:		Information Systems:		Professionals:		Technical/Scientific:	
Mgmt. Trainees:		Mktg. Professionals:	Y	Gen. Writing/Editing:		Info. Management:	Y	Finance/Acct.:	Y	Engineers, Elec.:	
Experienced Mgmt.:	Y	Retail Sales:		Technical Writing:	Y	Software Dev.:	Y	Law:	Y	Engineers, Other:	
Int'l Business:		Commercial/Industrial:	Y	Graphic Arts/Photog.:		Hardware Dev.:		HR/Other:	Y	Health/Lab	Y
MBA Graduates:	Y	Sales Trainees:	Y	Music:		Consulting/Other:		Training:	Y	Scientists/Research:	Y
		Advertising Pros.:		Broadcasting:				Health Care:	Y	Petroleum/Chemicals:	Y
				Other:				Consulting:		Math/Other:	Y

TYPES OF BUSINESS:

Pharmaceuticals Discovery & Development
Cancer Treatments
HIV Treatments
Cancer Diagnostics

BRANDS/DIVISIONS/AFFILIATES:

Myriad Pharmaceuticals, Inc.
TheraGuide 5-FU
Prezeon
BRACAnalysis
COLARIS
MELARIS
COLARIS AP
Melanoma Diagnostics, Inc.

CONTACTS: *Note: Officers with more than one job title may be intentionally listed here more than once.*

Peter D. Meldrum, CEO
Peter D. Meldrum, Pres.
James S. Evans, CFO
Jayne B.Hart, Exec. VP-Human Resources
Jerry Lanchbury, Chief Scientific Officer
Robert G. Harrison, CIO
Richard Marsh, General Counsel/Exec. VP/Corp. Sec.
William A. Hockett, III, Exec. VP-Corp. Comm.
Mark C. Capone, Pres., Myriad Genetic Laboratories, Inc.
John T. Henderson, Chmn.
Gary A. King, Exec. VP-Int'l Oper.

Phone: 801-584-3600	**Fax:** 801-584-3640
Toll-Free:	
Address: 320 Wakara Way, Salt Lake City, UT 84108 US	

GROWTH PLANS/SPECIAL FEATURES:

Myriad Genetics, Inc. is a biopharmaceutical company that develops and markets novel therapeutic and molecular diagnostic products. The company develops a number of proprietary technologies that are aimed at understanding the genetic basis of human disease in order to effectively treat them. Myriad's molecular diagnostic business is focused on both predictive and personalized medicine. Predictive medicine analyzes genes to assess an individual's potential risk of developing while personalized medicine works to assess a patient's risk in disease progression, recurrence and drug response. The company currently owns seven commercial predictive medicine products: BRACAnalysis for breast and ovarian cancer; COLARIS for colon and uterine cancer; COLARIS AP for polyp-forming syndromes of colon cancer; MELARIS for melanoma; TheraGuide 5-FU for determining the risk of toxic reaction to 5-FU chemotherapy; Prezeon for assessing PTEN function in cancer patients; and OnDose for optimizing 5-FU chemotherapy dosage. The company works with its wholly-owned subsidiary Myriad Pharmaceuticals, Inc. to develop novel small molecule drugs. The lead product pipeline includes Azixa for the treatment of melanoma, glioblastoma and anaplastic glioma; MPC-3100 for inhibiting Heat shock protein 90 (Hsp90) in cancer patients; MPC-9528 for the treatment of cancer; as well as other preclinical treatments for cancer and HIV. In December 2010, the firm acquired the early melanoma detection technology of Melanoma Diagnostics, Inc.

Myriad offers its employees medical, dental, life and AD&D insurance; an employee stock purchase plan; short- and long-term disability coverage; a 401(k) plan; and tax-free reimbursements.

FINANCIALS: Sales and profits are in thousands of dollars—add 000 to get the full amount. 2011 Note: Financial information for 2011 was not available for all companies at press time.

2011 Sales: $402,084	2011 Profits: $100,710	**U.S. Stock Ticker: MYGN**
2010 Sales: $362,648	2010 Profits: $152,303	**Int'l Ticker:**
2009 Sales: $326,527	2009 Profits: $84,615	Int'l Exchange:
2008 Sales: $222,855	2008 Profits: $47,845	Employees: 1,057 Fiscal Year Ends: 6/30
2007 Sales: $145,285	2007 Profits: $-34,962	Parent Company:

SALARIES/BENEFITS:

Pension Plan:	ESOP Stock Plan:	Profit Sharing:	Top Exec. Salary: $800,552	Bonus: $1,000,812
Savings Plan: Y	Stock Purch. Plan: Y		Second Exec. Salary: $551,465	Bonus: $415,812

OTHER THOUGHTS:

Apparent Women Officers or Directors: 2
Hot Spot for Advancement for Women/Minorities:

LOCATIONS: ("Y" = Yes)

West:	Southwest:	Midwest:	Southeast:	Northeast:	International:
Y					

NANOMETRICS INC

www.nanometrics.com

Industry Group Code: 3345

Management:		Sales/Marketing:		Liberal Arts:		Information Systems:		Professionals:		Technical/Scientific:	
Mgmt. Trainees:		Mktg. Professionals:	Y	Gen. Writing/Editing:		Info. Management:	Y	Finance/Acct.:	Y	Engineers, Elec.:	Y
Experienced Mgmt.:	Y	Retail Sales:		Technical Writing:	Y	Software Dev.:	Y	Law:	Y	Engineers, Other:	Y
Int'l Business:	Y	Commercial/Industrial:	Y	Graphic Arts/Photog.:		Hardware Dev.:	Y	HR/Other:	Y	Health/Lab	Y
MBA Graduates:	Y	Sales Trainees:	Y	Music:		Consulting/Other:		Training:	Y	Scientists/Research:	Y
		Advertising Pros.:		Broadcasting:				Health Care:		Petroleum/Chemicals:	
				Other:				Consulting:		Math/Other:	Y

TYPES OF BUSINESS:

Research & Development-Nanotechnology
Process Control Metrology Systems

BRANDS/DIVISIONS/AFFILIATES:

Atlas
Caliper
NanoSpec
NanoCD
NanoDiffract
NanoGen
VerteX
Nanda Technologies GmbH

CONTACTS: *Note: Officers with more than one job title may be intentionally listed here more than once.*

Timothy J. Stultz, CEO
Bruce A. Crawford, COO
Timothy J. Stultz, Pres.
Ronald W. Kisling, CFO
Nancy E. Egan, General Counsel
Bruce C. Rhine, Chmn.

Phone: 408-545-6000 | **Fax:** 408-232-5910
Toll-Free:
Address: 1550 Buckeye Dr., Milpitas, CA 95035 US

GROWTH PLANS/SPECIAL FEATURES:

Nanometrics, Inc. designs, manufactures and markets process control metrology systems used in the manufacture of silicon and compound semiconductor substrates, devices and integrated circuits. Metrology systems measure thin film properties, critical dimensions, overlay control and optical, electrical and material properties, including the structural composition of silicon and compound semiconductor devices, during the manufacturing process. The company's metrology systems fall into three categories: standalone, fully automated systems, which are used for high-volume manufacturing process control; integrated systems built into semiconductor processing equipment, which provide real-time measurements to improve process control and increase throughput; and materials characterization products that are used to monitor the physical, optical, electrical and material characteristics of HB-LED, compound semiconductor, strained silicon and silicon-on-insulator devices. Nanometrics offers products with such diverse applications as film analysis, Fourier transform infrared, inspection, mask metrology, overlay metrology and scatterometry. It also provides contamination/defect process control and carrier concentration applications. The firm's automated standalone systems products are sold under the Atlas, Caliper and NanoSpec brands. The NanoCD suite of products includes NanoDiffract, an optical CD (OCD) modeling and analysis software and NanoGen, a server-based library generation system. Integrated systems products include the 9000 series, which are ultra-compact measurement systems designed for integration into semiconductor processing equipment; the 9010b metrology platform, which incorporates both ultra violet OCD spectroscopic ellipsometry and deep ultra violet spectroscoptic reflectometry; and the IMPULSE series, which measures and profiles OCD, as well as employs a DUV channel for film thickness. The company also offers a line of manual and semi-automated thin film thickness, critical dimension, defect inspection and composition measurement systems under the VerteX and NanoSpec brands. Nanometrics has offices in the U.S., China, Japan, Taiwan, Israel, Korea and Singapore. In May 2011, Nanometrics opened a new advanced metrology facility in Singaore. In November 2011, the firm acquired German company Nanda Technologies, GmbH.

FINANCIALS: **Sales and profits are in thousands of dollars—add 000 to get the full amount. 2011 Note: Financial information for 2011 was not available for all companies at press time.**

2011 Sales: $	2011 Profits: $
2010 Sales: $188,065	2010 Profits: $55,948
2009 Sales: $76,707	2009 Profits: $-16,305
2008 Sales: $102,101	2008 Profits: $-82,726
2007 Sales: $146,290	2007 Profits: $-4,008

U.S. Stock Ticker: NANO
Int'l Ticker:
Int'l Exchange:
Employees: 456 Fiscal Year Ends: 12/31
Parent Company:

SALARIES/BENEFITS:

Pension Plan:	ESOP Stock Plan:	Profit Sharing: Y	Top Exec. Salary: $395,473	Bonus: $600,000
Savings Plan: Y	Stock Purch. Plan: Y		Second Exec. Salary: $324,986	Bonus: $515,000

OTHER THOUGHTS:

Apparent Women Officers or Directors: 1
Hot Spot for Advancement for Women/Minorities:

LOCATIONS: ("Y" = Yes)

West:	Southwest:	Midwest:	Southeast:	Northeast:	International:
Y					Y

NATIONAL BEVERAGE CORP

www.nationalbeverage.com

Industry Group Code: 3121

Management:		**Sales/Marketing:**		**Liberal Arts:**		**Information Systems:**		**Professionals:**		**Technical/Scientific:**	
Mgmt. Trainees:	Y	Mktg. Professionals:	Y	Gen. Writing/Editing:	Y	Info. Management:	Y	Finance/Acct.:	Y	Engineers, Elec.:	
Experienced Mgmt.:	Y	Retail Sales:		Technical Writing:		Software Dev.:		Law:	Y	Engineers, Other:	
Int'l Business:		Commercial/Industrial:	Y	Graphic Arts/Photog.:	Y	Hardware Dev.:		HR/Other:	Y	Health/Lab	
MBA Graduates:	Y	Sales Trainees:	Y	Music:		Consulting/Other:		Training:	Y	Scientists/Research:	
		Advertising Pros.:	Y	Broadcasting:				Health Care:		Petroleum/Chemicals:	
				Other:				Consulting:		Math/Other:	

TYPES OF BUSINESS:

Beverages-Soft Drinks Manufacturing
Juice Drinks
Bottled Water
Energy Drinks

BRANDS/DIVISIONS/AFFILIATES:

Shasta
Faygo
Asante
LaCROIX
Rip It
Ohana
Mr. Pure
Mt. Shasta

CONTACTS:

Note: Officers with more than one job title may be intentionally listed here more than once.

Nick A. Caporella, CEO
Joseph G. Caporella, Pres.
Dean A. McCoy, Chief Acct. Officer/Sr. VP
George R. Bracken, Sr. VP-Finance
Nick A. Caporella, Chmn.
Edward F. Knecht, Exec. VP-Procurement

Phone: 954-581-0922 **Fax:** 954-475-8780
Toll-Free: 877-622-3499
Address: 8100 SW 10th St., Ste. 4000, Ft. Lauderdale, FL 33324 US

GROWTH PLANS/SPECIAL FEATURES:

National Beverage Corp. develops, manufactures, markets and distributes carbonated and non-carbonated beverage products throughout the U.S. The company's products emphasize distinctive flavor variety and include its flagship brands Shasta and Faygo, which encompass complete lines of multi-flavored and cola soft drinks. Shasta, a 120-year-old brand, is the largest of the company's brands and includes multiple flavors as well as bottled spring and drinking waters. Established over 100 years ago, Faygo products are primarily distributed east of the Mississippi River and include a multi-flavored product line. Additionally, National Beverage offers an assortment of premium beverages geared toward health-conscious consumers, including Everfresh, Home Juice and Mr. Pure 100% juice and juice-based products; and LaCROIX, Mt. Shasta, Crystal Bay and ClearFruit flavored and spring water products. Asante is a new bottled vitamin water line. The company also produces specialty products, including Ohana fruit-flavored drinks; Rip It and PowerBlast energy drinks available in both liquid and powdered form; and St. Nick's holiday soft drinks. Additionally, the firm makes beverage enhancers, available in powder and effervescent tablets, under the NutraFizz name, which is a functional powder/tablet with amino acids and vitamins that can be added to drinks. National Beverage's brands are produced in its 12 manufacturing facilities, which are located in major metropolitan markets throughout the continental U.S. The company also develops and produces soft drinks for retail grocery chains, warehouse clubs, mass-merchandisers and wholesalers, as well as soft drinks for other beverage companies. National Beverage distributes products to convenience stores, gas stations and other small establishments through its own direct-store delivery fleets, along with those of independent distributors, and distributes to hospitals, schools, military bases, airlines and hotels primarily through independent distributors.

FINANCIALS:

Sales and profits are in thousands of dollars—add 000 to get the full amount. 2011 Note: Financial information for 2011 was not available for all companies at press time.

2011 Sales: $600,193	2011 Profits: $40,754	**U.S. Stock Ticker: FIZZ**
2010 Sales: $592,465	2010 Profits: $32,853	**Int'l Ticker:**
2009 Sales: $575,177	2009 Profits: $24,742	Int'l Exchange:
2008 Sales: $566,001	2008 Profits: $22,480	Employees: 1,200 Fiscal Year Ends: 4/30
2007 Sales: $539,030	2007 Profits: $24,682	Parent Company:

SALARIES/BENEFITS:

Pension Plan: Y	ESOP Stock Plan:	Profit Sharing:	Top Exec. Salary: $495,000	Bonus: $369,132
Savings Plan: Y	Stock Purch. Plan:		Second Exec. Salary: $186,500	Bonus: $60,000

OTHER THOUGHTS:

Apparent Women Officers or Directors:
Hot Spot for Advancement for Women/Minorities:

LOCATIONS: ("Y" = Yes)

West:	Southwest:	Midwest:	Southeast:	Northeast:	International:
Y	Y	Y	Y		

NATIONAL DENTEX CORP

www.nationaldentex.com

Industry Group Code: 33911

Management:		Sales/Marketing:		Liberal Arts:		Information Systems:		Professionals:		Technical/Scientific:	
Mgmt. Trainees:		Mktg. Professionals:	Y	Gen. Writing/Editing:		Info. Management:	Y	Finance/Acct.:	Y	Engineers, Elec.:	
Experienced Mgmt.:	Y	Retail Sales:		Technical Writing:	Y	Software Dev.:		Law:	Y	Engineers, Other:	Y
Int'l Business:	Y	Commercial/Industrial:	Y	Graphic Arts/Photog.:		Hardware Dev.:		HR/Other:	Y	Health/Lab	Y
MBA Graduates:	Y	Sales Trainees:	Y	Music:		Consulting/Other:		Training:	Y	Scientists/Research:	Y
		Advertising Pros.:		Broadcasting:				Health Care:	Y	Petroleum/Chemicals:	
				Other:				Consulting:		Math/Other:	

TYPES OF BUSINESS:

Dental Prosthetic Appliances
Dental Laboratories

BRANDS/DIVISIONS/AFFILIATES:

GeoDigm Corporation
Keller Group, Inc.
Green Dental Laboratories, Inc.
NDX Laboratories
NTI-tss

CONTACTS: *Note: Officers with more than one job title may be intentionally listed here more than once.*

David L. Brown, CEO
Josh Green, COO
Josh Green, Pres.
Wayne M. Coll, CFO/VP
Lynn D. Dine, VP-R&D
Richard G. Mariacher, VP-Tech. Svcs.
Donald H. Siegel, Sec.
Doug Baker, VP-Oper.
Richard F. Becker, Jr., Treas./Exec. VP
Dean Ribeiro, VP-Client Rel.
David V. Harkins, Chmn.

Phone: 508-907-7800 **Fax:** 508-907-6050
Toll-Free:
Address: 2 Vision Dr., Natick, MA 01760 US

GROWTH PLANS/SPECIAL FEATURES:

National Dentex Corp., a subsidiary of GeoDigm Corporation, designs, manufactures, markets and sells dentures, crowns, fixed bridges and other dental prosthetic appliances. The company owns and operates 42 full-service dental laboratories and four branch laboratories located throughout 28 states and one Canadian province, serving a customer base of over 28,000 dentists. The firm operates in three segments: Green Dental, representing the operations of Green Dental Laboratories, Inc., located in Arkansas; Keller, representing the operations of Keller Group, Inc. in Missouri and Kentucky; and NDX Laboratories, which represents the company's remaining laboratories. National Dentex's products are grouped into three main categories: restorative products such as crowns and bridges; reconstructive, which consist primarily of partial dentures and full dentures; and cosmetic products, comprised primarily of porcelain veneers and ceramic crowns. Additionally, the firm manufactures and markets a laboratory version of the NTI-tss plus device used as an alternative to full-coverage bite guards in the treatment of migraine pain and jaw disorders. The products are manufactured from materials such as high noble, noble and predominantly base alloys; zirconia; dental resins; composites; and porcelain. Trained technicians produce the dental products from work orders and cases, such as impressions, models and occlusal registrations of a patient's teeth. The company maintains a direct sales force to market and sell its products to dentists. In mid 2010, the firm merged with GeoDigm Corporation and began operating as GeoDigm's subsidiary.

The company offers its employees medical and dental insurance; educational assistance; dependent care flexible spending accounts; a 401(k); and life insurance.

FINANCIALS: **Sales and profits are in thousands of dollars—add 000 to get the full amount. 2011 Note: Financial information for 2011 was not available for all companies at press time.**

2011 Sales: $ 2011 Profits: $
2010 Sales: $ 2010 Profits: $
2009 Sales: $ 2009 Profits: $
2008 Sales: $ 2008 Profits: $
2007 Sales: $ 2007 Profits: $

U.S. Stock Ticker: Subsidiary
Int'l Ticker:
Int'l Exchange:
Employees: Fiscal Year Ends: 12/31
Parent Company: GEODIGM CORPORATION

SALARIES/BENEFITS:

Pension Plan: ESOP Stock Plan: Profit Sharing: Top Exec. Salary: $371,154 Bonus: $
Savings Plan: Y Stock Purch. Plan: Second Exec. Salary: $350,000 Bonus: $

OTHER THOUGHTS:

Apparent Women Officers or Directors: 1
Hot Spot for Advancement for Women/Minorities:

LOCATIONS: ("Y" = Yes)

West:	Southwest:	Midwest:	Southeast:	Northeast:	International:
	Y	Y	Y	Y	Y

NATIONAL WINE & SPIRITS INC

www.nwscorp.com

Industry Group Code: 4248

Management:		Sales/Marketing:		Liberal Arts:		Information Systems:		Professionals:		Technical/Scientific:	
Mgmt. Trainees:	Y	Mktg. Professionals:	Y	Gen. Writing/Editing:	Y	Info. Management:	Y	Finance/Acct.:	Y	Engineers, Elec.:	
Experienced Mgmt.:	Y	Retail Sales:		Technical Writing:		Software Dev.:	Y	Law:	Y	Engineers, Other:	
Int'l Business:		Commercial/Industrial:	Y	Graphic Arts/Photog.:	Y	Hardware Dev.:		HR/Other:	Y	Health/Lab	
MBA Graduates:	Y	Sales Trainees:	Y	Music:		Consulting/Other:		Training:	Y	Scientists/Research:	
		Advertising Pros.:	Y	Broadcasting:				Health Care:		Petroleum/Chemicals:	
				Other:				Consulting:		Math/Other:	

TYPES OF BUSINESS:

Wine & Spirits Distribution

BRANDS/DIVISIONS/AFFILIATES:

NWS Illinois LLC
NWS Inc
NWS Michigan Inc
Union Beverage Company
Chicago Wine Merchants

CONTACTS: *Note: Officers with more than one job title may be intentionally listed here more than once.*

James E. LaCrosse, CEO
John J. Baker, COO/Exec. VP
James E. LaCrosse, Pres.
James E. LaCrosse, CFO
Gregory J. Mauloff, Exec. VP-Sales & Mktg.
Dwight P. Deming, Corp. VP-Info. Systems
John J. Baker, Corp. Sec.
Steven A. Null, VP-Oper.
Catherine M. LaCrosse, Sr. VP-Corp. Dev. & Fine Wine
Patrick A. Trefun, Controller/Treas.
Harold McGovern, Pres., NWS Michigan, Inc.
James E. LaCrosse, Chmn.

Phone: 317-636-6092 **Fax:** 317-917-1210
Toll-Free: 800-562-7359
Address: 700 W. Morris St., Indianapolis, IN 46206 US

GROWTH PLANS/SPECIAL FEATURES:

National Wine & Spirits, Inc. (NWS) is a distributor of wine and spirits predominantly in the Midwest. Headquartered in Indianapolis, Indiana, NWS also maintains a hyper-terminal and office in South Bend and branch offices in Crown Point, Fort Wayne and Evansville. NWS sells wine through a distribution network consisting of master warehouses, hyper-terminals and cross-docking facilities located throughout Indiana, Kentucky and Michigan. It offers over 7,000 products from more than 350 suppliers; selling its products to over 12,000 retail businesses. The firm has a number of subsidiaries including NWS Illinois, LLC; NWS, Inc.; NWS Michigan, Inc.; Union Beverage Company; and Chicago Wine Merchants, among others.

FINANCIALS: **Sales and profits are in thousands of dollars—add 000 to get the full amount. 2011 Note: Financial information for 2011 was not available for all companies at press time.**

2011 Sales: $ | 2011 Profits: $
2010 Sales: $ | 2010 Profits: $
2009 Sales: $ | 2009 Profits: $
2008 Sales: $ | 2008 Profits: $
2007 Sales: $ | 2007 Profits: $

U.S. Stock Ticker: Private
Int'l Ticker:
Int'l Exchange:
Employees: Fiscal Year Ends: 3/31
Parent Company:

SALARIES/BENEFITS:

Pension Plan: ESOP Stock Plan: Profit Sharing: Top Exec. Salary: $ Bonus: $
Savings Plan: Stock Purch. Plan: Second Exec. Salary: $ Bonus: $

OTHER THOUGHTS:

Apparent Women Officers or Directors: 3
Hot Spot for Advancement for Women/Minorities: Y

LOCATIONS: ("Y" = Yes)

West:	Southwest:	Midwest:	Southeast:	Northeast:	International:
		Y			

NATUS MEDICAL INC

www.natus.com

Industry Group Code: 33911

Management:		Sales/Marketing:		Liberal Arts:		Information Systems:		Professionals:		Technical/Scientific:	
Mgmt. Trainees:		Mktg. Professionals:	Y	Gen. Writing/Editing:		Info. Management:	Y	Finance/Acct.:	Y	Engineers, Elec.:	Y
Experienced Mgmt.:	Y	Retail Sales:		Technical Writing:	Y	Software Dev.:	Y	Law:	Y	Engineers, Other:	Y
Int'l Business:	Y	Commercial/Industrial:	Y	Graphic Arts/Photog.:		Hardware Dev.:	Y	HR/Other:	Y	Health/Lab	Y
MBA Graduates:	Y	Sales Trainees:	Y	Music:		Consulting/Other:		Training:	Y	Scientists/Research:	Y
		Advertising Pros.:		Broadcasting:				Health Care:	Y	Petroleum/Chemicals:	
				Other:				Consulting:		Math/Other:	

TYPES OF BUSINESS:

Medical Diagnostics Manufacturer
Newborn Care Products

BRANDS/DIVISIONS/AFFILIATES:

Medix
Embla Systems, LLC

CONTACTS:

Note: Officers with more than one job title may be intentionally listed here more than once.

James B. Hawkins, CEO
John T. Buhler, COO
John T. Buhler, Pres.
Steven J. Murphy, CFO
Kenneth M. Traverso, VP-Mktg. & Sales
William L. Mince, VP-North American Oper.
Steven J. Murphy, VP-Finance
D. Christopher Chung, VP-Medical Affairs, Quality & Regulatory
Robert A. Gunst, Chmn.

Phone: 650-802-0400 **Fax:** 650-802-0401
Toll-Free: 800-255-3901
Address: 1501 Industrial Rd., San Carlos, CA 94070 US

GROWTH PLANS/SPECIAL FEATURES:

Natus Medical, Inc. is a provider of healthcare products used for the screening, detection, treatment, monitoring and tracking of common medical ailments. These ailments concern newborn care, hearing impairment, neurological dysfunction, epilepsy, sleep disorders and balance and mobility disorders. Natus divides its products into three categories: hearing products; monitoring systems for neurology; and newborn care. The company's hearing products use auditory brainstem response (ABR) technology, as well as otoacoustic emissions. The ABR test analyzes brainwaves from the inner ear and brainstem to determine hearing loss characteristics that cannot be provided by verbal or motor response tests. Hearing products include those for newborn hearing screening, diagnostic hearing assessment products and hearing screening supply kits. The firm's monitoring systems for neurology are used in the diagnosis and monitoring of central and peripheral nervous system disorders, as well as in monitoring patients during surgery, under sedation and in post-operative care. This segment includes products for diagnostic electroencephalography, diagnostic sleep analysis (polysomnography), electromyography, intra-operative monitoring, newborn brain monitoring and assessment of balance and mobility disorders. Finally, the company's newborn care segment offers products for the treatment of newborn brain injuries; the management of newborn jaundice; medical devices such as photometers, patient warming lamps, pediatric scales and oxygen hoods; and disposable products such as pacifiers, sucrose solution and heel lancets. In October 2010, Natus acquired Latin American newborn care device specialist Medix. In September 2011, the firm acquired sleep apnea diagnostic device company Embla Systems, LLC.

FINANCIALS:

Sales and profits are in thousands of dollars—add 000 to get the full amount. 2011 Note: Financial information for 2011 was not available for all companies at press time.

2011 Sales: $	2011 Profits: $
2010 Sales: $218,655	2010 Profits: $11,919
2009 Sales: $166,425	2009 Profits: $11,382
2008 Sales: $161,831	2008 Profits: $17,473
2007 Sales: $118,374	2007 Profits: $9,780

U.S. Stock Ticker: BABY
Int'l Ticker:
Int'l Exchange:
Employees: 750 Fiscal Year Ends: 12/31
Parent Company:

SALARIES/BENEFITS:

Pension Plan:	ESOP Stock Plan:	Profit Sharing:	Top Exec. Salary: $425,000	Bonus: $270,000
Savings Plan:	Stock Purch. Plan:		Second Exec. Salary: $322,874	Bonus: $60,000

OTHER THOUGHTS:

Apparent Women Officers or Directors: 1
Hot Spot for Advancement for Women/Minorities:

LOCATIONS: ("Y" = Yes)

West:	Southwest:	Midwest:	Southeast:	Northeast:	International:
Y		Y		Y	Y

NEKTAR THERAPEUTICS

www.nektar.com

Industry Group Code: 325412A

Management:		Sales/Marketing:		Liberal Arts:		Information Systems:		Professionals:		Technical/Scientific:	
Mgmt. Trainees:		Mktg. Professionals:	Y	Gen. Writing/Editing:		Info. Management:	Y	Finance/Acct.:	Y	Engineers, Elec.:	
Experienced Mgmt.:	Y	Retail Sales:		Technical Writing:	Y	Software Dev.:	Y	Law:	Y	Engineers, Other:	
Int'l Business:	Y	Commercial/Industrial:	Y	Graphic Arts/Photog.:		Hardware Dev.:		HR/Other:	Y	Health/Lab	Y
MBA Graduates:	Y	Sales Trainees:	Y	Music:		Consulting/Other:		Training:	Y	Scientists/Research:	Y
		Advertising Pros.:		Broadcasting:				Health Care:	Y	Petroleum/Chemicals:	
				Other:				Consulting:		Math/Other:	Y

TYPES OF BUSINESS:

Drug Delivery Systems
PEG-Based Delivery Systems
Molecular & Particle Engineering
Equipment-Inhalers

BRANDS/DIVISIONS/AFFILIATES:

Nektar PEGylation Technology
PEG-INTRON
Macugen
PEGASYS
Somavert
Neulasta
NKTR-118
NKTR-119

CONTACTS:

Note: Officers with more than one job title may be intentionally listed here more than once.

Howard W. Robin, CEO
Howard W. Robin, Pres.
John Nicholson, CFO/Sr. VP
Dorian Rinella, Sr. VP-Human Resources & Facilities
Stephen K. Doberstein, Chief Scientific Officer/Sr. VP
Maninder Hora, Sr. VP-Pharmaceutical Dev.
Maninder Hora, Sr. VP-Mftg. Oper.
Gil M. Labrucherie, General Counsel/Sec./Sr. VP
Rinko Ghosh, Chief Business Officer/Sr. VP
Jennifer Ruddock, VP-Corp. Affairs
Jennifer Ruddock, VP-Investor Rel.
Jillian B Thomsen, Sr. VP-Finance/Chief Acct. Officer
Robert Medve, Chief Medical Officer/VP
Timothy A. Riley, Sr. VP-Global Research
Robert B. Chess, Chmn.

Phone: 415-482-5300 **Fax:**
Toll-Free:
Address: 455 Mission Bay Blvd. S., San Francisco, CA 94158 US

GROWTH PLANS/SPECIAL FEATURES:

Nektar Therapeutics is a biopharmaceutical company focused on developing technology for unmet medical needs. Nektar Therapeutics creates potential breakthrough products in two ways: by developing products in collaboration with pharmaceutical and biotechnology companies that seek to improve and differentiate their products; and by applying its technologies to already approved drugs. The company has two leading technology platforms: PEGylation technology and advanced polymer conjugate technology. PEGylation technology is a chemical process designed to enhance the performance of most drug classes with the potential to improve solubility and stability; increase drug half-life; reduce immune responses to an active drug; and improve the efficacy and/or safety of a molecule in certain instances. Leading products approved by the U.S. Food and Drug Administration (FDA) include Macugen treatment for macular degeneration; PEGASYS for chronic Hepatitis C; Somavert, a human growth hormone receptor antagonist; PEG-INTRON for treating Hepatitis C; and Neulasta for the treatment of neutropenia, a condition where the body produces too few white blood cells. Most of these have been developed in collaboration with other pharmaceutical companies, including Amgen; Novartis Pharma; Bayer; Pfizer; and Merck. The firm's drug portfolio also contains NKTR-118 and NKTR-119 to treat pain without the side effect of constipation associated with opioid therapy; BAY41-6551 to treat Gram-negative pneumonias; NKTR-102 for cancer indications such as breast, colorectal and ovarian; NKTR-181, a mu opioid analgesic with allegedly reduced potential for abuse and fewer side effects than traditional opioid therapies; and NKTR-105, a chemotherapy agent, among others.

Nektar Therapeutics offers its employees medical, dental and vision plans; accident and life insurance; retirement and investment plans; and life enrichment programs, including tuition reimbursement and fitness membership discounts.

FINANCIALS:

Sales and profits are in thousands of dollars—add 000 to get the full amount. 2011 Note: Financial information for 2011 was not available for all companies at press time.

2011 Sales: $	2011 Profits: $	**U.S. Stock Ticker: NKTR**
2010 Sales: $159,039	2010 Profits: $-37,938	**Int'l Ticker:**
2009 Sales: $71,931	2009 Profits: $-102,519	Int'l Exchange:
2008 Sales: $90,185	2008 Profits: $-34,336	Employees: 408 Fiscal Year Ends: 12/31
2007 Sales: $273,027	2007 Profits: $-32,761	Parent Company:

SALARIES/BENEFITS:

Pension Plan:	ESOP Stock Plan:	Profit Sharing:	Top Exec. Salary: $758,581	Bonus: $700,000
Savings Plan: Y	Stock Purch. Plan: Y		Second Exec. Salary: $478,417	Bonus: $288,000

OTHER THOUGHTS:

Apparent Women Officers or Directors: 3
Hot Spot for Advancement for Women/Minorities: Y

LOCATIONS: ("Y" = Yes)

West:	Southwest:	Midwest:	Southeast:	Northeast:	International:
Y			Y		Y

NEOGEN CORPORATION

Industry Group Code: 325413

www.neogen.com

Management:		Sales/Marketing:		Liberal Arts:		Information Systems:		Professionals:		Technical/Scientific:	
Mgmt. Trainees:		Mktg. Professionals:	Y	Gen. Writing/Editing:		Info. Management:	Y	Finance/Acct.:	Y	Engineers, Elec.:	
Experienced Mgmt.:	Y	Retail Sales:		Technical Writing:	Y	Software Dev.:	Y	Law:	Y	Engineers, Other:	Y
Int'l Business:	Y	Commercial/Industrial:	Y	Graphic Arts/Photog.:		Hardware Dev.:	Y	HR/Other:	Y	Health/Lab	Y
MBA Graduates:	Y	Sales Trainees:	Y	Music:		Consulting/Other:		Training:	Y	Scientists/Research:	Y
		Advertising Pros.:		Broadcasting:				Health Care:	Y	Petroleum/Chemicals:	Y
				Other:				Consulting:		Math/Other:	Y

TYPES OF BUSINESS:

Sanitary & Livestock Diagnostic Products
Food Safety Test Kits
Animal Health Test Kits
Pharmacology Test Kits
Agricultural Test Kits
Veterinary Instruments
Veterinary Pharmaceuticals

BRANDS/DIVISIONS/AFFILIATES:

GeneSeek, Inc.
BetaStar Plus
Neogen do Brasil
AmVet
PanaKare
RenaKare
NeogenVet
Vita-15

CONTACTS: *Note: Officers with more than one job title may be intentionally listed here more than once.*

James L. Herbert, CEO
Lon M. Bohannon, COO
Lon M. Bohannon, Pres.
Steven J. Quinlan, CFO/VP
Mark A. Mozola, VP-R&D
Kenneth V. Kodilla, VP-Mfg.
Richard R. Current, Sec.
Edward L. Bradley, VP-Food Safety Oper.
Anthony E. Maltese, VP-Corp. Dev.
Joseph M. Madden, VP-Scientific Affairs
James L. Herbert, Chmn.

Phone: 517-372-9200 **Fax:** 517-372-2006
Toll-Free: 800-234-5333
Address: 620 Lesher Pl., Lansing, MI 48912 US

GROWTH PLANS/SPECIAL FEATURES:

Neogen Corporation and its subsidiaries develop, manufacture and market a diverse line of products for food and animal safety. Its two operating segments are food safety and animal safety. The company's food safety segment primarily sells diagnostic test kits and complementary products marketed to food and feed producers and processors to detect food-borne pathogens, spoilage organisms, natural toxins, food allergens, genetic modifications, ruminant by-products, drug residues, pesticide residues and general sanitation concerns. Many of its food safety test kits use immunoassay technology to rapidly detect target substances. This segment also includes bioluminescence-based diagnostic technology. Revenue from the food safety segment generated 54.4% of the firm's total 2010 revenue. Neogen's animal safety segment, which generated approximately 45.6% of its 2010 revenue, primarily develops, manufactures and markets pharmaceuticals, rodenticides, disinfectants, vaccines, veterinary instruments, topicals and diagnostic products to the worldwide animal safety market. This segment's brands include AmVet, PanaKare, RenaKare, NeogenVet, Vita-15 and Liver 7. Its line of approximately 100 drug detection immunoassay test kits are sold worldwide for the detection of approximately 300 abused and therapeutic drugs in racing animals, such as horses, greyhounds and camels, as well as for testing farm animals. The company has a sales network of over 120 distributors in 100 countries. The firm manufactures its products in Lansing, Michigan; Lexington, Kentucky; Randolph, Wisconsin; and Ayr, Scotland. Additionally, the firm maintains Neogen do Brasil to distribute its food safety products throughout Brazil. In early 2010, Neogen acquired GeneSeek, Inc., a commercial agricultural genetics laboratory, for $13.8 million. In June 2011, the firm acquired VeroMara, a seafood testing laboratory from GlycoMar Ltd. Also In June 2011, the firm's product, BetaStar Plus, which is used to detect dairy antibiotic residues, was approved by the FDA.

FINANCIALS: **Sales and profits are in thousands of dollars—add 000 to get the full amount. 2011 Note: Financial information for 2011 was not available for all companies at press time.**

2011 Sales: $172,683	2011 Profits: $22,839
2010 Sales: $140,509	2010 Profits: $17,521
2009 Sales: $118,721	2009 Profits: $13,874
2008 Sales: $102,418	2008 Profits: $12,098
2007 Sales: $86,138	2007 Profits: $9,125

U.S. Stock Ticker: NEOG
Int'l Ticker:
Int'l Exchange:
Employees: 654 Fiscal Year Ends: 5/31
Parent Company:

SALARIES/BENEFITS:

Pension Plan:	ESOP Stock Plan:	Profit Sharing:	Top Exec. Salary: $322,000	Bonus: $155,000
Savings Plan: Y	Stock Purch. Plan:		Second Exec. Salary: $224,000	Bonus: $90,000

OTHER THOUGHTS:

Apparent Women Officers or Directors: 1
Hot Spot for Advancement for Women/Minorities:

LOCATIONS: ("Y" = Yes)

West:	Southwest:	Midwest:	Southeast:	Northeast:	International:
		Y			Y

NETFLIX INC

www.netflix.com

Industry Group Code: 532230

Management:		Sales/Marketing:		Liberal Arts:		Information Systems:		Professionals:		Technical/Scientific:	
Mgmt. Trainees:	Y	Mktg. Professionals:	Y	Gen. Writing/Editing:	Y	Info. Management:	Y	Finance/Acct.:	Y	Engineers, Elec.:	
Experienced Mgmt.:	Y	Retail Sales:		Technical Writing:		Software Dev.:	Y	Law:	Y	Engineers, Other:	
Int'l Business:	Y	Commercial/Industrial:		Graphic Arts/Photog.:	Y	Hardware Dev.:		HR/Other:	Y	Health/Lab	
MBA Graduates:	Y	Sales Trainees:		Music:		Consulting/Other:		Training:	Y	Scientists/Research:	
		Advertising Pros.:	Y	Broadcasting:				Health Care:		Petroleum/Chemicals:	
				Other:	Y			Consulting:		Math/Other:	

TYPES OF BUSINESS:

Online DVD Rental
Video on Demand

BRANDS/DIVISIONS/AFFILIATES:

CONTACTS: *Note: Officers with more than one job title may be intentionally listed here more than once.*

Reed Hastings, CEO
David Wells, CFO
Leslie Kilgore, Chief Mktg. Officer
Patty McCord, Chief Talent Officer
Neil Hunt, Chief Prod. Officer
David Hyman, General Counsel
Andrew Rendich, Chief Service & Oper. Officer
Ted Sarandos, Chief Content Officer
Reed Hastings, Chmn.

Phone: 408-540-3700 **Fax:**
Toll-Free: 1-877-742-1480
Address: 100 Winchester Cir., Los Gatos, CA 95032 US

GROWTH PLANS/SPECIAL FEATURES:

Netflix, Inc. is one of the largest online movie rental subscription services, providing access to a library of movie, television and other filmed entertainment titles on DVD to nearly 25 million subscribers in the U.S., Canada and Latin America. The company offers subscription plans starting at $7.99 a month. There are no due dates, late fees or shipping costs. In the U.S., subscribers select titles at Netflix's web site, receive the movies by mail and return them using prepaid mailers. Netflix then mails the next available DVD in a subscriber's queue. The firm operates distribution centers nationwide, allowing delivery of DVDs to most subscribers in about one business day. The company also offers a Watch Instantly feature, allowing subscribers to view a growing library of movies and television episodes over the Internet or on Netflix-ready devices such as Blu-ray disc players, Internet-connected TVs, digital video players and game consoles. These devices include the PlayStation 3; the Xbox 360; the Nintendo Wii; the Apple iPhone, iPad and iTouch; Apple TV; and Google TV. Over 700 devices that stream Netflix content are available in the U.S. The firm's proprietary recommendation service enables it to create a customized store for each subscriber and generate personalized recommendations. The Netflix streaming content library includes media acquired through deals with corporations such as: ABC, Nickelodeon, Disney, Twentieth Century Fox, Paramount, Miramax, Lionsgate, MGM and CBS. In July 2011, the company launched services in Latin America and the Caribbean. Additionally, Netflix attempted to separate its unlimited streaming and unlimited DVD plans in the U.S., but quickly abandoned the idea. In October 2011, Netflix announced the expansion of services to the U.K. and Ireland. In November 2011, the company announced that a Netflix app will be preloaded on Barnes & Noble NOOK Tablets for access to instant streaming movies and TV shows.

FINANCIALS: **Sales and profits are in thousands of dollars—add 000 to get the full amount. 2011 Note: Financial information for 2011 was not available for all companies at press time.**

2011 Sales: $3,204,600 — 2011 Profits: $231,600
2010 Sales: $2,162,625 — 2010 Profits: $160,853
2009 Sales: $1,670,269 — 2009 Profits: $115,860
2008 Sales: $1,364,661 — 2008 Profits: $83,026
2007 Sales: $1,205,340 — 2007 Profits: $66,952

U.S. Stock Ticker: NFLX
Int'l Ticker:
Int'l Exchange:
Employees: 2,180 Fiscal Year Ends: 12/31
Parent Company:

SALARIES/BENEFITS:

Pension Plan: ESOP Stock Plan: Profit Sharing: Top Exec. Salary: $900,000 Bonus: $
Savings Plan: Stock Purch. Plan: Second Exec. Salary: $864,103 Bonus: $

OTHER THOUGHTS:

Apparent Women Officers or Directors: 2
Hot Spot for Advancement for Women/Minorities:

LOCATIONS: ("Y" = Yes)

West:	Southwest:	Midwest:	Southeast:	Northeast:	International:
Y	Y	Y	Y	Y	Y

NETGEAR INC

Industry Group Code: 33411

www.netgear.com

Management:		Sales/Marketing:		Liberal Arts:		Information Systems:		Professionals:		Technical/Scientific:	
Mgmt. Trainees:		Mktg. Professionals:	Y	Gen. Writing/Editing:		Info. Management:	Y	Finance/Acct.:	Y	Engineers, Elec.:	Y
Experienced Mgmt.:	Y	Retail Sales:		Technical Writing:	Y	Software Dev.:	Y	Law:	Y	Engineers, Other:	
Int'l Business:	Y	Commercial/Industrial:	Y	Graphic Arts/Photog.:		Hardware Dev.:	Y	HR/Other:	Y	Health/Lab	
MBA Graduates:	Y	Sales Trainees:	Y	Music:		Consulting/Other:		Training:	Y	Scientists/Research:	Y
		Advertising Pros.:		Broadcasting:				Health Care:		Petroleum/Chemicals:	
				Other:				Consulting:		Math/Other:	

TYPES OF BUSINESS:

Networking Equipment
Wireless Networking Products
Broadband Products
Entertainment Management Software
Security Products
Wi-Fi Phones

BRANDS/DIVISIONS/AFFILIATES:

CONTACTS: *Note: Officers with more than one job title may be intentionally listed here more than once.*

Patrick C.S. Lo, CEO
Christine M. Gorjanc, CFO
Michael Werdann, VP-Americas Sales
Tamesa Rogers, VP-Human Resources
Mark Merrill, CTO
Charles T. Olson, Sr. VP-Eng.
Andrew Kim, VP-Legal/Corp. Sec.
Michael Falcon, Sr. VP-Oper. & Support
Andrew Kim, VP-Corp. Dev.
Patrick C.S. Lo, Chmn.
David Soares, Sr. VP-Worldwide Sales & SMB Business

Phone: 408-907-8000	**Fax:** 408-907-8097
Toll-Free: 888-638-4327	
Address: 350 E. Plumeria Dr., San Jose, CA 95134-1911 US	

GROWTH PLANS/SPECIAL FEATURES:

NETGEAR, Inc. designs, develops and markets networking products for commercial businesses, home users and broadband service providers. NETGEAR has offices in California in the U.S. and 22 other countries around the world. The firm's products allow users to share Internet access, peripherals, files, digital multimedia content and applications among multiple networked devices and other Internet-enabled devices. NETGEAR's products are grouped into three major lines: commercial business networking, broadband access products and network connectivity products. Commercial businesses networking products include Ethernet switches, which can connect multiple PCs and network devices to a connection; wireless controllers, which can manage and control WiFi networks; Internet security appliances, such as anti-virus and anti-spam tools; and network attached storage, which can facilitate file sharing across multiple PCs over a local area network. Broadband access products include routers, which connect home or office networks to the Internet via broadband modems; gateways, which integrate routers with modems; IP telephony products, which transmit voice data over a network; and media servers, which stores multimedia content for PCs, laptops and other devices. Network connectivity products consist of wireless access points and wireless network interface cards, which enable wireless connections; Ethernet network interface cards, which allow devices to connect to an Ethernet network; media adapters, which connect TVs and PCs to a network; powerline adapters, which allow devices to connect to a network over existing electrical wiring; and Multimedia over Coax alliance adapters and bridges, which allows devices to connect to a network over existing coaxial wiring. NETGEAR sells its products through multiple sales channels worldwide, including traditional retailers, online retailers, direct market resellers, value-added resellers and broadband service providers. Domestic sales make up the majority of the company's net revenue, contributing 52% in 2010. Two of its most significant customers include Ingram Micro, Inc. and Best Buy Co., Inc.

FINANCIALS: **Sales and profits are in thousands of dollars—add 000 to get the full amount. 2011 Note: Financial information for 2011 was not available for all companies at press time.**

2011 Sales: $1,181,000 | 2011 Profits: $91,400
2010 Sales: $902,052 | 2010 Profits: $50,909
2009 Sales: $686,595 | 2009 Profits: $9,333
2008 Sales: $743,344 | 2008 Profits: $17,719
2007 Sales: $727,787 | 2007 Profits: $45,954

U.S. Stock Ticker: NTGR
Int'l Ticker:
Int'l Exchange:
Employees: 654 Fiscal Year Ends: 12/31
Parent Company:

SALARIES/BENEFITS:

Pension Plan: ESOP Stock Plan: Profit Sharing: Top Exec. Salary: $600,000 Bonus: $870,000
Savings Plan: Stock Purch. Plan: Second Exec. Salary: $360,616 Bonus: $213,639

OTHER THOUGHTS:

Apparent Women Officers or Directors: 4
Hot Spot for Advancement for Women/Minorities: Y

LOCATIONS: ("Y" = Yes)

West:	Southwest:	Midwest:	Southeast:	Northeast:	International:
Y					Y

NETSCOUT SYSTEMS INC

www.netscout.com

Industry Group Code: 511210B

Management:		**Sales/Marketing:**		**Liberal Arts:**		**Information Systems:**		**Professionals:**		**Technical/Scientific:**	
Mgmt. Trainees:		Mktg. Professionals:	Y	Gen. Writing/Editing:		Info. Management:	Y	Finance/Acct.:	Y	Engineers, Elec.:	Y
Experienced Mgmt.:	Y	Retail Sales:		Technical Writing:	Y	Software Dev.:	Y	Law:	Y	Engineers, Other:	
Int'l Business:	Y	Commercial/Industrial:	Y	Graphic Arts/Photog.:		Hardware Dev.:		HR/Other:	Y	Health/Lab	
MBA Graduates:	Y	Sales Trainees:	Y	Music:		Consulting/Other:		Training:	Y	Scientists/Research:	
		Advertising Pros.:		Broadcasting:				Health Care:		Petroleum/Chemicals:	
				Other:				Consulting:		Math/Other:	

TYPES OF BUSINESS:

Performance Management Systems
Application Management Solutions

BRANDS/DIVISIONS/AFFILIATES:

nGenius
nGenius Service Assurance Solution
nGenius Analytics
Psytechnics, Inc.
Sniffer

CONTACTS: *Note: Officers with more than one job title may be intentionally listed here more than once.*

Anil K. Singhal, CEO
Michael Szabados, COO
Anil K. Singhal, Pres.
David Sommers, CFO/Treas.
Steven Shalita, VP-Mktg.
Victor Becker, VP-Human Resources
Ashwani Singhal, Sr. VP-R&D
Ken Boyd, CIO/Sr. VP-Svcs.
Bruce Kelley, Jr., CTO/VP
Tracy Steele, VP-Mfg. & Bus. Oper.
Jeff Levinson, General Counsel/VP
David Sommers, Sr. VP-Gen. Oper.
Bruce Sweet, VP-Bus. Dev.
Stephanie Xavier, Sr. Mgr.-Public Rel.
Jean Bua, VP-Finance/Chief Acct. Officer
Anil K. Singhal, Chmn.
John Downing, Sr. VP-Worldwide Sales Oper.

Phone: 978-614-4000 **Fax:** 978-614-4004
Toll-Free: 800-357-7666
Address: 310 Littleton Rd., Westford, MA 01886 US

GROWTH PLANS/SPECIAL FEATURES:

NetScout Systems, Inc. designs, develops, manufactures, markets, sells and supports a family of products that assures the performance and availability of critical business applications and services in complex, high-speed networks. The company manufactures and markets these products as an integrated hardware and software solution that is used by enterprises, governmental agencies and service providers worldwide. The firm's nGenius Service Assurance Solution software product is a multi-function performance management solution implemented in a single, integrated application that monitors and reports on network, service and application traffic; troubleshoots performance problems; and provides precise information for capacity planning. It integrates real-time and historical information in a single management application. The system collects data from nGenius Probes, routers, switches and other flow-based information sources, such as NetFlow, and provides in-depth system-wide views of all applications on the network infrastructure. Other nGenius products include nGenius Performance Manager, which analyzes and correlates the meta-data delivered by an array of intelligent data sources; nGenius Analytics, one of the first intelligent early warning systems in the performance management marketplace. NetScout's Sniffer line of products offer more efficient troubleshooting and advanced network analysis. The firm sells its products to corporations, government agencies, other non-profit entities and other organizations with large- and medium-sized high-speed computer networks. The company's products have been sold to customers operating in industries such as financial services, technology, telecommunications, manufacturing, service provider, healthcare and retail. In April 2011, NetScout Systems acquired performance management technology provider Psytechnics, Inc.

FINANCIALS: **Sales and profits are in thousands of dollars—add 000 to get the full amount. 2011 Note: Financial information for 2011 was not available for all companies at press time.**

2011 Sales: $290,540 — 2011 Profits: $37,265
2010 Sales: $260,342 — 2010 Profits: $27,917
2009 Sales: $267,604 — 2009 Profits: $20,048
2008 Sales: $168,956 — 2008 Profits: $-2,088
2007 Sales: $102,472 — 2007 Profits: $7,737

U.S. Stock Ticker: NTCT
Int'l Ticker:
Int'l Exchange:
Employees: 845 Fiscal Year Ends: 3/31
Parent Company:

SALARIES/BENEFITS:

Pension Plan: ESOP Stock Plan: Profit Sharing: Top Exec. Salary: $318,747 Bonus: $750,000
Savings Plan: Stock Purch. Plan: Second Exec. Salary: $268,747 Bonus: $313,000

OTHER THOUGHTS:

Apparent Women Officers or Directors: 1
Hot Spot for Advancement for Women/Minorities:

LOCATIONS: ("Y" = Yes)

West:	Southwest:	Midwest:	Southeast:	Northeast:	International:
Y	Y			Y	Y

NETSUITE INC

www.netsuite.com

Industry Group Code: 511210H

Management:		Sales/Marketing:		Liberal Arts:		Information Systems:		Professionals:		Technical/Scientific:	
Mgmt. Trainees:		Mktg. Professionals:	Y	Gen. Writing/Editing:	Y	Info. Management:	Y	Finance/Acct.:	Y	Engineers, Elec.:	Y
Experienced Mgmt.:	Y	Retail Sales:		Technical Writing:	Y	Software Dev.:	Y	Law:	Y	Engineers, Other:	
Int'l Business:	Y	Commercial/Industrial:	Y	Graphic Arts/Photog.:		Hardware Dev.:		HR/Other:	Y	Health/Lab	
MBA Graduates:	Y	Sales Trainees:		Music:		Consulting/Other:		Training:	Y	Scientists/Research:	
		Advertising Pros.:	Y	Broadcasting:				Health Care:		Petroleum/Chemicals:	
				Other:				Consulting:		Math/Other:	

TYPES OF BUSINESS:

Business Management Application Suites
Enterprise Resource Planning
Customer Relationship Management
E-Commerce Capabilities

BRANDS/DIVISIONS/AFFILIATES:

NetSuite
NetSuite CRM+
NetSuite OneWorld
OpenAir Inc
QuickArrow Inc

CONTACTS: *Note: Officers with more than one job title may be intentionally listed here more than once.*

Zach Nelson, CEO
Jim McGeever, COO
Zach Nelson, Pres.
Ron Gill, CFO
James Ramsey, Sr. VP-Worldwide Sales
Evan Goldberg, CTO
Douglas P. Solomon, General Counsel/Sr. VP/Corp. Sec.
Mei Li, Sr. VP-Corp. Comm.
Tim Dilley, Exec. VP-Worldwide Svcs./Chief Customer Officer
Evan Goldberg, Chmn.
James Ramsey, Sr. VP-Worldwide Dist.

Phone: 650-627-1000 **Fax:** 650-627-1001
Toll-Free:
Address: 2955 Campus Dr., Ste. 100, San Mateo, CA 94403-2511 US

GROWTH PLANS/SPECIAL FEATURES:

NetSuite, Inc. is a leading vendor of on-demand, integrated business management application suites for small and medium-sized businesses and large company divisions. It provides a suite of enterprise resource planning (ERP), customer relationship management (CRM) and e-commerce capabilities that enables customers to manage their back-office, front-office and web operations in a single application. The company's main offering is NetSuite, which is designed to provide the integrated core business management capabilities that most of its customers require. NetSuite, NetSuite CRM+ and NetSuite OneWorld are designed for use by most types of businesses. In addition, the firm offers industry-specific configurations for use by wholesale/distribution, services and software companies, as well as additional on-demand application modules that provide functionality for unique industry needs. All elements of the company's application suite share the same customer and transaction data, enabling cross-departmental business process automation and real-time monitoring of core business metrics. In addition, the integrated ERP, CRM and e-commerce capabilities provide users with real-time visibility and appropriate functionality through dashboards tailored to their particular job function and access rights. The firm delivers its suite over the Internet as a subscription service using the Software-as-a-Service (SaaS) model. NetSuite has customers in 80 countries and derives roughly 25% of its revenues from sales outside of North America. Through its OpenAir and QuickArrow subsidiaries, the company offers professional services automation and project portfolio management services. In February 2011, NetSuite opened a new office in Melbourne, Australia.

FINANCIALS: **Sales and profits are in thousands of dollars—add 000 to get the full amount. 2011 Note: Financial information for 2011 was not available for all companies at press time.**

2011 Sales: $236,326 — 2011 Profits: $-32,007
2010 Sales: $193,149 — 2010 Profits: $-27,480
2009 Sales: $166,540 — 2009 Profits: $-24,112
2008 Sales: $152,476 — 2008 Profits: $-15,864
2007 Sales: $108,541 — 2007 Profits: $-23,906

U.S. Stock Ticker: N
Int'l Ticker:
Int'l Exchange:
Employees: 1,084 Fiscal Year Ends: 12/31
Parent Company:

SALARIES/BENEFITS:

Pension Plan: ESOP Stock Plan: Profit Sharing: Top Exec. Salary: $450,000 Bonus: $577,127
Savings Plan: Stock Purch. Plan: Second Exec. Salary: $375,000 Bonus: $238,829

OTHER THOUGHTS:

Apparent Women Officers or Directors: 3
Hot Spot for Advancement for Women/Minorities: Y

LOCATIONS: ("Y" = Yes)

West:	Southwest:	Midwest:	Southeast:	Northeast:	International:
Y	Y			Y	Y

NETWORK ENGINES INC

www.networkengines.com

Industry Group Code: 511210B

Management:		Sales/Marketing:		Liberal Arts:		Information Systems:		Professionals:		Technical/Scientific:	
Mgmt. Trainees:		Mktg. Professionals:	Y	Gen. Writing/Editing:		Info. Management:	Y	Finance/Acct.:	Y	Engineers, Elec.:	Y
Experienced Mgmt.:	Y	Retail Sales:		Technical Writing:	Y	Software Dev.:	Y	Law:	Y	Engineers, Other:	
Int'l Business:	Y	Commercial/Industrial:	Y	Graphic Arts/Photog.:		Hardware Dev.:		HR/Other:	Y	Health/Lab	
MBA Graduates:	Y	Sales Trainees:		Music:		Consulting/Other:		Training:		Scientists/Research:	
		Advertising Pros.:		Broadcasting:				Health Care:		Petroleum/Chemicals:	
				Other:				Consulting:		Math/Other:	

TYPES OF BUSINESS:

Server Applications
Storage & Security Software & Equipment
Supply Chain Services

BRANDS/DIVISIONS/AFFILIATES:

CONTACTS:

Note: Officers with more than one job title may be intentionally listed here more than once.

Gregory A. Shortell, CEO
Gregory A. Shortell, Pres.
Douglas G. Bryant, CFO
Charles N. Cone, III, Sr. VP-Sales & Mktg.
Austin Hipes, VP-Tech.
Rich Graber, Sr. VP-Eng.
Douglas G. Bryant, Corp. Sec.
Rich Graber, Sr. VP-Oper.
Douglas G. Bryant, Treas.
John A. Blaeser, Chmn.

Phone: 781-332-1000	**Fax:** 781-770-2000
Toll-Free:	
Address: 25 Dan Rd., Canton, MA 02021 US	

GROWTH PLANS/SPECIAL FEATURES:

Network Engines, Inc. (NEI) is a leading international developer, manufacturer and distributor of storage equipment, network security devices and services to original equipment manufacturers (OEM) and independent software vendors. The firm offers a comprehensive suite of services, including development, manufacturing, fulfillment and post-sale support. This enables customers to accelerate the time to market for their products, to optimize their server appliance solutions and in some cases enable them to utilize the company's infrastructure for fulfillment of server appliance solutions. The firm can fulfill orders from its software partners to their end-user base or to their channels. NEI produces equipment branded for its customers, who in turn resell the products to their own customers. Prominent clients include AVST, Inc., Bomgar, Inc.; Mavenir Systems; Bradford Networks; Symantec Corporation; Endace Measurement Systems, Ltd.; EMC Corporation; Sepaton, Inc.; Sophos, Plc.; and Tektronix, Inc.

Employees are offered medical, dental, vision, life and disability insurance and tuition reimbursement.

FINANCIALS:

Sales and profits are in thousands of dollars—add 000 to get the full amount. 2011 Note: Financial information for 2011 was not available for all companies at press time.

2011 Sales: $272,470
2010 Sales: $221,620
2009 Sales: $148,722
2008 Sales: $197,495
2007 Sales: $119,627

2011 Profits: $36,700
2010 Profits: $1,529
2009 Profits: $-3,198
2008 Profits: $-8,477
2007 Profits: $2,502

U.S. Stock Ticker: NEI
Int'l Ticker:
Int'l Exchange:
Employees: 237
Fiscal Year Ends: 9/30
Parent Company:

SALARIES/BENEFITS:

Pension Plan:
Savings Plan: Y
ESOP Stock Plan:
Stock Purch. Plan: Y
Profit Sharing:
Top Exec. Salary: $375,000
Bonus: $123,845
Second Exec. Salary: $341,840
Bonus: $7,927

OTHER THOUGHTS:

Apparent Women Officers or Directors:
Hot Spot for Advancement for Women/Minorities:

LOCATIONS: ("Y" = Yes)

West:	Southwest:	Midwest:	Southeast:	Northeast:	International:
				Y	Y

NEUSTAR INC

www.neustar.biz

Industry Group Code: 518210

Management:		Sales/Marketing:		Liberal Arts:		Information Systems:		Professionals:		Technical/Scientific:	
Mgmt. Trainees:		Mktg. Professionals:		Gen. Writing/Editing:	Y	Info. Management:	Y	Finance/Acct.:	Y	Engineers, Elec.:	
Experienced Mgmt.:	Y	Retail Sales:		Technical Writing:		Software Dev.:	Y	Law:	Y	Engineers, Other:	
Int'l Business:	Y	Commercial/Industrial:		Graphic Arts/Photog.:		Hardware Dev.:		HR/Other:	Y	Health/Lab	
MBA Graduates:	Y	Sales Trainees:		Music:		Consulting/Other:		Training:		Scientists/Research:	
		Advertising Pros.:		Broadcasting:				Health Care:		Petroleum/Chemicals:	
				Other:				Consulting:		Math/Other:	

TYPES OF BUSINESS:

Clearinghouse Services
Addressing Services
Domain Name Directories
Interoperability Services
Infrastructure

BRANDS/DIVISIONS/AFFILIATES:

CONTACTS:

Note: Officers with more than one job title may be intentionally listed here more than once.

Jeffrey Ganek, CEO
Lisa Hook, Pres.
Paul Lalljie, CFO/Sr. VP
Douglas S. Arnold, Sr. VP-Human Resources
Martin Lowen, General Counsel/Sr. VP/Sec.
Alex Tulchinsky, Sr. VP-Neustar Tech.
Gerald J. Kovach, Sr. VP-External Affairs
Steve J. Edwards, Sr. VP-Carrier Svcs., North America
Alexander L. Berry, Sr. VP-Internet Infrastructure Svcs.
James G. Cullen, Chmn.
Guenter H. Krauss, Sr. VP-Int'l Div., Carrier Svcs.

Phone: 571-434-5400 **Fax:**
Toll-Free: 855-683-2677
Address: 21575 Ridgetop Circle, Sterling, VA 20166 US

GROWTH PLANS/SPECIAL FEATURES:

NeuStar, Inc. provides directory and policy management services to communications carriers and commercial businesses. The company began as a sort of clearinghouse for maintaining telephone number portability standards, but has more recently transitioned into Internet services and high technology. The firm operates two primary divisions of services: carrier services and enterprise services. The carrier services segment maintains comprehensive databases for the dynamic routing of telecommunications data throughout the U.S. and Canada. These databases are geographically dispersed in multiple datacenters throughout North America and enable seamless connections between different carriers. The carrier services segment also enables optimized management and routing for IP (Internet Protocol) communications. The enterprise service segment primarily provides domain name system (DNS) services to enterprise customers, such as commercial businesses. Its services include Internet infrastructure services, which direct Internet traffic flow, resolve Internet queries, provide geolocation services and manage security protections; and registry services, which maintain registries for the .biz, .us, .co, .tel, .travel, .cn (China) and .tw (Taiwan) domains. NeuStar operates an exclusive contract with CTIA (originally known as the Cellular Telecommunications Industry Association) to serve the as the registry operator for the administration of U.S. Common Short Codes, which are short strings of numbers to which text messages can be addressed over participating wireless networks. In April 2011, the company announced plans to acquire the numbering management assets of Evolving Systems, Inc.

FINANCIALS:

Sales and profits are in thousands of dollars—add 000 to get the full amount. 2011 Note: Financial information for 2011 was not available for all companies at press time.

2011 Sales: $620,500 — 2011 Profits: $160,823
2010 Sales: $488,845 — 2010 Profits: $106,209
2009 Sales: $480,385 — 2009 Profits: $101,141
2008 Sales: $488,845 — 2008 Profits: $4,294
2007 Sales: $429,172 — 2007 Profits: $92,335

U.S. Stock Ticker: NSR
Int'l Ticker:
Int'l Exchange:
Employees: 1,022 Fiscal Year Ends: 12/31
Parent Company:

SALARIES/BENEFITS:

Pension Plan: ESOP Stock Plan: Profit Sharing: Top Exec. Salary: $593,848 Bonus: $591,000
Savings Plan: Stock Purch. Plan: Second Exec. Salary: $470,041 Bonus: $550,000

OTHER THOUGHTS:

Apparent Women Officers or Directors: 1
Hot Spot for Advancement for Women/Minorities:

LOCATIONS: ("Y" = Yes)

West:	Southwest:	Midwest:	Southeast:	Northeast:	International:
Y				Y	Y

NEW JERSEY RESOURCES CORPORATION www.njresources.com

Industry Group Code: 221210

Management:		Sales/Marketing:		Liberal Arts:		Information Systems:		Professionals:		Technical/Scientific:	
Mgmt. Trainees:		Mktg. Professionals:	Y	Gen. Writing/Editing:	Y	Info. Management:	Y	Finance/Acct.:	Y	Engineers, Elec.:	Y
Experienced Mgmt.:	Y	Retail Sales:		Technical Writing:		Software Dev.:		Law:	Y	Engineers, Other:	Y
Int'l Business:		Commercial/Industrial:	Y	Graphic Arts/Photog.:		Hardware Dev.:		HR/Other:	Y	Health/Lab	
MBA Graduates:	Y	Sales Trainees:		Music:		Consulting/Other:		Training:	Y	Scientists/Research:	
		Advertising Pros.:		Broadcasting:				Health Care:		Petroleum/Chemicals:	Y
				Other:				Consulting:		Math/Other:	

TYPES OF BUSINESS:

Utilities-Natural Gas
Energy-Related Services
Appliance Repair
Storage Management
Pipeline Capacity
Energy Investments

BRANDS/DIVISIONS/AFFILIATES:

New Jersey Natural Gas Company
NJR Home Services Company
NJR Energy Services Company
NJR Energy Investments
NJR Clean Energy Ventures
NJR Energy Corporation
Commercial Realty & Resources
NJR Plumbing Services

CONTACTS: *Note: Officers with more than one job title may be intentionally listed here more than once.*

Laurence M. Downes, CEO
Glenn C. Lockwood, CFO/Exec. VP
Mariellen Dugan, General Counsel/Sr. VP
Dennis Puma, Dir.-Investor Rel.
William Foley, Treas.
Rhonda M. Figueroa, Corp. Sec.
Kathleen T. Ellis, Exec. VP/COO-New Jersey Natural Gas
Stephen D. Westhoven, Sr. VP-NJR Energy Svcs.
Stan Kosierowski, Pres., NJR Clean Energy Ventures/NJR Home Svcs.
Laurence M. Downes, Chmn.

Phone: 732-938-1480 **Fax:** 732-938-3154
Toll-Free:
Address: 1415 Wyckoff Rd., Wall, NJ 07719 US

GROWTH PLANS/SPECIAL FEATURES:

New Jersey Resources Corporation (NJR) is an energy services holding company providing retail and wholesale natural gas and energy-related services from the Gulf Coast to New England, the Mid-Continent region, the West Coast and Canada. NJR operates through three segments: natural gas distribution; energy services and retail and other operations. The natural gas distribution segment consists of wholly-owned subsidiary New Jersey Natural Gas Company (NJNG), a provider of natural gas to roughly 490,000 residential and commercial customers in New Jersey's Monmouth, Ocean, Middlesex, Morris and Burlington counties, as well as a participant in off-system sales and capacity release markets. NJNG purchases its gas supply in long-term, winter-term and short-term contracts from 100 suppliers. The energy services segment consists of subsidiary NJR Energy Services Company, which provides unregulated wholesale energy services and natural gas storage and transportation asset optimization services. The retail and other operations segment includes NJR's various retail and service subsidiaries. These include NJR Energy Investments, which consolidates the firm's unregulated energy investments, such as NJR Clean Energy Ventures, NJR Investment and NJR Energy Corporation. Additionally, subsidiary NJR Retail Holdings consolidates NJR Home Services Company, which offers repair services for heating, ventilation and cooling (HVAC) appliances; NJR Plumbing Services, a plumbing repair and installation service company; and Commercial Realty & Resources, a commercial real estate developer. Additionally, NJR maintains a number of midstream asset investments, including a 5.53% equity interest in the Iroquois Pipeline.

NJR's employee benefits include medical, dental and life insurance; a 401(k) plan; a pension plan; disability protection; long-term care coverage; and flexible spending accounts.

FINANCIALS: **Sales and profits are in thousands of dollars—add 000 to get the full amount. 2011 Note: Financial information for 2011 was not available for all companies at press time.**

2011 Sales: $3,009,209 — 2011 Profits: $101,299
2010 Sales: $2,639,304 — 2010 Profits: $117,457
2009 Sales: $2,592,460 — 2009 Profits: $27,242
2008 Sales: $3,816,210 — 2008 Profits: $113,910
2007 Sales: $3,021,765 — 2007 Profits: $65,281

U.S. Stock Ticker: NJR
Int'l Ticker:
Int'l Exchange:
Employees: 891 Fiscal Year Ends: 9/30
Parent Company:

SALARIES/BENEFITS:

Pension Plan: Y | ESOP Stock Plan: | Profit Sharing: | Top Exec. Salary: $709,800 | Bonus: $
Savings Plan: Y | Stock Purch. Plan: | Second Exec. Salary: $291,923 | Bonus: $185,000

OTHER THOUGHTS:

Apparent Women Officers or Directors: 7
Hot Spot for Advancement for Women/Minorities: Y

LOCATIONS: ("Y" = Yes)

West:	Southwest:	Midwest:	Southeast:	Northeast:	International:
	Y			Y	

NEW YORK MERCANTILE EXCHANGE INC

www.cmegroup.com

Industry Group Code: 523210

Management:		**Sales/Marketing:**		**Liberal Arts:**		**Information Systems:**		**Professionals:**		**Technical/Scientific:**	
Mgmt. Trainees:		Mktg. Professionals:	Y	Gen. Writing/Editing:	Y	Info. Management:	Y	Finance/Acct.:	Y	Engineers, Elec.:	
Experienced Mgmt.:	Y	Retail Sales:		Technical Writing:		Software Dev.:	Y	Law:	Y	Engineers, Other:	
Int'l Business:	Y	Commercial/Industrial:		Graphic Arts/Photog.:		Hardware Dev.:		HR/Other:	Y	Health/Lab	
MBA Graduates:	Y	Sales Trainees:		Music:		Consulting/Other:		Training:	Y	Scientists/Research:	
		Advertising Pros.:	Y	Broadcasting:				Health Care:		Petroleum/Chemicals:	
				Other:				Consulting:		Math/Other:	Y

TYPES OF BUSINESS:

Futures Exchange
Clearing & Settlement Services
Electronic Trading
Market Data

BRANDS/DIVISIONS/AFFILIATES:

McGraw-Hill
CME Group Inc
Commodity Exchange Inc

CONTACTS:

Note: Officers with more than one job title may be intentionally listed here more than once.

Craig S. Donohue, CEO
Bryan T. Durkin, COO
Phupinder Gill, Pres.
James E. Parisi, CFO/Managing Dir.-Fiance & Corp. Dev.
Hilda Harris Piell, Chief Human Resources Officer/Managing Dir.
Kevin Kometer, CIO/Managing Dir.
Laurent Paulhac, Managing Dir.-Prod. & Svcs.
Kathleen M. Cronin, General Counsel/Corp. Sec./Managing Dir.
Julie Holzrichter, Managing Dir.-Global Oper.
John Pietroqicz, Managing Dir.-Bus. Dev. & Corp. Finance
James V. Pieper, Chief Acct. Officer/Managing Dir.
Derek Sammann, Managing Dir.-Foreign Exchange & Interest Rate
Kimberly Taylor, Pres., CME Clearing House Div.
Scot E. Warren, Managing Dir.-Equity Index Prod. & Svcs.
Kendal Vroman, Managing Dir.-Commodity, Info. Prod. & OTC Svcs.
Terrence A. Duffy, Chmn.

Phone: 212-299-2000 **Fax:** 212-301-4623
Toll-Free: 866-716-7274
Address: 1 N. End Ave., World Financial Ctr., New York, NY 10282 US

GROWTH PLANS/SPECIAL FEATURES:

New York Mercantile Exchange, Inc. (NYMEX) is one of the largest exchanges in the world for the trading of energy futures and options contracts. The company is a subsidiary of CME Group, Inc. (formerly Chicago Mercantile Exchange Holdings), a diverse international derivatives exchange located in Chicago. NYMEX offers clients different types of memberships, including corporate, individual and clearing. NYMEX is a designated contract market that offers the trade of futures and options contracts across the agriculture and energy markets and includes commodities such as crude oil, coal, natural gas, ethanol, heating oil, gasoline, propane and electricity. It also offers exchange for steel, palladium, platinum and uranium contracts, as well as certain agriculture futures such as cocoa, coffee, cotton and sugar. NYMEX provides physical facilities necessary for an open-outcry auction market, electronic trading systems and systems for matching and clearing all trades executed on the exchanges. The firm derives significant revenues from the sale of market data. It is also a major provider of financial services to the energy and metals industries.Subsidiary Commodity Exchange, Inc. (COMEX) offers contracts on gold, silver and copper futures and options. In November 2011, CME Group and McGraw-Hill formed a partnership for the purpose of entering the index services business, where $6 trillion in assets are to be benchmarked against leading indices.

FINANCIALS:

Sales and profits are in thousands of dollars—add 000 to get the full amount. 2011 Note: Financial information for 2011 was not available for all companies at press time.

2011 Sales: $ | 2011 Profits: $
2010 Sales: $ | 2010 Profits: $
2009 Sales: $ | 2009 Profits: $
2008 Sales: $ | 2008 Profits: $
2007 Sales: $ | 2007 Profits: $

U.S. Stock Ticker: Subsidiary
Int'l Ticker:
Int'l Exchange:
Employees: Fiscal Year Ends: 12/31
Parent Company: CME GROUP INC

SALARIES/BENEFITS:

Pension Plan: ESOP Stock Plan: Profit Sharing: Top Exec. Salary: $ Bonus: $
Savings Plan: Stock Purch. Plan: Second Exec. Salary: $ Bonus: $

OTHER THOUGHTS:

Apparent Women Officers or Directors: 4
Hot Spot for Advancement for Women/Minorities: Y

LOCATIONS: ("Y" = Yes)

West:	Southwest:	Midwest:	Southeast:	Northeast:	International:
				Y	Y

NIC INC

www.egov.com

Industry Group Code: 518210

Management:		Sales/Marketing:		Liberal Arts:		Information Systems:		Professionals:		Technical/Scientific:	
Mgmt. Trainees:		Mktg. Professionals:	Y	Gen. Writing/Editing:	Y	Info. Management:	Y	Finance/Acct.:	Y	Engineers, Elec.:	Y
Experienced Mgmt.:	Y	Retail Sales:		Technical Writing:	Y	Software Dev.:	Y	Law:	Y	Engineers, Other:	
Int'l Business:		Commercial/Industrial:	Y	Graphic Arts/Photog.:	Y	Hardware Dev.:		HR/Other:	Y	Health/Lab	
MBA Graduates:	Y	Sales Trainees:	Y	Music:		Consulting/Other:		Training:	Y	Scientists/Research:	
		Advertising Pros.:		Broadcasting:				Health Care:		Petroleum/Chemicals:	
				Other:				Consulting:		Math/Other:	

TYPES OF BUSINESS:

E-Government Services
Internet Portal Services
Electronic Filing Software
Application Development
Online Campaign Expenditure Development

BRANDS/DIVISIONS/AFFILIATES:

NIC Technologies
NIC Conquest
Uniform Commercial Code

CONTACTS: *Note: Officers with more than one job title may be intentionally listed here more than once.*

Harry H. Herington, CEO
William F. Bradley, Jr., COO
Stephen M. Kovzan, CFO
Ron Thornburgh, Sr. VP-Mktg. & Sales
William F. Bradley, Jr., General Counsel
Angela Skinner, Dir.-Comm.
Angela Skinner, Dir.-Investor Rel.
Aimi Daughtery, Chief Acct. Officer
Robert Knapp, Exec. VP
Harry H. Herington, Chmn.

Phone:	**Fax:** 913-498-3472
Toll-Free: 877-234-3468	
Address: 25501 W. Valley Pkwy., Ste. 300, Olathe, KS 66061 US	

GROWTH PLANS/SPECIAL FEATURES:

NIC, Inc. provides eGovernment services that help governments use the Internet to increase internal efficiencies and provide a higher level of service to businesses and citizens. It operates in two divisions: portal outsourcing and software and services. The portal outsourcing segment enters into long-term contracts with governments to design, build and operate web-based portals on their behalf. These portals consist of web sites and applications that allow businesses and citizens to access government information online and complete transactions, including applying for permits, retrieving driver's license records or filing a government-mandated form or report. The self-funding business model allows the firm to generate revenues by sharing in the fees its collects from eGovernment transactions. NIC currently has contracts to provide portal outsourcing services to over 25 states. The company typically enters into three- to five-year contracts with government partners and manages operations for each contractual relationship through separate local subsidiaries. The software and services segment primarily includes the company's Uniform Commercial Code (UCC) and corporate filings software development, as well as its ethics and elections businesses. The UCC and corporate filings software development business, NIC Conquest, is a provider of software applications and services for electronic filings and document management solutions for governments. This business is primarily engaged in servicing its contract with the California Secretary of State and is not actively marketing its applications and services in respect of new engagements. The ethics and elections business, NIC Technologies, designs and develops online campaign expenditure and ethics compliance systems for federal and state government agencies. This business is primarily engaged in servicing its contracts with the Federal Election Commission (FEC) and the State of Michigan. In 2011, NIC received new contracts to manage the online government portals for Mississippi, Delaware and Oregon.

Employees are offered medical and dental insurance; life insurance; disability coverage; and an educational reimbursement.

FINANCIALS: **Sales and profits are in thousands of dollars—add 000 to get the full amount. 2011 Note: Financial information for 2011 was not available for all companies at press time.**

2011 Sales: $	2011 Profits: $	**U.S. Stock Ticker: EGOV**
2010 Sales: $161,534	2010 Profits: $18,363	**Int'l Ticker:**
2009 Sales: $132,885	2009 Profits: $13,946	Int'l Exchange:
2008 Sales: $100,575	2008 Profits: $11,921	Employees: 596 Fiscal Year Ends: 12/31
2007 Sales: $85,755	2007 Profits: $11,955	Parent Company:

SALARIES/BENEFITS:

Pension Plan:	ESOP Stock Plan:	Profit Sharing:	Top Exec. Salary: $390,450	Bonus: $197,846
Savings Plan: Y	Stock Purch. Plan: Y		Second Exec. Salary: $267,150	Bonus: $235,368

OTHER THOUGHTS:

Apparent Women Officers or Directors: 2
Hot Spot for Advancement for Women/Minorities:

LOCATIONS: ("Y" = Yes)

West:	Southwest:	Midwest:	Southeast:	Northeast:	International:
Y	Y	Y	Y	Y	

NORTHWESTERN CORPORATION

www.northwesternenergy.com

Industry Group Code: 221

Management:		Sales/Marketing:		Liberal Arts:		Information Systems:		Professionals:		Technical/Scientific:	
Mgmt. Trainees:		Mktg. Professionals:	Y	Gen. Writing/Editing:	Y	Info. Management:	Y	Finance/Acct.:	Y	Engineers, Elec.:	Y
Experienced Mgmt.:	Y	Retail Sales:		Technical Writing:		Software Dev.:		Law:	Y	Engineers, Other:	Y
Int'l Business:		Commercial/Industrial:	Y	Graphic Arts/Photog.:		Hardware Dev.:		HR/Other:	Y	Health/Lab	
MBA Graduates:	Y	Sales Trainees:		Music:		Consulting/Other:		Training:	Y	Scientists/Research:	
		Advertising Pros.:		Broadcasting:				Health Care:		Petroleum/Chemicals:	Y
				Other:				Consulting:		Math/Other:	

TYPES OF BUSINESS:

Utilities-Electricity & Natural Gas
Energy Transmission & Distribution
Natural Gas Transmission & Distribution
Pipelines
Electricity Generation

BRANDS/DIVISIONS/AFFILIATES:

Northwestern Energy

CONTACTS:

Note: Officers with more than one job title may be intentionally listed here more than once.

Robert C. Rowe, CEO
Robert C. Rowe, Pres.
Brian B. Bird, CFO/VP/Treas.
Bobbi L. Schroeppel, VP-Human Resources
Heather H. Grahame, General Counsel/VP
Bobbi L. Schroeppel, VP-Customer Care & Comm.
Kendall G. Kliewer, Controller/VP
Michael R. Cashell, VP-Transmission
Curtis T. Pohl, VP-Dist.
Patrick R. Corcoran, VP-Gov't & Regulatory Affairs
E. Linn Draper, Jr., Chmn.
John D. Hines, VP-Supply

Phone: 605-978-2900	**Fax:** 605-978-2910
Toll-Free:	
Address: 3010 W. 69th St., Sioux Falls, SD 57108 US	

GROWTH PLANS/SPECIAL FEATURES:

NorthWestern Corporation, doing business as NorthWestern Energy, is one of the largest providers of electricity and natural gas in the upper Midwest and Northwest, serving roughly 665,000 customers in Montana, South Dakota and Nebraska. The company operates in three segments: regulated electric operations; regulated natural gas operations; and all other. Through the regulated electric operations segment, the firm generates, transmits and delivers electricity to about 337,600 customers in 187 communities in Montana; and more than 60,800 customers in 110 communities in South Dakota. In Montana, the firm's transmission system consists of approximately 7,000 miles of transmission lines and 125,000 transmission poles. Most of the electricity supplied in Montana is purchased from unaffiliated generating companies. In South Dakota, where Northwestern maintains approximately 3,300 miles of overhead and underground transmission and distribution lines as well as 123 substations, electricity is supplied from three power plants in which the firm has a minority interest. Through the regulated natural gas operations segment, the company distributes natural gas to 181,300 customers in 105 Montana communities and 85,300 customers in 60 South Dakota and four Nebraska communities. The all other segment primarily consists of an unregulated natural gas contract, the wind down of its captive insurance subsidiary and miscellaneous service activities. In 2010, NorthWestern acquired a majority stake in the Battle Creek Natural Gas Field in Blaine County, Montana, with estimated net proven developed producing reserves of 7.6 billion cubic feet. In January 2011, it completed the construction of the Mill Creek Generating Station, a 150 Megawatt natural gas-fired facility in Montana.

The company offers its employees medical, dental, vision and prescription drug coverage; flexible spending accounts; life and accident insurance; short- and long-term disability coverage; an employee assistance program; tuition reimbursement; a 401(k); and adoption benefits.

FINANCIALS:

Sales and profits are in thousands of dollars—add 000 to get the full amount. 2011 Note: Financial information for 2011 was not available for all companies at press time.

2011 Sales: $1,362,500	2011 Profits: $115,200
2010 Sales: $1,110,720	2010 Profits: $77,376
2009 Sales: $1,141,910	2009 Profits: $73,420
2008 Sales: $1,260,793	2008 Profits: $67,601
2007 Sales: $1,200,060	2007 Profits: $53,191

U.S. Stock Ticker: NWE
Int'l Ticker:
Int'l Exchange:
Employees: 1,363 Fiscal Year Ends: 12/31
Parent Company:

SALARIES/BENEFITS:

Pension Plan:	ESOP Stock Plan:	Profit Sharing:	Top Exec. Salary: $500,000	Bonus: $276,500
Savings Plan: Y	Stock Purch. Plan:		Second Exec. Salary: $328,008	Bonus: $154,164

OTHER THOUGHTS:

Apparent Women Officers or Directors: 5
Hot Spot for Advancement for Women/Minorities: Y

LOCATIONS: ("Y" = Yes)

West:	Southwest:	Midwest:	Southeast:	Northeast:	International:
Y		Y			

NOTIFY TECHNOLOGY CORP

www.notifycorp.com

Industry Group Code: 511210C

Management:		**Sales/Marketing:**		**Liberal Arts:**		**Information Systems:**		**Professionals:**		**Technical/Scientific:**	
Mgmt. Trainees:		Mktg. Professionals:	Y	Gen. Writing/Editing:	Y	Info. Management:	Y	Finance/Acct.:	Y	Engineers, Elec.:	Y
Experienced Mgmt.:	Y	Retail Sales:		Technical Writing:	Y	Software Dev.:	Y	Law:	Y	Engineers, Other:	
Int'l Business:	Y	Commercial/Industrial:	Y	Graphic Arts/Photog.:		Hardware Dev.:		HR/Other:	Y	Health/Lab	
MBA Graduates:	Y	Sales Trainees:	Y	Music:		Consulting/Other:		Training:	Y	Scientists/Research:	
		Advertising Pros.:		Broadcasting:				Health Care:		Petroleum/Chemicals:	
				Other:				Consulting:		Math/Other:	

TYPES OF BUSINESS:

E-Mail Notification Systems
Messaging Services
Device Management Software

BRANDS/DIVISIONS/AFFILIATES:

NotifyLink On-Demand
NotifyLink On-Premise
NotifySync
NotifyMDM

CONTACTS:

Note: Officers with more than one job title may be intentionally listed here more than once.

Paul F. DePond, CEO
Paul F. DePond, Pres.
Gerald W. Rice, CFO
Rhonda Chicone-Shick, CTO
Rhonda Chicone-Shick, VP-Prod. Dev.
Rhonda Chicone-Shick, VP-Eng.
Gerald W. Rice, Corp. Sec.
Paul F. DePond, Chmn.

Phone: 408-777-7930 **Fax:** 408-996-7405
Toll-Free:
Address: 1054 S. De Anza Blvd., Ste. 202, San Jose, CA 95129 US

GROWTH PLANS/SPECIAL FEATURES:

Notify Technology Corp. is a software developer providing secure, wireless synchronization of e-mail and personal information management (PIM) across a variety of wireless devices and e-mail collaboration suites. The company's products provide secure wireless mobile access using handheld wireless devices, such as the BlackBerry; Apple iPhone, iPod Touch and iPad; Palm; Windows Mobile; Android devices; and Symbian, to manage e-mail, calendar appointments, address books and task information. Supported e-mail collaboration systems include Novell GroupWise, Microsoft Exchange and a variety of other collaboration suites, such as Mirapoint, CommuniGate Pro, Scalix, Oracle OCS, Oracle Beehive, Google, Kerio, MDaemon, Zimbra, FirstClass, Sun and Meeting Maker. In addition, its software supports wireless devices from different manufacturers and different network carriers around the world. The company sells its products primarily through direct sales in the U.S. and through resellers internationally. Notify's software solutions include NotifyLink On-Premise, which allows mobile users to read, compose, reply, forward and delete e-mails, view and edit attachments and perform PIM tasks; NotifyLink On-Demand, which provides the same wireless synchronization of e-mail, calendar, contacts and task information as NotifyLink On-Premise Edition without the need of on-premise hardware or software; and NotifySync, which provides wireless synchronization of e-mail and PIM between any BlackBerry and its ActiveSync server. In February 2011, the firm introduced its newest software tool, NotifyMDM, a mobile device management solution for large organizations.

FINANCIALS:

Sales and profits are in thousands of dollars—add 000 to get the full amount. 2011 Note: Financial information for 2011 was not available for all companies at press time.

2011 Sales: $6,800	2011 Profits: $- 500	**U.S. Stock Ticker: NTFY**
2010 Sales: $7,246	2010 Profits: $ 616	**Int'l Ticker:**
2009 Sales: $6,032	2009 Profits: $ 71	Int'l Exchange:
2008 Sales: $4,641	2008 Profits: $- 288	Employees: 85 Fiscal Year Ends: 9/30
2007 Sales: $3,947	2007 Profits: $- 426	Parent Company:

SALARIES/BENEFITS:

Pension Plan:	ESOP Stock Plan:	Profit Sharing:	Top Exec. Salary: $275,923	Bonus: $127,394
Savings Plan:	Stock Purch. Plan:		Second Exec. Salary: $187,622	Bonus: $63,697

OTHER THOUGHTS:

Apparent Women Officers or Directors: 1
Hot Spot for Advancement for Women/Minorities:

LOCATIONS: ("Y" = Yes)

West:	Southwest:	Midwest:	Southeast:	Northeast:	International:
Y		Y			

NOVAMED INC

www.surgerypartners.com

Industry Group Code: 6214

Management:		Sales/Marketing:		Liberal Arts:		Information Systems:		Professionals:		Technical/Scientific:	
Mgmt. Trainees:		Mktg. Professionals:	Y	Gen. Writing/Editing:		Info. Management:	Y	Finance/Acct.:	Y	Engineers, Elec.:	
Experienced Mgmt.:	Y	Retail Sales:		Technical Writing:	Y	Software Dev.:	Y	Law:	Y	Engineers, Other:	
Int'l Business:		Commercial/Industrial:		Graphic Arts/Photog.:		Hardware Dev.:		HR/Other:	Y	Health/Lab	Y
MBA Graduates:	Y	Sales Trainees:	Y	Music:		Consulting/Other:		Training:	Y	Scientists/Research:	
		Advertising Pros.:	Y	Broadcasting:				Health Care:	Y	Petroleum/Chemicals:	
				Other:				Consulting:		Math/Other:	

TYPES OF BUSINESS:

Outpatient Surgery
Eye-Care Services
Laser Vision Correction
Corrective Lenses Labs
Eye-Care Products Distribution
Purchasing and Supply Chain Services
Marketing Services

BRANDS/DIVISIONS/AFFILIATES:

H.I.G. Capital LLC
Surgery Center Holdings, Inc.

CONTACTS:

Note: Officers with more than one job title may be intentionally listed here more than once.

Mike Doyle, CEO
Mike Doyle, Pres.
Scott T. Macomber, CFO/Exec. VP
William Milo, VP-Admin.
John W. Lawrence, Jr., General Counsel/Sr. VP
Jeff Parks, VP-Oper. & Anesthesiology Svcs.
Christy Mistler, VP-Bus. Dev.
John P. Hart, Corp. Controller/VP
Thomas J. Chirillo, Sr. VP-Dev.

Phone: 312-664-4100 **Fax:** 312-664-4250
Toll-Free: 888-668-2633
Address: 333 W. Wacker Dr., Ste. 1010, Chicago, IL 60606 US

GROWTH PLANS/SPECIAL FEATURES:

NovaMed, Inc. is a health care services company and an owner and operator of ambulatory surgery centers (ASCs). The firm's primary focus is the acquisition, development and operation of ASCs in joint ownership with physicians throughout the U.S. The company owns and operates 37 ASCs located in 19 states. Historically, most of NovaMed's ASCs have been single-specialty ophthalmic surgical facilities where ophthalmologists perform surgical procedures, primarily cataract surgery. Over the past six years, however, the firm has focused on expanding into other specialties such as orthopedics (including podiatry), pain management, gastroenterology, urology, otolaryngology (ENT), plastic surgery and gynecology. NovaMed offers surgical services in specialties other than ophthalmology in 13 of its ASCs. It owns a majority interest in 35 of its ASCs, two of which it fully owns. The company also owns and operates optical laboratories, which specialize in surfacing, finishing and distributing corrective lenses and eyeglass lenses; an optical products purchasing organization, which offers optical products through more than 275 suppliers; and a marketing products and services business, which provides brochures, videos, advertising and web site design, education and training programs and consulting services to eye care professionals and optical product vendors. The firm provides business, information technology, administrative, support, billing, procurement and financial services to two eye care practices in Chicago and Atlanta pursuant to long-term agreements. Of surgical procedures performed in NovaMed's facilities in 2010, 55% were ophthalmic, 19% were pain management, 10% were orthopedic, 5% were gastroenterology, 4% were ENT and 2% were urology. Elective plastic surgery accounted about 1% of its total procedures. Other procedures accounted for the remaining 4%. In May 2011, the company was acquired by Surgery Center Holdings, Inc., an affiliate of private equity firm H.I.G. Capital LLC.

FINANCIALS:

Sales and profits are in thousands of dollars—add 000 to get the full amount. 2011 Note: Financial information for 2011 was not available for all companies at press time.

2011 Sales: $	2011 Profits: $
2010 Sales: $92,640	2010 Profits: $
2009 Sales: $156,444	2009 Profits: $7,511
2008 Sales: $141,220	2008 Profits: $7,218
2007 Sales: $128,621	2007 Profits: $-5,594

U.S. Stock Ticker: Subsidiary
Int'l Ticker:
Int'l Exchange:
Employees: 772 Fiscal Year Ends: 12/31
Parent Company: SURGERY CENTER HOLDINGS INC

SALARIES/BENEFITS:

Pension Plan:	ESOP Stock Plan:	Profit Sharing:	Top Exec. Salary: $553,725	Bonus: $415,294
Savings Plan:	Stock Purch. Plan:		Second Exec. Salary: $290,000	Bonus: $145,000

OTHER THOUGHTS:

Apparent Women Officers or Directors: 1
Hot Spot for Advancement for Women/Minorities:

LOCATIONS: ("Y" = Yes)

West:	Southwest:	Midwest:	Southeast:	Northeast:	International:
Y	Y	Y	Y	Y	

NOVEN PHARMACEUTICALS INC

www.noven.com

Industry Group Code: 325412A

Management:		Sales/Marketing:		Liberal Arts:		Information Systems:		Professionals:		Technical/Scientific:	
Mgmt. Trainees:		Mktg. Professionals:	Y	Gen. Writing/Editing:		Info. Management:	Y	Finance/Acct.:	Y	Engineers, Elec.:	
Experienced Mgmt.:	Y	Retail Sales:		Technical Writing:	Y	Software Dev.:	Y	Law:	Y	Engineers, Other:	
Int'l Business:	Y	Commercial/Industrial:	Y	Graphic Arts/Photog.:		Hardware Dev.:		HR/Other:	Y	Health/Lab	Y
MBA Graduates:	Y	Sales Trainees:	Y	Music:		Consulting/Other:		Training:	Y	Scientists/Research:	Y
		Advertising Pros.:		Broadcasting:				Health Care:	Y	Petroleum/Chemicals:	
				Other:				Consulting:		Math/Other:	Y

TYPES OF BUSINESS:

Drug Delivery Systems
Hormone Replacement Products
Pain Management Products
Central Nervous System Products
Transdermal Drug Delivery Systems

BRANDS/DIVISIONS/AFFILIATES:

Novogyne Pharmaceuticals
Menorest
Daytrana
DOT Matrix
Estalis
Noven Therapeutics
Estradot
Stavzor

CONTACTS: *Note: Officers with more than one job title may be intentionally listed here more than once.*

Jeffrey F. Eisenberg, CEO
Jeffrey F. Eisenberg, Pres.
Michael D. Price, CFO/VP
Andrew C. Panagy, VP-Mktg. & Sales
Lance D. Williams, VP-Human Resources
Steven F. Dinh, Chief Scientific Officer/VP
Joel S. Lippman, Exec. VP-Prod. Dev.
Jeff T. Mihm, Chief Admin. Officer
Jeff T. Mihm, General Counsel/VP
Richard Gilbert, VP-Oper.
Patrick Gallagher, VP-Bus. Dev.
Joseph C. Jones, VP-Corp. Affairs
Peter G. Amanatides, VP-Quality Assurance & Quality Control
Joel S. Lippman, Chief Medical Officer

Phone: 305-253-5099	**Fax:** 305-251-1887
Toll-Free:	
Address: 11960 S.W. 144th St., Miami, FL 33186 US	

GROWTH PLANS/SPECIAL FEATURES:

Noven Pharmaceuticals, Inc. develops and manufactures advanced transdermal drug delivery systems and prescription transdermal products. Its principal commercialized products are transdermal drug delivery systems designed with its DOT Matrix technology for use in hormone replacement therapy. The firm's first product was an estrogen patch for the treatment of menopausal symptoms, marketed under the name Vivelle in the U.S. and Canada, and under the name Menorest in Europe and other markets. The company also launched the smallest transdermal estrogen patch ever approved by the U.S. FDA, Vivelle-Dot, and markets the product in several foreign countries under the name Estradot. The firm also markets its Lidocaine/DentiPatch for dental pain associated with dental procedures. Other Noven products include Pexeva for depression, panic disorder, obsessive compulsive disorder (OCD) and generalized anxiety disorder (GAD); Lithobid for bipolar disorder; Stavzor for bipolar disorder, migraine and epilepsy; Daytrana for ADHD; and its fentanyl transdermal system for chronic pain. The company also has four products in development: Lithium QD for bipolar disorder; Stavzor ER (extended release) for bipolar disorder, migraines and epilepsy; Mesafem for hot flashes; and a treatment for ADHD. Noven has partial ownership of a joint venture formed with Novartis Pharmaceuticals, Vivelle Ventures, doing business under the name Novogyne Pharmaceuticals. Novogyne markets Vivelle, Vivelle-Dot and CombiPatch (a combination estrogen/progestin transdermal patch for the treatment of menopausal symptoms) in the U.S. Beyond Novartis, Noven collaborates with a number of other pharmaceutical companies, such as Aventis, Shire, and Procter & Gamble.

FINANCIALS: **Sales and profits are in thousands of dollars—add 000 to get the full amount. 2011 Note: Financial information for 2011 was not available for all companies at press time.**

2011 Sales: $	2011 Profits: $
2010 Sales: $	2010 Profits: $
2009 Sales: $	2009 Profits: $
2008 Sales: $108,175	2008 Profits: $21,412
2007 Sales: $83,161	2007 Profits: $-45,376

U.S. Stock Ticker: Subsidiary
Int'l Ticker:
Int'l Exchange:
Employees: 650 Fiscal Year Ends: 12/31
Parent Company: HISAMITSU PHARMACEUTICAL CO INC

SALARIES/BENEFITS:

Pension Plan:	ESOP Stock Plan:	Profit Sharing:	Top Exec. Salary: $483,524	Bonus: $182,500
Savings Plan: Y	Stock Purch. Plan:		Second Exec. Salary: $422,500	Bonus: $365,625

OTHER THOUGHTS:

Apparent Women Officers or Directors:
Hot Spot for Advancement for Women/Minorities:

LOCATIONS: ("Y" = Yes)

West:	Southwest:	Midwest:	Southeast:	Northeast:	International:
			Y	Y	

NTELOS HOLDING CORP

www.ntelos.com

Industry Group Code: 517110

Management:		Sales/Marketing:		Liberal Arts:		Information Systems:		Professionals:		Technical/Scientific:	
Mgmt. Trainees:		Mktg. Professionals:	Y	Gen. Writing/Editing:	Y	Info. Management:	Y	Finance/Acct.:	Y	Engineers, Elec.:	Y
Experienced Mgmt.:	Y	Retail Sales:		Technical Writing:		Software Dev.:	Y	Law:	Y	Engineers, Other:	
Int'l Business:		Commercial/Industrial:	Y	Graphic Arts/Photog.:		Hardware Dev.:		HR/Other:	Y	Health/Lab	
MBA Graduates:	Y	Sales Trainees:	Y	Music:		Consulting/Other:		Training:	Y	Scientists/Research:	
		Advertising Pros.:		Broadcasting:				Health Care:		Petroleum/Chemicals:	
				Other:				Consulting:		Math/Other:	

TYPES OF BUSINESS:

Wireless & Wireline Services
Digital PCS Services
Paging Services
Internet Services

BRANDS/DIVISIONS/AFFILIATES:

Sprint Spectrum L.P.
Sprint Nextel Corp
FRAWG
nTouch

CONTACTS:

Note: Officers with more than one job title may be intentionally listed here more than once.

James A. Hyde, CEO
James A. Hyde, Pres.
Michael B. Moneymaker, CFO/Exec. VP
Mary McDermott, Sr. VP-Legal & Regulatory Affairs
Michael B. Moneymaker, Treas./Corp. Sec.
Conrad J. Hunter, Exec. VP/Pres., Wireless Oper.
Frank L. Berry, Exec. VP/Pres., Wireline Oper.
Michael Huber, Chmn.

Phone: 540-946-3500 **Fax:**
Toll-Free: 877-468-3567
Address: 401 Spring Ln., Ste. 300, Waynesboro, VA 22980 US

GROWTH PLANS/SPECIAL FEATURES:

nTelos Holding Corp. is a leading provider of wireless and wireline communications services to consumers and businesses primarily in Virginia, West Virginia and parts of Maryland and Pennsylvania. The company's wireless operations are composed of its nTelos-branded retail and wholesale businesses that it operates under an exclusive contract with Sprint Spectrum L.P., a subsidiary of Sprint Nextel Corporation. The firm's prepaid wireless services are offered under the FRAWG brand name. Its wireless business operates a code division multiple access (CDMA) digital PCS (personal communications service) network in Virginia, West Virginia and portions of Pennsylvania, Kentucky, Maryland, Ohio and North Carolina, with a total covered population of 5.8 million people. Postpay plans are the most popular service offerings, accounting for 71% of the firm's wireless customers, with prepay plans accounting for 29%. The company's wireline business is supported by a 5,800-mile regional fiber optic network. nTelos conducts its wireline business through two subsidiaries that qualify as rural local exchange carriers (RLEC). The company operates 129,700 RLEC telephone access lines and participates in partnerships that directly connect its networks with many of the largest markets in the mid-Atlantic region. nTelos markets and sells local and long distance, voice and data services almost exclusively to business customers through its competitive local exchange carrier (CLEC) and Internet service provider (ISP) operation, with 34,900 CLEC access line connections. It also offers DSL services in over 98% of its RLEC service area and operates 33,500 broadband access connections in its markets. In April 2010, nTelos launched the nTouch, a unified mobile communications product to link nTelos business desk and wireless phones using IP Centrex technology. In December 2010, the firm agreed to spin off its wireline operations to create a separate company; and acquired the FiberNet operations of One Communications Corp. In February 2011, nTelos opened a new location in Richmond, Virginia.

FINANCIALS:

Sales and profits are in thousands of dollars—add 000 to get the full amount. 2011 Note: Financial information for 2011 was not available for all companies at press time.

2011 Sales: $422,600 — 2011 Profits: $-23,700
2010 Sales: $545,684 — 2010 Profits: $46,345
2009 Sales: $549,700 — 2009 Profits: $64,175
2008 Sales: $535,906 — 2008 Profits: $44,877
2007 Sales: $500,394 — 2007 Profits: $32,453

U.S. Stock Ticker: NTLS
Int'l Ticker:
Int'l Exchange:
Employees: 1,445 Fiscal Year Ends: 12/31
Parent Company:

SALARIES/BENEFITS:

Pension Plan: ESOP Stock Plan: Profit Sharing: Top Exec. Salary: $575,000 Bonus: $549,585
Savings Plan: Stock Purch. Plan: Second Exec. Salary: $332,121 Bonus: $190,465

OTHER THOUGHTS:

Apparent Women Officers or Directors: 2
Hot Spot for Advancement for Women/Minorities:

LOCATIONS: ("Y" = Yes)

West:	Southwest:	Midwest:	Southeast:	Northeast:	International:
				Y	

NUGGET MARKET

www.nuggetmarket.com

Industry Group Code: 445110

Management:		Sales/Marketing:		Liberal Arts:		Information Systems:		Professionals:		Technical/Scientific:	
Mgmt. Trainees:	Y	Mktg. Professionals:	Y	Gen. Writing/Editing:	Y	Info. Management:	Y	Finance/Acct.:	Y	Engineers, Elec.:	
Experienced Mgmt.:	Y	Retail Sales:	Y	Technical Writing:		Software Dev.:	Y	Law:	Y	Engineers, Other:	
Int'l Business:		Commercial/Industrial:		Graphic Arts/Photog.:	Y	Hardware Dev.:		HR/Other:	Y	Health/Lab	
MBA Graduates:	Y	Sales Trainees:	Y	Music:		Consulting/Other:		Training:	Y	Scientists/Research:	
		Advertising Pros.:	Y	Broadcasting:				Health Care:		Petroleum/Chemicals:	
				Other:				Consulting:		Math/Other:	

TYPES OF BUSINESS:

Supermarket

BRANDS/DIVISIONS/AFFILIATES:

FishWise
Price Survey
NuggetMarket.com
Food 4 Less

CONTACTS: *Note: Officers with more than one job title may be intentionally listed here more than once.*

Eric Stille, Pres.
Kate Stille, Dir.-Mktg.
Eugene N. Stille, Chmn.

Phone: 530-669-3300	**Fax:**
Toll-Free:	
Address: 168 Court St., Woodland, CA 95695 US	

GROWTH PLANS/SPECIAL FEATURES:

Nugget Market is a family-owned chain of nine Nugget Markets full-service grocery stores and three Food 4 Less price-impact grocery stores in the Sacramento, California area. The stores offer conventional and organic produce, provided through local partner Nor-Cal Produce; meat and seafood, including natural Angus beef, free-range chicken and Nugget's own sausage; specialty grocery items; over 400 varieties of specialty cheese; bakery products; adult beverages; staple grocery products; eco-friendly bath, body and hair-care products; and vitamins, herbs and supplements. The company's FishWise system is a color-coded labeling program designed to make customers aware of the sustainability and population health of particular seafood items sold. The stores also maintain kitchens with different prepared meals inspired by Asian and other international cuisines, as well as staples such as sandwiches and salads. Additionally, coffee and juice bars are located in each establishment. The company aims to offer the lowest prices in the area and provides a Price Survey for customers to compare Nugget prices to those of other stores. The number of people who believe Nugget provides the lowest prices are then posted above the front entrance. The firm provides recipes for entrees, appetizers, desserts, sides and condiments, as well as a calendar of store events on NuggetMarket.com. Such events include wine tastings, sponsorship and seasonal events and talks with health professionals.

Employee benefits include health, prescription, vision and dental coverage; a 401(k); a profit sharing plan; a flexible spending account; a flexible work schedule; and life insurance.

FINANCIALS: **Sales and profits are in thousands of dollars—add 000 to get the full amount. 2011 Note: Financial information for 2011 was not available for all companies at press time.**

2011 Sales: $	2011 Profits: $	**U.S. Stock Ticker: Private**
2010 Sales: $	2010 Profits: $	**Int'l Ticker:**
2009 Sales: $	2009 Profits: $	Int'l Exchange:
2008 Sales: $	2008 Profits: $	Employees: Fiscal Year Ends:
2007 Sales: $	2007 Profits: $	Parent Company:

SALARIES/BENEFITS:

Pension Plan:	ESOP Stock Plan:	Profit Sharing: Y	Top Exec. Salary: $	Bonus: $
Savings Plan: Y	Stock Purch. Plan:		Second Exec. Salary: $	Bonus: $

OTHER THOUGHTS:

Apparent Women Officers or Directors: 1
Hot Spot for Advancement for Women/Minorities:

LOCATIONS: ("Y" = Yes)

West:	Southwest:	Midwest:	Southeast:	Northeast:	International:
Y					

NUSTAR ENERGY LP

www.nustarenergy.com

Industry Group Code: 424710

Management:		Sales/Marketing:		Liberal Arts:		Information Systems:		Professionals:		Technical/Scientific:	
Mgmt. Trainees:		Mktg. Professionals:	Y	Gen. Writing/Editing:		Info. Management:	Y	Finance/Acct.:	Y	Engineers, Elec.:	
Experienced Mgmt.:	Y	Retail Sales:		Technical Writing:		Software Dev.:		Law:	Y	Engineers, Other:	Y
Int'l Business:	Y	Commercial/Industrial:	Y	Graphic Arts/Photog.:		Hardware Dev.:		HR/Other:	Y	Health/Lab	
MBA Graduates:	Y	Sales Trainees:	Y	Music:		Consulting/Other:		Training:	Y	Scientists/Research:	
		Advertising Pros.:		Broadcasting:				Health Care:		Petroleum/Chemicals:	Y
				Other:				Consulting:		Math/Other:	

TYPES OF BUSINESS:

Petroleum Pipeline Transportation
Anhydrous Ammonia Transportation
Refined Products Transportation

BRANDS/DIVISIONS/AFFILIATES:

Aves Oil
S-Oil
AGE Refining
NuStar Logistics, L.P.
NuStar Pipe Line Operating Partnership L.P
NuStar GP, LLC
NuStar GP Holdings, LLC

CONTACTS:

Note: Officers with more than one job title may be intentionally listed here more than once.

Curtis Anastasio, CEO
Curtis Anastasio, Pres.
Steve Blank, CFO/Sr. VP
Brad Barron, General Counsel/Sr. VP/Sec.
Steven Blank, Treas.
Tom Shoaf, Controller/VP
Bill Greehey, Chmn.

Phone: 210-918-2000	**Fax:**
Toll-Free:	
Address: 2330 N. Loop 1604 W., San Antonio, TX 78248 US	

GROWTH PLANS/SPECIAL FEATURES:

NuStar Energy L.P. (NuStar) provides terminaling, storage, refining, transporting and marketing services for petroleum, anhydrous ammonia and asphalt products. The company conducts its operations through its subsidiaries, NuStar Logistics L.P. and NuStar Pipe Line Operating Partnership, L.P. NuStar operates in three business segments: storage, transportation and asphalt and fuels marketing. The storage segment owns 60 crude oil and intermediate feedstock storage tanks in Texas and California that have a storage capacity of 12.5 million barrels. In addition, this segment operates pipelines in Texas and Oklahoma and 22 refining terminals throughout the U.S that have an aggregate capacity of 4.5 million barrels. The transportation segment transports refined petroleum products, crude oil and anhydrous ammonia through 3,795 miles of pipeline. Refined products are transported from Valero Energy's Corpus Christi, Mckee, Three Rivers and Ardmore refineries to destinations in Texas, Oklahoma, Colorado, New Mexico, Arizona and other mid-continent states. Refined products include gasoline, diesel and jet fuel, natural gas liquids and other petrochemicals. The asphalt and fuels marketing segment includes its asphalt refining and fuels marketing operations. It refines crude oil to produce asphalt and other refined products. The firm also buys and resells gasoline and other petroleum products. In February 2011, NuStar closed on a joint venture with Turkish oil companies S-Oil and Aves Oil that gives NuStar majority ownership and operational control of two petroleum terminals in Turkey. In April 2011, the firm acquired a portion of AGE Refining's terminal and refining assets in south Texas for $41 million.

The company offers its employees a health and wellness program; adoption assistance; and tuition reimbursement.

FINANCIALS:

Sales and profits are in thousands of dollars—add 000 to get the full amount. 2011 Note: Financial information for 2011 was not available for all companies at press time.

2011 Sales: $6,575,300	2011 Profits: $221,600
2010 Sales: $4,403,061	2010 Profits: $238,970
2009 Sales: $3,855,871	2009 Profits: $224,875
2008 Sales: $4,828,770	2008 Profits: $254,018
2007 Sales: $1,475,014	2007 Profits: $150,298

U.S. Stock Ticker: NS
Int'l Ticker:
Int'l Exchange:
Employees: 1,413 Fiscal Year Ends: 12/31
Parent Company:

SALARIES/BENEFITS:

Pension Plan: Y	ESOP Stock Plan:	Profit Sharing:	Top Exec. Salary: $480,900	Bonus: $385,000
Savings Plan: Y	Stock Purch. Plan:		Second Exec. Salary: $346,015	Bonus: $173,000

OTHER THOUGHTS:

Apparent Women Officers or Directors:
Hot Spot for Advancement for Women/Minorities:

LOCATIONS: ("Y" = Yes)

West:	Southwest:	Midwest:	Southeast:	Northeast:	International:
Y	Y	Y	Y	Y	Y

NUTRASWEET COMPANY (THE)

www.nutrasweet.com

Industry Group Code: 31194

Management:		Sales/Marketing:		Liberal Arts:		Information Systems:		Professionals:		Technical/Scientific:	
Mgmt. Trainees:		Mktg. Professionals:	Y	Gen. Writing/Editing:		Info. Management:	Y	Finance/Acct.:	Y	Engineers, Elec.:	
Experienced Mgmt.:	Y	Retail Sales:		Technical Writing:		Software Dev.:		Law:	Y	Engineers, Other:	
Int'l Business:	Y	Commercial/Industrial:	Y	Graphic Arts/Photog.:	Y	Hardware Dev.:		HR/Other:	Y	Health/Lab	
MBA Graduates:	Y	Sales Trainees:	Y	Music:		Consulting/Other:		Training:	Y	Scientists/Research:	
		Advertising Pros.:	Y	Broadcasting:				Health Care:		Petroleum/Chemicals:	
				Other:				Consulting:		Math/Other:	

TYPES OF BUSINESS:

Artificial Sweeteners

BRANDS/DIVISIONS/AFFILIATES:

NutraSweet
J.W. Childs Equity Patners II LP
Neotame

CONTACTS: *Note: Officers with more than one job title may be intentionally listed here more than once.*

Craig R. Petray, CEO
William L. DeFer, COO
William L. DeFer, Pres.
James Stanley, CFO

Phone: 312-873-5000 **Fax:** 312-873-5050
Toll-Free: 800-323-5321
Address: 10 S. Wacker Dr., Chicago, IL 60606 US

GROWTH PLANS/SPECIAL FEATURES:

The NutraSweet Company is one of the world's largest producers of the artificial sweetener aspartame, which is roughly 200 times sweeter than table sugar. The company is owned by private investment firm J.W. Childs Equity Partners II, L.P. The company's NutraSweet-brand sweetener is sold in over 100 countries and used by roughly 250 million consumers every year. Additionally, the sweetener is used in more than 5,000 consumer food and beverage products throughout the world, such as breath mints; chewing gum; ice cream; yogurts; juices; pie and bakery fillings, toppings and syrups; over-the-counter pharmaceuticals; sauces; and ready-to-eat refrigerated desserts. The company sells its sweetener in the retail, food service and restaurant markets. In addition, through agreements with some of the world's largest food producers, the sweetener can be found in many foods and beverages, including bakery products, carbonated drinks, tea, fruit juices, coffee, ice cream, yogurt, pie and bakery fillings, ready-to-eat desserts, dry mixes, cough lozenges, chewable vitamins, barbecue sauce and assorted syrups. The firm is heavily invested in research and development for enhancement and formulation to ensure the safety and quality of its product. NutraSweet's latest sweetener and flavor enhancer, Neotame, is a product that is 40 times sweeter than Nutrasweet, and 8,000 times sweeter than table sugar. The firm is headquartered in Chicago, Illinois and maintains a manufacturing facility in Augusta, Georgia.

FINANCIALS: **Sales and profits are in thousands of dollars—add 000 to get the full amount. 2011 Note: Financial information for 2011 was not available for all companies at press time.**

2011 Sales: $ | 2011 Profits: $
2010 Sales: $ | 2010 Profits: $
2009 Sales: $ | 2009 Profits: $
2008 Sales: $ | 2008 Profits: $
2007 Sales: $ | 2007 Profits: $

U.S. Stock Ticker: Private
Int'l Ticker:
Int'l Exchange:
Employees: Fiscal Year Ends: 12/31
Parent Company: JW CHILDS EQUITY PARTNERS II LP

SALARIES/BENEFITS:

Pension Plan: ESOP Stock Plan: Profit Sharing: Top Exec. Salary: $ Bonus: $
Savings Plan: Stock Purch. Plan: Second Exec. Salary: $ Bonus: $

OTHER THOUGHTS:

Apparent Women Officers or Directors:
Hot Spot for Advancement for Women/Minorities:

LOCATIONS: ("Y" = Yes)

West:	Southwest:	Midwest:	Southeast:	Northeast:	International:
		Y	Y		

NUVASIVE INC

www.nuvasive.com

Industry Group Code: 33911

Management:		Sales/Marketing:		Liberal Arts:		Information Systems:		Professionals:		Technical/Scientific:	
Mgmt. Trainees:		Mktg. Professionals:	Y	Gen. Writing/Editing:		Info. Management:	Y	Finance/Acct.:	Y	Engineers, Elec.:	Y
Experienced Mgmt.:	Y	Retail Sales:		Technical Writing:	Y	Software Dev.:	Y	Law:	Y	Engineers, Other:	Y
Int'l Business:		Commercial/Industrial:	Y	Graphic Arts/Photog.:		Hardware Dev.:	Y	HR/Other:	Y	Health/Lab	Y
MBA Graduates:	Y	Sales Trainees:		Music:		Consulting/Other:		Training:	Y	Scientists/Research:	Y
		Advertising Pros.:		Broadcasting:				Health Care:	Y	Petroleum/Chemicals:	
				Other:				Consulting:		Math/Other:	

TYPES OF BUSINESS:

Medical Equipment Development
Spinal Surgery Equipment

BRANDS/DIVISIONS/AFFILIATES:

Maximum Access Surgery (MAS)
NV M5
eXtreme Lateral Interbody Fusion (XLIF)
MaXcess
FormaGraft
Osteocel Plus
NeoDisc
NV JJB

CONTACTS: *Note: Officers with more than one job title may be intentionally listed here more than once.*

Alexis V. Lukianov, CEO
Keith C. Valentine, COO
Keith C. Valentine, Pres.
Michael J. Lambert, CFO/Exec. VP
Jeffrey P. Rydin, Exec. VP-U.S. Sales
Craig E. Hunsaker, Sr. VP-Global Human Resources
G. Bryan Cornwall, Sr. VP-Research & Clinical Resources
Jason M. Hannon, General Counsel/Exec. VP
William L. Reynolds, Sr. VP-Oper.
Michael J. Lambert, Contact-Investor Rel.
Patrick F. Williams, VP-Finance
Tyler P. Lipschultz, Exec. VP-Biologics
Stephen Siemers, Exec. VP-Europe
Patrick Miles, Pres., Americas
Alexis V. Lukianov, Chmn.
Takaaki Tanaka, Exec. VP-APAC

Phone: 858-909-1800 **Fax:** 800-475-9134
Toll-Free: 800-475-9131
Address: 7475 Lusk Blvd., San Diego, CA 92121 US

GROWTH PLANS/SPECIAL FEATURES:

NuVasive, Inc. designs, develops and markets minimally invasive products for the surgical treatment of spine disorders. Its principle products include the Maximum Access Surgery (MAS) minimally disruptive surgical platform, which combines five different product offerings: NV M5, NV JJB, MaXcess, biologics and specialized implants. NV M5 and NV JJB are proprietary, software-driven intraoperative nerve avoidance systems. They allows surgeons to perform fusion surgery through a process NuVasive calls the eXtreme Lateral Interbody Fusion (XLIF), meaning the surgeon enters the body from the side rather than front or back. These systems are compatible with numerous existing surgical instruments, meaning surgeons can use the products to augment machines they are already comfortable with. MaXcess is a unique tri-blade system that combines instrumentation and specialized implants that provide maximum surgical spinal access while disrupting the soft tissue as little as possible. The firm's line of biologics includes FormaGraft synthetic collagen product, used to provide a scaffold for bone growth; and Osteocel Plus, an allograft (meaning not derived from the patient's own body) mesenchymal stem cell (MSC) matrix, a bone graft substitute. Specialized implants designed to function with the MAS platform are used for interbody disc height restoration to facilitate fusion and stabilization of the spine, and have been developed to be delivered through the MaXcess system, which minimizes the invasiveness of implant procedures. Its products include SpheRx and Armada pedicle screw systems and CoRoent implants. The company currently trains around 400-500 surgeons annually in its MAS platform and associated techniques. NuVasive is also developing NeoDisc, a nucleus-like total disc replacement device for cervical spine applications.

FINANCIALS: **Sales and profits are in thousands of dollars—add 000 to get the full amount. 2011 Note: Financial information for 2011 was not available for all companies at press time.**

2011 Sales: $540,506	2011 Profits: $-69,849
2010 Sales: $478,237	2010 Profits: $78,285
2009 Sales: $370,340	2009 Profits: $5,808
2008 Sales: $250,082	2008 Profits: $-27,528
2007 Sales: $154,290	2007 Profits: $-11,265

U.S. Stock Ticker: NUVA
Int'l Ticker:
Int'l Exchange:
Employees: 789 Fiscal Year Ends: 12/31
Parent Company:

SALARIES/BENEFITS:

Pension Plan:	ESOP Stock Plan:	Profit Sharing:	Top Exec. Salary: $800,000	Bonus: $650,000
Savings Plan:	Stock Purch. Plan:		Second Exec. Salary: $500,000	Bonus: $350,000

OTHER THOUGHTS:

Apparent Women Officers or Directors: 1
Hot Spot for Advancement for Women/Minorities:

LOCATIONS: ("Y" = Yes)

West:	Southwest:	Midwest:	Southeast:	Northeast:	International:
Y			Y		

ODYSSEY RE HOLDINGS CORP

www.odysseyre.com

Industry Group Code: 524130

Management:		Sales/Marketing:		Liberal Arts:		Information Systems:		Professionals:		Technical/Scientific:	
Mgmt. Trainees:		Mktg. Professionals:	Y	Gen. Writing/Editing:	Y	Info. Management:	Y	Finance/Acct.:	Y	Engineers, Elec.:	
Experienced Mgmt.:	Y	Retail Sales:		Technical Writing:	Y	Software Dev.:		Law:	Y	Engineers, Other:	
Int'l Business:	Y	Commercial/Industrial:	Y	Graphic Arts/Photog.:		Hardware Dev.:		HR/Other:	Y	Health/Lab	
MBA Graduates:	Y	Sales Trainees:	Y	Music:		Consulting/Other:		Training:	Y	Scientists/Research:	
		Advertising Pros.:		Broadcasting:				Health Care:		Petroleum/Chemicals:	
				Other:				Consulting:		Math/Other:	Y

TYPES OF BUSINESS:

Insurance-Reinsurance
Property & Casualty
Treaty Reinsurance
Facultative Reinsurance
Business Liability

BRANDS/DIVISIONS/AFFILIATES:

Clearwater Insurance Company
Newline Insurance Company Limited
Odyssey America Reinsurance Corporation
Newline Holdings UK Limited
Newline Syndicate at Lloyd's
Fairfax Financial Holdings Ltd

CONTACTS: *Note: Officers with more than one job title may be intentionally listed here more than once.*

Brian D. Young, CEO
Brian D. Young, Pres.
Jan Christiansen, CFO/Exec. VP
Alane R. Carey, Dir.-Global Mktg./Exec. VP
Peter H. Lovell, General Counsel/Sr. VP/Corp. Sec.
Philippe E. Mallier, Sr. VP-Latin American Reinsurance Oper.
Michael G. Wacek, Exec. VP-Global Risk Strategies
Christopher L. Gallagher, CEO-U.S. Insurance Div.
Robert S. Bennet, Chief Actuary/Exec. VP
Carl A. Overy, CEO-London Market Div.
Jeffrey M. Rubin, Sr. VP/Dir.-Global Claims
V. Prem Watsa, Chmn.
Lucien Pietropoli, CEO-EuroAsia Div.

Phone: 203-977-8000	**Fax:** 203-356-0196
Toll-Free:	
Address: 300 First Stamford Pl., Stamford, CT 06902 US	

GROWTH PLANS/SPECIAL FEATURES:

Odyssey Re Holdings Corp., a wholly-owned subsidiary of Fairfax Financial Holdings, Ltd., is an international underwriter of reinsurance, providing a full range of property and casualty products. The company, which operates through several subsidiaries, offers a range of both treaty and facultative reinsurance to property and casualty insurers/reinsurers; and writes specialty and non-traditional lines of reinsurance, including professional liability, marine and aerospace. The firm's operations are managed through four divisions: Americas, EuroAsia, London market and U.S. insurance. The Americas division (38% of gross written premiums) includes U.S. and Canadian treaty property, general casualty, specialty casualty, surety and facultative casualty reinsurance; and the firm's Latin American treaty and facultative businesses. The EuroAsia division (49.5% of written premiums) is composed of offices in Paris, Stockholm, Singapore and Tokyo and writes primarily treaty and facultative property policies. Odyssey's London market division (12.5% of written premiums) operates through its London branch, which provides worldwide property and casualty reinsurance; and Newline Syndicate at Lloyd's and Newline Insurance Company Limited, which focus on casualty insurance. The company's U.S. Insurance segment writes specialty insurance in the U.S., including medical professional liability, professional liability and crop business insurance. The company's main subsidiaries include Odyssey America Reinsurance Corporation, a property and casualty reinsurance company; Newline Holdings U.K. Limited, a Europe-based operation controlling the firm's Newline operation; and the Clearwater Insurance Company, a firm which holds insurance licenses in 43 states.

FINANCIALS: **Sales and profits are in thousands of dollars—add 000 to get the full amount. 2011 Note: Financial information for 2011 was not available for all companies at press time.**

2011 Sales: $	2011 Profits: $	**U.S. Stock Ticker: Subsidiary**
2010 Sales: $2,383,938	2010 Profits: $333,275	**Int'l Ticker:**
2009 Sales: $2,431,257	2009 Profits: $372,314	Int'l Exchange:
2008 Sales: $3,023,822	2008 Profits: $549,008	Employees: 738 Fiscal Year Ends: 12/31
2007 Sales: $2,989,095	2007 Profits: $595,575	Parent Company: FAIRFAX FINANCIAL HOLDINGS LTD

SALARIES/BENEFITS:

Pension Plan:	ESOP Stock Plan:	Profit Sharing:	Top Exec. Salary: $1,000,000	Bonus: $1,250,000
Savings Plan:	Stock Purch. Plan:		Second Exec. Salary: $706,731	Bonus: $675,000

OTHER THOUGHTS:

Apparent Women Officers or Directors: 1
Hot Spot for Advancement for Women/Minorities:

LOCATIONS: ("Y" = Yes)

West:	Southwest:	Midwest:	Southeast:	Northeast:	International:
Y		Y	Y	Y	Y

OMNOVA SOLUTIONS INC

www.omnova.com

Industry Group Code: 313

Management:		Sales/Marketing:		Liberal Arts:		Information Systems:		Professionals:		Technical/Scientific:	
Mgmt. Trainees:		Mktg. Professionals:	Y	Gen. Writing/Editing:	Y	Info. Management:	Y	Finance/Acct.:	Y	Engineers, Elec.:	
Experienced Mgmt.:	Y	Retail Sales:		Technical Writing:		Software Dev.:		Law:	Y	Engineers, Other:	
Int'l Business:	Y	Commercial/Industrial:	Y	Graphic Arts/Photog.:	Y	Hardware Dev.:		HR/Other:	Y	Health/Lab	
MBA Graduates:	Y	Sales Trainees:		Music:		Consulting/Other:		Training:		Scientists/Research:	
		Advertising Pros.:		Broadcasting:				Health Care:		Petroleum/Chemicals:	
				Other:	Y			Consulting:		Math/Other:	

TYPES OF BUSINESS:

Wall Coverings, Fabrics & Laminates
Roofing Systems
Performance Chemicals
Specialty Chemicals

BRANDS/DIVISIONS/AFFILIATES:

NovaCryl
Murek
GenFlo
GenGlaze
StyleCoat
PolyFox
DiversiWall
DuraMAX Flat Laminates

CONTACTS: *Note: Officers with more than one job title may be intentionally listed here more than once.*

Kevin M. McMullen, CEO
Kevin M. McMullen, Pres.
Michael E. Hicks, CFO/Sr. VP
Kris C. Syrvalin, VP-Human Resources Admin.
Douglas E. Wenger, CIO/Sr. VP
James C. LeMay, General Counsel
James C. LeMay, Sr. VP-Corp. Dev.
Chester W. Fox, Treas./VP
Robert H. Coleman, Pres., Decorative Prod.
James J. Hohman, VP/Pres., Performance Chemicals
Kris C. Syrvalin, Sec.
Kevin M. McMullen, Chmn.

Phone: 330-869-4200 | **Fax:** 330-869-4288
Toll-Free:
Address: 175 Ghent Rd., Fairlawn, OH 44333 US

GROWTH PLANS/SPECIAL FEATURES:

OMNOVA Solutions, Inc. designs, develops, produces and markets emulsion polymers, specialty chemicals, and decorative and functional surfaces for a variety of commercial, industrial and residential end uses. The firm utilizes about 20 strategically located manufacturing, development and design facilities in North America, Europe and Asia. OMNOVA operates in two business segments: performance chemicals, accounting for approximately 79% of the company's revenues, and decorative products, accounting for 21%. The performance chemicals segment is a North American leader in emulsion polymers and specialty chemicals. Its products include styrene butadiene carpet binders marketed under the NovaGreen and GenFlo brands; in-mold coating primers under the GenGlaze and StyleCoat brands; and paper chemicals such as coating binders and coating chemicals, which are developed by the firm's joint venture with Rohm and Haas, RohmNova. The segment's specialty chemicals include PolyFox fluorosurfactants for high gloss coatings; NovaCryl adhesives; Sunbond nonwoven materials used for disposable hygiene products; AcryGen acrylic top coats used in rubberized running tracks; and GenTac latex for tire and rubber goods. The decorative products segment develops, designs, produces and markets a broad line of decorative and functional surfacing products, such as commercial wall coverings; wall services; paper, flat and 3D laminates; digital wall murals; upholstery products; ceiling tile surfaces; pool liner films; and performance films, such as awnings, tents, banners, security shades for cars and movie screens. Brands within this segment include Bolta, Genon, Scion, Tower, Avant, Murek, Buflon, radiance, EFX, viewnique and DiversiWall. In 2011, OMNOVA released several new products, including duraMAX Flat Laminates; NovaCryl PS-R 30, a pressure sensitive adhesive; and Pliotec SC55, a self-crosslinking acrylic latex solution. In December 2011, the firm sold some of its North American commercial wall covering operations to J. Josephson, Inc.

OMNOVA offers its employees medical, dental and vision coverage; a 401(k) plan; life and AD&D insurance; adoption assistance; and more.

FINANCIALS: **Sales and profits are in thousands of dollars—add 000 to get the full amount. 2011 Note: Financial information for 2011 was not available for all companies at press time.**

2011 Sales: $1,201,100 — 2011 Profits: $-2,800
2010 Sales: $846,200 — 2010 Profits: $107,900
2009 Sales: $696,400 — 2009 Profits: $26,200
2008 Sales: $869,400 — 2008 Profits: $ 2,200
2007 Sales: $745,500 — 2007 Profits: $-6,700

U.S. Stock Ticker: OMN
Int'l Ticker:
Int'l Exchange:
Employees: 2,430 Fiscal Year Ends: 11/30
Parent Company:

SALARIES/BENEFITS:

Pension Plan: | ESOP Stock Plan: | Profit Sharing: | Top Exec. Salary: $690,727 | Bonus: $1,908,327
Savings Plan: Y | Stock Purch. Plan: | | Second Exec. Salary: $324,327 | Bonus: $280,697

OTHER THOUGHTS:

Apparent Women Officers or Directors: 1
Hot Spot for Advancement for Women/Minorities:

LOCATIONS: ("Y" = Yes)

West:	Southwest:	Midwest:	Southeast:	Northeast:	International:
		Y	Y	Y	Y

ONLINE RESOURCES CORP

www.orcc.com

Industry Group Code: 511210

Management:		Sales/Marketing:		Liberal Arts:		Information Systems:		Professionals:		Technical/Scientific:	
Mgmt. Trainees:		Mktg. Professionals:	Y	Gen. Writing/Editing:		Info. Management:	Y	Finance/Acct.:	Y	Engineers, Elec.:	Y
Experienced Mgmt.:	Y	Retail Sales:		Technical Writing:	Y	Software Dev.:	Y	Law:	Y	Engineers, Other:	
Int'l Business:		Commercial/Industrial:	Y	Graphic Arts/Photog.:		Hardware Dev.:		HR/Other:	Y	Health/Lab	
MBA Graduates:	Y	Sales Trainees:	Y	Music:		Consulting/Other:		Training:	Y	Scientists/Research:	
		Advertising Pros.:		Broadcasting:				Health Care:		Petroleum/Chemicals:	
				Other:				Consulting:		Math/Other:	

TYPES OF BUSINESS:

Software-Electronic Banking
Online Banking Services

BRANDS/DIVISIONS/AFFILIATES:

CONTACTS:

Note: Officers with more than one job title may be intentionally listed here more than once.

Joseph L. Cowan, CEO
Joseph L. Cowan, Pres.
Catherine A. Graham, CFO/Exec. VP
Janie M. West, Chief Mktg. Officer
Jeffrey L. Kissling, CTO
Eric M. Labiak, Chief Sales Officer
Stephen W. Ryan, Exec. VP-Software Solutions & Svcs.
John C. Dorman, Chmn.

Phone: 703-653-3100 **Fax:** 703-653-3105
Toll-Free:
Address: 4795 Meadow Wood Ln., Ste. 300, Chantilly, VA 20151 US

GROWTH PLANS/SPECIAL FEATURES:

Online Resources Corp. provides outsourced, web- and phone-based financial technology services to financial institution, biller, card issuer and creditor clients. The company serves nearly 2,000 credit unions, banks, account receivables management providers, billers, credit card issuers and other credit providers. End users may access and view their accounts online and perform various web-based, self-service functions. They may also make electronic bill payments and funds transfers, utilizing the firm's debit architecture, ACH and other payment methods. The company divides its products and services into two business lines: banking services and e-commerce services. The banking services business line, serving banks, credit unions and other depository financial institutions, provides electronic bill payment and online banking services, including an integrated suite of web-based account presentation, payment, relationship management and professional services. This segment accounts for roughly 80% of Online Resource Corp.'s revenues. The e-commerce business line (the remaining 20% of the firm's revenues), serving billers, card issuers and credit providers, provides web- and phone-based account presentation, payment, relationship management and professional services. The company's clients offer these services to end-users under their own brand names. Headquartered in Virginia, Online Resources Corp. has additional operations in New Jersey, California and Ohio.

The company offers employees medical, dental, vision and prescription drug coverage; 401(k) and employee stock purchase plans; tuition reimbursement; credit union membership; a college savings plan; an employee assistance program; and on-site fitness, dry cleaning and hairstyling facilities.

FINANCIALS:

Sales and profits are in thousands of dollars—add 000 to get the full amount. 2011 Note: Financial information for 2011 was not available for all companies at press time.

2011 Sales: $	2011 Profits: $	**U.S. Stock Ticker: ORCC**
2010 Sales: $149,513	2010 Profits: $5,376	**Int'l Ticker:**
2009 Sales: $151,863	2009 Profits: $5,130	Int'l Exchange:
2008 Sales: $151,642	2008 Profits: $1,919	Employees: 603 Fiscal Year Ends: 12/31
2007 Sales: $135,132	2007 Profits: $10,946	Parent Company:

SALARIES/BENEFITS:

Pension Plan:	ESOP Stock Plan:	Profit Sharing:	Top Exec. Salary: $266,611	Bonus: $269,877
Savings Plan: Y	Stock Purch. Plan: Y		Second Exec. Salary: $243,245	Bonus: $

OTHER THOUGHTS:

Apparent Women Officers or Directors: 2
Hot Spot for Advancement for Women/Minorities:

LOCATIONS: ("Y" = Yes)

West:	Southwest:	Midwest:	Southeast:	Northeast:	International:
Y		Y		Y	

ONSTREAM MEDIA CORPORATION

www.onstreammedia.com

Industry Group Code: 541810E

Management:		**Sales/Marketing:**		**Liberal Arts:**		**Information Systems:**		**Professionals:**		**Technical/Scientific:**	
Mgmt. Trainees:		Mktg. Professionals:	Y	Gen. Writing/Editing:	Y	Info. Management:	Y	Finance/Acct.:	Y	Engineers, Elec.:	
Experienced Mgmt.:	Y	Retail Sales:		Technical Writing:		Software Dev.:	Y	Law:	Y	Engineers, Other:	
Int'l Business:		Commercial/Industrial:	Y	Graphic Arts/Photog.:	Y	Hardware Dev.:		HR/Other:	Y	Health/Lab	
MBA Graduates:	Y	Sales Trainees:		Music:		Consulting/Other:		Training:		Scientists/Research:	
		Advertising Pros.:		Broadcasting:				Health Care:		Petroleum/Chemicals:	
				Other:	Y			Consulting:		Math/Other:	

TYPES OF BUSINESS:

Online Video Management Services
Webcasting Services
Networking Services
Media Presentations
Systems Integration
Engineering Services

BRANDS/DIVISIONS/AFFILIATES:

Digital Media Services Group
Audio and Web Conferencing Services Group
Infinite Conferencing
EDNet
Digital Media Services Platform
Auction Video
Smart Encoding
MarketPlace365.com

CONTACTS: *Note: Officers with more than one job title may be intentionally listed here more than once.*

Randy S. Selman, CEO
Alan M. Saperstein, COO/Exec. VP
Randy S. Selman, Pres.
Robert E. Tomlinson, CFO
David Glassman, Chief Mktg. Officer/Sr. VP
Clifford Friedland, Sr. VP-Bus. Dev.
Alan M. Saperstein, Treas.
Randy S. Selman, Chmn.

Phone: 954-917-6655 **Fax:** 954-917-6660
Toll-Free: 866-857-1960
Address: 1291 S.W. 29th Ave., Pompano Beach, FL 33069 US

GROWTH PLANS/SPECIAL FEATURES:

Onstream Media Corporation is an online services provider of live and on-demand Internet video, corporate audio and web communications and content management applications. Onstream's operations are organized into two groups: the Digital Media Services Group and the Audio and Web Conferencing Services Group. Generating approximately 45.9% of the company's revenue, the Digital Media Services Group consists of the Webcasting division, the Digital Media Services Platform (DMSP) division, the User Generated Content (UGC) division and the Smart Encoding division. The Webcasting division provides corporate-oriented, web-based media services to the corporate market, including live audio and video webcasting and on-demand audio and video streaming. The DMSP division provides online, subscription-based services that include access to enabling technologies and features for clients to acquire, store, index, secure, manage, distribute and transform digital assets into saleable commodities. The UGC division, which also operates as Auction Video, provides a video ingestion and flash encoder that can be used on a stand-alone basis or in conjunction with the DMSP. The Smart Encoding division provides both automated and manual encoding and editorial services for processing, searching, retrieving and streaming digital media, which can include photos, videos, audio, engineering specs, architectural plans, web pages and other pieces of business collateral. Onstream's Audio and Web Conferencing Services Group, which generates approximately 54.1% of its revenue, includes the Infinite Conferencing division, which provides reservationless and operator-assisted audio and web conferencing services; and the EDNet division, which provides connectivity within the entertainment and advertising industries through its managed network, which includes production and post-production companies, advertisers, producers and directors. In May 2011, Onstream Media launched new web portal MarketPlace365.com, which features online virtual tradeshows and communities in order to increase traffic for marketplace exhibitors.

FINANCIALS: **Sales and profits are in thousands of dollars—add 000 to get the full amount. 2011 Note: Financial information for 2011 was not available for all companies at press time.**

2011 Sales: $17,701	2011 Profits: $-5,195
2010 Sales: $16,694	2010 Profits: $-9,281
2009 Sales: $16,927	2009 Profits: $-11,831
2008 Sales: $17,587	2008 Profits: $-6,561
2007 Sales: $12,115	2007 Profits: $-14,758

U.S. Stock Ticker: ONSM
Int'l Ticker:
Int'l Exchange:
Employees: 94 Fiscal Year Ends: 9/30
Parent Company:

SALARIES/BENEFITS:

Pension Plan:	ESOP Stock Plan:	Profit Sharing:	Top Exec. Salary: $271,751	Bonus: $
Savings Plan: Y	Stock Purch. Plan:		Second Exec. Salary: $247,047	Bonus: $

OTHER THOUGHTS:

Apparent Women Officers or Directors:
Hot Spot for Advancement for Women/Minorities:

LOCATIONS: ("Y" = Yes)

West:	Southwest:	Midwest:	Southeast:	Northeast:	International:
Y			Y	Y	

OPENTV CORP

www.opentv.com

Industry Group Code: 511210C

Management:		Sales/Marketing:		Liberal Arts:		Information Systems:		Professionals:		Technical/Scientific:	
Mgmt. Trainees:		Mktg. Professionals:	Y	Gen. Writing/Editing:		Info. Management:	Y	Finance/Acct.:	Y	Engineers, Elec.:	Y
Experienced Mgmt.:	Y	Retail Sales:		Technical Writing:	Y	Software Dev.:	Y	Law:	Y	Engineers, Other:	
Int'l Business:	Y	Commercial/Industrial:	Y	Graphic Arts/Photog.:		Hardware Dev.:		HR/Other:	Y	Health/Lab	
MBA Graduates:	Y	Sales Trainees:	Y	Music:		Consulting/Other:		Training:	Y	Scientists/Research:	
		Advertising Pros.:		Broadcasting:				Health Care:		Petroleum/Chemicals:	
				Other:				Consulting:		Math/Other:	

TYPES OF BUSINESS:

Software-Interactive Television

BRANDS/DIVISIONS/AFFILIATES:

OpenTV Core Middleware
OpenTV PVR
OpenTV Spyglass
OpenTV EclipsePlus
OpenTV iAd
Kudelski Group (The)
OpenTV Participate

CONTACTS: *Note: Officers with more than one job title may be intentionally listed here more than once.*

Nigel W. Bennett, CEO
Christine Oury, Sr. Dir.-Comm.
Andre Kudelski, Chmn.

Phone: 415-962-5000	**Fax:** 415-962-5300
Toll-Free:	
Address: 275 Sacramento St., San Francisco, CA 94111 US	

GROWTH PLANS/SPECIAL FEATURES:

OpenTV Corp., a wholly-owned subsidiary of The Kudelski Group, provides software, services and applications for digital interactive television (iTV). The company's software has been shipped with or installed in more than 145 million set-top boxes worldwide and has been selected by over 58 network operators worldwide. OpenTV licenses its set-top box software to more than 40 digital set-top box manufacturers and licenses its authoring tools to hundreds of independent developers and content and service providers. The firm operates in two segments: middleware and advertising. The middleware segment is composed of set-top box middleware and embedded browser technologies, as well as software components that are deployed at the network operator's headend. Its primary software technology is the OpenTV Core Middleware. Other products include OpenTV PVR, which enables network operators to deliver advanced personal video recording services to their subscribers; and OpenTV Spyglass, a customizable HTML browser designed specifically for information appliances. The advertising segment provides software for the creation and delivery of advertising for digital television systems. Services in this segment include OpenTV EclipsePlus, an advertising campaign management system; OpenTV iAd, a suite of products that allow customers to create, enable and display interactive advertising applications as an overlay to broadcast advertising content; OpenTV SpotOn, a service that allows customization of advertising deployment based on geographic, demographic or psychographic profiles; and OpenTV Participate, which allows viewers to interact with programming through competitions, quizzes, auctions, voting and games.

FINANCIALS: **Sales and profits are in thousands of dollars—add 000 to get the full amount. 2011 Note: Financial information for 2011 was not available for all companies at press time.**

2011 Sales: $	2011 Profits: $	**U.S. Stock Ticker: Subsidiary**
2010 Sales: $	2010 Profits: $	**Int'l Ticker:**
2009 Sales: $120,012	2009 Profits: $6,242	Int'l Exchange:
2008 Sales: $116,474	2008 Profits: $9,613	Employees: 589 Fiscal Year Ends: 12/31
2007 Sales: $109,977	2007 Profits: $-5,161	Parent Company: KUDELSKI GROUP (THE)

SALARIES/BENEFITS:

Pension Plan:	ESOP Stock Plan:	Profit Sharing:	Top Exec. Salary: $475,000	Bonus: $
Savings Plan: Y	Stock Purch. Plan: Y		Second Exec. Salary: $334,223	Bonus: $

OTHER THOUGHTS:

Apparent Women Officers or Directors: 1
Hot Spot for Advancement for Women/Minorities:

LOCATIONS: ("Y" = Yes)

West:	Southwest:	Midwest:	Southeast:	Northeast:	International:
Y					Y

ORION MARINE GROUP INC

www.orionmarinegroup.com

Industry Group Code: 2389

Management:		**Sales/Marketing:**		**Liberal Arts:**		**Information Systems:**		**Professionals:**		**Technical/Scientific:**	
Mgmt. Trainees:		Mktg. Professionals:	Y	Gen. Writing/Editing:		Info. Management:	Y	Finance/Acct.:	Y	Engineers, Elec.:	
Experienced Mgmt.:	Y	Retail Sales:		Technical Writing:	Y	Software Dev.:		Law:	Y	Engineers, Other:	Y
Int'l Business:		Commercial/Industrial:	Y	Graphic Arts/Photog.:		Hardware Dev.:		HR/Other:	Y	Health/Lab	
MBA Graduates:	Y	Sales Trainees:		Music:		Consulting/Other:		Training:		Scientists/Research:	
		Advertising Pros.:		Broadcasting:				Health Care:		Petroleum/Chemicals:	
				Other:				Consulting:		Math/Other:	

TYPES OF BUSINESS:

Marine Construction & Specialty Services
Dredging Services

BRANDS/DIVISIONS/AFFILIATES:

TW LaQuay Dredging LLC

CONTACTS:

Note: Officers with more than one job title may be intentionally listed here more than once.

J. Michael Pearson, CEO
J. Michael Pearson, Pres.
Mark R. Stauffer, CFO/Exec. VP
Pete Buchler, General Counsel/Exec. VP/Corp. Sec.
Elliott J. Kennedy, Exec. VP-Gulf Coast
James L. Rose, Exec. VP-Atlantic Seaboard & Caribbean
Richard L. Daerr, Jr., Chmn.

Phone: 713-852-6500	**Fax:** 713-852-6530
Toll-Free:	
Address: 12000 Aerospace, Ste. 300, Houston, TX 77034 US	

GROWTH PLANS/SPECIAL FEATURES:

Orion Marine Group, Inc. is a marine specialty contractor that serves the heavy civil marine infrastructure industry. The firm offers an array of marine construction services on, over and under the water along the Atlantic Seaboard, Canada, the West Coast, the Gulf Coast and in the Caribbean Basin. The company's customers, for which Orion Marine acts as a single-source turnkey solution, include private commercial and industrial enterprises; and federal, state and municipal governments. The firm offers three types of services: marine construction, dredging and specialty services. Its marine construction services include construction of marine transportation facilities, bridges, causeways, marine pipelines and marine environmental structures. Marine transportation facility construction projects include public port facilities; private and special-use Navy terminals; cruise ship port facilities; and recreational use marinas and docks. The firm's bridge and causeway projects include the construction, repair and maintenance of bridges and causeways; and the development of fendering systems in marine environments. Its marine pipeline service projects generally include the installation and removal of underwater buried pipeline transmission lines; installation of pipeline intakes and outfalls for industrial facilities; construction of pipeline outfalls for wastewater and industrial discharges; river crossing and directional drilling; creation of hot taps and tie-ins; and inspection, maintenance and repair services. Orion Marine's dredging services involve removing mud and silt from the channel floor by means of pipeline systems and a mechanical backhoe, crane/bucket or cutter suction dredge. The company's specialty services include demolition; surveying; diving; salvage; towing; and underwater inspection, excavation and repair. In recent years, the firm acquired specialty dredging services firm T.W. LaQuay Dredging, LLC.

The firm offers employees medical, dental, vision, life, AD&D and disability insurance; an employee assistance plan; and a 401(k).

FINANCIALS:

Sales and profits are in thousands of dollars—add 000 to get the full amount. 2011 Note: Financial information for 2011 was not available for all companies at press time.

2011 Sales: $259,852	2011 Profits: $-13,114
2010 Sales: $353,135	2010 Profits: $21,882
2009 Sales: $293,494	2009 Profits: $20,030
2008 Sales: $261,802	2008 Profits: $14,475
2007 Sales: $210,360	2007 Profits: $16,617

U.S. Stock Ticker: ORN
Int'l Ticker:
Int'l Exchange:
Employees: 1,470 Fiscal Year Ends: 12/31
Parent Company:

SALARIES/BENEFITS:

Pension Plan:	ESOP Stock Plan:	Profit Sharing:	Top Exec. Salary: $498,385	Bonus: $285,000
Savings Plan: Y	Stock Purch. Plan:		Second Exec. Salary: $323,846	Bonus: $148,200

OTHER THOUGHTS:

Apparent Women Officers or Directors:
Hot Spot for Advancement for Women/Minorities:

LOCATIONS: ("Y" = Yes)

West:	Southwest:	Midwest:	Southeast:	Northeast:	International:
	Y		Y	Y	

PACIFIC BIOMARKERS INC

www.pacbio.com

Industry Group Code: 541712

Management:		**Sales/Marketing:**		**Liberal Arts:**		**Information Systems:**		**Professionals:**		**Technical/Scientific:**	
Mgmt. Trainees:		Mktg. Professionals:	Y	Gen. Writing/Editing:		Info. Management:	Y	Finance/Acct.:	Y	Engineers, Elec.:	Y
Experienced Mgmt.:	Y	Retail Sales:		Technical Writing:	Y	Software Dev.:	Y	Law:	Y	Engineers, Other:	Y
Int'l Business:		Commercial/Industrial:	Y	Graphic Arts/Photog.:		Hardware Dev.:		HR/Other:	Y	Health/Lab	Y
MBA Graduates:	Y	Sales Trainees:		Music:		Consulting/Other:	Y	Training:	Y	Scientists/Research:	Y
		Advertising Pros.:		Broadcasting:				Health Care:	Y	Petroleum/Chemicals:	
				Other:				Consulting:		Math/Other:	Y

TYPES OF BUSINESS:

Clinical Trials
Laboratory Services
Contract Research & Development
Diagnostic Tests
DNA Amplification Systems

BRANDS/DIVISIONS/AFFILIATES:

PBI Technology Inc
Pacific Biometrics Inc

CONTACTS: *Note: Officers with more than one job title may be intentionally listed here more than once.*

Ronald R. Helm, CEO
Michael Murphy, COO
Elizabeth Teng Leary, Chief Scientific Officer
Dave Swezey, Dir.-Laboratory Oper.
Sheri Dumond, Dir.-Bus. Dev.
John Jensen, VP-Finance/Controller
Ken Waters, Dir.-Strategic Planning
Edwin Merrifield, Dir.-Immunogenicity Biomarker Svcs.
Timothy Carlson, Dir.-Laboratory
Tonya Aggoune, Dir.-Project Svcs.
Ronald R. Helm, Chmn.

Phone: 206-298-0068	**Fax:** 206-298-9838
Toll-Free:	
Address: 220 W. Harrison St., Seattle, WA 98119 US	

GROWTH PLANS/SPECIAL FEATURES:

Pacific Biomarkers, Inc. (PBI), formerly known as Pacific Biometrics, Inc., provides specialty laboratory and clinical research services to pharmaceutical, biotechnology and laboratory diagnostic manufacturers. Laboratory services are offered primarily in support of clinical trials and diagnostic product development. In clinical trial support, tailored databases are customized for each clinical research study protocol while a data analyst facilitates adapted data management plans for all clients. Diagnostic product development services include the development and improvement of reagents and point-of-care devices for diagnostic companies. PBI's areas of specialty include cardiovascular disease, diabetes and bone and joint diseases. Services offered include the measurement of cardiovascular disease markers through lipoprotein components, cholesterol, triglycerides, phospholipids and apolipoproteins. One of PBI's wholly-owned subsidiaries, PBI Technology, Inc., develops and commercializes molecular diagnostic technologies, non-invasive diagnostic devices and early-stage drug candidates. PBI Technology also owns DNA-based proprietary technologies, processes and equipment, including a proprietary isothermal DNA amplification method (LIDA) and a genetic method for distinguishing live cells from dead cells (Cell Viability).

PBI offers its employees medical, dental and vision coverage; life and AD&D insurance; an employee stock purchase plan; a 401(k) plan; and flexible spending accounts.

FINANCIALS: **Sales and profits are in thousands of dollars—add 000 to get the full amount. 2011 Note: Financial information for 2011 was not available for all companies at press time.**

2011 Sales: $	2011 Profits: $	**U.S. Stock Ticker: Subsidiary**
2010 Sales: $9,665	2010 Profits: $-1,383	**Int'l Ticker:**
2009 Sales: $10,881	2009 Profits: $1,236	Int'l Exchange:
2008 Sales: $8,265	2008 Profits: $- 571	Employees: 57 Fiscal Year Ends: 6/30
2007 Sales: $8,480	2007 Profits: $-1,213	Parent Company: NorWes Tech

SALARIES/BENEFITS:

Pension Plan:	ESOP Stock Plan:	Profit Sharing:	Top Exec. Salary: $285,417	Bonus: $56,250
Savings Plan: Y	Stock Purch. Plan: Y		Second Exec. Salary: $170,231	Bonus: $21,852

OTHER THOUGHTS:

Apparent Women Officers or Directors: 3
Hot Spot for Advancement for Women/Minorities: Y

LOCATIONS: ("Y" = Yes)

West:	Southwest:	Midwest:	Southeast:	Northeast:	International:
Y					

PAR PHARMACEUTICAL COMPANIES INC

www.parpharm.com

Industry Group Code: 325412

Management:		Sales/Marketing:		Liberal Arts:		Information Systems:		Professionals:		Technical/Scientific:	
Mgmt. Trainees:		Mktg. Professionals:	Y	Gen. Writing/Editing:		Info. Management:	Y	Finance/Acct.:	Y	Engineers, Elec.:	
Experienced Mgmt.:	Y	Retail Sales:		Technical Writing:	Y	Software Dev.:	Y	Law:	Y	Engineers, Other:	
Int'l Business:	Y	Commercial/Industrial:	Y	Graphic Arts/Photog.:		Hardware Dev.:		HR/Other:	Y	Health/Lab	Y
MBA Graduates:	Y	Sales Trainees:	Y	Music:		Consulting/Other:		Training:	Y	Scientists/Research:	Y
		Advertising Pros.:		Broadcasting:				Health Care:	Y	Petroleum/Chemicals:	Y
				Other:				Consulting:		Math/Other:	Y

TYPES OF BUSINESS:

Drugs-Generic & Branded
Pharmaceutical Intermediates

BRANDS/DIVISIONS/AFFILIATES:

Pharmaceutical Resources, Inc.
Par Pharmaceutical, Inc.
Megace ES
Nascobal
Strativa Pharmaceuticals
Androgel
Oravig
Zuplenz

CONTACTS:

Note: Officers with more than one job title may be intentionally listed here more than once.

Patrick G. LePore, CEO
Patrick G. LePore, Pres.
Michael A. Tropiano, CFO/Exec. VP
Stephen Montalto, Sr. VP-Human Resources
Thomas J. Haughey, Chief Admin. Officer/Exec. VP
Thomas J. Haughey, General Counsel/Corp. Sec.
Allison Wey, VP-Corp. Affairs
Allison Wey, VP-Investor Rel.
Paul V. Campanelli, Exec. VP/Pres., Par Pharmaceutical
Patrick G. LePore, Chmn.

Phone: 201-802-4000 **Fax:** 201-802-4600
Toll-Free:
Address: 300 Tice Blvd., Woodcliff Lake, NJ 07677 US

GROWTH PLANS/SPECIAL FEATURES:

Par Pharmaceutical Companies, Inc. develops, manufactures and markets branded and generic pharmaceuticals through its principal wholly-owned subsidiary, Par Pharmaceutical, Inc. The firm operates in two segments: Par Pharmaceutical, the company's generic products division; and Strativa Pharmaceuticals, the firm's branded products division. Par Pharmaceutical's product line comprises prescription drugs consisting of approximately 50 product names (molecules), each with an associated Abbreviated New Drug Application (ANDA) approved by the U.S. Food and Drug Administration and approximately 175 SKUs (packaging sizes). Par Pharmaceutical's products are manufactured principally in solid oral dosage form (tablet, caplet and two-piece hard shell capsule). In addition, it also markets several oral suspension products and products in the semi-solid form of a cream. Some products are the result of license agreements with the branded drug's manufacturer, including generics of metoprolol succinate ER (Toprol XL) and zafirlukast (Accolate) licensed through AstraZeneca. Par markets its generic products primarily to wholesalers, drug store chains, supermarket chains, mass merchandisers, distributors, managed health care organizations, mail order accounts and government, principally through its internal staff. Strativa Pharmaceuticals markets four products: Megace ES, which is approved for the treatment of anorexia, cachexia or any unexplained, significant weight loss in patients with a diagnosis of AIDS; Nascobal Nasal Spray; a prescription vitamin B12 treatment indicated for maintenance of remission in certain pernicious anemia patients, as well as a supplement for a variety of B12 deficiencies; Oravig buccal tablets, an antifungal therapy for the treatment of oropharyngeal candidiasis; and Zuplenz oral soluble film, a novel formulation of ondansetron for the prevention of chemotherapy-induced nausea and vomiting. In January 2011, Par Pharmaceuticals released the generic forms of Lotrel and Rythmol SR.

FINANCIALS:

Sales and profits are in thousands of dollars—add 000 to get the full amount. 2011 Note: Financial information for 2011 was not available for all companies at press time.

2011 Sales: $926,100 — 2011 Profits: $-26,100
2010 Sales: $1,008,874 — 2010 Profits: $92,731
2009 Sales: $1,193,159 — 2009 Profits: $76,928
2008 Sales: $578,115 — 2008 Profits: $-55,171
2007 Sales: $769,666 — 2007 Profits: $49,898

U.S. Stock Ticker: PRX
Int'l Ticker:
Int'l Exchange:
Employees: 686 Fiscal Year Ends: 12/31
Parent Company:

SALARIES/BENEFITS:

Pension Plan: ESOP Stock Plan: Profit Sharing: Top Exec. Salary: $847,500 Bonus: $1,300,000
Savings Plan: Y Stock Purch. Plan: Second Exec. Salary: $382,885 Bonus: $350,000

OTHER THOUGHTS:

Apparent Women Officers or Directors: 1
Hot Spot for Advancement for Women/Minorities:

LOCATIONS: ("Y" = Yes)

West:	Southwest:	Midwest:	Southeast:	Northeast:	International:
				Y	

PATAGONIA INC

www.patagonia.com

Industry Group Code: 315211

Management:		Sales/Marketing:		Liberal Arts:		Information Systems:		Professionals:		Technical/Scientific:	
Mgmt. Trainees:		Mktg. Professionals:	Y	Gen. Writing/Editing:		Info. Management:	Y	Finance/Acct.:	Y	Engineers, Elec.:	
Experienced Mgmt.:	Y	Retail Sales:		Technical Writing:		Software Dev.:		Law:	Y	Engineers, Other:	
Int'l Business:	Y	Commercial/Industrial:	Y	Graphic Arts/Photog.:	Y	Hardware Dev.:		HR/Other:	Y	Health/Lab	
MBA Graduates:	Y	Sales Trainees:		Music:		Consulting/Other:		Training:		Scientists/Research:	
		Advertising Pros.:	Y	Broadcasting:				Health Care:		Petroleum/Chemicals:	
				Other:	Y			Consulting:		Math/Other:	

TYPES OF BUSINESS:

Outdoor Apparel, Manufacturing
Outdoor Equipment
Catalog Sales
Surfing Apparel
Surfing Equipment

BRANDS/DIVISIONS/AFFILIATES:

Lotus Designs
Point Blanks Surfboards
Water Girl USA
Lost Arrow Corporation
Beneficial T's
PCR Clothing

CONTACTS: *Note: Officers with more than one job title may be intentionally listed here more than once.*

Casey Sheahan, CEO
Rose Macario, COO
Casey Sheahan, Pres.
Rose Macario, CFO
Rob BonDurant, VP-Mktg.
Mike Busch, Dir.-IT
Jen Rapp, Contact-Corp. Comm.
Rick Ridgeway, VP-Environmental Initiatives

Phone: 805-643-8616 **Fax:** 800-543-5522
Toll-Free: 800-638-6464
Address: 259 W. Santa Clara St., Ventura, CA 93001 US

GROWTH PLANS/SPECIAL FEATURES:

Patagonia, Inc., the primary subsidiary and brand name of the Lost Arrow Corporation, markets and sells outdoor clothing and equipment developed and designed for a broad range of extreme sports, such as rock climbing, mountaineering, white-water kayaking, mountain biking, surfing and skiing. Patagonia sells its products through 30 Patagonia specific retail outlets in the U.S. and over 20 abroad, including stores in the U.K., France, Italy, Germany, Ireland, Japan, Korea, Hong Kong, Argentina and Chile, as well as through hundreds of other outdoor gear and clothing stores. Patagonia has pioneered many materials now considered essential for outdoor enthusiasts, such as polypropylene, Capilene and Synchilla, which are designed to retain warmth even when the material becomes moist from precipitation or sweat. The firm's Regulator System combines soft shells, insulation and moisture transition layers into jackets and pants to create an integrated clothing system designed to keep people warm and dry even in the most adverse weather conditions. The company also introduced Beneficial T's, made from organically grown cotton, and PCR Clothing, a fleece product line made from recycled plastic soda bottles. Patagonia also markets gear specifically for whitewater paddling under the Lotus Designs brand name and gear for surfing under the Point Blanks name. Water Girl USA, Inc. is the company's subsidiary dedicated to making surfing, paddling, swimming and kayaking clothing for women. Newer products include an expanded surfing line with wet suits and surfboards designed by the company.

Patagonia employees at the company's headquarters have access to an on-site child care facility, among other benefits.

FINANCIALS: **Sales and profits are in thousands of dollars—add 000 to get the full amount. 2011 Note: Financial information for 2011 was not available for all companies at press time.**

2011 Sales: $	2011 Profits: $
2010 Sales: $330,000	2010 Profits: $
2009 Sales: $315,000	2009 Profits: $
2008 Sales: $300,000	2008 Profits: $
2007 Sales: $290,000	2007 Profits: $

U.S. Stock Ticker: Subsidiary
Int'l Ticker:
Int'l Exchange:
Employees: 1,350 Fiscal Year Ends: 4/30
Parent Company: LOST ARROW CORPORATION

SALARIES/BENEFITS:

Pension Plan:	ESOP Stock Plan:	Profit Sharing:	Top Exec. Salary: $	Bonus: $
Savings Plan: Y	Stock Purch. Plan:		Second Exec. Salary: $	Bonus: $

OTHER THOUGHTS:

Apparent Women Officers or Directors: 2
Hot Spot for Advancement for Women/Minorities:

LOCATIONS: ("Y" = Yes)

West:	Southwest:	Midwest:	Southeast:	Northeast:	International:
Y	Y	Y	Y	Y	Y

PC CONNECTION INC

Industry Group Code: 423430

www.pcconnection.com

Management:		Sales/Marketing:		Liberal Arts:		Information Systems:		Professionals:		Technical/Scientific:	
Mgmt. Trainees:	Y	Mktg. Professionals:	Y	Gen. Writing/Editing:	Y	Info. Management:	Y	Finance/Acct.:	Y	Engineers, Elec.:	
Experienced Mgmt.:	Y	Retail Sales:	Y	Technical Writing:	Y	Software Dev.:	Y	Law:	Y	Engineers, Other:	
Int'l Business:		Commercial/Industrial:	Y	Graphic Arts/Photog.:	Y	Hardware Dev.:		HR/Other:	Y	Health/Lab	
MBA Graduates:	Y	Sales Trainees:	Y	Music:		Consulting/Other:		Training:	Y	Scientists/Research:	
		Advertising Pros.:	Y	Broadcasting:				Health Care:		Petroleum/Chemicals:	
				Other:				Consulting:		Math/Other:	

TYPES OF BUSINESS:

Computer Products, Direct Selling
Computer Accessories
Software
IT Services
Online Sales
Catalog Sales

BRANDS/DIVISIONS/AFFILIATES:

MoreDirect Inc
GovConnection Inc
Traxx
ProConnection
PC Connection Express Inc
ValCom Technology

CONTACTS: *Note: Officers with more than one job title may be intentionally listed here more than once.*

Timothy McGrath, CEO
Timothy McGrath, Pres.
Jack Ferguson, CFO/Exec. VP
Jack Ferguson, Treas.
Patricia Gallup, Chmn.

Phone: 603-683-2000	**Fax**: 603-423-5748
Toll-Free: 800-800-0009	
Address: 730 Milford Rd., Merrimack, NH 03054 US	

GROWTH PLANS/SPECIAL FEATURES:

PC Connection, Inc. is a direct marketer of information technology (IT) products and services, including computer systems, software and peripheral equipment, networking communications and other products and accessories. The company offers a selection of over 300,000 products, purchased from manufacturers, distributers and other suppliers, targeted for business use. It also offers a range of services including installation, configuration and repair, performed by company and third-party personnel. The company operates through four primary business segments: SMB, serving small- to medium-sized businesses and individual consumers; large accounts, responsible for sales to large enterprise customers through MoreDirect, Inc.; public sector, managing sales to federal, state and local governments and educational institutions through GovConnection, Inc.; and consumers and small office/home office customers through subsidiary PC Connection Express, Inc. MoreDirect operates the Traxx Internet-based transaction system, an integrated application that provides sales order processing, supply chain visibility and full electronic data interchange (EDI) links. PC Connection sells products through a combination of outbound telemarketing, field sales, targeted direct mail catalogs, web sites, Internet advertising and selected computer magazines. Its most frequently ordered products are carried in inventory and are typically shipped to customers the same day the order is received. Additionally, through ProConnection, the company provides complete IT solutions for its clients, including designing, developing and managing the integration of products and services to implement IT projects. PC Connection's net sales by business segment are as follows: SMB, 42%; large accounts, 31%; public sector; 23%; and consumer markets, 4%. In March 2011, the firm acquired ValCom Technology for roughly $11.6 million.

PC Connection offers its employees medical, vision, dental, life and disability coverage; tuition reimbursement; a 401(k); a discount stock purchase plan; adoption assistance; fitness reimbursement; legal services; computer loans; various product discounts; chair massages; and on-site dry cleaning services.

FINANCIALS: **Sales and profits are in thousands of dollars—add 000 to get the full amount. 2011 Note: Financial information for 2011 was not available for all companies at press time.**

2011 Sales: $2,103,300	2011 Profits: $28,800	**U.S. Stock Ticker: PCCC**
2010 Sales: $1,974,198	2010 Profits: $22,961	**Int'l Ticker:**
2009 Sales: $1,569,656	2009 Profits: $-1,222	Int'l Exchange:
2008 Sales: $1,753,680	2008 Profits: $10,366	Employees: 1,556 Fiscal Year Ends: 12/31
2007 Sales: $1,785,379	2007 Profits: $22,995	Parent Company:

SALARIES/BENEFITS:

Pension Plan:	ESOP Stock Plan:	Profit Sharing:	Top Exec. Salary: $750,000	Bonus: $1,000,000
Savings Plan: Y	Stock Purch. Plan: Y		Second Exec. Salary: $532,692	Bonus: $825,000

OTHER THOUGHTS:

Apparent Women Officers or Directors: 2
Hot Spot for Advancement for Women/Minorities:

LOCATIONS: ("Y" = Yes)

West:	Southwest:	Midwest:	Southeast:	Northeast:	International:
	Y	Y	Y	Y	

PEAPOD LLC

www.peapod.com

Industry Group Code: 445110E

Management:		Sales/Marketing:		Liberal Arts:		Information Systems:		Professionals:		Technical/Scientific:	
Mgmt. Trainees:	Y	Mktg. Professionals:	Y	Gen. Writing/Editing:	Y	Info. Management:	Y	Finance/Acct.:	Y	Engineers, Elec.:	
Experienced Mgmt.:	Y	Retail Sales:	Y	Technical Writing:		Software Dev.:	Y	Law:	Y	Engineers, Other:	
Int'l Business:		Commercial/Industrial:		Graphic Arts/Photog.:	Y	Hardware Dev.:		HR/Other:	Y	Health/Lab	
MBA Graduates:	Y	Sales Trainees:	Y	Music:		Consulting/Other:		Training:	Y	Scientists/Research:	
		Advertising Pros.:	Y	Broadcasting:				Health Care:		Petroleum/Chemicals:	
				Other:				Consulting:		Math/Other:	

TYPES OF BUSINESS:

Groceries, Online Retail
Grocery Delivery Services
Media & Research Services

BRANDS/DIVISIONS/AFFILIATES:

Ahold USA Inc
Royal Ahold NV
Peapod by Giant
Peapod by Stop & Shop
PeapodMobile

CONTACTS: *Note: Officers with more than one job title may be intentionally listed here more than once.*

Andrew B. Parkinson, CEO
Mike Brennan, COO/Sr. VP
Andrew B. Parkinson, Pres.
John Burchard, CIO/Sr. VP
Thomas L. Parkinson, CTO/Sr. VP
John Burchard, Chief Admin. Officer
Scott DeGraeve, Sr. VP/Gen. Mgr.-Washington & Chicago

Phone: 847-583-9400 **Fax:** 847-583-9494
Toll-Free: 800-573-2763
Address: 9933 Woods Dr., Skokie, IL 60077 US

GROWTH PLANS/SPECIAL FEATURES:

Peapod, LLC, a subsidiary of Royal Ahold, delivers groceries that consumers order over the Internet. The company's grocery delivery service, with costs ranging from $6.95 to $9.95 per order depending on the dollar value of the order, provides consumers with a virtual supermarket, personalized shopping, delivery and responsive telephone and e-mail support. A typical order totals $150, with customers shopping on average twice a month. Peapod provides more than 8,000 products in produce; meat and seafood; deli items; prepared foods; natural and organic foods; Kosher foods; office and school supplies; seasonal items; video products; pet items; health and beauty aids; and wine, beer and spirits. The firm has partnerships with Ahold's U.S. properties, Stop & Shop and Giant Food stores, offering their private label food products and using their facilities as secondary fulfillment spaces. Peapod also provides consumer goods companies with a forum for targeted interactive advertising, electronic coupons and extensive product research. The company operates through centralized distribution from its two warehouses in Chicago and Washington, D.C., which together total 150,000 square feet. It also owns 7,000 square-foot warerooms adjacent to its partner stores in Connecticut, Massachusetts, New York, New Jersey and Rhode Island. Peapod delivers to 1,500 zip codes and more than 12 million households. The firm has a supermarket presence in 22 major cities and suburban areas, including markets in Massachusetts, Virginia, Maryland, Wisconsin, Washington, D.C., Connecticut, New York, Rhode Island, Illinois, Indiana and New Jersey. Peapod has delivered more than 15 million orders since its inception. In 2011, it introduced PeapodMobile, a mobile shopping application for users of iPhones and iPads.

Employees receive medical, dental and prescription health benefits; a 401(k); short- and long-term disability coverage; life and accidental death and dismemberment insurance; and paid time off.

FINANCIALS: **Sales and profits are in thousands of dollars—add 000 to get the full amount. 2011 Note: Financial information for 2011 was not available for all companies at press time.**

2011 Sales: $	2011 Profits: $	**U.S. Stock Ticker: Subsidiary**
2010 Sales: $	2010 Profits: $	**Int'l Ticker:**
2009 Sales: $	2009 Profits: $	Int'l Exchange:
2008 Sales: $	2008 Profits: $	Employees: Fiscal Year Ends: 12/31
2007 Sales: $	2007 Profits: $	Parent Company: ROYAL AHOLD NV

SALARIES/BENEFITS:

Pension Plan:	ESOP Stock Plan:	Profit Sharing:	Top Exec. Salary: $	Bonus: $
Savings Plan: Y	Stock Purch. Plan:		Second Exec. Salary: $	Bonus: $

OTHER THOUGHTS:

Apparent Women Officers or Directors:
Hot Spot for Advancement for Women/Minorities:

LOCATIONS: ("Y" = Yes)

West:	Southwest:	Midwest:	Southeast:	Northeast:	International:
		Y		Y	

PEGASYSTEMS INC

www.pega.com

Industry Group Code: 511210H

Management:		Sales/Marketing:		Liberal Arts:		Information Systems:		Professionals:		Technical/Scientific:	
Mgmt. Trainees:		Mktg. Professionals:	Y	Gen. Writing/Editing:		Info. Management:	Y	Finance/Acct.:	Y	Engineers, Elec.:	
Experienced Mgmt.:	Y	Retail Sales:		Technical Writing:	Y	Software Dev.:	Y	Law:	Y	Engineers, Other:	
Int'l Business:	Y	Commercial/Industrial:	Y	Graphic Arts/Photog.:		Hardware Dev.:		HR/Other:	Y	Health/Lab	
MBA Graduates:	Y	Sales Trainees:		Music:		Consulting/Other:		Training:	Y	Scientists/Research:	
		Advertising Pros.:		Broadcasting:				Health Care:		Petroleum/Chemicals:	
				Other:				Consulting:		Math/Other:	

TYPES OF BUSINESS:

Business Process Management Software
Consulting

BRANDS/DIVISIONS/AFFILIATES:

PegaRULES Process Commander (The)
Pega BPM Suite (The)
Pega CRM
Pega Decision Management
Pega Cloud

CONTACTS: *Note: Officers with more than one job title may be intentionally listed here more than once.*

Alan Trefler, CEO
Craig A. Dynes, CFO/Sr. VP
Grant Johnson, Chief Mktg. Officer
Jeff Yanagi, Sr. VP-Human Capital
Mike Pyle, Sr. VP-Prod. Dev.
Mike Pyle, Sr. VP-Eng.
Shawn Hoyt, General Counsel/VP
Max Mayer, Sr. VP-Corp. Dev.
Brian Callahan, Dir.-Corp. Comm.
Leon Trefler, Sr. VP-Global Sales, Alliances & Vertical Dev.
Douglas Kra, Sr. VP-Global Svcs.
Alan Trefler, Chmn.

Phone: 617-374-9600	**Fax:** 617-374-9620
Toll-Free:	
Address: 101 Main St, Cambridge, MA 02142-1590 US	

GROWTH PLANS/SPECIAL FEATURES:

Pegasystems, Inc. develops, markets, licenses and supports business process management (BPM) software. The firm's Build for Change software technology directly captures business objectives, automating programming and automating work, enabling groups to build, deploy and change enterprise applications. Build for Change is standards-based and can leverage existing technology investments to reduce implementation time. The PegaRULES Process Commander, a rules engine that offers features such as a business process application, browser-based graphical development environment, execution engine and management dashboard. The Pega BPM Suite adds content management, process simulation, enterprise integration, process analysis, portal integration and case management capabilities to the PegaRULES Process Commander. The Pega CRM software allows for automated customer service inquiries and marketing. Pega Decision Management products are used to help in cross-channel decision-making. Pega Cloud is a cloud computing solution that allows for the quick development and deployment of dynamic business applications. Additionally, the firm's software supports secondary frameworks for industry specific purposes, such as financial services, healthcare and insurance, as well as exceptions management, including transactions that are not automatically processed by existing systems. The company also offers customer support and training/professional services. Pegasystems markets its products to customers in the financial services, healthcare, insurance, telecommunications, life sciences, travel, manufacturing and government sectors. The company maintains strategic partnerships with numerous companies, including IBM, Infosys, Wipro and Tata Consultancy Services. Its major clients include HSBC Holdings PLC, Citigroup, American National Insurance Group, Advanced Micro Devices, Inc., Novartis International AG and The British Airport Authority.

Employee benefits include healthcare coverage; additional training and certification programs; and retirement savings/pension plans.

FINANCIALS: **Sales and profits are in thousands of dollars—add 000 to get the full amount. 2011 Note: Financial information for 2011 was not available for all companies at press time.**

2011 Sales: $416,700	2011 Profits: $10,100	**U.S. Stock Ticker: PEGA**
2010 Sales: $336,599	2010 Profits: $-5,891	**Int'l Ticker:**
2009 Sales: $264,013	2009 Profits: $32,212	Int'l Exchange:
2008 Sales: $211,647	2008 Profits: $10,977	Employees: 1,031 Fiscal Year Ends: 12/31
2007 Sales: $161,949	2007 Profits: $6,595	Parent Company:

SALARIES/BENEFITS:

Pension Plan: Y	ESOP Stock Plan:	Profit Sharing:	Top Exec. Salary: $344,000	Bonus: $247,918
Savings Plan: Y	Stock Purch. Plan:		Second Exec. Salary: $313,000	Bonus: $145,812

OTHER THOUGHTS:

Apparent Women Officers or Directors:
Hot Spot for Advancement for Women/Minorities:

LOCATIONS: ("Y" = Yes)

West:	Southwest:	Midwest:	Southeast:	Northeast:	International:
Y	Y	Y	Y	Y	Y

PERFICIENT INC

www.perficient.com

Industry Group Code: 541512

Management:		Sales/Marketing:		Liberal Arts:		Information Systems:		Professionals:		Technical/Scientific:	
Mgmt. Trainees:		Mktg. Professionals:	Y	Gen. Writing/Editing:	Y	Info. Management:	Y	Finance/Acct.:	Y	Engineers, Elec.:	Y
Experienced Mgmt.:	Y	Retail Sales:		Technical Writing:	Y	Software Dev.:	Y	Law:	Y	Engineers, Other:	
Int'l Business:	Y	Commercial/Industrial:	Y	Graphic Arts/Photog.:		Hardware Dev.:		HR/Other:	Y	Health/Lab	
MBA Graduates:	Y	Sales Trainees:		Music:		Consulting/Other:	Y	Training:	Y	Scientists/Research:	
		Advertising Pros.:		Broadcasting:				Health Care:		Petroleum/Chemicals:	
				Other:	Y			Consulting:	Y	Math/Other:	

TYPES OF BUSINESS:

Consulting-On-Site Technical Services
Middleware
Web Services
Content Management Software
Enterprise Portal Services
IT Outsourcing

BRANDS/DIVISIONS/AFFILIATES:

Exervio Inc
JCB Partners LLC

CONTACTS:

Note: Officers with more than one job title may be intentionally listed here more than once.

Jeffrey S. Davis, CEO
Kathy Henely, COO
Jeffrey S. Davis, Pres.
Paul E. Martin, CFO
Don Kasica, VP-Field Oper.
Chris Gianattasio, VP-Field Oper.
John Jenkins, VP-Field Oper.
James R. Kackley, Chmn.

Phone: 314-529-3600	**Fax:** 314-529-3640
Toll-Free: 314-529-3555	
Address: 520 Maryville Center Dr., Ste. 400, St. Louis, MO 63141 US	

GROWTH PLANS/SPECIAL FEATURES:

Perficient, Inc. is an information technology (IT) consulting firm providing large enterprise companies with Internet-based technology using third party software products developed by its partners. Its products include custom applications; portals and collaboration; e-commerce; online customer management (CRM); enterprise customer management (ECM); business integration; mobile technology; technology platform implementations; and service oriented architectures. Perficient's experience with platforms including J2EE, .Net and open-source enables it to design, develop, implement and integrate custom application solutions that provide enterprise-specific functionality. The firm's technology solutions include business integration and service oriented architectures; enterprise portals, including searchable data systems, collaborative systems and transaction processing; custom application solutions; customer relationship management; technology platform implementations; business intelligence; enterprise content management, including Enterprise Imagine and Document Management and Enterprise Records Management; enterprise performance management; business process management and analysis; interactive design; and maintenance and support features. Perficient, headquartered in St, Louis, Missouri, serves its customers from a network of 18 markets throughout the U.S., Canada, Eastern Europe, China and India. In 2011, the firm acquired Exervio, Inc. and JCB Partners, LLC. In June 2011, the company opened a new facility in Hangzhou, China.

Employee benefits include medical and childcare flexible spending accounts; medical, dental and vision insurance; short- and long-term disability insurance; referral bonuses; a 401(k); a stock purchase plan; and mobile and connectivity allowances.

FINANCIALS:

Sales and profits are in thousands of dollars—add 000 to get the full amount. 2011 Note: Financial information for 2011 was not available for all companies at press time.

2011 Sales: $	2011 Profits: $	**U.S. Stock Ticker: PRFT**
2010 Sales: $214,950	2010 Profits: $6,480	**Int'l Ticker:**
2009 Sales: $188,150	2009 Profits: $1,463	Int'l Exchange:
2008 Sales: $231,488	2008 Profits: $10,000	Employees: 1,088 Fiscal Year Ends: 12/31
2007 Sales: $218,148	2007 Profits: $16,230	Parent Company:

SALARIES/BENEFITS:

Pension Plan:	ESOP Stock Plan:	Profit Sharing:	Top Exec. Salary: $285,000	Bonus: $479,000
Savings Plan: Y	Stock Purch. Plan: Y		Second Exec. Salary: $225,000	Bonus: $151,000

OTHER THOUGHTS:

Apparent Women Officers or Directors: 1
Hot Spot for Advancement for Women/Minorities:

LOCATIONS: ("Y" = Yes)

West:	Southwest:	Midwest:	Southeast:	Northeast:	International:
Y	Y	Y	Y	Y	Y

PERRY ELLIS INTERNATIONAL INC

www.pery.com

Industry Group Code: 31522

Management:		**Sales/Marketing:**		**Liberal Arts:**		**Information Systems:**		**Professionals:**		**Technical/Scientific:**	
Mgmt. Trainees:	Y	Mktg. Professionals:	Y	Gen. Writing/Editing:	Y	Info. Management:	Y	Finance/Acct.:	Y	Engineers, Elec.:	
Experienced Mgmt.:	Y	Retail Sales:		Technical Writing:		Software Dev.:		Law:	Y	Engineers, Other:	
Int'l Business:	Y	Commercial/Industrial:	Y	Graphic Arts/Photog.:	Y	Hardware Dev.:		HR/Other:	Y	Health/Lab	
MBA Graduates:	Y	Sales Trainees:	Y	Music:		Consulting/Other:		Training:	Y	Scientists/Research:	
		Advertising Pros.:	Y	Broadcasting:				Health Care:		Petroleum/Chemicals:	
				Other:	Y			Consulting:		Math/Other:	

TYPES OF BUSINESS:

Men's & Women's Apparel
Retail Stores
Golf Apparel
Swimwear
Accessories & Fragrances

BRANDS/DIVISIONS/AFFILIATES:

Perry Ellis America
Axis
Jantzen
Cubavera
Havanera Co
Original Penguin
C&C California
Rafaella Apparel Group Inc

CONTACTS: *Note: Officers with more than one job title may be intentionally listed here more than once.*

George Feldenkreis, CEO
Oscar Feldenkreis, COO
Oscar Feldenkreis, Pres.
Anita Britt, CFO
Brett Dean, Chief Mktg. Officer
Luis Paez, CIO
Cory Shade, General Counsel/Sr. VP
Gary Rubin, Pres., Retail & e-commerce
Fanny Hanono, Treas./Corp. Sec.
Steve Harriman, Pres., Perry Ellis Bottoms Div.
George Feldenkreis, Chmn.

Phone: 305-592-2830	**Fax:** 305-594-2307
Toll-Free: 800-994-0073	
Address: 3000 N.W. 107th Ave., Miami, FL 33172 US	

GROWTH PLANS/SPECIAL FEATURES:

Perry Ellis International, Inc. is a leading designer, distributor and licensor of a broad line of men's and women's apparel, accessories and fragrances. Its products include dress and casual shirts, golf sportswear, sweaters, dress and casual pants and shorts, jeans wear, active wear and men's and women's swimwear for all major levels of retail distribution. The company maintains a diversified portfolio of more than 30 brands, including Perry Ellis, Perry Ellis America, Axis, Jantzen, Cubavera, Havanera Co., Natural Issue, Grand Slam, C&C California, Laundry, Original Penguin and Manhattan. The company also licenses the Nike and JAG brands for swimwear and accessories and the PGA Tour brand for golf apparel. The firm's wholesale business accounts for 97% of the company's total revenues, and the licensing business for 3%. Perry Ellis sources its products from Asia (84%), the Americas (8%) and the Middle East (8%). The company distributes apparel primarily to department stores, national and regional chains, mass merchants, specialty stores, sporting goods stores, the corporate wear market and independent retailers in the U.S., Canada, and the U.K. In addition, the firm operates 39 Perry Ellis retail outlet stores, eight Original Penguin retail stores and one Cubavera retail location. Perry Ellis is currently the licensor in 134 license agreements (three worldwide, 37 domestic and 94 international) for various products. In early 2011, the firm acquired Rafaella Apparel Group, Inc. for $80 million.

Employees are offered health insurance; short- and long-term disability coverage; life insurance; a 401(k) plan; flexible spending accounts; an employee assistance program; and tuition reimbursement.

FINANCIALS: **Sales and profits are in thousands of dollars—add 000 to get the full amount. 2011 Note: Financial information for 2011 was not available for all companies at press time.**

2011 Sales: $790,288	2011 Profits: $24,112
2010 Sales: $729,217	2010 Profits: $13,167
2009 Sales: $825,868	2009 Profits: $-12,890
2008 Sales: $838,465	2008 Profits: $28,173
2007 Sales: $807,616	2007 Profits: $22,409

U.S. Stock Ticker: PERY
Int'l Ticker:
Int'l Exchange:
Employees: 2,400 Fiscal Year Ends: 1/31
Parent Company:

SALARIES/BENEFITS:

Pension Plan:	ESOP Stock Plan:	Profit Sharing:	Top Exec. Salary: $1,000,000	Bonus: $1,650,591
Savings Plan: Y	Stock Purch. Plan:		Second Exec. Salary: $1,000,000	Bonus: $1,650,591

OTHER THOUGHTS:

Apparent Women Officers or Directors: 3
Hot Spot for Advancement for Women/Minorities: Y

LOCATIONS: ("Y" = Yes)

West:	Southwest:	Midwest:	Southeast:	Northeast:	International:
Y	Y	Y	Y	Y	Y

PETMED EXPRESS INC

www.1800petmeds.com

Industry Group Code: 453910

Management:		Sales/Marketing:		Liberal Arts:		Information Systems:		Professionals:		Technical/Scientific:	
Mgmt. Trainees:	Y	Mktg. Professionals:	Y	Gen. Writing/Editing:	Y	Info. Management:	Y	Finance/Acct.:	Y	Engineers, Elec.:	
Experienced Mgmt.:	Y	Retail Sales:	Y	Technical Writing:		Software Dev.:	Y	Law:	Y	Engineers, Other:	
Int'l Business:		Commercial/Industrial:		Graphic Arts/Photog.:	Y	Hardware Dev.:		HR/Other:	Y	Health/Lab	
MBA Graduates:	Y	Sales Trainees:	Y	Music:		Consulting/Other:		Training:	Y	Scientists/Research:	
		Advertising Pros.:	Y	Broadcasting:				Health Care:		Petroleum/Chemicals:	
				Other:				Consulting:		Math/Other:	

TYPES OF BUSINESS:

Prescription & Non-Prescription Pet Drugs
Mail Order Pet Pharmacy
Veterinary Medications
Animal Vitamins & Nutraceuticals
Pet Care Products

BRANDS/DIVISIONS/AFFILIATES:

1-800-PetMeds
PetHealth101.com

CONTACTS: *Note: Officers with more than one job title may be intentionally listed here more than once.*

Menderes Akdag, CEO
Menderes Akdag, Pres.
Bruce S. Rosenbloom, CFO
Bruce S. Rosenbloom, Treas.
Robert C. Schweitzer, Chmn.

Phone: 954-979-5995	**Fax:** 954-971-0544
Toll-Free: 800-738-6337	
Address: 1441 S.W. 29th Ave., Pompano Beach, FL 33069 US	

GROWTH PLANS/SPECIAL FEATURES:

PetMed Express, Inc., doing business as 1-800-PetMeds, is a nationwide pet pharmacy that markets prescription/non-prescription pet medications and other health products for dogs, cats and horses. PetMed markets its products through national television, online and through direct mail/print and e-mail advertising campaigns. The 1-800-PetMeds catalog is a full-color catalog featuring the firm's most popular products and is produced by a combination of in-house writers, production artists and independent contractors. The firm offers roughly 1,200 products, including such brands as Frontline Plus, K9 Advantix, Advantage, Heartgard Plus, Sentinel, Interceptor, Program, Revolution, Deramaxx and Rimadyl. Non-prescription medications include flea and tick control products; bone and joint care products; vitamins and nutritional supplements; and hygiene products. Prescription medications offered by the company include heartworm preventatives; thyroid and arthritis medications; antibiotics; and other specialty medications, as well as generic substitutes. In addition to pet medications, the firm also sells grooming tools, odor controllers, beds, bowls, leashes, training aids and treats. Sales of non-prescription medications generate approximately 61% of PetMed's total sales, while prescription medications account for 38% and shipping and handling charges generate 1%. The company's average retail purchase is approximately $79. The company attracts approximately 16 million visitors to its web site annually, of whom roughly 14% place an order. Internet sales generate 71% of the company's total sales. Approximately 50% of the firm's customers reside in California, Florida, Texas, New York, Pennsylvania, Virginia, North Carolina and Georgia. PetMed additionally sponsors PetHealth101.com, which provides information regarding pet behavior, illness and natural and pharmaceutical remedies for pet problems.

FINANCIALS: **Sales and profits are in thousands of dollars—add 000 to get the full amount. 2011 Note: Financial information for 2011 was not available for all companies at press time.**

2011 Sales: $231,642	2011 Profits: $20,871	**U.S. Stock Ticker: PETS**
2010 Sales: $238,266	2010 Profits: $26,002	**Int'l Ticker:**
2009 Sales: $219,412	2009 Profits: $22,976	Int'l Exchange:
2008 Sales: $188,336	2008 Profits: $20,022	Employees: 204 Fiscal Year Ends: 3/31
2007 Sales: $162,246	2007 Profits: $14,443	Parent Company:

SALARIES/BENEFITS:

Pension Plan:	ESOP Stock Plan:	Profit Sharing:	Top Exec. Salary: $550,000	Bonus: $
Savings Plan: Y	Stock Purch. Plan:		Second Exec. Salary: $245,340	Bonus: $

OTHER THOUGHTS:

Apparent Women Officers or Directors:
Hot Spot for Advancement for Women/Minorities:

LOCATIONS: ("Y" = Yes)

West:	Southwest:	Midwest:	Southeast:	Northeast:	International:
			Y		

PETROLEUM DEVELOPMENT CORPORATION

www.petd.com

Industry Group Code: 211111

Management:		Sales/Marketing:		Liberal Arts:		Information Systems:		Professionals:		Technical/Scientific:	
Mgmt. Trainees:		Mktg. Professionals:		Gen. Writing/Editing:		Info. Management:	Y	Finance/Acct.:	Y	Engineers, Elec.:	
Experienced Mgmt.:	Y	Retail Sales:		Technical Writing:		Software Dev.:		Law:	Y	Engineers, Other:	Y
Int'l Business:	Y	Commercial/Industrial:		Graphic Arts/Photog.:		Hardware Dev.:		HR/Other:	Y	Health/Lab	
MBA Graduates:	Y	Sales Trainees:		Music:		Consulting/Other:		Training:	Y	Scientists/Research:	
		Advertising Pros.:		Broadcasting:				Health Care:		Petroleum/Chemicals:	Y
				Other:				Consulting:		Math/Other:	

TYPES OF BUSINESS:

Oil & Gas Production
Gas Marketing

BRANDS/DIVISIONS/AFFILIATES:

Riley Natural Gas
PDC Energy
PDC Mountaineer LLC

CONTACTS: *Note: Officers with more than one job title may be intentionally listed here more than once.*

James M. Trimble, CEO
James M. Trimble, Pres.
Gysle R. Shellum, CFO
George B. Courcier, VP-Mktg. & Midstream
John A. DeLawder, VP-Human Resources
James F. Gaulke, VP-IT
Susan A. Foster, Dir.-Reserve Eng.
John A. DeLawder, VP-Admin.
Daniel W. Amidon, General Counsel
Scott J. Reasoner, VP-Western Oper.
Lance A. Lauck, Sr. VP-Bus. Dev.
Ronald O. Wirth, Dir.-Investor Rel.
Peter G. Schreck, VP-Finance/Treas.
Barton R. Brookman, Sr. VP-Exploration & Prod.
Celesta M. Miracle, VP-Strategic Planning
R. Scott Meyers, Chief Acct. Officer
James R. Schaff, VP-Land
Jeffrey C. Swoveland, Chmn.

Phone: 303-860-5800	**Fax:** 303-860-5838
Toll-Free:	
Address: 1775 Sherman St., Ste. 3000, Denver, CO 80203 US	

GROWTH PLANS/SPECIAL FEATURES:

Petroleum Development Corporation, doing business as PDC Energy, is an independent energy company engaged in the exploration, acquisition, development, production and marketing of natural gas and oil. The company owns interest in approximately 5,048 wells, located primarily in the Rocky Mountain Region and the Appalachian Basin. PDC Energy's wells have net proved reserves of roughly 860.6 billion cubic feet of natural gas equivalent. About 68% of the company's production consists of natural gas and 32% of a combination of crude oil and natural gas liquids. The Rocky Mountain Region accounts for 91% of the firm's total annual production, with 7% coming from its Appalachian Basin properties (the remaining 2% comes from various other properties). PDC Energy operates in two segments: natural gas and oil sales; and natural gas marketing. The natural gas and oil sales segment primarily constitutes revenues and expenses from the production and sale of natural gas and oil. The natural gas marketing segment operates through Riley Natural Gas (RNG), which purchases, aggregates and resells natural gas developed by the firm and other producers. PDC Mountaineer LLC, a joint venture with Lime Rock Partners, is developing the Marcellus Shale resource play in the Appalachian region. During 2010, PDC Energy drilled 213 gross wells (170.1 net), with plans to drill 168 wells during 2011. In December 2010, the firm acquired four partnerships of wells on its Wattenberg Field and Piceance Basin properties for roughly $36.5 million. In June 2011, PDC Energy acquired three additional partnerships in these fields for approximately $43.3 million and agreed to acquire five more partnerships on these properties. In September 2011, PDC Mountaineer LLC agreed to acquire 90,000 acres in the Marcellus Shale resource play for $152.5 million.

FINANCIALS: **Sales and profits are in thousands of dollars—add 000 to get the full amount. 2011 Note: Financial information for 2011 was not available for all companies at press time.**

2011 Sales: $395,960	2011 Profits: $13,437	**U.S. Stock Ticker: PETD**
2010 Sales: $347,647	2010 Profits: $6,214	**Int'l Ticker:**
2009 Sales: $254,800	2009 Profits: $-79,300	Int'l Exchange:
2008 Sales: $473,900	2008 Profits: $113,300	Employees: 327 Fiscal Year Ends: 12/31
2007 Sales: $305,235	2007 Profits: $33,209	Parent Company:

SALARIES/BENEFITS:

Pension Plan:	ESOP Stock Plan:	Profit Sharing:	Top Exec. Salary: $550,000	Bonus: $825,000
Savings Plan:	Stock Purch. Plan:		Second Exec. Salary: $290,000	Bonus: $270,000

OTHER THOUGHTS:

Apparent Women Officers or Directors: 8
Hot Spot for Advancement for Women/Minorities: Y

LOCATIONS: ("Y" = Yes)

West:	Southwest:	Midwest:	Southeast:	Northeast:	International:
Y				Y	

PHAZAR CORP

www.phazarcorp.com

Industry Group Code: 3342

Management:		Sales/Marketing:		Liberal Arts:		Information Systems:		Professionals:		Technical/Scientific:	
Mgmt. Trainees:		Mktg. Professionals:	Y	Gen. Writing/Editing:	Y	Info. Management:	Y	Finance/Acct.:	Y	Engineers, Elec.:	Y
Experienced Mgmt.:	Y	Retail Sales:		Technical Writing:	Y	Software Dev.:	Y	Law:	Y	Engineers, Other:	Y
Int'l Business:		Commercial/Industrial:	Y	Graphic Arts/Photog.:		Hardware Dev.:	Y	HR/Other:	Y	Health/Lab	
MBA Graduates:	Y	Sales Trainees:		Music:		Consulting/Other:		Training:		Scientists/Research:	
		Advertising Pros.:		Broadcasting:				Health Care:		Petroleum/Chemicals:	
				Other:				Consulting:		Math/Other:	

TYPES OF BUSINESS:

Antenna Systems & Towers
Wireless Equipment
Contract Manufacturing

BRANDS/DIVISIONS/AFFILIATES:

Antenna Products Corporation
Phazar Antenna Corporation
Thirco, Inc.
Tumche, Inc.

CONTACTS:

Note: Officers with more than one job title may be intentionally listed here more than once.

Garland P. Asher, CEO
Garland P. Asher, Pres.
Deborah A. Inzer, CFO/VP
Garland P. Asher, Chmn.

Phone: 940-325-3301	**Fax:** 940-325-0716
Toll-Free:	
Address: 101 SE 25th Ave., Mineral Wells, TX 76067 US	

GROWTH PLANS/SPECIAL FEATURES:

Phazar Corp. is a holding company for antenna design, manufacturing and marketing subsidiaries Antenna Products Corporation (APC) and Phazar Antenna Corp. Additional subsidiaries include Thirco, Inc., which serves as a leasing company to Phazar's operating units; and Tumche Corp., which is essentially non-operational. APC, operating primarily as a build-to-order company, designs, manufactures and markets products such as instrument landing systems; commercial wireless devices; antennas; collinear antennas; mesh network radio technologies; towers and masts; shipboard equipment; and spare parts. Customers of APC include both military and civil agencies of the U.S. government; prime contractors of the U.S. government; and commercial clients. APC's customer base has been primarily government and government prime contractor focused, although this has been slowly changing in recent years as the company continues to develop and market new commercial products. Approximately 26% of the firm's 2010 sales were to the U.S. government. Products APC provides to the U.S. government include ground to air collinear antennas; instrument landing antennas and towers; fixed system multi-port antenna arrays; tactical quick erect antennas and masts; shipboard antenna tilting devices; surveillance antennas; antenna rotators, positioners and controls; high power broadcast baluns; and tactical military mesh radio wireless networking systems. Commercial products provided by APC include first responder emergency mesh radio systems; commercial mesh radio systems; panel, sector, omnidirectional and closed loop telecommunications antennas; automatic meter reading (AMR), instrument scientific medical (ISM), cellular, paging and yagi antennas; guyed towers; and self supported towers. Another subsidiary, Phazar Antenna Corp., provides commercial wireless fixed and mobile antennas for ISM (instrument scientific medical), wireless Internet, wireless LAN, wireless local loop, fixed global positioning system (GPS), MMDS (fixed wireless) and WiMAX market applications.

FINANCIALS:

Sales and profits are in thousands of dollars—add 000 to get the full amount. 2011 Note: Financial information for 2011 was not available for all companies at press time.

2011 Sales: $8,400	2011 Profits: $- 327
2010 Sales: $7,639	2010 Profits: $- 938
2009 Sales: $7,310	2009 Profits: $- 582
2008 Sales: $9,247	2008 Profits: $ 623
2007 Sales: $5,221	2007 Profits: $- 303

U.S. Stock Ticker: ANTP
Int'l Ticker:
Int'l Exchange:
Employees: 64 Fiscal Year Ends: 5/31
Parent Company:

SALARIES/BENEFITS:

Pension Plan:	ESOP Stock Plan:	Profit Sharing:	Top Exec. Salary: $189,520	Bonus: $
Savings Plan:	Stock Purch. Plan:		Second Exec. Salary: $115,000	Bonus: $

OTHER THOUGHTS:

Apparent Women Officers or Directors: 2
Hot Spot for Advancement for Women/Minorities:

LOCATIONS: ("Y" = Yes)

West:	Southwest:	Midwest:	Southeast:	Northeast:	International:
	Y				

PHILADELPHIA CONSOLIDATED HOLDING CORP www.phly.com

Industry Group Code: 524126

Management:		Sales/Marketing:		Liberal Arts:		Information Systems:		Professionals:		Technical/Scientific:	
Mgmt. Trainees:	Y	Mktg. Professionals:	Y	Gen. Writing/Editing:	Y	Info. Management:	Y	Finance/Acct.:	Y	Engineers, Elec.:	
Experienced Mgmt.:	Y	Retail Sales:		Technical Writing:	Y	Software Dev.:		Law:	Y	Engineers, Other:	
Int'l Business:	Y	Commercial/Industrial:	Y	Graphic Arts/Photog.:		Hardware Dev.:		HR/Other:	Y	Health/Lab	
MBA Graduates:	Y	Sales Trainees:	Y	Music:		Consulting/Other:		Training:	Y	Scientists/Research:	
		Advertising Pros.:		Broadcasting:				Health Care:		Petroleum/Chemicals:	
				Other:				Consulting:		Math/Other:	Y

TYPES OF BUSINESS:

Direct Property & Casualty Insurance
Commercial, Personal & Specialty Lines
Auto Insurance

BRANDS/DIVISIONS/AFFILIATES:

Tokio Marine Holdings, Inc.

CONTACTS:

Note: Officers with more than one job title may be intentionally listed here more than once.

James J. Maguire, Jr., CEO
Sean S. Sweeney, Pres.
Craig P. Keller, CFO/Exec. VP
Craig P. Keller, Corp. Sec.
Bill Procopio, Mgr.-Corp. Comm.
Craig P. Keller, Treas.
William J. Benecke, Chief Claims Officer/Exec. VP
John Glomb, Chief Underwriting Officer
Robert D. O'Leary, Exec. VP-Mktg.
James J. Maguire, Jr., Chmn.

Phone: 610-617-7900 **Fax:** 610-617-7940
Toll-Free: 800-873-4552
Address: 231 St. Asaph's Rd., Ste. 100, Bala Cynwyd, PA 19004 US

GROWTH PLANS/SPECIAL FEATURES:

Philadelphia Consolidated Holding Corp. designs, markets and underwrites specialty commercial and personal property and casualty insurance products incorporating value-added coverages and services for select target markets or niches. The company operates in four segments: commercial; management and professional liability, formerly called the specialty segment; personal lines underwriting and loss control. The commercial lines segment provides commercial multi-peril packages, commercial automobile, specialty property and inland marine and antique/collector care insurance products. The management and professional liability group offers a comprehensive list of insurance products that include directors and officers liability; coverages for organizations with up to 4,000 employees; crime protection and cyber security; and many other coverages. The personal lines underwriting segment provides antique car/collector car insurance and personal property insurance products. The personal property insurance is targeted at homeowners and the manufactured housing market in Florida, with flood programs available in all 50 states. The loss control services segment is designed for businesses. The firm offers trend analysis, client training in loss prevention, safety practices and risk management programs. The company is a subsidiary of Tokio Marine Holdings, Inc and has locations in approximately 432 cities in 38 countries and regions. In July 2011, Philadelphia Consolidated launched, through a strategic alliance with Ullico Casualty Company and Ullico Casualty Group, Inc., a new Surety Bond business group.

Employees of the firm are offered medical and vision insurance; life and AD&D insurance; disability insurance; 401(k); a variety of voluntary benefits; and tuition reimbursement, among many other benefits.

FINANCIALS:

Sales and profits are in thousands of dollars—add 000 to get the full amount. 2011 Note: Financial information for 2011 was not available for all companies at press time.

2011 Sales: $	2011 Profits: $
2010 Sales: $2,108,038	2010 Profits: $265,585
2009 Sales: $1,943,564	2009 Profits: $259,076
2008 Sales: $1,665,637	2008 Profits: $140,186
2007 Sales: $1,529,594	2007 Profits: $326,813

U.S. Stock Ticker: Subsidiary
Int'l Ticker:
Int'l Exchange:
Employees: 1,400 Fiscal Year Ends: 12/31
Parent Company: TOKIO MARINE HOLDINGS INC

SALARIES/BENEFITS:

Pension Plan:	ESOP Stock Plan:	Profit Sharing: Y	Top Exec. Salary: $	Bonus: $
Savings Plan: Y	Stock Purch. Plan: Y		Second Exec. Salary: $	Bonus: $

OTHER THOUGHTS:

Apparent Women Officers or Directors:
Hot Spot for Advancement for Women/Minorities:

LOCATIONS: ("Y" = Yes)

West:	Southwest:	Midwest:	Southeast:	Northeast:	International:
Y	Y	Y	Y	Y	Y

PHOENIX COMPANIES INC (THE)

www.phoenixwm.com

Industry Group Code: 524113

Management:		Sales/Marketing:		Liberal Arts:		Information Systems:		Professionals:		Technical/Scientific:	
Mgmt. Trainees:	Y	Mktg. Professionals:	Y	Gen. Writing/Editing:	Y	Info. Management:	Y	Finance/Acct.:	Y	Engineers, Elec.:	
Experienced Mgmt.:	Y	Retail Sales:		Technical Writing:	Y	Software Dev.:		Law:	Y	Engineers, Other:	
Int'l Business:	Y	Commercial/Industrial:		Graphic Arts/Photog.:		Hardware Dev.:		HR/Other:	Y	Health/Lab	
MBA Graduates:	Y	Sales Trainees:	Y	Music:		Consulting/Other:		Training:	Y	Scientists/Research:	
		Advertising Pros.:	Y	Broadcasting:				Health Care:	Y	Petroleum/Chemicals:	
				Other:				Consulting:		Math/Other:	Y

TYPES OF BUSINESS:

Insurance-Life
Mutual Funds
Annuities
Brokerage Services
Wealth Management
Trust Services
Investment

BRANDS/DIVISIONS/AFFILIATES:

Saybrus Partners, Inc.
PHL Variable Insurance Company
Phoenix Life Insurance Company

CONTACTS: *Note: Officers with more than one job title may be intentionally listed here more than once.*

James D. Wehr, CEO
James D. Wehr, Pres.
Peter A. Hofmann, CFO/Sr. Exec. VP
Bonnie J. Malley, Exec. VP-Human Resources
Deborah M. Zawisza, CIO/Sr. VP
Thomas Buckingham, Sr. VP-Prod. Implementation & Oper.
Bonnie J. Malley, Chief Admin. Officer/Exec. VP-Admin.
John T. Mulrain, General Counsel/Exec. VP/Sec.
William Hayward, Sr. VP-Oper.
Philip K. Polkinghorn, Sr. Exec. VP-Bus. Dev.
John V. LaGrasse, Exec. VP-Alternative Retirement Solutions
Edward W. Cassidy, Managing Principal-Saybrus Partners, Inc.
Christopher M. Wilkos, Chief Investment Officer/Exec. VP
David R. Pellerin, Chief Risk Officer/Sr. VP
Thomas S. Johnson, Chmn.
Edward W. Cassidy, Exec. VP-Dist.

Phone: 860-403-5000	**Fax:** 860-403-5534
Toll-Free:	
Address: 1 American Row, Hartford, CT 06102 US	

GROWTH PLANS/SPECIAL FEATURES:

The Phoenix Companies, Inc. is a provider of wealth management products and services designed specifically for affluent and high-net-worth clients, along with additional services for the broader middle market. Products offered by the company include universal life insurance; variable universal life insurance; fixed annuities; variable annuities; and single premium annuities. Through a variety of select advisors and financial services firms, the company serves the accumulation, preservation and wealth transfer needs of individuals and families, business owners, senior corporate executives and institutions. Phoenix's primary subsidiaries include PHL Variable Insurance Company and Phoenix Life Insurance Company. The company offers services to middle market customers through its Saybrus Partners, Inc. subsidiary. The firm currently has $49.4 billion of net life insurance in force and $4 billion of annuity assets under management. In mid 2010, Phoenix sold its PFG Holdings, Inc. division, which included the subsidiaries Philadelphia Financial Group, Inc. and AGL Life Assurance Company, to Tiptree Financial Partners LP. In October 2010, the firm sold Phoenix Life and Reassurance Company of New York to Tiptree Financial Partners. In July 2011, The Phoenix Companies and Legacy Marketing Group agreed to jointly develop new annuity products. In September 2011, the company agreed to sell subsidiary Goodwin Capital Advisers, Inc. to Conning Holdings Corp.

The company offers its employees flexible work schedules; a retirement plan; a 401(k) plan; a discount stock purchase plan; benefits for same-sex domestic partners; paternity leave; adoption assistance; flexible spending accounts; disability programs; and tuition reimbursement.

FINANCIALS: **Sales and profits are in thousands of dollars—add 000 to get the full amount. 2011 Note: Financial information for 2011 was not available for all companies at press time.**

2011 Sales: $1,849,700	2011 Profits: $8,100	**U.S. Stock Ticker: PNX**
2010 Sales: $2,084,900	2010 Profits: $-12,600	**Int'l Ticker:**
2009 Sales: $2,016,800	2009 Profits: $-319,000	Int'l Exchange:
2008 Sales: $2,008,300	2008 Profits: $-726,000	Employees: 625 Fiscal Year Ends: 12/31
2007 Sales: $2,572,800	2007 Profits: $123,900	Parent Company:

SALARIES/BENEFITS:

Pension Plan: Y	ESOP Stock Plan:	Profit Sharing:	Top Exec. Salary: $650,000	Bonus: $604,500
Savings Plan: Y	Stock Purch. Plan: Y		Second Exec. Salary: $475,000	Bonus: $574,275

OTHER THOUGHTS:

Apparent Women Officers or Directors: 3
Hot Spot for Advancement for Women/Minorities: Y

LOCATIONS: ("Y" = Yes)

West:	Southwest:	Midwest:	Southeast:	Northeast:	International:
				Y	

PIEDMONT NATURAL GAS COMPANY INC www.piedmontng.com

Industry Group Code: 221210

Management:		Sales/Marketing:		Liberal Arts:		Information Systems:		Professionals:		Technical/Scientific:	
Mgmt. Trainees:		Mktg. Professionals:	Y	Gen. Writing/Editing:	Y	Info. Management:	Y	Finance/Acct.:	Y	Engineers, Elec.:	Y
Experienced Mgmt.:	Y	Retail Sales:		Technical Writing:		Software Dev.:		Law:	Y	Engineers, Other:	Y
Int'l Business:		Commercial/Industrial:	Y	Graphic Arts/Photog.:		Hardware Dev.:		HR/Other:	Y	Health/Lab Scientists/Research:	
MBA Graduates:	Y	Sales Trainees:		Music:		Consulting/Other:		Training:	Y	Petroleum/Chemicals:	Y
		Advertising Pros.:		Broadcasting:				Health Care:		Math/Other:	
				Other:				Consulting:			

TYPES OF BUSINESS:

Utilities-Natural Gas
Pipelines
Gas Transportation & Storage
Natural Gas Marketing

BRANDS/DIVISIONS/AFFILIATES:

SouthStar Energy Services

CONTACTS:

Note: Officers with more than one job title may be intentionally listed here more than once.

Thomas E. Skains, CEO
Thomas E. Skains, Pres.
Karl W. Newlin, CFO/Sr. VP
Bill Williams, VP-Sales & Delivery Svcs.
Brad Merlie, VP-Info. Systems
Rodney Myers, VP-Eng.
Kevin M. O'Hara, Chief Admin. Officer/Sr. VP
Jane R. Lewis-Raymond, General Counsel/Sr. VP/Sec.
Rodney Myers, VP-Oper. Svcs.
Ken Valentine, VP-Bus. Dev. & Carbon Mgmt. Strategies
Robert O. Pritchard, Chief Risk Officer/Treas./VP
Jose Simon, VP/Controller
Michael H. Yount, Chief Utility Oper. Officer/Sr. VP
Franklin H. Yoho, Chief Commercial Oper. Officer/Sr. VP
Ranelle Warfield, VP-Customer Service
Thomas E. Skains, Chmn.

Phone: 704-364-3120	**Fax:** 704-365-3849
Toll-Free:	
Address: 4720 Piedmont Row Dr., Charlotte, NC 28210 US	

GROWTH PLANS/SPECIAL FEATURES:

Piedmont Natural Gas Company, Inc. (Piedmont) is an energy services company primarily engaged in the distribution of natural gas to residential, commercial and industrial customers in North Carolina, South Carolina and Tennessee. With over 1 million customers, it is one of the largest natural gas utilities in the Southeast. Piedmont owns approximately 2,600 miles of transmission pipelines and 28,900 miles of distribution mains. The company also maintains interests in several non-utility, energy-related businesses, including unregulated retail natural gas marketing and interstate and intrastate natural gas storage and transportation. Piedmont has 15% interest in SouthStar Energy Services, which offers a combination of unregulated energy products and services to industrial, commercial and residential customers in the southeastern U.S. Business strategies for Piedmont include focusing on core-utility businesses, pursuing new construction markets and converting existing homes and businesses to natural energy. The company, together with Progress Energy Carolinas, is constructing a 38-mile pipeline, along with an additional compression facility, to provide natural gas delivery service to the Progress Energy Carolina plant in Wayne County, North Carolina. The pipeline and compression facility, with an estimated price tag of $85 million, is expected to be operational by 2012.

FINANCIALS:

Sales and profits are in thousands of dollars—add 000 to get the full amount. 2011 Note: Financial information for 2011 was not available for all companies at press time.

2011 Sales: $1,433,905	2011 Profits: $113,568	**U.S. Stock Ticker: PNY**
2010 Sales: $1,552,295	2010 Profits: $141,954	**Int'l Ticker:**
2009 Sales: $1,638,116	2009 Profits: $122,824	Int'l Exchange:
2008 Sales: $2,089,108	2008 Profits: $110,007	Employees: 1,782 Fiscal Year Ends: 10/31
2007 Sales: $1,711,292	2007 Profits: $104,387	Parent Company:

SALARIES/BENEFITS:

Pension Plan: Y	ESOP Stock Plan: Y	Profit Sharing:	Top Exec. Salary: $802,139	Bonus: $508,182
Savings Plan: Y	Stock Purch. Plan:		Second Exec. Salary: $428,943	Bonus: $230,196

OTHER THOUGHTS:

Apparent Women Officers or Directors: 3
Hot Spot for Advancement for Women/Minorities: Y

LOCATIONS: ("Y" = Yes)

West:	Southwest:	Midwest:	Southeast:	Northeast:	International:
			Y	Y	

PIONEER NATURAL RESOURCES COMPANY www.pioneernrc.com

Industry Group Code: 211111

Management:		Sales/Marketing:	Liberal Arts:	Information Systems:		Professionals:		Technical/Scientific:	
Mgmt. Trainees:		Mktg. Professionals:	Gen. Writing/Editing:	Info. Management:	Y	Finance/Acct.:	Y	Engineers, Elec.:	
Experienced Mgmt.:	Y	Retail Sales:	Technical Writing:	Software Dev.:		Law:	Y	Engineers, Other:	Y
Int'l Business:	Y	Commercial/Industrial:	Graphic Arts/Photog.:	Hardware Dev.:		HR/Other:	Y	Health/Lab	
MBA Graduates:	Y	Sales Trainees:	Music:	Consulting/Other:		Training:	Y	Scientists/Research:	
		Advertising Pros.:	Broadcasting:			Health Care:		Petroleum/Chemicals:	Y
			Other:			Consulting:		Math/Other:	

TYPES OF BUSINESS:

Oil & Gas Exploration & Production

BRANDS/DIVISIONS/AFFILIATES:

CONTACTS:

Note: Officers with more than one job title may be intentionally listed here more than once.

Scott D. Sheffield, CEO
Timothy L. Dove, COO
Timothy L. Dove, Pres.
Richard P. Dealy, CFO/Exec. VP
Thomas C. Halbouty, CIO/VP
Thomas C. Halbouty, CTO
Larry N. Paulsen, VP-Admin. & Risk Mgmt.
Mark S. Berg, General Counsel/Exec. VP
Jay P. Still, Exec. VP-Domestic Oper.
Chris J. Cheatwood, Exec. VP-Bus. Dev. & Tech.
Susan A. Spratlen, VP-Corp. Comm. & Sustainable Dev.
Frank E. Hopkins, VP-Investor Rel.
Frank W. Hall, Chief Acct. Officer/VP
Danny L. Kellum, Exec. VP-Permian Oper.
William F. Hannes, Exec. VP-South Texas Oper.
Robert C. Hagens, VP-Land
Mark H. Kleinman, Chief Compliance Officer/VP/Corp. Sec.
Scott D. Sheffield, Chmn.
David McManus, Exec. VP-Int'l Oper.

Phone: 972-444-9001 **Fax:** 972-969-3576
Toll-Free:
Address: 5205 N. O'Connor Blvd., Ste. 200, Irving, TX 75039 US

GROWTH PLANS/SPECIAL FEATURES:

Pioneer Natural Resources Company (Pioneer) is one of the largest independent exploration and production companies in the U.S. The company owns interests in oil, natural gas liquids (NGL) and gas properties located in the U.S. and South Africa. The firm has total proved reserves of about 1.01 billion barrels of oil equivalent (boe), and produces approximately 115,000 boe per day. It owns over 9,200 producing wells and controls approximately $9.7 billion in assets. Pioneer's operations are split between domestic and international divisions. The domestic division includes the Spraberry field in west Texas; the Hugoton gas field in southwest Kansas and Oklahoma; the West Panhandle gas field in Texas; the Raton field gas operations in southern Colorado; the Pawnee gas field production and exploration wells in the Edwards Reef expansion in southern Texas; and a 70% interest in the Oooguruk project on Alaska's north slope. The firm's international operations are centered in Africa, with exploration projects offshore South Africa. Pioneer focuses its production efforts toward increasing its average daily production of oil and gas through development drilling, production enhancement activities and acquisitions of producing properties. Pioneer's drilling activities seek to increase its oil/gas reserves, production and cash flow by concentrating on drilling low-risk development wells and by conducting additional development activities such as well recompletions. During 2010, the firm's U.S. operations accounted for 90% of its total average daily production levels, with operations in South Africa and Tunisia representing about 5% each. In February 2011, Pioneer sold all of its share holdings in its Tunisian subsidiaries to a wholly-owned subsidiary of OMV AG for $866 million.

FINANCIALS:

Sales and profits are in thousands of dollars—add 000 to get the full amount. 2011 Note: Financial information for 2011 was not available for all companies at press time.

2011 Sales: $2,294,100	2011 Profits: $834,500
2010 Sales: $2,471,590	2010 Profits: $605,208
2009 Sales: $1,711,516	2009 Profits: $-52,106
2008 Sales: $2,284,841	2008 Profits: $210,020
2007 Sales: $1,785,018	2007 Profits: $372,728

U.S. Stock Ticker: PXD
Int'l Ticker:
Int'l Exchange:
Employees: 2,248 Fiscal Year Ends: 12/31
Parent Company:

SALARIES/BENEFITS:

Pension Plan:	ESOP Stock Plan:	Profit Sharing:	Top Exec. Salary: $956,001	Bonus: $2,007,600
Savings Plan: Y	Stock Purch. Plan:		Second Exec. Salary: $531,001	Bonus: $1,062,000

OTHER THOUGHTS:

Apparent Women Officers or Directors: 1
Hot Spot for Advancement for Women/Minorities:

LOCATIONS: ("Y" = Yes)

West:	Southwest:	Midwest:	Southeast:	Northeast:	International:
Y	Y	Y			Y

PIPER JAFFRAY COMPANIES

www.piperjaffray.com

Industry Group Code: 523110

Management:		**Sales/Marketing:**		**Liberal Arts:**		**Information Systems:**		**Professionals:**		**Technical/Scientific:**	
Mgmt. Trainees:		Mktg. Professionals:		Gen. Writing/Editing:	Y	Info. Management:	Y	Finance/Acct.:	Y	Engineers, Elec.:	
Experienced Mgmt.:	Y	Retail Sales:		Technical Writing:		Software Dev.:	Y	Law:	Y	Engineers, Other:	
Int'l Business:	Y	Commercial/Industrial:		Graphic Arts/Photog.:		Hardware Dev.:		HR/Other:	Y	Health/Lab	
MBA Graduates:	Y	Sales Trainees:		Music:		Consulting/Other:		Training:		Scientists/Research:	
		Advertising Pros.:		Broadcasting:				Health Care:		Petroleum/Chemicals:	
				Other:				Consulting:		Math/Other:	

TYPES OF BUSINESS:

Investment Banking
Venture Capital
Health Care Research & Investment
Investment Management
Investment Research
Private Equity Funds

BRANDS/DIVISIONS/AFFILIATES:

Piper Jaffray Private Capital LLC
Piper Jaffray Investment Management LLC
Fiduciary Asset Management Inc
Advisory Research Co

CONTACTS:

Note: Officers with more than one job title may be intentionally listed here more than once.

Andrew S. Duff, CEO
Thomas P. Schnettler, COO
Thomas P. Schnettler, Pres.
Debbra L. Schoneman, CFO
Chris Crawshaw, Head-Advisory Research
Shawn Quant, CIO
James L. Chosy, General Counsel/Sec.
Thomas G. Smith, Managing Dir.-Corp. Dev.
Brad Winges, Managing Dir./Head-Fixed Income Svcs.
R. Todd Firebaugh, Managing Dir./Co-Head-Public Finance
Robert Peterson, Managing Dir./Head-Global Equities
Brien O'Brien, Head-Asset Mgmt.
Andrew S. Duff, Chmn.
Alex Ko Po Ming, CEO-Piper Jaffray Asia

Phone: 612-303-6000	**Fax:** 612-303-8199
Toll-Free: 800-333-6000	
Address: 800 Nicollet Mall, Ste. 800, Minneapolis, MN 55402 US	

GROWTH PLANS/SPECIAL FEATURES:

Piper Jaffray Companies (PJC) is international asset management, institutional securities and middle-market investment firm that serves the needs of corporations, private equity groups, public entities, nonprofit clients and institutional investors. The company operates in four divisions: investment banking, equity and fixed income institutional brokerage, asset management and other income. The investment banking segment raises capital through equity financing in addition to providing advisory services relating to mergers and acquisitions for corporate clients. The segment focuses on seven different industries, including business services; clean technology and renewables; consumer; financial institutions; healthcare; industrial growth; and media, telecommunications and technology. Government and non-profit clients can obtain underwriting debt issuances and financial advisory and interest rate risk management from the firm. The equity and fixed finance institutional brokerage division offers equity and fixed income advisory and trade execution services for institutional investors, public entities and non-profit clients. The firm's asset management segment provides businesses with separately managed accounts, partnerships and open and closed-end mutual fund services. Other income includes gains and losses from investments in private equity and venture capital funds, as well as income associated with the forfeiture of stock-based competition. Investment banking is marketed under a single name-Piper Jaffray- for brand consistency, whereas asset management is marketed under two subsidiaries Advisory Research Co. (ARI) and Fiduciary Asset Management., Inc. (FAMCO). The company also offers asset management through Piper Jaffray Private Capital LLC and Piper Jaffray Investment Management LLC.

Employees of Piper Jaffray receive medical, dental and vision benefits; life and disability insurance; a 401(k) plan; tuition reimbursement; adoption assistance; a profit sharing plan; paid time off; and discounts on financial products and services.

FINANCIALS:

Sales and profits are in thousands of dollars—add 000 to get the full amount. 2011 Note: Financial information for 2011 was not available for all companies at press time.

2011 Sales: $458,125	2011 Profits: $-102,020
2010 Sales: $530,074	2010 Profits: $18,929
2009 Sales: $468,790	2009 Profits: $24,888
2008 Sales: $326,397	2008 Profits: $-182,975
2007 Sales: $182,497	2007 Profits: $21,943

U.S. Stock Ticker: PJC
Int'l Ticker:
Int'l Exchange:
Employees: 1,053 Fiscal Year Ends: 12/31
Parent Company:

SALARIES/BENEFITS:

Pension Plan:	ESOP Stock Plan:	Profit Sharing: Y	Top Exec. Salary: $608,333	Bonus: $3,525,398
Savings Plan: Y	Stock Purch. Plan:		Second Exec. Salary: $508,333	Bonus: $995,834

OTHER THOUGHTS:

Apparent Women Officers or Directors: 5
Hot Spot for Advancement for Women/Minorities: Y

LOCATIONS: ("Y" = Yes)

West:	Southwest:	Midwest:	Southeast:	Northeast:	International:
Y	Y	Y		Y	Y

PLAINS EXPLORATION AND PRODUCTION COMPANY

www.plainsxp.com

Industry Group Code: 211111

Management:		Sales/Marketing:		Liberal Arts:		Information Systems:		Professionals:		Technical/Scientific:	
Mgmt. Trainees:		Mktg. Professionals:		Gen. Writing/Editing:		Info. Management:	Y	Finance/Acct.:	Y	Engineers, Elec.:	
Experienced Mgmt.:	Y	Retail Sales:		Technical Writing:		Software Dev.:		Law:	Y	Engineers, Other:	Y
Int'l Business:		Commercial/Industrial:		Graphic Arts/Photog.:		Hardware Dev.:		HR/Other:	Y	Health/Lab	
MBA Graduates:	Y	Sales Trainees:		Music:		Consulting/Other:		Training:	Y	Scientists/Research:	
		Advertising Pros.:		Broadcasting:				Health Care:		Petroleum/Chemicals:	Y
				Other:				Consulting:		Math/Other:	

TYPES OF BUSINESS:

Oil & Gas Exploration & Production

BRANDS/DIVISIONS/AFFILIATES:

GROWTH PLANS/SPECIAL FEATURES:

Plains Exploration and Production Company (PXP) is an independent upstream energy company that acquires, develops, exploits, explores for and produces oil and gas in the U.S. Its principal operations in the U.S. are in the Los Angeles and San Joaquin Basins and the Arroyo Grande Field in California; the Santa Maria Basin offshore California; the Gulf Coast region, including the Haynesville Shale and areas of South and East Texas; the Gulf of Mexico, including areas of Louisiana; the Mid-Continent region, including parts of northern Texas and western Oklahoma; and the Wind River Basin in the Wyoming Rocky Mountains. It also has an interest in an exploration block offshore Vietnam. The company's focus areas include mature properties with long-lived reserves, as well as newer properties with development, exploitation and exploration potential. The firm has estimated proved reserves of 416.1 million barrels of oil equivalent (54% oil), of which 60% is proved developed. In 2010, PXP participated in 559 exploratory wells, of which 540 were successful. In December of the same year, the company sold its properties located in Gulf of Mexico shallow water to McMoRan Exploration Co. for roughly $86.1 million. Also in late 2010, the firm acquired about 60,000 acres in South Texas, part of the Eagle Ford oil and gas condensate area, for roughly $596.3 million.

CONTACTS: *Note: Officers with more than one job title may be intentionally listed here more than once.*

James C. Flores, CEO
James C. Flores, Pres.
Winston M. Talbert, CFO/Exec. VP
Doss R. Bourgeois, Exec. VP-Exploration & Prod.
Hance V. Myers, III, Dir.-Corp. Info./VP
John F. Wombwell, General Counsel/Exec. VP/Sec.
Steven P. Rusch, VP-Gov't Affairs
Joanna Pankey, Mgr.-Shareholder Svcs.
Steven P. Rusch, VP-Environmental, Health & Safety
James C. Flores, Chmn.

Phone: 713-579-6000 **Fax:** 713-579-6611
Toll-Free: 800-934-6083
Address: 700 Milam St., Ste. 3100, Houston, TX 77002 US

FINANCIALS: **Sales and profits are in thousands of dollars—add 000 to get the full amount. 2011 Note: Financial information for 2011 was not available for all companies at press time.**

2011 Sales: $1,964,488 | 2011 Profits: $84,325
2010 Sales: $1,544,595 | 2010 Profits: $103,265
2009 Sales: $1,187,130 | 2009 Profits: $136,305
2008 Sales: $2,403,471 | 2008 Profits: $-709,094
2007 Sales: $1,272,840 | 2007 Profits: $158,751

U.S. Stock Ticker: PXP
Int'l Ticker:
Int'l Exchange:
Employees: 826 Fiscal Year Ends: 12/31
Parent Company:

SALARIES/BENEFITS:

Pension Plan: ESOP Stock Plan: Profit Sharing: Top Exec. Salary: $1,400,000 Bonus: $1,400,000
Savings Plan: Stock Purch. Plan: Second Exec. Salary: $675,000 Bonus: $675,000

OTHER THOUGHTS:

Apparent Women Officers or Directors: 1
Hot Spot for Advancement for Women/Minorities:

LOCATIONS: ("Y" = Yes)

West:	Southwest:	Midwest:	Southeast:	Northeast:	International:
Y	Y		Y		

PLATO LEARNING INC

www.plato.com

Industry Group Code: 511210P

Management:		Sales/Marketing:		Liberal Arts:		Information Systems:		Professionals:		Technical/Scientific:	
Mgmt. Trainees:		Mktg. Professionals:	Y	Gen. Writing/Editing:	Y	Info. Management:	Y	Finance/Acct.:	Y	Engineers, Elec.:	Y
Experienced Mgmt.:	Y	Retail Sales:		Technical Writing:	Y	Software Dev.:	Y	Law:	Y	Engineers, Other:	
Int'l Business:	Y	Commercial/Industrial:	Y	Graphic Arts/Photog.:	Y	Hardware Dev.:		HR/Other:	Y	Health/Lab	
MBA Graduates:	Y	Sales Trainees:	Y	Music:		Consulting/Other:		Training:	Y	Scientists/Research:	
		Advertising Pros.:	Y	Broadcasting:				Health Care:		Petroleum/Chemicals:	
				Other:	Y			Consulting:		Math/Other:	

TYPES OF BUSINESS:

Educational Software
E-Learning Services

BRANDS/DIVISIONS/AFFILIATES:

PLATO
Straight Curve
PLATO eduTest
PLATO Test Packs with Prescriptions
Academic Systems
PLATO Learning Environment
Educational Options Inc

CONTACTS: *Note: Officers with more than one job title may be intentionally listed here more than once.*

Vincent (Vin) Riera, CEO
Vincent (Vin) Riera, Pres.
Robert J. Rueckl, CFO/VP/Corp. Sec.
Mary Schneider, Dir.-Mktg.
Stacey Herteux, Dir.-Human Resources
Mark Allen, CTO/VP
Jamie Candee, VP-Prod. & Mktg.
Ian Kees, Corp. Counsel/VP
Denise Schuenke, Sr. VP-Sales
Jennifer Morgans, VP-Customer Experience
Dave Adams, VP-Education Strategy & Content
David W. Smith, Chmn.

Phone: 952-832-1000 **Fax:** 952-832-1200
Toll-Free: 800-447-5286
Address: 5600 W. 83rd St., Ste. 300, 8200 Tower, Bloomington, MN 55437 US

GROWTH PLANS/SPECIAL FEATURES:

PLATO Learning, Inc. primarily develops and markets educational software and related services. It operates according to a SaaS (Software-as-a-Service) model, with the majority of its products delivered on a hosted, subscription service basis. The company provides online instruction, curriculum management, assessment and related professional development services to K-12 schools, community colleges and other educational institutions across the U.S. Its flagship products are the PLATO brand Elementary Solutions and Secondary Solutions self-paced tutoring programs, which include coursework in reading, writing, language arts, mathematics, science and social studies. The firm also offers Straight Curve, a set of multimedia instructional materials designed to be integrated into normal classroom instruction. For assessment, the company offers PLATO eduTest, PLATO Test Packs with Prescriptions, Simulated Test Systems and Simulated Certification Tests. The firm also markets the Academic Systems brand of post-secondary materials, mainly products for students who have completed high school but are not yet ready for college coursework. In addition to elementary and secondary education products, it offers post-secondary programs for college and adult students, such as developmental education courses, educator preparation and adult education. Through its web-based platform, the PLATO Learning Environment (PLE), the firm delivers all of the products mentioned above, while also allowing teachers to upload their own content. Besides products, the firm offers certain professional services, including consulting; professional development; curriculum and assessment management; funding recovery; data and support services; and field engineering. In November 2011, PLATO acquired the Virginia-based education technology firm Educational Options, Inc.

The company offers its employees medical and dental insurance, flexible spending accounts, a 529 College Savings Plan, a 401(k) and tuition reimbursement.

FINANCIALS: **Sales and profits are in thousands of dollars—add 000 to get the full amount. 2011 Note: Financial information for 2011 was not available for all companies at press time.**

2011 Sales: $	2011 Profits: $
2010 Sales: $	2010 Profits: $
2009 Sales: $65,183	2009 Profits: $ 957
2008 Sales: $68,401	2008 Profits: $-91,897
2007 Sales: $69,632	2007 Profits: $-14,876

U.S. Stock Ticker: Private
Int'l Ticker:
Int'l Exchange:
Employees: Fiscal Year Ends: 10/31
Parent Company: THOMA BRAVO LLC

SALARIES/BENEFITS:

Pension Plan:	ESOP Stock Plan:	Profit Sharing:	Top Exec. Salary: $390,000	Bonus: $233,883
Savings Plan: Y	Stock Purch. Plan:		Second Exec. Salary: $262,080	Bonus: $104,780

OTHER THOUGHTS:

Apparent Women Officers or Directors: 4
Hot Spot for Advancement for Women/Minorities: Y

LOCATIONS: ("Y" = Yes)

West:	Southwest:	Midwest:	Southeast:	Northeast:	International:
		Y		Y	

PMA COMPANIES INC

www.pmacompanies.com

Industry Group Code: 524126

Management:		Sales/Marketing:		Liberal Arts:		Information Systems:		Professionals:		Technical/Scientific:	
Mgmt. Trainees:	Y	Mktg. Professionals:	Y	Gen. Writing/Editing:	Y	Info. Management:	Y	Finance/Acct.:	Y	Engineers, Elec.:	
Experienced Mgmt.:	Y	Retail Sales:		Technical Writing:	Y	Software Dev.:		Law:	Y	Engineers, Other:	
Int'l Business:		Commercial/Industrial:	Y	Graphic Arts/Photog.:		Hardware Dev.:		HR/Other:	Y	Health/Lab	Y
MBA Graduates:	Y	Sales Trainees:	Y	Music:		Consulting/Other:		Training:	Y	Scientists/Research:	
		Advertising Pros.:		Broadcasting:				Health Care:	Y	Petroleum/Chemicals:	
				Other:				Consulting:		Math/Other:	Y

TYPES OF BUSINESS:

Insurance, Direct Property & Casualty
Workers' Compensation Insurance
Auto Insurance
Specialty Insurance

BRANDS/DIVISIONS/AFFILIATES:

PMA Capital Corporation
PMA Insurance Group
Manufacturers Alliance Insurance Company
Pennsylvania Manufacturers Indemnity Company
PMA Management Co.
PMA Management Corp. of New England, Inc.
Midlands Management Corporation
Old Republic International Corp

CONTACTS: *Note: Officers with more than one job title may be intentionally listed here more than once.*

Vincent T. Donnelly, CEO
Vincent T. Donnelly, Pres.
John M. Cochrane, CFO/Sr. VP
Jennifer J. Johnston, Chief Strategic Mktg. Officer/Sr. VP
Andrew J. McGill, Sr. VP-Human Resources & Facilities Mgmt.
Stephen L. Kibblehouse, General Counsel/Exec. VP/Sec.
Diane Nafranowicz, Mgr.-Corp. Comm. & Advertising
John Santulli, III, Exec. VP-Risk Svcs. & Sales
Anthony J. Ciofani, Exec. VP/Chief Underwriting Officer-PMA Insurance
Kevin M. Brady, Chief Corp. Actuary/Sr. VP
Mario Spina, VP-Georgia & Alabama Oper.

Phone: 610-397-5298	**Fax:** 610-397-5422
Toll-Free:	
Address: 380 Sentry Pkwy., Blue Bell, PA 19422 US	

GROWTH PLANS/SPECIAL FEATURES:

PMA Companies, Inc. (PMA), formerly PMA Capital Corporation, is an insurance holding company specializing in property & casualty and workers' compensation insurance. The firm writes workers' compensation and other standard lines of commercial insurance, including commercial general liability, commercial automobile and commercial multi-peril. The group focuses primarily on workers' compensation, which accounts for more than 80% of its net written premiums. PMA conducts business in the insurance sector through PMA Insurance Group. PMA Insurance Group is mainly comprised of the company's insurance subsidiaries: Manufacturers Alliance Insurance Company, Pennsylvania Manufacturers Indemnity Company and Pennsylvania Manufacturers' Association Insurance Company. Additional operations are conducted through subsidiaries PMA Management Co., which provides the firm with accounting, actuarial, administrative, claims-handling, legal, human resources and underwriting services; PMA Management Corp. of New England, Inc., which provides risk management and third party administration (TPA) services form workers' compensation products; and Midlands Management Corporation, which offers TPA, general management and program administration services. In October 2010, PMA was acquired by the insurance underwriting holding company Old Republic International Corp. In May 2011, it opened an office in Schaumburg, Illinois to offer property & casualty insurance and TPA services to employers throughout the state.

FINANCIALS: **Sales and profits are in thousands of dollars—add 000 to get the full amount. 2011 Note: Financial information for 2011 was not available for all companies at press time.**

2011 Sales: $
2010 Sales: $
2009 Sales: $531,715
2008 Sales: $494,157
2007 Sales: $455,777

2011 Profits: $
2010 Profits: $
2009 Profits: $21,213
2008 Profits: $5,689
2007 Profits: $-42,528

U.S. Stock Ticker: Subsidiary
Int'l Ticker:
Int'l Exchange:
Employees: 1,362 Fiscal Year Ends: 12/31
Parent Company: OLD REPUBLIC INTERNATIONAL CORP

SALARIES/BENEFITS:

Pension Plan: Y ESOP Stock Plan: Profit Sharing: Top Exec. Salary: $715,000 Bonus: $235,521
Savings Plan: Stock Purch. Plan: Second Exec. Salary: $435,016 Bonus: $134,184

OTHER THOUGHTS:

Apparent Women Officers or Directors: 2
Hot Spot for Advancement for Women/Minorities:

LOCATIONS: ("Y" = Yes)

West:	Southwest:	Midwest:	Southeast:	Northeast:	International:
		Y	Y	Y	

POLYPORE INTERNATIONAL INC

www.polypore.net

Industry Group Code: 3261

Management:		**Sales/Marketing:**		**Liberal Arts:**		**Information Systems:**		**Professionals:**		**Technical/Scientific:**	
Mgmt. Trainees:		Mktg. Professionals:		Gen. Writing/Editing:		Info. Management:	Y	Finance/Acct.:	Y	Engineers, Elec.:	
Experienced Mgmt.:	Y	Retail Sales:		Technical Writing:	Y	Software Dev.:	Y	Law:	Y	Engineers, Other:	Y
Int'l Business:	Y	Commercial/Industrial:	Y	Graphic Arts/Photog.:		Hardware Dev.:		HR/Other:	Y	Health/Lab	
MBA Graduates:	Y	Sales Trainees:		Music:		Consulting/Other:		Training:	Y	Scientists/Research:	Y
		Advertising Pros.:		Broadcasting:				Health Care:		Petroleum/Chemicals:	Y
				Other:				Consulting:		Math/Other:	Y

TYPES OF BUSINESS:

Polymer-Based Membranes
Battery Separators
Medical Equipment
Filtration Membranes

BRANDS/DIVISIONS/AFFILIATES:

Celgard LLC
Daramic LLC
Membrana GmbH
Liqui-Cel

CONTACTS: *Note: Officers with more than one job title may be intentionally listed here more than once.*

Robert B. Toth, CEO
Robert B. Toth, Pres.
Lynn Amos, CFO
John O'Malley, Sr. VP-Human Resources
Phillip Bryson, General Counsel
Lynn Amos, Contact-Investor Rel.
Lynn Amos, Treas./Corp. Sec.
Mitch Pulwer, VP/Gen. Mgr.-Calgard LLC
Pierre Hauswald, Pres., Daramic-Asia
Josef Sauer, VP/Gen Mgr.-Membrana GmbH
Pierre Hauswald, Gen. Mgr.-Daramic LLC
Michael Graff, Chmn.

Phone: 704-587-8409 **Fax:** 704-587-8796
Toll-Free:
Address: 11430 N. Community House Rd., Ste. 350, Charlotte, NC 28277-1591 US

GROWTH PLANS/SPECIAL FEATURES:

Polypore International, Inc. develops, manufactures and markets specialized polymer-based microporous membranes used in separation and filtration processes. The company operates in two business segments: energy storage and separations media. The energy storage segment makes membranes for use as separators in lead-acid and lithium batteries. These membranes regulate ion exchange in batteries used in laptops, cell phones, hybrid electric vehicles, energy storage systems and industrial and transportation applications,. These products are manufactured and distributed by two subsidiaries: Celgard LLC and Daramic LLC. Polypore's separations media segment manufactures filtration membranes for use in healthcare, high-performance industrial and specialty filtration applications, including the removal of submicron particles and degasification. Healthcare applications include hemodialysis, blood oxygenation and plasmapheresis. This segment includes the operations of subsidiary Membrana GmbH, a supplier of membrane products to the medical, semiconductor, power, pharmaceutical, food and beverage and photographic industries, and the Liqui-Cel brand of membranes for liquid degasification in microelectronics, industrial, ink, analytical and other applications. The energy storage segment accounts for approximately 71% of the firm's total sales, with the separations media segment making up the remaining 29%. Considered regionally, North America accounts for about 24% of sales, Europe 32%, Asia 34% and the rest of the world 10%. Polypore operates 14 manufacturing sites and 13 sales offices in the Americas, Europe and Asia. In recent years, Polypore's Celgard LLC business unit was granted $49 million from the U.S. Department of Energy to expand the production capacity of its lithium-ion separator manufacturing facility in Charlotte, North Carolina, and to construct a new manufacturing facility.

FINANCIALS: **Sales and profits are in thousands of dollars—add 000 to get the full amount. 2011 Note: Financial information for 2011 was not available for all companies at press time.**

2011 Sales: $763,074 | 2011 Profits: $105,240
2010 Sales: $616,600 | 2010 Profits: $63,600
2009 Sales: $516,900 | 2009 Profits: $-117,300
2008 Sales: $610,500 | 2008 Profits: $-15,200
2007 Sales: $534,700 | 2007 Profits: $ 500

U.S. Stock Ticker: PPO
Int'l Ticker:
Int'l Exchange:
Employees: 2,200 Fiscal Year Ends: 12/31
Parent Company:

SALARIES/BENEFITS:

Pension Plan: Y | ESOP Stock Plan: | Profit Sharing: | Top Exec. Salary: $580,000 | Bonus: $1,160,000
Savings Plan: Y | Stock Purch. Plan: Y | | Second Exec. Salary: $296,385 | Bonus: $420,000

OTHER THOUGHTS:

Apparent Women Officers or Directors: 1
Hot Spot for Advancement for Women/Minorities:

LOCATIONS: ("Y" = Yes)

West:	Southwest:	Midwest:	Southeast:	Northeast:	International:
				Y	Y

POWERSECURE INTERNATIONAL INC

www.powersecure.com

Industry Group Code: 335

Management:		Sales/Marketing:		Liberal Arts:		Information Systems:		Professionals:		Technical/Scientific:	
Mgmt. Trainees:		Mktg. Professionals:	Y	Gen. Writing/Editing:		Info. Management:	Y	Finance/Acct.:	Y	Engineers, Elec.:	Y
Experienced Mgmt.:	Y	Retail Sales:		Technical Writing:	Y	Software Dev.:	Y	Law:	Y	Engineers, Other:	Y
Int'l Business:	Y	Commercial/Industrial:	Y	Graphic Arts/Photog.:		Hardware Dev.:	Y	HR/Other:	Y	Health/Lab	
MBA Graduates:	Y	Sales Trainees:		Music:		Consulting/Other:		Training:	Y	Scientists/Research:	
		Advertising Pros.:		Broadcasting:				Health Care:		Petroleum/Chemicals:	
				Other:				Consulting:		Math/Other:	

TYPES OF BUSINESS:

Energy Metering Products & Services
Data Management Systems
Wireless Devices
Energy Analysis & Consulting

BRANDS/DIVISIONS/AFFILIATES:

WaterSecure Holdings, Inc.
PowerSecure, Inc.
Interactive Distributed Generation

CONTACTS:

Note: Officers with more than one job title may be intentionally listed here more than once.

Sidney Hinton, CEO
Sidney Hinton, Pres.
Chris Hutter, CFO/Exec. VP/Treas.
Gary J. Zuiderveen, Corp. Sec.
Gary J. Zuiderveen, VP-Financial Reporting
Gary J. Zuiderveen, Chief Acct. Officer/Controller

Phone: 919-556-3056 **Fax:** 919-556-3596
Toll-Free: 866-347-5455
Address: 1609 Heritage Commerce Court, Wake Forest, NC 27587 US

GROWTH PLANS/SPECIAL FEATURES:

PowerSecure International, Inc. (PSII) is an energy holding company. The firm provides energy technology measurement products, services and data management systems to industrial/commercial consumers and suppliers of natural gas and electricity. PSII conducts business through two subsidiaries: PowerSecure, Inc.; and WaterSecure Holdings, Inc. PowerSecure engineers, sells and manages distributed generation systems marketed primarily to industrial and commercial users of electricity; it also provides energy management, engineering and consulting services. PowerSecure's Interactive Distributed Generation systems provide on-site power generation that supplements or bypasses the public power grid by generating power at the customer's site, in order to take advantage of peak-shaving and load interruption incentives. The subsidiary's turnkey program provides system design; generator and switch gear acquisition and installation; financing; operation; rate analysis; and contract negotiation with utilities. WaterSecure owns and operates water processing, recycling and disposal facilities in northeastern Colorado. It serves oil and natural gas production firms in that area. PSII also offers a utility infrastructure unit, which provides utilities with power system engineering/construction, regulatory consulting and rate design services. In January 2011, the firm sold subsidiary Southern Flow Companies, Inc. to Zedi, Inc.

FINANCIALS:

Sales and profits are in thousands of dollars—add 000 to get the full amount. 2011 Note: Financial information for 2011 was not available for all companies at press time.

2011 Sales: $
2010 Sales: $97,514
2009 Sales: $102,540
2008 Sales: $135,440
2007 Sales: $111,112

2011 Profits: $
2010 Profits: $3,462
2009 Profits: $2,793
2008 Profits: $10,658
2007 Profits: $-1,608

U.S. Stock Ticker: POWR
Int'l Ticker:
Int'l Exchange:
Employees: 390 Fiscal Year Ends: 12/31
Parent Company:

SALARIES/BENEFITS:

Pension Plan: ESOP Stock Plan: Profit Sharing: Top Exec. Salary: $550,000 Bonus: $547,500
Savings Plan: Stock Purch. Plan: Second Exec. Salary: $312,000 Bonus: $147,000

OTHER THOUGHTS:

Apparent Women Officers or Directors:
Hot Spot for Advancement for Women/Minorities:

LOCATIONS: ("Y" = Yes)

West:	Southwest:	Midwest:	Southeast:	Northeast:	International:
	Y		Y	Y	

PREMIERE GLOBAL SERVICES INC

www.pgi.com

Industry Group Code: 518210

Management:		Sales/Marketing:		Liberal Arts:		Information Systems:		Professionals:		Technical/Scientific:	
Mgmt. Trainees:		Mktg. Professionals:	Y	Gen. Writing/Editing:		Info. Management:	Y	Finance/Acct.:	Y	Engineers, Elec.:	Y
Experienced Mgmt.:	Y	Retail Sales:		Technical Writing:	Y	Software Dev.:	Y	Law:	Y	Engineers, Other:	
Int'l Business:	Y	Commercial/Industrial:	Y	Graphic Arts/Photog.:		Hardware Dev.:		HR/Other:	Y	Health/Lab	
MBA Graduates:	Y	Sales Trainees:	Y	Music:		Consulting/Other:		Training:	Y	Scientists/Research:	
		Advertising Pros.:		Broadcasting:				Health Care:		Petroleum/Chemicals:	
				Other:				Consulting:		Math/Other:	

TYPES OF BUSINESS:

Message Management & Distribution Services
Conferencing Services
Document Management

BRANDS/DIVISIONS/AFFILIATES:

PGiCos
iMeet
GlobalMeet
ReadyConference

CONTACTS: *Note: Officers with more than one job title may be intentionally listed here more than once.*

Boland T. Jones, CEO
Theodore P. Schrafft, Pres.
David E. Trine, CFO
J. Scott Tap, Exec. VP-Mktg. & Sales
David M. Guthrie, CTO
Scott Askins Leonard, General Counsel/Sec./Sr. VP-Legal
Sean O'Brien, Exec. VP-Strategy
Sean O'Brien, Exec. VP-Corp. Comm.
John Stone, Exec. VP-European Oper.
Erik Petrik, Chief Creative Officer
Michele Dobnikar, Exec. VP-Customer Care
Boland T. Jones, Chmn.
Dennis Choo, Managing Dir.-Asia Pacific

Phone: 404-262-8400 **Fax:** 404-262-8540
Toll-Free: 866-548-3203
Address: 3280 Peachtree Rd. NE, Ste. 1000, Atlanta, GA 30305 US

GROWTH PLANS/SPECIAL FEATURES:

Premiere Global Services, Inc. (PGi) develops and markets a comprehensive suite of applied communication technologies. PGi has a global presence in 24 countries with a base of more than 30,000 customers, which includes nearly 75% of the Fortune 500. The firm's proprietary business applications are delivered through the PGi communications operating system (PGiCOS), an on-demand communications platform that delivers software-as-a-service (SaaS) meaning the applications are available without pre-existing software or hardware installations. The company has three primary applications. The iMeet service gives users their own personal meeting room online that combines video conferencing, social networking and media and file sharing. The GlobalMeet service integrates web and audio conferencing into one complete application. The ReadyConference audio conferencing suite includes automated conferencing, global conferencing with 140 access points and operator-assisted event conferencing. The firm offers open standards access to its technology applications via the company application programming interface suite, enabling its customers and technology partners to integrate its PGiCOS capabilities directly into their enterprise systems and existing business processes.

The company offers medical, dental and vision insurance; short- and long-term disability coverage; life and AD&D insurance; flexible spending accounts; an employee assistance program; legal assistance; a 401(k) plan; and identity theft coverage.

FINANCIALS: **Sales and profits are in thousands of dollars—add 000 to get the full amount. 2011 Note: Financial information for 2011 was not available for all companies at press time.**

2011 Sales: $473,800 — 2011 Profits: $21,400
2010 Sales: $441,753 — 2010 Profits: $4,831
2009 Sales: $453,962 — 2009 Profits: $13,609
2008 Sales: $620,400 — 2008 Profits: $36,103
2007 Sales: $559,706 — 2007 Profits: $33,355

U.S. Stock Ticker: PGI
Int'l Ticker:
Int'l Exchange:
Employees: 1,700 Fiscal Year Ends: 12/31
Parent Company:

SALARIES/BENEFITS:

Pension Plan: | ESOP Stock Plan: | Profit Sharing: | Top Exec. Salary: $900,000 | Bonus: $779,890
Savings Plan: Y | Stock Purch. Plan: | | Second Exec. Salary: $500,000 | Bonus: $649,908

OTHER THOUGHTS:

Apparent Women Officers or Directors: 2
Hot Spot for Advancement for Women/Minorities:

LOCATIONS: ("Y" = Yes)

West:	Southwest:	Midwest:	Southeast:	Northeast:	International:
Y		Y	Y	Y	Y

PRIMEENERGY CORPORATION

www.primeenergy.com

Industry Group Code: 211111

Management:		Sales/Marketing:		Liberal Arts:		Information Systems:		Professionals:		Technical/Scientific:	
Mgmt. Trainees:		Mktg. Professionals:		Gen. Writing/Editing:		Info. Management:	Y	Finance/Acct.:	Y	Engineers, Elec.:	
Experienced Mgmt.:	Y	Retail Sales:		Technical Writing:		Software Dev.:		Law:	Y	Engineers, Other:	Y
Int'l Business:	Y	Commercial/Industrial:		Graphic Arts/Photog.:		Hardware Dev.:		HR/Other:	Y	Health/Lab	
MBA Graduates:	Y	Sales Trainees:		Music:		Consulting/Other:		Training:	Y	Scientists/Research:	
		Advertising Pros.:		Broadcasting:				Health Care:		Petroleum/Chemicals:	Y
				Other:				Consulting:		Math/Other:	

TYPES OF BUSINESS:

Oil & Gas Exploration & Production
Oil Field Services & Construction

BRANDS/DIVISIONS/AFFILIATES:

PrimeEnergy Management Corporation
Prime Operating Company
Southwest Oilfield Construction Company
EOWS Midland Company
Eastern Oil Well Service Company

CONTACTS: *Note: Officers with more than one job title may be intentionally listed here more than once.*

Charles E. Drimal, Jr., CEO
Charles E. Drimal, Jr., Pres.
Beverly A. Cummings, CFO
James F. Gilbert, Corp. Sec.
Beverly A. Cummings, Treas./Exec. VP
Charles E. Drimal, Jr., Chmn.

Phone: 203-358-5700	**Fax:** 203-358-5786
Toll-Free:	
Address: 1 Landmark Sq., Ste. 100, Stamford, CT 06901 US	

GROWTH PLANS/SPECIAL FEATURES:

PrimeEnergy Corporation is engaged in the acquisition, exploration, development and production of crude oil and natural gas. The company currently operates oil and gas wells primarily located in Texas, Oklahoma, the Gulf of Mexico, New Mexico, Colorado, Louisiana and West Virginia. Subsidiary PrimeEnergy Management Corporation (PEMC) acts as the managing general partner in 18 oil and gas limited partnerships and as the managing trustee of two asset and income business trusts. As such, PEMC is responsible for all partnership and trust activities, including the review and analysis of oil and gas properties for acquisition, the drilling of development wells and the production and sale of oil and gas from producing wells. PrimeEnergy provides well servicing support operations and acts as operator for many of the onshore oil and gas wells in which the company has an interest, as well as for third parties, through its wholly-owned subsidiaries: Prime Operating Company; Southwest Oilfield Construction Company; EOWS Midland Company; and Eastern Oil Well Service Company. The firm also acquires producing oil and gas properties through joint ventures with industry partners and private investors. Southwest Oilfield Construction Company serves both PrimeEnergy and third parties with site preparation and construction services for oil and gas drilling and re-working operations. The firm has proved reserves of approximately 101 billion cubic feet equivalent of natural gas, 73% of which was developed, while 27% was still undeveloped. At present, the company does not own any refineries or marketing or bulk storage facilities and the only owned pipelines are those used in connection with producing wells and the interests in certain gas gathering systems. During 2010, PrimeEnergy participated in drilling a total of 47 gross (19.96 net) wells with a 100% success rate.

FINANCIALS: **Sales and profits are in thousands of dollars—add 000 to get the full amount. 2011 Note: Financial information for 2011 was not available for all companies at press time.**

2011 Sales: $	2011 Profits: $	**U.S. Stock Ticker: PNRG**
2010 Sales: $118,169	2010 Profits: $2,753	**Int'l Ticker:**
2009 Sales: $89,992	2009 Profits: $-22,665	Int'l Exchange:
2008 Sales: $169,338	2008 Profits: $ 541	Employees: 229 Fiscal Year Ends: 12/31
2007 Sales: $146,455	2007 Profits: $7,920	Parent Company:

SALARIES/BENEFITS:

Pension Plan:	ESOP Stock Plan:	Profit Sharing:	Top Exec. Salary: $360,500	Bonus: $1,000,000
Savings Plan:	Stock Purch. Plan:		Second Exec. Salary: $360,500	Bonus: $400,000

OTHER THOUGHTS:

Apparent Women Officers or Directors: 1
Hot Spot for Advancement for Women/Minorities:

LOCATIONS: ("Y" = Yes)

West:	Southwest:	Midwest:	Southeast:	Northeast:	International:
Y	Y	Y	Y	Y	

PROASSURANCE CORP

www.proassurance.com

Industry Group Code: 524126

Management:		Sales/Marketing:		Liberal Arts:		Information Systems:		Professionals:		Technical/Scientific:	
Mgmt. Trainees:	Y	Mktg. Professionals:	Y	Gen. Writing/Editing:	Y	Info. Management:	Y	Finance/Acct.:	Y	Engineers, Elec.:	
Experienced Mgmt.:	Y	Retail Sales:		Technical Writing:	Y	Software Dev.:		Law:	Y	Engineers, Other:	
Int'l Business:		Commercial/Industrial:	Y	Graphic Arts/Photog.:		Hardware Dev.:		HR/Other:	Y	Health/Lab	Y
MBA Graduates:	Y	Sales Trainees:	Y	Music:		Consulting/Other:		Training:	Y	Scientists/Research:	
		Advertising Pros.:		Broadcasting:				Health Care:	Y	Petroleum/Chemicals:	
				Other:				Consulting:		Math/Other:	Y

TYPES OF BUSINESS:

Professional Liability Insurance
Medical Liability Insurance

BRANDS/DIVISIONS/AFFILIATES:

ProAssurance Indemnity Company, Inc.
ProAssurance Casualty Company
ProAssurance National Capital Insurance Company
ProAssurance Wisconsin Insurance Company
ProAssurance Specialty Insurance Company, Inc.
American Physicians Service Group, Inc.
Podiatry Insurance Company of America

CONTACTS:

Note: Officers with more than one job title may be intentionally listed here more than once.

W. Stancil Starnes, CEO
Victor T. Adamo, Pres.
Edward L. Rand, Jr., CFO/Sr. VP
Jeffrey P. Lisenby, General Counsel/Corp. Sec./Sr. VP
Frank B. O'Neil, Sr. VP-Corp. Comm.
Frank B. O'Neil, Sr. VP-Investor Rel.
Howard H. Friedman, Chief Underwriting Officer/Chief Actuary/Sr. VP
Hayes V. Whiteside, Chief Medical Officer/Sr. VP
Darryl K. Thoman, Chief Claims Officer/Sr. VP
Jeffrey L. Bowlby, Chief Mktg. Officer-Liability Group/Sr. VP
W. Stancil Starnes, Chmn.

Phone: 205-877-4400 **Fax:** 205-868-4073
Toll-Free: 800-282-6242
Address: 100 Brookwood Pl., Birmingham, AL 35209 US

GROWTH PLANS/SPECIAL FEATURES:

ProAssurance Corp. is a holding company for property and casualty insurance companies. These companies provide professional liability insurance to physicians, dentists, other healthcare providers and healthcare facilities primarily in the mid-Atlantic, Midwest and Southeast U.S. The firm also has a small book of other professional liability business in the Midwest. ProAssurance generates the majority of its premiums from individual and small group practices, but also insures major physician groups as well as hospitals. While most of the firm's business is written in the standard market, the company also offers medical professional liability insurance on an excess and surplus lines basis. The company's top five states (Alabama, Ohio, Florida, Indiana and Michigan) represent about 46% of its gross premiums. The company maintains 20 claims and underwriting offices in 14 states and Washington, D.C., in order to keep a local market presence. ProAssurance's subsidiaries include ProAssurance Indemnity Company, Inc.; ProAssurance Casualty Company; ProAssurance National Capital Insurance Company; ProAssurance Wisconsin Insurance Company; Podiatry Insurance Company of America (PICA); and ProAssurance Specialty Insurance Company, Inc., its excess and supply lines carrier. ProAssurance is licensed to do business in every state. In November 2010, ProAssurance acquired American Physicians Service Group, Inc., a medical professional liability insurance company operating in Texas, Arkansas and Oklahoma.

FINANCIALS:

Sales and profits are in thousands of dollars—add 000 to get the full amount. 2011 Note: Financial information for 2011 was not available for all companies at press time.

2011 Sales: $716,784	2011 Profits: $287,096
2010 Sales: $692,065	2010 Profits: $231,598
2009 Sales: $672,683	2009 Profits: $222,026
2008 Sales: $567,162	2008 Profits: $177,725
2007 Sales: $706,068	2007 Profits: $168,186

U.S. Stock Ticker: PRA
Int'l Ticker:
Int'l Exchange:
Employees: 739 Fiscal Year Ends: 12/31
Parent Company:

SALARIES/BENEFITS:

Pension Plan:	ESOP Stock Plan:	Profit Sharing:	Top Exec. Salary: $821,940	Bonus: $1,034,378
Savings Plan:	Stock Purch. Plan:		Second Exec. Salary: $542,692	Bonus: $519,046

OTHER THOUGHTS:

Apparent Women Officers or Directors: 1
Hot Spot for Advancement for Women/Minorities:

LOCATIONS: ("Y" = Yes)

West:	Southwest:	Midwest:	Southeast:	Northeast:	International:
		Y	Y	Y	

PROTECTIVE LIFE CORP

www.protective.com

Industry Group Code: 524113

Management:		Sales/Marketing:		Liberal Arts:		Information Systems:		Professionals:		Technical/Scientific:	
Mgmt. Trainees:	Y	Mktg. Professionals:	Y	Gen. Writing/Editing:	Y	Info. Management:	Y	Finance/Acct.:	Y	Engineers, Elec.:	
Experienced Mgmt.:	Y	Retail Sales:		Technical Writing:	Y	Software Dev.:		Law:	Y	Engineers, Other:	
Int'l Business:		Commercial/Industrial:		Graphic Arts/Photog.:		Hardware Dev.:		HR/Other:	Y	Health/Lab	
MBA Graduates:	Y	Sales Trainees:	Y	Music:		Consulting/Other:		Training:	Y	Scientists/Research:	
		Advertising Pros.:	Y	Broadcasting:				Health Care:	Y	Petroleum/Chemicals:	
				Other:				Consulting:		Math/Other:	Y

TYPES OF BUSINESS:

Insurance-Life
Credit & Disability Insurance
Vehicle & Marine Insurance
Retirement Products
Annuity Products
Guaranteed Investment Contracts
Asset Protection Products and Services

BRANDS/DIVISIONS/AFFILIATES:

Protective Life Insurance Company
West Coast Life Insurance Company
Protective Life & Annuity Insurance Company
United Investors Life Insurance Company
Protective OneStep Life
West Coast Life OneStep Life

CONTACTS: *Note: Officers with more than one job title may be intentionally listed here more than once.*

John D. Johns, CEO
Carolyn M. Johnson, COO/Exec. VP
John D. Johns, Pres.
Richard J. Bielen, CFO/Vice Chmn.
Eric Miller, Dir.-Nat'l Mktg./VP
D. Scott Adams, Chief Human Resources Officer/Sr. VP
Deborah J. Long, General Counsel/Exec. VP/Sec.
Carolyn King, Sr. VP-Corp. Dev. & Acquisitions
Eva Robertson, VP-Investor Rel.
Steven G. Walker, Chief Acct. Officer/Sr. VP/Controller
Carl S. Thigpen, Chief Investment Officer/Exec. VP
Brent E. Griggs, Sr. VP-Asset Protection
Judy Wilson, Sr. VP-Stable Value Prod.
Edward M. Berko, Chief Risk Officer/Exec. VP
John D. Johns, Chmn.

Phone: 205-268-1000 **Fax:** 205-268-5547
Toll-Free: 800-866-3555
Address: 2801 Hwy. 280 S., Birmingham, AL 35223 US

GROWTH PLANS/SPECIAL FEATURES:

Protective Life Corp. is a holding company that offers various insurance and investment products through three main subsidiaries: Protective Life Insurance Company; West Coast Life Insurance Company; and Protective Life and Annuity Insurance Company. It operates through six segments: life marketing; acquisitions; annuities; stable value products; asset protection; and corporate and other. Its life marketing segment markets level premium term insurance, universal life, variable universal life and bank-owned life insurance products. Protective Life's acquisitions segment acquires, converts and services policies, primarily individual life insurance and annuities, from other companies. Its annuities segment manufactures and supports fixed and variable annuity products, including modified guaranteed annuities, single premium deferred annuities, single premium immediate annuities and equity indexed annuities. The firm's stable value products segment markets guaranteed funding agreements to special purpose entities; and fixed and floating rate funding agreements directly to the trustees of municipal bond proceeds, institutional investors, bank trust departments and money market funds. The asset protection segment markets extended service contracts and credit life and disability insurance to protect customer investments in automobiles, watercraft, and recreational vehicles; and a guaranteed asset protection product. The company's corporate and other segment consists of earnings from business lines the company is not actively marketing, such as cancer insurance, surety insurance and group annuities. In December 2010, Protective Life Insurance Company acquired United Investors Life Insurance Company for about $316 million. In June 2011, the firm introduced new flexible premium universal life insurance policies Protective OneStep Life and West Coast Life OneStep Life.

The company offers its employees vision, medical and dental coverage; life and disability insurance; flexible spending accounts; a 401(k) plan; a stock purchase plan; an employee stock ownership plan; a pension plan; an employee assistance program; and tuition reimbursement.

FINANCIALS: **Sales and profits are in thousands of dollars—add 000 to get the full amount. 2011 Note: Financial information for 2011 was not available for all companies at press time.**

2011 Sales: $3,566,000
2010 Sales: $3,097,755
2009 Sales: $3,068,026
2008 Sales: $2,505,564
2007 Sales: $3,051,700

2011 Profits: $339,070
2010 Profits: $260,241
2009 Profits: $271,488
2008 Profits: $-41,855
2007 Profits: $289,566

U.S. Stock Ticker: PL
Int'l Ticker:
Int'l Exchange:
Employees: 2,303 Fiscal Year Ends: 12/31
Parent Company:

SALARIES/BENEFITS:

Pension Plan: Y	ESOP Stock Plan: Y	Profit Sharing:	Top Exec. Salary: $866,667	Bonus: $
Savings Plan: Y	Stock Purch. Plan: Y		Second Exec. Salary: $448,333	Bonus: $

OTHER THOUGHTS:

Apparent Women Officers or Directors: 7
Hot Spot for Advancement for Women/Minorities: Y

LOCATIONS: ("Y" = Yes)

West:	Southwest:	Midwest:	Southeast:	Northeast:	International:
Y	Y	Y	Y	Y	

PURPLE COMMUNICATIONS INC

www.purple.us

Industry Group Code: 5172

Management:		Sales/Marketing:		Liberal Arts:		Information Systems:		Professionals:		Technical/Scientific:	
Mgmt. Trainees:		Mktg. Professionals:	Y	Gen. Writing/Editing:	Y	Info. Management:	Y	Finance/Acct.:	Y	Engineers, Elec.:	Y
Experienced Mgmt.:	Y	Retail Sales:		Technical Writing:	Y	Software Dev.:	Y	Law:	Y	Engineers, Other:	
Int'l Business:		Commercial/Industrial:	Y	Graphic Arts/Photog.:		Hardware Dev.:		HR/Other:	Y	Health/Lab	
MBA Graduates:	Y	Sales Trainees:		Music:		Consulting/Other:		Training:	Y	Scientists/Research:	
		Advertising Pros.:	Y	Broadcasting:				Health Care:		Petroleum/Chemicals:	
				Other:				Consulting:		Math/Other:	

TYPES OF BUSINESS:

Wireless Data Products
Deaf & Speech-Impaired Communications Systems

BRANDS/DIVISIONS/AFFILIATES:

i711.com
IP-Relay.com
Purple Language Services
Hands On VRS
ClearCaptions

CONTACTS:

Note: Officers with more than one job title may be intentionally listed here more than once.

Daniel Luis, Pres.
Tony LaRosa, CIO
Michael J. Pendergast, General Counsel/VP
Kelby Brick, VP-Regulatory & Strategic Policy
Fran Cummings, VP-VRS & Community Ops
Mark Bella, VP-Outreach
Ronald Obray, Chmn.

Phone:	**Fax:**
Toll-Free: 800-900-9478	
Address: 595 Menlo Dr., Rocklin, CA 94765 US	

GROWTH PLANS/SPECIAL FEATURES:

Purple Communications Inc., formerly GoAmerica, Inc., is a provider of video relay and text relay services, and professional interpreting services for individuals with hearing or speech disabilities. The company offers both major categories of relay services: traditional telecommunications and Internet-based services. Traditional relay service enables a person with a hearing or speech disability to utilize a text-telephone or captioned telephone device, to initiate calls to, and receive calls from, hearing enabled persons. Internet-based relay services include Internet protocol text relay (IP text relay) and video relay service. IP text relay is a text-based form of relay service that uses the Internet, rather than traditional telephone lines, for the leg of the call between the person with a hearing or speech disability and the communications assistant. Video relay service is an Internet-based form of relay service that enables persons whose primary language is American Sign Language (ASL) to communicate with a communications assistant in ASL using video conferencing equipment. The user accesses the communications assistant over an Internet-based device such as a webcam or videophone. The communications assistant receives the ASL communication, and then voices that communication to the hearing party, and vice versa. Video relay service currently represents both the most widely used and the fastest growing form of relay service. Services offered by Purple Communications include IP-Relay.com, which enables deaf people the ability to place calls over the Internet; Hands On VRS, is a tool that enables deaf people to communicate through ASL via video conferencing equipment; i711.com, which allows deaf people to using a computer, wireless handheld device or similar unit, though an operator that intercepts text to voice and vice versa; and Purple Language Services, which is a service that provides sign language, oral transliteration, low-vision and tactile interpreting. In April 2011, the company introduced ClearCaptions, a new product which displays captions of telephone calls in near-real-time on a web browser or through an application on the iPhone, iPad, or iPod Touch

FINANCIALS:

Sales and profits are in thousands of dollars—add 000 to get the full amount. 2011 Note: Financial information for 2011 was not available for all companies at press time.

2011 Sales: $	2011 Profits: $
2010 Sales: $	2010 Profits: $
2009 Sales: $109,166	2009 Profits: $-128,683
2008 Sales: $119,357	2008 Profits: $-15,740
2007 Sales: $18,625	2007 Profits: $-3,750

U.S. Stock Ticker: PRPL.PK
Int'l Ticker:
Int'l Exchange:
Employees: 428 Fiscal Year Ends: 12/31
Parent Company:

SALARIES/BENEFITS:

Pension Plan:	ESOP Stock Plan:	Profit Sharing:	Top Exec. Salary: $271,538	Bonus: $100,000
Savings Plan:	Stock Purch. Plan:		Second Exec. Salary: $142,947	Bonus: $40,000

OTHER THOUGHTS:

Apparent Women Officers or Directors: 1
Hot Spot for Advancement for Women/Minorities:

LOCATIONS: ("Y" = Yes)

West:	Southwest:	Midwest:	Southeast:	Northeast:	International:
				Y	

QUAKER CHEMICAL CORP

www.quakerchem.com

Industry Group Code: 325

Management:		Sales/Marketing:		Liberal Arts:		Information Systems:		Professionals:		Technical/Scientific:	
Mgmt. Trainees:		Mktg. Professionals:	Y	Gen. Writing/Editing:		Info. Management:	Y	Finance/Acct.:	Y	Engineers, Elec.:	
Experienced Mgmt.:	Y	Retail Sales:		Technical Writing:	Y	Software Dev.:		Law:	Y	Engineers, Other:	
Int'l Business:	Y	Commercial/Industrial:		Graphic Arts/Photog.:		Hardware Dev.:		HR/Other:	Y	Health/Lab Scientists/Research:	
MBA Graduates:	Y	Sales Trainees:		Music:		Consulting/Other:		Training:		Petroleum/Chemicals:	Y
		Advertising Pros.:		Broadcasting:				Health Care:		Math/Other:	
				Other:				Consulting:			

TYPES OF BUSINESS:

Specialty Chemicals
Chemical Management Services
Coatings
Construction Products
Lubricants
Corrosion Preventatives
Metalworking Compounds
Hydraulic Fluids

BRANDS/DIVISIONS/AFFILIATES:

Summit Lubricants, Inc.

CONTACTS: *Note: Officers with more than one job title may be intentionally listed here more than once.*

Michael F. Barry, CEO
Michael F. Barry, Pres.
Mark A. Featherstone, CFO/VP
D. Jeffry Benoliel, General Counsel/Corp. Sec.
D. Jeffry Benoliel, VP-Global Strategy
Irene M. Kisleiko, Mgr.-Investor Rel.
Mark A. Featherstone, Treas.
Joseph A. Berquist, VP/Managing Dir.-North America
Jan F. Nieman, VP/Managing Dir.-APAC
Wilbert Platzer, VP/Managing Dir.-Europe
George H. Hill, Global Controller
Michael F. Barry, Chmn.
Jose Luiz Bregolato, VP/Managing Dir.-South America

Phone: 610-832-4000 **Fax:** 610-832-4495
Toll-Free:
Address: 901 E. Hector St., 1 Quaker Pk., Conshohocken, PA 19428-2380 US

GROWTH PLANS/SPECIAL FEATURES:

Quaker Chemical Corp. develops, produces and markets a broad range of formulated chemical specialty products for various heavy industrial and manufacturing applications. The firm also offers chemical management services (CMS). Quaker Chemical's products are divided in three segments: metalworking process chemicals, which consist of industrial process fluids for various heavy industrial and manufacturing application; coatings, which consist of temporary and permanent coatings for metal and concrete products and chemical milling maskants; and other chemical products. The company's principal products include machining and grinding compounds, used by metalworking customers in cutting, shaping and grinding metal parts; forming compounds, used to facilitate the drawing and extrusion of metal products; hydraulic fluids, used by customers to operate hydraulically activated equipment; rolling lubricants, used by manufacturers of steel and aluminum; corrosion preventives, used by steel and metalworking customers to protect metal during manufacture, storage and shipment; metal finishing compounds, used to prepare metal surfaces for special treatments such as galvanizing and tin plating; technology for the removal of hydrogen sulfide; chemical milling maskants for the aerospace industry and for coatings of metal and concrete products; and construction products such as flexible sealants and protective coatings. A significant amount of the firm's sales worldwide are made directly through its employees and CMS programs; the remainder are made by resellers and agents. Rolling lubricants account for roughly 21.2% of Quaker Chemical's total revenues; machining and grinding compounds, 20.3%; hydraulic fluids, 13.7%; corrosion preventives, 11.5%; and chemical management services, 3.5%. The firm's largest customer is Arcelor-Mittal Group, accounting for approximately 9% of net sales. In July 2010, Quaker Chemical acquired the aluminum hot rolling oil operations of D.A. Stuart from Houghton International. In January 2011, the firm acquired specialty grease manufacturer Summit Lubricants, Inc.

FINANCIALS: **Sales and profits are in thousands of dollars—add 000 to get the full amount. 2011 Note: Financial information for 2011 was not available for all companies at press time.**

2011 Sales: $
2010 Sales: $544,063
2009 Sales: $451,490
2008 Sales: $581,641
2007 Sales: $545,597

2011 Profits: $
2010 Profits: $31,807
2009 Profits: $16,220
2008 Profits: $11,132
2007 Profits: $15,471

U.S. Stock Ticker: KWR
Int'l Ticker:
Int'l Exchange:
Employees: 1,385 Fiscal Year Ends: 12/31
Parent Company:

SALARIES/BENEFITS:

Pension Plan: ESOP Stock Plan: Profit Sharing: Top Exec. Salary: $489,583 Bonus: $701,853
Savings Plan: Y Stock Purch. Plan: Second Exec. Salary: $452,782 Bonus: $289,272

OTHER THOUGHTS:

Apparent Women Officers or Directors: 2
Hot Spot for Advancement for Women/Minorities:

LOCATIONS: ("Y" = Yes)

West:	Southwest:	Midwest:	Southeast:	Northeast:	International:
Y	Y	Y		Y	Y

QUALCOMM ATHEROS INC

Industry Group Code: 33441

www.qca.qualcomm.com

Management:		Sales/Marketing:		Liberal Arts:		Information Systems:		Professionals:		Technical/Scientific:	
Mgmt. Trainees:		Mktg. Professionals:	Y	Gen. Writing/Editing:		Info. Management:	Y	Finance/Acct.:	Y	Engineers, Elec.:	Y
Experienced Mgmt.:	Y	Retail Sales:		Technical Writing:	Y	Software Dev.:	Y	Law:	Y	Engineers, Other:	Y
Int'l Business:	Y	Commercial/Industrial:	Y	Graphic Arts/Photog.:		Hardware Dev.:	Y	HR/Other:	Y	Health/Lab	
MBA Graduates:	Y	Sales Trainees:	Y	Music:		Consulting/Other:		Training:	Y	Scientists/Research:	Y
		Advertising Pros.:		Broadcasting:				Health Care:		Petroleum/Chemicals:	
				Other:				Consulting:		Math/Other:	Y

TYPES OF BUSINESS:

Wireless Chip Manufacturing
Semiconductor Systems

BRANDS/DIVISIONS/AFFILIATES:

Super G
Super AG
XSPAN
Qualcomm Inc
Atheros Communications Inc

CONTACTS:

Note: Officers with more than one job title may be intentionally listed here more than once.

Craig H. Barratt, CEO
Craig H. Barratt, Pres.
Jack R. Lazar, CFO
Reynette Au, VP-Mktg. & Alliances
Sharon Thompson, VP-Global Human Resources
William J. McFarland, CTO
Richard G. Bahr, VP-Eng.
Adam H. Tachner, General Counsel/VP
Hing Chu, VP-Oper.
Jack R. Lazar, VP-Corp. Dev.
Molly Mulloy, Sr. Mgr.-Corp. Comm.
David Allen, Dir.-Investor Rel.
David D. Torre, Chief Acct. Officer/VP
Rick Hegberg, VP-Worldwide Sales
Amir Faintuch, Sr. VP/Gen. Mgr.-Consumer Bus. Unit
Dan Rabinovitsj, Sr. VP/Gen. Mgr.-Networking Bus. Unit
Gary L. Szilagyi, VP-Consumer Bus. Unit
John L. Hennessy, Chmn.
Jason Zheng, Sr. VP/Gen. Mgr.-Asia Pacific

Phone: 408-773-5200 **Fax:** 408-773-9940
Toll-Free:
Address: 1700 Technology Dr., San Jose, CA 95110 US

GROWTH PLANS/SPECIAL FEATURES:

Qualcomm Atheros, Inc., formerly Atheros Communications, Inc., develops semiconductor system technologies for wireless communications products such as computing and networking equipment, digital entertainment, broadband access and mobile devices. The firm combines its wireless systems expertise with high-performance radio frequency (RF), mixed-signal and digital semiconductor design to create integrated chipsets for complementary metal-oxide semiconductor (CMOS) processes. The company's product portfolio ranges from entry-level wireless networking products for homes and small offices to sophisticated wireless infrastructure systems-on-chip with advanced network management capabilities for the enterprise market. These wireless system technologies are used in a variety of applications in the personal computer (PC), enterprise access, small office and branch office networking, home networking, hotspot, wireless broadband, voice, mobile computing devices and consumer electronics markets. Qualcomm Atheros currently provides five basic types of semiconductors: radio-on-a-chip (RoC), consisting of one or more CMOS radio transmitters and receivers; MAC + Baseband, consisting of low frequency analog circuits and data converters integrated through a digital interface; stand-alone network processing unit (NPU) chips, supporting a variety of clock speeds and network interfaces; wireless system-on-a-chip (WiSoC); and integrated single chip offerings, which are designed to include substantially all necessary digital and analog circuitry within a single chip structure. The company's chipsets can be incorporated into WLAN devices to provide end users extended range, longer battery life and network management tools that reduce the overall cost of operating wireless networks. The firm's trademarks include Align, AMP, ETHOS, FYX, ROCm and XSPAN. Qualcomm Atheros sells its products to original equipment manufacturers (OEMs) in three primary channels: networking, which accounted for 51% of its 2010 revenue; computing, 26%; and consumer, 23%. In 2011, Atheros Communications was acquired by Qualcomm, Inc. for $3.1 billion.

FINANCIALS:

Sales and profits are in thousands of dollars—add 000 to get the full amount. 2011 Note: Financial information for 2011 was not available for all companies at press time.

2011 Sales: $ — 2011 Profits: $
2010 Sales: $926,832 — 2010 Profits: $54,373
2009 Sales: $542,468 — 2009 Profits: $46,407
2008 Sales: $472,396 — 2008 Profits: $18,872
2007 Sales: $416,960 — 2007 Profits: $39,980

U.S. Stock Ticker: Subsidiary
Int'l Ticker:
Int'l Exchange:
Employees: 1,778 Fiscal Year Ends: 12/31
Parent Company: QUALCOM INC

SALARIES/BENEFITS:

Pension Plan: ESOP Stock Plan: Profit Sharing: Top Exec. Salary: $370,000 Bonus: $629,000
Savings Plan: Stock Purch. Plan: Second Exec. Salary: $310,000 Bonus: $237,150

OTHER THOUGHTS:

Apparent Women Officers or Directors: 4
Hot Spot for Advancement for Women/Minorities: Y

LOCATIONS: ("Y" = Yes)

West:	Southwest:	Midwest:	Southeast:	Northeast:	International:
Y					Y

QUALITY SYSTEMS INC

www.qsii.com

Industry Group Code: 511210D

Management:		Sales/Marketing:		Liberal Arts:		Information Systems:		Professionals:		Technical/Scientific:	
Mgmt. Trainees:		Mktg. Professionals:	Y	Gen. Writing/Editing:		Info. Management:	Y	Finance/Acct.:	Y	Engineers, Elec.:	Y
Experienced Mgmt.:	Y	Retail Sales:		Technical Writing:	Y	Software Dev.:	Y	Law:	Y	Engineers, Other:	
Int'l Business:	Y	Commercial/Industrial:	Y	Graphic Arts/Photog.:		Hardware Dev.:		HR/Other:	Y	Health/Lab	
MBA Graduates:	Y	Sales Trainees:	Y	Music:		Consulting/Other:		Training:	Y	Scientists/Research:	
		Advertising Pros.:		Broadcasting:				Health Care:		Petroleum/Chemicals:	
				Other:				Consulting:		Math/Other:	

TYPES OF BUSINESS:

Software-Practice Management

BRANDS/DIVISIONS/AFFILIATES:

QSI Dental
Clinical Product Suite
Opus Healthcare Solutions Inc
NextGen Sphere LLC
NextGen Clinicals
CQI Solutions Inc
NextGen Healthcare Information Systems Inc
Healthcare Strategic Initiatives

CONTACTS: *Note: Officers with more than one job title may be intentionally listed here more than once.*

Steven T. Plochocki, CEO
Patrick B. Cline, Pres.
Paul A. Holt, CFO
James J. Sullivan, General Counsel/Exec. VP/Corp. Sec.
Scott D. Decker, Pres., NextGen Healthcare Info. Systems
Donn Neufeld, Exec. VP-EDI & Dental
Monte Sandler, Exec. VP-NextGen Practice Solutions
Steve Puckett, Exec. VP-NextGen Inpatient Solutions
Sheldon Razin, Chmn.

Phone: 949-255-2600 **Fax:** 949-255-2605
Toll-Free: 800-888-7955
Address: 18111 Von Karman, Ste. 700, Irvine, CA 92612 US

GROWTH PLANS/SPECIAL FEATURES:

Quality Systems, Inc. develops and provides computer-based practice management, medical records and e-business applications. The company is headquartered in Irvine, California, and has major facilities in Horsham, Pennsylvania and Atlanta, Georgia; and additional facilities in Maryland, Missouri and Texas. Quality Systems operates through three divisions: QSI Dental, Inpatient Solutions, NextGen and Practice Solutions. All three develop and market products that streamline patient records and administrative functions such as billing and scheduling. The divisions offer these services to medical and dental group practices, management service organizations, ambulatory care centers, community health centers and medical/dental schools. The QSI Dental division focuses on developing, marketing and supporting software suites for dental and niche medical practices. Its Clinical Product Suite is a UNIX-based medical practice management software suite that incorporates clinical tools including periodontal charting and digital imaging of x-ray and inter-oral camera images. The Inpatient Solutions division, formed through the recent acquisitions of Opus Healthcare Solutions, Inc. and NextGen Sphere, LLC, offers the solutions NextGen Clinicals and NextGen Financials. The NextGen division, operated by NextGen Healthcare Information Systems, Inc., develops and sells proprietary electronic medical records software and practice management systems. Its NextGen product line includes NextGen Electronic Health Records; NextGen Patient Portal; and NextGuard. The group's EDI/Connectivity products automate a number of manual, often paper-based or telephony intensive communications between patients and providers, such as insurance claim forwards. NextGen products can operate in a client-server environment as well as via private intranet, the Internet or in an ASP environment. The firm's Practice Solutions segment, operated by subsidiaries Healthcare Strategic Initiatives and Practice Management Partners, primarily provides billing and collection services for medical practices through a combination of web-based software as a service (SaaS) and the NextGen software platform. In August 2011, Quality Systems agreed to acquire CQI Solutions, Inc.

FINANCIALS: **Sales and profits are in thousands of dollars—add 000 to get the full amount. 2011 Note: Financial information for 2011 was not available for all companies at press time.**

2011 Sales: $353,363	2011 Profits: $61,606
2010 Sales: $291,811	2010 Profits: $48,379
2009 Sales: $245,515	2009 Profits: $46,119
2008 Sales: $186,500	2008 Profits: $40,078
2007 Sales: $157,165	2007 Profits: $33,232

U.S. Stock Ticker: QSII
Int'l Ticker:
Int'l Exchange:
Employees: 1,537 Fiscal Year Ends: 3/31
Parent Company:

SALARIES/BENEFITS:

Pension Plan: ESOP Stock Plan: Profit Sharing: Top Exec. Salary: $800,000 Bonus: $628,571
Savings Plan: Y Stock Purch. Plan: Second Exec. Salary: $522,500 Bonus: $156,750

OTHER THOUGHTS:

Apparent Women Officers or Directors: 1
Hot Spot for Advancement for Women/Minorities:

LOCATIONS: ("Y" = Yes)

West:	Southwest:	Midwest:	Southeast:	Northeast:	International:
Y	Y	Y	Y	Y	

QUANTUM CORP

Industry Group Code: 334112

www.quantum.com

Management:		Sales/Marketing:		Liberal Arts:		Information Systems:		Professionals:		Technical/Scientific:	
Mgmt. Trainees:		Mktg. Professionals:	Y	Gen. Writing/Editing:		Info. Management:	Y	Finance/Acct.:	Y	Engineers, Elec.:	Y
Experienced Mgmt.:	Y	Retail Sales:		Technical Writing:	Y	Software Dev.:	Y	Law:	Y	Engineers, Other:	Y
Int'l Business:	Y	Commercial/Industrial:	Y	Graphic Arts/Photog.:		Hardware Dev.:	Y	HR/Other:	Y	Health/Lab	
MBA Graduates:	Y	Sales Trainees:		Music:		Consulting/Other:	Y	Training:	Y	Scientists/Research:	
		Advertising Pros.:		Broadcasting:				Health Care:		Petroleum/Chemicals:	
				Other:				Consulting:		Math/Other:	

TYPES OF BUSINESS:

Data Storage Equipment
Tape Drives
Media Cartridges
Tape Automation Systems

BRANDS/DIVISIONS/AFFILIATES:

iLayer
SuperLoader
Pancetera Software Inc
StorNext
DXi-Series

CONTACTS: *Note: Officers with more than one job title may be intentionally listed here more than once.*

Jon Gacek, CEO
Jon Gacek, Pres.
Linda Breard, CFO/Sr. VP
Bill Britts, Sr. VP-Worldwide Mktg.
Barbara Barrett, Sr. VP-Human Resources
Rob Clark, Sr. VP-Disk & Tape Backup Prod. Group
Don Martella, Sr. VP-Eng.
Shawn Hall, General Counsel/Sr. VP/Sec.
Ted Stinson, Sr. VP-Oper.
Bill Britts, Sr. VP-Bus. Dev. & Service
Janae Stow Lee, Sr. VP-File System & Archive Prod. Group
Richard E. Belluzzo, Exec. Chmn.
Ted Stinson, Sr. VP-Worldwide Sales

Phone: 408-944-4000 **Fax:** 408-944-4040
Toll-Free: 800-677-6268
Address: 1650 Technology Dr., Ste. 800, San Jose, CA 95110 US

GROWTH PLANS/SPECIAL FEATURES:

Quantum Corp. is a global storage company specializing in backup, recovery and archive applications. It provides an integrated range of disk, tape and software products. The company aims to provide information technology (IT) departments with tools for protecting, retaining and accessing digital assets. The firm's products are divided into three categories: tape automation systems; data management software and disk-based backup systems; and devices and media. The tape automation systems portfolio includes autoloaders under the SuperLoader name, as well as entry-level, midrange and enterprise libraries. These products integrate tape drives into a system with automation technology, advanced connectivity and management tools. The autoloaders range from products with one tape drive and up to 16 cartridges to large enterprise-class libraries with hundreds of drives and thousands of cartridges. The midrange and enterprise libraries leverage a common, integrated software management approach known as iLayer, which provides monitoring, alerts and diagnostics. Data management software products, designed for open system computing environments, improve workflow efficiencies, storage consolidation and archive management. StorNext, Quantum's primary data management product, provides shared access to data across different operating systems and storage platforms, and automatically copies and moves data between different tiers of storage based on business value. Disk-based backup system products include the DXi-Series disk-based backup appliances featuring data deduplication and replication technologies. Data deduplication technology increases effective disk capacity, enabling longer use of fast recovery disk. Devices and media products include removable disk drives, standalone tape drives and media products in multiple tape technology formats. Quantum sells its products via its branded channels through more than 20 distributors and 5,000 resellers worldwide, as well as through original equipment manufacturers (OEMS). The company serves customers in approximately 100 countries, with multi-language technical support centers in North America, Europe and Asia. In June 2011, Quantum acquired Pancetera Software, Inc.

FINANCIALS: **Sales and profits are in thousands of dollars—add 000 to get the full amount. 2011 Note: Financial information for 2011 was not available for all companies at press time.**

2011 Sales: $672,270 — 2011 Profits: $4,541
2010 Sales: $681,427 — 2010 Profits: $16,634
2009 Sales: $808,972 — 2009 Profits: $-358,264
2008 Sales: $975,702 — 2008 Profits: $-60,234
2007 Sales: $1,016,174 — 2007 Profits: $-64,094

U.S. Stock Ticker: QTM
Int'l Ticker:
Int'l Exchange:
Employees: 1,830 Fiscal Year Ends: 3/31
Parent Company:

SALARIES/BENEFITS:

Pension Plan: ESOP Stock Plan: Profit Sharing: Top Exec. Salary: $700,000 Bonus: $90,000
Savings Plan: Stock Purch. Plan: Second Exec. Salary: $413,025 Bonus: $60,000

OTHER THOUGHTS:

Apparent Women Officers or Directors: 3
Hot Spot for Advancement for Women/Minorities: Y

LOCATIONS: ("Y" = Yes)

West:	Southwest:	Midwest:	Southeast:	Northeast:	International:
Y	Y	Y	Y	Y	Y

QUESTCOR PHARMACEUTICALS INC

www.questcor.com

Industry Group Code: 325412

Management:		**Sales/Marketing:**		**Liberal Arts:**		**Information Systems:**		**Professionals:**		**Technical/Scientific:**	
Mgmt. Trainees:		Mktg. Professionals:	Y	Gen. Writing/Editing:		Info. Management:	Y	Finance/Acct.:	Y	Engineers, Elec.:	
Experienced Mgmt.:	Y	Retail Sales:		Technical Writing:	Y	Software Dev.:	Y	Law:	Y	Engineers, Other:	
Int'l Business:		Commercial/Industrial:	Y	Graphic Arts/Photog.:		Hardware Dev.:		HR/Other:	Y	Health/Lab	Y
MBA Graduates:	Y	Sales Trainees:		Music:		Consulting/Other:		Training:	Y	Scientists/Research:	Y
		Advertising Pros.:		Broadcasting:				Health Care:	Y	Petroleum/Chemicals:	Y
				Other:	Y			Consulting:		Math/Other:	Y

TYPES OF BUSINESS:

Drugs-Neurology
Multiple Sclerosis Treatment
Kidney Proteinuria (Nephritic Syndrome) Treatment

BRANDS/DIVISIONS/AFFILIATES:

HP Acthar Gel
Doral

CONTACTS:

Note: Officers with more than one job title may be intentionally listed here more than once.

Don M. Bailey, CEO
Don M. Bailey, Pres.
Michael H. Mulroy, CFO/Sr. VP
James Knight, VP-Strategic Mktg.
David Young, Chief Scientific Officer
Timothy O'Neill, VP-Contract Mfg.
Michael H. Mulroy, General Counsel/Corp. Sec.
Dave Medieros, Sr. VP-Pharmaceutical Oper.
Steve Cartt, Chief Business Officer/Exec. VP
Gary Sawka, Sr. VP-Finance
Sian Bigora, Sr. VP-Regulatory Affairs
Eldon Mayer, VP-Commercial Oper.
Virgil D. Thompson, Chmn.

Phone: 714-786-4200 **Fax:**

Toll-Free:

Address: 1300 North Kellogg Dr., Ste. D, Anaheim, CA 92807 US

GROWTH PLANS/SPECIAL FEATURES:

Questcor Pharmaceuticals, Inc. is a biopharmaceutical company that focuses on novel therapeutics for the treatment of diseases and disorders of the central nervous system (CNS). The company currently owns and markets two commercial products: H.P. Acthar Gel (Acthar) and Doral. Acthar is a natural source, highly purified preparation of the adrenal corticotropin hormone, which is specially formulated to provide prolonged release after intramuscular or subcutaneous injection. The product is indicated for use in acute exacerbations of multiple sclerosis (MS) and is prescribed for patients that have MS and experience painful, episodic flares. It is also FDA-approved for treatment in patients with nephrotic syndrome. Doral (quazepam) is a non-narcotic, selective benzodiazepine receptor agonist that is indicated for the treatment of insomnia. Sleep disturbance and insomnia are very common side effects of many neurological diseases and disorders such as multiple sclerosis, Epilepsy, Parkinson's disease and Alzheimer's disease. In October 2010, Questcor Pharmaceuticals received FDA approval of Acthar approved for infantile spasms.

Employees are offered medical, dental and vision benefits; short- and long-term disability plans; life insurance; flexible spending accounts; and an employee assistance program.

FINANCIALS:

Sales and profits are in thousands of dollars—add 000 to get the full amount. 2011 Note: Financial information for 2011 was not available for all companies at press time.

2011 Sales: $	2011 Profits: $	**U.S. Stock Ticker: QSC**
2010 Sales: $115,131	2010 Profits: $35,071	**Int'l Ticker:**
2009 Sales: $88,320	2009 Profits: $26,629	Int'l Exchange:
2008 Sales: $95,248	2008 Profits: $40,532	Employees: 152 Fiscal Year Ends: 12/31
2007 Sales: $49,768	2007 Profits: $36,449	Parent Company:

SALARIES/BENEFITS:

Pension Plan:	ESOP Stock Plan:	Profit Sharing:	Top Exec. Salary: $562,380	Bonus: $487,710
Savings Plan: Y	Stock Purch. Plan: Y		Second Exec. Salary: $408,000	Bonus: $326,610

OTHER THOUGHTS:

Apparent Women Officers or Directors:
Hot Spot for Advancement for Women/Minorities:

LOCATIONS: ("Y" = Yes)

West:	Southwest:	Midwest:	Southeast:	Northeast:	International:
Y					

QUICKSILVER RESOURCES INC

www.qrinc.com

Industry Group Code: 211111

Management:		Sales/Marketing:		Liberal Arts:		Information Systems:		Professionals:		Technical/Scientific:	
Mgmt. Trainees:		Mktg. Professionals:		Gen. Writing/Editing:		Info. Management:	Y	Finance/Acct.:	Y	Engineers, Elec.:	
Experienced Mgmt.:	Y	Retail Sales:		Technical Writing:		Software Dev.:		Law:	Y	Engineers, Other:	Y
Int'l Business:	Y	Commercial/Industrial:		Graphic Arts/Photog.:		Hardware Dev.:		HR/Other:	Y	Health/Lab	
MBA Graduates:	Y	Sales Trainees:		Music:		Consulting/Other:		Training:	Y	Scientists/Research:	
		Advertising Pros.:		Broadcasting:				Health Care:		Petroleum/Chemicals:	Y
				Other:				Consulting:		Math/Other:	

TYPES OF BUSINESS:
Oil & Gas Exploration & Production
Shale Gas
Coal Bed Methane
Tight Sand Gas

BRANDS/DIVISIONS/AFFILIATES:
Quicksilver Resources Canada, Inc.
BreiBurn Energy Partners L.P.

CONTACTS:
Note: Officers with more than one job title may be intentionally listed here more than once.
Glenn Darden, CEO
Glenn Darden, Pres.
Philip W. Cook, CFO/Sr. VP
John C. Cirone, General Counsel/Sr. VP
Jeff Cook, Exec. VP-Oper.
Thomas F. Darden, Chmn.

Phone: 817-665-5000 **Fax:** 817-665-5005
Toll-Free: 877-665-5000
Address: 801 Cherry St., Ste. 3700, Unit 19, Fort Worth, TX 76102 US

GROWTH PLANS/SPECIAL FEATURES:
Quicksilver Resources, Inc. (Quicksilver) is engaged in the onshore exploration, development and production of unconventional reservoirs such as shale gas, coal bed methane and tight gas sands in North America. The Company has total proved reserves of approximately 3 trillion cubic feet equivalent of resources. Quicksilver operates in two segments: the U.S and Canada. The U.S segment operates in Texas, Colorado, Wyoming and Montana. This segment's principal areas of operation are the Fort Worth Basin of Texas; and the Green River Basin of Colorado. Quicksilver's Barnett Shale in Texas contains 90% of the company's proved reserves and accounts for 79% of its total average daily production. The company's assets in Southern Alberta Basin and the Greater Green River Basin regions are primarily oil reserves with depths ranging from 1,000 feet to 17,000 feet. The Canadian segment operates through the subsidiary Quicksilver Resources Canada, Inc. Its principal areas of operation are the Horn River Basin and the Western Canadian Sedimentary Basin. This segment has proved reserves of 266 billion cubic feet of natural gas equivalents. In April 2011, the company acquired 26% of BreiBurn Energy Partners L.P. In October 2011, Quicksilver announced plans to create a master limited partnership with a portion of its Barnett Shale assets.

FINANCIALS:
Sales and profits are in thousands of dollars—add 000 to get the full amount. 2011 Note: Financial information for 2011 was not available for all companies at press time.

2011 Sales: $	2011 Profits: $
2010 Sales: $928,331	2010 Profits: $435,069
2009 Sales: $832,725	2009 Profits: $-545,239
2008 Sales: $800,641	2008 Profits: $-373,994
2007 Sales: $561,258	2007 Profits: $479,378

U.S. Stock Ticker: KWK
Int'l Ticker:
Int'l Exchange:
Employees: 452 Fiscal Year Ends: 12/31
Parent Company:

SALARIES/BENEFITS:
Pension Plan: ESOP Stock Plan: Profit Sharing: Top Exec. Salary: $440,000 Bonus: $653,400
Savings Plan: Stock Purch. Plan: Second Exec. Salary: $385,000 Bonus: $381,150

OTHER THOUGHTS:
Apparent Women Officers or Directors:
Hot Spot for Advancement for Women/Minorities:

LOCATIONS: ("Y" = Yes)

West:	Southwest:	Midwest:	Southeast:	Northeast:	International:
Y	Y				Y

QUIDEL CORP

www.quidel.com

Industry Group Code: 325413

Management:		Sales/Marketing:		Liberal Arts:		Information Systems:		Professionals:		Technical/Scientific:	
Mgmt. Trainees:		Mktg. Professionals:	Y	Gen. Writing/Editing:		Info. Management:	Y	Finance/Acct.:	Y	Engineers, Elec.:	
Experienced Mgmt.:	Y	Retail Sales:		Technical Writing:	Y	Software Dev.:	Y	Law:	Y	Engineers, Other:	Y
Int'l Business:	Y	Commercial/Industrial:	Y	Graphic Arts/Photog.:		Hardware Dev.:		HR/Other:	Y	Health/Lab	Y
MBA Graduates:	Y	Sales Trainees:	Y	Music:		Consulting/Other:		Training:	Y	Scientists/Research:	Y
		Advertising Pros.:	Y	Broadcasting:				Health Care:	Y	Petroleum/Chemicals:	
				Other:				Consulting:		Math/Other:	Y

TYPES OF BUSINESS:

Rapid Diagnosis Products
Point-of-Care Diagnostic Tests
Research Products

BRANDS/DIVISIONS/AFFILIATES:

QuickVue
MicroVue
QuickVue+
Diagnostic Hybrids, Inc.
Molecular Influenza A+B Real-Time RT-PCR Assay

CONTACTS: *Note: Officers with more than one job title may be intentionally listed here more than once.*

Douglas C. Bryant, CEO
Douglas C. Bryant, Pres.
John M. Radak, CFO
Tim Stenzel, Chief Scientific Officer
Robert J. Bujarski, General Counsel
Scot M. McLeod, Sr. VP-Oper.
Robert J. Bujarski, Sr. VP-Bus. Dev.
John D. Tamerius, Sr. VP-Clinical & Regulatory Affairs
David Scholl, Sr. VP-Commercial Oper./Pres., DHI
Mark A. Pulido, Chmn.

Phone: 858-552-1100 **Fax:** 858-453-4338
Toll-Free: 800-874-1517
Address: 10165 McKellar Ct., San Diego, CA 92121 US

GROWTH PLANS/SPECIAL FEATURES:

Quidel Corp. develops, manufactures and markets rapid diagnostic products at the professional point-of-care level in infectious diseases and reproductive and women's health. The firm's products detect and manage medical conditions and illnesses such as pregnancy, infectious diseases, general health screening, oncology, autoimmune disorders and osteoporosis. Quidel sells its products to professionals for use in physician offices, hospitals, clinical laboratories, reference laboratories, leading universities, retail clinics and wellness screening centers. Approximately 89% of the firm's revenues are derived from sales of infectious disease and women's health products. Brand names include Quidel, MicroVue, QuickVue and QuickVue+. The company markets its products in the U.S. through a network of national and regional distributors, supported by a direct sales force. Internationally, the company sells and markets primarily in Japan, Europe and the Middle East through exclusive distributor agreements. During 2010, four distributors accounted for approximately 31% of Quidel's revenues: Cardinal Healthcare Corporation, McKesson Corporation, Fisher Scientific Corporation and Physician Sales & Services Corporation. In early 2010, Quidel acquired Diagnostic Hybrids, Inc., a manufacturer of direct fluorescent in vitro assays used in diagnosing viral respiratory infections, herpes, chlamydia and thyroid diseases. In August 2011, it received CE Mark for the Quidel Molecular Influenza A+B Real-Time RT-PCR Assay, the firm's first molecular diagnostic test.

The company offers its employees life, medical, dental and vision insurance; flexible spending accounts; tuition reimbursement; discounted gym memberships; a 401(k); an employee assistance program; and a stock purchase plan.

FINANCIALS: **Sales and profits are in thousands of dollars—add 000 to get the full amount. 2011 Note: Financial information for 2011 was not available for all companies at press time.**

2011 Sales: $
2010 Sales: $113,339
2009 Sales: $164,282
2008 Sales: $128,132
2007 Sales: $118,065

2011 Profits: $
2010 Profits: $-11,271
2009 Profits: $32,883
2008 Profits: $18,848
2007 Profits: $13,631

U.S. Stock Ticker: QDEL
Int'l Ticker:
Int'l Exchange:
Employees: 532 Fiscal Year Ends: 12/31
Parent Company:

SALARIES/BENEFITS:

Pension Plan: ESOP Stock Plan: Profit Sharing: Top Exec. Salary: $482,538 Bonus: $
Savings Plan: Y Stock Purch. Plan: Y Second Exec. Salary: $311,261 Bonus: $

OTHER THOUGHTS:

Apparent Women Officers or Directors: 1
Hot Spot for Advancement for Women/Minorities:

LOCATIONS: ("Y" = Yes)

West:	Southwest:	Midwest:	Southeast:	Northeast:	International:
Y		Y			

RAYTHEON APPLIED SIGNAL TECHNOLOGY INC www.appsig.com

Industry Group Code: 334210

Management:		Sales/Marketing:		Liberal Arts:		Information Systems:		Professionals:		Technical/Scientific:	
Mgmt. Trainees:		Mktg. Professionals:	Y	Gen. Writing/Editing:	Y	Info. Management:	Y	Finance/Acct.:	Y	Engineers, Elec.:	Y
Experienced Mgmt.:	Y	Retail Sales:		Technical Writing:	Y	Software Dev.:	Y	Law:	Y	Engineers, Other:	Y
Int'l Business:	Y	Commercial/Industrial:	Y	Graphic Arts/Photog.:		Hardware Dev.:	Y	HR/Other:	Y	Health/Lab	
MBA Graduates:	Y	Sales Trainees:	Y	Music:		Consulting/Other:		Training:	Y	Scientists/Research:	
		Advertising Pros.:		Broadcasting:				Health Care:		Petroleum/Chemicals:	
				Other:				Consulting:		Math/Other:	

TYPES OF BUSINESS:

Telecommunications Equipment-Signal Reconnaissance
Defense Communication Products
Digital Signal Processing Equipment
Analysis & System Software

BRANDS/DIVISIONS/AFFILIATES:

Pegasus
neu-VISION
Pyxis Engineering
Seismic LLC
Applied Signal Technology Inc
Raytheon Co

CONTACTS: *Note: Officers with more than one job title may be intentionally listed here more than once.*

William B. Van Vleet III, Pres.
John R. Treichler, CTO
Joseph Leonelli, VP-Strategic Initiatives
James E. Doyle, VP-Finance
R. Fred Roscher, Exec. VP-Broadband Comm. Systems
John F. Pesaturo, VP-Surveillance Systems
Roger W. Anderson, VP-Network Intelligence

Phone: 408-749-1888 **Fax:** 408-522-2800
Toll-Free:
Address: 460 W. California Ave., Sunnyvale, CA 94086 US

GROWTH PLANS/SPECIAL FEATURES:

Raytheon Applied Signal Technology, Inc. (Raytheon AST), formerly Applied Signal Technology, Inc., provides advanced digital signal processing products and systems that support intelligence, surveillance and reconnaissance (ISR) activities for the U.S. government. It designs, develops and manufactures its own systems and equipment through centralized facilities and provides training and support for its products. Raytheon AST's main area of operations is signal intelligence (SIGINT), which is subdivided into manmade signals, such as electronic intelligence (ELINT), and communications intelligence (COMINT). It also offers processors for naturally occurring signals, including sonar, radar, magnetic and chemical sensors. ELINT operations, which fall primarily under its Pegasus line, are similar to its COMINT operations, but acquire electronic signals mainly from weapon systems. ELINT products function both automatically and through manual control, supporting battlefield mapping; threat detection such as from incoming missiles; and emitter collection and analysis. The firm's COMINT operations include products such as wideband processors, which prepare telecommunication signals for further processing by voice-grade channel (VGC) processors by adjusting for signal distortions that commonly occur during transmission; and collection products, which consist of low-cost, small receivers that collect information in complex signaling formats and optimize multiple antenna inputs to overcome co-channel interference and multi-path interference. Its neu-VISION technology is an advanced neutron imaging system that can detect and classify explosives and other harmful elements through concrete, vehicles and other barriers. Besides its SIGINT solutions, the firm offers secure broadband communication systems primarily used in battlefield and other limited resource situations. In 2010, the company acquired Seismic LLC, a privately-held cyber security applications developer. In January 2011, Applied Signal Technology was acquired by, and became a wholly-owned subsidiary of, Raytheon Co.

Employees are offered medical, dental and vision insurance; an employee assistance program; disability coverage; life insurance; flexible spending accounts; and tuition reimbursement.

FINANCIALS: **Sales and profits are in thousands of dollars—add 000 to get the full amount. 2011 Note: Financial information for 2011 was not available for all companies at press time.**

2011 Sales: $	2011 Profits: $
2010 Sales: $225,229	2010 Profits: $13,223
2009 Sales: $202,615	2009 Profits: $14,529
2008 Sales: $186,331	2008 Profits: $8,017
2007 Sales: $170,375	2007 Profits: $6,812

U.S. Stock Ticker: Subsidiary
Int'l Ticker:
Int'l Exchange:
Employees: 856 Fiscal Year Ends: 10/31
Parent Company: RAYTHEON CO

SALARIES/BENEFITS:

Pension Plan:	ESOP Stock Plan:	Profit Sharing:	Top Exec. Salary: $445,969	Bonus: $266,069
Savings Plan: Y	Stock Purch. Plan:		Second Exec. Salary: $328,494	Bonus: $149,388

OTHER THOUGHTS:

Apparent Women Officers or Directors:
Hot Spot for Advancement for Women/Minorities:

LOCATIONS: ("Y" = Yes)

West:	Southwest:	Midwest:	Southeast:	Northeast:	International:
Y	Y			Y	

REALNETWORKS INC

www.realnetworks.com

Industry Group Code: 511210F

Management:		Sales/Marketing:		Liberal Arts:		Information Systems:		Professionals:		Technical/Scientific:	
Mgmt. Trainees:		Mktg. Professionals:	Y	Gen. Writing/Editing:		Info. Management:	Y	Finance/Acct.:	Y	Engineers, Elec.:	Y
Experienced Mgmt.:	Y	Retail Sales:		Technical Writing:	Y	Software Dev.:	Y	Law:	Y	Engineers, Other:	
Int'l Business:	Y	Commercial/Industrial:	Y	Graphic Arts/Photog.:		Hardware Dev.:		HR/Other:	Y	Health/Lab	
MBA Graduates:	Y	Sales Trainees:	Y	Music:		Consulting/Other:		Training:	Y	Scientists/Research:	
		Advertising Pros.:		Broadcasting:				Health Care:		Petroleum/Chemicals:	
				Other:				Consulting:		Math/Other:	

TYPES OF BUSINESS:

Digital Media Services
Computer Software-Streaming Audio & Video
Online Retail-Digital Media
Mobile Games
Mobile Music
Mobile Video

BRANDS/DIVISIONS/AFFILIATES:

RealPlayer
ClipSync
Unifi
RealArcade
SuperPass
Gamehouse
Atrativa
Zylom

CONTACTS: *Note: Officers with more than one job title may be intentionally listed here more than once.*

Thomas Nielsen, CEO
Thomas Nielsen, Pres.
Michael Eggers, CFO/Sr. VP
Judith Bitterli, Chief Mktg. Officer/Sr. VP-Unifi
Tracy D. Daw, Chief Legal Officer/Corp. Sec.
Scott Uomoto, Sr. VP-Helix, Sales & Oper.
Mike Lunsford, Exec. VP
Matt Hulett, Sr. VP-Games
Vern Poyner, Sr. VP-SaaS
Robert Glaser, Chmn.
DJ (Dongjin) Lee, Sr. VP-Asia SaaS

Phone: 206-674-2700	**Fax:** 206-674-2696
Toll-Free:	
Address: 2601 Elliott Ave., Ste. 1000, Seattle, WA 98121 US	

GROWTH PLANS/SPECIAL FEATURES:

RealNetworks, Inc. is a creator of digital media services and software. The company operates in three segments: core products, games and emerging products. The firm's core products segment offers Software-as-a-Service (SaaS) services, such as ring back tones, music-on-demand, video-on-demand, inter-carrier messages, professional services and system integration services to carriers and mobile handset firms. The core products segment also licenses its software products, including consumer subscriptions such as SuperPass, Helix for handsets and international radio subscriptions. RealNetworks' games segment creates, distributes and sells game licenses; advertising on game sites and social networking sites; micro-transactions from online and social games; online games subscription services; games syndication services; and sales of mobile games. The company develops original game content through the game studios Gamehouse, RealArcade, Atrativa and Zylom. The emerging products division manages the firm's RealPlayer media player software and the newly launched Unifi personal media cloud service. RealPlayer enables consumers to discover, play and manage audio and video programming on the Internet. Unifi allows users the ability to organize and access their digital media automatically from any network-enabled device. In September 2011, the firm announced a partnership agreement with AOL UK, in which AOL UK will provide its content to RealNetwork's RealPlayer throughout the UK market. In October 2011, the firm partnered with nToklo to incorporate nToklo's personalized recommendation platform and social discovery tools into RealNetworks white-label Music-On-Demand feature throughout the European market.

FINANCIALS: **Sales and profits are in thousands of dollars—add 000 to get the full amount. 2011 Note: Financial information for 2011 was not available for all companies at press time.**

2011 Sales: $335,700	2011 Profits: $-2,800
2010 Sales: $401,733	2010 Profits: $5,038
2009 Sales: $562,264	2009 Profits: $-216,764
2008 Sales: $604,810	2008 Profits: $-243,878
2007 Sales: $567,620	2007 Profits: $48,315

U.S. Stock Ticker: RNWK
Int'l Ticker:
Int'l Exchange:
Employees: 1,319 Fiscal Year Ends: 12/31
Parent Company:

SALARIES/BENEFITS:

Pension Plan:	ESOP Stock Plan:	Profit Sharing:	Top Exec. Salary: $469,902	Bonus: $100,000
Savings Plan:	Stock Purch. Plan:		Second Exec. Salary: $397,219	Bonus: $

OTHER THOUGHTS:

Apparent Women Officers or Directors: 2
Hot Spot for Advancement for Women/Minorities:

LOCATIONS: ("Y" = Yes)

West:	Southwest:	Midwest:	Southeast:	Northeast:	International:
Y				Y	Y

RECYCLED ENERGY DEVELOPMENT LLC www.recycled-energy.com

Industry Group Code: 541690

Management:		Sales/Marketing:		Liberal Arts:		Information Systems:		Professionals:		Technical/Scientific:	
Mgmt. Trainees:		Mktg. Professionals:	Y	Gen. Writing/Editing:		Info. Management:	Y	Finance/Acct.:	Y	Engineers, Elec.:	Y
Experienced Mgmt.:	Y	Retail Sales:		Technical Writing:	Y	Software Dev.:	Y	Law:	Y	Engineers, Other:	
Int'l Business:		Commercial/Industrial:	Y	Graphic Arts/Photog.:		Hardware Dev.:		HR/Other:	Y	Health/Lab	
MBA Graduates:	Y	Sales Trainees:	Y	Music:		Consulting/Other:	Y	Training:	Y	Scientists/Research:	Y
		Advertising Pros.:		Broadcasting:				Health Care:		Petroleum/Chemicals:	
				Other:				Consulting:		Math/Other:	

TYPES OF BUSINESS:

Co-Generation Technology
Waste Heat-to-Energy

BRANDS/DIVISIONS/AFFILIATES:

Turbosteam LLC

CONTACTS: *Note: Officers with more than one job title may be intentionally listed here more than once.*

Sean Casten, CEO
Sean Casten, Pres.
Aaron Walters, CFO
Gary Hoppenrath, VP-Eng. & Construction
Myra Karegianes, General Counsel/Sr. VP
Eric Gottung, VP-Bus. Dev.
Dick Munson, Sr. VP-Public Affairs
Scott Kerrigan, Controller/VP
Andres Pena, Sr. VP-Projects & Construction
Leif Bergquist, VP-Bus. Dev.
John Wilson, VP-Bus. Dev.
John Whitehouse, VP-Bus. Dev.
Thomas R. Casten, Chmn.

Phone: 630-590-6030	**Fax:** 630-590-6037
Toll-Free:	
Address: 640 Quail Ridge Dr., Westmont, IL 60559 US	

GROWTH PLANS/SPECIAL FEATURES:

Recycled Energy Development, LLC (RED) is a clean energy provider focused on developing combined heat and power (cogeneration) facilities and providing waste heat recovery services to existing power plants. The firm aims to reduce greenhouse-gas emissions, as well as reduce energy costs and increase power generation by using waste heat to produce thermal power and electricity. The company also aims to create increased profits for industrial partners by reducing costs, increasing output and providing the possibility of carbon credits. RED provides all of the necessary equipment, capital and services for the development, installation and long-term operation of recycled energy projects, which include combined heat and power plants (CHP) and waste energy recovery. It builds CHP facilities for industrial operations and other large institutions, allowing them to recycle excess heat emitted in the power generation process and use it to power their own operations and resulting in lower electricity costs. The firm's waste energy recovery operations similarly capture energy that manufacturers emit as waste and recycle it into useful forms of heating and cooling. In exchange for RED supplying the capital and operating the energy equipment, customers generally enter into a long-term power purchase agreement with RED. Turbosteam, the company's wholly-owned subsidiary, is a converter of waste energy into electricity. It has installed more than 180 systems in 32 states and 18 countries, saved customers $200 million and lowered global CO_2 emissions by over 4 million tons. Turbostream's services include detailed site engineering; design optimization; and capital equipment and turnkey installations.

FINANCIALS: **Sales and profits are in thousands of dollars—add 000 to get the full amount. 2011 Note: Financial information for 2011 was not available for all companies at press time.**

2011 Sales: $	2011 Profits: $	**U.S. Stock Ticker: Private**
2010 Sales: $	2010 Profits: $	**Int'l Ticker:**
2009 Sales: $	2009 Profits: $	Int'l Exchange:
2008 Sales: $	2008 Profits: $	Employees: Fiscal Year Ends:
2007 Sales: $	2007 Profits: $	Parent Company:

SALARIES/BENEFITS:

Pension Plan:	ESOP Stock Plan:	Profit Sharing:	Top Exec. Salary: $	Bonus: $
Savings Plan:	Stock Purch. Plan:		Second Exec. Salary: $	Bonus: $

OTHER THOUGHTS:

Apparent Women Officers or Directors: 1
Hot Spot for Advancement for Women/Minorities:

LOCATIONS: ("Y" = Yes)

West:	Southwest:	Midwest:	Southeast:	Northeast:	International:
		Y		Y	

Sales, profits and employees may be estimates. Financial information, benefits and other data can change quickly and may vary from those stated here.

REDBOX AUTOMATED RETAIL LLC

www.redbox.com

Industry Group Code: 532230

Management:		**Sales/Marketing:**		**Liberal Arts:**		**Information Systems:**		**Professionals:**		**Technical/Scientific:**	
Mgmt. Trainees:	Y	Mktg. Professionals:	Y	Gen. Writing/Editing:	Y	Info. Management:	Y	Finance/Acct.:	Y	Engineers, Elec.:	
Experienced Mgmt.:	Y	Retail Sales:		Technical Writing:		Software Dev.:	Y	Law:	Y	Engineers, Other:	
Int'l Business:	Y	Commercial/Industrial:	Y	Graphic Arts/Photog.:	Y	Hardware Dev.:		HR/Other:	Y	Health/Lab	
MBA Graduates:	Y	Sales Trainees:		Music:		Consulting/Other:		Training:	Y	Scientists/Research:	
		Advertising Pros.:	Y	Broadcasting:				Health Care:		Petroleum/Chemicals:	
				Other:	Y			Consulting:		Math/Other:	

TYPES OF BUSINESS:

DVD Rentals

BRANDS/DIVISIONS/AFFILIATES:

Redbox
Coinstar Inc

CONTACTS:

Note: Officers with more than one job title may be intentionally listed here more than once.

Mitch Lowe, Pres.
Paul Davis, CEO-Coinstar, Inc.
Gregg Kaplan, Pres./COO-Coinstar, Inc.
Raquel Karls, Chief People Officer-Coinstar, Inc.
J. Scott Di Valerio, CFO-Coinstar, Inc.

Phone: 630-756-8000 **Fax:** 630-756-8888
Toll-Free:
Address: 1 Tower Ln., Ste. 1200, Oak Brook Terrace, IL 60181 US

GROWTH PLANS/SPECIAL FEATURES:

Redbox Automated Retail LLC is one of the largest renters of DVDs in the U.S. The firm is a wholly-owned subsidiary of Coinstar, Inc. It vends DVDs through kiosks in locations such as McDonald's, Albertsons grocery stores and Stop & Shops. Redbox has a total of roughly 34,400 kiosks in 28,400 locations. Certain Wal-Mart stores also have kiosks installed in a trial program. With movies priced at roughly $1.20 to $1.50 per day, the kiosks average over 50 rentals a day. The kiosks offer up to 200 titles and hold 630 DVDs. Movies can also be rented online and picked up at Redbox locations. Customers can return the movies to any Redbox location. The firm offers several features, including the ability to use the Redbox web site to reserve a movie at a kiosk to pick up later. The company has distribution agreements with several major studios, including Summit Entertainment, Universal Studios, Paramount Home Entertainment, Warner Home Video, 20th Century Fox, Lionsgate and Sony Pictures Home Entertainment. Redbox offers video games for rent in several test markets. In June 2011, Redbox began carrying video game rentals for about $2.00 per day..

FINANCIALS:

Sales and profits are in thousands of dollars—add 000 to get the full amount. 2011 Note: Financial information for 2011 was not available for all companies at press time.

2011 Sales: $1,561,598 — 2011 Profits: $284,932
2010 Sales: $1,160,110 — 2010 Profits: $190,850
2009 Sales: $773,000 — 2009 Profits: $
2008 Sales: $450,000 — 2008 Profits: $
2007 Sales: $ — 2007 Profits: $

U.S. Stock Ticker: Subsidiary
Int'l Ticker:
Int'l Exchange:
Employees: Fiscal Year Ends:
Parent Company: COINSTAR INC

SALARIES/BENEFITS:

Pension Plan: ESOP Stock Plan: Profit Sharing: Top Exec. Salary: $ Bonus: $
Savings Plan: Stock Purch. Plan: Second Exec. Salary: $ Bonus: $

OTHER THOUGHTS:

Apparent Women Officers or Directors: 1
Hot Spot for Advancement for Women/Minorities:

LOCATIONS: ("Y" = Yes)

West:	Southwest:	Midwest:	Southeast:	Northeast:	International:
Y	Y	Y	Y	Y	Y

REGENERON PHARMACEUTICALS INC

www.regeneron.com

Industry Group Code: 325412

Management:		Sales/Marketing:		Liberal Arts:		Information Systems:		Professionals:		Technical/Scientific:	
Mgmt. Trainees:		Mktg. Professionals:	Y	Gen. Writing/Editing:		Info. Management:	Y	Finance/Acct.:	Y	Engineers, Elec.:	
Experienced Mgmt.:	Y	Retail Sales:		Technical Writing:	Y	Software Dev.:	Y	Law:	Y	Engineers, Other:	
Int'l Business:		Commercial/Industrial:	Y	Graphic Arts/Photog.:		Hardware Dev.:		HR/Other:	Y	Health/Lab	Y
MBA Graduates:	Y	Sales Trainees:	Y	Music:		Consulting/Other:		Training:	Y	Scientists/Research:	Y
		Advertising Pros.:		Broadcasting:				Health Care:	Y	Petroleum/Chemicals:	Y
				Other:				Consulting:		Math/Other:	Y

TYPES OF BUSINESS:

Drugs-Diversified
Protein-Based Drugs
Small-Molecule Drugs
Genetics & Transgenic Mouse Technologies

BRANDS/DIVISIONS/AFFILIATES:

VelocImmune
VelociGene
VelociMouse
VEGF Trap
VEGF Trap-Eye
VelociMab
ARCALYST
REGN88

CONTACTS: *Note: Officers with more than one job title may be intentionally listed here more than once.*

Leonard S. Schleifer, CEO
Leonard S. Schleifer, Pres.
Murray A. Goldberg, CFO
George D. Yancopoulos, Chief Scientific Officer/Exec. VP
Murray A. Goldberg, Sr. VP-Admin.
Daniel Van Plew, Sr. VP/Gen. Mgr.-Industrial Oper.
Murray A. Goldberg, Sr. VP-Finance/Treas.
George D. Yancopoulos, Pres., Regeneron Research Laboratories
Neil Stahl, Sr. VP-R&D Sciences
Peter Powchik, Sr. VP-Clinical Dev.
Robert J. Terifay, Sr. VP-Commercial
P. Roy Vagelos, Chmn.
Daniel Van Plew, Gen. Mgr.-Prod. Supply

Phone: 914-345-7400 **Fax:**
Toll-Free:
Address: 777 Old Saw Mill River Rd., Tarrytown, NY 10591 US

GROWTH PLANS/SPECIAL FEATURES:

Regeneron Pharmaceuticals, Inc. is a biopharmaceutical company that discovers, develops and commercializes pharmaceutical drugs for the treatment of serious medical conditions. The company's sole marketed product is Arcalyst, a therapy for the treatment of Cryopyrin-Associated Periodic Syndromes (CAPS), a rare, inherited inflammatory condition. The firm currently has three late-stage clinical development programs: aflibercept (VEGF Trap) in oncology; VEGF Trap eye formulation (VEGF Trap-Eye) in eye diseases using intraocular delivery; and rilonacept (IL-1 Trap) in gout. The VEGF Trap oncology development program is being developed jointly with the sanofi-aventis Group. Also in collaboration with sanofi-aventis is REGN88, an antibody to the Interleukin-6 receptor (IL-6R) for treatment of rheumatoid arthritis, developed using VelocImmune technologies. Regeneron's preclinical research programs are in the areas of oncology, angiogenesis, ophthalmology, metabolic and related diseases, muscle diseases and disorders, inflammation and immune diseases, bone and cartilage, pain, metabolic diseases, infectious diseases and cardiovascular diseases. The company expects that its next generation of product candidates will be based on its proprietary technologies for developing Traps and Human Monoclonal Antibodies. Regeneron's proprietary technologies include VelociGene, VelociMouse and VelocImmune, among others. The VelociGene technology allows precise DNA manipulation and gene staining, helping to identify where a particular gene is active in the body. VelociMouse technology allows for the direct and immediate generation of genetically altered mice from ES cells, avoiding the lengthy process involved in generating and breeding knock-out mice from chimeras. VelocImmune is a novel mouse technology platform for producing fully human monoclonal antibodies. Additionally, the VelociMab suite of technologies allows rapid screenings of therapeutic antibodies and eliminates the need for slower development techniques.

Regeneron employee benefits include medical, dental, vision, prescription, life and AD&D insurance; short- and long-term disability; flexible spending accounts, and tuition reimbursement.

FINANCIALS: **Sales and profits are in thousands of dollars—add 000 to get the full amount. 2011 Note: Financial information for 2011 was not available for all companies at press time.**

2011 Sales: $445,824 | 2011 Profits: $-221,760
2010 Sales: $459,074 | 2010 Profits: $-104,468
2009 Sales: $379,268 | 2009 Profits: $-67,830
2008 Sales: $238,457 | 2008 Profits: $-86,249
2007 Sales: $125,024 | 2007 Profits: $-115,373

U.S. Stock Ticker: REGN
Int'l Ticker:
Int'l Exchange:
Employees: 1,432 Fiscal Year Ends: 12/31
Parent Company:

SALARIES/BENEFITS:

Pension Plan: | ESOP Stock Plan: | Profit Sharing: | Top Exec. Salary: $759,370 | Bonus: $222,560
Savings Plan: Y | Stock Purch. Plan: | | Second Exec. Salary: $630,600 | Bonus: $654,540

OTHER THOUGHTS:

Apparent Women Officers or Directors:
Hot Spot for Advancement for Women/Minorities:

LOCATIONS: ("Y" = Yes)

West:	Southwest:	Midwest:	Southeast:	Northeast:	International:
				Y	

REINSURANCE GROUP OF AMERICA INC

www.rgare.com

Industry Group Code: 524130

Management:		Sales/Marketing:		Liberal Arts:		Information Systems:		Professionals:		Technical/Scientific:	
Mgmt. Trainees:		Mktg. Professionals:	Y	Gen. Writing/Editing:	Y	Info. Management:	Y	Finance/Acct.:	Y	Engineers, Elec.:	
Experienced Mgmt.:	Y	Retail Sales:		Technical Writing:	Y	Software Dev.:		Law:	Y	Engineers, Other:	
Int'l Business:	Y	Commercial/Industrial:	Y	Graphic Arts/Photog.:		Hardware Dev.:		HR/Other:	Y	Health/Lab	
MBA Graduates:	Y	Sales Trainees:	Y	Music:		Consulting/Other:		Training:	Y	Scientists/Research:	
		Advertising Pros.:		Broadcasting:				Health Care:		Petroleum/Chemicals:	
				Other:				Consulting:		Math/Other:	Y

TYPES OF BUSINESS:

Reinsurance
Life Reinsurance
International Life & Disability

BRANDS/DIVISIONS/AFFILIATES:

Reinsurance Company of Missouri, Inc.
RGA Barbados
RGA Canada
RGA Americas
RGA Reinsurance
RGA Atlantic
RGA U.K.
RGA Australia

CONTACTS: *Note: Officers with more than one job title may be intentionally listed here more than once.*

A. Greig Woodring, CEO
A. Greig Woodring, Pres.
Jack B. Lay, CFO/Sr. Exec. VP
Allan E. O'Bryant, Head-Oper./Exec. VP
Paul A. Schuster, Sr. Exec. VP-Group, Health & Long-Term Care
Alain Neemeh, CEO/Pres., RGA Life Reinsurance Co. Canada
Anna Manning, Exec. VP/Head-U.S. Markets
Scott D. Cochran, Exec. VP-Global Financial Solutions & Acquisitions
J. Cliff Eason, Chmn.
Allan E. O'Bryant, Head-Int'l Markets/Exec. VP

Phone: 636-736-7000 **Fax:** 636-736-7100
Toll-Free: 888-736-5445
Address: 1370 Timberlake Manor Pkwy., Chesterfield, MO 63017 US

GROWTH PLANS/SPECIAL FEATURES:

Reinsurance Group of America, Inc. (RGA) is an insurance holding company that is engaged primarily in traditional life, asset-intensive, critical illness and financial reinsurance. The company's principal assets are the Reinsurance Company of Missouri, Inc.; RGA Barbados; RGA U.K.; RGA Canada; RGA Atlantic; RGA Australia; and RGA Americas. Additionally, the firm has investments in several other wholly-owned subsidiaries. RGA's international operations include subsidiaries, branch operations and 27 representative offices in approximately 23 countries in the Americas, Europe, Asia-Pacific and Africa. RGA is one of the largest life reinsurers in the world, with approximately $2.5 trillion of life insurance in force and assets of $29.1 billion. The U.S. operations of the company market life reinsurance, reinsurance of asset-intensive products and financial reinsurance to the largest life insurance companies in the U.S. The Canadian operations assist clients with capital management activity and mortality risk management and provide traditional individual life reinsurance, including preferred underwriting products, as well as creditor and critical illness products. Combined, the U.S. and Canadian operations account for approximately 69% of RGA's net premiums. The company's European and South African operations provide life and critical illness reinsurance to clients throughout Europe and South Africa through yearly renewable term and coinsurance agreements. Its Asia-Pacific operations conduct reinsurance business in the Asia-Pacific region through branch operations in Hong Kong and representative offices in Japan, Taiwan and South Korea. The firm also conducts reinsurance business in the Latin American region through RGA Reinsurance. In September 2011, RGA opened a new office in Dubai.

FINANCIALS: **Sales and profits are in thousands of dollars—add 000 to get the full amount. 2011 Note: Financial information for 2011 was not available for all companies at press time.**

2011 Sales: $8,829,538	2011 Profits: $599,620
2010 Sales: $8,261,730	2010 Profits: $574,402
2009 Sales: $7,066,800	2009 Profits: $407,100
2008 Sales: $5,681,200	2008 Profits: $176,800
2007 Sales: $5,718,400	2007 Profits: $293,800

U.S. Stock Ticker: RGA
Int'l Ticker:
Int'l Exchange:
Employees: 1,535 Fiscal Year Ends: 12/31
Parent Company:

SALARIES/BENEFITS:

Pension Plan: Y	ESOP Stock Plan:	Profit Sharing: Y	Top Exec. Salary: $919,288	Bonus: $1,405,819
Savings Plan: Y	Stock Purch. Plan:		Second Exec. Salary: $560,959	Bonus: $699,769

OTHER THOUGHTS:

Apparent Women Officers or Directors: 2
Hot Spot for Advancement for Women/Minorities:

LOCATIONS: ("Y" = Yes)

West:	Southwest:	Midwest:	Southeast:	Northeast:	International:
		Y			Y

RENTRAK CORP

www.rentrak.com

Industry Group Code: 512110

Management:		**Sales/Marketing:**		**Liberal Arts:**		**Information Systems:**		**Professionals:**		**Technical/Scientific:**	
Mgmt. Trainees:		Mktg. Professionals:	Y	Gen. Writing/Editing:	Y	Info. Management:	Y	Finance/Acct.:	Y	Engineers, Elec.:	
Experienced Mgmt.:	Y	Retail Sales:		Technical Writing:	Y	Software Dev.:	Y	Law:	Y	Engineers, Other:	
Int'l Business:	Y	Commercial/Industrial:	Y	Graphic Arts/Photog.:		Hardware Dev.:		HR/Other:	Y	Health/Lab	
MBA Graduates:	Y	Sales Trainees:		Music:		Consulting/Other:		Training:	Y	Scientists/Research:	
		Advertising Pros.:	Y	Broadcasting:				Health Care:		Petroleum/Chemicals:	
				Other:	Y			Consulting:		Math/Other:	

TYPES OF BUSINESS:

Video Distribution
Information Management

BRANDS/DIVISIONS/AFFILIATES:

OnDemand Essentials
TV Essentials
StationView Essentials
Internet TV Essentials
Digital Download Essentials
Mobile Essentials
Media Salvation Inc
PPT System

CONTACTS: *Note: Officers with more than one job title may be intentionally listed here more than once.*

Bill P. Livek, CEO
David I. Chemerow, COO
David I. Chemerow, CFO
Bruce Goerlich, Chief Research Officer
Amir Yazdani, CIO/Exec. VP-IT
Cathy Hetzel, Pres., AMI Div.
Rom Giambra, Pres., Theatrical Worldwide
Chris Wilson, Pres., National Linear Television
Marty Graham, Pres., Home Entertainment Div.
Paul A. Rosenbaum, Chmn.

Phone: 503-284-7581 **Fax:**
Toll-Free: 866-333-6210
Address: 7700 NE Ambassador Place, 3rd Fl., Portland, OR 97220 US

GROWTH PLANS/SPECIAL FEATURES:

Rentrak Corp. is an information management and video distribution company that operates in two business divisions: Advanced Media and Information (AMI) and Home Entertainment (HE). The AMI division includes the firm's media measurement services, which are delivered to customers through web-based products within the firm's Entertainment Essentials business line. The primary content measurement services include television content, which is distributed by software brands OnDemand Essentials, TV Essentials and StationView Essentials; internet and mobile device content, distributed by brands Internet TV Essentials, Digital Download Essentials and Mobile Essentials; and theatrical box office content, which is distributed by the Box Office Essentials brand. Clients subscribing to the firm's media measurement services include movie studios, TV networks, cable operators and advertising agencies. The HE division utilizes the firm's Pay-Per -Transaction (PPT) System to lease home entertainment products such as DVDs, Blu-Ray disks and video games to regional chain and independent retailers. After an initial one-time upfront fee, Rentrak, the retailer and the supplier of the entertainment products share the revenue. The PPT System is sold throughout the United States and Canada. Rentrak supplies titles to retailers from such suppliers as Anchor Bay Entertainment LLC; Lionsgate Films, Inc.; Paramount Home Entertainment, Inc; and Sony Pictures Home Entertainment, Inc. In January 2011, the firm acquired Media Salvation, Inc. In June 2011, the company partnered with Anderson Merchandisers, who will begin marketing DVD and Blu-Ray content for rental from Arc Entertainment through Rentrak's revenue sharing program.

Employees are offered medical, dental and vision insurance; flexible spending accounts; educational assistance; life insurance; prescription drug coverage; a 401(k) plan; and vacation packages.

FINANCIALS: **Sales and profits are in thousands of dollars—add 000 to get the full amount. 2011 Note: Financial information for 2011 was not available for all companies at press time.**

2011 Sales: $97,088 — 2011 Profits: $- 767
2010 Sales: $91,076 — 2010 Profits: $ 576
2009 Sales: $94,966 — 2009 Profits: $5,363
2008 Sales: $93,188 — 2008 Profits: $4,594
2007 Sales: $105,721 — 2007 Profits: $5,887

U.S. Stock Ticker: RENT
Int'l Ticker:
Int'l Exchange:
Employees: 307 Fiscal Year Ends: 3/31
Parent Company:

SALARIES/BENEFITS:

Pension Plan: ESOP Stock Plan: Profit Sharing: Top Exec. Salary: $254,925 Bonus: $
Savings Plan: Y Stock Purch. Plan: Second Exec. Salary: $231,750 Bonus: $

OTHER THOUGHTS:

Apparent Women Officers or Directors: 2
Hot Spot for Advancement for Women/Minorities:

LOCATIONS: ("Y" = Yes)

West:	Southwest:	Midwest:	Southeast:	Northeast:	International:
Y			Y	Y	Y

RICELAND FOODS INC

www.riceland.com

Industry Group Code: 3112

Management:		Sales/Marketing:		Liberal Arts:		Information Systems:		Professionals:		Technical/Scientific:	
Mgmt. Trainees:		Mktg. Professionals:	Y	Gen. Writing/Editing:	Y	Info. Management:	Y	Finance/Acct.:	Y	Engineers, Elec.:	
Experienced Mgmt.:	Y	Retail Sales:		Technical Writing:		Software Dev.:		Law:	Y	Engineers, Other:	
Int'l Business:		Commercial/Industrial:	Y	Graphic Arts/Photog.:		Hardware Dev.:		HR/Other:	Y	Health/Lab	
MBA Graduates:	Y	Sales Trainees:	Y	Music:		Consulting/Other:		Training:		Scientists/Research:	
		Advertising Pros.:	Y	Broadcasting:				Health Care:		Petroleum/Chemicals:	
				Other:				Consulting:		Math/Other:	

TYPES OF BUSINESS:

Agricultural Services-Marketing
Farming Cooperative
Rice
Soybeans
Wheat
Oil Products
Feed Products

BRANDS/DIVISIONS/AFFILIATES:

Riceland

CONTACTS:

Note: Officers with more than one job title may be intentionally listed here more than once.

K. Daniel Kennedy, CEO
John B. Ruff, VP-Soybean & Grains

Phone: 870-673-5500	**Fax:** 870-673-3366
Toll-Free: 800-226-9522	
Address: 2120 S. Park Ave., Stuttgart, AR 72160 US	

GROWTH PLANS/SPECIAL FEATURES:

Riceland Foods, Inc. is a farming cooperative that provides marketing services for rice, soybeans and wheat grown by its members. The firm has approximately 9,000 farmer-members in Arkansas, Louisiana, Mississippi, Missouri and Texas. The company has a total of 55 storage facilities dispersed among its member states, capable of storing up to 103 million bushels of grain which is professionally monitored until needed at processing plants or moved into marketing channels. Riceland Foods receives, stores, transports, processes and markets more than 125 million bushels of grain each year, making it one of the world's largest rice producer that both mills and markets its own rice. The company has eight milling facilities. The firm markets packaged and flavored rice products under Riceland and private label brands. It also packages rice for private label and store brands. The co-op also sells oil and shortening products and processes soybeans, edible oils and lecithin to major food manufacturers. Defatted rice bran, rice bran oil, mill feed and hulls are sold to both the livestock and pet food industries as ingredients. Some rice hulls are burned for energy and the ash is used as an absorbent. Rice hulls are also used as a pressing aid in fruit juices extraction and as bedding in poultry houses. The firm sells soybeans domestically; wheat to Mexico and Egypt; and rice to Mexico and Central America. Processed rice products are sold nationwide and to 75 foreign markets, mainly in the Caribbean, Central America, the Middle East, Asia, Africa and Europe. The firm operates a research and technical center as well as a training and education center at its headquarters in Arkansas.

FINANCIALS:

Sales and profits are in thousands of dollars—add 000 to get the full amount. 2011 Note: Financial information for 2011 was not available for all companies at press time.

2011 Sales: $	2011 Profits: $	**U.S. Stock Ticker: Cooperative**
2010 Sales: $	2010 Profits: $	**Int'l Ticker:**
2009 Sales: $	2009 Profits: $	Int'l Exchange:
2008 Sales: $	2008 Profits: $	Employees: Fiscal Year Ends: 7/31
2007 Sales: $	2007 Profits: $	Parent Company:

SALARIES/BENEFITS:

Pension Plan:	ESOP Stock Plan:	Profit Sharing:	Top Exec. Salary: $	Bonus: $
Savings Plan:	Stock Purch. Plan:		Second Exec. Salary: $	Bonus: $

OTHER THOUGHTS:

Apparent Women Officers or Directors:
Hot Spot for Advancement for Women/Minorities:

LOCATIONS: ("Y" = Yes)

West:	Southwest:	Midwest:	Southeast:	Northeast:	International:
	Y	Y	Y		

RIGHTNOW TECHNOLOGIES INC

www.rightnow.com

Industry Group Code: 511210K

Management:		Sales/Marketing:		Liberal Arts:		Information Systems:		Professionals:		Technical/Scientific:	
Mgmt. Trainees:		Mktg. Professionals:	Y	Gen. Writing/Editing:		Info. Management:	Y	Finance/Acct.:	Y	Engineers, Elec.:	Y
Experienced Mgmt.:	Y	Retail Sales:		Technical Writing:	Y	Software Dev.:	Y	Law:	Y	Engineers, Other:	
Int'l Business:	Y	Commercial/Industrial:	Y	Graphic Arts/Photog.:		Hardware Dev.:		HR/Other:	Y	Health/Lab	
MBA Graduates:	Y	Sales Trainees:	Y	Music:		Consulting/Other:		Training:	Y	Scientists/Research:	
		Advertising Pros.:		Broadcasting:				Health Care:		Petroleum/Chemicals:	
				Other:	Y			Consulting:		Math/Other:	

TYPES OF BUSINESS:

Software-Customer Relationship Management
Sales & Marketing Software
Professional Services

BRANDS/DIVISIONS/AFFILIATES:

RightNow Service
RightNow Sales
RightNow Marketing
RightNow Feedback
RightNow Voice
RightNow Analytics
Q-go.com BV
Oracle Corp

CONTACTS: *Note: Officers with more than one job title may be intentionally listed here more than once.*

Greg R. Gianforte, CEO
Wayne Huyard, COO
Wayne Huyard, Pres.
Jeffery C. Davison, CFO
Jason Mittelstaedt, Chief Mktg. Officer
Julie Rich, Sr. VP-Human Resources
Laef Olson, CIO
Mike A. Myer, CTO
Alan A. Rassaby, General Counsel/Sr. VP/Corp. Sec.
Brian Curran, VP-Web Solutions
Jeffery C. Davison, Treas.
David Vap, Chief Solutions Officer
Susan Carstensen, Sr. VP-Customer Experience
Marcus Bragg, Sr. VP-Global Sales
Greg R. Gianforte, Chmn.

Phone: 406-522-4200 **Fax:** 406-522-4227
Toll-Free: 877-363-5678
Address: 136 Enterprise Blvd., Bozeman, MT 59718-9300 US

GROWTH PLANS/SPECIAL FEATURES:

RightNow Technologies, Inc. is a leading provider of on-demand customer relationship management (CRM) products and professional services that help organizations of all sizes build customer-focused businesses. RightNow's technology enables an organization's service, marketing and sales personnel to leverage a common application platform for phone, e-mail and chat functions. Additionally, through its on-demand delivery approach, RightNow's is able to reduce the complexity associated with traditional on-premise solutions and offer its products at lower prices than competitors. Products are designed to integrate with traditional enterprise applications and are available in several languages and dialects. The firm's CRM products include several branded lines. RightNow Service, which generates between 80% and 90% of the company's software, hosting and support revenues, is a multi-channel product that handles customer interactions in both traditional and online channels. RightNow Sales, a sales automation solution, maximizes sales efficiency and productivity. RightNow Marketing reduces the complexity of marketing campaign administration. RightNow Voice offers businesses voice automation services such as call routing, survey tools and customer self-service options. RightNow Feedback increases a firm's real-time customer feedback capture and response options. RightNow CX is intended to aid organizations in offering Internet, contact center and social customer experiences. RightNow Analytics offers service, sales, marketing and feedback analytics tools. The firm's professional services consist of business process optimization, integration services, customer development consultations and customer relations training for contact center staff. Besides its several U.S. offices, the company has international locations in Australia, Japan, the U.K., the Netherlands and Germany. In January 2011, the firm acquired the natural language search solutions provider Q-go.com BV. In October 2011, Oracle Corporation announced plans to acquire RightNow for approximately $1.5 billion.

FINANCIALS: **Sales and profits are in thousands of dollars—add 000 to get the full amount. 2011 Note: Financial information for 2011 was not available for all companies at press time.**

2011 Sales: $	2011 Profits: $
2010 Sales: $185,522	2010 Profits: $28,390
2009 Sales: $152,700	2009 Profits: $5,900
2008 Sales: $140,400	2008 Profits: $-7,300
2007 Sales: $112,077	2007 Profits: $-18,641

U.S. Stock Ticker: RNOW
Int'l Ticker:
Int'l Exchange:
Employees: 978 Fiscal Year Ends: 12/31
Parent Company:

SALARIES/BENEFITS:

Pension Plan:	ESOP Stock Plan:	Profit Sharing:	Top Exec. Salary: $350,000	Bonus: $386,400
Savings Plan:	Stock Purch. Plan:		Second Exec. Salary: $256,539	Bonus: $241,980

OTHER THOUGHTS:

Apparent Women Officers or Directors: 1
Hot Spot for Advancement for Women/Minorities:

LOCATIONS: ("Y" = Yes)

West:	Southwest:	Midwest:	Southeast:	Northeast:	International:
Y	Y	Y		Y	Y

RIVERBED TECHNOLOGY INC

www.riverbed.com

Industry Group Code: 33411

Management:		Sales/Marketing:		Liberal Arts:		Information Systems:		Professionals:		Technical/Scientific:	
Mgmt. Trainees:		Mktg. Professionals:	Y	Gen. Writing/Editing:		Info. Management:	Y	Finance/Acct.:	Y	Engineers, Elec.:	Y
Experienced Mgmt.:	Y	Retail Sales:		Technical Writing:	Y	Software Dev.:	Y	Law:	Y	Engineers, Other:	
Int'l Business:	Y	Commercial/Industrial:	Y	Graphic Arts/Photog.:		Hardware Dev.:		HR/Other:	Y	Health/Lab	
MBA Graduates:	Y	Sales Trainees:		Music:		Consulting/Other:	Y	Training:		Scientists/Research:	
		Advertising Pros.:		Broadcasting:				Health Care:		Petroleum/Chemicals:	
				Other:				Consulting:		Math/Other:	

TYPES OF BUSINESS:

Wide Area Data Services

BRANDS/DIVISIONS/AFFILIATES:

Riverbed Optimization System
Application Streamlining
Transport Streamlining
Steelhead
Central Management Console
Cascade
Aptimize Limited
Expand Networks

CONTACTS:

Note: Officers with more than one job title may be intentionally listed here more than once.

Jerry M. Kennelly, CEO
Randy S. Gottfried, CFO/Exec. VP-Bus. Svcs.
Eric Wolford, Sr. VP-Mktg.
Mark S. Day, Chief Scientist
Steve McCanne, CTO/Exec. VP
Gordon Chaffee, Sr. VP-Eng.
David Olson, Sr. VP-Mfg. & Oper.
Brett A. Nissenberg, General Counsel/Sr. VP
Stephen R. Smoot, VP-Tech. Oper.
Paul O'Farrell, VP-Corp. Dev. & Strategy
Eric Wolford, Exec. VP-GM Prod. Group
Paul Brady, GM-Cascade Bus. Unit/Sr. VP
Jerry M. Kennelly, Chmn.
David M. Peranich, Sr. VP-Worldwide Sales

Phone: 415-247-8800 **Fax:** 415-247-8801
Toll-Free:
Address: 199 Fremont St., San Francisco, CA 94105 US

GROWTH PLANS/SPECIAL FEATURES:

Riverbed Technology, Inc. provides wide-area data service (WDS) products designed to enable organizations with more than one office to overcome such problems as poor application performance and insufficient bandwidth at remote sites. Riverbed's Steelhead appliances improve the performance of applications and access to data across wide area networks (WANs), typically increasing transmission speeds by 5-50 times, by reducing application protocol inefficiencies through its proprietary Application Streamlining techniques, reducing network protocol inefficiencies through its proprietary Transport Streamlining techniques and reducing bandwidth requirements through its proprietary Data Streamlining techniques and data compression. The company's Steelhead appliances, which consist of its Riverbed Optimization System (RiOS) software embedded on a general purpose hardware computing platform, are installed at both ends of a WAN connection and are designed to be more easily and transparently integrated into existing networks than alternative products. Riverbed's Central Management Console (CMC) is a complimentary product designed to centrally manage many Steelhead appliances distributed across a WAN, simplifying the tasks of deploying, configuring, monitoring, reporting and upgrading large numbers of Steelhead appliances. The Cascade product line, including the Express, Cascade Pilot and Shark products, allow for the management, security and performance optimization of global applications. The Whitewater appliances and Virtual Whitewater product line are cloud storage accelerators, created to allow users the ability to accelerate, re-duplicate and to secure data that is stored in public clouds. Riverbed's products have been sold to over 8,700 customers worldwide in such industries as manufacturing, finance, technology, government, architecture, engineering, professional services, utilities, healthcare, media and retail. In July 2011, the firm acquired Aptimize Limited and Zeus Technology. In January 2012, the firm purchased Expand Networks.

FINANCIALS:

Sales and profits are in thousands of dollars—add 000 to get the full amount. 2011 Note: Financial information for 2011 was not available for all companies at press time.

2011 Sales: $726,476 — 2011 Profits: $63,807
2010 Sales: $551,889 — 2010 Profits: $34,158
2009 Sales: $394,146 — 2009 Profits: $7,085
2008 Sales: $333,349 — 2008 Profits: $10,601
2007 Sales: $236,406 — 2007 Profits: $14,798

U.S. Stock Ticker: RVBD
Int'l Ticker:
Int'l Exchange:
Employees: 1,244 Fiscal Year Ends: 12/31
Parent Company:

SALARIES/BENEFITS:

Pension Plan: ESOP Stock Plan: Profit Sharing: Top Exec. Salary: $463,333 Bonus: $1,007,194
Savings Plan: Y Stock Purch. Plan: Y Second Exec. Salary: $344,444 Bonus: $360,075

OTHER THOUGHTS:

Apparent Women Officers or Directors:
Hot Spot for Advancement for Women/Minorities:

LOCATIONS: ("Y" = Yes)

West:	Southwest:	Midwest:	Southeast:	Northeast:	International:
Y	Y	Y		Y	Y

ROBERT W BAIRD & CO INC

www.rwbaird.com

Industry Group Code: 523110

Management:		Sales/Marketing:		Liberal Arts:		Information Systems:		Professionals:		Technical/Scientific:	
Mgmt. Trainees:		Mktg. Professionals:		Gen. Writing/Editing:	Y	Info. Management:	Y	Finance/Acct.:	Y	Engineers, Elec.:	
Experienced Mgmt.:	Y	Retail Sales:		Technical Writing:		Software Dev.:	Y	Law:	Y	Engineers, Other:	
Int'l Business:	Y	Commercial/Industrial:		Graphic Arts/Photog.:		Hardware Dev.:		HR/Other:	Y	Health/Lab	
MBA Graduates:	Y	Sales Trainees:		Music:		Consulting/Other:		Training:	Y	Scientists/Research:	
		Advertising Pros.:		Broadcasting:				Health Care:		Petroleum/Chemicals:	
				Other:				Consulting:		Math/Other:	

TYPES OF BUSINESS:

Investment Banking
Investment Management
Stock Brokerage
Research
Financial Advising
Private Equity
Venture Capital

BRANDS/DIVISIONS/AFFILIATES:

Baird
Baird Capital Partners Asia
Baird Financial Advisors
Baird Capital Partners
Baird Venture Partners
Baird Advisors
Baird Investment Management
Harris Research

CONTACTS: *Note: Officers with more than one job title may be intentionally listed here more than once.*

Paul E. Purcell, CEO
Russell P. Schwei, COO
Paul E. Purcell, Pres.
Dominick P. Zarcone, CFO
Leslie H. Dixon, Chief Human Capital Officer
Glen F. Hackmann, General Counsel/Corp. Sec.
John D. Rumpf, Dir.-Corp. Comm.
Keith A. Kolb, Dir.-Public Finance
Mary Ellen Stanek, Chief Investment Officer
Mark A. Roble, Dir.-Risk Mgmt.
Steven G. Booth, Dir.-Investment Banking
Paul J. Carbone, Dir.-Private Equity Group
Paul E. Purcell, Chmn.
John A. Fordham, Chmn.-Baird Int'l

Phone: 414-765-3500 **Fax:** 414-765-3912
Toll-Free: 800-792-2473
Address: 777 E. Wisconsin Ave., Milwaukee, WI 53202 US

GROWTH PLANS/SPECIAL FEATURES:

Robert W. Baird & Co., Inc. is a Wisconsin-based wealth management, capital markets, private equity and asset management firm. Doing business as Baird, the firm serves corporate, institutional and high-net-worth clients in the U.S., Europe and Asia. The company has over $88 billion under management. The employee-owned firm specializes in the areas of public finance and equity research. Baird operates in five segments: private wealth management, equity capital markets, private equity, fixed income capital markets and asset management. The private wealth management group provides personalized financial advice to help corporate and individual investors grow and preserve their wealth and address client concerns such as wealth transfer, tax management, financial planning and asset allocation. Baird's equity capital markets group offers research, institutional equity services and investment banking. The private equity division, operating through Baird Capital Partners, Baird Venture Partners, Baird Capital Partners Asia and Baird Capital Partners Europe, focuses on smaller, high-potential firms and strives to maximize the value creation opportunities of its portfolio companies. The fixed income capital markets group provides fixed income sales and trading, and houses a public finance division. Baird provides asset management through Baird Advisors, Baird Public Investment Advisors and Baird Investment Management. In January 2011, Baird sold Aston Carter Group Limited to Allegis Group. In June 2011, Baird Capital Partners Asia made an investment in Chinese instrumentation valve and fitting producer Jiangsu Xinghe Valve Co. In mid 2011, Baird Venture Partners sold Accuri Cytometers to Becton, Dickinson and Company. In 2011, Baird Capital Partners acquired Justrite Manufacturing Company, L.L.C.; sold its interest in Medical Education Technologies, Inc. to CAE; and acquired Harris Research, Inc. from The Home Depot.

The firm offers employee benefits including medical, dental, vision, life, accident and disability coverage.

FINANCIALS: **Sales and profits are in thousands of dollars—add 000 to get the full amount. 2011 Note: Financial information for 2011 was not available for all companies at press time.**

2011 Sales: $ — 2011 Profits: $
2010 Sales: $ — 2010 Profits: $
2009 Sales: $718,000 — 2009 Profits: $
2008 Sales: $680,000 — 2008 Profits: $
2007 Sales: $729,000 — 2007 Profits: $

U.S. Stock Ticker: Private
Int'l Ticker:
Int'l Exchange:
Employees: Fiscal Year Ends: 12/31
Parent Company:

SALARIES/BENEFITS:

Pension Plan: ESOP Stock Plan: Profit Sharing: Y Top Exec. Salary: $ Bonus: $
Savings Plan: Y Stock Purch. Plan: Second Exec. Salary: $ Bonus: $

OTHER THOUGHTS:

Apparent Women Officers or Directors: 3
Hot Spot for Advancement for Women/Minorities: Y

LOCATIONS: ("Y" = Yes)

West:	Southwest:	Midwest:	Southeast:	Northeast:	International:
Y	Y	Y	Y	Y	Y

ROCKY BRANDS INC

www.rockyboots.com

Industry Group Code: 316219

Management:		Sales/Marketing:		Liberal Arts:		Information Systems:		Professionals:		Technical/Scientific:	
Mgmt. Trainees:		Mktg. Professionals:	Y	Gen. Writing/Editing:	Y	Info. Management:	Y	Finance/Acct.:	Y	Engineers, Elec.:	
Experienced Mgmt.:	Y	Retail Sales:		Technical Writing:		Software Dev.:		Law:	Y	Engineers, Other:	
Int'l Business:		Commercial/Industrial:	Y	Graphic Arts/Photog.:	Y	Hardware Dev.:		HR/Other:	Y	Health/Lab	
MBA Graduates:	Y	Sales Trainees:	Y	Music:		Consulting/Other:		Training:	Y	Scientists/Research:	
		Advertising Pros.:	Y	Broadcasting:				Health Care:		Petroleum/Chemicals:	
				Other:	Y			Consulting:		Math/Other:	

TYPES OF BUSINESS:

Footwear
Outdoor & Work Apparel, Footwear & Accessories
Duty & Western Apparel, Footwear & Accessories
Retail Stores

BRANDS/DIVISIONS/AFFILIATES:

Rocky
Durango
Georgia Boot
Lehigh
Rocky Outdoor Gear

CONTACTS: *Note: Officers with more than one job title may be intentionally listed here more than once.*

Mike Brooks, CEO
David Sharp, COO
David Sharp, Pres.
James E. McDonald, CFO/Exec. VP
Curtis Loveland, Sec.
James E. McDonald, Treas.
Mike Brooks, Chmn.

Phone: 740-753-1951	**Fax:** 740-753-4024
Toll-Free: 877-795-2410	
Address: 39 E. Canal St., Nelsonville, OH 45764 US	

GROWTH PLANS/SPECIAL FEATURES:

Rocky Brands, Inc. is a designer, manufacturer and marketer of footwear. The firm's portfolio of brand names includes Rocky Outdoor Gear, Georgia Boot, Durango and Lehigh. The company also licenses the Michelin and Mossy Oak brands. Its products are organized around four target markets: outdoor, work, duty and western. The outdoor product lines consist of footwear, apparel and accessory items, which are typically waterproof and insulated. The work product lines consist of footwear and apparel marketed to industrial and construction workers, as well as workers in the hospitality industry. The duty product line consists of footwear products marketed to law enforcement, security personnel and postal employees who are required to spend a majority of time at work on their feet. The western product line consists of authentic footwear products marketed to farmers and ranchers who generally live in rural communities in North America. The firm's products are distributed through three distinct business segments: wholesale, retail and military. The wholesale segment distributes products through a wide range of distribution channels representing over 10,000 retail store locations in the U.S. and Canada. Wholesale channels vary by product line and include sporting goods stores, outdoor retailers, independent shoe retailers, hardware stores, catalogs, mass merchants, uniform stores, farm store chains and other specialty retailers. The retail business includes direct sales of products to consumers through the Lehigh Safety Shoes mobile and retail stores (including a fleet of trucks supported by small warehouses that include retail stores); the Rocky outlet store; and the company's web site. The military division sells footwear under the Rocky label to the U.S. military.

FINANCIALS: **Sales and profits are in thousands of dollars—add 000 to get the full amount. 2011 Note: Financial information for 2011 was not available for all companies at press time.**

2011 Sales: $239,600	2011 Profits: $8,300	**U.S. Stock Ticker: RCKY**
2010 Sales: $252,792	2010 Profits: $7,684	**Int'l Ticker:**
2009 Sales: $229,486	2009 Profits: $1,175	Int'l Exchange:
2008 Sales: $259,538	2008 Profits: $1,167	Employees: 2,450 Fiscal Year Ends: 12/31
2007 Sales: $275,267	2007 Profits: $-23,105	Parent Company:

SALARIES/BENEFITS:

Pension Plan:	ESOP Stock Plan:	Profit Sharing:	Top Exec. Salary: $475,000	Bonus: $441,763
Savings Plan: Y	Stock Purch. Plan:		Second Exec. Salary: $398,100	Bonus: $308,537

OTHER THOUGHTS:

Apparent Women Officers or Directors:
Hot Spot for Advancement for Women/Minorities:

LOCATIONS: ("Y" = Yes)

West:	Southwest:	Midwest:	Southeast:	Northeast:	International:
		Y			

ROGERS CORPORATION

Industry Group Code: 3261

www.rogerscorp.com

Management:		Sales/Marketing:		Liberal Arts:		Information Systems:		Professionals:		Technical/Scientific:	
Mgmt. Trainees:		Mktg. Professionals:	Y	Gen. Writing/Editing:		Info. Management:	Y	Finance/Acct.:	Y	Engineers, Elec.:	
Experienced Mgmt.:	Y	Retail Sales:		Technical Writing:	Y	Software Dev.:		Law:	Y	Engineers, Other:	
Int'l Business:	Y	Commercial/Industrial:	Y	Graphic Arts/Photog.:		Hardware Dev.:		HR/Other:	Y	Health/Lab	
MBA Graduates:	Y	Sales Trainees:		Music:		Consulting/Other:		Training:	Y	Scientists/Research:	Y
		Advertising Pros.:		Broadcasting:				Health Care:		Petroleum/Chemicals:	
				Other:				Consulting:		Math/Other:	Y

TYPES OF BUSINESS:

Specialty Polymer Composite Materials
Printed Circuit Materials
High-Performance Foams
Polymer Materials & Components
Elastomers

BRANDS/DIVISIONS/AFFILIATES:

PORON
BISCO
RO-LINX
DUREL
NITROPHYL
ENDUR
Rogers Chan Chung Technologies, Inc.
Curamik Electronics GmbH

CONTACTS: *Note: Officers with more than one job title may be intentionally listed here more than once.*

Robert D. Wachob, CEO
Robert D. Wachob, Pres.
Dennis M. Loughran, CFO
Jeffrey Grudzien, VP-Mktg. & Sales
Robert C. Daigle, CTO/Sr. VP
Robert Soffer, Sec./VP
Dennis M. Loughran, VP-Finance
Debra Granger, VP-Corp. Compliance & Controls
Michael D. Bessette, VP-Advanced Circuit Materials Div.
Luc Van Eenaeme, VP-Rogers Europe
Peter G. Kaczmarek, Sr. VP
Michael N. Sehnert, VP-Rogers Asia
Michael L. Cooper, VP-Logistics

Phone: 860-774-9605	**Fax:** 860-779-5509
Toll-Free: 800-227-6437	
Address: 1 Technology Dr., Rogers, CT 06263-0188 US	

GROWTH PLANS/SPECIAL FEATURES:

Rogers Corporation, founded in 1832, manufactures and sells specialty polymer composite materials and components. Rogers operates in three business segments: Core Strategic, Development Stage, and Other. The Core Strategic segment is comprised of three divisions: Printed Circuit Materials (PCM), High Performance Foams (HPF) and Power Distribution Systems (PDS). PCM includes flexible and rigid printed circuit board (PCB) laminates for high-frequency, high-performance applications. Rigid PCB materials brands include RO3000, RO4000, DUROID, RO2800 and TMM laminates. These laminates are used for making circuitry that receive, transmit and process high frequency communications signals. High Performance Foams includes several brands of polyurethane and silicone foams. The PORON brand includes urethane foams used to manufacture high-performance gaskets and seals in vehicles, communications devices, computers and peripherals; cushion insole materials for footwear and related products; healthcare and medical materials for body cushioning and orthotic appliances; and compressible printing plate backing and mounting products for cushioning flexographic plates for printing on packaging materials. BISCO brand silicone foams are used to manufacture flame-retardant gaskets and seals in communications infrastructure equipment, aircraft, trains and automobiles. The PDS division includes the firm's busbar products, which are primarily used in power distribution system products in mass transit and renewable energy applications. Rogers' Development Stage segment includes two divisions: Printed and Electronic Solutions, which manufactures manufacture DUREL electroluminescent lamps and sells inverters that power the EL lamps; and Thermal Management Solutions, a start-up group that aims to eventually serve markets where thermal heat management is a priority, such as heat dissipation in electronic devices. The company's Other segment is involved in elastomer components, polyimide laminate systems and nonwoven composite materials. In late 2010, the firm sold its 50% ownership of joint venture Rogers Chan Chung Technologies, Inc. to venture partner Chan Chung Plastics Co., Ltd. In January 2011, Rogers acquired Curamik Electronics GmbH.

FINANCIALS: **Sales and profits are in thousands of dollars—add 000 to get the full amount. 2011 Note: Financial information for 2011 was not available for all companies at press time.**

2011 Sales: $553,150	2011 Profits: $37,055
2010 Sales: $379,188	2010 Profits: $34,571
2009 Sales: $291,821	2009 Profits: $-62,870
2008 Sales: $365,362	2008 Profits: $21,617
2007 Sales: $412,698	2007 Profits: $20,625

U.S. Stock Ticker: ROG
Int'l Ticker:
Int'l Exchange:
Employees: 1,940 Fiscal Year Ends: 12/31
Parent Company:

SALARIES/BENEFITS:

Pension Plan:	ESOP Stock Plan:	Profit Sharing:	Top Exec. Salary: $500,032	Bonus: $1,168,075
Savings Plan: Y	Stock Purch. Plan: Y		Second Exec. Salary: $290,480	Bonus: $384,277

OTHER THOUGHTS:

Apparent Women Officers or Directors: 3
Hot Spot for Advancement for Women/Minorities: Y

LOCATIONS: ("Y" = Yes)

West:	Southwest:	Midwest:	Southeast:	Northeast:	International:
	Y	Y		Y	Y

ROSETTA STONE INC

www.rosettastone.com

Industry Group Code: 511210P

Management:		Sales/Marketing:		Liberal Arts:		Information Systems:		Professionals:		Technical/Scientific:	
Mgmt. Trainees:		Mktg. Professionals:	Y	Gen. Writing/Editing:	Y	Info. Management:	Y	Finance/Acct.:	Y	Engineers, Elec.:	
Experienced Mgmt.:	Y	Retail Sales:		Technical Writing:		Software Dev.:	Y	Law:	Y	Engineers, Other:	
Int'l Business:		Commercial/Industrial:		Graphic Arts/Photog.:	Y	Hardware Dev.:		HR/Other:	Y	Health/Lab	
MBA Graduates:	Y	Sales Trainees:		Music:		Consulting/Other:		Training:	Y	Scientists/Research:	
		Advertising Pros.:	Y	Broadcasting:				Health Care:		Petroleum/Chemicals:	
				Other:	Y			Consulting:		Math/Other:	

TYPES OF BUSINESS:

Language Learning Software

BRANDS/DIVISIONS/AFFILIATES:

Rosetta Stone
Dynamic Immersion
Rosetta Stone Version 4TOTALe
Rosetta Stone ReFLEX

CONTACTS:

Note: Officers with more than one job title may be intentionally listed here more than once.

Tom P.H. Adams, CEO
Steve Swad, CFO
Michaela Oliver, Sr. VP-Human Resources
Pradeep Mannakkara, CIO
Mike Fulkerson, CTO
Michael Wu, General Counsel/Corp. Sec.
Jay Topper, Sr. VP-Customer Success
Judy Verses, Pres., Global Institutions
Greg Keim, Chief Innovation Officer
Laurence Franklin, Chmn.
Tak Shiohama, Pres., Rosetta Stone Japan, Inc.

Phone: **Fax:**
Toll-Free: 1-800-811-2755
Address: 1919 N. Lynn St., 7th Fl., Arlington, VA 22209 US

GROWTH PLANS/SPECIAL FEATURES:

Rosetta Stone, Inc. is a leading provider of technology-based language learning programs. The company develops, markets and sells learning systems consisting of software, online services and audio practice tools primarily under its Rosetta Stone brand. The company's teaching method, known as Dynamic Immersion, is designed to leverage the natural language learning ability that children use to learn their native language. Its interactive courses are based on proprietary technology and pedagogical content and utilize sequences of images, texts and sounds to teach a new language without translation or grammar explanation. By using over 10,000 photographic images and 15,000 professionally recorded sound files per software version, Rosetta Stone programs are more easily deployed across many languages. The company's proprietary student management system allows teachers and administrators to configure their own lesson plans using the Rosetta Stone content and allows for the capability of easily reviewing the student's progress. The firm's courses cover 34 languages and its customers include individuals, educational institutions, branches of the armed forces, government agencies and corporations. Approximately 79% of the firm's revenue in 2010 was generated through its consumer sales channels, which include call centers, web sites, retail resellers and over 300 kiosk locations. In August 2011, the company launched their Rosetta Stone ReFLEX and Rosetta Stone Version 4TOTALe products in Korea. In November 2011, the firm announced contracts with educational and government institutions in Colombia, Panama, Mexico and the Caribbean.

FINANCIALS:

Sales and profits are in thousands of dollars—add 000 to get the full amount. 2011 Note: Financial information for 2011 was not available for all companies at press time.

2011 Sales: $268,400	2011 Profits: $-20,000	**U.S. Stock Ticker: RST**
2010 Sales: $258,686	2010 Profits: $13,284	**Int'l Ticker:**
2009 Sales: $252,271	2009 Profits: $13,363	Int'l Exchange:
2008 Sales: $209,380	2008 Profits: $13,892	Employees: 1,800 Fiscal Year Ends: 12/31
2007 Sales: $	2007 Profits: $	Parent Company:

SALARIES/BENEFITS:

Pension Plan:	ESOP Stock Plan:	Profit Sharing:	Top Exec. Salary: $425,000	Bonus: $
Savings Plan:	Stock Purch. Plan:		Second Exec. Salary: $240,000	Bonus: $

OTHER THOUGHTS:

Apparent Women Officers or Directors: 5
Hot Spot for Advancement for Women/Minorities: Y

LOCATIONS: ("Y" = Yes)

West:	Southwest:	Midwest:	Southeast:	Northeast:	International:
Y	Y	Y	Y	Y	

ROVI CORPORATION

www.rovicorp.com

Industry Group Code: 511210L

Management:		Sales/Marketing:		Liberal Arts:		Information Systems:		Professionals:		Technical/Scientific:	
Mgmt. Trainees:		Mktg. Professionals:	Y	Gen. Writing/Editing:	Y	Info. Management:	Y	Finance/Acct.:	Y	Engineers, Elec.:	Y
Experienced Mgmt.:	Y	Retail Sales:		Technical Writing:	Y	Software Dev.:	Y	Law:	Y	Engineers, Other:	
Int'l Business:	Y	Commercial/Industrial:	Y	Graphic Arts/Photog.:		Hardware Dev.:		HR/Other:	Y	Health/Lab Scientists/Research:	
MBA Graduates:	Y	Sales Trainees:	Y	Music:		Consulting/Other:		Training:		Petroleum/Chemicals:	
		Advertising Pros.:		Broadcasting:				Health Care:		Math/Other:	
				Other:				Consulting:			

TYPES OF BUSINESS:

Software-Video Copyright Protection
Digital Rights Management Technologies

BRANDS/DIVISIONS/AFFILIATES:

Sonic Solutions
Analog Copy Protection (ACP)
RipGuard
BD+
TotalGuide
M7 Group S.A.

CONTACTS:

Note: Officers with more than one job title may be intentionally listed here more than once.

Tom Carson, CEO
Tom Carson, Pres.
James Budge, CFO
Corey Ferengul, Exec. VP-Products
Eileen Schloss, Exec. VP-Human Resources
Stephen Yu, General Counsel/Exec. VP/Corp. Sec.
Jim Wickett, Exec. VP-Corp. Dev.
Andrew K. Ludwick, Chmn.

Phone: 408-562-8400	**Fax:**
Toll-Free:	
Address: 2830 De La Cruz Blvd., Santa Clara, CA 95050 US	

GROWTH PLANS/SPECIAL FEATURES:

Rovi Corporation provides a broad set of technologies and services that enable businesses to protect, enhance and distribute their digital goods to consumers across multiple channels. The company's products include embedded licensing technologies such as recommendations and search capability; interactive program guides (IPGs) including the firm's TotalGuide applications; digital rights management products and technologies; embedded licensing technologies; and licensing of the firm's extensive information database. Rovi Corporation also allows customers to license patents and deploy their own IPG or a third party IPG. The firm's products are deployed in three market divisions: consumer electronics (CE) manufacturers, including set-top box manufacturers, digital TV providers, DVD player manufacturers, PC DVD drive suppliers and network-attached storage device providers; service providers, such as satellite, cable, mobile, telecommunications and Internet service providers; and other. The other division includes the company's entertainment company content protection products and services such as Analog Copy Protection (ACP), RipGuard and BD+ for digital content owners and system operators. Its content security technology customers have included Columbia-TriStar, Twentieth Century Fox Home Entertainment, Buena Vista Home Video, HBO Studio Productions and Warner Home Video DVD. The other segment also handles the licensing of Rovi Corporation's database of descriptive information about television, movie, music and game content. The database includes 450,000 movies; over 3.5 million television series episodes; searchable data on nearly every television show produced since 1960; and information regarding roughly 2.4 million music albums, 22 million music tracks, 65,000 video games and 8 million books. In March 2011, M7 Group S.A. joined the company's patent licensing program. In June 2011, the firm and Cogeco Cable formed a partnership agreement to launch the Rovi TotalGuide applications in Canada.

Rovi Corporation's employees receive life, disability, medical, dental and vision insurance; educational assistance; 11 paid holidays; and flexible spending accounts.

FINANCIALS:

Sales and profits are in thousands of dollars—add 000 to get the full amount. 2011 Note: Financial information for 2011 was not available for all companies at press time.

2011 Sales: $690,810	2011 Profits: $-41,286
2010 Sales: $541,490	2010 Profits: $212,884
2009 Sales: $483,911	2009 Profits: $-52,951
2008 Sales: $330,045	2008 Profits: $-114,060
2007 Sales: $155,685	2007 Profits: $31,500

U.S. Stock Ticker: ROVI
Int'l Ticker:
Int'l Exchange:
Employees: 1,200 Fiscal Year Ends: 12/31
Parent Company:

SALARIES/BENEFITS:

Pension Plan:	ESOP Stock Plan:	Profit Sharing:	Top Exec. Salary: $550,000	Bonus: $440,250
Savings Plan: Y	Stock Purch. Plan: Y		Second Exec. Salary: $447,352	Bonus: $48,929

OTHER THOUGHTS:

Apparent Women Officers or Directors: 1
Hot Spot for Advancement for Women/Minorities:

LOCATIONS: ("Y" = Yes)

West:	Southwest:	Midwest:	Southeast:	Northeast:	International:
Y	Y	Y		Y	Y

RPC INC

www.rpc.net

Industry Group Code: 213112

Management:		Sales/Marketing:		Liberal Arts:		Information Systems:		Professionals:		Technical/Scientific:	
Mgmt. Trainees:		Mktg. Professionals:	Y	Gen. Writing/Editing:		Info. Management:	Y	Finance/Acct.:	Y	Engineers, Elec.:	Y
Experienced Mgmt.:	Y	Retail Sales:		Technical Writing:		Software Dev.:		Law:	Y	Engineers, Other:	Y
Int'l Business:	Y	Commercial/Industrial:	Y	Graphic Arts/Photog.:		Hardware Dev.:		HR/Other:	Y	Health/Lab	
MBA Graduates:	Y	Sales Trainees:		Music:		Consulting/Other:		Training:	Y	Scientists/Research:	
		Advertising Pros.:		Broadcasting:				Health Care:		Petroleum/Chemicals:	Y
				Other:				Consulting:		Math/Other:	

TYPES OF BUSINESS:

Oil & Gas Technical & Support Services
Equipment Rental
Oilfield Services

BRANDS/DIVISIONS/AFFILIATES:

Bronco Oilfield Services
Patterson Rental & Fishing Tools
Well Control School
Cudd Energy Services
Thru Tubing Solutions

CONTACTS: *Note: Officers with more than one job title may be intentionally listed here more than once.*

Richard A. Hubbell, CEO
Richard A. Hubbell, Pres.
Ben M. Palmer, CFO/VP/Treas.
Linda H. Graham, Sec./VP
Sharon A. Lennon, Mgr.-Corp. Comm.
Sharon A. Lennon, Mgr.-Investor Rel.
James C. Landers, VP-Corp. Finance
R. Randall Rollins, Chmn.

Phone: 404-321-2140 **Fax:** 404-321-5483
Toll-Free:
Address: 2801 Buford Hwy., Ste. 520, Atlanta, GA 30329 US

GROWTH PLANS/SPECIAL FEATURES:

RPC, Inc. is an energy holding company whose operating units provide specialized oilfield services and equipment. The firm primarily serves independent and major oil and gas companies engaged in the exploration, production and development of oil and gas properties. Its clients operate in the Gulf of Mexico, mid-continent, southwest, Rocky Mountain and Appalachian regions, and in certain international markets including Canada, Cameroon, Egypt, Gabon, South Africa, Bolivia, Mexico, New Zealand, Oman and the United Arab Emirates. RPC services and equipment offered include pressure pumping services; coiled tubing services; snubbing services; nitrogen services; drill pipe and other specialized oilfield equipment rental services; downhole tool rental services; and firefighting and well control. The company operates in two segments: technical services and support services. The technical services segment handles the firm's oil and gas service lines, which perform value-added completion, production and maintenance services directly to customer wells. This segment's equipment and services offerings include pressure pumping, coiled tubing, snubbing, nitrogen, well control, downhole tools, wireline and fishing. RPC's support services division includes the company's oil and gas service lines that primarily provide equipment for customer use or services to assist client operations. Equipment and service offerings include drill pipe and related tools; pipe handling; pipe inspection; storage services; and oilfield training services. Both technical services and support services division customers primarily include certain nationally owned oil companies and domestic producers of major multi-national and independent oil and gas firms. RPC operates through units including Cudd Energy Services; Patterson Rental and Fishing Tools; Bronco Oilfield Services; Thru Tubing Solutions; and Well Control School.

FINANCIALS: **Sales and profits are in thousands of dollars—add 000 to get the full amount. 2011 Note: Financial information for 2011 was not available for all companies at press time.**

2011 Sales: $1,809,800
2010 Sales: $1,096,384
2009 Sales: $587,863
2008 Sales: $876,977
2007 Sales: $690,226

2011 Profits: $296,400
2010 Profits: $146,742
2009 Profits: $-22,745
2008 Profits: $83,403
2007 Profits: $87,049

U.S. Stock Ticker: RES
Int'l Ticker:
Int'l Exchange:
Employees: 2,500 Fiscal Year Ends: 12/31
Parent Company:

SALARIES/BENEFITS:

Pension Plan:
Savings Plan:
ESOP Stock Plan:
Stock Purch. Plan:
Profit Sharing:
Top Exec. Salary: $669,375 Bonus: $1,050,000
Second Exec. Salary: $573,750 Bonus: $900,000

OTHER THOUGHTS:

Apparent Women Officers or Directors: 2
Hot Spot for Advancement for Women/Minorities:

LOCATIONS: ("Y" = Yes)

West:	Southwest:	Midwest:	Southeast:	Northeast:	International:
Y	Y		Y	Y	

RSA SECURITY INC

www.rsa.com

Industry Group Code: 511210E

Management:		Sales/Marketing:		Liberal Arts:		Information Systems:		Professionals:		Technical/Scientific:	
Mgmt. Trainees:		Mktg. Professionals:	Y	Gen. Writing/Editing:		Info. Management:	Y	Finance/Acct.:	Y	Engineers, Elec.:	Y
Experienced Mgmt.:	Y	Retail Sales:		Technical Writing:	Y	Software Dev.:	Y	Law:	Y	Engineers, Other:	
Int'l Business:	Y	Commercial/Industrial:	Y	Graphic Arts/Photog.:		Hardware Dev.:		HR/Other:	Y	Health/Lab	
MBA Graduates:	Y	Sales Trainees:	Y	Music:		Consulting/Other:		Training:	Y	Scientists/Research:	
		Advertising Pros.:	Y	Broadcasting:				Health Care:		Petroleum/Chemicals:	
				Other:				Consulting:		Math/Other:	

TYPES OF BUSINESS:

Computer Software-Security
Data Encryption Tools
Web Access Management Products

BRANDS/DIVISIONS/AFFILIATES:

NetWitness Corporation
RSA Authentication Manager
RSA BSAFE
RSA Certificate Manager
RSA Access Manager
RSA SecurID Token
RSA Data Security System
RSA Data Loss Prevention Suite

CONTACTS: *Note: Officers with more than one job title may be intentionally listed here more than once.*

Thomas P. Heiser, Pres.
Bret Hartman, CTO
Dan Schiappa, Sr. VP-Prod.
Arthur W. Coviello, Jr., Exec. Chmn.

Phone: 781-515-5000	**Fax:** 781-515-5010
Toll-Free: 800-495-1095	
Address: 174 Middlesex Turnpike, Bedford, MA 01730 US	

GROWTH PLANS/SPECIAL FEATURES:

RSA Security, Inc., a subsidiary of EMC Corporation, is a provider of e-business security solutions in the telecommunications, pharmaceutical, financial and health care industries. RSA also caters to academic institutions, research laboratories and government organizations. The firm's secure mobile and remote access products include RSA SecurID authenticators and RSA Key Manager server software. They provide centrally managed two-factor user authentication systems for enterprise networks, operating systems, e-business web sites and other information technology infrastructures. SecurID software protects network resources by ensuring that only authorized users are granted access to information resources. RSA's secure enterprise access products manage and secure access to business-critical information resources within the enterprise. The company provides identity and access management capabilities through its RSA Access Manager, which provides a secure environment for web-based resources and centrally controls user access privileges to web-based resources. Other products include RSA BSAFE, a software security solution utilized by the U.S. Department of Defense; RSA enVision, a log, security and information event management solution; and RSA Certificate Manager, which enables organizations to issue, validate and manage digital certificates. The firm also uses its products to provide consumer identity protection and authentication services to the customers of online merchants and financial institutions. RSA Laboratories, which specializes in cryptography and data security, is the company's research center. Recent developments include new capabilities in the RSA Data Security System's encryption and key management suite, designed to secure sensitive data in file systems; the RSA SecurID Token for BlackBerry smartphones; RSA Entitlements Policy Manager for the security of branch offices and large infrastructures; and RSA Data Loss Prevention Suite, which protects sensitive data from loss and misuse. In April 2011, EMC acquired NetWitness Corporation and incorporated it into RSA Security.

FINANCIALS: **Sales and profits are in thousands of dollars—add 000 to get the full amount. 2011 Note: Financial information for 2011 was not available for all companies at press time.**

2011 Sales: $
2010 Sales: $729,400
2009 Sales: $606,000
2008 Sales: $581,300
2007 Sales: $

2011 Profits: $
2010 Profits: $
2009 Profits: $
2008 Profits: $
2007 Profits: $

U.S. Stock Ticker: Subsidiary
Int'l Ticker:
Int'l Exchange:
Employees: Fiscal Year Ends: 12/31
Parent Company: EMC CORP

SALARIES/BENEFITS:

Pension Plan:	ESOP Stock Plan:	Profit Sharing:	Top Exec. Salary: $	Bonus: $
Savings Plan:	Stock Purch. Plan:		Second Exec. Salary: $	Bonus: $

OTHER THOUGHTS:

Apparent Women Officers or Directors:
Hot Spot for Advancement for Women/Minorities:

LOCATIONS: ("Y" = Yes)

West:	Southwest:	Midwest:	Southeast:	Northeast:	International:
Y				Y	Y

S1 CORPORATION

www.s1.com

Industry Group Code: 511201

Management:		Sales/Marketing:		Liberal Arts:		Information Systems:		Professionals:		Technical/Scientific:	
Mgmt. Trainees:		Mktg. Professionals:	Y	Gen. Writing/Editing:	Y	Info. Management:	Y	Finance/Acct.:	Y	Engineers, Elec.:	Y
Experienced Mgmt.:	Y	Retail Sales:		Technical Writing:	Y	Software Dev.:	Y	Law:	Y	Engineers, Other:	
Int'l Business:	Y	Commercial/Industrial:	Y	Graphic Arts/Photog.:		Hardware Dev.:		HR/Other:	Y	Health/Lab	
MBA Graduates:	Y	Sales Trainees:	Y	Music:		Consulting/Other:		Training:	Y	Scientists/Research:	
		Advertising Pros.:		Broadcasting:				Health Care:		Petroleum/Chemicals:	
				Other:				Consulting:		Math/Other:	

TYPES OF BUSINESS:

Software-Financial Services
Internet Banking Applications

BRANDS/DIVISIONS/AFFILIATES:

Banking: Large FI
Banking: Community FI
ACI Worldwide, Inc.
Payments

CONTACTS: *Note: Officers with more than one job title may be intentionally listed here more than once.*

Johann Dreyer, CEO
Paul M. Parrish, CFO
Greg Orenstein, Chief Legal Officer/Sec.
Greg D. Orenstein, Sr. VP-Corp. Dev.
Francois van Schoor, Pres., Global Payments Bus.
Pierre Naude, Pres., U.S. Branch & Community Financial Bus.
John W. Spiegel, Chmn.
Jan Kruger, Pres., Global Large Financial Institutions

Phone: 404-923-3500 **Fax:** 404-923-6727
Toll-Free: 888-457-2237
Address: 705 Westech Dr., Norcross, GA 30092 US

GROWTH PLANS/SPECIAL FEATURES:

S1 Corporation is a global provider of software and related services that automate the processing of financial transactions. The firm's solutions are designed for financial organizations including banks, credit unions, insurance companies, transaction processors, payment card associations and retailers. S1 operates in three segments: Banking: Large FI; Banking: Community FI; and Payments. The Banking: Large FI segment represents global banking and insurance products and services primarily targeting larger financial institutions. It supports channels that a bank uses to interact with its customers, including self-service channels like the Internet for personal, business and corporate banking, as well as trade finance and mobile banking; and full service channels such as teller, branch, sales and service and call centers. The Banking: Community FI segment represents the community financial, full service banking and lending businesses in North America and global payment processing and management products and services. It provides Internet personal and business banking, voice banking and mobile banking products to community banks and credit unions, as well as payment processing and management offerings that drive ATMs (automated teller machines) and point-of-sale (POS) devices, to financial institutions, retailers, third-party processors, payments associations and other transaction generating endpoints. S1 licenses its suite of online, telephone and mobile banking applications primarily on a subscription only basis. The firm's Payments division provides ATM and point-of-sale driving, card management and merchant acquiring solutions to financial institutions, retailers and transaction processors of all sizes internationally. In October 2011, S1 agreed to be acquired by ACI Worldwide, Inc.

S1 offers its employees a 401(k) plan, and medical, prescription, dental, disability, life, accidental death and travel accident insurance benefits.

FINANCIALS: **Sales and profits are in thousands of dollars—add 000 to get the full amount. 2011 Note: Financial information for 2011 was not available for all companies at press time.**

2011 Sales: $
2010 Sales: $209,086
2009 Sales: $238,927
2008 Sales: $228,435
2007 Sales: $204,925

2011 Profits: $
2010 Profits: $-6,283
2009 Profits: $30,423
2008 Profits: $21,850
2007 Profits: $19,495

U.S. Stock Ticker: SONE
Int'l Ticker:
Int'l Exchange:
Employees: 1,670 Fiscal Year Ends: 12/31
Parent Company:

SALARIES/BENEFITS:

Pension Plan: ESOP Stock Plan: Profit Sharing: Top Exec. Salary: $415,000 Bonus: $
Savings Plan: Y Stock Purch. Plan: Second Exec. Salary: $325,000 Bonus: $

OTHER THOUGHTS:

Apparent Women Officers or Directors:
Hot Spot for Advancement for Women/Minorities:

LOCATIONS: ("Y" = Yes)

West:	Southwest:	Midwest:	Southeast:	Northeast:	International:
Y	Y			Y	Y

SACRAMENTO MUNICIPAL UTILITY DISTRICT www.smud.org

Industry Group Code: 221119

Management:		**Sales/Marketing:**		**Liberal Arts:**		**Information Systems:**		**Professionals:**		**Technical/Scientific:**	
Mgmt. Trainees:		Mktg. Professionals:	Y	Gen. Writing/Editing:	Y	Info. Management:	Y	Finance/Acct.:	Y	Engineers, Elec.:	Y
Experienced Mgmt.:	Y	Retail Sales:		Technical Writing:		Software Dev.:		Law:	Y	Engineers, Other:	Y
Int'l Business:		Commercial/Industrial:	Y	Graphic Arts/Photog.:		Hardware Dev.:		HR/Other:	Y	Health/Lab	
MBA Graduates:	Y	Sales Trainees:	Y	Music:		Consulting/Other:		Training:	Y	Scientists/Research:	
		Advertising Pros.:		Broadcasting:				Health Care:		Petroleum/Chemicals:	Y
				Other:				Consulting:		Math/Other:	

TYPES OF BUSINESS:

Electric Utility
Hydroelectric Generation
Solar Generation
Wind Generation

BRANDS/DIVISIONS/AFFILIATES:

CONTACTS:

Note: Officers with more than one job title may be intentionally listed here more than once.

John DiStasio, CEO/Gen. Mgr.
James Tracy, CFO
Gary King, Dir.-Workforce Mgmt.
Paul Lau, Assistant Gen. Mgr.-Tech.
Arlen Orchard, General Counsel
Elisabeth Brinton, Public Affairs Officer
Jim Shelter, Assistant Gen. Mgr.-Energy Supply
Michael Gianunzio, Dir.-Legislative & Regulatory
Phil West, Dir.-Customer Svcs.

Phone: 916-452-3211 **Fax:** 916-732-5835
Toll-Free:
Address: 6201 S St., Sacramento, CA 95817 US

GROWTH PLANS/SPECIAL FEATURES:

Sacramento Municipal Utility District (SMUD) is one of the largest electric utilities in the U.S. that is owned by a local government. The company serves a 900-square-mile area in the counties of Sacramento and Placer, California. It has approximately 595,076 customers, 529,695 of which are residential and 68,510 of which are commercial customers. SMUD owns over 450 circuit miles of transmission lines and 10,257 circuit miles of distribution lines. The firm, whose peak single day demand has been 3,299 megawatts (MW), uses hydroelectric and cogeneration power plants to create more than half of its electricity and purchases the remainder from alternative energy generation plants. SMUD has one of the largest solar energy distribution systems in the U.S. and operates a solar energy plant with a 3.2-MW capacity. The company has increased generation capacity and created its own transmission control area in order to decrease dependence on third-party energy generators and compete in California's deregulated power market. The firm also has been selected to test hydrogen fuel vehicles. SMUD plans on investing money in methane-generated electricity.

The company offers its employees benefits that include health insurance; the California Public Employees Retirement System defined benefit retirement plan; 401(k) and 457 savings plans; an on-site child care and fitness center; credit union membership; the CalPERS long-term care program; a paid education and employee development program; employee discounts; a personal computer purchase program; an employee social and recreational association; camping privileges in the Sierra Nevada; an employee assistance program; and a rideshare program with commuter vans.

FINANCIALS:

Sales and profits are in thousands of dollars—add 000 to get the full amount. 2011 Note: Financial information for 2011 was not available for all companies at press time.

2011 Sales: $ 2011 Profits: $
2010 Sales: $ 2010 Profits: $
2009 Sales: $ 2009 Profits: $
2008 Sales: $ 2008 Profits: $
2007 Sales: $ 2007 Profits: $

U.S. Stock Ticker: Government-Owned
Int'l Ticker:
Int'l Exchange:
Employees: Fiscal Year Ends: 12/31
Parent Company:

SALARIES/BENEFITS:

Pension Plan: Y ESOP Stock Plan: Profit Sharing: Top Exec. Salary: $ Bonus: $
Savings Plan: Y Stock Purch. Plan: Second Exec. Salary: $ Bonus: $

OTHER THOUGHTS:

Apparent Women Officers or Directors: 1
Hot Spot for Advancement for Women/Minorities:

LOCATIONS: ("Y" = Yes)

West:	Southwest:	Midwest:	Southeast:	Northeast:	International:
Y					

Sales, profits and employees may be estimates. Financial information, benefits and other data can change quickly and may vary from those stated here.

SALIX PHARMACEUTICALS

www.salix.com

Industry Group Code: 325412

Management:		Sales/Marketing:		Liberal Arts:		Information Systems:		Professionals:		Technical/Scientific:	
Mgmt. Trainees:		Mktg. Professionals:	Y	Gen. Writing/Editing:		Info. Management:	Y	Finance/Acct.:	Y	Engineers, Elec.:	
Experienced Mgmt.:	Y	Retail Sales:		Technical Writing:	Y	Software Dev.:	Y	Law:	Y	Engineers, Other:	
Int'l Business:	Y	Commercial/Industrial:	Y	Graphic Arts/Photog.:		Hardware Dev.:		HR/Other:	Y	Health/Lab	Y
MBA Graduates:	Y	Sales Trainees:	Y	Music:		Consulting/Other:		Training:	Y	Scientists/Research:	Y
		Advertising Pros.:		Broadcasting:				Health Care:	Y	Petroleum/Chemicals:	Y
				Other:				Consulting:		Math/Other:	Y

TYPES OF BUSINESS:

Pharmaceuticals Development & Manufacturing
Drugs-Gastroenterology

BRANDS/DIVISIONS/AFFILIATES:

Colazal
Azasan
Proctocort
Anusol-HC
OsmoPrep
Xifaxan
Visicol
Lupin Ltd

CONTACTS:

Note: Officers with more than one job title may be intentionally listed here more than once.

Carolyn J. Logan, CEO
Carolyn J. Logan, Pres.
Adam C. Derbyshire, CFO
William P. Forbes, Exec. VP-R&D
Adam C. Derbyshire, Sr. VP-Admin.
William P. Forbes, Chief Dev. Officer
G. Michael Freeman, VP-Investor Rel.
Adam C. Derbyshire, Exec. VP-Finance
Thomas W. D'Alonzo, Chmn.

Phone: 919-862-1000 | **Fax:** 919-862-1095
Toll-Free: 888-802-9956
Address: 1700 Perimeter Park Dr., Morrisville, NC 27560 US

GROWTH PLANS/SPECIAL FEATURES:

Salix Pharmaceuticals is a specialty pharmaceutical company dedicated to acquiring, developing and commercializing prescription drugs used in the treatment of a variety of gastrointestinal diseases. The company seeks to identify late-stage or approved proprietary therapeutics for in-licensing, which subsequently advances the new drugs through regulatory procedures and final product development stages. The firm's products are divided into three segments GI, Colonoscopy preps and other Salix products. In the GI segment, the company sells Metozolv ODT, a orally indigested metoclopramide tablet; Apriso, a once-a-day tablet for ulcerative colitis; Colazal (balsalazide disodium) treats ulcerative colitis; Xifaxan, an antibiotic for the gut; and Pepcid Oral Suspension, short-term treatment of gastroesophageal reflux disease. In the Colonoscopy prep segment, Salix sells OsmoPrep tablets; MoviPrep oral solution a gastrointestinal-specific oral antibiotic; and Visicol, a product indicated for cleansing of the bowel as a preparation for colonoscopy. Other Salix Products include, Azasan (azathioprine tablets), is intended to suppress immune response in organ transplant recipients; Anusol-HC rectal suppositories; Proctocort, which is available in a cream form that is indicated for the relief of the inflammation and in a suppository form, which is indicated for use in inflamed hemorrhoids and postirradiation proclitis; and Diuril Oral Suspension, treats high blood pressure. The primary product candidates Salix is developing are balsalazide disodium tablets, which the company intends to sell for the treatment of ulcerative colitis; a patented, granulated formula of mesalamine, which it intends to sell for the treatment of ulcerative colitis; Metoclopramide, for short-term therapy following gastroesophageal reflux; budesonide, a foam preparation for the treatment of mild to moderate forms of distal ulcerative colitis; and Vapreotide Acetate Powder, for the treatment of acute esophageal variceal bleeding. In October 2010, the firm acquired Lumacan, a product utilized for early detection of precancerous and cancerous lesions in the colon, from Photocure ASA.

FINANCIALS:

Sales and profits are in thousands of dollars—add 000 to get the full amount. 2011 Note: Financial information for 2011 was not available for all companies at press time.

2011 Sales: $540,488	2011 Profits: $87,399
2010 Sales: $336,973	2010 Profits: $-27,061
2009 Sales: $232,890	2009 Profits: $-43,619
2008 Sales: $178,766	2008 Profits: $-47,037
2007 Sales: $235,792	2007 Profits: $8,225

U.S. Stock Ticker: SLXP
Int'l Ticker:
Int'l Exchange:
Employees: 390 Fiscal Year Ends: 12/31
Parent Company:

SALARIES/BENEFITS:

Pension Plan: | ESOP Stock Plan: | Profit Sharing: Y | Top Exec. Salary: $741,500 | Bonus: $650,683
Savings Plan: Y | Stock Purch. Plan: | Second Exec. Salary: $410,000 | Bonus: $235,750

OTHER THOUGHTS:

Apparent Women Officers or Directors: 1
Hot Spot for Advancement for Women/Minorities:

LOCATIONS: ("Y" = Yes)

West:	Southwest:	Midwest:	Southeast:	Northeast:	International:
				Y	

SANDRIDGE ENERGY INC

www.sandridgeenergy.com

Industry Group Code: 211111

Management:		Sales/Marketing:		Liberal Arts:		Information Systems:		Professionals:		Technical/Scientific:	
Mgmt. Trainees:		Mktg. Professionals:		Gen. Writing/Editing:		Info. Management:	Y	Finance/Acct.:	Y	Engineers, Elec.:	
Experienced Mgmt.:	Y	Retail Sales:		Technical Writing:		Software Dev.:		Law:	Y	Engineers, Other:	Y
Int'l Business:		Commercial/Industrial:		Graphic Arts/Photog.:		Hardware Dev.:		HR/Other:	Y	Health/Lab	
MBA Graduates:	Y	Sales Trainees:		Music:		Consulting/Other:		Training:	Y	Scientists/Research:	
		Advertising Pros.:		Broadcasting:				Health Care:		Petroleum/Chemicals:	Y
				Other:				Consulting:		Math/Other:	

TYPES OF BUSINESS:

Oil & Gas Exploration & Production
Oil Well Drilling Services
Oilfield Services
Natural Gas Gathering & Compression
Carbon Dioxide Treatment
Oil Recovery Services

BRANDS/DIVISIONS/AFFILIATES:

Lariat Services, Inc.
SandRidge Midstream, Inc.
SandRidge Tertiary, LLC.
Arena Resources Inc

CONTACTS:

Note: Officers with more than one job title may be intentionally listed here more than once.

Tom L. Ward, CEO
Matthew K. Grubb, COO
Matthew K. Grubb, Pres.
James D. Bennet, CFO/Exec. VP
Mary L. Whitson, Sr. VP-Human Resources
Thomas L. Winton, CIO/Sr. VP-IT
Rodney E. Johnson, Exec. VP-Resevoir Eng.
Philip Warman, General Counsel/Corp. Sec./Sr. VP
David C. Lawler, Exec. VP-Oper.
Kevin R. White, Sr. VP-Bus. Dev.
Randall D. Cooley, Sr. VP-Acct.
Wayne C. Chang, Sr. VP-SandRidge Energy, Inc.
Todd N. Tipton, Exec. VP-Exploration
Craig A. Johnson, Sr. VP-Oper.
Tom L. Ward, Chmn.

GROWTH PLANS/SPECIAL FEATURES:

SandRidge Energy, Inc. (SE), based in Oklahoma City, is an oil exploration and production company. The firm operates in three business segments: exploration and production, drilling and oilfield services and midstream gas services. The exploration and production segment focuses on shallow, conventional, domestic on-shore oil basins. Primary areas of operations are in west Texas and east Texas, the Permian Basin and the Mid-Continent, Gulf Coast and Gulf of Mexico regions of the U.S. SE owns over 200,000 acres of leasehold in the Permian Basin and 900,000 acres of leasehold in the Mid-Continent region. The drilling and oilfield services segment operates through a wholly-owned subsidiary Lariat Services, Inc., which owns and operates drilling rigs primarily in West Texas. Lariat Services drills wells for both SE and third parties. Its fleet comprises 31 rigs. Lariat Services also provides oilfield services, including pulling unit provision, trucking, rental tools, location and road construction and roustabout services. The midstream gas services segment operates through two subsidiaries: SandRidge Midstream, Inc. and SandRidge Tertiary, LLC. The former subsidiary provides engineering, construction and operations for measurement facilities, pipelines, compressor stations, treating facilities and processing plants to other energy companies; it is also responsible for marketing the company's crude oil and natural gas products. The latter subsidiary is responsible for producing C02 to use for oil recovery operations. In February 2011, SE agreed to sell 23,000 net acres in New Mexico to an unnamed buyer for $200 million dollars.

SandRidge offers its employees medical, dental and vision coverage, flexible spending accounts, life and disability insurance, a 401(k) plan and restricted stock benefits.

Phone: 405-429-5500	**Fax:**
Toll-Free:	
Address: 123 Robert S. Kerr, Oklahoma City, OK 73102 US	

FINANCIALS:

Sales and profits are in thousands of dollars—add 000 to get the full amount. 2011 Note: Financial information for 2011 was not available for all companies at press time.

2011 Sales: $1,415,213	2011 Profits: $108,065
2010 Sales: $903,400	2010 Profits: $190,600
2009 Sales: $591,044	2009 Profits: $-1,773,332
2008 Sales: $1,181,814	2008 Profits: $-1,440,425
2007 Sales: $	2007 Profits: $

U.S. Stock Ticker: SD
Int'l Ticker:
Int'l Exchange:
Employees: 2,192 Fiscal Year Ends: 12/31
Parent Company:

SALARIES/BENEFITS:

Pension Plan:	ESOP Stock Plan:	Profit Sharing:	Top Exec. Salary: $1,500,000	Bonus: $1,500,000
Savings Plan: Y	Stock Purch. Plan:		Second Exec. Salary: $755,770	Bonus: $855,000

OTHER THOUGHTS:

Apparent Women Officers or Directors: 1
Hot Spot for Advancement for Women/Minorities:

LOCATIONS: ("Y" = Yes)

West:	Southwest:	Midwest:	Southeast:	Northeast:	International:
	Y				

SBA COMMUNICATIONS CORP

www.sbasite.com

Industry Group Code: 237130

Management:		**Sales/Marketing:**		**Liberal Arts:**		**Information Systems:**		**Professionals:**		**Technical/Scientific:**	
Mgmt. Trainees:		Mktg. Professionals:	Y	Gen. Writing/Editing:		Info. Management:	Y	Finance/Acct.:	Y	Engineers, Elec.:	Y
Experienced Mgmt.:	Y	Retail Sales:		Technical Writing:	Y	Software Dev.:	Y	Law:	Y	Engineers, Other:	
Int'l Business:	Y	Commercial/Industrial:	Y	Graphic Arts/Photog.:		Hardware Dev.:		HR/Other:	Y	Health/Lab	
MBA Graduates:	Y	Sales Trainees:		Music:		Consulting/Other:		Training:	Y	Scientists/Research:	
		Advertising Pros.:		Broadcasting:				Health Care:		Petroleum/Chemicals:	
				Other:	Y			Consulting:		Math/Other:	

TYPES OF BUSINESS:

Antenna Tower Operator
Antenna Space Leasing
Tower Site Development

BRANDS/DIVISIONS/AFFILIATES:

CONTACTS:

Note: Officers with more than one job title may be intentionally listed here more than once.

Jeffrey A. Stoops, CEO
Jeffrey A. Stoops, Pres.
Brendan T. Cavanagh, CFO/Sr. VP
Jo Carol Rutherford, VP-Human Resources
Jorge Grau, CIO/VP
Thomas P. Hunt, General Counsel/Sr. VP
Mark Ciarfella, Sr. VP-Oper.
Bill Bates, VP-Bus. Dev.
Brian D. Lazarus, Chief Acct. Officer/VP
Don Mueller, VP-Managed Sites
Pamela J. Kline, VP-Capital Markets
Joseph M. Lane, VP-Site Mgmt.
David Tribble, VP-Construction Svcs.
Steven Bernstein, Chmn.
Kurt Bagwell, Pres., Int'l

Phone: 561-995-7670 **Fax:** 561-998-3448
Toll-Free: 800-487-7483
Address: 5900 Broken Sound Pkwy. N.W., Boca Raton, FL 33487 US

GROWTH PLANS/SPECIAL FEATURES:

SBA Communications Corp. is an owner and operator of wireless communications towers in the contiguous U.S., as well as Canada, Puerto Rico and the U.S. Virgin Islands. The firm operates through two businesses: site leasing, which generated roughly 95.4% of 2010 operating profit, and site development. In the site leasing business, SBA leases antenna space on communication sites it manages or on its multi-tenant towers that it constructs, acquires, leases, subleases or manages for third parties to a variety of wireless service providers under long-term lease contracts. SBA owns 9,111 towers and manages or leases roughly 5,300 actual or potential communications sites, of which 500 are revenue producing. It averages 2.4 tenants per tower. SBA receives its site leasing revenues primarily from wireless service provider tenants, including Bell Canada, AT&T, Sprint, T-Mobile and Verizon Wireless. In its new build program, the company constructs towers for wireless service providers at locations that they have identified. SBA's site development business enables it to keep in close contact with the wireless service providers who generate substantially all of its site leasing revenue and to capture ancillary revenues. The development business comprises two segments, consulting and construction. In the consulting segment of its development business, SBA offers network pre-design; site audits; identification of potential locations for towers and antennas; support in buying or leasing of the location; and assistance in obtaining zoning approvals and permits. In the construction segment of its development business, the company provides tower and related site construction; antenna installation; and radio equipment installation, commissioning and maintenance.

SBA offers its employees medical, dental and vision insurance; short- and long-term disability; life and AD&D insurance; pet insurance; a 401(k) plan; a discount car purchase program; gym memberships; and an employee stock purchase program.

FINANCIALS:

Sales and profits are in thousands of dollars—add 000 to get the full amount. 2011 Note: Financial information for 2011 was not available for all companies at press time.

2011 Sales: $698,200	2011 Profits: $-126,500
2010 Sales: $626,619	2010 Profits: $-194,674
2009 Sales: $555,513	2009 Profits: $-140,871
2008 Sales: $474,954	2008 Profits: $-67,164
2007 Sales: $408,201	2007 Profits: $-77,879

U.S. Stock Ticker: SBAC
Int'l Ticker:
Int'l Exchange:
Employees: 720 Fiscal Year Ends: 12/31
Parent Company:

SALARIES/BENEFITS:

Pension Plan:	ESOP Stock Plan:	Profit Sharing:	Top Exec. Salary: $520,000	Bonus: $494,000
Savings Plan: Y	Stock Purch. Plan: Y		Second Exec. Salary: $320,000	Bonus: $304,000

OTHER THOUGHTS:

Apparent Women Officers or Directors: 2
Hot Spot for Advancement for Women/Minorities:

LOCATIONS: ("Y" = Yes)

West:	Southwest:	Midwest:	Southeast:	Northeast:	International:
Y			Y	Y	Y

SCANSOURCE INC

www.scansourceinc.com

Industry Group Code: 423430

Management:		Sales/Marketing:		Liberal Arts:		Information Systems:		Professionals:		Technical/Scientific:	
Mgmt. Trainees:		Mktg. Professionals:	Y	Gen. Writing/Editing:		Info. Management:	Y	Finance/Acct.:	Y	Engineers, Elec.:	Y
Experienced Mgmt.:	Y	Retail Sales:		Technical Writing:	Y	Software Dev.:	Y	Law:	Y	Engineers, Other:	
Int'l Business:	Y	Commercial/Industrial:	Y	Graphic Arts/Photog.:		Hardware Dev.:	Y	HR/Other:	Y	Health/Lab	
MBA Graduates:	Y	Sales Trainees:	Y	Music:		Consulting/Other:	Y	Training:	Y	Scientists/Research:	
		Advertising Pros.:		Broadcasting:				Health Care:		Petroleum/Chemicals:	
				Other:				Consulting:		Math/Other:	

TYPES OF BUSINESS:

Data Capture Products, Distribution
Bar Code & Point-of-Sale Products
Telephony Products Distribution
Business Communications Systems

BRANDS/DIVISIONS/AFFILIATES:

Catalyst Telecom
ScanSource Communications
ScanSource Security Distribution
ScanSource POS and Barcoding
ScanSource Communications GmbH
CDC Brasil, S.A.

CONTACTS: *Note: Officers with more than one job title may be intentionally listed here more than once.*

Michael L. Baur, CEO
Richard P. Cleys, CFO
Marsha Madore, VP-Human Resources
John J. Ellsworth, General Counsel/VP/Corp. Sec.
Andrea D. Meade, Exec. VP-Oper.
Andrea D. Meade, Exec. VP-Corp. Dev.
Melissa Andrews, Contact-Media Rel.
Richard P. Cleys, VP-Finance
Scott Benbenek, Pres., Worldwide Oper.
John Black, Pres., Catalyst Telecom
Jeff Yelton, Pres., ScanSource POS & Barcoding
Buck Baker, Pres., ScanSource Comm.
Steven R. Fischer, Chmn.
Elias Botbol, Pres., Latin America

Phone: 864-288-2432	**Fax:** 864-288-1165
Toll-Free: 800-944-2439	
Address: 6 Logue Ct., Greenville, SC 29615 US	

GROWTH PLANS/SPECIAL FEATURES:

ScanSource, Inc. is a wholesale distributor of specialty technology products, providing value-added distribution sales to resellers in the specialty technology markets. The firm currently markets more than 65,000 products from roughly 200 hardware and software vendors to over 20,000 reseller customers primarily from its central warehouses in Mississippi, Florida, Mexico, Belgium and Germany. The company has two geographic distribution segments: one segment serving North America from a Mississippi distribution center, the other serving Latin America (from distribution centers located in Florida and Mexico) and Europe (from the U.K. and Belgium). The North American distribution segment markets automatic identification and data capture (AIDC) and point-of-sale (POS) products through its ScanSource POS and Barcoding division (also utilized by the international segment); voice, data and converged communications equipment through its Catalyst Telecom sales unit; voice, data and converged communications products through its Paracon sales unit; and electronic security products through its ScanSource Security Distribution unit. AIDC and POS products interface with computer systems used to automate the collection, processing and communication of information for commercial and industrial applications, including retail sales, distribution, shipping, inventory control, materials handling and warehouse management. The Catalyst Telecom sales division is a distributor of Avaya communications products, including Small and Medium Enterprise, Avaya Aura Unified Communications, Avaya Global Communication Solutions and Internet protocol (IP) solutions; and Motorola wireless products. The ScanSource Communications sales division markets business converged communications and computer communication integration products from manufacturers including Dialogic, Polycom, Audiocodes and Plantronics. Subsidiary ScanSource Communications GmbH (formerly Algol Europe, GmbH) is a German distributor of convergence communications solutions. In April 2011, ScanSource acquired CDC Brasil, S.A.

ScanSource offers employees medical, dental, vision, disability, life and accident insurance; a 401(k) plan; an employee assistance program; an employee stock purchase plan; and other benefits.

FINANCIALS: **Sales and profits are in thousands of dollars—add 000 to get the full amount. 2011 Note: Financial information for 2011 was not available for all companies at press time.**

2011 Sales: $2,666,531	2011 Profits: $73,523
2010 Sales: $2,114,979	2010 Profits: $48,812
2009 Sales: $1,847,969	2009 Profits: $47,688
2008 Sales: $2,175,485	2008 Profits: $55,632
2007 Sales: $1,986,927	2007 Profits: $42,626

U.S. Stock Ticker: SCSC
Int'l Ticker:
Int'l Exchange:
Employees: 1,370 Fiscal Year Ends: 6/30
Parent Company:

SALARIES/BENEFITS:

Pension Plan:	ESOP Stock Plan:	Profit Sharing:	Top Exec. Salary: $750,000	Bonus: $1,060,860
Savings Plan: Y	Stock Purch. Plan: Y		Second Exec. Salary: $324,000	Bonus: $238,693

OTHER THOUGHTS:

Apparent Women Officers or Directors: 1
Hot Spot for Advancement for Women/Minorities:

LOCATIONS: ("Y" = Yes)

West:	Southwest:	Midwest:	Southeast:	Northeast:	International:
	Y	Y	Y	Y	Y

SCHICK TECHNOLOGIES INC

www.schicktech.com

Industry Group Code: 33911

Management:		Sales/Marketing:		Liberal Arts:		Information Systems:		Professionals:		Technical/Scientific:	
Mgmt. Trainees:		Mktg. Professionals:	Y	Gen. Writing/Editing:		Info. Management:	Y	Finance/Acct.:	Y	Engineers, Elec.:	Y
Experienced Mgmt.:	Y	Retail Sales:		Technical Writing:	Y	Software Dev.:	Y	Law:	Y	Engineers, Other:	Y
Int'l Business:	Y	Commercial/Industrial:	Y	Graphic Arts/Photog.:		Hardware Dev.:	Y	HR/Other:	Y	Health/Lab	Y
MBA Graduates:	Y	Sales Trainees:	Y	Music:		Consulting/Other:		Training:	Y	Scientists/Research:	Y
		Advertising Pros.:		Broadcasting:				Health Care:	Y	Petroleum/Chemicals:	
				Other:				Consulting:		Math/Other:	

TYPES OF BUSINESS:

Equipment-Medical & Dental Digital Imaging Products
Dental X-Ray Devices

BRANDS/DIVISIONS/AFFILIATES:

Sirona Dental Systems, Inc.
CDR
CDR Wireless
USBCam
accuDEXA
CDRPanX
CDRPanElite
iPan

CONTACTS: *Note: Officers with more than one job title may be intentionally listed here more than once.*

Michael Stone, Pres.
Jack Connelly, VP-Mktg.
Lynn Blankenship, VP-Human Resources & Svcs.
Ari Neugroschl, VP-IT & Quality Assurance
Stan Manelkern, VP-Eng.
Will Autz, VP-Mfg.
Ronald Rosner, Dir.-Admin. & Finance
Kevin McNulty, VP-Service Oper.
Susan Murphy, VP-Finance
Linda Ruggiero Gehringer, VP-U.S. Sales
Pio Cervi, VP-Int'l Sales

Phone: 718-937-5765 **Fax:** 718-937-5962
Toll-Free:
Address: 30-30 47th Ave., Long Island City, NY 11101 US

GROWTH PLANS/SPECIAL FEATURES:

Schick Technologies, Inc. designs, develops and manufactures digital radiographic imaging systems and devices for the dental and medical markets. It is a wholly-owned subsidiary of Sirona Dental Systems, Inc. operating in Sirona's Imaging Systems division. Schick's products, which are based on proprietary digital imaging technologies, create instant high-resolution radiographs with reduced levels of radiation. Specific products include the following. The CDR system, which has slowly become the firm's leading product, uses an intra-oral sensor to produce instant, full-size, high-resolution dental X-ray images on a color computer monitor without the use of film or the need for chemical development, while reducing the radiation dose by up to 80% compared to conventional X-rays. The firm also manufactures and sells CDR Wireless, a wireless radiography sensor for use with an existing CDR system; and digital panoramic imaging devices, including the entry model CDRPanX, the premium CDRPanElite and the iPan digital pan retrofit. The USBCam and USBCam 2 are small, toothbrush-sized intraoral cameras that use LED lighting to produce high-quality video images of a patient's mouth. In the field of medical radiography, the company manufactures and sells the accuDEXA bone densitometer, which allows physicians to assess bone mineral density and fracture risk. Core products are based primarily on proprietary active-pixel sensor imaging technology, in addition to enhanced charged coupled device technology.

Employees of Schick receive paid time off; a 401(k) plan; medical, dental and disability coverage; life insurance; and educational reimbursement.

FINANCIALS: Sales and profits are in thousands of dollars—add 000 to get the full amount. 2011 Note: Financial information for 2011 was not available for all companies at press time.

2011 Sales: $ 2011 Profits: $
2010 Sales: $ 2010 Profits: $
2009 Sales: $ 2009 Profits: $
2008 Sales: $ 2008 Profits: $
2007 Sales: $ 2007 Profits: $

U.S. Stock Ticker: Subsidiary
Int'l Ticker:
Int'l Exchange:
Employees: Fiscal Year Ends: 9/30
Parent Company: SIRONA DENTAL SYSTEMS INC

SALARIES/BENEFITS:

Pension Plan: ESOP Stock Plan: Profit Sharing: Top Exec. Salary: $ Bonus: $
Savings Plan: Y Stock Purch. Plan: Second Exec. Salary: $ Bonus: $

OTHER THOUGHTS:

Apparent Women Officers or Directors: 3
Hot Spot for Advancement for Women/Minorities: Y

LOCATIONS: ("Y" = Yes)

West:	Southwest:	Midwest:	Southeast:	Northeast:	International:
				Y	

SCHIFF NUTRITION INTERNATIONAL INC www.schiffnutrition.com

Industry Group Code: 325411

Management:		Sales/Marketing:		Liberal Arts:		Information Systems:		Professionals:		Technical/Scientific:	
Mgmt. Trainees:	Y	Mktg. Professionals:	Y	Gen. Writing/Editing:	Y	Info. Management:	Y	Finance/Acct.:	Y	Engineers, Elec.:	
Experienced Mgmt.:	Y	Retail Sales:		Technical Writing:	Y	Software Dev.:		Law:	Y	Engineers, Other:	
Int'l Business:	Y	Commercial/Industrial:	Y	Graphic Arts/Photog.:	Y	Hardware Dev.:		HR/Other:	Y	Health/Lab	Y
MBA Graduates:	Y	Sales Trainees:	Y	Music:		Consulting/Other:		Training:	Y	Scientists/Research:	Y
		Advertising Pros.:	Y	Broadcasting:				Health Care:	Y	Petroleum/Chemicals:	Y
				Other:				Consulting:		Math/Other:	

TYPES OF BUSINESS:

Vitamins/Nutrition Manufacturing & Specialty Retailing
Sports Nutrition Products
Weight Management Products
Nutrition Bars

BRANDS/DIVISIONS/AFFILIATES:

Tiger's Milk
Schiff Digestive Advantage
Fi-Bar
Weider Health and Fitness
Move Free
Schiff Sustenex
MegaRed
TPG

CONTACTS: *Note: Officers with more than one job title may be intentionally listed here more than once.*

Tarang Amin, CEO
Tarang Amin, Pres.
Joseph W. Baty, CFO/Exec. VP
Jennifer Steeves-Kiss, Chief Mktg. Officer/Sr. VP
Shane Durkee, Sr. VP-R&D
Scott K. Milsten, General Counsel/Sr. VP/Corp. Sec.
Jon Fieldman, Sr. VP-Oper.
Eric Weider, Chmn.

Phone: 801-975-5000 **Fax:** 801-972-2223
Toll-Free:
Address: 2002 S. 5070 W., Salt Lake City, UT 84104 US

GROWTH PLANS/SPECIAL FEATURES:

Schiff Nutrition International, Inc. develops, manufactures, markets, distributes and sells vitamins, nutritional supplements, weight management products and sports nutrition products in the form of capsules, tablets and nutritional bars. Schiff sells and distributes its products through mass volume retailers, health food stores and distributors, drug stores, supermarkets and health clubs. Its leading domestic product brands include Schiff, Tiger's Milk, Schiff Sustenex, Schiff Digestive Advantage, MegaRed, Move Free and Fi-Bar. Schiff brand vitamin products include multivitamins, such as Single Day; individual vitamins, such as Vitamin B, Vitamin C and Vitamin D; minerals, such as calcium and iron; specialty formulas for men and women, such as Prostate Health and Folic Acid; other specialty formulas, such as Melatonin Plus, Niacin and Lutein; and omega-3 products, such as Fish Oil and MegaRed. Manufactured private label products are sold to key retailers for distribution under their store brand names. Private label products include vitamins and minerals; specialty supplements, such as joint care products; and calcium. Schiff's two largest customers are Costco and Wal-Mart, which combined account for 73% of the firm's sales. The firm's largest investors include Weider Health and Fitness and TPG. In June 2011, the company acquired the rights to Sustenex and Digestive Advantage, as well as probiotic technology GanedenBC (used in the two acquired brands) from Ganeden Biotech, Inc. for roughly $40 million.

FINANCIALS: **Sales and profits are in thousands of dollars—add 000 to get the full amount. 2011 Note: Financial information for 2011 was not available for all companies at press time.**

2011 Sales: $213,648	2011 Profits: $12,642
2010 Sales: $204,887	2010 Profits: $18,446
2009 Sales: $190,691	2009 Profits: $10,330
2008 Sales: $176,914	2008 Profits: $11,302
2007 Sales: $172,656	2007 Profits: $12,436

U.S. Stock Ticker: WNI
Int'l Ticker:
Int'l Exchange:
Employees: 414 Fiscal Year Ends: 5/31
Parent Company:

SALARIES/BENEFITS:

Pension Plan:	ESOP Stock Plan:	Profit Sharing:	Top Exec. Salary: $432,673	Bonus: $
Savings Plan:	Stock Purch. Plan:		Second Exec. Salary: $300,000	Bonus: $181,440

OTHER THOUGHTS:

Apparent Women Officers or Directors: 1
Hot Spot for Advancement for Women/Minorities:

LOCATIONS: ("Y" = Yes)

West:	Southwest:	Midwest:	Southeast:	Northeast:	International:
Y					Y

SCICLONE PHARMACEUTICALS INC

www.sciclone.com

Industry Group Code: 325412

Management:		Sales/Marketing:		Liberal Arts:		Information Systems:		Professionals:		Technical/Scientific:	
Mgmt. Trainees:		Mktg. Professionals:	Y	Gen. Writing/Editing:		Info. Management:	Y	Finance/Acct.:	Y	Engineers, Elec.:	
Experienced Mgmt.:	Y	Retail Sales:		Technical Writing:	Y	Software Dev.:	Y	Law:	Y	Engineers, Other:	
Int'l Business:	Y	Commercial/Industrial:	Y	Graphic Arts/Photog.:		Hardware Dev.:		HR/Other:	Y	Health/Lab	Y
MBA Graduates:	Y	Sales Trainees:	Y	Music:		Consulting/Other:		Training:	Y	Scientists/Research:	Y
		Advertising Pros.:		Broadcasting:				Health Care:	Y	Petroleum/Chemicals:	Y
				Other:				Consulting:		Math/Other:	Y

TYPES OF BUSINESS:

Pharmaceuticals Acquisition & Development
Immune System Enhancers
Infectious Disease Therapies
Cancer Therapies

BRANDS/DIVISIONS/AFFILIATES:

NovaMed Pharmaceuticals, Inc.
ZADAXIN
SCV-07
RapidFilm
DC Bead
SciClone China

CONTACTS: *Note: Officers with more than one job title may be intentionally listed here more than once.*

Friedhelm Blobel, CEO
Friedhelm Blobel, Pres.
Gary Titus, CFO/Sr. VP
Cynthia W. Tuthill, Chief Scientific Officer
Robert King, VP-Prod. Dev.
Robert King, VP-Mftg.
Jeffery Lange, VP-Bus. Dev.
Gary Titus, Sr. VP-Finance
Israel Rios, Chief Medical Officer/Sr. VP-Medical Affairs
Cynthia W. Tuthill, Sr. VP-Scientific Affairs
Jon S. Saxe, Chmn.
Mark Lotter, CEO-China Oper.

Phone: 650-358-3456	**Fax:** 650-358-3469
Toll-Free:	
Address: 950 Tower Ln., Ste. 900, Foster City, CA 94404 US	

GROWTH PLANS/SPECIAL FEATURES:

SciClone Pharmaceuticals, Inc. develops and commercializes pharmaceutical and biological therapeutic compounds for oncology and infectious diseases. ZADAXIN (thymosin alpha 1), the firm's lead primary product, is used for treatment of the hepatitis B and hepatitis C viruses, certain cancers and as a vaccine adjuvant. ZADAXIN is approved for sale in over 30 countries, primarily in Asia, Eastern Europe, the Middle East and Latin America, with 96% of the company's sales of ZADAXIN coming from China through SciClone China. The company also markets DC Bead, a novel treatment for advanced liver cancer that is currently approved in 40 countries, including Europe and the U.S. The firm obtained the Chinese marketing rights for the treatment from Biocompatibles International PLC. RapidFilm, the firm's other marketed product, is an oral thin film formulation of ondansetron, commonly used to treat and prevent nausea and vomiting caused by chemotherapy, radiotherapy and surgery. RapidFilm is currently being evaluated for regulatory approval in Europe, and the company has commercialization rights for RapidFilm in China and Vietnam. SciClone's proprietary drug development candidate is SCV-07, which is used to treat infectious diseases and in oncology applications. SCV-07 is a synthetic dipeptide that has demonstrated immunomodulatory activity by increasing T-cell differentiation and function, biological processes that are necessary for the body to fight infection. The firm has conducted Phase II clinical trial to assess the safety and efficacy of SCV-07 for the severity of severe oral mucositis in subjects receiving chemoradiation therapy for head and neck cancers. The company acquired exclusive worldwide rights outside of Russia to SCV-07 from Verta, Ltd. In April 2011, SciClone acquired Chinese pharmaceutical firm NovaMed Pharmaceuticals, Inc.

SciClone offers employees medical, dental, vision and life insurance; short- and long-term disability coverage; flexible spending accounts; a 401(k) plan; and an employee stock purchase program.

FINANCIALS: **Sales and profits are in thousands of dollars—add 000 to get the full amount. 2011 Note: Financial information for 2011 was not available for all companies at press time.**

2011 Sales: $	2011 Profits: $	**U.S. Stock Ticker: SCLN**
2010 Sales: $85,112	2010 Profits: $21,081	**Int'l Ticker:**
2009 Sales: $72,411	2009 Profits: $11,945	Int'l Exchange:
2008 Sales: $54,113	2008 Profits: $-8,348	Employees: 261 Fiscal Year Ends: 12/31
2007 Sales: $37,058	2007 Profits: $-9,948	Parent Company:

SALARIES/BENEFITS:

Pension Plan:	ESOP Stock Plan:	Profit Sharing:	Top Exec. Salary: $462,000	Bonus: $
Savings Plan: Y	Stock Purch. Plan: Y		Second Exec. Salary: $353,600	Bonus: $160,000

OTHER THOUGHTS:

Apparent Women Officers or Directors: 1
Hot Spot for Advancement for Women/Minorities:

LOCATIONS: ("Y" = Yes)

West:	Southwest:	Midwest:	Southeast:	Northeast:	International:
Y					Y

SCIOS INC

www.sciosinc.com

Industry Group Code: 325412

Management:		Sales/Marketing:		Liberal Arts:		Information Systems:		Professionals:		Technical/Scientific:	
Mgmt. Trainees:		Mktg. Professionals:	Y	Gen. Writing/Editing:		Info. Management:	Y	Finance/Acct.:	Y	Engineers, Elec.:	
Experienced Mgmt.:	Y	Retail Sales:		Technical Writing:	Y	Software Dev.:	Y	Law:	Y	Engineers, Other:	
Int'l Business:		Commercial/Industrial:	Y	Graphic Arts/Photog.:		Hardware Dev.:		HR/Other:	Y	Health/Lab	Y
MBA Graduates:	Y	Sales Trainees:	Y	Music:		Consulting/Other:		Training:	Y	Scientists/Research:	Y
		Advertising Pros.:		Broadcasting:				Health Care:	Y	Petroleum/Chemicals:	Y
				Other:				Consulting:		Math/Other:	Y

TYPES OF BUSINESS:

Cardiovascular Drugs

BRANDS/DIVISIONS/AFFILIATES:

Natrecor
ADHERE
Johnson & Johnson

CONTACTS:

Note: Officers with more than one job title may be intentionally listed here more than once.

William C. Weldon, CEO-Johnson & Johnson
William C. Weldon, Chmn.-Johnson & Johnson

Phone: 732-524-0400	**Fax:**
Toll-Free:	
Address: 1 Johnson & Johnson Plz., New Brunswick, NJ 08933 US	

GROWTH PLANS/SPECIAL FEATURES:

Scios, Inc., a subsidiary of Johnson & Johnson, is a biopharmaceutical company developing treatments for cardiovascular diseases. The firm's technology platform fuses classical medicinal chemistry with the most recent advances in disease-based gene array, bioinformatics and computational chemistry. The company's lead product, Natrecor, is an intravenous cardiovascular drug approved to treat acutely decompensated congestive heart failure (ADHF) for patients who have dyspnea (shortness of breath) at rest or with minimal activity, such as talking, eating or bathing. Natrecor is a recombinant form of the human B-type natriuretic peptide (hBNP), which is normally produced by the heart. The firm's current research and development program focuses on the discovery of new therapeutics for other cardiovascular diseases. Scios also has a program call ADHERE, Acute Decompensated Heart Failure National Registry, which is an observational registry that lists data on heart failure patient treatment and associated outcomes.

The firm offers employees benefits including life, disability, medical, dental, long-term care and accident insurance; paid time off; savings and pension plans; and health and wellness services.

FINANCIALS:

Sales and profits are in thousands of dollars—add 000 to get the full amount. 2011 Note: Financial information for 2011 was not available for all companies at press time.

2011 Sales: $ | 2011 Profits: $
2010 Sales: $ | 2010 Profits: $
2009 Sales: $ | 2009 Profits: $
2008 Sales: $ | 2008 Profits: $
2007 Sales: $ | 2007 Profits: $

U.S. Stock Ticker: Subsidiary
Int'l Ticker:
Int'l Exchange:
Employees: Fiscal Year Ends: 12/31
Parent Company: JOHNSON & JOHNSON

SALARIES/BENEFITS:

Pension Plan: Y	ESOP Stock Plan:	Profit Sharing:	Top Exec. Salary: $	Bonus: $
Savings Plan: Y	Stock Purch. Plan:		Second Exec. Salary: $	Bonus: $

OTHER THOUGHTS:

Apparent Women Officers or Directors:
Hot Spot for Advancement for Women/Minorities:

LOCATIONS: ("Y" = Yes)

West:	Southwest:	Midwest:	Southeast:	Northeast:	International:
				Y	

SCOULAR COMPANY (THE)

www.scoular.com

Industry Group Code: 11511

Management:		Sales/Marketing:		Liberal Arts:		Information Systems:		Professionals:		Technical/Scientific:	
Mgmt. Trainees:		Mktg. Professionals:	Y	Gen. Writing/Editing:		Info. Management:	Y	Finance/Acct.:	Y	Engineers, Elec.:	
Experienced Mgmt.:	Y	Retail Sales:		Technical Writing:		Software Dev.:		Law:	Y	Engineers, Other:	
Int'l Business:	Y	Commercial/Industrial:	Y	Graphic Arts/Photog.:		Hardware Dev.:		HR/Other:	Y	Health/Lab	
MBA Graduates:	Y	Sales Trainees:		Music:		Consulting/Other:		Training:	Y	Scientists/Research:	
		Advertising Pros.:		Broadcasting:				Health Care:		Petroleum/Chemicals:	
				Other:				Consulting:		Math/Other:	

TYPES OF BUSINESS:

Grain Trade & Transport
Livestock Marketing
Ingredients
Animal Feed
Ethanol Production
Grain Elevators Operations
Transportation Services

BRANDS/DIVISIONS/AFFILIATES:

Gateway Plant LLC

CONTACTS: *Note: Officers with more than one job title may be intentionally listed here more than once.*

Chuck Elsea, CEO
Bob Ludington, COO
David Faith, Pres.
Nancy Todd, Head-Human Resources
Joan Maclin, General Counsel/Corp. Sec.
Todd McQueen, Sr. VP-Oper.
John Heck, Sr. VP-Asset Mgmt. & Bus. Dev.
Joan Maclin, Sr. VP-Comm.
Roger Barber, Treas./VP
Curt Engel, VP-Oper.
Steve Dunn, VP-Oper.
Tom DiGiorgio, VP-Asset Mgmt. & Loss Control
Randall Foster, VP-Acct. & Control
Marshall Faith, Chmn.

Phone: 402-342-3500 **Fax:**
Toll-Free: 800-487-1474
Address: 2027 Dodge St., Omaha, NE 68102 US

GROWTH PLANS/SPECIAL FEATURES:

The Scoular Company provides worldwide marketing and procurement services related to trading, transporting, handling and storing of grain, feed and food ingredients. The company has 57 grain handling facilities; a grain storage capacity of over 100 million bushels; and handles 376 million bushels every year. Markets served by Scoular include aquaculture; flour milling; food manufacturing and processing; grain production; identity-preserved (IP) grain; industrial agricultural marketing; livestock feeding and feed manufacturing; pet food manufacturing; renewable fuels; container and vessel transportation; and rail, truck and barge transportation. In the aquaculture market, the company supplies aqua feed producers with all types of marine proteins and fats; non-marine proteins and fats; grains and grain by-products; and specialized spray-dried ingredients, which act as attractants and palatability enhancers. The company sources and supplies a range of ingredients for food manufacturers, including starches, proteins, lactates, fibers, textured proteins, specialty flours and trans-fat reductions. In the grain production market, Scoular buys, stores, handles and transports corn, hay, millet, rice, sorghum, soybean and wheat. The company supplies IP corn, white corn, soybeans, wheat and other grains for the IP grain market. Scoular provides industrial agricultural processors with grain; end-use markets for by-products and co-products; and risk management strategies. For pet food manufacturing, Scoular identifies, buys, sells and ships pet food ingredients, as well as providing blending and secondary manufacturing, packaging and logistics. The company provides risk management, grain origination, logistics and marketing in the renewable fuels market, and also invests in plants and serves as the lead developer for new plant projects. In early 2011, the firm opened a new facility in South Carolina; and acquired the assets of Gateway Plant LLC, including a combined 55-million gallon ethanol and 1.8 million bushel shuttle train plant located in Kansas.

FINANCIALS: **Sales and profits are in thousands of dollars—add 000 to get the full amount. 2011 Note: Financial information for 2011 was not available for all companies at press time.**

2011 Sales: $4,900,000	2011 Profits: $	**U.S. Stock Ticker: Private**
2010 Sales: $4,000,000	2010 Profits: $	**Int'l Ticker:**
2009 Sales: $3,500,000	2009 Profits: $	Int'l Exchange:
2008 Sales: $4,300,000	2008 Profits: $	Employees: 660 Fiscal Year Ends: 5/31
2007 Sales: $4,300,000	2007 Profits: $	Parent Company:

SALARIES/BENEFITS:

Pension Plan:	ESOP Stock Plan:	Profit Sharing: Y	Top Exec. Salary: $	Bonus: $
Savings Plan: Y	Stock Purch. Plan:		Second Exec. Salary: $	Bonus: $

OTHER THOUGHTS:

Apparent Women Officers or Directors: 1
Hot Spot for Advancement for Women/Minorities:

LOCATIONS: ("Y" = Yes)

West:	Southwest:	Midwest:	Southeast:	Northeast:	International:
Y	Y	Y	Y	Y	Y

SEACHANGE INTERNATIONAL INC

www.schange.com

Industry Group Code: 511210C

Management:		Sales/Marketing:		Liberal Arts:		Information Systems:		Professionals:		Technical/Scientific:	
Mgmt. Trainees:		Mktg. Professionals:	Y	Gen. Writing/Editing:	Y	Info. Management:	Y	Finance/Acct.:	Y	Engineers, Elec.:	Y
Experienced Mgmt.:	Y	Retail Sales:		Technical Writing:	Y	Software Dev.:	Y	Law:	Y	Engineers, Other:	
Int'l Business:	Y	Commercial/Industrial:	Y	Graphic Arts/Photog.:		Hardware Dev.:		HR/Other:	Y	Health/Lab	
MBA Graduates:	Y	Sales Trainees:	Y	Music:		Consulting/Other:		Training:	Y	Scientists/Research:	
		Advertising Pros.:		Broadcasting:				Health Care:		Petroleum/Chemicals:	
				Other:				Consulting:		Math/Other:	

TYPES OF BUSINESS:

On Demand Video Systems & Services
Broadband & Broadcast Products
Media Content Services
Technical Support & Other Services

BRANDS/DIVISIONS/AFFILIATES:

VOD Link
Axiom
Spot System
SeaChange AdPulse On-Demand
MediaCluster System
SeaChange AdPulse On-Demand Advertising
SeaChange Nucleus Hybrid Gateway

CONTACTS: *Note: Officers with more than one job title may be intentionally listed here more than once.*

Raghu Rau, CEO
Yvette M. Kanouff, Pres.
Kevin M. Bisson, CFO
Ira Goldfarb, Sr. VP-Worldwide Sales
Steven M. Davi, Sr. VP-Advanced Tech.
Bruce E. Mann, Sr. VP-Network Storage Eng.
Kevin M. Bisson, Sr. VP-Admin.
Kevin M. Bisson, Sec.
Yvette Kanouff, Chief Strategy Officer
Kevin M. Bisson, Sr. VP-Finance/Treas.
Erwin van Dommelen, Pres., SeaChange Software
Thomas Kracz, VP-Professional Svcs.
Maria Duquette, VP-Customer Svcs.
Anthony W. Kelly, Sr. VP
Thomas F. Olson, Chmn.
Zheng Gao, Pres., SeaChange China & ZQ Interactive

Phone: 978-897-0100	**Fax:** 978-897-0132
Toll-Free:	
Address: 50 Nagog Park, Acton, MA 01720 US	

GROWTH PLANS/SPECIAL FEATURES:

SeaChange International, Inc. develops, manufactures and markets digital video systems and services. The company operates in three segments: software, which generated 72% of 2011 revenue; servers and storage, 15%; and media services, 13%. The software segment includes the video-on-demand (VOD) platform suite VODlink, which digitally manages, stores and distributes digital video. The system allows cable system operators and telecommunications companies to offer VOD and other interactive television services, including interactive electronic advertising and retrieval of Internet content. VODlink is comprised of hardware in the form of servers that store and deliver video content, as well as software that manages the video assets, the network and the back-office functions of the service. The division sells Axiom, its VOD software, independent of the hardware and offers subscription services for the software. The segment also includes the Spot System for the insertion of advertisements and other short-form video into television network streams; and the SeaChange AdPulse On-Demand Advertising software platform, which allows operators to insert advertisements into on-demand content. The servers and storage segment includes the MediaCluster System, which allows broadcast television companies to directly transmit content, such as commercials and other programming, to viewers through either single, multichannel or satellite delivery systems. The media services segment offers development and interactive media services throughout Europe and to mobile service operators, such as Vodacom, O2, 3UK and 3Italia. The firm maintains 24 hour service centers in locations such as the United States, France, Italy and Ireland. In June 2011, the firm announced an integration and distribution agreement with Civolution to offer NexGuard Video Watermarking for premium video-on-demand. In January 2012, the firm launched the SeaChange Nucleus Hybrid Gateway software.

Employee benefits include medical and dental insurance; flexible spending accounts; a 401(k) savings plan; education assistance programs; and an employee assistance program.

FINANCIALS: **Sales and profits are in thousands of dollars—add 000 to get the full amount. 2011 Note: Financial information for 2011 was not available for all companies at press time.**

2011 Sales: $216,727	2011 Profits: $29,468
2010 Sales: $201,665	2010 Profits: $1,323
2009 Sales: $201,836	2009 Profits: $9,974
2008 Sales: $179,893	2008 Profits: $2,902
2007 Sales: $161,334	2007 Profits: $-8,237

U.S. Stock Ticker: SEAC
Int'l Ticker:
Int'l Exchange:
Employees: 1,202 Fiscal Year Ends: 1/31
Parent Company:

SALARIES/BENEFITS:

Pension Plan:	ESOP Stock Plan:	Profit Sharing:	Top Exec. Salary: $452,083	Bonus: $
Savings Plan: Y	Stock Purch. Plan:		Second Exec. Salary: $359,081	Bonus: $49,918

OTHER THOUGHTS:

Apparent Women Officers or Directors: 2
Hot Spot for Advancement for Women/Minorities: Y

LOCATIONS: ("Y" = Yes)

West:	Southwest:	Midwest:	Southeast:	Northeast:	International:
Y				Y	Y

SEATTLE GENETICS

www.seagen.com

Industry Group Code: 325412

Management:		Sales/Marketing:		Liberal Arts:		Information Systems:		Professionals:		Technical/Scientific:	
Mgmt. Trainees:		Mktg. Professionals:	Y	Gen. Writing/Editing:		Info. Management:	Y	Finance/Acct.:	Y	Engineers, Elec.:	
Experienced Mgmt.:	Y	Retail Sales:		Technical Writing:	Y	Software Dev.:	Y	Law:	Y	Engineers, Other:	
Int'l Business:		Commercial/Industrial:	Y	Graphic Arts/Photog.:		Hardware Dev.:		HR/Other:	Y	Health/Lab	Y
MBA Graduates:	Y	Sales Trainees:	Y	Music:		Consulting/Other:		Training:	Y	Scientists/Research:	Y
		Advertising Pros.:		Broadcasting:				Health Care:	Y	Petroleum/Chemicals:	Y
				Other:				Consulting:		Math/Other:	Y

TYPES OF BUSINESS:

Biopharmaceuticals Development
Cancer Treatments
Monoclonal Antibodies
Autoimmune Diseases

BRANDS/DIVISIONS/AFFILIATES:

SGN-40 (Dacetuzumab)
SGN-75
SGN-33 (Lintuzumab)
SGN-35 (Brentuximab Vedotin)
SGN-70
Antibody-Drug Conjugates (ADCs)
Sugar Engineered Antibody (SEA)

CONTACTS: *Note: Officers with more than one job title may be intentionally listed here more than once.*

Clay B. Siegall, CEO
Eric L. Dobmeier, COO
Clay B. Siegall, Pres.
Todd S. Simpson, CFO
Chris Boerner, VP-Mktg.
Christopher Pawlowicz, Sr. VP-Human Resources
Jonathan Drachman, Sr. VP-Research & Translational Medicine
Vaughn B. Himes, Exec. VP-Tech. Oper.
Kirk D. Schumacher, General Counsel/VP-Legal Affairs & Compliance
Natasha Hernday, VP-Corp. Dev.
Thomas C. Reynolds, Chief Medical Officer
Charles R. Romp, VP-Sales
Bruce J. Seeley, Exec. VP-Commercial
Peter D. Senter, VP-Chemistry
Clay B. Siegall, Chmn.

Phone: 425-527-4000	**Fax:** 425-527-4001
Toll-Free:	
Address: 21823 30th Dr. SE, Bothell, WA 98021 US	

GROWTH PLANS/SPECIAL FEATURES:

Seattle Genetics develops monoclonal antibody (mAb)-based therapies for the treatment of cancer and autoimmune diseases. Its research and development activities focus on mAb-based (monoclonal antibodies) therapies for human cancers including lung, renal cell, Hodgkin's disease, non-Hodgkin's lymphoma, multiple myeloma and melanoma. Products in the developmental stage include SGN-40 (dacetuzumab), in testing for multiple myeloma, diffuse large B-cell lymphoma and non-Hodgkin's lymphoma; SGN-35, in testing for relapsed Hodgkin's lymphoma and systemic anaplastic large cell lymphoma; SGN-70, an IND for autoimmune diseases; SGN-75, a trial drug for non-Hodgkin lymphoma and renal cell carcinoma; SGN-19A, a preclinical candidate for the treatment of hematological malignancies; ASG-5ME, a preclinical drug for the treatment of prostate and pancreatic cancer, developed jointly with Agensys. These product candidates represent applications of Seattle Genetics' primary platform technologies: genetically engineered monoclonal antibodies and antibody-drug conjugates (ADC). Each of these platforms is designed to support therapies that are able to identify and kill cancer cells while limiting damage to normal tissue. The company also has a sugar engineered antibody (SEA) technology, which can increase the potency of monoclonal antibodies through enhanced effector function. Seattle Genetics currently has license agreements for its proprietary ADC technology with Genentech; Bayer Pharmaceuticals, Inc.; Progenics; Daiichi Sankyo; GlaxoSmithKline; Millennium Pharmaceuticals; and MedImmune, Inc. The company has a co-development agreement with Agensys to research and develop ADC products. In September 2010, Seattle Genetics discontinued its development of SGN-33 (lintuzumab), a test for acute myeloid leukemia (AML) and myelodysplastic syndromes (MDS).

Seattle Genetics offers its employees medical, dental and vision coverage; a flexible spending plan; short- and long-term disability; and life and AD&D coverage.

FINANCIALS: **Sales and profits are in thousands of dollars—add 000 to get the full amount. 2011 Note: Financial information for 2011 was not available for all companies at press time.**

2011 Sales: $	2011 Profits: $
2010 Sales: $107,470	2010 Profits: $-66,265
2009 Sales: $51,965	2009 Profits: $-81,683
2008 Sales: $35,236	2008 Profits: $-85,501
2007 Sales: $22,420	2007 Profits: $-48,932

U.S. Stock Ticker: SGEN
Int'l Ticker:
Int'l Exchange:
Employees: 348 Fiscal Year Ends: 12/31
Parent Company:

SALARIES/BENEFITS:

Pension Plan:	ESOP Stock Plan:	Profit Sharing:	Top Exec. Salary: $627,696	Bonus: $472,500
Savings Plan: Y	Stock Purch. Plan: Y		Second Exec. Salary: $394,129	Bonus: $201,346

OTHER THOUGHTS:

Apparent Women Officers or Directors: 2
Hot Spot for Advancement for Women/Minorities:

LOCATIONS: ("Y" = Yes)

West:	Southwest:	Midwest:	Southeast:	Northeast:	International:
Y					

SELECTICA INC

www.selectica.com

Industry Group Code: 511210K

Management:		Sales/Marketing:		Liberal Arts:		Information Systems:		Professionals:		Technical/Scientific:	
Mgmt. Trainees:		Mktg. Professionals:	Y	Gen. Writing/Editing:		Info. Management:	Y	Finance/Acct.:	Y	Engineers, Elec.:	
Experienced Mgmt.:	Y	Retail Sales:		Technical Writing:	Y	Software Dev.:	Y	Law:	Y	Engineers, Other:	
Int'l Business:	Y	Commercial/Industrial:	Y	Graphic Arts/Photog.:		Hardware Dev.:		HR/Other:	Y	Health/Lab	
MBA Graduates:	Y	Sales Trainees:		Music:		Consulting/Other:		Training:	Y	Scientists/Research:	
		Advertising Pros.:		Broadcasting:				Health Care:		Petroleum/Chemicals:	
				Other:				Consulting:		Math/Other:	

TYPES OF BUSINESS:

Contract Lifecycle Management Software
Interactive Sales Software
Professional & Technical Services
Sales Execution Software
Pricing Management

BRANDS/DIVISIONS/AFFILIATES:

Selectica Sales Configuration
Selectica Contract Lifecycle Management

CONTACTS:

Note: Officers with more than one job title may be intentionally listed here more than once.

Jason Stern, CEO
Leonard Rainow, COO
Jason Stern, Pres.
Todd Spartz, CFO
Rob Milks, Dir.-Sales
Steven Gans, Chief Tech. Officer
Leo Sigal, VP-Eng.
Jennifer Bomze, VP-Mktg.
Kamal Ahluwalia, Chief Strategy Officer
Rajesh Kamat, VP-Professional Svcs. Tech. Oper.
Joe Lipple, VP-Prod. Mgmt.
Doug Bell, Chief Commercial Officer
Jim Bleakley, VP-Worldwide Channel Sales & Alliances

Phone: 408-570-9700 **Fax:** 408-570-9705
Toll-Free: 877-712-9560
Address: 2121 S. El Camino Real, 10th Fl., San Mateo, CA 94403 US

GROWTH PLANS/SPECIAL FEATURES:

Selectica, Inc. provides sales configuration and contract lifecycle management software. Its products and services include software, on-demand hosting and professional services that enable clients to manage the pricing and sale of complex business products. Selectica's Sales Configuration solution consolidates pricing, configuration and quoting functions into a single platform, enabling companies to streamline the opportunity-to-order process for service providers, manufacturers and financial services firms. The Selectica Contract Lifecycle Management solution is a contract authoring, analysis, repository and process automation product that helps companies take control of their contract management processes by converting from paper-based to electronic repositories and by unlocking multiple layers of critical business data. Additionally, the company offers consulting, training and implementation services, as well as ongoing customer support and maintenance for its software. It serves a range of industries, including, telecommunications, high tech, manufacturing, healthcare and financial services. In 2011, the firm expanded its international business with the creation of a research and operations facility in Odessa, Ukraine.

Employment benefits include medical, dental and vision coverage; life insurance plans; flexible spending accounts; 401(k) plans; and on-site gyms as well as discount gym memberships.

FINANCIALS:

Sales and profits are in thousands of dollars—add 000 to get the full amount. 2011 Note: Financial information for 2011 was not available for all companies at press time.

2011 Sales: $14,523	2011 Profits: $-1,486
2010 Sales: $15,159	2010 Profits: $-4,644
2009 Sales: $16,445	2009 Profits: $-8,422
2008 Sales: $16,003	2008 Profits: $-23,901
2007 Sales: $14,721	2007 Profits: $-20,944

U.S. Stock Ticker: SLTC
Int'l Ticker:
Int'l Exchange:
Employees: 51 Fiscal Year Ends: 3/31
Parent Company:

SALARIES/BENEFITS:

Pension Plan:	ESOP Stock Plan:	Profit Sharing:	Top Exec. Salary: $262,384	Bonus: $43,750
Savings Plan: Y	Stock Purch. Plan:		Second Exec. Salary: $252,521	Bonus: $61,650

OTHER THOUGHTS:

Apparent Women Officers or Directors: 1
Hot Spot for Advancement for Women/Minorities:

LOCATIONS: ("Y" = Yes)

West:	Southwest:	Midwest:	Southeast:	Northeast:	International:
Y					Y

SENIOR HOUSING PROPERTIES

www.snhreit.com

Industry Group Code: 531120

Management:		Sales/Marketing:		Liberal Arts:		Information Systems:		Professionals:		Technical/Scientific:	
Mgmt. Trainees:	Y	Mktg. Professionals:		Gen. Writing/Editing:	Y	Info. Management:	Y	Finance/Acct.:	Y	Engineers, Elec.:	
Experienced Mgmt.:	Y	Retail Sales:		Technical Writing:		Software Dev.:		Law:	Y	Engineers, Other:	
Int'l Business:	Y	Commercial/Industrial:		Graphic Arts/Photog.:		Hardware Dev.:		HR/Other:	Y	Health/Lab Scientists/Research:	
MBA Graduates:	Y	Sales Trainees:		Music:		Consulting/Other:		Training:		Petroleum/Chemicals:	
		Advertising Pros.:	Y	Broadcasting:				Health Care:		Math/Other:	
				Other:				Consulting:			

TYPES OF BUSINESS:

Real Estate Investment Trust
Senior Housing Properties

BRANDS/DIVISIONS/AFFILIATES:

Reit Management and Research LLC

CONTACTS:

Note: Officers with more than one job title may be intentionally listed here more than once.

David J. Hegarty, COO
David J. Hegarty, Pres.
Richard A. Doyle, Jr., CFO
Jennifer B. Clark, Sec.
Richard A. Doyle, Jr., Treas.
William J. Sheehan, Dir.-Internal Audit & Compliance

Phone: 617-796-8350 **Fax:** 617-796-8349
Toll-Free:
Address: 255 Washington St., 2 Newton Place, Newton, MA 02458 US

GROWTH PLANS/SPECIAL FEATURES:

Senior Housing Properties (SHP) is a real estate investment trust (REIT) that invests in properties such as apartments for aged residents, assisted living facilities and nursing homes. SHP owns 320 properties in 36 states and Washington, D.C. The firm's portfolio consists of 226 senior living properties, with 26,380 units; two rehabilitation hospitals with 364 licensed beds; 82 medical office, clinic and biotech laboratory buildings, totaling 5.2 million square feet; and 10 wellness centers, with approximately 812,000 square feet of space. SHP's properties include senior apartments, in which residents care for themselves; independent living properties, which include services such as meals and maid service; assisted living properties, typically offering private units with 24-hour availability of various types of assistance to residents; nursing homes, which generally provide extensive nursing and healthcare services; rehabilitation hospitals, which provide services such as physical therapy, occupational therapy and speech language pathology; and wellness centers, which offer features such as gymnasiums, strength and cardiovascular equipment areas, tennis and racquet sports facilities, pools and spas. All SHP properties are triple net leased, meaning that each tenant pays rent and is also responsible for expenses such as taxes, insurance and maintenance costs. Approximately 87% of the firm's annual rent revenues come from properties where 80% or more of operating revenues are derived from residents who pay from private resources rather than from Medicare or Medicaid. The company's day to day operations are conducted by Reit Management & Research LLC (RMR), a real estate management company that oversees a large portfolio of publicly owned real estate in the U.S., Puerto Rico and Canada. In March 2011, the company agreed to acquire 20 senior living communities in five states for $304 million. In February 2012, the company announced its purchase of 9 senior living rental properties for $314 million.

FINANCIALS:

Sales and profits are in thousands of dollars—add 000 to get the full amount. 2011 Note: Financial information for 2011 was not available for all companies at press time.

2011 Sales: $450,017 | 2011 Profits: $151,419
2010 Sales: $339,009 | 2010 Profits: $116,485
2009 Sales: $296,777 | 2009 Profits: $109,715
2008 Sales: $233,210 | 2008 Profits: $106,511
2007 Sales: $188,022 | 2007 Profits: $85,303

U.S. Stock Ticker: SNH
Int'l Ticker:
Int'l Exchange:
Employees: 650 Fiscal Year Ends: 12/31
Parent Company:

SALARIES/BENEFITS:

Pension Plan: ESOP Stock Plan: Profit Sharing: Top Exec. Salary: $230,945 Bonus: $
Savings Plan: Stock Purch. Plan: Second Exec. Salary: $145,860 Bonus: $

OTHER THOUGHTS:

Apparent Women Officers or Directors: 1
Hot Spot for Advancement for Women/Minorities:

LOCATIONS: ("Y" = Yes)

West:	Southwest:	Midwest:	Southeast:	Northeast:	International:
Y	Y	Y	Y	Y	Y

SERACARE LIFE SCIENCES INC

Industry Group Code: 325414

www.seracare.com

Management:		Sales/Marketing:		Liberal Arts:		Information Systems:		Professionals:		Technical/Scientific:	
Mgmt. Trainees:		Mktg. Professionals:	Y	Gen. Writing/Editing:		Info. Management:	Y	Finance/Acct.:	Y	Engineers, Elec.:	
Experienced Mgmt.:	Y	Retail Sales:		Technical Writing:	Y	Software Dev.:	Y	Law:	Y	Engineers, Other:	
Int'l Business:	Y	Commercial/Industrial:	Y	Graphic Arts/Photog.:		Hardware Dev.:		HR/Other:	Y	Health/Lab	Y
MBA Graduates:	Y	Sales Trainees:		Music:		Consulting/Other:		Training:	Y	Scientists/Research:	Y
		Advertising Pros.:		Broadcasting:				Health Care:	Y	Petroleum/Chemicals:	
				Other:				Consulting:		Math/Other:	Y

TYPES OF BUSINESS:

Diagnostics Products
Blood & Plasma Collection & Processing
Research Support Services
Plasma-based Products
Biological Product Database

BRANDS/DIVISIONS/AFFILIATES:

ACCURUN
ACCUTYPE H1N1
ACCURUN 106 Series 1000 Positive Control
AccuCell Human PBMC-Basic
AccuCell Human PBMC-Characterized

CONTACTS: *Note: Officers with more than one job title may be intentionally listed here more than once.*

Susan L. N. Vogt, CEO
Susan L. N. Vogt, Pres.
Gregory A. Gould, CFO
Bill Smutny, VP-Mktg. & Sales
Kathi Benjamin, VP-Human Resources
Ron Dilling, VP-Mfg. Oper.
Gregory A. Gould, Sec.
Katheryn E. Shea, VP-BioServices Oper.
Mike Steele, VP-Bus. Dev.
Gregory A. Gould, Treas.
David M. Olsen, VP-Corp. Quality
Eugene I. Davis, Chmn.

Phone: 508-244-6400 **Fax:** 508-634-3394
Toll-Free: 800-676-1881
Address: 37 Birch St., Milford, MA 01757 US

GROWTH PLANS/SPECIAL FEATURES:

SeraCare Life Sciences, Inc. develops, manufactures and sells a broad range of biological based materials and services, which facilitate the discovery, development and production of diagnostic and therapeutic products. The company's portfolio includes plasma-based reagents; diagnostic controls; and molecular biomarkers, biobanking and contract research services. SeraCare's business is divided into two segments: the Diagnostic and Biopharmaceutical Products division; and the BioServices division. The Diagnostic and Biopharmaceutical Products division includes two product lines: controls and panels; and reagents and bioprocessing products. Controls and panels include the manufacture of products used for the evaluation and quality control of infectious disease testing in hospital and clinical testing labs and blood banks, and by in vitro diagnostic ("IVD") manufacturers. The firm offers over 100 control and panel products for infectious diseases including HIV, hepatitis A, HBV, HCV, West Nile Virus, Chagas and HPV. Most of the control products are sold under the ACCURUN brand name, and its panel products are called seroconversion and performance panels. The reagents and bioprocessing products line includes the manufacture and supply of biological materials used in the research, development and manufacturing of human and animal diagnostics, therapeutics and vaccines. Its products include diagnostic intermediates, therapeutic grade albumin, purified viable human cells and cell culture additives and media. The BioServices segment includes biobanking, sample processing and testing services for research and clinical trials; and contract research services in molecular biology, virology, immunology and biochemistry. Some of SeraCare's latest products include the ACCURUN 1 Series 2700 Multi-Market Positive Control; the ACCURUN 106 Series 1000 Positive Control; the AccuCell Human PBMC-Basic and AccuCell Human PBMC-Characterized products; and the ACCUTYPE H1N1.

SeraCare offers its employees health and dental coverage; short- and long-term disability; life and travel insurance; a 401(k) plan; a flexible spending account; and an employee assistance program.

FINANCIALS: **Sales and profits are in thousands of dollars—add 000 to get the full amount. 2011 Note: Financial information for 2011 was not available for all companies at press time.**

2011 Sales: $43,484	2011 Profits: $2,667
2010 Sales: $50,380	2010 Profits: $6,705
2009 Sales: $44,434	2009 Profits: $-15,379
2008 Sales: $48,967	2008 Profits: $-11,963
2007 Sales: $47,304	2007 Profits: $-13,165

U.S. Stock Ticker: SRLS
Int'l Ticker:
Int'l Exchange:
Employees: 193 Fiscal Year Ends: 9/30
Parent Company:

SALARIES/BENEFITS:

Pension Plan:	ESOP Stock Plan:	Profit Sharing:	Top Exec. Salary: $383,779	Bonus: $350,000
Savings Plan: Y	Stock Purch. Plan:		Second Exec. Salary: $274,128	Bonus: $250,000

OTHER THOUGHTS:

Apparent Women Officers or Directors: 5
Hot Spot for Advancement for Women/Minorities: Y

LOCATIONS: ("Y" = Yes)

West:	Southwest:	Midwest:	Southeast:	Northeast:	International:
				Y	Y

Sales, profits and employees may be estimates. Financial information, benefits and other data can change quickly and may vary from those stated here.

SHARED TECHNOLOGIES

www.sharedtechnologies.com

Industry Group Code: 561210

Management:		Sales/Marketing:		Liberal Arts:		Information Systems:		Professionals:		Technical/Scientific:	
Mgmt. Trainees:		Mktg. Professionals:	Y	Gen. Writing/Editing:		Info. Management:	Y	Finance/Acct.:	Y	Engineers, Elec.:	
Experienced Mgmt.:	Y	Retail Sales:		Technical Writing:	Y	Software Dev.:	Y	Law:	Y	Engineers, Other:	Y
Int'l Business:		Commercial/Industrial:	Y	Graphic Arts/Photog.:		Hardware Dev.:		HR/Other:	Y	Health/Lab	
MBA Graduates:	Y	Sales Trainees:		Music:		Consulting/Other:	Y	Training:	Y	Scientists/Research:	
		Advertising Pros.:		Broadcasting:				Health Care:		Petroleum/Chemicals:	
				Other:				Consulting:		Math/Other:	

TYPES OF BUSINESS:

Telecommunications Systems Services
Systems Installation
Unified Communications Systems
Network Security
Call Center Solutions

BRANDS/DIVISIONS/AFFILIATES:

Arrow Electronics, Inc.
KtWare
Sys-View Services
IPTFM

CONTACTS:

Note: Officers with more than one job title may be intentionally listed here more than once.

Glenn Means, Pres.
Tim Kick, CFO
Sean Shaughnessy, Sr. VP-Sales
Louis Burrell, VP-Human Resources
Jon M. Baird, CIO
Jeff Graham, CTO
Judy Vandoorne, VP-Training & Sales Admin.
Kelleye Martin Chube, General Counsel
Jack Sanders, Sr. VP- Oper.
Greg Bosworth, Corp. Comm.
Helen Cetrulo, VP-Customer Care
John Colvin, VP-Mktg. & Sales Oper.
Denise Crane, VP-Bus. Oper.
Jimmie Morton, VP-Project & Program Mgmt.
Anthony J. Parella, Chmn.
Ed Root, VP-Supply Chain

Phone: 972-462-5800	**Fax:**
Toll-Free: 888-835-4444	
Address: 2425 Gateway Dr., Irving, TX 75063 US	

GROWTH PLANS/SPECIAL FEATURES:

Shared Technologies, a subsidiary of Arrow Electronics, Inc., is a technology and enterprise solutions provider within the U.S. The firm focuses on three primary divisions: professional services, system maintenance services and system support customer care services. The professional services segment consists of the firm's converged network services, offering conversion from legacy networks to common IP-based architecture in network management. The system maintenance services segment offers the KtWare system, a customer business portal solution; Sys-View Services, which provides a snapshot of a customer's entire switching system; disaster recovery services; onsite technical support services; and maintenance services through partnerships with several industry partners. The system support customer care services division offers local office technical support and a national technical support call center as well as several online applications that enable customers to access real-time account information and activity, and IPTFM, a remote monitoring and alarm notification system. Technical support is offered 24 hours a day, seven days a week. In total, Shared Technologies' solutions encompass data networking, converged networking, network security, customized applications, unified communications, managed services, contact center solutions, unified messaging and disaster recovery. The firm has developed several working partnerships with industry leaders, such as Avaya, LevelX, Siemens, NEC, Mitel and Microsoft. These partnerships allow Shared Technologies to provide a variety of solutions to meet clients' needs.

Employees of the firm are offered medical, dental and vision plans; short- and long-term disability; life insurance; accidental death and dismemberment (AD&D) insurance; long-term care; flexible spending accounts; tuition reimbursement; adoption assistance; an employee assistance program; and a 401(k) plan.

FINANCIALS:

Sales and profits are in thousands of dollars—add 000 to get the full amount. 2011 Note: Financial information for 2011 was not available for all companies at press time.

2011 Sales: $	2011 Profits: $	**U.S. Stock Ticker: Subsidiary**
2010 Sales: $	2010 Profits: $	**Int'l Ticker:**
2009 Sales: $	2009 Profits: $	Int'l Exchange:
2008 Sales: $	2008 Profits: $	Employees: Fiscal Year Ends: 1/31
2007 Sales: $	2007 Profits: $	Parent Company: ARROW ELECTRONICS INC

SALARIES/BENEFITS:

Pension Plan:	ESOP Stock Plan:	Profit Sharing:	Top Exec. Salary: $	Bonus: $
Savings Plan: Y	Stock Purch. Plan:		Second Exec. Salary: $	Bonus: $

OTHER THOUGHTS:

Apparent Women Officers or Directors: 4
Hot Spot for Advancement for Women/Minorities: Y

LOCATIONS: ("Y" = Yes)

West:	Southwest:	Midwest:	Southeast:	Northeast:	International:
Y	Y	Y	Y	Y	

SHENANDOAH TELECOMMUNICATIONS CO

www.shentel.com

Industry Group Code: 517110

Management:		Sales/Marketing:		Liberal Arts:		Information Systems:		Professionals:		Technical/Scientific:	
Mgmt. Trainees:		Mktg. Professionals:	Y	Gen. Writing/Editing:	Y	Info. Management:	Y	Finance/Acct.:	Y	Engineers, Elec.:	Y
Experienced Mgmt.:	Y	Retail Sales:		Technical Writing:		Software Dev.:	Y	Law:	Y	Engineers, Other:	
Int'l Business:		Commercial/Industrial:	Y	Graphic Arts/Photog.:		Hardware Dev.:		HR/Other:	Y	Health/Lab	
MBA Graduates:	Y	Sales Trainees:	Y	Music:		Consulting/Other:		Training:	Y	Scientists/Research:	
		Advertising Pros.:		Broadcasting:				Health Care:		Petroleum/Chemicals:	
				Other:				Consulting:		Math/Other:	

TYPES OF BUSINESS:

Local Exchange Carrier
Long-Distance Service
Paging Services
Cellular Services
Equipment Leasing
Internet Access
Cable Television Service
Equipment Sales

BRANDS/DIVISIONS/AFFILIATES:

Shenandoah Personal Communications Company
Shenandoah Telephone Company
Shenandoah Cable Television Company
ShenTel Service Company
Shenandoah Mobile Company
Shenandoah Long Distance Company
Shenandoah Network Company
ShenTel Communications Company

CONTACTS: *Note: Officers with more than one job title may be intentionally listed here more than once.*

Earle A. MacKenzie, COO/Exec. VP
Christopher E. French, Pres.
Adele M. Skolits, CFO
William L. Pirtle, VP-Mktg. & Sales, Wireless & Wireline
Richard A. Baughman, VP-IT
Edward H. McKay, VP-Eng.
Ann E. Flowers, General Counsel/Corp. Sec./VP-Legal
Tom Whitaker, VP-Oper.
Edward H. McKay, VP-Planning
Adele M. Skolits, VP-Finance
David E. Ferguson, VP-Customer Svcs.
Chris Kyle, VP-Mktg. & Sales, Cable
Christopher E. French, Chmn.

Phone: 540-984-4141 **Fax:** 540-984-8192
Toll-Free: 800-743-6835
Address: 500 Shentel Way, Edinburg, VA 22824 US

GROWTH PLANS/SPECIAL FEATURES:

Shenandoah Telecommunications Co. (STC) is a diversified telecommunications holding company. Through its operating subsidiaries, provides both regulated and unregulated telecommunications services to end-user customers and other communications providers. The company offers a comprehensive suite of voice, video and data communications services. STC operates in three business segments: Wireless, Wireline and Cable TV. The Wireless segment, operated by subsidiary Shenandoah Personal Communications Company, provides digital service to a portion of a four-state area covering the region from Harrisburg, York and Altoona, Pennsylvania, to Harrisonburg, Virginia. Through the firm's Shenandoah Mobile Company subsidiary, the segment provides tower rental space to affiliates and non-affiliates in the company's personal communications services (PCS) market. The Wireline segment, conducted primarily by the Shenandoah Telephone Company, provides regulated and unregulated telephone services and leases fiber optic facilities primarily throughout the Northern Shenandoah Valley in Virginia. Other subsidiaries in this segment include ShenTel Service Company, which offers telecommunications equipment, information services and Internet access to customers in the Northern Shenandoah Valley and surrounding areas; Shenandoah Network Company, which owns and operates the Maryland and West Virginia portions of a fiber optic network; and Shenandoah Long Distance Company, which offers resale of long distance service for calls placed to locations outside the regulated telephone service area by telephone customers. The Cable Television segment's operations are carried out by the Shenandoah Cable Television Company, which provides coaxial cable-based television service throughout Shenandoah County. In July 2010, the company acquired the cable operations of JetBroadband Holdings, LLC for $147.4 million. In December 2010, STC acquired the cable business of Cequel III Communications II LLC (which does business as Suddenlink Communications) for $4.5 million.

The firm offers its employees medical, vision and dental insurance; life insurance; flexible spending accounts; bonus programs; educational assistance; and an employee assistance plan.

FINANCIALS: **Sales and profits are in thousands of dollars—add 000 to get the full amount. 2011 Note: Financial information for 2011 was not available for all companies at press time.**

2011 Sales: $ | 2011 Profits: $
2010 Sales: $194,889 | 2010 Profits: $18,075
2009 Sales: $160,616 | 2009 Profits: $15,092
2008 Sales: $144,424 | 2008 Profits: $24,405
2007 Sales: $130,365 | 2007 Profits: $18,803

U.S. Stock Ticker: SHEN
Int'l Ticker:
Int'l Exchange:
Employees: 636 Fiscal Year Ends: 12/31
Parent Company:

SALARIES/BENEFITS:

Pension Plan:	ESOP Stock Plan:	Profit Sharing:	Top Exec. Salary: $380,069	Bonus: $120,655
Savings Plan: Y	Stock Purch. Plan:		Second Exec. Salary: $309,389	Bonus: $98,109

OTHER THOUGHTS:

Apparent Women Officers or Directors: 4
Hot Spot for Advancement for Women/Minorities: Y

LOCATIONS: ("Y" = Yes)

West:	Southwest:	Midwest:	Southeast:	Northeast:	International:
				Y	

SHUTTERFLY INC

www.shutterfly.com

Industry Group Code: 519130

Management:		Sales/Marketing:		Liberal Arts:		Information Systems:		Professionals:		Technical/Scientific:	
Mgmt. Trainees:		Mktg. Professionals:	Y	Gen. Writing/Editing:	Y	Info. Management:	Y	Finance/Acct.:	Y	Engineers, Elec.:	
Experienced Mgmt.:	Y	Retail Sales:		Technical Writing:	Y	Software Dev.:	Y	Law:	Y	Engineers, Other:	
Int'l Business:		Commercial/Industrial:	Y	Graphic Arts/Photog.:	Y	Hardware Dev.:		HR/Other:	Y	Health/Lab	
MBA Graduates:	Y	Sales Trainees:	Y	Music:		Consulting/Other:		Training:	Y	Scientists/Research:	
		Advertising Pros.:	Y	Broadcasting:				Health Care:		Petroleum/Chemicals:	
				Other:	Y			Consulting:		Math/Other:	

TYPES OF BUSINESS:

Online Photographic Service
Photo Printing
Gifts-Retail

BRANDS/DIVISIONS/AFFILIATES:

shutterfly.com
weddingpaperdivas.com
tinyprints.com
Tiny Prints Inc

CONTACTS: *Note: Officers with more than one job title may be intentionally listed here more than once.*

Jeffrey T. Housenbold, CEO
Jeffrey T. Housenbold, Pres.
Mark J. Rubash, CFO/Sr. VP
Peter Elarde, Chief Mktg. Officer/Sr. VP
Peter Navin, Sr. VP-Human Resources
Neil Day, CTO/Sr. VP
Dan McCormick, Sr. VP-Prod. & Svcs.
Dwayne A. Black, Sr. VP-Oper.
Ed Han, Gen. Mgr.-Tiny Prints/VP
Philip A. Marineau, Chmn.

Phone: 650-610-5200 **Fax:** 650-654-1299
Toll-Free: 888-225-7159
Address: 2800 Bridge Pkwy., Redwood City, CA 94065 US

GROWTH PLANS/SPECIAL FEATURES:

Shutterfly, Inc. is a leading Internet-based photograph publishing service, operating shutterfly.com, weddingpaperdivas.com and tinyprints.com. Through Shutterfly, consumers can upload, edit, share and print their photos. The company's revenue is primarily generated through the sale of personalized products such as professionally-bound photo books, calendars, high-quality prints, greeting cards and stationary, which accounted for 71% of its 2010 revenue. Customers may choose to print pictures in a range of sizes from wallet-sized prints to jumbo 20x30-inch enlargements, as well as on a number of consumer goods, including mugs, mouse pads, tote bags, coasters, desk organizers, puzzles, playing cards, multi-media DVDs, magnets, keepsake boxes and ancillary products, such as frames, photo albums and scrap-booking accessories. The firm's Storytelling tool allows users to publish professional-looking photo books and digital scrapbooks. Additionally, the tool features photography and design tips, personal interviews and articles and the firm's favorite photo book style picks. The firm maintains facilities in Redwood City, California, Charlotte, North Carolina and Phoenix, Arizona. In March 2011, the company acquired Tiny Prints, Inc., the operator of tinyprints.com and weddingpaperdivas.com.

Employee benefits include performance-based merit increases, bonuses and equity awards; health and welfare programs; a flexible spending account; a 401(k) plan; gym and ski discounts; over $2,000 of free merchandise annually; and a free camera loan program.

FINANCIALS: **Sales and profits are in thousands of dollars—add 000 to get the full amount. 2011 Note: Financial information for 2011 was not available for all companies at press time.**

2011 Sales: $473,270	2011 Profits: $14,048
2010 Sales: $307,707	2010 Profits: $17,127
2009 Sales: $246,432	2009 Profits: $5,853
2008 Sales: $213,480	2008 Profits: $3,660
2007 Sales: $186,727	2007 Profits: $10,095

U.S. Stock Ticker: SFLY
Int'l Ticker:
Int'l Exchange:
Employees: 611 Fiscal Year Ends: 12/31
Parent Company:

SALARIES/BENEFITS:

Pension Plan:	ESOP Stock Plan:	Profit Sharing:	Top Exec. Salary: $505,833	Bonus: $688,250
Savings Plan: Y	Stock Purch. Plan:		Second Exec. Salary: $308,333	Bonus: $114,300

OTHER THOUGHTS:

Apparent Women Officers or Directors: 1
Hot Spot for Advancement for Women/Minorities:

LOCATIONS: ("Y" = Yes)

West:	Southwest:	Midwest:	Southeast:	Northeast:	International:
Y	Y			Y	

SIGMA DESIGNS INC

www.sigmadesigns.com

Industry Group Code: 33441

Management:		Sales/Marketing:		Liberal Arts:		Information Systems:		Professionals:		Technical/Scientific:	
Mgmt. Trainees:		Mktg. Professionals:	Y	Gen. Writing/Editing:		Info. Management:	Y	Finance/Acct.:	Y	Engineers, Elec.:	Y
Experienced Mgmt.:	Y	Retail Sales:		Technical Writing:	Y	Software Dev.:	Y	Law:	Y	Engineers, Other:	Y
Int'l Business:	Y	Commercial/Industrial:	Y	Graphic Arts/Photog.:		Hardware Dev.:	Y	HR/Other:	Y	Health/Lab	
MBA Graduates:	Y	Sales Trainees:		Music:		Consulting/Other:		Training:		Scientists/Research:	
		Advertising Pros.:		Broadcasting:				Health Care:		Petroleum/Chemicals:	
				Other:				Consulting:		Math/Other:	Y

TYPES OF BUSINESS:

Digital Media Processing Hardware & Software

BRANDS/DIVISIONS/AFFILIATES:

CONTACTS: *Note: Officers with more than one job title may be intentionally listed here more than once.*

Thinh Q. Tran, CEO
Thomas E. Gay, III, CFO
Sal Cobar, VP-Worldwide Sales
Jacques Martinella, VP-Eng.
Sal Cobar, VP-Bus. Dev.
Kenneth A. Lowe, VP-Strategic Mktg.
Gabi Hilevitz, VP/Gen. Mgr.-Home Connectivity Group
David Lynch, VP/Gen. Mgr.-Media Processor Group
Thinh Q. Tran, Chmn.
Kit Tsui, Managing Dir.-Sigma Designs Tech. Singapore

Phone: 408-262-9003 **Fax:** 408-957-9740
Toll-Free:
Address: 1778 McCarthy Blvd., Milpitas, CA 95035 US

GROWTH PLANS/SPECIAL FEATURES:

Sigma Designs, Inc. is a fabless semiconductor firm that provides system-on-chip (SoC) products. Its SoC products, combining semiconductors and software, are critical components of digital video/audio processing equipment, including Internet Protocol television (IPTV) set-top boxes, HDTVs and portable media players. Generally, the semiconductors function as the central processing unit (CPU) for the media system, providing HD video decoding for various compression standards, graphics acceleration, audio decoding and display control. The software provides control of the media processing and system security management. Specific products include Sigma's latest generation SoC media processor, the SMP8910, primarily serving the IPTV gateways; the SMP8670, used in IPTV set-top boxes and thin clients; the SMP8656, which serves the IPTV set-top boxes and supports 3D graphics; the SMP8634, which provides a highly-integrated solution for IPTV, Blu-ray, HDTV and digital media applications; and the ZW4102 for home security. Sigma serves customers in Asia, Europe and North America, including telecommunications carriers such as AT&T, Deutsche Telekom and Freebox; and consumer electronics producers such as Netgear, Sharp, and Sony. Customers outside North America account for approximately 95% of the firm's annual revenue.

Sigma offers its employees health and dental insurance, life insurance, a 401(k) savings plan, a stock purchase plan and a cafeteria 125 plan.

FINANCIALS: **Sales and profits are in thousands of dollars—add 000 to get the full amount. 2011 Note: Financial information for 2011 was not available for all companies at press time.**

2011 Sales: $286,915 2011 Profits: $9,147
2010 Sales: $206,083 2010 Profits: $2,455
2009 Sales: $209,160 2009 Profits: $26,423
2008 Sales: $221,206 2008 Profits: $70,209
2007 Sales: $91,218 2007 Profits: $6,244

U.S. Stock Ticker: SIGM
Int'l Ticker:
Int'l Exchange:
Employees: 592 Fiscal Year Ends: 1/31
Parent Company:

SALARIES/BENEFITS:

Pension Plan: ESOP Stock Plan: Profit Sharing: Top Exec. Salary: $550,175 Bonus: $100,000
Savings Plan: Y Stock Purch. Plan: Y Second Exec. Salary: $265,175 Bonus: $30,000

OTHER THOUGHTS:

Apparent Women Officers or Directors: 1
Hot Spot for Advancement for Women/Minorities:

LOCATIONS: ("Y" = Yes)

West:	Southwest:	Midwest:	Southeast:	Northeast:	International:
Y					Y

SILICON LABORATORIES INC

www.silabs.com

Industry Group Code: 33441

Management:		**Sales/Marketing:**		**Liberal Arts:**		**Information Systems:**		**Professionals:**		**Technical/Scientific:**	
Mgmt. Trainees:		Mktg. Professionals:	Y	Gen. Writing/Editing:		Info. Management:	Y	Finance/Acct.:	Y	Engineers, Elec.:	Y
Experienced Mgmt.:	Y	Retail Sales:		Technical Writing:	Y	Software Dev.:	Y	Law:	Y	Engineers, Other:	
Int'l Business:	Y	Commercial/Industrial:	Y	Graphic Arts/Photog.:		Hardware Dev.:	Y	HR/Other:	Y	Health/Lab	
MBA Graduates:	Y	Sales Trainees:		Music:		Consulting/Other:		Training:		Scientists/Research:	
		Advertising Pros.:		Broadcasting:				Health Care:		Petroleum/Chemicals:	
				Other:				Consulting:		Math/Other:	Y

TYPES OF BUSINESS:

Integrated Circuits
Mixed-Signal Integrated Circuits
Microcontrollers
Radio USB Products

BRANDS/DIVISIONS/AFFILIATES:

ISOmodem
ProSLIC
EZRadioPRO
Si85xx
Si3217x ProSLIC
Si84xx ISOpro
Si2170
SpectraLinear

CONTACTS: *Note: Officers with more than one job title may be intentionally listed here more than once.*

Necip Sayiner, CEO
Tyson Tuttle, COO/Sr. VP
Necip Sayiner, Pres.
Paul Walsh, CFO
Kurt Hoff, VP-Worldwide Sales
Diane Williams, VP-Human Resources
Everett G. Plante, Jr., CIO
Mark Thompson, VP-Embedded Mixed Signal Prod.
William Bock, Sr. VP-Admin.
Jon Ivester, Sr. VP-Worldwide Oper.
Mark Downing, VP-Bus. Dev. & Strategy
David Bresemann, VP-Broadcast Prod.
Carlos Garcia, VP-Wireline Prod.
Navdeep S. Sooch, Chmn.

Phone: 512-416-8500	**Fax:** 512-416-9669
Toll-Free: 877-444-3032	
Address: 400 W. Cesar Chavez, Austin, TX 78701 US	

GROWTH PLANS/SPECIAL FEATURES:

Silicon Laboratories, Inc. designs and develops proprietary, analog-intensive mixed-signal integrated circuits (ICs). Mixed-signal ICs are electronic components that convert real-world analog signals, such as sound and radio waves, into digital signals that electronic products are able to process. The firm's mixed-signal ICs are utilized as components in a variety of industries, including the medical, industrial, automotive, communications, consumer and power management markets. Silicon Laboratories' products use standard complementary metal oxide semiconductor technology to dramatically reduce the cost, size and system power requirements of devices that its customers sell to end-users. Its product applications include portable devices; motor control and sensors; satellite set top boxes; industrial monitoring and control; central office telephone equipment; FM/AM radios; customer premises equipment; test and measurement equipment; personal video recorders; and networking equipment. The company groups its products into the following categories: broad-based products, including EZRadio short-range wireless transceivers, 8-bit mixed-signal microcontrollers, ProSLIC subscriber line interface circuits, ISOmodem embedded modems and voice direct access arrangement (DAA); broadcast products, including video demodulators, broadcast radio receivers/ transmitters, satellite set-top box receivers and satellite radio tuners; mature products, including DSL analog front end ICs, silicon DAA for PC modems, optical physical layer transceivers and RF Synthesizers; and broad-based products, including clocks, recovery ICs/oscillators, isolators and current sensors. Silicon Laboratories' largest customers include Huawei, Philips, Samsung, Sony Ericsson, LG Electronics, 2Wire, Apple, Nokia, Thomson and Varian Medical Systems. The company maintains sales offices in North America, Europe and Asia. Recently released Silicon products include the EZRadioPRO embedded wireless radio series; the Si84xx ISOpro series of digital isolators; the Si3217x ProSLIC family of single-channel foreign exchange station solutions; the Si2170 hybrid television tuner; and the Si85xx ac current sensor. In January 2011, Silicon Laboratories acquired integrated timing solutions specialist SpectraLinear.

FINANCIALS: **Sales and profits are in thousands of dollars—add 000 to get the full amount. 2011 Note: Financial information for 2011 was not available for all companies at press time.**

2011 Sales: $491,625	2011 Profits: $35,472	**U.S. Stock Ticker: SLAB**
2010 Sales: $493,341	2010 Profits: $73,242	**Int'l Ticker:**
2009 Sales: $441,020	2009 Profits: $73,092	Int'l Exchange:
2008 Sales: $415,630	2008 Profits: $32,935	Employees: 845 Fiscal Year Ends: 12/31
2007 Sales: $337,461	2007 Profits: $204,836	Parent Company:

SALARIES/BENEFITS:

Pension Plan:	ESOP Stock Plan:	Profit Sharing:	Top Exec. Salary: $571,154	Bonus: $479,415
Savings Plan:	Stock Purch. Plan:		Second Exec. Salary: $328,615	Bonus: $250,129

OTHER THOUGHTS:

Apparent Women Officers or Directors: 1
Hot Spot for Advancement for Women/Minorities:

LOCATIONS: ("Y" = Yes)

West:	Southwest:	Midwest:	Southeast:	Northeast:	International:
Y	Y			Y	Y

SL GREEN REALTY CORP

www.slgreen.com

Industry Group Code: 531120

Management:		**Sales/Marketing:**		**Liberal Arts:**	**Information Systems:**		**Professionals:**		**Technical/Scientific:**
Mgmt. Trainees:		Mktg. Professionals:	Y	Gen. Writing/Editing:	Info. Management:	Y	Finance/Acct.:	Y	Engineers, Elec.:
Experienced Mgmt.:	Y	Retail Sales:		Technical Writing:	Software Dev.:		Law:	Y	Engineers, Other:
Int'l Business:		Commercial/Industrial:		Graphic Arts/Photog.:	Hardware Dev.:		HR/Other:	Y	Health/Lab
MBA Graduates:	Y	Sales Trainees:		Music:	Consulting/Other:		Training:		Scientists/Research:
		Advertising Pros.:		Broadcasting:			Health Care:		Petroleum/Chemicals:
				Other:			Consulting:		Math/Other:

TYPES OF BUSINESS:

Real Estate Investment Trust
Commercial Properties
Property Management

BRANDS/DIVISIONS/AFFILIATES:

CONTACTS:

Note: Officers with more than one job title may be intentionally listed here more than once.

Marc Holliday, CEO
Gregory F. Hughes, COO
Andrew W. Mathias, Pres.
James Mead, CFO
Edward V. Piccinich, Exec. VP-Property Mgmt. & Construction
Andrew S. Levine, Chief Legal Officer
Neil H. Kessner, Exec. VP-Leasing Counsel
Steven M. Durels, Exec. VP/Dir.-Leasing
Stephen L. Green, Chmn.

Phone: 212-594-2700	**Fax:** 212-216-1785
Toll-Free:	
Address: 420 Lexington Ave., New York, NY 10170 US	

GROWTH PLANS/SPECIAL FEATURES:

SL Green Realty Corp. is a self-managed REIT (Real Estate Investment Trust). The firm specializes in property management, acquisitions, financing, development, construction and leasing. The company's portfolio consists of fee and lease based ownership in 30 properties in Manhattan, totaling 22.3 million square feet; and 31 properties in the New York Metro area, including Long Island, Brooklyn, Queens, Westchester County, Connecticut and New Jersey, totaling 6.8 million square feet. Additionally, the firm invests in three land interests; 11 retail properties, totaling 405,362 square feet; four office properties, totaling 1.3 million square feet; and four development properties, totaling 465,441 square feet. Under operating sublease agreements, SL Green is responsible for collecting rent from subtenants, as well as payment of all expenses relating to the property. In 2011, the firm acquired 521 Fifth Avenue, an office condominium at 110 East 42nd Street, as well as a Times Square property located at 1552 Broadway. In February 2012, the company acquired 724 Fifth Avenue.

FINANCIALS:

Sales and profits are in thousands of dollars—add 000 to get the full amount. 2011 Note: Financial information for 2011 was not available for all companies at press time.

2011 Sales: $1,265,000	2011 Profits: $647,400	**U.S. Stock Ticker: SLG**
2010 Sales: $1,101,246	2010 Profits: $270,826	**Int'l Ticker:**
2009 Sales: $995,847	2009 Profits: $37,669	Int'l Exchange:
2008 Sales: $1,065,015	2008 Profits: $360,935	Employees: 1,027 Fiscal Year Ends: 12/31
2007 Sales: $974,830	2007 Profits: $626,355	Parent Company:

SALARIES/BENEFITS:

Pension Plan:	ESOP Stock Plan:	Profit Sharing:	Top Exec. Salary: $750,000	Bonus: $3,737,500
Savings Plan:	Stock Purch. Plan:		Second Exec. Salary: $725,000	Bonus: $4,062,500

OTHER THOUGHTS:

Apparent Women Officers or Directors:
Hot Spot for Advancement for Women/Minorities:

LOCATIONS: ("Y" = Yes)

West:	Southwest:	Midwest:	Southeast:	Northeast:	International:
				Y	

SMART MODULAR TECHNOLOGIES INC

www.smartm.com

Industry Group Code: 334111

Management:		Sales/Marketing:		Liberal Arts:		Information Systems:		Professionals:		Technical/Scientific:	
Mgmt. Trainees:		Mktg. Professionals:	Y	Gen. Writing/Editing:		Info. Management:	Y	Finance/Acct.:	Y	Engineers, Elec.:	Y
Experienced Mgmt.:	Y	Retail Sales:		Technical Writing:	Y	Software Dev.:	Y	Law:	Y	Engineers, Other:	
Int'l Business:	Y	Commercial/Industrial:	Y	Graphic Arts/Photog.:		Hardware Dev.:	Y	HR/Other:	Y	Health/Lab	
MBA Graduates:	Y	Sales Trainees:		Music:		Consulting/Other:	Y	Training:		Scientists/Research:	
		Advertising Pros.:		Broadcasting:				Health Care:		Petroleum/Chemicals:	
				Other:				Consulting:		Math/Other:	

TYPES OF BUSINESS:

Computer Hardware, Manufacturing
Logistics Services
Design Services

BRANDS/DIVISIONS/AFFILIATES:

Xceed
Silver Lake Partners

CONTACTS:

Note: Officers with more than one job title may be intentionally listed here more than once.

Iain MacKenzie, CEO
Jack Pacheco, COO/Sr. VP
Iain MacKenzie, Pres.
Jack Pacheco, CFO/Sr. VP
Wayne Eisenberg, VP-Worldwide Sales
Jack Moyer, VP-Human Resources
Bernie Rub, CTO/VP
Mike Rubino, VP-Eng.
Bruce Goldberg, General Counsel/VP/Chief Compliance Officer
Alan Marten, Sr. VP/Gen. Mgr.-Memory Bus. Unit
John Scaramuzzo, Sr. VP/Gen. Mgr.-Storage Bus. Unit
Frank Perezalonso, VP/Gen. Mgr.-SSD Defense Prod. Line
Anjali Rubino, VP-Worldwide Materials
Ajay Shah, Chmn.
Kiwan Kim, Pres., SMART Brazil/Sr. VP-Emerging Markets

Phone: 510-623-1231	**Fax:** 510-623-1434
Toll-Free:	
Address: 39870 Eureka Dr., Newark, CA 94560 US	

GROWTH PLANS/SPECIAL FEATURES:

SMART Modular Technologies, Inc. (SMART) is an independent designer, manufacturer and supplier of value added subsystems to original equipment manufacturers (OEMs). The company offers an array of standard and custom products to such OEMs as Cisco Systems; Dell; and Hewlett-Packard, which together accounted for over 50% of the company's 2010 net sales. Its products fall into two principal categories: Memory products and services and solid state storage products. Memory products include Dynamic Random Access Memory (DRAM) modules, flash memory cards and modules; Static Random Access Memory (SRAM) based single in-line memory modules (SIMMs), dual in-line memory modules (DIMMs) and small outline dual in-line memory modules (SO-DIMMs). It also offers product-related logistics and supply chain services. Solid state storage products include solid state drives (SSDs) and embedded storage products. SSDs are offered to multiple markets under the Xceed brand name and range in capacity from 4GB to 400GB. Embedded storage products, such as flash memory cards and modules, are manufactured in a variety of form factors and capacities, ranging from CompactFlash, PC Card and Key Drives to Embedded USB (EUSB), iSATA Drives and uSATA Drives, among other form factors. SMART has offices and manufacturing facilities in the U.S., Malaysia, Scotland, Korea and Brazil. In August 2011, the firm was acquired by Silver Lake Partners and Silver Lake Sumeru for approximately $645 million, making the firm a privately-owned company.

FINANCIALS:

Sales and profits are in thousands of dollars—add 000 to get the full amount. 2011 Note: Financial information for 2011 was not available for all companies at press time.

2011 Sales: $	2011 Profits: $	**U.S. Stock Ticker: Private**
2010 Sales: $703,090	2010 Profits: $52,571	**Int'l Ticker:**
2009 Sales: $441,317	2009 Profits: $-11,403	Int'l Exchange:
2008 Sales: $670,151	2008 Profits: $8,974	Employees: 1,223 Fiscal Year Ends: 8/31
2007 Sales: $844,627	2007 Profits: $57,733	Parent Company: SILVER LAKE PARTNERS

SALARIES/BENEFITS:

Pension Plan:	ESOP Stock Plan:	Profit Sharing:	Top Exec. Salary: $416,770	Bonus: $675,000
Savings Plan:	Stock Purch. Plan:		Second Exec. Salary: $335,769	Bonus: $368,040

OTHER THOUGHTS:

Apparent Women Officers or Directors: 1
Hot Spot for Advancement for Women/Minorities:

LOCATIONS: ("Y" = Yes)

West:	Southwest:	Midwest:	Southeast:	Northeast:	International:
Y	Y			Y	Y

SOLARRESERVE

www.solar-reserve.com

Industry Group Code: 237130

Management:		Sales/Marketing:		Liberal Arts:		Information Systems:		Professionals:		Technical/Scientific:	
Mgmt. Trainees:		Mktg. Professionals:	Y	Gen. Writing/Editing:		Info. Management:	Y	Finance/Acct.:	Y	Engineers, Elec.:	Y
Experienced Mgmt.:	Y	Retail Sales:		Technical Writing:	Y	Software Dev.:	Y	Law:	Y	Engineers, Other:	Y
Int'l Business:	Y	Commercial/Industrial:	Y	Graphic Arts/Photog.:	Y	Hardware Dev.:	Y	HR/Other:	Y	Health/Lab	
MBA Graduates:	Y	Sales Trainees:	Y	Music:		Consulting/Other:		Training:	Y	Scientists/Research:	Y
		Advertising Pros.:		Broadcasting:				Health Care:		Petroleum/Chemicals:	
				Other:				Consulting:		Math/Other:	Y

TYPES OF BUSINESS:

Concentrated Solar Power Technology
Energy Storage Technology

BRANDS/DIVISIONS/AFFILIATES:

United Technologies Corp.
US Renewables Group
Rocketdyne
Hamilton Sundstrand
Solar Power Tower
Good Energies
Nazarian Enterprises
Argonaut Private Equity

CONTACTS:

Note: Officers with more than one job title may be intentionally listed here more than once.

Kevin Smith, CEO
Michael Whalen, CFO
William R. Gould, Jr., CTO
Tim J. Connor, VP-Eng.
Chris Costanzo, Dir.-Legal
Tom Georgis, VP-Dev.
Chris Gerlach, Dir.-Finance
Matt Held, VP-Project Mgmt. & Construction
Alistair Jessop, VP-Dev.
Tim J. Connor, VP-Tech
Andrew Wang, Dir.-Dev.
Lee Bailey, Chmn.

Phone: 310-315-2200 **Fax:** 310-315-2201
Toll-Free: 866-622-2778
Address: 2425 Olympic Blvd., Ste. E. 500, Santa Monica, CA 90404 US

GROWTH PLANS/SPECIAL FEATURES:

SolarReserve develops solar energy power plants that generate and store electricity using molten salt Solar Power Tower technology. The company's founding partners are United Technologies, a leading advanced technology company, and US Renewables Group, an investment firm dedicated to renewable power and clean fuel ventures. Molten salt technology, originally developed by the Rocketdyne division of Hamilton Sundstrand, a wholly-owned subsidiary of United Technologies Corporation, uses thousands of tracking mirrors (called heliostats) to focus solar energy onto the top of a Power Tower. Within the receiver, the concentrated sunlight heats molten salt, a mixture of sodium and potassium nitrate, to over 1,000 degrees Fahrenheit. Because molten salt maintains 98% thermal efficiency, the energy stored within it can be used 24 hours per day, without needing constant sunlight. No fossil fuels are required to operate the molten salt plants. SolarReserve holds the exclusive worldwide license to build Concentrated Solar Power (CSP) plants using molten salt technology. The company's target regions for CSP development include the Southwest U.S., southern Europe, Australia and Africa. The firm's other partners include Citi's Sustainable Development Investors, Good Energies, Nazarian Enterprises, Argonaut Private Equity, Credit Suisse, and the PCG Clean Energy Fund.

FINANCIALS:

Sales and profits are in thousands of dollars—add 000 to get the full amount. 2011 Note: Financial information for 2011 was not available for all companies at press time.

2011 Sales: $	2011 Profits: $	**U.S. Stock Ticker: Private**
2010 Sales: $	2010 Profits: $	**Int'l Ticker:**
2009 Sales: $	2009 Profits: $	Int'l Exchange:
2008 Sales: $	2008 Profits: $	Employees: Fiscal Year Ends: 12/31
2007 Sales: $	2007 Profits: $	Parent Company:

SALARIES/BENEFITS:

Pension Plan:	ESOP Stock Plan:	Profit Sharing:	Top Exec. Salary: $	Bonus: $
Savings Plan:	Stock Purch. Plan:		Second Exec. Salary: $	Bonus: $

OTHER THOUGHTS:

Apparent Women Officers or Directors:
Hot Spot for Advancement for Women/Minorities:

LOCATIONS: ("Y" = Yes)

West:	Southwest:	Midwest:	Southeast:	Northeast:	International:
Y					Y

SOLFOCUS INC

www.solfocus.com

Industry Group Code: 334413

Management:		Sales/Marketing:		Liberal Arts:		Information Systems:		Professionals:		Technical/Scientific:	
Mgmt. Trainees:		Mktg. Professionals:	Y	Gen. Writing/Editing:		Info. Management:	Y	Finance/Acct.:	Y	Engineers, Elec.:	Y
Experienced Mgmt.:	Y	Retail Sales:		Technical Writing:	Y	Software Dev.:	Y	Law:	Y	Engineers, Other:	Y
Int'l Business:	Y	Commercial/Industrial:	Y	Graphic Arts/Photog.:	Y	Hardware Dev.:	Y	HR/Other:	Y	Health/Lab	
MBA Graduates:	Y	Sales Trainees:	Y	Music:		Consulting/Other:		Training:	Y	Scientists/Research:	Y
		Advertising Pros.:		Broadcasting:				Health Care:		Petroleum/Chemicals:	
				Other:				Consulting:		Math/Other:	Y

TYPES OF BUSINESS:

Concentrated Solar Power Technology
CPV

BRANDS/DIVISIONS/AFFILIATES:

CONTACTS:

Note: Officers with more than one job title may be intentionally listed here more than once.

Mark Crowley, CEO
Robert Legendre, COO
Robert Legendre, Pres.
Bob Raybuck, CFO
Nancy Hartsoch, VP-Mktg.
Steve Horne, CTO
Bob Raybuck, VP-Admin.
Nancy Hartsoch, VP-Bus. Dev.
Bill Heck, VP-Sales
Osvaldo Regalado, VP-Program Mgmt.
Gary D. Conley, Chmn.
Christian Herrero de Egana Y Daucik, Managing Dir.-SolFocus EMEA

Phone: 650-623-7100	**Fax:** 650-623-7101
Toll-Free:	
Address: 510 Logue Ave., Mountain View, CA 94043 US	

GROWTH PLANS/SPECIAL FEATURES:

SolFocus, Inc. is a solar energy company and a supplier of concentrator photovoltaic (CPV) technology. The firm aims to generate solar energy at a cost competitive to traditional fossil fuel sources. The company's CPV technology combines high-efficiency solar cells and advanced optics to offer a solar energy alternative that is capable of delivering clean, renewable and affordable energy. Its units consist of highly reflective power units, durable CPV panels, and dual-axis trackers to follow the sun and maximize energy output. Unlike traditional silicon-based photovoltaics, the firm uses aluminum, glass and steel to create a unit that requires less energy to manufacture and is more durable. Based in Mountain View, California, SolFocus has a manufacturing facility in Mesa, Arizona; maintains European operations in Madrid, Spain; and maintains additional manufacturing partnerships with firms based in India and China. The company has installations located in California, Colorado, Hawaii, Mexico, Spain, Italy, Greece and Australia, including at Palo Alto Water Treatment facility in California; NELHA in Hawaii; APS Star Center in Arizona; and Mesa Water in Arizona.

FINANCIALS:

Sales and profits are in thousands of dollars—add 000 to get the full amount. 2011 Note: Financial information for 2011 was not available for all companies at press time.

2011 Sales: $	2011 Profits: $	**U.S. Stock Ticker: Private**
2010 Sales: $	2010 Profits: $	**Int'l Ticker:**
2009 Sales: $	2009 Profits: $	Int'l Exchange:
2008 Sales: $	2008 Profits: $	Employees: 150 Fiscal Year Ends: 12/31
2007 Sales: $	2007 Profits: $	Parent Company:

SALARIES/BENEFITS:

Pension Plan:	ESOP Stock Plan:	Profit Sharing:	Top Exec. Salary: $	Bonus: $
Savings Plan:	Stock Purch. Plan:		Second Exec. Salary: $	Bonus: $

OTHER THOUGHTS:

Apparent Women Officers or Directors: 1
Hot Spot for Advancement for Women/Minorities:

LOCATIONS: ("Y" = Yes)

West:	Southwest:	Midwest:	Southeast:	Northeast:	International:
Y					Y

SOTHEBYS

www.sothebys.com

Industry Group Code: 453998

Management:		Sales/Marketing:		Liberal Arts:		Information Systems:		Professionals:		Technical/Scientific:	
Mgmt. Trainees:	Y	Mktg. Professionals:	Y	Gen. Writing/Editing:	Y	Info. Management:	Y	Finance/Acct.:	Y	Engineers, Elec.:	
Experienced Mgmt.:	Y	Retail Sales:		Technical Writing:		Software Dev.:	Y	Law:	Y	Engineers, Other:	
Int'l Business:	Y	Commercial/Industrial:		Graphic Arts/Photog.:	Y	Hardware Dev.:		HR/Other:	Y	Health/Lab	
MBA Graduates:	Y	Sales Trainees:		Music:		Consulting/Other:		Training:	Y	Scientists/Research:	
		Advertising Pros.:	Y	Broadcasting:				Health Care:		Petroleum/Chemicals:	
				Other:				Consulting:		Math/Other:	

TYPES OF BUSINESS:

Auctions, Retail
Art, Jewelry, Antiquities & Collectibles
Financial Services
Appraisal Services
Catalogs & Online Sales
Real Estate
Trust & Estate Services

BRANDS/DIVISIONS/AFFILIATES:

Sotheby's Trusts, Estates & Appraisals Services
Sothebys.com
Noortman Master Paintings

CONTACTS:

Note: Officers with more than one job title may be intentionally listed here more than once.

William F. Ruprecht, CEO
Bruno Vinciguerra, COO/Exec. VP
William F. Ruprecht, Pres.
William S. Sheridan, CFO/Exec. VP
Susan Alexander, Head-Human Resources/Exec. VP
David Ulmer, CTO/Sr. VP
Gilbert L. Klemann, II, General Counsel/Exec. VP/Corp. Sec.
David Ulmer, Chief Strategy Officer
Diana Phillips, Dir.-Press & Corp. Affairs/Exec. VP
Kevin M. Delaney, Chief Acct. Officer/Sr. VP/Controller
Mitchell Zuckerman, Pres., Sotheby's Ventures, LLC
Maarten ten Holder, Managing Dir.-Sotheby's Americas
Patrick van Maris van Dijk, Managing Dir.-Sotheby's Europe
Kevin Ching, CEO-Sotheby's Asia
Michael I. Sovern, Chmn.
Robin G. Woodhead, Chmn.-Sotheby's Int'l/Exec. VP

Phone: 212-606-7000	**Fax:** 212-606-7107
Toll-Free: 800-813-5968	
Address: 1334 York Ave., New York, NY 10021 US	

GROWTH PLANS/SPECIAL FEATURES:

Sotheby's is one of the world's largest auctioneers of fine arts, antiques and collectibles. It operates in three segments: auction, dealer and finance. Through its global auction division, the company offers property in over 70 collecting categories and holds roughly 250 sales each year at its nine auction centers. With operations in 40 countries, auction houses are located in New York, London, Paris, Geneva, Milan, Zurich, Doha in Qatar, Hong Kong and Toronto. As an auctioneer, Sotheby's principal role is to identify, evaluate and appraise works of art through Sotheby's Trusts, Estates and Appraisals Services, an international staff of specialists based in New York; increase purchaser interest through professional marketing techniques, such as its famous catalogs; and match sellers and buyers through the auction process. Upon the completion of a sale, the company collects commission fees from both the buyer and the seller. In addition to auctioneering, the auction division is engaged in several related services, including the purchase and resale of art and other collectibles and the brokering of private treaty sales. The company's catalogs include ancient and ethnographic art; Asian art; books and manuscripts; memorabilia; furniture and decorative arts; jewelry; paintings; photographs; stamps and coins; vintage wine and spirits; and timepieces. Sotheby's was one of the first global art auction houses to do business over the Internet. The company's dealer segment operates primarily through Noortman Master Paintings, an art dealer that specializes in Dutch/Flemish Old Master Paintings as well as French Impressionist and Post-Impressionist paintings. The finance division offers certain collectors and art dealers with financing, secured by works of art it either has in its possession or permits borrowers to possess. The firm also conducts limited art education activities and real estate brokerage activities outside of the U.S. and offers graduate degree programs in the arts in London and New York.

FINANCIALS:

Sales and profits are in thousands of dollars—add 000 to get the full amount. 2011 Note: Financial information for 2011 was not available for all companies at press time.

2011 Sales: $831,836	2011 Profits: $171,416
2010 Sales: $774,309	2010 Profits: $160,950
2009 Sales: $484,958	2009 Profits: $-6,528
2008 Sales: $691,559	2008 Profits: $26,456
2007 Sales: $917,722	2007 Profits: $213,139

U.S. Stock Ticker: BID
Int'l Ticker:
Int'l Exchange:
Employees: 1,380 Fiscal Year Ends: 12/31
Parent Company:

SALARIES/BENEFITS:

Pension Plan:	ESOP Stock Plan:	Profit Sharing:	Top Exec. Salary: $691,667	Bonus: $2,650,000
Savings Plan: Y	Stock Purch. Plan:		Second Exec. Salary: $632,800	Bonus: $1,096,138

OTHER THOUGHTS:

Apparent Women Officers or Directors: 3
Hot Spot for Advancement for Women/Minorities: Y

LOCATIONS: ("Y" = Yes)

West:	Southwest:	Midwest:	Southeast:	Northeast:	International:
				Y	Y

SOUTHERN UNION COMPANY

www.sug.com

Industry Group Code: 221210

Management:		Sales/Marketing:		Liberal Arts:		Information Systems:		Professionals:		Technical/Scientific:	
Mgmt. Trainees:		Mktg. Professionals:	Y	Gen. Writing/Editing:	Y	Info. Management:	Y	Finance/Acct.:	Y	Engineers, Elec.:	Y
Experienced Mgmt.:	Y	Retail Sales:		Technical Writing:		Software Dev.:		Law:	Y	Engineers, Other:	Y
Int'l Business:		Commercial/Industrial:	Y	Graphic Arts/Photog.:		Hardware Dev.:		HR/Other:	Y	Health/Lab	
MBA Graduates:	Y	Sales Trainees:		Music:		Consulting/Other:		Training:	Y	Scientists/Research:	
		Advertising Pros.:		Broadcasting:				Health Care:		Petroleum/Chemicals:	Y
				Other:				Consulting:		Math/Other:	

TYPES OF BUSINESS:

Utilities-Electricity & Natural Gas
Natural Gas Pipelines
Gas Appliances & Appliance Service
Electricity Generation

BRANDS/DIVISIONS/AFFILIATES:

Panhandle Eastern Pipeline Company LP
Citrus Corp.
Florida Gas Transmission Company, LLC
Missouri Gas Energy
New England Gas Co.
Southern Union Gas Services
Energy Transfer Equity LP

CONTACTS: *Note: Officers with more than one job title may be intentionally listed here more than once.*

George L. Lindemann, CEO
Eric D. Herschmann, COO
Eric D. Herschmann, Pres.
Richard N. Marshall, CFO/Sr. VP
Monica M. Gaudiosi, General Counsel/Sr. VP
Robert O. Bond, Sr. VP-Pipeline Oper.
John Barnett, Dir.-External Affairs
Jack Walsh, VP-Investor Rel.
Robert O. Bond, Pres./COO-Panhandle Energy & Crosscountry Energy
Roger A. Farrell, Sr. VP-Midstream Oper.
Roger A. Farrell, Pres./COO-Southern Union Gas Svcs.
Robert J. Hack, COO-Missouri Gas Energy
George L. Lindemann, Chmn.

Phone: 713-989-2000	**Fax:**
Toll-Free:	
Address: 5444 Westheimer Rd., Houston, TX 77056-5306 US	

GROWTH PLANS/SPECIAL FEATURES:

Southern Union Company (SUG) owns and operates assets in the regulated and unregulated natural gas industry and gathers, processes, transports, stores and distributes natural gas in the U.S. The company operates in three reportable segments: transportation and storage; gathering and processing; and distribution. The transportation and storage segment's operations include interstate transportation and storage of natural gas to Midwest, Southwest and Florida markets; and liquefied natural gas terminalling and regasification services. This segment operates through Panhandle Eastern Pipe Line Company, LP and its subsidiaries (Panhandle) and its 50% interest in Florida Gas Transmission Company LLC through Citrus Corp. The gathering and processing segment is primarily engaged in the gathering, treating, processing and redelivery of natural gas and natural gas liquids (NGLs) in Texas and New Mexico. Its operations are conducted through Southern Union Gas Services (SUGS), which controls a network of approximately 5,500 miles of natural gas and NGL pipelines; four cryogenic processing plants, with a combined capacity of 415 million cubic feet per day (MMcf/d); and five natural gas treating plants, with a combined capacity of 585 MMcf/d. SUGS activities include connecting natural gas wells to its gathering system; treating natural gas to remove impurities and NGL; and redelivering natural gas and NGLs to various markets. SUGS' primary resources are located in the Permian Basin of Texas and New Mexico. SUG's distribution segment primarily distributes natural gas locally in Missouri and Massachusetts, serving over 550,000 residential, commercial and industrial customers through 9,182 miles of mains, 5,928 miles of service lines and 45 miles of transmission lines. It operates through Missouri Gas Energy and New England Gas Company. In June 2011, the company agreed to be purchased by Energy Transfer Equity LP for $8.9 billion.

SUG offers its employees benefits including health, dental, vision, group term and dependent life insurance.

FINANCIALS: **Sales and profits are in thousands of dollars—add 000 to get the full amount. 2011 Note: Financial information for 2011 was not available for all companies at press time.**

2011 Sales: $2,665,954	2011 Profits: $255,424	**U.S. Stock Ticker: SUG**
2010 Sales: $2,489,913	2010 Profits: $216,213	**Int'l Ticker:**
2009 Sales: $2,179,018	2009 Profits: $170,897	Int'l Exchange:
2008 Sales: $3,070,154	2008 Profits: $279,412	Employees: 2,437 Fiscal Year Ends: 12/31
2007 Sales: $2,616,665	2007 Profits: $211,346	Parent Company:

SALARIES/BENEFITS:

Pension Plan:	ESOP Stock Plan:	Profit Sharing:	Top Exec. Salary: $1,000,000	Bonus: $3,250,000
Savings Plan: Y	Stock Purch. Plan:		Second Exec. Salary: $950,000	Bonus: $3,150,000

OTHER THOUGHTS:

Apparent Women Officers or Directors: 1
Hot Spot for Advancement for Women/Minorities:

LOCATIONS: ("Y" = Yes)

West:	Southwest:	Midwest:	Southeast:	Northeast:	International:
Y	Y	Y	Y	Y	

SOUTHWEST GAS CORP

www.swgas.com

Industry Group Code: 221210

Management:		Sales/Marketing:		Liberal Arts:		Information Systems:		Professionals:		Technical/Scientific:	
Mgmt. Trainees:		Mktg. Professionals:	Y	Gen. Writing/Editing:	Y	Info. Management:	Y	Finance/Acct.:	Y	Engineers, Elec.:	Y
Experienced Mgmt.:	Y	Retail Sales:		Technical Writing:		Software Dev.:		Law:	Y	Engineers, Other:	Y
Int'l Business:		Commercial/Industrial:	Y	Graphic Arts/Photog.:		Hardware Dev.:		HR/Other:	Y	Health/Lab	
MBA Graduates:	Y	Sales Trainees:		Music:		Consulting/Other:		Training:	Y	Scientists/Research:	
		Advertising Pros.:		Broadcasting:				Health Care:		Petroleum/Chemicals:	Y
				Other:				Consulting:		Math/Other:	

TYPES OF BUSINESS:

Utilities-Natural Gas
Pipeline Construction Services

BRANDS/DIVISIONS/AFFILIATES:

Northern Pipeline Construction Co.

CONTACTS: *Note: Officers with more than one job title may be intentionally listed here more than once.*

Jeffrey W. Shaw, CEO
James P. Kane, Pres.
Roy R. Centrella, CFO/Sr. VP
James F. Wunderlin, Sr. VP-Tech. Support
James F. Wunderlin, Sr. VP-Eng.
Laura Lopez Hobbs, VP-Admin.
Karen S. Haller, General Counsel/VP/Chief Compliance Officer
James F. Wunderlin, Sr. VP-Bus. Oper.
Edward A. Janov, Sr. VP-Corp. Dev.
Kenneth J. Kenny, VP-Finance/Treas.
John P. Hester, Sr. VP-Regulatory Affairs & Energy Resources
Gregory J. Peterson, VP/Controller/Chief Acct. Officer
George C. Biehl, Exec. VP
James J. Kropid, Chmn.

Phone: 702-876-7237 **Fax:**
Toll-Free: 800-331-1119
Address: 5241 Spring Mountain Rd., Las Vegas, NV 89193-8510 US

GROWTH PLANS/SPECIAL FEATURES:

Southwest Gas Corp. purchases, transports and distributes natural gas to approximately 1.837 million residential, commercial and industrial customers in Arizona, Nevada and California. Approximately 86% of the firm's customers are residential and small business customers; 10% are transportation companies; and 4% are industrial or other customers. The company operates in two segments: natural gas operations and construction services. The natural gas segment is one of the largest distributors in Arizona, selling and transporting natural gas in most of central and southern Arizona, including the Phoenix and Tucson metropolitan areas. It is also one of the largest suppliers of natural gas in Nevada, serving the Las Vegas metropolitan area and northern Nevada. In California, the company serves regions such as the Lake Tahoe area and the high desert and mountain areas in San Bernardino County. Southwest Gas acquires its gas supplies from about 46 suppliers. The firm transports much of its gas through the pipelines of El Paso Natural Gas Company; Northwest Pipeline Corp.; Kern River Gas Transmission Company; Tuscarora Gas Pipeline Company.; Transwestern Pipeline Company; Southern California Gas Co.; and Paiute. The construction services segment, through Northern Pipeline Construction Co. (NPL), is an underground piping contractor that provides utility companies with trenching and installation, replacement and maintenance services for energy distribution systems. NPL contracts primarily with local distribution companies to install, repair and maintain energy distribution systems from the town border station to the end-user. Construction operations are conducted from 17 field locations, with sales to Southwest Gas accounting for 19% of NPL's revenues.

FINANCIALS: **Sales and profits are in thousands of dollars—add 000 to get the full amount. 2011 Note: Financial information for 2011 was not available for all companies at press time.**

2011 Sales: $ — 2011 Profits: $
2010 Sales: $1,830,371 — 2010 Profits: $103,877
2009 Sales: $1,893,824 — 2009 Profits: $87,482
2008 Sales: $2,144,743 — 2008 Profits: $60,973
2007 Sales: $2,152,088 — 2007 Profits: $83,246

U.S. Stock Ticker: SWX
Int'l Ticker:
Int'l Exchange:
Employees: 2,349 Fiscal Year Ends: 12/31
Parent Company:

SALARIES/BENEFITS:

Pension Plan: ESOP Stock Plan: Profit Sharing: Top Exec. Salary: $673,644 Bonus: $403,098
Savings Plan: Stock Purch. Plan: Second Exec. Salary: $388,576 Bonus: $180,823

OTHER THOUGHTS:

Apparent Women Officers or Directors: 3
Hot Spot for Advancement for Women/Minorities: Y

LOCATIONS: ("Y" = Yes)

West:	Southwest:	Midwest:	Southeast:	Northeast:	International:
Y	Y				

SOUTHWESTERN ENERGY CO

www.swn.com

Industry Group Code: 211111

Management:		Sales/Marketing:		Liberal Arts:		Information Systems:		Professionals:		Technical/Scientific:	
Mgmt. Trainees:		Mktg. Professionals:		Gen. Writing/Editing:		Info. Management:	Y	Finance/Acct.:	Y	Engineers, Elec.:	
Experienced Mgmt.:	Y	Retail Sales:		Technical Writing:		Software Dev.:		Law:	Y	Engineers, Other:	Y
Int'l Business:	Y	Commercial/Industrial:		Graphic Arts/Photog.:		Hardware Dev.:		HR/Other:	Y	Health/Lab	
MBA Graduates:	Y	Sales Trainees:		Music:		Consulting/Other:		Training:	Y	Scientists/Research:	
		Advertising Pros.:		Broadcasting:				Health Care:		Petroleum/Chemicals:	Y
				Other:				Consulting:		Math/Other:	

TYPES OF BUSINESS:

Oil & Gas Exploration & Production
Natural Gas Marketing & Transportation

BRANDS/DIVISIONS/AFFILIATES:

SEECO, Inc.
Southwestern Energy Production, Co.
Southwestern Energy Services, Co.
DeSoto Gathering Co., LLC
DeSoto Drilling, Inc.
Angelina Gathering Company, LLC

CONTACTS: *Note: Officers with more than one job title may be intentionally listed here more than once.*

Steven L. Mueller, CEO
William J. Way, COO/Exec. VP
Steven L. Mueller, Pres.
Greg D. Kerley, CFO/Exec. VP
Jennifer N. McCauley, Sr. VP-Human Resources
Dee W. Hency, CIO/Sr. VP
Dee W. Hency, Sr. VP-Admin.
Mark K. Boling, General Counsel/Exec. VP/Sec.
J. Alan Stubblefield, VP-Oper., SEECO, Inc.
Jeffrey B. Sherrick, Sr. VP-Corp. Dev.
Timothy J. O'Donnell, VP-Corp. Affairs
Bradley D. Sylvester, VP-Investor Rel.
Robert C. Owen, Chief Acct. Officer/Controller
Gene A. Hammons, Pres., Southwestern Midstream Services Co.
William N. Banks, VP/Treas.
Danny W. Ferguson, VP-Gov't & Community Rel.
James L. Bolander, Jr., VP-Health, Safety & Environmental
Harold M. Korell, Chmn.

Phone: 281-618-4700 **Fax:** 281-618-4818
Toll-Free:
Address: 2350 N. Sam Houston Pkwy. E., Ste. 125, Houston, TX 77032 US

GROWTH PLANS/SPECIAL FEATURES:

Southwestern Energy Co. is an integrated energy company primarily engaged in the exploration, development and production of crude oil and natural gas. The company also focuses on creating and capturing additional value through its drilling and gathering businesses. Southwestern Energy operates in two segments: exploration and production; and midstream services. The firm conducts the majority of its exploration and production operations in the Arkoma Basin of Arkansas (called Fayetteville Shale play); Texas; Pennsylvania; and Oklahoma. The exploration and production segment engages in natural gas and oil exploration and production through its wholly-owned subsidiaries SEECO, Inc., and Southwestern Energy Production Co. (SEPCO). SEECO, which operates exclusively in Arkansas, holds a large base of both developed and undeveloped gas reserves and conducts both the ongoing conventional drilling program in the Arkansas part of the Arkoma Basin and the drilling program for the Fayetteville Shale play. SEPCO conducts development drilling and exploration programs in Oklahoma's Arkoma basin, Texas and Pennsylvania. DeSoto Drilling, Inc., a wholly-owned subsidiary of SEPCO, operates drilling rigs in East Texas and in the Fayetteville Shale play. The midstream services segment markets and transports the firm's gas production, as well as limited amounts of third-party natural gas. The segment operates through Southwestern Energy Services, Co., a marketing subsidiary; and gathering subsidiaries Angelina Gathering Company, LLC and DeSoto Gathering Co., LLC.

The company offers employee benefits such as life, long-term disability, health, dental and vision insurance; an employee assistance program; a 401(k); paid vacation and holidays; and educational assistance.

FINANCIALS: **Sales and profits are in thousands of dollars—add 000 to get the full amount. 2011 Note: Financial information for 2011 was not available for all companies at press time.**

2011 Sales: $2,952,900 — 2011 Profits: $637,800
2010 Sales: $2,610,663 — 2010 Profits: $604,118
2009 Sales: $2,145,779 — 2009 Profits: $-35,792
2008 Sales: $2,311,552 — 2008 Profits: $567,946
2007 Sales: $1,255,131 — 2007 Profits: $221,174

U.S. Stock Ticker: SWN
Int'l Ticker:
Int'l Exchange:
Employees: 2,088 Fiscal Year Ends: 12/31
Parent Company:

SALARIES/BENEFITS:

Pension Plan: Y ESOP Stock Plan: Profit Sharing: Top Exec. Salary: $720,000 Bonus: $2,105,000
Savings Plan: Y Stock Purch. Plan: Second Exec. Salary: $460,000 Bonus: $1,657,500

OTHER THOUGHTS:

Apparent Women Officers or Directors: 4
Hot Spot for Advancement for Women/Minorities: Y

LOCATIONS: ("Y" = Yes)

West:	Southwest:	Midwest:	Southeast:	Northeast:	International:
	Y		Y		

Sales, profits and employees may be estimates. Financial information, benefits and other data can change quickly and may vary from those stated here.

SOVRAN SELF STORAGE INC

www.unclebobs.com

Industry Group Code: 531120

Management:		**Sales/Marketing:**		**Liberal Arts:**		**Information Systems:**		**Professionals:**		**Technical/Scientific:**	
Mgmt. Trainees:	Y	Mktg. Professionals:		Gen. Writing/Editing:	Y	Info. Management:	Y	Finance/Acct.:	Y	Engineers, Elec.:	
Experienced Mgmt.:	Y	Retail Sales:		Technical Writing:		Software Dev.:		Law:	Y	Engineers, Other:	
Int'l Business:		Commercial/Industrial:		Graphic Arts/Photog.:		Hardware Dev.:		HR/Other:	Y	Health/Lab	
MBA Graduates:	Y	Sales Trainees:		Music:		Consulting/Other:		Training:		Scientists/Research:	
		Advertising Pros.:	Y	Broadcasting:				Health Care:		Petroleum/Chemicals:	
				Other:				Consulting:		Math/Other:	

TYPES OF BUSINESS:

Real Estate Investment Trust
Self-Storage Properties
Truck Rental
Moving & Storage Products
Property Management

BRANDS/DIVISIONS/AFFILIATES:

Uncle Bob's Self Storage
Dri-guard
Uncle Bob's Rental Trucks
AllBoxes.com
HHF Storage Holdings II LLC

CONTACTS: *Note: Officers with more than one job title may be intentionally listed here more than once.*

Robert J. Attea, CEO
Kenneth F. Myszka, COO
Kenneth F. Myszka, Pres.
David L. Rogers, CFO/Sec.
Edward Killeen, Exec. VP-Sales
Jennifer Kozub, Dir.-Human Resources
Jeffrey O'Donnell, Dir.-IT
Sandra Herberger, VP-Admin.
Sandra Herberger, VP-Legal Compliance
Edward Killeen, Exec. VP-Oper.
John Rogers, VP-Bus. Dev.
Diane Piegza, VP-Corp. Comm.
Andrew Gregoire, VP-Finance
Kevin Driscoll, Controller
Michael Rogers, VP-Real Estate & Asset Mgmt.
Paul Powell, Exec. VP-Real Estate
Robert J. Attea, Chmn.

Phone: 716-633-1850 **Fax:** 716-633-3397
Toll-Free: 800-242-1715
Address: 6467 Main St., Williamsville, NY 14221 US

GROWTH PLANS/SPECIAL FEATURES:

Sovran Self Storage, Inc. is a self-administered and self-managed REIT (Real Estate Investment Trust) that acquires, owns and manages self-storage properties. It owns and manages 435 self-storage facilities, comprising over 25 million square feet, making it one of the largest self-storage companies in the U.S. Sovran operates its stores under the trade name Uncle Bob's Self Storage, serving over 160,000 customers in 25 states. The states with the largest number of Uncle Bob's stores include Texas, with 90 stores; Florida, 56; New York, 28; Georgia, 23; Ohio, 23; Alabama, 22; Virginia, 18; North Carolina, 18; Louisiana, 14; Massachusetts, 12; and Mississippi, 12. Stores range in size from 23,000-181,000 rentable square feet, with an average size of 65,000 rentable square feet. Sovran's stores typically offer various value-added products and services. Dri-guard, its state-of-the art centrally controlled dehumidification system, is available either singly or paired with the firm's climate controlled storage system. Dri-guard has been used by the Smithsonian, Boeing, Volvo and the U.S. Military, including for the storage of Air Force One and Two. Uncle Bob's Rental Trucks offers moving trucks with 14 feet by 8 feet of storage space on a two-way, local basis only. The firm also sells locks, boxes, tarps and other ancillary items used by its customers, offering these products both at its stores and through its affiliate web site, AllBoxes.com. In August 2011, the firm formed the joint venture company HHF Storage Holdings II, LLC with Heitman LLC.

FINANCIALS: **Sales and profits are in thousands of dollars—add 000 to get the full amount. 2011 Note: Financial information for 2011 was not available for all companies at press time.**

2011 Sales: $	2011 Profits: $
2010 Sales: $192,072	2010 Profits: $40,642
2009 Sales: $191,040	2009 Profits: $19,916
2008 Sales: $196,286	2008 Profits: $37,399
2007 Sales: $190,013	2007 Profits: $37,958

U.S. Stock Ticker: SSS
Int'l Ticker:
Int'l Exchange:
Employees: 1,027 Fiscal Year Ends: 12/31
Parent Company:

SALARIES/BENEFITS:

Pension Plan:	ESOP Stock Plan:	Profit Sharing:	Top Exec. Salary: $419,000	Bonus: $209,500
Savings Plan: Y	Stock Purch. Plan:		Second Exec. Salary: $408,000	Bonus: $204,000

OTHER THOUGHTS:

Apparent Women Officers or Directors: 6
Hot Spot for Advancement for Women/Minorities: Y

LOCATIONS: ("Y" = Yes)

West:	Southwest:	Midwest:	Southeast:	Northeast:	International:
	Y	Y	Y	Y	

SPARTAN MOTORS INC

www.spartanmotors.com

Industry Group Code: 3363

Management:		**Sales/Marketing:**		**Liberal Arts:**		**Information Systems:**		**Professionals:**		**Technical/Scientific:**	
Mgmt. Trainees:		Mktg. Professionals:	Y	Gen. Writing/Editing:		Info. Management:	Y	Finance/Acct.:	Y	Engineers, Elec.:	
Experienced Mgmt.:	Y	Retail Sales:		Technical Writing:	Y	Software Dev.:		Law:	Y	Engineers, Other:	Y
Int'l Business:	Y	Commercial/Industrial:	Y	Graphic Arts/Photog.:	Y	Hardware Dev.:		HR/Other:	Y	Health/Lab	
MBA Graduates:	Y	Sales Trainees:	Y	Music:		Consulting/Other:		Training:	Y	Scientists/Research:	
		Advertising Pros.:	Y	Broadcasting:				Health Care:		Petroleum/Chemicals:	
				Other:				Consulting:		Math/Other:	

TYPES OF BUSINESS:

Heavy-Duty Chassis Manufacturing
Custom Chassis
Aerial Ladder Components

BRANDS/DIVISIONS/AFFILIATES:

Spartan Motors Chassis, Inc.
Utilimaster Corp.
Crimson Fire Aerials, Inc.
Crimson Fire, Inc.
Classic Fire LLC

CONTACTS: *Note: Officers with more than one job title may be intentionally listed here more than once.*

John E. Sztykiel, CEO
Thomas W. Gorman, COO
John E. Sztykiel, Pres.
Joseph M. Nowicki, CFO/Chief Compliance Officer
Thomas T. Kivell, General Counsel/VP/Corp. Sec.
William Foster, VP
Hugh Sloan, Chmn.

Phone: 517-543-6400	**Fax:** 517-543-9269
Toll-Free:	
Address: 1541 Reynolds Rd., Charlotte, MI 48813 US	

GROWTH PLANS/SPECIAL FEATURES:

Spartan Motors, Inc. is a world leader in the engineering, design and manufacturing of heavy-duty custom platforms and emergency vehicles. The firm has two operating segments: Specialty Vehicles, which accounted for 77% of its 2010 revenue; and Service and Delivery Vehicles, which generated the remaining 23%. The Specialty Vehicles segment consists of three wholly-owned subsidiaries: Spartan Motors Chassis, Inc. (Spartan Chassis); Crimson Fire, Inc. (Crimson); and Crimson Fire Aerials, Inc. (Crimson Aerials). Spartan Chassis engineers, manufactures and markets chassis for fire trucks, motor homes and specialty applications such as military vehicles, trolleys, utility trucks and crash-rescue vehicles. The chassis consist of a frame assembly, engine, transmission, electrical system, running gear and some specialty chassis applications. Spartan Chassis markets its custom manufactured chassis throughout the U.S. and Canada, primarily through the direct contact of its sales department with original equipment manufacturers (OEMs), dealers and end users. Crimson engineers and manufactures emergency vehicles, including pumpers and aerial fire apparatus, heavy- and light-duty rescue units, tankers and quick attack units. Crimson Aerials engineers and manufactures aerial ladder components for fire trucks. The Service and Delivery Vehicles segment operates exclusively through the company's Utilimaster Corp. subsidiary. Utilimaster manufactures customer specific specialty vehicles in the delivery and service market, including walk-in and hi-cube vans for use in the package delivery, one-way truck rental, bakery/snack delivery, utility and linen/uniform rental businesses. In 2010, the firm was awarded a contract from Isuzu Motors to assemble its 2012 gasoline-powered Isuzu N-Series trucks at its Charlotte, Michigan manufacturing facility. In September 2010, the company divested substantially all of the assets of its Road Rescue, Inc. subsidiary. In April 2011, the firm acquired Classic Fire LLC, a designer and manufacturer of fire apparatus.

FINANCIALS: **Sales and profits are in thousands of dollars—add 000 to get the full amount. 2011 Note: Financial information for 2011 was not available for all companies at press time.**

2011 Sales: $426,010	2011 Profits: $ 773	**U.S. Stock Ticker: SPAR**
2010 Sales: $480,736	2010 Profits: $4,141	**Int'l Ticker:**
2009 Sales: $429,926	2009 Profits: $11,772	Int'l Exchange:
2008 Sales: $844,390	2008 Profits: $42,714	Employees: 1,345 Fiscal Year Ends: 12/31
2007 Sales: $681,922	2007 Profits: $24,504	Parent Company:

SALARIES/BENEFITS:

Pension Plan:	ESOP Stock Plan:	Profit Sharing:	Top Exec. Salary: $318,977	Bonus: $40,275
Savings Plan:	Stock Purch. Plan:		Second Exec. Salary: $287,079	Bonus: $33,493

OTHER THOUGHTS:

Apparent Women Officers or Directors:
Hot Spot for Advancement for Women/Minorities:

LOCATIONS: ("Y" = Yes)

West:	Southwest:	Midwest:	Southeast:	Northeast:	International:
	Y	Y		Y	

SPECTRANETICS CORP

www.spectranetics.com

Industry Group Code: 33911

Management:		Sales/Marketing:		Liberal Arts:		Information Systems:		Professionals:		Technical/Scientific:	
Mgmt. Trainees:		Mktg. Professionals:	Y	Gen. Writing/Editing:		Info. Management:	Y	Finance/Acct.:	Y	Engineers, Elec.:	Y
Experienced Mgmt.:	Y	Retail Sales:		Technical Writing:	Y	Software Dev.:	Y	Law:	Y	Engineers, Other:	Y
Int'l Business:	Y	Commercial/Industrial:	Y	Graphic Arts/Photog.:		Hardware Dev.:	Y	HR/Other:	Y	Health/Lab	Y
MBA Graduates:	Y	Sales Trainees:	Y	Music:		Consulting/Other:		Training:	Y	Scientists/Research:	Y
		Advertising Pros.:		Broadcasting:				Health Care:	Y	Petroleum/Chemicals:	
				Other:				Consulting:		Math/Other:	

TYPES OF BUSINESS:

Equipment-Laser Systems
Coronary & Vascular Blockage Treatments

BRANDS/DIVISIONS/AFFILIATES:

LACI
ELCA Laser Ablation Catheter
CVX-300
Spectranetics Laser Sheath
LLD Lead Locking Device

CONTACTS: *Note: Officers with more than one job title may be intentionally listed here more than once.*

Scott Drake, CEO
Scott Drake, Pres.
Guy A. Childs, CFO/VP
Jason D. Hein, Sr. VP-Mktg. & Sales
Roger W. Wertheimer, VP-Human Resources
Wade A. Bowe, VP-R&D & Oper.
Shahriar Matin, Sr. VP-Prod. Dev.
Roger W. Wertheimer, General Counsel/Sec.
Shahriar Matin, Sr. VP-Oper.
Donald C. Fletcher, Jr., VP-Quality System
Thomas M. Rasmussen, VP-Clinical Affairs
Renee Boehme, VP-Sales, U.S. Lead Mgmt.
Francisco T. Rivas, VP/Chief Compliance Officer
R. John Fletcher, Chmn.
Shahriar Matin, Sr. VP-Int'l

Phone: 719-447-2000 **Fax:** 719-447-2022
Toll-Free: 800-633-0960
Address: 9965 Federal Dr., Colorado Springs, CO 80921 US

GROWTH PLANS/SPECIAL FEATURES:

Spectranetics Corp. develops, manufactures, markets and distributes single-use medical devices used in minimally invasive cardiovascular procedures in 40 countries. The firm's proprietary excimer laser system, CVX-300, is approved in the U.S., Canada, Japan and Europe for use in multiple, minimally invasive cardiovascular procedures. Its laser catheters contain up to 250 fiber-optic strands that can access difficult to reach peripheral and coronary anatomy and produce evenly distributed laser energy at the tip of the catheter. Excimer lasers deliver a relatively cool ultraviolet light in short, controlled energy pulses to remove tissue. The system is used in atherectomy procedures that open clogged or obstructed arteries; and in removing infected, defective or abandoned lead wires from patients with pacemakers or implantable cardiac defibrillators (ICD). It currently has approximately 942 installed laser systems, the majority of which are located in hospitals in the U.S. Spectranetics also markets vascular intervention products such as the Laser Angioplasty for Critical Limb Ischemia (LACI) system, which treats total blockages in leg arteries; lead removal products including the Spectranetics Laser Sheath and Lead Locking Device; and the ELCA Laser Ablation Catheter line for treatment of total occlusions of the superior femoral artery. Approximately 60% of the firm's revenue comes from the sale of CVX-300. Spectranetics has 62 issued U.S. patents and holds the rights to 15 additional U.S. patents under license agreements. The firm also holds approximately 52 international patents. In April 2011, Spectranetics received approval to sell its LLD Lead Locking Device in Japan.

Spectranetics offers its employees life, AD&D, disability, medical, dental and vision insurance; a 401 (k); a stock purchase plan; and an employee assistance program.

FINANCIALS: **Sales and profits are in thousands of dollars—add 000 to get the full amount. 2011 Note: Financial information for 2011 was not available for all companies at press time.**

2011 Sales: $	2011 Profits: $
2010 Sales: $117,917	2010 Profits: $-13,063
2009 Sales: $114,837	2009 Profits: $-13,373
2008 Sales: $104,010	2008 Profits: $-3,955
2007 Sales: $82,874	2007 Profits: $7,229

U.S. Stock Ticker: SPNC
Int'l Ticker:
Int'l Exchange:
Employees: 470 Fiscal Year Ends: 12/31
Parent Company:

SALARIES/BENEFITS:

Pension Plan:	ESOP Stock Plan:	Profit Sharing:	Top Exec. Salary: $446,462	Bonus: $
Savings Plan: Y	Stock Purch. Plan: Y		Second Exec. Salary: $259,087	Bonus: $43,063

OTHER THOUGHTS:

Apparent Women Officers or Directors: 2
Hot Spot for Advancement for Women/Minorities:

LOCATIONS: ("Y" = Yes)

West:	Southwest:	Midwest:	Southeast:	Northeast:	International:
Y					Y

SPECTRUM PHARMACEUTICALS INC

www.spectrumpharm.com

Industry Group Code: 325412

Management:		**Sales/Marketing:**		**Liberal Arts:**		**Information Systems:**		**Professionals:**		**Technical/Scientific:**	
Mgmt. Trainees:		Mktg. Professionals:	Y	Gen. Writing/Editing:		Info. Management:	Y	Finance/Acct.:	Y	Engineers, Elec.:	
Experienced Mgmt.:	Y	Retail Sales:		Technical Writing:	Y	Software Dev.:	Y	Law:	Y	Engineers, Other:	
Int'l Business:	Y	Commercial/Industrial:	Y	Graphic Arts/Photog.:		Hardware Dev.:		HR/Other:	Y	Health/Lab	Y
MBA Graduates:	Y	Sales Trainees:		Music:		Consulting/Other:		Training:	Y	Scientists/Research:	Y
		Advertising Pros.:		Broadcasting:				Health Care:	Y	Petroleum/Chemicals:	Y
				Other:	Y			Consulting:		Math/Other:	Y

TYPES OF BUSINESS:

Oncology & Urology Drugs
Cancer Treatments

BRANDS/DIVISIONS/AFFILIATES:

Fusilev
Elsamitrucin
Lucanthone
EOquin
RenaZorb
Ozarelix
Satraplatin

CONTACTS:

Note: Officers with more than one job title may be intentionally listed here more than once.

Rajesh C. Shrotriya, CEO
Rajesh C. Shrotriya, Pres.
Brett L. Scott, Interim CFO/Sr. VP
Steven M. Fruchtman, Chief Medical Officer
Shyam Kumaria, Sr. VP-Finance
James E. Shields, Chief Commercial Officer/ Sr. VP
Steven M. Fruchtman, VP-Medical & Regulatory Affairs
Nozar Azarnia, VP-Biostatistics & Data Mgmt.
Rajesh C. Shrotriya, Chmn.

Phone: 702-260-7421 **Fax:**
Toll-Free:
Address: 11500 S. Eastern Ave., Ste. 240, Henderson, NV 89052 US

GROWTH PLANS/SPECIAL FEATURES:

Spectrum Pharmaceuticals, Inc. is a biopharmaceutical company that develops, acquires and advances a diversified portfolio of drug candidates, with a focus on oncology, urology and other critical health challenges. The company has two drugs currently on the U.S. market and several others in development. Fusilev (levoleucovorin), its first approved drug, is a novel folate analog formulation that is marketed for patients with osteosarcoma after high-dose methotrexate therapy, a common cancer treatment that can cause toxicity or inadvertent overdose of folic acid antagonists. Fusilev has also been approved for the treatment of colorectal cancer. Spectrum's other marketed drug, Zevalin, is a treatment for patients with relapsed or refractory low-grade or follicular B-cell non-Hodgkin's lymphoma (NHL). The drug has also been submitted as an NDA for first-line therapy in NHL. The company currently has 10 drugs in various developmental stages. The firm's late-stage development products are EOquin, an anti-cancer agent for the treatment of non-invasive bladder cancer; and Belinostat, a histone deacetylase (HDAC) inhibitor for peripheral t-cell lymphoma. The company's Phase I and II drug candidates include Ortataxel, a treatment for solid tumors; SPI-1620, an adjunct to chemotherapy; Lucanthone, a chemo sensitizer in malignant brain tumors; and RenaZorb, a second-generation lanthanum-based treatment for hyperphosphatemia.

FINANCIALS:

Sales and profits are in thousands of dollars—add 000 to get the full amount. 2011 Note: Financial information for 2011 was not available for all companies at press time.

2011 Sales: $	2011 Profits: $
2010 Sales: $74,113	2010 Profits: $-48,844
2009 Sales: $38,025	2009 Profits: $-19,046
2008 Sales: $28,725	2008 Profits: $-14,196
2007 Sales: $7,672	2007 Profits: $-21,981

U.S. Stock Ticker: SPPI
Int'l Ticker:
Int'l Exchange:
Employees: 139 Fiscal Year Ends: 12/31
Parent Company:

SALARIES/BENEFITS:

Pension Plan: ESOP Stock Plan: Profit Sharing: Top Exec. Salary: $650,000 Bonus: $950,000
Savings Plan: Y Stock Purch. Plan: Second Exec. Salary: $290,000 Bonus: $100,000

OTHER THOUGHTS:

Apparent Women Officers or Directors:
Hot Spot for Advancement for Women/Minorities:

LOCATIONS: ("Y" = Yes)

West:	Southwest:	Midwest:	Southeast:	Northeast:	International:
Y					Y

SPIRE CORPORATION

www.spirecorp.com

Industry Group Code: 33441

Management:		**Sales/Marketing:**		**Liberal Arts:**		**Information Systems:**		**Professionals:**		**Technical/Scientific:**	
Mgmt. Trainees:		Mktg. Professionals:	Y	Gen. Writing/Editing:		Info. Management:	Y	Finance/Acct.:	Y	Engineers, Elec.:	Y
Experienced Mgmt.:	Y	Retail Sales:		Technical Writing:	Y	Software Dev.:	Y	Law:	Y	Engineers, Other:	Y
Int'l Business:	Y	Commercial/Industrial:	Y	Graphic Arts/Photog.:	Y	Hardware Dev.:	Y	HR/Other:	Y	Health/Lab	
MBA Graduates:	Y	Sales Trainees:	Y	Music:		Consulting/Other:		Training:	Y	Scientists/Research:	Y
		Advertising Pros.:		Broadcasting:				Health Care:		Petroleum/Chemicals:	
				Other:				Consulting:		Math/Other:	Y

TYPES OF BUSINESS:

Photovoltaic Module Manufacturing
Biomedical Products & Technologies
Electric Utility
Solar Power Generation
Optoelectronics

BRANDS/DIVISIONS/AFFILIATES:

Spire Solar
Spire Solar Systems
Spire Biomedical, Inc.
Spire Semiconductor LLC
Spire Solar India LLC
Spire Taiwan LLC
Spire Solar Technologies Private Limited
Spi-EL Electroluminescence Solar Module Tester

CONTACTS:
Note: Officers with more than one job title may be intentionally listed here more than once.

Roger G. Little, CEO
Rodger W. LaFavre, COO
Roger G. Little, Pres.
Robert S. Lieberman, CFO
Robert S. Lieberman, Treas.
Stephen J. Hogan, Exec. VP/Gen. Mgr.-Spire Solar
Mark C. Little, CEO-Spire Biomedical
Roger G. Little, Chmn.

Phone: 781-275-6000 **Fax:** 781-275-7470
Toll-Free: 800-510-4815
Address: 1 Patriots Park, Bedford, MA 01730-2396 US

GROWTH PLANS/SPECIAL FEATURES:

Spire Corporation develops, manufactures and markets highly engineered products and services in three principal business areas: capital equipment for the PV solar industry; biomedical; and optoelectronics. Spire Solar (84% of revenues), operating in the PV solar area, develops, manufactures and markets specialized equipment for the production of terrestrial photovoltaic modules from solar cells. Its solar production lines include turnkey module, turnkey cell, turnkey thin film and module development lines. Spire's equipment, for which the firm has 26 patents, has been installed in roughly 200 factories in 50 countries. Through Spire Solar Systems, the company provides solar system design and engineering services, offering commercial and federal clients grid-connected distributed photovoltaic systems and custom modules. Spire Biomedical, operating in the biomedical area, provides value-added surface treatments to manufacturers of orthopedic and other medical devices that enhance the durability, antimicrobial or other material characteristics of their products; and performs sponsored research programs into applications of advanced biomedical and biophotonic technologies. Spire Semiconductor, operating in the optoelectronics area, provides custom compound semiconductor foundry and fabrication services on a merchant basis to customers involved in biomedical/biophotonics instruments, telecommunications and defense applications. Services include compound semiconductor wafer growth, other thin film processes and related device processing and fabrication services. This subsidiary also produces gallium arsenide concentrator cells (GaAs). International subsidiaries include Spire Solar India LLC and Spire Taiwan LLC. In February 2011, the firm released new product Spi-EL Electroluminescence Solar Module Tester, an advanced metrology offering. In August 2011, Spire Corporation established new Indian subsidiary Spire Solar Technologies Private Limited.

FINANCIALS:
Sales and profits are in thousands of dollars—add 000 to get the full amount. 2011 Note: Financial information for 2011 was not available for all companies at press time.

2011 Sales: $	2011 Profits: $
2010 Sales: $79,842	2010 Profits: $- 408
2009 Sales: $69,871	2009 Profits: $-5,282
2008 Sales: $64,964	2008 Profits: $4,775
2007 Sales: $37,068	2007 Profits: $-1,933

U.S. Stock Ticker: SPIR
Int'l Ticker:
Int'l Exchange:
Employees: 194 Fiscal Year Ends: 12/31
Parent Company:

SALARIES/BENEFITS:

Pension Plan: ESOP Stock Plan: Profit Sharing: Top Exec. Salary: $515,500 Bonus: $2,480
Savings Plan: Stock Purch. Plan: Second Exec. Salary: $190,000 Bonus: $12,000

OTHER THOUGHTS:

Apparent Women Officers or Directors:
Hot Spot for Advancement for Women/Minorities:

LOCATIONS: ("Y" = Yes)

West:	Southwest:	Midwest:	Southeast:	Northeast:	International:
				Y	Y

SPORT SUPPLY GROUP INC

www.sportsupplygroup.com

Industry Group Code: 454113

Management:		Sales/Marketing:		Liberal Arts:		Information Systems:		Professionals:		Technical/Scientific:	
Mgmt. Trainees:	Y	Mktg. Professionals:	Y	Gen. Writing/Editing:	Y	Info. Management:	Y	Finance/Acct.:	Y	Engineers, Elec.:	
Experienced Mgmt.:	Y	Retail Sales:		Technical Writing:		Software Dev.:	Y	Law:	Y	Engineers, Other:	
Int'l Business:		Commercial/Industrial:		Graphic Arts/Photog.:	Y	Hardware Dev.:		HR/Other:	Y	Health/Lab	
MBA Graduates:	Y	Sales Trainees:	Y	Music:		Consulting/Other:		Training:	Y	Scientists/Research:	
		Advertising Pros.:	Y	Broadcasting:				Health Care:		Petroleum/Chemicals:	
				Other:				Consulting:		Math/Other:	

TYPES OF BUSINESS:

Sporting Goods, Direct Sales
Online Sales
Catalogs
Telemarketing
Physical Education Products

BRANDS/DIVISIONS/AFFILIATES:

Onex Corporation
BSN Sports
Tomark Sports
New England Camp
Dixie Sporting Goods
Kessler Team Sports
Salkeld Sports
ONCAP Investment Partners II LP

CONTACTS:

Note: Officers with more than one job title may be intentionally listed here more than once.

Adam Blumenfeld, CEO
Terrence M. Babilla, COO
Terrence M. Babilla, Pres.
John E. Pitts, CFO
Kurt Hagen, Exec. VP-Sales & Mktg.
Terrence M. Babilla, General Counsel/Sec.

Phone: 972-484-9484	**Fax:**
Toll-Free:	
Address: 1901 Diplomat Dr., Farmers Branch, TX 75234 US	

GROWTH PLANS/SPECIAL FEATURES:

Sport Supply Group, Inc. (SSG) manufactures, distributes and markets sporting related goods. The company primary products include sporting goods equipment, soft good athletic apparel, recreational and leisure products, physical education products and footwear. The firm primarily sells its products through direct catalogs, e-commerce sites, telemarketers and a direct sales team. SSG offers brand name and private-label products, including Nike, Wilson, Rawlings and Under Armour, among others. Catalogs include BSN Sports, League Direct, Tomark Sports and New England Camp. The company's web sites, each of which is targeted to a specific customer group or product line, enable consumers to place orders, access account information, track orders and perform routine customer service inquiries. In addition, the company has licenses and marketing alliances with national organizations such as YMCA, YWCA, Little League Baseball and American Youth Football. Through its dealer division, SSG offers sporting goods and equipment to the institutional market. The division consists of four regional dealers: Dixie Sporting Goods, based in Richmond, Virginia, supplies customers in Virginia, North Carolina, South Carolina, Ohio, Maryland and West Virginia; Orlando Team Sports serves the Florida market; Kessler Team Sports covers the Midwest and South Central regions; and Salkeld Sports serves Illinois. The company markets over 50,000 products to the U.S. institutional market, which comprises schools, colleges, universities, government agencies, military facilities, athletic clubs, athletic teams and dealers, youth sports leagues and recreational organizations. The firm is owned by private equity firm ONCAP Investment Partners II L.P., an investment platform of Onex Corporation.

Employees are offered health benefits as well as a 401(k) plan.

FINANCIALS:

Sales and profits are in thousands of dollars—add 000 to get the full amount. 2011 Note: Financial information for 2011 was not available for all companies at press time.

2011 Sales: $	2011 Profits: $	**U.S. Stock Ticker: Private**
2010 Sales: $	2010 Profits: $	**Int'l Ticker:**
2009 Sales: $250,227	2009 Profits: $11,916	Int'l Exchange:
2008 Sales: $251,394	2008 Profits: $9,733	Employees: Fiscal Year Ends: 3/31
2007 Sales: $236,855	2007 Profits: $3,860	Parent Company: ONEX CORPORATION

SALARIES/BENEFITS:

Pension Plan:	ESOP Stock Plan:	Profit Sharing:	Top Exec. Salary: $450,000	Bonus: $158,424
Savings Plan: Y	Stock Purch. Plan:		Second Exec. Salary: $415,000	Bonus: $146,102

OTHER THOUGHTS:

Apparent Women Officers or Directors:
Hot Spot for Advancement for Women/Minorities:

LOCATIONS: ("Y" = Yes)

West:	Southwest:	Midwest:	Southeast:	Northeast:	International:
	Y	Y	Y	Y	

SPORTSMAN'S GUIDE INC (THE)

www.sportsmansguide.com

Industry Group Code: 451110

Management:		Sales/Marketing:		Liberal Arts:		Information Systems:		Professionals:		Technical/Scientific:	
Mgmt. Trainees:	Y	Mktg. Professionals:	Y	Gen. Writing/Editing:	Y	Info. Management:	Y	Finance/Acct.:	Y	Engineers, Elec.:	
Experienced Mgmt.:	Y	Retail Sales:	Y	Technical Writing:		Software Dev.:	Y	Law:	Y	Engineers, Other:	
Int'l Business:		Commercial/Industrial:		Graphic Arts/Photog.:	Y	Hardware Dev.:		HR/Other:	Y	Health/Lab	
MBA Graduates:	Y	Sales Trainees:	Y	Music:		Consulting/Other:		Training:	Y	Scientists/Research:	
		Advertising Pros.:	Y	Broadcasting:				Health Care:		Petroleum/Chemicals:	
				Other:				Consulting:		Math/Other:	

TYPES OF BUSINESS:

Outdoor & Hunting Products
Online & Catalog Sales
Outdoor Apparel & Footwear
Boating Supplies

BRANDS/DIVISIONS/AFFILIATES:

Redcats USA
workwearsavings.com
The Buyers' Club
Buyer's Advantage Catalog

CONTACTS:

Note: Officers with more than one job title may be intentionally listed here more than once.

Jay Berlin, CEO
John M. Casler, Exec. VP-Mktg. & Creative Svcs.
Dale D. Monson, CIO/Sr. VP
John M. Casler, Exec. VP-Merch.
Dale D. Monson, Sr. VP-Oper.

Phone: 651-451-3030 **Fax:** 651-450-6130
Toll-Free: 888-844-0667
Address: 411 Farwell Ave. S., St. Paul, MN 55075 US

GROWTH PLANS/SPECIAL FEATURES:

The Sportsman's Guide, Inc., a subsidiary of Redcats USA (which is owned by Redcats Group), is a multi-channel direct marketer of value-priced outdoor gear and clothing, golf equipment and general merchandise. The company sells its products through main and specialty catalogs and several e-commerce sites, including SportsmansGuide.com and BargainOutfitters.com, a liquidation outlet. The firm's main catalog is mailed monthly and offers merchandise across a broad range of categories. Additional specialized catalogs are also offered during the course of each year and focus on individual categories such as camping, government surplus, ammunition and shooting supplies, gifts and hunting. The Buyers' Club, which customers can join for an annual fee, offers 10% discounts on most merchandise (5% on ammunition), a monthly Buyer's Advantage Catalog and exclusive special offers. The Sportsman's Guide e-commerce site offers a selection similar to its print catalog in addition to certain specialty catalogs available exclusively online. More than 65% of the company's sales come through its web site. An online resource center features a variety of articles, advice columns and information about outdoor lifestyles and pursuits, including a section specifically aimed at female outdoor enthusiasts. In addition, customers can find maps, fish and game forecasts, local guide and outfitter listings, ballistics charts, useful links and other information on the web site. Merchandise orders can be placed 24-hours-a-day by phone or online, and the company ships all orders directly from its 330,000-square-foot warehouse. In August 2010, the firm launched its new e-commerce web site, WorkwearSavings.com, which features name brand products at discounted prices.

FINANCIALS:

Sales and profits are in thousands of dollars—add 000 to get the full amount. 2011 Note: Financial information for 2011 was not available for all companies at press time.

2011 Sales: $ 2011 Profits: $
2010 Sales: $ 2010 Profits: $
2009 Sales: $ 2009 Profits: $
2008 Sales: $ 2008 Profits: $
2007 Sales: $ 2007 Profits: $

U.S. Stock Ticker: Subsidiary
Int'l Ticker:
Int'l Exchange:
Employees: Fiscal Year Ends: 12/31
Parent Company: REDCATS USA

SALARIES/BENEFITS:

Pension Plan: ESOP Stock Plan: Profit Sharing: Top Exec. Salary: $ Bonus: $655,000
Savings Plan: Stock Purch. Plan: Second Exec. Salary: $ Bonus: $

OTHER THOUGHTS:

Apparent Women Officers or Directors:
Hot Spot for Advancement for Women/Minorities:

LOCATIONS: ("Y" = Yes)

West:	Southwest:	Midwest:	Southeast:	Northeast:	International:
		Y			

SPROUTS FARMERS MARKET LLC

www.sprouts.com

Industry Group Code: 445110

Management:		Sales/Marketing:		Liberal Arts:		Information Systems:		Professionals:		Technical/Scientific:	
Mgmt. Trainees:	Y	Mktg. Professionals:	Y	Gen. Writing/Editing:	Y	Info. Management:	Y	Finance/Acct.:	Y	Engineers, Elec.:	
Experienced Mgmt.:	Y	Retail Sales:	Y	Technical Writing:		Software Dev.:	Y	Law:	Y	Engineers, Other:	
Int'l Business:		Commercial/Industrial:		Graphic Arts/Photog.:	Y	Hardware Dev.:		HR/Other:	Y	Health/Lab	
MBA Graduates:	Y	Sales Trainees:	Y	Music:		Consulting/Other:		Training:	Y	Scientists/Research:	
		Advertising Pros.:	Y	Broadcasting:				Health Care:		Petroleum/Chemicals:	
				Other:				Consulting:		Math/Other:	

TYPES OF BUSINESS:

Supermarkets

BRANDS/DIVISIONS/AFFILIATES:

Sprouts Magazine
Sprouts.com

CONTACTS:

Note: Officers with more than one job title may be intentionally listed here more than once.

Shon Boney, CEO
Doug Sanders, COO/Sr. VP
Shon Boney, Pres.
Brad Denton, CFO
Dana From, Mgr.-Media Rel.

Phone: 480-814-8016 **Fax:** 480-814-8017
Toll-Free: 888-577-7688
Address: 11811 N. Tatum Blvd., Ste. 2400, Phoenix, AZ 85028 US

GROWTH PLANS/SPECIAL FEATURES:

Sprouts Farmers Market LLC is an Arizona based independent natural foods retailer. The firm operates approximately 101 locations throughout California, Arizona, Texas and Colorado. The company's stores typically average between 23,000 to 37,000 square feet in size. The firm's products include baked goods, beer, wine, over 200 bulk food bins (rice and other grains, nuts, spices, dried fruit and old fashioned candies), dairy products, meat, poultry, produce, seafood, vitamins and supplements. In addition to Sprouts' own private label natural and organic foods, the company acquires products primarily from U.S. suppliers, emphasizing local buying practices. However, the company purchases certain seasonal fruits and vegetables from growers around the world. The firm's stores host a variety of events, such as cooking classes, health screenings and health information sessions. The company's web site (Sprouts.com) offers recipes, gift cards, nutritional information and a health guide. Additionally, the firm publishes a bimonthly magazine featuring articles on health, recipes and items of seasonal interest.

The company offers employees accidental death, short-term disability, critical illness, health, dental, vision and life insurance; a 401(k) plan after 90 days of employment; a 10% discount on all store purchases; paid time off; flexible spending account programs; weekly pay; pre-paid legal services; and bus cards.

FINANCIALS:

Sales and profits are in thousands of dollars—add 000 to get the full amount. 2011 Note: Financial information for 2011 was not available for all companies at press time.

2011 Sales: $	2011 Profits: $	**U.S. Stock Ticker: Private**
2010 Sales: $575,000	2010 Profits: $	**Int'l Ticker:**
2009 Sales: $	2009 Profits: $	Int'l Exchange:
2008 Sales: $	2008 Profits: $	Employees: Fiscal Year Ends:
2007 Sales: $	2007 Profits: $	Parent Company:

SALARIES/BENEFITS:

Pension Plan:	ESOP Stock Plan:	Profit Sharing:	Top Exec. Salary: $	Bonus: $
Savings Plan: Y	Stock Purch. Plan:		Second Exec. Salary: $	Bonus: $

OTHER THOUGHTS:

Apparent Women Officers or Directors: 1
Hot Spot for Advancement for Women/Minorities:

LOCATIONS: ("Y" = Yes)

West:	Southwest:	Midwest:	Southeast:	Northeast:	International:
Y	Y				

SRS LABS INC

www.srslabs.com

Industry Group Code: 334310

Management:		Sales/Marketing:		Liberal Arts:		Information Systems:		Professionals:		Technical/Scientific:	
Mgmt. Trainees:		Mktg. Professionals:		Gen. Writing/Editing:		Info. Management:	Y	Finance/Acct.:	Y	Engineers, Elec.:	Y
Experienced Mgmt.:	Y	Retail Sales:		Technical Writing:	Y	Software Dev.:	Y	Law:	Y	Engineers, Other:	
Int'l Business:	Y	Commercial/Industrial:	Y	Graphic Arts/Photog.:		Hardware Dev.:	Y	HR/Other:	Y	Health/Lab	
MBA Graduates:	Y	Sales Trainees:		Music:		Consulting/Other:		Training:		Scientists/Research:	
		Advertising Pros.:		Broadcasting:				Health Care:		Petroleum/Chemicals:	
				Other:				Consulting:		Math/Other:	

TYPES OF BUSINESS:

Audio & Video Equipment Technology
Technology Licensing
Audio Processing Systems

BRANDS/DIVISIONS/AFFILIATES:

Circle Surround
TruSurround
TruVolume
WOW

CONTACTS:

Note: Officers with more than one job title may be intentionally listed here more than once.

Thomas C. K. Yuen, CEO
Thomas C. K. Yuen, Pres.
Walter McBride, CFO
Alan Gharapetein, Sr. VP-Mktg.
David Walker, Sr. VP-Human Resources
Alan D. Kraemer, CTO
Sarah Yang, Sr. VP-Software Eng.
Maria Oppgard, Chief Acct. Officer
Bob Lyle, VP-Mobile Solutions Group
Thomas C. K. Yuen, Chmn.
Jeff Klaas, Sr. VP-Global Sales

Phone: 949-442-1070 **Fax:** 949-852-1099
Toll-Free: 800-243-2733
Address: 2909 Daimler St., Santa Ana, CA 92705 US

GROWTH PLANS/SPECIAL FEATURES:

SRS Labs, Inc. is a leading developer and provider of psychoacoustic applications. The firm's audio and voice technology solutions are utilized by the home entertainment, portable media device, personal telecommunications, personal computer, automotive and broadcast markets. SRS Labs develops and licenses audio, voice and surround sound technology solutions to leading original equipment manufacturers (OEMs), software providers and semiconductor companies worldwide. The company also licenses and markets hardware and software products to the PC and broadcast audio markets. SRS Labs' WOW playback enhancement technology improves the dynamics and bass performance of mono or stereo audio when used with smaller speakers or headphones or when the audio has been digitally compressed. This technology is particularly useful in mobile phones and home entertainment. The company's TruSurround XT technology processes up to seven channels of audio for playback over two speakers. Circle Surround, the company's encoding and decoding format, enables the distribution of up to 6.1 channels of audio over two-channel carriers. TruVolume is an intelligent volume control solution that eliminates fluctuations in volume in television broadcasts. SRS Labs' surround sound and voice processing technologies have been used in over 1 billion electronic products, including high-definition televisions (HDTVs), mobile phones, portable media devices, PCs and automotive entertainment systems. The home entertainment industry accounts for approximately 64% of SRS Labs' licensing revenues; PC applications, 16%; personal telecommunications, 10%; automotive, 7%; and portable media devices, 3%. Sales to Samsung and its affiliates accounted for approximately 38% of SRS Labs' sales.

FINANCIALS:

Sales and profits are in thousands of dollars—add 000 to get the full amount. 2011 Note: Financial information for 2011 was not available for all companies at press time.

2011 Sales: $	2011 Profits: $	**U.S. Stock Ticker: SRSL**
2010 Sales: $31,220	2010 Profits: $3,006	**Int'l Ticker:**
2009 Sales: $24,965	2009 Profits: $2,136	Int'l Exchange:
2008 Sales: $18,333	2008 Profits: $ 271	Employees: 106 Fiscal Year Ends: 12/31
2007 Sales: $18,852	2007 Profits: $5,414	Parent Company:

SALARIES/BENEFITS:

Pension Plan:	ESOP Stock Plan:	Profit Sharing: Y	Top Exec. Salary: $330,000	Bonus: $101,826
Savings Plan: Y	Stock Purch. Plan:		Second Exec. Salary: $314,000	Bonus: $82,140

OTHER THOUGHTS:

Apparent Women Officers or Directors: 2
Hot Spot for Advancement for Women/Minorities:

LOCATIONS: ("Y" = Yes)

West:	Southwest:	Midwest:	Southeast:	Northeast:	International:
Y					Y

SS&C TECHNOLOGIES HOLDINGS INC

www.ssctech.com

Industry Group Code: 511210

Management:		Sales/Marketing:		Liberal Arts:		Information Systems:		Professionals:		Technical/Scientific:	
Mgmt. Trainees:		Mktg. Professionals:	Y	Gen. Writing/Editing:		Info. Management:	Y	Finance/Acct.:	Y	Engineers, Elec.:	Y
Experienced Mgmt.:	Y	Retail Sales:		Technical Writing:	Y	Software Dev.:	Y	Law:	Y	Engineers, Other:	
Int'l Business:	Y	Commercial/Industrial:	Y	Graphic Arts/Photog.:		Hardware Dev.:		HR/Other:	Y	Health/Lab	
MBA Graduates:	Y	Sales Trainees:	Y	Music:		Consulting/Other:		Training:	Y	Scientists/Research:	
		Advertising Pros.:		Broadcasting:				Health Care:		Petroleum/Chemicals:	
				Other:				Consulting:		Math/Other:	

TYPES OF BUSINESS:

Financial and Investment Management Software
Business Process Outsourcing Services
Application Service Provider Solutions
Financial Education & Simulation Products
Hedge Fund Management Services

BRANDS/DIVISIONS/AFFILIATES:

SS&C Technologies Inc
BANC Mall
Antares
BenefitsXML
SSCFundServices.com
AdvisorWare

CONTACTS: *Note: Officers with more than one job title may be intentionally listed here more than once.*

William C. Stone, CEO
Normand A. Boulanger, COO
Normand A. Boulanger, Pres.
Patrick J.Pedonti, CFO/Sr. VP
Stephen V.R. Whitman, General Counsel/Sr. VP
Steve H. Kremidas, Chief Dev. Officer/Sr. VP
Phil Banas, Managing Dir.-SS&C Australia
Andrew Sexton, Managing Dir.-SS&C EMEA
Alex Marasco, Sr. VP/Gen. Mgr.-Asset Mgmt.
Colleen Nelsen, Sr. VP/Gen. Mgr.-Treasury, Banks & Credit Unions
William C. Stone, Chmn.
Tee Arasoo, Managing Dir.-SS&C Asia Pacific

Phone: 860-298-4500	**Fax:** 860-298-4900
Toll-Free: 800-234-0556	
Address: 80 Lamberton Rd., Windsor, CT 06095 US	

GROWTH PLANS/SPECIAL FEATURES:

SS&C Technologies Holdings, Inc., operating through SS&C Technologies, Inc., is an international company offering a family of highly specialized, mission-critical software and services. These services help automate and simplify information management, analysis, accounting, reporting and compliance for investment professionals in a broad range of financial services segments. The company's products allow clients to rapidly access, manage and analyze large amounts of transactions-based data both in the aggregate and in detail. The firm serves over 4,500 clients globally. The company's over 60 products and services cover eight main industry segments: alternative investments; asset management; insurance and pension funds; commercial lending; treasury, banks and credit unions; financial institutions; municipal finance; and real estate property management. Various branded products/services within the SS&C product lines include AdvisorWare, a software that supports hedge funds, funds of funds and family offices with sophisticated global investment, trading and management concerns; BANC Mall, an Internet-based research and lending tool for loan administration; and Antares, a real-time, event-driven trading and profit and loss reporting system designed to integrate trade modeling with trade order management. The firm's software-as-a-service business accounts for roughly 86% of total revenues, with approximately 83% of its business coming from North America. SS&C has expanded through acquisitions, acquiring 31 businesses since 1995 with the goal of obtaining companies that provide complementary products, address highly specialized niche markets, have strategic geographical presences, offer expertise that is amenable to software delivered services and possess proven technologies that can be further exploited. In March 2011, the firm acquired enterprise software solutions provider BenefitsXML. In June 2011, SS&C introduced new cloud-based platform SSCFundServices.com.

Employees are offered health benefits; flexible spending accounts; life and disability insurance; a 401(k); and tuition reimbursement.

FINANCIALS: **Sales and profits are in thousands of dollars—add 000 to get the full amount. 2011 Note: Financial information for 2011 was not available for all companies at press time.**

2011 Sales: $370,828	2011 Profits: $51,021	**U.S. Stock Ticker: SSNC**
2010 Sales: $328,905	2010 Profits: $32,413	**Int'l Ticker:**
2009 Sales: $270,915	2009 Profits: $19,018	Int'l Exchange:
2008 Sales: $280,006	2008 Profits: $18,801	Employees: 1,399 Fiscal Year Ends: 12/31
2007 Sales: $248,168	2007 Profits: $6,575	Parent Company:

SALARIES/BENEFITS:

Pension Plan:	ESOP Stock Plan:	Profit Sharing:	Top Exec. Salary: $	Bonus: $
Savings Plan: Y	Stock Purch. Plan:		Second Exec. Salary: $	Bonus: $

OTHER THOUGHTS:

Apparent Women Officers or Directors: 1
Hot Spot for Advancement for Women/Minorities:

LOCATIONS: ("Y" = Yes)

West:	Southwest:	Midwest:	Southeast:	Northeast:	International:
Y		Y		Y	Y

STAAR SURGICAL CO

www.staar.com

Industry Group Code: 33911

Management:		Sales/Marketing:		Liberal Arts:		Information Systems:		Professionals:		Technical/Scientific:	
Mgmt. Trainees:		Mktg. Professionals:	Y	Gen. Writing/Editing:		Info. Management:	Y	Finance/Acct.:	Y	Engineers, Elec.:	
Experienced Mgmt.:	Y	Retail Sales:		Technical Writing:	Y	Software Dev.:	Y	Law:	Y	Engineers, Other:	Y
Int'l Business:	Y	Commercial/Industrial:	Y	Graphic Arts/Photog.:		Hardware Dev.:	Y	HR/Other:	Y	Health/Lab	Y
MBA Graduates:	Y	Sales Trainees:	Y	Music:		Consulting/Other:		Training:	Y	Scientists/Research:	Y
		Advertising Pros.:		Broadcasting:				Health Care:	Y	Petroleum/Chemicals:	
				Other:				Consulting:		Math/Other:	

TYPES OF BUSINESS:

Equipment-Ophthalmic Surgery
Intraocular Lenses

BRANDS/DIVISIONS/AFFILIATES:

Collamer
Visian ICL
Visian Toric ICL
AquaFlow
Visian Implantable Collamer Lens V4

CONTACTS:

Note: Officers with more than one job title may be intentionally listed here more than once.

Barry Caldwell, CEO
Barry Caldwell, Pres.
Deborah Andrews, CFO/VP
Robin Hughes, VP-Global Mktg.
William Goodmen, VP-Global Human Resources
Craig Felberg, VP-Global R&D
Charles S. Kaufman, General Counsel/VP/Corp. Sec.
Paul Hambrick, VP-Global Oper.
Hans M. Blickensdoerfer, Pres., EMEA & Latin America
Philippe Subrin, VP-Switzerland Oper.
Donald Todd, Pres., Asia Pacific
Donald Lee Fagan, VP-North America Sales
Don M. Bailey, Chmn.
David Bailey, Pres., Int'l Oper.

Phone: 626-303-7902 **Fax:** 626-359-8402
Toll-Free: 800-352-7842
Address: 1911 Walker Ave., Monrovia, CA 91016 US

GROWTH PLANS/SPECIAL FEATURES:

STAAR Surgical Co. develops, produces and markets medical devices used to improve or correct vision in patients with refractive conditions, cataracts and glaucoma. Based in California, the firm operates primarily in the U.S., Switzerland and Japan; approximately 73% of its revenues are derived from international operations. The company's main product line consists of one-piece and three-piece foldable silicone and Collamer intraocular lenses (IOLs), used after cataract extraction. The lens is folded and implanted into the eye behind the iris and in front of the natural lens using minimally invasive techniques. This procedure is performed with topical anesthesia on an outpatient basis, with visual recovery within one to 24 hours. The firm has developed two implantable Collamer lenses (ICLs), the Visian ICL and Visian Toric ICL, to treat astigmatic abnormalities, myopia (near-sightedness) and hypermyopia (far-sightedness). These products are sold to ophthalmologists, surgical centers, hospitals, managed care providers, health maintenance organizations and group purchasing organizations in over 50 countries. The firm's Japanese subsidiary, STAAR Japan, Inc., manufactures and markets a preloaded injector system for deploying intraocular lenses in the eye. Sales of IOLs account for approximately 50% of STAAR's revenues, while ICLs account for 44%. STAAR also offers AquaFlow, an implant used in the treatment of glaucoma. These products are designed to improve patient outcomes, minimize patient risk and discomfort and simplify ophthalmic procedures and post-operative care. In June 2011, the firm received permission to market Visian Implantable Collamer Lens V4 in Brazil.

The company offers employees medical, dental, life, long-term disability and vision insurance.

FINANCIALS:

Sales and profits are in thousands of dollars—add 000 to get the full amount. 2011 Note: Financial information for 2011 was not available for all companies at press time.

2011 Sales: $	2011 Profits: $	**U.S. Stock Ticker: STAA**
2010 Sales: $54,958	2010 Profits: $ 53	**Int'l Ticker:**
2009 Sales: $51,060	2009 Profits: $-6,200	Int'l Exchange:
2008 Sales: $74,894	2008 Profits: $-23,195	Employees: 279 Fiscal Year Ends: 12/31
2007 Sales: $59,363	2007 Profits: $-15,999	Parent Company:

SALARIES/BENEFITS:

Pension Plan:	ESOP Stock Plan:	Profit Sharing:	Top Exec. Salary: $428,462	Bonus: $180,000
Savings Plan: Y	Stock Purch. Plan:		Second Exec. Salary: $325,274	Bonus: $

OTHER THOUGHTS:

Apparent Women Officers or Directors: 1
Hot Spot for Advancement for Women/Minorities:

LOCATIONS: ("Y" = Yes)

West:	Southwest:	Midwest:	Southeast:	Northeast:	International:
Y					Y

STATE AUTO FINANCIAL CORP

www.stateauto.com

Industry Group Code: 524126

Management:		Sales/Marketing:		Liberal Arts:		Information Systems:		Professionals:		Technical/Scientific:	
Mgmt. Trainees:	Y	Mktg. Professionals:	Y	Gen. Writing/Editing:	Y	Info. Management:	Y	Finance/Acct.:	Y	Engineers, Elec.:	
Experienced Mgmt.:	Y	Retail Sales:		Technical Writing:	Y	Software Dev.:		Law:	Y	Engineers, Other:	
Int'l Business:		Commercial/Industrial:	Y	Graphic Arts/Photog.:		Hardware Dev.:		HR/Other:	Y	Health/Lab	
MBA Graduates:	Y	Sales Trainees:	Y	Music:		Consulting/Other:		Training:	Y	Scientists/Research:	
		Advertising Pros.:		Broadcasting:				Health Care:		Petroleum/Chemicals:	
				Other:				Consulting:		Math/Other:	Y

TYPES OF BUSINESS:

Direct Property & Casualty Insurance
Investment Management
Insurance Processing Software
Financial Services
Real Estate

BRANDS/DIVISIONS/AFFILIATES:

Farmers Casualty Insurance Co
State Auto Property & Casualty Insurance
State Auto National Insurance Company
State Automobile Mutual Insurance Co
Milbank Insurance Co
Stateco Financial Services
518 Property Management & Leasing LLC

CONTACTS: *Note: Officers with more than one job title may be intentionally listed here more than once.*

Robert P. Restrepo Jr., CEO
Robert P. Restrepo Jr., Pres.
Steven E. English, CFO/VP
Clyde H. Fitch, Jr., Chief Sales Officer/Sr. VP
Doug E. Allen, VP/Dir.-IT
James A. Yano, General Counsel/VP/Sec.
Larry D. Williams, VP/Dir.-Middle Market Oper.
Cathy B. Miley, VP/Dir.-Corp. Dev.
Kyle Anderson, Dir.-Corp. Comm.
Terrence L. Bowshier, VP/Dir.-Investor Rel.
Cynthia A. Powell, Chief Acct. Officer/VP/Treas.
Joel E. Brown, VP/Dir.-Standard Lines
James E. Duemey, VP-Investment Officer
John M. Petrucci, VP/Dir.-Sales
Jean Reynolds, VP/Dir.-Budgeting & Planning
Robert P. Restrepo Jr., Chmn.

Phone: 614-464-5000 **Fax:** 614-464-5325
Toll-Free: 800-444-9950
Address: 518 E. Broad St., Columbus, OH 43215-3976 US

GROWTH PLANS/SPECIAL FEATURES:

State Auto Financial Corp. (STFC) is a super-regional property and casualty insurance holding company. The firm is primarily engaged in writing business and personal lines of insurance. It has three significant reportable segments: personal insurance, business insurance and specialty insurance. The insurance segments are managed separately because of the differences in types of customers served, products provided or services offered. The personal insurance segment provides primarily personal auto (standard and nonstandard) and homeowners to the personal insurance market. The business insurance segment provides primarily commercial auto, commercial multi-peril, fire and allied lines, other and product liability and workers' compensation insurance to small to mid-sized businesses within the commercial insurance market. The specialty insurance segment offers commercial coverages that require specialized product underwriting, claims handling or risk management services. It has three units: RED, which markets and underwrites small-to-medium commercial exposures; Rockhill, which markets and underwrites commercial exposures which have unique insurance requirements; and Workers' Compensation, which serves the small-to-medium account and association business. The firm's operations are carried out in 34 states by four subsidiaries: State Auto Property and Casualty Insurance (P&C); Milbank Insurance Co.; Farmers Casualty Insurance Co.; and State Auto Insurance Co. of Ohio. The firm and its subsidiaries are affiliated with State Automobile Mutual Insurance Co., which owns approximately 63% of the firm's outstanding common shares. STFC also has two non-insurance subsidiaries: Stateco Financial Services, which provides investment management services to company affiliates and customers; and 518 Property Management and Leasing, LLC (owned through State Auto P&C and Stateco Financial Services) which owns and leases real estate and personal property to the company and its affiliates. In December 2010, SATFC sold State Auto National Insurance Company, a non-standard automobile insurance subsidiary, to Hallmark Insurance Company.

The company offers employees benefits including life and health insurance; a 401(k); tuition assistance; and a stock purchase plan.

FINANCIALS: **Sales and profits are in thousands of dollars—add 000 to get the full amount. 2011 Note: Financial information for 2011 was not available for all companies at press time.**

2011 Sales: $1,315,811 — 2011 Profits: $-146,800
2010 Sales: $1,355,110 — 2010 Profits: $24,500
2009 Sales: $1,256,900 — 2009 Profits: $10,200
2008 Sales: $1,181,900 — 2008 Profits: $-31,100
2007 Sales: $1,011,600 — 2007 Profits: $119,100

U.S. Stock Ticker: STFC
Int'l Ticker:
Int'l Exchange:
Employees: 2,483 Fiscal Year Ends: 12/31
Parent Company:

SALARIES/BENEFITS:

Pension Plan: Y ESOP Stock Plan: Profit Sharing: Top Exec. Salary: $750,192 Bonus: $528,481
Savings Plan: Y Stock Purch. Plan: Y Second Exec. Salary: $473,077 Bonus: $305,769

OTHER THOUGHTS:

Apparent Women Officers or Directors: 7
Hot Spot for Advancement for Women/Minorities: Y

LOCATIONS: ("Y" = Yes)

West:	Southwest:	Midwest:	Southeast:	Northeast:	International:
Y	Y	Y	Y	Y	

STEPAN COMPANY

www.stepan.com

Industry Group Code: 325

Management:		**Sales/Marketing:**		**Liberal Arts:**		**Information Systems:**		**Professionals:**		**Technical/Scientific:**	
Mgmt. Trainees:		Mktg. Professionals:	Y	Gen. Writing/Editing:		Info. Management:	Y	Finance/Acct.:	Y	Engineers, Elec.:	Y
Experienced Mgmt.:	Y	Retail Sales:		Technical Writing:	Y	Software Dev.:		Law:	Y	Engineers, Other:	Y
Int'l Business:	Y	Commercial/Industrial:	Y	Graphic Arts/Photog.:		Hardware Dev.:		HR/Other:	Y	Health/Lab	
MBA Graduates:	Y	Sales Trainees:	Y	Music:		Consulting/Other:		Training:	Y	Scientists/Research:	Y
		Advertising Pros.:		Broadcasting:				Health Care:		Petroleum/Chemicals:	Y
				Other:				Consulting:		Math/Other:	

TYPES OF BUSINESS:

Specialty & Intermediate Chemicals
Surfactants
Polymers

BRANDS/DIVISIONS/AFFILIATES:

BIO-SOFT
NACCONOL
STEOL
Stepan Philippines, Inc.

CONTACTS:

Note: Officers with more than one job title may be intentionally listed here more than once.

F. Quinn Stepan, Jr., CEO
F. Quinn Stepan, Jr., Pres.
James E. Hurlbutt, CFO/VP
Mark F. Mydlach, VP-Surfactant Sales
Greg Servatius, VP-Human Resources
Frank Pacholec, VP-R&D
Matthew I. Levinson, VP-Global Process Dev.
Robert S. Mangold, VP-Eng.
Robert S. Mangold, VP-Mfg.
H. Edward Wynn, General Counsel/VP/Sec.
Kyle Montgomery, VP-Plant Oper., Americas
James S. Pall, VP-Corp. Dev.
John V. Venegoni, VP/Gen. Mgr.-Surfactants
Robert J. Wood, VP/Gen. Mgr.-Polymers
Anthony Martin, VP-Europe
Debra A. Stefaniak, VP-Global Logistics
F. Quinn Stepan, Chmn.
Charles A. Brown, VP-Latin America
Scott C. Mason, VP-Supply Chain

Phone: 847-446-7500	**Fax:** 847-501-2100
Toll-Free:	
Address: Edens and Winnetka Rd., Northfield, IL 60093 US	

GROWTH PLANS/SPECIAL FEATURES:

Stepan Company produces specialty and intermediate chemicals used in consumer products and industrial applications. The company operates through three segments: surfactants, polymers and specialty products. Surfactants are chemical agents that affect the interaction between two surfaces, causing actions such as detergency, wetting and foaming, dispersing, emulsification, demulsification, viscosity modifications and biocidal disinfectants. Surfactants are the basic cleaning agent in products such as detergents, shampoos and conditioners, fabric softeners, toothpastes, floor polishes, latex foams and coatings, cosmetics and other personal care products. Some of Stepan's surfactants brands, including BIO-SOFT, NACCONOL and STEOL, are found in laundry and dishwashing detergents, all-purpose cleaners, disinfectants, vehicle cleaning compounds, heavy duty commercial and industrial cleaners. Polymers, which include phthalic anhydride, polyols and polyurethane foam systems, are used in plastics, building materials and refrigeration industries. Polymers are also used in coating, adhesive, sealant and elastomer applications. Stepan is a principal provider of polymers used in construction, refrigeration, automotive, boating and other consumer product industries. Specialty products include chemicals used in food, flavoring and pharmaceutical applications. In July 2010, the firm acquired a Singapore methyl ester plant with a 100,000 ton-per-year production capacity from Peter Cremer GmbH. In July 2010, the company increased its ownership interest in joint venture Stepan Philippines, Inc. (with United Coconut Chemicals, Inc.) from 50% to 88.8%.

Stepan offers its employees medical, dental and vision insurance; flexible spending accounts; a 401(k) plan; a pension plan; a profit sharing plan; an employee stock ownership plan; life, AD&D and disability insurance; tuition reimbursement; an employee stock purchase plan; an employee assistance program; a quality recognition program; and the Stepan into wellness initiative.

FINANCIALS:

Sales and profits are in thousands of dollars—add 000 to get the full amount. 2011 Note: Financial information for 2011 was not available for all companies at press time.

2011 Sales: $1,843,092	2011 Profits: $71,976
2010 Sales: $1,431,122	2010 Profits: $65,427
2009 Sales: $1,276,382	2009 Profits: $63,049
2008 Sales: $1,600,130	2008 Profits: $37,172
2007 Sales: $1,329,901	2007 Profits: $15,118

U.S. Stock Ticker: SCL
Int'l Ticker:
Int'l Exchange:
Employees: 1,768 Fiscal Year Ends: 12/31
Parent Company:

SALARIES/BENEFITS:

Pension Plan: Y	ESOP Stock Plan: Y	Profit Sharing: Y	Top Exec. Salary: $683,333	Bonus: $450,795
Savings Plan: Y	Stock Purch. Plan:		Second Exec. Salary: $500,000	Bonus: $245,100

OTHER THOUGHTS:

Apparent Women Officers or Directors: 2
Hot Spot for Advancement for Women/Minorities:

LOCATIONS: ("Y" = Yes)

West:	Southwest:	Midwest:	Southeast:	Northeast:	International:
Y		Y	Y	Y	Y

STERLING AUTOBODY CENTERS

www.sterlingautobody.com

Industry Group Code: 8111

Management:		Sales/Marketing:		Liberal Arts:		Information Systems:		Professionals:		Technical/Scientific:	
Mgmt. Trainees:	Y	Mktg. Professionals:	Y	Gen. Writing/Editing:	Y	Info. Management:	Y	Finance/Acct.:	Y	Engineers, Elec.:	
Experienced Mgmt.:	Y	Retail Sales:		Technical Writing:	Y	Software Dev.:	Y	Law:	Y	Engineers, Other:	
Int'l Business:	Y	Commercial/Industrial:		Graphic Arts/Photog.:		Hardware Dev.:		HR/Other:	Y	Health/Lab	
MBA Graduates:	Y	Sales Trainees:		Music:		Consulting/Other:		Training:	Y	Scientists/Research:	
		Advertising Pros.:	Y	Broadcasting:				Health Care:		Petroleum/Chemicals:	
				Other:				Consulting:		Math/Other:	

TYPES OF BUSINESS:

Automotive Repair & Maintenance
Collision Repair

BRANDS/DIVISIONS/AFFILIATES:

Allstate Insurance Corporation (The)
Enterprise Rent-A-Car
Sterling University

CONTACTS:

Note: Officers with more than one job title may be intentionally listed here more than once.

Nick Notte, Pres.
Mike Nuxoll, VP-Human Resources & Training
Dan Lajoie, VP-Store Admin. & Construction
Roger Wright, VP-Oper.
Sharon Mazanec, VP-Corp. Comm.
Tony Giannola, VP-Finance
Bob Benjamin, VP-Strategic Design & Process Implementation
Sharon Mazanec, VP-Real Estate
Lou DiLisio, VP-Oper.
Tony Giannola, VP-Procurement

Phone:	**Fax:** 508-653-9538
Toll-Free: 800-653-5310	
Address: 9 Tech Cir., Natick, MA 01760 US	

GROWTH PLANS/SPECIAL FEATURES:

Sterling Autobody Centers, a subsidiary of The Allstate Corporation, operates over 60 automobile collision repair centers in 16 U.S. states, including California, Nevada, Arizona, Utah, Colorado, Texas, Illinois, Michigan, New York, Georgia and Florida. Known for its customer service, the company picks up damaged cars, delivers repaired cars, has all cars professionally cleaned and offers a limited lifetime warranty on all work performed. Through a partnership with Enterprise Rent-a-Car, the firm will also deliver and return rental cars for its customers. Sterling works exclusively with Enterprise Rent-A-Car for replacement cars during repair.

Sterling offers its employees medical, dental and vision care; short- and long-term disability; life insurance; and Sterling University, a company-wide program that teaches a variety of technical and managerial skills, to train and advance its employees.

FINANCIALS:

Sales and profits are in thousands of dollars—add 000 to get the full amount. 2011 Note: Financial information for 2011 was not available for all companies at press time.

2011 Sales: $	2011 Profits: $
2010 Sales: $	2010 Profits: $
2009 Sales: $	2009 Profits: $
2008 Sales: $	2008 Profits: $
2007 Sales: $	2007 Profits: $

U.S. Stock Ticker: Subsidiary
Int'l Ticker:
Int'l Exchange:
Employees: Fiscal Year Ends:
Parent Company: ALLSTATE CORPORATION (THE)

SALARIES/BENEFITS:

Pension Plan:	ESOP Stock Plan:	Profit Sharing:	Top Exec. Salary: $	Bonus: $
Savings Plan: Y	Stock Purch. Plan:		Second Exec. Salary: $	Bonus: $

OTHER THOUGHTS:

Apparent Women Officers or Directors: 1
Hot Spot for Advancement for Women/Minorities:

LOCATIONS: ("Y" = Yes)

West:	Southwest:	Midwest:	Southeast:	Northeast:	International:
Y	Y	Y	Y	Y	

STERLING CONSTRUCTION COMPANY

www.sterlingconstructionco.com

Industry Group Code: 237

Management:		**Sales/Marketing:**		**Liberal Arts:**		**Information Systems:**		**Professionals:**		**Technical/Scientific:**	
Mgmt. Trainees:	Y	Mktg. Professionals:	Y	Gen. Writing/Editing:		Info. Management:	Y	Finance/Acct.:	Y	Engineers, Elec.:	Y
Experienced Mgmt.:	Y	Retail Sales:		Technical Writing:	Y	Software Dev.:		Law:	Y	Engineers, Other:	Y
Int'l Business:		Commercial/Industrial:	Y	Graphic Arts/Photog.:	Y	Hardware Dev.:		HR/Other:	Y	Health/Lab	
MBA Graduates:	Y	Sales Trainees:	Y	Music:		Consulting/Other:		Training:		Scientists/Research:	
		Advertising Pros.:		Broadcasting:				Health Care:		Petroleum/Chemicals:	
				Other:				Consulting:		Math/Other:	

TYPES OF BUSINESS:

Heavy Construction & Reconstruction, Civil
Transportation & Water Infrastructure
Municipal Construction

BRANDS/DIVISIONS/AFFILIATES:

Texas Sterling Construction LP
Road and Highway Builders LLC
Ralph L. Wadsworth Construction Co LLC
Road and Highway Builders Inc
Road and Highway Builders of California Inc

CONTACTS: *Note: Officers with more than one job title may be intentionally listed here more than once.*

Patrick T. Manning, CEO
Joseph P. Harper, Sr., COO
Joseph P. Harper, Sr., Pres./Treas.
James H. Allen, Jr., CFO/Sr. VP
Roger M. Barzun, General Counsel/Sr. VP/Sec.
Anthony F. Colombo, Exec. VP-Oper.
Brian R. Manning, Chief Bus. Dev. Officer/Exec. VP
Joseph P. Harper, Jr., Exec. VP-Finance
Elizabeth D. Brumley, Chief Acct. Officer
Patrick T. Manning, Chmn.

Phone: 281-821-9091	**Fax:** 281-821-2995
Toll-Free:	
Address: 20810 Fernbush Ln., Houston, TX 77073 US	

GROWTH PLANS/SPECIAL FEATURES:

Sterling Construction Company is a civil construction company that builds and reconstructs water and transportation infrastructure in Nevada, Utah and Texas. It operates in the Texas markets of Houston, San Antonio, Dallas/Fort Worth and Austin; and provides services in Utah and Nevada. The firm operates entirely through five subsidiaries: Texas Sterling Construction, LP; Road and Highway Builders, LLC (Nevada); Road and Highway Builders, Inc.; Road and Highway Builders of California, Inc.; and Ralph L. Wadsworth Construction Company, LLC (Utah). Sterling Construction's activities include concrete and asphalt paving; concrete slip forming; concrete crushing; concrete batch plant operations; installation of large-diameter water and wastewater distribution systems; bridge construction; and the building of light rail infrastructure. The company provides general contracting services to both public sector and municipal clients, utilizing its own employees and equipment for activities including excavating, paving, pipe installation and concrete placement. The firm normally purchases its own materials, using subcontractors only for ancillary services. The Utah Department of Transportation, Sterling Construction's largest customer, accounts for approximately 26.2% of the company's revenue; the Texas Department of Transportation, its second largest customer, represents 20.7% of its total revenue.

FINANCIALS: **Sales and profits are in thousands of dollars—add 000 to get the full amount. 2011 Note: Financial information for 2011 was not available for all companies at press time.**

2011 Sales: $ | 2011 Profits: $
2010 Sales: $459,893 | 2010 Profits: $26,224
2009 Sales: $390,847 | 2009 Profits: $23,704
2008 Sales: $415,074 | 2008 Profits: $18,066
2007 Sales: $306,220 | 2007 Profits: $14,444

U.S. Stock Ticker: STRL
Int'l Ticker:
Int'l Exchange:
Employees: 1,300 Fiscal Year Ends: 12/31
Parent Company:

SALARIES/BENEFITS:

Pension Plan: ESOP Stock Plan: Profit Sharing: Top Exec. Salary: $365,000 Bonus: $325,000
Savings Plan: Stock Purch. Plan: Second Exec. Salary: $365,000 Bonus: $325,000

OTHER THOUGHTS:

Apparent Women Officers or Directors: 1
Hot Spot for Advancement for Women/Minorities:

LOCATIONS: ("Y" = Yes)

West:	Southwest:	Midwest:	Southeast:	Northeast:	International:
Y	Y				

STEVEN MADDEN LTD

www.stevemadden.com

Industry Group Code: 3162

Management:		**Sales/Marketing:**		**Liberal Arts:**		**Information Systems:**		**Professionals:**		**Technical/Scientific:**	
Mgmt. Trainees:		Mktg. Professionals:	Y	Gen. Writing/Editing:	Y	Info. Management:	Y	Finance/Acct.:	Y	Engineers, Elec.:	
Experienced Mgmt.:	Y	Retail Sales:		Technical Writing:		Software Dev.:		Law:	Y	Engineers, Other:	
Int'l Business:	Y	Commercial/Industrial:	Y	Graphic Arts/Photog.:	Y	Hardware Dev.:		HR/Other:	Y	Health/Lab	
MBA Graduates:	Y	Sales Trainees:	Y	Music:		Consulting/Other:		Training:	Y	Scientists/Research:	
		Advertising Pros.:	Y	Broadcasting:				Health Care:		Petroleum/Chemicals:	
				Other:	Y			Consulting:		Math/Other:	

TYPES OF BUSINESS:

Shoes, Manufacturing
Retail Stores
Online Sales
Women's Jewelry & Accessories
Brand Licensing

BRANDS/DIVISIONS/AFFILIATES:

Steve Madden
Steven
Elizabeth and James
Steven Maddden Retail Inc
Adesso-Madden Inc
Big Buddha
Betsey Johnson
Madden Girl

CONTACTS: *Note: Officers with more than one job title may be intentionally listed here more than once.*

Edward R. Rosenfeld, CEO
Awadesh Sinha, COO
Arvind Dharia, CFO
Robert Schmertz, Dir.-Brand
Arvind Dharia, Corp. Sec.
Amelia N. Varela, Exec. VP-Wholesale & Retail
Edward R. Rosenfeld, Chmn.

Phone: 718-446-1800	**Fax:** 718-446-5655
Toll-Free:	
Address: 52-16 Barnett Ave., Long Island City, NY 11104 US	

GROWTH PLANS/SPECIAL FEATURES:

Steven Madden, Ltd. designs, sources, markets and sells shoes for men, women and children. Headquartered in New York, it distributes products through its retail stores, its e-commerce web site and department and specialty stores throughout the U.S. and Canada, as well as Europe, Latin America and the Asia-Pacific. The company operates in five segments: wholesale footwear, wholesale accessories, retail, first cost and licensing. The wholesale footwear division is comprised of the Women's, Men's, Kid's, Madden Girl, Steven, International and Elizabeth and James segments. Madden Women's wholesale, the company's largest division, designs, sources and markets the Steve Madden brand to a variety of stores and boutiques. This division produces approximately 30% of the firm's net sales. Madden men's wholesale designs and markets men's casual and athletic shoes. The Kid's division designs shoes for young girls below the age of 13. Madden Girl markets young women's shoes geared for females ages 13-20. Steven designs, sources and markets footwear under the Steven brand. The International division handles the international shipment of all Madden footwear products. Through a license agreement with Dualstar Entertainment Group, LLC, the firm produces luxury footwear under the Elizabeth and James brand. The wholesale accessories segment designs, sources and markets name brand and private label fashion handbags and accessories. Its brands include Betsey Johnson, Big Buddha and Olsenboye, in addition to Steve Madden brands. The retail segment, operating through Steven Madden Retail, Inc., manages over 80 retail stores. The first cost division, through Adesso-Madden, Inc., acts as a buying agent for footwear products sold under private labels for mass merchandisers. The licensing segment is responsible for the licensing of the Steve Madden brand. In May 2011, the firm acquired Cejon, Inc., Cejon Accessories, Inc. and New East Designs, LLC for $30 million; and Topline Corporation for $55 million.

FINANCIALS: **Sales and profits are in thousands of dollars—add 000 to get the full amount. 2011 Note: Financial information for 2011 was not available for all companies at press time.**

2011 Sales: $968,549	2011 Profits: $97,319	**U.S. Stock Ticker: SHOO**
2010 Sales: $635,418	2010 Profits: $75,725	**Int'l Ticker:**
2009 Sales: $503,550	2009 Profits: $50,107	Int'l Exchange:
2008 Sales: $457,046	2008 Profits: $27,976	Employees: 1,440 Fiscal Year Ends: 12/31
2007 Sales: $431,050	2007 Profits: $35,690	Parent Company:

SALARIES/BENEFITS:

Pension Plan:	ESOP Stock Plan:	Profit Sharing:	Top Exec. Salary: $660,000	Bonus: $350,000
Savings Plan:	Stock Purch. Plan:		Second Exec. Salary: $539,963	Bonus: $175,500

OTHER THOUGHTS:

Apparent Women Officers or Directors: 1
Hot Spot for Advancement for Women/Minorities:

LOCATIONS: ("Y" = Yes)

West:	Southwest:	Midwest:	Southeast:	Northeast:	International:
Y	Y	Y	Y	Y	Y

STIEFEL LABORATORIES INC

Industry Group Code: 325412

www.stiefel.com

Management:		Sales/Marketing:		Liberal Arts:		Information Systems:		Professionals:		Technical/Scientific:	
Mgmt. Trainees:		Mktg. Professionals:	Y	Gen. Writing/Editing:		Info. Management:	Y	Finance/Acct.:	Y	Engineers, Elec.:	
Experienced Mgmt.:	Y	Retail Sales:		Technical Writing:	Y	Software Dev.:	Y	Law:	Y	Engineers, Other:	
Int'l Business:	Y	Commercial/Industrial:	Y	Graphic Arts/Photog.:		Hardware Dev.:		HR/Other:	Y	Health/Lab	Y
MBA Graduates:	Y	Sales Trainees:	Y	Music:		Consulting/Other:		Training:	Y	Scientists/Research:	Y
		Advertising Pros.:	Y	Broadcasting:				Health Care:	Y	Petroleum/Chemicals:	Y
				Other:				Consulting:		Math/Other:	Y

TYPES OF BUSINESS:

Dermatological & Skin Care Products

BRANDS/DIVISIONS/AFFILIATES:

Evoclin
Duac
Olux
MimyX
LUXIQ Foam
Verdeso
GlaxoSmithKline plc

CONTACTS:

Note: Officers with more than one job title may be intentionally listed here more than once.

Charles W. Stiefel, CEO
Bill Humphries, Pres.
Pascal Waucquez, VP-Global Mktg.
Michelle Biggs, Dir.-Human resources
Darren Coleman, VP-Oper.
Kristen Belmonte Slaoui, Head-Bus. Dev.
Stef Mendell, Head-Global Comm.
Chris Royal, Chief Compliance Officer
Salisa Hauptmann, VP-Regulatory Affairs
Francis Del Val, VP
Darren Coleman, VP-Strategy
Charles W. Stiefel, Chmn.

Phone: 305-443-3800	**Fax:** 305-443-3467
Toll-Free:	
Address: 20 T. W. Alexander Dr., Research Triangle Park, NC 33134-7412 US	

GROWTH PLANS/SPECIAL FEATURES:

Stiefel Laboratories, Inc., a subsidiary of GlaxoSmithKline plc, is a specialized pharmaceutical company that focuses on the advancement of dermatology and skin care. The company's sells hundreds of products that treat a wide range of dermatological ailments including acne, psoriasis, fungal infections, eczema, dry skin, oily skin, rosacea, seborrhea, pruritus and sun damaged and aging skin. Leading products include Evoclin and Duac, acne skin care products; MimyX, a cream that relieves dry and waxy skin for a variety of dermatoses; LUXIQ Foam, which reduces the signs of scalp dermatoses, such as scaling, redness, and plaques; Olux, also used for scalp treatment; and Verdeso, a treatment for eczema. The firm also offers pharmaceutical contract manufacturing of gels, creams, ointments, topical solutions and liquid orals, both prescription and over-the-counter. The company has subsidiaries in more than 30 countries and its products are available in more than 100 countries.

FINANCIALS:

Sales and profits are in thousands of dollars—add 000 to get the full amount. 2011 Note: Financial information for 2011 was not available for all companies at press time.

2011 Sales: $	2011 Profits: $	**U.S. Stock Ticker: Subsidiary**
2010 Sales: $	2010 Profits: $	**Int'l Ticker:**
2009 Sales: $	2009 Profits: $	Int'l Exchange:
2008 Sales: $	2008 Profits: $	Employees: Fiscal Year Ends:
2007 Sales: $	2007 Profits: $	Parent Company: GLAXOSMITHKLINE PLC

SALARIES/BENEFITS:

Pension Plan:	ESOP Stock Plan:	Profit Sharing:	Top Exec. Salary: $	Bonus: $
Savings Plan:	Stock Purch. Plan:		Second Exec. Salary: $	Bonus: $

OTHER THOUGHTS:

Apparent Women Officers or Directors: 4
Hot Spot for Advancement for Women/Minorities: Y

LOCATIONS: ("Y" = Yes)

West:	Southwest:	Midwest:	Southeast:	Northeast:	International:
Y			Y	Y	Y

SUN COMMUNITIES INC

www.suncommunities.com

Industry Group Code: 531120

Management:		Sales/Marketing:		Liberal Arts:		Information Systems:		Professionals:		Technical/Scientific:	
Mgmt. Trainees:	Y	Mktg. Professionals:	Y	Gen. Writing/Editing:	Y	Info. Management:	Y	Finance/Acct.:	Y	Engineers, Elec.:	
Experienced Mgmt.:	Y	Retail Sales:		Technical Writing:		Software Dev.:		Law:	Y	Engineers, Other:	
Int'l Business:		Commercial/Industrial:		Graphic Arts/Photog.:		Hardware Dev.:		HR/Other:	Y	Health/Lab	
MBA Graduates:	Y	Sales Trainees:		Music:		Consulting/Other:		Training:		Scientists/Research:	
		Advertising Pros.:	Y	Broadcasting:				Health Care:		Petroleum/Chemicals:	
				Other:				Consulting:		Math/Other:	

TYPES OF BUSINESS:

Real Estate Investment Trust
Manufactured Housing Communities
Recreational Vehicle Communities
Manufactured Home Sales
Property Management

BRANDS/DIVISIONS/AFFILIATES:

Sun Home Services Inc
Orange City RV Resort
Club Naples RV Resort LLC
Kountree RV Resort LLC
North Lake RV Resort LLC

CONTACTS: *Note: Officers with more than one job title may be intentionally listed here more than once.*

Gary A. Shiffman, CEO
John B. McLaren, COO/Exec. VP
Gary A. Shiffman, Pres.
Karen J. Dearing, CFO/Exec. VP
Karen J. Dearing, Sec.
Karen J. Dearing, Treas.
Jonathan M. Colman, Exec. VP
Gary A. Shiffman, Chmn.

Phone: 248-208-2500 **Fax:** 248-932-3072
Toll-Free:
Address: 27777 Franklin Rd., Ste. 200, Southfield, MI 48034 US

GROWTH PLANS/SPECIAL FEATURES:

Sun Communities, Inc. is a self-administered and self-managed Real Estate Investment Trust (REIT) that owns, operates and develops manufactured housing communities concentrated in the midwestern, southern and southeastern U.S. Sun, together with its affiliates and predecessors, has been in the business of acquiring, operating and expanding manufactured housing communities since 1975. The company owns and operates a portfolio of 136 properties in 18 states, including 124 manufactured housing communities; four recreational vehicle (RV) communities; and eight multi-use properties containing both manufactured housing and RV sites. The properties contain a total of 47,572 developed sites, including approximately 47,683 developed manufactured home sites, 3,209 permanent RV sites, 2,032 seasonal recreational vehicle sites and an additional 6,000 manufactured home sites suitable for development. The firm leases individual sites and utility access to customers for the placement of manufactured homes and RVs. Subsidiary Sun Home Services, Inc. markets, sells and leases new and pre-owned manufactured homes for placement in the properties. The firm expands primarily through the acquisition of manufactured housing and RV communities. In its acquisitions, Sun focuses on communities with a minimum of 200 home sites, located near large metropolitan areas; land/lease communities, rather than rental homes; RV communities with more than 50% annual leases; public utilities access; and the potential to expand. Headquartered in Southfield, Michigan, the company also maintains management offices in Texas, Ohio, Indiana and Florida. In May 2011, the firm acquired the Orange City RV Resort in Orange City, Florida from NHC-FL7 L.P. for approximately $6,470,000. In June 2011, the company acquired 17 manufactured home communities and one recreational vehicle community. In December 2011, the firm acquired three vehicle communities and certain assets from Club Naples RV Resort LLC, Kountree RV Resort LLC and North Lake RV Resort LLC.

Employees of Sun receive medical and prescription coverage; dental and vision plans; life, AD&D and identity theft insurance; a 401(k) plan; an employee assistance program; tuition reimbursement; and health and dependent care reimbursement accounts.

FINANCIALS: **Sales and profits are in thousands of dollars—add 000 to get the full amount. 2011 Note: Financial information for 2011 was not available for all companies at press time.**

2011 Sales: $289,185	2011 Profits: $-1,086	**U.S. Stock Ticker: SUI**
2010 Sales: $263,140	2010 Profits: $-2,883	**Int'l Ticker:**
2009 Sales: $256,609	2009 Profits: $-6,302	Int'l Exchange:
2008 Sales: $254,291	2008 Profits: $-34,448	Employees: 747 Fiscal Year Ends: 12/31
2007 Sales: $235,075	2007 Profits: $-16,643	Parent Company:

SALARIES/BENEFITS:

Pension Plan:	ESOP Stock Plan:	Profit Sharing:	Top Exec. Salary: $615,012	Bonus: $135,000
Savings Plan: Y	Stock Purch. Plan:		Second Exec. Salary: $290,096	Bonus: $

OTHER THOUGHTS:

Apparent Women Officers or Directors: 2
Hot Spot for Advancement for Women/Minorities:

LOCATIONS: ("Y" = Yes)

West:	Southwest:	Midwest:	Southeast:	Northeast:	International:
Y	Y	Y	Y	Y	

SUNOCO LOGISTICS PARTNERS LP

www.sunocologistics.com

Industry Group Code: 424710

Management:		Sales/Marketing:		Liberal Arts:		Information Systems:		Professionals:		Technical/Scientific:	
Mgmt. Trainees:		Mktg. Professionals:	Y	Gen. Writing/Editing:		Info. Management:	Y	Finance/Acct.:	Y	Engineers, Elec.:	
Experienced Mgmt.:	Y	Retail Sales:		Technical Writing:		Software Dev.:		Law:	Y	Engineers, Other:	
Int'l Business:	Y	Commercial/Industrial:	Y	Graphic Arts/Photog.:		Hardware Dev.:		HR/Other:	Y	Health/Lab	
MBA Graduates:	Y	Sales Trainees:		Music:		Consulting/Other:		Training:	Y	Scientists/Research:	
		Advertising Pros.:		Broadcasting:				Health Care:		Petroleum/Chemicals:	
				Other:				Consulting:		Math/Other:	

TYPES OF BUSINESS:

Pipelines
Crude Oil Refining & Marketing
Terminal & Storage Facilities

BRANDS/DIVISIONS/AFFILIATES:

Sunoco, Inc.
Mid-Valley Pipeline Company
Inland Corporation
Wolverine Pipe Line Co.
Yellowstone Pipe Line Co.
West Shore Pipe Line Co.
West Texas Gulf Pipe Line Company

CONTACTS: *Note: Officers with more than one job title may be intentionally listed here more than once.*

Lynn L. Elsenhans, CEO
Michael J. Hennigan, COO
Michael J. Hennigan, Pres.
Brian P. MacDonald, CFO/VP
Dennis Zeleny, Chief Human Resources Officer
Kathleen Shea-Ballay, General Counsel/VP/Sec.
David A. Justin, VP-Oper.
David A. Sexton, VP-Bus. Dev.
Peter J. Gvazdauskas, VP-Finance
Michael D. Galtman
Controller, Controller
Daniel J. Platt, Treas.
Lynn L. Elsenhans, Chmn.

Phone: 215-977-6350 **Fax:**
Toll-Free: 866-248-4344
Address: 1818 Market St., Ste. 1500, Philadelphia, PA 19103 US

GROWTH PLANS/SPECIAL FEATURES:

Sunoco Logistics Partners, L.P., formed by Sunoco, Inc., is an energy logistics company. The firm is principally engaged in the transport, terminalling and storage of refined products and crude oil; and the purchase and sale of crude oil in 17 states located in the Midwest, northwest, northeast and southwest regions of the U.S. The company operates in three segments: the refined products pipeline system, the crude oil pipeline system and terminal facilities. The refined products pipeline system primarily serves the northeast and Midwest U.S. and includes roughly 2,200 miles of refined product pipelines; about 140 miles of crude oil pipelines; a 31.5% interest in Wolverine Pipe Line Co.; a14% interest in Yellowstone Pipe Line Co.; and 12.3% interest in West Shore Pipe Line Co. The crude oil pipeline system gathers, purchases, sells and transports crude oil principally in Oklahoma and Texas and consists of roughly 4,900 miles of crude oil trunk pipelines. Through this segment, Sunoco Logistics owns 91% of Mid-Valley Pipeline Company; and 60.3% of West Texas Gulf Pipe Line Company. The terminal facilities segment includes 42 refined product terminals with an aggregate storage capacity of 7.2 million barrels, primarily serving the refined product pipeline system; the Nederland terminal, a 22 million marine crude oil terminal on the Texas Gulf Coast; one inland crude oil and two marine terminals with a combined capacity of 3.4 million barrels; a liquefied petroleum gas terminal near Michigan with a capacity of 1 million barrels; and a 2 million barrel refined product terminal in Pennsylvania. Sunoco, Inc. owns roughly 31% of the company and accounts for roughly 14% of the firm's revenues. In May 2011, Sunoco Logistics acquired Inland Corporation, operator of a 350-mile refined products pipeline.

FINANCIALS: **Sales and profits are in thousands of dollars—add 000 to get the full amount. 2011 Note: Financial information for 2011 was not available for all companies at press time.**

2011 Sales: $10,918,000 — 2011 Profits: $259,000
2010 Sales: $7,838,000 — 2010 Profits: $346,000
2009 Sales: $5,429,677 — 2009 Profits: $250,362
2008 Sales: $10,136,618 — 2008 Profits: $214,480
2007 Sales: $7,405,836 — 2007 Profits: $120,875

U.S. Stock Ticker: SXL
Int'l Ticker:
Int'l Exchange:
Employees: 1,400 Fiscal Year Ends: 12/31
Parent Company:

SALARIES/BENEFITS:

Pension Plan: ESOP Stock Plan: Profit Sharing: Top Exec. Salary: $296,051 Bonus: $312,883
Savings Plan: Stock Purch. Plan: Second Exec. Salary: $278,493 Bonus: $117,928

OTHER THOUGHTS:

Apparent Women Officers or Directors: 4
Hot Spot for Advancement for Women/Minorities: Y

LOCATIONS: ("Y" = Yes)

West:	Southwest:	Midwest:	Southeast:	Northeast:	International:
	Y	Y		Y	

SUPER MICRO COMPUTER INC

www.supermicro.com

Industry Group Code: 334111

Management:		Sales/Marketing:		Liberal Arts:		Information Systems:		Professionals:		Technical/Scientific:	
Mgmt. Trainees:		Mktg. Professionals:	Y	Gen. Writing/Editing:		Info. Management:	Y	Finance/Acct.:	Y	Engineers, Elec.:	Y
Experienced Mgmt.:	Y	Retail Sales:		Technical Writing:	Y	Software Dev.:	Y	Law:	Y	Engineers, Other:	Y
Int'l Business:	Y	Commercial/Industrial:	Y	Graphic Arts/Photog.:		Hardware Dev.:	Y	HR/Other:	Y	Health/Lab	
MBA Graduates:	Y	Sales Trainees:	Y	Music:		Consulting/Other:	Y	Training:	Y	Scientists/Research:	
		Advertising Pros.:		Broadcasting:				Health Care:		Petroleum/Chemicals:	
				Other:				Consulting:		Math/Other:	

TYPES OF BUSINESS:

Server Systems & Components

BRANDS/DIVISIONS/AFFILIATES:

CONTACTS:

Note: Officers with more than one job title may be intentionally listed here more than once.

Charles Liang, CEO
Charles Liang, Pres.
Howard Hideshima, CFO
Phidias Chou, VP-Worldwide Sales
Wally Liaw, Sec.
Sara Liu, VP-Oper.
Sara Liu, Treas.
Charles Liang, Chmn.
Wally Liaw, VP-Int'l Sales

Phone: 408-503-8000	**Fax:** 408-503-8008
Toll-Free:	
Address: 980 Rock Ave., San Jose, CA 95131 US	

GROWTH PLANS/SPECIAL FEATURES:

Super Micro Computer, Inc. (SMC) designs, develops, manufactures and sells application optimized, high-performance server systems based on modular and open-standard x86 architectures. Its products include a range of complete rackmount and blade server systems, as well as components such as serverboards, chassis, power supplies and system accessories. The firm offers its clients a high degree of flexibility and customization by providing a broad array of server components, which are interoperable and can be configured to create complete server systems. The company bases its offerings on open-standard components, such as processors from Intel and AMD, and its products are compatible with both Linux and Windows operating systems. The firm sells server systems in rack-mounted, standalone tower and blade form factors. It currently offers a complete range of server options with single, dual and quad CPU capability, supporting Intel Xeon and Pentium multi-core architectures in 1U, 2U, 3U and 4U, tower and blade form factors. Additionally, the firm offers complete server systems for AMD dual and quad Opteron in 1U, 2U, 4U and blade form factors. SMC offers over 4,500 SKUs, and for each system it provides multiple chassis designs and power supply options. The company also offers Supermicro Intelligent Management (SIM) card solutions to provide remote access and system monitoring. SMC sells its server systems and components primarily through distributors, which include value-added resellers and systems integrators, and, to a lesser extent, original equipment manufacturers (OEMs) and a direct sales force. In January 2012, the firm opened its new Science and Technology Park Taiwan.

The company offers its employees health, dental, vision, life AD&D and disability insurance, as well as a 401(k) plan.

FINANCIALS:

Sales and profits are in thousands of dollars—add 000 to get the full amount. 2011 Note: Financial information for 2011 was not available for all companies at press time.

2011 Sales: $942,582	2011 Profits: $40,213	**U.S. Stock Ticker: SMCI**
2010 Sales: $721,438	2010 Profits: $26,915	**Int'l Ticker:**
2009 Sales: $505,609	2009 Profits: $16,107	Int'l Exchange:
2008 Sales: $540,503	2008 Profits: $25,419	Employees: 1,239 Fiscal Year Ends: 6/30
2007 Sales: $420,393	2007 Profits: $19,339	Parent Company:

SALARIES/BENEFITS:

Pension Plan:	ESOP Stock Plan:	Profit Sharing:	Top Exec. Salary: $286,598	Bonus: $
Savings Plan: Y	Stock Purch. Plan:		Second Exec. Salary: $254,231	Bonus: $4,850

OTHER THOUGHTS:

Apparent Women Officers or Directors: 1
Hot Spot for Advancement for Women/Minorities:

LOCATIONS: ("Y" = Yes)

West:	Southwest:	Midwest:	Southeast:	Northeast:	International:
Y					Y

SUPERIOR UNIFORM GROUP INC

www.superioruniformgroup.com

Industry Group Code: 315299

Management:		**Sales/Marketing:**		**Liberal Arts:**		**Information Systems:**		**Professionals:**		**Technical/Scientific:**	
Mgmt. Trainees:		Mktg. Professionals:	Y	Gen. Writing/Editing:		Info. Management:	Y	Finance/Acct.:	Y	Engineers, Elec.:	
Experienced Mgmt.:	Y	Retail Sales:		Technical Writing:		Software Dev.:		Law:	Y	Engineers, Other:	
Int'l Business:		Commercial/Industrial:	Y	Graphic Arts/Photog.:	Y	Hardware Dev.:		HR/Other:	Y	Health/Lab	
MBA Graduates:	Y	Sales Trainees:	Y	Music:		Consulting/Other:		Training:	Y	Scientists/Research:	
		Advertising Pros.:	Y	Broadcasting:				Health Care:		Petroleum/Chemicals:	
				Other:				Consulting:		Math/Other:	

TYPES OF BUSINESS:

Uniform Design & Manufacture
Controlled Environment Wear
Online Sales
Uniform Accessories

BRANDS/DIVISIONS/AFFILIATES:

Fashion Seal Uniforms
Martin's Uniforms
UniVogue
Fashion Seal Healthcare
Worklon
TUGS!
Blade Sportswear Inc

CONTACTS:

Note: Officers with more than one job title may be intentionally listed here more than once.

Michael Benstock, CEO
Alan D. Schwartz, Pres.
Andrew D. Demott, Jr., CFO/Exec. VP
Jordan M. Alpert, General Counsel/Sec.
Andrew D. Demott, Jr., Treas.
Gerald M. Benstock, Chmn.

Phone: 727-397-9611	**Fax:** 727-397-9667
Toll-Free: 866-687-7118	
Address: 10055 Seminole Blvd., Seminole, FL 33772 US	

GROWTH PLANS/SPECIAL FEATURES:

Superior Uniform Group, Inc. manufactures and sells a range of uniforms, career apparel and accessories. Through its signature marketing brands, Fashion Seal Uniforms, Fashion Seal Healthcare, Martin's Uniforms, UniVogue, Worklon and TUGS!, the company provides uniform and clothing needs in the following markets: cleanroom; commercial; entertainment; government and public safety; healthcare; hospitality; laundry services; textile rental; promotional products; restaurant and food services; retail; and transportation. The firm's primary brands, Fashion Seal and Fashion Seal Healthcare, cater to lodging/hospitality employees as well as restaurant employees and healthcare providers. Martin's provides uniforms primarily to the public safety, transportation, governmental services, private security and commercial markets. UniVogue specializes in the lodging, hospitality and foodservice industries. The Worklon brand manufactures cleanroom, electrostatic-sensitive and controlled environment apparel and accessories for the automotive, semiconductor, food processing and pharmaceutical markets. TUGS! are slip-resistant shoes that the firm markets to customers in all of the industries it serves. Superior Uniform's inventory management system utilizes the latest forecasting and material requirements planning software and works with customers to analyze sales, establish forecasts, prioritize shipments and manage inventory levels. The company has manufacturing, warehousing and sales facilities within the U.S. and contracts out to manufacturers in Central America and Asia, including companies in Honduras, China, India, Bangladesh and Pakistan. Recently, Superior Uniform acquired Blade Sportswear, Inc., a manufacturer and distributor of uniforms that caters to major U.S. restaurants and foodservice chains.

The firm offers employees disability, medical and dental insurance; healthcare spending and dependent care accounts; life insurance; a 401(k) plan and pension plan; access to an onsite cafeteria; and an employee discount program.

FINANCIALS:

Sales and profits are in thousands of dollars—add 000 to get the full amount. 2011 Note: Financial information for 2011 was not available for all companies at press time.

2011 Sales: $	2011 Profits: $	**U.S. Stock Ticker: SGC**
2010 Sales: $105,878	2010 Profits: $3,807	**Int'l Ticker:**
2009 Sales: $102,802	2009 Profits: $1,967	Int'l Exchange:
2008 Sales: $123,745	2008 Profits: $2,134	Employees: 630 Fiscal Year Ends: 12/31
2007 Sales: $120,458	2007 Profits: $2,549	Parent Company:

SALARIES/BENEFITS:

Pension Plan: Y	ESOP Stock Plan:	Profit Sharing:	Top Exec. Salary: $410,000	Bonus: $301,335
Savings Plan: Y	Stock Purch. Plan:		Second Exec. Salary: $328,136	Bonus: $241,168

OTHER THOUGHTS:

Apparent Women Officers or Directors:
Hot Spot for Advancement for Women/Minorities: Y

LOCATIONS: ("Y" = Yes)

West:	Southwest:	Midwest:	Southeast:	Northeast:	International:
Y			Y	Y	

SUPERTEL HOSPITALITY INC

www.supertelinc.com

Industry Group Code: 531120

Management:		Sales/Marketing:		Liberal Arts:		Information Systems:		Professionals:		Technical/Scientific:	
Mgmt. Trainees:	Y	Mktg. Professionals:		Gen. Writing/Editing:	Y	Info. Management:	Y	Finance/Acct.:	Y	Engineers, Elec.:	
Experienced Mgmt.:	Y	Retail Sales:		Technical Writing:		Software Dev.:		Law:	Y	Engineers, Other:	
Int'l Business:		Commercial/Industrial:		Graphic Arts/Photog.:		Hardware Dev.:		HR/Other:	Y	Health/Lab	
MBA Graduates:	Y	Sales Trainees:		Music:		Consulting/Other:		Training:		Scientists/Research:	
		Advertising Pros.:		Broadcasting:				Health Care:		Petroleum/Chemicals:	
				Other:				Consulting:		Math/Other:	

TYPES OF BUSINESS:

Real Estate Investment Trust
Hotels & Motels

BRANDS/DIVISIONS/AFFILIATES:

Supertel Hospitality REIT Trust
E&P REIT Trust
Supertel Limited Partnership
E&P Financing Limited Partnership
Supertel Hospitality Management Inc
TRS Leasing Inc
Royco Hotels Inc
HLC Hotels Inc

CONTACTS: *Note: Officers with more than one job title may be intentionally listed here more than once.*

Kelly A. Walters, CEO
Stephen C. Gilbert, COO
Kelly A. Walters, Pres.
Corrine L. Scarpello, CFO
David L. Walter, Treas./Sr. VP
William C. Latham, Chmn.

Phone: 402-371-2520 **Fax:** 402-371-4229
Toll-Free:
Address: 1800 W. Pasewalk Ave., Ste. 200, Norfolk, NE 68701 US

GROWTH PLANS/SPECIAL FEATURES:

Supertel Hospitality, Inc. (SHI) is a self-administered REIT (Real Estate Investment Trust) primarily engaged in acquiring and owning hotels. Its portfolio includes 99 limited-service hotels in over 23 states under the following franchise brands: Super 8; Comfort Inn/Comfort Suites; Days Inn; Hampton Inn; Holiday Inn Express; Ramada, Ltd.; Tara Inn; Baymont Inn; Key West Inns; Savannah Suites; Masters Inn; Supertel Inn; Guest House Inn/Guesthouse Inn and Suites; and Sleep Inn. Standard guestroom amenities include high-speed wireless Internet; free local calls; cable TV, including movie channels; and an iron and ironing board. Select Supertel properties also have complimentary continental breakfast, pools, suites, conference centers and meeting facilities. Through its two wholly-owned subsidiaries, Supertel Hospitality REIT Trust and E&P REIT Trust, the firm owns a 99% interest in Supertel Limited Partnership and 100% of E&P Financing Limited Partnership. Together, these four firms, along with other subsidiaries and partnerships, own the firm's properties. Those other subsidiaries and partnerships include Supertel Hospitality Management, Inc.; SPPR-BMI Holdings, Inc.; and Solomon's Beacon Inn Limited Partnership. To enter into management agreements with independent contractors, in compliance with the REIT Modernization Act of 1999, SHI created TRS Leasing, Inc. and its subsidiaries TRS Subsidiary LLC; and SPPR TRS Subsidiary LLC. All SHI hotels are leased to TRS Leasing and are managed by Royco Hotels, Inc. and HLC Hotels, Inc. TRS also holds the firm's furniture, fixtures and equipment. In June 2011, the company sold Tara Inn located in Jonesboro, Georgia for approximately $1.85 million. In January 2012, the firm sold its Super 8 hotel in Fayetteville, Arkansas for approximately $1.56 million.

FINANCIALS: **Sales and profits are in thousands of dollars—add 000 to get the full amount. 2011 Note: Financial information for 2011 was not available for all companies at press time.**

2011 Sales: $
2010 Sales: $84,114
2009 Sales: $81,570
2008 Sales: $90,996
2007 Sales: $90,084

2011 Profits: $
2010 Profits: $-10,585
2009 Profits: $-27,395
2008 Profits: $6,656
2007 Profits: $4,078

U.S. Stock Ticker: SPPR
Int'l Ticker:
Int'l Exchange:
Employees: 1,664 Fiscal Year Ends: 12/31
Parent Company:

SALARIES/BENEFITS:

Pension Plan: ESOP Stock Plan: Profit Sharing: Top Exec. Salary: $262,000 Bonus: $
Savings Plan: Stock Purch. Plan: Second Exec. Salary: $145,000 Bonus: $

OTHER THOUGHTS:

Apparent Women Officers or Directors: 1
Hot Spot for Advancement for Women/Minorities:

LOCATIONS: ("Y" = Yes)

West:	Southwest:	Midwest:	Southeast:	Northeast:	International:
Y		Y	Y	Y	

SUPREME INDUSTRIES INC

Industry Group Code: 336211

www.supremeind.com

Management:		Sales/Marketing:		Liberal Arts:		Information Systems:		Professionals:		Technical/Scientific:	
Mgmt. Trainees:		Mktg. Professionals:	Y	Gen. Writing/Editing:	Y	Info. Management:	Y	Finance/Acct.:	Y	Engineers, Elec.:	
Experienced Mgmt.:	Y	Retail Sales:		Technical Writing:	Y	Software Dev.:		Law:	Y	Engineers, Other:	Y
Int'l Business:		Commercial/Industrial:	Y	Graphic Arts/Photog.:	Y	Hardware Dev.:		HR/Other:	Y	Health/Lab	
MBA Graduates:	Y	Sales Trainees:	Y	Music:		Consulting/Other:		Training:	Y	Scientists/Research:	
		Advertising Pros.:	Y	Broadcasting:				Health Care:		Petroleum/Chemicals:	
				Other:				Consulting:		Math/Other:	

TYPES OF BUSINESS:

Specialized Vehicles
Specialized Truck Bodies & Shuttle Buses
Vertically Integrated Fiberglass Products
Fiberglass Wind Deflectors

BRANDS/DIVISIONS/AFFILIATES:

Supreme Corp.
Signature Van
Iner-City
Spartan
Spartan MX
Supreme Specialty Vehicles
Kold King
Fuel Shark

CONTACTS: *Note: Officers with more than one job title may be intentionally listed here more than once.*

Kim Korth, CEO
Kim Korth, Pres.
Matthew W. Long, CFO
Bob Besse, VP-Mktg. & Sales
William J. Barrett, Corp. Sec./Exec. VP
Tom Beard, VP-Oper.
Matthew W. Long, Treas.
Mike Oium, VP-Systems Mgmt.
Herbert M. Gardner, Chmn.

Phone: 574-642-3070 **Fax:** 574-642-3208
Toll-Free: 800-642-4889
Address: 2581 E. Kercher Rd., Goshen, IN 46528 US

GROWTH PLANS/SPECIAL FEATURES:

Supreme Industries, Inc. manufactures specialized vehicles, including trucks, buses and armored vehicles. Supreme has manufacturing, distribution and service facilities in nine states across the continental U.S. The company has two operating segments: specialized vehicles and vertically integrated fiberglass products. The specialized vehicle industry consists of companies that manufacture and distribute specialized truck bodies and shuttle buses. Depending on the product, it is either built directly on a truck chassis or built separately and installed at a later date. The firm makes its own fiberglass wind deflectors under the Fuel Shark brand. Supreme's products include Signature Van bodies, which range from 10-28 feet in length; Iner-City cutaway van bodies, which are manufactured on cutaway chassis allowing access from the cab to the cargo area; Spartan cargo vans, which are available in lengths of 10-14 feet; Spartan MX insulated bodies, which are designed for companies making frequent hand-loaded refrigerated deliveries; Kold King insulated van bodies for temperature controlled applications; Stake bodies, which are flatbeds with various configurations of removable sides; Suburbans with armored protection against hostile fire; armored trucks, which are available in aluminum, galvaneal or stainless steel; and Supreme Specialty Vehicles (SSV), which are designed for emergency response and homeland security personnel. Additional products include StarTrans shuttle buses under the Senator and Candidate brands, which have seating capacities for 12-29 people; StarTrans mid-size buses under the President and Ambassador brands, which have seating capacities of up to 25 passengers; StarTrans trolleys, which are marketed to resort areas and theme parks; the StarTrans Tourliner, which provides transportation for up to 39 passengers; and the StarTrans Activity Bus, which is marketed to churches, schools and day care centers. In October 2010, through a restructuring, the company's former operating subsidiary, Supreme Corp., merged into Supreme Industries.

FINANCIALS: **Sales and profits are in thousands of dollars—add 000 to get the full amount. 2011 Note: Financial information for 2011 was not available for all companies at press time.**

2011 Sales: $	2011 Profits: $	**U.S. Stock Ticker: STS**
2010 Sales: $220,889	2010 Profits: $-11,529	**Int'l Ticker:**
2009 Sales: $192,036	2009 Profits: $-8,743	Int'l Exchange:
2008 Sales: $257,903	2008 Profits: $-3,061	Employees: 1,700 Fiscal Year Ends: 12/31
2007 Sales: $301,655	2007 Profits: $4,164	Parent Company:

SALARIES/BENEFITS:

Pension Plan:	ESOP Stock Plan:	Profit Sharing:	Top Exec. Salary: $162,500	Bonus: $
Savings Plan: Y	Stock Purch. Plan:		Second Exec. Salary: $95,850	Bonus: $

OTHER THOUGHTS:

Apparent Women Officers or Directors: 1
Hot Spot for Advancement for Women/Minorities:

LOCATIONS: ("Y" = Yes)

West:	Southwest:	Midwest:	Southeast:	Northeast:	International:
Y	Y	Y	Y	Y	

SVB FINANCIAL GROUP

www.svb.com

Industry Group Code: 522110

Management:		**Sales/Marketing:**		**Liberal Arts:**		**Information Systems:**		**Professionals:**		**Technical/Scientific:**	
Mgmt. Trainees:	Y	Mktg. Professionals:	Y	Gen. Writing/Editing:	Y	Info. Management:	Y	Finance/Acct.:	Y	Engineers, Elec.:	
Experienced Mgmt.:	Y	Retail Sales:		Technical Writing:		Software Dev.:		Law:	Y	Engineers, Other:	
Int'l Business:	Y	Commercial/Industrial:		Graphic Arts/Photog.:		Hardware Dev.:		HR/Other:	Y	Health/Lab	
MBA Graduates:	Y	Sales Trainees:		Music:		Consulting/Other:		Training:	Y	Scientists/Research:	
		Advertising Pros.:	Y	Broadcasting:				Health Care:		Petroleum/Chemicals:	
				Other:				Consulting:		Math/Other:	

TYPES OF BUSINESS:

Banking
Lending Services
Asset Management
Investment Banking
Online Banking
Trade & Foreign Exchange Services
Mutual Funds
Advisory Services

BRANDS/DIVISIONS/AFFILIATES:

Silicon Valley Bank
SVBeConnect
SVB Global
SVB Analytics
SVB Private Client Services
SVB Wine
eProsper

CONTACTS:

Note: Officers with more than one job title may be intentionally listed here more than once.

Gregory W. Becker, CEO
Bruce Wallace, COO
Gregory W. Becker, Pres.
Michael Descheneaux, CFO
Brian Dennehy, Chief Mktg. Officer
Chris Edmonds-Waters, Head-Human Resources
Mary Dent, General Counsel/Corp. Sec.
Marc Verissimo, Chief Strategy & Risk Officer
Carrie Merritt, Dir.-Public Rel.
Meghan O'Leary, Dir.-Investor Rel.
John China, Head-Relationship Mgmt.
Dave Jones, Chief Credit Officer
Joan Parsons, Head-U.S. Banking
Harry Kellogg, Head-Strategic Relationships
Alex W. Hart, Chmn.
Phil Cox, Head-Israel, U.K. & Europe

Phone: 408-654-7400 **Fax:** 408-496-2405
Toll-Free:
Address: 3003 Tasman Dr., Santa Clara, CA 95054 US

GROWTH PLANS/SPECIAL FEATURES:

SVB Financial Group (SVB) is a financial services/holding and bank holding company. Through principal subsidiary Silicon Valley Bank, the company aids entrepreneurs, specifically within the life science, private equity, technology and premium wine niches. The bank operates through four business segments: global commercial banking, SVB capital, relationship management and other business services. SVB's global commercial banking segment provides domestic and international cash management services including deposit services, collection services, disbursement services, electronic funds transfers and online banking through SVBeConnect. This segment also includes SVB Global, a provider of global banking products to non-U.S. clients. The SVB capital segment provides banking services to private equity and venture capital firms; makes private equity and venture capital fund investments; and establishes and maintains international alliances with venture capital firms. The firm's relationship management segment offers banking products and services to premium wine industry clients through SVB Wine and a range of private banking services targeted toward high-net-worth persons through SVB Private Client Services. The company's other business services division includes SVB Analytics, a provider of corporate equity tracking and administrative services to private venture capital-backed companies; as well as other debt and lending funds. SVB has approximately $17.5 billion in assets, $5.5 billion in loans and $14.3 billion in deposits. The firm maintains 26 U.S. offices and seven offices in the U.K., Israel, China and India. In December 2010, SVB acquired a 35% additional interest in eProsper; the firm now owns 100% of eProsper.

The company offers employees benefits such as life, dependent life, accident, disability, AD&D, medical, dental and vision insurance; access to a credit union; a 401(k); stock ownership, stock purchase and assistance plans; and paid time off.

FINANCIALS:

Sales and profits are in thousands of dollars—add 000 to get the full amount. 2011 Note: Financial information for 2011 was not available for all companies at press time.

2011 Sales: $902,500 — 2011 Profits: $171,900
2010 Sales: $709,261 — 2010 Profits: $94,951
2009 Sales: $528,969 — 2009 Profits: $48,010
2008 Sales: $610,416 — 2008 Profits: $78,628
2007 Sales: $664,770 — 2007 Profits: $123,638

U.S. Stock Ticker: SIVB
Int'l Ticker:
Int'l Exchange:
Employees: 1,428 Fiscal Year Ends: 12/31
Parent Company:

SALARIES/BENEFITS:

Pension Plan: — ESOP Stock Plan: Y — Profit Sharing: — Top Exec. Salary: $697,027 — Bonus: $
Savings Plan: Y — Stock Purch. Plan: Y — Second Exec. Salary: $416,618 — Bonus: $

OTHER THOUGHTS:

Apparent Women Officers or Directors: 6
Hot Spot for Advancement for Women/Minorities: Y

LOCATIONS: ("Y" = Yes)

West:	Southwest:	Midwest:	Southeast:	Northeast:	International:
Y	Y	Y	Y	Y	Y

SWIFT ENERGY CO

www.swiftenergy.com

Industry Group Code: 211111

Management:		**Sales/Marketing:**	**Liberal Arts:**	**Information Systems:**		**Professionals:**		**Technical/Scientific:**	
Mgmt. Trainees:		Mktg. Professionals:	Gen. Writing/Editing:	Info. Management:	Y	Finance/Acct.:	Y	Engineers, Elec.:	
Experienced Mgmt.:	Y	Retail Sales:	Technical Writing:	Software Dev.:		Law:	Y	Engineers, Other:	Y
Int'l Business:	Y	Commercial/Industrial:	Graphic Arts/Photog.:	Hardware Dev.:		HR/Other:	Y	Health/Lab	
MBA Graduates:	Y	Sales Trainees:	Music:	Consulting/Other:		Training:	Y	Scientists/Research:	
		Advertising Pros.:	Broadcasting:			Health Care:		Petroleum/Chemicals:	Y
			Other:			Consulting:		Math/Other:	

TYPES OF BUSINESS:
Oil & Gas Exploration & Production

BRANDS/DIVISIONS/AFFILIATES:
Lake Washington
Horseshoe Bayou
Bayou Penchant
Masters Creek
Sun TSH
Las Tiendas
AWP Olmos
Burr Ferry

CONTACTS: *Note: Officers with more than one job title may be intentionally listed here more than once.*
Terry E. Swift, CEO
Robert J. Banks, COO/Exec. VP
Bruce H. Vincent, Pres./Sec.
Alton D. Heckaman, Jr., CFO/Exec. VP
Stephen P. Schmitt, VP-Energy Mktg.
John C. Branca, VP-Exploration & Geosciences
Randy A. Bailey, VP-Prod.
Steven L. Tomberlin, VP-Eng.
Steven B. Yakle, VP-Corp. Admin.
Laurent A. Baillargeon, General Counsel/VP
James M. Kitterman, Sr. VP-Oper.
Paul Vincent, Mgr.-Investor Rel.
Adrian D. Shelley, Treas.
James P. Mitchell, Sr. VP-Commercial Transactions & Land
Barry S. Turcotte, VP-Acct./Controller
Homer A. Adams, Jr., VP-Drilling
Terry E. Swift, Chmn.
Robert J. Banks, VP-Int'l Oper., Swift Energy Int'l

Phone: 281-874-2700	**Fax:** 281-874-2726
Toll-Free: 800-777-2412	
Address: 16825 Northchase Dr., Ste. 400, Houston, TX 77060 US	

GROWTH PLANS/SPECIAL FEATURES:
Swift Energy Co., headquartered in Houston, Texas, is an independent exploration company. The firm develops, explores, acquires and operates oil and gas properties, focusing particularly on oil and natural gas reserves onshore and in the inland waters of Louisiana and Texas. The company has interests in several domestic wells. Swift Energy is currently focused on exploring and developing 15 fields in four areas: Lake Washington and Bay de Chene in southeastern Louisiana; Sun TSH, Hawkville AWP, Las Tiendas, Hawkville Artesia Wells, Hawkville Fasken and AWP in southern Texas; Cote Blanche Island, Horseshoe Bayou and Jeanerette in southern Louisiana; and Masters Creek, South Bearhead Creek, Burr Ferry and Brookeland in central Louisiana and eastern Texas. The firm has estimated proved reserves from continuing operations of 132.8 million barrels of oil equivalent. Of the company's total proved reserves, approximately 30% is crude oil, 53% is natural gas and 17% is made up of natural gas liquids. Roughly half of Swift Energy's total reserves are proved developed. Nearly all of these proved reserves are in Louisiana (40%) and Texas (59%). In recent years, Swift Energy sold its New Zealand assets to subsidiaries of Origin Energy Limited. In August 2011, the firm sold its interests in two fields in Texas, six in South Louisiana and one in Alabama to EnergyQuest II, LLC for roughly $53.5 million.

FINANCIALS: **Sales and profits are in thousands of dollars—add 000 to get the full amount. 2011 Note: Financial information for 2011 was not available for all companies at press time.**

2011 Sales: $599,131	2011 Profits: $98,821	**U.S. Stock Ticker: SFY**
2010 Sales: $438,429	2010 Profits: $46,294	**Int'l Ticker:**
2009 Sales: $370,445	2009 Profits: $-39,076	Int'l Exchange:
2008 Sales: $820,815	2008 Profits: $-257,130	Employees: 292 Fiscal Year Ends: 12/31
2007 Sales: $654,121	2007 Profits: $21,287	Parent Company:

SALARIES/BENEFITS:

Pension Plan:	ESOP Stock Plan:	Profit Sharing:	Top Exec. Salary: $627,270	Bonus: $1,254,540
Savings Plan: Y	Stock Purch. Plan:		Second Exec. Salary: $491,010	Bonus: $773,341

OTHER THOUGHTS:
Apparent Women Officers or Directors: 1
Hot Spot for Advancement for Women/Minorities:

LOCATIONS: ("Y" = Yes)

West:	Southwest:	Midwest:	Southeast:	Northeast:	International:
	Y		Y		

Sales, profits and employees may be estimates. Financial information, benefits and other data can change quickly and may vary from those stated here.

SYNAPTICS INC

www.synaptics.com

Industry Group Code: 334119

Management:		Sales/Marketing:		Liberal Arts:		Information Systems:		Professionals:		Technical/Scientific:	
Mgmt. Trainees:		Mktg. Professionals:	Y	Gen. Writing/Editing:		Info. Management:	Y	Finance/Acct.:	Y	Engineers, Elec.:	Y
Experienced Mgmt.:	Y	Retail Sales:		Technical Writing:	Y	Software Dev.:	Y	Law:	Y	Engineers, Other:	Y
Int'l Business:	Y	Commercial/Industrial:	Y	Graphic Arts/Photog.:	Y	Hardware Dev.:	Y	HR/Other:	Y	Health/Lab	
MBA Graduates:	Y	Sales Trainees:	Y	Music:		Consulting/Other:		Training:	Y	Scientists/Research:	
		Advertising Pros.:		Broadcasting:				Health Care:		Petroleum/Chemicals:	
				Other:				Consulting:		Math/Other:	

TYPES OF BUSINESS:

Electronic Components
User Interface Systems

BRANDS/DIVISIONS/AFFILIATES:

TouchPad
TouchStyk
OneTouch
TouchButtons
ClearButtons
TouchStyk
FlexPad
ClearPad

CONTACTS: *Note: Officers with more than one job title may be intentionally listed here more than once.*

Russ Knittel, Interim CEO
Russ Knittel, Interim Pres.
Kathleen Bayless, CFO/Sr. VP
Dave Long, Sr. VP-Worldwide Sales
James Harrington, Sr. VP-Global Human Resources
Shawn Day, CTO/VP
Kin Cheung, VP-Prod. Dev.
Kathleen Bayless, Sec.
Alex Wong, Sr. VP-Worldwide Oper.
Stanley Swearingen, Sr. VP-Corp. Dev. & Strategic Tech.
Kathleen Bayless, Treas.
Ruth Lutes, Sr. VP-Customer Care & Quality
Kevin Barber, Sr. VP/Gen. Mgr.-Handheld Div.
Mark Vena, Sr. VP/Gen. Mgr.-PC Bus. Unit
Ted Theocheung, VP-PC & Digital Home Div.
Francis Lee, Chmn.

Phone: 408-454-5100	**Fax:** 408-454-5200
Toll-Free:	
Address: 3120 Scott Blvd., Ste. 130, Santa Clara, CA 95054 US	

GROWTH PLANS/SPECIAL FEATURES:

Synaptics, Inc. (SYNA) is a worldwide developer of custom-designed user interface products for mobile computing, communications, entertainment and other electronic devices. These products emphasize ease of use, small size, low power consumption, advanced functionality, durability and reliability, making them applicable to a multitude of markets, including notebook computers, PC peripherals, mobile phones and portable entertainment devices such as MP3 players. SYNA's original equipment manufacturer (OEM) customers include most of the tier one PC OEMs and many of the world's largest OEMs for mobile smartphones and portable digital music players. The firm's OneTouch product enables customers to access the company's other technologies to develop their own interface designs for capacitive button and scrolling applications. Products for the PC market include the TouchPad, a touch-sensitive pad that senses movement of a person's finger on its surface; ClickPad, a multi-touch buttonless input device similar to the TouchPad; TouchStyk, a self-contained pointing stick module; NavPad, a directional button used in PDAs and ultra-mobile computers; Proximity Sensing devices, which detect a user's hand before it comes into contact; TouchButtons, which are non-physical buttons used in notebook computers; ClearPad, a full touchscreen system; ClearButtons, which are small resistive touchscreens used on cell phones; and FlexPad, a multi-use capacitive touchscreen. The company develops technologies for advanced touchscreen use, such as gesture recognition and multitouch capabilities. The firm holds 113 patents in force along with another 113 patents pending.

SYNA offers its employees medical, dental and vision coverage; life and disability insurance; a flexible spending account; an employee stock purchase plan; incentive stock options; a 401(k) plan; flexible time off; and an employee assistance program.

FINANCIALS: **Sales and profits are in thousands of dollars—add 000 to get the full amount. 2011 Note: Financial information for 2011 was not available for all companies at press time.**

2011 Sales: $598,538	2011 Profits: $63,796	**U.S. Stock Ticker: SYNA**
2010 Sales: $514,890	2010 Profits: $52,965	**Int'l Ticker:**
2009 Sales: $473,302	2009 Profits: $48,079	Int'l Exchange:
2008 Sales: $361,057	2008 Profits: $26,363	Employees: 676 Fiscal Year Ends: 6/30
2007 Sales: $266,787	2007 Profits: $26,534	Parent Company:

SALARIES/BENEFITS:

Pension Plan:	ESOP Stock Plan:	Profit Sharing:	Top Exec. Salary: $425,000	Bonus: $327,038
Savings Plan: Y	Stock Purch. Plan: Y		Second Exec. Salary: $319,000	Bonus: $212,321

OTHER THOUGHTS:

Apparent Women Officers or Directors: 2
Hot Spot for Advancement for Women/Minorities: Y

LOCATIONS: ("Y" = Yes)

West:	Southwest:	Midwest:	Southeast:	Northeast:	International:
Y	Y				Y

SYNIVERSE TECHNOLOGIES

www.syniverse.com

Industry Group Code: 517110

Management:		Sales/Marketing:		Liberal Arts:		Information Systems:		Professionals:		Technical/Scientific:	
Mgmt. Trainees:		Mktg. Professionals:	Y	Gen. Writing/Editing:		Info. Management:	Y	Finance/Acct.:	Y	Engineers, Elec.:	Y
Experienced Mgmt.:	Y	Retail Sales:		Technical Writing:		Software Dev.:	Y	Law:	Y	Engineers, Other:	
Int'l Business:	Y	Commercial/Industrial:	Y	Graphic Arts/Photog.:		Hardware Dev.:		HR/Other:	Y	Health/Lab	
MBA Graduates:	Y	Sales Trainees:	Y	Music:		Consulting/Other:		Training:		Scientists/Research:	
		Advertising Pros.:		Broadcasting:				Health Care:		Petroleum/Chemicals:	
				Other:				Consulting:		Math/Other:	

TYPES OF BUSINESS:

Telecommunications & Network Services
Communications Technology Services
Business Management Services

BRANDS/DIVISIONS/AFFILIATES:

Carlyle Group (The)

CONTACTS:

Note: Officers with more than one job title may be intentionally listed here more than once.

Tony Holcombe, CEO
Jeffrey S. Gordon, COO
Tony Holcombe, Pres.
David W. Hitchcock, CFO/Exec. VP
Janet Roberts, Chief Mktg. Officer
Leigh M. Hennen, Chief Human Resources Officer
Laura Binion, General Counsel/Sr. VP
Michael O'Brian, Sr. VP-Bus. Dev.
Jim Huseby, VP-Investor Rel.
Charles Landry, Sr. VP-Messaging
William McGee, Sr. VP-Mergers & Acquisitions
Mary Clark, Sr. VP-Roaming
John Wick, Sr. VP-Network
James A. Attwood, Chmn.
Pablo Mlikota, Sr. VP-Caribbean & Latin America

Phone: 813-637-5000	**Fax:**
Toll-Free: 800-892-2888	
Address: 8125 Highwoods Palm Way, Tampa, FL 33647 US	

GROWTH PLANS/SPECIAL FEATURES:

Syniverse Technologies (SVR) is a provider of wireless voice and data services for telecommunications companies worldwide. Its data clearinghouse, network and technology services solve technical and operational challenges for the wireless industry by translating incompatible communication standards and protocols and simplifying operator interconnectivity. The firm's fully integrated suite of transaction-based services allows carriers to deliver seamless voice, data and next generation services to wireless subscribers, including wireless voice and data roaming, Short Message Service (SMS), Multimedia Messaging Services (MMS), Mobile Instant Messaging (MIM), number portability and wireless value-added services. SVR currently provides services to more than 800 telecommunications service providers in over 160 countries. Demand for the company's services is driven primarily by wireless voice and data traffic, subscriber roaming activity, SMS and MMS messaging, number porting and next-generation IP applications. SVR's suite of services includes technology interoperability; network services; number portability; call processing; off-network database queries; and enterprise services. The company provides these services to most of the largest U.S. wireless carriers, including AT&T Mobility; Verizon Wireless; T-Mobile; and Sprint Nextel, as well as international carriers outside North America, including Vodafone, China Unicom, Telecom Italia and VimpelCom. SVR generates the majority of its revenue on a per-transaction basis, often producing multiple transactions from a single subscriber call or data sessions. The remainder of its revenue comes from custom software development fees, hardware sales, professional services and recurring, non-transaction fees for network connections and software maintenance. In January 2011, the company was acquired by The Carlyle Group for approximately $2.6 billion.

FINANCIALS:

Sales and profits are in thousands of dollars—add 000 to get the full amount. 2011 Note: Financial information for 2011 was not available for all companies at press time.

2011 Sales: $	2011 Profits: $	**U.S. Stock Ticker: Private**
2010 Sales: $	2010 Profits: $	**Int'l Ticker:**
2009 Sales: $482,991	2009 Profits: $65,677	Int'l Exchange:
2008 Sales: $506,356	2008 Profits: $78,464	Employees: 1,289 Fiscal Year Ends: 12/31
2007 Sales: $377,524	2007 Profits: $52,419	Parent Company: CARLYLE GROUP (THE)

SALARIES/BENEFITS:

Pension Plan:	ESOP Stock Plan:	Profit Sharing:	Top Exec. Salary: $526,923	Bonus: $535,000
Savings Plan:	Stock Purch. Plan:		Second Exec. Salary: $444,867	Bonus: $285,464

OTHER THOUGHTS:

Apparent Women Officers or Directors: 4
Hot Spot for Advancement for Women/Minorities: Y

LOCATIONS: ("Y" = Yes)

West:	Southwest:	Midwest:	Southeast:	Northeast:	International:
			Y		Y

SYNOVIS LIFE TECHNOLOGIES INC

www.synovislife.com

Industry Group Code: 33911

Management:		Sales/Marketing:		Liberal Arts:		Information Systems:		Professionals:		Technical/Scientific:	
Mgmt. Trainees:		Mktg. Professionals:	Y	Gen. Writing/Editing:		Info. Management:	Y	Finance/Acct.:	Y	Engineers, Elec.:	
Experienced Mgmt.:	Y	Retail Sales:		Technical Writing:	Y	Software Dev.:	Y	Law:	Y	Engineers, Other:	Y
Int'l Business:		Commercial/Industrial:	Y	Graphic Arts/Photog.:		Hardware Dev.:	Y	HR/Other:	Y	Health/Lab	Y
MBA Graduates:	Y	Sales Trainees:	Y	Music:		Consulting/Other:		Training:	Y	Scientists/Research:	Y
		Advertising Pros.:		Broadcasting:				Health Care:	Y	Petroleum/Chemicals:	
				Other:				Consulting:		Math/Other:	

TYPES OF BUSINESS:

Surgical & Interventional Treatment Products
Implantable Biomaterials

BRANDS/DIVISIONS/AFFILIATES:

Synovis Surgical Innovations
Synovis Micro Companies Alliance
Biover Microvascular Clamp
Microvascular Anastomotis COUPLER System
Peri-Strips
Veritas
Pegasus Biologics Inc
Synovis Orthopedic and Woundcare

CONTACTS: *Note: Officers with more than one job title may be intentionally listed here more than once.*

Richard W. Kramp, CEO
Richard W. Kramp, Pres.
Brett A. Reynolds, CFO
Daniel L. Mooradian, VP-R&D
Brett A. Reynolds, Corp. Sec.
Tim Floeder, VP-Corp. Dev.
Brett A. Reynolds, VP-Finance
Michael K. Campbell, Pres., Micro Companies Alliance, Inc.
Mary L. Frick, VP-Regulatory Affairs & Quality Assurance
Mary L. Frick, VP-Clinical Affairs
John D. Seaberg, Chmn.

Phone: 651-796-7300 **Fax:** 651-642-9018
Toll-Free: 800-255-4018
Address: 2575 University Ave. W., St. Paul, MN 55114-1024 US

GROWTH PLANS/SPECIAL FEATURES:

Synovis Life Technologies, Inc. is a diversified medical device firm engaged in developing, manufacturing and bringing to market products for the surgical treatment of disease. Its products are marketed for use in bariatric, cardiac, neurologic, thoracic, urogynecologic, vascular and general surgeries. The company operates through three subsidiaries: Synovis Surgical Innovations; Synovis Micro Companies Alliance; and Synovis Orthopedic and Woundcare. Synovis Surgical Innovations is focused on developing implantable biomaterial products designed to improve a patient's outcome in critical surgeries. The products are made from bovine pericardium, which easily assimilates into host tissue. Products offered by the firm include Peri-Strips, which are stapling buttresses used to reinforce surgical staple lines and reduce potential leakage; Dura-Guard, which is used by neurosurgeons in the treatment of tumors, brain trauma, cerebrovascular disorders and congenital disorders; and Veritas, for use in pelvic floor reconstruction, stress urinary incontinence treatment, vaginal and rectal prolapse repair, hernia repair as well as soft tissue repair. Synovis Micro Companies Alliance provides products to the niche microsurgery market. Products offered include the GEM Microvascular Anastomotic COUPLER System, which is used in small vessel anastomases; GEM Neurotube, which is used in primary or secondary nerve repair; GEM MicroClip, a hemostatic clip; GEM03 Focus Headlight, a rechargeable medical lamp; and the Biover Microvascular Clamp, a single use clamp for arteries and veins. Synovis Orthopedic and Woundcare is a medical device manufacturer that develops advanced biologic solutions for the repair, reinforcement, augmentation and reconstruction of soft tissues; and advanced wound management. Its products include Unite Biomatrix for chronic wounds and the OrthADAPT Bioimplant collagen scaffold.

FINANCIALS: **Sales and profits are in thousands of dollars—add 000 to get the full amount. 2011 Note: Financial information for 2011 was not available for all companies at press time.**

2011 Sales: $82,363	2011 Profits: $8,461	**U.S. Stock Ticker: SYNO**
2010 Sales: $68,565	2010 Profits: $4,876	**Int'l Ticker:**
2009 Sales: $58,211	2009 Profits: $2,706	Int'l Exchange:
2008 Sales: $49,800	2008 Profits: $11,485	Employees: 330 Fiscal Year Ends: 10/31
2007 Sales: $37,691	2007 Profits: $3,810	Parent Company:

SALARIES/BENEFITS:

Pension Plan:	ESOP Stock Plan:	Profit Sharing:	Top Exec. Salary: $375,032	Bonus: $151,670
Savings Plan: Y	Stock Purch. Plan:		Second Exec. Salary: $215,721	Bonus: $55,708

OTHER THOUGHTS:

Apparent Women Officers or Directors: 2
Hot Spot for Advancement for Women/Minorities:

LOCATIONS: ("Y" = Yes)

West:	Southwest:	Midwest:	Southeast:	Northeast:	International:
Y		Y	Y		

TAKE-TWO INTERACTIVE SOFTWARE INC www.take2games.com

Industry Group Code: 511210G

Management:		Sales/Marketing:		Liberal Arts:		Information Systems:		Professionals:		Technical/Scientific:	
Mgmt. Trainees:		Mktg. Professionals:	Y	Gen. Writing/Editing:	Y	Info. Management:	Y	Finance/Acct.:	Y	Engineers, Elec.:	Y
Experienced Mgmt.:	Y	Retail Sales:		Technical Writing:	Y	Software Dev.:	Y	Law:	Y	Engineers, Other:	
Int'l Business:	Y	Commercial/Industrial:	Y	Graphic Arts/Photog.:	Y	Hardware Dev.:		HR/Other:	Y	Health/Lab	
MBA Graduates:	Y	Sales Trainees:	Y	Music:	Y	Consulting/Other:		Training:		Scientists/Research:	
		Advertising Pros.:		Broadcasting:				Health Care:		Petroleum/Chemicals:	
				Other:	Y			Consulting:		Math/Other:	

TYPES OF BUSINESS:

Computer Software-Video Games
Software Distribution

BRANDS/DIVISIONS/AFFILIATES:

Rockstar Games
Grand Theft Auto
2K Games
2K Sports
2K Play

CONTACTS:

Note: Officers with more than one job title may be intentionally listed here more than once.

Strauss Zelnick, CEO
Karl Slatoff, COO
Lainie Goldstein, CFO
Seth Krauss, General Counsel/Exec. VP
Strauss Zelnick, Chmn.

Phone: 646-536-2842	**Fax:** 646-536-2926
Toll-Free:	
Address: 622 Broadway, New York, NY 10012 US	

GROWTH PLANS/SPECIAL FEATURES:

Take-Two Interactive Software, Inc. is a global publisher, developer and distributor of interactive entertainment software, hardware and accessories. Its publishing segment consists of Rockstar Games, 2K Games, 2K Sports and 2K Play publishing labels. The firm develops, markets and publishes software titles for the leading gaming and entertainment hardware platforms, including Sony's PlayStation 3; Microsoft's Xbox 360; Nintendo's Wii; personal computer (PC) games using Windows; and Apple iPhone, iPad and iPod Touch. The company digitally distributes some of its games through the Playstation Network for Playstation 3 games, Xbox LIVE Marketplace and Xbox LIVE Arcade for Xbox 360 games. The interactive software that it develops and publishes is broken down into two major categories: games developed by internal development studios and games that it publishes with, or markets and distributes on behalf of, third party developers. The firm has internal development studios located in the U.S., Canada, the U.K., the Czech Republic, Australia and China. The Rockstar Games titles are primarily internally developed and include the Grand Theft Auto series. Most of the firms third party developed titles are published by its 2K Games label. 2K Games has actively secured rights to publish popular entertainment properties including The Elder Scrolls IV: Oblivion, and its internally developed BioShock and Civilization franchises. Its 2K Sports titles include Major League Baseball 2K and NBA 2K. Its 2K Play publishes casual and family-friendly titles, including Carnival Games and Dora the Explorer. In 2010, Take-Two Interactive released several new games, including Major League Baseball 2K11; Top Spin 4; NBA 2K12; Grand Theft Auto V; L.A. Noire: The Complete Edition; and Grand Theft Auto III: 10 Year Anniversary Edition.

FINANCIALS:

Sales and profits are in thousands of dollars—add 000 to get the full amount. 2011 Note: Financial information for 2011 was not available for all companies at press time.

2011 Sales: $1,100,000 | 2011 Profits: $49,000
2010 Sales: $862,200 | 2010 Profits: $-28,802
2009 Sales: $701,057 | 2009 Profits: $-140,454
2008 Sales: $1,231,106 | 2008 Profits: $97,097
2007 Sales: $981,791 | 2007 Profits: $-138,406

U.S. Stock Ticker: TTWO
Int'l Ticker:
Int'l Exchange:
Employees: 2,228 Fiscal Year Ends: 3/31
Parent Company:

SALARIES/BENEFITS:

Pension Plan: | ESOP Stock Plan: | Profit Sharing: | Top Exec. Salary: $579,167 | Bonus: $563,562
Savings Plan: Y | Stock Purch. Plan: | | Second Exec. Salary: $520,549 | Bonus: $525,018

OTHER THOUGHTS:

Apparent Women Officers or Directors: 1
Hot Spot for Advancement for Women/Minorities:

LOCATIONS: ("Y" = Yes)

West:	Southwest:	Midwest:	Southeast:	Northeast:	International:
				Y	Y

TAMPA ELECTRIC COMPANY

www.tampaelectric.com

Industry Group Code: 2211

Management:		Sales/Marketing:		Liberal Arts:		Information Systems:		Professionals:		Technical/Scientific:	
Mgmt. Trainees:		Mktg. Professionals:	Y	Gen. Writing/Editing:	Y	Info. Management:	Y	Finance/Acct.:	Y	Engineers, Elec.:	Y
Experienced Mgmt.:	Y	Retail Sales:		Technical Writing:		Software Dev.:		Law:	Y	Engineers, Other:	Y
Int'l Business:		Commercial/Industrial:	Y	Graphic Arts/Photog.:		Hardware Dev.:		HR/Other:	Y	Health/Lab	
MBA Graduates:	Y	Sales Trainees:	Y	Music:		Consulting/Other:		Training:	Y	Scientists/Research:	
		Advertising Pros.:		Broadcasting:				Health Care:		Petroleum/Chemicals:	Y
				Other:				Consulting:		Math/Other:	

TYPES OF BUSINESS:

Utilities-Electricity & Natural Gas
Electric Generation
Solar Power
Coal Mining & Preparation
Synthetic Fuel
Ocean & River Shipping

BRANDS/DIVISIONS/AFFILIATES:

TECO Energy, Inc.
Peoples Gas System
Tampa Electric

CONTACTS: *Note: Officers with more than one job title may be intentionally listed here more than once.*

Gordon L. Gillette, Pres.
Bruce Narzissenfeld, VP-Mktg.
Bruce Narzissenfeld, VP-Fuels Oper.
Bruce Narzissenfeld, VP-Bus. Dev.
Charles O. Hinson, III, VP-Community & State Rel.
Bruce Narzissenfeld, VP-Customer Care
William T. Whale, VP-Electric & Gas Delivery
Thomas L. Hernandez, VP-Energy Supply

Phone: 813-228-1111 **Fax:** 813-228-1670
Toll-Free:
Address: 702 N. Franklin St., TECO Plz., Tampa, FL 33602 US

GROWTH PLANS/SPECIAL FEATURES:

Tampa Electric Company is the principal subsidiary of TECO Energy, Inc. The firm is a public utility that generates, purchases, transmits, distributes, markets and sells electric energy and natural gas in Florida. Founded in 1899, the company operates through two divisions: Tampa Electric and Peoples Gas System. Tampa Electric, with a total generating capacity of 4,684 megawatts, generates, transmits and distributes electric energy. The company serves over 672,000 customers in a 2,000 square mile operating service territory, including all of Hillsborough County and parts of Pasco, Polk and Pinellas counties in Florida. Tampa Electric derives roughly 50% of its revenue from residential sales; 30% from commercial sales; 9% from industrial sales; and 11% from other sales, including bulk power sales for resale. The company operates four generating plants with approximately 58% of the energy produced coming from its coal fired plants, approximately 42% coming from its gas fired plants and less than 1% coming from its oil fired plant. Peoples Gas System operates fossil-fueled power plants and distributes natural gas for more than 336,000 residential, commercial and industrial customers. Its distribution system consists of approximately 17,500 miles of pipe, including approximately 11,000 miles of mains and 6,500 miles of service line.

The company offers its employees life, long-term disability, medical, dental and vision insurance; a pension plan; a 401(k) plan; flexible spending accounts; tuition reimbursement; and paid time off.

FINANCIALS: **Sales and profits are in thousands of dollars—add 000 to get the full amount. 2011 Note: Financial information for 2011 was not available for all companies at press time.**

2011 Sales: $ | 2011 Profits: $
2010 Sales: $ | 2010 Profits: $
2009 Sales: $ | 2009 Profits: $
2008 Sales: $ | 2008 Profits: $
2007 Sales: $ | 2007 Profits: $

U.S. Stock Ticker: Subsidiary
Int'l Ticker:
Int'l Exchange:
Employees: Fiscal Year Ends: 12/31
Parent Company: TECO ENERGY INC

SALARIES/BENEFITS:

Pension Plan: Y | ESOP Stock Plan: | Profit Sharing: | Top Exec. Salary: $455,500 | Bonus: $284,694
Savings Plan: Y | Stock Purch. Plan: | | Second Exec. Salary: $245,640 | Bonus: $135,102

OTHER THOUGHTS:

Apparent Women Officers or Directors:
Hot Spot for Advancement for Women/Minorities:

LOCATIONS: ("Y" = Yes)

West:	Southwest:	Midwest:	Southeast:	Northeast:	International:
			Y		

TARGA RESOURCES PARTNERS LP

www.targaresources.com

Industry Group Code: 211111

Management:		Sales/Marketing:		Liberal Arts:		Information Systems:		Professionals:		Technical/Scientific:	
Mgmt. Trainees:		Mktg. Professionals:		Gen. Writing/Editing:		Info. Management:	Y	Finance/Acct.:	Y	Engineers, Elec.:	
Experienced Mgmt.:	Y	Retail Sales:		Technical Writing:		Software Dev.:		Law:	Y	Engineers, Other:	Y
Int'l Business:	Y	Commercial/Industrial:		Graphic Arts/Photog.:		Hardware Dev.:		HR/Other:	Y	Health/Lab Scientists/Research:	
MBA Graduates:	Y	Sales Trainees:		Music:		Consulting/Other:		Training:	Y		
		Advertising Pros.:		Broadcasting:				Health Care:		Petroleum/Chemicals:	Y
				Other:				Consulting:		Math/Other:	

TYPES OF BUSINESS:

Natural Gas Gathering & Compression
Natural & Gas Liquids Processing & Selling

BRANDS/DIVISIONS/AFFILIATES:

Natural Gas Gathering and Processing Division
NGL Logistics and Marketing Division
Targa Resources GP LLC

CONTACTS: *Note: Officers with more than one job title may be intentionally listed here more than once.*

Rene R. Joyce, CEO
Michael A. Heim, COO/Exec. VP
Joe Bob Perkins, Pres.
Matthew J. Meloy, CFO/Sr. VP
Jeffrey J. McParland, Pres.,Admin.
Paul W. Chung, General Counsel/Sec./Exec. VP
Jeffrey J. McParland, Pres.,Finance
Roy E. Johnson, Exec. VP
James W. Whalen, Exec. Chmn.

Phone: 713-584-1000 **Fax:**
Toll-Free:
Address: 1000 Louisiana St., Ste. 4300, Houston, TX 77002 US

GROWTH PLANS/SPECIAL FEATURES:

Targa Resources Partners LP, managed by its general partner Targa Resources GP LLC, owns, operates, acquires and develops midstream energy assets. Targa provides midstream natural gas and natural gas liquid services throughout the U.S. and in 40 countries, covering 18,100 square miles, and is involved in the gathering, compressing, treating, processing and sale of natural gas, and the storage, fractionating, treating, transportation and sale of natural gas liquid (NGL) and its associated products. The company operates under two primary divisions: natural gas gathering and processing, subsequently divided into the field and coastal gathering and processing segments, and the NGL logistics and marketing division, consisting of the logistics assets and marketing and distribution segments. The natural gas gathering and processing division deals with all aspects involved in the collection of natural gas produced from oil and gas wells, and processing the raw natural gas to produce a merchantable product. The NGL logistics and marketing division, also known as the Downstream Business, includes all activities involved in the process of fractionating the NGL into finished products, such as: ethane, propane, butane and gasoline. The Downstream Business also provides for the storage, terminaling, transportation, distribution and marketing of NGL. In March 2011, Targa agreed to acquire a refined products and crude oil storage and terminaling facility in Channelview, Texas. In May 2011, the company announced a 100,000 barrel per day fractionation expansion of the Cedar Bayou Fractionator in Mont Belvieu, Texas, and agreed to cosponsor the construction of a 700 mile pipeline running from the Permian Basin and Eagle Ford Shale to Mont Belvieu. In October 2011, Targa announced the construction of a new cryogenic processing plant to service North Texas.

Employee benefits include: life, medical, vision and dental insurance, disability coverage, flexible spending accounts and a 401(k) profit sharing plan.

FINANCIALS: **Sales and profits are in thousands of dollars—add 000 to get the full amount. 2011 Note: Financial information for 2011 was not available for all companies at press time.**

2011 Sales: $6,987,100 — 2011 Profits: $204,500
2010 Sales: $5,460,200 — 2010 Profits: $134,000
2009 Sales: $4,503,800 — 2009 Profits: $7,200
2008 Sales: $8,030,100 — 2008 Profits: $235,200
2007 Sales: $1,661,500 — 2007 Profits: $40,300

U.S. Stock Ticker: NGLS
Int'l Ticker:
Int'l Exchange:
Employees: 1,000 Fiscal Year Ends: 12/31
Parent Company:

SALARIES/BENEFITS:

Pension Plan: ESOP Stock Plan: Profit Sharing: Top Exec. Salary: $410,000 Bonus: $855,000
Savings Plan: Y Stock Purch. Plan: Second Exec. Salary: $361,250 Bonus: $593,280

OTHER THOUGHTS:

Apparent Women Officers or Directors: 4
Hot Spot for Advancement for Women/Minorities: Y

LOCATIONS: ("Y" = Yes)

West:	Southwest:	Midwest:	Southeast:	Northeast:	International:
Y	Y	Y	Y	Y	Y

TECHNE CORP

www.techne-corp.com

Industry Group Code: 325413

Management:		Sales/Marketing:		Liberal Arts:		Information Systems:		Professionals:		Technical/Scientific:	
Mgmt. Trainees:		Mktg. Professionals:	Y	Gen. Writing/Editing:		Info. Management:	Y	Finance/Acct.:	Y	Engineers, Elec.:	
Experienced Mgmt.:	Y	Retail Sales:		Technical Writing:	Y	Software Dev.:	Y	Law:	Y	Engineers, Other:	Y
Int'l Business:	Y	Commercial/Industrial:	Y	Graphic Arts/Photog.:		Hardware Dev.:	Y	HR/Other:	Y	Health/Lab	Y
MBA Graduates:	Y	Sales Trainees:	Y	Music:		Consulting/Other:		Training:	Y	Scientists/Research:	Y
		Advertising Pros.:	Y	Broadcasting:				Health Care:	Y	Petroleum/Chemicals:	
				Other:				Consulting:		Math/Other:	Y

TYPES OF BUSINESS:

Biotechnology Products
Reagents, Antibodies & Assay Kits
Hematology Products

BRANDS/DIVISIONS/AFFILIATES:

Research and Diagnostic Systems, Inc.
R&D Systems Europe, Ltd.
R&D Systems GmbH
R&D Systems China Co. Ltd.
Quantikine
BiosPacific
Tocris Holdings Limited

CONTACTS: *Note: Officers with more than one job title may be intentionally listed here more than once.*

Thomas Oland, CEO
Thomas Oland, Pres.
Gregory J. Melsen, CFO
Marcel Veronneau, VP-Hematology Oper.
Gregory J. Melsen, VP-Finance
Roger Lucas, Vice Chmn.
Thomas Oland, Chmn.

Phone: 612-379-8854	**Fax:** 612-379-6580
Toll-Free:	
Address: 614 McKinley Pl. NE, Minneapolis, MN 55413 US	

GROWTH PLANS/SPECIAL FEATURES:

Techne Corp. is a holding company involved in biotechnology and hematology products. The firm operates through two subsidiaries: Research and Diagnostic Systems, Inc. (R&D Systems) and R&D Systems Europe, Ltd. (R&D Europe). R&D Systems manufactures biological products in two major segments: hematology controls, which are used in clinical and hospital laboratories to monitor the accuracy of blood analysis instruments; and biotechnology products, which include purified proteins and antibodies that are sold exclusively to the research market and assay kits (under the trade name Quantikine) that are sold to the research and clinical diagnostic markets. R&D Europe distributes biotechnology products throughout Europe and operates sales offices in France and Germany through its German subsidiary, R&D Systems GmbH. The company also operates under its BiosPacific subsidiary, which supplies biologics to manufacturers of in vitro diagnostic systems and immunodiagnostic kits. In recent years, R&D Systems has also expanded its product portfolio to include enzymes and intracellular cell signaling reagents such as kinases, proteases and phosphatases; these reagents detect diseases such as cancer, Alzheimer's, arthritic, autoimmunity, diabetes, hypertension, obesity, AIDS and SARS. Techne also produces controls and calibrators for a variety of medical brands such as Abbott Diagnostics, Beckman Coulter, Siemens Healthcare Diagnostics and Sysmex. In the hematology sector, the company's Whole Blood Flow Cytometry Controls are used to identify and quantify white blood cells by their surface antigens while linearity and reportable range controls assess the linearity of hematology analyzers for white blood cells, red blood cells, platelets and reticulocytes. R&D Systems China Co. Ltd. is a wholly-owned subsidiary established to improve the level of service offered to R&D Systems' distributors and customers in Shanghai, China. In May 2011, the company acquired U.K.-based supplier of chemical, peptide and antibody products, Tocris Holdings Limited and its subsidiaries.

FINANCIALS: **Sales and profits are in thousands of dollars—add 000 to get the full amount. 2011 Note: Financial information for 2011 was not available for all companies at press time.**

2011 Sales: $289,962	2011 Profits: $112,302	**U.S. Stock Ticker: TECH**
2010 Sales: $269,047	2010 Profits: $109,776	**Int'l Ticker:**
2009 Sales: $263,956	2009 Profits: $105,242	Int'l Exchange:
2008 Sales: $257,420	2008 Profits: $103,558	Employees: 763 Fiscal Year Ends: 6/30
2007 Sales: $223,482	2007 Profits: $85,111	Parent Company:

SALARIES/BENEFITS:

Pension Plan:	ESOP Stock Plan:	Profit Sharing: Y	Top Exec. Salary: $275,100	Bonus: $19,478
Savings Plan: Y	Stock Purch. Plan:		Second Exec. Salary: $254,100	Bonus: $

OTHER THOUGHTS:

Apparent Women Officers or Directors: 1
Hot Spot for Advancement for Women/Minorities:

LOCATIONS: ("Y" = Yes)

West:	Southwest:	Midwest:	Southeast:	Northeast:	International:
Y		Y			Y

TEKELEC

www.tekelec.com

Industry Group Code: 334210

Management:		Sales/Marketing:		Liberal Arts:		Information Systems:		Professionals:		Technical/Scientific:	
Mgmt. Trainees:		Mktg. Professionals:	Y	Gen. Writing/Editing:		Info. Management:	Y	Finance/Acct.:	Y	Engineers, Elec.:	Y
Experienced Mgmt.:	Y	Retail Sales:		Technical Writing:	Y	Software Dev.:	Y	Law:	Y	Engineers, Other:	Y
Int'l Business:	Y	Commercial/Industrial:	Y	Graphic Arts/Photog.:		Hardware Dev.:	Y	HR/Other:	Y	Health/Lab	
MBA Graduates:	Y	Sales Trainees:	Y	Music:		Consulting/Other:		Training:	Y	Scientists/Research:	
		Advertising Pros.:		Broadcasting:				Health Care:		Petroleum/Chemicals:	
				Other:				Consulting:		Math/Other:	

TYPES OF BUSINESS:

Network Switching Equipment
Diagnostics Systems
Contact Center Products
IP Network Equipment
Mobile Messaging

BRANDS/DIVISIONS/AFFILIATES:

EAGLE 5
EAGLE XG

CONTACTS:

Note: Officers with more than one job title may be intentionally listed here more than once.

Ronald J. de Lange, CEO
Ronald J. de Lange, Pres.
Gregory Rush, CFO/Sr. VP
Susie Kim Riley, Chief Mktg. Officer
Marykay Wells, CIO/VP-IT
Vince Lesch, CTO
Stuart H. Kupinsky, General Counsel
David K. Rice, Sr. VP-Oper.
Stuart H. Kupinsky, Sr. VP-Corp. Affairs
Gregory S. Rush, Chief Acct. Officer
Luis Pajares, VP-Sales, Americas
Hubert de Pesquidoux, Chmn.
Boudewijn Pesch, VP-Sales, Europe & Asia

Phone: 919-460-5500 **Fax:** 919-460-0877
Toll-Free: 888-628-5521
Address: 5200 Paramount Pkwy., Morrisville, NC 27560 US

GROWTH PLANS/SPECIAL FEATURES:

Tekelec is an international provider of telecommunications network systems and software applications. The majority of the firm's 300 customers are traditional landline (wireline) telecommunications carriers and mobile (wireless) communications operators; however, the company also caters to emerging competitive service providers and cable television service providers who are offering communication services. These customers, including many of the largest service providers in the world, have deployed Tekelec systems and software applications in more than 100 countries. The network applications are designed to increase network efficiency and performance; provide basic and enhanced voice and data services to subscribers; and aid the transition from traditional networks to Internet Protocol- (IP) based networks. The firm's software and network solutions include signaling network applications, number portability applications and performance management and monitoring applications. The network signaling product portfolio enables service providers to establish, control and terminate voice and data communications calls or sessions. It utilizes EAGLE 5, a product family which offers flexible routing applications and voice, short message, multimedia message and prepaid services, and EAGLE XG, a platform which offers corrective dialing, number portability, SIP signaling routers, IP multimedia call control and electronic number mapping. Tekelec's performance management and monitoring applications work with EAGLE 5 and assist customers in measuring network and service performance, managing network and service efficiency and monetizing their networks and service offerings through the reduction of revenue loss. Tekelec's mobile messaging segment, which includes both 2G/3G and SIP-based networks, offers products and services such as SMS Personalized Services, SMS Advertising, Application Gateway, SMS Store, SMS Routing, SMS Security and a SIP Messaging Gateway.

Tekelec offers employees a bonus plan and business accident insurance.

FINANCIALS:

Sales and profits are in thousands of dollars—add 000 to get the full amount. 2011 Note: Financial information for 2011 was not available for all companies at press time.

2011 Sales: $	2011 Profits: $
2010 Sales: $423,963	2010 Profits: $15,009
2009 Sales: $469,261	2009 Profits: $47,402
2008 Sales: $460,564	2008 Profits: $55,039
2007 Sales: $431,800	2007 Profits: $-35,336

U.S. Stock Ticker: Private
Int'l Ticker:
Int'l Exchange:
Employees: 1,291 Fiscal Year Ends: 12/31
Parent Company: SIRIS CAPITAL GROUP LLC

SALARIES/BENEFITS:

Pension Plan: ESOP Stock Plan: Profit Sharing: Top Exec. Salary: $570,000 Bonus: $766,080
Savings Plan: Stock Purch. Plan: Y Second Exec. Salary: $627,099 Bonus: $

OTHER THOUGHTS:

Apparent Women Officers or Directors: 2
Hot Spot for Advancement for Women/Minorities:

LOCATIONS: ("Y" = Yes)

West:	Southwest:	Midwest:	Southeast:	Northeast:	International:
	Y	Y		Y	Y

TELIRIS

www.teliris.com

Industry Group Code: 561499

Management:		Sales/Marketing:		Liberal Arts:		Information Systems:		Professionals:		Technical/Scientific:	
Mgmt. Trainees:		Mktg. Professionals:	Y	Gen. Writing/Editing:	Y	Info. Management:	Y	Finance/Acct.:	Y	Engineers, Elec.:	Y
Experienced Mgmt.:	Y	Retail Sales:		Technical Writing:	Y	Software Dev.:	Y	Law:	Y	Engineers, Other:	Y
Int'l Business:	Y	Commercial/Industrial:	Y	Graphic Arts/Photog.:		Hardware Dev.:		HR/Other:	Y	Health/Lab	
MBA Graduates:	Y	Sales Trainees:	Y	Music:		Consulting/Other:		Training:	Y	Scientists/Research:	
		Advertising Pros.:	Y	Broadcasting:				Health Care:		Petroleum/Chemicals:	
				Other:				Consulting:		Math/Other:	

TYPES OF BUSINESS:

Video Conferencing Products & Services

BRANDS/DIVISIONS/AFFILIATES:

Teliris VirtuaLive Telepresence
Teliris Executive
Teliris Express Telepresence
Teliris Personal Telepresence
Teliris Telepresence Gateway
Teliris Lentaris
Teliris @nywhere
Teliris Ltd

CONTACTS: *Note: Officers with more than one job title may be intentionally listed here more than once.*

Neil Hobbs, CEO
Rick Glickman, CFO/Exec. VP
Jeff Tench, Chief Mktg. Officer
Steve Gage, CTO/Exec. VP
Jim Kaufold, Exec. VP-Oper.
Martyn Lewis, Chmn.-European Union
John Inglis, Exec. VP-Global Sales & Mktg.
Rodney Rogers, Chmn.
Tony Smith, Managing Dir.-European Union

Phone: 212-490-1065	**Fax:** 212-269-2869
Toll-Free:	
Address: 55 Broadway, 14th Fl., New York, NY 10006 US	

GROWTH PLANS/SPECIAL FEATURES:

Teliris offers corporate video conferencing and telepresence services. Its core technology is Teliris VirtuaLive Telepresence, with other main products including Teliris Express Telepresence and Teliris Personal Telepresence. VirtuaLive comprises a suite of installed technologies incorporated into a corporate meeting room. It includes anywhere from three to six screens, either 52-inches or 65-inches in size, and can accommodate up to 28 persons per room. Its broadcast is 720-1080 pixils high definition (HD) quality images at 30-60 frames per second (fps). The Express Telepresence offering is a small-scale offering that offers two to three 65-inch screens that can accommodate four to six people. The broadcast is displayed at 30-60 fps and at HD quality. The Personal Telepresence offering is a single 40-inch HD display offering 30 fps for one on one communication. The company's products also include Teliris Executive Telepresence, which offers a panoramic perspective of group meetings on a desktop; Teliris @nywhere, which allows users access to transmit telepresence technology from any general purpose network; and Teliris StarPoint, which allows any display to be telepresence-enabled. The company's Teliris Lentaris is a cloud-based interoperability platform that enables managed connectivity across many videoconferencing and telepresence endpoints. Teliris InfiNET is a global telepresence exchange that interconnects telepresence systems. All of the firm's products feature the Teliris Telepresence Gateway, making them compatible with other standards-based telepresence and videoconferencing systems. Besides its products, Teliris offers managed telepresence services and Teliris Working Practices, a compilation of best telepresence practices that offers customized services, solutions and policies. Co-headquartered in New York and London, the firm operates as Teliris, Inc. in the U.S. and as Teliris Ltd. in the U.K.

FINANCIALS: **Sales and profits are in thousands of dollars—add 000 to get the full amount. 2011 Note: Financial information for 2011 was not available for all companies at press time.**

2011 Sales: $	2011 Profits: $	**U.S. Stock Ticker: Private**
2010 Sales: $	2010 Profits: $	**Int'l Ticker:**
2009 Sales: $	2009 Profits: $	Int'l Exchange:
2008 Sales: $	2008 Profits: $	Employees: Fiscal Year Ends:
2007 Sales: $	2007 Profits: $	Parent Company:

SALARIES/BENEFITS:

Pension Plan:	ESOP Stock Plan:	Profit Sharing:	Top Exec. Salary: $	Bonus: $
Savings Plan:	Stock Purch. Plan:		Second Exec. Salary: $	Bonus: $

OTHER THOUGHTS:

Apparent Women Officers or Directors:
Hot Spot for Advancement for Women/Minorities:

LOCATIONS: ("Y" = Yes)

West:	Southwest:	Midwest:	Southeast:	Northeast:	International:
				Y	Y

TERREMARK WORLDWIDE INC

www.terremark.com

Industry Group Code: 517110

Management:		Sales/Marketing:		Liberal Arts:		Information Systems:		Professionals:		Technical/Scientific:	
Mgmt. Trainees:		Mktg. Professionals:	Y	Gen. Writing/Editing:		Info. Management:	Y	Finance/Acct.:	Y	Engineers, Elec.:	
Experienced Mgmt.:	Y	Retail Sales:		Technical Writing:		Software Dev.:	Y	Law:	Y	Engineers, Other:	
Int'l Business:	Y	Commercial/Industrial:	Y	Graphic Arts/Photog.:		Hardware Dev.:		HR/Other:	Y	Health/Lab	
MBA Graduates:	Y	Sales Trainees:	Y	Music:		Consulting/Other:		Training:	Y	Scientists/Research:	
		Advertising Pros.:	Y	Broadcasting:				Health Care:		Petroleum/Chemicals:	
				Other:				Consulting:		Math/Other:	

TYPES OF BUSINESS:

Internet Exchange Points
Managed Services

BRANDS/DIVISIONS/AFFILIATES:

Infinistructure
Enterprise Cloud
Peering Service
Exchange Point Services Platform
DS3 DataVaulting
vCloud Express
Verizon Communications Inc

CONTACTS:

Note: Officers with more than one job title may be intentionally listed here more than once.

Nelson Fonseca, COO
Kerry Bailey, Pres.
Jose A. Segrera, CFO
Barry Field, Sr. VP-U.S. Commercial Sales
Adam T. Smith, Chief Legal Officer
Marvin Wheeler, Chief Strategy Officer
Jamie Dos Santos, CEO/Pres., Terremark Federal Group
Herman Oggel, Pres., European Bus.

Phone: 305-961-3200	**Fax:** 305-961-8190
Toll-Free:	
Address: 2 S. Biscayne Blvd., 1 Biscayne Tower, Ste. 2800, Miami, FL 33131 US	

GROWTH PLANS/SPECIAL FEATURES:

Terremark Worldwide, Inc. is a global provider of managed IT infrastructure services. The firm leverages data centers throughout the U.S., Europe and Latin America and access to carrier-neutral network connectivity to cater to roughly 1,300 customers worldwide. Terremark provides managed hosting, collocation, connectivity, disaster recovery, security and cloud computing services. As a carrier-neutral provider, the company does not own or operate its own network and consequently its interconnection services enable its customers to exchange network traffic through direct connection with each other or through peering connections with multiple parties. Terremark's managed services are designed to support complex, transaction-intensive, mission-critical, line-of-business and Internet facing applications. It provides managed hosting services on dedicated servers located within its facilities or virtualized servers through its Infinistructure, digitalOps and Enterprise Cloud platforms. Additionally, the company provides managed storage and tape backup services. Terremark's managed services include device management; operating system and application platform management; patch management; monitoring services; problem and incident management; data storage; backup and restoration; security services, such as managed firewalls, intrusion detection and anti-virus services; database administration; application performance tuning; software installation and configuration; application testing; and deployment services. The company's collocation services offer clients the ability to deploy computing, network, storage and IT infrastructure through its data centers. Terremark's exchange point services enable the secure exchange of data, deliver Internet Protocol- (IP) based services and provide content between networks. In April 2011, the firm was acquired by Verizon Communications, Inc. The company is now a wholly-owned subsidiary of Verizon.

Terremark offers its employees medical, dental, disability, life and vision insurance.

FINANCIALS:

Sales and profits are in thousands of dollars—add 000 to get the full amount. 2011 Note: Financial information for 2011 was not available for all companies at press time.

2011 Sales: $	2011 Profits: $
2010 Sales: $292,347	2010 Profits: $-31,673
2009 Sales: $250,470	2009 Profits: $-10,569
2008 Sales: $187,414	2008 Profits: $-42,228
2007 Sales: $100,948	2007 Profits: $-14,952

U.S. Stock Ticker: Subsidiary
Int'l Ticker:
Int'l Exchange:
Employees: 712 Fiscal Year Ends: 3/31
Parent Company: VERIZON COMMUNICATIONS INC

SALARIES/BENEFITS:

Pension Plan:	ESOP Stock Plan:	Profit Sharing:	Top Exec. Salary: $490,808	Bonus: $
Savings Plan: Y	Stock Purch. Plan:		Second Exec. Salary: $425,000	Bonus: $378,250

OTHER THOUGHTS:

Apparent Women Officers or Directors: 1
Hot Spot for Advancement for Women/Minorities:

LOCATIONS: ("Y" = Yes)

West:	Southwest:	Midwest:	Southeast:	Northeast:	International:
Y	Y		Y	Y	Y

TESCO CORPORATION

www.tescocorp.com

Industry Group Code: 33313

Management:		**Sales/Marketing:**		**Liberal Arts:**		**Information Systems:**		**Professionals:**		**Technical/Scientific:**	
Mgmt. Trainees:		Mktg. Professionals:	Y	Gen. Writing/Editing:		Info. Management:	Y	Finance/Acct.:	Y	Engineers, Elec.:	Y
Experienced Mgmt.:	Y	Retail Sales:		Technical Writing:	Y	Software Dev.:	Y	Law:	Y	Engineers, Other:	
Int'l Business:	Y	Commercial/Industrial:	Y	Graphic Arts/Photog.:		Hardware Dev.:	Y	HR/Other:	Y	Health/Lab	
MBA Graduates:	Y	Sales Trainees:	Y	Music:		Consulting/Other:		Training:	Y	Scientists/Research:	
		Advertising Pros.:		Broadcasting:				Health Care:		Petroleum/Chemicals:	
				Other:				Consulting:		Math/Other:	

TYPES OF BUSINESS:

Oil & Gas Drilling Equipment
Equipment Maintenance
Casing Drilling Technology

BRANDS/DIVISIONS/AFFILIATES:

TESCO CASING DRILLING
Premiere Casing Services - Egypt S.A.E.

CONTACTS:

Note: Officers with more than one job title may be intentionally listed here more than once.

Julio M. Quintana, CEO
Julio M. Quintana, Pres.
Robert Kayl, CFO/Sr. VP
Fernando R. Assing, Sr. VP-Mktg.
Jonathan B. O'Blenes, VP-Surface Prod. Eng.
Jonathan B. O'Blenes, VP-Mfg.
Dean Ferris, General Counsel/Sr. VP/Corp. Sec.
Jeffrey L. Foster, Sr. VP-Oper.
Fernando R. Assing, Sr. VP-Bus. Dev.
John M. Dodson, Chief Acct. Officer/Corp. Controller/VP
Dietmar J. Neidhardt, Sr. VP-TESCO CASING DRILLING
Norman W. Robertson, Chmn.

Phone: 713-359-7000 **Fax:** 713-359-7001
Toll-Free:
Address: 3993 W. Sam Houston Pkwy. N., Ste. 100, Houston, TX 77043 US

GROWTH PLANS/SPECIAL FEATURES:

Tesco Corporation is a global designer, manufacturer and service deliverer of technology-based solutions for the upstream energy industry. The company operates in four segments: top drives; tubular services; casing drilling; and research and engineering. The top drive segment sells equipment and provides services to drilling contractors and oil and gas operating companies throughout the world. The division primarily manufactures top drives, which are used in drilling operations to rotate the drill string while suspended from the derrick above the rig floor. The segment also provides rental top drives on a day-rate basis for land and offshore drilling rigs. In addition, the segment provides after-market top drive sales and support services to customers on an ongoing basis and maintains regional stocks of high-demand parts as well as trained field and shop service personnel to support both its own rental units and units owned by customers. The tubular services segment offers conventional and proprietary casing and tubing running services. The casing drilling segment is focused on the firm's technology-based proprietary casing running solution, TESCO CASING DRILLING, which uses conventional oil well casing in well drilling but reduces drilling time and uncertainties. Casing is steel pipe installed in the well bore to maintain structural integrity; isolate water-bearing surface sands; and provide structural support of the wellhead and other casing and tubing strings in the well. The segment provides specialized equipment and personnel to operators and drilling contractors. The company's research and engineering segment comprises the firm's research and development activities. Its portfolio includes approximately 155 issued patents and 121 pending patent applications. Tesco has operations in 23 countries. In October 2011, the firm acquired Egyptian tubular services company Premiere Casing Services - Egypt S.A.E.

FINANCIALS:

Sales and profits are in thousands of dollars—add 000 to get the full amount. 2011 Note: Financial information for 2011 was not available for all companies at press time.

2011 Sales: $513,000	2011 Profits: $27,000
2010 Sales: $378,665	2010 Profits: $7,045
2009 Sales: $356,478	2009 Profits: $-5,265
2008 Sales: $543,942	2008 Profits: $49,923
2007 Sales: $462,378	2007 Profits: $32,302

U.S. Stock Ticker: TESO
Int'l Ticker:
Int'l Exchange:
Employees: 1,397 Fiscal Year Ends: 12/31
Parent Company:

SALARIES/BENEFITS:

Pension Plan: ESOP Stock Plan: Profit Sharing: Top Exec. Salary: $520,385 Bonus: $684,000
Savings Plan: Stock Purch. Plan: Second Exec. Salary: $296,873 Bonus: $295,500

OTHER THOUGHTS:

Apparent Women Officers or Directors:
Hot Spot for Advancement for Women/Minorities:

LOCATIONS: ("Y" = Yes)

West:	Southwest:	Midwest:	Southeast:	Northeast:	International:
	Y				Y

TESSCO TECHNOLOGIES INC

www.tessco.com

Industry Group Code: 423430

Management:		Sales/Marketing:		Liberal Arts:		Information Systems:		Professionals:		Technical/Scientific:	
Mgmt. Trainees:		Mktg. Professionals:	Y	Gen. Writing/Editing:		Info. Management:	Y	Finance/Acct.:	Y	Engineers, Elec.:	Y
Experienced Mgmt.:	Y	Retail Sales:		Technical Writing:	Y	Software Dev.:	Y	Law:	Y	Engineers, Other:	
Int'l Business:	Y	Commercial/Industrial:	Y	Graphic Arts/Photog.:		Hardware Dev.:		HR/Other:	Y	Health/Lab	
MBA Graduates:	Y	Sales Trainees:		Music:		Consulting/Other:		Training:		Scientists/Research:	
		Advertising Pros.:		Broadcasting:				Health Care:		Petroleum/Chemicals:	
				Other:				Consulting:		Math/Other:	

TYPES OF BUSINESS:

Wireless Communications Products Distributor
Supply Chain & Logistics Services
Network Infrastructure Products
Mobile Devices & Accessories
Test & Maintenance Products

BRANDS/DIVISIONS/AFFILIATES:

TerraWave
Ventev
Airstream
Wireless Solutions

CONTACTS: *Note: Officers with more than one job title may be intentionally listed here more than once.*

Robert B. Barnhill, Jr., CEO
Robert B. Barnhill, Jr., Pres.
David M. Young, CFO/Sr. VP
David M. Young, Corp. Sec.
Gerald T. Garland, Sr. VP-Solutions Dev. & Prod. Mgmt.
Douglas A. Rein, Sr. VP-Performance Systems Group
Robert B. Barnhill, Jr., Chmn.
Saeed Tofighi, Sr. VP-Customer Supply Chain

Phone: 410-229-1000 **Fax:** 410-527-0005
Toll-Free: 800-508-5444
Address: 11126 McCormick Rd., Hunt Valley, MD 21031 US

GROWTH PLANS/SPECIAL FEATURES:

TESSCO Technologies Inc. (TESSCO) is a distributor of telecommunications products and a provider of integrated product and supply chain services. The firm serves professionals that design, build, run, maintain and use wireless mobile, fixed and in-building systems. The company's operational platform, Knowledge, Configuration, Delivery and Control System (KCDC), allows customers and manufacturers to streamline the supply chain process and lower total inventories and costs by providing guaranteed availability and on-time delivery to the point of use throughout the world. TESSCO's offerings are classified into three business segments: network infrastructure; mobile devices and accessories; and installation, test and maintenance products. Network infrastructure products, accounting for 35% of revenue, include base station antennas, cable and transmission lines, fixed broadband equipment, filtering systems, small towers, lightning protection devices, connectors and miscellaneous hardware. Mobile devices and accessory products (55% of revenue) include cellular telephones and other data devices; pagers and two-way radios; and related accessories. Installation, test and maintenance products (10% of revenue) include sophisticated analysis equipment and various frequency, voltage and power measuring devices, as well as an assortment of tools, hardware, replacement and component parts and supplies required by service technicians. A majority of TESSCO's product purchases are concentrated on a small number of vendors. TESSCO primarily provides manufacturer brand-name products, but also offers some accessory products and infrastructure accessory components under the TESSCO-owned brands, including TerraWave, Ventev, Airstream and Wireless Solutions.

TESSCO offers its employees life, AD&D, disability, medical, dental, vision and prescription drug insurance; tuition subsidies; a 401(k) plan; profit sharing; flexible spending accounts; an employee stock purchase plan; referral rewards; adoption benefits; and access to a credit union.

FINANCIALS: **Sales and profits are in thousands of dollars—add 000 to get the full amount. 2011 Note: Financial information for 2011 was not available for all companies at press time.**

2011 Sales: $605,219	2011 Profits: $10,018
2010 Sales: $522,032	2010 Profits: $9,139
2009 Sales: $483,007	2009 Profits: $6,328
2008 Sales: $520,968	2008 Profits: $4,818
2007 Sales: $492,328	2007 Profits: $7,042

U.S. Stock Ticker: TESS
Int'l Ticker:
Int'l Exchange:
Employees: 874 Fiscal Year Ends: 3/31
Parent Company:

SALARIES/BENEFITS:

Pension Plan:	ESOP Stock Plan:	Profit Sharing: Y	Top Exec. Salary: $600,000	Bonus: $633,234
Savings Plan: Y	Stock Purch. Plan: Y		Second Exec. Salary: $300,000	Bonus: $203,411

OTHER THOUGHTS:

Apparent Women Officers or Directors:
Hot Spot for Advancement for Women/Minorities:

LOCATIONS: ("Y" = Yes)

West:	Southwest:	Midwest:	Southeast:	Northeast:	International:
Y				Y	Y

THERAGENICS CORP

www.theragenics.com

Industry Group Code: 33911

Management:		Sales/Marketing:		Liberal Arts:		Information Systems:		Professionals:		Technical/Scientific:	
Mgmt. Trainees:		Mktg. Professionals:	Y	Gen. Writing/Editing:		Info. Management:	Y	Finance/Acct.:	Y	Engineers, Elec.:	
Experienced Mgmt.:	Y	Retail Sales:		Technical Writing:	Y	Software Dev.:	Y	Law:	Y	Engineers, Other:	Y
Int'l Business:	Y	Commercial/Industrial:	Y	Graphic Arts/Photog.:		Hardware Dev.:		HR/Other:	Y	Health/Lab	Y
MBA Graduates:	Y	Sales Trainees:	Y	Music:		Consulting/Other:		Training:	Y	Scientists/Research:	Y
		Advertising Pros.:		Broadcasting:				Health Care:	Y	Petroleum/Chemicals:	
				Other:				Consulting:		Math/Other:	

TYPES OF BUSINESS:

Medical Devices
Surgical Products

BRANDS/DIVISIONS/AFFILIATES:

TheraSeed
Galt Medical Corp.
CP Medical Corp.
NeedleTech Products, Inc.
I-Seed

CONTACTS: *Note: Officers with more than one job title may be intentionally listed here more than once.*

M. Christine Jacobs, CEO
M. Christine Jacobs, Pres.
Frank J. Tarallo, CFO
C. Russell Small, Exec. VP-Sales & Mktg., Surgical Prod.
Bruce W. Smith, Corp. Sec.
Bruce W. Smith, Exec. VP-Strategy & Bus. Dev.
Frank J. Tarallo, Treas.
Joseph Plante, Pres., NeedleTech
Janet E. Zeman, Pres., CP Medical
M. Christine Jacobs, Chmn.

Phone: 770-271-0233	**Fax:**
Toll-Free:	
Address: 5203 Bristol Industrial Way, Buford, GA 30518 US	

GROWTH PLANS/SPECIAL FEATURES:

Theragenics Corp. is a medical device company serving the cancer treatment and surgical markets. The company operates in two segments: the brachytherapy seed business and the surgical products business. The brachytherapy seed business segment produces, markets and sells TheraSeed, the firm's premier palladium-103 prostate cancer treatment device; I-seed, its iodine-125 based prostrate cancer treatment device; and other related products and services. Theragenics is one of the world's largest producers of palladium-103, the radioactive isotope that supplies the therapeutic radiation for its TheraSeed device. TheraSeed is an implant the size of a grain of rice that is used primarily in treating localized prostate cancer with a one-time, minimally invasive procedure. The implant emits radiation within the immediate prostate area, killing the tumor while sparing surrounding organs from significant radiation exposure. Physicians, hospitals and other healthcare providers, primarily located in the U.S., utilize the TheraSeed device. The majority of TheraSeed sales are channeled through one third-party distributor. The surgical products business segment consists of wound closure, vascular access and specialty needle products. Wound closure products include sutures, needles and other surgical products with applications in, among other areas, urology, veterinary medicine, cardiology, orthopedics, plastic surgery and dental surgery. Vascular access products include introducers, guidewires and related products. Specialty needles include coaxial, biopsy, spinal and disposable veress needles; access trocars; and other needle-based products. The surgical products business sells its devices and components primarily to original equipment manufacturers (OEMs) and a network of distributors. The firm's wholly-owned subsidiaries CP Medical Corp., Galt Medical Corp. and NeedleTech Products, Inc. comprise the surgical products business. In October 2010, NeedleTech Products opened a new manufacturing facility in Massachusetts.

Employees are offered medical, dental and life insurance; short- and long-term disability coverage; a 401(k) plan; and an employee stock purchase plan.

FINANCIALS: **Sales and profits are in thousands of dollars—add 000 to get the full amount. 2011 Note: Financial information for 2011 was not available for all companies at press time.**

2011 Sales: $	2011 Profits: $	**U.S. Stock Ticker: TGX**
2010 Sales: $82,184	2010 Profits: $2,070	**Int'l Ticker:**
2009 Sales: $78,326	2009 Profits: $3,075	Int'l Exchange:
2008 Sales: $67,358	2008 Profits: $-58,540	Employees: 500 Fiscal Year Ends: 12/31
2007 Sales: $62,210	2007 Profits: $5,635	Parent Company:

SALARIES/BENEFITS:

Pension Plan:	ESOP Stock Plan:	Profit Sharing:	Top Exec. Salary: $555,000	Bonus: $457,842
Savings Plan: Y	Stock Purch. Plan: Y		Second Exec. Salary: $320,000	Bonus: $190,293

OTHER THOUGHTS:

Apparent Women Officers or Directors: 3
Hot Spot for Advancement for Women/Minorities: Y

LOCATIONS: ("Y" = Yes)

West:	Southwest:	Midwest:	Southeast:	Northeast:	International:
Y	Y		Y	Y	

THORATEC CORPORATION

www.thoratec.com

Industry Group Code: 33911

Management:		Sales/Marketing:		Liberal Arts:		Information Systems:		Professionals:		Technical/Scientific:	
Mgmt. Trainees:		Mktg. Professionals:	Y	Gen. Writing/Editing:		Info. Management:	Y	Finance/Acct.:	Y	Engineers, Elec.:	Y
Experienced Mgmt.:	Y	Retail Sales:		Technical Writing:	Y	Software Dev.:	Y	Law:	Y	Engineers, Other:	Y
Int'l Business:	Y	Commercial/Industrial:	Y	Graphic Arts/Photog.:		Hardware Dev.:	Y	HR/Other:	Y	Health/Lab	Y
MBA Graduates:	Y	Sales Trainees:	Y	Music:		Consulting/Other:		Training:	Y	Scientists/Research:	Y
		Advertising Pros.:		Broadcasting:				Health Care:	Y	Petroleum/Chemicals:	
				Other:				Consulting:		Math/Other:	

TYPES OF BUSINESS:

Medical Equipment-Ventricular Assistance Devices
Medical Equipment-Ventricular Assistance Devices
Circulatory Support Products
Vascular Graft Products

BRANDS/DIVISIONS/AFFILIATES:

Thoratec Paracorporeal Ventricular Assist Device
Thoratec Implantable Ventricular Assist Device
HeartMate Left Ventricular Assist System
HeartMate II Left Ventricular Assist System
CentriMag Blood Pumping System
Vectra

CONTACTS: *Note: Officers with more than one job title may be intentionally listed here more than once.*

Gerhard F. Burbach, CEO
Gerhard F. Burbach, Pres.
Roxanne Oulman, Interim CFO
David A. Lehman, General Counsel/Sr. VP/Corp. Sec.
Neil F. Dimick, Chmn.

Phone: 925-847-8600	**Fax:** 925-847-8571
Toll-Free: 800-456-1477	
Address: 6035 Stoneridge Dr., Pleasanton, CA 94588 US	

GROWTH PLANS/SPECIAL FEATURES:

Thoratec Corporation is a global manufacturer of mechanical circulatory support products for the treatment of heart failure. Thoratec's primary cardiovascular product lines are its ventricular assist devices (VADs), which may be placed inside or outside the body; can be used for left, right or biventricular support; and are suitable for patients of varying sizes and ages. VADs consist of four FDA-approved and CE Mark-approved products called the Thoratec Paracorporeal Ventricular Assist Device; the Thoratec Implantable Ventricular Assist Device; the HeartMate Left Ventricular Assist System; and the HeartMate II Left Ventricular Assist System. Thoratec also markets the CentriMag Blood Pumping System for acute heart failure and the Vectra vascular access graft for renal dialysis. Collectively, the firm's mechanical circulatory support devices are FDA-approved for bridge-to-transplant, long-term support for patients suffering from advanced stage heart failure who are not eligible for heart transplantation, post-cardiotomy myocardial recovery and support during cardiac surgery. Thoratec estimates that doctors have implanted more than 12,000 of its devices, primarily for patients awaiting a heart transplant or those who require permanent support. In November 2010, the company announced plans to sell its International Technidyne Corporation division to an affiliate of Pincus LLC.

Thoratec offers its employees a stock purchase plan; financial and wellness education; tuition reimbursement; fitness facility discounts; a 401(k) plan; and medical, dental, vision, disability, AD&D and life insurance.

FINANCIALS: **Sales and profits are in thousands of dollars—add 000 to get the full amount. 2011 Note: Financial information for 2011 was not available for all companies at press time.**

2011 Sales: $422,713	2011 Profits: $71,544	**U.S. Stock Ticker: THOR**
2010 Sales: $382,973	2010 Profits: $53,166	**Int'l Ticker:**
2009 Sales: $373,937	2009 Profits: $28,584	Int'l Exchange:
2008 Sales: $313,564	2008 Profits: $22,532	Employees: 662 Fiscal Year Ends: 12/31
2007 Sales: $234,780	2007 Profits: $3,235	Parent Company:

SALARIES/BENEFITS:

Pension Plan:	ESOP Stock Plan:	Profit Sharing:	Top Exec. Salary: $505,309	Bonus: $830,288
Savings Plan: Y	Stock Purch. Plan: Y		Second Exec. Salary: $373,439	Bonus: $496,825

OTHER THOUGHTS:

Apparent Women Officers or Directors: 1
Hot Spot for Advancement for Women/Minorities:

LOCATIONS: ("Y" = Yes)

West:	Southwest:	Midwest:	Southeast:	Northeast:	International:
Y		Y		Y	Y

TII NETWORK TECHNOLOGIES INC

www.tiinettech.com

Industry Group Code: 335

Management:		Sales/Marketing:		Liberal Arts:		Information Systems:		Professionals:		Technical/Scientific:	
Mgmt. Trainees:		Mktg. Professionals:		Gen. Writing/Editing:		Info. Management:	Y	Finance/Acct.:	Y	Engineers, Elec.:	Y
Experienced Mgmt.:	Y	Retail Sales:		Technical Writing:	Y	Software Dev.:	Y	Law:	Y	Engineers, Other:	
Int'l Business:		Commercial/Industrial:	Y	Graphic Arts/Photog.:		Hardware Dev.:	Y	HR/Other:	Y	Health/Lab	
MBA Graduates:	Y	Sales Trainees:	Y	Music:		Consulting/Other:		Training:		Scientists/Research:	
		Advertising Pros.:		Broadcasting:				Health Care:		Petroleum/Chemicals:	
				Other:				Consulting:		Math/Other:	

TYPES OF BUSINESS:

Overvoltage & Lightning Protection Devices
Network Interface Devices
Telecommunications Equipment
Station Electronics Products

BRANDS/DIVISIONS/AFFILIATES:

HomePlug
Frederick Fiber Optics

CONTACTS: *Note: Officers with more than one job title may be intentionally listed here more than once.*

Kenneth A. Paladino, CEO
Kenneth A. Paladino, Pres.
Jennifer E. Katsch, CFO
Walter Fay, VP-Mktg. & Sales
Nisar A. Chaudhry, Chief Scientist/VP
David E. Foley, VP-Tech. Dev.
Thomas Smith, VP-Eng.
Jennifer E. Katsch, Sec.
Jennifer E. Katsch, Head-Investor Rel.
Jennifer E. Katsch, VP-Finance/Treas.
Christopher James, VP-Quality
Monica Gonzalez-Greer, VP-Sales, Latin America & Caribbean
Brian J. Kelley, Chmn.
Michael Dawe, VP-Sales-Canada, U.K., Oceania, Europe & Asia

Phone: 631-789-5000 **Fax:** 631-789-5063
Toll-Free: 888-844-4720
Address: 141 Rodeo Dr., Edgewood, NY 11717 US

GROWTH PLANS/SPECIAL FEATURES:

TII Network Technologies, Inc. designs, manufactures and markets network interface devices (NID), broadband products, over-voltage surge protection and connectivity solutions for the communications industry. The company's NIDs connect and make use of surge protection technologies, electronics and DSL and fiber components. Along with its NIDs, TII also markets station electronic products that are installed with an NID. These products include a line of DSL station electronic items; for example, splitters that isolate the voice and data signals on a line to provide separate outputs for phone and data services, allowing for DSL services. Broadband products include Outrigger, the firm's intelligent NID that facilitates delivery of digital telephone, television and Internet data by telephone or cable service providers; and HomePlug, a technology that enables networking of voice, data and audio devices through the consumer's AC powerlines. The company's overvoltage products include gas tubes, which are the principal component of all of its overvoltage surge protectors; modular station protectors, the firm's most advanced overvoltage surge protectors; broadband coaxial protectors, which protect network powered coaxial lines that bring telephony and broadband services to homes and businesses; and AC powerline and dataline protectors for personal computers and home entertainment systems. TII's connectivity products include aerial and buried terminals as well as various VoIP (Voice over Internet Protocol) products. The company's principal VoIP products are a collection of passive products, which allow clients to consolidate multiple phone lines in one location in order to provide VoIP telephony to cable subscribers. TII sells its products through a network of multiple sales channels, principally to telecommunications providers, multi-system operators of communications services, including cable satellite service providers and original equipment manufacturers (OEMs). In March 2011, the firm acquired fiber optic product manufacturer Frederick Fiber Optics.

FINANCIALS: **Sales and profits are in thousands of dollars—add 000 to get the full amount. 2011 Note: Financial information for 2011 was not available for all companies at press time.**

2011 Sales: $
2010 Sales: $54,498
2009 Sales: $27,437
2008 Sales: $35,190
2007 Sales: $46,486

2011 Profits: $
2010 Profits: $2,230
2009 Profits: $ 73
2008 Profits: $ 578
2007 Profits: $6,440

U.S. Stock Ticker: TIII
Int'l Ticker:
Int'l Exchange:
Employees: 75 Fiscal Year Ends: 12/31
Parent Company:

SALARIES/BENEFITS:

Pension Plan: ESOP Stock Plan: Profit Sharing: Top Exec. Salary: $301,308 Bonus: $140,000
Savings Plan: Stock Purch. Plan: Second Exec. Salary: $195,785 Bonus: $65,000

OTHER THOUGHTS:

Apparent Women Officers or Directors: 2
Hot Spot for Advancement for Women/Minorities:

LOCATIONS: ("Y" = Yes)

West:	Southwest:	Midwest:	Southeast:	Northeast:	International:
				Y	

TOOTSIE ROLL INDUSTRIES INC

www.tootsie.com

Industry Group Code: 311320

Management:		Sales/Marketing:		Liberal Arts:		Information Systems:		Professionals:		Technical/Scientific:	
Mgmt. Trainees:	Y	Mktg. Professionals:	Y	Gen. Writing/Editing:	Y	Info. Management:	Y	Finance/Acct.:	Y	Engineers, Elec.:	
Experienced Mgmt.:	Y	Retail Sales:		Technical Writing:		Software Dev.:		Law:	Y	Engineers, Other:	Y
Int'l Business:	Y	Commercial/Industrial:	Y	Graphic Arts/Photog.:		Hardware Dev.:		HR/Other:	Y	Health/Lab	
MBA Graduates:	Y	Sales Trainees:	Y	Music:		Consulting/Other:		Training:	Y	Scientists/Research:	
		Advertising Pros.:	Y	Broadcasting:				Health Care:		Petroleum/Chemicals:	
				Other:	Y			Consulting:		Math/Other:	

TYPES OF BUSINESS:

Confectionery Product Manufacturing

BRANDS/DIVISIONS/AFFILIATES:

Tootsie Roll Pops
Caramel Apple Pops
Charms
Blow-Pop
Blue Razz
Cella's
Andes
Sugar Daddy

CONTACTS:

Note: Officers with more than one job title may be intentionally listed here more than once.

Melvin J. Gordon, CEO
Ellen R. Gordon, COO
Ellen R. Gordon, Pres.
Thomas E. Corr, VP-Mktg. & Sales
John W. Newlin, Jr., VP-Mfg.
G. Howard Ember, Jr., VP-Finance
Barry P. Bowen, Treas.
Melvin J. Gordon, Chmn.
John P. Majors, VP-Dist.

Phone: 773-838-3400	**Fax:** 773-838-3534
Toll-Free:	
Address: 7401 S. Cicero Ave., Chicago, IL 60629 US	

GROWTH PLANS/SPECIAL FEATURES:

Tootsie Roll Industries, Inc. is a manufacturer of confectionary products. Best known for the Tootsie Roll candy and Tootsie Roll Pop, the company's products include Cry Baby, Caramel Apple Pops, Charms, Blow-Pop, Blue Razz, Zip-a-Dee Pops, Cella's, Mason Dots, Mason Crows, Junior Mint, Charleston Chew, Sugar Daddy, Sugar Babies, Andes, Fluffy Stuff, Dubble Bubble, Razzles and Nik-L-Nip, as well as a variety pack called Child's Play. The company markets a variety of packages designed to be suitable for display and sale in different types of retail outlets. Products are distributed through approximately 100 candy and grocery brokers and by the firm itself to roughly15,000 customers throughout the U.S. These customers include wholesale distributors of candy and groceries, grocery stores, variety stores, dollar stores, drug chains, discount chains, cooperative grocery associations, warehouse and membership club stores, convenience stores, vending machine operators, the U.S. military and fund-raising charitable organizations. Tootsie Roll Industries' principal markets are in the U.S., Canada and Mexico, although the company maintains distribution channels in over 75 countries. The Mexican plant supplies a small percentage of the products marketed in the U.S. and Canada. The majority of the production from the Canadian plant is sold in the U.S.

FINANCIALS:

Sales and profits are in thousands of dollars—add 000 to get the full amount. 2011 Note: Financial information for 2011 was not available for all companies at press time.

2011 Sales: $532,505	2011 Profits: $43,938	**U.S. Stock Ticker: TR**
2010 Sales: $521,448	2010 Profits: $53,714	**Int'l Ticker:**
2009 Sales: $495,592	2009 Profits: $53,475	Int'l Exchange:
2008 Sales: $492,051	2008 Profits: $38,777	Employees: 2,200 Fiscal Year Ends: 12/31
2007 Sales: $492,742	2007 Profits: $51,625	Parent Company:

SALARIES/BENEFITS:

Pension Plan:	ESOP Stock Plan:	Profit Sharing:	Top Exec. Salary: $999,000	Bonus: $1,569,500
Savings Plan:	Stock Purch. Plan:		Second Exec. Salary: $999,000	Bonus: $1,469,500

OTHER THOUGHTS:

Apparent Women Officers or Directors: 2
Hot Spot for Advancement for Women/Minorities:

LOCATIONS: ("Y" = Yes)

West:	Southwest:	Midwest:	Southeast:	Northeast:	International:
		Y	Y	Y	Y

TOPPS COMPANY INC (THE)

www.topps.com

Industry Group Code: 311320

Management:		**Sales/Marketing:**		**Liberal Arts:**		**Information Systems:**		**Professionals:**		**Technical/Scientific:**	
Mgmt. Trainees:	Y	Mktg. Professionals:	Y	Gen. Writing/Editing:	Y	Info. Management:	Y	Finance/Acct.:	Y	Engineers, Elec.:	
Experienced Mgmt.:	Y	Retail Sales:		Technical Writing:		Software Dev.:		Law:	Y	Engineers, Other:	Y
Int'l Business:	Y	Commercial/Industrial:	Y	Graphic Arts/Photog.:		Hardware Dev.:		HR/Other:	Y	Health/Lab	
MBA Graduates:	Y	Sales Trainees:	Y	Music:		Consulting/Other:		Training:	Y	Scientists/Research:	
		Advertising Pros.:	Y	Broadcasting:				Health Care:		Petroleum/Chemicals:	
				Other:	Y			Consulting:		Math/Other:	

TYPES OF BUSINESS:

Candy & Gum Manufacturing
Collectibles
Trading Cards
Collectible Strategy Games

BRANDS/DIVISIONS/AFFILIATES:

Bazooka
Ring Pop
Push Pop
eTopps
Redemptions
ShopTOPPS.com
ToppsTown
Madison Dearborn Partners

CONTACTS: *Note: Officers with more than one job title may be intentionally listed here more than once.*

Ryan O'Hara, CEO
Ryan O'Hara, Pres.
Joseph Del Toro, CFO/VP
Ira Friedman, VP-New Product Dev. & Publishing
Andrew Gasper, General Counsel/VP
Steve Grimes, Chief Digital Officer/VP
Michael Bramlage, VP-Digital
Staci Weiss, Head-Entertainment
Stephen Carson, Gen. Mgr.-Int'l Confectionery
Christopher Rodman, VP-Europe

Phone: 212-376-0300	**Fax:** 212-376-0573
Toll-Free:	
Address: 1 Whitehall St., New York, NY 10004 US	

GROWTH PLANS/SPECIAL FEATURES:

The Topps Company, Inc. is a marketer of premium-branded confectionery products and collectible entertainment products. The firm markets a variety of products such as lollipops, including the Ring Pop, Push Pop and Baby Bottle Pop; Bazooka-brand bubble gum; and certain licensed candy items. In addition to candies and gum, the company markets products such as comic books; trading cards; sticker album collections featuring professional athletes, popular television shows, movies and other licensed characters; and collectible strategy games. The firm has subsidiaries in the U.K., Ireland, Canada, Italy and Argentina, as well as its U.S. headquarters located in New York City and operations center located in Duryea, Pennsylvania. The firm also operates an extensive web site that offers feature stories on various athletes and national sports teams; a direct link to connect to the company through Facebook; a shopping portal; and access to the firm's other sites such as eTopps, Redemptions, ShopTOPPS.com and ToppsTown. Its corporate partners include Major League Baseball; Mickey Mantle; Beckett Magazine; CMG Worldwide; Minor League Baseball; Major League Baseball Association; National Football League; WWE; UFC; and National Football League Players Association. The Topps Company is owned by former Disney CEO Michael Eisner's Tornante Company and private equity group Madison Dearborn Partners.

FINANCIALS: **Sales and profits are in thousands of dollars—add 000 to get the full amount. 2011 Note: Financial information for 2011 was not available for all companies at press time.**

2011 Sales: $	2011 Profits: $	**U.S. Stock Ticker: Private**
2010 Sales: $	2010 Profits: $	**Int'l Ticker:**
2009 Sales: $	2009 Profits: $	Int'l Exchange:
2008 Sales: $	2008 Profits: $	Employees: Fiscal Year Ends: 2/28
2007 Sales: $	2007 Profits: $	Parent Company: TORNANTE CO

SALARIES/BENEFITS:

Pension Plan:	ESOP Stock Plan:	Profit Sharing:	Top Exec. Salary: $	Bonus: $
Savings Plan:	Stock Purch. Plan:		Second Exec. Salary: $	Bonus: $

OTHER THOUGHTS:

Apparent Women Officers or Directors: 1
Hot Spot for Advancement for Women/Minorities:

LOCATIONS: ("Y" = Yes)

West:	Southwest:	Midwest:	Southeast:	Northeast:	International:
Y	Y	Y	Y	Y	Y

TRANSAMMONIA INC

www.transammonia.com

Industry Group Code: 486

Management:		Sales/Marketing:		Liberal Arts:		Information Systems:		Professionals:		Technical/Scientific:	
Mgmt. Trainees:		Mktg. Professionals:		Gen. Writing/Editing:		Info. Management:	Y	Finance/Acct.:	Y	Engineers, Elec.:	
Experienced Mgmt.:	Y	Retail Sales:		Technical Writing:		Software Dev.:		Law:	Y	Engineers, Other:	Y
Int'l Business:	Y	Commercial/Industrial:		Graphic Arts/Photog.:		Hardware Dev.:		HR/Other:	Y	Health/Lab	
MBA Graduates:	Y	Sales Trainees:		Music:		Consulting/Other:		Training:		Scientists/Research:	
		Advertising Pros.:		Broadcasting:				Health Care:		Petroleum/Chemicals:	Y
				Other:				Consulting:		Math/Other:	

TYPES OF BUSINESS:

Liquefied Petroleum Gas (LPG) Distribution
Marketing & Trading Operations
Distribution & Transport
Crude Oil & Oil Products
Methanol
Fertilizer Materials
Petrochemicals
Propane

BRANDS/DIVISIONS/AFFILIATES:

Transammonia
Trammochem
Trammo Gas
Sea-3
Transammonia DMCC
Trammo Gas International, Inc.
Trammochem Asia PTE
Transammonia Shanghai

CONTACTS:

Note: Officers with more than one job title may be intentionally listed here more than once.

Ronald P. Stanton, CEO
Edward G. Weiner, CFO/Sr. VP
Michel Dietlin, Head-Ammonia Div.
Ashok Kishore, Head-Petrochemicals Div.
Bill Cornell, Head-Propane Dist., Sea-3
Dave Smothermon, Head-Liquid Petroleum Gas Trading
Ronald P. Stanton, Chmn.
John Cugley, Head-Int'l Liquid Petroleum Gas Bus.

Phone: 212-223-3200	**Fax**: 212-759-1410
Toll-Free:	
Address: 320 Park Ave., New York, NY 10022 US	

GROWTH PLANS/SPECIAL FEATURES:

Transammonia, Inc., known as the Transammonia Group, is a marketer, trader, distributor and transporter of fertilizer materials, liquefied petroleum gas (LPG), petrochemicals (chiefly aromatics), methanol, crude oil and oil products internationally. The firm works through its four primary subsidiaries: Transammonia; Trammochem; Trammo Gas; and Sea-3. The company has international offices in 31 cities in 20 countries. The firm began as a producer and transporter of fertilizers, raw materials and ammonia and continues operations in these markets through the Transammonia subsidiary. Petrochemicals are created, bought and sold for the firm through subsidiary Trammochem. Through Trammochem, the firm trades methyl tertiary-butyl ether (MTBE), benzene, methanol, olefins, gasoline blend components, styrene monomers, toluene, ethanol, xylenes and isomers internationally, with annual traded volumes at about 2.7 million tons. Trammo Gas, headquartered in Houston, Texas, is focused solely on the U.S. and sells LPG, including propane, ethane, butane, iso butane and natural gas. The subsidiary trades approximately 8.0 million metric tons of all its products annually. Trammo Gas International, Inc., part of Trammo Gas, operates three gas carriers under long term time charters and provides international transportation of LPG for third parties. The Sea-3 subsidiary is a leading importer and distributor of liquefied propane in the northeastern U.S. and parts of Florida, and it also participates in gas marketing on the Gulf Coast and other areas of the U.S. Its customers include thousands of homes, businesses, industries, schools and hospitals. Recently, the firm established Trammochem Asia PTE in Singapore; Transammonia DMCC in the United Arab Emirates; and Transammonia Shanghai in China.

FINANCIALS:

Sales and profits are in thousands of dollars—add 000 to get the full amount. 2011 Note: Financial information for 2011 was not available for all companies at press time.

2011 Sales: $8,420,000	2011 Profits: $	**U.S. Stock Ticker: Private**
2010 Sales: $8,500,000	2010 Profits: $	**Int'l Ticker:**
2009 Sales: $5,490,000	2009 Profits: $	Int'l Exchange:
2008 Sales: $11,200,000	2008 Profits: $	Employees: 403 Fiscal Year Ends: 12/31
2007 Sales: $8,300,000	2007 Profits: $	Parent Company:

SALARIES/BENEFITS:

Pension Plan:	ESOP Stock Plan:	Profit Sharing:	Top Exec. Salary: $	Bonus: $
Savings Plan:	Stock Purch. Plan:		Second Exec. Salary: $	Bonus: $

OTHER THOUGHTS:

Apparent Women Officers or Directors:
Hot Spot for Advancement for Women/Minorities:

LOCATIONS: ("Y" = Yes)

West:	Southwest:	Midwest:	Southeast:	Northeast:	International:
	Y	Y	Y	Y	Y

TRANSATLANTIC HOLDINGS INC

www.transre.com

Industry Group Code: 524130

Management:		Sales/Marketing:		Liberal Arts:		Information Systems:		Professionals:		Technical/Scientific:	
Mgmt. Trainees:	Y	Mktg. Professionals:	Y	Gen. Writing/Editing:	Y	Info. Management:	Y	Finance/Acct.:	Y	Engineers, Elec.:	
Experienced Mgmt.:	Y	Retail Sales:		Technical Writing:	Y	Software Dev.:		Law:	Y	Engineers, Other:	
Int'l Business:	Y	Commercial/Industrial:	Y	Graphic Arts/Photog.:		Hardware Dev.:		HR/Other:	Y	Health/Lab	Y
MBA Graduates:	Y	Sales Trainees:	Y	Music:		Consulting/Other:		Training:	Y	Scientists/Research:	
		Advertising Pros.:		Broadcasting:				Health Care:		Petroleum/Chemicals:	
				Other:				Consulting:		Math/Other:	Y

TYPES OF BUSINESS:

Property & Casualty Reinsurance
Life Reinsurance
Marine & Aerospace Reinsurance
Surety & Credit Reinsurance

BRANDS/DIVISIONS/AFFILIATES:

American International Group (AIG)
Transatlantic Reinsurance Co
Trans Re Zurich
Putnam Reinsurance Co
Kuwait Reinsurance Co

CONTACTS: *Note: Officers with more than one job title may be intentionally listed here more than once.*

Robert F. Orlich, CEO
Michael C. Sapnar, COO
Michael C. Sapnar, Pres.
Steven S. Skalicky, CFO/Exec. VP
Gary A. Schwartz, General Counsel/Sr. VP
Thomas V. Cholnoky, Sr. VP-Investor Rel.
Paul A. Bonny, Exec. VP/Pres., Int'l Oper.
Javier E. Vijil, Exec. VP/Pres., Latin America & Caribbean Div.
Kenneth Apfel, Exec. VP/Chief Actuary
Amy M. Cinquegrana, Corp. Sec.
Richard S. Press, Chmn.
Lynda Wood, Chief Admin. Officer, Int'l/Sr. VP

Phone: 212-365-2200 **Fax:** 212-365-2360
Toll-Free:
Address: 80 Pine St., New York, NY 10005 US

GROWTH PLANS/SPECIAL FEATURES:

Transatlantic Holdings, Inc. offers reinsurance capacity for property and casualty products on both a treaty and facultative basis. The company operates through three wholly-owned subsidiaries: Transatlantic Reinsurance Co.; Trans Re Zurich; and Putnam Reinsurance Co. The company's principal lines of reinsurance include specialty liability, including directors' and officers' liability and errors and omissions coverages; ocean marine and aviation; medical malpractice; auto liability, including non-standard risks; accident and health; surety and credit; fire; allied lines; auto physical damage; and homeowners multiple peril lines. Casualty reinsurance constitutes the largest portion of the firm's business, accounting for 71% of net premiums written in 2010. Reinsurance is provided for most major lines of insurance on both excess-of-loss and pro rata bases. These products are provided directly and through brokers to insurance and reinsurance companies in both domestic and international markets. Transatlantic and its subsidiaries are licensed, accredited, authorized or can serve as a reinsurer in North America (including all 50 states), Puerto Rico, China, Japan, Hong Kong, the Dominican Republic, the U.K., Australia and Europe. The company supplements its traditional revenues with investments in diversified taxable bonds and tax-exempt municipal bonds. Additionally, the firm owns a 40% interest in Kuwait Reinsurance Co., which provides property, casualty and life reinsurance products to clients in the Middle Eastern and North African markets.

FINANCIALS: **Sales and profits are in thousands of dollars—add 000 to get the full amount. 2011 Note: Financial information for 2011 was not available for all companies at press time.**

2011 Sales: $4,365,600 | 2011 Profits: $-99,200
2010 Sales: $4,362,153 | 2010 Profits: $402,201
2009 Sales: $4,445,712 | 2009 Profits: $477,662
2008 Sales: $4,082,549 | 2008 Profits: $102,254
2007 Sales: $4,381,830 | 2007 Profits: $487,141

U.S. Stock Ticker: TRH
Int'l Ticker:
Int'l Exchange:
Employees: 640 Fiscal Year Ends: 12/31
Parent Company:

SALARIES/BENEFITS:

Pension Plan: Y | ESOP Stock Plan: | Profit Sharing: | Top Exec. Salary: $1,000,000 | Bonus: $2,400,000
Savings Plan: | Stock Purch. Plan: Y | | Second Exec. Salary: $660,000 | Bonus: $1,056,000

OTHER THOUGHTS:

Apparent Women Officers or Directors: 2
Hot Spot for Advancement for Women/Minorities:

LOCATIONS: ("Y" = Yes)

West:	Southwest:	Midwest:	Southeast:	Northeast:	International:
Y		Y	Y	Y	Y

TRANSCEND SERVICES INC

www.transcendservices.com

Industry Group Code: 518210

Management:		**Sales/Marketing:**		**Liberal Arts:**		**Information Systems:**		**Professionals:**		**Technical/Scientific:**	
Mgmt. Trainees:		Mktg. Professionals:	Y	Gen. Writing/Editing:	Y	Info. Management:	Y	Finance/Acct.:	Y	Engineers, Elec.:	
Experienced Mgmt.:	Y	Retail Sales:		Technical Writing:	Y	Software Dev.:	Y	Law:	Y	Engineers, Other:	
Int'l Business:		Commercial/Industrial:	Y	Graphic Arts/Photog.:		Hardware Dev.:		HR/Other:	Y	Health/Lab	
MBA Graduates:	Y	Sales Trainees:	Y	Music:		Consulting/Other:		Training:	Y	Scientists/Research:	
		Advertising Pros.:		Broadcasting:				Health Care:		Petroleum/Chemicals:	
				Other:				Consulting:		Math/Other:	

TYPES OF BUSINESS:

Data Processing Services
Internet-Based Medical Transcription Services

BRANDS/DIVISIONS/AFFILIATES:

BeyondTXT
BeyondAlerts
Salar, Inc.
DTS America, Inc.
Encore

CONTACTS:

Note: Officers with more than one job title may be intentionally listed here more than once.

Larry G. Gerdes, CEO
Susan McGrogan, COO
Susan McGrogan, Pres.
Lance Cornell, CFO
Scott Robertson, VP-Tech.
Lance Cornell, Corp. Sec.
Jeff Felshaw, Sr. VP-Bus. Dev.
Neil Berkman, Contact-Investor Rel.
Lance Cornell, Chief Acct. Officer/Treas.
Shailendra Sharma, VP-Professional & Support Svcs.
Larry G. Gerdes, Chmn.

Phone: 678-808-0600 **Fax:** 678-808-0601
Toll-Free: 800-555-8727
Address: 1 Glenlake Parkway, Ste. 1325, Atlanta, GA 30328 US

GROWTH PLANS/SPECIAL FEATURES:

Transcend Services, Inc. provides medical transcription services to the healthcare industry. Customers include hospitals, hospital systems, multi-specialty clinics and physician group practices. Transcend provides services to approximately 331 hospitals and clinics, with typical customers providing an average annual revenue of about $344,000, and several larger customers contributing annual revenues exceeding $1.5 million. The company offers two primary options to its customers: for customers without transcription technology available, Transcend offers BeyondTXT; alternatively, Transcend can access a customer's existing system to provide transcription services. BeyondTXT is a web-enabled voice and data distribution technology that allows a physician to dictate reports into several dictation products on the market, including handheld devices; hospital- or clinic-based transcription stations; and home phones or cell phones. This information is captured digitally by Transcend's central voice hub in Atlanta, Georgia, where the digital files are compressed, encrypted and stored. The audio recordings are then accessed by home-based medical transcription professionals through the Internet, who either transcribe the physicians' voice recordings directly or edit an electronic document created by BeyondTXT's voice recognition tool. After transcription, documents are returned to the Atlanta hub over the Internet, and are then distributed securely to hospital information systems via fax, printers or the Internet. Documents are generally produced and delivered within 24 hours, but may be delivered in as little as four hours for premium prices. The company's operations run 24-hours-a-day, 365-days-a-year. Transcend also offers point of care solutions for clinicians such as BeyondAlerts, which searches for predetermined keyword patterns in a physician's transcribed dictation, then triggers alerts to caregivers when the keywords are found. In April 2011, Transcend acquired DTS America, Inc. In June 2011, the firm released Encore, a software-as-a-service solution that offers customers who have in-house transcription departments a speech-recognition enabled platform. In August 2011, the company acquired Salar, Inc.

FINANCIALS:

Sales and profits are in thousands of dollars—add 000 to get the full amount. 2011 Note: Financial information for 2011 was not available for all companies at press time.

2011 Sales: $
2010 Sales: $94,307
2009 Sales: $71,764
2008 Sales: $48,696
2007 Sales: $42,454

2011 Profits: $
2010 Profits: $8,520
2009 Profits: $6,759
2008 Profits: $5,768
2007 Profits: $11,479

U.S. Stock Ticker: TRCR
Int'l Ticker:
Int'l Exchange:
Employees: 1,955 Fiscal Year Ends: 12/31
Parent Company:

SALARIES/BENEFITS:

Pension Plan: ESOP Stock Plan: Profit Sharing: Top Exec. Salary: $340,000 Bonus: $146,000
Savings Plan: Y Stock Purch. Plan: Second Exec. Salary: $275,000 Bonus: $120,000

OTHER THOUGHTS:

Apparent Women Officers or Directors: 1
Hot Spot for Advancement for Women/Minorities:

LOCATIONS: ("Y" = Yes)

West:	Southwest:	Midwest:	Southeast:	Northeast:	International:
Y			Y	Y	

TRAVELZOO INC

www.travelzoo.com

Industry Group Code: 5615E

Management:		Sales/Marketing:		Liberal Arts:		Information Systems:		Professionals:		Technical/Scientific:	
Mgmt. Trainees:		Mktg. Professionals:	Y	Gen. Writing/Editing:	Y	Info. Management:	Y	Finance/Acct.:	Y	Engineers, Elec.:	
Experienced Mgmt.:	Y	Retail Sales:		Technical Writing:		Software Dev.:	Y	Law:	Y	Engineers, Other:	
Int'l Business:	Y	Commercial/Industrial:	Y	Graphic Arts/Photog.:	Y	Hardware Dev.:		HR/Other:	Y	Health/Lab	
MBA Graduates:	Y	Sales Trainees:		Music:		Consulting/Other:		Training:	Y	Scientists/Research:	
		Advertising Pros.:	Y	Broadcasting:				Health Care:		Petroleum/Chemicals:	
				Other:	Y			Consulting:		Math/Other:	

TYPES OF BUSINESS:

Travel Services-Online

BRANDS/DIVISIONS/AFFILIATES:

Travelzoo Top 20
Newsflash
SuperSearch
Travelzoo Network
Fly.com

CONTACTS: *Note: Officers with more than one job title may be intentionally listed here more than once.*

Christopher Loughlin, CEO
Glen Ceremony, CFO
Christie McConnel, Sr. Mgr.-Mktg.
Max Rayner, CIO
Christie McConnel, Contact-Media
Shirley Tafoya, Pres., North America
Vivian Ho, Pres., China
Jorge Carulla, Mgr.-Spain
Holger Bartel, Chmn.
Melanie Bower, VP-Network, Entertainment, & Destinations, Europe

Phone: 212-484-4900	**Fax:**
Toll-Free:	
Address: 590 Madison Ave., 37th Fl., New York, NY 10022 US	

GROWTH PLANS/SPECIAL FEATURES:

Travelzoo, Inc. is a global Internet media company that publishes travel and entertainment offers from travel and entertainment companies. Its publications and products, which serve over 23 million subscribers, include the Travelzoo web sites, the Travelzoo Top 20 e-mail newsletter and the Newsflash e-mail alert service. Travelzoo operates in two geographical segments: North America and Europe. The firm's European segment, which consists of its operations in France, Germany, Spain and the U.K., generates approximately 22% of its revenue. Travelzoo provides versions of its web site for the U.S., Canada, France, Germany, Spain, and the U.K., and through a license agreement with Azzurro Capital, for Hong Kong, Japan, Taiwan, Australia, and China through Azzuro's subsidiaries Travel (Asia) Limited and Travelzoo Japan.K.K. These sites attract 10.4 million unique visitors per month. The firm operates SuperSearch, a pay-per-click travel search tool; Fly.com, a travel search engine that enables users to find and compare flight options from hundreds of airlines and online travel agencies; and the Travelzoo Network, a network of third-party web sites that lists deals published by Travelzoo. The firm has approximately 18.1 million subscribers to its Travelzoo Top 20 newsletter and 16.5 million subscribers to its Newsflash e-mail alert service. Approximately 6 million searches are conducted per month on Travelzoo's SuperSearch tool. More than 2,000 companies purchase Travelzoo's advertising services, sales of which generate all of the company's revenue.

FINANCIALS: **Sales and profits are in thousands of dollars—add 000 to get the full amount. 2011 Note: Financial information for 2011 was not available for all companies at press time.**

2011 Sales: $148,300	2011 Profits: $23,319	**U.S. Stock Ticker: TZOO**
2010 Sales: $112,784	2010 Profits: $13,157	**Int'l Ticker:**
2009 Sales: $93,973	2009 Profits: $8,618	Int'l Exchange:
2008 Sales: $80,817	2008 Profits: $-4,116	Employees: 255 Fiscal Year Ends: 12/31
2007 Sales: $78,911	2007 Profits: $9,109	Parent Company:

SALARIES/BENEFITS:

Pension Plan:	ESOP Stock Plan:	Profit Sharing:	Top Exec. Salary: $522,906	Bonus: $352,369
Savings Plan: Y	Stock Purch. Plan:		Second Exec. Salary: $435,608	Bonus: $399,912

OTHER THOUGHTS:

Apparent Women Officers or Directors: 5
Hot Spot for Advancement for Women/Minorities: Y

LOCATIONS: ("Y" = Yes)

West:	Southwest:	Midwest:	Southeast:	Northeast:	International:
Y		Y	Y	Y	Y

TREX COMPANY INC

www.trex.com

Industry Group Code: 326199

Management:		Sales/Marketing:		Liberal Arts:		Information Systems:		Professionals:		Technical/Scientific:	
Mgmt. Trainees:		Mktg. Professionals:	Y	Gen. Writing/Editing:		Info. Management:	Y	Finance/Acct.:	Y	Engineers, Elec.:	
Experienced Mgmt.:	Y	Retail Sales:		Technical Writing:	Y	Software Dev.:		Law:	Y	Engineers, Other:	
Int'l Business:		Commercial/Industrial:	Y	Graphic Arts/Photog.:		Hardware Dev.:		HR/Other:	Y	Health/Lab	
MBA Graduates:	Y	Sales Trainees:	Y	Music:		Consulting/Other:		Training:	Y	Scientists/Research:	
		Advertising Pros.:		Broadcasting:				Health Care:		Petroleum/Chemicals:	
				Other:				Consulting:		Math/Other:	

TYPES OF BUSINESS:

Wood-Alternative Decking, Railing & Fencing Products

BRANDS/DIVISIONS/AFFILIATES:

Trex
Iron Deck Corporation
Trex Contours
Trex Origins
Trex Accents
Trex Accents Fire Defense
Trex Brasilia
Trex Escapes

CONTACTS: *Note: Officers with more than one job title may be intentionally listed here more than once.*

Ronald W. Kaplan, CEO
Ronald W. Kaplan, Pres.
James E. Cline, CFO/VP
Adam D. Zamba, VP-Mktg.
William R. Gupp, Chief Admin. Officer
William R. Gupp, General Counsel/VP
F. Timothy Reese, VP-Oper.
J. Mitchell Cox, VP-Sales
Ronald W. Kaplan, Chmn.

Phone: 540-542-6300 **Fax:**
Toll-Free: 800-289-8739
Address: 160 Exeter Dr., Winchester, VA 22603-8605 US

GROWTH PLANS/SPECIAL FEATURES:

Trex Company, Inc. manufactures wood-alternative decking, railing, fencing and trim products. The majority of its products are made using a process supported by technology that combines waste wood fibers and reclaimed polyethylene. Trex purchases millions of pounds of recycled and reclaimed plastic and waste wood each year and uses them in Trex products. Its products are used primarily for residential and commercial decking, railing, fencing and trim. The firm's product lines include Trex Contours, which has a deep wood grain surface; Trex Origins, which features a smooth surface; Trex Accents, which offers a smooth surface on one side and subtle wood grain on the other; Trex Accents Fire Defense, which is a deck board that meets stringent fire resistant requirements in certain areas of the Western U.S.; Trex Brasilia, which replicates the look of tropical hardwoods with a smooth surface and subtle color variations; Trex Escapes, which is a low maintenance cellular PVC deck board; and Trex Transcend, which features a protective shell for enhanced protection against fading, staining and scratching. The company also offers Trex Hideaway, which is a hidden fastening system for specially grooved boards. Trex's railing product lines are Trex Designer Series Railing, consisting of a decorative top and bottom rail, refined balusters, Trex RailPost and post caps and skirts; and Trex Transcend Railing. Trex sells and distributes its products through wholesale distribution and through retail lumber dealers, retail building material specialty builders, Home Depot and Lowe's. Additionally, the firm owns a 35% interest in Denplax S.A., which operates a plant in El Ejido, Spain. In November 2010, Trex released LED dimmable deck lighting product Trex Deck Lighting. In May 2011, the company acquired Iron Deck Corporation and introduced new steel deck framing system Trex Elevations Steel Deck Framing.

FINANCIALS: **Sales and profits are in thousands of dollars—add 000 to get the full amount. 2011 Note: Financial information for 2011 was not available for all companies at press time.**

2011 Sales: $266,800 2011 Profits: $-11,600
2010 Sales: $317,690 2010 Profits: $-10,066
2009 Sales: $272,286 2009 Profits: $-16,449
2008 Sales: $329,194 2008 Profits: $13,552
2007 Sales: $328,952 2007 Profits: $-75,912

U.S. Stock Ticker: TREX
Int'l Ticker:
Int'l Exchange:
Employees: 550 Fiscal Year Ends: 12/31
Parent Company:

SALARIES/BENEFITS:

Pension Plan: ESOP Stock Plan: Profit Sharing: Y Top Exec. Salary: $500,000 Bonus: $626,250
Savings Plan: Y Stock Purch. Plan: Y Second Exec. Salary: $275,000 Bonus: $241,106

OTHER THOUGHTS:

Apparent Women Officers or Directors: 1
Hot Spot for Advancement for Women/Minorities:

LOCATIONS: ("Y" = Yes)

West:	Southwest:	Midwest:	Southeast:	Northeast:	International:
Y				Y	

TRIZETTO GROUP INC (THE)

www.trizetto.com

Industry Group Code: 511210D

Management:		Sales/Marketing:		Liberal Arts:		Information Systems:		Professionals:		Technical/Scientific:	
Mgmt. Trainees:		Mktg. Professionals:	Y	Gen. Writing/Editing:		Info. Management:	Y	Finance/Acct.:	Y	Engineers, Elec.:	Y
Experienced Mgmt.:	Y	Retail Sales:		Technical Writing:	Y	Software Dev.:	Y	Law:	Y	Engineers, Other:	
Int'l Business:	Y	Commercial/Industrial:	Y	Graphic Arts/Photog.:	Y	Hardware Dev.:		HR/Other:	Y	Health/Lab	
MBA Graduates:	Y	Sales Trainees:	Y	Music:		Consulting/Other:		Training:	Y	Scientists/Research:	
		Advertising Pros.:		Broadcasting:				Health Care:		Petroleum/Chemicals:	
				Other:				Consulting:		Math/Other:	

TYPES OF BUSINESS:

Software-Medical Billing & Administration
Health Care Internet Portal
IT Staffing & Consulting Services
Hosted Services
Consulting Services

BRANDS/DIVISIONS/AFFILIATES:

Apax Partners LLP
QicLink
CareAdvance Enterprise
QNXT
Gateway EDI
Tela Sourcing Inc
Medical Data Express
Kocsis Consulting Group

CONTACTS: *Note: Officers with more than one job title may be intentionally listed here more than once.*

Trace Devanny, CEO
Trace Devanny, Pres.
Regina Paolillo, CFO/Exec. VP-Enterprise Svcs.
Dan Spirek, Chief Mktg. Officer
Maureen Brennan, VP-Human Capital Mgmt.
Jeff Rideout, Chief Medical Officer/Sr. VP-Cost & Care Mgmt.
Alan Cullop, CIO/Sr. VP
Pierre Samec, CTO
Rich Kerian, Sr. VP-Prod. Dev. & Support
Jim Sullivan, General Counsel/Sr. VP/Sec.
Dan Spirek, Chief Strategy Officer
Loren Finkelstein, Dir.-Public Rel.
Marc Arseneau, Sr. VP-Finance & Acct.
John Jordan, Pres., Regional Healthcare Market
Rob Scavo, Pres., Emerging Market
Linda Fenton, Sr. VP-Enterprise Risk Mgmt. & Finance
Tim Fogerty, CEO-Gateway EDI
Trace Devanny, Chmn.

Phone: 303-495-7000 **Fax:** 303-495-7001
Toll-Free: 800-569-1222
Address: 6061 S. Willow Dr., Ste. 310, Denver, CO 80111 US

GROWTH PLANS/SPECIAL FEATURES:

The TriZetto Group, Inc. provides software application services to the health care industry. The company's software solutions include enterprise core administration, care management, network management, consumer retail healthcare and government programs. Software packages include the Facets, QicLink, CareAdvance Enterprise, QNXT and NetworX Suite. Facets is a scalable, enterprise-wide core administration product for healthcare payers, allowing them to meet various business requirements, including claims processing, claims re-pricing, risk fund accounting, referral management and customer service. QicLink allows benefits administrators to handle enrollment, customer service, claims adjudication, billing, accounts receivable, re-pricing and payment processes. The CareAdvance Enterprise suite of applications allows health plans to automate various aspects of care management, including member identification and assessment, guideline-based care planning, member and provider communications, task and team management, ongoing member monitoring and personalized health content. The QNXT enterprise application system is a user-configurable system that aids healthcare payers in adapting to market changes in a rapid and efficient manner. NetworX Suite is a group of software applications that provides execution, claims pricing, network operations and complete automation of contract modeling. The company can host and manage customer applications from its own data center or remotely manage on-site applications; and allows customers to outsource non-critical functions, including claims administration, enrollment and rules configuration. TriZetto's consulting staff provides project management, technology consulting and other customer-specific solutions to health plans and benefits administrators. The company is owned by global private equity advisory firm Apax Partners. In February 2011, TriZetto acquired the healthcare revenue management company Gateway EDI. In March 2011, the firm completed the acquisition of Tela Sourcing, Inc. In January 2012, TriZetto acquired Medical Data Express and Kocsis Consulting Group.

TriZetto offers employees benefits including life, disability, medical, dental and vision insurance; tuition reimbursement; a group legal plan; and an employee assistance program.

FINANCIALS: **Sales and profits are in thousands of dollars—add 000 to get the full amount. 2011 Note: Financial information for 2011 was not available for all companies at press time.**

2011 Sales: $	2011 Profits: $	**U.S. Stock Ticker: Private**
2010 Sales: $	2010 Profits: $	**Int'l Ticker:**
2009 Sales: $	2009 Profits: $	Int'l Exchange:
2008 Sales: $	2008 Profits: $	Employees: Fiscal Year Ends: 12/31
2007 Sales: $	2007 Profits: $	Parent Company: APAX PARTNERS LLP

SALARIES/BENEFITS:

Pension Plan:	ESOP Stock Plan:	Profit Sharing:	Top Exec. Salary: $	Bonus: $
Savings Plan: Y	Stock Purch. Plan:		Second Exec. Salary: $	Bonus: $

OTHER THOUGHTS:

Apparent Women Officers or Directors: 4
Hot Spot for Advancement for Women/Minorities: Y

LOCATIONS: ("Y" = Yes)

West:	Southwest:	Midwest:	Southeast:	Northeast:	International:
Y	Y	Y		Y	

TRUE RELIGION APPAREL INC

www.truereligionbrandjeans.com

Industry Group Code: 448

Management:		**Sales/Marketing:**		**Liberal Arts:**		**Information Systems:**		**Professionals:**		**Technical/Scientific:**	
Mgmt. Trainees:	Y	Mktg. Professionals:	Y	Gen. Writing/Editing:	Y	Info. Management:	Y	Finance/Acct.:	Y	Engineers, Elec.:	
Experienced Mgmt.:	Y	Retail Sales:	Y	Technical Writing:		Software Dev.:	Y	Law:	Y	Engineers, Other:	
Int'l Business:	Y	Commercial/Industrial:		Graphic Arts/Photog.:	Y	Hardware Dev.:		HR/Other:	Y	Health/Lab	
MBA Graduates:	Y	Sales Trainees:	Y	Music:		Consulting/Other:		Training:	Y	Scientists/Research:	
		Advertising Pros.:	Y	Broadcasting:				Health Care:		Petroleum/Chemicals:	
				Other:				Consulting:		Math/Other:	

TYPES OF BUSINESS:

Jeans & Apparel Retail

BRANDS/DIVISIONS/AFFILIATES:

True Religion Brand Jeans
True Religion Japan KK
TrueReligionBrandJeans.com
True Religion Brand Jeans Germany GmbH

CONTACTS: *Note: Officers with more than one job title may be intentionally listed here more than once.*

Jeffrey Lubell, CEO
Lynne Koplin, Pres.
Peter Collins, CFO
Jordan Daly, VP-Mktg.
Jeffrey Lubell, Chief Merchant
Kelly Gvildys, Sr. VP-Oper.
Jordan Daly, VP-Brand Strategy
Jordan Daly, VP-Public Rel.
David Chiovetti, Sr. VP-Retail, North America
Jeffrey Lubell, Chmn.

Phone: 323-266-3072	**Fax:** 323-266-8060
Toll-Free:	
Address: 2263 E. Vernon Ave., Vernon, CA 90058 US	

GROWTH PLANS/SPECIAL FEATURES:

True Religion Apparel, Inc. is a designer, manufacturer and marketer of the True Religion Brand Jeans brand. This brand includes high fashion designer jeans and related sportswear apparel. True Religion products fall into three categories: knits, including hoodies, t-shirts and sweats; denim fabrics, which includes its line of jeans; and non-denim fabrics, such as corduroy and twill. The firm's jeans usually sell for $172-350 per pair. True Religion operates in four segments: U.S. Wholesale, International, U.S. Consumer Direct and Other. The U.S. Wholesale division, which accounts for approximately 28.8% of the company's net sales, markets the firm's products to approximately 750 boutique and specialty stores; and major retail chains such as Saks Fifth Avenue, Neiman Marcus, Nordstrom and Bloomingdale's. The International segment (17.7% of sales) distributes products through subsidiary True Religion Japan, K.K. and joint venture True Religion Brand Jeans Germany GmbH (40%-owned by UNIFA Premium GmbH); and distributors/sales agents who sell to upscale boutiques in their respective geographic areas. The division markets its products in 50 countries on six continents. It also operates nine retail and four outlet locations in Japan, Germany, the U.K., the Netherlands and Canada. The U.S. Consumer Direct segment (52% of sales) includes True Religion Apparel's e-commerce web site (TrueReligionBrandJeans.com) and its 105 self-branded retail locations (including 27 outlets). The company's Other division handles its licensing business, including the licensing of the True Religion brand and logo to other companies. True Religion's average branded retail store measures approximately 1,700 square feet, while its outlet stores measure roughly 2,500 square feet. Roughly 48% of the firm's sales are derived from women's attire; 48% are derived from men's products; and 4% from children's items. In 2010, True Religion opened 24 new retail locations.

FINANCIALS: **Sales and profits are in thousands of dollars—add 000 to get the full amount. 2011 Note: Financial information for 2011 was not available for all companies at press time.**

2011 Sales: $419,800	2011 Profits: $45,000
2010 Sales: $363,714	2010 Profits: $43,496
2009 Sales: $311,001	2009 Profits: $47,332
2008 Sales: $270,000	2008 Profits: $44,371
2007 Sales: $173,256	2007 Profits: $27,845

U.S. Stock Ticker: TRLG
Int'l Ticker:
Int'l Exchange:
Employees: 1,663 Fiscal Year Ends: 12/31
Parent Company:

SALARIES/BENEFITS:

Pension Plan:	ESOP Stock Plan:	Profit Sharing:	Top Exec. Salary: $937,750	Bonus: $3,368,836
Savings Plan:	Stock Purch. Plan:		Second Exec. Salary: $510,773	Bonus: $180,839

OTHER THOUGHTS:

Apparent Women Officers or Directors: 2
Hot Spot for Advancement for Women/Minorities:

LOCATIONS: ("Y" = Yes)

West:	Southwest:	Midwest:	Southeast:	Northeast:	International:
Y	Y	Y	Y	Y	Y

UDR INC

www.udr.com

Industry Group Code: 531110

Management:		Sales/Marketing:		Liberal Arts:		Information Systems:		Professionals:		Technical/Scientific:	
Mgmt. Trainees:		Mktg. Professionals:	Y	Gen. Writing/Editing:	Y	Info. Management:	Y	Finance/Acct.:	Y	Engineers, Elec.:	
Experienced Mgmt.:	Y	Retail Sales:		Technical Writing:		Software Dev.:		Law:	Y	Engineers, Other:	
Int'l Business:		Commercial/Industrial:		Graphic Arts/Photog.:		Hardware Dev.:		HR/Other:	Y	Health/Lab	
MBA Graduates:	Y	Sales Trainees:		Music:		Consulting/Other:		Training:		Scientists/Research:	
		Advertising Pros.:		Broadcasting:				Health Care:		Petroleum/Chemicals:	
				Other:				Consulting:		Math/Other:	

TYPES OF BUSINESS:

Real Estate Investment Trust
Apartment Communities

BRANDS/DIVISIONS/AFFILIATES:

Heritage Communities LP
United Dominion Realty LP
RE3

CONTACTS: *Note: Officers with more than one job title may be intentionally listed here more than once.*

Thomas W. Toomey, CEO
Thomas W. Toomey, Pres.
David L. Messenger, CFO/Sr. VP
Steven H. Taraborelli, VP/Dir.-Mktg. & Sales
Mari A. Akers, VP-Human Resources
R. Scott Wesson, CIO/Sr. VP
Jerry A. Davis, Sr. VP-Property Oper.
Mark M. Culwell Jr., Sr. VP-Dev.
Christopher G. Van Ens, VP-Investor Rel.
William T. O'Shields, III, Treas./VP
H. Andrew Cantor, VP-Acquisitions & Dispositions
Richard A. Giannotti, Sr. VP-Redevelopment
Warren L. Troupe, Sr. Exec. VP
Harry G. Alcock, Sr. VP-Asset Mgmt.
James D. Klingbeil, Chmn.

Phone: 720-283-6120	**Fax:** 720-283-2451
Toll-Free:	
Address: 1745 Shea Center Dr., Ste. 200, Highlands Ranch, CO 80129 US	

GROWTH PLANS/SPECIAL FEATURES:

UDR, Inc. is a self-administered real estate investment trust (REIT) that owns, acquires, renovates, develops and manages multifamily apartment communities nationwide. UDR's property portfolio includes 172 communities located in 23 markets in 10 U.S. states and Washington, D.C. The firm currently owns 48,553 completed apartment homes and maintains an ownership interest in 9,891 apartment units (37 communities) through joint ventures. Its subsidiaries include two operating partnerships: Heritage Communities L.P. and United Dominion Realty L.P. Another subsidiary, RE3, provides development, land entitlement and short-term hold investment services. UDR's upgrade and rehabilitation programs enable it to raise rents and attract residents with higher levels of disposable income who are more likely to accept the transfer of expenses, such as water and sewer costs, from the landlord to the resident. It focuses on the middle-market segment of the apartment market, generally renters-by-necessity, including young professionals, blue-collar families, single-parent households, singles, immigrants and families renting while waiting to purchase a home. The company believes this renting-by-necessity population provides the highest profit potential in terms of rent growth, stability of occupancy and investment opportunities. In the future, UDR will continue to emphasize aggressive lease management, improved expense control, increased resident retention efforts and the realignment of employee incentive plans tied to its bottom line performance. In March 2011, the company agreed to acquire a 493-unit community in New York City from Witkoff Group for $260.8 million. In August 2011, UDR acquired a 210-home luxury apartment community in New York City. In September 2011, the firm acquired a 507-home luxury apartment community, also located in New York City, from The Moinian Group. Also in September 2011, UDR acquired a 217-home luxury apartment community in Virginia through joint venture Kuwait Finance House.

UDR offers its employees benefits including life, disability, medical, dental and vision coverage.

FINANCIALS: **Sales and profits are in thousands of dollars—add 000 to get the full amount. 2011 Note: Financial information for 2011 was not available for all companies at press time.**

2011 Sales: $684,900	2011 Profits: $20,000	**U.S. Stock Ticker: UDR**
2010 Sales: $632,249	2010 Profits: $-112,362	**Int'l Ticker:**
2009 Sales: $600,702	2009 Profits: $-95,858	Int'l Exchange:
2008 Sales: $561,073	2008 Profits: $688,708	Employees: 1,632 Fiscal Year Ends: 12/31
2007 Sales: $501,618	2007 Profits: $198,958	Parent Company:

SALARIES/BENEFITS:

Pension Plan:	ESOP Stock Plan:	Profit Sharing:	Top Exec. Salary: $500,000	Bonus: $2,136,000
Savings Plan: Y	Stock Purch. Plan: Y		Second Exec. Salary: $450,000	Bonus: $1,650,000

OTHER THOUGHTS:

Apparent Women Officers or Directors: 10
Hot Spot for Advancement for Women/Minorities: Y

LOCATIONS: ("Y" = Yes)

West:	Southwest:	Midwest:	Southeast:	Northeast:	International:
Y	Y		Y	Y	

UIL HOLDINGS CORPORATION

www.uil.com

Industry Group Code: 2211

Management:		**Sales/Marketing:**		**Liberal Arts:**		**Information Systems:**		**Professionals:**		**Technical/Scientific:**	
Mgmt. Trainees:		Mktg. Professionals:	Y	Gen. Writing/Editing:	Y	Info. Management:	Y	Finance/Acct.:	Y	Engineers, Elec.:	Y
Experienced Mgmt.:	Y	Retail Sales:		Technical Writing:		Software Dev.:		Law:	Y	Engineers, Other:	Y
Int'l Business:		Commercial/Industrial:	Y	Graphic Arts/Photog.:		Hardware Dev.:		HR/Other:	Y	Health/Lab	
MBA Graduates:	Y	Sales Trainees:	Y	Music:		Consulting/Other:		Training:	Y	Scientists/Research:	
		Advertising Pros.:		Broadcasting:				Health Care:		Petroleum/Chemicals:	Y
				Other:				Consulting:		Math/Other:	

TYPES OF BUSINESS:

Utilities-Electricity
Electricity Generation & Distribution
Electrical Systems Design

BRANDS/DIVISIONS/AFFILIATES:

The United Illuminating Co
GenConn Energy LLC
Connecticut Gas Compnay (SCG)
The Berkshire Gas Company (BGC)
NRG Energy, Inc.
NRG Energy, Inc.

CONTACTS: *Note: Officers with more than one job title may be intentionally listed here more than once.*

James P. Torgerson, CEO
Anthony Vallillo, COO/Exec. VP
James P. Torgerson, Pres.
Richard J. Nicholas, CFO/Exec. VP
Linda Randell, General Counsel/Sr. VP/Corp. Sec.
Steven P. Favuzza, Controller/VP

Phone: 203-499-3333	**Fax:** 203-499-3626
Toll-Free: 800-722-5584	
Address: 157 Church St., New Haven, CT 06506 US	

GROWTH PLANS/SPECIAL FEATURES:

UIL Holdings Corporation is a holding company that primarily operates in the regulated utility business. The utility business consists of the electric transmission and distribution operations of The United Illuminating Company (UI). UI is a regional distribution utility that provides electricity to the greater New Haven and Bridgeport areas of Connecticut. It purchases, transmits, distributes and sells electricity for residential, commercial and industrial purposes. UI has approximately 690,000 electric and gas utility customers in 66 communities across two states. UI also maintains a 50-50 joint venture with NRG Energy, Inc. called GenConn Energy, LLC, which was created to build power plants in Connecticut. UI invests in projects that earn above-average returns and form logical extensions to its current energy and subsidiary businesses. Investments include Ironwood Mezzanine Fund, a small business investment fund that partially invests in minority-owned and women-owned businesses, as well as in companies located in low to moderate income areas.

FINANCIALS: **Sales and profits are in thousands of dollars—add 000 to get the full amount. 2011 Note: Financial information for 2011 was not available for all companies at press time.**

2011 Sales: $1,570,447	2011 Profits: $99,710	**U.S. Stock Ticker: UIL**
2010 Sales: $997,666	2010 Profits: $54,854	**Int'l Ticker:**
2009 Sales: $896,550	2009 Profits: $54,317	Int'l Exchange:
2008 Sales: $948,720	2008 Profits: $48,148	Employees: 1,824 Fiscal Year Ends: 12/31
2007 Sales: $981,999	2007 Profits: $44,697	Parent Company:

SALARIES/BENEFITS:

Pension Plan:	ESOP Stock Plan:	Profit Sharing:	Top Exec. Salary: $625,000	Bonus: $459,375
Savings Plan:	Stock Purch. Plan:		Second Exec. Salary: $400,275	Bonus: $275,520

OTHER THOUGHTS:

Apparent Women Officers or Directors: 1
Hot Spot for Advancement for Women/Minorities: Y

LOCATIONS: ("Y" = Yes)

West:	Southwest:	Midwest:	Southeast:	Northeast:	International:
				Y	

ULTIMATE SOFTWARE GROUP INC

www.ultimatesoftware.com

Industry Group Code: 511210H

Management:		**Sales/Marketing:**		**Liberal Arts:**		**Information Systems:**		**Professionals:**		**Technical/Scientific:**	
Mgmt. Trainees:		Mktg. Professionals:	Y	Gen. Writing/Editing:		Info. Management:	Y	Finance/Acct.:	Y	Engineers, Elec.:	Y
Experienced Mgmt.:	Y	Retail Sales:		Technical Writing:	Y	Software Dev.:	Y	Law:	Y	Engineers, Other:	
Int'l Business:	Y	Commercial/Industrial:	Y	Graphic Arts/Photog.:		Hardware Dev.:		HR/Other:	Y	Health/Lab	
MBA Graduates:	Y	Sales Trainees:	Y	Music:		Consulting/Other:		Training:	Y	Scientists/Research:	
		Advertising Pros.:		Broadcasting:				Health Care:		Petroleum/Chemicals:	
				Other:				Consulting:		Math/Other:	

TYPES OF BUSINESS:

Employee Management Software

BRANDS/DIVISIONS/AFFILIATES:

UltiPro
UltiPro Workplace
UltiPro Enterprise
Ultimate Software Group of Canada Inc (The)
Ultimate Benefits Inc

CONTACTS: *Note: Officers with more than one job title may be intentionally listed here more than once.*

Scott Scherr, CEO
Marc D. Scherr, COO/Vice Chmn.
Scott Scherr, Pres.
Mitchell K. Dauerman, CFO/Exec. VP
Darlene Marcroft, Dir.-Public Rel.
Mitchell K. Dauerman, Treas.
Scott Scherr, Chmn.

Phone: 954-266-1000 **Fax:** 954-331-7300
Toll-Free: 800-432-1729
Address: 2000 Ultimate Way, Weston, FL 33326 US

GROWTH PLANS/SPECIAL FEATURES:

Ultimate Software Group, Inc. designs, markets, implements and supports human resources (HR), payroll and talent management solutions principally in the U.S. and Canada. The company main product is UltiPro, a web-based employee management program offered in two suites: UltiPro Enterprise, designed for large enterprises, defined as companies with more than 1,000 employees; and UltiPro Workplace, developed for medium-sized and smaller companies with less than 1,000 employees. Ultimate also offers a software-as-a-service (SaaS) version of UltiPro, meaning it is available on-demand as a subscription service, rather than being purchased outright. To manage the SaaS offering of UltiPro, the company contracts three data centers in Miami, Atlanta and Toronto. The two data centers in the United States are owned and operated by third party company Quality Technology Services (QTS), while the data center in Toronto is owned and operated by Verizon. In addition to standard UltiPro services, customers have the option to purchase optional features on a per-employee-per-month basis. These optional features include talent management products, benefits enrollment, time, attendance and scheduling, time management, tax filing, wage attachments and other features. The firm has two wholly-owned subsidiaries: The Ultimate Software Group of Canada, Inc. and Ultimate Benefits, Inc. The firm serves approximately 2,200 businesses. Customers include Adobe Systems, Inc.; Major League Baseball; P.F. Chang's; The Container Store; the Chicago Cubs; the New York Yankees; the City of Ann Arbor; and Ruth's Chris Steak House. In August 2011, Ultimate announced the opening of a new office in Santa Ana, California; thus expanding its west coast presence.

Ultimate offers its employees medical and dental benefits, tuition reimbursement, life insurance, flexible spending accounts and credit union membership. Additionally, the company provides on-site massage services, dry-cleaning services, inter-department bowling contests and more.

FINANCIALS: **Sales and profits are in thousands of dollars—add 000 to get the full amount. 2011 Note: Financial information for 2011 was not available for all companies at press time.**

2011 Sales: $
2010 Sales: $227,811
2009 Sales: $196,579
2008 Sales: $178,572
2007 Sales: $151,464

2011 Profits: $
2010 Profits: $2,157
2009 Profits: $-1,142
2008 Profits: $-2,897
2007 Profits: $33,129

U.S. Stock Ticker: ULTI
Int'l Ticker:
Int'l Exchange:
Employees: 1,134 Fiscal Year Ends: 12/31
Parent Company:

SALARIES/BENEFITS:

Pension Plan: ESOP Stock Plan: Profit Sharing: Top Exec. Salary: $700,000 Bonus: $
Savings Plan: Y Stock Purch. Plan: Second Exec. Salary: $625,000 Bonus: $

OTHER THOUGHTS:

Apparent Women Officers or Directors: 1
Hot Spot for Advancement for Women/Minorities:

LOCATIONS: ("Y" = Yes)

West:	Southwest:	Midwest:	Southeast:	Northeast:	International:
		Y	Y		Y

ULTRALIFE CORPORATION

www.ultralifecorporation.com

Industry Group Code: 33591

Management:		Sales/Marketing:		Liberal Arts:		Information Systems:		Professionals:		Technical/Scientific:	
Mgmt. Trainees:		Mktg. Professionals:	Y	Gen. Writing/Editing:		Info. Management:	Y	Finance/Acct.:	Y	Engineers, Elec.:	Y
Experienced Mgmt.:	Y	Retail Sales:		Technical Writing:	Y	Software Dev.:		Law:	Y	Engineers, Other:	Y
Int'l Business:	Y	Commercial/Industrial:	Y	Graphic Arts/Photog.:		Hardware Dev.:		HR/Other:	Y	Health/Lab	
MBA Graduates:	Y	Sales Trainees:		Music:		Consulting/Other:		Training:		Scientists/Research:	
		Advertising Pros.:		Broadcasting:				Health Care:		Petroleum/Chemicals:	
				Other:				Consulting:		Math/Other:	

TYPES OF BUSINESS:

Batteries
Lithium Ion Batteries
Rechargers & Accessories
Standby Power Systems
Integrated Communications Systems

BRANDS/DIVISIONS/AFFILIATES:

Ultralife Batteries
McDowell Research
ABLE
RedBlack Communications
Sationary Power Services
RPS Power Systems Inc.
Ultralife Batteries
US Energy Systems

CONTACTS: *Note: Officers with more than one job title may be intentionally listed here more than once.*

Michael D. Popielec, CEO
Michael D. Popielec, Pres.
Philip A. Fain, CFO
Peter F. Comerford, VP-Admin.
Peter F. Comerford, General Counsel
Philip A. Fain, Treas.
Patrick R. Hanna, Jr., VP/Corp. Compliance Officer
Bradford T. Whitmore, Chmn.

Phone: 315-332-7100 **Fax:** 315-331-7800
Toll-Free: 800-332-5000
Address: 2000 Technology Pkwy., Newark, NY 14513 US

GROWTH PLANS/SPECIAL FEATURES:

Ultralife Corporation is a provider of portable and standby power solutions for communications and electronics systems. The company designs, manufactures, installs and maintains power and communications systems, including rechargeable and non-rechargeable batteries, standby power systems, communications and electronics systems and accessories and custom engineered systems, solutions and services. The firm operates through two segments: battery & energy products and communication systems. The battery & energy products segment includes non-rechargeable and rechargeable product lines. It manufactures and/or markets a non-rechargeable family of lithium-manganese dioxide non-rechargeable batteries including nine-volt, HiRate cylindrical, Thin Cell and other chemistries and form factors; as well as lithium-thionyl chloride non-rechargeable batteries. Its rechargeable products include lithium ion rechargeable batteries, which are used in communications, medical and other portable electronic device applications. Additionally, the company offers lead-acid batteries and uninterruptable power supplies for the standby power market. The communications systems segment designs and manufactures a line of power solutions and accessories to support military communications systems including power supplies, power cables, connector assemblies, RF amplifiers, amplified speakers, equipment mounts, case equipment and integrated communication systems. Ultralife's brands include Ultralife Batteries, ABLE, McDowell Research, RedBlack Communications, Stationary Power Services, U.S. Energy Systems, RPS Power Systems and AMTI. In March 2011, Ultralife announced it will close its Energy Services business segment, formerly in charge of design, installation, integration and maintenance of communication electronics and standby power systems.

FINANCIALS: **Sales and profits are in thousands of dollars—add 000 to get the full amount. 2011 Note: Financial information for 2011 was not available for all companies at press time.**

2011 Sales: $ | 2011 Profits: $
2010 Sales: $178,577 | 2010 Profits: $-6,179
2009 Sales: $172,109 | 2009 Profits: $-9,241
2008 Sales: $254,700 | 2008 Profits: $13,663
2007 Sales: $137,596 | 2007 Profits: $5,583

U.S. Stock Ticker: ULBI
Int'l Ticker:
Int'l Exchange:
Employees: 1,169 Fiscal Year Ends: 12/31
Parent Company:

SALARIES/BENEFITS:

Pension Plan: | ESOP Stock Plan: | Profit Sharing: | Top Exec. Salary: $840,000 | Bonus: $270,000
Savings Plan: Y | Stock Purch. Plan: | | Second Exec. Salary: $675,000 | Bonus: $

OTHER THOUGHTS:

Apparent Women Officers or Directors: 1
Hot Spot for Advancement for Women/Minorities:

LOCATIONS: ("Y" = Yes)

West:	Southwest:	Midwest:	Southeast:	Northeast:	International:
Y	Y		Y	Y	Y

UNISOURCE ENERGY CORPORATION

www.uns.com

Industry Group Code: 221

Management:		Sales/Marketing:		Liberal Arts:		Information Systems:		Professionals:		Technical/Scientific:	
Mgmt. Trainees:		Mktg. Professionals:	Y	Gen. Writing/Editing:	Y	Info. Management:	Y	Finance/Acct.:	Y	Engineers, Elec.:	Y
Experienced Mgmt.:	Y	Retail Sales:		Technical Writing:		Software Dev.:		Law:	Y	Engineers, Other:	Y
Int'l Business:	Y	Commercial/Industrial:	Y	Graphic Arts/Photog.:		Hardware Dev.:		HR/Other:	Y	Health/Lab	
MBA Graduates:	Y	Sales Trainees:		Music:		Consulting/Other:		Training:	Y	Scientists/Research:	
		Advertising Pros.:		Broadcasting:				Health Care:		Petroleum/Chemicals:	Y
				Other:				Consulting:		Math/Other:	

TYPES OF BUSINESS:

Utilities-Electricity & Natural Gas
Investments

BRANDS/DIVISIONS/AFFILIATES:

Tucson Electric Power Co.
UniSource Energy Services, Inc.
Millennium Energy Holdings, Inc.
UniSource Energy Development Co.
Southwest Energy Solutions, Inc.
UNS Electric, Inc.
UNS Gas, Inc.

CONTACTS: *Note: Officers with more than one job title may be intentionally listed here more than once.*

Paul J. Bonavia, CEO
Paul J. Bonavia, Pres.
Kevin P. Larson, CFO/Sr. VP/Treas.
Lou Boltik, Dir.-Mktg. Comm.
Catherine E. Ries, VP-Human Resources
Thomas A. McKenna, VP-Eng. & UniSource Energy Svcs.
Todd C. Hixon, General Counsel/VP
Michael J. DeConcini, Sr. VP-Oper.
Joe Salkowski, Dir.-Corp. Comm.
Jo Smith, Dir.-Investor Rel.
Kentton C. Grant, VP-Finance & Rates
Philip J. Dion, VP-Public Policy
David G. Hutchens, Exec. VP
Herlinda H. Kennedy, Corp. Sec.
Karen G. Kissinger, Chief Compliance Officer/VP/Controller
Paul J. Bonavia, Chmn.

Phone: 520-571-4000 **Fax:** 520-884-3602
Toll-Free:
Address: 1 S. Church Ave., Ste. 100, Tucson, AZ 85701 US

GROWTH PLANS/SPECIAL FEATURES:

UniSource Energy Corporation is a diverse energy company. It is the holding company for UniSource Energy Services, Inc. (UES) and Tucson Electric Power Co. (TEP). The firm conducts its business in four primary business segments: TEP, UNS Gas, UNS Electric and Millennium Energy Holdings, Inc. TEP, which generates roughly 77% of the firm's revenue, is an electric utility that provides electric service to approximately 403,000 customers in the Tucson, Arizona, metropolitan area. Its principal fuel for electric generation is low-sulfur, bituminous or sub-bituminous coal from mines in Arizona, New Mexico and Colorado. The majority of the coal supplies are purchased under long-term contracts. TEP also holds a franchise to provide electric distribution service to customers in the city of Tucson and south Tucson. UES, through its subsidiaries UNS Gas, Inc. and UNS Electric, Inc., provides gas and electric service to 30 communities in Northern and Southern Arizona. UNS Gas has approximately 146,500 retail customers and UNS Electric has approximately 91,000 retail customers. UES subsidiary Millennium Energy Holdings, Inc. invests in unregulated businesses and emerging technology companies. Southwest Energy Solutions, Inc., a wholly-owned subsidiary of Millennium, provides UNS Electric and TEP with services such as line locating, facilities maintenance, meter reading, transmitting, distributing, dusk to dawn lighting and general supplemental support. Another UES subsidiary, UniSource Energy Development Co., develops generating resources and other project development activities, including the expansion of the Springerville Generating Station. TEP plans to open a new 25 megawatt (MW) photovoltaic array and a 5 MW concentrating solar power plant in Tucson by early 2012.

FINANCIALS: **Sales and profits are in thousands of dollars—add 000 to get the full amount. 2011 Note: Financial information for 2011 was not available for all companies at press time.**

2011 Sales: $1,509,515 | 2011 Profits: $109,975
2010 Sales: $1,453,677 | 2010 Profits: $111,477
2009 Sales: $1,394,424 | 2009 Profits: $104,258
2008 Sales: $1,397,511 | 2008 Profits: $14,021
2007 Sales: $1,381,373 | 2007 Profits: $58,373

U.S. Stock Ticker: UNS
Int'l Ticker:
Int'l Exchange:
Employees: 1,993 Fiscal Year Ends: 12/31
Parent Company:

SALARIES/BENEFITS:

Pension Plan: ESOP Stock Plan: Profit Sharing: Top Exec. Salary: $611,815 Bonus: $546,400
Savings Plan: Stock Purch. Plan: Second Exec. Salary: $342,027 Bonus: $183,000

OTHER THOUGHTS:

Apparent Women Officers or Directors: 5
Hot Spot for Advancement for Women/Minorities: Y

LOCATIONS: ("Y" = Yes)

West:	Southwest:	Midwest:	Southeast:	Northeast:	International:
	Y				

UNIT CORP

Industry Group Code: 213111

www.unitcorp.com

Management:		Sales/Marketing:		Liberal Arts:		Information Systems:		Professionals:		Technical/Scientific:	
Mgmt. Trainees:		Mktg. Professionals:		Gen. Writing/Editing:		Info. Management:	Y	Finance/Acct.:	Y	Engineers, Elec.:	
Experienced Mgmt.:	Y	Retail Sales:		Technical Writing:		Software Dev.:		Law:	Y	Engineers, Other:	Y
Int'l Business:	Y	Commercial/Industrial:		Graphic Arts/Photog.:		Hardware Dev.:		HR/Other:	Y	Health/Lab	
MBA Graduates:	Y	Sales Trainees:		Music:		Consulting/Other:		Training:	Y	Scientists/Research:	
		Advertising Pros.:		Broadcasting:				Health Care:		Petroleum/Chemicals:	Y
				Other:				Consulting:		Math/Other:	

TYPES OF BUSINESS:

Oil & Gas Exploration & Production
Contract Drilling Services
Natural Gas Wholesales

BRANDS/DIVISIONS/AFFILIATES:

Unit Petroleum Company
Unit Drilling Co
Unit Texas Drilling LLC
Superior Pipeline LLC

CONTACTS: *Note: Officers with more than one job title may be intentionally listed here more than once.*

Larry D. Pinkston, CEO
Larry D. Pinkston, Pres.
David T. Merrill, CFO
Brad Guidry, Sr. VP-Exploration, Unit Petroleum Co.
Mark E. Schell, General Counsel/Sr. VP/Corp. Sec.
David T. Merrill, Treas.
Richard E. Heck, VP-Safety, Health & Environment
John Cromling, Sr. VP-Drilling Oper., Unit Drilling Co.
Mark Colclasure, Sr. VP-Oper., Unit Petroleum Co.
Robert Parks, Pres., Superior Pipeline Co., LLC
John G. Nikkel, Chmn.

Phone: 918-493-7700 **Fax:** 918-493-7711
Toll-Free:
Address: 7130 S. Lewis Ave., Ste. 1000, Tulsa, OK 74136 US

GROWTH PLANS/SPECIAL FEATURES:

Unit Corp. is a diversified energy company. The firm contracts to drill onshore oil and natural gas wells; explores, develops, acquires and produces oil and natural gas properties; and buys, sells, processes and treats natural gas. The company's contract drilling business is conducted through subsidiary Unit Drilling Co. and its subsidiary Unit Texas Drilling, L.L.C. Through these companies, Unit Corp. drills onshore natural gas and oil wells for its own account as well as for other oil and gas companies. Its operations are mainly located in the Texas and Louisiana Gulf Coast; East Texas; the Oklahoma and Texas areas of the Anadarko and Arkoma Basins; the North Texas Barnett Shale; and the Rocky Mountain regions of Wyoming, Colorado, Utah and Montana. Subsidiary Unit Petroleum Company conducts the exploration and production activities. Its producing oil and natural gas properties, undeveloped leaseholds and related assets are located mainly in Oklahoma, Texas, Louisiana and New Mexico. It also operates in 11 other states and a small portion in Canada. Through this subsidiary, Unit Corp. owns over 454.1 billion cubic feet of oil equivalent of reserves. The company also owns about 121 drilling rigs, three natural gas treatment plants, eight operating processing plants and 34 active natural gas gathering systems. In addition, it has interests in roughly 7,999 wells. Its rig fleet is leveraged towards natural gas drilling, with one of the largest percentages of deep rated premium rigs in the industry. Unit Corp.'s rigs have maximum drilling capacities from 5,000 to 40,000 feet. Another subsidiary, Superior Pipeline, L.L.C., buys, sells, gathers, processes and treats natural gas for the company's own account, as well as for third parties. In December 2010, Superior Pipeline opened a new gas processing plant in Tulsa, Oklahoma.

FINANCIALS: **Sales and profits are in thousands of dollars—add 000 to get the full amount. 2011 Note: Financial information for 2011 was not available for all companies at press time.**

2011 Sales: $1,208,371	2011 Profits: $195,867	**U.S. Stock Ticker: UNT**
2010 Sales: $881,845	2010 Profits: $146,484	**Int'l Ticker:**
2009 Sales: $709,898	2009 Profits: $-55,500	Int'l Exchange:
2008 Sales: $1,358,093	2008 Profits: $143,625	Employees: 2,259 Fiscal Year Ends: 12/31
2007 Sales: $1,158,754	2007 Profits: $266,258	Parent Company:

SALARIES/BENEFITS:

Pension Plan:	ESOP Stock Plan:	Profit Sharing:	Top Exec. Salary: $637,000	Bonus: $425,000
Savings Plan: Y	Stock Purch. Plan:		Second Exec. Salary: $318,000	Bonus: $143,000

OTHER THOUGHTS:

Apparent Women Officers or Directors:
Hot Spot for Advancement for Women/Minorities:

LOCATIONS: ("Y" = Yes)

West:	Southwest:	Midwest:	Southeast:	Northeast:	International:
Y	Y		Y		

UNITED ONLINE INC

www.unitedonline.net

Industry Group Code: 517110

Management:		Sales/Marketing:		Liberal Arts:		Information Systems:		Professionals:		Technical/Scientific:	
Mgmt. Trainees:		Mktg. Professionals:	Y	Gen. Writing/Editing:	Y	Info. Management:	Y	Finance/Acct.:	Y	Engineers, Elec.:	Y
Experienced Mgmt.:	Y	Retail Sales:		Technical Writing:		Software Dev.:	Y	Law:	Y	Engineers, Other:	
Int'l Business:	Y	Commercial/Industrial:	Y	Graphic Arts/Photog.:		Hardware Dev.:		HR/Other:	Y	Health/Lab	
MBA Graduates:	Y	Sales Trainees:	Y	Music:		Consulting/Other:		Training:	Y	Scientists/Research:	
		Advertising Pros.:	Y	Broadcasting:				Health Care:		Petroleum/Chemicals:	
				Other:				Consulting:		Math/Other:	

TYPES OF BUSINESS:

Internet Service Provider
Social Networking Web Sites
Online Loyalty Marketing
Floral Delivery Services

BRANDS/DIVISIONS/AFFILIATES:

Juno
NetZero
Interflora
MyPoints.com
Trombi
StayFriends
FTD
MemoryLane.com

CONTACTS: *Note: Officers with more than one job title may be intentionally listed here more than once.*

Mark R. Goldston, CEO
Mark R. Goldston, Pres.
Scott H. Ray, CFO/Exec. VP
Jeremy Helfand, Chief Sales Officer/Exec. VP
Paul E. Jordan, Chief Personnel Officer/Exec. VP
Charles B. Ammann, General Counsel/Exec. VP/Sec.
Frederic A. Randall, Jr., Chief Strategy Officer/Exec. VP
Robert J. Taragan, Pres., Comm. Segment
Robert S. Apatoff, Pres., FTD Segment
Mark R. Goldston, Chmn.

Phone: 818-287-3000	**Fax:** 818-287-3001
Toll-Free:	
Address: 21301 Burbank Blvd., Woodland Hills, CA 91367 US	

GROWTH PLANS/SPECIAL FEATURES:

United Online, Inc. is a nationwide provider of consumer Internet and media services formed from the merger of NetZero, Inc. and Juno Online Services, Inc. The company operates in three segments: Content/Media, Communications and FTD. The Content and Media segment, which accounts for roughly 22% of United Online's revenues, offers online social networking through its web site MemoryLnae.com (ClassMates.com) and through five international social networking services including StayFriends web sites in Switzerland, Austria, Germany and Sweden and the Trombi web site in France. Through the social networking web sites, the company serves more than 60 million registered accounts, including 5.5 million pay accounts. This segment also provides online loyalty marketing through MyPoints.com. The MyPoints program provides consumers with points-based rewards for responding to e-mail offers, completing online surveys, shopping online and completing other online activities. The rewards points can be traded in for third-party gift cards and benefits from over 75 merchants. The Communications segment (18% of revenues) is primarily comprised of dial-up Internet and e-mail access through NetZero and Juno. The company's dial-up services, which are available in more than 12,000 North American cities, consist in accelerated dial-up Internet access, standard dial-up Internet access and a free dial-up Internet access service that is subject to hourly limitations. This segment also offers DSL services in certain areas that are purchased from third-parties and resold under the NetZero and Juno brands. The firm has roughly 1 million Communications pay accounts (700,000 of which are dial-up Internet clients). In addition to billable accounts, United Online derives revenues from selling online advertising space and services on its web sites and in e-mails. FTD (60% of revenues) provides floral product and services for consumers, retail florists and other retail locations in the U.S., Canada, the U.K. and Ireland through brands FTD and Interflora.

FINANCIALS: **Sales and profits are in thousands of dollars—add 000 to get the full amount. 2011 Note: Financial information for 2011 was not available for all companies at press time.**

2011 Sales: $897,685	2011 Profits: $51,730	**U.S. Stock Ticker: UNTD**
2010 Sales: $920,553	2010 Profits: $50,454	**Int'l Ticker:**
2009 Sales: $990,132	2009 Profits: $65,438	Int'l Exchange:
2008 Sales: $669,403	2008 Profits: $-94,657	Employees: 1,606 Fiscal Year Ends: 12/31
2007 Sales: $513,503	2007 Profits: $57,777	Parent Company:

SALARIES/BENEFITS:

Pension Plan:	ESOP Stock Plan:	Profit Sharing:	Top Exec. Salary: $989,394	Bonus: $
Savings Plan: Y	Stock Purch. Plan:		Second Exec. Salary: $560,769	Bonus: $

OTHER THOUGHTS:

Apparent Women Officers or Directors:
Hot Spot for Advancement for Women/Minorities:

LOCATIONS: ("Y" = Yes)

West:	Southwest:	Midwest:	Southeast:	Northeast:	International:
Y		Y	Y	Y	Y

UNITED THERAPEUTICS CORP

www.unither.com

Industry Group Code: 325412

Management:		Sales/Marketing:		Liberal Arts:		Information Systems:		Professionals:		Technical/Scientific:	
Mgmt. Trainees:		Mktg. Professionals:	Y	Gen. Writing/Editing:		Info. Management:	Y	Finance/Acct.:	Y	Engineers, Elec.:	
Experienced Mgmt.:	Y	Retail Sales:		Technical Writing:	Y	Software Dev.:	Y	Law:	Y	Engineers, Other:	
Int'l Business:	Y	Commercial/Industrial:	Y	Graphic Arts/Photog.:		Hardware Dev.:		HR/Other:	Y	Health/Lab	Y
MBA Graduates:	Y	Sales Trainees:	Y	Music:		Consulting/Other:		Training:	Y	Scientists/Research:	Y
		Advertising Pros.:		Broadcasting:				Health Care:	Y	Petroleum/Chemicals:	Y
				Other:				Consulting:		Math/Other:	Y

TYPES OF BUSINESS:

Cardiovascular, Cancer & Infectious Diseases Therapeutics
Dietary Supplements
Telecardiology Products

BRANDS/DIVISIONS/AFFILIATES:

Unither Biotheque Inc
Unither Therapeutik GmbH
Unither Biotech Inc
Remodulin
Unither Neuroscience Inc
Lung Rx, Inc
Unither Pharmaceuticals LLC

CONTACTS: *Note: Officers with more than one job title may be intentionally listed here more than once.*

Martine Rothblatt, CEO
Roger Jeffs, COO
Roger Jeffs, Pres.
John M. Ferrari, CFO
Paul A. Mahon, General Counsel/Exec. VP/Corp. Sec.
John M. Ferrari, Treas.
Martine Rothblatt, Chmn.

Phone: 301-608-9292	**Fax:** 301-608-9291
Toll-Free:	
Address: 1040 Spring St., Silver Spring, MD 20910 US	

GROWTH PLANS/SPECIAL FEATURES:

United Therapeutics Corp. (UTC) is a biotechnology company focused on the development and commercialization of therapeutic products for patients with cancer, cardiovascular diseases and other infectious diseases. Remodulin, the company's lead product, is an FDA-approved, treprostinil-based compound designed for the treatment of pulmonary arterial hypertension (PAH) for patients with negative symptoms associated with exercise. UTC has commercial rights for Remodulin in most European Union countries, Israel, Australia, Mexico, Argentina and Peru. The firm manufactures the treprostinil-based compound in an inhaled form, TYVASO; while Adcirca is the tablet form. Both are used in the treatment of pulmonary arterial hypertension to improve exercise ability. In addition, the company has a joint venture with Toray Industries, Inc., to develop Beraprost-MR, a prostacyclin analog drug designed to treat cardiovascular diseases. Subsidiary Unither Biotheque Inc., distributes and sells the company's products in Canada. The firm's other pharmaceutical subsidiaries include Unither Pharmaceuticals LLC.; Unither Neuroscience Inc.; Lung Rx, Inc.; Unither Telmed, Ltd.; United Therapeutics Europe, Ltd.; Unither Therapeutik GmbH; and Unither Virology, LLC. In 2011, UTC sold subsidiary Medicomp, Inc. to a group of private investors.

FINANCIALS: **Sales and profits are in thousands of dollars—add 000 to get the full amount. 2011 Note: Financial information for 2011 was not available for all companies at press time.**

2011 Sales: $743,183	2011 Profits: $217,868	**U.S. Stock Ticker: UTHR**
2010 Sales: $603,831	2010 Profits: $105,916	**Int'l Ticker:**
2009 Sales: $369,848	2009 Profits: $19,462	Int'l Exchange:
2008 Sales: $281,497	2008 Profits: $-42,789	Employees: 520 Fiscal Year Ends: 12/31
2007 Sales: $210,943	2007 Profits: $19,859	Parent Company:

SALARIES/BENEFITS:

Pension Plan:	ESOP Stock Plan:	Profit Sharing:	Top Exec. Salary: $874,768	Bonus: $900,000
Savings Plan: Y	Stock Purch. Plan:		Second Exec. Salary: $725,000	Bonus: $550,000

OTHER THOUGHTS:

Apparent Women Officers or Directors: 1
Hot Spot for Advancement for Women/Minorities:

LOCATIONS: ("Y" = Yes)

West:	Southwest:	Midwest:	Southeast:	Northeast:	International:
			Y	Y	Y

UNIVERSAL HOSPITAL SERVICES INC

www.uhs.com

Industry Group Code: 5324

Management:		Sales/Marketing:		Liberal Arts:		Information Systems:		Professionals:		Technical/Scientific:	
Mgmt. Trainees:		Mktg. Professionals:	Y	Gen. Writing/Editing:		Info. Management:	Y	Finance/Acct.:	Y	Engineers, Elec.:	
Experienced Mgmt.:	Y	Retail Sales:		Technical Writing:	Y	Software Dev.:		Law:	Y	Engineers, Other:	
Int'l Business:		Commercial/Industrial:	Y	Graphic Arts/Photog.:		Hardware Dev.:		HR/Other:	Y	Health/Lab	
MBA Graduates:	Y	Sales Trainees:	Y	Music:		Consulting/Other:		Training:	Y	Scientists/Research:	
		Advertising Pros.:		Broadcasting:				Health Care:	Y	Petroleum/Chemicals:	
				Other:				Consulting:		Math/Other:	

TYPES OF BUSINESS:

Medical Equipment Outsourcing & Services
Technical & Professional Services
Medical Equipment Sales & Remarketing

BRANDS/DIVISIONS/AFFILIATES:

Asset Recovery and Equipment Sales
Asset360 Program
UHS Holdco, Inc.
Medical Equipment Outsourcing
Emergent Group, Inc.
PRI Medical Technologies, Inc.

CONTACTS: *Note: Officers with more than one job title may be intentionally listed here more than once.*

Gary D. Blackford, CEO
Timothy W. Kuck, COO/Exec. VP
Rex T. Clevenger, CFO/Exec. VP
Jeffrey L. Singer, Exec. VP-Sales & Mktg.
Walter T. Chesley, Sr. VP-Human Resources & Dev.
David G. Lawson, Sr. VP-Info. & Strategic Resources
Diana Vance-Bryan, Exec. VP-Oper.
Timothy Kuck, Exec. VP-Bus. Dev. & Strategy
Scott M. Madson, Chief Acct. Officer/VP/Controller
David Holland, VP-Oper., East Region
Phil Zeller, VP-Oper., Central Region
Debbie Norman, VP-Oper., West Region
Robert Brooks, Sr. VP-Field Oper.
Gary D. Blackford, Chmn.

Phone: 952-893-3200	**Fax:** 952-893-0704
Toll-Free: 800-847-7368	
Address: 7700 France Ave. S., Ste. 275, Edina, MN 55435 US	

GROWTH PLANS/SPECIAL FEATURES:

Universal Hospital Services, Inc. (UHS) is a provider of medical equipment outsourcing and lifecycle services to the healthcare industry. The firm services roughly 8,600 customers through 84 offices across the U.S. and partners with 175 equipment manufacturers. UHS customers include national, regional and local acute and long-term acute care hospitals, alternate site providers (such as skilled nursing facilities, specialty hospitals, large physician clinics and home care providers) and medical equipment manufacturers. UHS owns or manages over 570,000 pieces of medical equipment, including products such as bariatric equipment and suites; critical care products; patient-monitoring products; newborn care equipment; respiratory and infusion therapy products; orthopedics equipment; and support surfaces. The company operates in three segments: medical equipment outsourcing; technical and professional services; and medical equipment sales and remarketing. Its medical equipment outsourcing customer base includes more than 4,250 acute care hospitals and approximately 4,350 alternate site providers. The medical equipment outsourcing segment accounts for roughly 78.9% of the company's revenue. The company offers various programs designed to provide patient care while meeting the facility's financial goals, including the Asset360 Program, Asset Recovery and Equipment Sales and the Medical Equipment Outsourcing program, among others. The Asset360 Program focuses on reducing capital expenditures; increasing equipment productivity; and improving quality of care and nursing satisfaction. The Asset Recovery and Equipment Sales program offers identification, purchasing and removal services for underutilized pieces of medical equipment. Medical Equipment Outsourcing offers solutions that maximize utilization, increase productivity and support patient care and safety. In April 2011, the firm acquired Emergent Group, Inc. and Emergent's wholly-owned subsidiary, PRI Medical Technologies, Inc.

FINANCIALS: **Sales and profits are in thousands of dollars—add 000 to get the full amount. 2011 Note: Financial information for 2011 was not available for all companies at press time.**

2011 Sales: $	2011 Profits: $	**U.S. Stock Ticker: Private**
2010 Sales: $317,400	2010 Profits: $-29,100	**Int'l Ticker:**
2009 Sales: $297,204	2009 Profits: $-18,573	Int'l Exchange:
2008 Sales: $289,119	2008 Profits: $-23,496	Employees: 1,330 Fiscal Year Ends: 12/31
2007 Sales: $263,976	2007 Profits: $-63,570	Parent Company: UHS HOLDCO INC

SALARIES/BENEFITS:

Pension Plan:	ESOP Stock Plan:	Profit Sharing:	Top Exec. Salary: $479,820	Bonus: $407,800
Savings Plan:	Stock Purch. Plan:		Second Exec. Salary: $348,504	Bonus: $291,400

OTHER THOUGHTS:

Apparent Women Officers or Directors: 2
Hot Spot for Advancement for Women/Minorities:

LOCATIONS: ("Y" = Yes)

West:	Southwest:	Midwest:	Southeast:	Northeast:	International:
Y	Y	Y	Y	Y	

UQM TECHNOLOGIES INC

www.uqm.com

Industry Group Code: 335

Management:		**Sales/Marketing:**		**Liberal Arts:**		**Information Systems:**		**Professionals:**		**Technical/Scientific:**	
Mgmt. Trainees:		Mktg. Professionals:	Y	Gen. Writing/Editing:		Info. Management:	Y	Finance/Acct.:	Y	Engineers, Elec.:	Y
Experienced Mgmt.:	Y	Retail Sales:		Technical Writing:	Y	Software Dev.:		Law:	Y	Engineers, Other:	Y
Int'l Business:		Commercial/Industrial:	Y	Graphic Arts/Photog.:		Hardware Dev.:	Y	HR/Other:	Y	Health/Lab	
MBA Graduates:	Y	Sales Trainees:		Music:		Consulting/Other:		Training:		Scientists/Research:	
		Advertising Pros.:		Broadcasting:				Health Care:		Petroleum/Chemicals:	
				Other:				Consulting:		Math/Other:	

TYPES OF BUSINESS:

Electric Motors
Research & Development
Electronic Propulsion Systems
Hybrid Engine Technology
Power Generator Control Systems
Software

BRANDS/DIVISIONS/AFFILIATES:

UQM Power Products Inc

CONTACTS: *Note: Officers with more than one job title may be intentionally listed here more than once.*

Eric R. Ridenour, CEO
Eric R. Ridenour, Pres.
Donald A. French, CFO
Adrian Schaffer, VP-Sales
Jon F. Lutz, VP-Eng.
Donald A. French, Sec.
Ronald M. Burton, Exec. VP-Oper.
Adrian Schaffer, VP-Bus. Dev.
Donald A. French, Treas.
William G. Rankin, Chmn.

Phone: 303-682-4900	**Fax:** 303-682-4901
Toll-Free:	
Address: 4120 Specialty Pl., Longmont, CO 80504 US	

GROWTH PLANS/SPECIAL FEATURES:

UQM Technologies, Inc. (UQM) is a developer and manufacturer of power dense, high efficiency electric motors, generators and power electronic controllers for the automotive, aerospace, military and industrial markets. The company's emphasis is on developing alternative energy technologies including propulsion systems for electric, hybrid electric and fuel cell electric vehicles. The firm operates out of a 129,304-square-foot manufacturing facility in Longmont, Colorado and a 28,000-square-foot manufacturing plant in Frederick, Colorado. The company's revenue is derived from two primary sources: funded contract research and development services performed for strategic partners, customers and the U.S. government; and the manufacture and sale of the products it designs. UQM's technology base includes a number of proprietary technologies and patents relating to brushless permanent magnet motors, generators and power electronic controllers, together with software code to intelligently manage the operation of its systems. The firm also manufactures motors and electronic products. In April 2011, UQM Technologies merged subsidiary UQM Power Products, Inc. into its existing operations.

UQM offers its employees a 401(k) plan and an employee stock purchase plan.

FINANCIALS: **Sales and profits are in thousands of dollars—add 000 to get the full amount. 2011 Note: Financial information for 2011 was not available for all companies at press time.**

2011 Sales: $9,021	2011 Profits: $-1,992	**U.S. Stock Ticker: UQM**
2010 Sales: $8,692	2010 Profits: $-4,141	**Int'l Ticker:**
2009 Sales: $8,728	2009 Profits: $-4,402	Int'l Exchange:
2008 Sales: $7,508	2008 Profits: $-4,586	Employees: 79 Fiscal Year Ends: 3/31
2007 Sales: $6,653	2007 Profits: $-3,431	Parent Company:

SALARIES/BENEFITS:

Pension Plan:	ESOP Stock Plan:	Profit Sharing:	Top Exec. Salary: $238,765	Bonus: $100,000
Savings Plan: Y	Stock Purch. Plan: Y		Second Exec. Salary: $236,568	Bonus: $270,000

OTHER THOUGHTS:

Apparent Women Officers or Directors:
Hot Spot for Advancement for Women/Minorities:

LOCATIONS: ("Y" = Yes)

West:	Southwest:	Midwest:	Southeast:	Northeast:	International:
Y					

US PHYSICAL THERAPY INC

www.usph.com

Industry Group Code: 6214

Management:		Sales/Marketing:		Liberal Arts:		Information Systems:		Professionals:		Technical/Scientific:	
Mgmt. Trainees:	Y	Mktg. Professionals:	Y	Gen. Writing/Editing:	Y	Info. Management:	Y	Finance/Acct.:	Y	Engineers, Elec.:	
Experienced Mgmt.:	Y	Retail Sales:		Technical Writing:	Y	Software Dev.:		Law:	Y	Engineers, Other:	
Int'l Business:		Commercial/Industrial:	Y	Graphic Arts/Photog.:		Hardware Dev.:		HR/Other:	Y	Health/Lab	Y
MBA Graduates:	Y	Sales Trainees:	Y	Music:		Consulting/Other:		Training:	Y	Scientists/Research:	
		Advertising Pros.:	Y	Broadcasting:				Health Care:	Y	Petroleum/Chemicals:	
				Other:				Consulting:		Math/Other:	

TYPES OF BUSINESS:

Occupational & Physical Therapy Clinics

BRANDS/DIVISIONS/AFFILIATES:

CONTACTS:

Note: Officers with more than one job title may be intentionally listed here more than once.

Christopher J. Reading, CEO
Glenn D. McDowell, COO
Christopher J. Reading, Pres.
Lawrance W. McAfee, CFO/Exec. VP
Jerald L. Pullins, Chmn.

Phone: 713-297-7000 **Fax:** 713-297-7090
Toll-Free: 800-580-6285
Address: 1300 W. Sam Houston Pkwy. S., Ste. 300, Houston, TX 77042 US

GROWTH PLANS/SPECIAL FEATURES:

U.S. Physical Therapy, Inc. (UPT) is a holding company engaged in the operation of outpatient physical therapy and occupational therapy clinics. These clinics provide pre- and post-operative care/treatment of orthopedic-related disorders, sports-injuries, preventive care, rehabilitation of injured workers and neurological-related injuries. UPT operates through subsidiary clinic partnerships, in which the firm generally owns a 1% general partnership interest and 64% limited partnership interest. The managing therapists of the clinics own the remaining limited partnership interest in the majority of the clinics. UPT also operates some clinics through wholly-owned subsidiaries, under profit sharing arrangements with therapists. There are approximately 392 outpatient physical and occupational therapy clinics (102 of which are wholly-owned) in 42 states. The average age of these clinics is roughly 7.5 years. Each clinic's staff typically includes one or more licensed physical or occupational therapists along with assistants, aides, exercise physiologists and athletic trainers. The clinics initially perform an evaluation of each patient, which is then followed by a treatment plan specific to the injury as prescribed by the patient's physician. The treatment plan may include procedures such as ultrasound, electrical stimulation, therapeutic exercise, hot packs, iontophoresis, daily life skills management and home exercise programs. A clinic's business primarily comes from referrals by local physicians. UPT also manages 15 physical therapy practices for third parties. The company receives most of its revenues from managed care programs (approximately 31.6%); insurance (25.2%); Medicare and Medicaid (20.9%); workers' compensation (17.6%); and other (4.7%). In 2010, the firm opened 19, closed 15, acquired 25 and sold 5 clinics. In January 2011, UPT acquired majority ownership of 14 clinics located in the southeastern U.S.

The company offers its employees life, disability, AD&D, medical, dental and vision insurance; paid time off; a 401(k); and education assistance.

FINANCIALS:

Sales and profits are in thousands of dollars—add 000 to get the full amount. 2011 Note: Financial information for 2011 was not available for all companies at press time.

2011 Sales: $	2011 Profits: $
2010 Sales: $211,233	2010 Profits: $15,645
2009 Sales: $201,409	2009 Profits: $11,767
2008 Sales: $187,686	2008 Profits: $10,004
2007 Sales: $151,686	2007 Profits: $8,738

U.S. Stock Ticker: USPH
Int'l Ticker:
Int'l Exchange:
Employees: 1,876 Fiscal Year Ends: 12/31
Parent Company:

SALARIES/BENEFITS:

Pension Plan:	ESOP Stock Plan:	Profit Sharing:	Top Exec. Salary: $392,596	Bonus: $393,000
Savings Plan: Y	Stock Purch. Plan:		Second Exec. Salary: $374,231	Bonus: $279,750

OTHER THOUGHTS:

Apparent Women Officers or Directors:
Hot Spot for Advancement for Women/Minorities:

LOCATIONS: ("Y" = Yes)

West:	Southwest:	Midwest:	Southeast:	Northeast:	International:
Y	Y	Y	Y	Y	

USANA HEALTH SCIENCES INC

www.usana.com

Industry Group Code: 325411

Management:		**Sales/Marketing:**		**Liberal Arts:**		**Information Systems:**		**Professionals:**		**Technical/Scientific:**	
Mgmt. Trainees:		Mktg. Professionals:	Y	Gen. Writing/Editing:	Y	Info. Management:	Y	Finance/Acct.:	Y	Engineers, Elec.:	
Experienced Mgmt.:	Y	Retail Sales:		Technical Writing:	Y	Software Dev.:		Law:	Y	Engineers, Other:	
Int'l Business:	Y	Commercial/Industrial:	Y	Graphic Arts/Photog.:	Y	Hardware Dev.:		HR/Other:	Y	Health/Lab	Y
MBA Graduates:	Y	Sales Trainees:	Y	Music:		Consulting/Other:		Training:	Y	Scientists/Research:	Y
		Advertising Pros.:	Y	Broadcasting:				Health Care:	Y	Petroleum/Chemicals:	Y
				Other:				Consulting:		Math/Other:	

TYPES OF BUSINESS:

Vitamins & Nutritional Supplements
Hair & Skin Care Products
Nutrition & Energy Drinks & Bars

BRANDS/DIVISIONS/AFFILIATES:

Sense
Nutritionals
Usanimals
Gentle Daily Cleanser
Firming Body Nourisher
Fibergy
Hydrating Toner
Proflavanol

CONTACTS: *Note: Officers with more than one job title may be intentionally listed here more than once.*

David Wentz, CEO
Roy W. Truett, COO
Fred Cooper, Pres.
Doug Hekking, CFO
Kevin Guest, Chief Mktg. Officer
Timothy E. Wood, Exec. VP-R&D
Roy W. Truett, CIO
James Bramble, General Counsel/Corp. Sec./Chief Legal Officer
Dan Macuga, Chief Comm. Officer
Mark H. Wilson, Exec. VP-Sales
Kevin Guest, Pres., North America
Myron W. Wentz, Chmn.
Deborah Woo, Pres., APAC

Phone: 801-954-7100 **Fax:** 801-954-7300
Toll-Free:
Address: 3838 W. Parkway Blvd., Salt Lake City, UT 84120 US

GROWTH PLANS/SPECIAL FEATURES:

USANA Health Sciences, Inc. develops, manufactures and distributes science-based nutritional and personal care products. The company sells products through two primary product lines: USANA Nutritionals, which includes supplements and functional foods; and Sense, a line of personal care products. USANA Nutritionals' product line falls into three classifications: essentials, optimizers and USANA Foods. Essentials include core vitamin and mineral supplements that provide a foundation of nutrition to each age group. Products include Usanimals, a formulation of vitamins, minerals and antioxidants in a chewable tablet form for children 13 months to 12 years old; Mega Antioxidant, a blend of 30 vitamins, antioxidants and other nutrients to support cellular metabolism and to counteract free-radical damage; Body Rox, a nutritional supplement containing 31 essential vitamins, minerals, antioxidants and cofactors for adolescents 12-18 years old; and HealthPak 100, a combination of USANA supplements and key optimizers packaged in pillow packs. Optimizers are targeted supplements designed to meet individual health and nutritional needs. Products include Proflavanol, Poly C, CoQuinone 30, BiOmega-3, E-Prime, Active Calcium, PhytoEstrin, Garlic EC, Rev3 Energy Drink and TenX Antioxidant Blast. USANA Foods include healthy, low-glycemic functional foods such as Fibergy drink mixes, as well as Nutrition and Fibergy Bars. The division also offers sales and marketing tools designed to assist customers in building their businesses and selling the firm's products. USANA Health Science's Sense line includes brands such as Perfecting Essence, Nourishing Conditioner, Firming Body Nourisher, Gentle Daily Cleanser, Hydrating Toner, Eye Nourisher, Daytime Protective Emulsion, Night Renewal, Serum Intensive, Rice Bran Polisher, Crème Masque, Revitalizing Shampoo, Energizing Shower Gel and Intensive Hand Therapy. Products are sold in the U.S., the U.K., Canada, Mexico, China, Australia, New Zealand, Singapore, Malaysia, the Philippines, Hong Kong, Taiwan, Japan and South Korea.

FINANCIALS: **Sales and profits are in thousands of dollars—add 000 to get the full amount. 2011 Note: Financial information for 2011 was not available for all companies at press time.**

2011 Sales: $581,900 | 2011 Profits: $50,800
2010 Sales: $517,644 | 2010 Profits: $45,651
2009 Sales: $436,940 | 2009 Profits: $33,556
2008 Sales: $429,012 | 2008 Profits: $29,945
2007 Sales: $423,149 | 2007 Profits: $45,030

U.S. Stock Ticker: USNA
Int'l Ticker:
Int'l Exchange:
Employees: 1,240 Fiscal Year Ends: 12/31
Parent Company:

SALARIES/BENEFITS:

Pension Plan: ESOP Stock Plan: Profit Sharing: Top Exec. Salary: $588,462 Bonus: $411,885
Savings Plan: Stock Purch. Plan: Second Exec. Salary: $578,353 Bonus: $396,527

OTHER THOUGHTS:

Apparent Women Officers or Directors: 1
Hot Spot for Advancement for Women/Minorities:

LOCATIONS: ("Y" = Yes)

West:	Southwest:	Midwest:	Southeast:	Northeast:	International:
Y					Y

UTAH MEDICAL PRODUCTS INC

www.utahmed.com

Industry Group Code: 33911

Management:		**Sales/Marketing:**		**Liberal Arts:**		**Information Systems:**		**Professionals:**		**Technical/Scientific:**	
Mgmt. Trainees:		Mktg. Professionals:	Y	Gen. Writing/Editing:		Info. Management:	Y	Finance/Acct.:	Y	Engineers, Elec.:	
Experienced Mgmt.:	Y	Retail Sales:		Technical Writing:	Y	Software Dev.:	Y	Law:	Y	Engineers, Other:	Y
Int'l Business:	Y	Commercial/Industrial:	Y	Graphic Arts/Photog.:		Hardware Dev.:		HR/Other:	Y	Health/Lab	Y
MBA Graduates:	Y	Sales Trainees:	Y	Music:		Consulting/Other:		Training:	Y	Scientists/Research:	Y
		Advertising Pros.:		Broadcasting:				Health Care:	Y	Petroleum/Chemicals:	
				Other:				Consulting:		Math/Other:	

TYPES OF BUSINESS:

Equipment-Obstetrics & Gynecology
Disposable Products
Electrosurgical Systems
Neonatal Intensive Care Equipment

BRANDS/DIVISIONS/AFFILIATES:

Intran
Intran Plus
Disposa-Hood
Deltran
Gesco
Filtresse
Liberty
Femcare Holdings Limited

CONTACTS: *Note: Officers with more than one job title may be intentionally listed here more than once.*

Kevin L. Cornwell, CEO
Kevin L. Cornwell, Pres.
Paul O. Richins, CFO
Paul O. Richins, Chief Admin. Officer
Kevin L. Cornwell, Corp. Sec.
Paul O. Richins, Chief Acct. Officer
Kevin L. Cornwell, Chmn.

Phone: 801-566-1200	**Fax:** 801-566-7305
Toll-Free: 866-754-9789	
Address: 7043 S. 300 W., Midvale, UT 84047 US	

GROWTH PLANS/SPECIAL FEATURES:

Utah Medical Products, Inc. (UTMD) produces proprietary disposable medical devices for hospital use. It markets medical devices used in critical care, especially in neonatal intensive care units (NICU) and labor and delivery departments in hospitals, as well as outpatient clinics and physicians' offices. UTMD's products include obstetrics products, such as fetal monitoring accessories and vacuum-assisted delivery systems; NICU products; gynecology, urology and electrosurgery products; and blood pressure monitoring and accessories. The firm's primary fetal monitoring accessories include Intran, the first disposable, intrauterine pressure catheter that places the pressure transducer at the pressure source within the uterine cavity, and Intran Plus, which has refined tip design, a zero switch and a dedicated amnio lumen, providing immediate access to amniotic fluid. For NICUs, the firm manufactures the Disposa-Hood, an infant respiratory hood, and Gesco umbilical vessel catheters. Additional offerings include the LETZ system for cervical intraepithelial neoplasia; Finesse filters and electrosurgical generators; the Pathfinder endoscopic bulb irrigator; the Liberty pelvic floor stimulator and Filtresse smoke evacuators. Neonatal blood pressure monitoring equipment includes Deltran systems, Hemo-Nate blood filtration systems and Delta-Flow flush devices. UTMD's products are sold directly to end users in the U.S. domestic market by the company's own direct sales representatives, independent manufacturers' representatives, specialty distributors, national hospital distribution companies and other medical device manufacturers. Internationally, products are sold through other medical device companies and through independent medical products distributors. 6% of the company's sales are made to OEMs; 64% are direct sales to U.S.-based end users; and roughly 31% are sold to international firms and distributors. In March 2011, UTMD acquired U.K.-based female surgical contraception device marketer Femcare Holdings Limited.

UTMD offers its employees life, AD&D, medical, dental, vision, disability and prescription drug coverage; a medical expense, health insurance premium and dependent care 125 plan; paid military, bereavement and jury duty leave; and educational assistance.

FINANCIALS: **Sales and profits are in thousands of dollars—add 000 to get the full amount. 2011 Note: Financial information for 2011 was not available for all companies at press time.**

2011 Sales: $	2011 Profits: $	**U.S. Stock Ticker: UTMD**
2010 Sales: $25,121	2010 Profits: $6,014	**Int'l Ticker:**
2009 Sales: $25,916	2009 Profits: $6,258	Int'l Exchange:
2008 Sales: $27,782	2008 Profits: $7,205	Employees: 367 Fiscal Year Ends: 12/31
2007 Sales: $28,502	2007 Profits: $7,905	Parent Company:

SALARIES/BENEFITS:

Pension Plan:	ESOP Stock Plan:	Profit Sharing:	Top Exec. Salary: $256,100	Bonus: $185,250
Savings Plan: Y	Stock Purch. Plan: Y		Second Exec. Salary: $102,649	Bonus: $11,255

OTHER THOUGHTS:

Apparent Women Officers or Directors: 1
Hot Spot for Advancement for Women/Minorities:

LOCATIONS: ("Y" = Yes)

West:	Southwest:	Midwest:	Southeast:	Northeast:	International:
Y					Y

VARIAN SEMICONDUCTOR EQUIPMENT ASSOCIATES INC

www.vsea.com

Industry Group Code: 33441

Management:		Sales/Marketing:		Liberal Arts:		Information Systems:		Professionals:		Technical/Scientific:	
Mgmt. Trainees:		Mktg. Professionals:	Y	Gen. Writing/Editing:		Info. Management:	Y	Finance/Acct.:	Y	Engineers, Elec.:	Y
Experienced Mgmt.:	Y	Retail Sales:		Technical Writing:	Y	Software Dev.:	Y	Law:	Y	Engineers, Other:	Y
Int'l Business:	Y	Commercial/Industrial:	Y	Graphic Arts/Photog.:		Hardware Dev.:	Y	HR/Other:	Y	Health/Lab	
MBA Graduates:	Y	Sales Trainees:		Music:		Consulting/Other:		Training:		Scientists/Research:	
		Advertising Pros.:		Broadcasting:				Health Care:		Petroleum/Chemicals:	
				Other:				Consulting:		Math/Other:	Y

TYPES OF BUSINESS:

Semiconductor Manufacturing Equipment

BRANDS/DIVISIONS/AFFILIATES:

VIISta
Varian Control System (VCS)
Varian Positioning System (VPS)
Applied Materials Inc

CONTACTS:

Note: Officers with more than one job title may be intentionally listed here more than once.

Gary E. Dickerson, CEO
Robert J. Halliday, CFO/Exec. VP
Richard A. Aurelio, Chmn.

Phone: 978-281-2000 **Fax:**
Toll-Free:
Address: 35 Dory Rd., Gloucester, MA 01930 US

GROWTH PLANS/SPECIAL FEATURES:

Varian Semiconductor Equipment Associates, Inc. (VSEA) is a leading supplier of ion implantation systems used to build the transistors in semiconductor chips. It designs, manufactures, markets and services semiconductor processing equipment for virtually all of the major semiconductor manufacturers worldwide. Ion implanters work by creating ions of a given atomic element, called the dopant, and shooting those ions a given depth into a silicon wafer according to the circuit pattern. The amount of dopant, or dose, together with the depth of the implant into the wafer, or energy, constitutes the two variables that characterize VSEA's implanters. The company offers four implanters: high current, with high dose and low energy; ultra high dose, with very high dose and very low energy; medium current, with low dose and medium energy; and high energy, with low dose and very high energy. High current and medium current implanters are used in logic, memory and foundry manufacturing applications. Ultra high dose implanters are used in memory and certain new flash memory applications. High energy implanters are predominantly used by memory manufacturers, as well as in most wafer fabrication facilities. All of the firm's implanters are built upon the same technology platform and are sold under the VIISta brand name. Additionally, they all feature the Varian Control System (VCS), the Varian Positioning System (VPS) and the VIISta single wafer end station. The VCS monitors and maintains the precise conditions required for semiconductor manufacturing; the VPS increases beam accuracy, allowing for smaller, more compact semiconductor design; and the single wafer end station enhances the final processing of the wafer. The firm has more than 3,300 implanters installed worldwide, with a combined daily implant capacity of 5 million wafers. Besides its locations in the U.S., the firm has offices in Israel and seven European countries. In November 2011, the company was acquired by manufacturing company Applied Materials, Inc.

FINANCIALS:

Sales and profits are in thousands of dollars—add 000 to get the full amount. 2011 Note: Financial information for 2011 was not available for all companies at press time.

2011 Sales: $	2011 Profits: $
2010 Sales: $831,780	2010 Profits: $159,584
2009 Sales: $362,081	2009 Profits: $-37,998
2008 Sales: $834,061	2008 Profits: $99,516
2007 Sales: $1,054,864	2007 Profits: $144,409

U.S. Stock Ticker: Subsidiary
Int'l Ticker:
Int'l Exchange:
Employees: 1,462 Fiscal Year Ends: 9/30
Parent Company: APPLIED MATERIALS INC

SALARIES/BENEFITS:

Pension Plan: ESOP Stock Plan: Profit Sharing: Top Exec. Salary: $628,617 Bonus: $1,266,840
Savings Plan: Y Stock Purch. Plan: Y Second Exec. Salary: $356,846 Bonus: $642,218

OTHER THOUGHTS:

Apparent Women Officers or Directors:
Hot Spot for Advancement for Women/Minorities:

LOCATIONS: ("Y" = Yes)

West:	Southwest:	Midwest:	Southeast:	Northeast:	International:
Y	Y			Y	Y

VASCO DATA SECURITY INTERNATIONAL INC www.vasco.com

Industry Group Code: 511210E

Management:		**Sales/Marketing:**		**Liberal Arts:**		**Information Systems:**		**Professionals:**		**Technical/Scientific:**	
Mgmt. Trainees:		Mktg. Professionals:	Y	Gen. Writing/Editing:		Info. Management:	Y	Finance/Acct.:	Y	Engineers, Elec.:	Y
Experienced Mgmt.:	Y	Retail Sales:		Technical Writing:	Y	Software Dev.:	Y	Law:	Y	Engineers, Other:	
Int'l Business:	Y	Commercial/Industrial:	Y	Graphic Arts/Photog.:		Hardware Dev.:		HR/Other:	Y	Health/Lab	
MBA Graduates:	Y	Sales Trainees:	Y	Music:		Consulting/Other:		Training:	Y	Scientists/Research:	
		Advertising Pros.:		Broadcasting:				Health Care:		Petroleum/Chemicals:	
				Other:				Consulting:		Math/Other:	

TYPES OF BUSINESS:

Security Software
Authentication Devices
Banking Transaction Support Products
Credit Card Verification Products
Remote Verification Products
Anti-Fraud Services

BRANDS/DIVISIONS/AFFILIATES:

Digipass
VACMAN Controller
VACMAN Middleware
aXs GUARD
Identikey
DigipassPlus
DigiNotar B.V.
Alfa & Ariss B.V.

CONTACTS: *Note: Officers with more than one job title may be intentionally listed here more than once.*

T. Kendall Hunt, CEO
Jan Valcke, COO
Jan Valcke, Pres.
Clifford K. Bown, CFO/Exec. VP
Clifford K. Brown, Sec.
T. Kendall Hunt, Chmn.

Phone: 630-932-8844 **Fax:** 630-932-8852
Toll-Free:
Address: 1901 S. Meyers Rd., Ste. 210, Oakbrook Terrace, IL 60181 US

GROWTH PLANS/SPECIAL FEATURES:

VASCO Data Security International, Inc. designs, develops, markets and supports open-standards-based hardware and software security systems that manage and secure access to information assets. The company's products provide mission-critical security to corporate customers' internal and external infrastructures. The firm also secures financial transactions made over private enterprise networks and the Internet. VASCO's primary product line is the VACMAN Controller, which supports all VASCO authentication technologies including passwords, dynamic password technology (Digipass), certificates and biometrics. Other products include VACMAN Middleware security software; aXs GUARD, an authentication appliance; and Digipass, a suite of over 50 multi-application client e-signature software products based on the world's most widely spread electronic client platforms. Digipass is used in a wide variety of applications, the largest of which is banking, both corporate and retail banking. Another application of the Digipass is to secure access to corporate networks for home-based, traveling and other remote users. Digipass 110, a zero-footprint e-signature application, is aimed at the large volume e-commerce and retail e-banking markets. Another key product is IdentiKey. With this product, a credit card customer is given a small token on which a password constantly changes. The password can be used to securely authorize ATM transactions or credit card purchases, including online purchases. Targeted markets are the applications that use fixed passwords as security. The company's top 10 customers account for roughly 37% of its total revenue. The firm currently serves roughly 11,000 companies in over 100 countries, including over 1,700 international financial institutions. In January 2011, VASCO acquired DigiNotar B.V., a Netherlands-based Internet trust services firm. In April 2011, the company acquired Netherlands-based open identity and access management group Alfa & Ariss B.V.

FINANCIALS: **Sales and profits are in thousands of dollars—add 000 to get the full amount. 2011 Note: Financial information for 2011 was not available for all companies at press time.**

2011 Sales: $	2011 Profits: $	**U.S. Stock Ticker: VDSI**
2010 Sales: $107,963	2010 Profits: $12,390	**Int'l Ticker:**
2009 Sales: $101,695	2009 Profits: $12,632	Int'l Exchange:
2008 Sales: $132,977	2008 Profits: $24,291	Employees: 342 Fiscal Year Ends: 12/31
2007 Sales: $119,980	2007 Profits: $20,963	Parent Company:

SALARIES/BENEFITS:

Pension Plan:	ESOP Stock Plan:	Profit Sharing:	Top Exec. Salary: $425,376	Bonus: $225,325
Savings Plan:	Stock Purch. Plan:		Second Exec. Salary: $375,000	Bonus: $169,444

OTHER THOUGHTS:

Apparent Women Officers or Directors:
Hot Spot for Advancement for Women/Minorities:

LOCATIONS: ("Y" = Yes)

West:	Southwest:	Midwest:	Southeast:	Northeast:	International:
		Y		Y	Y

VENTANA MEDICAL SYSTEMS INC

www.ventanamed.com

Industry Group Code: 33911

Management:		**Sales/Marketing:**		**Liberal Arts:**		**Information Systems:**		**Professionals:**		**Technical/Scientific:**	
Mgmt. Trainees:		Mktg. Professionals:	Y	Gen. Writing/Editing:		Info. Management:	Y	Finance/Acct.:	Y	Engineers, Elec.:	
Experienced Mgmt.:	Y	Retail Sales:		Technical Writing:	Y	Software Dev.:	Y	Law:	Y	Engineers, Other:	Y
Int'l Business:	Y	Commercial/Industrial:	Y	Graphic Arts/Photog.:		Hardware Dev.:	Y	HR/Other:	Y	Health/Lab	Y
MBA Graduates:	Y	Sales Trainees:	Y	Music:		Consulting/Other:		Training:	Y	Scientists/Research:	Y
		Advertising Pros.:		Broadcasting:				Health Care:	Y	Petroleum/Chemicals:	
				Other:				Consulting:		Math/Other:	

TYPES OF BUSINESS:

Instrument-Reagent Systems
Discovery Systems
Clinical Systems
Consumable Products

BRANDS/DIVISIONS/AFFILIATES:

Roche Holding Ltd
VIAS
Discovery
BenchMark
NexES
EBAR
BioImagene, Inc.
mtm laboratories AG.

CONTACTS:

Note: Officers with more than one job title may be intentionally listed here more than once.

Mara G. Aspinall, Pres.
Eric Walk, Chief Medical Officer/Sr. VP
Daniel O'Day, COO-Roche Diagnostics

Phone: 520-887-2155 **Fax:** 520-229-6855
Toll-Free: 800-227-2155
Address: 1910 E. Innovation Park Dr., Tucson, AZ 85755 US

GROWTH PLANS/SPECIAL FEATURES:

Ventana Medical Systems, Inc., a subsidiary of Roche Holding Ltd., develops, manufactures and markets tissue-based diagnostic solutions for patients worldwide. The company specializes in medical diagnostic instrument and reagent systems used in automation technology for use in the slide-based diagnosis of cancer and infectious disease. Although focused on products to standardize slide staining and preparation with the aim of speeding the discovery of new drug targets, the firm also offers workflow solutions and patient information management tools. Its products are split into two main categories: instruments and reagents. The company's instruments consist of equipment intended to standardize the preparation and staining of human tissue or cells mounted on a microscope slide, such as the SYMPHONY system, a one-touch slide preparation machine. The company also sells instruments under the VIAS, BenchMark, NexES, EBAR, VANTAGE and Discovery brand names. The company also markets reagents optimized for the automation of diagnostic and drug discovery procedures. Reagent products include monoclonal antibodies and detection systems; blocking reagents, which give excellent color separation and elimination of non-specific staining; and specialty stains. The firm operates subsidiaries in the U.S., Europe, Japan and Australia, and its instruments are installed in 63 companies. The company's customers include hospital-based histology laboratories, independent reference laboratories and the drug discovery laboratories of pharmaceutical and biotechnology companies, government labs and medical research centers. It has 225 worldwide patents and 200 patents pending. In late 2010, the firm acquired BioImagene, Inc., provider of digital pathology workflow and analysis, for roughly $100 million. In July 2011, Ventana Medical acquired mtm laboratories AG.

Employees receive medical, dental, vision, life and accident insurance; short- and long-term disability coverage; an education assistance program; a family travel assistance program; and an employee assistance program.

FINANCIALS:

Sales and profits are in thousands of dollars—add 000 to get the full amount. 2011 Note: Financial information for 2011 was not available for all companies at press time.

2011 Sales: $	2011 Profits: $
2010 Sales: $	2010 Profits: $
2009 Sales: $	2009 Profits: $
2008 Sales: $	2008 Profits: $
2007 Sales: $	2007 Profits: $

U.S. Stock Ticker: Subsidiary
Int'l Ticker:
Int'l Exchange:
Employees: 1,300 Fiscal Year Ends: 12/31
Parent Company: ROCHE HOLDING LTD

SALARIES/BENEFITS:

Pension Plan: Y	ESOP Stock Plan:	Profit Sharing:	Top Exec. Salary: $	Bonus: $
Savings Plan: Y	Stock Purch. Plan:		Second Exec. Salary: $	Bonus: $

OTHER THOUGHTS:

Apparent Women Officers or Directors: 1
Hot Spot for Advancement for Women/Minorities:

LOCATIONS: ("Y" = Yes)

West:	Southwest:	Midwest:	Southeast:	Northeast:	International:
	Y				Y

VERENIUM CORPORATION

www.verenium.com

Industry Group Code: 541712

Management:		Sales/Marketing:		Liberal Arts:		Information Systems:		Professionals:		Technical/Scientific:	
Mgmt. Trainees:		Mktg. Professionals:		Gen. Writing/Editing:		Info. Management:	Y	Finance/Acct.:	Y	Engineers, Elec.:	Y
Experienced Mgmt.:	Y	Retail Sales:		Technical Writing:	Y	Software Dev.:	Y	Law:	Y	Engineers, Other:	Y
Int'l Business:		Commercial/Industrial:	Y	Graphic Arts/Photog.:		Hardware Dev.:		HR/Other:	Y	Health/Lab	Y
MBA Graduates:	Y	Sales Trainees:		Music:		Consulting/Other:		Training:		Scientists/Research:	Y
		Advertising Pros.:		Broadcasting:				Health Care:		Petroleum/Chemicals:	Y
				Other:				Consulting:		Math/Other:	

TYPES OF BUSINESS:

Specialty Enzyme Production
Biofuels Research

BRANDS/DIVISIONS/AFFILIATES:

Deltazym GA L-E5
Cottonase
Fuelzyme-LF
Purifine
Luminase
Phyzyme XP

CONTACTS:

Note: Officers with more than one job title may be intentionally listed here more than once.

James Levine, CEO
Janet Roemer, COO
James Levine, Pres.
Jeffrey G. Black, CFO/Exec. VP
David Weiner, VP-R&D Strategy
Kevin Bracken, VP-Mfg.
Alex Fitzpatrick, General Counsel/Sr. VP/Sec.
Ken Barrett, VP-Bus. Dev. & Strategy
Kelly Lindenboom, VP-Corp. Comm.
David Weiner, VP-Innovation & Partnerships
James Cavanaugh, Chmn.

Phone: 858-431-8500 **Fax:**
Toll-Free:
Address: 4955 Directors Pl., San Diego, CA 92121 US

GROWTH PLANS/SPECIAL FEATURES:

Verenium Corporation is an alternative energy and bioenzymes company. The firm operates in two segments: Specialty Enzymes and a Research and Development business unit that supports the Specialty Enzymes segment. The Specialty Enzymes segment manufactures chemicals for three target markets: alternative fuels, specialty industrial processes and animal health and nutrition. Its commercial enzymes for the biofuels market include Fuelzyme-LF, used to increase the efficiency of corn ethanol production, and Purifine, used to convert vegetable oils to biodiesel and oilseed into edible oils. For the industrial market, Luminase makes pulp more susceptible to bleaching and Cottonase is designed to provide better cleaning of cotton that traditional methods like chemical scouring. For the animal health & nutrition market, the Phzyme enzyme helps phosphorous and other nutrients in animal feed become more digestible. In September 2010, BP Biofuels North America acquired all of Vernium's cellulosic biofuels business. Verenium retains its enzyme business and certain research and development capabilities. Also in September 2010, the firm began marketing Deltazym GA L-E5, an enzyme that saccharifies liquefied starch in the process of fuel ethanol production. In June 2011, Verenium and Novus International Inc., agreed to jointly develop and market new animal nutrition enzyme products.

Employees are offered health insurance and stock options.

FINANCIALS:

Sales and profits are in thousands of dollars—add 000 to get the full amount. 2011 Note: Financial information for 2011 was not available for all companies at press time.

2011 Sales: $	2011 Profits: $	**U.S. Stock Ticker: VRNM**
2010 Sales: $52,073	2010 Profits: $19,933	**Int'l Ticker:**
2009 Sales: $48,819	2009 Profits: $-21,891	Int'l Exchange:
2008 Sales: $69,659	2008 Profits: $-185,542	Employees: 89 Fiscal Year Ends: 12/31
2007 Sales: $46,273	2007 Profits: $-107,585	Parent Company:

SALARIES/BENEFITS:

Pension Plan:	ESOP Stock Plan:	Profit Sharing:	Top Exec. Salary: $495,000	Bonus: $504,900
Savings Plan: Y	Stock Purch. Plan: Y		Second Exec. Salary: $318,077	Bonus: $273,550

OTHER THOUGHTS:

Apparent Women Officers or Directors: 3
Hot Spot for Advancement for Women/Minorities: Y

LOCATIONS: ("Y" = Yes)

West:	Southwest:	Midwest:	Southeast:	Northeast:	International:
Y			Y	Y	

VIASAT INC

www.viasat.com

Industry Group Code: 334220

Management:		Sales/Marketing:		Liberal Arts:		Information Systems:		Professionals:		Technical/Scientific:	
Mgmt. Trainees:		Mktg. Professionals:	Y	Gen. Writing/Editing:	Y	Info. Management:	Y	Finance/Acct.:	Y	Engineers, Elec.:	Y
Experienced Mgmt.:	Y	Retail Sales:		Technical Writing:	Y	Software Dev.:	Y	Law:	Y	Engineers, Other:	Y
Int'l Business:	Y	Commercial/Industrial:	Y	Graphic Arts/Photog.:		Hardware Dev.:	Y	HR/Other:	Y	Health/Lab	
MBA Graduates:	Y	Sales Trainees:	Y	Music:		Consulting/Other:		Training:	Y	Scientists/Research:	
		Advertising Pros.:		Broadcasting:				Health Care:		Petroleum/Chemicals:	
				Other:				Consulting:		Math/Other:	

TYPES OF BUSINESS:

Telecommunications Equipment-Digital Satellite Networking & Wireless Signal Processing

BRANDS/DIVISIONS/AFFILIATES:

SurfBeam
WildBlue Communications, Inc.
SKYLink

CONTACTS: *Note: Officers with more than one job title may be intentionally listed here more than once.*

Mark D. Dankberg, CEO
Richard A. Baldridge, COO
Richard A. Baldridge, Pres.
Ron G. Wangerin, CFO/VP
H. Stephen Estes, VP-Human Resources
Stephan R. Hart, Co-CTO/VP
Gregory D. Monahan, Sr. VP-Admin. & New Facilities Acquisition
Keven K. Lippert, General Counsel/Sec./VP
Kevin R. Hunter, VP-Oper.
Thomas E. Moore, Sr. VP/Pres., WildBlue
Mark J. Miller, Co-CTO/VP
Mark D. Dankberg, Chmn.

Phone: 760-476-2200	**Fax:** 760-929-3941
Toll-Free:	
Address: 6155 El Camino Real, Carlsbad, CA 92009 US	

GROWTH PLANS/SPECIAL FEATURES:

ViaSat, Inc. provides advanced satellite and wireless communications and secure networking systems, products and services. The company operates in three segments: Government Systems, Commercial Networks and Satellite Services. The Government Systems segment encompasses products serving defense customers, including its tactical data link product line; tactical networking and information assurance, enabling the government and military to secure information up to Top Secret levels; and mobile satellite communication systems. Current defense products include a multifunction information distribution system (MIDS); simulation and test equipment for airborne radio systems; and UHF DAMA satellite communications products, such as modems, terminals and network control systems. The Commercial Networks segment includes consumer satellite broadband systems, powered by ViaSat's SurfBeam; antenna systems, which are used for terrestrial and satellite communications; mobile broadband systems, including the design and development of airborne, maritime and ground mobile terminals and systems; enterprise VSAT (Very Small Aperture Terminal) networks; and satellite communications, MMIC (monolithic microwave integrated circuit) and enterprise network technology design and development. The Satellite Services segment, similar to the Commercial Networks segment, offers wholesale and retail broadband services through the WildBlue brand to about 424,000 subscribers; mobile satellite broadband services to airborne- and marine-based customers; and managed broadband wireless networking services. In October 2010, the company acquired the SKYLink airborne broadband system from ARINC, Inc., which allows aircraft in motion to access high speed Internet services.

ViaSat offers its employees medical, dental and vision coverage; life and AD&D insurance; an employee assistance plan; flexible spending accounts; an employee stock purchase plan; tuition reimbursement; wellness benefits; and a 401(k) plan.

FINANCIALS: **Sales and profits are in thousands of dollars—add 000 to get the full amount. 2011 Note: Financial information for 2011 was not available for all companies at press time.**

2011 Sales: $802,206	2011 Profits: $36,115
2010 Sales: $688,080	2010 Profits: $30,839
2009 Sales: $628,179	2009 Profits: $38,331
2008 Sales: $574,650	2008 Profits: $33,513
2007 Sales: $516,566	2007 Profits: $30,166

U.S. Stock Ticker: VSAT
Int'l Ticker:
Int'l Exchange:
Employees: 2,200 Fiscal Year Ends: 3/31
Parent Company:

SALARIES/BENEFITS:

Pension Plan:	ESOP Stock Plan:	Profit Sharing:	Top Exec. Salary: $700,000	Bonus: $800,000
Savings Plan: Y	Stock Purch. Plan: Y		Second Exec. Salary: $530,000	Bonus: $600,000

OTHER THOUGHTS:

Apparent Women Officers or Directors:
Hot Spot for Advancement for Women/Minorities:

LOCATIONS: ("Y" = Yes)

West:	Southwest:	Midwest:	Southeast:	Northeast:	International:
Y					Y

VIBRANT MEDIA INC

www.vibrantmedia.com

Industry Group Code: 541810E

Management:		Sales/Marketing:		Liberal Arts:		Information Systems:		Professionals:		Technical/Scientific:	
Mgmt. Trainees:		Mktg. Professionals:	Y	Gen. Writing/Editing:	Y	Info. Management:	Y	Finance/Acct.:	Y	Engineers, Elec.:	
Experienced Mgmt.:	Y	Retail Sales:		Technical Writing:		Software Dev.:	Y	Law:	Y	Engineers, Other:	
Int'l Business:	Y	Commercial/Industrial:	Y	Graphic Arts/Photog.:	Y	Hardware Dev.:		HR/Other:	Y	Health/Lab	
MBA Graduates:	Y	Sales Trainees:	Y	Music:		Consulting/Other:		Training:	Y	Scientists/Research:	
		Advertising Pros.:	Y	Broadcasting:				Health Care:		Petroleum/Chemicals:	
				Other:	Y			Consulting:		Math/Other:	

TYPES OF BUSINESS:

Online Advertising

BRANDS/DIVISIONS/AFFILIATES:

Vibrant In-Text ADs
IntelliTXT
Vibrant InterestAD
SmartAD
Image Space Media

CONTACTS: *Note: Officers with more than one job title may be intentionally listed here more than once.*

Cella Irvine, CEO
Jeff Babka, COO
Jeff Babka, CFO
Anna Kassoway, Sr. VP-Mktg. & Creative
Kristina Nakanishi, VP-Human Resources
Jason Richman, VP-Prod. Mgmt.
Derrick Horner, General Counsel
Paul Joachim, Sr. VP-Oper.
Derrick Horner, Sr. VP-Corp. Strategy
Stacey Hafers, Sr. VP-Finance
Brian White, Sr. VP-Publisher Solutions
Paul Joachim, Sr. VP/Managing Dir.-Americas
Martin Forbes, Sr. VP/Managing Dir.-Europe

Phone: 646-312-6100 **Fax:** 212-867-4925
Toll-Free:
Address: 565 5th Ave., 15th Fl., New York, NY 10017 US

GROWTH PLANS/SPECIAL FEATURES:

Vibrant Media, Inc. offers video and contextual advertising services. The firm's core offering consists of Vibrant In-Text ADs, which includes Vibrant Video and Vibrant InterestADs. The firm's SmartAD software uses Vibrant's IntelliTXT technology to scan and double-underline web page key words, with customer advertisements appearing when moved over with a cursor. Vibrant Video allows customers to deliver video, movie trailers, TV ads or music videos through the In-Text link, while Vibrant InterestADs allows customers to deliver static images, flash animation, MPU (Message Plus Unit) or animated .gif files. Vibrant In-Text ADs usually provide a link that users may follow to learn more about, or in some cases actually purchase a client's product. Vibrant has a creative department, media account planners and an optimization team to assist customers in designing their In-Text ad, including converting flash to video and choosing key words. After a customer has purchased and installed an In-Text service, Vibrant provides continuous, web-based reports on the campaign's performance. The company also offers Vibrant Related Content, which lists links similar to a user's target destination with the goal of keeping visitors within a client's page. The firm only serves customers with sites receiving over 500,000 page views per month and has strict content standards, refusing to offer In-Text ads for sites containing, promoting or linking directly to gambling, violent content, drugs or pornography, for example. Vibrant Media serves more than 6,500 premium publishers that receive a combined 250 million unique users per month. In January 2012, the firm acquired in-image advertising technology group Image Space Media.

FINANCIALS: **Sales and profits are in thousands of dollars—add 000 to get the full amount. 2011 Note: Financial information for 2011 was not available for all companies at press time.**

2011 Sales: $	2011 Profits: $	**U.S. Stock Ticker: Private**
2010 Sales: $	2010 Profits: $	**Int'l Ticker:**
2009 Sales: $	2009 Profits: $	Int'l Exchange:
2008 Sales: $	2008 Profits: $	Employees: Fiscal Year Ends: 12/31
2007 Sales: $	2007 Profits: $	Parent Company:

SALARIES/BENEFITS:

Pension Plan:	ESOP Stock Plan:	Profit Sharing:	Top Exec. Salary: $	Bonus: $
Savings Plan:	Stock Purch. Plan:		Second Exec. Salary: $	Bonus: $

OTHER THOUGHTS:

Apparent Women Officers or Directors: 4
Hot Spot for Advancement for Women/Minorities: Y

LOCATIONS: ("Y" = Yes)

West:	Southwest:	Midwest:	Southeast:	Northeast:	International:
Y				Y	Y

VIROPHARMA INC

www.viropharma.com

Industry Group Code: 325412

Management:		Sales/Marketing:		Liberal Arts:		Information Systems:		Professionals:		Technical/Scientific:	
Mgmt. Trainees:		Mktg. Professionals:	Y	Gen. Writing/Editing:		Info. Management:	Y	Finance/Acct.:	Y	Engineers, Elec.:	
Experienced Mgmt.:	Y	Retail Sales:		Technical Writing:	Y	Software Dev.:	Y	Law:	Y	Engineers, Other:	
Int'l Business:		Commercial/Industrial:	Y	Graphic Arts/Photog.:		Hardware Dev.:		HR/Other:	Y	Health/Lab	Y
MBA Graduates:	Y	Sales Trainees:	Y	Music:		Consulting/Other:		Training:	Y	Scientists/Research:	Y
		Advertising Pros.:		Broadcasting:				Health Care:	Y	Petroleum/Chemicals:	Y
				Other:				Consulting:		Math/Other:	Y

TYPES OF BUSINESS:

Oral Antibiotics
Hepatitis C Drugs
Infectious Diseases Drugs

BRANDS/DIVISIONS/AFFILIATES:

Cinryze
Vancocin
CINRYZESolutions
Ryze Above

CONTACTS:

Note: Officers with more than one job title may be intentionally listed here more than once.

Vincent J. Milano, CEO
Daniel B. Soland, COO/VP
Vincent J. Milano, Pres.
Charles A Rowland, CFO/VP
Colin Broom, Chief Scientific Officer/VP
J. Peter Wolf, General Counsel/VP/Sec.
Robert C. Fletcher, VP-Bus. Dev. & Project Mgmt.
Richard S. Morris, Controller/Chief Acct. Officer
Thomas F. Doyle, VP-Strategic Initiatives
Vincent J. Milano, Chmn.
Robert G. Pietrusko, VP-Global Regulatory Affairs & Quality

Phone: 610-458-7300 **Fax:** 610-458-7380
Toll-Free: 888-651-0201
Address: 730 Stockton Dr., Exton, PA 19341 US

GROWTH PLANS/SPECIAL FEATURES:

ViroPharma, Inc. is a biopharmaceutical company that develops and commercializes products that address serious infectious diseases, with a focus on products used by physician specialists or in hospital settings. The firm has two marketed products and two development programs. ViroPharma's marketed products include Cinryze and Vancocin. ViroPharma markets and sells Cinryze in the U.S. for routine prophylaxis against angioedema attacks in adolescent and adult patients with hereditary angioedema (HAE). Cinryze is a C1 esterase inhibitor therapy for routine prohylaxis against HAE, also known as C1 inhibitor (C1-INH), a life-threatening genetic disorder. The firm recently obtained expanded rights to commercialize Cinryze and future C1-INH derived products in certain European countries and other territories throughout the world, as well as rights to develop future C1-INH derived products for additional indications. ViroPharma also markets and sells Vancocin HCl capsules in the U.S. Vancocin is an antibiotic that is used to treat pseudomembranous colitis and enterocolitis, including methicillin-resistant strains. ViroPharma's development programs include C1 esterase inhibitor to identify therapeutic uses and potential additional indications and other modes of administration for the treatment of HAE and other C1 mediated diseases; and a non-toxigenic strain of C. difficile (NTCD) for the treatment and prevention of CDI, currently in Phase I. The firm licensed the U.S. and Canadian rights for a further product development candidate, an intranasal formulation of pleconaril, to Merck & Co., Inc. for the treatment of picornavirus infections. In June 2011, ViroPharma was granted permission to commercialize Cinryze in Europe.

The company offers its employees medical and dental benefits; a 401(k) plan; and stock options.

FINANCIALS:

Sales and profits are in thousands of dollars—add 000 to get the full amount. 2011 Note: Financial information for 2011 was not available for all companies at press time.

2011 Sales: $544,374	2011 Profits: $140,659
2010 Sales: $439,012	2010 Profits: $125,608
2009 Sales: $310,449	2009 Profits: $-11,077
2008 Sales: $232,307	2008 Profits: $67,617
2007 Sales: $203,770	2007 Profits: $95,353

U.S. Stock Ticker: VPHM
Int'l Ticker:
Int'l Exchange:
Employees: 232 Fiscal Year Ends: 12/31
Parent Company:

SALARIES/BENEFITS:

Pension Plan:	ESOP Stock Plan:	Profit Sharing:	Top Exec. Salary: $500,000	Bonus: $244,972
Savings Plan: Y	Stock Purch. Plan: Y		Second Exec. Salary: $365,000	Bonus: $193,360

OTHER THOUGHTS:

Apparent Women Officers or Directors:
Hot Spot for Advancement for Women/Minorities:

LOCATIONS: ("Y" = Yes)

West:	Southwest:	Midwest:	Southeast:	Northeast:	International:
				Y	

VOLCOM INC

www.volcom.com

Industry Group Code: 315

Management:		Sales/Marketing:		Liberal Arts:		Information Systems:		Professionals:		Technical/Scientific:	
Mgmt. Trainees:		Mktg. Professionals:	Y	Gen. Writing/Editing:	Y	Info. Management:	Y	Finance/Acct.:	Y	Engineers, Elec.:	
Experienced Mgmt.:	Y	Retail Sales:		Technical Writing:		Software Dev.:		Law:	Y	Engineers, Other:	
Int'l Business:	Y	Commercial/Industrial:	Y	Graphic Arts/Photog.:	Y	Hardware Dev.:		HR/Other:	Y	Health/Lab	
MBA Graduates:	Y	Sales Trainees:	Y	Music:		Consulting/Other:		Training:	Y	Scientists/Research:	
		Advertising Pros.:	Y	Broadcasting:				Health Care:		Petroleum/Chemicals:	
				Other:	Y			Consulting:		Math/Other:	

TYPES OF BUSINESS:

Activewear
Sports-Specific Apparel
Music & Film Production
Sporting Events

BRANDS/DIVISIONS/AFFILIATES:

Volcom
Electric Visual Evolution LLC
Laguna Surf & Sport
Volcom Entertainment
Veeco Productions
Volcom Pipehouse
PPR SA

CONTACTS: *Note: Officers with more than one job title may be intentionally listed here more than once.*

Richard Woolcott, CEO
Jason W. Steris, COO
Jason W. Steris, Pres.
Tom Ruiz, Exec. VP-Sales
David A. Unter, VP-Finance
Ryan N. Immegart, VP-Mktg.
Ethan F. Anderson, Exec. VP/Creative Dir.
Richard R. Woolcott, Chmn.

Phone: 949-646-2175	**Fax:** 949-646-5247
Toll-Free:	
Address: 1740 Monrovia Ave., Costa Mesa, CA 92627 US	

GROWTH PLANS/SPECIAL FEATURES:

Volcom, Inc. is a designer, marketer and distributor of lifestyle clothing, footwear and accessories for young men and women. Its products are sold throughout the U.S. and in over 40 countries worldwide through traditional and online retailers, as well as 20 company-operated Volcom branded retail stores and additional licensed stores worldwide. Volcom products, marketed under the Volcom brand name, are targeted at participants of boardsports, including skateboarding, snowboarding and surfing. Products are organized into six primary categories: mens, girls, boys, footwear, girls swim and snow. Principal products include t-shirts, fleece, swimwear, denim, boardshorts, bottoms, tops, jackets, outerwear, slip-on footwear, music and film. The firm's executive, warehousing and distribution offices are located in Costa Mesa, California. Volcom employs a multi-faceted advertising and promotion strategy through internal marketing and art departments that create its advertisements and manage its various grassroots programs. These include an athlete sponsorship program; Volcom sponsored sporting events; Volcom Entertainment, the firm's own music label; Film, through Veeco Productions; and the Volcom Pipehouse located in front of the renowned Pipeline surf break on the North Shore of Oahu Hawaii, which serves as a headquarters for marketing, research and development for top Volcom-sponsored riders. Additionally, the company owns two Laguna Surf & Sport stores that sell a variety of brands and Electric Visual Evolution LLC, an action sports lifestyle brand. In June 2011, Volcom was acquired by French apparel group PPR SA.

FINANCIALS: **Sales and profits are in thousands of dollars—add 000 to get the full amount. 2011 Note: Financial information for 2011 was not available for all companies at press time.**

2011 Sales: $	2011 Profits: $	**U.S. Stock Ticker: Subsidiary**
2010 Sales: $323,181	2010 Profits: $22,290	**Int'l Ticker:**
2009 Sales: $280,639	2009 Profits: $21,744	Int'l Exchange:
2008 Sales: $334,304	2008 Profits: $21,709	Employees: 543 Fiscal Year Ends: 12/31
2007 Sales: $268,613	2007 Profits: $33,335	Parent Company: PPR SA

SALARIES/BENEFITS:

Pension Plan:	ESOP Stock Plan:	Profit Sharing:	Top Exec. Salary: $392,553	Bonus: $
Savings Plan: Y	Stock Purch. Plan:		Second Exec. Salary: $322,989	Bonus: $

OTHER THOUGHTS:

Apparent Women Officers or Directors:
Hot Spot for Advancement for Women/Minorities:

LOCATIONS: ("Y" = Yes)

West:	Southwest:	Midwest:	Southeast:	Northeast:	International:
Y				Y	Y

VOX INTERNATIONAL CORPORATION

www.voxintl.com

Industry Group Code: 334310

Management:		Sales/Marketing:		Liberal Arts:		Information Systems:		Professionals:		Technical/Scientific:	
Mgmt. Trainees:		Mktg. Professionals:		Gen. Writing/Editing:	Y	Info. Management:	Y	Finance/Acct.:	Y	Engineers, Elec.:	Y
Experienced Mgmt.:	Y	Retail Sales:		Technical Writing:	Y	Software Dev.:	Y	Law:	Y	Engineers, Other:	
Int'l Business:	Y	Commercial/Industrial:		Graphic Arts/Photog.:		Hardware Dev.:	Y	HR/Other:	Y	Health/Lab	
MBA Graduates:	Y	Sales Trainees:		Music:		Consulting/Other:		Training:	Y	Scientists/Research:	
		Advertising Pros.:		Broadcasting:				Health Care:		Petroleum/Chemicals:	
				Other:				Consulting:		Math/Other:	

TYPES OF BUSINESS:

Mobile & Consumer Electronics
Automotive Electronics
Radio Products

BRANDS/DIVISIONS/AFFILIATES:

American Radio Corp.
Audiovox Accessories Corp.
Audiovox Consumer Electronics, Inc.
Audiovox Electronics Corporation
Audiovox German Holdings GmbH
Audiovox Venezuela, C.A.
Entretenimiento Digital Mexico, S. de C.V.
Klipsch Group Inc

CONTACTS: *Note: Officers with more than one job title may be intentionally listed here more than once.*

Patrick Lavelle, CEO
Patrick Lavelle, Pres.
Charles Stoehr, CFO/Sr. VP
Ann Boutcher, Chief Mktg. Officer/VP
Chris L. Johnson, VP/Sec.
Richard A. Maddia, Sr. VP
Thomas C. Malone, Sr. VP
C. David Geise, Sr. VP
Loriann Shelton, Sr. VP
John J. Shalam, Chmn.

Phone: 631-231-7750	**Fax:**
Toll-Free:	
Address: 180 Marcus Blvd., Hauppauge, NY 11788 US	

GROWTH PLANS/SPECIAL FEATURES:

Voxx International Corporation (formerly Audiovox Corporation) designs and markets a diverse line of mobile, accessory and consumer electronics products. The company operates through two segments: electronic products and accessories products. The electronics products segment includes mobile multi-media video products; autosound products; satellite radios; automotive security and remote start systems; automotive power accessories; rear observation and collision avoidance systems; home and portable stereos; camcorders; clock-radios; digital voice recorders; e-readers; digital picture frames; portable DVD players; and home speaker systems. The accessories products segment includes HDTV and Wi-Fi antennas; home electronic accessories; universal TV remotes; wireless headphones; rechargeable battery backups; power supply systems; electronic equipment cleaning products; and set-top boxes. The firm conducts business through 11 wholly-owned subsidiaries: American Radio Corp.; Audiovox Accessories Corp.; Audiovox Consumer Electronics, Inc.; Audiovox Electronics Corporation; Audiovox Canada Limited; Audiovox German Holdings GmbH; Audiovox Venezuela, C.A.; Entretenimiento Digital Mexico; Code Systems, Inc.; Schwaiger GmbH; and Invision Automotive Systems, Inc. The company markets its equipment through a large domestic and international distribution network under the Audiovox brand name, as well as the Acoustic Research, Advent, Ambico, Car Link, Chapman, Code-Alarm, Discwasher, Energizer, Heco, Incaar, Invision, Jensen, Mac Audio, Movies2Go, Oehlbach, Phase Linear, Prestige, Pursuit, RCA, RCA Accessories, Recoton, Road Gear, Schwaiger, Spikemaster and Terk brands and private labels. Voxx is also an original equipment manufacturer (OEM) supplier through several distribution channels. Audiovox's products are sold to power retailers; mass merchants; regional chain stores; specialty and Internet retailers; distributors; new car dealers; vehicle equipment manufacturers; and the U.S. military. In February 2010, Invision Automotive Systems, Inc. acquired Invision Industries, Inc. In March 2011, the firm acquired Klipsch Group, Inc., an audio equipment manufacturer, for $166 million.

FINANCIALS: **Sales and profits are in thousands of dollars—add 000 to get the full amount. 2011 Note: Financial information for 2011 was not available for all companies at press time.**

2011 Sales: $561,672	2011 Profits: $23,031	**U.S. Stock Ticker: VOXX**
2010 Sales: $550,695	2010 Profits: $22,483	**Int'l Ticker:**
2009 Sales: $603,099	2009 Profits: $-71,029	Int'l Exchange:
2008 Sales: $591,355	2008 Profits: $8,465	Employees: 970 Fiscal Year Ends: 2/28
2007 Sales: $456,690	2007 Profits: $2,936	Parent Company:

SALARIES/BENEFITS:

Pension Plan:	ESOP Stock Plan:	Profit Sharing:	Top Exec. Salary: $925,160	Bonus: $
Savings Plan:	Stock Purch. Plan:		Second Exec. Salary: $360,000	Bonus: $

OTHER THOUGHTS:

Apparent Women Officers or Directors: 2
Hot Spot for Advancement for Women/Minorities:

LOCATIONS: ("Y" = Yes)

West:	Southwest:	Midwest:	Southeast:	Northeast:	International:
Y		Y	Y	Y	Y

WABASH NATIONAL CORP

www.wabashnational.com

Industry Group Code: 33611

Management:		Sales/Marketing:		Liberal Arts:		Information Systems:		Professionals:		Technical/Scientific:	
Mgmt. Trainees:		Mktg. Professionals:		Gen. Writing/Editing:	Y	Info. Management:	Y	Finance/Acct.:	Y	Engineers, Elec.:	
Experienced Mgmt.:	Y	Retail Sales:		Technical Writing:	Y	Software Dev.:		Law:	Y	Engineers, Other:	Y
Int'l Business:	Y	Commercial/Industrial:	Y	Graphic Arts/Photog.:	Y	Hardware Dev.:		HR/Other:	Y	Health/Lab	
MBA Graduates:	Y	Sales Trainees:	Y	Music:		Consulting/Other:		Training:		Scientists/Research:	
		Advertising Pros.:		Broadcasting:				Health Care:		Petroleum/Chemicals:	
				Other:				Consulting:		Math/Other:	

TYPES OF BUSINESS:

Trailer Manufacturer
Trailer Dealerships
Repair Parts
Leasing & Financing
Trailer Rental

BRANDS/DIVISIONS/AFFILIATES:

Wabash National Trailer Center
DuraPlate
Benson
RoadRailer
FreightPro
SolarGuard
Eagle
Transcraft Corporation

CONTACTS:

Note: Officers with more than one job title may be intentionally listed here more than once.

Richard J. Giromini, CEO
Richard J. Giromini, Pres.
Mark J. Weber, CFO/Sr. VP
Bruce N. Ewald, Sr. VP-Mktg. & Sales
Timothy J. Monahan, Sr. VP-Human Resources
Rodney P. Ehrich, CTO/Sr. VP
Joe Zachman, Sr. VP-Mfg.
Erin J. Roth, General Counsel/Sr. VP/Corp. Sec.
Martin C. Jischke, Chmn.

Phone: 765-771-5300	**Fax:** 765-771-5474
Toll-Free: 800-937-4784	
Address: 1000 Sagamore Pkwy. S., Lafayette, IN 47905 US	

GROWTH PLANS/SPECIAL FEATURES:

Wabash National Corp. designs, manufactures and markets standard and customized truck trailers and related transportation equipment. This equipment includes dry vans, refrigerated vans, flat trailers, dump trailers, tank trailers and container chassis. Company operations are conducted through two wholly-owned subsidiaries: Transcraft Corporation, which develops and manufactures flatbed and drop deck trailers; and Wabash National Trailer Centers, which markets and sells new and used trailers as well as parts for the industry. The products are distributed through 11 company-owned dealerships, as well as through a network of 112 independent dealers with 185 locations. The firm also sells used trailers from other manufacturers. Wabash supplies trailers to Schneider National, Werner Enterprises, Heartland Express, Swift Transportation, FedEx Corporation, Crete Carrier Corporation, Safeway, U.S. Xpress Enterprises, Knight Transportation and others. The company markets freight trailer brands from Wabash, including the DuraPlate dry van trailer and the RoadRailer bi-modal system, which is able to travel on highways and railways. The firm also offers FreightPro smooth aluminum trailers; Transcraft, Eagle and Benson platform trailers; dump equipment; and SolarGuard refrigerated trailers, which enables customers to achieve lower costs through reduced fuel consumption and reduced operating hours. The firm has an agreement with PODS Enterprises to use the Wabash DuraPlate segment to produce and service PODS mobile storage containers.

FINANCIALS:

Sales and profits are in thousands of dollars—add 000 to get the full amount. 2011 Note: Financial information for 2011 was not available for all companies at press time.

2011 Sales: $1,187,200	2011 Profits: $15,000
2010 Sales: $640,372	2010 Profits: $-167,214
2009 Sales: $337,840	2009 Profits: $-101,765
2008 Sales: $836,213	2008 Profits: $-125,826
2007 Sales: $1,102,544	2007 Profits: $16,285

U.S. Stock Ticker: WNC
Int'l Ticker:
Int'l Exchange:
Employees: 1,800 Fiscal Year Ends: 12/31
Parent Company:

SALARIES/BENEFITS:

Pension Plan:	ESOP Stock Plan:	Profit Sharing:	Top Exec. Salary: $516,150	Bonus: $498,710
Savings Plan:	Stock Purch. Plan:		Second Exec. Salary: $245,587	Bonus: $104,706

OTHER THOUGHTS:

Apparent Women Officers or Directors: 1
Hot Spot for Advancement for Women/Minorities:

LOCATIONS: ("Y" = Yes)

West:	Southwest:	Midwest:	Southeast:	Northeast:	International:
Y	Y	Y	Y	Y	Y

WADDELL & REED FINANCIAL INC

www.waddell.com

Industry Group Code: 523920

Management:		Sales/Marketing:		Liberal Arts:		Information Systems:		Professionals:		Technical/Scientific:	
Mgmt. Trainees:		Mktg. Professionals:	Y	Gen. Writing/Editing:		Info. Management:	Y	Finance/Acct.:	Y	Engineers, Elec.:	
Experienced Mgmt.:	Y	Retail Sales:		Technical Writing:	Y	Software Dev.:		Law:	Y	Engineers, Other:	
Int'l Business:	Y	Commercial/Industrial:		Graphic Arts/Photog.:		Hardware Dev.:		HR/Other:	Y	Health/Lab	
MBA Graduates:	Y	Sales Trainees:		Music:		Consulting/Other:		Training:		Scientists/Research:	
		Advertising Pros.:	Y	Broadcasting:				Health Care:		Petroleum/Chemicals:	
				Other:				Consulting:		Math/Other:	Y

TYPES OF BUSINESS:

Investment Management/Mutual Funds
Life Insurance & Annuities, Distribution
Financial Planning

BRANDS/DIVISIONS/AFFILIATES:

Waddell & Reed Investment Management Co
Ivy Investment Management Co
Legend Advisory Corp
Waddell & Reed Inc
Ivy Funds Distributor Inc
Legend Equities Corp
Advisors Fund

CONTACTS:

Note: Officers with more than one job title may be intentionally listed here more than once.

Henry J. Herrmann, CEO
Michael D. Strohm, COO/Sr. VP
Michael L. Avery, Pres./Portfolio Mgr.
Daniel P. Connealy, CFO/Sr. VP
Thomas W. Butch, Chief Mktg. Officer/Exec. VP
Philip J. Sanders, CIO
John E. Sundeen, Chief Admin. Officer/Sr. VP
Daniel C. Shulte, Chief Legal Officer/Sr. VP
Henry J. Herrmann, Chmn.

Phone: 913-236-2000	**Fax:**
Toll-Free: 888-923-3355	
Address: 6300 Lamar Ave., Overland Park, KS 66202 US	

GROWTH PLANS/SPECIAL FEATURES:

Waddell & Reed Financial, Inc. is an investment management firm with approximately $84 billion in assets under management. It provides investment management operations as well as underwriting and distribution services primarily through registered investment advisory subsidiaries Waddell & Reed Investment Management Company, Ivy Investment Management Company and Legend Advisory Corporation. The firm divides its operations into three distribution channels: the advisors channel, the wholesale channel and the institutional channel. The advisors channel, serving 517,000 mutual fund customers, consists of a sales force of 1,847 financial advisors who sell investment products advised by the company to middle-income and mass affluent individuals, families and businesses. The wholesale channel manages $40.9 billion in assets and focuses on retail fund distribution through brokers and dealers, registered investment advisors and retirement platforms. The institutional channel manages assets for defined benefit pension plans, other investment companies, defined contribution plans, endowments and high net worth clients. 60% of the institutional channel's assets are developed from subadvisory relationships. The firm's underwriting and distribution services are offered through broker/dealers Waddell & Reed, Inc., Ivy Funds Distributor, Inc. and Legend Equities Corporation. The firm is the exclusive underwriter and distributor of 82 open-end mutual fund portfolios, including offerings in the Advisors Funds; Ivy Funds; Ivy Funds VIP; and InvestEd.

FINANCIALS:

Sales and profits are in thousands of dollars—add 000 to get the full amount. 2011 Note: Financial information for 2011 was not available for all companies at press time.

2011 Sales: $	2011 Profits: $
2010 Sales: $1,032,162	2010 Profits: $156,959
2009 Sales: $839,089	2009 Profits: $105,505
2008 Sales: $919,120	2008 Profits: $96,163
2007 Sales: $837,554	2007 Profits: $125,497

U.S. Stock Ticker: WDR
Int'l Ticker:
Int'l Exchange:
Employees: 1,485 Fiscal Year Ends: 12/31
Parent Company:

SALARIES/BENEFITS:

Pension Plan:	ESOP Stock Plan:	Profit Sharing:	Top Exec. Salary: $1,000,000	Bonus: $3,000,000
Savings Plan:	Stock Purch. Plan:		Second Exec. Salary: $650,000	Bonus: $1,500,000

OTHER THOUGHTS:

Apparent Women Officers or Directors: 1
Hot Spot for Advancement for Women/Minorities:

LOCATIONS: ("Y" = Yes)

West:	Southwest:	Midwest:	Southeast:	Northeast:	International:
Y	Y	Y	Y	Y	

WEBEX COMMUNICATIONS INC

www.webex.com

Industry Group Code: 561499

Management:		Sales/Marketing:		Liberal Arts:		Information Systems:		Professionals:		Technical/Scientific:	
Mgmt. Trainees:		Mktg. Professionals:	Y	Gen. Writing/Editing:	Y	Info. Management:	Y	Finance/Acct.:	Y	Engineers, Elec.:	Y
Experienced Mgmt.:	Y	Retail Sales:		Technical Writing:	Y	Software Dev.:	Y	Law:	Y	Engineers, Other:	
Int'l Business:	Y	Commercial/Industrial:	Y	Graphic Arts/Photog.:		Hardware Dev.:		HR/Other:	Y	Health/Lab	
MBA Graduates:	Y	Sales Trainees:	Y	Music:		Consulting/Other:		Training:	Y	Scientists/Research:	
		Advertising Pros.:	Y	Broadcasting:				Health Care:		Petroleum/Chemicals:	
				Other:				Consulting:		Math/Other:	

TYPES OF BUSINESS:

Online Collaboration Services
Online Conferencing Services & Software

BRANDS/DIVISIONS/AFFILIATES:

Cisco Systems Inc
Cisco WebEx Meeting Center
Cisco WebEx Event Center
Cisco WebEx Training Center
Cisco WebEx Remote Support
Cisco WebEx Remote Access
Cisco WebEx System Management

CONTACTS: *Note: Officers with more than one job title may be intentionally listed here more than once.*

Frank Calderoni, CFO/Exec. VP
Joe Schwartz, Dir.-Mktg.
Ismael Hassa, Dir.-WebEx Oper., Cisco

Phone: 408-435-7048	**Fax:** 408-496-4353
Toll-Free: 877-509-3239	
Address: 3979 Freedom Cir., Santa Clara, CA 95054 US	

GROWTH PLANS/SPECIAL FEATURES:

WebEx Communications, Inc., a subsidiary of Cisco Systems, Inc., provides conferencing services that allow users to share presentations, applications, documents and desktops, including video and audio content, online using a standard web browser. The company's flagship product is Cisco WebEx Meeting Center, a multimedia communications service that allows users to make presentations, share applications, update spreadsheets, share desktops, conduct training sessions and record meetings among multiple participants using variable platforms and browsers. Advanced options and other products include Cisco WebEx Event Center, which allows customers to host and manage multimedia events for up to 3,000 participants; Cisco WebEx Training Center, an online classroom that allows presentation sharing, multimedia streaming and live video delivery for remote employees, customers, partners and students; Cisco WebEx Remote Support, which facilitates internal IT support to reduce company downtime; Cisco WebEx Remote Access, for the provision of support services to unattended computers; Cisco WebEx System Management, for remote IT infrastructure control; and additional WebEx Voice and Unified Communication solutions for enterprises. WebEx provides services to customers in the financial services, high-tech, healthcare, pharmaceutical, communications, manufacturing, government and management consulting industries. In August 2011, the firm introduced WebEx 8, a smaller meeting room for $19 a month.

FINANCIALS: **Sales and profits are in thousands of dollars—add 000 to get the full amount. 2011 Note: Financial information for 2011 was not available for all companies at press time.**

2011 Sales: $ | 2011 Profits: $
2010 Sales: $ | 2010 Profits: $
2009 Sales: $ | 2009 Profits: $
2008 Sales: $ | 2008 Profits: $
2007 Sales: $ | 2007 Profits: $

U.S. Stock Ticker: Subsidiary
Int'l Ticker:
Int'l Exchange:
Employees: Fiscal Year Ends: 12/31
Parent Company: CISCO SYSTEMS INC

SALARIES/BENEFITS:

Pension Plan:	ESOP Stock Plan:	Profit Sharing:	Top Exec. Salary: $	Bonus: $
Savings Plan:	Stock Purch. Plan:		Second Exec. Salary: $	Bonus: $

OTHER THOUGHTS:

Apparent Women Officers or Directors:
Hot Spot for Advancement for Women/Minorities:

LOCATIONS: ("Y" = Yes)

West:	Southwest:	Midwest:	Southeast:	Northeast:	International:
Y					

WEBMD HEALTH CORP

www.webmd.com

Industry Group Code: 519130

Management:		Sales/Marketing:		Liberal Arts:		Information Systems:		Professionals:		Technical/Scientific:	
Mgmt. Trainees:		Mktg. Professionals:	Y	Gen. Writing/Editing:	Y	Info. Management:	Y	Finance/Acct.:	Y	Engineers, Elec.:	
Experienced Mgmt.:	Y	Retail Sales:		Technical Writing:	Y	Software Dev.:	Y	Law:	Y	Engineers, Other:	
Int'l Business:	Y	Commercial/Industrial:	Y	Graphic Arts/Photog.:	Y	Hardware Dev.:		HR/Other:	Y	Health/Lab	
MBA Graduates:	Y	Sales Trainees:	Y	Music:		Consulting/Other:		Training:	Y	Scientists/Research:	
		Advertising Pros.:	Y	Broadcasting:				Health Care:		Petroleum/Chemicals:	
				Other:	Y			Consulting:		Math/Other:	

TYPES OF BUSINESS:

Health Care Internet Portals
Content Licensing

BRANDS/DIVISIONS/AFFILIATES:

WebMD Health Network
WebMD Health
RxList.com
Medscape from WebMD
TheHeart.org
MedicineNet.com
eMedicineHealth.com

CONTACTS:

Note: Officers with more than one job title may be intentionally listed here more than once.

Wayne T. Gattinella, CEO
Anthony Vuolo, COO
Wayne T. Gattinella, Pres.
Anthony Vuolo, CFO
William Pence, CTO/Exec. VP
Douglas W. Wamsley, General Counsel/Exec. VP/Corp. Sec.
Kate Hahn, Contact-Media Rel.
Risa Fisher, Contact-Investor Rel.
Gregory A. Mason, Exec. VP-Consumer Svcs.
Steven Zatz, Exec. VP-Professional Svcs.
Martin J. Wygood, Chmn.

Phone: 212-624-3700	**Fax:**
Toll-Free:	
Address: 111 8th Ave., New York, NY 10011 US	

GROWTH PLANS/SPECIAL FEATURES:

WebMD Health Corp. provides health information services to consumers, physicians, healthcare professionals, employers and health plan providers via the Internet. The firm's public online service, WebMD Health Network, offers WebMD Health, the company's primary public portal; and Medscape from WebMD, a public portal for physicians and health care professionals. WebMD Health provides health and wellness articles and features, and decision-support services to help consumers make informed decisions about health care providers, health risks and treatment options. Available information and interactive tools include detailed data on specific diseases or conditions, physician location and individual health care data storage. Medscape from WebMD assists physicians and health care professionals in improving clinical knowledge with original content such as daily news, commentary, conference coverage and continuing medical education. The WebMD Health Network has an approximate monthly average of 83 million unique users, with an aggregate 7 billion page views in 2010. The firm generates revenue from its public offerings primarily through advertising sales and sponsorships. Private portals offered by WebMD enable employees and health plan members to learn about benefits, providers and treatment decisions, customized to a user's health insurance plan. Additional web sites in the WebMD Health Network include MedicineNet.com, eMedicineHealth.com, RxList.com and TheHeart.org. The company also provides personalized telephonic health coaching. Revenue is generated from the private side through content and technology licensed to employers and health plans, either directly or through distributors.

FINANCIALS:

Sales and profits are in thousands of dollars—add 000 to get the full amount. 2011 Note: Financial information for 2011 was not available for all companies at press time.

2011 Sales: $558,800	2011 Profits: $74,600	**U.S. Stock Ticker: WBMD**
2010 Sales: $534,519	2010 Profits: $54,072	**Int'l Ticker:**
2009 Sales: $439,536	2009 Profits: $117,336	Int'l Exchange:
2008 Sales: $373,462	2008 Profits: $560,223	Employees: 1,630 Fiscal Year Ends: 12/31
2007 Sales: $319,232	2007 Profits: $12,585	Parent Company:

SALARIES/BENEFITS:

Pension Plan: Y	ESOP Stock Plan:	Profit Sharing:	Top Exec. Salary: $560,000	Bonus: $403,099
Savings Plan:	Stock Purch. Plan:		Second Exec. Salary: $450,000	Bonus: $376,341

OTHER THOUGHTS:

Apparent Women Officers or Directors: 2
Hot Spot for Advancement for Women/Minorities:

LOCATIONS: ("Y" = Yes)

West:	Southwest:	Midwest:	Southeast:	Northeast:	International:
Y		Y	Y	Y	

WEBMEDIA BRANDS INC

www.webmediabrands.com

Industry Group Code: 519130

Management:		Sales/Marketing:		Liberal Arts:		Information Systems:		Professionals:		Technical/Scientific:	
Mgmt. Trainees:		Mktg. Professionals:	Y	Gen. Writing/Editing:	Y	Info. Management:	Y	Finance/Acct.:	Y	Engineers, Elec.:	
Experienced Mgmt.:	Y	Retail Sales:		Technical Writing:		Software Dev.:	Y	Law:	Y	Engineers, Other:	
Int'l Business:	Y	Commercial/Industrial:	Y	Graphic Arts/Photog.:	Y	Hardware Dev.:		HR/Other:	Y	Health/Lab	
MBA Graduates:	Y	Sales Trainees:	Y	Music:		Consulting/Other:		Training:	Y	Scientists/Research:	
		Advertising Pros.:	Y	Broadcasting:				Health Care:		Petroleum/Chemicals:	
				Other:	Y			Consulting:		Math/Other:	

TYPES OF BUSINESS:

Business & Technology News Portal
Online Image Library
Market Research
Trade Shows

BRANDS/DIVISIONS/AFFILIATES:

MediaBistro.com
SocialTimes
AllFacebook
Graphics.com
AdsoftheWorld.com
FacebookMarketing.de
SemanticOverflow.com
Inside Network Inc

CONTACTS:

Note: Officers with more than one job title may be intentionally listed here more than once.

Alan M. Meckler, CEO
Donald J. O'Neil, CFO/VP
Alan M. Meckler, Chmn.

Phone: 212-389-2000 **Fax:** 866-880-1429
Toll-Free:
Address: 475 Park Ave. S., 4th Floor, New York, NY 10016 US

GROWTH PLANS/SPECIAL FEATURES:

WebMedia Brands, Inc. is a global provider of original information, job boards and events for information technology (IT), business and creative professionals. WebMedia Brands' online business includes MediaBistro.com, a blog network that provides content about major media markets for media professionals. MediaBistro.com is dedicated to anyone who creates or works with content, or who is a professional working in a content/creative industry. This includes editors, writers, producers, graphic designers, book publishers and others in industries such as magazines, television, film, radio, newspapers, book publishing, online media, advertising, public relations and design. MediaBistro.com's blog network includes: SocialTimes and AllFacebook. SocialTimes follows trends and news in the realm of social media and games, as well as viral video and marketing. AllFacebook covers news and stories regarding Facebook as well as its millions of users and the content they generate. The company's other web sites include Graphics.com, AdsoftheWorld.com, BrandsoftheWorld.com, LiquidTreat.com, StepInsideDesign.com, Creativebits.com and GraphicsDesignForum.com. The company also holds trade shows including: the Semantic Technology Conference; Socialize: Monetizing Social Media; SMOC: Social Media Optimizing Conference; Social Gaming Summit & Virtual Goods Summit; and AF Expo and Publishing App Expo. In February 2011, division Mediabistro.com acquired the trade show and assets of the European Semantic Technology Conference from Semantic Technology Institute Int'l of Vienna, Austria. Additionally, Mediabistro.com acquired the assets of the Twittercism.com blog. In March 2011, Mediabistro.com formed a joint venture with pedigital GmbH to launch AllFacebookStats.com. Mediabistro.com also acquired the FacebookMarketing.de blog and SemanticOverflow.com. In May 2011, the firm acquired social media research firm Inside Network Inc.

WebMedia Brands offers its employees flexible spending accounts; dental and medical coverage; paid holidays and personal days; and short and long term disability.

FINANCIALS:

Sales and profits are in thousands of dollars—add 000 to get the full amount. 2011 Note: Financial information for 2011 was not available for all companies at press time.

2011 Sales: $	2011 Profits: $
2010 Sales: $8,987	2010 Profits: $-3,020
2009 Sales: $6,013	2009 Profits: $-26,201
2008 Sales: $8,858	2008 Profits: $-116,681
2007 Sales: $	2007 Profits: $

U.S. Stock Ticker: WEBM
Int'l Ticker:
Int'l Exchange:
Employees: 69 Fiscal Year Ends: 12/31
Parent Company:

SALARIES/BENEFITS:

Pension Plan:	ESOP Stock Plan:	Profit Sharing:	Top Exec. Salary: $294,980	Bonus: $
Savings Plan: Y	Stock Purch. Plan:		Second Exec. Salary: $200,608	Bonus: $

OTHER THOUGHTS:

Apparent Women Officers or Directors:
Hot Spot for Advancement for Women/Minorities:

LOCATIONS: ("Y" = Yes)

West:	Southwest:	Midwest:	Southeast:	Northeast:	International:
				Y	

WEBSENSE INC

www.websense.com

Industry Group Code: 511210E

Management:		Sales/Marketing:		Liberal Arts:		Information Systems:		Professionals:		Technical/Scientific:	
Mgmt. Trainees:		Mktg. Professionals:	Y	Gen. Writing/Editing:		Info. Management:	Y	Finance/Acct.:	Y	Engineers, Elec.:	Y
Experienced Mgmt.:	Y	Retail Sales:		Technical Writing:	Y	Software Dev.:	Y	Law:	Y	Engineers, Other:	
Int'l Business:	Y	Commercial/Industrial:	Y	Graphic Arts/Photog.:		Hardware Dev.:		HR/Other:	Y	Health/Lab	
MBA Graduates:	Y	Sales Trainees:	Y	Music:		Consulting/Other:		Training:	Y	Scientists/Research:	
		Advertising Pros.:	Y	Broadcasting:				Health Care:		Petroleum/Chemicals:	
				Other:				Consulting:		Math/Other:	

TYPES OF BUSINESS:

Software-Employee Internet Management
Network & Internet Security Software

BRANDS/DIVISIONS/AFFILIATES:

Websense Web Security Gateway
Websense Web Filter
Websense Hosted Email Security
Websense Triton
Websense Data Security Suite

CONTACTS:

Note: Officers with more than one job title may be intentionally listed here more than once.

Gene Hodges, CEO
John R. McCormack, Pres.
Michael Newman, Interim CFO
Didier Guibal, Exec. VP-Worldwide Sales
Michael Newman, Chief Admin. Officer
Michael Newman, General Counsel/Sr. VP
Kate Patterson, VP-Investor Rel.
John B. Carrington, Chmn.

Phone: 858-320-8000	**Fax:** 858-458-2950
Toll-Free: 800-723-1166	
Address: 10240 Sorrento Valley Rd., San Diego, CA 92121 US	

GROWTH PLANS/SPECIAL FEATURES:

Websense, Inc. is a leading provider of unified web, data and email content security solutions that are designed to protect data and users from modern cyber-threats, information leaks, legal liability and productivity loss. It organizes its offerings into three categories: web security; e-mail and messaging; and data security products, available as server-based software or hosted (on-demand) solutions. The company's products are designed to provide web, data and e-mail security by preventing employee access to unwanted and dangerous web elements, such as sites that contain inappropriate content or sites that download malicious code; filtering unwanted e-mails out of incoming traffic; filtering viruses and other malicious attachments out of e-mails and instant messages; managing the use of non-web Internet traffic, such as peer-to-peer communications and instant messaging; restricting the unauthorized use and loss of sensitive data, such as customer or employee information; and controlling misuse of computing resources, including the unauthorized download of high-bandwidth content. Some of the company's products include Websense Triton, offering a unified content analysis, a unified platform and unified management capabilities to deploy Web, data and email security solutions in one architecture; Websense Web Filter, which allows employers to analyze, report and manage employee access to the Internet; Websense Web Security Gateway, which secures Internet traffic while enabling web-based applications; the Websense Data Security Suite, which discovers, protects and monitors information on a network; and Websense Hosted E-mail Security, which blocks inbound and outbound e-mail threats. Websense maintains R&D facilities in San Diego and Los Gatos, California; Reading, England; Beijing, China; and Ra'anana, Israel.

FINANCIALS:

Sales and profits are in thousands of dollars—add 000 to get the full amount. 2011 Note: Financial information for 2011 was not available for all companies at press time.

2011 Sales: $364,183 — 2011 Profits: $30,994
2010 Sales: $332,762 — 2010 Profits: $18,652
2009 Sales: $262,907 — 2009 Profits: $-10,697
2008 Sales: $288,274 — 2008 Profits: $-26,779
2007 Sales: $210,307 — 2007 Profits: $-16,481

U.S. Stock Ticker: WBSN
Int'l Ticker:
Int'l Exchange:
Employees: 1,455 Fiscal Year Ends: 12/31
Parent Company:

SALARIES/BENEFITS:

Pension Plan: ESOP Stock Plan: Profit Sharing: Top Exec. Salary: $557,000 Bonus: $273,821
Savings Plan: Stock Purch. Plan: Second Exec. Salary: $395,673 Bonus: $145,885

OTHER THOUGHTS:

Apparent Women Officers or Directors: 2
Hot Spot for Advancement for Women/Minorities:

LOCATIONS: ("Y" = Yes)

West:	Southwest:	Midwest:	Southeast:	Northeast:	International:
Y					Y

WESTAR ENERGY

www.westarenergy.com

Industry Group Code: 2211

Management:		Sales/Marketing:		Liberal Arts:		Information Systems:		Professionals:		Technical/Scientific:	
Mgmt. Trainees:		Mktg. Professionals:	Y	Gen. Writing/Editing:	Y	Info. Management:	Y	Finance/Acct.:	Y	Engineers, Elec.:	Y
Experienced Mgmt.:	Y	Retail Sales:		Technical Writing:		Software Dev.:		Law:	Y	Engineers, Other:	Y
Int'l Business:	Y	Commercial/Industrial:	Y	Graphic Arts/Photog.:		Hardware Dev.:		HR/Other:	Y	Health/Lab	
MBA Graduates:	Y	Sales Trainees:	Y	Music:		Consulting/Other:		Training:	Y	Scientists/Research:	
		Advertising Pros.:		Broadcasting:				Health Care:		Petroleum/Chemicals:	Y
				Other:				Consulting:		Math/Other:	

TYPES OF BUSINESS:

Utilities-Electricity & Natural Gas
Nuclear Power Plants

BRANDS/DIVISIONS/AFFILIATES:

Kansas Gas & Electric Co.
Wolf Creek Generating Station
Wolf Creek Nuclear Operating Corp.

CONTACTS: *Note: Officers with more than one job title may be intentionally listed here more than once.*

Mark A. Ruelle, CEO
Doug Sterbenz, COO/Exec. VP
Mark A. Ruelle, Pres.
Tony Somma, CFO/Sr. VP
Jerl Banning, VP-Human Resources
Larry Irick, General Counsel/VP/Corp. Sec.
Kelly B. Harrison, VP-Transmission Oper.
Greg A. Greenwood, Sr. VP-Strategy
James Ludwig, Exec. VP-Public Affairs & Consumer Svcs.
Bruce Burns, Dir.-Investor Rel.
Tony Somma, Treas.
Leroy P. Wages, VP/Controller
Jeff Beasley, VP-Corp. Compliance & Internal Audit
Greg A. Greenwood, VP-Major Construction Projects
Michael Lennen, VP-Regulatory Affairs
Charles Q. Chandler, IV, Chmn.

Phone: 785-575-6300 **Fax:** 785-575-1796
Toll-Free:
Address: 818 S. Kansas Ave., Topeka, KS 66612 US

GROWTH PLANS/SPECIAL FEATURES:

Westar Energy is an electric utility providing electric generation, transmission and distribution services to approximately 687,000 customers in central and northeastern Kansas. This area includes the cities of Topeka, Lawrence, Manhattan, Salina and Hutchinson. Wholly-owned subsidiary Kansas Gas & Electric Co. (KGE) provides the same services for the south-central and southeastern Kansas areas, including the Wichita metropolitan area. Both Westar Energy and KGE conduct business under the Westar Energy name. Westar also supplies wholesale electric energy to electric distribution systems in 55 Kansas cities and four rural electric cooperatives and has contracts for the sale, purchase or exchange of wholesale electricity with other utilities. Along with utility supplies, KGE owns a 47% interest in the Wolf Creek Generating Station, a nuclear power plant located near Burlington, Kansas, and a 47% interest in Wolf Creek Nuclear Operating Corp., the operating company for the generating station. Westar owns 92% interest in three coal-fired units at Jeffrey Energy Center. Approximately 51% of the company's total energy capacity (6,756 megawatts) comes from coal; 41% from natural gas or oil; 8% from nuclear energy; and less than 1% from wind power. Westar also provides energy generating capacity to other companies. The firm has two wind farms at Jeffrey Energy Center in Kansas. In December 2010, Westar Energy agreed to purchase a combined 369 megawatts of wind energy from two wind development groups.

The company offers its employees medical and dental insurance; flexible spending accounts; life and disability insurance; a retirement plan; a 401(k) plan; tuition reimbursement; and an employee assistance program.

FINANCIALS: **Sales and profits are in thousands of dollars—add 000 to get the full amount. 2011 Note: Financial information for 2011 was not available for all companies at press time.**

2011 Sales: $2,170,991 — 2011 Profits: $230,239
2010 Sales: $2,056,171 — 2010 Profits: $202,926
2009 Sales: $1,858,231 — 2009 Profits: $175,075
2008 Sales: $1,838,996 — 2008 Profits: $177,170
2007 Sales: $1,726,834 — 2007 Profits: $167,384

U.S. Stock Ticker: WR
Int'l Ticker:
Int'l Exchange:
Employees: 2,416 Fiscal Year Ends: 12/31
Parent Company:

SALARIES/BENEFITS:

Pension Plan: Y | ESOP Stock Plan: | Profit Sharing: | Top Exec. Salary: $655,000 | Bonus: $
Savings Plan: Y | Stock Purch. Plan: | | Second Exec. Salary: $451,667 | Bonus: $

OTHER THOUGHTS:

Apparent Women Officers or Directors: 4
Hot Spot for Advancement for Women/Minorities: Y

LOCATIONS: ("Y" = Yes)

West:	Southwest:	Midwest:	Southeast:	Northeast:	International:
	Y	Y			Y

WGL HOLDINGS INC

www.wglholdings.com

Industry Group Code: 221

Management:		Sales/Marketing:		Liberal Arts:		Information Systems:		Professionals:		Technical/Scientific:	
Mgmt. Trainees:		Mktg. Professionals:	Y	Gen. Writing/Editing:	Y	Info. Management:	Y	Finance/Acct.:	Y	Engineers, Elec.:	Y
Experienced Mgmt.:	Y	Retail Sales:		Technical Writing:		Software Dev.:		Law:	Y	Engineers, Other:	Y
Int'l Business:		Commercial/Industrial:	Y	Graphic Arts/Photog.:		Hardware Dev.:		HR/Other:	Y	Health/Lab	
MBA Graduates:	Y	Sales Trainees:		Music:		Consulting/Other:		Training:	Y	Scientists/Research:	
		Advertising Pros.:		Broadcasting:				Health Care:		Petroleum/Chemicals:	Y
				Other:				Consulting:		Math/Other:	

TYPES OF BUSINESS:

Natural Gas Utility
Energy Marketing
Residential & Light Commercial Services
Energy Systems Design & Engineering
Energy Systems Upgrading
Renewable Energy Services

BRANDS/DIVISIONS/AFFILIATES:

Washington Gas Light Co.
Hampshire Gas Co.
Crab Run Gas Co.
Washington Gas Resources Corp.
Washington Gas Energy Services, Inc.
Washington Gas Energy Systems, Inc.
Washington Gas Credit Corp.

CONTACTS: *Note: Officers with more than one job title may be intentionally listed here more than once.*

Terry McCallister, CEO
Adrian P. Chapman, COO
Adrian P. Chapman, Pres.
Vincent L. Ammann, Jr., CFO/VP
Leslie T. Thornton, General Counsel/VP
Gautam Chandra, VP-Bus. Dev., Strategy & Bus. Process Outsourcing
Douglas Bonawitz, Head-Investor Rel.
Anthony Nee, Treas.
William R. Ford, Controller
Arden T. Phillips, Sec./Corp. Governance Officer
Terry McCallister, Chmn.

Phone: 703-750-2000	**Fax:**
Toll-Free:	
Address: 101 Constitution Ave. N.W., Washington, DC 20080 US	

GROWTH PLANS/SPECIAL FEATURES:

WGL Holdings, Inc. is a public utility holding company that, through its subsidiaries, sells and delivers natural gas and provides a variety of energy-related products and services to customers primarily in Washington, D.C. and the surrounding metropolitan areas in Maryland and Virginia. The firm operates in three business segments: regulated utility; retail energy marketing; and design-build energy systems, through subsidiaries Washington Gas Light Co.; Washington Gas Resources Corp.; Hampshire Gas Co.; and Crab Run Gas Co. Washington Gas is a regulated public utility that delivers and sells natural gas to more than 1 million customers in Washington, D.C. and the surrounding region. Washington Gas Resources owns most of the company's unregulated subsidiaries, including Washington Gas Energy Services, Inc. (WGES); Washington Gas Energy Systems, Inc. (WGE Systems); and Washington Gas Credit Corp. WGES is engaged solely in the sale of natural gas and electricity to residential, commercial and industrial customers; it does not own or operate any natural gas or electric generation, production, transmission or distribution assets. It serves approximately 350,000 customers in Maryland, Virginia, Delaware, Washington D.C. and Pennsylvania. WGE Systems is a provider of design-build energy efficient and sustainable solutions to government and commercial clients. It focuses on upgrading the mechanical, electrical, water and energy-related systems of large government and commercial facilities in Maryland, Virginia and Washington, D.C. Hampshire Gas is a regulated utility that operates underground natural gas storage facilities, including pipeline delivery facilities, in West Virginia. Crab Run is an exploration and production company.

FINANCIALS: **Sales and profits are in thousands of dollars—add 000 to get the full amount. 2011 Note: Financial information for 2011 was not available for all companies at press time.**

2011 Sales: $2,751,501	2011 Profits: $118,370	**U.S. Stock Ticker: WGL**
2010 Sales: $2,708,876	2010 Profits: $111,205	**Int'l Ticker:**
2009 Sales: $2,706,856	2009 Profits: $120,373	Int'l Exchange:
2008 Sales: $2,628,194	2008 Profits: $116,523	Employees: 1,384 Fiscal Year Ends: 9/30
2007 Sales: $2,646,008	2007 Profits: $107,900	Parent Company:

SALARIES/BENEFITS:

Pension Plan:	ESOP Stock Plan:	Profit Sharing:	Top Exec. Salary: $620,000	Bonus: $572,880
Savings Plan: Y	Stock Purch. Plan:		Second Exec. Salary: $405,000	Bonus: $314,685

OTHER THOUGHTS:

Apparent Women Officers or Directors: 4
Hot Spot for Advancement for Women/Minorities: Y

LOCATIONS: ("Y" = Yes)

West:	Southwest:	Midwest:	Southeast:	Northeast:	International:
				Y	

WHITEWAVE FOODS COMPANY

www.whitewave.com

Industry Group Code: 3115

Management:		**Sales/Marketing:**		**Liberal Arts:**		**Information Systems:**		**Professionals:**		**Technical/Scientific:**	
Mgmt. Trainees:		Mktg. Professionals:	Y	Gen. Writing/Editing:	Y	Info. Management:	Y	Finance/Acct.:	Y	Engineers, Elec.:	
Experienced Mgmt.:	Y	Retail Sales:		Technical Writing:		Software Dev.:		Law:	Y	Engineers, Other:	Y
Int'l Business:		Commercial/Industrial:	Y	Graphic Arts/Photog.:		Hardware Dev.:		HR/Other:	Y	Health/Lab	
MBA Graduates:	Y	Sales Trainees:	Y	Music:		Consulting/Other:		Training:	Y	Scientists/Research:	
		Advertising Pros.:	Y	Broadcasting:				Health Care:		Petroleum/Chemicals:	
				Other:	Y			Consulting:		Math/Other:	

TYPES OF BUSINESS:

Soymilk & Soy-Based Products
Dairy Products

BRANDS/DIVISIONS/AFFILIATES:

Dean Foods Company
Silk
International Delight
Land O' Lakes
Horizon Organic
Horizon Organic Producer Education

CONTACTS: *Note: Officers with more than one job title may be intentionally listed here more than once.*

Blaine McPeak, Pres.
Kelly Haecker, CFO
Doug Behrens, Chief Customer Officer/Sr. VP-Sales
Thomas N. Zanetich, Sr. VP-Human Resources
Roger Theodoredis, General Counsel/Sr. VP
Jim Peacock, VP-Oper.
Jason Vieth, VP-Bus. Dev. & Corp. Strategy
Jarod Ballentine, Contact-Media Rel.
Kelly Shea, VP-Industry Rel. & Organic Stewardship
Mike Keown, Pres., Indulgent Brands
Mike Ferry, Pres., Horizon
Craig Shiesley, Gen. Mgr.-Silk Soymilk

Phone: 303-635-4000	**Fax:**
Toll-Free:	
Address: 12002 Airport Way, Broomfield, CO 80021 US	

GROWTH PLANS/SPECIAL FEATURES:

WhiteWave Foods Company, a division of Dean Foods Co., manufactures and sells soy-based products and dairy products throughout the U.S. The company's brands include Silk, a line of soymilks, almondmilks, soy yogurts and soy creamers; Horizon Organic, a certified organic brand that produces milk, yogurt, cheese, cream, ice cream, sour cream, cream cheese, eggs, cottage cheese and butter; International Delight, which produces flavored non-dairy creamers; and Land O' Lakes, producing butter, margarine and spreads, eggs, cheese, half and half, whipping cream, seasonings and hot chocolate and cappuccino mixes. All of WhiteWave's soy products are made from certified organic soybeans and are certified Kosher. Silk, Horizon, International Delights and the company's headquarters use renewable wind-powered energy sources in their production and supply chain operations. Silk soymilk is produced with non-genetically modified soy sourced in the U.S. Horizon works with more than 600 family farmers in the U.S., who produce most of the milk the company sells. The remaining milk is produced at company-owned farms in Maryland and Idaho. The firm maintains the Horizon Organic Producer Education (HOPE) program, a sponsorship program for farmers transitioning to organic farming practices. WhiteWave's web site provides information on its products and ingredients, as well as organic certification requirements and issues, green power news, soy-based recipes and cooking tips. In 2011, WhiteWave converted it Organic Cow brand to Horizon; released new product Horizon Fat-Free Milk Plus DHA Omega-3; and released Silk Pure Coconut coconut milk.

FINANCIALS: **Sales and profits are in thousands of dollars—add 000 to get the full amount. 2011 Note: Financial information for 2011 was not available for all companies at press time.**

2011 Sales: $	2011 Profits: $	**U.S. Stock Ticker: Subsidiary**
2010 Sales: $	2010 Profits: $	**Int'l Ticker:**
2009 Sales: $	2009 Profits: $	Int'l Exchange:
2008 Sales: $	2008 Profits: $	Employees: Fiscal Year Ends: 12/31
2007 Sales: $	2007 Profits: $	Parent Company: DEAN FOODS CO

SALARIES/BENEFITS:

Pension Plan:	ESOP Stock Plan:	Profit Sharing:	Top Exec. Salary: $	Bonus: $
Savings Plan:	Stock Purch. Plan:		Second Exec. Salary: $	Bonus: $

OTHER THOUGHTS:

Apparent Women Officers or Directors: 1
Hot Spot for Advancement for Women/Minorities:

LOCATIONS: ("Y" = Yes)

West:	Southwest:	Midwest:	Southeast:	Northeast:	International:
Y	Y		Y	Y	

WIKIMEDIA FOUNDATION

www.wikimediafoundation.org

Industry Group Code: 519130

Management:		Sales/Marketing:		Liberal Arts:		Information Systems:		Professionals:		Technical/Scientific:	
Mgmt. Trainees:		Mktg. Professionals:		Gen. Writing/Editing:	Y	Info. Management:	Y	Finance/Acct.:	Y	Engineers, Elec.:	
Experienced Mgmt.:	Y	Retail Sales:		Technical Writing:	Y	Software Dev.:	Y	Law:	Y	Engineers, Other:	
Int'l Business:	Y	Commercial/Industrial:		Graphic Arts/Photog.:		Hardware Dev.:		HR/Other:	Y	Health/Lab	
MBA Graduates:	Y	Sales Trainees:		Music:		Consulting/Other:		Training:		Scientists/Research:	
		Advertising Pros.:		Broadcasting:				Health Care:		Petroleum/Chemicals:	
				Other:	Y			Consulting:		Math/Other:	

TYPES OF BUSINESS:

Online Dictionary
Online Encyclopedia
Online Educational Content

BRANDS/DIVISIONS/AFFILIATES:

Wikipedia
Wikiversity
Wikibooks
Wiktionary
Wikisource
Wikiquote
Wikinews
Mediawiki

CONTACTS: *Note: Officers with more than one job title may be intentionally listed here more than once.*

Sue Gardner, Exec. Dir.
Garfield Byrd, CFO
Gayle Karen Young, Chief Talent & Culture Officer
Mani Pande, Head-Global Dev. Research
Danese Cooper, CTO
Rob Lanphier, Dir.-Platform Eng.
Garfield Byrd, Chief Admin. Officer
Geoff Brigham, General Counsel
Kul Wadhwa, Head-Bus. Dev. & Mobile
Zack Exley, Chief Community Officer
Jay Walsh, Head-Comm.
Tony Le, Controller
Barry Newstead, Chief Global Dev. Officer
Frank Schulenburg, Head-Public Outreach
Philippe Beaudette, Head-Reader Rel.
Erik Moller, Deputy Dir.
Ting Chen, Chmn.

Phone: 415-839-6885 **Fax:** 415-882-0495
Toll-Free:
Address: 149 New Montgomery St., 3rd Fl., San Francisco, CA 94105 US

GROWTH PLANS/SPECIAL FEATURES:

Wikimedia Foundation is a non-profit charitable organization that operates Wikipedia, a free online encyclopedia that contains over 20 million articles and is offered in more than 270 languages. Wikipedia receives over 477 million unique visitors each month. The foundation also administers a number of other resources, including Wikiversity, a source for tutorials and learning development; Wikibooks, a source for free content textbooks; Wiktionary, an online dictionary; Wikisource, a collection of published texts; Wikiquote, a collection of quotations; Wikinews, a source for news entries written as in the style of news stories; Wikispecies, a comprehensive catalog of species aimed at scientists; Mediawiki, a software application engine that manages Wiki content; and Wikimedia Commons, a collection of images and other media. Article contribution and editing of Wiki content is open to anyone, from anonymous volunteers to highly specialized professionals. The aim of the foundation is to foster the collection and development of educational content by people all over the world, and to provide a free and public domain for the issuing of information. Because Wikipedia owns all of the servers that run each project, the sites feature no advertisements. Wikimedia is run by a staff with the help of numerous volunteers either contributing content, participating through committees or acting as interns. The foundation relies heavily on donations from individuals, but also receives money from grants, gifts of servers and fundraising. Wikimedia has chapters in 38 countries that support the aims of Wikimedia but do not share control of Wikimedia sites.

FINANCIALS: **Sales and profits are in thousands of dollars—add 000 to get the full amount. 2011 Note: Financial information for 2011 was not available for all companies at press time.**

2011 Sales: $24,785 — 2011 Profits: $
2010 Sales: $16,578 — 2010 Profits: $
2009 Sales: $8,658 — 2009 Profits: $
2008 Sales: $5,033 — 2008 Profits: $
2007 Sales: $2,734 — 2007 Profits: $

U.S. Stock Ticker: Nonprofit
Int'l Ticker:
Int'l Exchange:
Employees: 80 Fiscal Year Ends: 6/30
Parent Company:

SALARIES/BENEFITS:

Pension Plan: ESOP Stock Plan: Profit Sharing: Top Exec. Salary: $ Bonus: $
Savings Plan: Stock Purch. Plan: Second Exec. Salary: $ Bonus: $

OTHER THOUGHTS:

Apparent Women Officers or Directors: 12
Hot Spot for Advancement for Women/Minorities: Y

LOCATIONS: ("Y" = Yes)

West:	Southwest:	Midwest:	Southeast:	Northeast:	International:
Y				Y	Y

WIND RIVER SYSTEMS INC

www.windriver.com

Industry Group Code: 511210I

Management:		Sales/Marketing:		Liberal Arts:		Information Systems:		Professionals:		Technical/Scientific:	
Mgmt. Trainees:		Mktg. Professionals:	Y	Gen. Writing/Editing:		Info. Management:	Y	Finance/Acct.:	Y	Engineers, Elec.:	Y
Experienced Mgmt.:	Y	Retail Sales:		Technical Writing:	Y	Software Dev.:	Y	Law:	Y	Engineers, Other:	
Int'l Business:	Y	Commercial/Industrial:	Y	Graphic Arts/Photog.:		Hardware Dev.:		HR/Other:	Y	Health/Lab	
MBA Graduates:	Y	Sales Trainees:	Y	Music:		Consulting/Other:		Training:	Y	Scientists/Research:	
		Advertising Pros.:		Broadcasting:				Health Care:		Petroleum/Chemicals:	
				Other:				Consulting:		Math/Other:	

TYPES OF BUSINESS:

Computer Software-Embedded Systems
Consulting Services
Operating Systems
Device Software Optimization

BRANDS/DIVISIONS/AFFILIATES:

Intel Corp.
Wind River Workbench
VxWorks
Wind River Simic 4.6
Wind River Linux Secure

CONTACTS: *Note: Officers with more than one job title may be intentionally listed here more than once.*

Barry Mainz, COO
Ken Klein, Pres.
Jim Douglas, Sr. VP-Mktg.
Jeff Loehr, Sr. VP-Human Resources
Tomas Evensen, CTO/Gen. Mgr.-Common Tech. Prod. Div.
Scot Morrison, Sr. VP-Prod.
Vincent Rerolle, Chief Strategy Officer
Tomas Evensen, VP/Gen. Mgr.-Wind River Tools
Amit Ronen, VP/Gen. Mgr.-Device Mgmt. Prod. Div.
Roger Williams, VP-Bus. Dev. & Alliances
Michael Krutz, VP-Worldwide Solutions & Svcs.

Phone: 510-748-4100 **Fax:** 510-749-2010
Toll-Free: 800-545-9463
Address: 500 Wind River Way, Alameda, CA 94501 US

GROWTH PLANS/SPECIAL FEATURES:

Wind River Systems, Inc., a wholly-owned subsidiary of Intel Corp., is a leader in device software optimization (DSO). The firm develops, markets and sells operating systems, middleware and software development tools for embedded systems to be used in a diverse range of products, including set-top boxes; automobile braking and navigation systems; mobile handsets; Internet routers; avionics control panels; and coronary pacemakers. Because the company's solutions are hardware-agnostic, they may be deployed on several architectures, including Intel, ARM, PowerPC, Freescale, MIPS and others. Wind River offers five primary services: VxWorks, which consists of the firm's proprietary VxWorks real-time operating system and related products; Linux, which comprises Wind River's open-source-based, commercial-grade Linux operating systems and related products; Windriver Workbench, an Eclipse-based software development suite, which allows customers to manage the design, development, debugging and testing of their device software systems; Industry solutions, which offers solutions to the consumer electronics, automotive, aerospace/defense, network infrastructure and industrial markets; and on-chip debugging tools, which simplify the hardware development process and integrate firmware, hardware and software debugging. Wind River technology is deployed in more than 500 million devices worldwide. The company offers solutions to the aerospace and defense, automotive, consumer, industrial and network equipment industries. In May 2011, the company introduced Wind River Simics 4.6, a new electronic systems simulator; and Wind River Linux Secure, a new security solution.

FINANCIALS: **Sales and profits are in thousands of dollars—add 000 to get the full amount. 2011 Note: Financial information for 2011 was not available for all companies at press time.**

2011 Sales: $	2011 Profits: $	**U.S. Stock Ticker: Subsidiary**
2010 Sales: $	2010 Profits: $	**Int'l Ticker:**
2009 Sales: $	2009 Profits: $	Int'l Exchange:
2008 Sales: $	2008 Profits: $	Employees: Fiscal Year Ends: 1/31
2007 Sales: $	2007 Profits: $	Parent Company: INTEL CORP

SALARIES/BENEFITS:

Pension Plan:	ESOP Stock Plan:	Profit Sharing:	Top Exec. Salary: $650,000	Bonus: $280,000
Savings Plan:	Stock Purch. Plan:		Second Exec. Salary: $350,000	Bonus: $98,000

OTHER THOUGHTS:

Apparent Women Officers or Directors:
Hot Spot for Advancement for Women/Minorities:

LOCATIONS: ("Y" = Yes)

West:	Southwest:	Midwest:	Southeast:	Northeast:	International:
Y	Y	Y	Y	Y	Y

WMS INDUSTRIES INC

www.wms.com

Industry Group Code: 329999

Management:		Sales/Marketing:		Liberal Arts:		Information Systems:		Professionals:		Technical/Scientific:	
Mgmt. Trainees:		Mktg. Professionals:	Y	Gen. Writing/Editing:		Info. Management:	Y	Finance/Acct.:	Y	Engineers, Elec.:	Y
Experienced Mgmt.:	Y	Retail Sales:		Technical Writing:	Y	Software Dev.:	Y	Law:	Y	Engineers, Other:	
Int'l Business:	Y	Commercial/Industrial:	Y	Graphic Arts/Photog.:	Y	Hardware Dev.:	Y	HR/Other:	Y	Health/Lab	
MBA Graduates:	Y	Sales Trainees:	Y	Music:	Y	Consulting/Other:		Training:		Scientists/Research:	
		Advertising Pros.:	Y	Broadcasting:				Health Care:		Petroleum/Chemicals:	
				Other:	Y			Consulting:		Math/Other:	

TYPES OF BUSINESS:

Gaming Machines
Video Lottery Terminals
Game Manufacturing

BRANDS/DIVISIONS/AFFILIATES:

CONTACTS:
Note: Officers with more than one job title may be intentionally listed here more than once.

Brian R. Gamache, CEO
Kenneth Lochiatto, COO/Exec. VP
Orrin J. Edidin, Pres.
Scott D. Schweinfurth, CFO/Exec. VP
Amy Lipton, VP-Mktg.
Larry J. Pacey, Chief Innovation Officer/Exec. VP-Global Prod.
Kathleen J. McJohn, General Counsel/VP/Sec.
Scott D. Schweinfurth, Treas.
John P. McHicholas, Jr., Chief Acct. Officer/Controller/VP
Brian R. Gamache, Chmn.

Phone: 847-785-3000 **Fax:** 847-785-3058
Toll-Free:
Address: 800 S. Northpoint Blvd., Waukegan, IL 60085 US

GROWTH PLANS/SPECIAL FEATURES:

WMS Industries, Inc. designs, manufactures and distributes video & reel-spinning gaming machines and video lottery terminals (VLTs). The company also derives revenue from the sale of spare parts, conversion kits and amusement-with-prize (AWP) gaming machines, as well as from licensing its gaming themes and other intellectual property. The company's game library includes licensed brands such as Monopoly, Battleship, The Wizard of Oz and The Lord of the Rings. The firm utilizes its proprietary Player Driven Innovation approach in development of new games and products. WMS typically designs its games with secondary bonus rounds that allow players the opportunity to win additional bonuses without additional wagering. The firm's Wide-Area Progressive (WAP) technology games allow players to compete amongst multiple casinos, whereas the Local-Area Progressive (LAP) technology feature joins games within a single location. The company offers video gaming machines, mechanical reel gaming machines and video poker gaming machines. In 2011, video gaming machines generated approximately 64.8% of the firm's product sales, mechanical reel gaming machines generated 17.6%, conversion kits generated 6.3% and used gaming machines generated 7.6%. WMS operates its primary manufacturing facility in the U.S., with additional development and distribution offices located in the U.K., Australia, Canada, India, Mexico, Spain, Argentina, South Africa and China. The company's gaming machines are installed in all of the major regulated gaming jurisdictions in the U.S. and it is authorized to conduct business in over 140 international gaming jurisdictions. In June 2011, the firm sold the Orion Gaming manufacturing facility. In July 2011, WMS sold subsidiary Systems in Progress GmbH (SiP).

FINANCIALS:
Sales and profits are in thousands of dollars—add 000 to get the full amount. 2011 Note: Financial information for 2011 was not available for all companies at press time.

2011 Sales: $783,300 | 2011 Profits: $81,000
2010 Sales: $765,100 | 2010 Profits: $112,900
2009 Sales: $706,400 | 2009 Profits: $92,200
2008 Sales: $650,100 | 2008 Profits: $67,500
2007 Sales: $539,800 | 2007 Profits: $48,900

U.S. Stock Ticker: WMS
Int'l Ticker:
Int'l Exchange:
Employees: 1,880 Fiscal Year Ends: 6/30
Parent Company:

SALARIES/BENEFITS:

Pension Plan: | ESOP Stock Plan: | Profit Sharing: | Top Exec. Salary: $945,790 | Bonus: $
Savings Plan: Y | Stock Purch. Plan: Y | | Second Exec. Salary: $636,883 | Bonus: $

OTHER THOUGHTS:

Apparent Women Officers or Directors: 2
Hot Spot for Advancement for Women/Minorities: Y

LOCATIONS: ("Y" = Yes)

West:	Southwest:	Midwest:	Southeast:	Northeast:	International:
		Y			Y

WRIGHT MEDICAL GROUP INC

www.wmt.com

Industry Group Code: 33911

Management:		**Sales/Marketing:**		**Liberal Arts:**		**Information Systems:**		**Professionals:**		**Technical/Scientific:**	
Mgmt. Trainees:		Mktg. Professionals:	Y	Gen. Writing/Editing:		Info. Management:	Y	Finance/Acct.:	Y	Engineers, Elec.:	
Experienced Mgmt.:	Y	Retail Sales:		Technical Writing:	Y	Software Dev.:	Y	Law:	Y	Engineers, Other:	Y
Int'l Business:	Y	Commercial/Industrial:	Y	Graphic Arts/Photog.:		Hardware Dev.:		HR/Other:	Y	Health/Lab	Y
MBA Graduates:	Y	Sales Trainees:	Y	Music:		Consulting/Other:		Training:	Y	Scientists/Research:	Y
		Advertising Pros.:		Broadcasting:				Health Care:	Y	Petroleum/Chemicals:	
				Other:				Consulting:		Math/Other:	

TYPES OF BUSINESS:

Orthopedic Implants
Reconstructive Joint Devices
Biologics Materials

BRANDS/DIVISIONS/AFFILIATES:

Wright Medical Technology, Inc.
Wright Medical Autralia Pty, Ltd
EZ Frame
A-CLASS
CHARLOTTE
ADVANCE
XPANSION
GRAFTJACKET

CONTACTS: *Note: Officers with more than one job title may be intentionally listed here more than once.*

David D. Stevens, Interim CEO
Lance A. Berry, CFO/Sr. VP
John T. Treace, Sr. VP-Global Mktg. & U.S. Sales
Edward A. Steiger, Sr. VP-Human Resources
Frank S. Bono, CTO/Sr. VP
Kyle M. Joines, VP-Mfg.
Raymond C. Kills, General Counsel/VP/Corp. Sec.
William L. Griffin, Sr. VP-Global Oper.
Timothy E. Davis, Jr., Sr. VP-Bus. Dev.
Joyce B. Jones, Treas./VP
Max K. Mortensen, VP-Quality, Clinical & Regulatory Affairs
Rhonda L. Fellows, Sr. VP-Gov't Affairs & Reimbursement
Karen L. Harris-Coleman, Sr. VP-Sales & Mktg, Japan, Latin America, Pacific
Lisa L. Michael, VP/Chief Compliance Officer
David D. Stevens, Chmn.
Cary P. Hagan, Sr. VP-Comm. Oper., EMEA
William J. Flannery, VP-Logistics & Materials

Phone: 901-867-9971 **Fax:** 901-867-9534
Toll-Free: 800-238-7117
Address: 5677 Airline Rd., Arlington, TN 38002 US

GROWTH PLANS/SPECIAL FEATURES:

Wright Medical Group, Inc., primarily through its Wright Medical Technology, Inc. subsidiary, is a global orthopedic medical device company that specializes in the design, manufacture and marketing of reconstructive joint devices and biologics products. Wright offers products in four primary market sectors: knee reconstruction, hip reconstruction, extremity hardware and biologics. The company's knee reconstruction portfolio includes total knee reconstruction products, revision replacement implants and limb preservation products. The ADVANCE knee system made with BIOFOAM material is its primary knee product line offering, featuring the ADVANCE medial pivot knee, designed to approximate the movement and function of a healthy knee by using a unique spherical medial feature. Wright's hip joint reconstruction portfolio provides offerings in the areas of bone-conserving implants, total hip reconstruction, revision replacement implants and limb preservation. The CONSERVE family of products incorporates anatomically-replicating large diameter bearings and its A-CLASS advanced metal technology, which is designed to result in significantly less wear than traditional metal-on-metal hip implants. Wright's extremity products include its CHARLOTTE foot and ankle system; MICRONAIL intramedullary wrist fracture repair system; and the SIDEKICK line of external fixators, a less invasive form of bone compression. The company offers biologics products used to replace and repair damaged or diseased bone, tendons and soft tissues utilizing synthetic and human tissue-based materials. Products include its GRAFTJACKET soft tissue graft designed for augmentation of tendon and ligament repairs; OSTEOSET bone graft substitute; and ALLOMATRIX injectable putty. Subsidiary Wright Medical Australia Pty, Ltd. manages all of the company's extremity and biologics distribution in Australia and New Zealand. In June 2010, the company launched the XPANSION micrografting system, a disposable kit for the application of skin grafts. In October 2010, Wright Medical acquired the rights to the EZ Frame external foot fixator from EZ Concept Surgical Device Corporation.

FINANCIALS: **Sales and profits are in thousands of dollars—add 000 to get the full amount. 2011 Note: Financial information for 2011 was not available for all companies at press time.**

2011 Sales: $512,947	2011 Profits: $-5,143
2010 Sales: $518,973	2010 Profits: $17,841
2009 Sales: $487,508	2009 Profits: $12,131
2008 Sales: $465,547	2008 Profits: $3,197
2007 Sales: $386,850	2007 Profits: $ 961

U.S. Stock Ticker: WMGI
Int'l Ticker:
Int'l Exchange:
Employees: 1,390 Fiscal Year Ends: 12/31
Parent Company:

SALARIES/BENEFITS:

Pension Plan: ESOP Stock Plan: Profit Sharing: Top Exec. Salary: $517,650 Bonus: $160,043
Savings Plan: Y Stock Purch. Plan: Y Second Exec. Salary: $312,650 Bonus: $57,996

OTHER THOUGHTS:

Apparent Women Officers or Directors: 7
Hot Spot for Advancement for Women/Minorities: Y

LOCATIONS: ("Y" = Yes)

West:	Southwest:	Midwest:	Southeast:	Northeast:	International:
			Y		Y

XETA TECHNOLOGIES INC

Industry Group Code: 334210

www.xeta.com

Management:		Sales/Marketing:		Liberal Arts:		Information Systems:		Professionals:		Technical/Scientific:	
Mgmt. Trainees:		Mktg. Professionals:	Y	Gen. Writing/Editing:		Info. Management:	Y	Finance/Acct.:	Y	Engineers, Elec.:	Y
Experienced Mgmt.:	Y	Retail Sales:		Technical Writing:	Y	Software Dev.:	Y	Law:	Y	Engineers, Other:	Y
Int'l Business:		Commercial/Industrial:	Y	Graphic Arts/Photog.:		Hardware Dev.:	Y	HR/Other:	Y	Health/Lab	
MBA Graduates:	Y	Sales Trainees:	Y	Music:		Consulting/Other:	Y	Training:	Y	Scientists/Research:	
		Advertising Pros.:		Broadcasting:				Health Care:		Petroleum/Chemicals:	
				Other:				Consulting:		Math/Other:	

TYPES OF BUSINESS:

Communications Systems & Solutions
Communication technology for Hospitality Industry
Advanced Communication Technology
Voice over Internet Protocol (VoIP)

BRANDS/DIVISIONS/AFFILIATES:

Virtual XL
Virtual XL.2
Hotel Technology Soulutions, Inc.
Pyramid Communication Services, Inc.
PAETEC Holding Corp.
Data-Com Telecommunications, Inc.

CONTACTS: *Note: Officers with more than one job title may be intentionally listed here more than once.*

Greg D. Forrest, CEO
Paul R. Comeau, COO
Greg D. Forrest, Pres.
Robert B. Wagner, CFO
Donald Reigel, Chief Sales Officer
Robert B. Wagner, Corp. Sec.
Tom Luce, Exec. Dir.-Strategic Relationships & Managed Svcs.

Phone: 918-664-8200	**Fax:**
Toll-Free: 800-845-9145	
Address: 1814 W. Tacoma St., Broken Arrow, OK 74012 US	

GROWTH PLANS/SPECIAL FEATURES:

XETA Technologies, Inc. provides enterprise-class communications technologies. The firm specializes in assisting customers transitioning from traditional voice telephony to Internet Protocol based telephony (VoIP). The company markets applications for its customers' contact centers, message management systems and integrated multi-media applications, dividing its products into two lines: commercial systems and hospitality products. The commercial system applications include message management systems that integrate voicemail and fax messages with existing e-mail systems; speech recognition systems; and multimedia applications such as streaming audio and video systems. XETA sells these systems under dealer agreements with several companies including: Avaya; Nortel; Cisco Systems Inc.; Juniper Systems; Hewlett-Packard Company and Samsung. The products that the company supplies to the hospitality market include communications systems, which are equipped with hospitality-specific software; related products such as voicemail systems, analog telephones, uninterrupted power supplies and announcement systems; and call accounting products, offering customers nearly comprehensive integration of their operations. These products are marketed under the Virtual XL and Virtual XL.2 names. In addition to these products, XETA offers services that include nation-wide customer service, project management, installation, structured cabling implementation and consulting. The company provides its products and services primarily through its direct sales force to a wide variety of customers including: Large national companies, mid-size companies, the Federal government, as well as the healthcare and hospitality industries. In May 2010, XETA acquired Hotel Technology Solutions, Inc. In August 2010, it acquired Pyramid Communication Services, Inc., a provider of communications equipment, applications and related services. In September 2010, it purchased the operating assets of Data-Com Telecommunications, Inc., a provider of communications equipment to the greater NYC area. In May 2011, the company was acquired by PAETEC Holding Corp. and began operating in PAETEC's Managed Services division.

FINANCIALS: **Sales and profits are in thousands of dollars—add 000 to get the full amount. 2011 Note: Financial information for 2011 was not available for all companies at press time.**

2011 Sales: $	2011 Profits: $	**U.S. Stock Ticker: Subsidiary**
2010 Sales: $85,678	2010 Profits: $1,373	**Int'l Ticker:**
2009 Sales: $71,572	2009 Profits: $-10,317	Int'l Exchange:
2008 Sales: $84,321	2008 Profits: $2,056	Employees: 467 Fiscal Year Ends: 10/31
2007 Sales: $70,093	2007 Profits: $1,432	Parent Company: PAETEC HOLDING CORP

SALARIES/BENEFITS:

Pension Plan:	ESOP Stock Plan:	Profit Sharing:	Top Exec. Salary: $212,039	Bonus: $49,650
Savings Plan:	Stock Purch. Plan:		Second Exec. Salary: $145,000	Bonus: $40,575

OTHER THOUGHTS:

Apparent Women Officers or Directors:
Hot Spot for Advancement for Women/Minorities:

LOCATIONS: ("Y" = Yes)

West:	Southwest:	Midwest:	Southeast:	Northeast:	International:
Y	Y	Y			

XO GROUP INC

www.xogroupinc.com

Industry Group Code: 519130

Management:		Sales/Marketing:		Liberal Arts:		Information Systems:		Professionals:		Technical/Scientific:	
Mgmt. Trainees:		Mktg. Professionals:	Y	Gen. Writing/Editing:	Y	Info. Management:	Y	Finance/Acct.:	Y	Engineers, Elec.:	
Experienced Mgmt.:	Y	Retail Sales:		Technical Writing:		Software Dev.:	Y	Law:	Y	Engineers, Other:	
Int'l Business:		Commercial/Industrial:	Y	Graphic Arts/Photog.:	Y	Hardware Dev.:		HR/Other:	Y	Health/Lab	
MBA Graduates:	Y	Sales Trainees:	Y	Music:		Consulting/Other:		Training:	Y	Scientists/Research:	
		Advertising Pros.:	Y	Broadcasting:				Health Care:		Petroleum/Chemicals:	
				Other:	Y			Consulting:		Math/Other:	

TYPES OF BUSINESS:

Online Resource for Wedding Planning
Online Gift Registry
Wedding Books & Magazines
Online Community
Wedding Supplies

BRANDS/DIVISIONS/AFFILIATES:

LilaGuide.com
Knot Weddings Magazine (The)
TheKnot.com
TheNest.com
IJie.com
BreastFeeding.com
Knot Wedding Shop (The)
TheBump.com

CONTACTS: *Note: Officers with more than one job title may be intentionally listed here more than once.*

David Liu, CEO
Carol Koh Evans, COO
David Liu, Pres.
John Mueller, CFO
Nic Dilorio, CTO
Jeremy Lechtzin, General Counsel
Jacalyn Lee, Dir.-Public Rel.
Carley Roney, Editor-in-Chief
David Liu, Chmn.

Phone: 212-219-8555 | **Fax:** 212-219-1929
Toll-Free: 877-843-5668
Address: 462 Broadway, 6th Fl., New York, NY 10013 US

GROWTH PLANS/SPECIAL FEATURES:

XO Group, Inc., formerly The Knot, Inc., is one of the world's leading wedding media and services companies. The firm provides couples with planning information, interactive tools and a vast array of online resources. The company's web site, TheKnot.com, has been utilized by over 20 million couples. The Knot Wedding Shop is one of the largest online wedding retailers in the world, offering supplies, favors and attendant gifts, among other items. The company's online services include gift registries, searchable databases, planning tools, a guest list manager, a budgeter and advice columns. It owns and operates several additional online properties, including wedding registry web site WeddingChannel.com; TheNest.com, for newlyweds; LilaGuide.com, a site with resources for parents; TheBump.com, providing print and online guides to fertility, pregnancy, birth and baby resources; BreastFeeding.com, an online resource for first-time parents; IJie.com, a Chinese web site that offers advice on relationships, weddings and pregnancy; and WedSnap, the developer of Weddingbook, a FaceBook application for weddings. Additionally, it is the exclusive wedding content provider to Internet portals including MSN and Yahoo. In physical media, the company publishes The Knot Weddings Magazine, a quarterly national publication that features editorial content covering every major wedding planning decision; and authors a book series on wedding planning and a gift-book series on wedding gowns and flowers.

Employees are offered life, disability, medical and dental insurance; flexible spending accounts; and an assistance program.

FINANCIALS: **Sales and profits are in thousands of dollars—add 000 to get the full amount. 2011 Note: Financial information for 2011 was not available for all companies at press time.**

2011 Sales: $	2011 Profits: $	**U.S. Stock Ticker: XOXO**
2010 Sales: $112,881	2010 Profits: $3,654	**Int'l Ticker:**
2009 Sales: $106,416	2009 Profits: $-4,874	Int'l Exchange:
2008 Sales: $103,897	2008 Profits: $4,129	Employees: 605 Fiscal Year Ends: 12/31
2007 Sales: $98,688	2007 Profits: $11,869	Parent Company:

SALARIES/BENEFITS:

Pension Plan:	ESOP Stock Plan:	Profit Sharing:	Top Exec. Salary: $370,000	Bonus: $185,000
Savings Plan: Y	Stock Purch. Plan: Y		Second Exec. Salary: $350,000	Bonus: $161,875

OTHER THOUGHTS:

Apparent Women Officers or Directors: 3
Hot Spot for Advancement for Women/Minorities: Y

LOCATIONS: ("Y" = Yes)

West:	Southwest:	Midwest:	Southeast:	Northeast:	International:
Y	Y	Y		Y	

XOMA LTD

Industry Group Code: 325412

www.xoma.com

Management:		Sales/Marketing:		Liberal Arts:		Information Systems:		Professionals:		Technical/Scientific:	
Mgmt. Trainees:		Mktg. Professionals:	Y	Gen. Writing/Editing:		Info. Management:	Y	Finance/Acct.:	Y	Engineers, Elec.:	
Experienced Mgmt.:	Y	Retail Sales:		Technical Writing:	Y	Software Dev.:	Y	Law:	Y	Engineers, Other:	
Int'l Business:		Commercial/Industrial:	Y	Graphic Arts/Photog.:		Hardware Dev.:		HR/Other:	Y	Health/Lab	Y
MBA Graduates:	Y	Sales Trainees:	Y	Music:		Consulting/Other:		Training:	Y	Scientists/Research:	Y
		Advertising Pros.:		Broadcasting:				Health Care:	Y	Petroleum/Chemicals:	Y
				Other:				Consulting:		Math/Other:	Y

TYPES OF BUSINESS:

Therapeutic Antibodies

BRANDS/DIVISIONS/AFFILIATES:

Raptiva
Lucentis
CIMZIA
XOMA 3AB
XOMA 052
HCD 122
Novartis AG
Takeda Pharmaceutical Company Ltd.

CONTACTS:

Note: Officers with more than one job title may be intentionally listed here more than once.

Steven B. Engle, CEO
Fred Kurland, CFO
Charles C. Wells, VP-Human Resources
Charles C. Wells, VP-IT
Christopher J. Margolin, General Counsel/VP/Corp. Sec.
Robert S. Tenerowicz, VP-Oper.
Jim Neal, VP-Bus. Dev.
Fred Kurland, VP-Finance
Patrick J. Scannon, Chief Medical Officer/Exec. VP
Daniel P. Cafaro, VP-Regulatory Affairs & Compliance
Susan Kramer, VP-Project & Alliance Mgmt.
Calvin C. McGoogan, VP-Quality & Facilities
Steven B. Engle, Chmn.

Phone: 510-204-7200	**Fax:** 510-644-2011
Toll-Free: 800-246-9662	
Address: 2910 7th St., Berkeley, CA 94710 US	

GROWTH PLANS/SPECIAL FEATURES:

Xoma, Ltd. is a biopharmaceutical company that discovers, develops and manufactures therapeutic antibodies designed to treat inflammatory, autoimmune, infectious and oncological diseases. Xoma's product development pipeline includes proprietary products and collaborative programs at various stages of preclinical and clinical development. Products in the development pipeline include XOMA 052, an anti-interleukin-1 beta (anti-IL-1 beta) antibody being evaluated as a treatment for type 1 and type 2 diabetes and cardiovascular disease; XOMA 3AB, a biodefense anti-botulism antibody candidate; HCD 122, a fully human antibody being developed with Novartis AG as a treatment for B-cell cancers such as lymphoma; and several antibodies in preclinical development. Xoma has collaborations with several companies, including Takeda Pharmaceutical Company Limited; Schering-Plough Research Institute; and Novartis. In 2010, Xoma disposed of its royalty interests in CIMZIA, approved for the treatment of Crohn's disease and rheumatoid arthritis. In December 2010, the firm formed a license and collaboration agreement with Les Laboratoires Servier to jointly develop and market XOMA 052.

Xoma offers its employees medical, dental and vision plans, flexible spending accounts, short- and long-term disability programs, life insurance, a stock purchase plan, an employee assistance program, educational assistance, a commuter checks program, concierge services, ticket discounts and credit union membership.

FINANCIALS:

Sales and profits are in thousands of dollars—add 000 to get the full amount. 2011 Note: Financial information for 2011 was not available for all companies at press time.

2011 Sales: $	2011 Profits: $
2010 Sales: $33,641	2010 Profits: $-68,756
2009 Sales: $98,430	2009 Profits: $ 550
2008 Sales: $67,987	2008 Profits: $-45,245
2007 Sales: $84,252	2007 Profits: $-12,326

U.S. Stock Ticker: XOMA
Int'l Ticker:
Int'l Exchange:
Employees: 240 Fiscal Year Ends: 12/31
Parent Company:

SALARIES/BENEFITS:

Pension Plan: Y	ESOP Stock Plan:	Profit Sharing:	Top Exec. Salary: $551,550	Bonus: $246,130
Savings Plan:	Stock Purch. Plan: Y		Second Exec. Salary: $399,040	Bonus: $179,539

OTHER THOUGHTS:

Apparent Women Officers or Directors: 1
Hot Spot for Advancement for Women/Minorities:

LOCATIONS: ("Y" = Yes)

West:	Southwest:	Midwest:	Southeast:	Northeast:	International:
Y					

XTO ENERGY INC

www.xtoenergy.com

Industry Group Code: 211111

Management:		**Sales/Marketing:**		**Liberal Arts:**		**Information Systems:**		**Professionals:**		**Technical/Scientific:**	
Mgmt. Trainees:		Mktg. Professionals:		Gen. Writing/Editing:		Info. Management:	Y	Finance/Acct.:	Y	Engineers, Elec.:	
Experienced Mgmt.:	Y	Retail Sales:		Technical Writing:		Software Dev.:		Law:	Y	Engineers, Other:	Y
Int'l Business:	Y	Commercial/Industrial:		Graphic Arts/Photog.:		Hardware Dev.:		HR/Other:	Y	Health/Lab	
MBA Graduates:	Y	Sales Trainees:		Music:		Consulting/Other:		Training:	Y	Scientists/Research:	
		Advertising Pros.:		Broadcasting:				Health Care:		Petroleum/Chemicals:	Y
				Other:				Consulting:		Math/Other:	

TYPES OF BUSINESS:

Oil & Gas Exploration & Production

BRANDS/DIVISIONS/AFFILIATES:

Exxon Mobil Corporation (Exxonmobil)

CONTACTS:
Note: Officers with more than one job title may be intentionally listed here more than once.

Jack Williams, Pres.
Louis G. Baldwin, CFO/Exec. VP
Bob Simpson, Chmn.

Phone: 817-870-2800	**Fax:** 817-870-1671
Toll-Free: 800-299-2800	
Address: 810 Houston St., Fort Worth, TX 76102-6298 US	

GROWTH PLANS/SPECIAL FEATURES:

XTO Energy, Inc., a wholly-owned subsidiary of Exxon Mobil Corporation (ExxonMobil), is engaged in the acquisition, development, exploitation and exploration of unconventional resources, as well as in the production, processing, marketing and transportation of oil and natural gas. The firm's proved reserves are concentrated in several regions that the company groups as follows: the Eastern Region, which includes the East Texas Basin, the Haynesville Shale and northwestern Louisiana and Mississippi; the North Texas Region, which includes the Barnett Shale; the Mid-Continent and Rocky Mountain Region, including the Fayetteville Shale, the Woodford Shale and the Bakken Shale; the San Juan Region, spanning parts of New Mexico, Colorado and Utah; the Permian Region, centered in West Texas; the South Texas and Gulf Coast Region, including reserves located offshore in the Gulf of Mexico; and other properties that include reserves in the Marcellus Shale in Pennsylvania and in the North Sea. XTO Energy became a subsidiary of ExxonMobil in 2010.

FINANCIALS:
Sales and profits are in thousands of dollars—add 000 to get the full amount. 2011 Note: Financial information for 2011 was not available for all companies at press time.

2011 Sales: $
2010 Sales: $
2009 Sales: $9,064,000
2008 Sales: $7,695,000
2007 Sales: $5,513,000

2011 Profits: $
2010 Profits: $
2009 Profits: $2,019,000
2008 Profits: $1,912,000
2007 Profits: $1,691,000

U.S. Stock Ticker: Subsidiary
Int'l Ticker:
Int'l Exchange:
Employees: Fiscal Year Ends: 12/31
Parent Company: EXXON MOBIL CORPORATION (EXXONMOBIL)

SALARIES/BENEFITS:

Pension Plan: ESOP Stock Plan: Profit Sharing: Top Exec. Salary: $3,600,000 Bonus: $
Savings Plan: Y Stock Purch. Plan: Second Exec. Salary: $1,400,000 Bonus: $3,125,000

OTHER THOUGHTS:

Apparent Women Officers or Directors:
Hot Spot for Advancement for Women/Minorities:

LOCATIONS: ("Y" = Yes)

West:	Southwest:	Midwest:	Southeast:	Northeast:	International:
Y	Y	Y	Y	Y	Y

YOUNG'S MARKET COMPANY LLC

www.youngsmarket.com

Industry Group Code: 4248

Management:		**Sales/Marketing:**		**Liberal Arts:**		**Information Systems:**		**Professionals:**		**Technical/Scientific:**	
Mgmt. Trainees:	Y	Mktg. Professionals:	Y	Gen. Writing/Editing:	Y	Info. Management:	Y	Finance/Acct.:	Y	Engineers, Elec.:	
Experienced Mgmt.:	Y	Retail Sales:	Y	Technical Writing:		Software Dev.:	Y	Law:	Y	Engineers, Other:	
Int'l Business:		Commercial/Industrial:	Y	Graphic Arts/Photog.:	Y	Hardware Dev.:		HR/Other:	Y	Health/Lab	
MBA Graduates:	Y	Sales Trainees:	Y	Music:		Consulting/Other:		Training:	Y	Scientists/Research:	
		Advertising Pros.:	Y	Broadcasting:				Health Care:		Petroleum/Chemicals:	
				Other:				Consulting:		Math/Other:	

TYPES OF BUSINESS:

Alcohol Distribution

BRANDS/DIVISIONS/AFFILIATES:

Young's Holdings Inc
Young's Market Company of Arizona LLC

CONTACTS:

Note: Officers with more than one job title may be intentionally listed here more than once.

Chris Underwood, CEO
John Klein, Pres.
Kevin Manion, CFO/Exec. VP
Valerie Gart, Sr. VP-Strategic Human Resources
Greg Franklin, CIO/Sr. VP
Don Robbins, General Counsel/Exec. VP
Dan Walker, Sr. VP-Bus. Dev.
Eric Dopkins, Pres., California
Eric Lake, Sr. VP-National Accounts On-Premise
Carl Carlson, Sr. VP-Spirits & Fine Beverages, California
Donald Mackey, Sr. VP-Wine
Vernon O. Underwood, Chmn.
Bob Richardson, Exec. VP-Corp. Logistics & Holdings

Phone: 714-283-4933 **Fax:** 714-283-6175
Toll-Free: 800-317-6150
Address: 2164 N. Batavia St., Orange, CA 92865 US

GROWTH PLANS/SPECIAL FEATURES:

Young's Market Company LLC, a California-based subsidiary of Young's Holdings, Inc., is one of the largest distributors of beer, wine and distilled spirits in the U.S., with operations in California, Oregon, Hawaii, Washington, Alaska, Idaho, Utah, Wyoming and Montana. The firm was founded in 1888 as a grocery and specialty food shop in California. Young's distributes products for Bacardi, Kenwood, Brown-Forman (including its Sonoma-Cutrer Vineyards and Foster's Group Australian Wines) and many other wineries and distilleries on the U.S. West Coast and abroad. It also distributes domestic and imported beers, with a total distribution portfolio of over 100 alcoholic beverage products. The firm conducts inventories, manages merchandising displays and performs other vital sales-related tasks, along with taking orders for stores and supplying stock. Customers include liquor stores, grocery stores, bars and other retail outlets. Recently, the firm signed distribution contracts with Winebow, an importer of wines and spirits, and Constellation Brands, Young's largest supplier in the Pacific Northwest. In August 2011, the company merged its alcohol beverage operations in Arizona with Republic National Distributing Company, launching Young's Market Company of Arizona, LLC.

FINANCIALS:

Sales and profits are in thousands of dollars—add 000 to get the full amount. 2011 Note: Financial information for 2011 was not available for all companies at press time.

2011 Sales: $2,300,000	2011 Profits: $	**U.S. Stock Ticker: Private**
2010 Sales: $2,300,000	2010 Profits: $	**Int'l Ticker:**
2009 Sales: $2,120,000	2009 Profits: $	Int'l Exchange:
2008 Sales: $2,050,000	2008 Profits: $	Employees: Fiscal Year Ends: 2/28
2007 Sales: $2,100,000	2007 Profits: $	Parent Company: YOUNGS HOLDINGS INC

SALARIES/BENEFITS:

Pension Plan:	ESOP Stock Plan:	Profit Sharing:	Top Exec. Salary: $	Bonus: $
Savings Plan:	Stock Purch. Plan:		Second Exec. Salary: $	Bonus: $

OTHER THOUGHTS:

Apparent Women Officers or Directors: 3
Hot Spot for Advancement for Women/Minorities: Y

LOCATIONS: ("Y" = Yes)

West:	Southwest:	Midwest:	Southeast:	Northeast:	International:
Y	Y				

ZAP JONWAY

www.zapworld.com

Industry Group Code: 336991

Management:		Sales/Marketing:		Liberal Arts:		Information Systems:		Professionals:		Technical/Scientific:	
Mgmt. Trainees:		Mktg. Professionals:		Gen. Writing/Editing:	Y	Info. Management:	Y	Finance/Acct.:	Y	Engineers, Elec.:	Y
Experienced Mgmt.:	Y	Retail Sales:		Technical Writing:	Y	Software Dev.:	Y	Law:	Y	Engineers, Other:	Y
Int'l Business:	Y	Commercial/Industrial:	Y	Graphic Arts/Photog.:	Y	Hardware Dev.:		HR/Other:	Y	Health/Lab	
MBA Graduates:	Y	Sales Trainees:		Music:		Consulting/Other:		Training:	Y	Scientists/Research:	
		Advertising Pros.:		Broadcasting:				Health Care:		Petroleum/Chemicals:	
				Other:				Consulting:		Math/Other:	

TYPES OF BUSINESS:

Light Electric Vehicles
Electric Bicycles & Scooters
Electric ATVs
Lithium Batteries
Electric Fleet Vehicle Manufacturing

BRANDS/DIVISIONS/AFFILIATES:

Zhejiang Jonway Automobile Co. Ltd.
A380
ALIAS EV
ZAPPY
Zapino
ZAP Dude
XEBRA
ZAP Manufacturing, Inc.

CONTACTS: *Note: Officers with more than one job title may be intentionally listed here more than once.*

Steven Schneider, Co-CEO
Gary Dodd, Pres.
Benjamin Zhu, CFO
Wang Gang, Co-CEO
Priscilla M. Lu, Chmn.

Phone: 707-525-8658	**Fax:**
Toll-Free: 800-251-4555	
Address: 501 Fourth St., Santa Rosa, CA 95401 US	

GROWTH PLANS/SPECIAL FEATURES:

ZAP Jonway, formerly ZAP, is a U.S.-China auto manufacturer focused on the development of electric vehicles (EVs). The new company was formed in January 2011, when ZAP acquired a 51% controlling interest in Chinese automaker Zhejiang Jonway Automobile Co. Ltd. (Jonway). The combined company is currently developing an electric version of Jonway's A380 SUV, with its initial target being the fleet and taxi markets. The firm's other development efforts consist of production and commercialization of its ALIAS EV roadster. The ALIAS, which the firm plans to launch commercially in late 2011, is a three-wheel EV with a range of 100 miles and top speeds of 85 mph. Historically, ZAP manufactured various EVs for the consumer and fleet markets, including the zero-emission ZAPPY and Zapino electric scooters; ZAP Dude electric ATVs; the XEBRA 100% electric sedan and utility pick-up truck; the ZAPTRUCK XL utility truck; and the ZAPVAN SHUTTLE. ZAP Jonway has a number of wholly-owned subsidiaries, such as Voltage Vehicles, engaged primarily in the distribution and sale of advanced technology and conventional automobiles; ZAPWorld Stores, Inc., engaged primarily in consumer sales of ZAP products; ZAP Manufacturing, Inc., primarily involved in the distribution of ZAP products; and ZAP Retail Outlet. The company has worked on projects for the taxi fleet market in China; qualified as a supplier for the U.S. General Service Administration; and designed electric vehicles for a proposal for the conversion to an all-electric USPS fleet. In November 2010, it signed a long-term supply and development agreement with Remy Electric Motors, LLC to use Remy's HVH 250 electric motor in its future cars and SUVs. The two firms will also collaborate on the development of a drivetrain for use in future vehicles.

FINANCIALS: **Sales and profits are in thousands of dollars—add 000 to get the full amount. 2011 Note: Financial information for 2011 was not available for all companies at press time.**

2011 Sales: $	2011 Profits: $
2010 Sales: $3,816	2010 Profits: $-19,018
2009 Sales: $4,068	2009 Profits: $-10,687
2008 Sales: $7,588	2008 Profits: $9,807
2007 Sales: $5,712	2007 Profits: $-28,006

U.S. Stock Ticker: ZAAP.OB
Int'l Ticker:
Int'l Exchange:
Employees: 555 Fiscal Year Ends: 12/31
Parent Company:

SALARIES/BENEFITS:

Pension Plan:	ESOP Stock Plan:	Profit Sharing:	Top Exec. Salary: $240,000	Bonus: $
Savings Plan:	Stock Purch. Plan:		Second Exec. Salary: $121,448	Bonus: $

OTHER THOUGHTS:

Apparent Women Officers or Directors: 1
Hot Spot for Advancement for Women/Minorities:

LOCATIONS: ("Y" = Yes)

West:	Southwest:	Midwest:	Southeast:	Northeast:	International:
				Y	Y

ZEP INC

Industry Group Code: 325

www.zepinc.com

Management:		Sales/Marketing:		Liberal Arts:		Information Systems:		Professionals:		Technical/Scientific:	
Mgmt. Trainees:		Mktg. Professionals:	Y	Gen. Writing/Editing:		Info. Management:	Y	Finance/Acct.:	Y	Engineers, Elec.:	
Experienced Mgmt.:	Y	Retail Sales:		Technical Writing:	Y	Software Dev.:		Law:	Y	Engineers, Other:	
Int'l Business:	Y	Commercial/Industrial:	Y	Graphic Arts/Photog.:		Hardware Dev.:		HR/Other:	Y	Health/Lab	
MBA Graduates:	Y	Sales Trainees:	Y	Music:		Consulting/Other:		Training:		Scientists/Research:	
		Advertising Pros.:		Broadcasting:				Health Care:		Petroleum/Chemicals:	Y
				Other:				Consulting:		Math/Other:	

TYPES OF BUSINESS:

Cleaning Products
Pesticides
Lawn & Garden Care Products
Car Care Products

BRANDS/DIVISIONS/AFFILIATES:

Zep
Enforcer
Zep Commercial
Zep Professional
Amrep, Inc.
EnviroEdge
GreenLink
Provisions

CONTACTS:

Note: Officers with more than one job title may be intentionally listed here more than once.

John K. Morgan, CEO
John K. Morgan, Pres.
Mark R. Bachmann, CFO/Exec. VP
Jeffrey J. Sorensen, Chief Mktg. Officer/VP
Stanley R. Weller, CTO/VP
Robert P. Collins, Chief Admin. Officer/VP
Philip A. Theodore, General Counsel/VP/Sec.
Thomas Moffet, Pres., Midwest Oper.
Tony Mezza, VP-Finance/Treas.
Lisa B. Malloy, Pres., Retail
Robert L. Droke II, Pres., Zep Central
John K. Morgan, Chmn.
Alessandro Brighenti, Pres, Europe Oper.
Jeffrey L. Fleck, Chief Supply Chain Officer/VP

Phone: 404-352-1680 **Fax:** 404-603-7958
Toll-Free:
Address: 1310 Seaboard Industrial Blvd., Atlanta, GA 30318-2825 US

GROWTH PLANS/SPECIAL FEATURES:

Zep, Inc. is a leading manufacturer and marketer of cleaning products for the commercial, industrial, institutional, and consumer end-markets. The company has over 4,000 distinct formulations used in the manufacture of its products. Zep produces more than 10,000 industrial maintenance and sanitation products, including hand cleaners, detergents, degreasers, floor finishes, disinfectants, pest control solutions, deodorizers and lubricants. It sells these products to a customer base including car washes; schools, municipalities and other governmental organizations; manufacturers; food preparers and processors; restaurants; hospitals; and hotels. Through its direct sales organization, the firm provides cleaning and maintenance solutions to more than 200,000 customers. Zep sells its products to customers primarily in the U.S. (80% of net sales), Canada (11%) and Europe (9%). Its proprietary brands include Zep, Zep Commercial, Zep Professional, Enforcer and Amrep. The company's flagship brand, Zep, represents the largest portfolio of industrial chemical products commercial, industrial and institutional customers. Zep Commercial provides professional cleaning and plumbing chemical products to contractors and small businesses and markets these products through various retailers. Zep Professional comprises products offered through the distribution channel. The Enforcer provides retail plumbing, as well as pest and weed control products sold through home improvement retailers. Zep licenses the brands ArmorAll Professional car care products from Clorox, and a line of cleaners under the Rubbermaid Commercial brand name. The company also produces many environmentally-conscious product lines based on renewable and environmentally preferred raw materials, such as the GreenLink, EnviroEdge and Provisions brands. In September 2010, Zep acquired certain assets of Waterbury Companies, Inc., including certain air-care brands. In October 2010, the firm acquired Niagara National, LLC.

The firm provides its employees with medical, dental and vision insurance benefits.

FINANCIALS:

Sales and profits are in thousands of dollars—add 000 to get the full amount. 2011 Note: Financial information for 2011 was not available for all companies at press time.

2011 Sales: $645,972 2011 Profits: $17,401
2010 Sales: $568,512 2010 Profits: $13,504
2009 Sales: $501,032 2009 Profits: $9,260
2008 Sales: $574,724 2008 Profits: $16,322
2007 Sales: $565,886 2007 Profits: $14,083

U.S. Stock Ticker: ZEP
Int'l Ticker:
Int'l Exchange:
Employees: 2,300 Fiscal Year Ends: 8/31
Parent Company:

SALARIES/BENEFITS:

Pension Plan: ESOP Stock Plan: Profit Sharing: Top Exec. Salary: $541,500 Bonus: $470,000
Savings Plan: Y Stock Purch. Plan: Y Second Exec. Salary: $296,434 Bonus: $181,245

OTHER THOUGHTS:

Apparent Women Officers or Directors: 1
Hot Spot for Advancement for Women/Minorities:

LOCATIONS: ("Y" = Yes)

West:	Southwest:	Midwest:	Southeast:	Northeast:	International:
			Y		Y

ZIEBART INTERNATIONAL CORP

www.ziebart.com

Industry Group Code: 8111

Management:		Sales/Marketing:		Liberal Arts:		Information Systems:		Professionals:		Technical/Scientific:	
Mgmt. Trainees:	Y	Mktg. Professionals:	Y	Gen. Writing/Editing:	Y	Info. Management:	Y	Finance/Acct.:	Y	Engineers, Elec.:	
Experienced Mgmt.:	Y	Retail Sales:		Technical Writing:	Y	Software Dev.:	Y	Law:	Y	Engineers, Other:	
Int'l Business:	Y	Commercial/Industrial:		Graphic Arts/Photog.:		Hardware Dev.:		HR/Other:	Y	Health/Lab	
MBA Graduates:	Y	Sales Trainees:		Music:		Consulting/Other:		Training:	Y	Scientists/Research:	
		Advertising Pros.:	Y	Broadcasting:				Health Care:		Petroleum/Chemicals:	
				Other:				Consulting:		Math/Other:	

TYPES OF BUSINESS:

Automotive Repair & Maintenance
Aftermarket Accessories Installation
Detailing
Paint & Fabric Protection
Window Tinting
Rust Protection

BRANDS/DIVISIONS/AFFILIATES:

Renu-A-Shine
Inner-Clean
Protect-A-Shine
Diamond Gloss
Inner Guard
ZeeGuard
Gold Shield
Formula Z

CONTACTS: *Note: Officers with more than one job title may be intentionally listed here more than once.*

Thomas E. Wolfe, CEO
Thomas E. Wolfe, Pres.
James F. Levagood, Dir.-Computer Oper.
William R. Patterson, Treas./VP

Phone: 248-588-4100	**Fax:** 248-588-1444
Toll-Free: 800-877-1312	
Address: 1290 E. Maple Rd., Troy, MI 48083 US	

GROWTH PLANS/SPECIAL FEATURES:

Ziebart International Corp. is a leading global provider of automotive appearance and protection services, with a network of 400 locations in 30 countries. The company's services include detailing; paint and fabric protection; window tinting; rust protection; and installation of electronic systems, sunroofs and alarm systems. The company specializes in truck accessories, such as bed liners, trailer hitches, toolboxes, bedrails, as well as scratch, and scuff paint repair for bed liners. Ziebart's detailing products include Aquapel, Renu-A-Shine and Inner-Clean. Its other brand names include Protect-A-Shine, Diamond Gloss, Z-Liner, Ziebart TidyCar, Ziebart Shield, ZeeGaurd, Formula Z, Express Shine, Preserv-A-Shine, Shatter Bloc, Artech, Gold Shield, Ziebart Anti-Bacterial Process and Inner Guard. The company also provides spray-on truck bed liners; glass repair and replacement; and remote starter installation. The firm maintains strategic business partnerships with groups including Speedy Auto Glass and Rhino Linings. Ziebart also offers management; marketing; construction design, location scouting, and layout of a new store; business development; grand opening support; monthly publications, ongoing support for franchise owners; marketing meetings and technical, sales and marketing training for its franchisees. The company has been named to Entrepreneur's list of the Top 500 Franchisers for 15 consecutive years; Success magazine's Franchise Gold 100 for four consecutive years; Income Opportunities' Platinum 200 list; and as one of Franchise Times magazine's Top 200.

FINANCIALS: **Sales and profits are in thousands of dollars—add 000 to get the full amount. 2011 Note: Financial information for 2011 was not available for all companies at press time.**

2011 Sales: $	2011 Profits: $	**U.S. Stock Ticker: Private**
2010 Sales: $	2010 Profits: $	**Int'l Ticker:**
2009 Sales: $	2009 Profits: $	Int'l Exchange:
2008 Sales: $	2008 Profits: $	Employees: Fiscal Year Ends:
2007 Sales: $	2007 Profits: $	Parent Company:

SALARIES/BENEFITS:

Pension Plan:	ESOP Stock Plan: Y	Profit Sharing:	Top Exec. Salary: $	Bonus: $
Savings Plan:	Stock Purch. Plan:		Second Exec. Salary: $	Bonus: $

OTHER THOUGHTS:

Apparent Women Officers or Directors:
Hot Spot for Advancement for Women/Minorities:

LOCATIONS: ("Y" = Yes)

West:	Southwest:	Midwest:	Southeast:	Northeast:	International:
Y	Y	Y	Y	Y	Y

ZOLL MEDICAL CORP

www.zoll.com

Industry Group Code: 33911

Management:		Sales/Marketing:		Liberal Arts:		Information Systems:		Professionals:		Technical/Scientific:	
Mgmt. Trainees:		Mktg. Professionals:	Y	Gen. Writing/Editing:		Info. Management:	Y	Finance/Acct.:	Y	Engineers, Elec.:	
Experienced Mgmt.:	Y	Retail Sales:		Technical Writing:	Y	Software Dev.:	Y	Law:	Y	Engineers, Other:	Y
Int'l Business:	Y	Commercial/Industrial:	Y	Graphic Arts/Photog.:		Hardware Dev.:	Y	HR/Other:	Y	Health/Lab	Y
MBA Graduates:	Y	Sales Trainees:	Y	Music:		Consulting/Other:		Training:	Y	Scientists/Research:	Y
		Advertising Pros.:		Broadcasting:				Health Care:	Y	Petroleum/Chemicals:	
				Other:				Consulting:		Math/Other:	

TYPES OF BUSINESS:

Cardiac Resuscitation Devices
Disposable Electrodes
Intravascular Temperature Management
Information Management

BRANDS/DIVISIONS/AFFILIATES:

Rectilinear Biphasic
Real CPR Help
LifeVest
AED Pro
AED Plus
AutoPulse Non-invasive Sudden Cardiac Support Pump
RescueNet
Alsius Corporation

CONTACTS: *Note: Officers with more than one job title may be intentionally listed here more than once.*

Richard A. Packer, CEO
Jonathan A. Rennert, Pres.
A. Ernest Whiton, CFO
Ward M. Hamilton, Sr. VP-Mktg.
E. Jane Wilson, VP-R&D
A. Ernest Whiton, VP-Admin.
Stephen Korn, General Counsel/VP/Corp. Sec.
Diane Egan, Contact-Investor Rel.
John P. Bergeron, Treas./VP
Steven K. Flora, Sr. VP-North American Sales
Benson F. Smith, Chmn.
Alex N. Moghadam, VP-Int'l Oper.

Phone: 978-421-9655	**Fax:** 978-421-0025
Toll-Free: 800-348-9011	
Address: 269 Mill Rd., Chelmsford, MA 01824 US	

GROWTH PLANS/SPECIAL FEATURES:

Zoll Medical Corp. designs, manufactures and markets non-invasive resuscitation devices and software solutions to help healthcare professionals, emergency medical service (EMS) providers and first responders advance and improve the practice of resuscitation. Zoll's products include three core technologies that are implemented throughout the product line: Rectilinear Biphasic waveform, which is utilized in its professional defibrillators and automated external defibrillators (AEDs); external pacing technology, which is used in its professional defibrillators; and Real CPR Help technology, which is used in its professional defibrillators and AEDs. The company developed a uniquely shaped biphasic waveform that achieves higher efficacy at lower current levels than monophasic waveforms, reducing the heart's exposure to high peak current. In addition, Zoll's biphasic waveform keeps the waveform shape and duration constant over a wide range of patients whose differing physiologies affect the conduction of current. Professional defibrillators include such as the M Series, E Series, R Series, and AED Pro with manual defibrillation capability. AED products are for use by minimally trained rescuers, including the AED Pro and the AED Plus. The ZOLL LifeVest is a wearable automatic defibrillator, designed for endovascular hypothermia. Zoll entered the intravascular temperature management sector for the first time with its recent acquisition of the assets of Alsius Corporation. The company and its subsidiaries currently hold approximately 250 U.S. and roughly 180 foreign patents, which relate to pacing, defibrillation, CPR, hypothermia and other resuscitation therapies. In August 2010, Zoll received FDA approval to sell a new model of its LifeVest wearable automatic defibrillator and for a new model of its E-Series Monitor/Defibrillator, a device designed to detect carbon monoxide poisoning for use by fire and rescue personnel.

FINANCIALS: **Sales and profits are in thousands of dollars—add 000 to get the full amount. 2011 Note: Financial information for 2011 was not available for all companies at press time.**

2011 Sales: $523,709	2011 Profits: $31,288	**U.S. Stock Ticker: ZOLL**
2010 Sales: $443,989	2010 Profits: $18,919	**Int'l Ticker:**
2009 Sales: $385,185	2009 Profits: $9,564	Int'l Exchange:
2008 Sales: $398,018	2008 Profits: $23,441	Employees: 1,908 Fiscal Year Ends: 9/30
2007 Sales: $309,451	2007 Profits: $16,662	Parent Company:

SALARIES/BENEFITS:

Pension Plan:	ESOP Stock Plan:	Profit Sharing:	Top Exec. Salary: $400,000	Bonus: $141,000
Savings Plan: Y	Stock Purch. Plan:		Second Exec. Salary: $310,000	Bonus: $88,000

OTHER THOUGHTS:

Apparent Women Officers or Directors: 2
Hot Spot for Advancement for Women/Minorities:

LOCATIONS: ("Y" = Yes)

West:	Southwest:	Midwest:	Southeast:	Northeast:	International:
Y				Y	Y

ZYNGA INC

www.zynga.com

Industry Group Code: 511210G

Management:		Sales/Marketing:		Liberal Arts:		Information Systems:		Professionals:		Technical/Scientific:	
Mgmt. Trainees:		Mktg. Professionals:	Y	Gen. Writing/Editing:	Y	Info. Management:	Y	Finance/Acct.:	Y	Engineers, Elec.:	Y
Experienced Mgmt.:	Y	Retail Sales:		Technical Writing:		Software Dev.:	Y	Law:	Y	Engineers, Other:	
Int'l Business:	Y	Commercial/Industrial:		Graphic Arts/Photog.:	Y	Hardware Dev.:		HR/Other:	Y	Health/Lab	
MBA Graduates:	Y	Sales Trainees:		Music:	Y	Consulting/Other:		Training:		Scientists/Research:	
		Advertising Pros.:	Y	Broadcasting:				Health Care:		Petroleum/Chemicals:	
				Other:	Y			Consulting:		Math/Other:	

TYPES OF BUSINESS:

Online Games
Social Media Gaming

BRANDS/DIVISIONS/AFFILIATES:

FarmVille
Mafia Wars
CafeWorld
FishVille
Zynga Poker
Words with Friends
Bonfire Studios
Newtoy Inc

CONTACTS:

Note: Officers with more than one job title may be intentionally listed here more than once.

Mark Pincus, CEO
John Schappert, COO
Dave Wehner, CFO
Jeff Karp, Chief Mktg. & Revenue Officer
Colleen McCreary, Chief People Officer/VP
Cadir Lee, CTO
Mark Pincus, Chief Prod. Officer
Reggie Davis, General Counsel
David Ko, Chief Mobile Officer
Steve Chiang, Exec. VP-Games
Mike Vardu, Chief Creative Officer
Mark Pincus, Chmn.

Phone: 855-449-9642 **Fax:** 302-636-5454
Toll-Free:
Address: 699 8th St., San Francisco, CA 94103 US

GROWTH PLANS/SPECIAL FEATURES:

Zynga, Inc. is a leading developer of online social games for social media sites, online networks and mobile devices. The company's games are hosted on a variety of social networks, including Facebook, MySpace and My Yahoo. Its products include casino games, word games, board games, role playing games and party games. Zynga's most successful games include FarmVille, Mafia Wars, Words with Friends, CafeWorld, FishVille, Zynga Poker and Vampire Wars. The company also administers Zynga.org, which donates money and educational goods to international nonprofits. The firm has received funding from Kleiner Perkins Caufield & Beyers, Foundry Group, Union Square Ventures, Institutional Venture Partners, Avalon Ventures, SoftBank and The Pilot Group. More than 227 million monthly unique visitors in 175 countries play Zynga's games each month. In late 2010, Zynga purchased Bonfire Studios, a developer of video games for PC and Microsoft's Xbox 360 console; and Newtoy, Inc., a developer of apps for mobile devices. In December 2011, the company held its initial public offering of stock.

FINANCIALS:

Sales and profits are in thousands of dollars—add 000 to get the full amount. 2011 Note: Financial information for 2011 was not available for all companies at press time.

2011 Sales: $1,140,100	2011 Profits: $-404,316	**U.S. Stock Ticker: ZNGA**
2010 Sales: $597,000	2010 Profits: $91,000	**Int'l Ticker:**
2009 Sales: $121,000	2009 Profits: $-53,000	Int'l Exchange:
2008 Sales: $	2008 Profits: $	Employees: 1,300 Fiscal Year Ends: 12/31
2007 Sales: $	2007 Profits: $	Parent Company:

SALARIES/BENEFITS:

Pension Plan:	ESOP Stock Plan:	Profit Sharing:	Top Exec. Salary: $	Bonus: $
Savings Plan:	Stock Purch. Plan:		Second Exec. Salary: $	Bonus: $

OTHER THOUGHTS:

Apparent Women Officers or Directors: 1
Hot Spot for Advancement for Women/Minorities:

LOCATIONS: ("Y" = Yes)

West:	Southwest:	Midwest:	Southeast:	Northeast:	International:
Y	Y			Y	Y

ADDITIONAL INDEXES

CONTENTS:

INDEX OF FIRMS NOTED AS HOT SPOTS FOR ADVANCEMENT FOR WOMEN & MINORITIES

INDEX OF SUBSIDIARIES, BRAND NAMES AND AFFILIATIONS

INDEX OF SUBSIDIARIES, BRAND NAMES AND AFFILIATIONS, CONT.

INDEX OF SUBSIDIARIES, BRAND NAMES AND AFFILIATIONS, CONT.

INDEX OF SUBSIDIARIES, BRAND NAMES AND AFFILIATIONS, CONT.

INDEX OF SUBSIDIARIES, BRAND NAMES AND AFFILIATIONS, CONT.

INDEX OF SUBSIDIARIES, BRAND NAMES AND AFFILIATIONS, CONT.

INDEX OF SUBSIDIARIES, BRAND NAMES AND AFFILIATIONS, CONT.

INDEX OF SUBSIDIARIES, BRAND NAMES AND AFFILIATIONS, CONT.

INDEX OF SUBSIDIARIES, BRAND NAMES AND AFFILIATIONS, CONT.

INDEX OF SUBSIDIARIES, BRAND NAMES AND AFFILIATIONS, CONT.

INDEX OF SUBSIDIARIES, BRAND NAMES AND AFFILIATIONS, CONT.

INDEX OF SUBSIDIARIES, BRAND NAMES AND AFFILIATIONS, CONT.

INDEX OF SUBSIDIARIES, BRAND NAMES AND AFFILIATIONS, CONT.

INDEX OF SUBSIDIARIES, BRAND NAMES AND AFFILIATIONS, CONT.

INDEX OF SUBSIDIARIES, BRAND NAMES AND AFFILIATIONS, CONT.

INDEX OF SUBSIDIARIES, BRAND NAMES AND AFFILIATIONS, CONT.

INDEX OF SUBSIDIARIES, BRAND NAMES AND AFFILIATIONS, CONT.

INDEX OF SUBSIDIARIES, BRAND NAMES AND AFFILIATIONS, CONT.

INDEX OF SUBSIDIARIES, BRAND NAMES AND AFFILIATIONS, CONT.

INDEX OF SUBSIDIARIES, BRAND NAMES AND AFFILIATIONS, CONT.

INDEX OF SUBSIDIARIES, BRAND NAMES AND AFFILIATIONS, CONT.

INDEX OF SUBSIDIARIES, BRAND NAMES AND AFFILIATIONS, CONT.

INDEX OF SUBSIDIARIES, BRAND NAMES AND AFFILIATIONS, CONT.

INDEX OF SUBSIDIARIES, BRAND NAMES AND AFFILIATIONS, CONT.

INDEX OF SUBSIDIARIES, BRAND NAMES AND AFFILIATIONS, CONT.

INDEX OF SUBSIDIARIES, BRAND NAMES AND AFFILIATIONS, CONT.

INDEX BY COMPANIES FOR SPECIFIC TYPES OF JOB SEEKERS

Indexed by the following categories:

Information Systems

Consulting/Other
ADEPT TECHNOLOGY INC
ADVISORY BOARD COMPANY (THE)
ALIEN TECHNOLOGY CORPORATION
AMERESCO INC
ARGON ST INC
CHANNELL COMMERCIAL CORP
CHINDEX INTERNATIONAL INC
COMVERGE INC
CORPORATE EXECUTIVE BOARD COMPANY (THE)
CRA INTERNATIONAL INC (CHARLES RIVER)
CRAY INC
DIAMOND ADVISORY SERVICES
EMULEX CORP
ENERNOC INC
EPAM SYSTEMS
FORRESTER RESEARCH INC
GALLUP ORGANIZATION (THE)
GLOBECOMM SYSTEMS INC
HARRIS INTERACTIVE INC
INTERACTIVE INTELLIGENCE GROUP INC
ISILON SYSTEMS INC
KEYNOTE SYSTEMS INC
KIMLEY-HORN AND ASSOCIATES INC
LCC INTERNATIONAL INC
LOGISTICARE INC
MANAGEMENT NETWORK GROUP INC (THE)
PACIFIC BIOMARKERS INC
PERFICIENT INC
QUANTUM CORP
RECYCLED ENERGY DEVELOPMENT LLC
RIVERBED TECHNOLOGY INC
SCANSOURCE INC
SHARED TECHNOLOGIES
SMART MODULAR TECHNOLOGIES INC
SUPER MICRO COMPUTER INC
XETA TECHNOLOGIES INC

Hardware Development
ABAXIS INC
ADEPT TECHNOLOGY INC
ADTRAN INC
ALIEN TECHNOLOGY CORPORATION
ALIGN TECHNOLOGY INC
AMERICAN MEDICAL SYSTEMS HOLDINGS INC
AMERICAN SCIENCE & ENGINEERING INC
AMTECH SYSTEMS INC
ANALOGIC CORP
ANAREN INC
AROTECH CORPORATION
ARRIS GROUP INC
ATRION CORPORATION
BIOSITE INC
CALIPER LIFE SCIENCES INC
CARDIONET INC
CEPHEID
CHANNELL COMMERCIAL CORP
CHOLESTECH CORP
CIRRUS LOGIC INC
CLEARONE COMMUNICATIONS INC
COHERENT INC
COMTECH TELECOMMUNICATIONS CORP
COMVERGE INC
CRAY INC
CYBERONICS INC
DEI HOLDINGS INC
DOLBY LABORATORIES INC
EMCORE CORP
EMS TECHNOLOGIES INC
EMULEX CORP
ENVIRONMENTAL TECTONICS CORP
FORTINET INC
FUEL SYSTEMS SOLUTIONS INC
GENERAL ATOMICS
GENOMIC HEALTH INC
GEN-PROBE INC
GLOBECOMM SYSTEMS INC
HAEMONETICS CORPORATION
HELIOVOLT CORP
I-FLOW CORPORATION
ILLUMINA INC
IMMUCOR INC
INTERMEC INC
INTUITIVE SURGICAL INC
IRIDEX CORP
IRIS INTERNATIONAL INC
IROBOT CORP
ISILON SYSTEMS INC
KEY TRONIC CORP
LIFECORE BIOMEDICAL INC
LOJACK CORPORTATION
LUMINEX CORPORATION
MERIDIAN BIOSCIENCE INC
MINDSPEED TECHNOLOGIES INC
NANOMETRICS INC
NATUS MEDICAL INC
NEOGEN CORPORATION
NETGEAR INC
NUVASIVE INC
PHAZAR CORP
POWERSECURE INTERNATIONAL INC
QUALCOMM ATHEROS INC
QUANTUM CORP
RAYTHEON APPLIED SIGNAL TECHNOLOGY INC
SCANSOURCE INC
SCHICK TECHNOLOGIES INC
SIGMA DESIGNS INC
SILICON LABORATORIES INC
SMART MODULAR TECHNOLOGIES INC
SOLARRESERVE
SOLFOCUS INC
SPECTRANETICS CORP
SPIRE CORPORATION
SRS LABS INC
STAAR SURGICAL CO
SUPER MICRO COMPUTER INC
SYNAPTICS INC
SYNOVIS LIFE TECHNOLOGIES INC
TECHNE CORP
TEKELEC
TESCO CORPORATION
THORATEC CORPORATION

TII NETWORK TECHNOLOGIES INC
UQM TECHNOLOGIES INC
VARIAN SEMICONDUCTOR EQUIPMENT ASSOCIATES INC
VENTANA MEDICAL SYSTEMS INC
VIASAT INC
VOX INTERNATIONAL CORPORATION
WMS INDUSTRIES INC
XETA TECHNOLOGIES INC
ZOLL MEDICAL CORP

Information Management
24/7 REAL MEDIA INC
AAMCO TRANSMISSIONS INC
ABAXIS INC
ACI WORLDWIDE INC
ACME PACKET INC
ACXIOM DIGITAL INC
ADEPT TECHNOLOGY INC
ADTRAN INC
ADVISORY BOARD COMPANY (THE)
AFFILIATED MANAGERS GROUP
AKAMAI TECHNOLOGIES INC
AKORN INC
AKQA INC
ALBANY MOLECULAR RESEARCH INC
ALEXANDER & BALDWIN INC
ALEXION PHARMACEUTICALS INC
ALIEN TECHNOLOGY CORPORATION
ALIGN TECHNOLOGY INC
ALLEGIANT TRAVEL COMPANY
ALLIED HEALTHCARE INTERNATIONAL INC
ALLSCRIPTS HEALTHCARE SOLUTIONS INC
AMAG PHARMACEUTICALS INC
AMCOL INTERNATIONAL CORP
AMCON DISTRIBUTING CO
AMERESCO INC
AMERICAN CAMPUS COMMUNITIES INC
AMERICAN FIDELITY ASSURANCE COMPANY
AMERICAN MEDICAL SYSTEMS HOLDINGS INC
AMERICAN SCIENCE & ENGINEERING INC
AMERICAN TIRE DISTRIBUTORS
AMERICAN TOWER CORP
AMERICAN VANGUARD CORP
AMERICA'S CAR-MART INC
AMTECH SYSTEMS INC
AMTRUST FINANCIAL SERVICES INC
ANALOGIC CORP
ANAREN INC
ANIKA THERAPEUTICS INC
APP PHARMACEUTICALS INC
ARCSIGHT INC
ARDEN GROUP INC
ARGON ST INC
ARIBA INC
ARIZONA CHEMICAL COMPANY
AROTECH CORPORATION
ARRAY BIOPHARMA INC
ARRIS GROUP INC
ARTHROCARE CORP
ARUBA NETWORKS INC
ASTEX PHARMACEUTICALS INC
ATHENAHEALTH INC
ATLANTIC CITY ELECTRIC COMPANY
ATLANTIC TELE-NETWORK INC
ATRION CORPORATION
AUDIBLE INC
AVALONBAY COMMUNITIES INC
AVIALL INC
AVISTA CORPORATION
B&G FOODS INC
BANKRATE INC
BERRY PETROLEUM CO
BIO REFERENCE LABORATORIES INC
BIOMARIN PHARMACEUTICAL INC
BIOSCRIP INC
BIOSITE INC
BLACK HILLS CORP
BLACKBOARD INC
BLUE COAT SYSTEMS INC
BLUE NILE INC
BOSTON BEER COMPANY INC (THE)
BOTTOMLINE TECHNOLOGIES INC
BRIGHTSTAR CORPORATION
CABOT OIL & GAS CORP
CACTUS FEEDERS INC
CAGLE'S INC
CALAVO GROWERS INC
CALGON CARBON CORPORATION
CALIBER HOLDINGS CORP
CALIPER LIFE SCIENCES INC
CAL-MAINE FOODS INC
CAMBREX CORP
CANTEL MEDICAL CORP
CANTOR FITZGERALD LP
CAPITOL FEDERAL FINANCIAL INC
CARACO PHARMACEUTICAL LABORATORIES LTD
CARBO CERAMICS INC
CARDIONET INC
CARDTRONICS INC
CARRIZO OIL & GAS INC
CATALYST HEALTH SOLUTIONS INC
CELLDEX THERAPEUTICS INC
CELSIS INTERNATIONAL PLC
CENTRAL VERMONT PUBLIC SERVICE CORP
CEPHEID
CERUS CORPORATION
CF INDUSTRIES HOLDINGS INC
CHANNELL COMMERCIAL CORP
CHATTEM INC
CHINDEX INTERNATIONAL INC
CHOICESTREAM INC
CHOLESTECH CORP
CIRRUS LOGIC INC
CKX INC
CLAYTON WILLIAMS ENERGY INC
CLEAN ENERGY FUELS CORP
CLEARONE COMMUNICATIONS INC
COGENT COMMUNICATIONS
COHERENT INC
COMDATA CORP
COMPASS DIVERSIFIED HOLDINGS
COMTECH TELECOMMUNICATIONS CORP
COMVERGE INC
CONCUR TECHNOLOGIES INC
CONSTANT CONTACT INC
CONTINENTAL RESOURCES INC
CONTINUCARE CORP
CORPORATE EXECUTIVE BOARD COMPANY (THE)
COSTAR GROUP INC
COUPONS INC
CRA INTERNATIONAL INC (CHARLES RIVER)
CRAY INC
CRITICAL CARE SYSTEMS
CROWN CASTLE INTERNATIONAL CORP
CRUM & FORSTER HOLDINGS INC

CRYOLIFE INC
CUBIST PHARMACEUTICALS INC
CULP INC
CUMULUS MEDIA INC
CYBERONICS INC
CYBERSOURCE CORP
DANNON COMPANY INC (THE)
DAWSON GEOPHYSICAL COMPANY
DEI HOLDINGS INC
DELPHI FINANCIAL GROUP INC
DENBURY RESOURCES INC
DIAMOND ADVISORY SERVICES
DIAMOND FOODS INC
DIGITAL GENERATION INC
DJO GLOBAL INC
DOLBY LABORATORIES INC
DORMAN PRODUCTS INC
DPL INC
DREAMWORKS ANIMATION SKG INC
DRUGSTORE.COM INC
EATON VANCE CORP
EBIX INC
ECHO GLOBAL LOGISTICS INC
ECHOSTAR CORP
ECOLLEGE.COM
EDELMAN FINANCIAL GROUP (THE)
EDGAR ONLINE INC
EDUCATIONAL DEVELOPMENT CORP
EHEALTH INC
EMBARCADERO TECHNOLOGIES INC
EMCORE CORP
EMS TECHNOLOGIES INC
EMULEX CORP
ENCORE CAPITAL GROUP INC
ENERGY TRANSFER PARTNERS LP
ENERNOC INC
ENVIRONMENTAL TECTONICS CORP
EOG RESOURCES INC
EPAM SYSTEMS
EQT CORPORATION
EQUINIX INC
ERESEARCH TECHNOLOGY INC
ESSEX PROPERTY TRUST INC
EVERCORE PARTNERS INC
EVEREST RE GROUP LTD
EXACTECH INC
F5 NETWORKS INC

FAIR ISAAC CORPORATION
FEDEX SUPPLY CHAIN SERVICES INC
FIRST FINANCIAL BANCORP (OH)
FNB CORP
FORRESTER RESEARCH INC
FORTINET INC
FRESHDIRECT LLC
FROZEN FOOD EXPRESS INDUSTRIES INC
FUEL SYSTEMS SOLUTIONS INC
FUEL TECH INC
GAIAM INC
GALLUP ORGANIZATION (THE)
GENCO SHIPPING & TRADING LIMITED
GENENCOR INTERNATIONAL INC
GENERAL ATOMICS
GENERAL COMMUNICATION INC (GCI)
GENESIS ENERGY LP
GENOMIC HEALTH INC
GEN-PROBE INC
GFI GROUP INC
G-III APPAREL GROUP
GLEACHER & COMPANY INC
GLOBAL PARTNERS LP
GLOBECOMM SYSTEMS INC
GLU MOBILE INC
GOLDEN ENTERPRISES INC
GOLFSMITH INTERNATIONAL HOLDINGS INC
GREAT AMERICAN FINANCIAL RESOURCES INC
GREAT LAKES CHEESE COMPANY INC
GREEN MOUNTAIN POWER CORPORATION
GTC BIOTHERAPEUTICS INC
GULFMARK OFFSHORE INC
HAEMONETICS CORPORATION
HAHN AUTOMOTIVE WAREHOUSE INC
HANCOCK HOLDING COMPANY
HANOVER FOODS CORPORATION
HARRIS INTERACTIVE INC
HCC INSURANCE HOLDINGS INC
HEALTH GRADES INC
HEALTH INSURANCE PLAN OF GREATER NEW YORK
HEALTHSTREAM INC
HEALTHTRONICS INC

HEARUSA INC
HELIOVOLT CORP
HELIX ENERGY SOLUTIONS GROUP INC
HESKA CORP
HICKORY TECH CORPORATION
HI-TECH PHARMACAL CO INC
HOLLYFRONTIER CORPORATION
HORACE MANN EDUCATORS CORPORATION
HOSPITALITY PROPERTIES TRUST
HOULIHAN LOKEY HOWARD & ZUKIN INC
HUB GROUP INC
HUDSON CITY BANCORP INC
IBASIS INC
ICONIX BRAND GROUP INC
ICU MEDICAL INC
IDACORP INC
I-FLOW CORPORATION
ILLUMINA INC
IMG WORLDWIDE INC
IMMUCOR INC
IMPAX LABORATORIES INC
INDEPENDENCE HOLDING CO
INFOSPACE INC
INNOPHOS HOLDINGS INC
INNOSPEC INC
INTEGRAL SYSTEMS INC
INTEGRAMED AMERICA INC
INTERACTIVE DATA CORPORATION
INTERACTIVE INTELLIGENCE GROUP INC
INTERCONTINENTALEXCHANGE INC (ICE)
INTERMEC INC
INTERNAP NETWORK SERVICES CORP
INTERNATIONAL CREATIVE MANAGEMENT INC (ICM)
INTERNATIONAL DAIRY QUEEN INC
INTUITIVE SURGICAL INC
INVESTMENT TECHNOLOGY GROUP INC (ITG)
INVESTORS REAL ESTATE TRUST
IRIDEX CORP
IRIS INTERNATIONAL INC
IROBOT CORP
ISILON SYSTEMS INC
IVILLAGE INC
J2 GLOBAL COMMUNICATIONS INC
JAZZ PHARMACEUTICALS INC

JOE'S JEANS INC
JOHN B SANFILIPPO & SON INC
KAMPGROUNDS OF AMERICA INC
KBW INC
KENDALL-JACKSON WINE ESTATES LTD
KENNETH COLE PRODUCTIONS INC
KEY TRONIC CORP
KEYNOTE SYSTEMS INC
KIMLEY-HORN AND ASSOCIATES INC
KIRBY CORP
KKR & CO LP (KOHLBERG KRAVIS ROBERTS & CO)
KNIGHT CAPITAL GROUP INC
KNOLOGY INC
KORN/FERRY INTERNATIONAL
KRONOS WORLDWIDE INC
LACLEDE GROUP INC (THE)
LAKELAND INDUSTRIES INC
LB FOSTER COMPANY
LCC INTERNATIONAL INC
LESLIE'S POOLMART INC
LIFECELL CORPORATION
LIFECORE BIOMEDICAL INC
LIVEPERSON INC
LOGISTICARE INC
LOJACK CORPORTATION
LUCASFILM LTD
LUCOR INC
LUMINEX CORPORATION
MAGELLAN MIDSTREAM PARTNERS LP
MAKO SURGICAL CORP
MALT-O-MEAL COMPANY
MANAGEMENT NETWORK GROUP INC (THE)
MANHATTAN ASSOCIATES INC
MAPFRE USA CORP
MARTEK BIOSCIENCES CORP
MARVEL ENTERTAINMENT LLC
MEDICINES CO (THE)
MEDICIS PHARMACEUTICAL CORP
MEDIFAST INC
MEDTOX SCIENTIFIC INC
MENTOR CORP
MERIDIAN BIOSCIENCE INC
MERIT MEDICAL SYSTEMS INC
MESIROW FINANCIAL HOLDINGS INC
METROPOLITAN HEALTH NETWORKS INC
MICHELINAS INC
MICROTEK MEDICAL HOLDINGS INC
MID-AMERICA APARTMENT COMMUNITIES INC
MIDAS INC
MILLENNIUM PHARMACEUTICALS INC
MINDSPEED TECHNOLOGIES INC
MOELIS & COMPANY
MONSTER BEVERAGE CORP
MOTORCAR PARTS OF AMERICA INC
MTR GAMING GROUP INC
MYRIAD GENETICS INC
NANOMETRICS INC
NATIONAL BEVERAGE CORP
NATIONAL DENTEX CORP
NATIONAL WINE & SPIRITS INC
NATUS MEDICAL INC
NEKTAR THERAPEUTICS
NEOGEN CORPORATION
NETFLIX INC
NETGEAR INC
NETSCOUT SYSTEMS INC
NETSUITE INC
NETWORK ENGINES INC
NEUSTAR INC
NEW JERSEY RESOURCES CORPORATION
NEW YORK MERCANTILE EXCHANGE INC
NIC INC
NORTHWESTERN CORPORATION
NOTIFY TECHNOLOGY CORP
NOVAMED INC
NOVEN PHARMACEUTICALS INC
NTELOS HOLDING CORP
NUGGET MARKET
NUSTAR ENERGY LP
NUTRASWEET COMPANY (THE)
NUVASIVE INC
ODYSSEY RE HOLDINGS CORP
OMNOVA SOLUTIONS INC
ONLINE RESOURCES CORP
ONSTREAM MEDIA CORPORATION
OPENTV CORP
ORION MARINE GROUP INC
PACIFIC BIOMARKERS INC
PAR PHARMACEUTICAL COMPANIES INC
PATAGONIA INC
PC CONNECTION INC
PEAPOD LLC
PEGASYSTEMS INC
PERFICIENT INC
PERRY ELLIS INTERNATIONAL INC
PETMED EXPRESS INC
PETROLEUM DEVELOPMENT CORPORATION
PHAZAR CORP
PHILADELPHIA CONSOLIDATED HOLDING CORP
PHOENIX COMPANIES INC (THE)
PIEDMONT NATURAL GAS COMPANY INC
PIONEER NATURAL RESOURCES COMPANY
PIPER JAFFRAY COMPANIES
PLAINS EXPLORATION AND PRODUCTION COMPANY
PLATO LEARNING INC
PMA COMPANIES INC
POLYPORE INTERNATIONAL INC
POWERSECURE INTERNATIONAL INC
PREMIERE GLOBAL SERVICES INC
PRIMEENERGY CORPORATION
PROASSURANCE CORP
PROTECTIVE LIFE CORP
PURPLE COMMUNICATIONS INC
QUAKER CHEMICAL CORP
QUALCOMM ATHEROS INC
QUALITY SYSTEMS INC
QUANTUM CORP
QUESTCOR PHARMACEUTICALS INC
QUICKSILVER RESOURCES INC
QUIDEL CORP
RAYTHEON APPLIED SIGNAL TECHNOLOGY INC
REALNETWORKS INC
RECYCLED ENERGY DEVELOPMENT LLC
REDBOX AUTOMATED RETAIL LLC
REGENERON PHARMACEUTICALS INC
REINSURANCE GROUP OF AMERICA INC
RENTRAK CORP
RICELAND FOODS INC
RIGHTNOW TECHNOLOGIES INC
RIVERBED TECHNOLOGY INC
ROBERT W BAIRD & CO INC
ROCKY BRANDS INC

ROGERS CORPORATION
ROSETTA STONE INC
ROVI CORPORATION
RPC INC
RSA SECURITY INC
S1 CORPORATION
SACRAMENTO MUNICIPAL UTILITY DISTRICT
SALIX PHARMACEUTICALS
SANDRIDGE ENERGY INC
SBA COMMUNICATIONS CORP
SCANSOURCE INC
SCHICK TECHNOLOGIES INC
SCHIFF NUTRITION INTERNATIONAL INC
SCICLONE PHARMACEUTICALS INC
SCIOS INC
SCOULAR COMPANY (THE)
SEACHANGE INTERNATIONAL INC
SEATTLE GENETICS
SELECTICA INC
SENIOR HOUSING PROPERTIES
SERACARE LIFE SCIENCES INC
SHARED TECHNOLOGIES
SHENANDOAH TELECOMMUNICATIONS CO
SHUTTERFLY INC
SIGMA DESIGNS INC
SILICON LABORATORIES INC
SL GREEN REALTY CORP
SMART MODULAR TECHNOLOGIES INC
SOLARRESERVE
SOLFOCUS INC
SOTHEBYS
SOUTHERN UNION COMPANY
SOUTHWEST GAS CORP
SOUTHWESTERN ENERGY CO
SOVRAN SELF STORAGE INC
SPARTAN MOTORS INC
SPECTRANETICS CORP
SPECTRUM PHARMACEUTICALS INC
SPIRE CORPORATION
SPORT SUPPLY GROUP INC
SPORTSMAN'S GUIDE INC (THE)
SPROUTS FARMERS MARKET LLC
SRS LABS INC
SS&C TECHNOLOGIES HOLDINGS INC
STAAR SURGICAL CO
STATE AUTO FINANCIAL CORP
STEPAN COMPANY
STERLING AUTOBODY CENTERS
STERLING CONSTRUCTION COMPANY
STEVEN MADDEN LTD
STIEFEL LABORATORIES INC
SUN COMMUNITIES INC
SUNOCO LOGISTICS PARTNERS LP
SUPER MICRO COMPUTER INC
SUPERIOR UNIFORM GROUP INC
SUPERTEL HOSPITALITY INC
SUPREME INDUSTRIES INC
SVB FINANCIAL GROUP
SWIFT ENERGY CO
SYNAPTICS INC
SYNIVERSE TECHNOLOGIES
SYNOVIS LIFE TECHNOLOGIES INC
TAKE-TWO INTERACTIVE SOFTWARE INC
TAMPA ELECTRIC COMPANY
TARGA RESOURCES PARTNERS LP
TECHNE CORP
TEKELEC
TELIRIS
TERREMARK WORLDWIDE INC
TESCO CORPORATION
TESSCO TECHNOLOGIES INC
THERAGENICS CORP
THORATEC CORPORATION
TII NETWORK TECHNOLOGIES INC
TOOTSIE ROLL INDUSTRIES INC
TOPPS COMPANY INC (THE)
TRANSAMMONIA INC
TRANSATLANTIC HOLDINGS INC
TRANSCEND SERVICES INC
TRAVELZOO INC
TREX COMPANY INC
TRIZETTO GROUP INC (THE)
TRUE RELIGION APPAREL INC
UDR INC
UIL HOLDINGS CORPORATION
ULTIMATE SOFTWARE GROUP INC
ULTRALIFE CORPORATION
UNISOURCE ENERGY CORPORATION
UNIT CORP
UNITED ONLINE INC
UNITED THERAPEUTICS CORP
UNIVERSAL HOSPITAL SERVICES INC
UQM TECHNOLOGIES INC
US PHYSICAL THERAPY INC
USANA HEALTH SCIENCES INC
UTAH MEDICAL PRODUCTS INC
VARIAN SEMICONDUCTOR EQUIPMENT ASSOCIATES INC
VASCO DATA SECURITY INTERNATIONAL INC
VENTANA MEDICAL SYSTEMS INC
VERENIUM CORPORATION
VIASAT INC
VIBRANT MEDIA INC
VIROPHARMA INC
VOLCOM INC
VOX INTERNATIONAL CORPORATION
WABASH NATIONAL CORP
WADDELL & REED FINANCIAL INC
WEBEX COMMUNICATIONS INC
WEBMD HEALTH CORP
WEBMEDIA BRANDS INC
WEBSENSE INC
WESTAR ENERGY
WGL HOLDINGS INC
WHITEWAVE FOODS COMPANY
WIKIMEDIA FOUNDATION
WIND RIVER SYSTEMS INC
WMS INDUSTRIES INC
WRIGHT MEDICAL GROUP INC
XETA TECHNOLOGIES INC
XO GROUP INC
XOMA LTD
XTO ENERGY INC
YOUNG'S MARKET COMPANY LLC
ZAP JONWAY
ZEP INC
ZIEBART INTERNATIONAL CORP
ZOLL MEDICAL CORP
ZYNGA INC

Software Development
24/7 REAL MEDIA INC
AAMCO TRANSMISSIONS INC
ABAXIS INC
ACI WORLDWIDE INC
ACME PACKET INC
ACXIOM DIGITAL INC
ADEPT TECHNOLOGY INC
ADTRAN INC
ADVISORY BOARD COMPANY (THE)
AKAMAI TECHNOLOGIES INC

AKORN INC
AKQA INC
ALBANY MOLECULAR RESEARCH INC
ALEXION PHARMACEUTICALS INC
ALIEN TECHNOLOGY CORPORATION
ALIGN TECHNOLOGY INC
ALLEGIANT TRAVEL COMPANY
ALLIED HEALTHCARE INTERNATIONAL INC
ALLSCRIPTS HEALTHCARE SOLUTIONS INC
AMCON DISTRIBUTING CO
AMERICAN MEDICAL SYSTEMS HOLDINGS INC
AMERICAN SCIENCE & ENGINEERING INC
AMERICA'S CAR-MART INC
AMTECH SYSTEMS INC
ANALOGIC CORP
ANAREN INC
ANIKA THERAPEUTICS INC
APP PHARMACEUTICALS INC
ARCSIGHT INC
ARDEN GROUP INC
ARGON ST INC
ARIBA INC
AROTECH CORPORATION
ARRAY BIOPHARMA INC
ARRIS GROUP INC
ARTHROCARE CORP
ARUBA NETWORKS INC
ATHENAHEALTH INC
ATLANTIC TELE-NETWORK INC
ATRION CORPORATION
AUDIBLE INC
BANKRATE INC
BIO REFERENCE LABORATORIES INC
BIOMARIN PHARMACEUTICAL INC
BIOSCRIP INC
BIOSITE INC
BLACKBOARD INC
BLUE COAT SYSTEMS INC
BLUE NILE INC
BOTTOMLINE TECHNOLOGIES INC
BRIGHTSTAR CORPORATION
CALIBER HOLDINGS CORP
CALIPER LIFE SCIENCES INC
CAMBREX CORP
CANTOR FITZGERALD LP

CARACO PHARMACEUTICAL LABORATORIES LTD
CARDTRONICS INC
CATALYST HEALTH SOLUTIONS INC
CELLDEX THERAPEUTICS INC
CELSIS INTERNATIONAL PLC
CEPHEID
CERUS CORPORATION
CHANNELL COMMERCIAL CORP
CHINDEX INTERNATIONAL INC
CHOICESTREAM INC
CHOLESTECH CORP
CIRRUS LOGIC INC
CLEARONE COMMUNICATIONS INC
COGENT COMMUNICATIONS
COHERENT INC
COMDATA CORP
COMTECH TELECOMMUNICATIONS CORP
COMVERGE INC
CONCUR TECHNOLOGIES INC
CONSTANT CONTACT INC
CONTINUCARE CORP
COSTAR GROUP INC
COUPONS INC
CRAY INC
CRITICAL CARE SYSTEMS
CROWN CASTLE INTERNATIONAL CORP
CUBIST PHARMACEUTICALS INC
CYBERONICS INC
CYBERSOURCE CORP
DAWSON GEOPHYSICAL COMPANY
DEI HOLDINGS INC
DIGITAL GENERATION INC
DOLBY LABORATORIES INC
DORMAN PRODUCTS INC
DREAMWORKS ANIMATION SKG INC
DRUGSTORE.COM INC
EBIX INC
ECHOSTAR CORP
ECOLLEGE.COM
EDELMAN FINANCIAL GROUP (THE)
EDGAR ONLINE INC
EDUCATIONAL DEVELOPMENT CORP
EHEALTH INC
EMBARCADERO TECHNOLOGIES INC
EMCORE CORP

EMS TECHNOLOGIES INC
EMULEX CORP
ENCORE CAPITAL GROUP INC
ENERNOC INC
ENVIRONMENTAL TECTONICS CORP
EPAM SYSTEMS
EQUINIX INC
ERESEARCH TECHNOLOGY INC
EVERCORE PARTNERS INC
F5 NETWORKS INC
FAIR ISAAC CORPORATION
FORRESTER RESEARCH INC
FORTINET INC
FRESHDIRECT LLC
FUEL TECH INC
GAIAM INC
GALLUP ORGANIZATION (THE)
GENCO SHIPPING & TRADING LIMITED
GENENCOR INTERNATIONAL INC
GENERAL ATOMICS
GENERAL COMMUNICATION INC (GCI)
GENOMIC HEALTH INC
GEN-PROBE INC
GFI GROUP INC
GLEACHER & COMPANY INC
GLOBECOMM SYSTEMS INC
GLU MOBILE INC
GOLFSMITH INTERNATIONAL HOLDINGS INC
GREAT AMERICAN FINANCIAL RESOURCES INC
GTC BIOTHERAPEUTICS INC
HAEMONETICS CORPORATION
HAHN AUTOMOTIVE WAREHOUSE INC
HARRIS INTERACTIVE INC
HEALTH GRADES INC
HEALTHSTREAM INC
HEALTHTRONICS INC
HEARUSA INC
HELIOVOLT CORP
HESKA CORP
HICKORY TECH CORPORATION
HI-TECH PHARMACAL CO INC
HOULIHAN LOKEY HOWARD & ZUKIN INC
HUB GROUP INC
IBASIS INC
ICU MEDICAL INC

I-FLOW CORPORATION
ILLUMINA INC
IMMUCOR INC
IMPAX LABORATORIES INC
INFOSPACE INC
INTEGRAL SYSTEMS INC
INTEGRAMED AMERICA INC
INTERACTIVE DATA CORPORATION
INTERACTIVE INTELLIGENCE GROUP INC
INTERCONTINENTALEXCHANGE INC (ICE)
INTERMEC INC
INTERNAP NETWORK SERVICES CORP
INTERNATIONAL DAIRY QUEEN INC
INTUITIVE SURGICAL INC
INVESTMENT TECHNOLOGY GROUP INC (ITG)
IRIDEX CORP
IRIS INTERNATIONAL INC
IROBOT CORP
ISILON SYSTEMS INC
IVILLAGE INC
J2 GLOBAL COMMUNICATIONS INC
JAZZ PHARMACEUTICALS INC
KBW INC
KEY TRONIC CORP
KEYNOTE SYSTEMS INC
KIRBY CORP
KNIGHT CAPITAL GROUP INC
KNOLOGY INC
KORN/FERRY INTERNATIONAL
LCC INTERNATIONAL INC
LESLIE'S POOLMART INC
LIFECELL CORPORATION
LIFECORE BIOMEDICAL INC
LIVEPERSON INC
LOGISTICARE INC
LOJACK CORPORTATION
LUCASFILM LTD
LUMINEX CORPORATION
MANHATTAN ASSOCIATES INC
MARVEL ENTERTAINMENT LLC
MEDICINES CO (THE)
MEDICIS PHARMACEUTICAL CORP
MEDIFAST INC
MEDTOX SCIENTIFIC INC
MERIDIAN BIOSCIENCE INC
MESIROW FINANCIAL HOLDINGS INC
METROPOLITAN HEALTH NETWORKS INC
MIDAS INC
MILLENNIUM PHARMACEUTICALS INC
MINDSPEED TECHNOLOGIES INC
MOELIS & COMPANY
MYRIAD GENETICS INC
NANOMETRICS INC
NATIONAL WINE & SPIRITS INC
NATUS MEDICAL INC
NEKTAR THERAPEUTICS
NEOGEN CORPORATION
NETFLIX INC
NETGEAR INC
NETSCOUT SYSTEMS INC
NETSUITE INC
NETWORK ENGINES INC
NEUSTAR INC
NEW YORK MERCANTILE EXCHANGE INC
NIC INC
NOTIFY TECHNOLOGY CORP
NOVAMED INC
NOVEN PHARMACEUTICALS INC
NTELOS HOLDING CORP
NUGGET MARKET
NUVASIVE INC
ONLINE RESOURCES CORP
ONSTREAM MEDIA CORPORATION
OPENTV CORP
PACIFIC BIOMARKERS INC
PAR PHARMACEUTICAL COMPANIES INC
PC CONNECTION INC
PEAPOD LLC
PEGASYSTEMS INC
PERFICIENT INC
PETMED EXPRESS INC
PHAZAR CORP
PIPER JAFFRAY COMPANIES
PLATO LEARNING INC
POLYPORE INTERNATIONAL INC
POWERSECURE INTERNATIONAL INC
PREMIERE GLOBAL SERVICES INC
PURPLE COMMUNICATIONS INC
QUALCOMM ATHEROS INC
QUALITY SYSTEMS INC
QUANTUM CORP
QUESTCOR PHARMACEUTICALS INC
QUIDEL CORP
RAYTHEON APPLIED SIGNAL TECHNOLOGY INC
REALNETWORKS INC
RECYCLED ENERGY DEVELOPMENT LLC
REDBOX AUTOMATED RETAIL LLC
REGENERON PHARMACEUTICALS INC
RENTRAK CORP
RIGHTNOW TECHNOLOGIES INC
RIVERBED TECHNOLOGY INC
ROBERT W BAIRD & CO INC
ROSETTA STONE INC
ROVI CORPORATION
RSA SECURITY INC
S1 CORPORATION
SALIX PHARMACEUTICALS
SBA COMMUNICATIONS CORP
SCANSOURCE INC
SCHICK TECHNOLOGIES INC
SCICLONE PHARMACEUTICALS INC
SCIOS INC
SEACHANGE INTERNATIONAL INC
SEATTLE GENETICS
SELECTICA INC
SERACARE LIFE SCIENCES INC
SHARED TECHNOLOGIES
SHENANDOAH TELECOMMUNICATIONS CO
SHUTTERFLY INC
SIGMA DESIGNS INC
SILICON LABORATORIES INC
SMART MODULAR TECHNOLOGIES INC
SOLARRESERVE
SOLFOCUS INC
SOTHEBYS
SPECTRANETICS CORP
SPECTRUM PHARMACEUTICALS INC
SPIRE CORPORATION
SPORT SUPPLY GROUP INC
SPORTSMAN'S GUIDE INC (THE)
SPROUTS FARMERS MARKET LLC
SRS LABS INC
SS&C TECHNOLOGIES HOLDINGS INC
STAAR SURGICAL CO
STERLING AUTOBODY CENTERS
STIEFEL LABORATORIES INC

SUPER MICRO COMPUTER INC
SYNAPTICS INC
SYNIVERSE TECHNOLOGIES
SYNOVIS LIFE TECHNOLOGIES INC
TAKE-TWO INTERACTIVE SOFTWARE INC
TECHNE CORP
TEKELEC
TELIRIS
TERREMARK WORLDWIDE INC
TESCO CORPORATION
TESSCO TECHNOLOGIES INC
THERAGENICS CORP
THORATEC CORPORATION
TII NETWORK TECHNOLOGIES INC
TRANSCEND SERVICES INC
TRAVELZOO INC
TRIZETTO GROUP INC (THE)
TRUE RELIGION APPAREL INC
ULTIMATE SOFTWARE GROUP INC
UNITED ONLINE INC
UNITED THERAPEUTICS CORP
UTAH MEDICAL PRODUCTS INC
VARIAN SEMICONDUCTOR EQUIPMENT ASSOCIATES INC
VASCO DATA SECURITY INTERNATIONAL INC
VENTANA MEDICAL SYSTEMS INC
VERENIUM CORPORATION
VIASAT INC
VIBRANT MEDIA INC
VIROPHARMA INC
VOX INTERNATIONAL CORPORATION
WEBEX COMMUNICATIONS INC
WEBMD HEALTH CORP
WEBMEDIA BRANDS INC
WEBSENSE INC
WIKIMEDIA FOUNDATION
WIND RIVER SYSTEMS INC
WMS INDUSTRIES INC
WRIGHT MEDICAL GROUP INC
XETA TECHNOLOGIES INC
XO GROUP INC
XOMA LTD
YOUNG'S MARKET COMPANY LLC
ZAP JONWAY
ZIEBART INTERNATIONAL CORP
ZOLL MEDICAL CORP
ZYNGA INC

Liberal Arts

Broadcasting
CUMULUS MEDIA INC

General Writing/Editing
24/7 REAL MEDIA INC
AAMCO TRANSMISSIONS INC
ACXIOM DIGITAL INC
ADVISORY BOARD COMPANY (THE)
AKAMAI TECHNOLOGIES INC
AKQA INC
ALIEN TECHNOLOGY CORPORATION
ALLEGIANT TRAVEL COMPANY
ALLIED HEALTHCARE INTERNATIONAL INC
AMERICAN CAMPUS COMMUNITIES INC
AMERICAN FIDELITY ASSURANCE COMPANY
AMERICA'S CAR-MART INC
AMTRUST FINANCIAL SERVICES INC
ANAREN INC
ARDEN GROUP INC
ARRIS GROUP INC
ATHENAHEALTH INC
ATLANTIC CITY ELECTRIC COMPANY
AUDIBLE INC
AVALONBAY COMMUNITIES INC
AVISTA CORPORATION
B&G FOODS INC
BANKRATE INC
BIOSCRIP INC
BLACK HILLS CORP
BLACKBOARD INC
BLUE NILE INC
BOSTON BEER COMPANY INC (THE)
BOTTOMLINE TECHNOLOGIES INC
CALIBER HOLDINGS CORP
CANTOR FITZGERALD LP
CAPITOL FEDERAL FINANCIAL INC
CARDTRONICS INC
CATALYST HEALTH SOLUTIONS INC
CENTRAL VERMONT PUBLIC SERVICE CORP
CHANNELL COMMERCIAL CORP
CHATTEM INC
CHOICESTREAM INC
CKX INC
CLEARONE COMMUNICATIONS INC
COMDATA CORP
COMTECH TELECOMMUNICATIONS CORP
CONSTANT CONTACT INC
CONTINUCARE CORP
CORPORATE EXECUTIVE BOARD COMPANY (THE)
COSTAR GROUP INC
COUPONS INC
CRA INTERNATIONAL INC (CHARLES RIVER)
CRITICAL CARE SYSTEMS
CRUM & FORSTER HOLDINGS INC
CULP INC
CUMULUS MEDIA INC
DANNON COMPANY INC (THE)
DEI HOLDINGS INC
DELPHI FINANCIAL GROUP INC
DIAMOND ADVISORY SERVICES
DIGITAL GENERATION INC
DPL INC
DREAMWORKS ANIMATION SKG INC
DRUGSTORE.COM INC
EATON VANCE CORP
EBIX INC
ECHO GLOBAL LOGISTICS INC
ECHOSTAR CORP
ECOLLEGE.COM
EDELMAN FINANCIAL GROUP (THE)
EDGAR ONLINE INC
EDUCATIONAL DEVELOPMENT CORP
EHEALTH INC
EMS TECHNOLOGIES INC
ENCORE CAPITAL GROUP INC
EPAM SYSTEMS
EQT CORPORATION
EVERCORE PARTNERS INC
EVEREST RE GROUP LTD
FAIR ISAAC CORPORATION
FEDEX SUPPLY CHAIN SERVICES INC
FIRST FINANCIAL BANCORP (OH)
FNB CORP
FORRESTER RESEARCH INC
FRESHDIRECT LLC
GAIAM INC
GALLUP ORGANIZATION (THE)
GENERAL COMMUNICATION INC (GCI)

G-III APPAREL GROUP	KNIGHT CAPITAL GROUP INC	PIEDMONT NATURAL GAS COMPANY INC
GLEACHER & COMPANY INC	KNOLOGY INC	PIPER JAFFRAY COMPANIES
GLOBECOMM SYSTEMS INC	LACLEDE GROUP INC (THE)	PLATO LEARNING INC
GOLDEN ENTERPRISES INC	LESLIE'S POOLMART INC	PMA COMPANIES INC
GOLFSMITH INTERNATIONAL HOLDINGS INC	LIVEPERSON INC	PROASSURANCE CORP
GREAT AMERICAN FINANCIAL RESOURCES INC	LOJACK CORPORTATION	PROTECTIVE LIFE CORP
GREAT LAKES CHEESE COMPANY INC	LUCASFILM LTD	PURPLE COMMUNICATIONS INC
GREEN MOUNTAIN POWER CORPORATION	LUCOR INC	RAYTHEON APPLIED SIGNAL TECHNOLOGY INC
HANCOCK HOLDING COMPANY	MALT-O-MEAL COMPANY	REDBOX AUTOMATED RETAIL LLC
HANOVER FOODS CORPORATION	MANAGEMENT NETWORK GROUP INC (THE)	REINSURANCE GROUP OF AMERICA INC
HARRIS INTERACTIVE INC	MAPFRE USA CORP	RENTRAK CORP
HCC INSURANCE HOLDINGS INC	MARTEK BIOSCIENCES CORP	RICELAND FOODS INC
HEALTH GRADES INC	MARVEL ENTERTAINMENT LLC	ROBERT W BAIRD & CO INC
HEALTH INSURANCE PLAN OF GREATER NEW YORK	MEDIFAST INC	ROCKY BRANDS INC
HEALTHSTREAM INC	MESIROW FINANCIAL HOLDINGS INC	ROSETTA STONE INC
HEARUSA INC	METROPOLITAN HEALTH NETWORKS INC	ROVI CORPORATION
HICKORY TECH CORPORATION	MICHELINAS INC	S1 CORPORATION
HORACE MANN EDUCATORS CORPORATION	MID-AMERICA APARTMENT COMMUNITIES INC	SACRAMENTO MUNICIPAL UTILITY DISTRICT
HOSPITALITY PROPERTIES TRUST	MIDAS INC	SCHIFF NUTRITION INTERNATIONAL INC
HOULIHAN LOKEY HOWARD & ZUKIN INC	MOELIS & COMPANY	SEACHANGE INTERNATIONAL INC
HUDSON CITY BANCORP INC	MONSTER BEVERAGE CORP	SENIOR HOUSING PROPERTIES
IBASIS INC	MTR GAMING GROUP INC	SHENANDOAH TELECOMMUNICATIONS CO
ICONIX BRAND GROUP INC	NATIONAL BEVERAGE CORP	SHUTTERFLY INC
IDACORP INC	NATIONAL WINE & SPIRITS INC	SOTHEBYS
INDEPENDENCE HOLDING CO	NETFLIX INC	SOUTHERN UNION COMPANY
INFOSPACE INC	NETSUITE INC	SOUTHWEST GAS CORP
INTERACTIVE DATA CORPORATION	NEUSTAR INC	SOVRAN SELF STORAGE INC
INTERCONTINENTALEXCHANGE INC (ICE)	NEW JERSEY RESOURCES CORPORATION	SPORT SUPPLY GROUP INC
INTERMEC INC	NEW YORK MERCANTILE EXCHANGE INC	SPORTSMAN'S GUIDE INC (THE)
INTERNAP NETWORK SERVICES CORP	NIC INC	SPROUTS FARMERS MARKET LLC
INTERNATIONAL DAIRY QUEEN INC	NORTHWESTERN CORPORATION	STATE AUTO FINANCIAL CORP
INVESTMENT TECHNOLOGY GROUP INC (ITG)	NOTIFY TECHNOLOGY CORP	STERLING AUTOBODY CENTERS
INVESTORS REAL ESTATE TRUST	NTELOS HOLDING CORP	STEVEN MADDEN LTD
IVILLAGE INC	NUGGET MARKET	SUN COMMUNITIES INC
J2 GLOBAL COMMUNICATIONS INC	ODYSSEY RE HOLDINGS CORP	SUPERTEL HOSPITALITY INC
JOHN B SANFILIPPO & SON INC	OMNOVA SOLUTIONS INC	SUPREME INDUSTRIES INC
KAMPGROUNDS OF AMERICA INC	ONSTREAM MEDIA CORPORATION	SVB FINANCIAL GROUP
KBW INC	PC CONNECTION INC	TAKE-TWO INTERACTIVE SOFTWARE INC
KENDALL-JACKSON WINE ESTATES LTD	PEAPOD LLC	TAMPA ELECTRIC COMPANY
KENNETH COLE PRODUCTIONS INC	PERFICIENT INC	TELIRIS
KKR & CO LP (KOHLBERG KRAVIS ROBERTS & CO)	PERRY ELLIS INTERNATIONAL INC	TOOTSIE ROLL INDUSTRIES INC
	PETMED EXPRESS INC	TOPPS COMPANY INC (THE)
	PHAZAR CORP	TRANSATLANTIC HOLDINGS INC
	PHILADELPHIA CONSOLIDATED HOLDING CORP	TRANSCEND SERVICES INC
	PHOENIX COMPANIES INC (THE)	TRAVELZOO INC

TRUE RELIGION APPAREL INC
UDR INC
UIL HOLDINGS CORPORATION
UNISOURCE ENERGY CORPORATION
UNITED ONLINE INC
US PHYSICAL THERAPY INC
USANA HEALTH SCIENCES INC
VIASAT INC
VIBRANT MEDIA INC
VOLCOM INC
VOX INTERNATIONAL CORPORATION
WABASH NATIONAL CORP
WEBEX COMMUNICATIONS INC
WEBMD HEALTH CORP
WEBMEDIA BRANDS INC
WESTAR ENERGY
WGL HOLDINGS INC
WHITEWAVE FOODS COMPANY
WIKIMEDIA FOUNDATION
XO GROUP INC
YOUNG'S MARKET COMPANY LLC
ZAP JONWAY
ZIEBART INTERNATIONAL CORP
ZYNGA INC

Graphic Arts/Photography
24/7 REAL MEDIA INC
ACXIOM DIGITAL INC
AKQA INC
ALLEGIANT TRAVEL COMPANY
ALLSCRIPTS HEALTHCARE SOLUTIONS INC
AMCON DISTRIBUTING CO
AMERICAN TIRE DISTRIBUTORS
ARCSIGHT INC
ARDEN GROUP INC
AUDIBLE INC
BLACKBOARD INC
BLUE NILE INC
BOSTON BEER COMPANY INC (THE)
CALAVO GROWERS INC
CAL-MAINE FOODS INC
CHOICESTREAM INC
CONSTANT CONTACT INC
COUPONS INC
CULP INC
DIAMOND FOODS INC
DREAMWORKS ANIMATION SKG INC
DRUGSTORE.COM INC
ECOLLEGE.COM
EDUCATIONAL DEVELOPMENT CORP
EMCORE CORP
FRESHDIRECT LLC
GAIAM INC
G-III APPAREL GROUP
GLU MOBILE INC
GOLDEN ENTERPRISES INC
GOLFSMITH INTERNATIONAL HOLDINGS INC
HAHN AUTOMOTIVE WAREHOUSE INC
HEALTH GRADES INC
HEALTHSTREAM INC
HELIOVOLT CORP
INFOSPACE INC
INTERMEC INC
INTERNATIONAL DAIRY QUEEN INC
IVILLAGE INC
JOE'S JEANS INC
JOHN B SANFILIPPO & SON INC
KAMPGROUNDS OF AMERICA INC
KENDALL-JACKSON WINE ESTATES LTD
KENNETH COLE PRODUCTIONS INC
KEY TRONIC CORP
LESLIE'S POOLMART INC
LUCASFILM LTD
MARVEL ENTERTAINMENT LLC
MEDIFAST INC
MONSTER BEVERAGE CORP
MTR GAMING GROUP INC
NATIONAL BEVERAGE CORP
NATIONAL WINE & SPIRITS INC
NETFLIX INC
NIC INC
NUGGET MARKET
NUTRASWEET COMPANY (THE)
OMNOVA SOLUTIONS INC
ONSTREAM MEDIA CORPORATION
PATAGONIA INC
PC CONNECTION INC
PEAPOD LLC
PERRY ELLIS INTERNATIONAL INC
PETMED EXPRESS INC
PLATO LEARNING INC
REDBOX AUTOMATED RETAIL LLC
ROCKY BRANDS INC
ROSETTA STONE INC
SCHIFF NUTRITION INTERNATIONAL INC
SHUTTERFLY INC
SOLARRESERVE
SOLFOCUS INC
SOTHEBYS
SPARTAN MOTORS INC
SPIRE CORPORATION
SPORT SUPPLY GROUP INC
SPORTSMAN'S GUIDE INC (THE)
SPROUTS FARMERS MARKET LLC
STERLING CONSTRUCTION COMPANY
STEVEN MADDEN LTD
SUPERIOR UNIFORM GROUP INC
SUPREME INDUSTRIES INC
SYNAPTICS INC
TAKE-TWO INTERACTIVE SOFTWARE INC
TRAVELZOO INC
TRIZETTO GROUP INC (THE)
TRUE RELIGION APPAREL INC
USANA HEALTH SCIENCES INC
VIBRANT MEDIA INC
VOLCOM INC
WABASH NATIONAL CORP
WEBMD HEALTH CORP
WEBMEDIA BRANDS INC
WMS INDUSTRIES INC
XO GROUP INC
YOUNG'S MARKET COMPANY LLC
ZAP JONWAY
ZYNGA INC

Music
CUMULUS MEDIA INC
DREAMWORKS ANIMATION SKG INC
GLU MOBILE INC
LUCASFILM LTD
TAKE-TWO INTERACTIVE SOFTWARE INC
WMS INDUSTRIES INC
ZYNGA INC

Other
24/7 REAL MEDIA INC
ACXIOM DIGITAL INC
ADVISORY BOARD COMPANY (THE)
ASTEX PHARMACEUTICALS INC
AUDIBLE INC

BLACKBOARD INC
BLUE NILE INC
BOSTON BEER COMPANY INC (THE)
CELLDEX THERAPEUTICS INC
CERUS CORPORATION
CHATTEM INC
CHOICESTREAM INC
CLEARONE COMMUNICATIONS INC
CORPORATE EXECUTIVE BOARD COMPANY (THE)
COUPONS INC
CULP INC
CUMULUS MEDIA INC
DIGITAL GENERATION INC
DOLBY LABORATORIES INC
DREAMWORKS ANIMATION SKG INC
ECOLLEGE.COM
EDUCATIONAL DEVELOPMENT CORP
EPAM SYSTEMS
FORRESTER RESEARCH INC
GALLUP ORGANIZATION (THE)
G-III APPAREL GROUP
GLU MOBILE INC
GOLDEN ENTERPRISES INC
HARRIS INTERACTIVE INC
ICONIX BRAND GROUP INC
IVILLAGE INC
JOE'S JEANS INC
KENDALL-JACKSON WINE ESTATES LTD
KENNETH COLE PRODUCTIONS INC
KEYNOTE SYSTEMS INC
LIVEPERSON INC
LUCASFILM LTD
MALT-O-MEAL COMPANY
MARVEL ENTERTAINMENT LLC
NETFLIX INC
OMNOVA SOLUTIONS INC
ONSTREAM MEDIA CORPORATION
PATAGONIA INC
PERFICIENT INC
PERRY ELLIS INTERNATIONAL INC
PLATO LEARNING INC
QUESTCOR PHARMACEUTICALS INC
REDBOX AUTOMATED RETAIL LLC
RENTRAK CORP
RIGHTNOW TECHNOLOGIES INC
ROCKY BRANDS INC
ROSETTA STONE INC
SBA COMMUNICATIONS CORP
SHUTTERFLY INC
SPECTRUM PHARMACEUTICALS INC
STEVEN MADDEN LTD
TAKE-TWO INTERACTIVE SOFTWARE INC
TOOTSIE ROLL INDUSTRIES INC
TOPPS COMPANY INC (THE)
TRAVELZOO INC
VIBRANT MEDIA INC
VOLCOM INC
WEBMD HEALTH CORP
WEBMEDIA BRANDS INC
WHITEWAVE FOODS COMPANY
WIKIMEDIA FOUNDATION
WMS INDUSTRIES INC
XO GROUP INC
ZYNGA INC

Technical Writing
AAMCO TRANSMISSIONS INC
ABAXIS INC
ACI WORLDWIDE INC
ACME PACKET INC
ADEPT TECHNOLOGY INC
ADTRAN INC
ADVISORY BOARD COMPANY (THE)
AKAMAI TECHNOLOGIES INC
AKORN INC
ALBANY MOLECULAR RESEARCH INC
ALEXION PHARMACEUTICALS INC
ALIEN TECHNOLOGY CORPORATION
ALIGN TECHNOLOGY INC
ALLIED HEALTHCARE INTERNATIONAL INC
ALLSCRIPTS HEALTHCARE SOLUTIONS INC
AMAG PHARMACEUTICALS INC
AMCOL INTERNATIONAL CORP
AMERESCO INC
AMERICAN FIDELITY ASSURANCE COMPANY
AMERICAN MEDICAL SYSTEMS HOLDINGS INC
AMERICAN SCIENCE & ENGINEERING INC
AMERICAN TIRE DISTRIBUTORS
AMERICAN TOWER CORP
AMTECH SYSTEMS INC
AMTRUST FINANCIAL SERVICES INC
ANALOGIC CORP
ANAREN INC
ANIKA THERAPEUTICS INC
APP PHARMACEUTICALS INC
ARCSIGHT INC
ARGON ST INC
ARIBA INC
ARIZONA CHEMICAL COMPANY
AROTECH CORPORATION
ARRAY BIOPHARMA INC
ARRIS GROUP INC
ARTHROCARE CORP
ARUBA NETWORKS INC
ASTEX PHARMACEUTICALS INC
ATHENAHEALTH INC
ATRION CORPORATION
AVIALL INC
BANKRATE INC
BIO REFERENCE LABORATORIES INC
BIOMARIN PHARMACEUTICAL INC
BIOSCRIP INC
BIOSITE INC
BLACKBOARD INC
BLUE COAT SYSTEMS INC
BOTTOMLINE TECHNOLOGIES INC
BRIGHTSTAR CORPORATION
CALGON CARBON CORPORATION
CALIBER HOLDINGS CORP
CALIPER LIFE SCIENCES INC
CAMBREX CORP
CANTEL MEDICAL CORP
CARACO PHARMACEUTICAL LABORATORIES LTD
CARBO CERAMICS INC
CARDIONET INC
CARDTRONICS INC
CATALYST HEALTH SOLUTIONS INC
CELLDEX THERAPEUTICS INC
CELSIS INTERNATIONAL PLC
CEPHEID
CERUS CORPORATION
CHANNELL COMMERCIAL CORP
CHATTEM INC
CHINDEX INTERNATIONAL INC
CHOLESTECH CORP
CIRRUS LOGIC INC
CLEARONE COMMUNICATIONS INC

COHERENT INC
COMDATA CORP
COMTECH TELECOMMUNICATIONS CORP
COMVERGE INC
CONCUR TECHNOLOGIES INC
CONTINUCARE CORP
CORPORATE EXECUTIVE BOARD COMPANY (THE)
COSTAR GROUP INC
CRAY INC
CRITICAL CARE SYSTEMS
CROWN CASTLE INTERNATIONAL CORP
CRUM & FORSTER HOLDINGS INC
CRYOLIFE INC
CUBIST PHARMACEUTICALS INC
CYBERONICS INC
CYBERSOURCE CORP
DAWSON GEOPHYSICAL COMPANY
DEI HOLDINGS INC
DELPHI FINANCIAL GROUP INC
DJO GLOBAL INC
DOLBY LABORATORIES INC
DORMAN PRODUCTS INC
EATON VANCE CORP
EBIX INC
ECHOSTAR CORP
ECOLLEGE.COM
EDGAR ONLINE INC
EHEALTH INC
EMBARCADERO TECHNOLOGIES INC
EMCORE CORP
EMS TECHNOLOGIES INC
EMULEX CORP
ENERNOC INC
ENVIRONMENTAL TECTONICS CORP
EPAM SYSTEMS
EQUINIX INC
ERESEARCH TECHNOLOGY INC
EVEREST RE GROUP LTD
EXACTECH INC
F5 NETWORKS INC
FAIR ISAAC CORPORATION
FEDEX SUPPLY CHAIN SERVICES INC
FORRESTER RESEARCH INC
FORTINET INC
FUEL SYSTEMS SOLUTIONS INC

FUEL TECH INC
GALLUP ORGANIZATION (THE)
GENENCOR INTERNATIONAL INC
GENERAL ATOMICS
GENOMIC HEALTH INC
GEN-PROBE INC
GLOBECOMM SYSTEMS INC
GLU MOBILE INC
GREAT AMERICAN FINANCIAL RESOURCES INC
GTC BIOTHERAPEUTICS INC
HAEMONETICS CORPORATION
HARRIS INTERACTIVE INC
HCC INSURANCE HOLDINGS INC
HEALTH GRADES INC
HEALTH INSURANCE PLAN OF GREATER NEW YORK
HEALTHSTREAM INC
HEALTHTRONICS INC
HEARUSA INC
HELIOVOLT CORP
HELIX ENERGY SOLUTIONS GROUP INC
HESKA CORP
HI-TECH PHARMACAL CO INC
HOLLYFRONTIER CORPORATION
HORACE MANN EDUCATORS CORPORATION
ICU MEDICAL INC
I-FLOW CORPORATION
ILLUMINA INC
IMMUCOR INC
IMPAX LABORATORIES INC
INDEPENDENCE HOLDING CO
INNOPHOS HOLDINGS INC
INNOSPEC INC
INTEGRAL SYSTEMS INC
INTEGRAMED AMERICA INC
INTERACTIVE DATA CORPORATION
INTERACTIVE INTELLIGENCE GROUP INC
INTERCONTINENTALEXCHANGE INC (ICE)
INTERMEC INC
INTERNAP NETWORK SERVICES CORP
INTUITIVE SURGICAL INC
INVESTMENT TECHNOLOGY GROUP INC (ITG)
IRIDEX CORP
IRIS INTERNATIONAL INC
IROBOT CORP

ISILON SYSTEMS INC
J2 GLOBAL COMMUNICATIONS INC
JAZZ PHARMACEUTICALS INC
KEY TRONIC CORP
KEYNOTE SYSTEMS INC
KIMLEY-HORN AND ASSOCIATES INC
KRONOS WORLDWIDE INC
LAKELAND INDUSTRIES INC
LB FOSTER COMPANY
LCC INTERNATIONAL INC
LIFECELL CORPORATION
LIFECORE BIOMEDICAL INC
LIVEPERSON INC
LOGISTICARE INC
LOJACK CORPORTATION
LUCASFILM LTD
LUCOR INC
LUMINEX CORPORATION
MAKO SURGICAL CORP
MANAGEMENT NETWORK GROUP INC (THE)
MANHATTAN ASSOCIATES INC
MAPFRE USA CORP
MARTEK BIOSCIENCES CORP
MEDICINES CO (THE)
MEDICIS PHARMACEUTICAL CORP
MEDTOX SCIENTIFIC INC
MENTOR CORP
MERIDIAN BIOSCIENCE INC
MERIT MEDICAL SYSTEMS INC
MESIROW FINANCIAL HOLDINGS INC
METROPOLITAN HEALTH NETWORKS INC
MICROTEK MEDICAL HOLDINGS INC
MIDAS INC
MILLENNIUM PHARMACEUTICALS INC
MINDSPEED TECHNOLOGIES INC
MOTORCAR PARTS OF AMERICA INC
MYRIAD GENETICS INC
NANOMETRICS INC
NATIONAL DENTEX CORP
NATUS MEDICAL INC
NEKTAR THERAPEUTICS
NEOGEN CORPORATION
NETGEAR INC
NETSCOUT SYSTEMS INC
NETSUITE INC

NETWORK ENGINES INC
NIC INC
NOTIFY TECHNOLOGY CORP
NOVAMED INC
NOVEN PHARMACEUTICALS INC
NUVASIVE INC
ODYSSEY RE HOLDINGS CORP
ONLINE RESOURCES CORP
OPENTV CORP
ORION MARINE GROUP INC
PACIFIC BIOMARKERS INC
PAR PHARMACEUTICAL COMPANIES INC
PC CONNECTION INC
PEGASYSTEMS INC
PERFICIENT INC
PHAZAR CORP
PHILADELPHIA CONSOLIDATED HOLDING CORP
PHOENIX COMPANIES INC (THE)
PLATO LEARNING INC
PMA COMPANIES INC
POLYPORE INTERNATIONAL INC
POWERSECURE INTERNATIONAL INC
PREMIERE GLOBAL SERVICES INC
PROASSURANCE CORP
PROTECTIVE LIFE CORP
PURPLE COMMUNICATIONS INC
QUAKER CHEMICAL CORP
QUALCOMM ATHEROS INC
QUALITY SYSTEMS INC
QUANTUM CORP
QUESTCOR PHARMACEUTICALS INC
QUIDEL CORP
RAYTHEON APPLIED SIGNAL TECHNOLOGY INC
REALNETWORKS INC
RECYCLED ENERGY DEVELOPMENT LLC
REGENERON PHARMACEUTICALS INC
REINSURANCE GROUP OF AMERICA INC
RENTRAK CORP
RIGHTNOW TECHNOLOGIES INC
RIVERBED TECHNOLOGY INC
ROGERS CORPORATION
ROVI CORPORATION
RSA SECURITY INC
S1 CORPORATION
SALIX PHARMACEUTICALS
SBA COMMUNICATIONS CORP
SCANSOURCE INC
SCHICK TECHNOLOGIES INC
SCHIFF NUTRITION INTERNATIONAL INC
SCICLONE PHARMACEUTICALS INC
SCIOS INC
SEACHANGE INTERNATIONAL INC
SEATTLE GENETICS
SELECTICA INC
SERACARE LIFE SCIENCES INC
SHARED TECHNOLOGIES
SHUTTERFLY INC
SIGMA DESIGNS INC
SILICON LABORATORIES INC
SMART MODULAR TECHNOLOGIES INC
SOLARRESERVE
SOLFOCUS INC
SPARTAN MOTORS INC
SPECTRANETICS CORP
SPECTRUM PHARMACEUTICALS INC
SPIRE CORPORATION
SRS LABS INC
SS&C TECHNOLOGIES HOLDINGS INC
STAAR SURGICAL CO
STATE AUTO FINANCIAL CORP
STEPAN COMPANY
STERLING AUTOBODY CENTERS
STERLING CONSTRUCTION COMPANY
STIEFEL LABORATORIES INC
SUPER MICRO COMPUTER INC
SUPREME INDUSTRIES INC
SYNAPTICS INC
SYNOVIS LIFE TECHNOLOGIES INC
TAKE-TWO INTERACTIVE SOFTWARE INC
TECHNE CORP
TEKELEC
TELIRIS
TESCO CORPORATION
TESSCO TECHNOLOGIES INC
THERAGENICS CORP
THORATEC CORPORATION
TII NETWORK TECHNOLOGIES INC
TRANSATLANTIC HOLDINGS INC
TRANSCEND SERVICES INC
TREX COMPANY INC
TRIZETTO GROUP INC (THE)
ULTIMATE SOFTWARE GROUP INC
ULTRALIFE CORPORATION
UNITED THERAPEUTICS CORP
UNIVERSAL HOSPITAL SERVICES INC
UQM TECHNOLOGIES INC
US PHYSICAL THERAPY INC
USANA HEALTH SCIENCES INC
UTAH MEDICAL PRODUCTS INC
VARIAN SEMICONDUCTOR EQUIPMENT ASSOCIATES INC
VASCO DATA SECURITY INTERNATIONAL INC
VENTANA MEDICAL SYSTEMS INC
VERENIUM CORPORATION
VIASAT INC
VIROPHARMA INC
VOX INTERNATIONAL CORPORATION
WABASH NATIONAL CORP
WADDELL & REED FINANCIAL INC
WEBEX COMMUNICATIONS INC
WEBMD HEALTH CORP
WEBSENSE INC
WIKIMEDIA FOUNDATION
WIND RIVER SYSTEMS INC
WMS INDUSTRIES INC
WRIGHT MEDICAL GROUP INC
XETA TECHNOLOGIES INC
XOMA LTD
ZAP JONWAY
ZEP INC
ZIEBART INTERNATIONAL CORP
ZOLL MEDICAL CORP

Management

Experienced Management
24/7 REAL MEDIA INC
AAMCO TRANSMISSIONS INC
ABAXIS INC
ACI WORLDWIDE INC
ACME PACKET INC
ACXIOM DIGITAL INC
ADEPT TECHNOLOGY INC
ADTRAN INC
ADVISORY BOARD COMPANY (THE)
AFFILIATED MANAGERS GROUP
AKAMAI TECHNOLOGIES INC

AKORN INC
AKQA INC
ALBANY MOLECULAR RESEARCH INC
ALEXANDER & BALDWIN INC
ALEXION PHARMACEUTICALS INC
ALIEN TECHNOLOGY CORPORATION
ALIGN TECHNOLOGY INC
ALLEGIANT TRAVEL COMPANY
ALLIED HEALTHCARE INTERNATIONAL INC
ALLSCRIPTS HEALTHCARE SOLUTIONS INC
AMAG PHARMACEUTICALS INC
AMCOL INTERNATIONAL CORP
AMCON DISTRIBUTING CO
AMERESCO INC
AMERICAN CAMPUS COMMUNITIES INC
AMERICAN FIDELITY ASSURANCE COMPANY
AMERICAN MEDICAL SYSTEMS HOLDINGS INC
AMERICAN SCIENCE & ENGINEERING INC
AMERICAN TIRE DISTRIBUTORS
AMERICAN TOWER CORP
AMERICAN VANGUARD CORP
AMERICA'S CAR-MART INC
AMTECH SYSTEMS INC
AMTRUST FINANCIAL SERVICES INC
ANALOGIC CORP
ANAREN INC
ANIKA THERAPEUTICS INC
APP PHARMACEUTICALS INC
ARCSIGHT INC
ARDEN GROUP INC
ARGON ST INC
ARIBA INC
ARIZONA CHEMICAL COMPANY
AROTECH CORPORATION
ARRAY BIOPHARMA INC
ARRIS GROUP INC
ARTHROCARE CORP
ARUBA NETWORKS INC
ASTEX PHARMACEUTICALS INC
ATHENAHEALTH INC
ATLANTIC CITY ELECTRIC COMPANY
ATLANTIC TELE-NETWORK INC

ATRION CORPORATION
AUDIBLE INC
AVALONBAY COMMUNITIES INC
AVIALL INC
AVISTA CORPORATION
B&G FOODS INC
BANKRATE INC
BERRY PETROLEUM CO
BIO REFERENCE LABORATORIES INC
BIOMARIN PHARMACEUTICAL INC
BIOSCRIP INC
BIOSITE INC
BLACK HILLS CORP
BLACKBOARD INC
BLUE COAT SYSTEMS INC
BLUE NILE INC
BOSTON BEER COMPANY INC (THE)
BOTTOMLINE TECHNOLOGIES INC
BRIGHTSTAR CORPORATION
CABOT OIL & GAS CORP
CACTUS FEEDERS INC
CAGLE'S INC
CALAVO GROWERS INC
CALGON CARBON CORPORATION
CALIBER HOLDINGS CORP
CALIPER LIFE SCIENCES INC
CAL-MAINE FOODS INC
CAMBREX CORP
CANTEL MEDICAL CORP
CANTOR FITZGERALD LP
CAPITOL FEDERAL FINANCIAL INC
CARACO PHARMACEUTICAL LABORATORIES LTD
CARBO CERAMICS INC
CARDIONET INC
CARDTRONICS INC
CARRIZO OIL & GAS INC
CATALYST HEALTH SOLUTIONS INC
CELLDEX THERAPEUTICS INC
CELSIS INTERNATIONAL PLC
CENTRAL VERMONT PUBLIC SERVICE CORP
CEPHEID
CERUS CORPORATION
CF INDUSTRIES HOLDINGS INC
CHANNELL COMMERCIAL CORP
CHATTEM INC
CHINDEX INTERNATIONAL INC
CHOICESTREAM INC
CHOLESTECH CORP

CIRRUS LOGIC INC
CKX INC
CLAYTON WILLIAMS ENERGY INC
CLEAN ENERGY FUELS CORP
CLEARONE COMMUNICATIONS INC
COGENT COMMUNICATIONS
COHERENT INC
COMDATA CORP
COMPASS DIVERSIFIED HOLDINGS
COMTECH TELECOMMUNICATIONS CORP
COMVERGE INC
CONCUR TECHNOLOGIES INC
CONSTANT CONTACT INC
CONTINENTAL RESOURCES INC
CONTINUCARE CORP
CORPORATE EXECUTIVE BOARD COMPANY (THE)
COSTAR GROUP INC
COUPONS INC
CRA INTERNATIONAL INC (CHARLES RIVER)
CRAY INC
CRITICAL CARE SYSTEMS
CROWN CASTLE INTERNATIONAL CORP
CRUM & FORSTER HOLDINGS INC
CRYOLIFE INC
CUBIST PHARMACEUTICALS INC
CULP INC
CUMULUS MEDIA INC
CYBERONICS INC
CYBERSOURCE CORP
DANNON COMPANY INC (THE)
DAWSON GEOPHYSICAL COMPANY
DEI HOLDINGS INC
DELPHI FINANCIAL GROUP INC
DENBURY RESOURCES INC
DIAMOND ADVISORY SERVICES
DIAMOND FOODS INC
DIGITAL GENERATION INC
DJO GLOBAL INC
DOLBY LABORATORIES INC
DORMAN PRODUCTS INC
DPL INC
DREAMWORKS ANIMATION SKG INC
DRUGSTORE.COM INC
EATON VANCE CORP
EBIX INC
ECHO GLOBAL LOGISTICS INC

ECHOSTAR CORP
ECOLLEGE.COM
EDELMAN FINANCIAL GROUP (THE)
EDGAR ONLINE INC
EDUCATIONAL DEVELOPMENT CORP
EHEALTH INC
EMBARCADERO TECHNOLOGIES INC
EMCORE CORP
EMS TECHNOLOGIES INC
EMULEX CORP
ENCORE CAPITAL GROUP INC
ENERGY TRANSFER PARTNERS LP
ENERNOC INC
ENVIRONMENTAL TECTONICS CORP
EOG RESOURCES INC
EPAM SYSTEMS
EQT CORPORATION
EQUINIX INC
ERESEARCH TECHNOLOGY INC
ESSEX PROPERTY TRUST INC
EVERCORE PARTNERS INC
EVEREST RE GROUP LTD
EXACTECH INC
F5 NETWORKS INC
FAIR ISAAC CORPORATION
FEDEX SUPPLY CHAIN SERVICES INC
FIRST FINANCIAL BANCORP (OH)
FNB CORP
FORRESTER RESEARCH INC
FORTINET INC
FRESHDIRECT LLC
FROZEN FOOD EXPRESS INDUSTRIES INC
FUEL SYSTEMS SOLUTIONS INC
FUEL TECH INC
GAIAM INC
GALLUP ORGANIZATION (THE)
GENCO SHIPPING & TRADING LIMITED
GENENCOR INTERNATIONAL INC
GENERAL ATOMICS
GENERAL COMMUNICATION INC (GCI)
GENESIS ENERGY LP
GENOMIC HEALTH INC
GEN-PROBE INC
GFI GROUP INC
G-III APPAREL GROUP
GLEACHER & COMPANY INC
GLOBAL PARTNERS LP
GLOBECOMM SYSTEMS INC
GLU MOBILE INC
GOLDEN ENTERPRISES INC
GOLFSMITH INTERNATIONAL HOLDINGS INC
GREAT AMERICAN FINANCIAL RESOURCES INC
GREAT LAKES CHEESE COMPANY INC
GREEN MOUNTAIN POWER CORPORATION
GTC BIOTHERAPEUTICS INC
GULFMARK OFFSHORE INC
HAEMONETICS CORPORATION
HAHN AUTOMOTIVE WAREHOUSE INC
HANCOCK HOLDING COMPANY
HANOVER FOODS CORPORATION
HARRIS INTERACTIVE INC
HCC INSURANCE HOLDINGS INC
HEALTH GRADES INC
HEALTH INSURANCE PLAN OF GREATER NEW YORK
HEALTHSTREAM INC
HEALTHTRONICS INC
HEARUSA INC
HELIOVOLT CORP
HELIX ENERGY SOLUTIONS GROUP INC
HESKA CORP
HICKORY TECH CORPORATION
HI-TECH PHARMACAL CO INC
HOLLYFRONTIER CORPORATION
HORACE MANN EDUCATORS CORPORATION
HOSPITALITY PROPERTIES TRUST
HOULIHAN LOKEY HOWARD & ZUKIN INC
HUB GROUP INC
HUDSON CITY BANCORP INC
IBASIS INC
ICONIX BRAND GROUP INC
ICU MEDICAL INC
IDACORP INC
I-FLOW CORPORATION
ILLUMINA INC
IMG WORLDWIDE INC
IMMUCOR INC
IMPAX LABORATORIES INC
INDEPENDENCE HOLDING CO
INFOSPACE INC
INNOPHOS HOLDINGS INC
INNOSPEC INC
INTEGRAL SYSTEMS INC
INTEGRAMED AMERICA INC
INTERACTIVE DATA CORPORATION
INTERACTIVE INTELLIGENCE GROUP INC
INTERCONTINENTALEXCHANGE INC (ICE)
INTERMEC INC
INTERNAP NETWORK SERVICES CORP
INTERNATIONAL CREATIVE MANAGEMENT INC (ICM)
INTERNATIONAL DAIRY QUEEN INC
INTUITIVE SURGICAL INC
INVESTMENT TECHNOLOGY GROUP INC (ITG)
INVESTORS REAL ESTATE TRUST
IRIDEX CORP
IRIS INTERNATIONAL INC
IROBOT CORP
ISILON SYSTEMS INC
IVILLAGE INC
J2 GLOBAL COMMUNICATIONS INC
JAZZ PHARMACEUTICALS INC
JOE'S JEANS INC
JOHN B SANFILIPPO & SON INC
KAMPGROUNDS OF AMERICA INC
KBW INC
KENDALL-JACKSON WINE ESTATES LTD
KENNETH COLE PRODUCTIONS INC
KEY TRONIC CORP
KEYNOTE SYSTEMS INC
KIMLEY-HORN AND ASSOCIATES INC
KIRBY CORP
KKR & CO LP (KOHLBERG KRAVIS ROBERTS & CO)
KNIGHT CAPITAL GROUP INC
KNOLOGY INC
KORN/FERRY INTERNATIONAL
KRONOS WORLDWIDE INC
LACLEDE GROUP INC (THE)
LAKELAND INDUSTRIES INC
LB FOSTER COMPANY
LCC INTERNATIONAL INC
LESLIE'S POOLMART INC
LIFECELL CORPORATION
LIFECORE BIOMEDICAL INC

LIVEPERSON INC
LOGISTICARE INC
LOJACK CORPORTATION
LUCASFILM LTD
LUCOR INC
LUMINEX CORPORATION
MAGELLAN MIDSTREAM PARTNERS LP
MAKO SURGICAL CORP
MALT-O-MEAL COMPANY
MANAGEMENT NETWORK GROUP INC (THE)
MANHATTAN ASSOCIATES INC
MAPFRE USA CORP
MARTEK BIOSCIENCES CORP
MARVEL ENTERTAINMENT LLC
MEDICINES CO (THE)
MEDICIS PHARMACEUTICAL CORP
MEDIFAST INC
MEDTOX SCIENTIFIC INC
MENTOR CORP
MERIDIAN BIOSCIENCE INC
MERIT MEDICAL SYSTEMS INC
MESIROW FINANCIAL HOLDINGS INC
METROPOLITAN HEALTH NETWORKS INC
MICHELINAS INC
MICROTEK MEDICAL HOLDINGS INC
MID-AMERICA APARTMENT COMMUNITIES INC
MIDAS INC
MILLENNIUM PHARMACEUTICALS INC
MINDSPEED TECHNOLOGIES INC
MOELIS & COMPANY
MONSTER BEVERAGE CORP
MOTORCAR PARTS OF AMERICA INC
MTR GAMING GROUP INC
MYRIAD GENETICS INC
NANOMETRICS INC
NATIONAL BEVERAGE CORP
NATIONAL DENTEX CORP
NATIONAL WINE & SPIRITS INC
NATUS MEDICAL INC
NEKTAR THERAPEUTICS
NEOGEN CORPORATION
NETFLIX INC
NETGEAR INC
NETSCOUT SYSTEMS INC
NETSUITE INC

NETWORK ENGINES INC
NEUSTAR INC
NEW JERSEY RESOURCES CORPORATION
NEW YORK MERCANTILE EXCHANGE INC
NIC INC
NORTHWESTERN CORPORATION
NOTIFY TECHNOLOGY CORP
NOVAMED INC
NOVEN PHARMACEUTICALS INC
NTELOS HOLDING CORP
NUGGET MARKET
NUSTAR ENERGY LP
NUTRASWEET COMPANY (THE)
NUVASIVE INC
ODYSSEY RE HOLDINGS CORP
OMNOVA SOLUTIONS INC
ONLINE RESOURCES CORP
ONSTREAM MEDIA CORPORATION
OPENTV CORP
ORION MARINE GROUP INC
PACIFIC BIOMARKERS INC
PAR PHARMACEUTICAL COMPANIES INC
PATAGONIA INC
PC CONNECTION INC
PEAPOD LLC
PEGASYSTEMS INC
PERFICIENT INC
PERRY ELLIS INTERNATIONAL INC
PETMED EXPRESS INC
PETROLEUM DEVELOPMENT CORPORATION
PHAZAR CORP
PHILADELPHIA CONSOLIDATED HOLDING CORP
PHOENIX COMPANIES INC (THE)
PIEDMONT NATURAL GAS COMPANY INC
PIONEER NATURAL RESOURCES COMPANY
PIPER JAFFRAY COMPANIES
PLAINS EXPLORATION AND PRODUCTION COMPANY
PLATO LEARNING INC
PMA COMPANIES INC
POLYPORE INTERNATIONAL INC
POWERSECURE INTERNATIONAL INC
PREMIERE GLOBAL SERVICES INC
PRIMEENERGY CORPORATION

PROASSURANCE CORP
PROTECTIVE LIFE CORP
PURPLE COMMUNICATIONS INC
QUAKER CHEMICAL CORP
QUALCOMM ATHEROS INC
QUALITY SYSTEMS INC
QUANTUM CORP
QUESTCOR PHARMACEUTICALS INC
QUICKSILVER RESOURCES INC
QUIDEL CORP
RAYTHEON APPLIED SIGNAL TECHNOLOGY INC
REALNETWORKS INC
RECYCLED ENERGY DEVELOPMENT LLC
REDBOX AUTOMATED RETAIL LLC
REGENERON PHARMACEUTICALS INC
REINSURANCE GROUP OF AMERICA INC
RENTRAK CORP
RICELAND FOODS INC
RIGHTNOW TECHNOLOGIES INC
RIVERBED TECHNOLOGY INC
ROBERT W BAIRD & CO INC
ROCKY BRANDS INC
ROGERS CORPORATION
ROSETTA STONE INC
ROVI CORPORATION
RPC INC
RSA SECURITY INC
S1 CORPORATION
SACRAMENTO MUNICIPAL UTILITY DISTRICT
SALIX PHARMACEUTICALS
SANDRIDGE ENERGY INC
SBA COMMUNICATIONS CORP
SCANSOURCE INC
SCHICK TECHNOLOGIES INC
SCHIFF NUTRITION INTERNATIONAL INC
SCICLONE PHARMACEUTICALS INC
SCIOS INC
SCOULAR COMPANY (THE)
SEACHANGE INTERNATIONAL INC
SEATTLE GENETICS
SELECTICA INC
SENIOR HOUSING PROPERTIES
SERACARE LIFE SCIENCES INC
SHARED TECHNOLOGIES
SHENANDOAH

TELECOMMUNICATIONS CO
SHUTTERFLY INC
SIGMA DESIGNS INC
SILICON LABORATORIES INC
SL GREEN REALTY CORP
SMART MODULAR TECHNOLOGIES INC
SOLARRESERVE
SOLFOCUS INC
SOTHEBYS
SOUTHERN UNION COMPANY
SOUTHWEST GAS CORP
SOUTHWESTERN ENERGY CO
SOVRAN SELF STORAGE INC
SPARTAN MOTORS INC
SPECTRANETICS CORP
SPECTRUM PHARMACEUTICALS INC
SPIRE CORPORATION
SPORT SUPPLY GROUP INC
SPORTSMAN'S GUIDE INC (THE)
SPROUTS FARMERS MARKET LLC
SRS LABS INC
SS&C TECHNOLOGIES HOLDINGS INC
STAAR SURGICAL CO
STATE AUTO FINANCIAL CORP
STEPAN COMPANY
STERLING AUTOBODY CENTERS
STERLING CONSTRUCTION COMPANY
STEVEN MADDEN LTD
STIEFEL LABORATORIES INC
SUN COMMUNITIES INC
SUNOCO LOGISTICS PARTNERS LP
SUPER MICRO COMPUTER INC
SUPERIOR UNIFORM GROUP INC
SUPERTEL HOSPITALITY INC
SUPREME INDUSTRIES INC
SVB FINANCIAL GROUP
SWIFT ENERGY CO
SYNAPTICS INC
SYNIVERSE TECHNOLOGIES
SYNOVIS LIFE TECHNOLOGIES INC
TAKE-TWO INTERACTIVE SOFTWARE INC
TAMPA ELECTRIC COMPANY
TARGA RESOURCES PARTNERS LP
TECHNE CORP
TEKELEC
TELIRIS

TERREMARK WORLDWIDE INC
TESCO CORPORATION
TESSCO TECHNOLOGIES INC
THERAGENICS CORP
THORATEC CORPORATION
TII NETWORK TECHNOLOGIES INC
TOOTSIE ROLL INDUSTRIES INC
TOPPS COMPANY INC (THE)
TRANSAMMONIA INC
TRANSATLANTIC HOLDINGS INC
TRANSCEND SERVICES INC
TRAVELZOO INC
TREX COMPANY INC
TRIZETTO GROUP INC (THE)
TRUE RELIGION APPAREL INC
UDR INC
UIL HOLDINGS CORPORATION
ULTIMATE SOFTWARE GROUP INC
ULTRALIFE CORPORATION
UNISOURCE ENERGY CORPORATION
UNIT CORP
UNITED ONLINE INC
UNITED THERAPEUTICS CORP
UNIVERSAL HOSPITAL SERVICES INC
UQM TECHNOLOGIES INC
US PHYSICAL THERAPY INC
USANA HEALTH SCIENCES INC
UTAH MEDICAL PRODUCTS INC
VARIAN SEMICONDUCTOR EQUIPMENT ASSOCIATES INC
VASCO DATA SECURITY INTERNATIONAL INC
VENTANA MEDICAL SYSTEMS INC
VERENIUM CORPORATION
VIASAT INC
VIBRANT MEDIA INC
VIROPHARMA INC
VOLCOM INC
VOX INTERNATIONAL CORPORATION
WABASH NATIONAL CORP
WADDELL & REED FINANCIAL INC
WEBEX COMMUNICATIONS INC
WEBMD HEALTH CORP
WEBMEDIA BRANDS INC
WEBSENSE INC
WESTAR ENERGY
WGL HOLDINGS INC
WHITEWAVE FOODS COMPANY

WIKIMEDIA FOUNDATION
WIND RIVER SYSTEMS INC
WMS INDUSTRIES INC
WRIGHT MEDICAL GROUP INC
XETA TECHNOLOGIES INC
XO GROUP INC
XOMA LTD
XTO ENERGY INC
YOUNG'S MARKET COMPANY LLC
ZAP JONWAY
ZEP INC
ZIEBART INTERNATIONAL CORP
ZOLL MEDICAL CORP
ZYNGA INC

International Business
24/7 REAL MEDIA INC
AAMCO TRANSMISSIONS INC
ABAXIS INC
ACI WORLDWIDE INC
ACME PACKET INC
ACXIOM DIGITAL INC
ADEPT TECHNOLOGY INC
ADTRAN INC
ADVISORY BOARD COMPANY (THE)
AFFILIATED MANAGERS GROUP
AKAMAI TECHNOLOGIES INC
AKQA INC
ALBANY MOLECULAR RESEARCH INC
ALEXANDER & BALDWIN INC
ALEXION PHARMACEUTICALS INC
ALIEN TECHNOLOGY CORPORATION
ALIGN TECHNOLOGY INC
ALLIED HEALTHCARE INTERNATIONAL INC
AMCOL INTERNATIONAL CORP
AMERESCO INC
AMERICAN CAMPUS COMMUNITIES INC
AMERICAN FIDELITY ASSURANCE COMPANY
AMERICAN MEDICAL SYSTEMS HOLDINGS INC
AMERICAN SCIENCE & ENGINEERING INC
AMERICAN TOWER CORP
AMERICAN VANGUARD CORP
AMERICA'S CAR-MART INC
AMTECH SYSTEMS INC
AMTRUST FINANCIAL SERVICES

INC
ANALOGIC CORP
ANAREN INC
APP PHARMACEUTICALS INC
ARCSIGHT INC
ARGON ST INC
ARIBA INC
ARIZONA CHEMICAL COMPANY
AROTECH CORPORATION
ARRIS GROUP INC
ARTHROCARE CORP
ARUBA NETWORKS INC
ATHENAHEALTH INC
ATLANTIC TELE-NETWORK INC
ATRION CORPORATION
AUDIBLE INC
AVIALL INC
B&G FOODS INC
BANKRATE INC
BERRY PETROLEUM CO
BIOMARIN PHARMACEUTICAL INC
BIOSITE INC
BLACKBOARD INC
BLUE COAT SYSTEMS INC
BLUE NILE INC
BOTTOMLINE TECHNOLOGIES INC
BRIGHTSTAR CORPORATION
CACTUS FEEDERS INC
CALAVO GROWERS INC
CALGON CARBON CORPORATION
CALIPER LIFE SCIENCES INC
CAMBREX CORP
CANTEL MEDICAL CORP
CANTOR FITZGERALD LP
CARBO CERAMICS INC
CARDTRONICS INC
CARRIZO OIL & GAS INC
CATALYST HEALTH SOLUTIONS INC
CELSIS INTERNATIONAL PLC
CENTRAL VERMONT PUBLIC SERVICE CORP
CEPHEID
CERUS CORPORATION
CF INDUSTRIES HOLDINGS INC
CHANNELL COMMERCIAL CORP
CHATTEM INC
CHINDEX INTERNATIONAL INC
CHOLESTECH CORP
CIRRUS LOGIC INC
CKX INC
CLEAN ENERGY FUELS CORP
CLEARONE COMMUNICATIONS INC
COGENT COMMUNICATIONS
COHERENT INC
COMTECH TELECOMMUNICATIONS CORP
CONCUR TECHNOLOGIES INC
CORPORATE EXECUTIVE BOARD COMPANY (THE)
COSTAR GROUP INC
COUPONS INC
CRA INTERNATIONAL INC (CHARLES RIVER)
CRAY INC
CROWN CASTLE INTERNATIONAL CORP
CRYOLIFE INC
CUBIST PHARMACEUTICALS INC
CULP INC
CYBERONICS INC
CYBERSOURCE CORP
DAWSON GEOPHYSICAL COMPANY
DEI HOLDINGS INC
DELPHI FINANCIAL GROUP INC
DENBURY RESOURCES INC
DIAMOND ADVISORY SERVICES
DIAMOND FOODS INC
DIGITAL GENERATION INC
DJO GLOBAL INC
DOLBY LABORATORIES INC
DORMAN PRODUCTS INC
DRUGSTORE.COM INC
EATON VANCE CORP
EBIX INC
ECHOSTAR CORP
ECOLLEGE.COM
EMBARCADERO TECHNOLOGIES INC
EMCORE CORP
EMS TECHNOLOGIES INC
EMULEX CORP
ENERNOC INC
ENVIRONMENTAL TECTONICS CORP
EOG RESOURCES INC
EPAM SYSTEMS
EQT CORPORATION
EQUINIX INC
ERESEARCH TECHNOLOGY INC
EVERCORE PARTNERS INC
EVEREST RE GROUP LTD
EXACTECH INC
F5 NETWORKS INC
FAIR ISAAC CORPORATION
FEDEX SUPPLY CHAIN SERVICES INC
FORRESTER RESEARCH INC
FORTINET INC
FUEL SYSTEMS SOLUTIONS INC
FUEL TECH INC
GALLUP ORGANIZATION (THE)
GENCO SHIPPING & TRADING LIMITED
GENENCOR INTERNATIONAL INC
GENERAL ATOMICS
GEN-PROBE INC
GFI GROUP INC
G-III APPAREL GROUP
GLEACHER & COMPANY INC
GLOBAL PARTNERS LP
GLOBECOMM SYSTEMS INC
GLU MOBILE INC
GOLFSMITH INTERNATIONAL HOLDINGS INC
GTC BIOTHERAPEUTICS INC
GULFMARK OFFSHORE INC
HAEMONETICS CORPORATION
HANOVER FOODS CORPORATION
HARRIS INTERACTIVE INC
HCC INSURANCE HOLDINGS INC
HEALTHTRONICS INC
HEARUSA INC
HELIX ENERGY SOLUTIONS GROUP INC
HESKA CORP
HI-TECH PHARMACAL CO INC
HOLLYFRONTIER CORPORATION
HOSPITALITY PROPERTIES TRUST
HOULIHAN LOKEY HOWARD & ZUKIN INC
HUB GROUP INC
IBASIS INC
ICONIX BRAND GROUP INC
ICU MEDICAL INC
IDACORP INC
I-FLOW CORPORATION
ILLUMINA INC
IMG WORLDWIDE INC
IMMUCOR INC
INFOSPACE INC
INNOPHOS HOLDINGS INC
INNOSPEC INC

INTEGRAL SYSTEMS INC
INTERACTIVE DATA CORPORATION
INTERACTIVE INTELLIGENCE GROUP INC
INTERCONTINENTALEXCHANGE INC (ICE)
INTERMEC INC
INTERNAP NETWORK SERVICES CORP
INTERNATIONAL CREATIVE MANAGEMENT INC (ICM)
INTERNATIONAL DAIRY QUEEN INC
INTUITIVE SURGICAL INC
INVESTMENT TECHNOLOGY GROUP INC (ITG)
IRIDEX CORP
IRIS INTERNATIONAL INC
IROBOT CORP
ISILON SYSTEMS INC
J2 GLOBAL COMMUNICATIONS INC
JOE'S JEANS INC
KAMPGROUNDS OF AMERICA INC
KBW INC
KENDALL-JACKSON WINE ESTATES LTD
KENNETH COLE PRODUCTIONS INC
KEY TRONIC CORP
KEYNOTE SYSTEMS INC
KIRBY CORP
KKR & CO LP (KOHLBERG KRAVIS ROBERTS & CO)
KNIGHT CAPITAL GROUP INC
KORN/FERRY INTERNATIONAL
KRONOS WORLDWIDE INC
LAKELAND INDUSTRIES INC
LCC INTERNATIONAL INC
LIFECELL CORPORATION
LIFECORE BIOMEDICAL INC
LIVEPERSON INC
LOJACK CORPORTATION
LUCASFILM LTD
LUMINEX CORPORATION
MANAGEMENT NETWORK GROUP INC (THE)
MANHATTAN ASSOCIATES INC
MARTEK BIOSCIENCES CORP
MARVEL ENTERTAINMENT LLC
MEDICINES CO (THE)
MEDICIS PHARMACEUTICAL CORP
MENTOR CORP
MERIDIAN BIOSCIENCE INC
MERIT MEDICAL SYSTEMS INC
MESIROW FINANCIAL HOLDINGS INC
MICHELINAS INC
MICROTEK MEDICAL HOLDINGS INC
MIDAS INC
MILLENNIUM PHARMACEUTICALS INC
MINDSPEED TECHNOLOGIES INC
MOELIS & COMPANY
MONSTER BEVERAGE CORP
MOTORCAR PARTS OF AMERICA INC
NANOMETRICS INC
NATIONAL DENTEX CORP
NATUS MEDICAL INC
NEKTAR THERAPEUTICS
NEOGEN CORPORATION
NETFLIX INC
NETGEAR INC
NETSCOUT SYSTEMS INC
NETSUITE INC
NETWORK ENGINES INC
NEUSTAR INC
NEW YORK MERCANTILE EXCHANGE INC
NOTIFY TECHNOLOGY CORP
NOVEN PHARMACEUTICALS INC
NUSTAR ENERGY LP
NUTRASWEET COMPANY (THE)
ODYSSEY RE HOLDINGS CORP
OMNOVA SOLUTIONS INC
OPENTV CORP
PAR PHARMACEUTICAL COMPANIES INC
PATAGONIA INC
PEGASYSTEMS INC
PERFICIENT INC
PERRY ELLIS INTERNATIONAL INC
PETROLEUM DEVELOPMENT CORPORATION
PHILADELPHIA CONSOLIDATED HOLDING CORP
PHOENIX COMPANIES INC (THE)
PIONEER NATURAL RESOURCES COMPANY
PIPER JAFFRAY COMPANIES
PLATO LEARNING INC
POLYPORE INTERNATIONAL INC
POWERSECURE INTERNATIONAL INC
PREMIERE GLOBAL SERVICES INC
PRIMEENERGY CORPORATION
QUAKER CHEMICAL CORP
QUALCOMM ATHEROS INC
QUALITY SYSTEMS INC
QUANTUM CORP
QUICKSILVER RESOURCES INC
QUIDEL CORP
RAYTHEON APPLIED SIGNAL TECHNOLOGY INC
REALNETWORKS INC
REDBOX AUTOMATED RETAIL LLC
REINSURANCE GROUP OF AMERICA INC
RENTRAK CORP
RIGHTNOW TECHNOLOGIES INC
RIVERBED TECHNOLOGY INC
ROBERT W BAIRD & CO INC
ROGERS CORPORATION
ROVI CORPORATION
RPC INC
RSA SECURITY INC
S1 CORPORATION
SALIX PHARMACEUTICALS
SBA COMMUNICATIONS CORP
SCANSOURCE INC
SCHICK TECHNOLOGIES INC
SCHIFF NUTRITION INTERNATIONAL INC
SCICLONE PHARMACEUTICALS INC
SCOULAR COMPANY (THE)
SEACHANGE INTERNATIONAL INC
SELECTICA INC
SENIOR HOUSING PROPERTIES
SERACARE LIFE SCIENCES INC
SIGMA DESIGNS INC
SILICON LABORATORIES INC
SMART MODULAR TECHNOLOGIES INC
SOLARRESERVE
SOLFOCUS INC
SOTHEBYS
SOUTHWESTERN ENERGY CO
SPARTAN MOTORS INC
SPECTRANETICS CORP
SPECTRUM PHARMACEUTICALS INC
SPIRE CORPORATION
SRS LABS INC
SS&C TECHNOLOGIES HOLDINGS INC
STAAR SURGICAL CO
STEPAN COMPANY

STERLING AUTOBODY CENTERS
STEVEN MADDEN LTD
STIEFEL LABORATORIES INC
SUNOCO LOGISTICS PARTNERS LP
SUPER MICRO COMPUTER INC
SVB FINANCIAL GROUP
SWIFT ENERGY CO
SYNAPTICS INC
SYNIVERSE TECHNOLOGIES
TAKE-TWO INTERACTIVE SOFTWARE INC
TARGA RESOURCES PARTNERS LP
TECHNE CORP
TEKELEC
TELIRIS
TERREMARK WORLDWIDE INC
TESCO CORPORATION
TESSCO TECHNOLOGIES INC
THERAGENICS CORP
THORATEC CORPORATION
TOOTSIE ROLL INDUSTRIES INC
TOPPS COMPANY INC (THE)
TRANSAMMONIA INC
TRANSATLANTIC HOLDINGS INC
TRAVELZOO INC
TRIZETTO GROUP INC (THE)
TRUE RELIGION APPAREL INC
ULTIMATE SOFTWARE GROUP INC
ULTRALIFE CORPORATION
UNISOURCE ENERGY CORPORATION
UNIT CORP
UNITED ONLINE INC
UNITED THERAPEUTICS CORP
USANA HEALTH SCIENCES INC
UTAH MEDICAL PRODUCTS INC
VARIAN SEMICONDUCTOR EQUIPMENT ASSOCIATES INC
VASCO DATA SECURITY INTERNATIONAL INC
VENTANA MEDICAL SYSTEMS INC
VIASAT INC
VIBRANT MEDIA INC
VOLCOM INC
VOX INTERNATIONAL CORPORATION
WABASH NATIONAL CORP
WADDELL & REED FINANCIAL INC
WEBEX COMMUNICATIONS INC
WEBMD HEALTH CORP
WEBMEDIA BRANDS INC
WEBSENSE INC
WESTAR ENERGY
WIKIMEDIA FOUNDATION
WIND RIVER SYSTEMS INC
WMS INDUSTRIES INC
WRIGHT MEDICAL GROUP INC
XTO ENERGY INC
ZAP JONWAY
ZEP INC
ZIEBART INTERNATIONAL CORP
ZOLL MEDICAL CORP
ZYNGA INC

Management Trainees
AAMCO TRANSMISSIONS INC
ALLIED HEALTHCARE INTERNATIONAL INC
AMCON DISTRIBUTING CO
AMERICAN CAMPUS COMMUNITIES INC
AMERICAN FIDELITY ASSURANCE COMPANY
AMERICAN TIRE DISTRIBUTORS
AMERICA'S CAR-MART INC
AMTRUST FINANCIAL SERVICES INC
ARDEN GROUP INC
ATHENAHEALTH INC
AUDIBLE INC
AVALONBAY COMMUNITIES INC
BIOSCRIP INC
BLACKBOARD INC
BLUE NILE INC
BOSTON BEER COMPANY INC (THE)
CALAVO GROWERS INC
CALIBER HOLDINGS CORP
CAL-MAINE FOODS INC
CANTOR FITZGERALD LP
CAPITOL FEDERAL FINANCIAL INC
CARDTRONICS INC
CATALYST HEALTH SOLUTIONS INC
CLEAN ENERGY FUELS CORP
COMDATA CORP
CONTINUCARE CORP
CRITICAL CARE SYSTEMS
CRUM & FORSTER HOLDINGS INC
DELPHI FINANCIAL GROUP INC
DIAMOND FOODS INC
DRUGSTORE.COM INC
ECOLLEGE.COM
EDELMAN FINANCIAL GROUP (THE)
EHEALTH INC
ENCORE CAPITAL GROUP INC
FIRST FINANCIAL BANCORP (OH)
FNB CORP
FRESHDIRECT LLC
GAIAM INC
G-III APPAREL GROUP
GOLFSMITH INTERNATIONAL HOLDINGS INC
GREAT AMERICAN FINANCIAL RESOURCES INC
HAHN AUTOMOTIVE WAREHOUSE INC
HANCOCK HOLDING COMPANY
HCC INSURANCE HOLDINGS INC
HEALTH INSURANCE PLAN OF GREATER NEW YORK
HEALTHSTREAM INC
HEARUSA INC
HORACE MANN EDUCATORS CORPORATION
HUDSON CITY BANCORP INC
INDEPENDENCE HOLDING CO
INTEGRAMED AMERICA INC
INTERNATIONAL DAIRY QUEEN INC
INVESTMENT TECHNOLOGY GROUP INC (ITG)
KAMPGROUNDS OF AMERICA INC
KENDALL-JACKSON WINE ESTATES LTD
KENNETH COLE PRODUCTIONS INC
LESLIE'S POOLMART INC
LUCOR INC
LUMINEX CORPORATION
MAPFRE USA CORP
MEDIFAST INC
METROPOLITAN HEALTH NETWORKS INC
MID-AMERICA APARTMENT COMMUNITIES INC
MIDAS INC
MONSTER BEVERAGE CORP
NATIONAL BEVERAGE CORP
NATIONAL WINE & SPIRITS INC
NETFLIX INC
NUGGET MARKET
PC CONNECTION INC
PEAPOD LLC
PERRY ELLIS INTERNATIONAL INC
PETMED EXPRESS INC
PHILADELPHIA CONSOLIDATED HOLDING CORP

PHOENIX COMPANIES INC (THE)
PMA COMPANIES INC
PROASSURANCE CORP
PROTECTIVE LIFE CORP
REDBOX AUTOMATED RETAIL LLC
SCHIFF NUTRITION INTERNATIONAL INC
SENIOR HOUSING PROPERTIES
SOTHEBYS
SOVRAN SELF STORAGE INC
SPORT SUPPLY GROUP INC
SPORTSMAN'S GUIDE INC (THE)
SPROUTS FARMERS MARKET LLC
STATE AUTO FINANCIAL CORP
STERLING AUTOBODY CENTERS
STERLING CONSTRUCTION COMPANY
SUN COMMUNITIES INC
SUPERTEL HOSPITALITY INC
SVB FINANCIAL GROUP
TOOTSIE ROLL INDUSTRIES INC
TOPPS COMPANY INC (THE)
TRANSATLANTIC HOLDINGS INC
TRUE RELIGION APPAREL INC
US PHYSICAL THERAPY INC
YOUNG'S MARKET COMPANY LLC
ZIEBART INTERNATIONAL CORP

MBA Graduates

24/7 REAL MEDIA INC
AAMCO TRANSMISSIONS INC
ABAXIS INC
ACI WORLDWIDE INC
ACME PACKET INC
ACXIOM DIGITAL INC
ADEPT TECHNOLOGY INC
ADTRAN INC
ADVISORY BOARD COMPANY (THE)
AFFILIATED MANAGERS GROUP
AKAMAI TECHNOLOGIES INC
AKORN INC
AKQA INC
ALBANY MOLECULAR RESEARCH INC
ALEXANDER & BALDWIN INC
ALEXION PHARMACEUTICALS INC
ALIEN TECHNOLOGY CORPORATION
ALIGN TECHNOLOGY INC
ALLEGIANT TRAVEL COMPANY
ALLIED HEALTHCARE INTERNATIONAL INC
ALLSCRIPTS HEALTHCARE SOLUTIONS INC
AMAG PHARMACEUTICALS INC
AMCOL INTERNATIONAL CORP
AMCON DISTRIBUTING CO
AMERESCO INC
AMERICAN CAMPUS COMMUNITIES INC
AMERICAN FIDELITY ASSURANCE COMPANY
AMERICAN MEDICAL SYSTEMS HOLDINGS INC
AMERICAN SCIENCE & ENGINEERING INC
AMERICAN TIRE DISTRIBUTORS
AMERICAN TOWER CORP
AMERICAN VANGUARD CORP
AMERICA'S CAR-MART INC
AMTECH SYSTEMS INC
AMTRUST FINANCIAL SERVICES INC
ANALOGIC CORP
ANAREN INC
ANIKA THERAPEUTICS INC
APP PHARMACEUTICALS INC
ARCSIGHT INC
ARDEN GROUP INC
ARGON ST INC
ARIBA INC
ARIZONA CHEMICAL COMPANY
AROTECH CORPORATION
ARRAY BIOPHARMA INC
ARRIS GROUP INC
ARTHROCARE CORP
ARUBA NETWORKS INC
ASTEX PHARMACEUTICALS INC
ATHENAHEALTH INC
ATLANTIC CITY ELECTRIC COMPANY
ATLANTIC TELE-NETWORK INC
ATRION CORPORATION
AUDIBLE INC
AVALONBAY COMMUNITIES INC
AVIALL INC
AVISTA CORPORATION
B&G FOODS INC
BANKRATE INC
BERRY PETROLEUM CO
BIO REFERENCE LABORATORIES INC
BIOMARIN PHARMACEUTICAL INC
BIOSCRIP INC
BIOSITE INC
BLACK HILLS CORP
BLACKBOARD INC
BLUE COAT SYSTEMS INC
BLUE NILE INC
BOSTON BEER COMPANY INC (THE)
BOTTOMLINE TECHNOLOGIES INC
BRIGHTSTAR CORPORATION
CABOT OIL & GAS CORP
CACTUS FEEDERS INC
CAGLE'S INC
CALAVO GROWERS INC
CALGON CARBON CORPORATION
CALIBER HOLDINGS CORP
CALIPER LIFE SCIENCES INC
CAL-MAINE FOODS INC
CAMBREX CORP
CANTEL MEDICAL CORP
CANTOR FITZGERALD LP
CAPITOL FEDERAL FINANCIAL INC
CARACO PHARMACEUTICAL LABORATORIES LTD
CARBO CERAMICS INC
CARDIONET INC
CARDTRONICS INC
CARRIZO OIL & GAS INC
CATALYST HEALTH SOLUTIONS INC
CELLDEX THERAPEUTICS INC
CELSIS INTERNATIONAL PLC
CENTRAL VERMONT PUBLIC SERVICE CORP
CEPHEID
CERUS CORPORATION
CF INDUSTRIES HOLDINGS INC
CHANNELL COMMERCIAL CORP
CHATTEM INC
CHINDEX INTERNATIONAL INC
CHOICESTREAM INC
CHOLESTECH CORP
CIRRUS LOGIC INC
CKX INC
CLAYTON WILLIAMS ENERGY INC
CLEAN ENERGY FUELS CORP
CLEARONE COMMUNICATIONS INC
COGENT COMMUNICATIONS
COHERENT INC
COMDATA CORP
COMPASS DIVERSIFIED HOLDINGS
COMTECH TELECOMMUNICATIONS CORP

COMVERGE INC
CONCUR TECHNOLOGIES INC
CONSTANT CONTACT INC
CONTINENTAL RESOURCES INC
CONTINUCARE CORP
CORPORATE EXECUTIVE BOARD COMPANY (THE)
COSTAR GROUP INC
COUPONS INC
CRA INTERNATIONAL INC (CHARLES RIVER)
CRAY INC
CRITICAL CARE SYSTEMS
CROWN CASTLE INTERNATIONAL CORP
CRUM & FORSTER HOLDINGS INC
CRYOLIFE INC
CUBIST PHARMACEUTICALS INC
CULP INC
CUMULUS MEDIA INC
CYBERONICS INC
CYBERSOURCE CORP
DANNON COMPANY INC (THE)
DAWSON GEOPHYSICAL COMPANY
DEI HOLDINGS INC
DELPHI FINANCIAL GROUP INC
DENBURY RESOURCES INC
DIAMOND ADVISORY SERVICES
DIAMOND FOODS INC
DIGITAL GENERATION INC
DJO GLOBAL INC
DOLBY LABORATORIES INC
DORMAN PRODUCTS INC
DPL INC
DREAMWORKS ANIMATION SKG INC
DRUGSTORE.COM INC
EATON VANCE CORP
EBIX INC
ECHO GLOBAL LOGISTICS INC
ECHOSTAR CORP
ECOLLEGE.COM
EDELMAN FINANCIAL GROUP (THE)
EDGAR ONLINE INC
EDUCATIONAL DEVELOPMENT CORP
EHEALTH INC
EMBARCADERO TECHNOLOGIES INC
EMCORE CORP
EMS TECHNOLOGIES INC
EMULEX CORP
ENCORE CAPITAL GROUP INC
ENERGY TRANSFER PARTNERS LP
ENERNOC INC
ENVIRONMENTAL TECTONICS CORP
EOG RESOURCES INC
EPAM SYSTEMS
EQT CORPORATION
EQUINIX INC
ERESEARCH TECHNOLOGY INC
ESSEX PROPERTY TRUST INC
EVERCORE PARTNERS INC
EVEREST RE GROUP LTD
EXACTECH INC
F5 NETWORKS INC
FAIR ISAAC CORPORATION
FEDEX SUPPLY CHAIN SERVICES INC
FIRST FINANCIAL BANCORP (OH)
FNB CORP
FORRESTER RESEARCH INC
FORTINET INC
FRESHDIRECT LLC
FROZEN FOOD EXPRESS INDUSTRIES INC
FUEL SYSTEMS SOLUTIONS INC
FUEL TECH INC
GAIAM INC
GALLUP ORGANIZATION (THE)
GENCO SHIPPING & TRADING LIMITED
GENENCOR INTERNATIONAL INC
GENERAL ATOMICS
GENERAL COMMUNICATION INC (GCI)
GENESIS ENERGY LP
GENOMIC HEALTH INC
GEN-PROBE INC
GFI GROUP INC
G-III APPAREL GROUP
GLEACHER & COMPANY INC
GLOBAL PARTNERS LP
GLOBECOMM SYSTEMS INC
GLU MOBILE INC
GOLDEN ENTERPRISES INC
GOLFSMITH INTERNATIONAL HOLDINGS INC
GREAT AMERICAN FINANCIAL RESOURCES INC
GREAT LAKES CHEESE COMPANY INC
GREEN MOUNTAIN POWER CORPORATION
GTC BIOTHERAPEUTICS INC
GULFMARK OFFSHORE INC
HAEMONETICS CORPORATION
HAHN AUTOMOTIVE WAREHOUSE INC
HANCOCK HOLDING COMPANY
HANOVER FOODS CORPORATION
HARRIS INTERACTIVE INC
HCC INSURANCE HOLDINGS INC
HEALTH GRADES INC
HEALTH INSURANCE PLAN OF GREATER NEW YORK
HEALTHSTREAM INC
HEALTHTRONICS INC
HEARUSA INC
HELIOVOLT CORP
HELIX ENERGY SOLUTIONS GROUP INC
HESKA CORP
HICKORY TECH CORPORATION
HI-TECH PHARMACAL CO INC
HOLLYFRONTIER CORPORATION
HORACE MANN EDUCATORS CORPORATION
HOSPITALITY PROPERTIES TRUST
HOULIHAN LOKEY HOWARD & ZUKIN INC
HUB GROUP INC
HUDSON CITY BANCORP INC
IBASIS INC
ICONIX BRAND GROUP INC
ICU MEDICAL INC
IDACORP INC
I-FLOW CORPORATION
ILLUMINA INC
IMG WORLDWIDE INC
IMMUCOR INC
IMPAX LABORATORIES INC
INDEPENDENCE HOLDING CO
INFOSPACE INC
INNOPHOS HOLDINGS INC
INNOSPEC INC
INTEGRAL SYSTEMS INC
INTEGRAMED AMERICA INC
INTERACTIVE DATA CORPORATION
INTERACTIVE INTELLIGENCE GROUP INC
INTERCONTINENTALEXCHANGE INC (ICE)
INTERMEC INC

INTERNAP NETWORK SERVICES CORP
INTERNATIONAL CREATIVE MANAGEMENT INC (ICM)
INTERNATIONAL DAIRY QUEEN INC
INTUITIVE SURGICAL INC
INVESTMENT TECHNOLOGY GROUP INC (ITG)
INVESTORS REAL ESTATE TRUST
IRIDEX CORP
IRIS INTERNATIONAL INC
IROBOT CORP
ISILON SYSTEMS INC
IVILLAGE INC
J2 GLOBAL COMMUNICATIONS INC
JAZZ PHARMACEUTICALS INC
JOE'S JEANS INC
JOHN B SANFILIPPO & SON INC
KAMPGROUNDS OF AMERICA INC
KBW INC
KENDALL-JACKSON WINE ESTATES LTD
KENNETH COLE PRODUCTIONS INC
KEY TRONIC CORP
KEYNOTE SYSTEMS INC
KIMLEY-HORN AND ASSOCIATES INC
KIRBY CORP
KKR & CO LP (KOHLBERG KRAVIS ROBERTS & CO)
KNIGHT CAPITAL GROUP INC
KNOLOGY INC
KORN/FERRY INTERNATIONAL
KRONOS WORLDWIDE INC
LACLEDE GROUP INC (THE)
LAKELAND INDUSTRIES INC
LB FOSTER COMPANY
LCC INTERNATIONAL INC
LESLIE'S POOLMART INC
LIFECELL CORPORATION
LIFECORE BIOMEDICAL INC
LIVEPERSON INC
LOGISTICARE INC
LOJACK CORPORTATION
LUCASFILM LTD
LUCOR INC
LUMINEX CORPORATION
MAGELLAN MIDSTREAM PARTNERS LP
MAKO SURGICAL CORP
MALT-O-MEAL COMPANY
MANAGEMENT NETWORK GROUP INC (THE)
MANHATTAN ASSOCIATES INC
MAPFRE USA CORP
MARTEK BIOSCIENCES CORP
MARVEL ENTERTAINMENT LLC
MEDICINES CO (THE)
MEDICIS PHARMACEUTICAL CORP
MEDIFAST INC
MEDTOX SCIENTIFIC INC
MENTOR CORP
MERIDIAN BIOSCIENCE INC
MERIT MEDICAL SYSTEMS INC
MESIROW FINANCIAL HOLDINGS INC
METROPOLITAN HEALTH NETWORKS INC
MICHELINAS INC
MICROTEK MEDICAL HOLDINGS INC
MID-AMERICA APARTMENT COMMUNITIES INC
MIDAS INC
MILLENNIUM PHARMACEUTICALS INC
MINDSPEED TECHNOLOGIES INC
MOELIS & COMPANY
MONSTER BEVERAGE CORP
MOTORCAR PARTS OF AMERICA INC
MTR GAMING GROUP INC
MYRIAD GENETICS INC
NANOMETRICS INC
NATIONAL BEVERAGE CORP
NATIONAL DENTEX CORP
NATIONAL WINE & SPIRITS INC
NATUS MEDICAL INC
NEKTAR THERAPEUTICS
NEOGEN CORPORATION
NETFLIX INC
NETGEAR INC
NETSCOUT SYSTEMS INC
NETSUITE INC
NETWORK ENGINES INC
NEUSTAR INC
NEW JERSEY RESOURCES CORPORATION
NEW YORK MERCANTILE EXCHANGE INC
NIC INC
NORTHWESTERN CORPORATION
NOTIFY TECHNOLOGY CORP
NOVAMED INC
NOVEN PHARMACEUTICALS INC
NTELOS HOLDING CORP
NUGGET MARKET
NUSTAR ENERGY LP
NUTRASWEET COMPANY (THE)
NUVASIVE INC
ODYSSEY RE HOLDINGS CORP
OMNOVA SOLUTIONS INC
ONLINE RESOURCES CORP
ONSTREAM MEDIA CORPORATION
OPENTV CORP
ORION MARINE GROUP INC
PACIFIC BIOMARKERS INC
PAR PHARMACEUTICAL COMPANIES INC
PATAGONIA INC
PC CONNECTION INC
PEAPOD LLC
PEGASYSTEMS INC
PERFICIENT INC
PERRY ELLIS INTERNATIONAL INC
PETMED EXPRESS INC
PETROLEUM DEVELOPMENT CORPORATION
PHAZAR CORP
PHILADELPHIA CONSOLIDATED HOLDING CORP
PHOENIX COMPANIES INC (THE)
PIEDMONT NATURAL GAS COMPANY INC
PIONEER NATURAL RESOURCES COMPANY
PIPER JAFFRAY COMPANIES
PLAINS EXPLORATION AND PRODUCTION COMPANY
PLATO LEARNING INC
PMA COMPANIES INC
POLYPORE INTERNATIONAL INC
POWERSECURE INTERNATIONAL INC
PREMIERE GLOBAL SERVICES INC
PRIMEENERGY CORPORATION
PROASSURANCE CORP
PROTECTIVE LIFE CORP
PURPLE COMMUNICATIONS INC
QUAKER CHEMICAL CORP
QUALCOMM ATHEROS INC
QUALITY SYSTEMS INC
QUANTUM CORP
QUESTCOR PHARMACEUTICALS INC
QUICKSILVER RESOURCES INC
QUIDEL CORP

RAYTHEON APPLIED SIGNAL TECHNOLOGY INC
REALNETWORKS INC
RECYCLED ENERGY DEVELOPMENT LLC
REDBOX AUTOMATED RETAIL LLC
REGENERON PHARMACEUTICALS INC
REINSURANCE GROUP OF AMERICA INC
RENTRAK CORP
RICELAND FOODS INC
RIGHTNOW TECHNOLOGIES INC
RIVERBED TECHNOLOGY INC
ROBERT W BAIRD & CO INC
ROCKY BRANDS INC
ROGERS CORPORATION
ROSETTA STONE INC
ROVI CORPORATION
RPC INC
RSA SECURITY INC
S1 CORPORATION
SACRAMENTO MUNICIPAL UTILITY DISTRICT
SALIX PHARMACEUTICALS
SANDRIDGE ENERGY INC
SBA COMMUNICATIONS CORP
SCANSOURCE INC
SCHICK TECHNOLOGIES INC
SCHIFF NUTRITION INTERNATIONAL INC
SCICLONE PHARMACEUTICALS INC
SCIOS INC
SCOULAR COMPANY (THE)
SEACHANGE INTERNATIONAL INC
SEATTLE GENETICS
SELECTICA INC
SENIOR HOUSING PROPERTIES
SERACARE LIFE SCIENCES INC
SHARED TECHNOLOGIES
SHENANDOAH TELECOMMUNICATIONS CO
SHUTTERFLY INC
SIGMA DESIGNS INC
SILICON LABORATORIES INC
SL GREEN REALTY CORP
SMART MODULAR TECHNOLOGIES INC
SOLARRESERVE
SOLFOCUS INC
SOTHEBYS
SOUTHERN UNION COMPANY

SOUTHWEST GAS CORP
SOUTHWESTERN ENERGY CO
SOVRAN SELF STORAGE INC
SPARTAN MOTORS INC
SPECTRANETICS CORP
SPECTRUM PHARMACEUTICALS INC
SPIRE CORPORATION
SPORT SUPPLY GROUP INC
SPORTSMAN'S GUIDE INC (THE)
SPROUTS FARMERS MARKET LLC
SRS LABS INC
SS&C TECHNOLOGIES HOLDINGS INC
STAAR SURGICAL CO
STATE AUTO FINANCIAL CORP
STEPAN COMPANY
STERLING AUTOBODY CENTERS
STERLING CONSTRUCTION COMPANY
STEVEN MADDEN LTD
STIEFEL LABORATORIES INC
SUN COMMUNITIES INC
SUNOCO LOGISTICS PARTNERS LP
SUPER MICRO COMPUTER INC
SUPERIOR UNIFORM GROUP INC
SUPERTEL HOSPITALITY INC
SUPREME INDUSTRIES INC
SVB FINANCIAL GROUP
SWIFT ENERGY CO
SYNAPTICS INC
SYNIVERSE TECHNOLOGIES
SYNOVIS LIFE TECHNOLOGIES INC
TAKE-TWO INTERACTIVE SOFTWARE INC
TAMPA ELECTRIC COMPANY
TARGA RESOURCES PARTNERS LP
TECHNE CORP
TEKELEC
TELIRIS
TERREMARK WORLDWIDE INC
TESCO CORPORATION
TESSCO TECHNOLOGIES INC
THERAGENICS CORP
THORATEC CORPORATION
TII NETWORK TECHNOLOGIES INC
TOOTSIE ROLL INDUSTRIES INC
TOPPS COMPANY INC (THE)
TRANSAMMONIA INC
TRANSATLANTIC HOLDINGS INC
TRANSCEND SERVICES INC

TRAVELZOO INC
TREX COMPANY INC
TRIZETTO GROUP INC (THE)
TRUE RELIGION APPAREL INC
UDR INC
UIL HOLDINGS CORPORATION
ULTIMATE SOFTWARE GROUP INC
ULTRALIFE CORPORATION
UNISOURCE ENERGY CORPORATION
UNIT CORP
UNITED ONLINE INC
UNITED THERAPEUTICS CORP
UNIVERSAL HOSPITAL SERVICES INC
UQM TECHNOLOGIES INC
US PHYSICAL THERAPY INC
USANA HEALTH SCIENCES INC
UTAH MEDICAL PRODUCTS INC
VARIAN SEMICONDUCTOR EQUIPMENT ASSOCIATES INC
VASCO DATA SECURITY INTERNATIONAL INC
VENTANA MEDICAL SYSTEMS INC
VERENIUM CORPORATION
VIASAT INC
VIBRANT MEDIA INC
VIROPHARMA INC
VOLCOM INC
VOX INTERNATIONAL CORPORATION
WABASH NATIONAL CORP
WADDELL & REED FINANCIAL INC
WEBEX COMMUNICATIONS INC
WEBMD HEALTH CORP
WEBMEDIA BRANDS INC
WEBSENSE INC
WESTAR ENERGY
WGL HOLDINGS INC
WHITEWAVE FOODS COMPANY
WIKIMEDIA FOUNDATION
WIND RIVER SYSTEMS INC
WMS INDUSTRIES INC
WRIGHT MEDICAL GROUP INC
XETA TECHNOLOGIES INC
XO GROUP INC
XOMA LTD
XTO ENERGY INC
YOUNG'S MARKET COMPANY LLC
ZAP JONWAY
ZEP INC

ZIEBART INTERNATIONAL CORP
ZOLL MEDICAL CORP
ZYNGA INC

Professionals

Consulting
ADVISORY BOARD COMPANY (THE)
AMERESCO INC
ARGON ST INC
CORPORATE EXECUTIVE BOARD COMPANY (THE)
CRA INTERNATIONAL INC (CHARLES RIVER)
DIAMOND ADVISORY SERVICES
EPAM SYSTEMS
FORRESTER RESEARCH INC
GALLUP ORGANIZATION (THE)
HARRIS INTERACTIVE INC
KEYNOTE SYSTEMS INC
KORN/FERRY INTERNATIONAL
LCC INTERNATIONAL INC
LOGISTICARE INC
MANAGEMENT NETWORK GROUP INC (THE)
PERFICIENT INC

Finance/Accounting
24/7 REAL MEDIA INC
AAMCO TRANSMISSIONS INC
ABAXIS INC
ACI WORLDWIDE INC
ACME PACKET INC
ACXIOM DIGITAL INC
ADEPT TECHNOLOGY INC
ADTRAN INC
ADVISORY BOARD COMPANY (THE)
AFFILIATED MANAGERS GROUP
AKAMAI TECHNOLOGIES INC
AKORN INC
AKQA INC
ALBANY MOLECULAR RESEARCH INC
ALEXANDER & BALDWIN INC
ALEXION PHARMACEUTICALS INC
ALIEN TECHNOLOGY CORPORATION
ALIGN TECHNOLOGY INC
ALLEGIANT TRAVEL COMPANY
ALLIED HEALTHCARE INTERNATIONAL INC
ALLSCRIPTS HEALTHCARE SOLUTIONS INC
AMAG PHARMACEUTICALS INC
AMCOL INTERNATIONAL CORP
AMCON DISTRIBUTING CO
AMERESCO INC
AMERICAN CAMPUS COMMUNITIES INC
AMERICAN FIDELITY ASSURANCE COMPANY
AMERICAN MEDICAL SYSTEMS HOLDINGS INC
AMERICAN SCIENCE & ENGINEERING INC
AMERICAN TIRE DISTRIBUTORS
AMERICAN TOWER CORP
AMERICAN VANGUARD CORP
AMERICA'S CAR-MART INC
AMTECH SYSTEMS INC
AMTRUST FINANCIAL SERVICES INC
ANALOGIC CORP
ANAREN INC
ANIKA THERAPEUTICS INC
APP PHARMACEUTICALS INC
ARCSIGHT INC
ARDEN GROUP INC
ARGON ST INC
ARIBA INC
ARIZONA CHEMICAL COMPANY
AROTECH CORPORATION
ARRAY BIOPHARMA INC
ARRIS GROUP INC
ARTHROCARE CORP
ARUBA NETWORKS INC
ASTEX PHARMACEUTICALS INC
ATHENAHEALTH INC
ATLANTIC CITY ELECTRIC COMPANY
ATLANTIC TELE-NETWORK INC
ATRION CORPORATION
AUDIBLE INC
AVALONBAY COMMUNITIES INC
AVIALL INC
AVISTA CORPORATION
B&G FOODS INC
BANKRATE INC
BERRY PETROLEUM CO
BIO REFERENCE LABORATORIES INC
BIOMARIN PHARMACEUTICAL INC
BIOSCRIP INC
BIOSITE INC
BLACK HILLS CORP
BLACKBOARD INC
BLUE COAT SYSTEMS INC
BLUE NILE INC
BOSTON BEER COMPANY INC (THE)
BOTTOMLINE TECHNOLOGIES INC
BRIGHTSTAR CORPORATION
CABOT OIL & GAS CORP
CACTUS FEEDERS INC
CAGLE'S INC
CALAVO GROWERS INC
CALGON CARBON CORPORATION
CALIBER HOLDINGS CORP
CALIPER LIFE SCIENCES INC
CAL-MAINE FOODS INC
CAMBREX CORP
CANTEL MEDICAL CORP
CANTOR FITZGERALD LP
CAPITOL FEDERAL FINANCIAL INC
CARACO PHARMACEUTICAL LABORATORIES LTD
CARBO CERAMICS INC
CARDIONET INC
CARDTRONICS INC
CARRIZO OIL & GAS INC
CATALYST HEALTH SOLUTIONS INC
CELLDEX THERAPEUTICS INC
CELSIS INTERNATIONAL PLC
CENTRAL VERMONT PUBLIC SERVICE CORP
CEPHEID
CERUS CORPORATION
CF INDUSTRIES HOLDINGS INC
CHANNELL COMMERCIAL CORP
CHATTEM INC
CHINDEX INTERNATIONAL INC
CHOICESTREAM INC
CHOLESTECH CORP
CIRRUS LOGIC INC
CKX INC
CLAYTON WILLIAMS ENERGY INC
CLEAN ENERGY FUELS CORP
CLEARONE COMMUNICATIONS INC
COGENT COMMUNICATIONS
COHERENT INC
COMDATA CORP
COMPASS DIVERSIFIED HOLDINGS
COMTECH TELECOMMUNICATIONS CORP
COMVERGE INC

CONCUR TECHNOLOGIES INC
CONSTANT CONTACT INC
CONTINENTAL RESOURCES INC
CONTINUCARE CORP
CORPORATE EXECUTIVE BOARD COMPANY (THE)
COSTAR GROUP INC
COUPONS INC
CRA INTERNATIONAL INC (CHARLES RIVER)
CRAY INC
CRITICAL CARE SYSTEMS
CROWN CASTLE INTERNATIONAL CORP
CRUM & FORSTER HOLDINGS INC
CRYOLIFE INC
CUBIST PHARMACEUTICALS INC
CULP INC
CUMULUS MEDIA INC
CYBERONICS INC
CYBERSOURCE CORP
DANNON COMPANY INC (THE)
DAWSON GEOPHYSICAL COMPANY
DEI HOLDINGS INC
DELPHI FINANCIAL GROUP INC
DENBURY RESOURCES INC
DIAMOND ADVISORY SERVICES
DIAMOND FOODS INC
DIGITAL GENERATION INC
DJO GLOBAL INC
DOLBY LABORATORIES INC
DORMAN PRODUCTS INC
DPL INC
DREAMWORKS ANIMATION SKG INC
DRUGSTORE.COM INC
EATON VANCE CORP
EBIX INC
ECHO GLOBAL LOGISTICS INC
ECHOSTAR CORP
ECOLLEGE.COM
EDELMAN FINANCIAL GROUP (THE)
EDGAR ONLINE INC
EDUCATIONAL DEVELOPMENT CORP
EHEALTH INC
EMBARCADERO TECHNOLOGIES INC
EMCORE CORP
EMS TECHNOLOGIES INC
EMULEX CORP
ENCORE CAPITAL GROUP INC
ENERGY TRANSFER PARTNERS LP
ENERNOC INC
ENVIRONMENTAL TECTONICS CORP
EOG RESOURCES INC
EPAM SYSTEMS
EQT CORPORATION
EQUINIX INC
ERESEARCH TECHNOLOGY INC
ESSEX PROPERTY TRUST INC
EVERCORE PARTNERS INC
EVEREST RE GROUP LTD
EXACTECH INC
F5 NETWORKS INC
FAIR ISAAC CORPORATION
FEDEX SUPPLY CHAIN SERVICES INC
FIRST FINANCIAL BANCORP (OH)
FNB CORP
FORRESTER RESEARCH INC
FORTINET INC
FRESHDIRECT LLC
FROZEN FOOD EXPRESS INDUSTRIES INC
FUEL SYSTEMS SOLUTIONS INC
FUEL TECH INC
GAIAM INC
GALLUP ORGANIZATION (THE)
GENCO SHIPPING & TRADING LIMITED
GENENCOR INTERNATIONAL INC
GENERAL ATOMICS
GENERAL COMMUNICATION INC (GCI)
GENESIS ENERGY LP
GENOMIC HEALTH INC
GEN-PROBE INC
GFI GROUP INC
G-III APPAREL GROUP
GLEACHER & COMPANY INC
GLOBAL PARTNERS LP
GLOBECOMM SYSTEMS INC
GLU MOBILE INC
GOLDEN ENTERPRISES INC
GOLFSMITH INTERNATIONAL HOLDINGS INC
GREAT AMERICAN FINANCIAL RESOURCES INC
GREAT LAKES CHEESE COMPANY INC
GREEN MOUNTAIN POWER
CORPORATION
GTC BIOTHERAPEUTICS INC
GULFMARK OFFSHORE INC
HAEMONETICS CORPORATION
HAHN AUTOMOTIVE WAREHOUSE INC
HANCOCK HOLDING COMPANY
HANOVER FOODS CORPORATION
HARRIS INTERACTIVE INC
HCC INSURANCE HOLDINGS INC
HEALTH GRADES INC
HEALTH INSURANCE PLAN OF GREATER NEW YORK
HEALTHSTREAM INC
HEALTHTRONICS INC
HEARUSA INC
HELIOVOLT CORP
HELIX ENERGY SOLUTIONS GROUP INC
HESKA CORP
HICKORY TECH CORPORATION
HI-TECH PHARMACAL CO INC
HOLLYFRONTIER CORPORATION
HORACE MANN EDUCATORS CORPORATION
HOSPITALITY PROPERTIES TRUST
HOULIHAN LOKEY HOWARD & ZUKIN INC
HUB GROUP INC
HUDSON CITY BANCORP INC
IBASIS INC
ICONIX BRAND GROUP INC
ICU MEDICAL INC
IDACORP INC
I-FLOW CORPORATION
ILLUMINA INC
IMG WORLDWIDE INC
IMMUCOR INC
IMPAX LABORATORIES INC
INDEPENDENCE HOLDING CO
INFOSPACE INC
INNOPHOS HOLDINGS INC
INNOSPEC INC
INTEGRAL SYSTEMS INC
INTEGRAMED AMERICA INC
INTERACTIVE DATA CORPORATION
INTERACTIVE INTELLIGENCE GROUP INC
INTERCONTINENTALEXCHANGE INC (ICE)
INTERMEC INC
INTERNAP NETWORK SERVICES

CORP
INTERNATIONAL CREATIVE MANAGEMENT INC (ICM)
INTERNATIONAL DAIRY QUEEN INC
INTUITIVE SURGICAL INC
INVESTMENT TECHNOLOGY GROUP INC (ITG)
INVESTORS REAL ESTATE TRUST
IRIDEX CORP
IRIS INTERNATIONAL INC
IROBOT CORP
ISILON SYSTEMS INC
IVILLAGE INC
J2 GLOBAL COMMUNICATIONS INC
JAZZ PHARMACEUTICALS INC
JOE'S JEANS INC
JOHN B SANFILIPPO & SON INC
KAMPGROUNDS OF AMERICA INC
KBW INC
KENDALL-JACKSON WINE ESTATES LTD
KENNETH COLE PRODUCTIONS INC
KEY TRONIC CORP
KEYNOTE SYSTEMS INC
KIMLEY-HORN AND ASSOCIATES INC
KIRBY CORP
KKR & CO LP (KOHLBERG KRAVIS ROBERTS & CO)
KNIGHT CAPITAL GROUP INC
KNOLOGY INC
KORN/FERRY INTERNATIONAL
KRONOS WORLDWIDE INC
LACLEDE GROUP INC (THE)
LAKELAND INDUSTRIES INC
LB FOSTER COMPANY
LCC INTERNATIONAL INC
LESLIE'S POOLMART INC
LIFECELL CORPORATION
LIFECORE BIOMEDICAL INC
LIVEPERSON INC
LOGISTICARE INC
LOJACK CORPORTATION
LUCASFILM LTD
LUCOR INC
LUMINEX CORPORATION
MAGELLAN MIDSTREAM PARTNERS LP
MAKO SURGICAL CORP
MALT-O-MEAL COMPANY
MANAGEMENT NETWORK GROUP INC (THE)
MANHATTAN ASSOCIATES INC
MAPFRE USA CORP
MARTEK BIOSCIENCES CORP
MARVEL ENTERTAINMENT LLC
MEDICINES CO (THE)
MEDICIS PHARMACEUTICAL CORP
MEDIFAST INC
MEDTOX SCIENTIFIC INC
MENTOR CORP
MERIDIAN BIOSCIENCE INC
MERIT MEDICAL SYSTEMS INC
MESIROW FINANCIAL HOLDINGS INC
METROPOLITAN HEALTH NETWORKS INC
MICHELINAS INC
MICROTEK MEDICAL HOLDINGS INC
MID-AMERICA APARTMENT COMMUNITIES INC
MIDAS INC
MILLENNIUM PHARMACEUTICALS INC
MINDSPEED TECHNOLOGIES INC
MOELIS & COMPANY
MONSTER BEVERAGE CORP
MOTORCAR PARTS OF AMERICA INC
MTR GAMING GROUP INC
MYRIAD GENETICS INC
NANOMETRICS INC
NATIONAL BEVERAGE CORP
NATIONAL DENTEX CORP
NATIONAL WINE & SPIRITS INC
NATUS MEDICAL INC
NEKTAR THERAPEUTICS
NEOGEN CORPORATION
NETFLIX INC
NETGEAR INC
NETSCOUT SYSTEMS INC
NETSUITE INC
NETWORK ENGINES INC
NEUSTAR INC
NEW JERSEY RESOURCES CORPORATION
NEW YORK MERCANTILE EXCHANGE INC
NIC INC
NORTHWESTERN CORPORATION
NOTIFY TECHNOLOGY CORP
NOVAMED INC
NOVEN PHARMACEUTICALS INC
NTELOS HOLDING CORP
NUGGET MARKET
NUSTAR ENERGY LP
NUTRASWEET COMPANY (THE)
NUVASIVE INC
ODYSSEY RE HOLDINGS CORP
OMNOVA SOLUTIONS INC
ONLINE RESOURCES CORP
ONSTREAM MEDIA CORPORATION
OPENTV CORP
ORION MARINE GROUP INC
PACIFIC BIOMARKERS INC
PAR PHARMACEUTICAL COMPANIES INC
PATAGONIA INC
PC CONNECTION INC
PEAPOD LLC
PEGASYSTEMS INC
PERFICIENT INC
PERRY ELLIS INTERNATIONAL INC
PETMED EXPRESS INC
PETROLEUM DEVELOPMENT CORPORATION
PHAZAR CORP
PHILADELPHIA CONSOLIDATED HOLDING CORP
PHOENIX COMPANIES INC (THE)
PIEDMONT NATURAL GAS COMPANY INC
PIONEER NATURAL RESOURCES COMPANY
PIPER JAFFRAY COMPANIES
PLAINS EXPLORATION AND PRODUCTION COMPANY
PLATO LEARNING INC
PMA COMPANIES INC
POLYPORE INTERNATIONAL INC
POWERSECURE INTERNATIONAL INC
PREMIERE GLOBAL SERVICES INC
PRIMEENERGY CORPORATION
PROASSURANCE CORP
PROTECTIVE LIFE CORP
PURPLE COMMUNICATIONS INC
QUAKER CHEMICAL CORP
QUALCOMM ATHEROS INC
QUALITY SYSTEMS INC
QUANTUM CORP
QUESTCOR PHARMACEUTICALS INC
QUICKSILVER RESOURCES INC
QUIDEL CORP
RAYTHEON APPLIED SIGNAL

TECHNOLOGY INC
REALNETWORKS INC
RECYCLED ENERGY DEVELOPMENT LLC
REDBOX AUTOMATED RETAIL LLC
REGENERON PHARMACEUTICALS INC
REINSURANCE GROUP OF AMERICA INC
RENTRAK CORP
RICELAND FOODS INC
RIGHTNOW TECHNOLOGIES INC
RIVERBED TECHNOLOGY INC
ROBERT W BAIRD & CO INC
ROCKY BRANDS INC
ROGERS CORPORATION
ROSETTA STONE INC
ROVI CORPORATION
RPC INC
RSA SECURITY INC
S1 CORPORATION
SACRAMENTO MUNICIPAL UTILITY DISTRICT
SALIX PHARMACEUTICALS
SANDRIDGE ENERGY INC
SBA COMMUNICATIONS CORP
SCANSOURCE INC
SCHICK TECHNOLOGIES INC
SCHIFF NUTRITION INTERNATIONAL INC
SCICLONE PHARMACEUTICALS INC
SCIOS INC
SCOULAR COMPANY (THE)
SEACHANGE INTERNATIONAL INC
SEATTLE GENETICS
SELECTICA INC
SENIOR HOUSING PROPERTIES
SERACARE LIFE SCIENCES INC
SHARED TECHNOLOGIES
SHENANDOAH TELECOMMUNICATIONS CO
SHUTTERFLY INC
SIGMA DESIGNS INC
SILICON LABORATORIES INC
SL GREEN REALTY CORP
SMART MODULAR TECHNOLOGIES INC
SOLARRESERVE
SOLFOCUS INC
SOTHEBYS
SOUTHERN UNION COMPANY
SOUTHWEST GAS CORP
SOUTHWESTERN ENERGY CO
SOVRAN SELF STORAGE INC
SPARTAN MOTORS INC
SPECTRANETICS CORP
SPECTRUM PHARMACEUTICALS INC
SPIRE CORPORATION
SPORT SUPPLY GROUP INC
SPORTSMAN'S GUIDE INC (THE)
SPROUTS FARMERS MARKET LLC
SRS LABS INC
SS&C TECHNOLOGIES HOLDINGS INC
STAAR SURGICAL CO
STATE AUTO FINANCIAL CORP
STEPAN COMPANY
STERLING AUTOBODY CENTERS
STERLING CONSTRUCTION COMPANY
STEVEN MADDEN LTD
STIEFEL LABORATORIES INC
SUN COMMUNITIES INC
SUNOCO LOGISTICS PARTNERS LP
SUPER MICRO COMPUTER INC
SUPERIOR UNIFORM GROUP INC
SUPERTEL HOSPITALITY INC
SUPREME INDUSTRIES INC
SVB FINANCIAL GROUP
SWIFT ENERGY CO
SYNAPTICS INC
SYNIVERSE TECHNOLOGIES
SYNOVIS LIFE TECHNOLOGIES INC
TAKE-TWO INTERACTIVE SOFTWARE INC
TAMPA ELECTRIC COMPANY
TARGA RESOURCES PARTNERS LP
TECHNE CORP
TEKELEC
TELIRIS
TERREMARK WORLDWIDE INC
TESCO CORPORATION
TESSCO TECHNOLOGIES INC
THERAGENICS CORP
THORATEC CORPORATION
TII NETWORK TECHNOLOGIES INC
TOOTSIE ROLL INDUSTRIES INC
TOPPS COMPANY INC (THE)
TRANSAMMONIA INC
TRANSATLANTIC HOLDINGS INC
TRANSCEND SERVICES INC
TRAVELZOO INC
TREX COMPANY INC
TRIZETTO GROUP INC (THE)
TRUE RELIGION APPAREL INC
UDR INC
UIL HOLDINGS CORPORATION
ULTIMATE SOFTWARE GROUP INC
ULTRALIFE CORPORATION
UNISOURCE ENERGY CORPORATION
UNIT CORP
UNITED ONLINE INC
UNITED THERAPEUTICS CORP
UNIVERSAL HOSPITAL SERVICES INC
UQM TECHNOLOGIES INC
US PHYSICAL THERAPY INC
USANA HEALTH SCIENCES INC
UTAH MEDICAL PRODUCTS INC
VARIAN SEMICONDUCTOR EQUIPMENT ASSOCIATES INC
VASCO DATA SECURITY INTERNATIONAL INC
VENTANA MEDICAL SYSTEMS INC
VERENIUM CORPORATION
VIASAT INC
VIBRANT MEDIA INC
VIROPHARMA INC
VOLCOM INC
VOX INTERNATIONAL CORPORATION
WABASH NATIONAL CORP
WADDELL & REED FINANCIAL INC
WEBEX COMMUNICATIONS INC
WEBMD HEALTH CORP
WEBMEDIA BRANDS INC
WEBSENSE INC
WESTAR ENERGY
WGL HOLDINGS INC
WHITEWAVE FOODS COMPANY
WIKIMEDIA FOUNDATION
WIND RIVER SYSTEMS INC
WMS INDUSTRIES INC
WRIGHT MEDICAL GROUP INC
XETA TECHNOLOGIES INC
XO GROUP INC
XOMA LTD
XTO ENERGY INC
YOUNG'S MARKET COMPANY LLC
ZAP JONWAY
ZEP INC
ZIEBART INTERNATIONAL CORP

ZOLL MEDICAL CORP
ZYNGA INC

Health Care
ABAXIS INC
AKORN INC
ALBANY MOLECULAR RESEARCH INC
ALEXION PHARMACEUTICALS INC
ALIGN TECHNOLOGY INC
AMERICAN FIDELITY ASSURANCE COMPANY
AMERICAN MEDICAL SYSTEMS HOLDINGS INC
AMTRUST FINANCIAL SERVICES INC
ANALOGIC CORP
ANIKA THERAPEUTICS INC
APP PHARMACEUTICALS INC
ARRAY BIOPHARMA INC
ARTHROCARE CORP
ASTEX PHARMACEUTICALS INC
ATRION CORPORATION
BIO REFERENCE LABORATORIES INC
BIOMARIN PHARMACEUTICAL INC
BIOSCRIP INC
BIOSITE INC
CALIPER LIFE SCIENCES INC
CAMBREX CORP
CANTEL MEDICAL CORP
CARACO PHARMACEUTICAL LABORATORIES LTD
CARDIONET INC
CATALYST HEALTH SOLUTIONS INC
CELLDEX THERAPEUTICS INC
CELSIS INTERNATIONAL PLC
CEPHEID
CERUS CORPORATION
CHATTEM INC
CHINDEX INTERNATIONAL INC
CHOLESTECH CORP
COHERENT INC
CONTINUCARE CORP
CRITICAL CARE SYSTEMS
CRUM & FORSTER HOLDINGS INC
CRYOLIFE INC
CUBIST PHARMACEUTICALS INC
CYBERONICS INC
DELPHI FINANCIAL GROUP INC
DJO GLOBAL INC
EHEALTH INC
ENVIRONMENTAL TECTONICS CORP
EXACTECH INC
GENENCOR INTERNATIONAL INC
GENOMIC HEALTH INC
GEN-PROBE INC
GREAT AMERICAN FINANCIAL RESOURCES INC
GTC BIOTHERAPEUTICS INC
HAEMONETICS CORPORATION
HCC INSURANCE HOLDINGS INC
HEALTH INSURANCE PLAN OF GREATER NEW YORK
HEALTHTRONICS INC
HEARUSA INC
HESKA CORP
HI-TECH PHARMACAL CO INC
ICU MEDICAL INC
I-FLOW CORPORATION
ILLUMINA INC
IMMUCOR INC
IMPAX LABORATORIES INC
INDEPENDENCE HOLDING CO
INTEGRAMED AMERICA INC
INTUITIVE SURGICAL INC
IRIDEX CORP
IRIS INTERNATIONAL INC
JAZZ PHARMACEUTICALS INC
LIFECELL CORPORATION
LIFECORE BIOMEDICAL INC
LUMINEX CORPORATION
MAKO SURGICAL CORP
MARTEK BIOSCIENCES CORP
MEDICINES CO (THE)
MEDICIS PHARMACEUTICAL CORP
MEDTOX SCIENTIFIC INC
MENTOR CORP
MERIDIAN BIOSCIENCE INC
MERIT MEDICAL SYSTEMS INC
METROPOLITAN HEALTH NETWORKS INC
MICROTEK MEDICAL HOLDINGS INC
MILLENNIUM PHARMACEUTICALS INC
MYRIAD GENETICS INC
NATIONAL DENTEX CORP
NATUS MEDICAL INC
NEKTAR THERAPEUTICS
NEOGEN CORPORATION
NOVAMED INC
NOVEN PHARMACEUTICALS INC
NUVASIVE INC
PACIFIC BIOMARKERS INC
PAR PHARMACEUTICAL COMPANIES INC
PHOENIX COMPANIES INC (THE)
PMA COMPANIES INC
PROASSURANCE CORP
PROTECTIVE LIFE CORP
QUESTCOR PHARMACEUTICALS INC
QUIDEL CORP
REGENERON PHARMACEUTICALS INC
SALIX PHARMACEUTICALS
SCHICK TECHNOLOGIES INC
SCHIFF NUTRITION INTERNATIONAL INC
SCICLONE PHARMACEUTICALS INC
SCIOS INC
SEATTLE GENETICS
SERACARE LIFE SCIENCES INC
SPECTRANETICS CORP
SPECTRUM PHARMACEUTICALS INC
STAAR SURGICAL CO
STIEFEL LABORATORIES INC
SYNOVIS LIFE TECHNOLOGIES INC
TECHNE CORP
THERAGENICS CORP
THORATEC CORPORATION
UNITED THERAPEUTICS CORP
UNIVERSAL HOSPITAL SERVICES INC
US PHYSICAL THERAPY INC
USANA HEALTH SCIENCES INC
UTAH MEDICAL PRODUCTS INC
VENTANA MEDICAL SYSTEMS INC
VIROPHARMA INC
WRIGHT MEDICAL GROUP INC
XOMA LTD
ZOLL MEDICAL CORP

Human Resources/Other
24/7 REAL MEDIA INC
AAMCO TRANSMISSIONS INC
ABAXIS INC
ACI WORLDWIDE INC
ACME PACKET INC
ACXIOM DIGITAL INC
ADEPT TECHNOLOGY INC

ADTRAN INC
ADVISORY BOARD COMPANY (THE)
AFFILIATED MANAGERS GROUP
AKAMAI TECHNOLOGIES INC
AKORN INC
AKQA INC
ALBANY MOLECULAR RESEARCH INC
ALEXANDER & BALDWIN INC
ALEXION PHARMACEUTICALS INC
ALIEN TECHNOLOGY CORPORATION
ALIGN TECHNOLOGY INC
ALLEGIANT TRAVEL COMPANY
ALLIED HEALTHCARE INTERNATIONAL INC
ALLSCRIPTS HEALTHCARE SOLUTIONS INC
AMAG PHARMACEUTICALS INC
AMCOL INTERNATIONAL CORP
AMCON DISTRIBUTING CO
AMERESCO INC
AMERICAN CAMPUS COMMUNITIES INC
AMERICAN FIDELITY ASSURANCE COMPANY
AMERICAN MEDICAL SYSTEMS HOLDINGS INC
AMERICAN SCIENCE & ENGINEERING INC
AMERICAN TIRE DISTRIBUTORS
AMERICAN TOWER CORP
AMERICAN VANGUARD CORP
AMERICA'S CAR-MART INC
AMTECH SYSTEMS INC
AMTRUST FINANCIAL SERVICES INC
ANALOGIC CORP
ANAREN INC
ANIKA THERAPEUTICS INC
APP PHARMACEUTICALS INC
ARCSIGHT INC
ARDEN GROUP INC
ARGON ST INC
ARIBA INC
ARIZONA CHEMICAL COMPANY
AROTECH CORPORATION
ARRAY BIOPHARMA INC
ARRIS GROUP INC
ARTHROCARE CORP
ARUBA NETWORKS INC
ASTEX PHARMACEUTICALS INC

ATHENAHEALTH INC
ATLANTIC CITY ELECTRIC COMPANY
ATLANTIC TELE-NETWORK INC
ATRION CORPORATION
AUDIBLE INC
AVALONBAY COMMUNITIES INC
AVIALL INC
AVISTA CORPORATION
B&G FOODS INC
BANKRATE INC
BERRY PETROLEUM CO
BIO REFERENCE LABORATORIES INC
BIOMARIN PHARMACEUTICAL INC
BIOSCRIP INC
BIOSITE INC
BLACK HILLS CORP
BLACKBOARD INC
BLUE COAT SYSTEMS INC
BLUE NILE INC
BOSTON BEER COMPANY INC (THE)
BOTTOMLINE TECHNOLOGIES INC
BRIGHTSTAR CORPORATION
CABOT OIL & GAS CORP
CACTUS FEEDERS INC
CAGLE'S INC
CALAVO GROWERS INC
CALGON CARBON CORPORATION
CALIBER HOLDINGS CORP
CALIPER LIFE SCIENCES INC
CAL-MAINE FOODS INC
CAMBREX CORP
CANTEL MEDICAL CORP
CANTOR FITZGERALD LP
CAPITOL FEDERAL FINANCIAL INC
CARACO PHARMACEUTICAL LABORATORIES LTD
CARBO CERAMICS INC
CARDIONET INC
CARDTRONICS INC
CARRIZO OIL & GAS INC
CATALYST HEALTH SOLUTIONS INC
CELLDEX THERAPEUTICS INC
CELSIS INTERNATIONAL PLC
CENTRAL VERMONT PUBLIC SERVICE CORP
CEPHEID
CERUS CORPORATION
CF INDUSTRIES HOLDINGS INC
CHANNELL COMMERCIAL CORP

CHATTEM INC
CHINDEX INTERNATIONAL INC
CHOICESTREAM INC
CHOLESTECH CORP
CIRRUS LOGIC INC
CKX INC
CLAYTON WILLIAMS ENERGY INC
CLEAN ENERGY FUELS CORP
CLEARONE COMMUNICATIONS INC
COGENT COMMUNICATIONS
COHERENT INC
COMDATA CORP
COMPASS DIVERSIFIED HOLDINGS
COMTECH TELECOMMUNICATIONS CORP
COMVERGE INC
CONCUR TECHNOLOGIES INC
CONSTANT CONTACT INC
CONTINENTAL RESOURCES INC
CONTINUCARE CORP
CORPORATE EXECUTIVE BOARD COMPANY (THE)
COSTAR GROUP INC
COUPONS INC
CRA INTERNATIONAL INC (CHARLES RIVER)
CRAY INC
CRITICAL CARE SYSTEMS
CROWN CASTLE INTERNATIONAL CORP
CRUM & FORSTER HOLDINGS INC
CRYOLIFE INC
CUBIST PHARMACEUTICALS INC
CULP INC
CUMULUS MEDIA INC
CYBERONICS INC
CYBERSOURCE CORP
DANNON COMPANY INC (THE)
DAWSON GEOPHYSICAL COMPANY
DEI HOLDINGS INC
DELPHI FINANCIAL GROUP INC
DENBURY RESOURCES INC
DIAMOND ADVISORY SERVICES
DIAMOND FOODS INC
DIGITAL GENERATION INC
DJO GLOBAL INC
DOLBY LABORATORIES INC
DORMAN PRODUCTS INC
DPL INC
DREAMWORKS ANIMATION SKG INC

DRUGSTORE.COM INC
EATON VANCE CORP
EBIX INC
ECHO GLOBAL LOGISTICS INC
ECHOSTAR CORP
ECOLLEGE.COM
EDELMAN FINANCIAL GROUP (THE)
EDGAR ONLINE INC
EDUCATIONAL DEVELOPMENT CORP
EHEALTH INC
EMBARCADERO TECHNOLOGIES INC
EMCORE CORP
EMS TECHNOLOGIES INC
EMULEX CORP
ENCORE CAPITAL GROUP INC
ENERGY TRANSFER PARTNERS LP
ENERNOC INC
ENVIRONMENTAL TECTONICS CORP
EOG RESOURCES INC
EPAM SYSTEMS
EQT CORPORATION
EQUINIX INC
ERESEARCH TECHNOLOGY INC
ESSEX PROPERTY TRUST INC
EVERCORE PARTNERS INC
EVEREST RE GROUP LTD
EXACTECH INC
F5 NETWORKS INC
FAIR ISAAC CORPORATION
FEDEX SUPPLY CHAIN SERVICES INC
FIRST FINANCIAL BANCORP (OH)
FNB CORP
FORRESTER RESEARCH INC
FORTINET INC
FRESHDIRECT LLC
FROZEN FOOD EXPRESS INDUSTRIES INC
FUEL SYSTEMS SOLUTIONS INC
FUEL TECH INC
GAIAM INC
GALLUP ORGANIZATION (THE)
GENCO SHIPPING & TRADING LIMITED
GENENCOR INTERNATIONAL INC
GENERAL ATOMICS
GENERAL COMMUNICATION INC (GCI)
GENESIS ENERGY LP
GENOMIC HEALTH INC
GEN-PROBE INC
GFI GROUP INC
G-III APPAREL GROUP
GLEACHER & COMPANY INC
GLOBAL PARTNERS LP
GLOBECOMM SYSTEMS INC
GLU MOBILE INC
GOLDEN ENTERPRISES INC
GOLFSMITH INTERNATIONAL HOLDINGS INC
GREAT AMERICAN FINANCIAL RESOURCES INC
GREAT LAKES CHEESE COMPANY INC
GREEN MOUNTAIN POWER CORPORATION
GTC BIOTHERAPEUTICS INC
GULFMARK OFFSHORE INC
HAEMONETICS CORPORATION
HAHN AUTOMOTIVE WAREHOUSE INC
HANCOCK HOLDING COMPANY
HANOVER FOODS CORPORATION
HARRIS INTERACTIVE INC
HCC INSURANCE HOLDINGS INC
HEALTH GRADES INC
HEALTH INSURANCE PLAN OF GREATER NEW YORK
HEALTHSTREAM INC
HEALTHTRONICS INC
HEARUSA INC
HELIOVOLT CORP
HELIX ENERGY SOLUTIONS GROUP INC
HESKA CORP
HICKORY TECH CORPORATION
HI-TECH PHARMACAL CO INC
HOLLYFRONTIER CORPORATION
HORACE MANN EDUCATORS CORPORATION
HOSPITALITY PROPERTIES TRUST
HOULIHAN LOKEY HOWARD & ZUKIN INC
HUB GROUP INC
HUDSON CITY BANCORP INC
IBASIS INC
ICONIX BRAND GROUP INC
ICU MEDICAL INC
IDACORP INC
I-FLOW CORPORATION
ILLUMINA INC
IMG WORLDWIDE INC
IMMUCOR INC
IMPAX LABORATORIES INC
INDEPENDENCE HOLDING CO
INFOSPACE INC
INNOPHOS HOLDINGS INC
INNOSPEC INC
INTEGRAL SYSTEMS INC
INTEGRAMED AMERICA INC
INTERACTIVE DATA CORPORATION
INTERACTIVE INTELLIGENCE GROUP INC
INTERCONTINENTALEXCHANGE INC (ICE)
INTERMEC INC
INTERNAP NETWORK SERVICES CORP
INTERNATIONAL CREATIVE MANAGEMENT INC (ICM)
INTERNATIONAL DAIRY QUEEN INC
INTUITIVE SURGICAL INC
INVESTMENT TECHNOLOGY GROUP INC (ITG)
INVESTORS REAL ESTATE TRUST
IRIDEX CORP
IRIS INTERNATIONAL INC
IROBOT CORP
ISILON SYSTEMS INC
IVILLAGE INC
J2 GLOBAL COMMUNICATIONS INC
JAZZ PHARMACEUTICALS INC
JOE'S JEANS INC
JOHN B SANFILIPPO & SON INC
KAMPGROUNDS OF AMERICA INC
KBW INC
KENDALL-JACKSON WINE ESTATES LTD
KENNETH COLE PRODUCTIONS INC
KEY TRONIC CORP
KEYNOTE SYSTEMS INC
KIMLEY-HORN AND ASSOCIATES INC
KIRBY CORP
KKR & CO LP (KOHLBERG KRAVIS ROBERTS & CO)
KNIGHT CAPITAL GROUP INC
KNOLOGY INC
KORN/FERRY INTERNATIONAL
KRONOS WORLDWIDE INC
LACLEDE GROUP INC (THE)
LAKELAND INDUSTRIES INC
LB FOSTER COMPANY

LCC INTERNATIONAL INC
LESLIE'S POOLMART INC
LIFECELL CORPORATION
LIFECORE BIOMEDICAL INC
LIVEPERSON INC
LOGISTICARE INC
LOJACK CORPORTATION
LUCASFILM LTD
LUCOR INC
LUMINEX CORPORATION
MAGELLAN MIDSTREAM PARTNERS LP
MAKO SURGICAL CORP
MALT-O-MEAL COMPANY
MANAGEMENT NETWORK GROUP INC (THE)
MANHATTAN ASSOCIATES INC
MAPFRE USA CORP
MARTEK BIOSCIENCES CORP
MARVEL ENTERTAINMENT LLC
MEDICINES CO (THE)
MEDICIS PHARMACEUTICAL CORP
MEDIFAST INC
MEDTOX SCIENTIFIC INC
MENTOR CORP
MERIDIAN BIOSCIENCE INC
MERIT MEDICAL SYSTEMS INC
MESIROW FINANCIAL HOLDINGS INC
METROPOLITAN HEALTH NETWORKS INC
MICHELINAS INC
MICROTEK MEDICAL HOLDINGS INC
MID-AMERICA APARTMENT COMMUNITIES INC
MIDAS INC
MILLENNIUM PHARMACEUTICALS INC
MINDSPEED TECHNOLOGIES INC
MOELIS & COMPANY
MONSTER BEVERAGE CORP
MOTORCAR PARTS OF AMERICA INC
MTR GAMING GROUP INC
MYRIAD GENETICS INC
NANOMETRICS INC
NATIONAL BEVERAGE CORP
NATIONAL DENTEX CORP
NATIONAL WINE & SPIRITS INC
NATUS MEDICAL INC
NEKTAR THERAPEUTICS
NEOGEN CORPORATION

NETFLIX INC
NETGEAR INC
NETSCOUT SYSTEMS INC
NETSUITE INC
NETWORK ENGINES INC
NEUSTAR INC
NEW JERSEY RESOURCES CORPORATION
NEW YORK MERCANTILE EXCHANGE INC
NIC INC
NORTHWESTERN CORPORATION
NOTIFY TECHNOLOGY CORP
NOVAMED INC
NOVEN PHARMACEUTICALS INC
NTELOS HOLDING CORP
NUGGET MARKET
NUSTAR ENERGY LP
NUTRASWEET COMPANY (THE)
NUVASIVE INC
ODYSSEY RE HOLDINGS CORP
OMNOVA SOLUTIONS INC
ONLINE RESOURCES CORP
ONSTREAM MEDIA CORPORATION
OPENTV CORP
ORION MARINE GROUP INC
PACIFIC BIOMARKERS INC
PAR PHARMACEUTICAL COMPANIES INC
PATAGONIA INC
PC CONNECTION INC
PEAPOD LLC
PEGASYSTEMS INC
PERFICIENT INC
PERRY ELLIS INTERNATIONAL INC
PETMED EXPRESS INC
PETROLEUM DEVELOPMENT CORPORATION
PHAZAR CORP
PHILADELPHIA CONSOLIDATED HOLDING CORP
PHOENIX COMPANIES INC (THE)
PIEDMONT NATURAL GAS COMPANY INC
PIONEER NATURAL RESOURCES COMPANY
PIPER JAFFRAY COMPANIES
PLAINS EXPLORATION AND PRODUCTION COMPANY
PLATO LEARNING INC
PMA COMPANIES INC
POLYPORE INTERNATIONAL INC

POWERSECURE INTERNATIONAL INC
PREMIERE GLOBAL SERVICES INC
PRIMEENERGY CORPORATION
PROASSURANCE CORP
PROTECTIVE LIFE CORP
PURPLE COMMUNICATIONS INC
QUAKER CHEMICAL CORP
QUALCOMM ATHEROS INC
QUALITY SYSTEMS INC
QUANTUM CORP
QUESTCOR PHARMACEUTICALS INC
QUICKSILVER RESOURCES INC
QUIDEL CORP
RAYTHEON APPLIED SIGNAL TECHNOLOGY INC
REALNETWORKS INC
RECYCLED ENERGY DEVELOPMENT LLC
REDBOX AUTOMATED RETAIL LLC
REGENERON PHARMACEUTICALS INC
REINSURANCE GROUP OF AMERICA INC
RENTRAK CORP
RICELAND FOODS INC
RIGHTNOW TECHNOLOGIES INC
RIVERBED TECHNOLOGY INC
ROBERT W BAIRD & CO INC
ROCKY BRANDS INC
ROGERS CORPORATION
ROSETTA STONE INC
ROVI CORPORATION
RPC INC
RSA SECURITY INC
S1 CORPORATION
SACRAMENTO MUNICIPAL UTILITY DISTRICT
SALIX PHARMACEUTICALS
SANDRIDGE ENERGY INC
SBA COMMUNICATIONS CORP
SCANSOURCE INC
SCHICK TECHNOLOGIES INC
SCHIFF NUTRITION INTERNATIONAL INC
SCICLONE PHARMACEUTICALS INC
SCIOS INC
SCOULAR COMPANY (THE)
SEACHANGE INTERNATIONAL INC
SEATTLE GENETICS
SELECTICA INC

SENIOR HOUSING PROPERTIES
SERACARE LIFE SCIENCES INC
SHARED TECHNOLOGIES
SHENANDOAH TELECOMMUNICATIONS CO
SHUTTERFLY INC
SIGMA DESIGNS INC
SILICON LABORATORIES INC
SL GREEN REALTY CORP
SMART MODULAR TECHNOLOGIES INC
SOLARRESERVE
SOLFOCUS INC
SOTHEBYS
SOUTHERN UNION COMPANY
SOUTHWEST GAS CORP
SOUTHWESTERN ENERGY CO
SOVRAN SELF STORAGE INC
SPARTAN MOTORS INC
SPECTRANETICS CORP
SPECTRUM PHARMACEUTICALS INC
SPIRE CORPORATION
SPORT SUPPLY GROUP INC
SPORTSMAN'S GUIDE INC (THE)
SPROUTS FARMERS MARKET LLC
SRS LABS INC
SS&C TECHNOLOGIES HOLDINGS INC
STAAR SURGICAL CO
STATE AUTO FINANCIAL CORP
STEPAN COMPANY
STERLING AUTOBODY CENTERS
STERLING CONSTRUCTION COMPANY
STEVEN MADDEN LTD
STIEFEL LABORATORIES INC
SUN COMMUNITIES INC
SUNOCO LOGISTICS PARTNERS LP
SUPER MICRO COMPUTER INC
SUPERIOR UNIFORM GROUP INC
SUPERTEL HOSPITALITY INC
SUPREME INDUSTRIES INC
SVB FINANCIAL GROUP
SWIFT ENERGY CO
SYNAPTICS INC
SYNIVERSE TECHNOLOGIES
SYNOVIS LIFE TECHNOLOGIES INC
TAKE-TWO INTERACTIVE SOFTWARE INC
TAMPA ELECTRIC COMPANY
TARGA RESOURCES PARTNERS LP
TECHNE CORP
TEKELEC
TELIRIS
TERREMARK WORLDWIDE INC
TESCO CORPORATION
TESSCO TECHNOLOGIES INC
THERAGENICS CORP
THORATEC CORPORATION
TII NETWORK TECHNOLOGIES INC
TOOTSIE ROLL INDUSTRIES INC
TOPPS COMPANY INC (THE)
TRANSAMMONIA INC
TRANSATLANTIC HOLDINGS INC
TRANSCEND SERVICES INC
TRAVELZOO INC
TREX COMPANY INC
TRIZETTO GROUP INC (THE)
TRUE RELIGION APPAREL INC
UDR INC
UIL HOLDINGS CORPORATION
ULTIMATE SOFTWARE GROUP INC
ULTRALIFE CORPORATION
UNISOURCE ENERGY CORPORATION
UNIT CORP
UNITED ONLINE INC
UNITED THERAPEUTICS CORP
UNIVERSAL HOSPITAL SERVICES INC
UQM TECHNOLOGIES INC
US PHYSICAL THERAPY INC
USANA HEALTH SCIENCES INC
UTAH MEDICAL PRODUCTS INC
VARIAN SEMICONDUCTOR EQUIPMENT ASSOCIATES INC
VASCO DATA SECURITY INTERNATIONAL INC
VENTANA MEDICAL SYSTEMS INC
VERENIUM CORPORATION
VIASAT INC
VIBRANT MEDIA INC
VIROPHARMA INC
VOLCOM INC
VOX INTERNATIONAL CORPORATION
WABASH NATIONAL CORP
WADDELL & REED FINANCIAL INC
WEBEX COMMUNICATIONS INC
WEBMD HEALTH CORP
WEBMEDIA BRANDS INC
WEBSENSE INC
WESTAR ENERGY
WGL HOLDINGS INC
WHITEWAVE FOODS COMPANY
WIKIMEDIA FOUNDATION
WIND RIVER SYSTEMS INC
WMS INDUSTRIES INC
WRIGHT MEDICAL GROUP INC
XETA TECHNOLOGIES INC
XO GROUP INC
XOMA LTD
XTO ENERGY INC
YOUNG'S MARKET COMPANY LLC
ZAP JONWAY
ZEP INC
ZIEBART INTERNATIONAL CORP
ZOLL MEDICAL CORP
ZYNGA INC

Law
24/7 REAL MEDIA INC
AAMCO TRANSMISSIONS INC
ABAXIS INC
ACI WORLDWIDE INC
ACME PACKET INC
ACXIOM DIGITAL INC
ADEPT TECHNOLOGY INC
ADTRAN INC
ADVISORY BOARD COMPANY (THE)
AFFILIATED MANAGERS GROUP
AKAMAI TECHNOLOGIES INC
AKORN INC
AKQA INC
ALBANY MOLECULAR RESEARCH INC
ALEXANDER & BALDWIN INC
ALEXION PHARMACEUTICALS INC
ALIEN TECHNOLOGY CORPORATION
ALIGN TECHNOLOGY INC
ALLEGIANT TRAVEL COMPANY
ALLIED HEALTHCARE INTERNATIONAL INC
ALLSCRIPTS HEALTHCARE SOLUTIONS INC
AMAG PHARMACEUTICALS INC
AMCOL INTERNATIONAL CORP
AMCON DISTRIBUTING CO
AMERESCO INC
AMERICAN CAMPUS COMMUNITIES INC

AMERICAN FIDELITY ASSURANCE COMPANY
AMERICAN MEDICAL SYSTEMS HOLDINGS INC
AMERICAN SCIENCE & ENGINEERING INC
AMERICAN TIRE DISTRIBUTORS
AMERICAN TOWER CORP
AMERICAN VANGUARD CORP
AMERICA'S CAR-MART INC
AMTECH SYSTEMS INC
AMTRUST FINANCIAL SERVICES INC
ANALOGIC CORP
ANAREN INC
ANIKA THERAPEUTICS INC
APP PHARMACEUTICALS INC
ARCSIGHT INC
ARDEN GROUP INC
ARGON ST INC
ARIBA INC
ARIZONA CHEMICAL COMPANY
AROTECH CORPORATION
ARRAY BIOPHARMA INC
ARRIS GROUP INC
ARTHROCARE CORP
ARUBA NETWORKS INC
ASTEX PHARMACEUTICALS INC
ATHENAHEALTH INC
ATLANTIC CITY ELECTRIC COMPANY
ATLANTIC TELE-NETWORK INC
ATRION CORPORATION
AUDIBLE INC
AVALONBAY COMMUNITIES INC
AVIALL INC
AVISTA CORPORATION
B&G FOODS INC
BANKRATE INC
BERRY PETROLEUM CO
BIO REFERENCE LABORATORIES INC
BIOMARIN PHARMACEUTICAL INC
BIOSCRIP INC
BIOSITE INC
BLACK HILLS CORP
BLACKBOARD INC
BLUE COAT SYSTEMS INC
BLUE NILE INC
BOSTON BEER COMPANY INC (THE)
BOTTOMLINE TECHNOLOGIES INC
BRIGHTSTAR CORPORATION
CABOT OIL & GAS CORP
CACTUS FEEDERS INC
CAGLE'S INC
CALAVO GROWERS INC
CALGON CARBON CORPORATION
CALIBER HOLDINGS CORP
CALIPER LIFE SCIENCES INC
CAL-MAINE FOODS INC
CAMBREX CORP
CANTEL MEDICAL CORP
CANTOR FITZGERALD LP
CAPITOL FEDERAL FINANCIAL INC
CARACO PHARMACEUTICAL LABORATORIES LTD
CARBO CERAMICS INC
CARDIONET INC
CARDTRONICS INC
CARRIZO OIL & GAS INC
CATALYST HEALTH SOLUTIONS INC
CELLDEX THERAPEUTICS INC
CELSIS INTERNATIONAL PLC
CENTRAL VERMONT PUBLIC SERVICE CORP
CEPHEID
CERUS CORPORATION
CF INDUSTRIES HOLDINGS INC
CHANNELL COMMERCIAL CORP
CHATTEM INC
CHINDEX INTERNATIONAL INC
CHOICESTREAM INC
CHOLESTECH CORP
CIRRUS LOGIC INC
CKX INC
CLAYTON WILLIAMS ENERGY INC
CLEAN ENERGY FUELS CORP
CLEARONE COMMUNICATIONS INC
COGENT COMMUNICATIONS
COHERENT INC
COMDATA CORP
COMPASS DIVERSIFIED HOLDINGS
COMTECH TELECOMMUNICATIONS CORP
COMVERGE INC
CONCUR TECHNOLOGIES INC
CONSTANT CONTACT INC
CONTINENTAL RESOURCES INC
CONTINUCARE CORP
CORPORATE EXECUTIVE BOARD COMPANY (THE)
COSTAR GROUP INC
COUPONS INC
CRA INTERNATIONAL INC (CHARLES RIVER)
CRAY INC
CRITICAL CARE SYSTEMS
CROWN CASTLE INTERNATIONAL CORP
CRUM & FORSTER HOLDINGS INC
CRYOLIFE INC
CUBIST PHARMACEUTICALS INC
CULP INC
CUMULUS MEDIA INC
CYBERONICS INC
CYBERSOURCE CORP
DANNON COMPANY INC (THE)
DAWSON GEOPHYSICAL COMPANY
DEI HOLDINGS INC
DELPHI FINANCIAL GROUP INC
DENBURY RESOURCES INC
DIAMOND ADVISORY SERVICES
DIAMOND FOODS INC
DIGITAL GENERATION INC
DJO GLOBAL INC
DOLBY LABORATORIES INC
DORMAN PRODUCTS INC
DPL INC
DREAMWORKS ANIMATION SKG INC
DRUGSTORE.COM INC
EATON VANCE CORP
EBIX INC
ECHO GLOBAL LOGISTICS INC
ECHOSTAR CORP
ECOLLEGE.COM
EDELMAN FINANCIAL GROUP (THE)
EDGAR ONLINE INC
EDUCATIONAL DEVELOPMENT CORP
EHEALTH INC
EMBARCADERO TECHNOLOGIES INC
EMCORE CORP
EMS TECHNOLOGIES INC
EMULEX CORP
ENCORE CAPITAL GROUP INC
ENERGY TRANSFER PARTNERS LP
ENERNOC INC
ENVIRONMENTAL TECTONICS CORP
EOG RESOURCES INC
EPAM SYSTEMS

EQT CORPORATION
EQUINIX INC
ERESEARCH TECHNOLOGY INC
ESSEX PROPERTY TRUST INC
EVERCORE PARTNERS INC
EVEREST RE GROUP LTD
EXACTECH INC
F5 NETWORKS INC
FAIR ISAAC CORPORATION
FEDEX SUPPLY CHAIN SERVICES INC
FIRST FINANCIAL BANCORP (OH)
FNB CORP
FORRESTER RESEARCH INC
FORTINET INC
FRESHDIRECT LLC
FROZEN FOOD EXPRESS INDUSTRIES INC
FUEL SYSTEMS SOLUTIONS INC
FUEL TECH INC
GAIAM INC
GALLUP ORGANIZATION (THE)
GENCO SHIPPING & TRADING LIMITED
GENENCOR INTERNATIONAL INC
GENERAL ATOMICS
GENERAL COMMUNICATION INC (GCI)
GENESIS ENERGY LP
GENOMIC HEALTH INC
GEN-PROBE INC
GFI GROUP INC
G-III APPAREL GROUP
GLEACHER & COMPANY INC
GLOBAL PARTNERS LP
GLOBECOMM SYSTEMS INC
GLU MOBILE INC
GOLDEN ENTERPRISES INC
GOLFSMITH INTERNATIONAL HOLDINGS INC
GREAT AMERICAN FINANCIAL RESOURCES INC
GREAT LAKES CHEESE COMPANY INC
GREEN MOUNTAIN POWER CORPORATION
GTC BIOTHERAPEUTICS INC
GULFMARK OFFSHORE INC
HAEMONETICS CORPORATION
HAHN AUTOMOTIVE WAREHOUSE INC
HANCOCK HOLDING COMPANY

HANOVER FOODS CORPORATION
HARRIS INTERACTIVE INC
HCC INSURANCE HOLDINGS INC
HEALTH GRADES INC
HEALTH INSURANCE PLAN OF GREATER NEW YORK
HEALTHSTREAM INC
HEALTHTRONICS INC
HEARUSA INC
HELIOVOLT CORP
HELIX ENERGY SOLUTIONS GROUP INC
HESKA CORP
HICKORY TECH CORPORATION
HI-TECH PHARMACAL CO INC
HOLLYFRONTIER CORPORATION
HORACE MANN EDUCATORS CORPORATION
HOSPITALITY PROPERTIES TRUST
HOULIHAN LOKEY HOWARD & ZUKIN INC
HUB GROUP INC
HUDSON CITY BANCORP INC
IBASIS INC
ICONIX BRAND GROUP INC
ICU MEDICAL INC
IDACORP INC
I-FLOW CORPORATION
ILLUMINA INC
IMG WORLDWIDE INC
IMMUCOR INC
IMPAX LABORATORIES INC
INDEPENDENCE HOLDING CO
INFOSPACE INC
INNOPHOS HOLDINGS INC
INNOSPEC INC
INTEGRAL SYSTEMS INC
INTEGRAMED AMERICA INC
INTERACTIVE DATA CORPORATION
INTERACTIVE INTELLIGENCE GROUP INC
INTERCONTINENTALEXCHANGE INC (ICE)
INTERMEC INC
INTERNAP NETWORK SERVICES CORP
INTERNATIONAL CREATIVE MANAGEMENT INC (ICM)
INTERNATIONAL DAIRY QUEEN INC
INTUITIVE SURGICAL INC
INVESTMENT TECHNOLOGY GROUP INC (ITG)

INVESTORS REAL ESTATE TRUST
IRIDEX CORP
IRIS INTERNATIONAL INC
IROBOT CORP
ISILON SYSTEMS INC
IVILLAGE INC
J2 GLOBAL COMMUNICATIONS INC
JAZZ PHARMACEUTICALS INC
JOE'S JEANS INC
JOHN B SANFILIPPO & SON INC
KAMPGROUNDS OF AMERICA INC
KBW INC
KENDALL-JACKSON WINE ESTATES LTD
KENNETH COLE PRODUCTIONS INC
KEY TRONIC CORP
KEYNOTE SYSTEMS INC
KIMLEY-HORN AND ASSOCIATES INC
KIRBY CORP
KKR & CO LP (KOHLBERG KRAVIS ROBERTS & CO)
KNIGHT CAPITAL GROUP INC
KNOLOGY INC
KORN/FERRY INTERNATIONAL
KRONOS WORLDWIDE INC
LACLEDE GROUP INC (THE)
LAKELAND INDUSTRIES INC
LB FOSTER COMPANY
LCC INTERNATIONAL INC
LESLIE'S POOLMART INC
LIFECELL CORPORATION
LIFECORE BIOMEDICAL INC
LIVEPERSON INC
LOGISTICARE INC
LOJACK CORPORTATION
LUCASFILM LTD
LUCOR INC
LUMINEX CORPORATION
MAGELLAN MIDSTREAM PARTNERS LP
MAKO SURGICAL CORP
MALT-O-MEAL COMPANY
MANAGEMENT NETWORK GROUP INC (THE)
MANHATTAN ASSOCIATES INC
MAPFRE USA CORP
MARTEK BIOSCIENCES CORP
MARVEL ENTERTAINMENT LLC
MEDICINES CO (THE)
MEDICIS PHARMACEUTICAL CORP

MEDIFAST INC
MEDTOX SCIENTIFIC INC
MENTOR CORP
MERIDIAN BIOSCIENCE INC
MERIT MEDICAL SYSTEMS INC
MESIROW FINANCIAL HOLDINGS INC
METROPOLITAN HEALTH NETWORKS INC
MICHELINAS INC
MICROTEK MEDICAL HOLDINGS INC
MID-AMERICA APARTMENT COMMUNITIES INC
MIDAS INC
MILLENNIUM PHARMACEUTICALS INC
MINDSPEED TECHNOLOGIES INC
MOELIS & COMPANY
MONSTER BEVERAGE CORP
MOTORCAR PARTS OF AMERICA INC
MTR GAMING GROUP INC
MYRIAD GENETICS INC
NANOMETRICS INC
NATIONAL BEVERAGE CORP
NATIONAL DENTEX CORP
NATIONAL WINE & SPIRITS INC
NATUS MEDICAL INC
NEKTAR THERAPEUTICS
NEOGEN CORPORATION
NETFLIX INC
NETGEAR INC
NETSCOUT SYSTEMS INC
NETSUITE INC
NETWORK ENGINES INC
NEUSTAR INC
NEW JERSEY RESOURCES CORPORATION
NEW YORK MERCANTILE EXCHANGE INC
NIC INC
NORTHWESTERN CORPORATION
NOTIFY TECHNOLOGY CORP
NOVAMED INC
NOVEN PHARMACEUTICALS INC
NTELOS HOLDING CORP
NUGGET MARKET
NUSTAR ENERGY LP
NUTRASWEET COMPANY (THE)
NUVASIVE INC
ODYSSEY RE HOLDINGS CORP
OMNOVA SOLUTIONS INC
ONLINE RESOURCES CORP
ONSTREAM MEDIA CORPORATION
OPENTV CORP
ORION MARINE GROUP INC
PACIFIC BIOMARKERS INC
PAR PHARMACEUTICAL COMPANIES INC
PATAGONIA INC
PC CONNECTION INC
PEAPOD LLC
PEGASYSTEMS INC
PERFICIENT INC
PERRY ELLIS INTERNATIONAL INC
PETMED EXPRESS INC
PETROLEUM DEVELOPMENT CORPORATION
PHAZAR CORP
PHILADELPHIA CONSOLIDATED HOLDING CORP
PHOENIX COMPANIES INC (THE)
PIEDMONT NATURAL GAS COMPANY INC
PIONEER NATURAL RESOURCES COMPANY
PIPER JAFFRAY COMPANIES
PLAINS EXPLORATION AND PRODUCTION COMPANY
PLATO LEARNING INC
PMA COMPANIES INC
POLYPORE INTERNATIONAL INC
POWERSECURE INTERNATIONAL INC
PREMIERE GLOBAL SERVICES INC
PRIMEENERGY CORPORATION
PROASSURANCE CORP
PROTECTIVE LIFE CORP
PURPLE COMMUNICATIONS INC
QUAKER CHEMICAL CORP
QUALCOMM ATHEROS INC
QUALITY SYSTEMS INC
QUANTUM CORP
QUESTCOR PHARMACEUTICALS INC
QUICKSILVER RESOURCES INC
QUIDEL CORP
RAYTHEON APPLIED SIGNAL TECHNOLOGY INC
REALNETWORKS INC
RECYCLED ENERGY DEVELOPMENT LLC
REDBOX AUTOMATED RETAIL LLC
REGENERON PHARMACEUTICALS INC
REINSURANCE GROUP OF AMERICA INC
RENTRAK CORP
RICELAND FOODS INC
RIGHTNOW TECHNOLOGIES INC
RIVERBED TECHNOLOGY INC
ROBERT W BAIRD & CO INC
ROCKY BRANDS INC
ROGERS CORPORATION
ROSETTA STONE INC
ROVI CORPORATION
RPC INC
RSA SECURITY INC
S1 CORPORATION
SACRAMENTO MUNICIPAL UTILITY DISTRICT
SALIX PHARMACEUTICALS
SANDRIDGE ENERGY INC
SBA COMMUNICATIONS CORP
SCANSOURCE INC
SCHICK TECHNOLOGIES INC
SCHIFF NUTRITION INTERNATIONAL INC
SCICLONE PHARMACEUTICALS INC
SCIOS INC
SCOULAR COMPANY (THE)
SEACHANGE INTERNATIONAL INC
SEATTLE GENETICS
SELECTICA INC
SENIOR HOUSING PROPERTIES
SERACARE LIFE SCIENCES INC
SHARED TECHNOLOGIES
SHENANDOAH TELECOMMUNICATIONS CO
SHUTTERFLY INC
SIGMA DESIGNS INC
SILICON LABORATORIES INC
SL GREEN REALTY CORP
SMART MODULAR TECHNOLOGIES INC
SOLARRESERVE
SOLFOCUS INC
SOTHEBYS
SOUTHERN UNION COMPANY
SOUTHWEST GAS CORP
SOUTHWESTERN ENERGY CO
SOVRAN SELF STORAGE INC
SPARTAN MOTORS INC
SPECTRANETICS CORP
SPECTRUM PHARMACEUTICALS INC

SPIRE CORPORATION
SPORT SUPPLY GROUP INC
SPORTSMAN'S GUIDE INC (THE)
SPROUTS FARMERS MARKET LLC
SRS LABS INC
SS&C TECHNOLOGIES HOLDINGS INC
STAAR SURGICAL CO
STATE AUTO FINANCIAL CORP
STEPAN COMPANY
STERLING AUTOBODY CENTERS
STERLING CONSTRUCTION COMPANY
STEVEN MADDEN LTD
STIEFEL LABORATORIES INC
SUN COMMUNITIES INC
SUNOCO LOGISTICS PARTNERS LP
SUPER MICRO COMPUTER INC
SUPERIOR UNIFORM GROUP INC
SUPERTEL HOSPITALITY INC
SUPREME INDUSTRIES INC
SVB FINANCIAL GROUP
SWIFT ENERGY CO
SYNAPTICS INC
SYNIVERSE TECHNOLOGIES
SYNOVIS LIFE TECHNOLOGIES INC
TAKE-TWO INTERACTIVE SOFTWARE INC
TAMPA ELECTRIC COMPANY
TARGA RESOURCES PARTNERS LP
TECHNE CORP
TEKELEC
TELIRIS
TERREMARK WORLDWIDE INC
TESCO CORPORATION
TESSCO TECHNOLOGIES INC
THERAGENICS CORP
THORATEC CORPORATION
TII NETWORK TECHNOLOGIES INC
TOOTSIE ROLL INDUSTRIES INC
TOPPS COMPANY INC (THE)
TRANSAMMONIA INC
TRANSATLANTIC HOLDINGS INC
TRANSCEND SERVICES INC
TRAVELZOO INC
TREX COMPANY INC
TRIZETTO GROUP INC (THE)
TRUE RELIGION APPAREL INC
UDR INC
UIL HOLDINGS CORPORATION
ULTIMATE SOFTWARE GROUP INC
ULTRALIFE CORPORATION
UNISOURCE ENERGY CORPORATION
UNIT CORP
UNITED ONLINE INC
UNITED THERAPEUTICS CORP
UNIVERSAL HOSPITAL SERVICES INC
UQM TECHNOLOGIES INC
US PHYSICAL THERAPY INC
USANA HEALTH SCIENCES INC
UTAH MEDICAL PRODUCTS INC
VARIAN SEMICONDUCTOR EQUIPMENT ASSOCIATES INC
VASCO DATA SECURITY INTERNATIONAL INC
VENTANA MEDICAL SYSTEMS INC
VERENIUM CORPORATION
VIASAT INC
VIBRANT MEDIA INC
VIROPHARMA INC
VOLCOM INC
VOX INTERNATIONAL CORPORATION
WABASH NATIONAL CORP
WADDELL & REED FINANCIAL INC
WEBEX COMMUNICATIONS INC
WEBMD HEALTH CORP
WEBMEDIA BRANDS INC
WEBSENSE INC
WESTAR ENERGY
WGL HOLDINGS INC
WHITEWAVE FOODS COMPANY
WIKIMEDIA FOUNDATION
WIND RIVER SYSTEMS INC
WMS INDUSTRIES INC
WRIGHT MEDICAL GROUP INC
XETA TECHNOLOGIES INC
XO GROUP INC
XOMA LTD
XTO ENERGY INC
YOUNG'S MARKET COMPANY LLC
ZAP JONWAY
ZEP INC
ZIEBART INTERNATIONAL CORP
ZOLL MEDICAL CORP
ZYNGA INC

Training
24/7 REAL MEDIA INC
AAMCO TRANSMISSIONS INC
ABAXIS INC
ACI WORLDWIDE INC
ACME PACKET INC
ACXIOM DIGITAL INC
ADEPT TECHNOLOGY INC
ADTRAN INC
ADVISORY BOARD COMPANY (THE)
AKAMAI TECHNOLOGIES INC
AKORN INC
AKQA INC
ALBANY MOLECULAR RESEARCH INC
ALEXION PHARMACEUTICALS INC
ALIEN TECHNOLOGY CORPORATION
ALIGN TECHNOLOGY INC
ALLEGIANT TRAVEL COMPANY
ALLIED HEALTHCARE INTERNATIONAL INC
ALLSCRIPTS HEALTHCARE SOLUTIONS INC
AMAG PHARMACEUTICALS INC
AMCOL INTERNATIONAL CORP
AMCON DISTRIBUTING CO
AMERESCO INC
AMERICAN FIDELITY ASSURANCE COMPANY
AMERICAN MEDICAL SYSTEMS HOLDINGS INC
AMERICAN SCIENCE & ENGINEERING INC
AMERICAN TIRE DISTRIBUTORS
AMERICAN TOWER CORP
AMERICAN VANGUARD CORP
AMERICA'S CAR-MART INC
AMTECH SYSTEMS INC
AMTRUST FINANCIAL SERVICES INC
ANALOGIC CORP
ANAREN INC
ANIKA THERAPEUTICS INC
APP PHARMACEUTICALS INC
ARCSIGHT INC
ARDEN GROUP INC
ARGON ST INC
ARIBA INC
ARIZONA CHEMICAL COMPANY
AROTECH CORPORATION
ARRIS GROUP INC
ARTHROCARE CORP
ARUBA NETWORKS INC
ASTEX PHARMACEUTICALS INC

ATHENAHEALTH INC
ATLANTIC CITY ELECTRIC COMPANY
ATRION CORPORATION
AUDIBLE INC
AVIALL INC
AVISTA CORPORATION
B&G FOODS INC
BERRY PETROLEUM CO
BIO REFERENCE LABORATORIES INC
BIOMARIN PHARMACEUTICAL INC
BIOSCRIP INC
BIOSITE INC
BLACK HILLS CORP
BLACKBOARD INC
BLUE COAT SYSTEMS INC
BLUE NILE INC
BOSTON BEER COMPANY INC (THE)
BOTTOMLINE TECHNOLOGIES INC
BRIGHTSTAR CORPORATION
CABOT OIL & GAS CORP
CAGLE'S INC
CALAVO GROWERS INC
CALIBER HOLDINGS CORP
CALIPER LIFE SCIENCES INC
CAL-MAINE FOODS INC
CAMBREX CORP
CANTEL MEDICAL CORP
CANTOR FITZGERALD LP
CAPITOL FEDERAL FINANCIAL INC
CARACO PHARMACEUTICAL LABORATORIES LTD
CARBO CERAMICS INC
CARDIONET INC
CARDTRONICS INC
CARRIZO OIL & GAS INC
CATALYST HEALTH SOLUTIONS INC
CENTRAL VERMONT PUBLIC SERVICE CORP
CEPHEID
CERUS CORPORATION
CHANNELL COMMERCIAL CORP
CHATTEM INC
CHINDEX INTERNATIONAL INC
CHOICESTREAM INC
CHOLESTECH CORP
CKX INC
CLAYTON WILLIAMS ENERGY INC
CLEARONE COMMUNICATIONS INC
COGENT COMMUNICATIONS

COHERENT INC
COMDATA CORP
COMTECH TELECOMMUNICATIONS CORP
CONCUR TECHNOLOGIES INC
CONTINENTAL RESOURCES INC
CONTINUCARE CORP
CORPORATE EXECUTIVE BOARD COMPANY (THE)
COUPONS INC
CRAY INC
CRITICAL CARE SYSTEMS
CROWN CASTLE INTERNATIONAL CORP
CRUM & FORSTER HOLDINGS INC
CRYOLIFE INC
CUBIST PHARMACEUTICALS INC
CYBERONICS INC
CYBERSOURCE CORP
DANNON COMPANY INC (THE)
DAWSON GEOPHYSICAL COMPANY
DEI HOLDINGS INC
DELPHI FINANCIAL GROUP INC
DENBURY RESOURCES INC
DIAMOND FOODS INC
DIGITAL GENERATION INC
DJO GLOBAL INC
DOLBY LABORATORIES INC
DORMAN PRODUCTS INC
DPL INC
DREAMWORKS ANIMATION SKG INC
DRUGSTORE.COM INC
EBIX INC
ECOLLEGE.COM
EHEALTH INC
EMBARCADERO TECHNOLOGIES INC
EMCORE CORP
EMS TECHNOLOGIES INC
EMULEX CORP
ENCORE CAPITAL GROUP INC
ENERNOC INC
ENVIRONMENTAL TECTONICS CORP
EOG RESOURCES INC
EPAM SYSTEMS
EQT CORPORATION
EQUINIX INC
ERESEARCH TECHNOLOGY INC
EVERCORE PARTNERS INC

EVEREST RE GROUP LTD
EXACTECH INC
F5 NETWORKS INC
FAIR ISAAC CORPORATION
FEDEX SUPPLY CHAIN SERVICES INC
FIRST FINANCIAL BANCORP (OH)
FNB CORP
FORRESTER RESEARCH INC
FRESHDIRECT LLC
FROZEN FOOD EXPRESS INDUSTRIES INC
FUEL SYSTEMS SOLUTIONS INC
FUEL TECH INC
GALLUP ORGANIZATION (THE)
GENENCOR INTERNATIONAL INC
GENERAL COMMUNICATION INC (GCI)
GENESIS ENERGY LP
GENOMIC HEALTH INC
GEN-PROBE INC
GLOBAL PARTNERS LP
GLOBECOMM SYSTEMS INC
GLU MOBILE INC
GOLDEN ENTERPRISES INC
GOLFSMITH INTERNATIONAL HOLDINGS INC
GREAT AMERICAN FINANCIAL RESOURCES INC
GREAT LAKES CHEESE COMPANY INC
GREEN MOUNTAIN POWER CORPORATION
GTC BIOTHERAPEUTICS INC
GULFMARK OFFSHORE INC
HAEMONETICS CORPORATION
HAHN AUTOMOTIVE WAREHOUSE INC
HANCOCK HOLDING COMPANY
HANOVER FOODS CORPORATION
HARRIS INTERACTIVE INC
HCC INSURANCE HOLDINGS INC
HEALTH GRADES INC
HEALTH INSURANCE PLAN OF GREATER NEW YORK
HEALTHSTREAM INC
HEALTHTRONICS INC
HEARUSA INC
HELIOVOLT CORP
HELIX ENERGY SOLUTIONS GROUP INC
HESKA CORP

HICKORY TECH CORPORATION
HI-TECH PHARMACAL CO INC
HOLLYFRONTIER CORPORATION
HORACE MANN EDUCATORS CORPORATION
HOULIHAN LOKEY HOWARD & ZUKIN INC
HUDSON CITY BANCORP INC
IBASIS INC
ICU MEDICAL INC
IDACORP INC
I-FLOW CORPORATION
ILLUMINA INC
IMG WORLDWIDE INC
IMMUCOR INC
IMPAX LABORATORIES INC
INDEPENDENCE HOLDING CO
INTEGRAL SYSTEMS INC
INTEGRAMED AMERICA INC
INTERACTIVE INTELLIGENCE GROUP INC
INTERCONTINENTALEXCHANGE INC (ICE)
INTERMEC INC
INTERNAP NETWORK SERVICES CORP
INTERNATIONAL CREATIVE MANAGEMENT INC (ICM)
INTERNATIONAL DAIRY QUEEN INC
INTUITIVE SURGICAL INC
INVESTMENT TECHNOLOGY GROUP INC (ITG)
IRIDEX CORP
IRIS INTERNATIONAL INC
IROBOT CORP
ISILON SYSTEMS INC
IVILLAGE INC
J2 GLOBAL COMMUNICATIONS INC
JAZZ PHARMACEUTICALS INC
JOHN B SANFILIPPO & SON INC
KAMPGROUNDS OF AMERICA INC
KENDALL-JACKSON WINE ESTATES LTD
KENNETH COLE PRODUCTIONS INC
KEY TRONIC CORP
KEYNOTE SYSTEMS INC
KIMLEY-HORN AND ASSOCIATES INC
KNIGHT CAPITAL GROUP INC
KORN/FERRY INTERNATIONAL
KRONOS WORLDWIDE INC
LACLEDE GROUP INC (THE)

LAKELAND INDUSTRIES INC
LCC INTERNATIONAL INC
LESLIE'S POOLMART INC
LIFECELL CORPORATION
LIFECORE BIOMEDICAL INC
LIVEPERSON INC
LOGISTICARE INC
LOJACK CORPORTATION
LUCASFILM LTD
LUCOR INC
LUMINEX CORPORATION
MAGELLAN MIDSTREAM PARTNERS LP
MAKO SURGICAL CORP
MALT-O-MEAL COMPANY
MANHATTAN ASSOCIATES INC
MAPFRE USA CORP
MARTEK BIOSCIENCES CORP
MARVEL ENTERTAINMENT LLC
MEDICINES CO (THE)
MEDICIS PHARMACEUTICAL CORP
MEDIFAST INC
MEDTOX SCIENTIFIC INC
MENTOR CORP
MERIDIAN BIOSCIENCE INC
MERIT MEDICAL SYSTEMS INC
METROPOLITAN HEALTH NETWORKS INC
MICHELINAS INC
MICROTEK MEDICAL HOLDINGS INC
MIDAS INC
MILLENNIUM PHARMACEUTICALS INC
MOELIS & COMPANY
MONSTER BEVERAGE CORP
MOTORCAR PARTS OF AMERICA INC
MYRIAD GENETICS INC
NANOMETRICS INC
NATIONAL BEVERAGE CORP
NATIONAL DENTEX CORP
NATIONAL WINE & SPIRITS INC
NATUS MEDICAL INC
NEKTAR THERAPEUTICS
NEOGEN CORPORATION
NETFLIX INC
NETGEAR INC
NETSCOUT SYSTEMS INC
NETSUITE INC
NEW JERSEY RESOURCES CORPORATION

NEW YORK MERCANTILE EXCHANGE INC
NIC INC
NORTHWESTERN CORPORATION
NOTIFY TECHNOLOGY CORP
NOVAMED INC
NOVEN PHARMACEUTICALS INC
NTELOS HOLDING CORP
NUGGET MARKET
NUSTAR ENERGY LP
NUTRASWEET COMPANY (THE)
NUVASIVE INC
ODYSSEY RE HOLDINGS CORP
ONLINE RESOURCES CORP
OPENTV CORP
PACIFIC BIOMARKERS INC
PAR PHARMACEUTICAL COMPANIES INC
PC CONNECTION INC
PEAPOD LLC
PEGASYSTEMS INC
PERFICIENT INC
PERRY ELLIS INTERNATIONAL INC
PETMED EXPRESS INC
PETROLEUM DEVELOPMENT CORPORATION
PHILADELPHIA CONSOLIDATED HOLDING CORP
PHOENIX COMPANIES INC (THE)
PIEDMONT NATURAL GAS COMPANY INC
PIONEER NATURAL RESOURCES COMPANY
PLAINS EXPLORATION AND PRODUCTION COMPANY
PLATO LEARNING INC
PMA COMPANIES INC
POLYPORE INTERNATIONAL INC
POWERSECURE INTERNATIONAL INC
PREMIERE GLOBAL SERVICES INC
PRIMEENERGY CORPORATION
PROASSURANCE CORP
PROTECTIVE LIFE CORP
PURPLE COMMUNICATIONS INC
QUALCOMM ATHEROS INC
QUALITY SYSTEMS INC
QUANTUM CORP
QUESTCOR PHARMACEUTICALS INC
QUICKSILVER RESOURCES INC
QUIDEL CORP

RAYTHEON APPLIED SIGNAL TECHNOLOGY INC
REALNETWORKS INC
RECYCLED ENERGY DEVELOPMENT LLC
REDBOX AUTOMATED RETAIL LLC
REGENERON PHARMACEUTICALS INC
REINSURANCE GROUP OF AMERICA INC
RENTRAK CORP
RIGHTNOW TECHNOLOGIES INC
ROBERT W BAIRD & CO INC
ROCKY BRANDS INC
ROGERS CORPORATION
ROSETTA STONE INC
RPC INC
RSA SECURITY INC
S1 CORPORATION
SACRAMENTO MUNICIPAL UTILITY DISTRICT
SALIX PHARMACEUTICALS
SANDRIDGE ENERGY INC
SBA COMMUNICATIONS CORP
SCANSOURCE INC
SCHICK TECHNOLOGIES INC
SCHIFF NUTRITION INTERNATIONAL INC
SCICLONE PHARMACEUTICALS INC
SCIOS INC
SCOULAR COMPANY (THE)
SEACHANGE INTERNATIONAL INC
SEATTLE GENETICS
SELECTICA INC
SERACARE LIFE SCIENCES INC
SHARED TECHNOLOGIES
SHENANDOAH TELECOMMUNICATIONS CO
SHUTTERFLY INC
SOLARRESERVE
SOLFOCUS INC
SOTHEBYS
SOUTHERN UNION COMPANY
SOUTHWEST GAS CORP
SOUTHWESTERN ENERGY CO
SPARTAN MOTORS INC
SPECTRANETICS CORP
SPECTRUM PHARMACEUTICALS INC
SPIRE CORPORATION
SPORT SUPPLY GROUP INC
SPORTSMAN'S GUIDE INC (THE)
SPROUTS FARMERS MARKET LLC
SS&C TECHNOLOGIES HOLDINGS INC
STAAR SURGICAL CO
STATE AUTO FINANCIAL CORP
STEPAN COMPANY
STERLING AUTOBODY CENTERS
STEVEN MADDEN LTD
STIEFEL LABORATORIES INC
SUNOCO LOGISTICS PARTNERS LP
SUPER MICRO COMPUTER INC
SUPERIOR UNIFORM GROUP INC
SUPREME INDUSTRIES INC
SVB FINANCIAL GROUP
SWIFT ENERGY CO
SYNAPTICS INC
SYNOVIS LIFE TECHNOLOGIES INC
TAMPA ELECTRIC COMPANY
TARGA RESOURCES PARTNERS LP
TECHNE CORP
TEKELEC
TELIRIS
TERREMARK WORLDWIDE INC
TESCO CORPORATION
THERAGENICS CORP
THORATEC CORPORATION
TOOTSIE ROLL INDUSTRIES INC
TOPPS COMPANY INC (THE)
TRANSATLANTIC HOLDINGS INC
TRANSCEND SERVICES INC
TRAVELZOO INC
TREX COMPANY INC
TRIZETTO GROUP INC (THE)
TRUE RELIGION APPAREL INC
UIL HOLDINGS CORPORATION
ULTIMATE SOFTWARE GROUP INC
UNISOURCE ENERGY CORPORATION
UNIT CORP
UNITED ONLINE INC
UNITED THERAPEUTICS CORP
UNIVERSAL HOSPITAL SERVICES INC
US PHYSICAL THERAPY INC
USANA HEALTH SCIENCES INC
UTAH MEDICAL PRODUCTS INC
VASCO DATA SECURITY INTERNATIONAL INC
VENTANA MEDICAL SYSTEMS INC
VIASAT INC
VIBRANT MEDIA INC
VIROPHARMA INC
VOLCOM INC
VOX INTERNATIONAL CORPORATION
WEBEX COMMUNICATIONS INC
WEBMD HEALTH CORP
WEBMEDIA BRANDS INC
WEBSENSE INC
WESTAR ENERGY
WGL HOLDINGS INC
WHITEWAVE FOODS COMPANY
WIND RIVER SYSTEMS INC
WRIGHT MEDICAL GROUP INC
XETA TECHNOLOGIES INC
XO GROUP INC
XOMA LTD
XTO ENERGY INC
YOUNG'S MARKET COMPANY LLC
ZAP JONWAY
ZIEBART INTERNATIONAL CORP
ZOLL MEDICAL CORP

Sales/Marketing

Advertising Professionals
24/7 REAL MEDIA INC
AAMCO TRANSMISSIONS INC
ACXIOM DIGITAL INC
AKQA INC
ALLEGIANT TRAVEL COMPANY
AMERICAN FIDELITY ASSURANCE COMPANY
AMERICAN TIRE DISTRIBUTORS
AMERICAN VANGUARD CORP
AMERICA'S CAR-MART INC
ARDEN GROUP INC
ATHENAHEALTH INC
AUDIBLE INC
AVALONBAY COMMUNITIES INC
BANKRATE INC
BLACKBOARD INC
BLUE NILE INC
BOSTON BEER COMPANY INC (THE)
CALAVO GROWERS INC
CALIBER HOLDINGS CORP
CAL-MAINE FOODS INC
CAPITOL FEDERAL FINANCIAL INC
CARDTRONICS INC
CHATTEM INC
CHOICESTREAM INC
CHOLESTECH CORP

COMDATA CORP
CONTINUCARE CORP
COUPONS INC
CRITICAL CARE SYSTEMS
DANNON COMPANY INC (THE)
DEI HOLDINGS INC
DIAMOND FOODS INC
DIGITAL GENERATION INC
DREAMWORKS ANIMATION SKG INC
DRUGSTORE.COM INC
ECOLLEGE.COM
EDGAR ONLINE INC
EDUCATIONAL DEVELOPMENT CORP
EHEALTH INC
FIRST FINANCIAL BANCORP (OH)
FNB CORP
FRESHDIRECT LLC
GAIAM INC
G-III APPAREL GROUP
GOLDEN ENTERPRISES INC
GOLFSMITH INTERNATIONAL HOLDINGS INC
GREAT AMERICAN FINANCIAL RESOURCES INC
GREAT LAKES CHEESE COMPANY INC
HAHN AUTOMOTIVE WAREHOUSE INC
HANCOCK HOLDING COMPANY
HANOVER FOODS CORPORATION
HEALTH GRADES INC
HEALTHSTREAM INC
HEALTHTRONICS INC
HEARUSA INC
HOSPITALITY PROPERTIES TRUST
HUDSON CITY BANCORP INC
IBASIS INC
IMMUCOR INC
INDEPENDENCE HOLDING CO
INFOSPACE INC
INTERCONTINENTALEXCHANGE INC (ICE)
INTERNATIONAL DAIRY QUEEN INC
INVESTORS REAL ESTATE TRUST
IVILLAGE INC
JOHN B SANFILIPPO & SON INC
KAMPGROUNDS OF AMERICA INC
KENDALL-JACKSON WINE ESTATES LTD
KENNETH COLE PRODUCTIONS INC

LESLIE'S POOLMART INC
LIVEPERSON INC
LOJACK CORPORTATION
LUCASFILM LTD
LUCOR INC
MALT-O-MEAL COMPANY
MARTEK BIOSCIENCES CORP
MARVEL ENTERTAINMENT LLC
MEDIFAST INC
MERIDIAN BIOSCIENCE INC
MICHELINAS INC
MID-AMERICA APARTMENT COMMUNITIES INC
MIDAS INC
MONSTER BEVERAGE CORP
MTR GAMING GROUP INC
NATIONAL BEVERAGE CORP
NATIONAL WINE & SPIRITS INC
NETFLIX INC
NETSUITE INC
NEW YORK MERCANTILE EXCHANGE INC
NOVAMED INC
NUGGET MARKET
NUTRASWEET COMPANY (THE)
PATAGONIA INC
PC CONNECTION INC
PEAPOD LLC
PERRY ELLIS INTERNATIONAL INC
PETMED EXPRESS INC
PHOENIX COMPANIES INC (THE)
PLATO LEARNING INC
PROTECTIVE LIFE CORP
PURPLE COMMUNICATIONS INC
QUIDEL CORP
REDBOX AUTOMATED RETAIL LLC
RENTRAK CORP
RICELAND FOODS INC
ROCKY BRANDS INC
ROSETTA STONE INC
RSA SECURITY INC
SCHIFF NUTRITION INTERNATIONAL INC
SENIOR HOUSING PROPERTIES
SHUTTERFLY INC
SOTHEBYS
SOVRAN SELF STORAGE INC
SPARTAN MOTORS INC
SPORT SUPPLY GROUP INC
SPORTSMAN'S GUIDE INC (THE)
SPROUTS FARMERS MARKET LLC

STERLING AUTOBODY CENTERS
STEVEN MADDEN LTD
STIEFEL LABORATORIES INC
SUN COMMUNITIES INC
SUPERIOR UNIFORM GROUP INC
SUPREME INDUSTRIES INC
SVB FINANCIAL GROUP
TECHNE CORP
TELIRIS
TERREMARK WORLDWIDE INC
TOOTSIE ROLL INDUSTRIES INC
TOPPS COMPANY INC (THE)
TRAVELZOO INC
TRUE RELIGION APPAREL INC
UNITED ONLINE INC
US PHYSICAL THERAPY INC
USANA HEALTH SCIENCES INC
VIBRANT MEDIA INC
VOLCOM INC
WADDELL & REED FINANCIAL INC
WEBEX COMMUNICATIONS INC
WEBMD HEALTH CORP
WEBMEDIA BRANDS INC
WEBSENSE INC
WHITEWAVE FOODS COMPANY
WMS INDUSTRIES INC
XO GROUP INC
YOUNG'S MARKET COMPANY LLC
ZIEBART INTERNATIONAL CORP
ZYNGA INC

Commerical/Industrial
24/7 REAL MEDIA INC
ABAXIS INC
ACI WORLDWIDE INC
ACME PACKET INC
ACXIOM DIGITAL INC
ADEPT TECHNOLOGY INC
ADTRAN INC
ADVISORY BOARD COMPANY (THE)
AKAMAI TECHNOLOGIES INC
AKORN INC
AKQA INC
ALBANY MOLECULAR RESEARCH INC
ALEXANDER & BALDWIN INC
ALEXION PHARMACEUTICALS INC
ALIEN TECHNOLOGY CORPORATION
ALIGN TECHNOLOGY INC

ALLEGIANT TRAVEL COMPANY
ALLSCRIPTS HEALTHCARE SOLUTIONS INC
AMAG PHARMACEUTICALS INC
AMCOL INTERNATIONAL CORP
AMCON DISTRIBUTING CO
AMERESCO INC
AMERICAN MEDICAL SYSTEMS HOLDINGS INC
AMERICAN SCIENCE & ENGINEERING INC
AMERICAN TIRE DISTRIBUTORS
AMERICAN TOWER CORP
AMERICAN VANGUARD CORP
AMTECH SYSTEMS INC
AMTRUST FINANCIAL SERVICES INC
ANALOGIC CORP
ANAREN INC
ANIKA THERAPEUTICS INC
APP PHARMACEUTICALS INC
ARCSIGHT INC
ARGON ST INC
ARIBA INC
ARIZONA CHEMICAL COMPANY
AROTECH CORPORATION
ARRAY BIOPHARMA INC
ARRIS GROUP INC
ARTHROCARE CORP
ARUBA NETWORKS INC
ASTEX PHARMACEUTICALS INC
ATHENAHEALTH INC
ATLANTIC CITY ELECTRIC COMPANY
ATLANTIC TELE-NETWORK INC
ATRION CORPORATION
AVIALL INC
AVISTA CORPORATION
B&G FOODS INC
BANKRATE INC
BIO REFERENCE LABORATORIES INC
BIOMARIN PHARMACEUTICAL INC
BIOSCRIP INC
BIOSITE INC
BLACK HILLS CORP
BLACKBOARD INC
BLUE COAT SYSTEMS INC
BOSTON BEER COMPANY INC (THE)
BOTTOMLINE TECHNOLOGIES INC
BRIGHTSTAR CORPORATION
CACTUS FEEDERS INC
CAGLE'S INC
CALAVO GROWERS INC
CALGON CARBON CORPORATION
CALIPER LIFE SCIENCES INC
CAL-MAINE FOODS INC
CAMBREX CORP
CANTEL MEDICAL CORP
CARACO PHARMACEUTICAL LABORATORIES LTD
CARBO CERAMICS INC
CARDIONET INC
CARDTRONICS INC
CATALYST HEALTH SOLUTIONS INC
CELLDEX THERAPEUTICS INC
CELSIS INTERNATIONAL PLC
CENTRAL VERMONT PUBLIC SERVICE CORP
CEPHEID
CERUS CORPORATION
CF INDUSTRIES HOLDINGS INC
CHANNELL COMMERCIAL CORP
CHATTEM INC
CHINDEX INTERNATIONAL INC
CHOICESTREAM INC
CHOLESTECH CORP
CIRRUS LOGIC INC
CKX INC
CLEARONE COMMUNICATIONS INC
COGENT COMMUNICATIONS
COHERENT INC
COMDATA CORP
COMTECH TELECOMMUNICATIONS CORP
CONCUR TECHNOLOGIES INC
CONSTANT CONTACT INC
CONTINUCARE CORP
CORPORATE EXECUTIVE BOARD COMPANY (THE)
COSTAR GROUP INC
COUPONS INC
CRA INTERNATIONAL INC (CHARLES RIVER)
CRAY INC
CRITICAL CARE SYSTEMS
CROWN CASTLE INTERNATIONAL CORP
CRUM & FORSTER HOLDINGS INC
CRYOLIFE INC
CUBIST PHARMACEUTICALS INC
CULP INC
CUMULUS MEDIA INC
CYBERONICS INC
CYBERSOURCE CORP
DANNON COMPANY INC (THE)
DAWSON GEOPHYSICAL COMPANY
DEI HOLDINGS INC
DELPHI FINANCIAL GROUP INC
DIAMOND FOODS INC
DIGITAL GENERATION INC
DJO GLOBAL INC
DOLBY LABORATORIES INC
DORMAN PRODUCTS INC
DPL INC
DREAMWORKS ANIMATION SKG INC
EBIX INC
ECHO GLOBAL LOGISTICS INC
ECHOSTAR CORP
ECOLLEGE.COM
EDGAR ONLINE INC
EDUCATIONAL DEVELOPMENT CORP
EMBARCADERO TECHNOLOGIES INC
EMCORE CORP
EMS TECHNOLOGIES INC
EMULEX CORP
ENERNOC INC
ENVIRONMENTAL TECTONICS CORP
EPAM SYSTEMS
EQT CORPORATION
EQUINIX INC
ERESEARCH TECHNOLOGY INC
EVEREST RE GROUP LTD
EXACTECH INC
F5 NETWORKS INC
FAIR ISAAC CORPORATION
FEDEX SUPPLY CHAIN SERVICES INC
FORRESTER RESEARCH INC
FORTINET INC
FROZEN FOOD EXPRESS INDUSTRIES INC
FUEL SYSTEMS SOLUTIONS INC
FUEL TECH INC
GALLUP ORGANIZATION (THE)
GENCO SHIPPING & TRADING LIMITED
GENENCOR INTERNATIONAL INC
GENERAL ATOMICS
GENERAL COMMUNICATION INC

(GCI)
GENESIS ENERGY LP
GENOMIC HEALTH INC
GEN-PROBE INC
G-III APPAREL GROUP
GLOBAL PARTNERS LP
GLOBECOMM SYSTEMS INC
GLU MOBILE INC
GOLDEN ENTERPRISES INC
GOLFSMITH INTERNATIONAL HOLDINGS INC
GREAT LAKES CHEESE COMPANY INC
GREEN MOUNTAIN POWER CORPORATION
GTC BIOTHERAPEUTICS INC
GULFMARK OFFSHORE INC
HAEMONETICS CORPORATION
HANOVER FOODS CORPORATION
HARRIS INTERACTIVE INC
HCC INSURANCE HOLDINGS INC
HEALTH GRADES INC
HEALTH INSURANCE PLAN OF GREATER NEW YORK
HEALTHSTREAM INC
HEALTHTRONICS INC
HELIOVOLT CORP
HELIX ENERGY SOLUTIONS GROUP INC
HESKA CORP
HICKORY TECH CORPORATION
HI-TECH PHARMACAL CO INC
HOLLYFRONTIER CORPORATION
HORACE MANN EDUCATORS CORPORATION
HUB GROUP INC
IBASIS INC
ICONIX BRAND GROUP INC
ICU MEDICAL INC
IDACORP INC
I-FLOW CORPORATION
ILLUMINA INC
IMG WORLDWIDE INC
IMMUCOR INC
IMPAX LABORATORIES INC
INFOSPACE INC
INNOPHOS HOLDINGS INC
INTEGRAL SYSTEMS INC
INTERACTIVE DATA CORPORATION
INTERACTIVE INTELLIGENCE GROUP INC
INTERMEC INC

INTERNAP NETWORK SERVICES CORP
INTERNATIONAL CREATIVE MANAGEMENT INC (ICM)
INTUITIVE SURGICAL INC
INVESTMENT TECHNOLOGY GROUP INC (ITG)
IRIDEX CORP
IRIS INTERNATIONAL INC
IROBOT CORP
ISILON SYSTEMS INC
IVILLAGE INC
J2 GLOBAL COMMUNICATIONS INC
JAZZ PHARMACEUTICALS INC
JOE'S JEANS INC
JOHN B SANFILIPPO & SON INC
KENDALL-JACKSON WINE ESTATES LTD
KENNETH COLE PRODUCTIONS INC
KEY TRONIC CORP
KEYNOTE SYSTEMS INC
KIMLEY-HORN AND ASSOCIATES INC
KIRBY CORP
KORN/FERRY INTERNATIONAL
KRONOS WORLDWIDE INC
LACLEDE GROUP INC (THE)
LAKELAND INDUSTRIES INC
LB FOSTER COMPANY
LCC INTERNATIONAL INC
LIFECELL CORPORATION
LIFECORE BIOMEDICAL INC
LIVEPERSON INC
LOGISTICARE INC
LOJACK CORPORTATION
LUCASFILM LTD
LUMINEX CORPORATION
MAGELLAN MIDSTREAM PARTNERS LP
MAKO SURGICAL CORP
MALT-O-MEAL COMPANY
MANAGEMENT NETWORK GROUP INC (THE)
MANHATTAN ASSOCIATES INC
MAPFRE USA CORP
MARTEK BIOSCIENCES CORP
MEDICINES CO (THE)
MEDICIS PHARMACEUTICAL CORP
MEDTOX SCIENTIFIC INC
MENTOR CORP
MERIDIAN BIOSCIENCE INC
MERIT MEDICAL SYSTEMS INC

METROPOLITAN HEALTH NETWORKS INC
MICHELINAS INC
MICROTEK MEDICAL HOLDINGS INC
MILLENNIUM PHARMACEUTICALS INC
MINDSPEED TECHNOLOGIES INC
MONSTER BEVERAGE CORP
MOTORCAR PARTS OF AMERICA INC
MYRIAD GENETICS INC
NANOMETRICS INC
NATIONAL BEVERAGE CORP
NATIONAL DENTEX CORP
NATIONAL WINE & SPIRITS INC
NATUS MEDICAL INC
NEKTAR THERAPEUTICS
NEOGEN CORPORATION
NETGEAR INC
NETSCOUT SYSTEMS INC
NETSUITE INC
NETWORK ENGINES INC
NEW JERSEY RESOURCES CORPORATION
NIC INC
NORTHWESTERN CORPORATION
NOTIFY TECHNOLOGY CORP
NOVEN PHARMACEUTICALS INC
NTELOS HOLDING CORP
NUSTAR ENERGY LP
NUTRASWEET COMPANY (THE)
NUVASIVE INC
ODYSSEY RE HOLDINGS CORP
OMNOVA SOLUTIONS INC
ONLINE RESOURCES CORP
ONSTREAM MEDIA CORPORATION
OPENTV CORP
ORION MARINE GROUP INC
PACIFIC BIOMARKERS INC
PAR PHARMACEUTICAL COMPANIES INC
PATAGONIA INC
PC CONNECTION INC
PEGASYSTEMS INC
PERFICIENT INC
PERRY ELLIS INTERNATIONAL INC
PHAZAR CORP
PHILADELPHIA CONSOLIDATED HOLDING CORP
PIEDMONT NATURAL GAS COMPANY INC
PLATO LEARNING INC

PMA COMPANIES INC
POLYPORE INTERNATIONAL INC
POWERSECURE INTERNATIONAL INC
PREMIERE GLOBAL SERVICES INC
PROASSURANCE CORP
PURPLE COMMUNICATIONS INC
QUALCOMM ATHEROS INC
QUALITY SYSTEMS INC
QUANTUM CORP
QUESTCOR PHARMACEUTICALS INC
QUIDEL CORP
RAYTHEON APPLIED SIGNAL TECHNOLOGY INC
REALNETWORKS INC
RECYCLED ENERGY DEVELOPMENT LLC
REDBOX AUTOMATED RETAIL LLC
REGENERON PHARMACEUTICALS INC
REINSURANCE GROUP OF AMERICA INC
RENTRAK CORP
RICELAND FOODS INC
RIGHTNOW TECHNOLOGIES INC
RIVERBED TECHNOLOGY INC
ROCKY BRANDS INC
ROGERS CORPORATION
ROVI CORPORATION
RPC INC
RSA SECURITY INC
S1 CORPORATION
SACRAMENTO MUNICIPAL UTILITY DISTRICT
SALIX PHARMACEUTICALS
SBA COMMUNICATIONS CORP
SCANSOURCE INC
SCHICK TECHNOLOGIES INC
SCHIFF NUTRITION INTERNATIONAL INC
SCICLONE PHARMACEUTICALS INC
SCIOS INC
SCOULAR COMPANY (THE)
SEACHANGE INTERNATIONAL INC
SEATTLE GENETICS
SELECTICA INC
SERACARE LIFE SCIENCES INC
SHARED TECHNOLOGIES
SHENANDOAH TELECOMMUNICATIONS CO
SHUTTERFLY INC

SIGMA DESIGNS INC
SILICON LABORATORIES INC
SMART MODULAR TECHNOLOGIES INC
SOLARRESERVE
SOLFOCUS INC
SOUTHERN UNION COMPANY
SOUTHWEST GAS CORP
SPARTAN MOTORS INC
SPECTRANETICS CORP
SPECTRUM PHARMACEUTICALS INC
SPIRE CORPORATION
SRS LABS INC
SS&C TECHNOLOGIES HOLDINGS INC
STAAR SURGICAL CO
STATE AUTO FINANCIAL CORP
STEPAN COMPANY
STERLING CONSTRUCTION COMPANY
STEVEN MADDEN LTD
STIEFEL LABORATORIES INC
SUNOCO LOGISTICS PARTNERS LP
SUPER MICRO COMPUTER INC
SUPERIOR UNIFORM GROUP INC
SUPREME INDUSTRIES INC
SYNAPTICS INC
SYNIVERSE TECHNOLOGIES
SYNOVIS LIFE TECHNOLOGIES INC
TAKE-TWO INTERACTIVE SOFTWARE INC
TAMPA ELECTRIC COMPANY
TECHNE CORP
TEKELEC
TELIRIS
TERREMARK WORLDWIDE INC
TESCO CORPORATION
TESSCO TECHNOLOGIES INC
THERAGENICS CORP
THORATEC CORPORATION
TII NETWORK TECHNOLOGIES INC
TOOTSIE ROLL INDUSTRIES INC
TOPPS COMPANY INC (THE)
TRANSATLANTIC HOLDINGS INC
TRANSCEND SERVICES INC
TRAVELZOO INC
TREX COMPANY INC
TRIZETTO GROUP INC (THE)
UIL HOLDINGS CORPORATION
ULTIMATE SOFTWARE GROUP INC

ULTRALIFE CORPORATION
UNISOURCE ENERGY CORPORATION
UNITED ONLINE INC
UNITED THERAPEUTICS CORP
UNIVERSAL HOSPITAL SERVICES INC
UQM TECHNOLOGIES INC
US PHYSICAL THERAPY INC
USANA HEALTH SCIENCES INC
UTAH MEDICAL PRODUCTS INC
VARIAN SEMICONDUCTOR EQUIPMENT ASSOCIATES INC
VASCO DATA SECURITY INTERNATIONAL INC
VENTANA MEDICAL SYSTEMS INC
VERENIUM CORPORATION
VIASAT INC
VIBRANT MEDIA INC
VIROPHARMA INC
VOLCOM INC
WABASH NATIONAL CORP
WEBEX COMMUNICATIONS INC
WEBMD HEALTH CORP
WEBMEDIA BRANDS INC
WEBSENSE INC
WESTAR ENERGY
WGL HOLDINGS INC
WHITEWAVE FOODS COMPANY
WIND RIVER SYSTEMS INC
WMS INDUSTRIES INC
WRIGHT MEDICAL GROUP INC
XETA TECHNOLOGIES INC
XO GROUP INC
XOMA LTD
YOUNG'S MARKET COMPANY LLC
ZAP JONWAY
ZEP INC
ZOLL MEDICAL CORP

Marketing Professionals
24/7 REAL MEDIA INC
AAMCO TRANSMISSIONS INC
ABAXIS INC
ACI WORLDWIDE INC
ACME PACKET INC
ACXIOM DIGITAL INC
ADEPT TECHNOLOGY INC
ADTRAN INC
ADVISORY BOARD COMPANY (THE)
AFFILIATED MANAGERS GROUP

AKAMAI TECHNOLOGIES INC
AKORN INC
AKQA INC
ALBANY MOLECULAR RESEARCH INC
ALEXANDER & BALDWIN INC
ALEXION PHARMACEUTICALS INC
ALIEN TECHNOLOGY CORPORATION
ALIGN TECHNOLOGY INC
ALLEGIANT TRAVEL COMPANY
ALLIED HEALTHCARE INTERNATIONAL INC
ALLSCRIPTS HEALTHCARE SOLUTIONS INC
AMCOL INTERNATIONAL CORP
AMCON DISTRIBUTING CO
AMERESCO INC
AMERICAN FIDELITY ASSURANCE COMPANY
AMERICAN MEDICAL SYSTEMS HOLDINGS INC
AMERICAN SCIENCE & ENGINEERING INC
AMERICAN TIRE DISTRIBUTORS
AMERICAN TOWER CORP
AMERICA'S CAR-MART INC
AMTECH SYSTEMS INC
AMTRUST FINANCIAL SERVICES INC
ANALOGIC CORP
ANAREN INC
ANIKA THERAPEUTICS INC
APP PHARMACEUTICALS INC
ARCSIGHT INC
ARDEN GROUP INC
ARGON ST INC
ARIBA INC
ARIZONA CHEMICAL COMPANY
AROTECH CORPORATION
ARRAY BIOPHARMA INC
ARRIS GROUP INC
ARTHROCARE CORP
ARUBA NETWORKS INC
ATHENAHEALTH INC
ATLANTIC CITY ELECTRIC COMPANY
ATLANTIC TELE-NETWORK INC
ATRION CORPORATION
AUDIBLE INC
AVALONBAY COMMUNITIES INC
AVIALL INC

AVISTA CORPORATION
B&G FOODS INC
BANKRATE INC
BIO REFERENCE LABORATORIES INC
BIOMARIN PHARMACEUTICAL INC
BIOSCRIP INC
BIOSITE INC
BLACK HILLS CORP
BLACKBOARD INC
BLUE COAT SYSTEMS INC
BLUE NILE INC
BOSTON BEER COMPANY INC (THE)
BOTTOMLINE TECHNOLOGIES INC
BRIGHTSTAR CORPORATION
CAGLE'S INC
CALAVO GROWERS INC
CALIBER HOLDINGS CORP
CALIPER LIFE SCIENCES INC
CAL-MAINE FOODS INC
CAMBREX CORP
CANTEL MEDICAL CORP
CAPITOL FEDERAL FINANCIAL INC
CARACO PHARMACEUTICAL LABORATORIES LTD
CARBO CERAMICS INC
CARDIONET INC
CARDTRONICS INC
CATALYST HEALTH SOLUTIONS INC
CENTRAL VERMONT PUBLIC SERVICE CORP
CEPHEID
CHANNELL COMMERCIAL CORP
CHATTEM INC
CHINDEX INTERNATIONAL INC
CHOICESTREAM INC
CHOLESTECH CORP
CIRRUS LOGIC INC
CKX INC
CLEARONE COMMUNICATIONS INC
COGENT COMMUNICATIONS
COHERENT INC
COMDATA CORP
COMTECH TELECOMMUNICATIONS CORP
CONCUR TECHNOLOGIES INC
CONTINUCARE CORP
CORPORATE EXECUTIVE BOARD COMPANY (THE)
COSTAR GROUP INC
COUPONS INC

CRAY INC
CRITICAL CARE SYSTEMS
CROWN CASTLE INTERNATIONAL CORP
CRUM & FORSTER HOLDINGS INC
CRYOLIFE INC
CUBIST PHARMACEUTICALS INC
CULP INC
CYBERONICS INC
CYBERSOURCE CORP
DANNON COMPANY INC (THE)
DAWSON GEOPHYSICAL COMPANY
DEI HOLDINGS INC
DELPHI FINANCIAL GROUP INC
DIAMOND FOODS INC
DIGITAL GENERATION INC
DJO GLOBAL INC
DOLBY LABORATORIES INC
DORMAN PRODUCTS INC
DPL INC
DREAMWORKS ANIMATION SKG INC
DRUGSTORE.COM INC
EATON VANCE CORP
EBIX INC
ECHO GLOBAL LOGISTICS INC
ECHOSTAR CORP
ECOLLEGE.COM
EDELMAN FINANCIAL GROUP (THE)
EDGAR ONLINE INC
EDUCATIONAL DEVELOPMENT CORP
EHEALTH INC
EMBARCADERO TECHNOLOGIES INC
EMCORE CORP
EMS TECHNOLOGIES INC
EMULEX CORP
ENCORE CAPITAL GROUP INC
ENERNOC INC
ENVIRONMENTAL TECTONICS CORP
EPAM SYSTEMS
EQT CORPORATION
EQUINIX INC
ERESEARCH TECHNOLOGY INC
ESSEX PROPERTY TRUST INC
EVEREST RE GROUP LTD
EXACTECH INC
F5 NETWORKS INC
FAIR ISAAC CORPORATION

FEDEX SUPPLY CHAIN SERVICES INC
FIRST FINANCIAL BANCORP (OH)
FNB CORP
FORRESTER RESEARCH INC
FORTINET INC
FRESHDIRECT LLC
FROZEN FOOD EXPRESS INDUSTRIES INC
FUEL SYSTEMS SOLUTIONS INC
FUEL TECH INC
GAIAM INC
GALLUP ORGANIZATION (THE)
GENCO SHIPPING & TRADING LIMITED
GENENCOR INTERNATIONAL INC
GENERAL COMMUNICATION INC (GCI)
GENESIS ENERGY LP
GENOMIC HEALTH INC
GEN-PROBE INC
G-III APPAREL GROUP
GLEACHER & COMPANY INC
GLOBAL PARTNERS LP
GLOBECOMM SYSTEMS INC
GLU MOBILE INC
GOLDEN ENTERPRISES INC
GOLFSMITH INTERNATIONAL HOLDINGS INC
GREAT AMERICAN FINANCIAL RESOURCES INC
GREAT LAKES CHEESE COMPANY INC
GREEN MOUNTAIN POWER CORPORATION
GTC BIOTHERAPEUTICS INC
GULFMARK OFFSHORE INC
HAEMONETICS CORPORATION
HAHN AUTOMOTIVE WAREHOUSE INC
HANOVER FOODS CORPORATION
HARRIS INTERACTIVE INC
HCC INSURANCE HOLDINGS INC
HEALTH GRADES INC
HEALTH INSURANCE PLAN OF GREATER NEW YORK
HEALTHSTREAM INC
HEALTHTRONICS INC
HEARUSA INC
HELIOVOLT CORP
HELIX ENERGY SOLUTIONS GROUP INC
HESKA CORP
HICKORY TECH CORPORATION
HI-TECH PHARMACAL CO INC
HOLLYFRONTIER CORPORATION
HORACE MANN EDUCATORS CORPORATION
HOSPITALITY PROPERTIES TRUST
HUB GROUP INC
HUDSON CITY BANCORP INC
IBASIS INC
ICONIX BRAND GROUP INC
ICU MEDICAL INC
IDACORP INC
I-FLOW CORPORATION
ILLUMINA INC
IMG WORLDWIDE INC
IMMUCOR INC
IMPAX LABORATORIES INC
INDEPENDENCE HOLDING CO
INFOSPACE INC
INNOPHOS HOLDINGS INC
INNOSPEC INC
INTEGRAL SYSTEMS INC
INTEGRAMED AMERICA INC
INTERACTIVE DATA CORPORATION
INTERACTIVE INTELLIGENCE GROUP INC
INTERCONTINENTALEXCHANGE INC (ICE)
INTERMEC INC
INTERNAP NETWORK SERVICES CORP
INTERNATIONAL CREATIVE MANAGEMENT INC (ICM)
INTERNATIONAL DAIRY QUEEN INC
INTUITIVE SURGICAL INC
INVESTMENT TECHNOLOGY GROUP INC (ITG)
IRIDEX CORP
IRIS INTERNATIONAL INC
IROBOT CORP
ISILON SYSTEMS INC
IVILLAGE INC
J2 GLOBAL COMMUNICATIONS INC
JAZZ PHARMACEUTICALS INC
JOE'S JEANS INC
JOHN B SANFILIPPO & SON INC
KAMPGROUNDS OF AMERICA INC
KENDALL-JACKSON WINE ESTATES LTD
KENNETH COLE PRODUCTIONS INC
KEY TRONIC CORP
KEYNOTE SYSTEMS INC
KIMLEY-HORN AND ASSOCIATES INC
KIRBY CORP
KKR & CO LP (KOHLBERG KRAVIS ROBERTS & CO)
KNIGHT CAPITAL GROUP INC
KNOLOGY INC
KORN/FERRY INTERNATIONAL
KRONOS WORLDWIDE INC
LACLEDE GROUP INC (THE)
LAKELAND INDUSTRIES INC
LB FOSTER COMPANY
LCC INTERNATIONAL INC
LESLIE'S POOLMART INC
LIFECELL CORPORATION
LIFECORE BIOMEDICAL INC
LIVEPERSON INC
LOGISTICARE INC
LOJACK CORPORTATION
LUCASFILM LTD
LUCOR INC
LUMINEX CORPORATION
MAGELLAN MIDSTREAM PARTNERS LP
MALT-O-MEAL COMPANY
MANAGEMENT NETWORK GROUP INC (THE)
MANHATTAN ASSOCIATES INC
MAPFRE USA CORP
MARTEK BIOSCIENCES CORP
MARVEL ENTERTAINMENT LLC
MEDICINES CO (THE)
MEDICIS PHARMACEUTICAL CORP
MEDIFAST INC
MEDTOX SCIENTIFIC INC
MENTOR CORP
MERIDIAN BIOSCIENCE INC
MERIT MEDICAL SYSTEMS INC
MESIROW FINANCIAL HOLDINGS INC
METROPOLITAN HEALTH NETWORKS INC
MICHELINAS INC
MICROTEK MEDICAL HOLDINGS INC
MID-AMERICA APARTMENT COMMUNITIES INC
MIDAS INC
MILLENNIUM PHARMACEUTICALS INC
MINDSPEED TECHNOLOGIES INC
MONSTER BEVERAGE CORP
MOTORCAR PARTS OF AMERICA

INC
MTR GAMING GROUP INC
MYRIAD GENETICS INC
NANOMETRICS INC
NATIONAL BEVERAGE CORP
NATIONAL DENTEX CORP
NATIONAL WINE & SPIRITS INC
NATUS MEDICAL INC
NEKTAR THERAPEUTICS
NEOGEN CORPORATION
NETFLIX INC
NETGEAR INC
NETSCOUT SYSTEMS INC
NETSUITE INC
NETWORK ENGINES INC
NEW JERSEY RESOURCES CORPORATION
NEW YORK MERCANTILE EXCHANGE INC
NIC INC
NORTHWESTERN CORPORATION
NOTIFY TECHNOLOGY CORP
NOVAMED INC
NOVEN PHARMACEUTICALS INC
NTELOS HOLDING CORP
NUGGET MARKET
NUSTAR ENERGY LP
NUTRASWEET COMPANY (THE)
NUVASIVE INC
ODYSSEY RE HOLDINGS CORP
OMNOVA SOLUTIONS INC
ONLINE RESOURCES CORP
ONSTREAM MEDIA CORPORATION
OPENTV CORP
ORION MARINE GROUP INC
PACIFIC BIOMARKERS INC
PAR PHARMACEUTICAL COMPANIES INC
PATAGONIA INC
PC CONNECTION INC
PEAPOD LLC
PEGASYSTEMS INC
PERFICIENT INC
PERRY ELLIS INTERNATIONAL INC
PETMED EXPRESS INC
PHAZAR CORP
PHILADELPHIA CONSOLIDATED HOLDING CORP
PHOENIX COMPANIES INC (THE)
PIEDMONT NATURAL GAS COMPANY INC
PLATO LEARNING INC
PMA COMPANIES INC
POWERSECURE INTERNATIONAL INC
PREMIERE GLOBAL SERVICES INC
PROASSURANCE CORP
PROTECTIVE LIFE CORP
PURPLE COMMUNICATIONS INC
QUAKER CHEMICAL CORP
QUALCOMM ATHEROS INC
QUALITY SYSTEMS INC
QUANTUM CORP
QUESTCOR PHARMACEUTICALS INC
QUIDEL CORP
RAYTHEON APPLIED SIGNAL TECHNOLOGY INC
REALNETWORKS INC
RECYCLED ENERGY DEVELOPMENT LLC
REDBOX AUTOMATED RETAIL LLC
REGENERON PHARMACEUTICALS INC
REINSURANCE GROUP OF AMERICA INC
RENTRAK CORP
RICELAND FOODS INC
RIGHTNOW TECHNOLOGIES INC
RIVERBED TECHNOLOGY INC
ROCKY BRANDS INC
ROGERS CORPORATION
ROSETTA STONE INC
ROVI CORPORATION
RPC INC
RSA SECURITY INC
S1 CORPORATION
SACRAMENTO MUNICIPAL UTILITY DISTRICT
SALIX PHARMACEUTICALS
SBA COMMUNICATIONS CORP
SCANSOURCE INC
SCHICK TECHNOLOGIES INC
SCHIFF NUTRITION INTERNATIONAL INC
SCICLONE PHARMACEUTICALS INC
SCIOS INC
SCOULAR COMPANY (THE)
SEACHANGE INTERNATIONAL INC
SEATTLE GENETICS
SELECTICA INC
SERACARE LIFE SCIENCES INC
SHARED TECHNOLOGIES
SHENANDOAH TELECOMMUNICATIONS CO
SHUTTERFLY INC
SIGMA DESIGNS INC
SILICON LABORATORIES INC
SL GREEN REALTY CORP
SMART MODULAR TECHNOLOGIES INC
SOLARRESERVE
SOLFOCUS INC
SOTHEBYS
SOUTHERN UNION COMPANY
SOUTHWEST GAS CORP
SPARTAN MOTORS INC
SPECTRANETICS CORP
SPECTRUM PHARMACEUTICALS INC
SPIRE CORPORATION
SPORT SUPPLY GROUP INC
SPORTSMAN'S GUIDE INC (THE)
SPROUTS FARMERS MARKET LLC
SS&C TECHNOLOGIES HOLDINGS INC
STAAR SURGICAL CO
STATE AUTO FINANCIAL CORP
STEPAN COMPANY
STERLING AUTOBODY CENTERS
STERLING CONSTRUCTION COMPANY
STEVEN MADDEN LTD
STIEFEL LABORATORIES INC
SUN COMMUNITIES INC
SUNOCO LOGISTICS PARTNERS LP
SUPER MICRO COMPUTER INC
SUPERIOR UNIFORM GROUP INC
SUPREME INDUSTRIES INC
SVB FINANCIAL GROUP
SYNAPTICS INC
SYNIVERSE TECHNOLOGIES
SYNOVIS LIFE TECHNOLOGIES INC
TAKE-TWO INTERACTIVE SOFTWARE INC
TAMPA ELECTRIC COMPANY
TECHNE CORP
TEKELEC
TELIRIS
TERREMARK WORLDWIDE INC
TESCO CORPORATION
TESSCO TECHNOLOGIES INC
THERAGENICS CORP
THORATEC CORPORATION

TOOTSIE ROLL INDUSTRIES INC
TOPPS COMPANY INC (THE)
TRANSATLANTIC HOLDINGS INC
TRANSCEND SERVICES INC
TRAVELZOO INC
TREX COMPANY INC
TRIZETTO GROUP INC (THE)
TRUE RELIGION APPAREL INC
UDR INC
UIL HOLDINGS CORPORATION
ULTIMATE SOFTWARE GROUP INC
ULTRALIFE CORPORATION
UNISOURCE ENERGY CORPORATION
UNITED ONLINE INC
UNITED THERAPEUTICS CORP
UNIVERSAL HOSPITAL SERVICES INC
UQM TECHNOLOGIES INC
US PHYSICAL THERAPY INC
USANA HEALTH SCIENCES INC
UTAH MEDICAL PRODUCTS INC
VARIAN SEMICONDUCTOR EQUIPMENT ASSOCIATES INC
VASCO DATA SECURITY INTERNATIONAL INC
VENTANA MEDICAL SYSTEMS INC
VIASAT INC
VIBRANT MEDIA INC
VIROPHARMA INC
VOLCOM INC
WADDELL & REED FINANCIAL INC
WEBEX COMMUNICATIONS INC
WEBMD HEALTH CORP
WEBMEDIA BRANDS INC
WEBSENSE INC
WESTAR ENERGY
WGL HOLDINGS INC
WHITEWAVE FOODS COMPANY
WIND RIVER SYSTEMS INC
WMS INDUSTRIES INC
WRIGHT MEDICAL GROUP INC
XETA TECHNOLOGIES INC
XO GROUP INC
XOMA LTD
YOUNG'S MARKET COMPANY LLC
ZEP INC
ZIEBART INTERNATIONAL CORP
ZOLL MEDICAL CORP
ZYNGA INC

Retail Sales
AMERICAN TIRE DISTRIBUTORS
AMERICA'S CAR-MART INC
ARDEN GROUP INC
AUDIBLE INC
BLUE NILE INC
DRUGSTORE.COM INC
FRESHDIRECT LLC
GAIAM INC
GOLFSMITH INTERNATIONAL HOLDINGS INC
HAHN AUTOMOTIVE WAREHOUSE INC
HEARUSA INC
LESLIE'S POOLMART INC
MEDIFAST INC
NUGGET MARKET
PC CONNECTION INC
PEAPOD LLC
PETMED EXPRESS INC
SPORTSMAN'S GUIDE INC (THE)
SPROUTS FARMERS MARKET LLC
TRUE RELIGION APPAREL INC
YOUNG'S MARKET COMPANY LLC

Sales Trainees
24/7 REAL MEDIA INC
ABAXIS INC
ACI WORLDWIDE INC
ACME PACKET INC
ACXIOM DIGITAL INC
ADEPT TECHNOLOGY INC
ADTRAN INC
ADVISORY BOARD COMPANY (THE)
AKAMAI TECHNOLOGIES INC
AKORN INC
AKQA INC
ALEXANDER & BALDWIN INC
ALEXION PHARMACEUTICALS INC
ALIEN TECHNOLOGY CORPORATION
ALIGN TECHNOLOGY INC
ALLEGIANT TRAVEL COMPANY
ALLSCRIPTS HEALTHCARE SOLUTIONS INC
AMCOL INTERNATIONAL CORP
AMCON DISTRIBUTING CO
AMERESCO INC
AMERICAN FIDELITY ASSURANCE COMPANY
AMERICAN MEDICAL SYSTEMS HOLDINGS INC
AMERICAN SCIENCE & ENGINEERING INC
AMERICAN TIRE DISTRIBUTORS
AMERICAN TOWER CORP
AMERICA'S CAR-MART INC
AMTECH SYSTEMS INC
AMTRUST FINANCIAL SERVICES INC
ANALOGIC CORP
ANAREN INC
ANIKA THERAPEUTICS INC
APP PHARMACEUTICALS INC
ARCSIGHT INC
ARDEN GROUP INC
ARGON ST INC
ARIBA INC
ARIZONA CHEMICAL COMPANY
AROTECH CORPORATION
ARRAY BIOPHARMA INC
ARRIS GROUP INC
ARTHROCARE CORP
ARUBA NETWORKS INC
ATHENAHEALTH INC
ATRION CORPORATION
AUDIBLE INC
AVIALL INC
B&G FOODS INC
BANKRATE INC
BIO REFERENCE LABORATORIES INC
BIOMARIN PHARMACEUTICAL INC
BIOSCRIP INC
BIOSITE INC
BLACK HILLS CORP
BLACKBOARD INC
BLUE COAT SYSTEMS INC
BLUE NILE INC
BOSTON BEER COMPANY INC (THE)
BOTTOMLINE TECHNOLOGIES INC
BRIGHTSTAR CORPORATION
CAGLE'S INC
CALAVO GROWERS INC
CALIPER LIFE SCIENCES INC
CAL-MAINE FOODS INC
CAMBREX CORP
CANTEL MEDICAL CORP
CARACO PHARMACEUTICAL LABORATORIES LTD
CARBO CERAMICS INC
CARDIONET INC

CARDTRONICS INC
CENTRAL VERMONT PUBLIC SERVICE CORP
CEPHEID
CHANNELL COMMERCIAL CORP
CHATTEM INC
CHINDEX INTERNATIONAL INC
CHOICESTREAM INC
CHOLESTECH CORP
CKX INC
CLEARONE COMMUNICATIONS INC
COGENT COMMUNICATIONS
COHERENT INC
COMDATA CORP
COMTECH TELECOMMUNICATIONS CORP
CONCUR TECHNOLOGIES INC
CONSTANT CONTACT INC
CONTINUCARE CORP
CORPORATE EXECUTIVE BOARD COMPANY (THE)
COSTAR GROUP INC
COUPONS INC
CRITICAL CARE SYSTEMS
CROWN CASTLE INTERNATIONAL CORP
CRUM & FORSTER HOLDINGS INC
CRYOLIFE INC
CUBIST PHARMACEUTICALS INC
CULP INC
CUMULUS MEDIA INC
CYBERONICS INC
CYBERSOURCE CORP
DANNON COMPANY INC (THE)
DEI HOLDINGS INC
DELPHI FINANCIAL GROUP INC
DIAMOND FOODS INC
DIGITAL GENERATION INC
DJO GLOBAL INC
DPL INC
DREAMWORKS ANIMATION SKG INC
DRUGSTORE.COM INC
ECOLLEGE.COM
EMBARCADERO TECHNOLOGIES INC
EMCORE CORP
EMS TECHNOLOGIES INC
EMULEX CORP
ENERNOC INC
EPAM SYSTEMS

EQT CORPORATION
EQUINIX INC
ERESEARCH TECHNOLOGY INC
EXACTECH INC
F5 NETWORKS INC
FAIR ISAAC CORPORATION
FEDEX SUPPLY CHAIN SERVICES INC
FORTINET INC
FRESHDIRECT LLC
FUEL SYSTEMS SOLUTIONS INC
GAIAM INC
GENENCOR INTERNATIONAL INC
GENERAL COMMUNICATION INC (GCI)
GENESIS ENERGY LP
GENOMIC HEALTH INC
GEN-PROBE INC
G-III APPAREL GROUP
GLOBAL PARTNERS LP
GLOBECOMM SYSTEMS INC
GLU MOBILE INC
GOLDEN ENTERPRISES INC
GOLFSMITH INTERNATIONAL HOLDINGS INC
GREAT AMERICAN FINANCIAL RESOURCES INC
GREAT LAKES CHEESE COMPANY INC
GREEN MOUNTAIN POWER CORPORATION
GTC BIOTHERAPEUTICS INC
GULFMARK OFFSHORE INC
HAEMONETICS CORPORATION
HAHN AUTOMOTIVE WAREHOUSE INC
HANOVER FOODS CORPORATION
HARRIS INTERACTIVE INC
HCC INSURANCE HOLDINGS INC
HEALTH GRADES INC
HEALTH INSURANCE PLAN OF GREATER NEW YORK
HEALTHSTREAM INC
HEALTHTRONICS INC
HEARUSA INC
HELIOVOLT CORP
HESKA CORP
HICKORY TECH CORPORATION
HI-TECH PHARMACAL CO INC
HORACE MANN EDUCATORS CORPORATION
HUB GROUP INC

IBASIS INC
ICONIX BRAND GROUP INC
ICU MEDICAL INC
IDACORP INC
I-FLOW CORPORATION
ILLUMINA INC
IMG WORLDWIDE INC
IMMUCOR INC
INDEPENDENCE HOLDING CO
INFOSPACE INC
INTEGRAL SYSTEMS INC
INTEGRAMED AMERICA INC
INTERACTIVE DATA CORPORATION
INTERACTIVE INTELLIGENCE GROUP INC
INTERMEC INC
INTERNAP NETWORK SERVICES CORP
INTERNATIONAL CREATIVE MANAGEMENT INC (ICM)
INTUITIVE SURGICAL INC
INVESTMENT TECHNOLOGY GROUP INC (ITG)
IRIDEX CORP
IRIS INTERNATIONAL INC
IVILLAGE INC
J2 GLOBAL COMMUNICATIONS INC
JAZZ PHARMACEUTICALS INC
JOE'S JEANS INC
JOHN B SANFILIPPO & SON INC
KENDALL-JACKSON WINE ESTATES LTD
KENNETH COLE PRODUCTIONS INC
KEY TRONIC CORP
KIRBY CORP
KORN/FERRY INTERNATIONAL
LAKELAND INDUSTRIES INC
LCC INTERNATIONAL INC
LESLIE'S POOLMART INC
LIFECELL CORPORATION
LIFECORE BIOMEDICAL INC
LIVEPERSON INC
LOGISTICARE INC
LOJACK CORPORTATION
LUCASFILM LTD
LUMINEX CORPORATION
MAGELLAN MIDSTREAM PARTNERS LP
MALT-O-MEAL COMPANY
MANAGEMENT NETWORK GROUP INC (THE)
MANHATTAN ASSOCIATES INC

MAPFRE USA CORP
MARTEK BIOSCIENCES CORP
MEDICINES CO (THE)
MEDICIS PHARMACEUTICAL CORP
MEDIFAST INC
MEDTOX SCIENTIFIC INC
MENTOR CORP
MERIDIAN BIOSCIENCE INC
MERIT MEDICAL SYSTEMS INC
MICHELINAS INC
MICROTEK MEDICAL HOLDINGS INC
MILLENNIUM PHARMACEUTICALS INC
MONSTER BEVERAGE CORP
MOTORCAR PARTS OF AMERICA INC
MYRIAD GENETICS INC
NANOMETRICS INC
NATIONAL BEVERAGE CORP
NATIONAL DENTEX CORP
NATIONAL WINE & SPIRITS INC
NATUS MEDICAL INC
NEKTAR THERAPEUTICS
NEOGEN CORPORATION
NETGEAR INC
NETSCOUT SYSTEMS INC
NIC INC
NOTIFY TECHNOLOGY CORP
NOVAMED INC
NOVEN PHARMACEUTICALS INC
NTELOS HOLDING CORP
NUGGET MARKET
NUSTAR ENERGY LP
NUTRASWEET COMPANY (THE)
ODYSSEY RE HOLDINGS CORP
ONLINE RESOURCES CORP
OPENTV CORP
PAR PHARMACEUTICAL COMPANIES INC
PC CONNECTION INC
PEAPOD LLC
PERRY ELLIS INTERNATIONAL INC
PETMED EXPRESS INC
PHILADELPHIA CONSOLIDATED HOLDING CORP
PHOENIX COMPANIES INC (THE)
PLATO LEARNING INC
PMA COMPANIES INC
PREMIERE GLOBAL SERVICES INC
PROASSURANCE CORP
PROTECTIVE LIFE CORP
QUALCOMM ATHEROS INC
QUALITY SYSTEMS INC
QUIDEL CORP
RAYTHEON APPLIED SIGNAL TECHNOLOGY INC
REALNETWORKS INC
RECYCLED ENERGY DEVELOPMENT LLC
REGENERON PHARMACEUTICALS INC
REINSURANCE GROUP OF AMERICA INC
RICELAND FOODS INC
RIGHTNOW TECHNOLOGIES INC
ROCKY BRANDS INC
ROVI CORPORATION
RSA SECURITY INC
S1 CORPORATION
SACRAMENTO MUNICIPAL UTILITY DISTRICT
SALIX PHARMACEUTICALS
SCANSOURCE INC
SCHICK TECHNOLOGIES INC
SCHIFF NUTRITION INTERNATIONAL INC
SCICLONE PHARMACEUTICALS INC
SCIOS INC
SEACHANGE INTERNATIONAL INC
SEATTLE GENETICS
SHENANDOAH TELECOMMUNICATIONS CO
SHUTTERFLY INC
SOLARRESERVE
SOLFOCUS INC
SPARTAN MOTORS INC
SPECTRANETICS CORP
SPIRE CORPORATION
SPORT SUPPLY GROUP INC
SPORTSMAN'S GUIDE INC (THE)
SPROUTS FARMERS MARKET LLC
SS&C TECHNOLOGIES HOLDINGS INC
STAAR SURGICAL CO
STATE AUTO FINANCIAL CORP
STEPAN COMPANY
STERLING CONSTRUCTION COMPANY
STEVEN MADDEN LTD
STIEFEL LABORATORIES INC
SUPER MICRO COMPUTER INC
SUPERIOR UNIFORM GROUP INC
SUPREME INDUSTRIES INC
SYNAPTICS INC
SYNIVERSE TECHNOLOGIES
SYNOVIS LIFE TECHNOLOGIES INC
TAKE-TWO INTERACTIVE SOFTWARE INC
TAMPA ELECTRIC COMPANY
TECHNE CORP
TEKELEC
TELIRIS
TERREMARK WORLDWIDE INC
TESCO CORPORATION
THERAGENICS CORP
THORATEC CORPORATION
TII NETWORK TECHNOLOGIES INC
TOOTSIE ROLL INDUSTRIES INC
TOPPS COMPANY INC (THE)
TRANSATLANTIC HOLDINGS INC
TRANSCEND SERVICES INC
TREX COMPANY INC
TRIZETTO GROUP INC (THE)
TRUE RELIGION APPAREL INC
UIL HOLDINGS CORPORATION
ULTIMATE SOFTWARE GROUP INC
UNITED ONLINE INC
UNITED THERAPEUTICS CORP
UNIVERSAL HOSPITAL SERVICES INC
US PHYSICAL THERAPY INC
USANA HEALTH SCIENCES INC
UTAH MEDICAL PRODUCTS INC
VASCO DATA SECURITY INTERNATIONAL INC
VENTANA MEDICAL SYSTEMS INC
VIASAT INC
VIBRANT MEDIA INC
VIROPHARMA INC
VOLCOM INC
WABASH NATIONAL CORP
WEBEX COMMUNICATIONS INC
WEBMD HEALTH CORP
WEBMEDIA BRANDS INC
WEBSENSE INC
WESTAR ENERGY
WHITEWAVE FOODS COMPANY
WIND RIVER SYSTEMS INC
WMS INDUSTRIES INC
WRIGHT MEDICAL GROUP INC
XETA TECHNOLOGIES INC
XO GROUP INC
XOMA LTD
YOUNG'S MARKET COMPANY LLC

ZEP INC
ZOLL MEDICAL CORP

Technical/Scientific

Engineers, Electrical
ABAXIS INC
ACI WORLDWIDE INC
ACME PACKET INC
ADEPT TECHNOLOGY INC
ADTRAN INC
AKAMAI TECHNOLOGIES INC
ALIEN TECHNOLOGY CORPORATION
ALLSCRIPTS HEALTHCARE SOLUTIONS INC
AMERESCO INC
AMERICAN SCIENCE & ENGINEERING INC
AMERICAN TOWER CORP
AMTECH SYSTEMS INC
ANALOGIC CORP
ANAREN INC
ARCSIGHT INC
ARGON ST INC
ARIBA INC
ARIZONA CHEMICAL COMPANY
AROTECH CORPORATION
ARRIS GROUP INC
ARTHROCARE CORP
ARUBA NETWORKS INC
ATLANTIC CITY ELECTRIC COMPANY
ATLANTIC TELE-NETWORK INC
ATRION CORPORATION
AVISTA CORPORATION
BIOSITE INC
BLACK HILLS CORP
BLUE COAT SYSTEMS INC
BOTTOMLINE TECHNOLOGIES INC
CALIPER LIFE SCIENCES INC
CARBO CERAMICS INC
CARDIONET INC
CENTRAL VERMONT PUBLIC SERVICE CORP
CEPHEID
CHANNELL COMMERCIAL CORP
CHOLESTECH CORP
CIRRUS LOGIC INC
CLEARONE COMMUNICATIONS INC
COGENT COMMUNICATIONS
COHERENT INC
COMTECH TELECOMMUNICATIONS CORP
COMVERGE INC
CONCUR TECHNOLOGIES INC
CRAY INC
CROWN CASTLE INTERNATIONAL CORP
CYBERONICS INC
CYBERSOURCE CORP
DAWSON GEOPHYSICAL COMPANY
DEI HOLDINGS INC
DJO GLOBAL INC
DOLBY LABORATORIES INC
DORMAN PRODUCTS INC
DPL INC
EBIX INC
ECHOSTAR CORP
EMBARCADERO TECHNOLOGIES INC
EMCORE CORP
EMS TECHNOLOGIES INC
EMULEX CORP
ENERNOC INC
ENVIRONMENTAL TECTONICS CORP
EQT CORPORATION
EQUINIX INC
ERESEARCH TECHNOLOGY INC
F5 NETWORKS INC
FORTINET INC
FUEL SYSTEMS SOLUTIONS INC
GENERAL ATOMICS
GENERAL COMMUNICATION INC (GCI)
GEN-PROBE INC
GLOBECOMM SYSTEMS INC
GLU MOBILE INC
GREEN MOUNTAIN POWER CORPORATION
HAEMONETICS CORPORATION
HELIOVOLT CORP
HICKORY TECH CORPORATION
HOLLYFRONTIER CORPORATION
IBASIS INC
IDACORP INC
I-FLOW CORPORATION
ILLUMINA INC
INTEGRAL SYSTEMS INC
INTERACTIVE INTELLIGENCE GROUP INC
INTERMEC INC
INTERNAP NETWORK SERVICES CORP
INTUITIVE SURGICAL INC
INVESTMENT TECHNOLOGY GROUP INC (ITG)
IRIDEX CORP
IRIS INTERNATIONAL INC
IROBOT CORP
ISILON SYSTEMS INC
J2 GLOBAL COMMUNICATIONS INC
KEY TRONIC CORP
KEYNOTE SYSTEMS INC
KIMLEY-HORN AND ASSOCIATES INC
KNOLOGY INC
LACLEDE GROUP INC (THE)
LCC INTERNATIONAL INC
LIVEPERSON INC
LOJACK CORPORTATION
LUMINEX CORPORATION
MAGELLAN MIDSTREAM PARTNERS LP
MANHATTAN ASSOCIATES INC
MINDSPEED TECHNOLOGIES INC
MOTORCAR PARTS OF AMERICA INC
NANOMETRICS INC
NATUS MEDICAL INC
NETGEAR INC
NETSCOUT SYSTEMS INC
NETSUITE INC
NETWORK ENGINES INC
NEW JERSEY RESOURCES CORPORATION
NIC INC
NORTHWESTERN CORPORATION
NOTIFY TECHNOLOGY CORP
NTELOS HOLDING CORP
NUVASIVE INC
ONLINE RESOURCES CORP
OPENTV CORP
PACIFIC BIOMARKERS INC
PERFICIENT INC
PHAZAR CORP
PIEDMONT NATURAL GAS COMPANY INC
PLATO LEARNING INC
POWERSECURE INTERNATIONAL INC
PREMIERE GLOBAL SERVICES INC
PURPLE COMMUNICATIONS INC
QUALCOMM ATHEROS INC

QUALITY SYSTEMS INC
QUANTUM CORP
RAYTHEON APPLIED SIGNAL TECHNOLOGY INC
REALNETWORKS INC
RECYCLED ENERGY DEVELOPMENT LLC
RIGHTNOW TECHNOLOGIES INC
RIVERBED TECHNOLOGY INC
ROVI CORPORATION
RPC INC
RSA SECURITY INC
S1 CORPORATION
SACRAMENTO MUNICIPAL UTILITY DISTRICT
SBA COMMUNICATIONS CORP
SCANSOURCE INC
SCHICK TECHNOLOGIES INC
SEACHANGE INTERNATIONAL INC
SHENANDOAH TELECOMMUNICATIONS CO
SIGMA DESIGNS INC
SILICON LABORATORIES INC
SMART MODULAR TECHNOLOGIES INC
SOLARRESERVE
SOLFOCUS INC
SOUTHERN UNION COMPANY
SOUTHWEST GAS CORP
SPECTRANETICS CORP
SPIRE CORPORATION
SRS LABS INC
SS&C TECHNOLOGIES HOLDINGS INC
STEPAN COMPANY
STERLING CONSTRUCTION COMPANY
SUPER MICRO COMPUTER INC
SYNAPTICS INC
SYNIVERSE TECHNOLOGIES
TAKE-TWO INTERACTIVE SOFTWARE INC
TAMPA ELECTRIC COMPANY
TEKELEC
TELIRIS
TESCO CORPORATION
TESSCO TECHNOLOGIES INC
THORATEC CORPORATION
TII NETWORK TECHNOLOGIES INC
TRIZETTO GROUP INC (THE)
UIL HOLDINGS CORPORATION
ULTIMATE SOFTWARE GROUP INC
ULTRALIFE CORPORATION
UNISOURCE ENERGY CORPORATION
UNITED ONLINE INC
UQM TECHNOLOGIES INC
VARIAN SEMICONDUCTOR EQUIPMENT ASSOCIATES INC
VASCO DATA SECURITY INTERNATIONAL INC
VERENIUM CORPORATION
VIASAT INC
VOX INTERNATIONAL CORPORATION
WEBEX COMMUNICATIONS INC
WEBSENSE INC
WESTAR ENERGY
WGL HOLDINGS INC
WIND RIVER SYSTEMS INC
WMS INDUSTRIES INC
XETA TECHNOLOGIES INC
ZAP JONWAY
ZYNGA INC

Engineers, Other
ABAXIS INC
ACME PACKET INC
ALIEN TECHNOLOGY CORPORATION
ALIGN TECHNOLOGY INC
AMCOL INTERNATIONAL CORP
AMERICAN MEDICAL SYSTEMS HOLDINGS INC
AMERICAN SCIENCE & ENGINEERING INC
AMERICAN TOWER CORP
AMERICAN VANGUARD CORP
AMTECH SYSTEMS INC
ANALOGIC CORP
ANAREN INC
ANIKA THERAPEUTICS INC
ARIZONA CHEMICAL COMPANY
AROTECH CORPORATION
ARRAY BIOPHARMA INC
ARRIS GROUP INC
ARTHROCARE CORP
ATLANTIC CITY ELECTRIC COMPANY
ATRION CORPORATION
AVIALL INC
AVISTA CORPORATION
B&G FOODS INC
BERRY PETROLEUM CO
BIOSITE INC
BLACK HILLS CORP
BOSTON BEER COMPANY INC (THE)
CABOT OIL & GAS CORP
CALIPER LIFE SCIENCES INC
CANTEL MEDICAL CORP
CARBO CERAMICS INC
CARRIZO OIL & GAS INC
CENTRAL VERMONT PUBLIC SERVICE CORP
CEPHEID
CHANNELL COMMERCIAL CORP
CHOLESTECH CORP
CIRRUS LOGIC INC
CLAYTON WILLIAMS ENERGY INC
COHERENT INC
COMTECH TELECOMMUNICATIONS CORP
CONTINENTAL RESOURCES INC
CROWN CASTLE INTERNATIONAL CORP
CYBERONICS INC
DANNON COMPANY INC (THE)
DAWSON GEOPHYSICAL COMPANY
DEI HOLDINGS INC
DENBURY RESOURCES INC
DJO GLOBAL INC
DOLBY LABORATORIES INC
DORMAN PRODUCTS INC
DPL INC
EMCORE CORP
EMS TECHNOLOGIES INC
ENERGY TRANSFER PARTNERS LP
ENVIRONMENTAL TECTONICS CORP
EOG RESOURCES INC
EQT CORPORATION
EXACTECH INC
FUEL SYSTEMS SOLUTIONS INC
GENENCOR INTERNATIONAL INC
GENERAL ATOMICS
GEN-PROBE INC
GLOBECOMM SYSTEMS INC
GREAT LAKES CHEESE COMPANY INC
GREEN MOUNTAIN POWER CORPORATION
HAEMONETICS CORPORATION
HANOVER FOODS CORPORATION
HELIOVOLT CORP
HELIX ENERGY SOLUTIONS GROUP INC

HOLLYFRONTIER CORPORATION
ICU MEDICAL INC
IDACORP INC
I-FLOW CORPORATION
ILLUMINA INC
IMMUCOR INC
INTERMEC INC
INTUITIVE SURGICAL INC
IRIDEX CORP
IRIS INTERNATIONAL INC
IROBOT CORP
ISILON SYSTEMS INC
KENDALL-JACKSON WINE ESTATES LTD
KEY TRONIC CORP
KEYNOTE SYSTEMS INC
KIMLEY-HORN AND ASSOCIATES INC
KRONOS WORLDWIDE INC
LACLEDE GROUP INC (THE)
LAKELAND INDUSTRIES INC
LCC INTERNATIONAL INC
LIFECELL CORPORATION
LIFECORE BIOMEDICAL INC
LOJACK CORPORTATION
LUMINEX CORPORATION
MAGELLAN MIDSTREAM PARTNERS LP
MALT-O-MEAL COMPANY
MENTOR CORP
MERIDIAN BIOSCIENCE INC
MERIT MEDICAL SYSTEMS INC
MICHELINAS INC
MICROTEK MEDICAL HOLDINGS INC
MINDSPEED TECHNOLOGIES INC
MOTORCAR PARTS OF AMERICA INC
NANOMETRICS INC
NATIONAL DENTEX CORP
NATUS MEDICAL INC
NEOGEN CORPORATION
NEW JERSEY RESOURCES CORPORATION
NORTHWESTERN CORPORATION
NUSTAR ENERGY LP
NUVASIVE INC
ORION MARINE GROUP INC
PACIFIC BIOMARKERS INC
PETROLEUM DEVELOPMENT CORPORATION
PHAZAR CORP
PIEDMONT NATURAL GAS COMPANY INC
PIONEER NATURAL RESOURCES COMPANY
PLAINS EXPLORATION AND PRODUCTION COMPANY
POLYPORE INTERNATIONAL INC
POWERSECURE INTERNATIONAL INC
PRIMEENERGY CORPORATION
QUALCOMM ATHEROS INC
QUANTUM CORP
QUICKSILVER RESOURCES INC
QUIDEL CORP
RAYTHEON APPLIED SIGNAL TECHNOLOGY INC
RPC INC
SACRAMENTO MUNICIPAL UTILITY DISTRICT
SANDRIDGE ENERGY INC
SCHICK TECHNOLOGIES INC
SHARED TECHNOLOGIES
SIGMA DESIGNS INC
SOLARRESERVE
SOLFOCUS INC
SOUTHERN UNION COMPANY
SOUTHWEST GAS CORP
SOUTHWESTERN ENERGY CO
SPARTAN MOTORS INC
SPECTRANETICS CORP
SPIRE CORPORATION
STAAR SURGICAL CO
STEPAN COMPANY
STERLING CONSTRUCTION COMPANY
SUPER MICRO COMPUTER INC
SUPREME INDUSTRIES INC
SWIFT ENERGY CO
SYNAPTICS INC
SYNOVIS LIFE TECHNOLOGIES INC
TAMPA ELECTRIC COMPANY
TARGA RESOURCES PARTNERS LP
TECHNE CORP
TEKELEC
TELIRIS
THERAGENICS CORP
THORATEC CORPORATION
TOOTSIE ROLL INDUSTRIES INC
TOPPS COMPANY INC (THE)
TRANSAMMONIA INC
UIL HOLDINGS CORPORATION
ULTRALIFE CORPORATION
UNISOURCE ENERGY CORPORATION
UNIT CORP
UQM TECHNOLOGIES INC
UTAH MEDICAL PRODUCTS INC
VARIAN SEMICONDUCTOR EQUIPMENT ASSOCIATES INC
VENTANA MEDICAL SYSTEMS INC
VERENIUM CORPORATION
VIASAT INC
WABASH NATIONAL CORP
WESTAR ENERGY
WGL HOLDINGS INC
WHITEWAVE FOODS COMPANY
WRIGHT MEDICAL GROUP INC
XETA TECHNOLOGIES INC
XTO ENERGY INC
ZAP JONWAY
ZOLL MEDICAL CORP

Health/Laboratory
ABAXIS INC
AKORN INC
ALBANY MOLECULAR RESEARCH INC
ALEXION PHARMACEUTICALS INC
ALIGN TECHNOLOGY INC
ALLIED HEALTHCARE INTERNATIONAL INC
AMAG PHARMACEUTICALS INC
AMERICAN MEDICAL SYSTEMS HOLDINGS INC
AMTRUST FINANCIAL SERVICES INC
ANALOGIC CORP
ANIKA THERAPEUTICS INC
APP PHARMACEUTICALS INC
ARRAY BIOPHARMA INC
ARTHROCARE CORP
ASTEX PHARMACEUTICALS INC
ATRION CORPORATION
BIO REFERENCE LABORATORIES INC
BIOMARIN PHARMACEUTICAL INC
BIOSITE INC
CALIPER LIFE SCIENCES INC
CAMBREX CORP
CANTEL MEDICAL CORP
CARACO PHARMACEUTICAL LABORATORIES LTD
CARDIONET INC
CELLDEX THERAPEUTICS INC

CELSIS INTERNATIONAL PLC
CEPHEID
CERUS CORPORATION
CHATTEM INC
CHOLESTECH CORP
COHERENT INC
CONTINUCARE CORP
CRITICAL CARE SYSTEMS
CRUM & FORSTER HOLDINGS INC
CRYOLIFE INC
CUBIST PHARMACEUTICALS INC
CYBERONICS INC
DELPHI FINANCIAL GROUP INC
DJO GLOBAL INC
EHEALTH INC
ENVIRONMENTAL TECTONICS CORP
EXACTECH INC
GENENCOR INTERNATIONAL INC
GENOMIC HEALTH INC
GEN-PROBE INC
GTC BIOTHERAPEUTICS INC
HAEMONETICS CORPORATION
HCC INSURANCE HOLDINGS INC
HEALTH INSURANCE PLAN OF GREATER NEW YORK
HEALTHTRONICS INC
HEARUSA INC
HESKA CORP
HI-TECH PHARMACAL CO INC
ICU MEDICAL INC
I-FLOW CORPORATION
ILLUMINA INC
IMMUCOR INC
IMPAX LABORATORIES INC
INTEGRAMED AMERICA INC
INTUITIVE SURGICAL INC
IRIDEX CORP
IRIS INTERNATIONAL INC
JAZZ PHARMACEUTICALS INC
LAKELAND INDUSTRIES INC
LIFECELL CORPORATION
LIFECORE BIOMEDICAL INC
LUMINEX CORPORATION
MAKO SURGICAL CORP
MARTEK BIOSCIENCES CORP
MEDICINES CO (THE)
MEDICIS PHARMACEUTICAL CORP
MEDTOX SCIENTIFIC INC
MENTOR CORP
MERIDIAN BIOSCIENCE INC
MERIT MEDICAL SYSTEMS INC
METROPOLITAN HEALTH NETWORKS INC
MICROTEK MEDICAL HOLDINGS INC
MILLENNIUM PHARMACEUTICALS INC
MYRIAD GENETICS INC
NANOMETRICS INC
NATIONAL DENTEX CORP
NATUS MEDICAL INC
NEKTAR THERAPEUTICS
NEOGEN CORPORATION
NOVAMED INC
NOVEN PHARMACEUTICALS INC
NUVASIVE INC
PACIFIC BIOMARKERS INC
PAR PHARMACEUTICAL COMPANIES INC
PMA COMPANIES INC
PROASSURANCE CORP
QUESTCOR PHARMACEUTICALS INC
QUIDEL CORP
REGENERON PHARMACEUTICALS INC
SALIX PHARMACEUTICALS
SCHICK TECHNOLOGIES INC
SCHIFF NUTRITION INTERNATIONAL INC
SCICLONE PHARMACEUTICALS INC
SCIOS INC
SEATTLE GENETICS
SERACARE LIFE SCIENCES INC
SPECTRANETICS CORP
SPECTRUM PHARMACEUTICALS INC
STAAR SURGICAL CO
STIEFEL LABORATORIES INC
SYNOVIS LIFE TECHNOLOGIES INC
TECHNE CORP
THERAGENICS CORP
THORATEC CORPORATION
TRANSATLANTIC HOLDINGS INC
UNITED THERAPEUTICS CORP
US PHYSICAL THERAPY INC
USANA HEALTH SCIENCES INC
UTAH MEDICAL PRODUCTS INC
VENTANA MEDICAL SYSTEMS INC
VERENIUM CORPORATION
VIROPHARMA INC
WRIGHT MEDICAL GROUP INC
XOMA LTD
ZOLL MEDICAL CORP

Math/Other
AFFILIATED MANAGERS GROUP
AKORN INC
ALBANY MOLECULAR RESEARCH INC
ALEXION PHARMACEUTICALS INC
AMERICAN FIDELITY ASSURANCE COMPANY
AMERICAN SCIENCE & ENGINEERING INC
AMTECH SYSTEMS INC
AMTRUST FINANCIAL SERVICES INC
ANIKA THERAPEUTICS INC
APP PHARMACEUTICALS INC
ARIBA INC
AROTECH CORPORATION
ARRAY BIOPHARMA INC
ARTHROCARE CORP
ASTEX PHARMACEUTICALS INC
BIOMARIN PHARMACEUTICAL INC
BIOSITE INC
CALIPER LIFE SCIENCES INC
CAMBREX CORP
CARACO PHARMACEUTICAL LABORATORIES LTD
CELLDEX THERAPEUTICS INC
CELSIS INTERNATIONAL PLC
CEPHEID
CERUS CORPORATION
CHATTEM INC
CHOLESTECH CORP
CIRRUS LOGIC INC
COHERENT INC
COMPASS DIVERSIFIED HOLDINGS
COMVERGE INC
CRUM & FORSTER HOLDINGS INC
CUBIST PHARMACEUTICALS INC
CYBERSOURCE CORP
DAWSON GEOPHYSICAL COMPANY
DELPHI FINANCIAL GROUP INC
EATON VANCE CORP
EHEALTH INC
EMCORE CORP
EMULEX CORP
EPAM SYSTEMS
EVEREST RE GROUP LTD
GALLUP ORGANIZATION (THE)
GENENCOR INTERNATIONAL INC

GENERAL ATOMICS
GENOMIC HEALTH INC
GEN-PROBE INC
GFI GROUP INC
GLOBECOMM SYSTEMS INC
GREAT AMERICAN FINANCIAL RESOURCES INC
GTC BIOTHERAPEUTICS INC
HARRIS INTERACTIVE INC
HCC INSURANCE HOLDINGS INC
HEALTH INSURANCE PLAN OF GREATER NEW YORK
HELIOVOLT CORP
HESKA CORP
HI-TECH PHARMACAL CO INC
HORACE MANN EDUCATORS CORPORATION
ILLUMINA INC
IMMUCOR INC
IMPAX LABORATORIES INC
INDEPENDENCE HOLDING CO
INTERCONTINENTALEXCHANGE INC (ICE)
IROBOT CORP
JAZZ PHARMACEUTICALS INC
KEYNOTE SYSTEMS INC
KKR & CO LP (KOHLBERG KRAVIS ROBERTS & CO)
KNIGHT CAPITAL GROUP INC
LCC INTERNATIONAL INC
LIFECELL CORPORATION
LIFECORE BIOMEDICAL INC
LUMINEX CORPORATION
MAPFRE USA CORP
MARTEK BIOSCIENCES CORP
MEDICINES CO (THE)
MEDICIS PHARMACEUTICAL CORP
MERIDIAN BIOSCIENCE INC
METROPOLITAN HEALTH NETWORKS INC
MILLENNIUM PHARMACEUTICALS INC
MINDSPEED TECHNOLOGIES INC
MYRIAD GENETICS INC
NANOMETRICS INC
NEKTAR THERAPEUTICS
NEOGEN CORPORATION
NEW YORK MERCANTILE EXCHANGE INC
NOVEN PHARMACEUTICALS INC
ODYSSEY RE HOLDINGS CORP
PACIFIC BIOMARKERS INC
PAR PHARMACEUTICAL COMPANIES INC
PHILADELPHIA CONSOLIDATED HOLDING CORP
PHOENIX COMPANIES INC (THE)
PMA COMPANIES INC
POLYPORE INTERNATIONAL INC
PROASSURANCE CORP
PROTECTIVE LIFE CORP
QUALCOMM ATHEROS INC
QUESTCOR PHARMACEUTICALS INC
QUIDEL CORP
REGENERON PHARMACEUTICALS INC
REINSURANCE GROUP OF AMERICA INC
ROGERS CORPORATION
SALIX PHARMACEUTICALS
SCICLONE PHARMACEUTICALS INC
SCIOS INC
SEATTLE GENETICS
SERACARE LIFE SCIENCES INC
SIGMA DESIGNS INC
SILICON LABORATORIES INC
SOLARRESERVE
SOLFOCUS INC
SPECTRUM PHARMACEUTICALS INC
SPIRE CORPORATION
STATE AUTO FINANCIAL CORP
STIEFEL LABORATORIES INC
TECHNE CORP
TRANSATLANTIC HOLDINGS INC
UNITED THERAPEUTICS CORP
VARIAN SEMICONDUCTOR EQUIPMENT ASSOCIATES INC
VIROPHARMA INC
WADDELL & REED FINANCIAL INC
XOMA LTD

Petroleum/Chemicals
AKORN INC
ALEXION PHARMACEUTICALS INC
AMCOL INTERNATIONAL CORP
AMERICAN VANGUARD CORP
ANIKA THERAPEUTICS INC
APP PHARMACEUTICALS INC
ARIZONA CHEMICAL COMPANY
ASTEX PHARMACEUTICALS INC
ATLANTIC CITY ELECTRIC COMPANY
AVISTA CORPORATION
BERRY PETROLEUM CO
BIOMARIN PHARMACEUTICAL INC
BLACK HILLS CORP
CABOT OIL & GAS CORP
CAMBREX CORP
CARACO PHARMACEUTICAL LABORATORIES LTD
CARBO CERAMICS INC
CARRIZO OIL & GAS INC
CELLDEX THERAPEUTICS INC
CELSIS INTERNATIONAL PLC
CENTRAL VERMONT PUBLIC SERVICE CORP
CERUS CORPORATION
CHATTEM INC
CLAYTON WILLIAMS ENERGY INC
CONTINENTAL RESOURCES INC
CUBIST PHARMACEUTICALS INC
DAWSON GEOPHYSICAL COMPANY
DENBURY RESOURCES INC
DPL INC
ENERGY TRANSFER PARTNERS LP
EOG RESOURCES INC
EQT CORPORATION
GENENCOR INTERNATIONAL INC
GENESIS ENERGY LP
GREEN MOUNTAIN POWER CORPORATION
GTC BIOTHERAPEUTICS INC
GULFMARK OFFSHORE INC
HELIX ENERGY SOLUTIONS GROUP INC
HESKA CORP
HI-TECH PHARMACAL CO INC
HOLLYFRONTIER CORPORATION
IDACORP INC
INNOPHOS HOLDINGS INC
INNOSPEC INC
JAZZ PHARMACEUTICALS INC
KRONOS WORLDWIDE INC
LACLEDE GROUP INC (THE)
MAGELLAN MIDSTREAM PARTNERS LP
MARTEK BIOSCIENCES CORP
MEDICINES CO (THE)
MEDICIS PHARMACEUTICAL CORP
MILLENNIUM PHARMACEUTICALS INC
MYRIAD GENETICS INC
NEOGEN CORPORATION

NEW JERSEY RESOURCES CORPORATION
NORTHWESTERN CORPORATION
NUSTAR ENERGY LP
PAR PHARMACEUTICAL COMPANIES INC
PETROLEUM DEVELOPMENT CORPORATION
PIEDMONT NATURAL GAS COMPANY INC
PIONEER NATURAL RESOURCES COMPANY
PLAINS EXPLORATION AND PRODUCTION COMPANY
POLYPORE INTERNATIONAL INC
PRIMEENERGY CORPORATION
QUAKER CHEMICAL CORP
QUESTCOR PHARMACEUTICALS INC
QUICKSILVER RESOURCES INC
REGENERON PHARMACEUTICALS INC
RPC INC
SACRAMENTO MUNICIPAL UTILITY DISTRICT
SALIX PHARMACEUTICALS
SANDRIDGE ENERGY INC
SCHIFF NUTRITION INTERNATIONAL INC
SCICLONE PHARMACEUTICALS INC
SCIOS INC
SEATTLE GENETICS
SOUTHERN UNION COMPANY
SOUTHWEST GAS CORP
SOUTHWESTERN ENERGY CO
SPECTRUM PHARMACEUTICALS INC
STEPAN COMPANY
STIEFEL LABORATORIES INC
SWIFT ENERGY CO
TAMPA ELECTRIC COMPANY
TARGA RESOURCES PARTNERS LP
TRANSAMMONIA INC
UIL HOLDINGS CORPORATION
UNISOURCE ENERGY CORPORATION
UNIT CORP
UNITED THERAPEUTICS CORP
USANA HEALTH SCIENCES INC
VERENIUM CORPORATION
VIROPHARMA INC
WESTAR ENERGY
WGL HOLDINGS INC
XOMA LTD
XTO ENERGY INC
ZEP INC

Scientists/Research
ABAXIS INC
AKORN INC
ALBANY MOLECULAR RESEARCH INC
ALEXION PHARMACEUTICALS INC
ALIGN TECHNOLOGY INC
AMAG PHARMACEUTICALS INC
AMERICAN MEDICAL SYSTEMS HOLDINGS INC
AMTECH SYSTEMS INC
ANALOGIC CORP
ANIKA THERAPEUTICS INC
APP PHARMACEUTICALS INC
ARRAY BIOPHARMA INC
ARTHROCARE CORP
ASTEX PHARMACEUTICALS INC
ATRION CORPORATION
BIO REFERENCE LABORATORIES INC
BIOMARIN PHARMACEUTICAL INC
BIOSITE INC
CALIPER LIFE SCIENCES INC
CAMBREX CORP
CANTEL MEDICAL CORP
CARACO PHARMACEUTICAL LABORATORIES LTD
CARDIONET INC
CELLDEX THERAPEUTICS INC
CELSIS INTERNATIONAL PLC
CEPHEID
CERUS CORPORATION
CHATTEM INC
CHOLESTECH CORP
COHERENT INC
CRYOLIFE INC
CUBIST PHARMACEUTICALS INC
CYBERONICS INC
DAWSON GEOPHYSICAL COMPANY
DJO GLOBAL INC
EMCORE CORP
EMULEX CORP
ENERNOC INC
ENVIRONMENTAL TECTONICS CORP
ERESEARCH TECHNOLOGY INC
EXACTECH INC
FUEL TECH INC
GENENCOR INTERNATIONAL INC
GENERAL ATOMICS
GENOMIC HEALTH INC
GEN-PROBE INC
GTC BIOTHERAPEUTICS INC
HAEMONETICS CORPORATION
HELIOVOLT CORP
HESKA CORP
HI-TECH PHARMACAL CO INC
ICU MEDICAL INC
I-FLOW CORPORATION
ILLUMINA INC
IMMUCOR INC
IMPAX LABORATORIES INC
INTUITIVE SURGICAL INC
IRIDEX CORP
IRIS INTERNATIONAL INC
IROBOT CORP
JAZZ PHARMACEUTICALS INC
LAKELAND INDUSTRIES INC
LIFECELL CORPORATION
LIFECORE BIOMEDICAL INC
LUMINEX CORPORATION
MAKO SURGICAL CORP
MARTEK BIOSCIENCES CORP
MEDICINES CO (THE)
MEDICIS PHARMACEUTICAL CORP
MEDTOX SCIENTIFIC INC
MENTOR CORP
MERIDIAN BIOSCIENCE INC
MERIT MEDICAL SYSTEMS INC
MICROTEK MEDICAL HOLDINGS INC
MILLENNIUM PHARMACEUTICALS INC
MYRIAD GENETICS INC
NANOMETRICS INC
NATIONAL DENTEX CORP
NATUS MEDICAL INC
NEKTAR THERAPEUTICS
NEOGEN CORPORATION
NETGEAR INC
NOVEN PHARMACEUTICALS INC
NUVASIVE INC
PACIFIC BIOMARKERS INC
PAR PHARMACEUTICAL COMPANIES INC
POLYPORE INTERNATIONAL INC
QUALCOMM ATHEROS INC
QUESTCOR PHARMACEUTICALS INC

QUIDEL CORP
RECYCLED ENERGY DEVELOPMENT LLC
REGENERON PHARMACEUTICALS INC
ROGERS CORPORATION
SALIX PHARMACEUTICALS
SCHICK TECHNOLOGIES INC
SCHIFF NUTRITION INTERNATIONAL INC
SCICLONE PHARMACEUTICALS INC
SCIOS INC
SEATTLE GENETICS
SERACARE LIFE SCIENCES INC
SOLARRESERVE
SOLFOCUS INC
SPECTRANETICS CORP
SPECTRUM PHARMACEUTICALS INC
SPIRE CORPORATION
STAAR SURGICAL CO
STEPAN COMPANY
STIEFEL LABORATORIES INC
SYNOVIS LIFE TECHNOLOGIES INC
TECHNE CORP
THERAGENICS CORP
THORATEC CORPORATION
UNITED THERAPEUTICS CORP
USANA HEALTH SCIENCES INC
UTAH MEDICAL PRODUCTS INC
VENTANA MEDICAL SYSTEMS INC
VERENIUM CORPORATION
VIROPHARMA INC
WRIGHT MEDICAL GROUP INC
XOMA LTD
ZOLL MEDICAL CORP

CPSIA information can be obtained at www.ICGtesting.com
Printed in the USA
LVOW030108140312

272954LV00001B/1/P

9 781608 796649